A DICTIONARY OF

CULTURAL AND CRITICAL THEORY

Editor
MICHAEL PAYNE

Associate editor
Meenakshi Ponnuswami

Assistant editor
Jennifer Payne

Advisory board
Simon Frith
Henry Louis Gates, Jr
David Rasmussen
Janet Todd
Peter Widdowson

Blackwell
Publishing

350 Main Street, Malden, MA 02148-5020, USA
108 Cowley Road, Oxford OX4 1JF, UK
550 Swanston Street, Carlton, Victoria 3053, Australia

First published 1996 by Blackwell Publishing Ltd
First published in paperback 1997
Reprinted 1998, 1999, 2000, 2001, 2003, 2004

Library of Congress Cataloging-in-Publication Data

A dictionary of cultural and critical theory / [edited by] Michael Payne
  p.   cm.
  Includes bibliographical references and index.
  ISBN 0–631–17197–5 (alk. paper)—ISBN 0–631–20753–8 (pbk)
  1. Culture—Dictionaries. 2. Critical theory—Dictionaries.
  I. Payne, Michael
  HM101.D527   1996   95–8003
  306'03—dc20   CIP

A catalogue record for this title is available from the British Library.

Set in 9 on 11pt Ehrhardt
by Graphicraft Typesetters Ltd, Hong Kong
Printed and bound in the United Kingdom
by Athenaeum Press Ltd, Gateshead, Tyne & Wear

For further information on
Blackwell Publishing, visit our website:
http://www.blackwellpublishing.com

Contents

Contributors

Toshihiko Aida
Komazawa University, Tokyo

Teresa Amott
Bucknell University, Lewisburg

R. Lanier Anderson
University of Pennsylvania

Oliver Arnold
Princeton University

Robin Attfield
University of Wales, Cardiff

Chris Baldick
Goldsmith's College, London

Susan E. Bassnett
University of Warwick

Robert Beard
Bucknell University, Lewisburg

Andrew Belsey
University of Wales, Cardiff

James R. Bennett
University of Arkansas

Ian H. Birchall
Middlesex University (retired)

Andrew Bowie
Anglia Polytechnic University, Cambridge

Malcolm Bowie
All Souls College, Oxford

Mary Ellen Bray
Rutgers University

Joseph Bristow
University of York

Michael Byram
University of Durham

John Callaghan
University of Wolverhampton

Colin Campbell
University of York

Glynis Carr
Bucknell University, Lewisburg

Erica Carter
University of Warwick

Howard Caygill
University of East Anglia

Lynn Cazabon
Bucknell University, Lewisburg

Danielle Clarke
Wadham College, Oxford

Greg Clingham
Bucknell University, Lewisburg

Mike Cole
University of Brighton

Steven Connor
Birkbeck College, London

David E. Cooper
University of Durham

Kathleen Creed-Page
Bucknell University, Lewisburg

Shadia B. Drury
University of Calgary, Alberta

Madhu Dubey
Northwestern University

Jonathan Dunsby
University of Reading

Alan Durant
Middlesex University

Gerald Eager
Bucknell University, Lewisburg

Andrew Edgar
University of Wales, Cardiff

Gregory Elliott
University of Brighton

Uzoma Esonwanne
St Mary's University, Halifax, Nova Scotia

Emmanuel Chukwudi Eze
Bucknell University, Lewisburg

Susan L. Fischer
Bucknell University, Lewisburg

Richard Fleming
Bucknell University, Lewisburg

Pauline Fletcher
Bucknell University, Lewisburg

Simon Frith
University of Strathclyde, Glasgow

Jeanne Garane
University of Evansville, Indiana

Susanne Gibson
University of Wales, Cardiff

Tara G. Gilligan
Johns Hopkins University

Thomas C. Greaves
Bucknell University, Lewisburg

Michael Green
University of Birmingham

Glyne A. Griffith
Bucknell University, Lewisburg

M.A.R. Habib
Rutgers University, Camden

Stephen Heath
Jesus College, Cambridge

Glenn A. Herdling
Marvel Comics, New York

William G. Holzberger
Bucknell University, Lewisburg

Paul Innes
University of Edinburgh

Shannon Jackson
Harvard University

John J. Joyce
Nazareth College at Rochester

May Joseph
New York University

Evelyne Keitel
Technische Universität, Chemnitz

Frank Kermode
King's College, Cambridge

Peter Karl Kresl
Bucknell University, Lewisburg

Sarah N. Lawall
University of Massachusetts at Amherst

Linden Lewis
Bucknell University, Lewisburg

David Macey
Leeds

Janet MacGaffey
Bucknell University, Lewisburg

Kirsten Malmkjær
Research Centre for English and Applied Linguistics, Cambridge

Joseph Margolis
Temple University, Philadelphia

Graham McCann
King's College, Cambridge

Andrew McNeillie
Blackwell Publishers, Oxford

J.N. Mohanty
Temple University, Philadelphia

Toril Moi
Duke University

Peter Morris-Keitel
Bucknell University, Lewisburg

Keith Morrison
University of Durham

Laura Mulvey
British Film Institute

John V. Murphy
Bucknell University, Lewisburg

Paul Norcross
Chichester Institute

Christopher Norris
University of Wales, Cardiff

G. Dennis O'Brien
University of Rochester

Tucker Orbison
Bucknell University, Lewisburg

Peter Osborne
University of Middlesex

Oyekan Owomoyela
University of Nebraska, Lincoln

Karl Patten
Bucknell University, Lewisburg

Michael Payne
Bucknell University, Lewisburg

Jean Peterson
Bucknell University, Lewisburg

James Phillips
Trinity University, San Antonio

Meenakshi Ponnuswami
Bucknell University, Lewisburg

Alice J. Poust
Bucknell University, Lewisburg

Laurence J. Ray
University of Lancaster

James P. Rice
Bucknell University, Lewisburg

John S. Rickard
Bucknell University, Lewisburg

K.K. Ruthven
University of Melbourne

Aparajita Sagar
Purdue University

Raphael Salkie
University of Brighton

Matthias Schubnell
The College of the Incarnate Word, San Antonio

Harold Schweizer
Bucknell University, Lewisburg

Peter R. Sedgwick
University of Wales, Cardiff

John Shand
University of Manchester

Andrew Shanks
University of Lancaster

Richard Shusterman
Temple University, Philadelphia

Susan R. Skand
Rutgers University

Barry Smart
University of Auckland

Shiva Kumar Srinivasan
University of Wales, Cardiff

Fred L. Standley
Florida State University, Tallahassee

Gary Steiner
Bucknell University, Lewisburg

Douglas Sturm
Bucknell University, Lewisburg

Radhika Subramaniam
New York University

Tony Tanner
King's College, Cambridge

Helen Taylor
University of Warwick

Jenny Bourne Taylor
University of Sussex

Demetrius Teigas
Darwin College, University of Kent

Janet Todd
University of East Anglia

J.B. Trapp
Warburg Institute, London

Jeffrey S. Turner
Bucknell University, Lewisburg

Kenneth J. Urban
Bucknell University, Lewisburg

Immanuel Wallerstein
Fernand Braudel Center, Binghamton University

Peter Widdowson
Cheltenham and Gloucester College of Higher Education

Barry Wilkins
University of Wales, Cardiff

Iain Wright
Australian National University, Canberra

Slava I. Yastremski
Bucknell University, Lewisburg

Preface

This dictionary provides a full and accessible reference guide to modern ideas in the broad interdisciplinary fields of cultural and critical theory, which have developed from interactions among modern linguistic, literary, anthropological, philosophical, political, and historical traditions of thought. The interdisciplinary focus of this book is on contemporary theory, reflecting the remarkable breaching during the past 20 years of many of the traditional barriers that once separated disciplines within and between the humanities and social sciences. Structuralist, post-structuralist, phenomenological, feminist, hermeneutical, psychoanalytic, Marxist, and formalist modes of theory have been especially influential; they are, therefore, prominent in the dictionary entries. Work in these fields that appeared before the twentieth century is included when it forms an important context for understanding later thinking.

The length of articles is not intended as a judgment of the relative importance of topics, but rather as an indication of either the extent of their current use by cultural and critical theorists or their difficulty and complexity. A special feature of the dictionary is the inclusion of several speculative or polemical essays on selected key topics and writers. Survey articles on area studies and period studies are also incorporated and help to give a sense of connection between topics that might otherwise seem simply discrete.

It understandably may appear premature to offer now a dictionary of cultural and critical theory, since both cultural studies and critical theory are yet protean innovations in the discourses of the humanities and human sciences. Indeed, there is good reason to question even whether the two sets of terms in the previous sentence – "cultural studies"/"critical theory" and "humanities"/"human sciences" – can sit comfortably side by side. Perhaps this dictionary might have been more accurately titled "a dictionary of mercurial discourse about the study of human beings at the end of the twentieth century." But such an all-embracing title would also have created false expectations. There is little here that would assist beginning students or general readers interested solely in the physical or managerial sciences, except in so far as those sciences intersect with the arts, the critical humanities, and the revisionary social sciences. There may also be little here to interest the traditional humanist, if such there be, who continues to cherish a sense of art removed from the vicissitudes of history, politics, economics, and the recent interventions of deconstruction, feminism, semiotics, Marxism, and psychoanalysis. Nevertheless, even those who have contributed to such interventions might be disturbed to find here articles on perennial topics in the history of ideas and on some authors who have been vilified, perhaps justifiably, by activist intellectuals who find it no longer possible to believe that history, politics, and economics can any more serve simply as "background" to the study of the humanities. Although the scope of this dictionary is wide, the individual entries are often purposefully polemical.

Current intellectual discourse in the humanities and human sciences is often messy, difficult, and dynamic. It embraces not only the greatest writers, artists, and thinkers of the past but also radio, film, blues, rap, and comics; it crosses the traditional boundaries that once (always uncertainly) separated the creative from the critical; it is *engagé* in ways that might have made even Sartre uncomfortable, because of its restless concern for the excluded and the marginalized; it is self-critical and self-conscious to the point where its language has occasionally seemed far too difficult, tortured, or obscure. This dictionary in part reflects the messy dynamics of current discourse about the human condition at the end of the twentieth century; nevertheless, it attempts to be useful by making that discourse more widely intelligible.

The authors of the following entries have been asked to write for a worldwide English-reading audience of students, scholars, and general readers. We have tried to be clear when clarity is possible, but not to avoid difficulty and uncertainty. Authors have also been asked to assume a point of view on their topics and to indicate that they have done so, when such seems to them appropriate. We have made every effort to gather an ecumenical and international authorship, but there is also represented here one fairly substantial group of contributions from a single academic institution in the United States. By this means an attempt has been made to take, as it were, a seismographic reading of the innovations in cultural and critical studies at one university and to play those off against work in many other institutions throughout the world, literally from Australia to Zimbabwe, in recognition of the cultural specificity of cultural studies.

It is hoped that the entries in this dictionary will be taken as provocative and provisional. Most of them include suggestions for further reading; there is a thorough cross-referencing system (words or names in capitals refer to full articles on these topics); and readers will find a comprehensive bibliography and index at the end of the volume. In the event of a second edition of this book, readers are encouraged to communicate with the editor concerning errors of fact or omission, by way of the publisher.

This book is dedicated to the memory of Raman Selden, who died very young soon after proposing this project. Where it has been possible to determine Professor Selden's original editorial intentions, those have been followed whenever feasible. The members of the advisory board have been exceptionally tolerant in agreeing to work with two general editors who unfortunately never met. I would like especially to thank several of my students who assisted with the bibliography and contributed in other ways to this book: Ruth Davies, Tara Gilligan (both Knight Fellows), David Barneda, Robert Woodward, and Ted Temple. Without the continuous support of Stephan Chambers, Alyn Shipton, Andrew McNeillie, and particularly Denise Rea at Blackwell Publishers, this project would never have been continued, much less completed. Sandra Raphael guided this project through the final stages of production with tactful and intelligent efficiency. Reference librarians at the British Library, the London Library, the Warburg Institute (London), Senate House Library (University of London), and the Ellen Clarke Bertrand Library (Bucknell University) were, as always, helpful and resourceful.

MICHAEL PAYNE

Introduction
Some Versions of Cultural and Critical Theory

> It is the trope of our times to locate the question of culture in the realm of the *beyond*. At the century's edge, we are less exercised by annihilation – the death of the author – or epiphany – the birth of the "subject." Our existence today is marked by a tenebrous sense of survival, living on the borderlines of the "present" for which there seems to be no proper name other than the current and controversial shiftiness of the prefix "post:" *postmodernism, postcolonialism, postfeminism*. (Bhabha, 1994, p. 1)

In one of his witty fictions of futile human efforts to give order to knowledge, Borges describes a Chinese encyclopedia's categories of animals as "(a) belonging to the Emperor, (b) embalmed, (c) tame, (d) sucking pigs, (e) sirens, (f) fabulous, (g) stray dogs, (h) included in the present classification, (i) frenzied, (j) innumerable, (k) drawn with a very fine camelhair brush, (l) *et cetera*, (m) having just broken the water pitcher, (n) that from a long way off look like flies" (Borges, 1974, p. 708). It is not surprising that the many recent attempts to define the field of cultural studies seem no less whimsical than this, since culture is simultaneously such an elusive and all-encompassing idea. In 1952 the distinguished anthropologists A.L. Kroeber and Clyde Kluckhohn published the most comprehensive assessment of culture as a term and an idea. They carefully distinguished definitions proposed by 110 authors according to 52 discrete concepts used in those definitions. However, like the Chinese encyclopedist in Borges's Celestial Emporium of Benevolent Knowledge, they added a further category of 25 additional terms not included in their primary list of 52, as though under the heading of *et cetera*. Raymond Williams obviously committed no exaggeration when he announced that "*culture* is one of the two or three most complicated words in the English language" (Williams, 1988, p. 87).

Definitions of Culture
In the humanities and human sciences, *culture* retains some of its Latinate connotation of physical nurture or cultivation, as the term is commonly used by biologists; but it was not applied to the historical and social organization of human beings until the mid-eighteenth century, in German. According to Kroeber and Kluckhohn's survey, the adoption of the term in Romance languages and in English was delayed by the currency of *civilization*, also a Latinate term (from *civis, civilis, civitas, civilitas*), where the reference is to the life of the citizen in politically sophisticated urban states, in contrast to the rural, barbaric, or pastoral life of the tribesman. As the concept of *culture* slowly began to eclipse that of *civilization* – from the mid-eighteenth to the mid-nineteenth century – it came to signify "a set of attributes and products of human societies, and therewith of mankind, which are extrasomatic and transmissible by mechanisms other than biological heredity, and are as essentially lacking in sub-human species as they are characteristic of the human species as it is aggregated in its societies" (Kroeber and Kluckhohn, 1952, p. 284). In 1871, at last, E.B. Tylor's then provocatively titled book *Primitive Culture* gave some stability to the term and clarity to its definition: "Culture, or civilization," he wrote, ". . . is that complex whole which includes knowledge, belief, art, law, morals, custom,

and any other capabilities and habits acquired by man as a member of society" (quoted by Kroeber and Kluckhohn, 1952, p. 81). Except for what we now would read as a perhaps unconsciously sexist nineteenth-century metonymy for human beings ("man"), Tylor's definition has not been improved.

Coordinates of Cultural and Critical Theory

The study of culture, or cultural theory, is no less a multiplicity than *culture*, even though cultural studies have generally come to be identified with the Centre for Contemporary Cultural Studies (CCCS) at the University of Birmingham and with the influence of Richard Hoggart's *The Uses of Literacy* (1957), Raymond Williams's *Culture and Society* (1958), and E.P. Thompson's *The Making of the English Working Class* (1968). Although published a decade later than the books by Hoggart and Williams, E.P. Thompson's work provided a meticulous social historical foundation for the earlier books, in which Hoggart and Williams find themselves caught between the disappearance of the working-class culture into which they were born and the commercial / capitalist/American assault on a literary culture into which they were educated. Although unemployment has understandably come to be thought a recent threat by those who suffer from it, anticipate it, or fear it, there were never fewer than a million unemployed in Britain's working class from the 1920s until the 1939–45 war, when suddenly Britain, like the United States, moved fitfully toward full employment, mainly because of the numbers of people then in military service. After 1945, with the introduction of new production techniques in industry, the possibility of an upwardly mobile, leisure culture, instead of a jobless one, seemed quite real. Founded on this belief, a massive effort began on both sides of the Atlantic, not only to educate former soldiers but also to dispense literature and the other arts in order to cultivate leisure in a manner previously unrealized. In the United States, for example, the Ford Foundation sponsored a highly successful Great Books program through local libraries. Somewhat later the Elderhostel program for people of retirement age made possible short university courses at little expense. In this spirit, Eric Hoffer, the philosopher of the International Longshoreman's Union in California, championed the creative use of leisure and even proposed, in an exuberant moment, that all of northern California be set aside for such cultivated leisure. Even before the war, the task of widespread cultural education had been taken up more soberly by the "New Critics," Cleanth Brooks, R.B. Heilman, and Robert Penn Warren, in the popular college textbooks they edited together, and in their influential criticism. Meanwhile in Britain I.A. Richards, F.R. Leavis, and William Empson set for themselves an even more ambitious task.

Leavis's work, as he may well have welcomed, has recently been subjected to careful and elaborate scrutiny (see Mulhern, 1979 and Baldick, 1983). Unlike the American New Critics, he promoted not only such a program of close reading as did Richards and Empson, but also a careful consideration of the importance of literature as a cultural product and as a force for moral education and informed judgment. In this respect Leavis continued a tradition of English criticism that extended from Sir Philip Sidney to Samuel Johnson, through William Blake and Matthew Arnold to T.S. Eliot. Although rarely examining this problem, recent champions of that moral tradition have assumed a connection between knowledge and virtue that has rarely, since Plato, gone uncontested. The hope had always been that knowledge would lead to virtue, although the realization of that hope continues to be elusive at best.

As cultural studies developed in Britain under the influence of Hoggart and Williams, a set of concepts came to determine much of the discourse of this new interdisciplinary or anti-disciplinary field. Human subjectivity and consciousness, ideology and hegemony, critique and polysemy provided then, as now, the key coordinates of cultural studies, especially, since the

1970s, as cultural theorists have become more fully responsive to continental European developments in semiotics, psychoanalysis, critical theory, and philosophy. Although debate has been passionate and complex concerning these matters – and continues unabated – many cultural and critical theorists either advocate or find their thinking clarified in opposition to the following three contentions:

(i) *Subjectivity and consciousness*   Much of the language that commonly refers to human beings as individuals with essential and determinate identities disguises the divided character of subjectivity and consciousness. As Hegel argued in *Phenomenology of the Mind*, consciousness operates not only by defining what falls within its scope but also by breaching what it previously thought to be its defining limitations and then incorporating those superseded definitions into a newly expanded structure of thought. An inescapable feature of consciousness is thus its capacity to think about a topic and simultaneously to assess critically how that topic is being thought about. Freud, however, in *The Interpretation of Dreams*, observed that centuries before Hegel poets and other writers had explored a vast expanse of mental activity that lies beyond consciousness – in dreams and fantasies – or that unexpectedly disrupts it – in jokes, slips of the tongue, and works of art. The determination of recent thinkers (such as Lacan, Derrida, and Kristeva) to refer to human beings as subjects manifests an effort to resist pre-Hegelian and pre-Freudian assumptions of human unity and ego identity. Subjectivity, however, also recalls a sense of subjection and a resistance to unthought assumptions about essential human freedom. Born into language, culture, and race, class and gender politics, the subject is never fully autonomous.

(ii) *Ideology and hegemony*   Marx, in his "Preface to *A Contribution to the Critique of Political Economy*" argued, "It is not the consciousness of men that determines their existence, but their social existence that determines their consciousness" (Marx and Engels, 1968, p. 173). A failure to recognize the ways in which the economic structure of society determines the social relations of human beings and curtails the independence of their will is to be in the grip of ideology. Indeed, the ruling ideas of an age, as Marx and Engels argued in *The German Ideology*, amount to little more than the idealization of then dominant economic class relationships. Forms of consciousness therefore constitute ideologies, which either hold subjects in their grip or form limitations that can be breached by critique or social revolution. An alternative (or supplement) to violent forms of suppressing or postponing revolutionary change is the manipulation of the superstructural forms of culture – education, media, religion, art – not only by government but also by those who are subject to such manipulation. Hegemony, in this sense, is complicity in oppression as normal or as necessarily a part of culture by those who are ruled by it. As Gramsci claimed in his *Prison Notebooks*, hegemony is woven out of a network of ideologies and is then transmitted by intellectuals in affiliation with the ruling class.

(iii) *Critique and polysemy*   A systematic program to perform a critique of ideology (*Ideologiekritik*) in order simultaneously to understand its processes and to resist its dominance has been the continuing project of the so-called Frankfurt school of social theorists (including Adorno, Horkheimer, the early Marcuse, and Habermas), whether these thinkers have worked in Vienna, California, New York, or Frankfurt. If indeed forms of consciousness can be understood as the substance of ideology, education as a conduit of hegemony, and intellectuals as unwitting or complicitous agents of non-violent oppression, then any attempt to know (or theorize) the processes of society must begin with a radical criticism of the dominating forces of ideology in order to disengage consciousness from what keeps it politically unconscious. The principal effort here is not simply to oppose those forces with moralizing criticism but also to discover a new form of knowledge that is distinct from empirical science, that is founded in radical criticism, and that is determined to be a force for social change. These features of *Ideologiekritik* are also common to many forms of feminist, postcolonial, and anti-racist criticism. One opening for this ambitious critique of ideology is provided by a cardinal principle of semiotics: language and all signifying structures are polysemous, not only in the sense that they mean many things at once, but also that they may say more than they want to say. Derrida, for example, in *Of Grammatology* argues that all texts (whether in written language or in other signifying forms) if read carefully enough can be shown to provide, often unwittingly, the resources for their own critique. If, however, polysemy provides such deconstructive resources for a critique of ideology, those same resources are to be found in critical texts for their appropriation by the dominant ideology. For this reason such pliant ideologies as liberal humanism would seem to be more of a threat to radical criticism than the authoritarian ideologies of closed societies.

The occasional papers published by the Birmingham Centre for Contemporary Cultural Studies during the 1960s and 1970s reveal a considerable struggle over these concepts and over the theoretical orientation of the Centre itself. Some of the themes of that debate were how much concern should be devoted to the disappearance of British working-class culture in England, especially during the years after the 1939–45 war; how much to the efforts to continue the development of English studies, which had sustained much opposition at both Cambridge and Oxford in its formative years; how much to a *rapprochement* with sociology; how much to an incorporation of continental thought, such as the work of Max Weber and Emile Durkheim; and how much – if any – to new cultural forms, such as cinema and television. Although the Centre, a recent victim of Thatcherism, unfortunately no longer exists as a research institute in its own right, there is a sense in which there never was or could be a center for cultural studies. A movement that began in the post-Leavis years at Cambridge, exemplified by Raymond Williams's *Culture and Society*, was taken to Birmingham by Richard Hoggart and to Oxford by Terry Eagleton. The famous Essex Conferences, the programs in cultural studies at Sussex and Cardiff, and the many programs in regional universities are eloquent signs of the eventual prevalence of cultural studies in Britain. If there was some uncertainty whether the words "cultural studies" should be followed by a singular or plural verb, there seems little doubt now of their protean plurality (Johnson, 1984, p. 1). Indeed, cultural studies in Britain began with the realization that a common working-class culture of reconciliation was dying or being destroyed, leaving the secular canon of literature and the other arts in an embattled relationship to popular and commercial culture. British cultural studies continue under renewed cuts in funding for higher education as a way to keep politically committed research and teaching alive in the major humanities and social science disciplines.

British Cultural Studies: Raymond Williams
Raymond Williams's *Culture and Society*, which is a founding text for both cultural theory and the New Left, provides the classic "map" of the effects of the Industrial Revolution as they imprint themselves on English literature. A key element in Williams's narrative of the transformation of British culture from Coleridge to Orwell is the change in the meanings of the word *art* from the last decades of the eighteenth through the nineteenth century:

> From its original sense of a human attribute, a "skill," it had come, by the period with which
> we are concerned, to be a kind of institution, a set body of activities of a certain kind. An *art*

had formerly been any human skill; but *Art*, now, signified a particular group of skills, the "imaginative" or "creative" arts. *Artist* had meant a skilled person, as had *artisan*; but *artist* now referred to these selected skills alone. Further, and most significantly, *Art* came to stand for a special kind of truth, "imaginative truth" and *artist* for a special kind of person, as the words *artistic* and *artistical*, to describe human beings, new in the 1840s show. A new name *aesthetics*, was found to describe the judgement of art, and this, in its turn, produced a name for a special kind of person – *aesthete*. *The arts* – literature, music, painting, sculpture, theatre – were grouped together, in this new phase, as having something essentially in common which distinguished them from other human skills. (Williams, 1958, pp. xv–xvi).

No sooner is this ideology of the supremacy or automony of artistic truth asserted (as in Keats's letters and in the final pages of Shelley's *Defence of Poetry*) than it begins to be overtaken by an earlier argument for the complex responsibility of poets to their readers, which began to be articulated by Wordsworth and Coleridge, in their *Preface to the Lyrical Ballads*, and was later more fully developed by Pugin, Ruskin, Arnold, and Morris. Not only does Morris stress the root sense of culture as a process of cultivation, but he also challenges the elevation of the artist above the artisan: "Any one," he wrote, "who professes to think that the question of art and cultivation must go before that of the knife and fork . . . does not understand what art means, or how that its roots must have a soil of a thriving and unanxious life." In his view, it is civilization, in opposition to culture, that "has reduced the workman to such a skinny and pitiful existence, that he scarcely knows how to frame a desire for any life much better than that which he now endures." Morris concludes that it is the responsibility of art to set before the members of the working class "the true ideal of a full and reasonable life" in which beauty and pleasure are as necessary to them as the material substance of their lives (Williams, 1958, pp. 150–6).

Society loses its root sense of companionship and fellowship and becomes an institutional abstraction when civilization, in its form as the ideological appropriation of culture, detaches art from its social and economic base (Williams, 1976, p. 291). In this view, art is not necessarily or naturally part of a superstructure but has been abstracted and alienated there by the politics of civilization, which here, as Morris thought, retains its sense of urban uprootedness. Williams virtually predicts a prime minister who denied that there was any such thing as society and a succession of American presidents who acted on such a denial (see Hall, 1988, pp. 271–83). Marx identifies the locus of this process of abstraction or alienation – the denial of the root sense of the social – in the transfer of the use-value of labour power to the capitalist, who consumes it before the laborer is compensated. As though anticipating Gramsci's concept of hegemony, Marx stresses that the laborer not only allows this alienating appropriation to occur, but "everywhere gives credit to the capitalist" (Marx, 1954, Vol. I, p. 170). Then by elevating itself to superstructure, art sacrifices its capacity for cultural reconciliation. Williams insists that Marx did not offer a fully articulated literary or artistic theory, not because he thought such a project irrelevant to his basic concerns or because he thought of literature and the other arts reductively, but because he foresaw much complexity in such an articulation that awaited further elaboration, which he welcomed. Williams reads Engels's later elaboration of Marx's distinction between economic base and cultural superstructure as a hardening of what for Marx was essentially a pliable metaphor (Marx and Engels, 1958, p. 167).

Williams's book concludes by bequeathing a powerful and rather intimidating legacy to cultural studies. One tangible consequence of the crisis of culture, conceived as cultivation, and the denial of society, conceived as companionship – both results of their ideological abstraction unwittingly launched by poets – is the rise of cultural studies. "The change in the whole form of our common life produced, as a necessary reaction, an emphasis on attention to this whole form" (Williams, 1958, p. 295). In Williams's view, cultural and critical theory is itself a cultural production, simultaneously committed to the processes of cultural critique and to the renewal of cultivation and companionship made possible by the reconciling potential of art that is actively resistant to ideological appropriation.

American New Historicism and Ethnography: Stephen Greenblatt and Clifford Geertz

Ambitious as Williams's program was, it was also deliberately narrow, both geographically and historically. Williams chose to confine his attention to English writers from 1780 to 1950 because of his determination to focus on the immediate effects of the Industrial Revolution on British culture (Williams, 1958, p. vi). The only continental European theorist of culture Williams considers is Marx. Although much indebted to British cultural studies, the New Historicism in America has a considerably wider geographical, historical, and theoretical focus, which results, however, in a less clearly articulated politics. In 1982 Stephen Greenblatt, a professor of English at the University of California at Berkeley, edited a collection of essays on Renaissance studies entitled *The Forms of Power and the Power of Forms*; in his introduction to that volume, Greenblatt used the phrase "new historicism" (Greenblatt, 1982, p. 1) in a way that seemed to many readers a call for a new movement in literary study. Two years earlier, he had published *Renaissance Self-Fashioning: From More to Shakespeare*, a book of lasting importance that significantly changed the landscape of English Renaissance studies. In that book Greenblatt argues that the idea of the self as an artifact to be fashioned by individual will is itself a cultural production of the Renaissance. Although a close approximation of this thesis can be found in Marx and Engels's discussion of individuality in the *Manifesto of the Communist Party* (Marx and Engels, 1958, pp. 47–8), Greenblatt's argument arises out of a uniquely "thick" description of the texts he examines. Despite the obvious significance for him of Michel Foucault, who visited Berkeley in 1980, and the scholars of the Warburg Institute, where Greenblatt has sometimes worked, he has been most powerfully influenced by the cultural theories of the American anthropologist Clifford Geertz. Indeed, the new historicism is solidly based on a new ethnography that proclaims itself both a fictional art and a social science.

Geertz's concept of culture, however, is fundamentally a semiotic one. He sees the task of anthropology as that of deciphering the complex webs of significance spun by human beings (Geertz, 1973, p. 5). Echoing the language of the American philosopher Stanley Cavell, he thinks of anthropology at its best as the acknowledgement of the meaningful ordinary life of another person, who is most often a member of a culture different from that of the ethnographer. Anthropology is thus an encounter with otherness in terms of the minute semiotic details of ordinary life. The essays collected in Geertz's *The Interpretation of Cultures*, first published in 1973, not only provide a retrospective of 15 years of his fieldwork but also his most fully presented theory of culture, which he insists is necessarily embedded in the microscopic details of ethnography. For him (with no apparent allusion to Heidegger), cultural theory is rooted in the soil of ordinary daily life and is discovered there when the ethnographer is about his professional task of "thick description."

Geertz takes the phrase "thick description" from Gilbert Ryle, who invites his reader, in the context of wondering what the sculpture of Rodin's *Thinker* is thinking, to consider the behavior of boys who are not thinking, but winking. One boy's wink may be in fact an involuntary twitch, another a conspiratorial wink, another – possibly in reaction to the second – a dismissive parody of a truly adequate conspiratorial wink, a fourth a preparation before a mirror to mock an inadequate conspiratorial wink. In all cases, here much simplified, a camera, if it were there, would simply record multiple winks, indistinguishable from parodies and rehearsals of parodies.

But, Geertz argues, using a carefully chosen example from the relevant anthropological literature, the ethnographer is professionally charged to render thick descriptions of the differences in meaning among these various winks. The ethnographer, as writer of the relevant ethnos, must write what it variously *means*. According to Geertz's formulation, there are, then, four characteristics of ethnographic description. First, it is interpretative; second, what it interprets is the "flow of social discourse" from winks to Javanese rituals to Balinese cockfights; third, the act of interpreting is an attempt to "rescue" the meaning of such discourse from the perishable occasions on which it occurs and to "fix" it in perusable terms; and fourth, it is microscopic in the sense that it confronts the same grand realities as the other human sciences – such as power, change, faith, oppression, beauty, love – but locates them in the homely details of everyday life (Geertz, 1973, pp. 20–1).

Geertz is openly contemptuous of the notion that the essence of complex national societies or great religions can be discovered in certain "typical" small towns or localities, whether Jonesville, Easter Island, or Montaillou. It is not the generality but the variation of cultural forms, he insists, that is both anthropology's greatest resource and the basis of its besetting theoretical dilemma: "how is such variation to be squared with the biological unity of the human species?" (Geertz, 1973, p. 22). Given this dilemma, it is not surprising to discover the major advances of cultural theory in specific studies by such ethnographers as Lévi-Strauss, Evans-Pritchard, Malinowski, and Benedict (Geertz, 1993).

Accordingly, it is not surprising to discover the most important achievements of new historicism in such particular cases as Greenblatt's studies of Walter Raleigh, Holbein's *The Ambassadors*, Spenser's "Mutability Cantos," and his account of the books that Christopher Columbus read. But Greenblatt's work also manifests a politics that is purposefully absent from Geertz's ethnographical project. At a critical point in his career Michel Foucault described the object of his work as "knowledge invested in complex systems of institutions" (quoted by Macey, 1993, p. 234). By carrying forward a project parallel to Foucault's, but one that brings to written texts the same attention to microscopic detail that Geertz brought to his fieldwork, Greenblatt's "New Historicism" is no less an engaged or committed criticism than Williams's. In a rare moment of explicit critical theory, Greenblatt wrote,

> The simple operation of any systematic order, any allocation method, will inevitably run the risk of exposing its own limitations, even (or perhaps especially) as it asserts its underlying moral principle. This exposure is at its most intense at moments in which a comfortably established ideology confronts unusual circumstances, moments when the moral value of a particular form of power is not merely assumed but explained. (Greenblatt, 1992, p. 92)

The context for this reflection on the implications of cultural poetics for cultural politics is Greenblatt's thick description of Thomas Harriot's *A Brief and True Report of the New Found Land of Virginia*, a text that reveals a critical instance of the social construction of European values in America, when the dynamics of subversion encompassed the colonialists no less than the native Americans whose land they had appropriated.

Critical Theory and Culture: Jürgen Habermas

The idea of critical theory is rightly associated with a group of German philosophers, including Horkheimer and Adorno, whose founding text for the Frankfurt school, *Dialectic of Enlightenment* (*Dialektik der Aufklärung* (1944)), was published long before any of the books by Raymond Williams, Clifford Geertz, or Stephen Greenblatt. The tradition of critical theory is now carried on by Jürgen Habermas, whose writing provides more comprehensively than his predecessors a powerful critique of modernity that reaches from Hegel and Marx to Nietzsche and Heidegger and on to Foucault and Derrida. No one, it appears, is more widely read in contemporary cultural and critical theory than Habermas, as *The Philosophical Discourse of Modernity* (*Der philosophische Diskurs der Moderne: Zwölf Vorlesungen* (1985)) amply demonstrates. In his view, modern philosophical discourse continues to struggle with the legacy of Hegel that Marx and other Left Hegelians inherited more than a century ago. Whereas Hegel in *Phenomenology of the Mind* attempted to purify the subject-centered reason of the Enlightenment in an effort to attain absolute knowledge, Marx and the Young Hegelians insisted on reason's inescapable impurity, on its being caught in history, politics, passion, and the body. Accordingly, Nietzsche proceeded to analyze "the fruitlessness of cultural tradition uncoupled from action and shoved into the sphere of interiority," and to announce the end of philosophy (Habermas, 1985, p. 85). Reading French poststructuralism – especially the writings of Derrida, Foucault, and Bataille – as the direct outcome of that proclamation, Habermas is determined to affirm reason as a form of communicative action that is conversant with such dark, banished antitheses to reason as madness and desire and that is determined to fulfill its communicative role actively and publicly.

Hegel himself briefly glimpsed this need for philosophy's full cultural engagement; if not the first modern, he was, in this sense, the first to see the problem of modernity. In the manuscript of his *Systemprogramm*, Hegel records the conviction, which he shared in Frankfurt with Hölderlin and Schelling, that philosophy needs to join with art to fashion a mythology that would make philosophy's cultural engagement possible and publicly accessible. Habermas describes this program as "the monotheism of reason and of the heart [that] is supposed to join itself to the polytheism of the imagination" (Habermas, 1985, p. 32). The German Romantic poetry that Hegel saw being written at the beginning of the nineteenth century, however, seemed inadequate to carry out the great cultural task he thought necessary. Despite his desire to overcome them, Hegel was thus caught in the fundamental alterities of modernity. He was transfixed by the divisions between private reflection and public engagement, between reason and imagination, between philosophy and literature. Nietzsche, Heidegger, and the French poststructuralists (in Habermas's view) set out to work within those alterities, while neoconservatives yield "uncritically to the rampaging dynamism of social modernity, inasmuch as it trivializes the modern consciousness of time and prunes reason back into understanding and rationality back into purposive rationality" (Habermas, 1987, p. 117).

During the 1939–45 war, Horkheimer and Adorno, working in the traditions of Kant and Hegel, developed critical theory as a way to think through the consequences of multiple historical tragedies: fascism in Germany, Stalinism in Soviet Russia, and the apparent mistake of Marx's prognosis for revolution worldwide. All of this they saw as "the self-destruction of the Enlightenment." They insisted, however, in *Dialectic of Enlightenment*:

> We are wholly convinced – and therein lies our *petitio principii* – that social freedom is inseparable from enlightened thought. Nevertheless, we believe that we have just as clearly recognized that the notion of this very way of thinking, no less than the actual historic forms – the social institutions – with which it is interwoven, already contains the seed of the reversal universally apparent today. If enlightenment does not accommodate reflection on this recidivist element, then it seals its own fate. If consideration of the destructive aspect of progress is left to its enemies, blindly pragmatized thought loses its transcending quality and its relation to truth. In the enigmatic readiness of the technologically educated masses to fall under the sway of any despotism, in its self-destructive affinity to popular paranoia, and in all uncomprehended absurdity, the weakness of the modern theoretical faculty is apparent. (Adorno and Horkheimer, pp. 243–4)

The threat of the enlightenment's self-destruction encompassed the fear that reason was being extinguished, leaving civilization in ruins (Habermas, 1987, p. 117). Furthermore, philosophy seemed impotent to deal with these threats; it knew "no workable or abstract rules or goals to replace those at present in force;" it was "simultaneously alien and sympathetic to the status quo" (Adorno and Horkheimer, pp. 243–4). Critical theory, however, seemed capable of rediscovering the power of dialectic, which philosophy had abandoned or forgotten (Habermas, 1987, p. 117).

The most important phrase in Adorno and Horkheimer's statement of their concern, as it now appears, is the observation that rational enlightenment, like other ways of thinking, includes "the seed of reversal." Habermas traces that reversal through Marx's ideological critique, which puts under suspicion the thought that the identities of bourgeois ideals are directly manifested in institutions – such as individual nation-states, corporate enterprises, universities, or established modes of thought in the media or in particular publishing houses. Although Habermas is understandably not willing to say so, his updating of critical theory incorporates Derridean deconstruction at precisely the point where Habermas may want to exclude it. Critical theory models itself on Marx's critique of ideology, which asserts that the meaning of institutions presents a "double face," showing not only the ideology of the dominant class, but also "the starting point for an immanent critique of structures that elevate to the status of the general interest." Habermas warns, however, that such critique may be appropriated to serve the interest of the "dominant part of society" (Habermas, 1987, p. 117).

Culture and Imperialism: Edward Said and the Legacy of Foucault

The project of critical theory rests on the conviction that the humanities and human sciences must be emancipatory in order to resist becoming ideological instruments of a post-Enlightenment state. Whether or not they give any overt recognition to the work of the Frankfurt school, such movements within cultural theory as feminism, postcolonialism, multiculturalism, and studies of racism share its epistemological politics. However, as these various longitudinal movements within cultural studies proceed to demonstrate a presiding sexism, colonialism, enthnocentrism, or racism within the various disciplines in the humanities and social sciences, each in turn promotes its critical project as *the* most effective or legitimately universal means of exposing a methodological Eurocentrism at work in the production of knowledge. In an important recent book on racist culture, for example, David Theo Goldberg proposes to show how, "through various primary ordering concepts and root metaphors, contemporary knowledge production reinvigorates racialized categories or launches new ones and so subtly orders anew the exclusiveness and exclusions of racist expression" (Goldberg, 1993, p. 149). Edward Said's *Culture and Imperialism* is one of the most ambitious recent efforts to expose such a politically tainted epistemology.

In the original preface to his *History of Madness*, Michel Foucault wrote:

> The Orient, thought of as the origin, dreamed of as the vertiginous point that gives birth to nostalgias and promises of return . . . the night of beginnings, in which the West was formed, but in which it traced a dividing line, the Orient is for the West all that the West is not, even though it is there that it must seek its primitive truth. A history of this division throughout its long western evolution should be written, followed in its continuity and its exchanges, but it must also be allowed to appear in its tragic hieratism. (Quoted by Macey, 1993, p. 146)

Beginning with his book *Orientalism*, Said set out to write that history, although he has recently been determined to deny or obscure his precise debt to Foucault. The object of Said's critical attention has not been simply attempts by the West to subdue the Orient by force or by economic exploitation; rather, he has argued that the Orient is virtually an invention of those European disciplines that have set out to study it. Orientalism, as a form of epistemological imperialism, is therefore, not a foreign, but "an integral part of European *material* civilization and culture" (Said, 1979, p. 1). Not only oriental studies but also linguistics, history, criticism, philosophy, religious studies, sociology, anthropology, psychology, political science, economics are all complicitous in the production of orientalism. Rather than simply continuing the argument of his earlier book, Said's *Culture and Imperialism* enlarges its thesis by setting out to demonstrate that orientalism is but one manifestation of imperialism and that in their pursuits of empire Europe and American have used their cultural forms, including such ideals as freedom and individualism, as means of conquest and domination. "Neither imperialism nor colonialism," he argues, "is a simple act of accumulation and acquisition. Both are supported and perhaps even impelled by impressive ideological formations that include notions that certain territories and people *require* and beseech domination, as well as forms of knowledge affiliated with domination" (Said, 1993, p. 8). Indeed, the imperial experience provided the focused opportunity for developing the new multidiscipline of cultural studies. Cultural theory, it would therefore seem, is compromised from its start.

In Said's view cultural and critical theory from Williams to Habermas has either been "blinded" to imperialism or unreliable in resisting it; indeed, the only French theorists he exempts from this judgment are Deleuze, Todorov, and Derrida (Said, 1993, p. 336). Said's theory of culture, however, attempts to disown what he sees as the contaminated beginnings of cultural studies. Apparently for this reason he uses the word "culture" in two strategically distinct ways. In one sense, it signifies for him "all those practices, like the arts of description, communication, and representation, that have relative autonomy from the economic, social, and political realms and that often exist in aesthetic forms, one of whose principal aims is pleasure." In a second sense, culture is a concept that, by suggesting refinement and elevation, extends from what a given society thinks to be the best that has been known and thought (as in Matthew Arnold's famous definition) to self-aggrandizing or xenophobic identification of a culture with what it thinks to be the best that the world has known (Said, 1993, pp. xii–xiii). The first category allows for the private pleasure Said finds in such texts as Conrad's *Heart of Darkness* or Verdi's *Aida*, while the second provides the opportunity to critique the manifestations of imperialist ideologies in those texts and in their corresponding appropriation by a dominating culture to promote the interests of empire. In order to account for the relationships between these two categories, Said resorts to a metaphor from music that seems designed to provide no conceptual resolution. He writes:

> I have been proposing the contrapuntal lines of a global analysis, in which texts and worldly institutions are seen working together, in which Dickens and Thackeray as London authors are read also as writers whose historical influence is informed by the colonial enterprises in India and Australia of which they were so aware, and in which the literature of one commonwealth is involved in the literatures of others. (Said, 1993, pp. 385–6)

Indeed, Said himself seems caught in what Habermas sees as the besetting modernist dilemma of multiple alterities: born into a Protestant family in the Middle East, educated in the West in preparation for returning to the cause of the Palestinians, teaching and writing about American and European imperialism at Columbia for a predominantly American and British audience, Said is eloquent in his honest inability to resolve these conflicts, which is what leads him to the final debilitating image of his troubled book. This is the way he captures the tragic hieratic that Foucault called for:

> There is a great difference ... between the optimistic mobility, the intellectual liveliness, and "the logic of daring" described by the various theoreticians on whose work I have drawn, and the massive dislocations, waste, misery, and horrors endured in our century's migrations and mutilated lives. Yet it is no exaggeration to say that liberation as an intellectual mission, born in the resistance and opposition to the confinements and ravages of imperialism, has now shifted from the settled, established, and domesticated dynamics of culture to its un-housed, decentred, and exilic energies, energies whose incarnation today is the migrant, and whose consciousness is that of the intellectual and artist in exile, the political figure between domains, between forms, between homes, and between languages. From this perspective then all things are indeed counter, original, spare, strange. From this perspective also, one can see "the complete consort dancing together" contrapuntally. (Said, 1993, p. 403)

From such an accomplished musical performer and music critic as Said, these images have the resonance of authenticity. But Said understandably fears that there might be something Panglossian in his conclusion. Is it possible to imagine or even to describe, in the manner of Clifford Geertz's "thick" precision, a dance of starving and dispossessed peoples from Africa, Europe, and elsewhere moving rhythmically with intellectual theorists – dislocated or otherwise – to some contrapuntal music that intermixes modernist private pleasure with massive cultural guilt? Said has the audacity to confront the challenge of how the aesthetic and the political can possibly coexist. That was, however, also the project of Foucault, which Said now condemns, based on his reading of Foucault's unfinished *History of Sexuality*, as an extended glorification of the self, a stigma he labors hard to avoid himself.

Cultural and critical theory has not yet found a means of crossing the impasse or aporia that divides aesthetic pleasure from social responsibility, however determinedly it works to do so. Its determination has been to chart the impact of major disruptions in the discourse of culture and the ideological appropriation of the arts – such as Said's uncovering of traces of imperialism in nineteenth-century fiction and opera or Williams's project for registering the literary impact of the Industrial Revolution – while simultaneously being determined to work for cultural change, whether for the literary enfranchisement of the working class that Williams proposed, or for an understanding, at last, of the recurring consequences of the social disruptions created by the 1939–45 war, which continue to manifest themselves throughout the world. Cultural and critical theory will have done little if it fails to bring some renewed reflection – accompanied by informed action – to these continuing treats to the project of the enlightenment.

Reading

Adorno, Theodor, and Horkheimer, Max 1979: *Dialectic of Enlightenment*.
Baldick, Chris 1983: *The Social Mission of English Criticism*.
Bhabha, Homi K. 1994: *The Location of Culture*.
Blundell, Valda, Shepherd, John, and Taylor, Ian, eds 1993: *Relocating Cultural Studies: Developments in Theory and Research*.
Borges, Jorge Luis 1974: *Obras Completas*.
Derrida, Jacques 1976: *Of Grammatology*.
During, Simon, ed. 1993: *The Cultural Studies Reader*.
Eagleton, Terry 1993: *The Crisis of Contemporary Culture*.
Geertz, Clifford 1973 (*1993*): *The Interpretation of Cultures*.
——1989: *Works and Lives: The Anthropologist as Author*.

Goldberg, David Theo 1993: *Racist Culture: Philosophy and the Politics of Meaning*.

Greenblatt, Stephen 1980: *Renaissance Self-Fashioning*.

——ed. 1982: *The Forms of Power and the Power of Forms*.

——1985 (*1992*): "Invisible bullets: Renaissance authority and its subversion. *Henry IV* and *Henry V*."

Habermas, Jürgen 1987: *The Philosophical Discourse of Modernity*.

Hall, Stuart 1988: *The Hard Road to Renewal: Thatcherism and the Crisis of the Left*.

Inglis, Fred 1993: *Cultural Studies*.

Jayawardena, Kumari 1986: *Feminism and Nationalism in the Third World*.

Johnson, Richard 1984: *What Is Cultural Studies Anyway?*

Kroeber, A.L. and Kluckhohn, Clyde 1952: *Culture: A Critical Review of Concepts and Definitions*.

Macey, David 1993: *The Lives of Michel Foucault*.

Marx, Karl *1954*: *Capital: A Critique of Political Economy*.

——and Engels, Frederick *1968*: *Selected Works in One Volume*.

Mulhern, Francis 1979: *The Moment of "Scrutiny."*

Said, Edward 1993: *Culture and Imperialism*.

——1979: *Orientalism*.

Williams, Raymond 1958 (*1993*): *Culture & Society: Coleridge to Orwell*.

——1976 (*1988*): *Keywords*.

MICHAEL PAYNE

A

actant A structural unit of NARRATOLOGY proposed in GREIMAS (1966). Sentences have six actants,
comprising three BINARY OPPOSITIONS. Each pair
epitomizes a fundamental narrative element: sub-
ject/object refers to desire, sender/receiver to communication, and helper/opponent to secondary
assistance or interference. This structure is posited
as basic to all narrative.

Reading
Greimas, A.J. 1966: *Semantique Structurale.*
—— 1970: *Du Sens.*
—— 1973: "Les Actants, les acteurs et les figures."
                                        PAUL INNES

Adorno, Theodor W. (1903–69) German philosopher, musicologist and cultural critic. A prominent member of the FRANKFURT SCHOOL of critical
theorists. Alongside Husserl, HEIDEGGER, GADAMER,
and WITTGENSTEIN, Adorno is one of the most important German-language philosophers of the
century. The range and volume of his output is
enormous (Adorno, 1970b). It includes studies of
central figures in the German philosophical tradition
(HEGEL, Kierkegaard, Husserl, Heidegger), mono-
graphs and essays on composers (Wagner, Mahler,
Schoenberg, Stravinsky, Berg), four volumes of
LITERARY CRITICISM, a variety of sociological writings, and numerous essays and fragments of cultural
criticism. Most significant, however, are three works
of outstanding philosophical originality: *Dialectic
of Enlightenment* (1944), cowritten with HORK-
HEIMER, *Negative Dialectics* (1966) and the posthumously published *Aesthetic Theory* (1970a).

Son of an assimilated Jewish wine merchant and
a Corsican Catholic mother, who was a professional
singer, Adorno's early years were comfortable and
precocious. Whereas BENJAMIN's childhood provided him with a model of the way frustration gives
rise to the power of the wish, Adorno's seems to
have furnished him with an experience of fulfillment
against which to measure the privations of later
life. (Symptomatically, perhaps, Adorno was his

mother's name. He exchanged it for his patro-
nymic Wiesengrund in the late 1930s.)

Adorno came to both music and philosophy young.
Having trained in piano as a child, and acquired
a doctorate (on Husserl's phenomenology) by the
age of 21, he studied composition for two years in
Vienna as a student of Alban Berg, before returning to Frankfurt to prepare his *Habilitationsschrift*
(the thesis required for a tenured position in a
German university) on "The concept of the unconscious in the transcendental theory of the mind"
(1927). This ambitious attempt at an unorthodox
NEO-KANTIAN reading of FREUD, with Marxist
conclusions, was unsuccessful in gaining Adorno
the right to teach, but it indicates the scope of his
interests at the time.

In 1928 he became the editor of the Viennese
musical journal *Anbruch*, and turned to a study of
Kierkegaard for a fresh attempt at his *Habilitation*.
Along with this study of Kierkegaard (Adorno,
1933), which was published in Germany on the
day Hitler came to power, two other early (posthumously published) pieces stand out as representative statements of Adorno's project: "The actuality
of philosophy," his inaugural lecture at the University of Frankfurt, and "The idea of natural history,"
a talk to the Frankfurt branch of the Kant Society
(Adorno, 1931; 1932). All three are characterized
by the methodological influence of Benjamin's
Origin of German Tragic Drama (1928a), hostility
to Heidegger's EXISTENTIALISM (which had already
achieved considerable impact by the early 1930s),
and a stylistic debt to Schoenberg's compositional
technique – features which Adorno's writings retained, in one way or another, to the end.

Adorno's philosophical position developed significantly during his period of exile from Germany
(1934–50), initially in Oxford, then later, along
with the rest of the Frankfurt school in the United
States; in part as a result of his collaboration with
Horkheimer, in part as a consequence of his ongoing
debate with Benjamin, which continued, internalized, long after the latter's death. Yet the broad

parameters of his thought remained remarkably stable. They may be summarized as follows: interrogation of the *possibility and form of philosophy* after the critique of idealism (the recognition of the insufficiency of thought to grasp "the totality of the real"); insistence on the historical character of philosophies as *idealized reflections of the logic of social forms*; preoccupation with the constitutive *separation of the enlightenment conception of "reason" from the sensuous particularity of the aesthetic*, and its deleterious effects on the formation of subjectivity.

At the centre of each lies a tension between the immanence of critique and the aspiration to transcendence inherent in the universality of the concept of reason. Adorno's overriding goal was the productive maintenance of this tension, in the exposition of cultural practices and products as manifestations of an historical reason. His means was a renewal of dialectical thought in the wake of the regression of the Marxist critique of Hegel, back into the sclerotic form of the system it had set out to explode.

To begin with, Adorno adopted an essentially hermeneutical model of philosophy as interpretation, derived from Benjamin's appropriation of the early German Romantics' conception of criticism. However, this was soon replaced with his own distinctive notion of philosophy as a particular kind of experience: "second reflection" or reflection upon the (reflective) relationship between subject and object constitutive of other types of experience. Like the concept of NEGATIVE DIALECTICS to which it gave rise, this idea may be viewed as a compromise formation midway between the thought of KANT and Hegel.

Philosophy aspires to the standpoint of the transcendental, the unconditioned, yet it exists only in historically specific and thus socially restricted forms. If it is to be true to itself, it must incorporate a consciousness of its own limitations into its reflections on other forms of experience. It must combat the delusion of an achieved universality, without falling back into an affirmation of the merely existent. This is the trick of a negative dialectics: to refuse to foreclose the endless movement of reflection between the universality of reason and the particularity of experience, whereby each corrects the one-sidedness of the other and renders it determinate in its historically specific form.

Adorno thus combines a Kantian emphasis on the *limits* of reason with Hegel's sense of dialectical reflection as *absolute productivity*. The difference from Hegel is that the absolute is never achieved.

It is the speculative horizon of all thought concerned with truth (as opposed to mere knowledge, which is the business of science), and as such is constitutive of philosophical experience. Yet as soon as it is given a positive charcterization, it is falsified. This is the meaning of two of Adorno's best-known aphorisms: "The whole is the untrue" (Adorno, 1951) and "Universal history must be constructed and denied" (Adorno, 1966).

In line with these ideas, Adorno's output may be divided into three basic kinds: social critiques of philosophies, philosophical criticism of culture, and more purely philosophical works in which the theoretical terms of the other writings are expounded in their own right. It is for his cultural criticism that Adorno is justly most famous. Yet this is more or less unintelligible without a sense of its philosophical rationale. The absence of such a sense has produced a grossly distorted image of Adorno's CULTURAL THEORY in English–language media studies and CULTURAL STUDIES to date, and precluded a productive engagement with it from within these disciplines. For them, it is simply another version of the pessimistic elitism of the mandarin defense of HIGH CULTURE (and its aspiration to a transcendent truth) against its "contamination" by mass culture.

Yet this is to overlook the fundamental principle of Adorno's cultural criticism: namely, that the "high" and the "low" are complementary parts of a larger whole. As Adorno put it in a letter to Benjamin: they are "torn halves of an integral freedom to which however they do not add up." Both, he argued, "bear the stigmata of capitalism" and both "contain elements of change." He thought it romantic to sacrifice one to the other, since it is "the division itself" which is the truth (Adorno, 1936).

However, within this framework, there is no doubt that Adorno himself had considerably more sympathy for the modernist avant-garde than he did for that part of the truth embodied in its mass-cultural other. He saw the former as guided by a moment of artistic autonomy (and hence as potentially critical of the existing state of affairs), while the latter was too dependent on preestablished conditions of reception to have more than a passive relationship to truth. This opposition is most notoriously summed up in the contrast between Adorno's intellectual enthusiasm for Schoenberg's "new music" and his brutal dimissal of jazz (Adorno, 1955).

Of particular note are the different ways in which the commodification of culture is taken to affect the two domains. In Schoenberg's case, the status of the music as a commodity is understood to be resisted internally, by the music itself. Its social form is incorporated into the musical materials, and critically reflected through its MEDIATION with the history of music, to which the music consequently contributes something new. Commodification is a part of what the music is *about*. In the case of jazz, on the other hand, the commodity form is taken to dominate the musical form, which provides its listeners with "a few simple recipes," gratifying a conformist desire for the reproduction of the familiar. In neither case is the criterion of judgment the affirmation of CULTURE (*Kultur*) as a spiritual VALUE. Rather, it is the capacity of the work to criticize the existing state of society. In this respect, the writings on jazz may be accused of failing to live up to Adorno's own model of *dialectical* criticism.

Adorno's cultural writings are distinctive in treating what is often thought of as "popular" culture as a product of the CULTURE INDUSTRIES. "Mass" culture is conceived as an industrial product, central to the ideological manipulation of desire and need. This raises the question of Adorno's relationships to MARXISM and PSYCHOANALYSIS.

On the one hand, in part because of his technical musicological knowledge, Adorno is probably the most important philosopher of musical modernism; on the other, he is the theorist who has most directly and consistently applied MARX's political economy to the analysis of cultural form. Marxist theory played two main roles in Adorno's work. It provided him with a materialist critique of traditional philosophy as a realm of alienated universality or "bad" abstraction, and it endowed him (via LUKÁCS) with the concept of REIFICATION – the development of an aspect of Marx's account of commodity fetishisms. (In commodity fetishism, the commodity is mystified by taking on attributes which properly belong to people. In reification, relations between people assume the form of relations between things.)

Adorno interpreted Marx's theory of value as a sociology of cultural form. Later (Adorno and Horkheimer, 1944), utilizing elements of NIETZSCHE's anthropology, he extended this reading into a critique of the structure of equivalence inherent in thought itself. The relationship of exchange between commodities, whereby each is reduced to its equivalent value (socially necessary labour time) becomes the interpretative model for the communicative dimension of instrumental reason, whereby each object is reduced to an common set of abstract properties (pragmatically defined by the interest of self-preservation). Adorno called this form of thought *identity-thinking*, in contrast to the nonidentity of negative dialectics.

Adorno's Marxism is thus at once apparently orthodox in its assertion of the law of value, yet radically heterodox in its allegorical expansion of its scope to cover the totality of human relations across the whole of human history. (For Marx, it applied only to the capitalist mode of production.) Originally developed by Lukács to explain the barriers to the emergence of a revolutionary subjectivity, at a particular stage of capitalist development, reification becomes descriptive of a permanent feature of the human condition, so far. This process reaches its apogee in the thesis of the "totally administered society," a nightmare scenario provocatively sketched by Adorno and Horkheimer as a warning of the developmental tendencies of capitalist and state socialist societies alike in the postwar period. (The thesis was popularized in the 1960s by MARCUSE in *One-Dimensional Man* (Marcuse, 1964).)

Abstracted from the broader context of Marxist theory (and particularly from its account of class relations, which Adorno considered empirically outdated) and generalized, the idea of reification has more in common with a paranoid version of Max WEBER's "iron cage" of societal rationalization than anything recognizably Marxist, although it does resonate with a certain Trotskyist hostility to bureaucracy. (Adorno shared an extremely hostile attitude to developments in the Soviet Union.) Adorno's use of psychoanalytic concepts is similarly unorthodox, yet also immensely suggestive.

Following the pioneering early work of Eric Fromm (1932), psychoanalytical concepts are transferred from the level of the individual to the domain of the social and historical, in a number of different ways. Sometimes the transference is allegorical – in the characterization of fascism as the "revenge of repressed nature," for example. Elsewhere it is more systematic, such as in the large collective empirical study *The Authoritarian Personality* (Adorno et al., 1950), although this work, through which Adorno was known in the English-speaking world until the late 1960s, is, ironically, methodologically extemely atypical of his thought.

Adorno's more grandiose historico-philosophical speculations were the product of his collaboration with Horkheimer: the "shared philosophy" to which he so often referred. They are highly ambiguous, for if they are read in the context of Adorno's prohibition on positive totalizations, either they violate it or they must be interpreted in another, more negative way: as provocations, perhaps, stylistically deliberate exaggerations. ("Only the exaggerations are true" is another of Adorno's well-known aphorisms about PSYCHOANALYSIS.) All of Adorno's writings display an acute sensitivity to the question of philosophical language. In this respect, it is *Minima Moralia: Reflections from Damaged Life* (1951), more of a cross between Friedrich Schlegel's *Philosophical Fragments* and Benjamin's *One-Way Street* (1928) than anything like a work in the philosophy of history, which is his most characteristic work.

Attacked from a variety of positions since the late 1960s for their pessimistic attitude to political change, and their rigorous theoretical negativity, Adorno's writings have recently been the object of a revived interest. This has mainly concerned the rich theoretical detail of Adorno's AESTHETICS, but the advent of POSTSTRUCTURALISM has provided a broader context for the reconsideration of Adorno's place in the history of philosophy. The relevance of his work to current debates in both philosophical and cultural theory remains a heated issue.

Reading

Adorno, Theodor W. 1951 (*1978*): *Minima Moralia. Reflections from Damaged Life.*
—— 1955 (*1982*): *Prisms.*
—— 1966 (*1990*): *Negative Dialectics.*
—— 1970a (*1984*): *Aesthetic Theory.*
—— 1991: *The Culture Industry: Selected Essays on Mass Culture.*
Adorno, Theodor W. and Horkheimer, Max 1944 (*1979*): *Dialectic of Enlightenment.*
Buck-Morss, Susan 1977: *The Origin of Negative Dialectics: Theodor W. Adorno, Walter Benjamin, and the Frankfurt Institute.*
Jameson, Frederic 1990: *Late Marxism: Adorno, or, The Persistence of Dialectic.*
Jay, Martin 1984a: *Adorno.*
Roberts, David 1991: *Art and Enlightenment: Aesthetic Theory After Adorno.*
Rose, Gillian 1978: *The Melancholy Science: An Introduction to the Thought of Theodor W. Adorno.*
Zuidervaart, Lambert 1991: *Adorno's Aesthetic Theory: The Redemption of Illusion.*

PETER OSBORNE

aesthetic, black *See* BLACK AESTHETIC

aesthetics The reflection on art and beauty is allegedly to be found in several different cultures at several different periods. The philosophical sophistication of such reflection in Ancient Greece is attested by Plato's *Hippias Major* and Aristotle's *Poetics*, which were formative texts for the Western tradition, but until very recently there was nothing in this tradition comparable with the level of Chinese reflection on painting reached in a text such as Chang Yen-yüan's ninth-century *Li-Tai Ming-hua Chi* (*Record of Famous Paintings*). Yet it would be extremely imprudent to collect these and other examples of reflection on art and beauty under the title of "aesthetics." The latter is not only of modern origin, but its preoccupations, direction of analysis, and consequently its internal system of division and classification are specifically European and should not be applied to either premodern or non-European materials.

The term is first used in connection with art and beauty by the German rationalist philosopher Alexander Gottlieb Baumgarten in his *Reflections on Poetry* (1735) and developed subsequently in his *Aesthetica* (1750–8). In the former Baumgarten introduced aesthetics at the very end of his analysis, referring to the Greek origins of the term in the contrast between *aestheta* or "things perceived" and *noeta* or "things known." The reasons for coining the new term were twofold. Baumgarten was a follower of the German rationalist philosopher Christian Wolff, and was responding to two problems in the Wolffian philosophy. The first was the place of ART within a rational system of philosophy; the second the relationship between reason and sensibility. He began writing the *Reflections* in the form of a commentary on Horace's *Ars Poetica* in order to solve the first problem, but realized in the course of composition that the two problems were related: beauty was none other than rational perfection expressed in sensuous form. The outcome in both the *Reflections* and the *Aesthetica* was a systematically equivocal definition of aesthetics as, on the one hand, a doctrine of sensibility, and on the other, a philosophy of art.

The equivocation persists in KANT's extremely influential use of the term: in the *Critique of Pure Reason* (1781) aesthetic refers to the analysis of sensibility and the forms of intuition space and time; yet in the *Critique of Judgement* (1790) it refers to the philosophical analysis of beauty. Kant's analysis in the latter text, seen by many as inaugurating modern European aesthetics, may be read in two ways. In the first reading, Kant presents a justification of the universality and necessity of aesthetic judgment, one concerned largely with the reception of art, but with hints of an account of its production in the discussion of "genius." In the second reading, however, Kant is seen as critically undermining the dominant, modern philosophical DISCOURSES on beauty and art – Baumgarten's "aesthetics" and the theory of "taste" – and leaving the outcome open, content to point to the paradoxes which inevitably beset modern philosophical reflection upon art and beauty.

At stake in the two readings of Kant is nothing less than the validity of the aesthetic form of reflection on art outside of the temporally and geographically specific confines of the culture from which it emerged. The first reading accepts that aesthetic judgments may be universally and necessarily valid, while the second is skeptical of any such claim. The latter view suggests that aesthetics as the philosophical discourse on art and beauty is inseparable from a system of culturally specific oppositions, of which the most significant are "sense and reason," "matter and form," "spirit and letter," "expression and expressed," "pleasure and finality," and "freedom and necessity." On this view aesthetics as a discourse on art and beauty remains firmly within the parameters of these oppositions, however ingeniously they may be refined or developed.

For this reason critics of aesthetics maintain that it should not uncritically be extended to the works of art and criticism of other cultures and periods. On this view, to speak of "medieval aesthetics" or the "aesthetics of Japanese calligraphy" is to subordinate these discourses and objects to a modern, Western European SYSTEM of values. It is of course possible to apply the aesthetic distinctions of "matter and form" or "sense and reason" to Tang dynasty painting or to Chang Yen-yüan's treatise, but only at the risk of losing much of its significance in the course of translation into the terms of aesthetics. For this reason twentieth-century meditations on art such as those of HEIDEGGER in his "Dialogue of language" and Beckett in "Three dialogues" choose deliberately to suspend the received framework of aesthetic oppositions and cautiously to develop new ways for thinking about art and beauty.

Reading
Benjamin, Andrew and Osborne Peter 1991: *Thinking Art: Beyond Traditional Aesthetics.*

Caygill, Howard 1989: *Art of Judgement.*
Eagleton, Terry 1990: *The Ideology of the Aesthetic.*
GREGORY ELLIOTT

affective fallacy   A term central to NEW CRITICISM, which derives from the title of an essay by W.K. Wimsatt and Monroe C. Beardsley, "The affective fallacy" (1949). The essay seeks to promote an "objective criticism" in which attention is directed exclusively to the artifact itself. Its purported "classical objectivity" (as against "romantic reader psychology") concerns itself with giving an account of the poem (the New Critics tend to privilege POETRY in their work, but the concept is equally applicable to other genres) as the cause of an emotion, rather than of the emotion expressed or effected by the poem.

Reading
Wimsatt, W.K. and Beardsley, Monroe C. 1949 (*1954*): "The affective fallacy."
PETER WIDDOWSON

African philosophy   The qualification of philosophy as "African" is consistent with the custom of naming philosophical traditions and practices according to their cultural, ethnic, national, or merely geographic origins, thus we have "American philosophy," "Jewish philosophy" "British philosophy," "German philosophy," or "French philosophy." Following Vincent Descombes (1980) who defines "contemporary French philosophy" as "coincident with the sum of the discourses elaborated in France and considered by the public of today as philosophical," African philosophy may be said to consist of all intellectual and discursive productions elaborated in Africa and considered "philosophical" by today's public. But this imitative definition fails to capture the historical, political, and cultural contradictions and complexities which animate the historical dynamics of "African philosophy" as an academic and professional tradition.

For example, when one attempts to extend the meaning of the qualifier "African" beyond the scope of its geographical meaning, it becomes notoriously difficult to define what kind of philosophical production is "African" or not. If the designation "African philosophy" is meant to highlight the ethnic/cultural origin of the philosophy in question, then should one not speak of African *philosophies* rather than philosophy in the singular, since Africa is made up of markedly diverse ethnic/cultural sources/traditions that constitute the philosophic originations? Or is the African identity of a philosopher – irrespective of method or content of her/his philosophy – necessary and/or sufficient to warrant the qualification of such philosophy as belonging to the African tradition? What are the credentials of an intellectual work that would be simultaneously "philosophy" and "African?"

Since the end of the 1939–45 war attempts by African (and non-African) philosophers to answer the above questions have generated debates that dominate contemporary discussions on African philosophy. Some thinkers have sought to write the history of African philosophy by appealing to the Egyptian origins of Western philosophy, and then arguing that ancient Egyptian philosophy and science represent the classical flourishing of civilizations that originated and remained influential in "the Heart of Negro lands" (the Nubia, Galla, Zimbabwe, Somalia, etc.) (Diop, 1974). In addition to Chiek Anta Diop, other scholars who take this "ancient Egypt" route in the (re)construction of the history of African philosophy include Theophilus Obenga (1973; 1990), Osabutey (1936), G. James (1954), and Henry Olela (1980), and their works have found considerable support from Martin Bernal's influential volumes *The Black Athena* (1987–). Other philosophers such as Lacinay Keita, however, (re)construct a history of African philosophy by tracing/documenting the trajectory of philosophical activities from ancient and medieval Islamic north Africa (Timbuktu, Songhai, the Ghana empire, and the Sudanic states of central Africa). It is pointed out that the north African–Arab Islamic scholarship of about the seventh century AD and onwards was instrumental in the translation and transmission of Greek philosophy, especially the "pagan" Aristotle and his (re)introduction into the European philosophical world. (In general, the contribution of the Arab philosophers such as Avicenna and Averroes are also highlighted in this connection.) For example, the efforts of Claude Sumner to translate, document, and analyze the works of the sixteenth-century Abyssinian rationalist philosopher Zär'a Ya'eqob (1599–1692), Wäldä Heywat, and Skendes, and the resurgent interests in the translation and analysis of the writings of William Amo, a Ghanaian philosopher who taught at the universities of Halle, Wittenberg, and Jena in eighteenth-century Germany, are PARADIGMatic of the quest for historical reconstruction of past philosophical enterprises in Africa.

Yet there is no disputing the fact that the single most important impetus that drives the contemporary field of African philosophy as a disciplinary and professional–academic enterprise goes beyond the technical desire to ascertain its Egyptian, Arab, or Abyssinian origins; rather, this motive must be traced to an experience of crisis. The brutal encounter of the African world with European modernity constitutes a crisis of indescribable proportions whose tragic reality and history is incarnated and marked in the institutions of slavery, colonialism, and the ideologies of European cultural and racial superiority.

Natural historians, anthropologists, and philosophers of the European ENLIGHTENMENT speculated widely on the nature of the African "mind" which they generally agreed was "magical," "mystical," "irrational," and therefore "inferior." For example, the philosophers Hume, KANT, and HEGEL each depicted the African world as "dark," "savage," primitive," etc. The institution of anthropology as a scientific discipline subsequently lent scientific respectability to these speculations, and so we have Lévy-Bruhl and Evans-Pritchard producing works that described the African mind as either prelogical or "mystical" (as opposed to "rational"). These anthropological productions, often commissioned after the military invasion of an African territory or after a rebellion against occupying European powers (Asad, 1973; Achebe, 1988), were intended to provide the European administrations and missionary cultural workers with information about the "primitive" African mind, so that they could properly inculcate into the African conscience European values and cultural attitudes. It is within this context that the significance of Father Placide Tempels's controversial book, *Bantu Philosophy* (1945), must be understood. As stated by the author, the aim of the book is to teach the colonialists the cultural "philosophy," or more strictly, the world view and the belief systems of the African in order that the European evangelization and "civilizatory" work will succeed, and succeed in a self-sustaining manner. Tempels's book is therefore predominantly a work of exposition of the ontological systems of the Baluba, an ethnic group in Zaire where Tempels, a Belgian Franciscan missionary, worked for many years. Tempels believed that the Baluba–African ontology grounds and regulates the daily ethical, political, and economic existence of the African, and therefore in order to elevate the "pagan" existence of the African to "civilization," one must work through this ontological system which grounds the existential interiority of the Bantu.

However, the historical significance of Tempels's work lies in the author's explicit use of the term "philosophy" in the title of the book to designate an intellectual product associated with the African, in this case the Bantu of Zaire. Whereas the anthropologist spoke of savage "mentality" or primitive "thought," Tempels spoke of *philosophy*; and this designation is crucial because philosophy, to the Western mind, is the honorific term symbolizing the highest exercise of the faculty of reason. To acknowledge the existence of an African philosophy, then, is to acknowledge the existence of African reason, and hence African humanity. This notion flies in the face of the entire edifice of colonialism which was built precisely on the negation of this possibility. The African is subhuman because s/he is "irrational," "prelogical," etc., and therefore can never produce philosophy: hence, the revolutionary potential of *Bantu Philosophy*.

Tempels's book, then, was fruitfully ambiguous. The author intended it to be a "handbook" for the missionary cultural worker: a plea to the European colonialist administrator or missionary that the African's "philosophy" and culture ought to be understood and respected in order for the "civilizing" mission to succeed. However, the ambiguous yet fruitful conjunction of "philosophy" as an implicit ontological system which underlies and sustains an African communal world view, and the honorific notion of "philosophy" as the highest rational (human) achievement was not lost on the emerging African intelligentsia. Tempels's book collapsed the ideological scaffold that had supported racism and colonialism, and the book became for these Africans a manual for revolt.

With the discovery in Africa of "Bantu philosophy," and the emergence in the United States of the Harlem Renaissance – with its philosophers and intellectuals, Alain Locke, Claude McKay, W.E.B. Dubois and others – where Africans in the diaspora were already engaged in the critique of African colonialism and the racism of the New World, a third movement in the history of African philosophy was born: Négritude. As a literary and cultural/philosophical movement originated in Paris by African and Afro-Caribbean students, Négritude, through Aimé Césaire and Leopold Sedar Senghor among others, found in *Bantu Philosophy* and in the pluralist anthropologies of Frobenius, Herskovits, and Delafosse sympathetic arguments to show that

Africa has "philosophy." Each of the three movements mentioned above prompted reexaminations of various European theorizings about Africa and the African "mind," such as those of Hume, Kant, Hegel and evolutionist anthropology. The idea of "African philosophy" as a field of inquiry thus has its contemporary roots in the effort of African thinkers to examine, question, and contest identities imposed upon them by Europeans; and the claims and counterclaims, justifications, and ALIENATIONS that characterize such contests indelibly mark the discipline.

Two of the earliest strands that developed out of this African attempt were both a counter DISCOURSE and a theoretical articulation and (re)construction of a historical and cultural autonomy: the "ethnophilosophy" strand remained faithful to Tempels and continued the traditions of exposing and analyzing African world views to elicit and distill ontologies, ETHICS, metaphysics, political and aesthetic theories from the languages and other cultural institutions of the African peoples. Since the West deemed philosophy or the possession of philosophic traditions as a sign of the attainment of full humanity, it is no wonder that, in the face of the denigration of their humanity, the impulse of the Africans thinkers was to research, using phenomenologic and interpretative methods, their native traditions, customs, languages, etc. to show the "philosophicness" of these practices. African philosophy, in this sense, became the analysis of cultural/oral institutional and linguistic traditions, such as Alexis Kagame's *La Philosophie Bantoue–Rwandaise de l'Être* (1956) or Barry Hallen and J.O. Sodipo's "analytic experiments" in Yoruba philosophy (1986). Kwame Gyekye's *An Essay in African Philosophical Thought: The Akan Conceptual Scheme* (1987) and William Abraham's *The Mind of Africa* (1962), or the Reverend John Mibiti's popular *African Philosophy and Religions* (1992) may be classified as belonging to this ethnophilosophic strand.

The second strand, inspired more indirectly by Tempels's work, developed more overtly political, anti-colonial, and ideological tendencies. Freedom fighters and political leaders such as Nnamdi Azikiwe and Obafemi Awolowo in Nigeria, Julius Nyerere in Tanzania, Leopold Sedar Senghor in Senegal, Oginga Odinga in Kenya, Kenneth Kaunda in Zambia, and most of all, Kwame Nkrumah of Ghana each produced varying amounts of philosophical-political works that have recourse to resilient elements of native African cultural traditions. In traditions such as communalism, these leaders and thinkers endeavored to elicit and develop various forms of "African socialism" and ideological theories of cultural "authenticity" that would empower Africa to emancipate itself and build an autonomous future. Representative works in this area are Nyerere's *Ujamma: Essays On Socialism* (1968), Nkrumah's *Consciencism: Philosophy and Ideology for Decolonization and Development with Particular Reference to the African Revolution* (1964), or Senghor's three-volume *Liberté* (1964; 1971; and 1977). This trend in the development of African philosophy is called "political-ideological philosophy."

Tempels and ethnophilosophy, however, have always had their critics (such as Franz Crahay, Robin Horton, etc.); but especially since the mid-1970s in Africa, there has arisen a loose group of African philosophers, highly trained in the techniques of modern Western philosophy, usually in French and British universities, who designated themselves as "professional philosophers" and who constituted themselves as a group in/through their mutual opposition to the idea of philosophy propagated by Tempels and his disciples. Included in this group are Paulin Houtondji, Odera Oruka, Kwasi Wiredu, and Peter Bodunrin, although each brings specific emphasis and nuances to his critique of Tempels and/or ethnophilosophy. This "school" of African philosophy maintains that, although philosophy operates within/on a culture, it is a *universal, scientific* discipline/method of inquiry, so that to speak of "African" philosophy is simply to identify either the geographic or the authorial origin of that particular philosophical work. This group of self-designated "professional" philosophers accuses ethnophilosophy of failing to be a "strict" philosophy because it is *communal*, relies on *unwritten* sources, and, in fact, it is (premodern), *unscientific*. For Houtondji (1983), for example, philosophy is born only where there is (modern) science, and one cannot (yet) speak of "African science." Yet, Oruka, although himself one of the "professional" philosophers, rejects the negative connotations of some of these conditions, such as those ascribed to orality. One can say that Oruka's well-known University of Nairobi "Sage Philosophy Project" is a sustained attempt to overcome the critical questions of orality and collectivism of thought implied in the criticism of ethnophilosophy by producing named individuals who do philosophy in the oral tradition. (See Oruka's *Sage Philosophy:*

Indigenous Thinkers and Modern Debates in Philosophy, 1990.) The other members of the "professional" philosophy quartet, Wiredu and Bodurin, however, conceive of philosophy as a specifically modern (European) invention with a universal method which can be applied to the analysis and critique of African CULTURES. Wiredu, for example, demonstrates this in his *Philosophy in an African Culture* (1980).

Critical ethnophilosophy, as well as works in line with the modernist streak of the self-proclaimed "professional" philosophers, are flourishing in philosophy departments in Africa, and in North America, an emerging growth area in the field of African philosophy is in the critical–hermeneutic and deconstructive trends, where emphasis is brought to bear on the historical understanding and interpretation of the African colonial and postcolonial situation in conjunction with, or linked to the DECONSTRUCTION of the Western ideological and philosophic–epistemological CANONS that theorize the African out of reason and denigrate African humanity. In this deconstructive vein, works by V.Y. Mudimbe (1988), Tsenay Serequeberhan (1994), Anthony Appiah (1992), Lucius Outlaw (1987), Emmanuel Eze (1993), among others, challenge the longstanding exclusion of Africa, or more accurately, its inclusion as the negative "OTHER" of reason and the Western World in the mainstream traditions of modern European philosophy. Their philosophies, in conjunction with, for example, the feminist and other marginalized clusters of progressive critique and critical resistance, excavate and problematize the significance of RACE, GENDER, and other cultural embeddedness of philosophical practice which have been long ignored. For most in this group, the rereading and reinterpreting of the precocious works of radical African philosophers and thinkers such as Frantz Fanon, Amilcar Cabral, and Aimé Césaire yield the fruits of *rapprochement* between African and Afro-American philosophy, as evidenced in the growing interest in the concept of "Africa*na* philosophy" as an organizing notion for the constellation of the traditions of philosophy in Africa and the diaspora.

Reading

Appiah, Kwame Anthony 1992: *In My Father's House: Africa in the Philosophy of Culture.*
Bernal, Martin 1987: *The Black Athena: The Afroasiatic Roots of Classical Civilization.*
Cabral, Amilcar 1973: *Return to the Source: Selected Speeches of Amilcar Cabral.*

Césaire, Aimé 1972: *Discourse On Colonialism*.

Diop, C.A. 1974: *The African Origin of Civilization*.

Fanon, Frantz 1952 *(1989)*: *Black Skin, White Masks*.

Floistad, G., ed. 1987: *Contemporary Philosophy: A New Survey*.

Harris, Leonard, ed. 1983: *Philosophy Born of Struggle: Anthology of Afro-American Philosophy from 1917*.

Houtondji, Paulin 1983: *African Philosophy: Myth or Reality*.

Kagame, Alexis 1975: *La philosophie bantoue–rwandaise de l'être*.

Masolo, D.A. 1994: *African Philosophy in Search of Identity*.

Mudimbe, V.Y. 1988: *The Invention of African: Gnosis, Philosophy and the Order of Knowledge*.

Nkrumah, Kwame 1964: *Consciencism: Philosophy and Ideology for Decolonization and Development with Particular Reference to the African Revolution*.

Oruka, Odera 1990b: *Sage Philosophy: Indigenous Thinkers and Modern Debates about African Philosophy*.

Serequberhan, Tsenay 1994: *The Hermeneutics of African Philosophy: Horizon and Discourse*.

——ed. 1992: *African Philosophy: The Essential Reading*.

Tempels, Placide 1969: *Bantu Philosophy*.

Wiredu, Kwasi 1980: *Philosophy in an African Culture*.

EMMANUEL CHUKWUDI EZE

AIDS and literature   Since the mid-1980s, there has been an artistic response to the AIDS crisis which crosses various modes of literary production in both the Western and non-Western worlds. Though many recent artistic endeavors reflect the changing ways in which we view sex and sexuality, a specific literary response addresses AIDS and its various representations. It is important to note that it is impossible and undesirable to create a "coherent" body of AIDS literature; the response is too varied. Yet, with such a disclaimer in mind, this entry will attempt to point out some of the literature and the critical work emerging in response to the disease, invariably making such generalizations as one desires to avoid.

In the West, the literary response to AIDS has largely taken the form of nonfiction and fiction writings (short stories, novels, and POETRY), while in non-Western countries, the response is more closely associated with performance-oriented forms of DISCOURSE. These responses to the AIDS crisis, in both the West and non-Western worlds, are intimately connected with theater and other means of "modern" representation, such as film, television, newspapers, magazines, informational pamphlets and, most recently, electronic newsgroups.

This entry will focus solely on the nonfiction and fiction WRITINGS, excluding drama, since it is too large a topic to approach here. However, in limiting the focus to written creative works, the intent is not to imply that such writings exist outside the sphere of other AIDS DISCOURSES, such as the medical research and media coverage of the disease or the academic sociological writings of activists such as Cindy Patton and Douglas Crimp. The writings discussed here are inevitably connected with such work; though television movies on AIDS such as *An Early Frost* or various brochures on "safe sex" are not explicitly discussed, such forms of AIDS representations inform and overlap in various ways with fiction and nonfiction writings. The interdisciplinary nature of AIDS discourse cannot be ignored when considering AIDS-related literature.

In Western countries, communities of gay men were among the most traumatized at the beginning of the crisis; therefore much of the writing, both fiction and nonfiction, is written by gay male authors, many of whom are suffering from AIDS or HIV infection. However, as Judith Lawrence Pastore (1993) points out, it is inaccurate to assume that literature dealing with AIDS is solely a gay male undertaking. For example, one of the first stories to deal with AIDS in a mainstream publication is Susan Sontag's 1986 short story "The way we live now." In the realm of nonfiction, some of the earliest writings are memoirs by mothers who have lost their sons, as well as wives coping with husbands dying from AIDS.

In recent years, there has emerged a substantial body of popular AIDS writing from an openly gay point of view. Writers such as David Feinberg, Sarah Schulman, and Thom Gunn, as well as younger writers whose work is published in compilations, are approaching AIDS with a sense of honesty and power, foregrounding vital issues of sexuality and GENDER during the time of an epidemic. The idea that AIDS is strictly a "gay disease" has led some recent gay male writers, such as Peter Cameron, to eschew the topic. Yet the absence of AIDS from some recent gay fiction does not necessarily connote indifference. Some critics feel that such an absence disrupts the representation of gay as a "high risk" group. In showing that there are only "high risk" behaviors, such absence prevents marginalization of gays. However, others feel the absence of any discussion of AIDS ultimately diminishes the work since it is not fully expressive of modern gay life. Regardless, AIDS has inevitably changed the way that gay literature and, quite possibly, all literature is written and read.

In terms of classification and Genre, literature dealing with AIDS can be seen as a "literature of crisis," a term denoting works emerging from moments of historical crises, such as the writings of Jews during the Holocaust as well as Afro-Americans during slavery. Emmanuel S. Nelson (1992) wishes to resist such comparisons; he notes that though there are "some formal similarities, ideological affinities, and spiritual connections among" other writings produced during historical moments of crises, there is a "uniqueness [in] the literature of AIDS" (p. 3). AIDS and its textual representations exist in a sphere of overlapping medical, social, and literary discourses associated mainly with those on the margins (primarily gays, intravenous drug users, and sex workers). This marginalized status makes it problematic to place a strict label such as "literature of crisis" on this body of literature.

This ambiguity in classification extends to placing such writings in a historical genre. Several essays collected in Nelson's book address the topic of genre. Laurel Brodsley finds Daniel Defoe's seventeenth-century novel *The Journal of the Plague Year* a suitable Paradigm for recent nonfiction works like Randy Shilts's *And the Band Played On* and Paul Monette's *Borrowed Time*, while Gregory Woods contextualizes poetry dealing with AIDS in the broader elegiac tradition of English poetry. However, critics such as Joseph Dewey problematize such stable models for the literature(s) of AIDS, since such genres as plague literature or elegies are anachronistic to the postmodern reality of AIDS and do not encompass the spirit of activist resistance present in such writings. Robert Franke (1993) feels that the characteristics of both fiction and nonfiction AIDS writing suggests the development of a new genre, one which acknowledges the failure of modern science to support the complex realities of human experience.

There is also much discussion on the political component necessary in literature addressing AIDS. Pastore assumes that "literary AIDS" must have clear-cut pedagogical goals, "to dispel unwarranted fears . . . [and] overcome homophobia" (pp. 3–4). Such politicized goals are indeed critical and addressed in many AIDS writings, emerging in large part from the activism with which many of these writers are concerned. However, such a limited view of literature dealing with AIDS dismisses the multifaceted levels on which such writings operate to merely a political and educational one; aesthetic

issues explored by recent writers are devalued in such a framework if such experimentation is not viewed as politically expedient. Such issues, as well as related questions like whether writings about AIDS have the ability to create compassion and understanding about the disease in its readers, remain highly debatable.

The magnitude of the literary response to AIDS makes it a difficult task to address in any significant capacity. Therefore, this overview inevitably leaves out critical issues and contributions of important writers. The literatures of AIDS are both omnipresent and unrecognizable in various degrees. In focusing on one aspect of the response, this entry cannot help but encounter the other fields responding to AIDS. Any study attempting an understanding of AIDS writing must recognize the impact of the media and the medical field in our understanding of this disease. Writing AIDS is much more than intertextual; it is a phenomenon of Culture situated in an overlapping area of discourse which is not merely a site of academic study, but rather a matter of life and death.

Reading

Avena, Thomas, ed. 1994: *Life Sentence: Writers, Artists, and AIDS*.
Cameron, Peter 1994: *The Weekend*.
Collard, Cyril 1989 (*1993*): *Savage Nights*.
Franke, Robert G. 1993: "Beyond good doctor, bad doctor: AIDS fiction and biography as a developing genre."
Gunn, Thom 1992: *The Man with Night Sweats*.
Klusacek, Allan, and Morrison, Ken, eds 1993: *A Leap in the Dark: AIDS, Art and Contemporary Culture*.
Miller, Timothy F. and Poirier, Suzanne, eds 1993: *Writing AIDS: Gay Literature, Language and Analysis*.
Monette, Paul 1988: *Borrowed Time: An AIDS Memoir*.
Nelson, Emmanuel S., ed. 1992: *AIDS: The Literary Response*.
Pastore, Judith Laurence, ed. 1993: *Confronting AIDS through Literature: The Responsibilities of Representation*.
Patton, Cindy 1990: *Inventing AIDS*.
Peck, Dale 1993: *Martin and John*.
Preston, John, ed. 1989: *Personal Dispatches: Writers Confront AIDS*.
Schulman, Sarah 1990: *People in Trouble*.
Shilts, Randy 1987: *And the Band Played On: Politics, People and the AIDS Epidemic*.
Sontag, Susan 1986 (*1988*): "The way we live now."
                                        KENNETH J. URBAN

alienation   As defined by Marx in the *Economic and Philosophical Manuscripts* (1844), alienation is a specific historical condition in which man experiences a separation from nature, other human beings, and especially the products of his labor. Since man creates himself through labor, all of these forms of alienation imply an alienation of man from himself. For HEGEL, alienation was a philosophical concept expressing one aspect of the process of self-objectification: in the dialectical process, Spirit objectified itself in nature (a stage in which it was alienated from itself) and then returned to itself. Marx regards alienation as a product of the evolution of division of labor, private property, and the state: when these phenomena reach an advanced stage, as in capitalist society, the individual experiences the entire objective world as a conglomeration of alien forces standing over and above him. In this sense, alienation can only be overcome by the revolutionary abolition of the economic system based on private property.

Alienation is also a central concept in sociology, a centrality deriving in part from Max Weber's recognition of the individual's feeling of helplessness in a "disenchanted" world governed by rational, bureacratic, and impersonal institutions. Existentialists, notably HEIDEGGER and SARTRE, have also centralized this concept, viewing it not as the symptom of given historical configurations but as a defining condition of existence. The concept of alienation has also reverberated widely through the various branches of psychology.

See also ESTRANGEMENT.

Reading
Geyer, R.F. 1992: *Alienation, Society and the Individual.*
Israel, J. 1971: *Alienation, from Marx to Modern Sociology.*
Meszaros, I. 1970: *Marx's Theory of Alienation.*
Schweitzer, D. and Geyer, R.F., eds 1989: *Alienation Theories and Alienation Strategies.*

SUSAN R. SKAND

alienation effect (*Verfremdungseffekt*)   A term first used by the German Marxist playwright, dramaturge, poet, literary theorist, and political thinker Bertolt BRECHT, deployed in a variety of contexts to suggest the idea of a deliberate break with those traditional values (verisimilitude, unity of action, audience participation, tragic catharsis, the imaginative "suspension of disbelief," etc.) which Brecht saw as deeply bound up with the hegemony of bourgeois aesthetic, social, and political institutions. Hence – he argued – the need for a truly revolutionary theater that would exploit every means of disrupting and subverting such routine habits of response. These might include the introduction of strikingly anomalous or anachronistic details in

order to break the realist illusion; the use of conspicuous devices (for example, on-stage commentary or actors speaking "out of character") to similar defamiliarizing effect; the juxtaposition of incongruous styles – including elements of dance and song – to undermine the classical norms and precepts of genre identity; and the large-scale "reworking" (*Umfunktionierung*) of plays from the established repertoire, such as Brecht's treatment of *Coriolanus* as a commentary on moral and political issues raised by the East German workers' rising of 1953. It could also entail the staging of didactic "parables" (*Lehrstücke*) which presented these issues in a starkly paradoxical form, and which thus held out against the audience's so-called "natural" tendency to identify vicariously with characters perceived as tragic protagonists or victims of social injustice. Brecht's purpose was not (of course) to lessen our sense of such injustice but to jolt us into thinking about the events on stage in a more critical, more detached, and thus (potentially) more activist mode of concern.

See also DEFAMILIARIZATION; FORMALISM.

Reading
Benjamin, Walter 1973: *Understanding Brecht.*
Brecht, Bertolt 1978: *Brecht on Theatre.*
Willett, John 1984: *Brecht in Context.*

CHRISTOPHER NORRIS

Althusser, Louis   (1918–90)   French Communist philosopher. One of the most notable Marxist theoreticians of the postwar period, Althusser's comprehensive reconstruction of Marxist philosophy and social theory won him a large intellectual following throughout Western Europe and Latin America in the 1960s and 1970s.

In *For Marx* and *Reading "Capital"* (1965), Althusser and his collaborators (including Etienne BALIBAR and Pierre MACHEREY) subjected actually existing Marxism to swingeing critique on account of its alleged HEGELIANISM. According to Althusser, the seemingly antithetical traditions of orthodox MARXISM (Kautsky or Stalin) and Western Marxism (LUKÁCS or SARTRE) exhibited the common vice of HISTORICISM. Whether in the guise of economism or HUMANISM, both tendencies cancelled Marx's departure from the German idealism of his youth by construing historical materialism as a philosophy of history. As pseudo-materialist inversions of Hegelian theodicy, they each depicted human history as an expressive totality or process, with an origin, a center, a subject, and a goal. Economism – typical of Stalinist orthodoxy from the mid-1920s – constituted a technological DETERMINISM, positing a metanarrative of the advance of the productive forces towards an ineluctable communism. Humanism – characteristic of the anti-Stalinist reaction in the 1950s and 1960s – represented a teleological philosophical anthropology, projecting an odyssey of the human essence, from its ALIENATION in CLASS society to its reappropriation in a classless future. Althusser's objections were at once analytical and political: abstracting from the specificities of concrete historical conjunctures, all such schematism precluded the requisite comprehension – hence possible transformation – of them.

The Althusserian reformation – the professed "return to Marx" – encompassed three interdependent endeavors: (i) an epistemological history of the foundation and development of Marxism – in the first instance, by a rereading of MARX's own heterogeneous *oeuvre*; (ii) the elaboration of a historical epistemology which would identify the substance, and clarify the status, of Marx's "materialist conception of history"; and (iii) the renovation of HISTORICAL MATERIALISM as a nonhistoricist theory of modes of production and SOCIAL FORMATIONS.

The SYMPTOMATIC READING of Marx conducted by Althusser revolved around the postulate of a profound conceptual and epistemological discontinuity between the supposedly non-Marxist "early works" of 1840–4 and the unevenly Marxist texts of 1845–6 onwards. The "epistemological break" effected in *The German Ideology* (Marx and Engels, 1932) separated distinct and irreconcilable theoretical "problematics" – the one, tributary to left-Hegelianism, amounting to nothing more than the repetition of an ideological philosophy of history; the other, peculiar to Marx, summing up to nothing less than the initiation of the science of history. However, this "theoretical revolution" had merely been commenced by Marx. He had opened up the "continent of History" to scientific exploration – above all, in the three volumes of *Capital* – founding a research program which remained to be developed, not bequeathing a fixed doctrine which need only be quoted, by his successors.

The import of Althusser's interpretation was affirmation of the scientificity of historical materialism, and yet insistence upon its incompletion, not only as a consequence of the inevitable limitations of Marx's own achievement, but also as a normal correlate of its scientific status. Althusser

renounced the materialist metaphysic of the Second and Third Internationals, according to which Marxism was a self-sufficient cosmology or "world view," the accomplished science of anything, everything and nothing. Instead, he conceived historical materialism as a "finite" theory of history, in principle committed to incessant development and susceptible to recurrent rectification, which did not own exclusive rights to the production of objective knowledge of human phenomena. As Francis Mulhern (1994, p. 160) observes, "[t]he theoretical field within which [Althusser] situated Marx's science was ... the new 'quadrivium' of history, ethnology, psychoanalysis and linguistics, and their lingua franca, 'structuralism'. The pursuit of scientificity here meant the repudiation of intellectual autarky."

Variously indebted to Spinozist rationalism and French conventionalist philosophy of science, Althusserian epistemology therefore rejected the canonical "dialectical materialism" systematized by Stalin as the general science of the laws of nature, history, and thought. Althusser's alternative – the "theory of theoretical practice" – sought to secure the cognitive autonomy of the sciences against the intrusions of politics. At the same time, it wished to recognize their RELATIVE AUTONOMY as sociohistorical products. It did so by maintaining that any society was "a complex unity of 'social practice'," which could be divided into four practices: economic, political, ideological, and theoretical. Each possessed the transformative structure of the labor process as dissected by Marx, entailing the three "moments" of raw material, means of production, and product. Thus, the production of knowledge was the fruit of theoretical practice, comprising raw material in the form of existing facts and concepts; means of production in the shape of a problematic (or theoretical matrix); and products, knowledge(s).

Contrary to the "empiricist conception of knowledge," Althusser conceived the cognitive process – the production of concepts by means of concepts – as wholly *intra*-theoretical. Its starting point and end product were conceptual "objects of knowledge." Via the "theoretical object" (for example, "Fordism"), knowledge of a "real object" (for example, contemporary British capitalism) was appropriated in thought. The theory of theoretical practice aspired to be both a "materialism," accepting the primacy of objective reality, which existed independently of theories of it; and an antiempiricism, asserting the indispensability of theory as the discursive construction of that reality. Furthermore, it maintained that, once theoretical practices had crossed the threshold of scientificity, they required neither philosophical guarantees nor external confirmation of their status; they had their own criteria of verification.

The Althusserian reconstruction of historical materialism consisted of four main themes. The first was a recasting of the Marxist "dialectic." Althusser criticized the traditional interpretation of the Marx–Hegel relationship as the materialist "inversion" of an idealist construct. For him any such operation preserved the incorrigibly teleological character of the HEGELian dialectic. This was true, for example, of economism, wherein the contradiction between the forces and relations of production supplied the trans-historical efficient cause of a unilinear social evolution. Instead, Althusser postulated the OVER-DETERMINATION of any CONTRADICTION. Although hierarchically organized in a determinate (if variable) order, each of the multiple contradictions active in any society was internally marked by the others, which provided its "conditions of existence." Each was ineliminably real and effective, simultaneously determinant and determined. Political revolutions were therefore not the punctual effects of an economic contradiction that had reached its maturity, but the contingent results of the "condensation" of social contradictions in a "ruptural unity."

A complementary reconceptualization of social formations (societies) aimed to respect their constitutive complexity, by displacing the inherited BASE AND SUPERSTRUCTURE topography, and differentiating the Marxist totality from the Hegelian. Any SOCIAL FORMATION – feudal, capitalist, communist – was a unified but DECENTERED STRUCTURE: a "structure of structures," subsuming economic, political, and ideological "instances." The Marxist totality secreted no essence to be expressed nor center to be reflected. Its regional structures were not heteronomous – secondary phenomena subject to an economic first cause. Each of them enjoyed relative autonomy and "specific effectivity." They were not, however, independent, for they were governed by a "structural causality" whereby economic "determination in the last instance" operated through the permutation of "dominance" between the various structures in different social formations (in feudal societies, for example, the political is dominant; in capitalist, the economic).

The third component of the Althusserian recasting of historical materialism (largely elaborated by Balibar) bore upon a nonevolutionist theory of modes of production. Abandoning technological determinism, Balibar reconfigured modes of production as articulated – and not inherently contradictory – combinations of forces and relations of production, under the primacy of the latter. Consequently, they were not transient phenomena whose sequential rise and fall were determined by iron laws of history, but self-reproducing totalities. According to Balibar's account of the transition from one mode of production to another, the ultimate "motor of history" was the struggle between contending social classes.

Yet Marxism was not a HUMANISM. On Althusser's understanding of history, it was a "process without a subject," in which social structures had primacy over the human agents who were their "bearers." Individuals were individuated, constituted as social identities by and in IDEOLOGY, materialized in IDEOLOGICAL STATE APPARATUSES (for example, the family and schools), via the mechanism of INTERPELLATION (1984, pp. 1–60). Althusser's fourth contribution to historical materialism drew upon the psychoanalysis of Jacques LACAN to theorize ideology as the realm of the "imaginary." In it the real relations between subject and society were inverted, such that individuals lived those relations as if they were the "subjects of" them, rather than "subject to" them. Ideology was the set of representations of people's "imaginary relations" to their conditions of existence requisite for them to function as social agents in any conceivable society. There would be no end to ideology under Communism.

The Althusserian enterprise was one of remarkable scope and originality, seductively combining political radicalism – a quasi-Maoist stance to the left of mainstream Communism – and philosophical modernism – selective affinities with structuralism. It came as a liberation to a younger generation and defined the terms of Marxist debate for a period. This was because Althusser reclaimed historical materialism as an open, underdeveloped research program, which did not reduce social phenomena to economic epiphenomena, but promised to grasp them in their concrete specificity, as the "synthesis of many determinations." As commentators have demonstrated (Elliott, 1987; Mulhern, 1994), Althusserianism sponsored a mass of research and contributed to a series of intellectual initiatives (for example, the literary criticism of Terry EAGLETON, the work of the CENTRE FOR

CONTEMPORARY CULTURAL STUDIES, the film theory of SCREEN, or the socialist feminism of Juliet MITCHELL).

In jettisoning much of Marx, as well as his successors, however, Althusserianism represented an "imaginary Marxism" (a fact its author subsequently acknowledged (1992, p. 221)). Indeed, in retrospect it can be seen to have constituted a transitional theoretical formation, precariously poised between Marxism and POSTSTRUCTURALISM, one of whose unintended consequences was to facilitate a transfer of intellectual allegiances from the one to the other. The principal determinant of this process was political – the series of reverses experienced by the European Left in the 1970s, which induced a general decline in the reputation of Marxism. However, it possessed a theoretical rationale. For whilst Althusser's innovations were extremely powerful as critiques, problematizing basic assumptions of the Marxist tradition, they were vulnerable as solutions, inviting countercritiques which soon ensued (see Benton, 1984).

Thus, for example, the theory of theoretical practice was identified as an unstable compromise between rationalism and conventionalism, from which the indicated escape for many was perspectivism. Anti-humanism met with both philosophical and political objections to its supposed structural determinism (especially in Thompson, 1978), which rendered social change inconceivable and inexplicable. The theory of ideology was convicted of functionalism and residual economism. Relative autonomy was deconstructed as a contradiction in terms, paving the way for "post-Marxist" pluralism.

Althusser's attempt to answer such criticisms and resolve some of the problems of high Althusserianism (see, for example, 1989) is generally agreed to have foundered. And with the ascendancy of "post-Marxism," which often effects an anti-Marxist radicalization of Althusserian theses, his star was eclipsed, if not quite extinguished. Nevertheless, whatever his current reputation, Althusser can be said to possess three indubitable historical merits (see Callinicos, in Kaplan and Sprinker, 1993). The first is that his rereading of the classics (re)connected Marxism with non-Marxist currents of thought (especially Lacanian PSYCHOANALYSIS and Saussurean linguistics), disclaiming a Marxist monopoly of social knowledge and sponsoring new departures across the disciplinary board. Second, his philosophy for science was a commendable endeavor to reconcile the conventionalist critique of EMPIRICISM and POSITIVISM with a realist theory of the natural and social sciences. Third, his assault upon the Hegelian heritage in Marxism released historical materialism from a set of false promissory notes, analytical and political. In these respects, the Althusserian intervention "for Marx" arguably remains part of the theoretical UNCONSCIOUS of much contemporary cultural and CRITICAL THEORY, and Althusser's future may last a long time.

Reading
Althusser, L. 1965b (1990): For Marx.
——1984 (1993): Essays on Ideology.
——1990: Philosophy and the Spontaneous Philosophy of the Scientists & Other Essays.
——1992 (1993): The Future Lasts A Long Time and The Facts.
——and Balibar, E. 1965 (1990): Reading "Capital."
Benton, T. 1984: The Rise and Fall of Structural Marxism.
Callinicos, A. 1976: Althusser's Marxism.
Elliott, G. 1987: Althusser: The Detour of Theory.
—— ed. 1994: Althusser: A Critical Reader.
Kaplan, E.A. and Sprinker, M., eds 1993: The Althusserian Legacy.
Mulhern, F. 1994: "Message in a bottle: Althusser in literary studies."
Sprinker, M. 1987: Imaginary Relations: Aesthetics and Ideology in the Theory of Historical Materialism.
Thompson, E.P. 1978: The Poverty of Theory and Other Essays.

GREGORY ELLIOTT

ambiguity   An expression is ambiguous if it contains two or more different (usually mutually exclusive) meanings between which the interpreter must choose. When Milton wrote that some of God's servants "also serve who only stand and wait", are we to picture them waiting *for* God's commands, or waiting *on* him, as servants?

In ordinary usage and in pre-twentieth-century literary criticism, ambiguity is usually seen as a flaw, but in modern criticism it becomes a term of praise. William EMPSON argued in *Seven Types of Ambiguity* (1930), "The machinations of ambiguity are among the very roots of poetry," and the NEW CRITICS subsequently took up this argument and made it a keystone of their theory.

Interest in ambiguity has recently been revived in DECONSTRUCTION, but now with an emphasis on the undecidable multiplicity of *all* linguistic meaning rather than as a specific literary device whose contradictions can in principle be resolved by Empsonian analysis.

See also EMPSON, WILLIAM; NEW CRITICISM.

Reading
Empson, William 1930 (*1973*): *Seven Types of Ambiguity*.
Bahti, Timothy 1986: "Ambiguity and indeterminacy: the juncture."

IAIN WRIGHT

Amin, Samir (1931–) Egyptian economic historian. Amin is a leading theorist on the economic predicament of Third World countries. A major contributor to United Nations economic dialog, he rejects explanations and development stratagems of the capitalist West. Arguing that capitalist or socialist models neither recognize the realities of the underdeveloped world nor offer solutions, Amin proposes alternative, "polycentric" development strategies under regional direction. Amin has published detailed analyses of economic prospects for West Africa and the Arab World.

Reading
Amin, Samir 1990: *Maldevelopment: Anatomy of a Global Failure*.

THOMAS C. GREAVES

analysis, genre *See* GENRE ANALYSIS

analysis, race–class–gender *See* RACE–CLASS–GENDER ANALYSIS

Anderson, Perry (1938–) Marxist political historian and theorist. One of the foremost contemporary Marxist thinkers, Perry Anderson has been centrally concerned with defining the unity, limitations, and prospects (in his own words, the "historical balance sheet") of Western MARXISM. As editor of the *New Left Review*, Anderson has spearheaded a project attempting to remedy the deficiency, identified in his essay "Components of a national culture" (1968), of a tradition of Marxism in his native England. This and other issues were to generate a sustained polemic between E.P. THOMPSON and Anderson, documented in their respective volumes *The Poverty of Theory* (1978) and *Arguments Within English Marxism* (1980).

Anderson has equally been concerned to investigate, from a historical materialist perspective, both the proximate and remote antecedents of capitalist society. His earlier works, *Passages from Antiquity to Feudalism* (1974a) and *Lineages of the Absolutist State* (1974b), attempt respectively to trace two neglected historical connections: between the classical world and feudalism, and between feudalism and the absolutist state. *Passages* explains the emergence of feudalism from the "convergent collapse" of two preceding but mutually distinct modes of production, the slave mode which had characterized the Greek and Roman worlds, and the "primitive–communal" modes of the Germanic invaders of the Roman Empire. The new feudal mode of production was "dominated by the land and a natural economy" and eventually produced a unified civilization which represented a huge advance on the "patchwork communities of the Dark Ages." Nevertheless, Feudalism's own structural contradictions, such as that between "its own rigorous tendency to a decomposition of sovereignty and the absolute exigencies of a final authority" contributed to its decline (Anderson, 1974a, pp. 147, 152, 183).

In *Lineages*, Anderson sees the absolutist state as the "legitimate political heir" of feudalism. The book's compass extends over the development of absolutism in Western and Eastern Europe, contrasting this with the structural development of the Ottoman Empire and Japan. Modifying MARX's own formulations, Anderson argues that the "unique passage to capitalism" in Europe was enabled by the concatenation of the ancient and feudal modes of production, rather than being the result of a linear transition from the former through the latter (Anderson, 1974b, pp. 420–2).

Perhaps Anderson's most influential (and controversial) works have been *Considerations on Western Marxism* (1976) and its "sequel" *In the Tracks of Historical Materialism* (1983). In the former, Anderson argues that, in contrast with the unity of theory and practice characterizing the generation of Lenin, Trotsky, and Luxemburg, whose theorizing was based "directly on the mass struggles of the proletariat" (Anderson, 1976, pp. 11, 13, 17), Western Marxism was born of the failure of proletarian revolutions in the advanced nations of European capitalism after the 1914–18 war and developed an "increasing scission between socialist theory and working-class practice" (1976, p. 92). Theory was secluded within the universities, its language achieving unprecedented sophistication yet becoming increasingly specialized, pessimistic and entering into "contradictory symbiosis" with non-Marxist and idealist systems of thought (1976, pp. 93–4).

In contrast with this Western tradition, Anderson traces a tradition of Marxism descending from Trotsky which, far from being academic, concentrated on politics and economics rather than philosophy, was internationalist, and spoke a language of "clarity and urgency" (1976, p. 100). But above all, it was not limited by Western Marxism's view of official Communism as the only incarnation of the revolutionary proletariat (1976, p. 96). Anderson sees this alternative tradition as central to any renaissance of internationalist revolutionary Marxism (1976, p. 100). In fact he predicts that, with the advent of a new phase in the workers' movement, signaled by the French revolt of 1968 and the successes of working-class insurgency in Britain, Italy, and Japan in the early 1970s, Western Marxism will fall into extinction once the divorce of theory and practice which called it into being is itself abolished (1976, pp. 95, 101). In *Tracks*, Anderson sees his prediction of the death of Western Marxism confirmed, its traditional site, Latin Europe, undergoing a rapid decline and being displaced by the emergent Marxist theory in England and America. However, he admits that his prediction of the reuniting of theory and practice has remained unfulfilled. Arguing that Western (Latin) Marxism has effectively been eclipsed by STRUCTURALISM and POSTSTRUCTURALISM, Anderson launches his own attack on the indiscriminate, ahistorical, and socially reductive linguistic model which constitutes the explanatory infrastructure offered by these. Anderson finally poses the question of the relationship between Marxism, socialism, and the process of human emancipation in general, which includes the struggle of feminism and the nuclear disarmament lobby. While Anderson implies the possibility of a dialog between these various struggles, he insists that such general emancipation cannot realize itself without socialism at its center.

Anderson's later collections of essays, *English Questions* (1992a) and *A Zone of Engagement* (1992b), continue his inquiry into the future of socialism in an environment bloodied by Thatcherism. He suggests that the "central case" against capitalism lies in its breeding a combination of ecological crisis and social polarization. The task before socialism is to realize itself in an adequate historical agent. It must overcome its own debilitating attachment to particular loyalties, working instead towards international CLASS solidarity motivated by universal ideals of freedom and equality. Affiliation with the nation-state must give way before the broader goal of a European federation.

Reading
Eagleton, T. 1986a: "Marxism, structuralism and post/structuralism."
Martin, J. 1984: *Marxism and Totality*.
Thompson, E.P. 1978: *The Poverty of Theory and Other Essays*.

M.A.R. HABIB

androgyny   Derived from the Greek *anēr*, *andros* (male) and *gynē* (female), "androgyny" literally refers to hermaphroditism, or the presence of both male and female reproductive organs in a single organism. Historically, the term has been most often used by biologists, especially botanists discussing certain plants. However, in the 1960s and 1970s, the concept of androgyny became popular among feminist theorists to describe the combination and expression of both masculine and feminine appearances, traits, qualities, characteristics, and virtues by human individuals.

The feminist argument for androgyny proceeded from the axiom that sex and GENDER are not identical. Sexist thinking, which is generally both dualistic and dichotomous in its approach to human nature, tends to conflate the two. Sexist cultural systems first establish two categories, "male" and "female," then ascribe the traits by which people are sorted into these categories, evaluate the categories and their traits (devaluing the female and traits associated with females), and finally, order the categories through a variety of cultural moves (such as situation, standardization, and distribution of perspectivity), ultimately to enforce relations of dominance and subordination between human beings classified as male and female (Messer-Davidow, 1987, pp. 81–3). Since sexism is only possible when human beings are able to distinguish between males and females of the species, human beings in sexist societies are prohibited from appearing to belong to the other sex, to neither sex, or to both sexes. Since the psychological and cultural reproduction of sexism is only possible when males and females are prohibited from performing the work or expressing the qualities associated with the other sex, appropriate gender behavior is rigorously enforced. Feminists claimed that the practice of androgyny would promote human freedom by asserting the right of individuals to develop according to their own innate logic, not one imposed by sexist culture; it would expose the social constructedness of gender and thus expose sites for the *re*construction of a genderless society; and finally, androgyny would attack sexism directly and effectively by undermining its foundation, the differentiation of human beings into male and female sex-classes.

Before the 1960s and 1970s, feminists explored androgyny only occasionally, such as when Elizabeth Cady Stanton asserted that the deity was androgynous in *The Woman's Bible* (1895) and Virginia Woolf prescribed in *A Room of One's Own* (1928) that writers be either "man-womanly" or "woman-manly." The fullest articulation of androgyny as a feminist popular cultural ideal is Carolyn Heilbrun's *Toward a Recognition of Androgyny* (1973). Interest in androgyny diminished by the 1980s, which might be called the "decade of difference." Radical feminists claimed that, in a male-dominated society, androgyny could never be realized, that "andro" would always prevail over "gyn." Radicals urged women not to flee from femaleness and femininity, but to emphasize and celebrate their difference from men. Black feminists also exerted cultural pressure to explore difference, urging greater attention to the racial and cultural specificity of notions of gender. Feminists influenced by DECONSTRUCTION also emphasized difference, the "difference within" analytical categories. They claimed that, because androgyny preserves the categories of male and female, it can never be an alternative to the sex–gender system, that "androgyny" is implicated in the very dualism it seeks to undermine.

"Androgyny," then, represents the road not taken in feminist theory and praxis, but certain interests of contemporary cultural critics – in hybridity and the transgression of boundaries – and a popular cultural movement to "gentle" or feminize men, suggest its lingering if subterranean appeal in the late 1980s and 1990s.
See also DECONSTRUCTION; GENDER.

Reading
Heilbrun, Carolyn 1973: *Toward a Recognition of Androgyny.*
Messer-Davidow, Ellen 1987: "The philosophical bases of feminist literary criticism."

GLYNIS CARR

Annales **historians** The journal *Annales d'histoire sociale et économique* was founded in 1929 by Lucien Febvre and Marc BLOCH, who at that time were professors of history at the University of Strasbourg.

The purpose of the journal was to revitalize the study of history, which at the Sorbonne had become trivialized to the point of extinction. The founders of the journal were determined to turn their discipline from a narrow conception of political and diplomatic history to a dynamic structural study of social and economic history. Febvre and Bloch moved to Paris during the 1930s, Febvre to the Collège de France and Bloch to the Sorbonne. During the 1939–45 war Febvre worked for the Resistance; Bloch was shot by the Germans. Even during the occupation of France, Febvre continued work on the journal. After the war it was given a new and even more specific title: *Annales: Economies, sociétés, civilisations.* Fernand BRAUDEL followed Febvre as editorial director in 1957. J.H. Hexter (1979, pp. 61–145) has written an exceptionally informative, though obnoxiously sarcastic, assessment of Braudel and the *Annales* historians.

MICHAEL PAYNE

anthropology, cultural *See* CULTURAL ANTHROPOLOGY

anxiety of influence A term in literary theory, used especially by Harold BLOOM to refer to a consequence of the impact of responsive reading on "strong" poets or readers. When a strong poet or reader, such as William Blake, registers the full impact of a precursor's work, Milton's *Paradise Lost* for example, the initial response is to feel genuinely overwhelmed by the earlier poet's achievement and momentarily to believe that nothing more is possible in the mode of such achievement, such as English epic POETRY. This state of anxiety of influence may make the later poet experience a condition of imaginative claustrophobia, or a sense of the exhaustion of imaginative opportunity by what has been previously written. Rather than being defeated by such a sense, a strong poet sets about the task of interpretatively reducing the predecessor's work by an act of willful misprision, thus claiming, as Blake did, that Milton was in chains when he wrote of God but free when he wrote of Satan, because he was a true poet and unconsciously of the Devil's party. Such productive MISREADING opens up the possibility of new creative activity in the reclaimed imaginative space. Although Bloom develops his theory on the basis of meticulous commentary on the practices of

English Romantic poets – initially Shelley and Blake – it roughly parallels DERRIDA's independent theory of DECONSTRUCTION. Although in its early formulation (Bloom, 1973), the anxiety of influence was a theory of post-Miltonic literary history that did not extend back to Shakespeare, it soon became a model for all literary history, at least since biblical times (Bloom, 1975a). As such, Bloom's anxiety of influence may be read as a productive response to Kabbalistic readings of the Bible, NIETZSCHE's theories of reading in *Ecce Homo*, and FREUD's theory of the agon characteristic of the Oedipal phase of human development.

Reading
Bloom, Harold 1973: *The Anxiety of Influence: A Theory of Poetry.*
Bloom, Harold 1975b: *A Map of Misreading.*
de Bolla, Peter 1988: *Harold Bloom: Towards Historical Rhetorics.*

MICHAEL PAYNE

aporia   A term from ancient philosophy denoting a problem which is difficult to solve owing to some CONTRADICTION either in the object itself or in the concept of it. Aristotle defined it as "equality between contrary deductions." It has enjoyed a revival in post-HEGELian thought because it registers the objectivity of contradiction without the implication of a prospective dialectical "overcoming".

PETER OSBORNE

archaeology of knowledge   A form of analysis associated with the work of Michel FOUCAULT and concerned with transformations in the field of knowledge. An alternative history of thought which places emphasis on analysis of the rules of formation through which groups of statements achieve a unity as a science, a theory, or a TEXT. The focus of analysis is on DISCURSIVE PRACTICES and relations. *See also* ARCHIVE; DISCURSIVE PRACTICES.

Reading
Foucault, M. 1974: *The Archaeology of Knowledge.*
—— 1989a: "The archaeology of knowledge."
—— 1989b: "The order of things."
Smart, B. 1985: *Michel Foucault.*

BARRY SMART

archetype   A term central to Jungian psychology, which derives from the Greek *arche*, meaning

"primal," and *typos*, meaning "imprint, stamp, pattern." The tendency to apprehend and experience life in a fashion conditioned by the past history of (wo)mankind JUNG terms archetypal, and archetypes are the "*a priori*, inborn forms of 'intuition'" (*Collected Works*, Vol. 8, p. 133). Nevertheless, archetypes are unconscious and exist only *in potentia*; they must be beckoned forth by circumstance, and different ones operate in different lives. Perhaps the phrase "*a priori* categories of possible functioning" best captures the Jungian essence of the term (*Collected Works*, Vol. 16, p. 34). The archetypes are experienced as emotions as well as images (often in dreams), and their effect is especially salient in typical and significant milestones such as birth and death, triumph over natural obstacles, transitional stages of life like adolescence, extreme danger, or awe-inspiring experiences. As a result of his study of dreams, mythologies, legends, religions, and alchemy, Jung came to classify two broad categories of archetypes. First, there are the *personifying archetypes*, which take on a human-like identity when they function in the psyche. For example, the *anima* in man and its counterpart in woman, the *animus*, are convenient designations for any number of interpersonal situations between the sexes. Thus, the anima represents all of man's ancestral experiences with woman and the animus all of woman's ancestral experiences with man. Secondly, there are the *transforming archetypes*, which are not necessarily personalities, but include typical situations, geometric figures, places, and other means that emerge when the personality is moving toward change, and particularly that balancing sort of transformation which will result in the experience of "wholeness" or "totality," the archetype of the *self*. The main archetypes of transformation discussed by Jung are the *mandala*, a Sanskrit word meaning magic circle, whose symbolism includes all concentrically arranged figures, all radial or spherical arrangements, and all circles or squares with a central point (for example, the wheel, eyes, flowers, the sun, a star, snakes holding their tails); and the *quaternity*, which has to do with geometrical figures being divisible by four, having four sides, or four directions. Mandala and quaternity SYMBOLS are often brought together, for instance, in the flower symbol (petals focusing our attention on the pistil), the wheel symbol (spokes focusing attention on the hub), but the most frequent symbol for the mandala is the cross (focusing attention on the union of the four-sided structure). Jung states: "It is no use at all to learn a list of archetypes by heart. Archetypes are complexes of experience that come upon us like fate, and their effects are felt in our most personal life" (*Collected Works*, Vol. 9. i, p. 30). *See also* COLLECTIVE UNCONSCIOUS; JUNG, CARL GUSTAV.

Reading
Jacobi, Jolande 1959: *Complex/Archetype/Symbol in the Psychology of C.G. Jung.*
Jung, C.G. 1969: *Four Archetypes: Mother/Rebirth/Spirit/Trickster.*
——ed. 1964: *Man and His Symbols.*

SUSAN L. FISCHER

archive A term associated with Michel FOUCAULT's archaeological analysis of forms of thought. The archive is "the general system of the formation and transformation of statements" (1974, p. 130) which exists during a given period within a particular society. It refers to the rules of DISCURSIVE PRACTICE through which past statements achieved both their enunciability as events and functioning as things. For Foucault the archive comprises "DISCOURSES that have just ceased to be ours," and its analysis serves to establish "that we are difference, that our reason is the difference of discourses, our history the difference of times, our selves the difference of masks" (ibid., p. 131). *See also* ARCHAEOLOGY OF KNOWLEDGE; DISCURSIVE PRACTICES.

Reading
Dreyfus, H.L. and Rabinow, P. 1982: *Michel Foucault: Beyond Structuralism and Hermeneutics.*
Foucault, M. 1974: *The Archaeology of Knowledge.*
——1978: "Politics and the study of discourse."
——1989a: "The archaeology of knowledge."
Smart, B. 1985: *Michel Foucault.*

BARRY SMART

Arendt, Hannah (1906–75) Political thinker. Arendt is notable, not least, for her radical critique of the whole tradition of political philosophy on the grounds that philosophy, as a *contemplative* discipline, intrinsically tends to inhibit any genuine feel for politics.

Although by nature a contemplative thinker herself, her life experience taught her to mistrust pure contemplation. Even so, she was equally averse to political orthodoxies. Thus, having originated

from a thoroughly assimilated German Jewish background, she nevertheless chose to celebrate –as the purest antithesis to the socially ambitious "parvenu" – the vocation of the politically conscious "pariah."

Her only direct participation in organized politics came during the period 1933–42, when she was active in the Zionist movement. This led her ⸗into exile, first in Paris, and then from 1941 in New York (where, ten years later, she became an American citizen). She had been a student of Martin HEIDEGGER and Karl JASPERS, and in 1929 had published her doctoral dissertation, "Der Liebesbegriff bei Augustin." The first of her major works, however, is her monumental study of *The Origins of Totalitarianism*, which appeared in 1951. Thereafter all her writings, although they take various forms, may be seen as following a consistent trajectory. *The Origins of Totalitarianism* has been criticized for its lopsidedness: by "totalitarianism" she means what Nazism had in common with Stalinism, but most of the book is concerned with the prehistory specifically of Nazism. Her original intention therefore was to supplement it with a critique of MARX, and Marxist tradition. What this eventually turned into, however, was *The Human Condition* – a systematic phenomenological study of the *vita activa*. Here, her critique of Marx is placed within the broader context of a general polemic against the prevailing modern subordination of politics to an ethos deriving from the experience of "labor," and is supplemented by a parallel attack on the reduction of politics to a mode of "work." By "labor" she means what we do to meet the most basic demands of living, and the corresponding ethos is one designed to maximize production and consumption. "Work" is what we do to construct a stable world in which to live. Philosophers naturally tend to idealize political stability as an optimum environment for their way of life. But true political wisdom, she suggests, lies rather in a proper appreciation of *"action"*: public performance, as such. Inasmuch as totalitarianism seeks to minimize the space for this, the lesson of the nightmare is that we should learn to love that space – for its own sake.

In *The Human Condition* she celebrates what Plato devalues, the public CULTURE of ancient Athens, as one embodiment of such wisdom; whilst in the works that follow, *Between Past and Future*, *On Revolution*, and *Crises of the Republic*, she traces its reappearance also in the initial ferment of modern revolutions, before they were hijacked by political parties, and in the student movement of the 1960s.

Arendt is not only an analyst of the *vita activa*, though. In her final, unfinished work, *The Life of the Mind*, she turns to the *vita contemplativa*. This stems from what she had observed in 1961 at the trial of the Nazi, Adolf Eichmann, for genocide. Her initial report, *Eichmann in Jerusalem*, caused a furore, because of her (incidental) criticisms of the Jewish community leadership, although its major theme is captured in the sub-title: "A report on the banality of evil." Above all, she insists, Eichmann's crimes derived from his radical incapacity to think, will, or judge for himself – and she therefore sets out systematically to consider the ethical dimensions of these three activities. (Sadly, she managed to complete only the first two volumes, *Thinking* and *Willing*.)

See also PHENOMENOLOGY.

Reading

Canovan, Margaret 1992: *Hannah Arendt: A Reinterpretation of Her Political Thought*.
Young-Bruehl, Elisabeth 1982: *Hannah Arendt: For Love of the World*.

ANDREW SHANKS

Arnold, Matthew (1822–88) British poet, educationalist, literary and cultural critic. The founder of the modern LIBERAL humanist tradition in British and American literary studies. In *Culture and Anarchy* (1869) and other works he campaigned in gracefully ironic fashion against insular utilitarian philistinism, under the slogans of "CULTURE" (that is, balanced self-perfection) and "criticism" (that is, disinterested pursuit of the best ideas), also predicting that dogmatic religion would be replaced with poetry as the bonding agent of modern society. His suspicion of democracy and individualism, and his extension of LITERARY CRITICISM into general cultural and social criticism later influenced ELIOT, RICHARDS, LEAVIS, and TRILLING.

See also HUMANISM; MORAL CRITICISM.

Reading

Carroll, Joseph 1982: *The Cultural Theory of Matthew Arnold*.
Collini, Stefan 1988: *Arnold*.

CHRIS BALDICK

art What is art? The working definition of art to be discussed here is that art is the subject of art historical writings, and specifically art is the subject of (i) Ernst GOMBRICH's *The Story of Art*, 1950 (*1995*) and (ii) Mieke Bal's *Reading "Rembrandt": Beyond the Word–Image Opposition* (1991). Gombrich's *The Story of Art* and Bal's *Reading "Rembrandt"* are used here because they occupy such distinct places along one spectrum of art historical WRITINGS. Gombrich's is certainly the most widely read and possibly the most generally acclaimed book associated with traditional art history, and Bal's is one of the most sharply focused and carefully reasoned books employing and developing ideas on what has been termed new art history. The books are also distinctive because they are directed at different levels of readership. Gombrich's is an introductory TEXT intended for the reader new to the study of art, while Bal's requires a reader/viewer who has experience in the study of art. But here Bal's book will be viewed as another introduction – or more precisely, as another idea of what art is. Gombrich's *The Story of Art* and Bal's *Reading "Rembrandt"* are widely divergent in their views of art, but taken together (though the discussion of their writings here does not approach, much less combine, the clarity of Gombrich's thought and the subtlety of Bal's ideas, which is to be discovered in these books themselves) they offer a broad basis for a discussion of what art is.

Ernst Gombrich begins his survey of the history of art, *The Story of Art*, by saying that there is no such thing as Art. (It may be helpful to point out now that the word "art" is used in three ways by Gombrich. When Art is spelled with a capital "A," he is referring to a universal aesthetic component in works, which for him is usually discussed with a combination of pomposity and vagueness. When Art is spelled with a lower-case "a," he means either routine image making – that is, works which would be of interest as artifacts, such as popular art and children's art – or he means what can be characterized as fine art – that is, those works which are the proper subject of art history.) One reason for saying that there is no such thing as Art is to prepare the young readers for whom the book is intended for the great variety of works that are to be encountered in a survey from prehistoric times to the present. From the painting of a bison in a cave in Altamira to the bronze sculpture of a horseman by Marino Marini, Gombrich's book describes more than 300 works that represent a vast range in materials and techniques, form and content, function and aim. Another reason for saying there is no such thing as Art is to point out to the reader that most of the works presented were made in response to specific purposes and particular occasions, and were not meant to be taken from this context and exhibited in a museum (or reproduced in a book) as Art. Gombrich's discussion restores to the works the context from which they emerged, describing, for example, the belief in magically insuring success in hunting that prompted the cave painting, and the sight of Italian peasants on farm horses fleeting the shelling of their villages during the 1939–45 war that brought about Marini's sculpture. However, perhaps the main reason for Gombrich to say that there is no such thing as Art is to prevent his readers from bringing with them predetermined expectations about how works should look. Gombrich's book encourages readers to be open to the various languages to be found in works from the past – from the classical beauty of Melozzo Da Forli's angels to the primitive strength of a Tuscan Master's crucified Christ. There are two expectations that readers might cling to about the appearance of works that Gombrich singles out for special attention. To the first of these – that works appear real – Gombrich suggests that the summary treatment in Rembrandt's charcoal drawing of an elephant is as convincing a statement as the detailed treatment in Dürer's watercolor of a hare. To the second – that works be like those with which the viewer is already familiar and comfortable – Gombrich points out that the honesty of Caravaggio's first and rejected version of *The Inspiration of St Matthew* may be preferable to the conventionality of his second and accepted version.

By saying at the outset that there is no such thing as Art, Gombrich gives the readers the opportunity to view with unprejudiced eyes the different responses that works show to different ideas and beliefs. But Gombrich also provides guidance for the readers as to the limits of the differences. For while Gombrich says there is no such thing as Art, he says that there are artists – individuals who give special care to thinking about and working on their responses in the work that they do. On a modest level, Gombrich says, we are able to recognize the artist because all of us from time to time have been concerned with making something look just right, even if it was only the simple task of arranging flowers in a vase. The difference between this modest artist in us all and the artists discussed in art history is that those artists devote most of their time to such work and thought, and the best of them are willing to make great sacrifices for what they think and do. There is a sameness in the different works discussed by Gombrich as fine art,

which is that they express deeply held values in a way that, no matter how much effort has gone into their creation, conveys a sense of effortless harmony. Three specific sign posts are set up by Gombrich to further define the limits of the works that will be encountered by the readers – one "go" sign and two "stop" signs. First, the well-known masterpieces (such as works by Leonardo da Vinci and Rembrandt) will be discussed because they exemplify supreme efforts in the expression of human values and in the appearance of visual harmony; second, works that follow fashion and popular taste (such as POP ART) are not to be included because they reflect passing rather than permanent values; and third, works that mock sincere works (such as dada art) are excluded because they do not deserve to be either seriously discussed or (like pop art) to be included alongside the work of masters such as Leonardo da Vinci and Rembrandt.

The statement that there is no such thing as Art coupled with the statement that there are artists make explicit in Gombrich's book what is implicit in all introductory histories of art – that is, that art is defined in its historical context, and by providing an idea of this context the historian can offer an understanding of what art is. As the title – story rather than history of art – conveys, Gombrich's book is not to be understood simply as a chronological record, but also as a planned narrative in which the works discussed are selected as one might choose characters for the telling of a tale. This is not to say that other histories of art are less a story than Gombrich's, but only that Gombrich's history does not pretend a pure objectivity about what art is. The principal characters of Gombrich's narrative are master works by master artists, which serve as the primary guidelines in marking out the territory of art over the course of its history. And the primary plot in his narrative is to provide an idea of the artist's intentions and the social and cultural conditions of the periods in which these artists lived. An example (if one is needed) is the work of Rembrandt, "one of the greatest painters who ever lived" and "the greatest painter of Holland" where, in the seventeenth century, Protestantism was victorious and where there was a stiff and bracing competition among artists for the attention of the middle-class picture-buying public. Specifically, a late self-portrait by Rembrandt is discussed as an example of what belongs in the history of art. It is art not because this work corresponds to some prevailing idea of Beauty, but because in it Rembrandt portrays himself with total honesty, adding a new dimension of psychic reality to the physical reality that has been achieved in the portraiture of earlier masters, such as Leonardo da Vinci's *Mona Lisa*.

The idea of what art is, into which the reader is initiated by Gombrich's *The Story of Art*, is viewed as being a severely limited one in the recent writing of a number of art historians and those from other areas of study who write about art. In this writing, which includes Mieke Bal's *Reading "Rembrandt": Beyond the Word–Image Opposition*, the kind of art history found in Gombrich's narrative is viewed as elitist, sexist, racist, Eurocentric, and one that focuses too exclusively on works selected with a theory of progressive development of representation in mind. The basic objection to Gombrich's narrative that lies behind these views is to the subjectivity of its method, which informs the works discussed by the point of view of the historian. But the objection is aimed less at the methodology of traditional art history than at the definition that methodology forces on art. Of the three specific guidelines cited by Gombrich to set the limits on what works are to be included and excluded in *Reading "Rembrandt,"* the first two of these (the use of masterpieces as primary landmarks in the history of art, and the exclusion of popular art from the history of fine art) are directly contradicted; the third (the refusal to treat art that is anti-art as fine art) is indirectly, but perhaps more fundamentally, called into question. Beginning with the third, Gombrich sees the work of Marcel Duchamp, such as the ready-made urinal entitled Fountain, and the "serious" writing about it as redefining art, as "trivialities." A work such as Duchamp's *L.H.O.O.Q.* is also an insult to traditional art history. The title, mustache, and goatee are a commentary (surely an adolescent one for Gombrich) on Leonardo da Vinci's work along the lines of Walter Pater's well-known description of *Mona Lisa* as "older than the rocks among which she sits" (the facial hair applied by Duchamp does age *Mona Lisa* somewhat), which Gombrich finds "blatantly subjective." However, Gombrich's own comment on *Mona Lisa* that she "looks alive" and "seems to change before our eyes" is different only in degree (though the degree for Gombrich is critical), not kind, from Pater's and Duchamp's. With the use of image (the hair and reproduction) and words (the title) Duchamp's mustached *Mona Lisa* is a kind of visual/verbal art history that parodies and caricatures traditional art history while it assaults fine art ideals.

Duchamp's *L.H.O.O.Q.* also can be taken to be, then, an emblem of the cultural history of Bal's *Reading "Rembrandt": Beyond the Word–Image Opposition* – not for what it is not in this case, but for what it is. First, in the spirit of Duchamp, a basic goal of Bal's study is to seek out connections between the verbal and the visual, examining the constant interactions between reading and viewing in cultural experience. Also, Bal finds that historical study is shaped and shaded by the background and standards of its writers that are projected on the material of the study. This is particularly true not only if the text of the study is art, which invites subjective reading, but also if the text of the study is the social context in which the art is enmeshed, because this entailed selection and interpretation that is subject to the presence of the writers. Additionally, like Duchamp in *L.H.O.O.Q.*, Bal in *Reading "Rembrandt"* raises the question of the validity of the master work by master artist approach to the understanding of the experience of art. While Bal chooses Rembrandt as the primary visual text in her study because he is a master artist responsible for what is seen as being "HIGH ART," her view of Rembrandt focuses on how that lofty positioning contributes to the response that his work elicits on issues that are of concern in contemporary Western CULTURE at large. Her interest lies not in Rembrandt as artistic genius (thus, one reason Rembrandt's name is put in quotation marks by Bal is because the question of whether one is dealing with works that can be attributed with certainty to his hand or not – a question for the elitist interests of connoisseurship – is not at issue), but rather in bringing POPULAR CULTURE to bear on "Rembrandt." Analogous to Duchamp's commentary on Leonardo da Vinci by using a reproduction of *Mona Lisa* in his *L.H.O.O.Q.* (which itself in turn is re-reproduced for further consumption), Bal deflates the concept of master artist and at the same time causes to collapse the hierarchy separating high and popular art.

Bal's reading of Rembrandt's self-portraits may serve as a specific example of what view of art is taken in recent CULTURAL STUDIES. Bal chooses an early, small self-portrait of the artist in his studio by "Rembrandt" as the focus of her discussion, rather than what might be considered a "major," "mature," or "characteristic" work by the artist. Her analysis reacts against the realism of the self-portrait to concentrate on its constructedness, so rather than viewing it in its sequential relationship to Renaissance portraiture, as Gombrich does, Bal examines it in tandem with Velázquez's *Maids of Honor*. Unlike Gombrich, who approaches the self-portrait by Rembrandt as a whole experience to suggest its basic and summary impact, for Bal it is frequently the small detail in a work (such as the palette hanging on the back wall in the "Rembrandt" self-portrait which is positioned like and functions as the mirror on the back wall in Velasquez's work) that is an index to a specific and often overlooked text in the work. The dialectic between artist as humble craftsman and artist as proud creator that can be seen in both "Rembrandt"'s and Velasquez's paintings of themselves in working situations reflects on the viewer of these paintings because of the presence of an implied or actual mirror. The question, "Where is the viewer positioned?," raised in the Velasquez painting by the mirror and the narrativity found in the other figures present has been the subject of much art historical/critical writing. With an intertextual reading of the early "Rembrandt" self-portrait (in which, even though the figure of the artist is still and alone, a narrativity may be discovered by the viewer's own work) and Velasquez's *Maids of Honor*, Bal is able to discern and describe different kinds of self-reflectedness in the writing about the Velasquez painting, unintended but no less real self-portraits of art historians and critics at work. In their discussions of Rembrandt's and "Rembrandt"'s self-portraits, Gombrich aims at making the viewer aware of what Rembrandt has achieved, while Bal's aim is to make the viewer/reader aware of how viewing and reading can interact, has interacted, and does interact with the accomplishments of "Rembrandt".

In her reading of "Rembrandt", Mieke Bal has followed the advice given by Ernst Gombrich in the *Story of Art*, looking at pictures with fresh eyes and embarking on a voyage of discovery. Although Gombrich would not agree with everything that she has brought back from her journey, he and Bal start their journeys from the same place, travel side by side through important places along the way, and journey in the same direction. Gombrich and Bal both begin by knowing that, while there are artists, there is no such thing as Art. They agree about the importance of being attentive to the social situations in which artists work, and about the significant role that the subjectivity of historians plays in their discussions of those situations and those works. Further, they agree on the profound transforming effect that verbal discussions,

including their own, have on visual images. Just as visitors to art museums easily can find themselves being drawn toward the labels beside the pictures and away from the pictures themselves, so too the discussion of pictures in art history and cultural history, like grossly extended labels, can obscure the pictures it is meant to bring closer to the viewer. Finally, Gombrich and Bal both understand the powerful effect that the work of art can have on its viewers, and both, in writing down their observations, thoughts, and beliefs from their own journeys in search of the sources of this power, have guided others in the continual discovery of what art is.

Reading
Bal, Mieke 1991: *Reading "Rembrandt": Beyond the Word–Image Opposition.*
Gombrich, Ernst 1950 (*1989*): *The Story of Art.*
                                                          GERALD EAGER

art, pop   *See* POP ART

art worlds   Term developed by the sociologist, Howard S. BECKER. For Becker, art entails the "joint activity" of a number of people, and an art work always shows "SIGNS of that cooperation" (1974). Art worlds, then, "consist of all the people whose activities are necessary to the production of the characteristic works which that world, and perhaps others as well, define as art" (1982, p. 34) Art worlds do not only produce works of art but also give them their aesthetic value.

Reading
Becker, Howard S. 1974: "Art as collective action."
—— 1982: *Art Worlds.*
                                                          SIMON FRITH

arts movement, black   *See* BLACK ARTS MOVEMENT

Auerbach, Erich (1892–1957) Philologist. Author of the landmark critical work *Mimesis*, Auerbach wrote extensively on Italian, French, and medieval Latin literature, the literary influences of Christian symbolism, and methods of historical criticism.

The product of an eclectic academic background in Germany, where he studied art history, law, and philology, Auerbach, as a leading philologist of Romance languages and literatures, established a metaphysical/historical interpretative perspective which constituted a new epistemological approach to historical LITERARY CRITICISM.

Discharged as professor of Romance philology at Marburg University by the Nazi regime in 1935, Auerbach spent the next 12 years in Istanbul, where his work became both driven and informed by a desire to define and, if possible, preserve Western literary and cultural traditions and values. The recurring framing device characterizing his work was the analysis of literary language and themes as a method of historical interpretation.

The subject of Auerbach's most important work, *Mimesis* (subtitled *The Representation of Reality in Western Literature*), was not so much realism in general as much as the manner in which realistic subjects were treated seriously, problematically, or tragically throughout the history of the development of European literature. In this respect – especially in light of Auerbach's methodology of isolating what he referred to as "levels of style" derived from textual interpretations unfettered by historical critical convention – his work presaged much of the poststructuralist critique of European literature and CULTURE which followed him.

Reading

Auerbach, Erich 1959: *Scenes from the Drama of European Literature.*
—— 1961: *Introduction to Romance Languages and Literature.*
—— 1968: *Mimesis.*
Green, Geoffrey 1982: *Literary Criticism and the Structures of History: Erich Auerbach and Leo Spitzer.*

JAMES P. RICE

aura A key term in Walter BENJAMIN's account of the historical development of the work of ART. The aura registers the irreducible specificity or uniqueness of the traditional art object. It derives from the origin of art in ritual. In MODERNITY, ART is characterized by the destruction and decay of the aura from technical reproduction.

PETER OSBORNE

Austin, John Langshaw (1911–60) Philosopher born in Lancaster, England, educated at Oxford University and a fellow of All Souls College (1933–5) and Magdalen College (1935–52). He was elected to the White's Professor of Moral Philosophy Chair at Oxford in 1952 and held the position until his death. He wrote little and published less (seven articles during his life), yet his name was

for decades synonymous with a philosophical approach that emphasized careful attention to ordinary language use, sometimes simply called Oxford philosophy.

Austin took pride in being a teacher and a university professor. He believed, however, that philosophy should be more than traditional academic lecturing and writing. Philosophy was for him something in which to engage, in which to participate actively. It should be a joint undertaking, not a solitary one; it is best done in groups as a cooperative enterprise. Philosophical inquiry, Austin believed, should include careful discussions with others about clearly set topics and have definitive goals.

Even though he stressed the cooperative and shared nature of philosophy, Austin had the reputation of being a terrifying person and made many an enemy at Oxford. His work was often dismissed as limited and unphilosophical. His use of philosophy was considered trivial by Bertrand Russell and nothing but extremely narrow wordplay by A.J. Ayer. Such sentiments are still to be found in discussions of Austin's philosophy, with it often being dismissed on the grounds that it simply represents overly refined Oxford tastes and an exaggerated preoccupation with language.

While there is no denying a specific focus to his mature work, a careful reading of his papers and lectures reveals an amazing breadth of interest. A sizable, though subtly used, number of literary, scientific, legal, and philosophical quotations and references populate his TEXTS. Even Austin's early lectures and papers belie criticisms of triviality and narrowness. As a young man he made a very careful study of the philosophy of Leibniz, and closely examined Greek philosophy, especially Aristotle's ethical works and Plato's *Republic*. He also translated Frege's *Foundations of Arithmetic* (published 1950). As his thought developed, he found himself reinterpreting philosophy in concerns and methods reminiscent of Socrates, and his interest in language was not separable from his interest in the nature of the world and the human character. Austin's interest in language was pursued with rigor, tenaciousness, and patience with the aim of achieving clarity and improvement of thought. Such qualities are well represented in his most notable (1946) article "Other minds" (Austin, 1979, pp. 76–116).

Much of the difficulty in appreciating Austin is due to his general refusal to provide comprehensive theses and conclusions to his work; and although repeated themes can easily be found (philosopher's fixation with a few words, the danger of oversimplified conclusions, lack of careful and correct descriptions, repeated phrases and half-studied facts, obsessive repetition of the same small range of tired examples), there is no grounding of his observations and assertions in a set of simple and unifying principles. Nevertheless, such a supposed lack is an important ingredient of his way of working. Each inquiry in which he engaged has an independence from others, and no one study or set of data or result is to serve as the basis or framework for other inquiries. We are to investigate our ordinary uses of language without the dogmatic restrictions of general principles and theories developed from other studies. If there is a single truth Austin thinks he finds in his many inquiries, it is that our ordinary words are much subtler in their use, and there are many more possible uses and distinctions of language than philosophers have realized. There is a complexity, specificity, and nontheoretical, many-voiced character to Austin's work that must not be missed in attempts to categorize and understand it.

While some philosophers find the study of ordinary language of little use, Austin felt that such attention can give philosophy a clear task and subject-matter. Its aim and goal might be as grand as finding ourselves and others in our language; or as simple (Austin's preference) as exposing distinctions, complexities, and subtleties of language we had not known or had not heeded. Whatever one's judgment about his procedures, Austin was convinced that his approach was productive for it afforded him "what philosophy is so often thought, and made, barren of – the fun of discovery, the pleasures of co-operation, and the satisfaction of reaching agreement" ("A plea for excuses," 1956, reprinted in Austin, 1979, p. 175).

Several of Austin's students have tried to recreate his method of work so that others, in Austin's absence, could understand and possibly use it; and so that others might better appreciate his written works, which were derived from these procedures. The most elaborate such discussion is found in J.O. Urmson's article entitled "J.L. Austin" (Urmson, 1965). That presentation has been enhanced by the written discussions of others and by the recreation of several Austin lectures and sets of teaching notes that have been published posthumously. (The most notable is *Sense and Sensibilia*, 1962.) Essentially the method of inquiry, which Austin –

somewhat hesitatingly – called "linguistic phenomenology," comprises the following steps:

(i)   Choose an area of DISCOURSE.
(ii)   Collect the complete vocabulary of this area.
(iii)   Provide examples of use and misuse of the collected data.
(iv)   Attempt to give general accounts of the various expressions under consideration.
(v)   Compare the accounts given with what philosophers have said.
(vi)   Examine traditional philosophical arguments in light of results.
(vii)   Return to number (i).

Austin thought of his method as an empirical inquiry necessitating the efforts of many. It was best employed by using a team of a dozen or so individuals working closely together. It was to provide a nondogmatic method of discovery rather than a theory of explanation. The method would show its worth and justification, like any laboratory technique, by its success in practice.

There is some value in such a organized view of Austin's method of inquiry, for if nothing else it provides insight into how his papers came to be written and why they have the form they do. Nonetheless such a presentation must be accompanied by several warnings (Cavell, 1965). Austin is not doing descriptive linguistics, for he intends to look as much at the world as at language in his procedures; he does not remain satisfied with describing what people say but also wants to know why people speak as they do; he is not revealing social conventions but seeking truths about the human condition; he is not giving priority to the speech of others but is interested in understanding where and why one does use, or hesitates to use, or feels uncomfortable in using particular words and expressions. ("Why do I feel this way?" tends to be a question at the centre of the method.) For all of its stress on empirical discovery and cooperative work, it must be said that advantageous and productive use of Austin's method requires a self-reflective intelligence and a lively imagination. Some have even said that the method was only of use to someone like Austin who had the scholarly patience and artistic creativity to make it work.

Austin's work uncovered the way language and action are intertwined, and much of his reputation still rests on his discussion of performative utterances (for example, promising, warning, apologizing); on the way that saying something entails doing something; on the way many things are created when we say something. An important question that Austin could not shy away from was "can saying make it so?" (*How To Do Things with Words*, 1981, pp. 7ff). This question sounds strange and we clearly are tempted to say no. However, Austin's work on performative utterances suggests that it is not as odd a query as might first appear. Saying something is not an isolated act but requires the appropriate fabric and circumstances of life to be meaningful and have the force it possesses. Hence being able to say something is closely related to the nature of things, and Austin, in this regard, stresses the need to consider the total SPEECH-ACT situation. In our examination of ordinary language, we study not simply a word or a sentence, but the breathing of, the issuing of, the very life of an utterance. Like WITTGENSTEIN, Austin's appeal to ordinary language is made to emphasize that what we say is said meaningfully in a definite context and is said by humans to humans – hence the obsession not with words or sentences, but with the use and life of language. The ordinariness of an expression is less important than the fact that an expression is said (written) by human beings, in a language they share. For Austin, there is nothing wrong with using technical or special terminology, and ordinary language is not to be treated as sacred. Nevertheless, he insisted that we must be clear about the language we use and the ways we use it.

Readings
Austin, J.L. 1979: *Philosophical Papers*.
Cavell, Stanley 1965: "Austin at criticism."
Urmson, J.O. 1965: "J.L. Austin."
RICHARD FLEMING

author, death of A theme in POSTSTRUCTURALISM decisively stated in Roland BARTHES's "The death of the author" (1967). Barthes identified a cultural investment in the author as explanatory source of TEXTS: the idea of the author-as-God originating meaning, against which he stressed the linguistic reality of the author – created only in language – and the plurality of any text – space of the interaction of a number of WRITINGS. Recognition of this is the condition of a modern literary practice (Barthes cites Mallarmé's desire to yield the initiative to words). The death of the author brings the liberation of the reader, no longer constrained to the authorial fiction of the single voice in mastery of its text. Subsequently, Barthes envisaged a poss-

ible "amicable" return of the author (made up in reading as a novelistic figure, a set of textual "charms") and explored ways in which the author's *I* might be written as itself a text (the "person" taken apart in writing, removed from all assertion of some expressive unity of "self ").

While reiterating some of Barthes's emphases, Michel FOUCAULT's "What is an author?" (1969) proposed the study of a historically variable "author-function" characterizing the existence and circulation of certain DISCOURSES within a society. Such a study leads to questions of *authorization* – who may figure as an author, which texts have authority, how are discourses "owned"? – that the dissolution of authorship into textuality can too easily avoid.

Reading
Barthes, Roland 1967 (*1977*): "The death of the author."
Burke, Sean 1992: *The Death and Return of the Author*.
Foucault, Michel 1969 (*1986*): "What is an author?"
STEPHEN HEATH

autonomy, relative   *See* RELATIVE AUTONOMY

avant-garde   This term, taken from French military usage designating the select corps which went out in advance of the main body of troops, is applied to the political and the cultural spheres (particularly the visual arts) to describe those individuals or groups whose ideas and work seem ahead of the times. The concept of an avant-garde functioned as a primary stratagem in the description of modern art, which was seen as a battleground where certain artists thrust toward new territory while conservative forces held fast to tradition. Surveys of modern art start at different times, but those written prior to the 1980s begin in the same place – with the notion of an artistic revolution against the established order led by an avant-garde. For John Canady, *Mainstreams of Modern Art* (1959), modernism begins with Jacques-Louis David, whose life and art are presented as part of the violent break that the French Revolution makes with the aristocratic tradition of the rococo. The pattern that Canady then describes is revolution followed by counterrevolution of the next avant-garde, with new forward positions continually being established in art throughout the nineteenth and twentieth centuries, from neoclassicism to abstract expressionism. At the time when the abstract expressionist avant-garde began to be eclipsed by the next avant-garde, Harold ROSENBERG sees a new historical pattern developing: the breaking with tradition becoming its own tradition, that is, the tradition of the new (1959). As E.H. GOMBRICH points out (1971), adopting this pattern of progress to tell the story of modern art, seeing each new generation of artists pushing the frontiers of art into a new territory, results in the perceived difference between antiquated and advanced art obscuring a real distinction between the serious and the frivolous in art. So for Gombrich, the anti-art of Marcel Duchamp and Dada, which exemplifies the frivolous misread as the serious, might have functioned to call attention to the pompousness of the notion of progress in art, if it was not itself mistaken for avant-garde. Clement GREENBERG, who felt that avant-garde art was the only protection against the evils of Kitsch (popular art for the masses) saw the seemingly difficult art of Duchamp and Dada as a pseudo-avant-garde art (later termed avant-gardes by Greenberg) that threatened authentic avant-garde art (1971). Hilton Kramer believed that the acceptance and popular recognition of abstract expressionism (itself becoming a form of Kitsch) marked the end of the avant-garde pattern in modernism (1973). T.J. CLARK, in writing about Gustave Courbet, cautions his readers not to view avant-garde as a monolithic force, but to see it as a secret and unstable action, more akin, one imagines, to a CIA operation than a military maneuver (1973 (1984)). Added to these views, which held that avant-garde patterns had changed, or ended altogether, or were not what they had been thought to be, was the view that the avant-garde had never existed in the first place. The shift in the perception of the avant-garde in modernism – from being a functioning principle of artistic development to being a complete fiction – was brought about by many factors. Among them are included: the shrinking of the time-lag between the creation of the avant-garde work and its acceptance by the art audience; the disbelief in artistic revolution as causing social change; the disgust at the shameless marketing of "new and improved" art; the distaste for the war imagery built into the term "avant-garde"; the dismay at the picture within the vanguard pattern of modernism that presented important artistic creation as essentially a white male activity; and the discovery in postmodern art of the deconstruction of the avant-garde. A modernism very different from that in Canady's book is described by Robert Hughes in *The Shock of the New* (1980 (*1991*)), because of the changed view of the avant-garde. Hughes does not see modern art as a series of successful revolutions, but as a set of ambitious, sometimes empty, though basically failed dreams. For Hughes the notion of an avant-garde becomes suspect primarily because of the abuse of the concept in the aesthetic ideology of the United States, which was based, he believed, on a shallow educational system, crass commercialism, addiction to change for its own sake, and an obsession with current fashion and fad. Rosalind Krauss argues that the various avant-gardes have in common a belief in the essential originality of their art. However, for Krauss, the strategy of appropriation in postmodern art reveals that repetition and recurrence play a part equally essential to that of originality in artistic creation, though their role is hidden by the discourse of originality (engaged in by galleries and museums, art critics and historians, and artists themselves) on which the existence of the avant-garde depends. Thus the pictures by Sherrie Levine, which are photographs of the photographs of Edward Weston and Eliot Porter (whose photographs are in turn based on models by other artists), disclose the fiction of pure originality and along with it expose the myth of the avant-garde (1981 (*1985*)). Donald Kuspit contends in *The Cult of the Avant-Garde Artist* (1993) that the appropriations of Levine not only deconstruct the original works that they copy, but also dismember them, stripping originality of its meaning. However, in the process of emasculating the works of Weston and Porter, Kuspit sees Eleven's copies as also acknowledging the potency of the originals, and thus her appropriations reaffirm the avant-garde of the past. For Kuspit, then, postmodernism not only marks the end of the avant-garde, but is also the beginning of a neo-avant-garde art, a decadent mannerism that castrates, but at the same time authenticates, the avant-garde.

Reading

Gombrich, Ernst 1971: *The Ideas of Progress and Their Impact on Art.*
Greenberg, Clement 1971: "Counter avant-garde."
Kramer, Hilton 1973: *The Age of the Avant-Garde: An Art Chronicle of 1956–72.*
Krauss, Rosalind 1981 (*1985*): "The originality of the avant-garde."
Kuspit, Donald 1993: *The Cult of the Avant-Garde Artist.*
Mann, Paul 1991: *The Theory-Death of the Avant-Garde.*
Rosenberg, Harold 1959: *The Tradition of the New.*

GERALD EAGER

B

Bachelard, Gaston (1884–1962) French scientist, philosopher, and literary theorist. Among the most comprehensive and sophisticated French thinkers of the twentieth century, Bachelard first completed his studies in mathematics and physics and was especially influenced by the scientific thinking of Einstein and Heisenberg and their respective theories of relativity and indeterminacy. Immediately following his scientific studies, Bachelard began to explore philosophy as a necessary complement to the evolution of thought that he recognized occurring in contemporary science. He then commenced teaching at the University of Dijon (1930–40), where he lectured on mathematics and physics and pursued his scientific writings, which are best represented by his book *The New Scientific Spirit* (1934). Increasingly concerned with the philosophy of science, he was subsequently invited to the Sorbonne as professor of the history and philosophy of science (1940–54). By the time he went to Paris, he had already published 13 books and many articles focusing mainly on issues related to physics.

Here began his rigorous investigations into the formation of scientific and humanistic knowledge, which, he argued, took place not simply by the accretion of facts, but rather by combat leading to conquest over conventional epistemological hindrances in perception, opinion, and reductive thinking that tended to become rigid or absolute. More than merely dialectical thinking, Bachelard's explorations could be termed "multilectical," for he refuses to be bound by preconceived ideas that avoid what he calls "unfixing" both traditional subject and object relationships. He seeks a philosophic stance, exemplified in *The Philosophy of No* (1940) (*1968*), that is decidedly open and capable of synthesizing the historical revolutions in thought that have distinguished human experience and knowledge. For Bachelard, this argumentative direction is not a leap toward the irrational or the capricious – just the opposite. His refusal to be "fixed" in finite certitudes can be seen as an informed, conscious statement for a higher rationality, what he calls a *rationalité appliqué*.

Besides Bachelard's numerous articles (approximately 70), a series of 12 books on science, 2 on time and consciousness, and 9 on poetic consciousness were written between 1928 and 1962. In these intellectually ambitious treatises he strives to identify, analyze, and argue for a coordinating opposition between scientific rationalism and poetic imagination, insisting that creativity must flourish in both domains by way of redefining the human project. Particularly by concentrated attention to language and a reinterpretation of SUBJECT–OBJECT RELATIONships, we will be able to affirm the interconnection between science and poetry and the rational and imaginative faculties. Thus, along with BARTHES, FOUCAULT, MERLEAU-PONTY, and SARTRE, Bachelard found himself in the center of what was termed the "humanist controversy" in France, and was responsible for inventing the concept of the "epistemological break," or, without incongruity, the capacity for discontinuity and indeterminacy in formal thought patterns. Furthermore, he is credited with having inspired literary critics and scholars, especially in the 1960s and after, by fostering and facilitating the theoretical directions for NEW CRITICISM, STRUCTURALISM, and POSTSTRUCTURALISM. According to Roland Barthes and Gilbert Durand, Bachelard not only provided the foundation for a new critical school, but also, and for the first time, forced French thinkers to take imagination seriously, thereby producing significant debate – precisely what he hoped intellectual tension would cultivate.

Bachelard's seeming inconsistency as he moves beyond conventional scientific and literary thinking is based on a failure by critics and theorists to recognize his aptitude for "debasing" his own and others' thought-in-progress, which he takes seriously as a willingness to allow mental images to assume a primacy in forming and de-forming the thinking process. Basically anti-Cartesian in philosophical outlook, but trained as a mathematician and physicist, he rigorously analyzes the way in which language and external phenomena interact abrasively to create our human reality, embracing both subjectivity and objectivity, becoming and being simultaneously. When the languages of mathematics and science, of PHENOMENOLOGY and PSYCHOANALYSIS, and of poetry, for example, consistently challenge our traditional assumptions, they can be seen as creative formulations to generate original thinking. Thus we constantly come to new thought patterns not through agreement or harmony, but rather by going against the grain of our knowledge, by "unfixing" or deconstructing our paradigmatic perspectives.

Because Bachelard's speculative approach to science, philosophy, and literature disavows categorization, he is looked upon with understandable suspicion by thinkers whose domains range from applied science to abstract literary theory. If imagination is given preeminence in the human ways of knowing, then obviously followers of all traditional epistemology will be forced to reexamine radically any claim concerning the nature of reality or truth. Although we assert the difference between rational and imaginative faculties – exemplified by scientific endeavors being opposed to poetic expression – none the less, Bachelard would have us explore the links between the two, particularly since this interchange is revealed by creativity shaped by the imagining process. For him, images and imagistic patterns are constantly and naturally forming in our consciousness, and his repeated reference to "psychoanalysis" calls attention to the phenomenological interrelationship humans establish with the world, and not to the "psyche" of writer and reader.

In essence, Bachelard considers himself to be one who incorporates scientific, philosophic, and literary principles in the service of *becoming* (not *being*) a serious reader of images: the "TEXT," which includes the physical universe we inhabit in conjunction with consciousness, is the dynamic starting point for revealing and developing the human project of imagining. In such works as *The Psychoanalysis of Fire* (1938), *Earth and Reveries of Will* (1948), and *The Poetics of Space* (1957), Bachelard does not direct us toward a theory of imagining; instead, he performs that act himself or indicates how other writers reveal it in their choice of imagery. Inhabited by a steady flow of images, the meditative mind that is revealed to us in a state of reverie illustrates our profound, complex, and natural affiliation with self and world – imagining

is not theoretical, abstract, nor problematic; it is actual, vital, and akin to what we do and are. Said in another way, humans are imagining beings whose deepest identity is created by the world of their inclusive experience. Bachelard, at least, would encourage us to imagine such a remarkable human condition.

See also IMAGINARY/SYMBOLIC/REAL; SCIENCE, PHILOSOPHY OF.

Reading

Bachelard, Gaston 1934 (*1985*): *The New Scientific Spirit.*
—— 1957 (*1969*): *The Poetics of Space.*
—— 1961 (*1988*): *The Flame of a Candle.*
Clark, John G. 1989: "The place of alchemy in Bachelard's oneiric criticism."
Grieder, Alfons 1986: "Gaston Bachelard – 'phénoménologue' of modern science."
Lafrance, Guy, ed. 1987: *Gaston Bachelard.*
McAllester, Mary 1990: "On science, poetry and the 'honey of being:' Bachelard's Shelley."
—— 1991: *Gaston Bachelard: Subversive Humanist.*
Smith, Roth C. 1985: "Bachelard's logosphere and Derrida's logocentrism: is there a differance [sic]?"
JOHN V. MURPHY

Bakhtin, Mikhail (1895–1975) and colleagues

An important group of Russian writers on literature, language and culture.

Bakhtin studied at St Petersburg University, reading widely in philosophy and literature at a time of high intellectual and political excitement. Later he taught in Nevel and then Vitebsk, where he worked with many other artists and intellectuals including V.N. VOLOSHINOV (1894–1936) and P.N. MEDVEDEV (1891–1938). From this circle emerged several TEXTS which arose from shared debates, touching on important and sensitive issues in the difficult and highly policed early years of the Soviet Union. Voloshinov died of an illness and Medvedev was shot, while Bakhtin, exiled for a period, often ill but extraordinarily hard-working as a teacher and writer, maintained his intellectual activities in the shadows despite a briefly positive reception for his book on Dostoevsky, published in 1929. His dissertation on Rabelais was controversial, and only much later in his life was he recognized and praised in the Soviet Union, even as some of the group's books began to appear in the West, where they have become highly influential.

All these circumstances – the need to tread warily, the flow of ideas which were exchanged and discussed, the disappearance of some texts, the emergence of others in translation, belatedly and in a different climate – have unfortunately created continual confusion about the group's work, which is still far from resolved. In part this results from the richness and many-sidedness of the arguments, which have been appropriated in different ways, but there is also serious scholarly disagreement about the extent of shared or disguised authorship so that writers have made different assumptions about authorship and even claimed that passages in the texts disguised the intentions of the group. These matters are largely unresolved and may remain so. Here texts are referred to in the names of the several writers but there can be no doubt of a common, at times highly indirect and ironic, play of ideas.

The work of the group is situated between that of the contemporary formalists and futurists on the one hand, and that of the official Party line on CULTURE on the other. It bears the marks of both but explores sophisticated ways forward from each. From the formalists had come an emphasis on the distinctive properties of language and conventional devices in literary work, close attention being paid to linguistic innovation and the formal properties of literary texts with little reference to other forms of language or the social circumstances of WRITING. By comparison orthodox Party MARXISM, increasingly intolerant and suspicious of deviation, proclaimed SOCIALIST REALISM as its approved cultural vehicle and argued that literature and language were reflections of social conditions and relations.

If there is a common program at all in the work of Bakhtin's group (which valued diversity), it concerned the study of ideologies in their "social qualities:" "what is lacking is a properly worked out *sociological* study of the specific properties of the material, forms and goals belonging to each of the domains of ideological creativity" (Medvedev, 1928); "the forms of signs are conditioned above all by the social organisation of the participants involved and also by the immediate conditions of their interaction" (Voloshinov, 1929); "primitive marketplace genres prepared the setting for the popular-festive forms and images of the language in which Rabelais expressed his own new truth about the world" (Bakhtin, 1965). Some of the group's studies are highly theoretical, offering critiques of psychology and PSYCHOANALYSIS for their misreading of the social being of individual consciousness; Bakhtin's own work includes detailed though boldly wide-ranging studies of Dostoevsky, Rabelais and his understanding of the novel, also a

number of difficult meditations upon forms of writing and much else.

Medvedev's work (probably written with Bakhtin, 1928) paid tribute to the formalists as worthy foes in the development of a more adequate account of literature in which the "concrete life" of a work of art should be seen in its literary milieu, that milieu within a larger ideological milieu, and both within their socioeconomic setting. The program attempted to dissolve the distinction between text and context, between properties intrinsic and others extrinsic to the literary work, by locating works within genres which at once required forms of LITERARY PRODUCTION and intended audiences which are inside, not outside, a genre's development.

A year later, Voloshinov's book on language attacked forcefully both a notion of individual consciousness and the REIFICATION of language (as potentially in SAUSSURE and many dominant forms of linguistics) as an objective SYSTEM. Instead language was neither merely subjective nor wholly objective. Words were an "index of social changes" and (controversially in Soviet Marxism) because "class does not coincide with the sign community . . . different classes will use one and the same language" so that "differently oriented accents intersect in every ideological sign" and SIGN "becomes an arena of the CLASS struggle." The study of language was that of "the particular situation of the utterance and its audience" within "genres of behavioural speech" ("the drawing-room causerie, urban carouses, workers' lunchtime chats"). Signs possessed a "social multiaccentuality" since they were constantly appropriated for different purposes even if "the inner dialectic quality of the sign comes out fully in the open only in times of social crises or revolutionary changes." Though this work became known only much later and in quite different intellectual settings, it staked out a distinctive agenda for a materialist study of language forms within a variety of social situations in culture, analyzing "speech performances" and their typical, yet open-ended characteristics as inextricably linked to transactions offering possibilities for exchange, conflict and struggle.

In work later known as Bakhtin's primarily or alone, references by Voloshinov to "the active reception of other speakers' speech" becomes a much larger study of a principle of social dialog (the internalization of and speaking to other positions) in forms of writing as well as speech. Equally, the "differently oriented social interests" extend to a dense celebration of cultural "heterogeneity." Utterances imply listeners and in Bakhtin's most valued writers different voices coexist, irrupting against each other in a ceaseless play. His study of Dostoevsky asserts that the author's work is distinctively polyphonic, articulating a number of positions and refusing to privilege any of them. In his long and densely referenced study of Rabelais, the typical forms of carnival (shows and pageants, parodies, cursing and swearing) are seen as the creative busting forth of a repressed world of folk culture, its interests in bodies and blasphemy, into the official medieval world: "the bodily lower stratum of grotesque realism still fulfilled its unifying, degrading, uncrowning and simultaneously regenerating functions." Both books locate literary work (as the Rabelais study puts it) within "the very depths of the life of that time" within which "an active plurality of languages . . . led to exceptional linguistic freedom."

Necessarily, Bakhtin's own "utterances" were sensitive to the presence of other voices in the increasingly grim circumstances of Soviet life. A difficult and cryptic strand of his work (1981) presented three models of possible language situations: monoglot, with a shared language and strong cohesion of values; polyglot, in which languages coexist; and heteroglot, where inside a unified common language there are divergent voices and registers. His own boldly wide-ranging form of the novel proclaimed those moments in which contradictory opinions could be voiced simultaneously, while his work on Rabelais and the carnival celebrated the productivity of popular pleasures against officialdom. In fact his writing has much in common with the contemporary music of Shostakovich, with whose situation and thus, in the group's analysis, utterances Bakhtin had much in common. In both, ambiguous and qualified presentations of official thinking are cut across by a huge, almost uncontrolled variety of other voices, often sardonic and ironic, in a "victory" over linguistic (or musical) "dogmatism."

Current knowledge of the writings of the Bakhtin group, its debates, and degree of shared purpose is tantalizingly incomplete and likely to remain so. It seems that the writings were of necessity "double coded," though that quality and the celebration of difference has brought Bakhtin into the field of postmodernist thought. It has been possible not only to see in the work a tactical retreat from key Marxist positions, but also to see Voloshinov's

writing on conflict through language and the ideological sign, and Bakhtin's on the social construction of literary voices, as crucial enrichments in contemporary Marxism against an economist reductionist tradition. Elsewhere, despite the constant ambiguity in the group's work towards the distinctiveness of literary strategies from other forms of utterance, Bakhtin has been noted for offering a distinctive poetics of texts as polyphonic: Todorov (1984) called him the "greatest theoretician of literature in the twentieth century."

If one user of the group's work values its analysis of intertextuality, others look outside the play of texts at their broader treatment of language and culture. The notion of dialog between DISCOURSES, however enigmatically and abstractly treated at times, is a fundamental contribution. Another is the treatment of a set of shifting relations between official and popular forms. A third is the approach to the grotesque not as a convention or form but as a registration of the body against the spirituality (and repression) of AESTHETICS and thought. A fourth is the interest in HETEROGLOSSIA and difference, "processes of decentralisation and disunification" next to "verbal–ideological centralisation and unification" (1981).

Bakhtin remarked at the end of his book on Rabelais (1965) that *belles lettres* and the modern novel were "born on the boundaries of two languages" and it is the group's exploration of this shifting position, and their own location between formalist aesthetics (to which they paid tribute) and Party Marxism (which they saw as a deformation even as they suffered from it) which has given their work its remarkable suggestiveness, breadth, and new relevance.

See also FORMALISM.

Reading
Bakhtin, M. 1929 (*1984*): *Problems of Dostoevsky's Poetics.*
—— 1965 (*1984*): *Rabelais and His World.*
—— 1975 (*1981*): *The Dialogic Imagination.*
—— 1979 (*1986*): *Speech Genres and Other Late Essays.*
Bennett, T. 1979: *Formalism and Marxism.*
Clark, K. and Holquist, M. 1984: *Mikhail Bakhtin.*
Hirschkop, K. and Shepherd, D., eds 1989: *Bakhtin and Cultural Theory.*
Medvedev, P.N. 1928 (*1978*): *The Formal Method in Literary Scholarship: A Critical Introduction to Sociological Poetics.*
Todorov, T. 1981b (*1984*): *Mikhail Bakhtin: The Dialogical Principle.*
Voloshinov, V.N. 1926 (*1976*): *Freudianism: A Marxist Critique.*
—— 1929 (*1973*): *Marxism and the Philosophy of Language.*

White, A. and Stallybrass, P. 1986: *The Politics and Poetics of Transgression.*

MICHAEL GREEN

Balibar, Etienne (1942–) French Marxist theoretician, former pupil and collaborator of Louis ALTHUSSER, and a lecturer in philosophy at the University of Paris (Sorbonne). For 20 years a member of the French Communist Party until his exclusion in 1981, Balibar has since been prominent in anti-racist campaigns in France. From the 1960s to the 1990s these political commitments have profoundly marked his intellectual engagements, which focused on four main, interrelated areas: (i) critical development of a "historical epistemology" – an anti-empiricist French tradition in the history and philosophy of science, associated with Gaston BACHELARD, Jean Cavaillès, and Georges Canguilhem; (ii) interrogation and reconstruction of theoretical MARXISM in light of the record of historical Communism – the joint, internationally influential enterprise of "Althusserianism," undertaken with Pierre MACHEREY and Michel PÉCHEUX among others; (iii) interpretation of the political actuality of the thought of Spinoza, classical philosopher-general of Althusserian Marxism; and (iv) reflections and interventions on contemporary nationalism and RACISM.

In his best-known work (1965), Balibar employed Bachelardian–Althusserian categories to reconstruct historical materialism as the general theory of social formations founded by Marx. Arguing that the concept of "mode of production," properly understood, effected an "epistemological break" with the prior tradition of the philosophy of history, initiating a "science of history" in its stead, Balibar sought to displace quasi-Hegelian formulations of Marxism. In particular, this meant rejection of the evolutionism of orthodox historical materialism which, basing itself upon Marx's 1859 Preface (*1976*), conceived the advent of communism as the preordained result of the autonomous, progressive development of the productive forces. Prioritizing the category of "reproduction" over that of "contradiction," and affirming the explanatory primacy of the social relations of production, Balibar advanced a theory of historical transition from one mode of production to another, in which the determinant instance was the CLASS struggle, and not the master contradiction between (advanced) productive forces and (retarded) property relations.

Balibar's insistence on the constitutive complexity of concrete social formations, irreducible to the "laws of motion" of a single mode of production, proved immensely fertile for subsequent Marxist research. However, in response to critiques of the rationalist epistemology informing *Reading "Capital,"* he abandoned the project of a "general theory" of modes of production (1974, pp. 227–45). Here, as in his defense of Leninism against the tactical adjustments of the PCF (1976), the influence of a certain Maoism, derived from the professed principles (though not the actual practices) of the Cultural Revolution, can be discerned, characteristic of the theoretico-political orientation of many French Marxists in the late 1960s and 1970s.

Amid the "crisis of Marxism," Balibar has refused the familiar options of sheer renunciation or mere reassertion of Marx, offering a nuanced appreciation of his enduring significance (1993b). His recent work, some of it undertaken via a dialog with the historical sociologist Immanuel Wallerstein (1988), has been preoccupied with the burning philosophical and political issues posed by the emergence throughout the advanced capitalist world of a new "integral nationalism" and neoracism, whose legitimating ideology is "cultural difference." Among the arresting theses of Balibar's successive interventions is that *theoretical* racism is a "*theoretical* humanism." Summoning his readers to "an effective anti-racism" (Balibar and Wallerstein, 1988, p. 13) as the precondition of a renewed class politics, Balibar evinces his commitment to a cosmopolitan vocation for political philosophy, as exemplified by Baruch Spinoza.

Reading
Balibar, Etienne 1965 (*1990*): "The basic concepts of historical materialism."
—— 1974: *Cinq études du matérialisme historique.*
—— 1976 (*1977*): *On the Dictatorship of the Proletariat.*
—— 1985: *Spinoza et la politique.*
—— 1991a: *Ecrits pour Althusser.*
—— 1993a: *Masses, Classes, Ideas.*
—— 1993b (*1995*): *The Philosophy of Marx.*
—— and Wallerstein, Immanuel 1988 (*1991*): *Race, Nation, Class.*

GREGORY ELLIOTT

Barthes, Roland (1915–80) French critic whose constantly innovative writings were greatly influential in literary and CULTURAL STUDIES. From 1960 Barthes taught at the Ecole Pratique des

Hautes Etudes in Paris, offering a seminar under the heading "Sociology of signs, symbols and representations." In 1976 he was elected to a chair in "literary semiology" at the Collège de France.

Barthes's work was wide-ranging in the topics it treated and the areas in which it was important. Individual books and articles made decisive contributions to the development of SEMIOLOGY, the structural analysis of narrative, the study of specific sign systems (that of fashion, for example), the redefinition of LITERARY CRITICISM, the reading of particular works or bodies of work (those of Sade, Michelet, Proust, Sollers, and numerous others, including artists and composers), the understanding of the social use and subjective experience of photographs (the list could be extended). It would be difficult to find many aspects of the contemporary CULTURE that did not somewhere receive consideration in the multitude of his texts and interviews, and this underlines the extent to which Barthes filled and helped define a certain role of the intellectual crucially and critically engaged in the demonstration and questioning of the culture's given realities as systems of meaning, as implicated in processes of signification which precisely structure and inform their "givenness." Over all its diversity, throughout its various stages of development, Barthes's work was characterized by this concern with conditions of meaning: with the ways in which meanings are made, presented, fixed, grounded, and then with the ways in which they can be unmade, challenged, displaced, pluralized. His approach was always in terms of language, the one unfailing object of his attention and investment, his curiosity and desire.

The initial writings dealt explicitly with social operations of language, the power of institutionalized forms of meaning. *Writing Degree Zero* (1953) took literature as such a form and described an inescapable sociality of language to which it is bound. Language exists not as a neutral instrument for the untrammeled expression of a writer's message, a channel for the passage of an independent content, but as so many orders of DISCOURSE, so many sociolects or "WRITINGS" which inform and shape that message and content. A writing – an *écriture* – is language loaded with a consistency of representation, bringing with it a ready-made version of "reality" that coercively runs together facts and norms, information and judgment. Such set forms make up – *are* – the society's intelligibility, "naturally" its vision of things. Literature is

part of this vision: a defined and regulated site of language use that holds a writer's TEXT to repetition of its constraining sense of "literature." Modern writers, from Flaubert onwards, are distinguished by an acute consciousness of this social occupation of language and engaged thereby in a struggle to write free of the forms of a society from which they are divided by that very consciousness (no longer any innocence of language), while at the same time inevitably returned to it in the very act of writing (no stepping outside its sociality). *Mythologies* (1957) focused on the objects and events of everyday life as replete with meaning, thick with a mythical discourse that seeks to convey as universal the particular values it represents. It is this conversion of cultural sense into essential nature which Barthes refers to as myth and identifies as the defining mode of the bourgeois IDEOLOGY of his society, tracking it down in a wrestling match or a poem (*Writing Degree Zero* was exactly a mythology of literary language), in an advertisement for spaghetti or the staging of a play (in a series of reviews contemporary with *Mythologies*, Barthes championed BRECHT's practice of *displaying* meanings, offering them frankly to be read as such, against that of a bourgeois theater that hides them in the naturalistic illusion of a presentation of "life").

Mythologies ended with a theoretical essay which drew on the linguistic notion of the SIGN to give an account of mythical DISCOURSE as a SYSTEM of CONNOTATION: myth takes over an initial SIGNIFYING system as the support – the signifier – for new meanings proposed as *motivated* by the initial system, simply "there." In what he would later characterize as a euphoric dream of scientificity, Barthes played a major part in the development of semiology, the science of signs envisaged by SAUSSURE, and in *Elements of Semiology* (1964) provided a synthesis of its terms and concepts. In fact, semiology was always for him a potentially critical discourse that, with its formal analyses of the systematic conditions of meanings in social life, contributed to the demystification of the workings of ideology that had been his first preoccupation. Semiology, that is, helped provide the tools for an effective critique of a "society of communication" dependent on a regime of meaning in which signs are proffered as closed unities of an exchange of sense from one SUBJECT to another. Insisting on an understanding of signification – the production of signs – and on the subject not as some full consciousness originating meaning but as set in place within signifying systems, Barthes was concerned semiologically with the demystification of the sign ("the great affair of MODERNITY"), but then too with that of semiology itself for its failure to question its own dependence on the sign as focus and limit of its analyses. Semiology describes signifying systems, but assumes in so doing the idea of the sign as the join of a signifer and a signified in a way that allows the latter to continue to be regarded as a prior content that the former comes to express and so the maintenance of the accepted terms of subject, meaning, and communication. As opposed to which, Barthes was concerned increasingly to stress the productive nature of signifying systems – their realization of subject positions and terms of meaning – and to acknowledge the all-pervasive fact – the everywhereness – of language: there is no object or content or ground of meaning outside of a signifying process giving it as such, and so no METALANGUAGE, inasmuch as no language can reach some objectivity outside of language and no metalinguistic representation can be more than a particular construction within the infinite movement of language, a productivity that can never be brought to an end – other than in some theological or metaphysical or scientistic imagination of closure (semiology fell too easily into the latter: a scientific discourse conceiving itself as science but refusing to consider itself as DISCOURSE).

As regards LITERARY CRITICISM, such an emphasis on language meant a challenge to beliefs in works as deriving their meaning from a reality they represent or a mind they express (in a famous essay of 1967 Barthes announced the DEATH OF THE AUTHOR) and a perception of the critic as creatively trying them out with different interpretative models. *On Racine* (1963) gave a structural and thematic reading of the corpus of Racine's plays through the languages of anthropology and PSYCHO-ANALYSIS, while *Criticism and Truth* (1966) defended this procedure against traditional literary-historical "author-and-works" attacks, and succinctly stated Barthes's critical premises: there is no impartial choice of a system of interpretation and objectivity is a choice of language institutionally sanctioned as such; what counts is the rigor with which the language chosen is applied, not the meaning of the work but the meaning of what the critic says of it; there is, indeed, no arriving at "the meaning of the work" (contrary assertions by certain academic approaches are yet another example of mythical discourse, attempts to hide *their* "objective"

meanings as those of "the work itself "), no final grounds for stopping the plurality into which, as language, works open. Traditional criticism submits works exactly to the regime of the sign and seeks the signified as a secret to be deciphered, brought out by a discipline of knowledge that thereby explains – represents – the work, settles its meaning. Against which, Barthes as critic assumes the materiality of the signifier and seeks to set works off into a multitude of readings, effecting displacements of meaning, realizing their plural potential.

Barthes puts this as the movement from *work* to *text*. The works of "literature" are themselves elaborated within the regime of the sign, bound up in given terms of meaning and making a powerful "readerly" representation. In *S/Z* (1970), Barthes demonstrates this readerliness through a detailed phrase-by-phrase account of a Balzac novella, showing the ways in which narrative and other codes combine to construct a particular, "natural" direction of reading in the interests of a particular coherence – precisely a settlement – of meaning. His demonstration, however, is simultaneously that of the novella's plurality which the limiting direction of reading cannot fully contain, since any hold over language is itself a linguistic production, exceeded by language; Barthes's reading, that is, returns Balzac's work to textuality, to a "writerliness" – its availability for a proliferation of meanings, for an experience of the signifier. What Barthes then understands by and values as *text* is at once the possibility of plurality in the classic work; the aim and achievement of modern avant-garde nonrepresentational practices of language; an apprehension of language and the signifier that can be had in the interstices of everyday life as well as in written works ("the living writing of the street"); a utopian vision of plurality. In connection with this, a second sense of *écriture* is developed by Barthes, contrary to that of *Writing Degree Zero*: writing now names a practice that unsettles forms of closure (the mythical instrumentalizations of language to which *écriture* earlier referred; writing in this new sense is intransitive, indeterminate in address, nonrepresentational). Such a practice breaks down the division between reader and writer: no longer communication from one to the other but a textual performance in which both instances are put in question, subject and signified dispersed across the "other scene" of language's infinite productivity.

The theory of the text finally can only coincide

with writing, can sustain no metalinguistic *distance*. Barthes the semiologist was overtaken by Barthes the writer, his work moving away from any representation of a knowledge, any possibility of codification into an externally applicable theoretical system (no equivalent, for instance, to the DECONSTRUCTION derived from DERRIDA). He talked of himself more and more as an *amateur*, writing not professionally, under some conception of a discipline, but perversely, under the sway of desire, shifting intellectual analysis to questions of enjoyment. *The Pleasure of the Text* (1973b) recast the readerly/writerly distinction of *S/Z* into a reflection on pleasure and JOUISSANCE, exploring in a series of brief notations the cultural enjoyments of language that works may produce and then the radical orgasmic abandonment of the subject that is the extreme experience – the JOUISSANCE – of texts. This writing desire, transgressing academic forms and procedures, distinguished Barthes's subsequent writings which variously engage the subject in language. *Roland Barthes by Roland Barthes* (1975) set Barthes out in a series of novelistic fragments, so many "biographemes" to capture and examine a certain imaginary construction of the writer; *A Lover's Discourse* (1977c) traced the different moments of the subjectivity of love through the various episodes of language in which it is deployed; *Camera Lucida* (*1980*) explored the terms of the subject engaged in the experience of photographs, again mixing analysis and biography. These books and other writings brought Barthes close to the novel, but the novel without any certainty of subject or representation, without any coherence of narrative action or narrating voice. The last course he taught concerned, indeed, the conditions on which a writer of today could conceive of undertaking a novel. The posthumously published *Incidents* (1987) contains reflections on ways of writing the novelistic surface of everyday existence, together with short diary entries for two different periods of Barthes's life. These are the first pieces in which Barthes is explicit about his homosexuality, but his work may be importantly read as inflected by a gay textual attention: in accordance with his overall refusal of imperatives of meaning, homosexuality is precisely not a signified in his texts but rather a matter of the signifier, a particular retreat from the rectitude of the fixed divisions of sexes and signs, all the ready sense of sexuality.

Barthes's work finally brings an ethical sensibility. The visceral dislike of the mass of communications, of the foregone conclusions of signs and meanings, goes along with the pleasure in the mobility of signs, the enchantment with the signifier. What is vital for Barthes is always the achievement of a space of movement, some play in the field of meaning: demystification and displacement of the fixtures of sense, access to plurality, desire in language (Barthes registers distress at what he sees as his society's giving up of language as a site of pleasure, not for any purpose, in perversion). The marginal (askew to given terms and positions), the individual (not unity of the person but a network of singularities), the neutral (the utopia of some peace from meanings) became the key words and topics of his last courses and writings. Literature – works read in their textuality, *for their writing* – was, as ever, the necessary reference here: literature as the experience of the freedom that it was Barthes's project as critic, theorist, and writer to propose.

See also SEMIOTICS; SIGN; STRUCTURALISM; TEXT.

Reading
Culler, J. 1983: *Barthes*.
Lavers, A. 1982: *Roland Barthes: Structuralism and After*.
Roger, P. 1986: *Roland Barthes, Roman*.

STEPHEN HEATH

base and superstructure   The concept of base and superstructure was first employed by Karl MARX and Frederick ENGELS in *The German Ideology* (1845) (*1976*), to posit the theory that the forces and relations of labor (the base) within a society determine its social consciousness (the superstructure) and class system, all of which in turn shape the entity of the state for the good of its ruling class.

The concept is defined in this passage from Marx's Preface to *A Contribution to the Critique of Political Economy* (1859) (*1976*):

> In the social production of their life, men enter into definite relations that are indispensable and independent of their will, *relations of production* which correspond to a definite stage of development of their material *forces*. The sum total of these relations of production constitutes the economic structure of a society, the real foundation, on which rises a legal and political superstructure and to which correspond definite forms of social consciousness. The mode of production

of material life conditions the social, political and intellectual life process in general. It is not the consciousness of men that determines their being, but on the contrary, their social being that determines consciousness. (Marx, 1976, p. 3)

In terms of the elements of the superstructure, Marx and Engels identify law, politics, religion, AESTHETICS, and ART as "definite forms of social consciousness," which they term "ideology." IDEOLOGY, which purports to represent the ideas of an entire society, (its "social consciousness"), actually serves to validate the power of the ruling social class, the owners of economic production. However, Marx and Engels also theorize that superstructure and ideology are not mere reflections of a society's economic base; both grow *from* the economic base, but may develop apart from it as well, often functioning with considerable autonomy. In addition, the sophistication of the base does not necessarily correspond to the sophistication of the superstructure. For example, a society which is economically underdeveloped may attain considerable artistic achievements. Marx uses the case of classic Greek civilization to press the issue that "in the case of the arts, it is well known that certain periods of their flowering are out of all proportion to the general development of society, hence also to the material foundation, the skeletal structure . . . of its organization." Engels in particular suggests that the relationship between the base and the superstructure is not an automatic or strictly linear one: the superstructure (or parts of it) can actually create change within the base, rather than merely reflect it (Marx and Engels, 1968, pp. 682–3).

Reading
Eagleton, T. 1976: *Marxism and Literary Criticism.*
Engels, F. 1968 (*1977*): "Letter to J. Bloch."
Marx, K. 1976: *Preface and Introduction to A Contribution to the Critique of Political Economy.*
—— and Engels, F. 1970 (*1982*): *The German Ideology: Part One.*

SUSAN R. SKAND

Bataille, Georges (1897–1962) Although his work as a novelist, philosopher, and theorist of ART and CULTURE is intimately related to the intellectual movements of the earlier part of this century, and especially French surrealism, Georges Bataille has exercised a powerful and continuing influence on much philosophy and CULTURAL THEORY during the 1960s, 1970s, and 1980s, including the work of Jacques DERRIDA, Michel FOUCAULT, Jean BAUDRILLARD, Roland BARTHES, and Julia KRISTEVA in his native France, as well as critical and cultural theorists elsewhere.

After an unpromising academic beginning, Bataille trained as a librarian at the Ecole des Chartes and in 1922 obtained a position at the Bibliothèque Nationale in Paris which he was to hold for 20 years until his resignation on grounds of ill-health in 1942. After meeting Michel Leiris in 1924, Bataille began an association with the surrealist movement. He was one of the founders in 1929 of *Documents*, a review devoted to subjects such as ART, ethnography, and PSYCHOANALYSIS, to which he contributed a number of rather disturbing and obsessional essays. These aroused the wrath of André Breton, the official leader of Parisian surrealism, with whom Bataille was to be locked in bitter dispute through the early years of the 1930s. During this period, Bataille espoused an anti-Stalinist Marxism, which he expressed in his contributions to the journal *La Critique Sociale* from 1931 to 1934 and in his interest in Contre-Attaque, a political group which he founded in 1935. From 1936 onwards, however, the influence of MARX gave way to that of NIETZSCHE, as Bataille joined a small secret society of intellectuals called Acéphale, after the title of the short-lived journal which they published, and a more public group, the Collège de Sociologie. The latter, with which Bataille was associated from 1937 to 1939, was committed to the exploration of the sacred in primitive social life, and had the aim of making its forms and energies available for developed societies. After the war, Bataille devoted himself to ethnographic investigations, theological and philosophical speculation, and the writing of fiction, much of it pornographic.

From the beginning of his absorption in surrealism Bataille had been deeply attracted by the movement's interest in the base, the degraded, and the carnal. The grounds of Bataille's argument with surrealism, at least as its principles were expounded by André Breton, were that its interest in such excessive and unspeakable forms was accessory to the aim of sublimating the real into the "sur-real," the higher reality apprehended by art. Bataille's interest was drawn by contrast to the degradation of carnality, and especially those portions or functions of the human body which cannot but pose a threat to the integrity of individual and social identity, and so must be expelled from consciousness or acknowledgement – the anus, the genitals, the big toe. This interest may be contrasted with that of the Soviet linguist and critic Mikhail BAKHTIN. Where Bakhtin's aim is to reintegrate a body politic which has split itself neurotically and repressively between upper and lower, Bataille refuses to allow the expulsive, subversive violence of the body to be safely recuperated in the larger integration of the person or the social group.

Bataille's interest in everything excessive to or unassimilable by official social forms, an interest which he called "heterology," received a decisive impetus from his reading in the late 1920s of the work of the French anthropologist Marcel MAUSS. Mauss's *The Gift* (1923) includes an analysis of the practice of *potlatch* among native people of the Northwestern American coast, a practice in which prodigious quantities of goods and property are ceremonially destroyed with no other purpose than the gratuitous exhilaration derived from the act. Bataille responded enthusiastically to Mauss's suggestion that the practice of *potlatch* pointed to an economic, social, and psychological principle in human life which was at odds with the principles of utility and rational self-interest which held sway in developed societies. The idea that the fundamental drive in all human life is towards glorious expenditure rather than prudent conservation is enlarged upon in Bataille's 1933 essay "The notion of expenditure" (Bataille, 1985, pp. 116–29). This idea made sense of Bataille's fascination up to that time with the laughable, the grotesque, and the formless, in fact with everything that official society stigmatized as wasteful or without value, and it remained the organizing idea behind Bataille's subsequent investigations into art, literature, politics, ethnology, archaeology, philosophy, theology, sexuality, psychology, and economics. His *Interior Experience* (1943, trans. *1988*) attempted to articulate the value of a form of mystical self-abasement which would not be a mere detour from the road to the positive benefits of salvation or enlightenment. His *Literature and Evil* (1957b, trans. *1985*) explored the principle of amoral intensity as he found it in the works of Emily Brontë, William Blake, the Marquis de Sade, and Jean Genet. In *Eroticism* (1957a, trans. *1962*), Bataille gathered evidence of the close association between sexuality, violence, and death, especially in practices of mutilation and bodily extremity; this is an association

which had been elaborated in Bataille's own extraordinary pornographic fable, *The Story of the Eye* (1928, trans. *1979*), which was much admired by Roland BARTHES for its conjoining of bodily and textual perversity. The most ambitious and encompassing statement of Bataille's economic theories is to be found in his *The Accursed Share* (1949, trans. *1988*), which argues that the principle of expenditure in fact governs the astrobiological economics of the physical cosmos; Bataille finds the enactment of this in the sun, which we are accustomed to think of as the principle of life and increase, but is in fact nothing more than a "ceaseless prodigality" of slow but glorious self-destruction (Bataille, 1988, p. 29).

Bataille's influence has been immense and far-reaching. His uneasy relationship with Marxism, for example, anticipates that of many later French cultural theorists. Bataille for a time was attracted by the possibility that Marxism might release the revolutionary energies of transgression, though he was increasingly repelled by the repressive bureaucracy of state Marxism in the Soviet Union. His fidelity to the idea of a politics of ecstatic excess, which went beyond the constraining forms of institutionalized politics, provided a powerful precedent for the "libidinal politics" of Jean-François LYOTARD, Gilles Deleuze, and Félix Guattari in the late 1960s. Bataille's interest in Nietzsche may have been partly responsible for transmitting the prestige of this writer to French poststructuralism, especially in the work of Michel FOUCAULT. Foucault is drawn in particular to the principle of transgression that is theorized in Bataille's work, a transgression of boundaries that Foucault believes goes beyond even the conventional divisions between the conventional and the transgressive, in its affirmation of "the limitlessness into which it leaps as it opens this zone to existence" (Foucault, 1997, p. 35). Jean BAUDRILLARD's investigation during the early 1970s of the nature of value in contemporary consumer society draws heavily on Baudrillard's writings on economics. Bataille's critique of what he saw as the inherent conservatism of the economic model of the psyche in Freudian psychoanalysis has been taken up in various ways in the rereading of Freud conducted by recent French psychoanalysts, such as Jacques LACAN and Julia KRISTEVA; the latter's exploration of the force of the "abject" in social and psychological life draws particularly on Bataille. Perhaps the most significant area of Bataille's influence on contemporary thought has been the impact of his writing on the work of Jacques DERRIDA. Derrida's essay on Bataille in his *Writing and Difference* explores the challenge which Bataille's work offers to the prestige of reason in the Hegelian tradition. Where, in the dialectical process described by HEGEL, reason encounters its opposite or negation, in order finally to assimilate that negativity to a heightened and enlarged self-knowledge, Bataille's work proposes the ways in which reason can negotiate its own forms of absolute undoing or, in the term which Bataille uses to run together the economic and the philosophical, "dé-pense." Such a procedure has much in common with the process of DECONSTRUCTION which Derrida goes on to develop in later work.

Reading
Bataille, Georges 1928 (*1979*): *The Story of the Eye.*
—— 1943 (*1988*): *Inner Experience.*
—— 1949 (*1988*): *The Accursed Share.*
—— 1957a (*1962*): *Eroticism: Death and Sensuality.*
—— 1957b (*1985*): *Literature and Evil.*
—— 1985: *Visions of Excess: Selected Writings 1927–1939.*
Derrida, Jacques 1978a: "An hegelianism without reserve: from restricted to general economy in Georges Bataille."
Foucault, Michel 1977b: "Preface to transgression."
Hollier, Denis, ed. 1979: *Le Collège de Sociologie: Textes de Georges Bataille et Autres.*
Mauss, Marcel 1923 (*1990*): *The Gift: Form and Reason for Exchange in Archaic Societies.*
Richman, Michele 1982: *Reading Georges Bataille: Beyond the Gift.*

STEVEN CONNOR

Baudrillard, Jean (1929–) Jean Baudrillard has moved from being a sociologist of consumer society to being the most notorious and immoderate of the thinkers associated with POSTMODERNISM. The account he develops of contemporary mass culture and the mass media is far-reaching and extravagant in its claims, and has had an important influence across a number of disciplines, especially CULTURAL STUDIES, FILM, and LITERARY CRITICISM. It would probably also be true to say that the very flamboyance and hyperbole of Baudrillard's writing, especially from the 1980s onwards, which has brought him in almost equal measure such widespread adulation and notoriety, has also prevented that work from receiving the serious and sustained critical attention which it deserves.

Baudrillard's writing career began, like that of many French theorists since the 1960s, with a complex argument with MARXISM, an argument which is given particular impetus by the euphoria and

defeat of the events of May 1968. The shape of Baudrillard's social theory is determined by the trajectory of his disaffiliation from MARXISM. In a series of books which appeared between 1968 and 1973, Baudrillard undertakes to free social analysis from the narrow determinism of a Marxism that reduced CULTURE to the secondary effect of economic factors and relations. In *Le Système des Objects* (1968) and *La Société de Consommation* (1970), he argues that in a society organized on the principle of consumption rather than production, the economic categories of need, supply, distribution, and profit are inadequate for analyzing the nature and function of objects and commodities. Baudrillard maintains that the circulation of material goods in late twentieth-century developed economies is comprehensible only as the operation and diversification of linguistic codes. Baudrillard's most important contribution to the theory of consumer society is his insistence that consumption has little to do with the satisfaction of needs, actual or artificial. His argument is that CONSUMER CULTURE creates and sustains a universal CODE or SYSTEM of exchangeability between commodities. The desire of the consumer is not for this or that object or element within the code, but rather for inclusion within the system of consumption as a whole. Such inclusion is a potent means of social control, and is a wholly logical and necessary extension of the rationalization of the means of production.

In *For a Critique of the Political Economy of the Sign* (1972) and *The Mirror of Production* (1973), Baudrillard mounts a devastating assault on the idea of production which is so central to Marxist sociology. He focuses in these two books on the Marxist theory of value, and especially on the fundamental distinction it draws between use values, which are held to be immediate, authentic, and unfalsifiable, and exchange values, which come into being with the institution of the market, and are artificial, distorted, and exploitative. Baudrillard's argument is that all needs of whatever kind are always produced as the effect of structures of exchange and, latterly, as an effect of the code of consumption. The notion of use value therefore offers no political promise of redemption from the artificialities and distortions of the market, since use value is produced as a derivative or precipitate of the market. "Use value has no autonomy, it is only the *satellite* and *alibi* of exchange value," writes Baudrillard (1981, p. 139).

Nevertheless, despite the hostility toward a

central principle of Marxist analysis of culture, Baudrillard still seems at this point to be trying to revive and radicalize Marxist analysis rather than to bury it. These works, as well as his next, *Symbolic Exchange and Death* (1976, trans. *1993*), show the strain of trying to maintain an ideal and a rhetoric of social critique while seemingly undermining all of the values and principles which might give such critique its point. If there is no possibility of defining authentic human needs and values under market conditions that seem so totally to have abolished the distinction between the authentic and the artificial, if, indeed, that dream is a production of the very system against which it seems to stand, then what kind of critique is possible, and in the name of what conceivable form of liberation? In some of the essays dealing with the revolutionary spectacles and events of May 1968 in *For a Critique of the Political Economy of the Sign*, Baudrillard had still seemed to glimpse some principle of resistance to or refusal of what he calls grimly "the code." But the conclusion towards which he moves inexorably in *L'Echange symbolique et la mort* (1976) is that the system of symbolic exchange at work in contemporary consumer society is so all-encompassing that the only principle of resistance lies in the destruction or negation of all value or utility whatsoever. The only alternative value is the negation of value itself; such that ultimately and in a political sense, highly unpromisingly, the only challenge to the dominance of symbolic value is death. In this period of his work, Baudrillard draws close to the extreme political and aesthetic position associated with the work of Georges BATAILLE, who similarly rejects the principle of value as such.

From this point on, Baudrillard begins to develop the theoretical analysis of the present with which he has come to be most clearly identified, the analysis of the regime of the simulacrum. The distance travelled in Baudrillard's analysis from his works of the 1970s may be measured by a judgment offered in "The last tango of value," the final essay of his volume *Simulacres et Simulation* (1981). There the institution of the university, which 13 years before had seemed like the laboratory of new social and political values, is now characterized as "the site of a desperate initiation into the empty form of value," an obedient replication of that emptying out of value into indifference which has become the general condition of contemporary culture.

The most influential of Baudrillard's works from the 1980s is the essay "The precession of simulacra" from the same collection. There, he suggests that the dominance of signs, images, and representations in the contemporary world is such that the real has been effectively obliterated, and "truth, reference and objective causes have ceased to exist" (Baudrillard, 1988, p. 168; n.b. this translation of Baudrillard's essay confusingly gives it the title of the volume from which it is derived, "Simulacra and simulations"). He provides a useful, if slightly tongue-in-cheek synopsis of the historical stages by which this condition has been reached. Initially, the sign is "the reflection of a basic reality. In the second stage, the sign "masks and perverts a basic reality" (this is perhaps the stage of IDEOLOGY and manufactured false consciousness). In a third stage, the sign "masks the *absence* of a basic reality." In the fourth stage, at which the contemporary world has arrived, and from which it can hope neither to progress nor retreat, the sign "bears no relation to any reality whatever; it is its own pure simulacrum" (Baudrillard, 1988, p. 170).

Baudrillard's argument is often misunderstood. It is sometimes objected, for example, that the disappearance of reality is scarcely something that can constitute a historical event. Either the real continues to exist, only masked and dissimulated beneath impenetrable layers of simulation, in which case Baudrillard's claims about its disappearance are merely rhetorical; or it has never really existed, so that the developments Baudrillard describes are really only the recognition that what counts as "real" is always dependent upon activities of representation. However, these objections rest on an assumed absolute contrast between the real and the fictive which it is precisely the purpose of Baudrillard's analysis to contest. Central to that analysis is his provocative distinguishing of simulation from imitation. If one imitates or counterfeits an illness, it may be difficult, but not in principle impossible to detect the fraud, for such imitation keeps the distinction between the real and the false intact, even as it masks it. But when an illness is simulated, as for example in certain hysterical or psychosomatic conditions, some of the symptoms of the "actual" illness may indeed be produced in the person of the simulator. In such a case, the either/or logic of real and false, truth and deceit is threatened. It is this condition which Baudrillard insists is that of the modern world. It is not that everything has become purely fictional, or without real effects, since the point about a simulation is that it is both real and unreal (the simulated illness is a simulation rather than an imposture precisely because it *does* produce real effects). The basis of Baudrillard's argument is therefore not shaken substantially by arguments such as those of Christopher NORRIS, who pours scorn on Baudrillard's apparently lunatic prophecy in an article in *The Guardian* newspaper in February 1991 that the Gulf War would not take place, and his serene assurance in an article of the following month that despite all bloody appearances, the Gulf War had not in fact taken place (see Norris, 1993; Baudrillard, 1991). To argue as Baudrillard did that the Gulf War was so completely designed and executed as a media spectacle that it could not be said to have taken place as other wars have is not to argue that the Gulf War was a simple fabrication (this is to fall back into the real/false pattern of thinking which Baudrillard claims is no longer adequate or even available). Rather it is to claim that it is a simulation, precisely to the degree that the reproductive technology which represented the war as a spectacle also *was* the war in actual fact (this was instanced grotesquely in the guided missiles which had cameras in their nose cones). A war that consists largely of its own representation is no longer a real war in the old sense, no matter how ghastly its human consequences.

Perhaps the most telling part of Baudrillard's analysis of the effect of the waning of the sense of reality in the age of the simulacrum is his account of the "escalation of the true" which takes place as a kind of panic-stricken compensation, "a proliferation of myths of origin and signs of reality; of second-hand truth, objectivity and authenticity" (Baudrillard, 1988, p. 171). The desire to believe in what is natural, primitive, "real," or otherwise beyond the reach of reproductive or simulacral technologies is heightened by the awareness of the fading of such unfalsifiable truth. Paradoxically, this very desire can only express itself through more energetic acts of simulation than ever before. The false feeds the dream of the true, which can appear only as the "hyperreal" or simulated true.

Baudrillard develops an impressive array of terms and metaphors, many of them drawn from science fiction, to dramatize the grim fascination of appearances in the contemporary world. He has construed the world in biological terms, as the operationalization of codes and models, just as every embodied form is an operationalization of the DNA

which precedes and determines it. Elsewhere, he speaks of the "satellization" of the world, to convey the idea that the world has been reassembled as a perfect replica, and put into orbit around itself. Military metaphors also feature, in so far as modern military strategy seems a perfect exemplification of much of his argument: the world of appearance and reproduction is said to be a kind of "deterrence" of the real. Baudrillard devotes a whole book to an analysis of the effect of "seduction" which he claims signs and images exercise in the modern world (1979). The overheated multiplication of these images and devices in the restless proliferation of brilliant analyses that Baudrillard has continued to conduct of different areas of contemporary art and culture almost seems like a secret enactment of the principle of resistance that his analysis coolly declares to be impossible; as though a form of theory and critique that denies itself the authority to speak on behalf of the truth continued to assert an aesthetic principle of value in the transcendence or intensification of the real.

Reading

Baudrillard, Jean 1968: *Le Système des objets.*
—— 1970: *La Société de consommation.*
——1972 *(1981)*: *For a Critique of the Political Economy of the Sign.*
——1973 *(1975)*: *The Mirror of Production.*
——1976 *(1993)*: *Symbolic Exchange and Death.*
——1979 *(1990)*: *Seduction.*
——1981 *(1983)*: *Simulacra and Simulations.*
——1988: *Selected Writings.*
——1990 *(1993)*: *The Transparency of Evil: Essays on Extreme Phenomena.*
——1991: *La Guerre du Golfe n'a pas lieu.*
Kellner, Douglas 1989: *Jean Baudrillard: From Marxism to Postmodernism and Beyond.*
Norris, Christopher 1992: *Uncritical Theory: Postmodernism, Intellectuals and the Gulf War.*

STEVEN CONNOR

Beauvoir, Simone de (1908–86) French philosopher and novelist. Simone de Beauvoir was a pioneering feminist philosopher who has been justly called "the emblematic intellectual woman of the twentieth century" (Moi, 1994, p. 1). Her reputation, which is secure virtually everywhere but in France, rests largely on her prolific work as a writer and social activist. Her more than 25 books include works of philosophy: *Pyrrhus et Cineas* (1944), *The Ethics of Ambiguity* (1947), *The Second Sex* (1949); fiction: *She Came to Stay* (1943), *The Mandarins* (1954), *The Woman Destroyed* (1968); and memoirs: *Memoirs of a Dutiful Daughter* (1958), *The Prime of Life* (1960), *Force of Circumstance* (1963), *All Said and Done* (1972).

Although she was unable to enter the Ecole Normale Supérieure, which did not grant full student status to women until 1927, Beauvoir first studied mathematics, classics, and literature, and then in 1929 passed the prestigious *agrégation* examination at the Sorbonne in philosophy. She was only the ninth woman ever to have passed that examination in philosophy and the youngest *agrégée* (man or woman) ever in that discipline. Furthermore, she received the second highest mark, the first that year going to Jean-Paul SARTRE, with whom she was to have a lifelong relationship. Despite the many obstacles she had to overcome or to circumvent in order to do philosophy and be an intellectual woman, it was not until 1946, in a conversation with Sartre, that she was fully struck by the consequences of the difference between being born a woman and being born a man. This realization led her to give full attention to finding out about the condition of woman in its broadest terms (Beauvoir, 1963, p. 103). The result of this search was her most influential book, *The Second Sex*, which echoes the opening words of ROUSSEAU's *Social Contract*, in its proclamation of the birth of the free woman.

Throughout the 1950s, *The Second Sex* was the only book by an intellectual woman that exposed the hypocrisies of patriarchal IDEOLOGY (for an account of the book's reception, see Moi, 1994, pp. 179–213). However, as soon as the first installments of *The Second Sex* began to appear in *Les Temps Modernes* in 1948/9, the French intellectual establishment, including Albert CAMUS and François Mauriac, launched a series of outraged attacks on its author. Beauvoir recalled the hysteria of many of her first French readers in *Force of Circumstance*: "Unsatisfied, cold, priapic, nymphomaniac, lesbian, a hundred times aborted, I was everything, even an unmarried mother. People offered to cure me of my frigidity or to satisfy my ghoulish appetites" (Beauvoir, 1963, p. 197). Despite the moral courage and intellectual achievement of her book, Beauvoir has been either ignored or vehemently dismissed by such prominent French feminists as Julia KRISTEVA, Luce IRIGARAY, and Hélène CIXOUS. An important recent exception to this treatment is the work of Michèle Le Dœuff, who in *Hipparchia's Choice* demonstrates the importance of *The Second Sex* as simultaneously a work of materialist feminism and philosophical critique.

Reading
Beauvoir, Simone de 1949 (*1984*): *The Second Sex.*
—— 1963 (*1987*): *Force of Circumstance.*
Le Dœuff, Michèle 1989 (*1991*): *Hipparchia's Choice: An Essay Concerning Women, Philosophy, etc.*
Moi, Toril 1994: *Simone de Beauvoir: The Making of an Intellectual Woman.*

MICHAEL PAYNE

Becker, Howard Saul (1928–) American sociologist trained in the Chicago school of symbolic interactionism. Becker's work has had a significant influence on CULTURAL THEORY in two areas. His initial research on jazz clubs and musicians, published as *Outsiders* (1963), was central to 1960s deviant theory and had a major impact on British studies of both SUBCULTURE and POPULAR CULTURE (Becker was one of the few academics to study popular music). And in his 1970s work on ART WORLDS, Becker, like Pierre Bourdieu, demonstrated the continuing value of a sociological approach to aesthetic questions.

Reading
Becker, Howard S. 1963: *Outsiders. Studies in the Sociology of Deviant.*
—— 1982: *Art Worlds.*

SIMON FRITH

Benjamin, Walter (1892–40) German-Jewish philosopher and literary critic. He committed suicide while attempting to cross from occupied France into Spain on his way to America. Probably the most important European theorist of CULTURE this century; certainly the most important to identify with the Marxist tradition. Benjamin's writings display an extraordinary range of interests, often combining what at first sight appear to be eccentric and incompatible approaches to their objects. They are resolutely cross-disciplinary, and as concerned with what were then the latest cultural technologies (photography, film, radio) as they are with both the classical forms of bourgeois culture (drama, POETRY, the novel) and its more neglected marginalia (such as nineteenth-century children's books and toys).

Benjamin's writings are associated with the theoretical combination of materialist and theological perspectives. Thus, while his work may in some respects be seen as a forerunner of the omnivorous pluralism of CULTURAL STUDIES, in others it belongs to a different world entirely – the world of

1920s Jewish MARXISM with its subtle meditations on the inextricability of truth and history.

This diversity of perspectives and concerns has produced a number of competing schools of interpretation, each with its own distinctive "Benjamin," between which there has been heated debate: Benjamin the Critic, Benjamin the Marxist, Benjamin the Modernist, Benjamin the Jew. These disputes are complicated by the fact that Benjamin's thought developed through a series of distinct phases, marked by close personal relationships with other thinkers (in particular, Scholem, ADORNO, and BRECHT). Ideas from earlier periods were never wholly rejected, but subjected to a continual and unfinished process of recasting.

The key to the continuity of this process lies in Benjamin's distinction between immediate, everyday experience (*Erlebnis*) and authentic or philosophical experience (*Erfahrung*). The practical goal of all Benjamin's work was to transform everyday experience into the experience of truth: to seek out the ecstatic within the everyday, to find "history" within the merely historical, in order to recover the repressed energies of the past for the construction of a better future. In this almost Manichean polarization of forms of experience, Benjamin's writings may be compared to the other great philosophical work of Weimar culture, HEIDEGGER's *Being and Time* (1927), with its central distinction between "authentic" and "inauthentic" existence. However, despite this structural parallel, Benjamin's work stands opposed to Heidegger's in almost every other respect, both theoretically and politically. Benjamin's concern throughout the 1930s with the interconnected themes of ART, truth, and history constitutes a direct reply to Heidegger's work: the counterposition of a revolutionary Marxist philosophy of historical time to the philosophy of time and "Being" of the conservative revolution of German fascism.

The best way to chart the continuities and ruptures in Benjamin's thinking is to follow the changes in his conception of truth. This delineates a path from an early ROMANTIC aestheticism, associated with a programmatic rejection of politics, to a theologically enriched historical materialism of cultural forms, in solidarity with a left-wing communism, via the "profane illumination" of "Surrealist experience" (Benjamin, 1929). Benjamin's thought developed under the cumulative impact of a series of models of cultural experience – Proust, Kafka, Baudelaire, Brecht (Benjamin, 1968) – which were

constantly reworked to provide the terms of a Marxist theory of MODERNITY. But it is surrealism which is the key to the practical hopes of Benjamin's later writings.

Son of a well-to-do Jewish businessman who had made his money as an art dealer, Benjamin began his intellectual career at the University of Freiburg in the years immediately preceding the 1914–18 war with a dual rejection: intellectual rejection of the NEO-KANTIANISM then dominant in the academy in favor of a esoteric metaphysics of values; political rejection of the values of Wilhelminian society (what he later called "the abyss of my own class"), in favor of the anarchic radicalism of the Free Student Movement. An important, if little studied work from this period is entitled "Metaphysics of youth" (Benjamin, 1913). At the same time, Benjamin committed himself to a type of cultural Zionism that was resolutely internationalist. Judaism was understood as the representative of spiritual values *per se*, rather than the basis for any kind of nationally specific project. His early writings include an esoteric PHILOSOPHY OF LANGUAGE, centered on a biblical theory of naming, and an interrogation of the "mystical premises" of the early Romantic concept of criticism, in which he claims that "the very centre of Romanticism" is its Messianism.

At this stage, Benjamin's project was to expand to infinity the range of philosophical experience and to comprehend such experience on the model of the experience of the work of art. Criticism was the key to such comprehension since, according to Benjamin, it is criticism which "completes" the work. Developing from his doctoral dissertation on *The Concept of Art Criticism in German Romanticism* (1919), Benjamin's essay on Goethe's *Elective Affinities* (1923) elaborates a systematic critique of the SYMBOL as the cognitive structure of the work of art, identifying truth with allegory and the absence of expression. (The polemical force of this argument in the context of expressionism is clear.) At this point, Benjamin understood truth as a quasi-Platonic realm of ideas, represented by works of art, but recoverable as experience only through the philosophical criticism of art.

This theory achieves its final form in the difficult Prologue to Benjamin's *Habilitation*, the higher degree required for a tenured position in a German university, *The Origin of German Trauerspiel* (Benjamin, 1928a). (*Trauerspiel* means "sorrow play." It is a little-studied baroque genre which

Benjamin distinguished in principle from classical TRAGEDY.) The reception of this work – it was withdrawn to avoid formal rejection by the University of Frankfurt – led to the abrupt termination of the academic phase of Benjamin's life. Henceforth he would earn his living from journalism and take his motivation from politics, although he never became a member of the German Communist Party, with which he sympathized.

In leaving the academy for politics and the press, Benjamin abandoned the esoteric aspirations of his early work, replacing them with reflection on the historical conditions of its failure, in the form of a theorization of MODERNITY as the destruction of tradition. It is this theorization, embodied in the developing frame of Benjamin's critical essays, which constitutes his most enduring contribution to CULTURAL THEORY. It derived its inspiration from the cultural and political AVANT-GARDE of West Berlin, but it includes among its resources materials from the very tradition it rejects as beyond recuperation: the mystical tradition of Jewish Messianism, as recovered by Gershom Scholem, Benjamin's friend from before the 1914–18 war.

Benjamin's mature work is a sustained reflection on the contradictory relations between modernity and tradition, in which a variety of cultural forms are subjected to historical interpretation within the terms of a philosophy of history which draws on the Marxist and Messianic traditions alike. Yet Benjamin is far from being an eclectic thinker. Rather, once he grasped the depth of what he called the "crisis in the arts" as symptomatic of a crisis in the very form of historical time (tradition) upon which the work of art depends for its social existence, he saw that the question of truth had been displaced by history from art onto the historical process itself. History becomes the whole to which experience must be related if it is to become an experience of truth.

It is at this point that the mystical motifs of Jewish Messianism reenter the picture, with their totalizing sense of redemption, not as an event *within* history, but *of* history, as a whole. In opposition to both the peremptory teleology of HEGELIANISM and the complacent chronologism of Ranke's HISTORICISM, Jewish Messianism offered Benjamin a structure of thought in which to think of history as a whole, while still maintaining the openness of the present to political action. The explosive tension of the later work, manifest most

clearly in the famous thesis "On the concept of history" (Benjamin, 1940), is generated by the attempt to render such thought consistent with historical MATERIALISM under rapidly degenerating political conditions. This project took the form of a critique of the concept of progress.

It is this aspect of Benjamin's work – a philosophy of history which is utopian and pessimistic in equal measure – which exerted most influence on the FRANKFURT SCHOOL. In Benjamin's own case, it led to the redefinition of historiography from a type of science to a form of remembrance (*Eingedenken*), in active opposition to the "forgetting" taken to suffuse the historical time-consciousness of modernity.

One-Way Street (1928), in which the new perspective emerges for the first time with all the force and excitement of "the new," is one of the great works of the Weimar avant-garde. "Significant literary work," it declares in the first of its series of fragments, "can only come into being in a strict alternation between writing and action; it must nurture the inconspicuous forms that better fit its influence in active communities than does the pretentious, universal gesture of the book – in leaflets, brochures, articles, and placards. Only this prompt language shows itself actively equal to the moment." Benjamin's production would henceforth be fagmentary and essayistic, not merely out of financial necessity, but also as a matter of joint aesthetic and political principle. In the slipstream of surrealism, Benjamin endowed what Ernst BLOCH called his "feel for the peripheral" with the weightiest claims of the philosophical tradition. In the process, he produced some of the most powerful critical writing of the century. His model for such writing – alternating between writing and action – was the film.

"All the problems of contemporary art," Benjamin wrote in his massive unfinished work on nineteenth-century Paris, the *Arcades Project*, "find their final formulation only in relation to film" (Benjamin, 1972, V). To understand this statement, one needs to appreciate the depth to which Benjamin understood all forms of cultural experience as having been transformed by technology and commodification (Benjamin, 1936). In its inherent "reproducibility," culture in twentieth-century capitalist societies distinguishes itself from all previous artistic forms, and contains a potentially progressive collective content. At the same time, however, this content is imprisoned within the fetish character of the commodity form, which cuts off the experience of the work from an appreciation of the social processes through which it is produced, received, and transmitted to future generations.

Benjamin took Brecht's epic theater as the model for an artistic practice which would combat this tendency toward self-enclosure by making the exposure of the conditions for the production of the work a part of the work itself. In this vein, he developed the idea of the author as a "producer," on the model of MARX's analysis of the labor process (Benjamin, 1934).

On the other hand, Benjamin set himself apart from other Marxist theorists of culture by refusing to dismiss the commodity form merely as a realm of false consciousness. Instead, he attempted its "dialectical redemption" as a form of historical consciousness by seeking, through its fetish character, access to a new (allegorical) form of experience of history as a fulfilled whole. The light cast by this essentially instantaneous experience of history as a whole – for which Benjamin used the term *Jetztzeit*, meaning "now-time" – is taken to reveal the present as unfulfilled, and thereby to provide an impulse to its radical transformation. The anarchic libertarianism of Benjamin's youth is thus reproduced in his mature theory in the explosive structure of the Messianic "now," although this is only the best known of a series of models of historical experience to be found in his later writings. (Benjamin did not intend his thesis "On the concept of history" to be published. In fact, he explicitly anticipated its miscomprehension.)

In the combination of a refusal to dismiss the commodity form as mere false consciousness with an interest in its character as representation and object of fantasy, Benjamin is taken by some to have anticipated the affirmative attitude towards commodification characteristic of POSTMODERNISM. Yet it is important to distinguish Benjamin's Marxist concept of phantasmagoria (the interpretation of the world of commodities as a dream-world), in principle, from such notions of BAUDRILLARD's as simulation and hyperreality, since Benjamin remained committed to a metaphysical conception of the objectivity of truth. Indeed, his entire *oeuvre* revolves around one. In this respect, he is better viewed as a baroque or even a gothic Marxist (Cohen, 1993) than any kind of postmodernist *avant la lettre*.

See also ART; MARXISM.

Reading
Benjamin, Walter 1968: *Illuminations*.
——1977: *Understanding Brecht*.
——1979: *One-Way Street and Other Writings*.
Buck-Morss, Susan 1989: *Dialectics of Seeing: Walter Benjamin and the Arcades Project*.
Lunn, Eugene 1982: *Marxism and Modernism: An Historical Study of Lukács, Brecht, Benjamin and Adorno*.
McCole, John 1993: *Walter Benjamin and the Antinomies of Tradition*.
Scholem, Gershom 1975 (*1982*): *Walter Benjamin: The Story of a Friendship*.
Smith, Gary, ed. 1988: *On Walter Benjamin: Critical Essays and Reflections*.
——ed. 1989: *Walter Benjamin: Philosophy, Aesthetics, History*.
Witte, Bernd 1985 (*1991*): *Walter Benjamin: An Intellectual Biography*.
Wolin, Richard 1982: *Walter Benjamin: An Aesthetic of Redemption*.

PETER OSBORNE

Benveniste, Emile (1902–76) French linguist. Benveniste is best known for his creative combination of historical linguistics with STRUCTURALISM, which extended linguistics into CULTURAL THEORY. His best-known works are *Problems of General Linguistics* (1966) and *Indo-European Language and Society* (1969). One of his most influential arguments is his qualified disagreement with Ferdinand de SAUSSURE's principle that the nature of the linguistic SIGN is arbitrary. By focusing much of his attention on the speaker of language, Benveniste resisted the tendency in linguistics to treat language as simply a formal SYSTEM. In this respect, his work had a significant impact on Julia KRISTEVA's SEMIOTICS and her efforts to close the gap between linguistics and PSYCHOANALYSIS.

Reading
Benveniste, Emile 1966 (*1971*): *Problems of General Linguistics*.
——1969 (*1973*): *Indo-European Language and Society*.
Kristeva, Julia 1974a (*1984*): *Revolution in Poetic Language*.
MICHAEL PAYNE

Bernstein, Leonard (1918–90) Musician, born in Lawrence, Massachusetts. One of the first US-born musicians to gain international esteem and reputation, essentially by means of his conducting. At the age of 40 he became the youngest music director hired by the New York Philharmonic Orchestra. Throughout his life he was guest conductor to the major orchestras of the world and recorded hundreds of performances, especially with the Vienna, Israel, and New York Philharmonics. His talents and creative endeavors were extensive in other areas as well, including the composition of symphonic music, Broadway musicals, ballets, songs, film and theatre scores. He made pioneering efforts in music education, much of which is found in his extremely popular and influential work in television (most notably his *Omnibus* programs and *Young People's Concerts*). His influence on others was extensive and his lasting work ranged from composer and conductor to pianist and scholar.

Bernstein's philosophical and cultural reflections can be found in numerous lectures, essays, correspondences, and critical musical studies. (Some of these are in his popular texts: *The Joy of Music*, 1959; *The Infinite Variety of Music*, 1966, and *Findings*, 1982; while others, including many of his public lectures and television scripts and presentations, are only now being published and made readily available.) The principal text, however, that unifies and situates Bernstein's work is his Harvard lectures of 1973, the Charles Eliot Norton Lectures, entitled *The Unanswered Question* (published in 1976). It is there that we find a direct and sustained attempt to understand the variety of questions and themes that pervaded Bernstein's life in all of its forms, including the nature of music, the human craving for universality, the problem of negation, the challenge to the musical perspectives of Theodor ADORNO, the introduction of interdisciplinary study to the intellectual and popular communities, and the value of personal exploration and expression of self.

Standing behind everything scholarly Bernstein did is his devotion to and expression of interdisciplinary study. When discussing his student days at Harvard and specifically his philosophical studies, Bernstein says, "the principal thing I absorbed from Professor Prall [his philosophy professor], and from Harvard in general, was a sense of interdisciplinary value – that the best way to 'know' a thing is in the context of another discipline." It is this epistemological interest in knowing one thing by means of the context of something else that guides and provides the method for much of Bernstein's work. In his attempts to understand music, for example, he sets it side by side with disciplines and concerns such as linguistics (CHOMSKY), poetry (ELIOT), physics (laws of sound), anthropological speculations about origins (ROUSSEAU, Schopenhauer), and philosophy (EXISTENTIALISM). His reason for such

a method is a belief that it will lead not only to a better perspective on the nature of music or any discipline so investigated, but just as importantly to an improved understanding of the self, of the human creature who creates and lives such a disciplined existence. Interdisciplinary study is finally, for Bernstein, an expression of the self and being we all share; an investigation of that (nonprivate) being we have in common with others.

This expression of a common being reflects Bernstein's efforts to exhibit the human craving (his own craving) for universal grounding of our being. Interdisciplinary attempts at understanding music are exemplary of other attempts at finding the universal grounding and impulses of any inquiry, music being one example of an expression of common human beingness. For Bernstein, the pursuit of our personal feelings and the expressions, the deeply confessional expressions, of these feelings reveal our shared being, and universal connection, with others. This claim requires a studied and holistic reading of *The Unanswered Question* to be truly appreciated. However, there is another way to come to recognize this perspective of Bernstein. The problem of how to speak to others about those things we have deeply studied and investigated continually concerned Bernstein. The Norton Lectures again and again ask: "Who is the audience?" "To whom am I speaking?" "How am I to make myself understood?" This concern was of immense importance when Bernstein thought about how to speak to "laymen," to a nondiscipline-specific audience, about music. He had no tolerance for the "music appreciation racket" as he sometimes called it, but he was well aware that a technical, discipline-bound discussion would fall flat and be of little interest to all but a few. So how is one to speak to others (about this or anything else)? Bernstein believed that he could do so only by investigating himself: by uncovering those ingredients and characteristics of a musical subject, or a musical composition, which were exciting to him and spoke to him personally. Investigations of the self can give us something to say, for we find in ourselves a possible common bond with others. These revealed feelings and findings are then expressed, with the help of interdisciplinary methods and examples, in standard, ordinary language, in that everyday language we all share. Importantly, for Bernstein, investigations of the self allow us to ask the perfectly ordinary questions: "Don't you feel as I feel?" "Don't you find in yourself the same experiences I find?" (Such questions were asked again and again in Bernstein's writings.) Our meaningful attempts to communicate with others must come from careful pursuits of self-knowledge expressed in the form of personal confession and feelings. (It is this devotion to study and expression of himself that made Bernstein's attempt to communicate with others so successful, whether it be *Young People's Concerts*, performances of Mahler, or investigations of negation and death in the Norton Lectures.) In his pursuit of himself Bernstein found others and his common bond with others.

Bernstein found the question of the nature of music closely tied to the question of the nature of the twentieth century. Both face crises of being that, when investigated, shed light on the inevitable crisis of self. When examining the twentieth-century crisis in music, in the Norton Lectures, one of Bernstein's central antagonists is Theodor Adorno, specifically Adorno's text, *The Philosophy of Modern Music* (1948). Bernstein's discussion throughout these lectures can be usefully read, as aspiring to be read, as an antithesis to Adorno's text. Many similar topics are discussed in the two: neoclassicism, music about music, the origins of tonality, subjectivity and objectivity, sincerity and inauthenticity. But whereas Adorno sees the crisis, represented in the compositions of Schoenberg and Stravinsky, in fairly stark terms, as a choice between good and evil, progress and stagnation, Bernstein sees both Stravinsky and Schoenberg searching for the same thing, just in different ways. They share the same motivation: increased expressive power. Bernstein believes the difficulties expressed in twentieth-century music are more complex than Adorno allows, and that Adorno simply misreads Stravinsky and lacks sufficient literary appreciation for what Stravinsky does. Irony, humor, literary indirections all escape the narrow and dogmatic approach taken by Adorno.

In his Norton Lectures, Bernstein attempts to confront honestly and nondogmatically, in broad interdisciplinary ways, the disappointments, negations, and threats of nihilism that confront him in the century his life spans (the century of death, as he calls it). The self-confidence exhibited at the beginning of the twentieth century is shattered, and a crisis of self and questioning of one's self follows. Bernstein tries to understand this crisis of self through questions about the nature of music, which as a discipline faces a similar crisis and search. Ultimately both face the reality of death.

Nevertheless, even in the face of this great negation of being, humans still create and struggle to express themselves. For Bernstein, musical expression shows the human desire to affirm human life and creativity directly in the face of nihilism and death. What more positive expression of our common being can there be, asks Bernstein, than such an impulse? It is such extreme passion and existential affirmation that pervades Bernstein's work and writing, and few have missed it. However, without an understanding of the scholarly work and methods that surround these characteristics we miss much of his real depth and value as a teacher, composer, and conductor.

Reading
Bernstein, Leonard 1976: *The Unanswered Question*.
Burton, Humphrey 1994: *Leonard Bernstein*.
Ewen, David 1960: *Leonard Bernstein*.
Gradenwitz, Peter 1987: *Leonard Bernstein: The Infinite Variety of a Musician*.
Ledbetter, Steven, ed. 1988: *Sennets and Tuckets: A Bernstein Celebration*.
Museum of Broadcasting, 1985: *Leonard Bernstein: The Television Work*.

RICHARD FLEMING

biblical studies   One of the most important and most controversial developments in biblical studies during the past 20 years has been the influence of literary and CRITICAL THEORY on the understanding of biblical TEXTS, the circumstances of their composition, and the history of their interpretation. Myth criticism, feminist theory, SEMIOTICS, STRUCTURALISM, DECONSTRUCTION, READER-RESPONSE CRITICISM have all been employed in readings of individual texts, as well as in an attempt to understand Hebrew Scripture, the New Testament, and the Old and New Testaments as a whole. Although Stephen D. Moore has demonstrated that "literary criticism has been a component of biblical criticism almost since its inception" (1989, p. xv), the dismissive phrase "the Bible as literature" has been often used defensively against biblical scholarship that draws on theories and practices of LITERARY CRITICISM. This has only partly been the consequence of an opposition between secular literary scholars and practicing Jews and Christians. It has also been the result of a theoretical clash between formalist literary critics determined to find aesthetic unity in every text and textual scholars whose documentary hypothesis leads them to see the Bible as a mosaic of texts composed at different times but later edited into a not quite seamless whole (see Gros Louis, 1982, pp. 13–34). Matthew ARNOLD set out the terms of this controversy in *God and the Bible*, when he wrote, "the language of the Bible is not scientific, but *literary*. That is, it is the language of poetry and emotion, approximate language thrown out, as it were, at certain great objects which the human mind augurs and feels after, and thrown out by men very liable, many of them to delusion and error" (*1978*, p. 228).

Northrop FRYE, while acknowledging openly his debt to Vico rather than perhaps a more profound one to Arnold, began a preliminary series of maps of the Bible's literary landscape, extending through seven phases of revelation that link the Old Testament (or Hebrew Bible) with the New Testament. (Frye also had to work under the shadow of T.S. ELIOT's condemnation of the literary study of the Bible in his essay "Religion and literature:" "The fact that men of letters now discuss [the Bible] as 'literature' probably indicates the *end* of its 'literary' influence" (Eliot, *1960*, p. 344)). In such books as *Anatomy of Criticism* (1957), *Creation and Recreation* (1980), and *The Great Code: The Bible and Literature* (1982), Frye provided the most comprehensive literary theoretical study of the Bible yet published. His discussion of typology within and between the Old and New Testaments is the key to Frye's view of the Bible and the poetics of its historiography. Typological reading sees an earlier story (the *typos*) as completed by – and achieving its meaning from – a later one (the *antitypos*). Cain and Abel by Jacob and Esau, Moses by Jesus, Jesus by Paul. An inescapable consequence of typological reading, however, is the cultural appropriation of what comes early (in the text or in history) by what comes later. Thus, the New Testament could be typologically read as the definitive antitype to the Old, and Jewish culture as merely a prologue to Christianity.

In *The Poetics of Biblical Narrative* (1985) Meir Sternberg does not condescend to mention Frye (perhaps as a consequence of Frye's typologies) even in the context of his many arguments with other literary critics of the Bible. Sternberg's ambitious book, which was the first volume in the Indiana Literary Biblical Series, uses modern literary criticism to illuminate the surface and the depths of biblical narrative, while it also turns scriptural texts back on literary criticism in an attempt to correct and augment the practices of literary theorists.

Sternberg believes that, while literary critics can contribute significantly to biblical study, they also will receive from the Bible beneficial instruction in the techniques of narrative and the ways to interpret it. The Bible thus generates its own NARRATOLOGY.

Critics are more likely than other students of the Bible, Sternberg suggests, to pose fundamental questions about the functional structure of narrative and to examine carefully the transaction between narrator and audience that produces the Bible's strategic effects. The methods of the NEW CRITICISM must, however, be supplemented by communication theory (or the rhetoric of fiction) and by READER-RESPONSE CRITICISM to produce a method that begins to be adequate for biblical study.

> To offer a poetics of biblical narrative is to claim that biblical narrative is a work of literature. Not just an artful work; not a work marked by some aesthetic property; not a work resorting to so-called literary devices; not a work that the interpreter may choose (or refuse) to consider from a literary viewpoint . . . but a literary work. (Sternberg, 1985, p. 2)

Biblical scholars ignorant of the complexities of modern literary criticism misleadingly refer to "*the* literary approach," as though literary studies were monolithic. Instead, Sternberg argues, the study of the Bible by those who see it as a literary work will necessarily generate a new poetics of literature as a whole, enlarging biblical and literary studies at the same time. In this respect, his argument converges with Frye's.

The essence of Sternberg's thesis is that the ideological, historical, and aesthetic dimensions of the Bible invite a dynamic response from those who work carefully with the text, a response in which reading becomes a dramatic act. The "ideological imperative" of scripture, in his view, is the celebration of God's mastery over creation, which takes the form of "the shift of ground from existence to epistemology" (p. 46). The crucial link between omniscient narrative form and theological content is that throughout the Bible God's omniscience is displayed against the background of man's limitations. Such a contrast between the divine and the human gives rise to the longing for a historical vision of sufficient power to place the facts of limited human experience within a panoramic, coherent context that can make the past retrospectively present in human consciousness. At the same time that the ideological dimension of the Bible gives rise to an aesthetic preference for omniscient narration consistent with the view of God's mastery, its historical dimension renders in realistic detail the intractable imperfection of human beings. Finally, the experience of reading the Bible casts "interpretation as an ordeal that enacts and distinguishes the human predicament" (p. 46) of limitation that reaches out to an infinite divinity, leading the reader to fresh or renewed understanding of divine and human creativity.

Sternberg's biblical criticism, much of it originally written in Hebrew, came to the attention of most Western readers through Robert Alter's generous citations in *The Art of Biblical Narrative* (1981). The following pastiche of quotations from Alter indicates the similarity between his and Sternberg's critical practices:

> It is important to move from the analysis of formal structures to a deeper understanding of the values, the moral vision embodied in a particular kind of narrative. . . . Meaning, perhaps for the first time in narrative literature, was conceived as a *process*, requiring continual revision – both in the ordinary sense and in the etymological sense of seeing-again – continual suspension of judgment, weighing of multiple possibilities, brooding over gaps in the information provided . . . The implicit theology of the Hebrew Bible dictates a complex moral and psychological realism in biblical narrative because God's purposes are always entrammeled in history, dependent on the acts of individual men and women for their continuing realization . . . [There is in the Bible] a complete interfusion of literary art with theological, moral, or historiosophical vision, the fullest perception of the latter dependent on the fullest grasp of the former. (Alter, 1981, pp. x, 12, 19)

Alter's book is still the best guide in English to the Hebrew Bible's narrative strategies.

In a subsequent volume, *The Art of Biblical Poetry* (1985), Alter supplies an equally comprehensive guide to the formal systems of biblical poetry. In the first three chapters of this book he explores the basic system of semantic parallelism in biblical poetry, which, unlike phonetic and syntactic elements, survives translation. Adopting Barbara Herrnstein Smith's proposal that POETRY is distinguished from prose by readers who perceive

"that a verbal sequence has a sustained rhythm, that it is formally structured according to a continuous operating principle of organization," Alter proceeds to show that what sets biblical poetry off from surrounding prose is "the strictly observed principle of parallelism" (Alter, 1985, p. 6). Biblical poetry relies on parallelism between two (or sometimes three) fractions of a line, called versets. Alter's account of this technique can easily be summarized by applying it to the opening lines of five psalms selected almost at random:

Ps. 46: God is our refuge and strength/
    a very present help in trouble.

Ps. 47: O clap your hands, all ye people:/
    shout unto God with the voice of
    triumph.

Ps. 49: Hear this, all ye people:/
    give ear, all ye inhabitants of the
    world.

Ps. 50: The mighty God even the Lord hath
    spoken./
    and called the earth from the rising of
    the sun to the going down thereof.

Ps. 51: Have mercy upon me, O God, according
    to thy loving-kindness/
    according unto the multitude of thy
    tender mercies blot out my
    transgressions.

There are essentially three kinds of parallelism in biblical poetry: parallelism of meaning (Pss 46 and 49); parallelism of stresses between the half-lines (Ps. 47): and syntactic parallelism – "the word order in each of the half-lines mirroring the other, with each corresponding term in the same syntactic position" (p. 7) – which often produces a chiastic structure (Ps. 51). Alter points out that modern scholarship has neglected J.G. Herder's important observation of the late eighteenth century that biblical parallelism is rarely used for synonymity; rather, "the two [parallel] members strengthen, heighten, empower each other" (p. 11). The examples from the Psalms illustrate how these intensifying effects are achieved: by an impulse to intensification, with an implied "how much more so" in the second half-line (Ps. 49); by focusing, in a movement from the general to the specific (Ps. 46); by linguistic intensification, in a movement from standard to literary diction (Ps. 51); by a movement toward narrativity, from metaphor to story (Ps. 50); and by a movement toward the extreme, or hyperbole (Ps. 47). Although he does not dwell on this point, Alter implies that the reliance of biblical Hebrew poetry on parallelism greatly contributed to the cultural transmission of the Bible in translation.

Gerald Hammond's *The Making of the English Bible* (1983) is a detailed examination of the evolution of the Bible in English during the sixteenth and seventeenth centuries, which culminated in the appearance of the Authorized (or King James) Version of 1611. By carefully comparing Renaissance and modern readings with the Hebrew and Greek texts, Hammond concludes that the practice and achievement of the earlier translators is in most ways preferable to the methods of subsequent modern scholarly translators of the Bible in English:

> To translate meaning while ignoring the way that meaning has been articulated is not translation at all but merely replacement – murdering the original instead of recreating it. It is partly a matter of the creative inferiority of the modern translators; normally they are scholars and exegetes whose instincts are to replace the dangerous ambiguities of poetry with the safer specificities of prose. They do not see that the life of anything written lies in the words and syntax. While the Renaissance Bible translator saw half of his task as reshaping English so that it could adapt itself to Hebraic idiom, the modern translator wants to make no demands on the language he translates into. (Hammond, 1983, p. 2)

Hammond gives his highest praise to William Tyndale's translations, which, despite the adverse conditions which then prevailed, achieve simplicity, flexibility, and surprising literalness, combined with "a fine capacity to tap the emotional resources of his original" (p. 43). The New English Bible, despite its translators' scholarly advantages over Tyndale, is the antithesis to the Authorized Version and "has, in effect, unmade [an English] Bible which took ninety years to make, and which held the imaginations and emotions of its readers for three hundred and fifty years" (p. 13). One might also add that many lives were sacrificed, including Tyndale's, for the Authorized Version.

In contrast to the negative example of the New English Bible, several features of Renaissance translations – especially the Authorized Version – stand out clearly. The early translators sought to preserve some of the alien features of the original instead of statically translating word for word or idiom for idiom. They celebrated and incorporated the difference of their primary text. The Renaissance versions accordingly reshaped English idiom to adapt it to the Hebrew original, they preserved poetic ambiguities, rather than reshaping them into prose, they maintained the word order of the original and often translated idioms literally, rather than searching for appropriate idiomatic English equivalents; with relative consistency they retained the same English word for the Hebrew, allowing for important comparisons between passages in different parts of the Bible; they recognized that the most literal rendering is often the most powerful (as in the construct form "to eat the *bread of sorrows*" noun + "of" + noun); and they relied on the imaginative and interpretive skills of readers (see RENAISSANCE STUDIES).

For his translation of the Old Testament, Tyndale worked from the Masoretic text that was first printed in 1488. Unlike modern translators who are aware of variants and emendations in the Hebrew, Tyndale saw his source as an immutable original. Because of this view, Tyndale was concerned to achieve fullness of translation, neither taking anything away nor adding anything to the original as he saw it, while at the same time conveying some of the nuances of Hebrew style. One of the most important of these stylistic features is a lack of variation in word order, which results from the ubiquitous use of *waw* (a coordinating suffix in biblical Hebrew) that produces predominately coordinating rather than subordinating clauses. This practice creates the effect of neutral narrative development (despite omniscient narration) in which events seem simply to unfold. This coordinated style is commonly associated with the unsophisticated and fluent ways children tell stories, reducing or conflating any separate sense of cause and consequence into simultaneity. Fidelity to this feature of biblical Hebrew runs counter to the highly interpretative and complex practices in the prose of Erasmus, More, Lyly, and Sidney. (Although Hammond does not dwell on this, coordinated prose style reinforces also the practice of poetic parallelism in the Bible.)

Because Old Testament Hebrew is a highly inflected language, it often uses separate pronouns for emphasis: "She, even she herself said, He is my brother." Such repetition for emphasis is a distinguishing feature of Tyndale's translation, even though he strikes a balance between stylistic variation and repetition. For example, the Hebrew text often matches a verb with its most directly derived noun: "God plagued Pharaoh . . . with great plagues." In reproducing these stylistic details, Tyndale displays his most distinctive quality, which Hammond describes as "his matching of simple and direct English to a care for the essential meaning of the original text" (p. 38). Tyndale was generally correct in his view that English is better suited than Latin as a language for translating Hebrew. Furthermore, two major syntactic differences between English and Hebrew are resolved by his translation: in Hebrew the verb normally precedes the subject (". . . and said Moses") and the adjective often follows the noun ("cities great and walled up to heaven"). Later sixteenth-century translators followed Tyndale in modifying the usual English syntax to retain the Hebrew word order. This balance between literalness and flexibility, Hammond observes, appears also in the fluidity of Tyndale's narrative style. The practice of separating the text into verses began with the Geneva Bible. As useful as that practice has become for purposes of reference, Tyndale appears to have thought beyond separate verses and thus more fluidly in paragraphs (now a rare feature in modern Bibles). To illustrate this point, Hammond offers the telling example of Tyndale's translation of Num. 14:22–5, where God explains why the Children of Israel will not see the promised land. Whereas the Authorized Version breaks up the narrative into sentences that closely correspond to the verse units, Tyndale turns three and a half verses into a controlled sentence of more than a hundred words, while retaining the Hebrew word order:

> For all of those men which have seen my glory and my miracles which I did in Egypt and in the Wilderness, and you have tempted me now this ten times, and have not harkened unto my voice, there shall not one see the land which I sware unto their fathers, neither shall any of them that railed upon me see it: but my servant Caleb, because there is another manner [of] spirit with him, and because he hath followed me unto the utmost, him will I bring into the land which he that waled in, and his seed shall conquer it, and also the Amalachites and Canaanites which dwell in the low countries.

Such a capacity to render biblical narrative, Hammond observes, had a major positive impact on the development of English prose, even though it soon began to lose ground first to the Authorized and then to later versions.

Because of Tyndale's imprisonment and execution, the English Reformation Bible was completed by Miles Coverdale, whose ignorance of Hebrew and Greek forced him to rely on his aesthetic judgment in choosing among translations. Tyndale had completed the Pentateuch, Jonah, the Old Testament historical books, and the New Testament, leaving most of the poetic books untranslated. These books, especially the Psalms, are Coverdale's great legacy. Coverdale's grasp of the essence of Hebrew poetry was intuitive but remarkably accurate, given his ignorance of Hebrew scholarship. His translations evolve toward a rendering of the parallel structure of Hebrew poetry, including such fine details as chiastic word order. Coverdale's 1535 Bible was the first complete Bible printed in English, and his 1539 Great Bible became the first authorized version. In making his 1539 revisions, he had access to the more scholarly Continental versions, which enabled him to bring his word order closer to the Hebrew and to make his word choices more exact. Despite the appearance of other English Bibles after the two Coverdale Bibles, the translations of Tyndale, Coverdale, and the Geneva Bible became the chief influences on the Authorized Version.

The major achievement of Hammond's book is that it tells the story of the English Bible's evolution from the inside out, comparing words and syntax of several versions with the original in order to show what the Bible is and why the legacy of Tyndale is so rich. However, in all of his attention to detail, Hammond wisely allows the versions he analyzes to make their own subtle case against contemporary claims of literalism and fundamentalism that are so adamantly opposed to modern biblical scholarship. "For is the Kingdome of God become words or syllables?" the Authorized Version's translators ask rhetorically in their Preface, as though anticipating twentieth-century biblical conservatism. Relying on the finest classical scholarship of their time and inspired by a loyalty to the Hebrew and Greek texts, while still retaining a respect for the achievements of their inspired predecessors, the 1611 translators achieved perhaps the finest thing ever produced by a committee. In its retention of parallelism and coordination, its treatment of the infinitive, its reproduction of a consecutive narrative syntax, and its use of the English equivalent of the construct form, the Authorized Version established an English biblical style that has had a powerful hold over English prose until modern times.

In an effort to recover the intersection of biblical narrative art with processes of its interpretation, several scholars have recently conducted investigations of the hermeneutical technique that incorporates interpretation into the retelling of the story that it sets out to explain. A rough approximation of the midrashic tradition can be captured from this delightful passage in the Talmud in which some rabbis are discussing the fourth verse of Psalm 2: "He that sitteth in the heavens shall laugh." Rabbi Isaac's somber reflection that God laughs only on that day described apocalyptically in the psalm prompts a discussion that includes Rabbi Judah's account of how God spends each day:

> The day consists of twelve hours: during the first three hours the Holy One, blessed be He, is occupying Himself with the Torah; during the second three He sits in judgment on the whole world, and when He sees that the World is so guilty as to deserve destruction, he transfers Himself from the seat of Justice to the seat of Mercy; during the third quarter, He is feeding the whole world, from the horned buffalo to the brood of vermin; during the fourth quarter He is sporting with the leviathan. (Abodah Zarah, p. 36)

Finally, Rabbi Nahman b. Isaac concludes the discussion by pointing out that God sports *with* His creatures and does not laugh *at* them except on the day mentioned in the psalm.

This passage in its own way suggests many of the topics explored in *Midrash and Literature*, edited by Geoffrey Hartman and Sanford Budick (1986). God is a close reader even of his own text and gives first priority each day to poring over it. There is humor and joy in His activities, just as there is in the rabbis' reading of the psalm. Then, as they interpret the psalm, the rabbis produce a kind of discourse that is the very essence of midrash in that their interpretation of an earlier text becomes embodied in a narrative within a new text, thus distinguishing midrash from typology. As David Stern puts it, "Midrash . . . touches upon literature not at the point where literature becomes exegesis but at what might be called its opposite

conjunction, where exegesis turns into literature and comes to possess its own language and voice" (Hartman and Budick, 1986, p. 105). In this volume and in *The Genesis of Secrecy* (1979), *The Art of Telling* (1983), and in his contributions to *The Literary Guide to the Bible* (Alter and Kermode, 1987), Frank KERMODE takes up one of the most perplexing questions concerning the Bible: Can we say anything we like about a text, or are there institutional controls on interpretation? This question poses an antithesis between *midrash* and *peshat*, or the plain sense of things. Taking his cue from Wallace Stevens's "The snow man," Kermode argues that the antithesis may be insubstantial, that the longing for the plain sense can never be satisfied, that "the plain sense depends . . . on imaginative activity of interpreters" (Hartman and Budick, p. 191). Finally, it is not the text but the institution of which he is a part that limits the interpreter's freedom. In this respect Christian interpreters have enjoyed less hermeneutical freedom than Jewish interpreters, for the Church "in some ways stood to the New Testament as the New Testament did to the Old" (p. 187). Even in our own time, Kermode argues, Protestant hermeneutics has insisted upon the necessity of understanding tradition as formative of the horizon from which we must seek some kind of encounter with ancient texts (188). (In "New Ways with Bible Stories" (Kermode, 1990, pp. 29–48) Kermode provides the best brief account available of recent biblical scholarship inspired by literary criticism and narrative theory.)

Of the several feminist critics who have set out to challenge the traditional institutional restraints on interpretation, which they see as essentially patriarchal, Mieke Bal's *Lethal Love: Feminist Literary Readings of Biblical Love Stories* (1987) and Alicia Ostriker's *Feminist Revision and the Bible* (1993) are among the most provocative. Ostriker puts her version of the challenge to traditional interpretation succinctly: "The biblical story of monotheism and covenant is, to use the language of politics, a cover-up; . . . when we lift the cover we find quite another story, an obsessively told and retold story of erased female power" (p. 30). A neglected text for the case that female power is most often erased when the Bible is read is the stunning example of Proverbs 8, in which an explicitly female wisdom announces that she was present with God at the beginning of creation, that even before the world was she was there, that those who ignore (or hate) her wisdom love only death. But here of course, as Sternberg observed, the Bible provides its own challenge to later interpretation. Proverbs 8 is a self-contained, chapter-length monologue, which awaits any reader who finds his or her way through the polyvocal texts of the Pentateuch, the histories, and the prophets to the long-preserved, deeply challenging wisdom literature. The Bible now seems a collection of texts determined to undermine each of its many affirmations; its declaration of the prerogatives of the first-born son inevitably give way to the younger child of love; its marginalization of women is most often undercut by their greater intelligence and subtler power; the high claims of the law and tradition are subverted long before the first book of the New Testament is written; but even with the coming of the new covenant, the authority of Hebrew scripture in its multiple and always uncertain interpretations never subsides.

Reading

Alter, Robert 1981: *The Art of Biblical Narrative.*
——1985: *The Art of Biblical Poetry.*
——and Kermode, Frank, eds 1987: *The Literary Guide to the Bible.*
Arnold, Matthew 1978: *God and the Bible.*
Bal, Mieke 1987: *Lethal Love: Feminist Literary Readings of Biblical Love Stories.*
Eliot, T.S. 1960: "Religion and literature."
Frye, Northrop 1957: *Anatomy of Criticism.*
——1980: *Creation and Recreation.*
——1982: *The Great Code: The Bible and Literature.*
Gros Louis, Kenneth R.R., ed. 1974, 1982: *Literary Interpretations of Biblical Narratives.* 2 vols.
Hammond, Gerald 1983: *The Making of the English Bible.*
Hartman, Geoffrey, and Budick, Sanford, eds 1986: *Midrash and Literature.*
Kermode, Frank 1979: *The Genesis of Secrecy.*
——1983: *The Art of Telling.*
——1990b: "New ways with Bible stories."
Moore, Stephen D. *Literary Criticism and the Gospels: The Theoretical Challenge.*
Ostriker, Alicia 1993: *Feminist Revision and the Bible.*
Sternberg, Meir 1985: *The Poetics of Biblical Narrative: Ideological Literature and the Drama of Reading.*
MICHAEL PAYNE

binary opposition A relationship of opposition and mutual exclusion between two elements: a crucial term in the theories of STRUCTURALISM. Examples of such oppositions would be masculine/feminine, cold/heat, or up/down.

The phrase appears in the work of the French structural anthropologist Claude LÉVI-STRAUSS on myths, particularly those of the indigenous American tribes. He analyzes their legends as embodying major oppositions between mythical archetypes of certain animals, such as the Frog and the Snake. Each animal has certain associations, and the relations between these associations are analyzed according to the relations between the mythic figures which epitomize them. In effect every mythic creature stands for certain meanings. From this maneuver is extracted a general rule: a pair of antagonists is the fundamental element of all mythic narratives, When one element of the relation is present, so too, and necessarily, is the other by means of an operation of difference predicated upon direct opposition. Binary oppositions occur in all myths and so can be seen to be the universal factor in the production of stories. Lévi-Strauss asks why this should be so, and his answer is that these binary oppositions so produced are the symptoms in myth of the way the human mind works, the way in which language and thought operate.

Many structuralist theorists take this position as a starting point, especially those concerned with NARRATOLOGY. Developing a theory of the operation of narrative from the work on myths, narratologists such as A.J. GREIMAS in his earlier work take binary oppositions as the basis for their attempts to theorize the fundamental structure of all narrative (for an example, see ACTANT). Others, for example, Roman JAKOBSON, find the concept useful in that it underpins other, more complex relationships, since it is assumed to be a structure which is inherent in language itself. Structuralists such as Householder, who are uncomfortable with an assumption that binary oppositions are universal, still utilize the concept because of its methodological rigor. The one element which all of these different uses of the concept have in common is its helpfulness in the operation of classification. Structuralist literary critics interpret TEXTS in terms of CODES which are composed of multiple binary oppositions, classifying the meanings they produce. It is this reading practice which is assumed to be, ultimately and universally, the way that meaning is produced, as the text weaves its way among sets of binary oppositions. Meaning is oppositional, but this opposition is stable, with the proviso that the only legitimate meanings are those which are constructed in terms of such oppositions.

The importance of binary oppositions as a crucial part of structuralist practice has led to a problematizing of the concept by critiques of the methods of

STRUCTURALISM as a whole. This is one of the concerns of the French philosopher Jacques DERRIDA in *Of Grammatology* (1976). He analyzes binary oppositions by means of a detailed investigation of the relations between the two supposedly opposed terms of the STRUCTURE. His procedure is to begin from the logic of SAUSSURE's structural linguistics, in which the lexical item (the SIGN) has meaning only by virtue of its difference from other pieces of vocabulary. Language is structured as a differential SYSTEM. The meaning of the sign therefore depends on what it is not, in other words precisely what it excludes. This insight is then applied to the structure of binary oppositions themselves, so that the logic of the mutual exclusion of the two terms is seen to be dependent on the differential structure. Derrida questions the rigor of this structure by suggesting that in fact each term of an opposition depends for its exclusivity upon the success of the operation which places the two terms in contradiction. He destabilizes this operation of simple binarism by showing that such terms can be analyzed as each containing elements of the other. For example, using this technique, it could be argued that the opposition between black and white is not so simple as structuralists would propose. Black is black by virtue of its not being white, in a relation of difference. But since it is precisely this difference which defines black, rather than its own blackness, it is forever haunted by white, its supplement. Meaning is not simple. This analytical operation is the maneuver which is characteristic of DECONSTRUCTION. It is this procedure underpinning Derrida's destabilization of the Western metaphysical tradition, which he notes as depending on binary oppositions such as writing/speech and absence/presence.

Avowedly materialist critics have also utilized the concept of the binary opposition as a useful point at which to interrogate structuralist practice. For example, in *Literary Theory: An Introduction* (1985) the English theorist and critic Terry EAGLETON produces just such a reading. He begins by noting that for structuralists cultural forms may change, but the universal oppositions uncovered by Lévi-Strauss remain. There is a kind of deeper reality underpinning the ephemeral changes which take place in the realm of the social, and this reality is palpably unchanging, eternal, rooted perhaps in the very biological structure of the human being. Eagleton criticizes this universal structure as utterly ahistorical, leading on to his more general observations about the structuralist model itself. He problematizes the separation performed in structuralist theory between the deeper reality of the structure on the one hand and the movement of contingency on the other, and in effect he categorizes the structuralist method as ideological. To separate a deeper universal meaning from the play of history and language is to replicate the Arnoldian maneuver which removes CULTURE from politics.

However, both deconstructionist and materialist critics acknowledge their own debts to the theorizing of binary oppositions made by structuralists, as a position from which to begin their own analyses. The "deconstruction" of these oppositions produced a decentering of presence and a reconstruction of the importance of the written sign. This operation has resulted in the emergence of POSTSTRUCTURALISM.

Reading
Culler, Jonathan 1975 (*1989*): *Structuralist Poetics*.
Derrida, Jacques 1967 (*1976*): *Of Grammatology*.
Eagleton, Terry 1983 (*1985*): *Literary Theory: An Introduction*.
Householder, Fred 1971: *Linguistic Speculations*.
Lévi-Strauss, Claude 1971 (*1981*): *The Naked Man*.
                                                    PAUL INNES

black aesthetic   The aesthetic program propagated by practitioners of the BLACK ARTS MOVEMENT during the 1960s. Committed to a radical revaluation of Western aesthetic ideology, black aesthetic theorists claimed to derive their conception of black art from traditional African aesthetics. Against the Western notion of great art as a category that transcends IDEOLOGY, the black aesthetic stridently declared its political intention of furthering the aims of black nationalism. Refusing the ideology of art for art's sake and fusing aesthetics with ETHICS, black aesthetic critics regarded artistic form as a transparent medium of moral and political messages, and could justify ART only if it served the function of raising the cultural consciousness of the black community. Elements of African culture (including clothing, hairstyles, language, music, dance, and religious practices) were appropriated and celebrated by numerous black artists during the 1960s in an attempt to recover an alternative cultural tradition that survived the middle passage and the ensuing history of slavery and political oppression. Affirming the cultural resources of the black community, black aesthetic theorists soundly condemned the Western aesthetic privileging of the individual artist as the source of creation. The collective emphasis of black aesthetic ideology motivated its promotion of certain literary genres over others as well as its perception of oral forms as the repositories of authentic black communal consciousness. Often elevating music in particular to a black cultural paradigm, black aesthetic critics preferred POETRY and drama as the genres which, because they are more amenable to public oral performances than fiction, are capable of achieving a direct, interactive relationship between the artist and the black community.

Perhaps the most profoundly transformative element of black aesthetic ideology was its redefinition of the category of blackness as a beautiful, natural, vital essence. However, this new mystique of blackness was often elaborated in highly dogmatic terms, discouraging literary explorations of the internal differences that complicate any unitary conception of black experience. Consequently, black writers and critics of the 1970s and 1980s have reacted sharply against black aesthetic theory on several grounds, including its essentialist and sternly prescriptive discourse on racial authenticity (see Gates, 1978), and its projection of black machismo, conjoined with its dismissal of black feminist ideology as a form of false Western consciousness that impedes the formation of a unified black community (see McDowell, 1989; Smith, 1989).
See also BLACK ARTS MOVEMENT.

Reading
Baker, Houston A., Jr 1980: *The Journey Back*.
Gates, Henry Louis, Jr 1978: "Preface to blackness: text and pretext."
Gayle, Addison, Jr, ed. 1971 (*1972*): *The Black Aesthetic*.
McDowell, Deborah 1989: "Reading family matters."
Smith, Valerie 1989: "Gender and Afro–Americanist literary theory and criticism."

MADHU DUBEY

black arts movement   A separatist black cultural movement developed during the middle and late 1960s by a variety of dramatists, poets, and critics in largely urban areas of the United States. Among its prominent practitioners and advocates were: Amiri Baraka, Ed Bullins, Mari Evans, Hoyt W. Fuller, Addison Gayle, Jr, Nikki Giovanni, Stephen Henderson, Ron Karenga, Haki Madhubuti, Ron Milner, Larry Neal, Carolyn Rodgers, and Sonia Sanchez. Explicitly committed to propagating the ideology of black cultural nationalism, the black arts movement was founded on the premise that black people in the United States share a unique set of aesthetic and cultural values which require indigenous modes of appreciation that must be developed completely separately from the surrounding white culture.

In order to raise black consciousness and to free the black community from the false consciousness produced by participation in mainstream American culture, black arts proponents attempted to create an autonomous black cultural community by various means. Several independent journals (*Journal of Black Poetry, Black Books Bulletin*), publishing houses (Broadside Press, Jihad Press, Third World Press), theater groups (Baraka's Harlem Black Arts Repertory Theater School, Barbara Ann Teer's National Black Theater), and other cultural organizations (such as Spirit House in Newark, or the Black Academy of Arts and Letters) were founded in the 1960s. Numerous cultural events including street plays and poetry readings, concerts, lectures, exhibitions, and creative writing workshops were organized during this period with the explicit goal of fashioning an alternative system of values for the black community. Although the BLACK AESTHETIC program developed by black arts advocates has been severely criticized by subsequent generations of black writers, the black arts movement enabled remarkable formal innovations in all genres of black literature, and undeniably succeeded in promoting a powerful sense of black cultural pride and solidarity.
See also BLACK AESTHETIC.

Reading
Baker, Houston A., Jr 1988: *Afro–American Poetics: Revisions of Harlem and the Black Aesthetic*.
Jones, LeRoi, and Neal, Larry, eds 1968: *Black Fire*.
Neal, Larry 1971 (*1972*): " The black arts movement."
Smith, David Lionel 1991: "The black arts movement and its critics."

MADHU DUBEY

black cultural studies   The notion of a black cultural studies is both problematic and locatable in a specific set of critical and cultural practices. While there is no definition of the term "black cultural studies," a wide range of WRITINGS, theories, cultural work, and performances have emerged as an informally defined area of inquiry within what has come to be called CULTURAL STUDIES.

Such DISCOURSES have been related to the histories and CULTURES of peoples historically invoked and produced as "black" or, at other times, more loosely as "Third World," in a postindependence, postcolonial and post-Civil Rights framework. A black cultural studies addresses the interests, concerns, ideologies, and contexts of black cultural work within a national and global context. While no particular set of theories proposes a separate area called black cultural studies, the analysis and critique of work dealing with questions of RACE and IDEOLOGY, race and CULTURE, race and material practice, race and GENDER, emerged out of and within the absences and legacies of existing critical and cultural studies. Where race was merely incidental to the axis around which different trajectories of cultural studies emerged, a black cultural studies accounts for the ways race plays a crucial part within feminist, Marxist, psychoanalytic, and postcolonial theories of culture.

There are different contingent developments within the broader area of cultural studies which have contributed to the emergence of race as a crucial component of a politically informed practice of culture. In Britain, the development of British cultural studies, in its many different inflections till the 1970s and the early 1980s, largely tended to overlook or include (in a peripheral fashion) the intersections of race, sexuality, and gender toward a primarily class and political economy-based critique of culture. While research and cultural work continually addressed concerns of race and gender within British cultural studies, it was the broad expanse of writings in informal spaces, as well as through centers like the Centre for Contemporary Cultural Studies at the University of Birmingham, journals such as *Race and Class*, and the dialogs within community centers, art communities, cultural workers, film and theater practitioners, and independent collectives such as the Sankofa, Ceddo, Retake, and Black Audio Film Collectives which brought about a more rigorous and popular shift in the cultural work being done from the 1970s to the 1990s.

In the United States, the popularization and diffusion of the term "cultural studies" has produced numerous versions of a United States-based form of cultural studies, with various genealogies or intellectual formations. The particular history of cultural work in the United States has produced a critical practice committed to exploring the cultural production of various legally constituted minorities as part of the broader development of cultural studies with the legacies of a postemancipation and post-Civil Rights discourse. Of these recent critical developments, which I am locating primarily within the Academy and other institutions of culture, the impact and pertinence of race in the study of POPULAR CULTURE has been an important though marginal aspect of the development of an American cultural studies.

The very term "black cultural studies" must be viewed as part of a larger movement toward both a moving away from traditional theoretical approaches to black culture, as well as an inflection within the US context of a rigorous minority discourse during the 1980s and the 1990s. While the expression could be regarded as a contradiction in terms from some viewpoints, it is also part of the historic formations of political and cultural frameworks within the United States. As such, the articulation of a black cultural studies has been in tandem with the emergence of an Asian–American cultural studies, a Latino/Chicana/o cultural studies, and so on, not as independent developments, but rather, as deeply imbricated by the political and legal rhetorics within the United States.

In Britain, publications such as *Policing the Crisis, The Empire Strikes Back, There Ain't No Black In the Union Jack, Charting the Journey*, the ICA Documents 6 and 7, *Race and Class*, the writings of C.L.R. James, Stuart Hall, Hazel Carby, Erroll Lawrence, Pratibha Parmar, Paul Gilroy, Homi Bhabha, Jim Pines, Kobena Mercer, and the films of the various film and video collectives such as Ceddo, Black Audio, Sankofa, Star, and Retake, and the various informal modes of exchange through the works of various black playwrights/performers such as Benjamin Zephaniah, Mustapha Matura, Yvonne Brewster, Hanif Khureishi, and black/Asian artists in Britain, created a milieu of cultural work that was locally based, committed, and theoretically engaged with questions of AESTHETICS, practice, audience, and IDEOLOGY.

In the United States since the 1980s, a number of publications have emerged that map, discuss, and debate the various implications of cultural studies in that country and its differing genealogies. *Marxism and the Interpretation of Culture, Cultural Studies* by Grossberg, Nelson, Treichler, various journals such as *Inscriptions, Cultural Studies, Transitions, Diaspora, Cultural Critique, Critical Inquiry, Black Popular Culture*, and the writings of people like Michele Wallace, bell hooks, Wahneema

Lubiano, Cornel West, Manthia Diawara, Herman Grey, Clyde Taylor, Michael Dyson, Tricia Rose, Houston Baker, and Henry Louis Gates among others, have discussed the practice of a black cultural studies which maintains "race" as a critical axis of inquiry.

See also CULTURAL STUDIES; DIASPORA; HALL, STUART; HYBRIDITY.

Reading

Centre for Contemporary Cultural Studies 1982: *The Empire Strikes Back.*
Cham, Mbye B. and Andrade-Watkins, Claire, eds 1988: *Blackframes: Critical Perspectives on Black Independent Cinema.*
Diawara, Manthia 1992: *African Cinema: Politics and Culture.*
Ferguson, Russell et al., eds 1990: *Out There: Marginalization and Contemporary Cultures.*
Gilroy, Paul 1987: *There Ain't No Black In The Union Jack. The Cultural Politics of Race and Nation.*
Grossberg, L., Nelson, L., and Treichler, P. 1992: *Cultural Studies.*
hooks, bell 1992: *Black Looks: Race and Representation.*
James, C.L.R. 1938 (*1980*): *The Black Jacobins: Toussaint L'Ouverture and the Saint Domingo Revolution.*
Mercer, Kobena, ed. 1988: *Black Film/British Cinema, ICA Document 7.*
Owusu, Kwesi, ed. 1988: *Storms of the Heart: An Anthology of Black Arts and Culture.*
Wallace, Michelle 1992: *Black Popular Culture.*
Williams, Patricia J. 1991: *The Alchemy of Race and Rights.*
                                          MAY JOSEPH

black nationalism   Black nationalist movements of various kinds have had a long and continuous history in the United States, from the back-to-Africa emigrationist societies of the late eighteenth century to the hip-hop nationalism of the 1990s. Despite sharp ideological differences, all types of black nationalism share the conviction that blacks exist in a relationship of colonial subordination to white America, and can attain economic, political, and cultural equality only through the development of a racial solidarity based on their common experience of oppression. Strategic separatism from mainstream American society is essential to all kinds of black nationalism, whether the ultimate goal be the establishment of a separate black nation or the achievement of full citizenship in the United States. For the sake of analytical clarity, the many black nationalist ideologies may be divided into the following categories.

Territorial separatism is perhaps the most extreme variety of black nationalism, represented by organizations such as the Republic of New Africa and the Revolutionary Action Movement, which demand the formation of geographically demarcated and sovereign all-black townships or states within the United States.

Closely affiliated to territorial separatism is *emigrationism*, which enjoyed its heyday during the late eighteenth, nineteenth, and early twentieth centuries, and whose most celebrated proponents include Martin Delany, Alexander Crummell, and Marcus Garvey. It called for the founding of a separate nation in Africa, Haiti, or even Canada, consisting of black *émigrés* from the United States.

Several black nationalist ideologies have been inspired and authorized by radical theologies of political emancipation. Whether Christian, Jewish, or Muslim, *religious nationalist* thinkers and organizations such as Albert Cleage, the National Committee of Black Churchmen, the Nation of Islam, and the Moorish American Science Temple maintain that blacks are a chosen people whose liberation is divinely ordained, but who must nevertheless form separatist religious organizations to work actively toward freedom.

Perhaps the most popular of all the nationalist ideologies is *cultural nationalism*, based on the belief that black people across the globe share a unique culture originating in Africa. The 1960s in America witnessed the spawning of numerous cultural nationalist organizations, among them Amiri Baraka's Congress of African Peoples and Ron Karenga's US Organization, all of which were committed to preserving and celebrating black cultural difference by recovering an unbroken cultural heritage rooting back to Africa. The cultural nationalists regard institutional separatism as a necessary precondition for developing alternative, indigenous interpretative systems that alone can fully comprehend and appreciate the non-Western modes of black American CULTURE.

During the 1960s, cultural nationalism was often sharply polarized against *revolutionary nationalism*, which was advocated by organizations such as the Black Panther Party, the Dodge Revolutionary Union Movement, and the League of Revolutionary Black Workers. The most significant point of disagreement between these two ideologies is that, while the cultural nationalists consider the cultural independence of the black community to be a prerequisite to its political liberation, the revolutionary nationalists, depending on homegrown variants of Marxist–Leninist IDEOLOGY, contend that black liberation requires the overthrow of American capitalism.

Economic autonomy has always formed a crucial component of black nationalist ideology, ranging from the socialist ideal of the revolutionary nationalists to the bourgeois nationalism of organizations like the United Negro Improvement Association and the Nation of Islam. The most widespread form of black *economic nationalism* in the United States has been bourgeois in its orientation, encouraging black-hiring and buy-black campaigns in the hope of establishing an independent black capitalist economy parallel to the American capitalist system.

Of course, in actuality none of these nationalist ideologies has operated in a pure state unmixed with the others. A rare kind of nationalism that lacks a historic relationship to a specific geographical territory, black nationalism in the United States has nevertheless derived its effective power and its ideological coherence from a profound sense of disaffection with the processes of American capitalism and democracy.

Reading
Bracey, John H., Jr, Meier, August, and Elliott, Rudwick, eds 1970: *Black Nationalism in America.*
Draper, Theodore 1970: *The Rediscovery of Black Nationalism.*
Moses, Wilson Jeremiah 1978: *The Golden Age of Black Nationalism, 1850–1925.*
Pinkney, Alphonso 1976: *Red, Black and Green: Black Nationalism in the United States.*
Stuckey, Sterling 1972: *The Ideological Origins of Black Nationalism.*

MADHU DUBEY

Bloch, Ernst (1885–1977) German Marxist philosopher.

Born in Ludwigshafen, the son of a railway worker, Bloch was educated in Munich, Würzburg, and Berlin (where he met Lukács) before moving to Heidelberg. In his first expressionistic book, *Geist der Utopia* (1918) Bloch sought to revitalize utopian thought, seemingly combining Marxist materialism with mystic and messianic elements. *Thomas Münzer als Theologe der Revolution* (1921) developed Bloch's concern with the revolutionary potential of religious thought, and indeed his perception of the inherently religious nature of humanity. In *Erbschaft dieser Ziet* (*Heritage of Our Times*) (1935) Bloch responded to the rise of Nazism with a series of cultural and social analyses that embraced physics alongside music, cinema, literature, and politics.

In 1938 Bloch was forced into exile in America. Although he had no academic post, it was there that he wrote his most important work, *Das Prinzip Hoffnung* (*The Principle of Hope*). This may be taken to underline the shift in emphasis of Bloch's concerns from the religious and messianic to a more broadly based social and cultural analysis of utopian aspiration and longing. In 1949 Bloch returned to Europe, to a post at Leipzig University. The following decade saw Bloch's increasing disillusionment with Eastern European Communism, and periodic but severe criticism by more orthodox or vulgar Marxists. By chance he was in West Germany in 1961 when the Berlin Wall was raised, and he applied for political asylum. He accepted a post at Tübingen. His extensive late publications include works on religion, metaphysics, materialism, and natural law.

Bloch's MARXISM rests within the tradition of process philosophy. The ontological structures of the human being and the world are "not yet" given or achieved. Bloch stresses the future orientation of Marxism, arguing that Marx transformed philosophy by making the recognition of present contradiction the ground for future orientated practice. Previously, philosophy had merely interpreted the past. Marxism is thereby presented, paradoxically, as an open SYSTEM. HEGEL's backward-looking system, characterized by *anamnesis*, is closed. It presupposes that truth has already been realized. Bloch's philosophy is in contrast open not merely to new particularistic content, but also to the possibility that such content will demand the rethinking of the system's categories. Yet the philosophy remains disciplined. It lacks the coherence of a closed system, because the world itself is not well ordered. Bloch frequently appeals to the fragments and montage techniques of expressionism in order to explore the tension and latency within contemporary society.

In diverse aspects of CULTURE, and specifically in imaginative yearning, be it for a better society or merely for such technological achievement as flight, Bloch finds evidence of humanity being "not yet conscious" of its truth and potential. The operator "not yet" (*noch nicht*) allows Bloch to transform concepts, and so highlight the complex future orientation concealed within overtly repressive social relationships. The "not yet" refers at once to that which is conceivable, but not yet possible; present now, but only problematically; that which is expected in the future and that which has "still not" occurred. The utopian future is obscurely glimpsed in its preappearance (*Vor-Schein*), through humanity's discontent with this world, and its hope for a better world. For Bloch such yearning is not empty but, through disciplined interpretation, serves as the point of departure for revolutionary practice. *See also* MARXISM AND MARXIST CRITICISM.

Reading
Bloch, E. (*1986*): *The Principle of Hope*, 3 vols.
——(*1988*): *Natural Law and Human Dignity.*
——(*1991*): *Heritage of Our Times.*
Hudson, W. (*1982*): *The Marxist Philosophy of Ernst Bloch.*
ANDREW EDGAR

Bloom, Harold (1930–) American literary theorist and critic. One of the most influential and widely read living theorists of POETRY, Bloom is an extraordinarily prolific, individualistic, and controversial writer and editor. Like many other North American theorists who came into prominence during the second half of the twentieth century, Bloom did his early work on English Romanticism (see ROMANTIC STUDIES). His writing falls roughly into four groups: (i) a series of studies in Romantic poetry: *Shelley's Mythmaking* (1959), *The Visionary Company* (1961), *Blake's Apocalypse* (1963), and the commentary and annotations for *The Poetry and Prose of William Blake*, edited by David Erdman (1965); (ii) six books on the theory of poetry: *The Anxiety of Influence: A Theory of Poetry* (1973), *A Map of Misreading* (1975b), *Kabbalah and Criticism* (1975a), *Poetry and Repression* (1976), *Agon: Towards a Theory of Revisionism* (1982), and *The Breaking of the Vessels* (1982); (iii) studies in the modernist inheritance of Romanticism and its transformation into "the American Sublime": *Yeats' "A Vision"* (1972), *Figures of Capable Imagination* (1976), and *Wallace Stevens: The Poems of Our Climate* (1977); and (iv) the Chelsea House series of literally several hundred volumes of criticism on major writers and texts, each volume selected, edited, and introduced by Bloom. This final project may be the most ambitious ever undertaken by a single literary critic. Although often considered a member of what was once the "Yale school" of criticism – which included Geoffrey Hartman, J. Hillis Miller, and Paul DE MAN – Bloom has often respectfully distanced himself from their work. He once announced his determination to find a middle way between the spiritualism of AUERBACH and FRYE and the deconstructive secularism of DERRIDA and Miller.

In the clarity and consistency of its vision, however, Bloom's theory of literature most closely resembles that of Frye. Not only do Bloom and Frye share a deep imaginative commitment to the work of William Blake, but also, like Blake, they see LITERARY CRITICISM, theory, and history at their best as poetic projects. As though in response to Blake's aphorism, "without contraries is no progression," Bloom's books read as if it were a progressive contrary to Frye's. Whereas Frye is at his best when writing about COMEDY and romance, Bloom is at his best in the modes of TRAGEDY and IRONY. For him the history of poetry is a NIETZSCHEan struggle (or agon) of powerful wills, but – in the manner of Blake's resolution of the Oedipal struggle between the repressive father Urizen and revolutionary son Orc – the triumph of the belated son eventually lies in his final embrace and incorporation of his progenitor. Creative belatedness for Bloom requires the embracing and revisionary appropriation of the past. Though the later strong poet revises his precursor in a willful MISREADING, responding to the ANXIETY OF INFLUENCE that comes to him from the work of earlier strong poets, the prolific outcome is a continuation of the poetic line of descent.

Also like Blake and Frye, Bloom's progeny have been anything but passive receivers of the will of the father. His most notorious follower is Camille Paglia, herself a prodigious scholar and outrageous bane of American feminists. However, as Bloom's best commentator Peter de Bolla has observed, the determined efforts of Sandra GILBERT and Susan GUBAR to write a comprehensive literary history of women is also a Bloomian legacy (de Bolla, 1988, p. 12). Despite Bloom's outrageous and deliberately provocative anti-feminism, he has written a detailed and brilliant commentary on Hebrew Scripture (*The Book of J*), suggesting that the Yahwist poet (J) was (or should have been) a woman (see BIBLICAL STUDIES).

Reading
Bloom, Harold 1961: *The Visionary Company.*
——1973: *The Anxiety of Influence: A Theory of Poetry.*
——1982: *The Breaking of the Vessels.*
——1991: *The Book of J.*
de Bolla, Peter 1988: *Harold Bloom: Towards Historical Rhetorics.*
MICHAEL PAYNE

Boas, Franz (1858–1942) North American anthropologist. Often regarded as the founder of modern anthropology in North America, Boas was also a major contributor to early twentieth-century studies of Native American CULTURES. Born in Westphalia, Germany, he studied geography, physics, and mathematics, receiving his doctorate at Kiel in 1881. The following year, he accompanied a meteorological expedition to Greenland, where "a year spent as an Eskimo among Eskimos . . . led me . . . towards a desire to understand what determines the behavior of human beings." Emigrating to the United States, Boas taught geography and anthropology at Clark University and then at Columbia University until 1937, where he remained Professor Emeritus until his death. His students included Alfred KROEBER, Margaret MEAD, and others who became major figures in twentieth-century American anthropology and CULTURAL STUDIES.

In place of grand theories or laws, Boas insisted instead upon the careful recording of even apparently small details of cultural expression as the only solid empirical basis for understanding and appreciating human behavior in all its diversity and richness – an approach which became known as historical particularism. Criticizing biological determinism ("nature"), he emphasized the primacy of culture ("nurture") in human development, engaging what became one of the crucial intellectual and ideological debates of the century. He also stressed the complexity, essential adequacy, and uniqueness of all human cultures and languages. Boas helped establish the methodological importance of direct, personal fieldwork, and he conducted extensive linguistic fieldwork among Native Americans on the Canadian Pacific coast. He was wary of popularizing scholarship because he feared its oversimplified use in political causes, and he condemned fascist pseudoscientific theories of racial superiority in the 1930s.

See also CULTURAL STUDIES; KROEBER, ALFRED L.; MEAD, MARGARET; NATIVE AMERICAN STUDIES; RACE.

Reading
Boas, Franz 1911: *The Mind of Primitive Man.*
Stocking, George, ed. 1974: *The Shaping of American Anthropology. 1883–1911: A Franz Boas Reader.*
JAMES PHILLIPS

body Although it may at first seem solidly a fixture of NATURE rather than CULTURE, the body is, nevertheless, both a biological entity and a social and philosophical construct. Because it is born,

feels pain and pleasure, ages, and dies, the physical body can never be completely appropriated by the SYMBOLic order. Although it may be "foundational of all symbolism" (Brooks, 1993, p. 7), the body is also precultural and prelinguistic. Whatever is not of the body, however, seems to demand that it be thought of in terms of the body. Thus, the poet William Blake in *The Marriage of Heaven and Hell* (1794) could refer to it as "the chief inlet of the soul in this age." As soon as the body becomes an object of thought, it is reshaped by the IDEOLOGY of DISCOURSE. Accordingly, Peter Brown (1988, pp. 9–11) has demonstrated that early Christians commonly thought of women as "failed males" because their bodies had not managed during coagulation in their mothers' wombs to amass the same quantities of heat and spiritual vitality that made men what they were. Just as the warmth of semen demonstrated the vital achievement of the male body, so menstruation was a sign of the failure of the female to process heat, which coagulated when it was not used. Still, a woman's surplus energy was necessary for its intended use in the nurturing of children, which did not, however, restrain Galen from observing that "the Creator had purposefully made one half of the whole race imperfect, and as it were, mutilated" (*De usu partium*, 14.6). The theory of female heat at least was a gesture toward overturning the idea spoken by no less than Apollo in Aeschylus's *Eumenides* that only the father is the true parent, the mother's body being merely an incubating receptacle of the male seed (see REPRODUCTIVE TECHNOLOGY). Perhaps with a sense of irony Shakespeare invoked some of this ancient anatomical theory to imply (in Sonnet 129) that spirit is conveyed by semen. He often plays, too, with the convention that the temperament of human beings is determined by the prominence of one of four fluids or "humours:" blood, phlegm, choler, or melancholy. The dominant humour was determined by the sign under which a person was born (Tillyard, 1943).

During the Enlightenment, as David Theo Goldberg has shown, classical values of bodily beauty were resurrected and equated with economic value. The poor were defined as lacking the racialized characteristics of "fair skin, straight hair, orgnathous jaw, skull shape and size, well-composed bodily proportions, and so on" (1993, p. 30). Later in even the most racially polarized societies, bodily skin color became but one mode of enculturated reference that included "modes of dress, bearing, gait, hairstyle, speech, and their relation" (Goldberg, 1993, p. 74). On such distinctions black slavery and anti-Semitism – to mention but two instances of RACISM – have been sustained. Even within racial groups, variations in skin color, hair texture, and other bodily features have been the basis on which CLASS distinctions have been maintained (see RACE).

Recent CULTURAL THEORY has explicitly emphasized the body's semiotic qualities. For KRISTEVA the first signifying process occurs in the womb (Payne, 1993, pp. 167–70), and for FOUCAULT the body is the site of an unidealized genealogical history that resists the abstractions of origin and emergence (Foucault, 1977, p. 147). Nevertheless, Kenneth Clark (1956) has shown that the depiction of the nude has been a manifestation of such abstractly idealized forms, at least since Vitruvius, and that artists have been ready to distort grotesquely the human body in order to make its representation conform to a culturally specific aesthetic ideal. Even so, somatic imagery has long been paradigmatic "for any forced, artful, contrived, and violent study of depths" (Stafford, 1991, p. 47). This accounts for Foucault's terse remark (1977, p. 154) that "knowledge is not made for understanding: it is made for cutting."

Reading

Brown, Peter 1988: *The Body and Society: Men, Women and Sexual Renunciation in Early Christianity.*
Clark, Kenneth 1956: *The Nude.*
Foucault, Michel 1972 (*1977*): "Nietzsche, genealogy, history."
Goldberg, David Theo 1993: *Racist Culture: Philosophy and the Politics of Meaning.*
Payne, Michael 1993: *Reading Theory: An Introduction to Lacan, Derrida, and Kristeva.*
Stafford, Barbara Maria 1991: *Body Criticism: Imaging the Unseen in Enlightenment Art and Medicine.*
Tillyard, E.M.W. 1943: *The Elizabethan World Picture.*

MICHAEL PAYNE

bolekaja criticism A term by which Chinweizu and Madubuike identify the corrective struggle of "men and of nations" with "the stiflers of their life" (1983). In Yoruba bolekaja means "Come down let's fight!" However, there is far more to bolekajarism than intellectual pugilism.

Committed to afrocentric cultural nationalism, "Issues and tasks," the final chapter of *Toward the Decolonization of African Literature* is a manifesto for African LITERARY PRODUCTION and interpretation. Earlier chapters consist of resolute critiques of the universalist assumptions of "eurocentric criticism" of African fiction and poetry. In contrast to eurocentrism, they propose a "supportive" role for the critic.

Supportive criticism provides writer and audience with the knowledge of "things valued in traditional African orature." A principal term in this HERMENEUTICS of support is imitation: just as writers must rely on African oral DISCOURSE to simulate "the flavor of African life," so critics should sustain their efforts by providing them with the raw material – "knowledge of things valued in traditional African orature, and why" – of their craft. Given their stress on oral discourse, their preference for "20th-century diction and idiom," and their insistence on the autonomy of African literature, it is hardly surprising that Chinweizu, Jemie, and Madubuike decry the impact of the "anglo-modernist sensibility" on some African poets and approve of the pursuit of traditionalism in others.

Bolekaja criticism has been called an "ethnic model" for its insistence on the "cultural specificity" of African literature and its "pursuit and defense of difference." But missing from this appraisal is the recognition that some of its political inspiration derives from nonethnic, supraethnic "imagined communities" – the nation, the continent. Equally unacknowledged are its other debts: its cognitive (us–them) apparatus, its mimeticism, its (cultural) nationalist IDEOLOGY. Many of these are owed, either directly or not, to European history, epistemologies, and theories of art. Bolekaja criticism is, like afrocentrism in North America, a form of nativism. Caught in the logic of eurocentrism, it cannot formulate a hermeneutic by which the generic, linguistic, and expressive eclecticism of African cultural practices can be most productively explicated.

Reading

Appiah, Kwame Anthony 1992: *In My Father's House: Africa in the Philosophy of Culture.*
Chinweizu, Onwuchekwa Jemie, and Madubuike, Ihechukwu, 1983: *Toward the Decolonization of African Literature.* Vol. 1.

UZOMA ESONWANNE

boundary 2 Since its inception at the State University of New York at Binghamton under the editorship of W.V. Spanos in 1972, *boundary 2* has been the leading journal of the literature and CRITICAL THEORY of POSTMODERNISM. In its early years, the journal was a vehicle for a very particular critique of the metaphysical bases of aesthetic modernism which was derived from the work of Martin HEIDEGGER. In a number of important articles, Spanos himself argued for a postmodernist literature and LITERARY CRITICISM which would acknowledge the open and unfinished condition of "being-in-time," thus abandoning the abstract will-to-power of the disinterested, or timeless work or critical interpretation. *boundary 2* has also provided a forum for postmodernist POETRY and fiction. More recently, under the editorship of Paul Bové, the journal has widened its focus to explore developments in postmodernism and attitudes towards it outside the Anglo-American mainstream, for example, in Ireland, Latin America, and Japan.

Reading
Bové, Paul 1990: "A conversation with William V. Spanos."
Pasanen, Outi 1986: "Postmodernism: an interview with William V. Spanos."
STEVEN CONNOR

Bourdieu, Pierre (1930–) French sociologist. Although Bourdieu graduated from the École Normale Supérieure as an *agrégé de philosophie*, in reaction against what he took to be the intellectually authoritarian and Stalinist orientation of the institution, he refused to write a thesis. Conscripted into the French Army in 1956, he spent four years in Algeria, publishing *Sociologie de l'Algérie* in 1958 and teaching at the University of Algiers until 1960 when he returned to France. After short periods at the University of Paris and the University of Lille, he assumed the post of Director of Studies at the Ecole Pratique des Hautes Etudes, where he soon established the Centre for European Sociology, which he continues to direct. Bourdieu was appointed to a chair at the Collège de France in 1981. Most of his publications reflect both his early engagement with philosophy and his meticulous anthropological fieldwork in Algeria. Like Michel FOUCAULT and Jacques DERRIDA, Bourdieu has been equally suspicious of the EXISTENTIALISM of Jean-Paul SARTRE and the STRUCTURALISM of Claude LÉVI-STRAUSS. In his generous but critical response to such thinkers as MARX, Weber, DURKHEIM, and WITTGENSTEIN, Bourdieu finds in each of them a means for overcoming the limitations of the others (Jenkins, 1992, p. 19).

Bourdieu has been persistently concerned with the problem of how an ethnographer can come to know the CULTURE he studies. It is not sufficient, he argues, simply for the investigator to distance himself from, or to objectify, the social reality he studies; it is also necessary that he sustain a continuing critique of his methods and epistemological PARADIGMS. The first critical distancing he calls "participant objectivation," and the second "the objectification of objectification." Although he is suspicious and ironically dismissive of theory (despite his several books and articles with "theory" in the title), Bourdieu has been attentive to the ways that theories, often unconsciously and uncritically, determine the cultural practices of people's everyday lives. Doing is what makes knowing possible, he argues (Jenkins, 1992, p. 69). A prolific writer, Bourdieu's interests range from sociological theory and education to literature, the visual arts, and philosophy. *The Logic of Practice* (1980) provides the best entrance into his work, and there is an excellent bibliography of his publications in *In Other Words* (1990).

Reading
Bourdieu, Pierre 1958 (*1962*): *The Algerians*.
——1980 (*1990*): *The Logic of Practice*.
——1990: *In Other Words*.
Jenkins, Richard 1992: *Pierre Bourdieu*.
Robbins, Derek 1991: *The Work of Pierre Bourdieu*.
MICHAEL PAYNE

bracketing The name of a philosophical method first introduced by the German philosopher Edmund HUSSERL in and around 1905. "Bracketing" means "putting out of operation." The phenomenologist, Husserl insisted, must "bracket," that is "suspend his belief in," "not make any use of" all presuppositions, all that he already believes in, in order to be able to do presuppositionless description of experience. "Bracketing" is not denying, nor does it amount to doubting. It amounts to "neutralizing" one's attitude toward what one brackets. When you "bracket" something, something else remains outside the bracket. Husserl called it the phenomenological "residue."
J.N. MOHANTY

Braudel, Fernand (1902–85) French historian who was first and foremost a critical theorist, although this is a phrase he would never have applied to himself. He regarded himself as a historian of the *longue durée*, one who thought that good history was *histoire pensée*, that is, history which provided responses to serious intellectual questions.

He is one of three towering figures of the *Annales* school of history, the leader of the so-called second generation (the first generation having been led by its founders, Lucien Febvre and Marc BLOCH). The *Annales* school stood for the coming together and mutual fructification of history and the social sciences. It stood in opposition to all forms of mindless EMPIRICISM, which Braudel termed *histoire événementielle*. It stood equally opposed to all structural universalisms that asserted generalizations purporting to hold true throughout time and space. In short, the *Annales* school refused to be trapped in the *Methodenstreit*, rejecting equally the nomothetic and idiographic stances. The *Annales* school was thus established on the basis of a profound critique of the major methodological and substantive premises of a very large part of the writings of historians and social scientists of the nineteenth and twentieth centuries.

Fernand Braudel made two stunning contributions to contemporary thought. They are to be found primarily in his two great (and very large) books: *The Mediterranean and the Mediterranean World in the Age of Philip II* (1949; 2nd edition, amplified, 2 vols, 1966); and *Civilization and Capitalism, 15th to 18th Century* (1979, 3 vols). The first contribution is the concept of multiple social temporalities. The second contribution is his upside-down analysis of capitalism as a mode of production and a civilization.

The Mediterranean began as an analysis of the regime of Philip II of Spain. In writing it, Braudel turned the story around. It became the story of the Mediterranean world as *a* (not *the*) world-economy. The hyphen in the word "world-economy" was crucial to Braudel, because in French he had coined the term *économie-monde* precisely to distinguish it from *économie mondiale*, usually translated into English as "world economy" without the hyphen (see discussion in Braudel, 1984, pp. 21–4).

The Mediterranean world was a world-economy in that it had a discernible division of labor with dominant cities and a hierarchy. It was a "world theatre," with boundaries and an identity, but one that bestrode political and cultural frontiers. A world-economy was a space–time zone with a history. Such a conception brought to the fore the essential intellectual question Braudel sought to address: If a given space–time zone has a history,

indeed if the space and the time form its history but its history defines its space and time as well, how can one know, how can one define categories of space and time? For most of modern thought, space and time were just there – implacable, unbudgeable, exogenous parameters to the lives and actions of individuals, groups, and social structures. One recorded the last in time and space. Time and space were not themselves empirical variables to study.

Braudel said no to this standard view. Time and space were, he argued, the central empirical variables to study, since they were social creations. He argued this by demonstration in *The Mediterranean*. He argued this theoretically in his key methodological article, "Histoire et les sciences sociales," published in *Annales E.S.C.* in 1958.

For Braudel, there were three real social temporalities and a fourth mythical one. The three real ones he termed STRUCTURE, conjuncture, and event, which correlated with long, medium, and short time. Short time, *histoire événementielle*, episodic history was the social temporality explored by most historians. It was the history of kings and battles, the history of dates and chronology, the history of infinite contingencies. But, said Braudel in *The Mediterranean*, "events are dust." They are dust because they matter little and change little. And they are dust because they prevent one from seeing the underlying real structures.

Structures exist in the *longue durée*, which may last hundreds, even thousands of years; but they are never eternal. Structures are those continuing underlying social patterns which provide the continuing constraints on our actions. They may represent patterned cultural, economic, or political modes of dealing with, and reacting to, natural phenomena (from climate to topography to parasites) or particular sociocultural modes of perceiving social reality (such as world views or normative rules governing social hierarchies). Their crucial aspect is that, in the *short* run, structures are fixed and therefore the framework within which the impact of events is limited.

And in between structures and events lie the *conjonctures* (inadequately translated into English as conjunctures). They represent the cyclical rhythms which are the normal fluctuations of all structures. Most of these fluctuations are middle-run, says Braudel, constituting discernible temporary but important shifts in the global context (such as periods of overall economic expansion versus periods of overall economic contraction).

Braudel's contribution was to insist that serious history, *histoire pensée*, was the explication of the structures and the conjunctures, and not of the events – and also not of that mythical time–space, the eternal time–space of the structural universalists (the prime example cited by Braudel being LÉVI-STRAUSS).

Braudel has become so associated with the concept of the *longue durée* that some of his readers have failed to notice the equally critical concept of capitalism. If *The Mediterranean* was organized as a tale told three times, about three time–spaces (structure, conjuncture, event), *Civilization and Capitalism* is organized as a tale told about three storeys in the building of economic life: the ground floor of everyday life, the middle floor of the market, and the upper storey of capitalism. In some ways, everyday life is akin to structures. Braudel is speaking here of patterns of very long duration whose reality constrains the actions of people and institutions in the shorter run. However, if "structures" seemed to refer to macrophenomena (the relationship of mountain-dwellers to plain-dwellers, the wind patterns, the Roman *limes* as a continuing cultural boundary), the economy of everyday life seemed to refer primarily to very microphenomena (the patterns of cooking food, growing staples, costume, and the use of farm animals). These patterns provided the unspoken, unanalyzed basis of real economic life.

The next storey, that of the market, was seen by Braudel in a very particular way. He defined the market as the zone of multiple buyers and sellers and therefore of "small" profits, of regularity, and of liberation from constraints. This may not seem exceptional, except that he quite explicitly saw the state as having played the role historically of preserving the freedom of the market by regulating it.

The great enemy of the market for Braudel, what he called the anti-market, was not the state but capitalism. Capitalism was the opaque zone on top of, imposed upon, the market, the zone of "exceptional" profits via monopolies, and via the state in so far as it was the guarantor of monopolies. Far from being regular, capitalism was speculative. Far from being the zone of supply and demand, capitalism was the zone of power and cunning.

Braudel turned upside down the classical picture of capitalism (that of both Adam Smith and Karl MARX) as normally competitive and only abnormally monopolistic. For Braudel, the whole point of capitalism – real capitalism, as seen historically in the *longue durée* – was the effort to suppress the freedom of the market in order to maximize profit.

The impact of these two critical concepts of Braudel – multiple social temporalities and the priority of structure and conjuncture over event; and capitalism as the anti-market – is only now beginning to show its impact on history and the social sciences. Braudel represents one of the most original readings of the modern world and one of those most likely to form the basis of conceptual analyses in the twenty-first century.

Reading
Braudel, Fernand 1958 (*1972*): "History and the social sciences: the longue durée."
—— 1949 (*1973*): *The Mediterranean and the Mediterranean World in the Age of Philip II.*
—— 1979 (*1981–4*): *Civilization and Capitalism, 15th–18th Century.*
Wallerstein, Immanuel 1991: *Unthinking Social Science: The Limits of Nineteenth-Century Paradigms.* Part V: "Revisiting Braudel."

IMMANUEL WALLERSTEIN

Brecht, Bertolt (1898–1956) German playwright, poet, director, and theoretician. One of the most influential theorists of drama in the twentieth century, especially in England and France, as well as in Germany, Brecht was born in Augsburg. His career generally divides into four stages: early plays, poems, and short stories, and his two operas (1914–30); his *Lehrstücke*, or learning plays (1930–33); plays written during his exile from Germany (1933–48); return to Germany, Austrian citizenship, establishment of the Berliner Ensemble, and adaptations of Shakespeare, Molière, and others.

Coming of age during the 1914–18 war, Brecht studied medicine at the university in Munich, was drafted, and suffered traumatic experiences as a hospital orderly during the last months of the war. As a result, he espoused pacifism and a generally nihilistic attitude toward life. Settling in Berlin during the chaotic years of the Weimar Republic, he came under two main influences, MARXISM and the theater. During his youth he had read the *Manifesto* and by 1926 he was studying *Das Kapital*. Though he never joined the Communist Party, he determined to change the world in accordance with MARXIST principles. His interest in the theater, for which he had already written two plays, led Brecht to become an assistant to Max Reinhardt. At this point he developed a familiarity with the work of

Erwin Piscator, a director who had evolved a mode of theater that he called epic drama. In 1928, Brecht produced *The Threepenny Opera*, a sardonic, pessimistic view of capitalism. The didactic plays of Brecht's second period followed, notably *The Mother* and *Saint Joan of the Stockyards*, both in 1932. By this time Brecht had become a serious student of dialectical materialism. Censored by the National Socialists in 1933, Brecht left Germany. After moving from one European city to another and writing *The Life of Galileo, The Good Person of Szechwan*, and *Mother Courage and Her Children*, he finally left for America in 1941. Living mainly in New York and Los Angeles, he wrote various pieces, *The Caucasian Chalk Circle* among them. He was forced to appear before the House Un-American Activities Committee in 1947, then left immediately for Switzerland. He ultimately settled in East Berlin and established the Berliner Ensemble in 1949, for which he wrote his adaptations and directed his plays until his death.

While not agreeing with some of Piscator's ideas, Brecht found in his predecessor's epic drama a way to communicate his social ideas to an audience, a way that the current modes of drama failed to accommodate. Realism fell short because, though he espoused the dramatic goal of revealing to the audience the truth about social conditions as he saw them, he rejected the notion that the stage should present a mere slice of life: peering through an imagined fourth wall allowed a spectator to submit himself or herself passively to a world of illusion. He needed an audience that was actively engaged in the the struggle against the capitalist organization and bourgeois values of society. Brecht also opposed naturalism because its view of the human being revealed him or her as determined by environment, whereas MARX had taught him that people were capable of change. Finally, expressionism failed to serve Brecht's purposes because it presented characters too subjectively. His theory of epic theater brilliantly resolved these objections to the drama of his day and forwarded his political agenda.

Epic theatre had the didactic purpose of making the audience think about the social conditions of their lives. In his notes to *The Rise and Fall of the City of Mahagonny* (1929), titled "The modern theatre is the epic theatre" (Willett, 1964, p. 37), Brecht provided a list of concepts, dramatic techniques, and stage devices that showed the change in emphasis from what he termed "dramatic theater," by which he meant theater that followed Aristotelian principles, to epic theater. The key items in the list point to Brecht's view of man's nature, the staging of this view, and the desired effect on the audience. Because environment does not determine man's nature, his identity is not fixed. This crucial conception allowed Brecht to treat the spectators as capable of thinking for themselves, and able to act on their new perceptions. His desire to bring his audience to the point of recognizing the truth about the inequalities of society led him to use every dramatic device at his command to effect this goal. The corollary consisted in avoiding any pattern of dramatic construction or staging that frustrated his aim. Thus Brecht rejected any aspect of performance that would create illusion, since in his view illusion acts as a kind of narcotic that prevents clear thinking. Emotion, too, clouds the mind and hence must be avoided if possible. Let the play be constructed as a succession of discrete scenes, each of which presents an argument that is addressed to the reason. The spectator must neither be allowed to empathize with the characters nor be permitted to develop an interest in an intriguing plot. Consequently, the audience must be forced to stand outside the action so as to become an objective observer. For sensation, experience, and feelings, the spectator was to substitute thought, understanding, and decisions. Brecht's termed this process *Verfremdung*, a word that is usually translated as "ALIENATION," but since that term often carries inappropriate overtones, others are sometimes substituted: estrangement, detachment, or distantiation. However translated, the word points to Brecht's desire to make the familiar strange. Were the spectator to perceive a character or an action as unfamiliar, even astonishing, he or she would be able to see it with fresh eyes. This ALIENATION EFFECT (A-effect) would allow the spectators first to escape from their social and political conditioning, then to perceive the truth in their social situation, and finally to act on it.

To illustrate how the epic play should be directed and acted, Brecht wrote an essay, "The street scene," subtitled "A basic model for an epic theatre" (Willett, 1964, pp. 121–9). Imagine, writes Brecht, that a person has seen an automobile accident and then tells others what he or she saw. Instead of attempting to reenact the event by impersonating the driver or the victim, he uses an objective, reportorial style to narrate the succession of events with an eye to revealing their social significance. In this way, avoiding illusion and emotion, the narrator estranges the action so that the listeners can draw their own conclusions about who was responsible. To achieve the A-effect, actors in epic theater must, in like manner, forgo impersonating character in the way that Stanislavski advocated; they must distance themselves from the character and the action, reading their lines as though reporting a historical event. One of their methods might consist in addressing the audience directly, not in an effort to solicit sympathy but with the goal of instructing them in reasoned choices. To communicate his social meaning, Brecht believed, following the example of Chinese acting, that the actor had to discover a social *Gestus*. Difficult to translate, *Gestus* (or gest) refers to a kind of fusion of substance, attitude, and gesture: any kind of sign, song, expression, or action. A *social* gest is one that allows the audience to understand the social attitudes and import of the scene in which it occurs. For Brecht, so important was the social gest that he wrote: "The object of the A-effect is to alienate the social gest underlying every incident" (Willett, 1964, p. 139). By way of illustration, the story is told of an incident during Brecht's rehearsal of his adaptation of Marlowe's *Edward II*. In one scene Baldock betrays Edward to the enemy by giving him a handkerchief. After many rehearsals Brecht shouted at the actor, "Not that way!" He then said to the actor, "*Baldock is a traitor . . . You must demonstrate the behavior of a traitor. Baldock goes about the betrayal with friendly outstretched arms, tenderly and submissively handing (Edward) the cloth with broad, projecting gestures . . . The public should note the behavior of a traitor and thereby pay attention!*" (McDowell, 1976, p. 113). Roland BARTHES (1977, p. 73) suggests the significance of the social gest: "[T]his Brechian concept [is] one of the clearest and most intelligent that dramatic theory has ever produced," and in a photo essay (1967) he acutely analyzed seven examples from *Mother Courage*.

Other alienating stage devices included the use of posters that set forth the resolution of the scene's key problem as well as the time and place of the scene. The spectator's attention was thus directed away from suspense and toward critical interpretation. To further this aim, Brecht used montage to construct the succession of episodic scenes, so that the actors had no through-line to follow and the audience would not be drawn into the action. Moreover, coherent development within each scene

was interrupted so that the social gest would be distanced (BENJAMIN, 1973, p. 18), and the songs were designed to arise only peripherally out of the situation. The musicians played in full view of the audience and the lighting equipment was set up in the audience's field of vision. The tone of the music was usually harsh, the songs sardonic and satiric, and the lighting flat and brilliant. In short, every aspect of Brecht's dramaturgy was designed to establish the alienating gest.

Some critics have pointed out that Brecht's instinct for drama often defeated his theory of epic theater, that to the extent the plays have been successful the theory has suffered accordingly. The stage history of *Mother Courage* provides an illustrative example. Brecht condemned the title character because, as a capitalist entrepreneur, she lives only to profit from the war. Her obsession with buying and selling causes her to lose her three beloved children, and at the play's end Brecht intended to show that, in getting back into harness to pull her wagon, she has learned nothing from her sorrow. At the play's first performance, however, the audience empathized with her noble determination to carry on and tended to see her as a heroine. Angered, Brecht rewrote some of the scenes so as to present Mother Courage more unsympathetically (for example, scene 5, in which she refuses to allow some shirts in her stock to be used as bandages for the wounded). In the later Berlin production, however, the audience still did not see Courage as a villain; in fact they pitied her. Blaming the audience for their enslavement to Aristotelian or what he called "culinary" theater, he gave up. Thus, while the A-effect apparently worked well in the play's opening scenes, Brecht had created characters and scenes that, toward the end of the play, prevented distancing. The play's last scene, in which Kattrin dies during her successful attempt to save the city, is almost universally seen as tragic in its effect. Brecht finally had to admit that some emotion could be allowed at Kattrin's death. The artist, the poet, and the Aristotelian dramatist in Brecht could, then, and sometimes did, override the theorist in him.

If we look back over all of Brecht's statements during his career, we can see that in fact he never took as firm a stand on the side of instruction as he sometimes seemed to. In fact, he always admitted that, in some way, a play should be entertaining. During his whole life, he never stood still, continually revising his plays and his ideas. As early as

1926 he was asserting that if he did not "get fun" out of his playwriting, he could not expect his audience to have "fun" (Willett, 1964, p. 7). Likewise, in 1927, he wrote that though epic theater "appeals less to the feelings than to the spectator's reason . . . it would be quite wrong to try and deny emotion to this kind of theatre" (Willett, 1964, p. 23). Even so, until 1939 Brecht held with the main goal of epic theater: to present the audience with instructive productions that would make them think critically. Then in "On experimental theatre" (1939) he began to see the need for balance: "How can the theatre be both instructive and entertaining?" (Willett, 1964, p. 135), and in 1948, when he wrote his major essay "A short organum for the theatre," he moved to full acceptance of "fun:" "From the first it has been the theater's business to entertain people. . . . Not even instruction can be demanded of it" (Willett, 1964, pp. 180–1). By this time Brecht had come to appreciate the shortcomings of his original concept of "epic theater," a phrase that he now understood as too vague to express his intention. He shifted to the descriptive phrase "theater of the scientific age" but discarded it as being too narrow (Willett, 1964, p. 276). He finally resorted to the designation "dialectical theater," though he had apparently not settled on it by the time he died.

Brecht's theory of drama will probably always be referred to as "epic theater," and the term is useful in SIGNIFYING an objectively narrated story intended to estrange the spectators so that they can ponder current social conditions. At the same time the phrase "dialectical theater" goes to the very heart of Brecht's practice (especially in his later plays), as it arises out of his theoretical assumptions, for he dramatizes each social situation as a process that is, as he wrote, "in disharmony with itself" (Willett, 1964, p. 193). He goes so far as to say, "The coherence of the character is in fact shown by the way its individual qualities contradict one another" (Willett, 1964, p. 196). Mother Courage, for example, is by turns courageous and cowardly, tenacious and pliant, harsh and loving. This dialectical technique appears in virtually all elements of his plays, perhaps most obviously in the bifurcated character Shen Te/Shui Ta of *The Good Person of Szechwan*, and in the drunk/sober Puntila of *Herr Puntila and His Man Matti*. Thus the actor must always act out what Brecht calls the "not . . . but" (Willett, 1964, p. 137): the actor performs a certain act, but that act must always imply

"what he is not doing." To cite Brecht's illustration, when the actor says, "You'll pay for that," he does not say, "I forgive you." All words, scenes, and characters contain their own internal contradictions. This dialectical method, then, was, from the beginning, crucial to Brecht's dramaturgy. In effect, Brecht found a dramatic form appropriate to his belief in dialectical materialism.

When collected, Brecht's essays, speeches, interviews, descriptions of productions, and other writings, constitute a fully developed theory of theater, one of the most influential, challenging, and provocative in this century. True, Brecht has been attacked or ignored at various times and in many places. He was of course censored when the Nazis came to power, and even during the 1950s, when he was working in the German Democratic Republic, he was heavily criticized by the Socialist Unity Party for, among other things, not presenting "positive heroes" (Wolfgang Emmerich, quoted in Kruger, 1994, p. 491). In the United States Brecht's politics have always caused concern (see Kushner, 1989). As for acting methods, American and British actors (Patterson, 1994, pp. 282–3), as well as French actors (Dort, 1990, p. 97), apparently prefer Stanislavski's method to Brecht's A-effect. In recent years Western Europe, except for England, has suffered so-called *Brecht-Müdigkeit* ("Brecht-fatigue"), owing, in part, to stodgy, museum-like productions such as those of the Berliner Ensemble (Brecht's heirs have restricted experimentation). Nevertheless, Brecht's influence has been pervasive, though, it should be said, Eric Bentley (1990) has raised serious questions on the problem of assigning influence. The Berliner Ensemble has toured a number of countries, for example, Poland in 1952, France in 1954 and 1955, England in 1956, Moscow in 1957, Venice in 1966, Toronto in 1986. During the 1970s the number of Brecht performances in the Federal Republic of Germany, Austria, and Switzerland outnumbered those of Schiller and Shakespeare (Weber, 1980, p. 97). Brecht has influenced such directors as Peter Brook, Joan Littlewood, Andrei Serban, Roger Planchon, Ariane Mnouchkine, Giorgio Strehler, Robert Woodruff, and Robert Wilson, and such playwrights as John Arden, Edward Bond, David Hare, Robert Bolt, Caryl Churchill, Peter Weiss, Heiner Muller, Helmut Baierl, Peter Hacks, Athol Fugard, and Dario Fo. American troupes, such as the Living Theater, the San Francisco Mime Troupe, and the Women's Experimental Theater have used Brechtian techniques. Scholarly interest in Brecht remains high: the annual bibliography in *Modern Drama* listed 66 Brecht items in 1992, 114 in 1993. *The Brecht Yearbook*, published by the International Brecht Society, gives essays on sources, theory, and interpretation, as well as book reviews. Critics continue to discover productive approaches to both theory and plays, especially along the lines of FEMINIST CRITICISM (for example, *The Brecht Yearbook*, vol. 12 (1983); Diamond, 1988; Geis, 1990; Reinelt, 1990; Laughlin, 1990; and Smith, 1991); and film study (for example, Willett, 1983; Copeland, 1987; Byg, 1990; and Kleber and Visser, 1990). Brecht's relation to POSTMODERNISM has been studied by Wright (1989), Silberman (1993), and Solich (1993). A 30-volume edition of Brecht's work has been under way since 1989, published by Suhrkamp Verlag (Frankfurt) and Aufbau Verlag (Berlin and Weimar), and the collected plays have been published by Vintage. Issues of journals have focused on Brecht: for example, *Tulane Drama Review*, 6 (1961); *The Drama Review* (*TDR*), 12, no. 1 (fall 1967); *The Drama Review* (*TDR*), 24, no. 1 (fall 1980); *Theatre* (Yale), 17 (spring 1986); *Theatre Journal*, 39 (1987); and *Modern Drama*, 31 (1988). The March 1993 issue of *Theatre Journal*, titled "German Theatre after the F/Wall," examines the state of German drama, and the situation of Brecht in particular, since November 1989.

The fall of the Berlin Wall appears to have had, so far, little effect *per se* on the way Brecht's theory has been perceived. True, some believe that because Communism appears to have been discredited, Brecht's politics have become irrelevant (see the discussion, pro and con, in Eddershaw, 1991, pp. 303–4), but one might well argue that as long as social inequity characterizes modern life, Brecht's goal of changing society will continue to require consideration. The extent to which feminist and postmodern approaches will shift our views of Brecht's theory and practice remains to be seen. Meanwhile, Silberman's report (1993, p. 19) that Berlin has provided financial support for the Berliner Ensemble, which, under new management committed to innovation "in Brecht's spirit," is experiencing a rebirth, augurs well. Naturally, directors, actors, and playwrights will continue to argue about Brecht's ideas, and some have discarded them, but Brecht's metatheatrical technique and the dialectical nature of his dramatic structures, especially perhaps his rejection of essentialist views of character, his acceptance of openendedness, and his inclusion of a critical audience, make him indispensable. Brecht remains a major presence, for his revolutionary dramaturgy, tied as it is to political awareness, has changed and enlarged our ways of perceiving theatre.

Reading

Bentley, Eric 1981: *The Brecht Commentaries, 1943–1980.*
Brooker, Peter 1988: *Bertolt Brecht: Dialectics, Poetry, Politics.*
Cohn, Ruby 1969: *Currents in Contemporary Drama.*
Esslin, Martin 1959 (*1971*): *Brecht: The Man and His Work.*
Fuegi, John 1972: *The Essential Brecht.*
Hill, Claude 1975: *Bertolt Brecht.*
Mews, Siegfried, ed. 1989: *Critical Essays on Bertolt Brecht.*
Mueller, Roswitha 1989: *Bertolt Brecht and the Theory of Media.*
Speirs, Ronald 1987: *Bertolt Brecht.*
Suvin, Darko 1984: *To Brecht and Beyond: Soundings in Modern Dramaturgy.*
Thomson, Peter, and Sacks, Glendyr, ed. 1994: *The Cambridge Companion to Brecht.*
Willett, John 1959: *The Theatre of Bertolt Brecht: A Study from Eight Aspects.*

TUCKER ORBISON

Bremond, Claude (1929–) French narratologist. Bremond interrogates the work of the Russian structuralist Vladimir PROPP on folktales. For Bremond the structuralist critic should pay attention to possible meanings other than those offered by the literary work. He theorizes that TEXTS contain points at which choices are made, the plot changes, or characters develop. By using the linguistics of SAUSSURE, of differential relations, he sees these points as producing meaning through the very choices which are excluded.

Reading

Bremond, Claude 1973: *Logique du récit.*
Propp, Vladimir 1958: *Morphology of the Folktale.*

PAUL INNES

bricolage A term associated with Claude LÉVI-STRAUSS, referring to the use of a roughly suited conceptual tool when no other means is available. In *The Elementary Structures of Kinship*, Lévi-Strauss (1969, pp. 2–4) defines "nature" as that which is universal, spontaneous, and not dependent on a particular culture or norm; and "CULTURE" as that which is dependent on a SYSTEM of socially regulating norms and which varies from one social structure to another. Nevertheless, having established this distinction between nature and culture, he proceeds to discuss incest prohibition, which appears to be both universal and natural, and normative and cultural. Although in a sense scandalously inadequate, the nature/culture distinction is nevertheless indispensable and its use an instance of *bricolage*. DERRIDA escalates the applicability of the term by observing that, if *bricolage* is the necessary borrowing of concepts from an incoherent or ruined heritage, then "every discourse is *bricoleur*" (1978, p. 285).

Reading
Derrida, Jacques 1967b (*1978*): *Writing and Difference.*
Lévi-Strauss, Claude 1949 (*1969*): *The Elementary Structures of Kinship.*

MICHAEL PAYNE

British Film Institute   Founded in 1933 amid bitter debate about the role of film education and film culture in Britain. Since then, it has had to struggle to maintain its independence as an institution that exists essentially within the public sphere, in the face of industry pressure and changing government policies. Throughout its history it has played a crucial innovative role in film culture. One of the Institute's first responsibilities was to set up a National Film Library (the origin of the present National Film and Television Archive). It also took over the journal *Sight and Sound* in 1934, and created an exhibition wing with the foundation of the National Film Theatre in 1952. From its inception, the BFI has been concerned with defining and promoting film education and it is primarily through these activities that its work has made a unique contribution to the development of film theory. Intellectual innovation and debate has always benefited from the backing and dissemination available through the BFI's different activities, most particularly the film distribution library, publishing, and the specialized information service and book library.

In the mid-1960s the Education Department of the British Film Insitute adopted a new, dynamic policy toward film criticism and FILM STUDIES that provided a crucible for emergent film theory. It is possible to date the new initiatives from the appointment of Paddy Whannel as the Institute's Education Officer in 1957. He then coauthored, with Stuart HALL, *The Popular Arts* (1964), a book whose title reflects the upheaval that his engagement with film culture would bring to the British Film Institute. The established approach to film criticism at the time is evident in the editorial policies of *Sight and Sound*. *Sight and Sound* had, particularly after 1948 when Gavin Lambert became editor, represented the best of the British tradition, concentrating its critical support and enthusiasm on the work of the international art cinema and some exceptional American films. It was under Whannel's aegis that the Hollywood studio system cinema first came to be taken seriously in the BFI.

The collaboration that produced *The Popular Arts* is, perhaps, symptomatic as both authors came from outside the English intellectual establishment, Whannel as a working-class Scot and Hall as an Oxford-educated Jamaican. Both were prepared to give intellectual attention and social analysis to cinema that had previously been at best critically neglected, and often received with active hostility by an elite which dismissed Hollywood as kitsch in its products and imperialist in its domination of the international entertainment market. Whannel initiated a critical concern with popular, particularly Hollywood, cinema and further confounded traditional attitudes by adopting this position with a left political commitment.

It is of great importance to establish Paddy Whannel's influence on these critical changes because he never again published. He encouraged and sustained critical polemic and passion, but it was his organizing energy that transformed ideas into policies. Most of all, he collected a group of like-minded people in the BFI Education Department. These were the writers, administrators, and educationalists who would launch the new approach to film theory. During the 1960s the influence of *Cahiers du Cinéma* had taken root in Britain, also initiating a new interest in Hollywood. Victor Perkins, of the *Movie* editorial board, and Peter Wollen, who had been writing about Hollywood cinema from an auteurist perspective in *New Left Review* under the pseudonym Lee Russell, both joined the Education Department in 1966. It was in the subsequent years that the Education Department's unique approach was hammered out at the BFI in seminars, screenings, and the enormously influential Education Department summer schools. Although the critical problems posed by studio system cinema were central to these debates, so was the work of pioneer film theorists such as Eisenstein and Bazin.

The need to develop a policy toward education, as the basis for a future film culture, provided the context in which questions of theory were first addressed. While film criticism had traditionally depended on concepts of value that were appropriate for high cultural products, particularly those of literary criticism, films produced by the Hollywood studio system demanded a new form of criticism and a new approach to value. It was out of this intellectual challenge that the BFI Education Department turned to theories of SEMIOTICS and STRUCTURALISM. And it was probably only in Britain that the passion for Hollywood cinema could be met with French ideas. The mix of low culture from across the Atlantic and high theory from across the Channel amounted to a slap in the face to traditional Englishness that was, in many ways, characteristic of this generation and its rejection of English isolationism and chauvinism. As the Education Department moved into publishing, Peter Wollen's *Signs and Meaning in the Cinema* (1969, BFI and Secker and Warburg; reissued 1972), Jim Kitses's *Horizons West* (1969, BFI and Secker and Warburg), and Colin McArthur's *Underworld USA* (1972, BFI and Secker and Warburg) all represent these trends toward theorization, while also continuing to address the *Cahiers* issues of auteurism and genre. At the same time, the British Film Institute funded the first university appointments dedicated to film studies, which were to provide the next means of expanding these ideas to a wider constitutency and a new generation. Robin Wood, who had played an important part in the Education Department debates from a rather different, more Leavisite position, was appointed to the first of these posts at Warwick University.

This "first wave" of film theory suffered a setback when Paddy Whannel and a number of his colleagues resigned their posts in 1971 over a change in policy toward education within the BFI. However, the Education Department position had accumulated support and its work continued, while other Departments forwarded the debates through their own activities. For instance, the critical decisions that lay behind the collection of 16 mm prints and study extracts enabled Hollywood cinema to be taught, seriously and analytically, along the lines of the Education Department policy. However, the cultural atmosphere was changing in the late 1960s, opening the way for new developments in film theory. The Vietnam War and the political events of 1968 shifted attention away from Hollywood

cinema, which was, in any case, going through profound crises of its own. The BFI-funded journal SCREEN continued, during this period, to expand and elaborate the film and theory conjuncture, particularly through ALTHUSSERian MARXISM and LACANian PSYCHOANALYSIS.

While the BFI's work with theory continued and consolidated in education and publishing, from the mid-1970s interest in film theory and AVANT-GARDE AESTHETICS started to influence production policy. With Peter Sainsbury's appointment as Head of the Production Board in 1976, the potential of 16 mm film making as the basis for an alternative cinema brought together previously uncoordinated aspirations. Although the Production Board's funding included films ranging from cinema *vérité* to the avant-garde, this period also produced work that attempted to create a theoretical cinema. Once again, the British context responded to hybrid influences, those of the New American Cinema movement represented, for instance, by Michael Snow and Hollis Frampton, and the radical European cinema represented, for instance, by Jean-Luc Godard and Jean-Marie Straub/Danielle Huillet. Sainsbury's policy funded films that responded to these trends, while also reflecting the impact of FEMINISM and work on representation and psychoanalytic theory.

The face of independent film changed in the 1980s, responding to the impact of Channel 4 as well as to cuts in government provision of funds. However, with coproductions, the BFI funded many directors whose work has become synonymous with British cinema today. New funding policies were designed, by the setting up of workshops, to create film-making opportunities in the regions, beyond metropolitan monopoly. The black film-making collectives (Ceddo, Sankofa, Black Audio Film Collective, Retake) began to produce work that extended and reconfigured the radical and theoretical tradition of the Production Board.

During the years of Thatcherite Conservatism, the BFI had to lobby to maintain its policies. Its success is confirmed by developments that have taken place on two fronts. First of all, awareness of film, and increasingly television, has been firmly established in schools, widening the availability of the theory that was pioneered in the earlier period. Media studies are now included in the core curiculum that must be taught in all schools. This impetus is also reflected in the ideas and presentation behind the BFI's Museum of the Moving Image, founded in 1988. Secondly, the BFI has made a commitment to wide-ranging research into new developments in the moving image culture. Drawing, for instance, on its historical collections (such as the National Film Archive, its Library, and its other resources) the BFI's research initiatives can cut across the culture and commerce divide that haunts film and television. In 1992 the BFI established (with Birkbeck College, London University) an MA in Film and Television History and Theory that is now at the heart of its research program.

The story of the BFI's support for radical ideas and innovations, in debate and in advance of their establishment or acceptance, bears witness to the crucial contribution of public sector institutions to a culture which can also affect and inform the commercial. The year of the centenary of cinema sees the BFI working in conjunction with the film industry, and achieving a cooperation that would have been inconceivable at the time of the Institute's birth, or even ten or so years ago. At this particular moment of history, when the very concept of the "public" has to be defended both theoretically and practically, the BFI is finding ways of keeping its tradition of conservation and innovation alive for future generations.

Reading
Houston, Penelope 1994: *Keepers of the Frame. The Film Archives.* London: BFI.
McArthur, Colin 1992: *The Big Heat.* London: BFI.
MacCabe, Colin 1993: *On the Eloquence of the Vulgar. A Justification of the Study of Film and Television.* London: BFI.

LAURA MULVEY

Brooks, Cleanth (1906–94) American critic. Brooks was the chief popularizer of NEW CRITICISM. A member of the second generation of the movement, he was not one of its seminal thinkers, describing his work as a "synthesis" of others' ideas, but his student handbook *Understanding Poetry* (with Robert Penn Warren, 1938) was enormously influential in spreading the gospel of New Criticism throughout American literature departments. *Modern Poetry and the Tradition* (1939) and *The Well-Wrought Urn* (1947) are the representative critical works of the movement, and *Literary Criticism: A Short History* (with William K. Wimsatt, 1957) also became a standard text.

Modern Poetry and the Tradition was the American equivalent of F.R. LEAVIS's *Revaluation* (1936),

an ambitious attempt to write a "Revised History of English Poetry" in terms of T.S. ELIOT's ideas, and simultaneously a spirited defense of modernist poetry. Brooks's work aimed at a "general theory of the history of English poetry implied by the practice of the modern poets." In other words, like Eliot and Leavis, Brooks in effect read literary history backwards, in the service of a polemic against "the scholars, the appointed custodians of the tradition." Their dismissal of modern poetry as "difficult" and overintellectual results from their being trapped in a defunct tradition, one which runs back to Romanticism and narrow eighteenth-century conceptions of "the poetic." In order for criticism to go forward, Brooks wants it go further back, reestablishing contact with an earlier tradition, that of the early seventeenth century, and reversing the process which "broke the tradition of wit."

There is a "significant relationship between the modernist poets and the seventeenth-century poets of wit." Both groups use a poetic language which expresses "mature" and "complex" attitudes, especially ironic ones, fusing intellect and feeling, as Eliot had described Donne. The greater part of the book is a demonstration of how the poet who has mastered this "serious wit" "is constantly remaking his world by relating into an organic whole the amorphous and heterogenous and contradictory." Brooks makes a strong case although it is also one which now looks alarmingly exclusive, since it suggests that all the poets between Donne and Eliot, lacking "wit" in this very special definition, were purveyors of simple-minded emotion or equally simple-minded rationalism.

The other questionable aspect of Brooks's essay derives from the fact that it is something much more than a revisionist literary history. Like his mentors Eliot, RICHARDS, RANSOM, and TATE, and like Leavis, Brooks is out to promote a particular vision of modern history, and it is a melodramatically gloomy and Spenglerian one. He endorses Allan Tate's descriptions of "our present disintegration," in which the mass of the population live experientially chaotic lives. He quotes with enthusiasm Eliot's snobbish description of "the ordinary man's experience" as "chaotic, irregular, fragmentary" (in contrast to the mind of the witty ideal poet, which "is constantly amalgamating disparate experience"), and when he applies his Eliotic "test" of good poets – "the scope and breadth of experience which their poetry assimilates" – not just to poetry but to the reading public, he comes to "a strange and perhaps illuminating conclusion, namely that it is the public which inhabits the Ivory Tower, separating its emotional life ... from the actual world." A strange conclusion indeed, and one which throws doubt on Brooks's (and the New Critics') whole enterprise.

The Well-Wrought Urn was published in 1947. In between the two books the 1939–45 war had intervened, and, according to Brooks, had led to increased attacks on the "difficulty" of modernist poetry. He therefore returned to the fray, with even more aggressive claims. PARADOX replaced IRONY and wit as the key term, and the book opens with the sweeping assertion that "paradox is the language appropriate and inevitable to poetry." The tactic was now different, however. Realizing perhaps that this criterion would yield an even narrower definition of the one true tradition, he conceded that some poetry worth reading was written between the English Civil War and T.S. Eliot. "The 'new criticism', so called, has tended to center around the rehabilitation of Donne, and the Donne tradition" but now critics should look further afield and seek "paradox" elsewhere too. He now found it in Wordsworth (who had been described in *Modern Poetry* as "inimical to intellect"), in Keats, and even in Tennyson ("perhaps the last English poet one would think of associating with the subtleties of paradox and ambiguity").

The increase in flexibility was welcome. Nevertheless, this was still an extraordinarily blinkered way of reading English poetry, and, despite the interest and subtlety of many of Brooks's individual close readings, it has not survived as a critical or historical theory.

See also NEW CRITICISM; ELIOT, T.S.; RANSOM, JOHN; IRONY; PARADOX.

Reading
Crane, R.S. 1952: "The critical monism of Cleanth Brooks."
Guillory, John 1983: "The ideology of canon-formation: T.S. Eliot and Cleanth Brooks."
Simpson, Lewis, ed. 1976: *The Possibilities of Order: Cleanth Brooks and His Works.*
Wellek, René 1986b: "Cleanth Brooks."

IAIN WRIGHT

Bryson, Norman (1949–) British scholar of comparative studies who brings polarities from literary theory (that is, CONNOTATION/DENOTATION; SYNTAGMATIC/PARADIGMATIC) to bear on the discipline of art history. In *Word and Image*, for example, Bryson examines French painting from LeBrun to David not as a succession of styles but as an interaction between the Discursive and the Figural. This view permits, for example, the painting of Chardin to be viewed not as a bad fit in the rococo style, but as a blend of the discursivity of LeBrun and the figurality of Watteau.

See also GAZE; GOMBRICH, ERNST; SEMIOTICS; STRUCTURALISM.

Reading
Bryson, Norman 1981 (*1986*): *Word and Image: French Painting of the Ancien Regime.*
——1983 (*1988*): *Vision and Painting: The Logic of the Gaze.*
——1984: *Tradition and Desire: From David to Delacroix.*
——1989: *Looking at the Overlooked: Four Essays on Still-life.*

GERALD EAGER

Burke, Kenneth (1897–) American literary critic. Although Burke is usually considered a literary critic – he has even been hailed as the foremost critic since Coleridge – his own definition of his project was that it constituted an investigation into symbolic motivations and linguistic action in general (Burke, 1966, p. 494). Burke was a prolific writer, translator, poet, short-story writer, and novelist. By concentrating much of his attention on the effects of texts on their audience, he both expanded and refined the art of rhetoric. The fierce independence of his thought, however, greatly limited his influence. His theoretical interests, which distinguish him from the NEW CRITICISM, ranged from PSYCHOANALYSIS and linguistics to MARXISM and pragmatism; but he was not systematically responsive to any of those disciplines. Nevertheless, as a model of the committed intellectual in America at a time when both political commitment and intellectualism were suspect, he has a secure place in the history of American letters. Critical assessments of his work are likely to be either fulsome or dismissive. His last major book, *Language as Symbolic Action* (1966), provides an excellent retrospective of his work.

Reading
Burke, Kenneth 1966: *Language as Symbolic Action.*
MICHAEL PAYNE

C

Cage, John Milton (1912–92) Musician, born in Los Angeles, California. An influential composer and a leading figure in the experimental art movements of the last half of the twentieth century, his compositions and ideas using chance, silence, and nonintentionality challenged the way music was made and heard. He wrote music in a variety of styles and investigated a vast array of compositional forms and methods of composing. His work extended beyond music to the areas of dance, painting, art, philosophy, and POETRY. His collaborators and friends included dancer Merce Cunningham, visual artists Robert Rauschenberg, Jasper Johns, Marcel Duchamp, pianist David Tudor, composers Pierre Boulez, Karlheinz Stockhausen, Morton Feldman, Christian Wolff, and Earle Brown.

Several individuals were important in Cage's early musical and intellectual development. In the early 1930s he studied composition with Henry Cowell at the New School in New York and with Arnold Schoenberg in Los Angeles. In 1938 and 1939 he worked with Bonnie Bird's dance company at the Cornish School in Seattle and there met Merce Cunningham, with whom he was to collaborate for the rest of his life, and for whose dance company he wrote numerous compositions. During the mid-1940s Cage began a serious study of non-Western thought. He studied Indian philosophy with the musician Gita Sarabhai, who introduced him to the writings of Ramakrishna. In the late 1940s Cage studied Zen Buddhism with Daisetz T. Suzuki at Columbia University in New York. In 1951 he was given a copy of the Chinese Book of Changes, the I Ching, by Christian Wolff. That TEXT proved important for Cage's thought and was used by him to assist the chance operations and compositional decisions required for many of his musical scores and writings. While these individuals and events helped shape his early life, his work with Schoenberg (although rather brief) produced several life-forming decisions and numerous interesting and often repeated anecdotes. Cage returned in 1934 to Los Angeles from New York and sought out Schoenberg, who agreed to give him lessons but only if he was ready to commit his life to music. Cage said that he was and he moved back to Los Angeles and began studying counterpoint with Schoenberg. Schoenberg expressed strong reservations about Cage's musical abilities. While he found Cage to be "an inventor of genius" he did not feel he had the necessary talents or proper sense of harmony to be a composer. On being confronted with this depressing prognosis about his musical future, Cage felt even more determined to push ahead. Schoenberg told him that he would reach a point where he would hit a wall and be unable to go any further. Cage's reply was that then he would spend his life banging his head against that wall. He had promised Schoenberg that he would devote his life to music and that is what he would do. And so he did. His complete catalogue of compositions numbers over 200. A list of the most important would include: Credo in Us (1942), Sonatas and Interludes (1948), Williams Mix (1952), 4'33" (1952), HPSCHD (1969), Roaratorio (1979), and Europeras 1 & 2 (1987). During his life he was internationally honored, receiving numerous artistic awards, and was commissioned by many of the most important orchestras and performing companies in the world. He authored several books including Silence (1961), A Year from Monday (1967), and Empty Words (1979); and he created many visual works, including 17 Drawings by Thoreau (1978), Ryoku (1985), and Eleven Stones (1989). He was the Charles Eliot Norton Lecturer at Harvard in 1988–9; those lectures, published in 1990 under the title I–VI, provide the best and most extensive example of a form of his poetic writing, a form he titled mesostic.

While original and provocative in much of what he did, Cage's work has roots in the early American artistic and intellectual traditions. In particular, his interests in experimentation and stretching the limits of human expression and artistic experience have important precedents in the music of Charles Ives and the writings of Henry David Thoreau and Ralph Waldo EMERSON. The following quotation might have come from any one of them: "let me remind the reader that I am only an experimenter. Do not set the least value on what I do, or the least discredit on what I do not, as if I pretended to settle anything as true or false. I unsettle all things. No facts are to me sacred; none are profane; I simply experiment, an endless seeker, with no Past at my back" ("Circles," Emerson). Cage's delight in experimentation can be traced to his father, a self-employed inventor who created one of the first submarines. On numerous occasions, Cage acknowledged this influence of his father and told the story of his destined-to-be-rejected submarine. "Dad is an inventor. In 1912 his submarine had the world's record for staying under water. Running as it did by means of a gasoline engine, it left bubbles on the surface, so it was not employed during World War I" (*Silence*, Wesleyan University Press, 1961, p. 12).

The experimental nature of Cage's work was often the direct result of factual necessity. His own limits, for instance, as a traditional composer (which Schoenberg had noted) forced him to investigate individual sounds and sustained duration of sound in ways others had not, and to give less importance to the standard relationships and harmony between sounds, and thereby to imagine and explore different ways of structuring the temporal dimension of music. It was physical limitations that brought about his invention of the prepared piano. Not having enough room on a stage for more than a standard piano yet needing sound the piano could not produce led Cage (in the late 1930s) to experiment with altering the sound of the piano. He placed bolts and nuts and strips of rubber on and between the strings inside the piano, thereby producing new possibilities of sound for the standard instrument. (Some of his most beautiful music was written for the prepared piano, for example, *The Perilous Night* (1943–4) and *Sonatas and Interludes*.) For Cage, the limits and necessities of our world are best treated as occasions for experimentation and opportunities to attempt new things that have not been tried before. Much of his devotion to experimentation was due to his belief that the obstacles and restrictions of our lives should be turned to our advantage rather than accepted as reasons for failure.

Experimenting with and composing for the prepared piano produced not only variable and new sounds, a new versatility, for this traditional instrument, but also made Cage realize that he had less control over the final sounds of the compositions he wrote for this new instrument. This understanding led to an interest in other kinds of compositions where the resulting sounds would be variable with each performance. He thus began to experiment with indeterminate composition by means of chance operations, a form of composition that was to mark his work like no other and was to cause many a former friend and colleague, like Boulez, to no longer feel comfortable with his work. The use of chance operations was not intended to introduce arbitrariness into musical performance, but to remove the decisions of the composer from the last stage of creation. Removing the personal desires and choices of the composer by chance operations was not intended to produce uncalculated acts of composition or a preference for random performances. If we simply do anything we wish in an arbitrary fashion, then we rely on memory or feelings or whatever is part of us at a given moment, whereas the use of carefully calculated chance operations provides an objective procedure for choosing the sounds for a composition. In much of his (especially later) work Cage sought a context of nonintentionality and removal of the personal self, and escape from the choices and desires of the self, a divorcing of the final product of composition from the conscious desires of the composer, and a coming to live with the silence (all the sounds we do not intend) of our world.

Silence was another important part of Cage's music. It was for him "all the sounds we don't intentionally make," and that which opens us fully to the world. It breaks the barrier between world and art in such a way that we no longer know the difference between them, and necessitates an active rather than a passive listener. Silence leads us out of the world of art and into the whole of life. It is not the opposite of sound, but the encompassing of all sound. The silence of the world was the music most preferred by Cage. "If you want to know the truth of the matter, the music I prefer, even to my own and everything, is what we hear if we are just quiet" (Kostelanetz, 1988, p. 23).

The desire to encompass all sound (silence) is most fully expressed in Cage's most talked about and notorious composition: *4'33"*. It is a piece, originally written in three movements and later adopted for any duration, consisting of four minutes and thirty-three seconds (a time determined by chance operations) of silence. The piece is the sounds that naturally happen during the time of performance; it is those sounds that occur in the concert hall (people moving, chairs squeaking) and in the outside environment (car horns honking, wind blowing) that make their way to the audience's ears. Most fully of all his compositions it represents his love and respect for the world as it is. *4'33"* expresses Cage's feeling that the main question before us is "How quickly will we say yes?" to our lives. Such a question uncovers another important interest of Cage, that of anarchism. A fundamental assumption of anarchism for Cage was that people are generally good and capable of taking care of themselves without hierarchical arrangements of their lives by others. In order to write music the way he did, Cage said you have to assume that people are good and able to take care of and think for themselves. Experimentation, chance, and silence are important ingredients and expressions of Cage's anarchistic way of composing and living. He sought to give all sound an equal footing and hearing in our lives; and he tried to compose and live so as "not to interfere with the music that is continuously going on around us." His was a music that expressed the natural goodness and livability of our ordinary lives.

Cage's work created and creates much controversy. One of the recurring conflicts is often presented as that between his music and his ideas (or his philosophy). Although such a dichotomy is almost inevitably used in writings about Cage (it is used several times in this present discussion), it can be quite misleading, and it has produced an important controversy in the ways we listen to, talk about, and write about Cage's work. There tend to be two somewhat extreme sides on this issue: one says "they can't stand his music but his ideas are important," and the other asserts "Cage was first and foremost a composer, not a philosopher, and to concentrate on his ideas is to demean and devalue his compositions." James Pritchett has usefully reanimated this discussion and overlays his text on Cage with the controversy. He insists that Cage be treated as a composer and that attempts to make him a philosopher simply undermine understanding him. He writes, "it has been stated on various occasions by various authorities that Cage was more a philosopher than a composer, that his ideas were more interesting than his music." However, asserts Pritchett, "Cage-as-philosopher is . . . an image that will not bear close scrutiny" and so he returns to what he says is "the obvious: Cage was a composer" (Pritchett, *The Music of John Cage*, pp. 1–3).

These two positions permeate much of the writing and talk about Cage. Choosing between them fairly easily leads to a preference for the second approach. It is difficult not to agree that without a healthy dose of listening to Cage and experiencing numerous of his compositions, one is not in a very good position to talk about his work (this seems obvious but is not so in discussion about Cage). However, that position does not finally leave one satisfied for it simply overstates the point. If one ignores or downplays the philosophy in Cage's work, then one is apt to miss questions and reflections embodied in the music which are capable of producing valuable thoughts about the nature of sound and provocations about how we live our lives, important parts of Cage's interest. The philosopher in us all benefits from listening to Cage. When we, for instance, listen to many of his compositions and hear (encounter) his idea that things need to be themselves and that our cravings for establishing relationships between things are best given up, we experience possible life-shaping challenges. (In different language it might be said that we hear how Cage's metaphysics places epistemology, or how his concerns with the nature of being establish and remove contexts for our attempts at knowing.) Cage's music encourages a reshaping of the questions we ask about music, our world, ourselves, and that is a philosophical enterprise. His music usually exemplifies rather than informs but what it exemplifies must not be ignored. Attempts to dismiss Cage the musician or Cage the philosopher fail in a similar way. The second encourages and tolerates a narrowness about philosophy and Cage that we need not accept, whereas the first assumes and works with a conception of music and ideas that unnecessarily confines us. Both positions, however, importantly uncover a question that naturally and inevitably must be confronted in facing Cage: Can ideas and sounds be separated? (Can philosophy and music be themselves?) It is not hard to guess that Cage knew we unhesitatingly answer yes, rather than silently admitting we do not know.

Reading

Fleming, Richard, and Duckworth, William, eds 1989: *John Cage at Seventy-Five*.
Kostelantez, Richard 1988: *Conversing with Cage*.
Pritchett, James 1993: *The Music of John Cage*.
Revill, David 1992: *The Roaring Silence: John Cage: A Life*.

RICHARD FLEMING

Cahiers du Cinéma Spanning more than four decades and composed of well over 400 issues, *Cahiers du Cinéma* has earned its place as one of the most influential and controversial journals of film criticism. Even today, the journal owes much of its reputation to the early days of its existence when, at the height of its popularity, *Cahiers du Cinéma* had a circulation of 13,000. As George Lellis, one of many writers to devote a whole text to analyzing the journal, observes, "*Cahiers du Cinéma* in the early 1980s is hardly the monolithic force it was in the late 1950s or early 1960s." In 1951 Lo Duca, André Bazin, and Jacques Doniol-Valcroze jointly edited the first issue. Within a few years, a group of young film critics who were later to become major directors of French New Wave cinema – Claude Chabrol, Jean-Luc Godard, Jacques Rivette, Eric Rohmer, François Truffaut – joined the magazine as regular contributors. In 1954 Truffaut submitted an essay, "Une certaine tendance du cinéma français," in which he introduced his *politique des auteurs*, the theory widely held within the *Cahiers* circle that a film bears the mark of the director, the film's true author (*auteur*). The notion itself was not entirely new; years earlier, an article in *Revue du Cinéma*, a forerunner of *Cahiers du Cinéma*, expressed a similar idea. But with Truffaut's article, the idea exploded onto the *Cahiers* agenda. Entwined in the *auteur* theory, *mise en scène*, a focus on the composition of individual shots rather than the effect created by cutting together many shots, became another central concept in the journal. Critics of *Cahiers du Cinéma* have complained that the journal gave too much credit to a select group of French and American directors experimenting with the *auteur* theory, and at least one American critic, John Hess, faults the journal for its partiality to films which are too much alike, all representing more or less the same world view.

For several reasons, the tone of the journal changed during the early 1960s until it was only a ghost of its earlier image. Some critics today suggest that, as the *auteurs* of the 1950s died or retired from film making, *Cahiers* writers were forced to turn elsewhere for subjects of their criticism. And, as the original critics began pursuing careers as directors – experimenting firsthand with the *auteur* theory and *mise en scène* – a new group of critics, more academic than the first, altered the journal's tone. *Cahiers du Cinéma* went through a slow time in the early 1960s; Godard suggested in 1962 that it no longer had any new ideas, that everyone simply agreed with each other. However, as the journal reacted to the French political turmoil of 1968, it stirred controversy anew. The controversy reached even the editorial board in 1969, when the journal changed ownership as the result of irreconcilable conflicts within the board. Around this time, Jacques LACAN, Roland BARTHES, and Christian Metz joined the board and pushed the journal into new areas. In the post-1968 era, *Cahiers du Cinéma*, deeply influenced by Brecht, presented a highly politicized and theoretical agenda of an increasingly militant tone, a marked contrast to its 1950s reverence for Hollywood *auteurs*. *Cahiers du Cinéma* supported the argument that commercial films reflect the dominant IDEOLOGY of capitalism.

TARA G. GILLIGAN

call and response A term central to BLACK CULTURAL STUDIES, which refers to the antiphonal exchange between performer and audience that characterizes a variety of black American oral forms. Occurring whenever a phrase, whether spoken, sung, or played by a solo performer, is repeated and answered by a chorus or an audience, the pattern of call and response establishes and affirms an interactive and participatory model of communication.

Reading
Smitherman, Geneva 1977: *Talkin and Testifyin: The Language of Black America*.

MADHU DUBEY

Camera Obscura Founded in 1974 by four women experimenting with feminist socialism and keenly interested in the relation between women and the cinema, especially AVANT-GARDE and experimental films made by women, *Camera Obscura* reflects the changing theoretical beliefs of its creators. Janet Bergstrom, Sandy Flitterman, Elisabeth Hart Lyon, and Constance Penley joined the editorial board of *Women and Film* one year before founding *Camera Obscura*. "The need to begin a new review arose out of longstanding and seemingly unresolvable controversies within *Women and Film*," they wrote in 1979. *Camera Obscura* provided a fresh outlet for their theories and a chance to practice a form of feminist socialism. For the first two years, the four women acted idealistically as a single unit, signing all of their work, whether created individually or by the team, as the *Camera Obscura* Collective. By 1976, the same year in which

Women and Film finally collapsed, forcing *Camera Obscura* to adopt the task of announcing information about women's film activities in a section entitled "Women Working," the founding editors realized that the collective model was not appropriate to their journal. In a later issue they wrote (collectively) that much of the audience of their first issue found the effect to be "monolithic" and to discourage the contributions of others beyond the editorial collective. For another decade the editorial collective still presided over the journal. In 1986 the editorial collective, minus Flitterman who left the journal in 1978, became simply "editors." The editors still collaborate on the occasional article, but they now sign their own names, or combination of names, to most articles.

The editors of *Camera Obscura* have used their journal as a place for writing about and experimenting with theories and ideologies. In their editorial for the fifth issue (Spring 1980), for example, their emphasis on feminism and the classical film, subjects which recur in issue upon issue, is undeniable: "it is clearly important for our project on the analysis of women and representation to understand the functioning of the structural and symbolic role of sexual difference in the classical film." As with any journal so firmly planted in IDEOLOGY, *Camera Obscura* has not been free of criticism. The *Camera Obscura* editors admit openly their reverence for Jean-Luc Godard's work; a triple issue (Nos 8–9–10, Fall 1982) is dedicated to a review of his recent work. But one critic, James Roy MacBean, writing for *Quarterly Review of Film Studies*, while pleased with some of the insights he finds in an otherwise "uneven volume," faults the editors for their "relative narrowness" in interpreting one of Godard's films. He accuses the editors, and is probably justified in doing so, of creating a "fictional world built up by the narrative" rather than interpreting the actual events of the film. Yet even after delivering some caustic blows, MacBean ends his comments with a bit of deserved flattery: "the *Camera Obscura* editors," he writes, "have made a significant contribution . . . to our ongoing appraisal of the work of Jean-Luc Godard." One might also claim that the editors have made a significant contribution to feminism and film theory.

TARA G. GILLIGAN

Canadian studies Canadian studies consists of a body of work which treats Canadian society and

CULTURE as its subject. It is to be distinguished from works by Canadians, such as those of Harry Johnson (economics) or Northrope FRYE (literary criticism) which have contributed to general knowledge or to their individual disciplines. Considered thus, Canadian studies is only about 25 years old, although many of the most important works which comment on, or which are descriptive of, Canadian culture and society were written or created decades before the late 1960s. It also follows that the work to be included should not be limited to that of Canadians but must also include the considerable body of work done by non-Canadian scholars.

Perhaps the event which was most crucial to the birth of Canadian studies was US participation in the war in Vietnam and the concomitant reaction to it by many Canadian intellectuals. Owing to the physical proximity to the United States and to an intense debate about Canada's role in that conflict, there was a profound examination of Canada as a nation and a serious effort to discern what was distinctive about Canada, and indeed, what differentiated it specifically from the United States.

This quest for Canadian uniqueness was further stimulated by publication of a study by Ronald and Paul Wonnacott extolling the benefits of a free trade pact between Canada and the United States, a work which gave birth to a vast number of specialized and econometric studies promoting this scheme. For the rapidly growing Canadian nationalist movement continental free trade was synonymous with *de facto* absorption of Canada into its larger neighbor, a perception such a policy measure would have on the Canadian economy.

The reaction of Canadians to these threats to their sense of self spanned the political spectrum. The Tory-heroic vision to Donald Creighton's biography of Canada's first Prime Minister, *John A. Macdonald* (1952 and 1955), George Grant's *Lament for a Nation* (1965), and poet Dennis Lee's *Civil Elegies* (1968) was matched on the left by the work of economists Mel Watkins, Kari Levitt, and Abraham Rotstein, and by a long list of cultural nationalists. Liberal historian Frank Underwood had earlier provided a metropolitan-based alternative for Canada to American historian Frederick Jackson Turner's "frontier thesis" and, with *The Vertical Mosaic* (1965), John Porter gave a Canadian counter to the American "melting pot," one which was later to give rise to the Department of Multicultural Affairs of the national government.

From the American Revolution onwards, many Canadians had always seen their nation as an alternative to their southern neighbor; an alternative which had its basis in Canada's origins as a colony of France and then of England. Many aspects of the social institutions, the law, and the culture of Quebec, which retained a distinctly non-North American character, and Canada's parliament, preference for political evolution rather than revolution, and the less individualistic social values were appreciated for their non-US character. However, as the post 1939–45 war realities of national power and the feasibility of international linkages with the United Kingdom became apparent, the power of these colonial identifications weakened markedly.

The universities became a central battlefield between those who sought to hire faculty according to their traditional practices and those who, endorsing the work of Robin Mathews and James Steele ("The universities: take-over of the mind," 1970), held that these traditional practices resulted in far too many foreign professors and far too many classes with little or no "Canadian content." The year 1975 saw publication of the so-called Symons Report (*To Know Ourselves*), in which a plea was made that increased curricular attention and funding be given to the study of Canadian society and culture at all levels of Canadian education. This proposal was instrumental in gaining support for Canadian studies both in Canada, through the office of the Secretary of State, and internationally, through the Department of External Affairs. The Secretary of State supports Canadian studies at all levels of education within Canada, and, among its other activities, it issues an extensive listing of curricular materials and publications relating to Canadian studies.

The Canadian studies community has developed into an extensive network of national associations in 16 countries in all parts of the world, including China, Japan, India, and Russia, as well as the major nations of North America and Europe. The International Council for Canadian Studies (located in Ottawa) has served the needs of these member associations since 1981. Most of the associations have their own journals and conferences. Much of the network receives some financial support from the Department of External Affairs, in addition to funding from foreign universities, foundations, and corporations.

The first (1971), and the largest (with 1,500 members), of the national associations was the Association for Canadian Studies in the United States. Given the proximity of the United States to Canada, the political and sovereignty concerns of Canadians since the late 1960s, and the interest in cross-border issues, it is perhaps natural that scholars in the United States should have been the first to give attention to Canadian studies. Strong associations soon followed in the United Kingdom (1975), France (1976), Italy (1977), and the German-speaking countries (1980), as well as in Canada itself (1973).

Canadian studies has had a checkered existence in Canada, as the study of Canada permeates much of what traditional scholars in Canada do. It has also been argued, more as an assertion than as a proven hypothesis, that support for Canadian studies abroad diverts funding from non-Canadian studies scholarship at home. Others have argued that scholarship done outside Canada is of lower quality than that done by Canadian scholars. But this argument is not unique to Canadian studies, and in addition one must evaluate the objectives of non-Canadian scholars as well as the impact of scholarship done abroad, both on the understanding internationally of Canada as a culture and a society and on Canada's perceived status abroad. Being accepted in international organizations as an important member has long been an objective of Canada's foreign policy, and one can argue that being seen as a nation with an internationally recognized literature and art, and as an important subject of social science research contributes toward that end. It is in recognition of this fact that the mandate for support for Canadian studies outside Canada has been given to the Department of External Affairs, rather than to the Secretary of State or the Canadian Council.

It has long been stated that Canada is long on geography and short on history. An exaggeration to be sure but topography, space, and climate have had powerful influences on all disciplines which examine Canada. Both literature and ART were dominated until recently by the need to come to terms with the forest, lakes, prairies, and mountains in which Canadians lived their lives. Cities were secondary. The Group of Seven painters portrayed the landscape as awesome and indifferent, but engaging in ways which were quite unlike that of painting in England, France, or the United States. Canadian writers, such as Gabrielle Roy (*The Tin Flute*, 1945), had often set their works in Canada's cities, but for Canadianists more of the Canadian psyche, at least in its Anglophone version, was to be found in the rural settings of the novels of W.O. Mitchell (*Who Has Seen The Wind*, 1974), Margaret Lawrence (*The Stone Angel*, 1964), Rudy Wiebe (*The Temptations of Big Bear*, 1973), and Robert Kroetsch (*Studhorse Man*, 1970), the short stories of Alice Munro, or in poetry such as Douglas LePan's "A country without a mythology" (1953). Indeed several important writers, such as Margaret Atwood (*Surfacing*, 1972), Marian Engel (*Bear*, 1976), and Aritha van Hirk (*Tent Peg*, 1981), give their primary characters a profound experience with the wilderness. Following Gabrielle Roy, writers in the French language of recent decades, such as Roger Lemellin (*The Town Below*, 1948), Marie-Claire Blais (*A Season in the Life of Emmanuel*, 1965), and Jacques Godbout (*Knife on the Table*, 1965) have tended to place their works in the urban settings of Montreal or Quebec City.

In the social sciences physical space had also had a dominant influence, with the "staples approach" of Harold Innis shaping the understanding Canadians had about the development and functioning of their economic and political institutions. The nation-building policies of the national government during the nineteenth century, known as National Policy (1879), focused policy initiative on establishing control over the land mass north of the 49th parallel, in competition with an expansionist United States, setting and establishing claim to the national territory, and producing and marketing its primary products. Immigration led to the strong and concentrated ethnic communities, especially in the West, which became Porter's mosaic.

Beyond Canada's borders, the country was seen as a small relatively developed nation where one could observe and evaluate experimentation with flexible exchange rates, or metropolitan-wide governance, or modifications of social welfare systems, or other policies which subsequently might be adopted elsewhere.

Since the the 1914–18 war, public policy scholars have given much attention to Canada's distinctive international role. In international relations Canada has been portrayed as the primary example of a "middle power" which is uniquely able to play a constructive role in international peacekeeping through its participation in several United Nations forces. Political scientists are intrigued with Canada as the smaller participant, with the United States, in a "disparate dyad," in which the small country

must seek to further its own national interest and sovereignty while linked powerfully with a large partner. Economists have found Canada to be a superb economy for study of the impacts of trade liberalization, especially on a regional basis with the United States and now with Mexico. For constitutional specialists, Canada's efforts to resolve its considerable tensions aver minority language rights, its never-ending federal–provincial and regional power-sharing disputes, its land claims disputes with native peoples, and its recent implementation of a Charter of Rights have made Canada a stimulating subject of study.

During the past decade some of these original conceptualizations of Canadian studies have broken down, largely owing to the fact that Canadian culture and society themselves have been transformed. This is seen most clearly in the growth of importance of Canada's major cities in relation to the forest, prairies, and small towns which had earlier captured the attention of Canadianists. Toronto, Montreal, and Vancouver have become exciting internationally engaged cities, contrasting with their dowdy, dull, and parochial images of earlier years. As a consequence, Canadian painting has become more fully integrated in international movements (Jean-Paul Riopelle and Emile Borduas), writers such as Robertson Davies, Margaret Atwood, and Michael Ondaatje have chosen urban settings for their works of fiction, and social scientists have focused their attention more on urban economies, manufacturing, and business and financial services, and less on agriculture and staples development. Native Americans have emerged from the landscape to become a distinct community and voice, and a powerful political force which can no longer be overlooked.

As a consequence of this, Canadian studies has expanded in focus beyond literature, history, political economy, and geography to include such specialized areas such as comparative urban development, the rights of native peoples, environmental policies, feminist literary and social criticism, cross-border policy issues and constitutional reform. However, in all of these areas the reality of the Canadian culture and society which is being studied continues to be marked by the country's "northernness," its proximity to the United States, its French and English colonial past, its geographic dimensions and characteristics, its distinctiveness as a player on the world's political stage, and the sociological characteristics of its population.

Reading

Atwood, Margaret 1972: *Survival: A Thematic Guide to Canadian Literature.*
Hurtig, Mel (Publ.) 1985: *The Canadian Encyclopedia.*
Clement, Wallace, and Williams, Glen, eds 1989: *The New Canadian Political Economy.*
International Council for Canadian Studies 1992: *International Directory of Canadian Studies.*
Lipset, Seymour Martin 1990: *Continental Divide: The Values and Institutions of the United States and Canada.*
Lord, Barry 1974: *The History of Painting in Canada: Towards a People's Art.*
Metcalf, William 1982: *Understanding Canada.*
Symons, T.H.B. 1975: *To Know Ourselves: The Report of the Commission on Canadian Studies.*

PETER KARL KRESL

canon   A collection or list of texts that are thought to be inspired or authoritative. Following from its primary definition of "canon" as "a rule, law, or decree of the Church; esp. a rule laid down by an ecclesiastical Council," the *Oxford English Dictionary* (*OED*) defines the term in a second sense, which in English has been used since 1382, as "the collection of books of the Bible accepted by the Christian Church as genuine and inspired" and by analogy (since 1870) as "any set of sacred books." Although it is tempting to link the primary and secondary definitions of "canon" by assuming that the New Testament, for example, came into being by a rule laid down by an ecclesiastical Council's determination of a restrictive list of texts, the historical process was quite otherwise. Nevertheless, much recent debate about canonical and noncanonical secular literature rests on such a false analogy, which Henry Louis Gates, Jr, set out to correct in his Foreword to the Schomburg Library of Nineteenth-Century Black Women Writers (1988, p. xviii): "Literary works configure into a tradition . . . because writers read other writers and ground their representations of experience in models of language provided largely by other writers to whom they feel akin."

The history of the New Testament canon does not serve the argument that canons are formed to exclude diversity. The crucial event that precipitated the formation of the New Testament was the failed effort of Marcion (*c*.AD 140) to purge Christian scripture of its Jewish inheritance (von Campenhausen, p. 148). Thinking he saw an irreconcilable antagonism between the Law and the Gospel and thus between Judaism and Christianity, Marcion and his followers denounced the non-Pauline epistles and all the gospels but Luke, which

also required careful editing to remove its Jewish elements. Although Marcion's beliefs are known mainly from Irenaeus's *Contra Haereses,* his efforts to produce a single-voiced testament led to the plurivocity of the New Testament, with its four gospels and interargumentative Pauline and non-Pauline epistles (see BIBLICAL STUDIES).

In *Forms of Attention* (1985) and *History and Value* (1988), Frank KERMODE has argued that pluralism has sustained the vitality of the literary canon. He admits, however, that this may be the "soft view" of canons. The "hard view" would then be attentive to the politics of interpretation, which associates canons with networks of institutions that may be viewed as oppressive (1990, p. 75). Here the relevant modern institutions seem to be publishing houses, school and university curricula, and such professional academic organizations as the Modern Language Association. Rather than thinking of canons as fixed or closed lists of texts, it may be more fruitful to ask, "By what means do we attribute value to works of art, and how do our valuations affect our ways of attending to them?" (Kermode, 1985, p. xiii).

See also VALUE IN LITERATURE.

Reading

Campenhausen, Hans von 1972: *The Formation of the Christian Bible.*
Gates, Henry Louis, Jr 1988: Foreword to Anna Julia Cooper, *A Voice from the South.*
——— 1992: *Loose Canons.*
Kermode, Frank 1985: *Forms of Attention.*
——— 1988: *History and Value.*
——— 1990: *Poetry, Narrative, History.*
Payne, Michael 1991: "Canon: New Testament to Derrida."

MICHAEL PAYNE

Caribbean studies   The Caribbean is that archipelago of countries curving gently from the tip of Florida in the north to the northernmost point of the South American continent. Its complex geopolitics allows for the inclusion of Guyana and arguably Venezuela as Caribbean territories, although they are part of the South American continent rather than islands. Its ideological and political diversity allows for the inclusion of Cuba. A history of Conquistadorial acquisitiveness, slavery, indentureship, colonialism, and the socioeconomic fallout from a declining empire has precipitated the diverse ethnic and racial admixture for which the region has become known. There is also great linguistic diversity for an area so small in global context. Spanish, English, French, Dutch, Portuguese, and their "New World" configurations, Papiamentu, Haitian language, St Lucian kweyol, Jamaican language, Rasta talk (to list just some of the indigenous linguistic configurations) mark this part of the globe as among the obvious choices for critiques which address cultural diversity.

As a result of what might be seen as a potentially fortuitous future thrown up ironically by a callous and often brutish past, the Caribbean has privileged countless hypotheses, theses, speculations, and indeed its fair share of superficial commentary by providing raw material for conscientious analysis and spurious scholarship alike. The region's nominal history of conquest, exploitation of natural and human resources, and subjugation by the myopia of eurocentricity brought Africa, Asia, and Europe together in this part of the so-called New World. Since this "meeting of cultures" did not occur in a mutually beneficial context, reflecting epistemological tolerance and respect, the challenge for the Caribbean has been to reconstruct itself out of the tragedy of its inauspicious beginnings. Caribbean studies as a discipline or perhaps more accurately as an interdisciplinary endeavor might be defined as the study and analysis of this region's coming into being, its modes of representation, and its strategies of survival and cultural reproduction. Such an obviously vast and complex interdisciplinary terrain is beyond the scope of this brief discussion. As a result, our discussion here will seek to present a rough sketch of aspects of the region's cultural diversity and focus in a general manner on some of the significant literary manifestations of Caribbean cultural identity.

Representations of Caribbean CULTURE might be said to fall into two camps. There are those who, like M.G. Smith, argue for cultural pluralism in the Caribbean (see, for example, Smith's *The Plural Society in the British West Indies*) and those who argue for creolization or cultural admixture, like Edward Kamau Braithwaite (see, for example, Braithwaite's *The Development of Creole Society in Jamaica: 1770–1820*). The former position sees the Caribbean existing in an uneasy tension of cultural groupings, held together by external political and economic forces rather than by internal cohesiveness. The latter position represents Caribbean cultural reality as an admixture where, certainly in Braithwaite's view, ex-African cultural vestiges underpin Caribbean cultural diversity.

Despite the sometimes radically different approaches to analyses and representations of Caribbean cultural diversity which still tend to revolve around these two early positions, most assessments of Caribbean reality generally endorse the view expressed by Rex Nettleford:

> If the people of the Caribbean own nothing else, they certainly can own their creative imagination which, viewed in a particular way, is a powerful means of production for much that brings meaning and purpose to human life. And it is the wide variety of products emanating from the free and ample exercise of this creative imagination which signifies to man his unique gift of culture. (Nettleford, 1978)

This creative imagination has been the mainstay of Caribbean peoples. It has ensured their survival through centuries of physical atrocities and material deprivation. With Anansi-like imaginative dexterity, they have wielded this metaphysical weapon of the weak to create being out of nothingness and personhood out of "otherness."

Perhaps the material symbol *par excellence* of this cultural creativity is the steel pan, a "New World" musical instrument fashioned from the discarded oil drum, in the hills of Laventille, Trinidad. Indeed Laventille itself might be seen as a symbol of that typically urban, social castaway, the ghetto. Out of these two discards, the "useless" oil drum and the "useless" ghetto, arises the steel pan as a twentieth-century reaffirmation of the indomitable spirit of Caribbean cultural creativity. This reaffirmation of the spirit of survival and creativity symbolized by the steel pan provides Trinidadian novelist Earl Lovelace with the narrative map for his novel *The Wine of Astonishment*. In similar fashion, Bob Marley, Peter Tosh, and Bunny Wailer create a haunting union of lyric and beat out of the "nothingness" of a Kingston, Jamaica ghetto, yet another "New World" cultural creation which would see Marley's name and music internationalized with such evangelistic fervor that the signifiers "Bob Marley" and "Reggae" resonate with the authority of synecdoche across national and linguistic boundaries to conjure up representations of the Caribbean. Challenged to construct personhood in the hostile, ontological wasteland of plantation America, Caribbean peoples have repeatedly defied historical odds and stereotypical representations of themselves as lack and void. Whether as Toussaint

L'Ouverture, rising out of slavery to challenge Europe's greatest generals and create the possibility for Haiti to become the first black independent state in the so-called New World, or as Garfield Sobers, rising out of the obscurity of humble beginnings in diminuitive Barbados to revolutionize and dominate the Commonwealth game of cricket, Caribbean peoples have, for a long time, salvaged their being from discarded nothingness.

The institutionalized study of Caribbean issues and affairs is perhaps most obviously embodied in the region by the University of the West Indies (UWI), and in the "diaspora" by the Caribbean Studies Association.

Established in 1948, partly as the colonial response to an increasingly restless and dissatisfied colonized population, the UWI has nurtured and been influenced by such figures as George Beckford, Derek Walcott, Orlando Patterson, Walter Rodney, Sir Philip Sherlock, Edward Kamau Braithwaite, Gordon Rohlehr, Rex Nettleford, Kenneth Ramchand, Elsa Goveia, Sir Frank Worrell, and a host of other intellectual workers whose steadfast vocation has been the Caribbean. It is ironically appropriate, given the Caribbean's history of creating value out of the resource of the mind, the creative imagination, that the site of the first of UWI's three campuses is located on a former plantation in Jamaica. A place of material deprivation and tortured dispossession, signified by slavery and indentureship, transformed into a place where Caribbean peoples would grapple with a colonial past and move beyond it to address the complexities of a postcolonial future.

The Caribbean Studies Association (CSA) is an organization of academics and other intellectual workers who came together in 1975 because they shared an interest in the study of the Caribbean. Since the first conference in Puerto Rico, the group has met annually in places such as Grenada, Barbados, Martinique, Jamaica, and other areas of the Caribbean. Another smaller group devoted to the study of the Caribbean is the Association of Caribbean Studies. This group, aware of the importance of regional links to the diaspora as well as ancestral homelands, has held conferences in several extraregional locations including the African continent. At the Jamaica campus of the UWI there is the Institute of Caribbean Studies which publishes a monthly newsletter about books, projects, conferences, and other items and activities related to Caribbean studies.

In addition to these institutional approaches to the study of the area, there are of course the critical contributions of intellectuals who have worked outside of institutional frameworks for the most part. The creative and critical work of C.L.R. JAMES is essential to any conscientious understanding and critical interpretation of the history and culture of this region. The fiction of George Lamming, Jean Rhys, Wilson Harris, Samuel Selvon, Erna Brodber, and several other anglophone Caribbean novelists might be considered essential reading in order to gain insight into the narrative construction of West Indian personhood. Similarly, the work of Alejo Carpentier, Aimé Césaire, Jacques Roumain and others provides a window into the physical and metaphysical struggles of embattled personhood from the hispanophone and francophone perspectives:

The traditional "organic intellectuals" of the region, the calypsonians provide a sense of the historical and contemporary struggles of Caribbean peoples through the popular medium of the calypso. Fine artists such as Edna Manley, Karl Broodhagen, and Stanley Greaves capture the traces of the indomitable Caribbean spirit in stone and on canvas. Rhythm poets like Mutabaruka, Jean Binta Breeze, Linton Kwesi Johnson, the late Mikey Smith, Winston Farrell, and Adisa Andwele capture the historical and contemporary anguish of Caribbean suffering and resistance in their poetry. The "mother" of them all, Louise Bennett-Coverly, smiled at Caribbean idiosyncrasy and satirized eurocentric foibles in her "rhythm" poetry long before either the form or content of such creativity was deemed serious and respectable. Similarly, Joe Tudor and Alfred Pragnell were exploring the artistic merit of oral tradition and folk humor before such activity was generally recognized as evidence of cultural and artistic creativity. In short, the Caribbean has never lacked the unfathomable resource of the creative and critical imagination, though it has lacked and still lacks much materially, at least from the perspective of the mass of ordinary folk comprising most of its population.

Privileging the power of the creative imagination as a resource is not tantamount to romanticizing the Caribbean. This is the resource which allowed Caribbean peoples to survive the material deprivation and psychological trauma of slavery, indentureship, and colonialism. It is the resource by which the Caribbean protects and sustains itself into the twenty-first century, despite claims to the contrary made by technocracy at the altar of technology. Caribbean studies is therefore essentially the study of this phenomenon, the Caribbean creative imagination.

Reading
Braithwaite, Edward Kamau 1978: *The Development of Creole Society in Jamaica: 1770–1820.*
Césaire, Aimé 1972: *Discourse on Colonialism.*
Devonish, Hubert 1986: *Language and Liberation: Creole Language Politics in the Caribbean.*
James, C.L.R. 1938: *The Black Jacobins: Toussaint L'Ouverture and the Saint Domingo Revolution.*
——1977: *The Future in the Present.*
Lewis, Gordon K. 1968: *The Growth of the Modern West Indies.*
——1983: *Main Currents in Caribbean Thought: The Historical Evolution of Caribbean Society in Its Ideological Aspects 1492–1900.*
Nettleford, Rex 1978: *Caribbean Cultural Identity: The Case of Jamaica.*
Smith, M.G. 1965: *The Plural Society in the British West Indies.*

GLYNE A. GRIFFITH

Castoriadis, Cornelius (1922–) French political/social theorist and psychoanalyst. Though born in Constantinople and educated in Athens, Castoriadis has lived in France since 1945. He founded the influential left-wing journal *Socialisme ou Barbarie* in 1949. Castoriadis began as a Marxist theorist interested in the questions of bureaucratic capitalism. His early contention that management by workers could serve as a check to Stalinism was confirmed by the events of the Hungarian Revolution in 1956. Castoriadis then went on to conduct a systematic inquiry into the foundations of MARXISM. This resulted in a rejection of the Marxist shibboleths of materialism and determinism. Castoriadis saw that the deterministic strain in Marxism was incompatible with MARX's own call for the autonomy of revolutionary action. Castoriadis argued that it was time to choose between loyalty to a DISCOURSE that had outworn its usefulness and the need to remain a revolutionary. He advanced instead a conception of the social-historical. By this he meant the world of human action that would not be restricted to a narrow conception of the political. The revolutionary project itself had to be decentered into a quest for autonomy in which all could participate. Such a project would have to move away from traditional teleologies of time that are deterministic. Castoriadis distinguishes between homogeneous and heterogeneous modes of temporality in capitalism. It is precisely this difference between the time of consolidation and crisis that distinguishes capitalism from other modes of economic organization. All societies, however, misrecognize the tension between the different modes of temporality by which they are constituted. This is, however, not a matter of "ontological necessity." The revolutionary agenda is predicated on the possibility of being able to switch between modes of temporality.

The permutational possibilities of the social-historical depend on the "social imaginary." The imaginary is not a mere reflection of some pre-existent reality. It is instead the very condition of possibility for a relation between the object and the image. The imaginary institutes the moment of singularity in any sociohistorical formation. It functions as a minimal coupling of signifier–signified without which it would not be possible to articulate the differences between what matters and what does not in any given epoch. The social imaginary cannot be reduced to a set of impersonal rules; the belief that it can be reduced to one is the illusion of theory. There is no such thing as a "rigorously rigorous theory" even in mathematics, let alone in politics. Hence the ethical necessity of admitting responsibility for any theory that is advanced by the theorist. The theorist cannot retire to his study and submit everything to systematic doubt. He/she is always already constituted through the social. That which is opposed to the social is not the individual SUBJECT but the psyche. Castoriadis advances the notion of a psychical monad. The monad is torn open only by socialization. But then again the social imaginary is accessed only through the psyche. A relation of mutual supplementarity is posited between the two.

Castoriadis brings a similar claim to bear on the scientific claims of PSYCHOANALYSIS. Neither psychoanalysis nor political theory can hope to become a science. These discourses are organized by fields of transference where the identity of the author continues to matter. Whereas the rough notes of a Newton or Einstein do not matter to the validity of their theories, it would not be possible to maintain the same claim in the case of, say, Freud's correspondence with Wilhelm Fliess. Referring to LACAN's comment that he had "discovered" Freud, Castoriadis writes that scientists discover things and not other scientists. Dirac did not claim to have discovered Planck but the positive electron. Psychoanalysis should not trap itself in the desire to be a science but should recognize that it cannot be anything more than a "practico-poetic" activity. Psychoanalysis does not actualize either the faculties or the potential of a SUBJECT directly; it seeks instead to actualize "a potential of the second degree, a capacity of a capacity to be." Psychoanalysis then, despite being confronted with the real, must come to terms with the impossibility of its formalization. Castoriadis's critique of Lacan stems precisely from the latter's attempt to formalize the real. He reads Lacan's use of topological objects like the Moebius strip as an attempt to evacuate history in the impossible attempt to emulate science. And again, Castoriadis argues vehemently that the question of doctrinal transmission cannot be addressed in a formulaic mode that will not seek recourse to a natural language. What psychoanalysis, pedagogy, and politics have in common is the attempt to create autonomous individuals. Autonomy, for Castoriadis, is a state where the subject is capable of self-reflexivity and deliberation. Autonomy, however, is not an end in itself but a means to other possibilities. The politics of autonomy should transcend modes of being that are specific to psychoanalysis, pedagogy, and social consciousness such that the subject continues to draw its creativity from "the radical imaginary of the anonymous collectivity."

Reading

Castoriadis, Cornelius 1984: *Crossroads in the Labyrinth.*
——1987: *The Imaginary Institution of Society.*
——1991: *Philosophy, Politics, Autonomy.*
——1993: *Political and Social Writings.*

SHIVA KUMAR SRINIVASAN

Cavell, Stanley (1926–) Philosopher, born in Atlanta, Georgia, professor of AESTHETICS and the general theory of value at Harvard University. His extensive writing is greatly influenced by his teacher J.L. AUSTIN and by the twentieth-century philosopher Ludwig WITTGENSTEIN. Hearing Austin give the William James lectures at Harvard in 1955 (later published in 1962 as *How To Do Things With Words*) caused Cavell to stop work on his dissertation and to choose a different path of research and topic for study. (That decision would delay the completion of his dissertation, *The Claim to Rationality*, until 1961.) His reading of Wittgenstein's *Philosophical Investigations* revealed a philosophy that was novel in its manner of WRITING and grounded in a KANTian and transcendental spirit

of inquiry, both of which gave Cavell's work a form and direction it was never to lose. Cavell was one of the earliest to note the Kantian spirit in Wittgenstein's work – see his essays "Must we mean what we say" and "The availability of Wittgenstein's later philosophy" – and to give Austin serious hearing in philosophical contexts; see his "Austin at criticism" (Cavell, 1969). His writings also include published texts on Shakespeare's plays and skepticism (*Disowning Knowledge*, 1987), on film study and the kind of object film presents to aesthetic inquiry (*The World Viewed*, 1979), and on Thoreau and Emerson and the need to recover the sometimes intentionally severed and largely neglected tradition of American philosophy they initiated (*The Senses of Walden*, 1972). Throughout these writings there is often expressed a desire to recognize the destruction wrought by dualistic conceptions of ourselves and our relations to others, and similarly to bridge the gap, to keep conversations open, between Anglo-American and Continental philosophy.

Cavell's work is most fully constituted by his *Claim of Reason* (1979). It is the one indispensable text for understanding and appreciating him. All the areas addressed in his writings are given a place in *The Claim of Reason* and his many recurring topics of interest are discussed there, for example, the denial by philosophy of an essential part of itself, the need to pursue self-knowledge (and thereby understand the value and limits of empirical knowledge), the hope for a facing of, and finally a living of, skepticism. While these topics are closely interrelated in Cavell's work and give way to numerous other concerns, they none the less can usefully serve as nodal points for engaging his writings.

The Nature of Philosophy The discipline (those who are part of it) must come to recognize the need to replace pursuits of certainty and empirical groundings of being with attempts at finding and situating itself (themselves). In our philosophical reflections, we need to embrace our finitude and ordinary existence rather than flee from them. It is important to ask what our lives would be like if we accepted, rather than fought with, the truth of skepticism, with the fact that we cannot obtain infallible groundings for our concerns. Philosophy must try to keep open the threat of and temptation to skepticism, rather than give it a less destructive face, and prize the inhuman. To face skepticism is to provide interpretation of human finitude, and for Cavell, following EMERSON, Austin, and Wittgenstein (among others) means understanding what is at stake in inhabiting our words and the language we use. Philosophy's task is not to defeat skepticism but to preserve it; to show why it has no end, at least none within philosophy. Cavell's call to live out skepticism is not simply an assertion of our natural condition as knowers (our nonknowing relationship to the world and others) but to encourage a way to inhabit our condition of doubt and thereby situate our lives. We must acknowledge the truth of skepticism rather than avoid or attempt to refute it.

Self-knowledge　If we do accept the position on skepticism and the perspective of philosophy given by Cavell, then he believes we will see, and the philosopher in us all will see, the proper place of self-knowledge for our interests. The quest for self-knowledge is prevalent in all of Cavell's writings and can be found investigated in each part of *The Claim of Reason*. Cavell attempts to uncover the motivations and reasons for traditional philosophy's (mainly the modern period's) rejection of the human and pursuit of self-knowledge. Philosophy, as Cavell tries to understand it, must push beyond saying that something is true or false, trying to grasp the argument, problem, or conclusion someone utters or writes. It must consider the finite human being who says what is true or false. Instead of confronting our everyday selves and work, Cavell finds that we substitute for it, exchange for it, the search for empirical knowledge (regardless of whether we believe in the final success of such knowledge). By placing self-knowledge in the forefront of the philosophical inquiry Cavell is not encouraging self-indulgence or a rejection of an objective (non-personal) perspective. One of the important themes of *The Claim of Reason* is that pursuit of the self reveals the other. It is not a narcissistic enterprise we engage in when seeking self-knowledge. The soul is impersonal and no matter how far we go in the investigations of the self we do not find anything special to us.

Skepticism　Wittgenstein's *Philosophical Investigations*, says Cavell, is endlessly struggling with skepticism. Cavell's own struggle with Wittgenstein's text, as well as with the nature of philosophy and concerns with self-knowledge, lead him to conclude that we must finally see skepticisim as a part

of what it is to be human. It is that part of our being which desires and obsessively demands a relationship of knowing to the world and others, yet is unable to succeed in achieving such knowledge. (This is Cavell's retelling of the peculiar fate of reason expressed by Kant in the opening sentence of *Critique of Pure Reason*.) We must not then try to refute skepticism or overcome it but learn to face it and live it, accept the fact of our intellectual, moral and ordinary finitude and limits. To live my skepticism, to face the truth of skepticism, is to recover the self and find my ordinary, human voice.

As these three topics indicate, Cavell offers definite challenges to such areas as analytical philosophy, deconstructive literary theory, epistemological foundationalism. While many have avoided reading and confronting Cavell and rest undisturbed at philosophy and intellectual studies forgoing their therapeutic, self-directed dimension, others find Cavell compelling yet cannot accept his seemingly overwrought way of writing and apparent abandoning of traditional philosophical argumentation. Cavell's writing is at times admittedly difficult and his attention to argument is to be sure not always the traditional one. Nevertheless, his writing is a far cry from argument abandonment. His way of writing encourages us to understand argument as one way of accepting full responsibilty for one's own discourse, confessing reasons why one uses the words one does and in the manner one does. His manner (call it his method) of writing and the context of that writing exhibit an attempt at reattaching our philosophical attention to what we say and mean.

Certainly many forms of philosophical investigation invite the perspectives provided in Cavell's work (most of which Cavell cites and draws from at length), but seldom to the ends or with the consistency found in Cavell. He attempts to show us that our words often do not mean what we say, that we easily lose control of them. Our loss of control is not over what words mean but what we mean in using them when and where we do. We easily lose a sense of ourselves and the context of language use in which we speak. (Cavell finds these concerns dominating that lost philosophical tradition in America voiced by Thoreau and EMERSON; he sees them underwriting the concerns of ordinary language philosophy, as it is found in Wittgenstein and Austin, and therefore tries to return them to a place of prominence in the philosophical tradition.) If we do not pay attention to our human forms of expression we lose ourselves (and thereby others and the world) and it is for that reason that Cavell places the attempt and the need to understand the self consistently before us.

Reading
Cavell, Stanley 1979a: *The Claim of Reason.*
Fischer, Michael 1989: *Stanley Cavell and Literary Scepticism.*
Fleming, Richard 1993: *The State of Philosophy; A Reading in Three Parts of Stanley Cavell's The Claim of Reason.*
——and Payne, Michael, eds 1987: *The Senses of Stanley Cavell. Bucknell Review.*
Mulhall, Stephen 1994: *Stanley Cavell: Philosophy's Recounting of the Ordinary.*

RICHARD FLEMING

Centre for Contemporary Cultural Studies A postgraduate unit of the University of Birmingham, important in the later development of CULTURAL STUDIES. The CCCS, founded in 1964 within an English Department by Richard HOGGART (subsequent Directors were Stuart HALL and Richard Johnson) instigated an energetic cross-disciplinary exploration of areas within media, youth culture, education, gender, and "race." It became widely known for its combination of engaged political critique (concerned with IDEOLOGY, HEGEMONY, and struggles over meanings in everyday life), work on texts but also through ethnographic studies inside a framework of political and social change, and a restless exploration of theoretical frameworks. A practice of group work and writing by staff and student members (many of whom taught and published elsewhere, so helping to register cultural studies as a space within education), resulted in a series of working papers, a journal, and various influential books. CCCS later (1988) became a Department of Cultural Studies (within Social Sciences), developing undergraduate as well as higher degrees and producing its own journal and books.

Reading
Agger, B. 1992: *Cultural Studies as Critical Theory.*
Brantlinger, P. 1990: *Crusoe's Footprints.*
Clarke, J. 1991: *New Times and Old Enemies.*
Hall, S., Hobson, D., Lowe, A., and Willis, P. 1980: *Culture, Media, Language.*

MICHAEL GREEN

Césaire, Aimé (1913–) Martinican poet, playwright, essayist, political figure, and cofounder of negritude. In his best-known work, *Notebook of a*

Return to My Native Land (1939), Césaire forever changed the course of Antillean literature. Whereas Césaire's predecessors emulated classical French poetic models and hid their own cultural specificity, Césaire both depicted the evils of colonialism in Martinique and confronted stereotypical images of blacks. Armed with a surrealist aesthetic, as the title of his *Miraculous Weapons* (1946) implies, Césaire set out to extinguish black alienation in Martinique and to replace it with a new pride in black cultural heritage (negritude).

Reading
Arnold, A. James 1981: *Modernism and Negritude: The Poetry and Poetics of Aimé Césaire.*
Césaire, Aimé 1939 *(1983): Cahier d'un Retour au Pays Natal (Notebook of a Return to My Native Land).*
Kesteloot, Lilyan 1963 *(1974): Black Writers in French. A Literary History of Negritude.*

JEANNE GARANE

Chicago school An influential body of sociological writing from the University of Chicago between the wars. The rapid growth and extreme diversity of Chicago combined with a concern for social reform to provide a common focus for diverse writers. Robert Park and others pioneered approaches to the study of contrasting CITY areas, using detailed ethnographies and life-history work to examine informal networks and shared values among even apparently "unattached" groups. Elements of future concerns with symbolic interaction, the sociology of deviance, and SUBCULTURES were strongly present. Despite later criticism of the use of ecological metaphors for urban form, and close attention to subordinate groups which neglected STRUCTURES of power and the worlds of the powerful, the early Chicago work and that of succeeding generations have produced debate and empirical analysis important in sociology and in urban studies.

Reading
Bulmer, M. 1984: *The Chicago School of Sociology.*
Park, R.E., Burgess, E.W., and McKenzie, R.D. 1925 *(1967): The City.*
Shaw, C.R. 1930 *(1966): The Jack-Roller: A Delinquent Boy's Own Story.*
Urban Life 1983: Special issue "The Chicago school: the tradition and the legacy."

MICHAEL GREEN

Chodorow, Nancy (1944–) US feminist sociologist and psychoanalytic critic. The central project

of Chodorow's most influential work, *The Reproduction of Mothering* (1978), was to explain the seemingly inevitable, trans-historical, and cross-culturally
universal fact of male dominance in terms that did
not assume biological determinism, but would instead allow intervention and transformation of the
sexual divisions of productive and reproductive
labor. Published at a time when most US feminists
were hostile to PSYCHOANALYSIS, *The Reproduction
of Mothering* made a strong case for its usefulness
to feminist inquiry. Drawing on the work of Karen
Horney and Melanie KLEIN, Chodorow revised traditional theories of OBJECT-RELATIONS and Freudian narratives of development, shifting the focus
from the father and the Oedipal complex to the
mother and the pre-Oedipal period to conclude
that GENDER identity is constructed differently for
men and women: "women's self more in relation
and involved with boundary negotiations, separation
and connection, men's self more distanced and based
on defensively firm boundaries and denials of self-
other connection" (1989, p. 2). Women's exclusive
responsibility for childrearing is a prime determinant of male dominance, for women who mother
(and men who do not) produce daughters "with
mothering capacities and the desire to mother"
and sons for whom masculinity means male superiority and "whose nurturant capacities and needs
have been systematically curtailed and repressed"
(1978, p. 7). Thus sexual asymmetry and inequality are not "natural" but sociological and psychological facts reproduced in and by each generation.
The political implications were clear: "a fundamental reorganization of parenting [is necessary],
so that primary parenting is shared between men
and women" (1978, p. 215).

In her later work, including essays collected
in *Feminism and Psychoanalytic Theory* (1989),
Chodorow no longer argues that male dominance
has a single cause, nor that gender differences are
always implicated in relations of inequality. Responding to materialists' criticism that psychoanalysis lacks historical and cultural specificity,
Chodorow has become more interested in understanding social change and in producing accounts
more attentive to differences among women (such
as RACE, CLASS, and ETHNICITY), the multivocality
of women's narratives, and the plurality of women's
social, psychological, and cultural identities.

See also FEMINIST CRITICISM; FREUD, SIGMUND;
MASCULINITY; PSYCHOANALYSIS AND PSYCHOAN-
ALYTIC CRITICISM.

Reading
Chodorow, Nancy 1978: *The Reproduction of Mothering:
Psychoanalysis and the Sociology of Gender.*
——1989: *Feminism and Psychoanalytic Theory.*

GLYNIS CARR

Chomsky, Noam (1928–) American linguist
and political campaigner. Born in Philadelphia in
the eastern United States, Chomsky first studied
linguistics under Zellig Harris (see HARRIS, Zellig)
at the University of Pennsylvania. After a short
spell at Harvard he moved to the Massachusetts
Institute of Technology (MIT) in Boston in 1955,
where he has been based ever since. In the mid-
1960s he actively opposed United States military
involvement in Vietnam and was arrested while
addressing a large anti-war demonstration in Washington. Subsequently he has been equally critical
of United States policy around the world, particularly the Pacific region, the Middle East, and Central America. Chomsky has lectured on linguistics
and politics in many countries and has received
many academic honours. He was once described as
"arguably the most important intellectual alive."

Chomsky is perhaps best known for his claim
that many properties of language are innate, that
is, the result of human genetic programming rather
than being learned from experience. He came to
prominence in the late 1950s when his work played
a major part in transforming linguistics from an
esoteric discipline into a central component of the
human and cognitive sciences. His vigorous critiques of structuralist linguistics (Chomsky, 1964a)
and the behaviorist psychology with which it was
linked (Chomsky, 1964b) helped to establish his
reputation (see LANGUAGE THEORIES).

Chomsky developed a new approach to the study
of language. His starting point was dissatisfaction
with the structuralist linguistics favored by Harris.
The structuralists had viewed a language as a collection of utterances. The English language, seen in
this way, was everything that speakers of English
said and wrote, taken as a whole. What, then, was
a grammar of a language? In abstract, mathematical
terms it was a set of formulae which specified the
structure of this collection of utterances. Chomsky's
early work investigated the mathematical properties
of this set of formulae. He argued that there are an
infinite number of possible utterances, but that the
grammar must be finite, containing within itself
recursive mechanisms which enable it to characterize
an infinite set of STRUCTURES. He further argued

that it is not possible to specify a "discovery procedure" which starts with a language and automatically produces a single correct grammar (hence the dream of the structuralists was not achievable).

Since a grammar is finite but a language is not, the next step for Chomsky was to take a grammar as the central object to be investigated, rather than a language. A further reason for this is that any language (considered as a set of utterances) will contain many errors, false starts, repetitions, coughs, splutters, and so on. The grammar, on the other hand, the thing that speakers of a language have in common, presumably does not contain any of these blemishes. But if a grammar is not a physical thing, like a set of utterances, what is it? The only sensible answer, Chomsky concluded, was this: a complete grammar of a language must be regarded as a model of the knowledge in the mind of a person who speaks that language (a "native speaker").

Now further questions arise, in particular, the question of how this grammar comes to be in the brain of a speaker of a language. The structuralist answer was that it was learned from experience, and it is true that a young person acquires the grammar of the language spoken around him or her. There are certain things about grammars, however, which suggest strongly that this cannot be the whole story. As we saw, a discovery procedure for a grammar is not feasible. If a grammar is learned, then it must be by trial and error on the part of young people, since they are certainly not "taught" their first language by adults (indeed, when adults attempt to do this they usually make the task harder rather than easier). But trial and error is not a plausible answer either, since despite very different experiences of language, all children exposed to English acquire the SAME grammar of English: different people's grammars are remarkably uniform, with much less variation than, say, in their hairstyles or tastes in music. What is more, the order in which different parts of grammar are acquired is remarkably constant across children and across languages.

Our genetic endowment accounts for the twofold uniformity of language acquisition, and also explains how certain rules of grammar are acquired in the absence of any data that would warrant them. Such rules (and there are many of them) could be learned only if young people were systematically taught that certain structures are NOT grammatical. But children are not taught this. Genetics is the only possible solution.

Chomsky's research program aims to specify the genetic properties of language. The first step is to provide a partial GENERATIVE GRAMMAR of a particular language. The second is to isolate those rules and principles of this generative grammar which could not have been learned. The third step is to generalize these rules and principles as widely as possible and to propose that they are part of Universal Grammar (UG), a model of the genetic properties of language (in earlier work UG was called the Language Acquisition Device (LAD). Finally, other languages are investigated to evaluate the proposals about UG. Any hypothesis about UG must be broad enough to allow for all human languages, but narrow enough to exclude things that are not possible human languages. It should be noted that devising a generative grammar is only one step in this process, and that UG is the ultimate goal. Using the term "generative grammar" as a label for Chomsky's approach to language is therefore misleading: a better name is "language as a biological system."

Chomsky's theoretical framework has been extremely influential, within both linguistics and neighboring fields such as psychology and philosophy. His ideas remain highly controversial, however (for an outline of the main criticisms see Salkie, 1990, pp. 96–120).

Reading

Chomsky, N. 1964a: *Current Issues in Linguistic Theory.*
—— 1964b: "Review of *Verbal Behaviour* by B.F. Skinner."
—— 1987: *On Power and Ideology.*
—— 1988: *Language and Problems of Knowledge.*
—— 1991a: *Deterring Democracy.*
Cook, V. 1988: *Chomsky's Universal Grammar: An Introduction.*
Peck, J., ed. 1987: *The Chomsky Reader.*
Salkie, R. 1990: *The Chomsky Update: Linguistics and Politics.*

RAPHAEL SALKIE

city The ancient world provides us with two mythic origins and originators for the city. There is Plutarch's Theseus, the legendary founder of Athens, whose city is organized, coherent, reasoned and reasonable, abstract, bound and guarded by laws. Then there is the city of Cain; for, in the Bible, it is Cain – a cursed and banished murderer, a marked man condemned to be a vagrant and vagabond – who builds the first city. Since Cain was a criminal, a fugitive, a nomad, we may think of a city full of aliens, vagrants; anonymity, randomness;

the lost and the damned. The city, particularly as it has developed during the last 200 years, has often aspired to the condition of Theseus's Athens; but it has more often been described as being more like a city of Cain.

The city and Western literature are effectively coeval. But the great literary concentration, exploration, and evocation of the city really starts in the nineteenth century. This was when the city started to become both mysterious and ubiquitous, unknowable and inescapable, housing the past and determining – or destroying – the future. Increasingly, meaning no longer comes from the church, the court, or the manor, but is produced – and reproduced – in the city.

Already Wordsworth was realizing that "the great city" was producing a new kind of experience, perhaps a new kind of person:

How often, in the overflowing streets,
Have I gone forward with the crowd and said
Unto myself, "The face of every one
That passes me is a mystery!"
(*Prelude*, Book VII)

Edgar Allan Poe caught this memorably in "The Man of the Crowd," the first story of urban *anomie*, which was to become a key text for Walter Benjamin. Poe also, effectively, invented the detective story ("The murders in the rue Morgue"), which turned out to prove an ideal genre for tracking the clues of the mysteries and crimes spawned by the modern metropolis. The miseries of this new crowd of strangers, particularly of the new urban proletariat, provoked different cries of outrage from principled Victorians, which could point towards a radical politics. As in the case of Engels: "however much one may be aware that this isolation of the individual, this narrow self-seeking is the fundamental principle of our society everywhere, it is nowhere so shamelessly barefaced, so self-conscious as just here in the crowding of the great city. The dissolution of mankind into monads . . . is here carried out to its utmost extremes" (*The Condition of the Working Class in England in 1844*). On a more personal level, James Thomson recorded how the city could become phantasmagoric, a nightmare of tormented consciousness, in *City of Dreadful Night* (1870).

The Futurist Manifesto of 1909 first identified the city as the preeminent theme of modern literature and painting; and it was Ezra Pound who pointed out that while "the life of the village is narrative . . . In a city the visual impressions succeed each other, overlap, overcross, they are cinematographic." A number of major twentieth-century novels give us just such a "cinematographic," disintegrative, discontinuous, explosive rendering of the city – for instance, Bely's *Petersburg* (1913), Döblin's *Berlin Alexanderplatz* (1929), and Céline's *Voyage au bout de la nuit* (1932). But the nineteenth century had already seen the growth of a rich tradition of a literature of the city. London is not the background or setting for Charles Dickens's novels – it is the protagonist, with a terrible energy and power, of which his human characters are simply more or less functioning fragments. (See the opening paragraph of *Bleak House*.) Honoré de Balzac immersed himself in Paris – the high life, the low life; the streets, the shops, the money, the clothes, the food; the crowds, the shocks, the collisions; and the endless circulation of peculiarly modern desires and dissatisfactions engendered by the modern city. Charles Baudelaire – who created the image of the poet as city *flâneur* – was, arguably, the first great poet of the city, and he saw Balzac's city-haunting characters as true heroes compared to the "pygmies" of the *Iliad*, and Balzac himself as the greatest hero of all.

Where the varied landscapes of the cultural past seemed relatively knowable and describable, the modern city, protean, amorphous, incoherent, always expanding and in flux, posed new problems of representation. And the city was coming to be felt to be *everywhere*; it seemed there was no place or point outside it from which it could be seen and comprehended as a whole (as pastoral and Romantic poets had often "surveyed" the landscapes stretching out before or beneath them). We may take T.S. Eliot and James Joyce as representing two ways of responding to, and representing, the modern city. Eliot's *The Waste Land* evokes the generic modern city as fragmented, polluted, sterile, collapsing – "unreal":

Falling towers
Jerusalem Athens Alexandria
Vienna London
Unreal.
(lines 373–6)

Joyce's *Ulysses*, with its massive recreation of the teeming life of one Dublin day, using the whole range of possible literary styles as it walks *through* the city, listening to its many *voices*, offers a much more fecund and festive sense of the modern city; though here, too, with intimations of ultimate meaninglessness:

> Cityful passing away, other cityful coming, passing away too: other coming on, passing on. Houses, lines of houses, streets, miles of pavements, piled up bricks, stones. . . . Piled up in cities, worn away age after age. Pyramids in sand. (Joyce, 1967, p. 208)

Yet the city offered writers a great deal to stimulate them. Robert Musil, whose city was Vienna, wrote, in his great work *The Man Without Qualities*, that the city afforded "irregularity, change, sliding forward, not keeping in step, collisions of things and affairs" – "a tangle of forces" generating "the well-known incoherency of ideas, with their way of spreading out without a central point . . . without a basic unity." More basically, the city offered cheap paper, easier publishing opportunities, and a growing market for books and magazines – not to mention a concentration of libraries, academies, museums, and galleries. In the city the writer could become, for the first time, his own master – independent of the uncertain patronage of an unpredictable court and a quixotic aristocracy. The relatively fixed and stable routines of rural life were superseded by new experiences of mobility, complexity, variety, openness, and change. The modern city saw new social, economic, and cultural relations being formed, along with enriched and facilitated intercultural communications, and new metropolitan sophistications. It is hardly too much to say that modern literature is predominantly an urban product. And yet, the response of many modern writers to the city has been antagonistic, adversarial, denunciatory; often provoking nostalgic yearnings for some imagined lost world – rural or pre-industrial – of stability, security, and reassuring familiarity. Rilke's *The Notebooks of Malta Laurids Brigge* (1910) records his experience of Paris, and it starts: "So this is where people come to live; I'd have thought it was a place to come and die." The city never sleeps, and never lets him sleep – "electric trams hurtle ringing through my room. Automobiles ride across me." But – being a writer – he is determined to find an appropriate mode of response: "I'm learning to see. Yes, I am beginning. It's not going very well yet. But I intend to make the most of my time." In the event, he makes

an imaginative journey back into his childhood. However, one may take a more general point. The modern city forced artists – writers; painters (Monet, Meidner, Munch, Kirchner, Boccioni, Delaunay, Grosz, Dix – painting the city as everything from a new technological Arcadia to a new kind of hell on earth); and of course film-makers (Fritz Lang's *Metropolis*, 1926) – to *see* in new ways. There was a major perceptual shift, and we can no longer look at the world with pre-city eyes.

Of course, artists create their own cities, as Henry James indicated when he wrote of "making a mere Rome of words, talking of a Rome of my own which was no Rome of reality . . . the whole thing was a rare state of the imagination." Ruskin recreated a whole lost Venice in *The Stones of Venice*, which was a rare state of the imagination indeed, and had an incalculable effect on subsequent literature. But the modern city seems not to lend itself to such confident recuperations. Kafka is perhaps the quintessential writer of experience in the modern city, and here is one of his complete fragments – fitting form for the city.

> I stand on the end platform of the tram and am completely unsure of my footing in this world, in this town, in my family. Not even casually could I indicate any claims that I might rightly advance in any direction. I have not even any defense to offer for standing on this platform, holding on to this strap, letting myself be carried along by this tram, nor for the people who give way to the tram or walk quietly along or stand gazing into shop windows. Nobody asks me to put up a defense, indeed, but that is irrelevant. . . . (On the Tram)

Reading
Benevolo, Leonardo 1993: *The European City*.
Benjamin, Walter 1928b *(1979)*: *One-way Street*.
Berman, Marshall 1982 *(1983)*: *All That is Solid Melts into Air. The Experience of Modernity*.
Jaye, Michael, and Watts, Ann Chalmers 1981: *Literature and the Urban Experience*.
Mumford, Lewis 1961: *The City in History: Its Origins, Its Transformations, Its Prospects*.
Prendergast, Christopher 1992: *Paris and the Nineteenth Century*.
Strauss, Leo 1964: *The City and Man*.
Tanner, Tony 1992: *Venice Desired*.
Timms, Edward, and Kelly, David 1985: *Unreal City: Urban Experience in Modern European Literature and Art*.
Weber, Max 1962: *The City*.
Williams, Raymond 1973: *The Country and the City*.

TONY TANNER

civil society A term which in contemporary discussion is generally used to mean a social sphere of freedom, voluntary association, and plurality of human relationships, identities, differences, and values as contrasted with the coercive political power of state and government (Keane, 1988b). Several social and political factors help to explain the current popularity of this idea: the rise of autonomous social movements (for example, peace and environmentalist movements, liberation movements of women, gays, and black people); the conspicuous failures of Western social-democratic parties and governments over the last 20 years; and the experience of political dictatorship and state oppression under the former Soviet and Eastern European regimes, the growth of opposition movements (for example, Solidarity in Poland), the overthrow/ collapse of those regimes, and the fragmentation of many of the states which they governed. Flowing from such experiences, the argument has been developed both in the West and in Eastern Europe that strengthening the associations, movements, and institutions of civil society is fundamental to the successful pursuit of increased freedom, equality, and democracy at the level of both society and the state (Keane, 1988a).

This usage of "civil society" partly derives from the revival of the term earlier this century by GRAMSCI. However, there is a vital difference. For Gramsci the concept is central to his critique of capitalist society (Gramsci, 1971). Western European capitalist societies, according to Gramsci, are governed not only by the coercive powers of the state, but also by the maintenance of consent to bourgeois HEGEMONY (roughly, intellectual and cultural leadership) in the realm of civil society. In the associations and institutions of civil society the bourgeoisie maintains its social dominance through the influence of its ideas and cultural products. Thus, for Gramsci, civil society is a vital terrain on which capitalism must be fought. While Gramsci's use of civil society here is not free from problems (Hunt, 1986), it is nevertheless intended as a central element in a critique of capitalism. However, this forthrightly anti-capitalist deployment of the concept has now largely fallen into abeyance. This is but the latest in a series of shifts of meaning which the idea of civil society has undergone, and the diversity of meanings which the term has carried since it originated in the seventeenth century has given it an elusive and ambiguous character (Honneth, 1993; Tester, 1992).

HEGEL was the first theorist to draw a clear distinction between civil society and the state (Hegel, 1821). Earlier writers, such as Hobbes, Locke, and Rousseau, despite the deep theoretical differences which divided them, had *identified* civil society with the creation of the modern state. But for Hegel, civil society is the social realm within which egoistic individuals pursue their "private" interests. Thus economic activities such as work, the production and exchange of goods, and the acquisition of property are central to Hegel's view of civil society, though he also includes other important elements such as ethical, cultural, and educational features. The state, on the other hand, is concerned with the pursuit of the general interest of the whole community. It is a structure of political authority which is separate from civil society and only very loosely representative of it. One of the main purposes of the state is to integrate disparate egoistic individuals into a unified community. Thus, for Hegel, despite this innovative distinction, the state remains fundamental to the existence and functioning of civil society.

In his early writings MARX accepted Hegel's distinction between civil society and the state while arguing against Hegel: first, that civil society is the foundation of the state and not vice versa; and second, for a radical democratization of the state. However, Marx became increasingly critical of the idea of civil society and a developed critique of it may be found in his later work (Hunt, 1987). Marx analyzes modern capitalist society as a social formation with a distinctive economic structure containing social classes of very unequal power. This implies that *social* relations, and not only the applications of state power, are systematically coercive in character, and that this coercion flows from the fundamental structure of society. While on the surface society appears to consist of free individuals pursuing their interests by entering into voluntary association with each other, the underlying reality, according to Marx's critique, is that with its monopoly of the means of production a wealthy minority coerces, oppresses, and exploits the majority. The concept of civil society as an expression of the surface appearances of capitalist society is thus profoundly misleading.

Contemporary proponents of civil society tend to reject this Marxist critique on the grounds that it is "reductionist" and "economistic" in locating the main source of coercive power in capitalist society in its economic and class structure (Keane,

1988a). They tend to argue that the sources of power in modern society are too pluralistic and heterogeneous to be accounted for in this way. Instead, society is seen as an arena within which individuals of diverse identities associate in a multiplicity of ways in pursuit of their goals, and engage in a variety of forms of resistance to the many different sources of power and coercion. Civil society is upheld as the key notion required to conceptualize the potential for freedom and liberation which this arena contains.

In viewing society as a sphere within which disparate individuals relate in diverse ways, and in understating (or even ignoring) questions of social structure and class, there is a strong tendency for this contemporary defence of civil society to remain confined within a liberal theoretical framework, despite the more radical language in which it is expressed. As against this, the relevance and validity of the Marxist critique continues to be upheld by some writers. One such critic is Wood, who argues that while the pursuit of freedom, equality, and democracy must certainly entail resistance to all forms of social and political oppression, crucially it must include opposition to the systematic coercion and exploitation inherent in capitalist social relations. She maintains that many contemporary theorists of civil society "conceptualize away the problem of capitalism" by dissolving it "into an unstructured and undifferentiated plurality of social institutions and relations" (Wood, 1990, pp. 60, 66–7), with the result that the idea of civil society obscures and mystifies vital social issues rather than illuminating them.

Reading
Gramsci, Antonio 1971: *Selections From the Prison Notebooks.*
Honneth, Axel 1993: "Conceptions of 'civil society.'"
Hunt, Geoffrey 1987: "The development of the concept of civil society in Marx."
Keane, John 1988a: *Democracy and Civil Society.*
——ed. 1988b: *Civil Society and the State: New European Perspectives.*
Tester, Keith 1992: *Civil Society.*
Wood, Ellen Meiksins 1990: "The uses and abuses of 'civil society.'"

BARRY WILKINS

Cixous, Hélène (1937–) French feminist, writer, and critic. Cixous is the leading French feminist associated with *écriture féminine*, a DISCOURSE which originates in the pre-Oedipal drives of the body. Writing these "bodily" sensations serves to disrupt the symbolic (male) language/order. Her work draws on a variety of intellectual influences, PSYCHOANALYSIS, DECONSTRUCTION, history, and criticism, but submits to none of them. Despite a wide range of published material, including her early work on James Joyce, in England and America, she is chiefly represented by three main essays: "Sorties," "The Laugh of the Medusa," and "Coming to Writing." The account that follows is based primarily on these works.

The disruptive potential of *écriture féminine* is predicated on the organization of CULTURE and representation around the primary term of the male/female opposition, "'the' couple, man/woman" (1975, p. 64), where the female is figured as the negative underside to the male HEGEMONY. This culture, Cixous argues, has resulted in the relegation of woman to the other, and the denial of her own access to the pleasure of her BODY, "Shut out of his system's space, she is the repressed that ensures the system's functioning" (1975, p. 67). This SYSTEM is one based on hierarchy and opposition, where the traditional equation of the male with activity, and the female with passivity, posits the female as nonexistent and unthought. Thus the opposition is *not* a couple, and the feminine is merely a space or a lack subjected to male desire. She is thus a nonpresence, even to herself, dislocated from her own body and its desire. Cixous uses her experience of colonization in Algeria as a metaphor to describe the power relations operative in this process of objectification and appropriation, whereby dominance requires the expulsion of the strange: the colonized body/country is the "dark continent," infinitely other, but with the power to threaten associated with the return of the repressed.

Like IRIGARAY, Cixous analyzes the dependence of the male economy of desire on looking – FREUD's theory (and that of LACAN) is "a voyeur's theory" (1975, p. 82) – and thus upon the objectification, expulsion, and fragmentation of the feminine. The operative distinction is between the "self-same" and the other, yet the other cannot be theorized without being assimilated into dialectic. She argues that the (male) SUBJECT goes out into the OTHER in order to come back to itself; thus desire for the other is really desire for the self; an economy refuted by the feminine, which is plural in its drives and desires.

The difference of woman from man lies not only in her status as repressed and "other," but also in her capacity for maternity, bisexuality, and plurality. Moreover, each of these also contains within it subversive and disruptive potential. The relation designated by Cixous as the "m/other relation" provides a model for the overturning of the "Empire of the Selfsame" (1975, p. 78): she argues that the sex-specific role of nurturing and giving birth facilitates the acceptance of disruptions to the self, characteristic of the encounter with the other (1975, pp. 74 and 90). This unregretful splitting apart of subjectivity marks her specific libidinal economy – her *jouissance*. The maternal relation functions without appropriation or the erasure of difference, and thus enables plurality to come into play; the "gift" economy where all is given, and nothing is expected in return. This celebration of the revolutionary potential of mothering is one part of Cixous's project of (re)gaining power from the male order; she argues that the maternal role has been assimilated into the paternal, so that the primary social and economic relation becomes that between father and child (1975, p. 101).

However, the feminine is not only repressed for women, but for men also, who have denied the FEMININITY of male sexuality. Thus bisexuality provides another model for disruption as it is "the location within oneself of the presence of both sexes . . . the nonexclusion of difference or a sex." This presence of the other, of difference, is particularly applicable to women, as within a Freudian system they *are* bisexual, owing to to the requirement that they change the object of desire from the mother to the father. It is this coexistence of the other and difference, and their endless interplay, which constitutes woman's "instinctual economy," or her *jouissance*, which cannot be referred to, or described, by masculine discourse.

For Cixous, writing itself is the place of the other, where identities are questioned and changed. Woman writing herself will enact a return to her confiscated body, the gateway to the unconscious. The WRITING of the body, via an unsettling of the speech/writing distinction and the return of the repressed, will serve to disrupt the binary, hierarchical structures, for this writing means "nonexclusion." Cixous insists upon the fact that this "feminine practice of writing" cannot be defined or theorized, for to do so would signal a return to the old systems of logic. Unlike Irigaray, she argues that *écriture féminine* is not exclusively tied to the biological sex of the writer, but to the capacity to include the other – Jean Genet is one of her examples of a "feminine" writer. This distinction would seem to confound those of her critics who have claimed that her ideas depend upon an unproblematized biological determinism.

The blowing up of the Law which has exiled the other is an event which will happen in language, by writing with "the unimpeded tongue that bursts partitions, classes and rhetorics, orders and codes" (1975, pp. 94–5). A model that exemplifies this revolutionary return of the repressed for Cixous is the hysteric, who confounded Freud's laws by fragmenting and disrupting language. Woman is to displace the opposing male signifier, to overturn it, but *not* to make it hers, for this would leave the structure itself intact. This demand to disrupt and borrow, but not to appropriate, is signalled by Cixous's complex puns and word-plays, for example, that on *voler* (in French the verb means both "to fly" and "to steal"): "To fly/steal is woman's gesture, to steal into language to make it fly." The woman writing will fly/steal her confiscated body, to which she will then return.

Cixous's belief in the power of writing to express a female Imaginary which will undo the BINARY OPPOSITIONS upon which her exclusion rests, draws upon much contemporary French philosophy – the work of DERRIDA in particular. Attention to the gaps and silences of language and texts will unsettle the HEGEMONY of male DISCOURSE and culture. Her own writing provides an example of this: her work resists definitions such as fiction or theory, as she collapses generic distinctions, and disrupts the linear logic of male language, breaking up the TEXT and destabilizing meaning. Often dismissed as utopian, Cixous does offer a theory which enacts the possibility for radical change, without simply reproducing the STRUCTURES which oppress.

Reading

Cixous, Hélène 1975a (*1987*): "Sorties: out and out: attacks/ways out/forays."
——1975b (*1981*): "The laugh of the Medusa."
——1991: *"Coming to Writing" and Other Essays.*
Moi, Toril 1985: *Sexual/Textual Politics: Feminist Literary Theory.*
Sellers, Susan 1991: *Language and Sexual Difference: Feminist Writing in France.*
Shiach, Morag 1989: "Their 'symbolic' exists, it holds power – we, the sowers of disorder, know it only too well."
——1991: *Hélène Cixous: A Politics of Writing.*
Wilcox, Helen, ed. 1990: *The Body and the Text: Hélène Cixous, Reading and Teaching.*

DANIELLE CLARKE

Clark, Timothy James   British-born and educated art historian, now working in the United
States. Clark gives new life to the study and
understanding of the social history of nineteenth-
century France in his trilogy on French painting
from 1848 to 1884 by viewing political event and
CLASS structure not as so many bones on which
loosely hang the skin of art works, but as the muscle
and sinew of experience which can be seen as giving shape and meaning to form and image in ART.
See also AVANT-GARDE; GREENBERG, CLEMENT.

Reading
Clark, T.J. 1973: The Absolute Bourgeois: Artists and Politics in France 1848-1851.
——— 1973 (1984): Image of the People: Gustave Courbet
   and the 1848 Revolution.
——— 1985: The Painting of Modern Life: Paris in the Art
   of Manet and his Followers.
                                              GERALD EAGER

class   During the Industrial Revolution, the term
came to refer both to a group of persons sharing
common social or economic status and to persons
engaged in common economic activities. The political economists of the eighteenth and nineteenth
centuries tied status more firmly to economic role
or function, with the discussion of the three great
classes (landlords, capitalists, and laborers) in J.S.
Mill and D. Ricardo. The decisive step from taxonomy to teleology was taken by Karl MARX and
Friedrich ENGELS, whose polemical writings divide
humankind under capitalism into two classes, wage-
laborers who produce surplus and capitalists who
appropriate it. The bourgeoisie and the proletariat,
each with its own consciousness and organization,
form "two great hostile camps," locked in a class
struggle whose inevitable outcome is the demise of
capitalism and the birth of socialism/communism.
Thus Marx and Engels wove together considerations of status, economic function, political consciousness, and human destiny into the well-known
revolutionary claim in the Communist Manifesto:
"The history of all hitherto existing society is the
history of class struggles" (Marx, Engels, 1848).
Much of the twentieth-century theorizing about
class has since wrestled with the two intertwined
problematics of the taxonomy of class and the teleology of class struggle. The taxonomic debate has
tended to remain bounded by the categories of
political economy, focusing on the functional classification of the new middle classes, while scholars

concerned with the teleology of class have addressed
issues of agency, CULTURE, and consciousness,
moving rather far afield from Marxist political
economy. Still, no matter how far from Capital
the debate has strayed, Marx's original conceptions continue to define the shape and logic of
the argument. In fact, one could argue that the
burden of twentieth-century thought on class has
been the task of rehabilitation, elaboration, DECON-
STRUCTION, and contestation of Marx's original
construction of class, that to criticize Marxist conceptions of class, one must stand in the space that
Marx cleared.

   The earliest to claim the terrain was Max Weber,
who shifted the analysis of class from the sphere of
production to that of consumption, focusing on
conflicts among status groups who share similar
material standards of living, and are thus differentiated on the basis of market relations and life
chances, and also on the role of political parties,
especially those organized along lines of ethnicity
and nationality. Thus, the subordinate place accorded to economic class by Weber, whose antagonism to MARXISM was marked and well known, stands
in contrast to the privileged position accorded class
by Marx and later neo-Marxists. Still, one should
not overstate the distinctions between Marxist and
Weberian taxonomies of class: neo-Weberians acknowledge the importance of class definitions based
on economic production, while neo-Marxists recognize the role played by status, party, and nation.
Commenting on the extent to which neo-Marxists
have come to acknowledge the role of other forms
of group identification, Frank Parkin (1979) noted,
"Inside every neo-Marxist there seems to be a
Weberian struggling to get out." Parkin worked
explicitly in the Weberian vein, focusing on the
notion of social closure as the key element of exclusion by which classes are constructed. In his
view, ruling classes achieve closure by monopoliz-
ing "exoteric" knowledge and armed force, not
only economic resources such as land or capital.
Anthony Giddens, standing simultaneously in the
Weberian and Marxist traditions, shifted the discussion from class boundaries to the process of
"class structuration," which depends not only on
the degree of closure in "distributive groupings,"
but also on the division of labor within organizations, and the mechanisms of control in the workplace. Pierre BOURDIEU (1984) further attenuated
the link between economic relations and class analysis in his notions of a class "habitus" and the

transmission of class capital, neither of which is exclusively material or centered on the workplace.

A substantial body of empirical and theoretical work has sought to rescue Marxist class analysis from the straitjacket of the two-class model. Much of this work has been motivated by the emergence of new middle groups of white-collar workers such as clerical, managerial, and professional employees who do not fit neatly into the simple polarities of polemical Marxism. For Nicos Poulantzas (1975), white-collar workers, whose work consists of the distribution and circulation of commodities rather than their production, constituted a new petty bourgeoisie whose class position must be understood as resting on political and ideological criteria alongside economic criteria. In placing this group on the capitalist side of the "boundary problem," however, Poulantzas destroyed the working class, whose tiny numbers hardly seem adequate to the task of building a revolution. Harry Braverman (1974) saw the process of "deskilling" as proceeding at such a pace that the new middle class would inevitably be proletarianized. Erik Olin Wright (1985) took up the question of white-collar work, seeking to retain the criteria of exploitation and appropriation as essential in any taxonomy of class. Wright introduced the notion of contradictory class locations to explain white-collar workers as simultaneously occupying positions in both the capitalist and the working class. Similarly, Wright defines mediated class relations, where an individual might occupy one class position as a result of her own class, but be linked to another by marriage, and temporal class locations, entailing changes in the nature of an individual's work over her career trajectory. As both his critics and his supporters acknowledge, Wright's theoretical moves are an attempt to provide greater complexity to the starkness of the picture painted by the *Manifesto*, while retaining the privileged status of class relations in the larger Marxist analysis (and project) of historical change.

Responding to his critics, Wright (1989) points out that the problem of understanding the middle class presents neo-Marxists with a "Weberian temptation" to abandon notions of exploitation and appropriation; the Weberian solution relieves Marxists of the theoretical "burdens" on class analysis that are present in a theory that must span historical modes of production and explain the logic of exploitation and class antagonism. But for Wright, the choice of Marxism over Weberian approaches is simultaneously the expression of a methodological preference for systematic rather than *ad hoc* specifications and a political decision to ally himself with the Marxist tradition, which in his view "remains the most comprehensive and productive general framework for developing macrostructural theory of large-scale emancipatory possibilities."

Thus, the taxonomic question is simultaneously political and teleological. In seeking to delimit class boundaries and to situate particular groups of workers, neo-Marxist theorists have hoped to understand why the working classes in Western industrialized countries have not organized themselves to overthrow capitalism and why other nonclass axes of organization, including religion or nationality, have proven so potent in recent decades. Michele Barrett (1991), writing about "Marxisant treatments of sociology, politics and economics," argues that "there has been a potential for engagement with the actuality of *non-class* divisions, but (to express the situation tactfully) this has remained in many instances a potential rather than a nettle to be grasped."

A more promising avenue for analysis of the role of class and nonclass divisions was opened up with the critique of economism, reductionism, and class essentialism that transformed Western Marxism in the twentieth century. As early as the 1920s, authors such as Antonio GRAMSCI, Georg LUKÁCS, and members of the FRANKFURT SCHOOL broke free of political economy to embrace studies of psychology, philosophy, culture, and politics. Focusing on class consciousness, most likely in response to the emergence of new middle classes and the reformist character of working-class parties in Western Europe, these authors developed a powerful critique of Soviet Marxism's POSITIVISM, economism, and teleological leanings, and in the process began to accord less pride of place to class analysis. While the extent to which Gramsci's analysis dethrones class is in dispute, his work on HEGEMONY has proven enormously influential in understanding political and cultural processes by which dominating classes achieve the consent of the dominated, and clearly contribute to the critique of economism. Stuart HALL's dissection of Thatcherism in *The Great Moving Right Show*, for instance, draws heavily on Gramsci to provide important, if controversial, insights into working-class support for Tory governments. Others contributing to the critique of class essentialism include Ernesto Laclau and Chantal Mouffe (1985), whose work has been hailed for its definitive break with reductionism. Declaring themselves to the "post-Marxist," they reject all "normative epistemologies" and "universal DISCOURSES" in *Hegemony and Socialist Strategy*. In their view, even Gramsci remained tied to economistic definitions of class and to necessary rather than contingent views of the role of the working class in history.

Critics of class essentialism have pointed to the rise in the latter half of the twentieth century of radical social movements that contest limits placed upon persons because of GENDER, race, nationality, ethnicity, or sexual orientation. The class position of women had long posed problems for Marxism, and led to a series of unsuccessful attempts, such as the domestic labor debate, to subsume gender into the terms of Marxist class categories. Feminists have attacked such attempts to restore the primacy of class, in analysis of autonomous gender interests as an explanation and motor for contemporary political and social events. In the process, a debate formed around the interaction of class and gender, or the systemic relationship between capitalism and PATRIARCHY, with one group of theorists arguing that these two operate autonomously (dual systems theory), while others seek to develop various versions of a unified theory. The salience of nationalities as motors of human history has also become ever more clear with the rise of religious and nationalistic movements around the world, and analysis of race, nationality, and ethnicity is proving to be an enormously rich terrain for cultural and political work.

The question that remains is whether class analysis has been "superseded." Certainly the critiques of class essentialism have shifted the focus away from class analysis in cultural studies, but political economy continues to accord class pride of place. Finally, it is perhaps ironic that alternative explanations of politics have arisen precisely at the moment when in both Britain and the United States the class nature of contemporary politics has become even more glaring, and at the moment when global capitalism and its monoculture appear to be on a triumphal march against cultural specificities of all types. As Barrett (1991) points out, the very term "new social movement" implies that a movement is new *because* it is not class based; that is, the logic of class continues to overshadow even the most determined rejection of class analytics. When standing in the space Marx has cleared, we continue to feel his presence.

See also BOURDIEU, PIERRE; FRANKFURT SCHOOL; GRAMSCI, ANTONIO; HEGEMONY; LUKÁCS, GEORG; MARX, KARL; MARXISM AND MARXIST CRITICISM; RACE, CLASS, GENDER ANALYSIS.

Reading
Barrett, Michele 1991: *The Politics of Truth*.
Bottomore, T.B. 1965 (*1991*): *Classes in Modern Society*.
Bourdieu, Pierre 1984: *Distinction: A Social Critique of the Judgement of Taste*.
Braverman, Harry 1974: *Labor and Monopoly Capital*.
Giddens, Anthony 1973 (*1980*): *The Class Structure of the Advanced Societies*.
Hall, Stuart 1988: *The Hard Road to Renewal: Thatcherism and the Crisis of the Left*.
Laclau, Ernesto, and Mouffe, Chantal 1985: *Hegemony and Socialist Strategy: Towards a Radical Democratic Politics*.
Marx, Karl, and Engels, Friedrich 1848: *The Manifesto of the Communist Party*.
Parkin, Frank 1971: *Class Inequality and Political Order*.
Poulantzas, Nicos 1975: *Classes in Contemporary Capitalism*.
Thompson, E.P. 1964: *The Making of the English Working Class*.
Weber, Max 1921 (*1968*): *Economy and Society*.
Wright, Erik Olin 1985: *Classes*.

TERESA AMOTT

classical realism   A term used mainly by MARXIST and poststructuralist critics to denote the various generic conventions that (supposedly) characterized fictional writing during the period of high bourgeois aesthetic and sociopolitical HEGEMONY. For some Marxists – LUKÁCS among them – such works still possessed a critical-emancipatory potential, a capacity to encompass (to "concretely portray") whole worlds of diverse historical and social experience, and thus to reveal the deep-laid conflicts of residual, dominant, and emergent ideologies. For others (for example, MACHEREY and EAGLETON) realism often functions as a mode of false consciousness, a smoothing-over of precisely those conflicts – those stress points in its own ideological project – which can emerge only through a reading in the "symptomatic" mode. This antagonism between rival schools of Marxist thought with regard to the nature, status, and value of nineteenth-century realism is reproduced in their respective (sharply polarized) attitudes toward literary MODERNISM and its programmatic break with realist modes of writing. Thus, where Lukács sees modernism as a symptom of late bourgeois cultural decline, Eagleton and Macherey take a modernizing lesson from Brecht in the various techniques of critical reworking (*Umfunktionierung*) which can draw out the ideological subtexts – the latent contradictions of meaning and structure – that inhabit the conventions of classic bourgeois realism.

For poststructuralists like Roland BARTHES these conventions are likewise a mere artifice, a ruse whereby the novel attempts to conceal or disavow all the signs of its own cultural production, and thus masquerades as a window upon (or a mirror held up to) reality. Worse still, it performs this work of ideological recruitment by surreptitiously transforming culture into nature, or passing off the values of its own time and place as transcendent, ahistorical truths. Thus the rise of the novel is seen as a cultural phenomenon that reflects – and promotes – the emergence of a dominant bourgeois ideology premised on those same "commonsense" values of autonomous selfhood, possessive individualism, transparent access to "the real," etc. The task of criticism, conversely, is to analyze the various narrative CODES and devices whereby such illusory values are created and made to appear nothing less than self-evident.

This project is carried through to most briliant effect in Barthes's *S/Z*, an exhaustive (almost word-by-word) textual exegesis of Balzac's novella *Sarrasine*. Here we see the "classic realist text" subjected to a process of disseminative reading which begins by breaking it down into 561 fragments that Barthes calls "lexemes," or minimal distinctive units of narrative meaning, by loose analogy with "phonemes" in the discourse of structural linguistics. (See also DISCOURSE, NARRATOLOGY, STRUCTURALISM.) Each of these is then assigned to one or more of the five "codes" – the proaieretic (code of actions and events), HERMENEUTIC (code of puzzles and enigmas), semic (code of character), cultural (code of commonplace or received wisdom), and symbolic (code of deep-laid collective unconscious (for example, gender-role) representation – which traverse the narrative in a ceaseless "polyphony" of intertextual echoes and allusions. Barthes's purpose in all this is to foreground those moments of crosscode interference or disruption which enable *Sarrasine* to figure as an exemplary "limit-text," that is, a work that undermines the conventions of classic bourgeois realism by exposing them to all manner of unresolved PARADOX, APORIA, self-deconstructive *mise-en-abîme* and suchlike obstacles to straightforward READERLY (*lisible*) consumption. To this extent at least it is a WRITERLY (*scriptible*) text, though one whose "parsimonious plurality" of meaning is acknowledged as placing certain constraints upon the range of possibilities thus opened up.

There is much that is brilliant, provocative, and liberating – as well as inspirational for the jaded teacher of those "classic realist texts" – in Barthes's idiosyncratic commentary on Balzac's once neglected, now celebrated novella. Unfortunately, as often happens, his *obiter dicta* have been turned by some poststructuralists into just the kind of ironcast orthodoxy that Barthes was so anxious to escape. At any rate there is more to be said in defense of "naive" (or "bourgeois") realism, some of it said rather effectively by old-school Marxists like Lukács.

Reading
Lukács, Georg 1962: *The Historical Novel.*
——1963: *The Meaning of Contemporary Realism.*
Barthes, Roland 1973a: *S/Z.*
——1982: *A Barthes Reader.*
MacCabe, Colin 1978: *James Joyce and the "Revolution of the World."*

CHRISTOPHER NORRIS

classification, primitive *See* PRIMITIVE CLASSIFICATION

codes organizing principles composed of BINARY OPPOSITIONS: a fundamental term in NARRATOLOGY. Derived from the work of Claude LÉVI-STRAUSS on myths, narratological theory specifies that codes function to organize the binary oppositions which constitute the functioning of language. They therefore comprise a homogenizing operation, one which seeks to render meaning into easily understood categories.

S/Z (1974) by Roland BARTHES is perhaps the literary critical work which most exhaustively employs codes as the foundation of an interpretative method. He reads Balzac's short story of the same name in terms of five codes: HERMENEUTICS (formal elements which are organized into binary oppositions such as question/answer): semes (elements of meaning which are constitutive of pieces of TEXT such as characters): the SYMBOLic (plurality of meaning as it is organized in the process of interpretation): the proaieretic (sequences of actions, or plot); and cultural (references to types of knowledge). For Barthes, the interweaving of these five codes is what constitutes the text, with no single code achieving any kind of overall preponderance. He reads through Balzac's story, sorting it into categories which are overdetermined by these codes, interspersing it with his own critical text. In so doing, he classifies pieces of text as elements of the codes. Nevertheless, there are points at which he invokes the reader as part of the production of meaning, implying that codes do not completely interpret the text. Since readers can vary, so too, therefore, can the meanings produced, and this problem threatens the provisional stability of his structural codes.

Barthes himself moved on from this kind of analysis into a concern with the multiplicity of meaning. His cultural code became more and more problematical, and was replaced with his particular use of the concept of INTERTEXTUALITY. In this respect he moves into the area covered by POSTSTRUCTURALISM.

Reading
Barthes, Roland 1973a (*1990*): *S/Z*.
Culler, Jonathan 1975 (*1989*): *Structuralist Poetics*.
PAUL INNES

collective unconscious   A term central to Jungian psychology, which refers to the continuum of age-old patterns central to human experience that are deeper than, prior to, and more fundamental than the individual personality. In the same way human beings share common instincts and common physical STRUCTURES, they also share a common – *collective* – stratum of the psyche. From those "objective" inner depths, which are not always gloomy and negative as in the Freudian vision of the subconscious, there emerge certain patterns often experienced by the ego-consciousness as *complexes* and *symptoms*, as well as the SYMBOLS and images of dreams, fantasies, and visions. In 1919 JUNG adopted the Platonic–Augustinian term *archetype* to account for the recurring expressions of the symbolic contents of the collective unconscious psyche.
See also ARCHETYPE; JUNG, CARL GUSTAV.

Reading
Jung, C.G. 1969b: *The Collective Works*, Volume 9, Part I: *The Archetypes and the Collective Unconscious*.
SUSAN L. FISCHER

comedy   A form of dramatic or narrative plot that emphasizes social integration. Whereas tragedy typically leads to the isolation of a character by accentuating suffering or death, comedy brings about the assimilation of characters into a changed or renewed social order that celebrates marriage, new life, or communal stability. Unlike the theory of tragedy, which has a long tradition that extends back to Aristotle's *Poetics*, the theory of comedy is largely a product of twentieth-century thought. Although it is commonly assumed that what is comic is the object of laughter, this is not necessarily so. While comic in the shape of its plot – because it traces the journey of the lost soul through the terrors of hell and the cleansing of purgatory in preparation for the union with God – the narrative of Dante's *Divine Comedy* is rarely humorous.

In his pioneering study "Laughter" (1900), however, Henri Bergson emphasized the dependence of humor on social organization. The typical object of laughter, he argued, is a human manifestation of mechanical inelasticity, or a rigidity of manner, belief, or personality. When the exposure of such inelasticity leads to laughter, two groups are immediately formed: those who laugh and those at whom the laughter is directed. Laughter is thus a form of social criticism or a force for social conformity, in which those who laugh see more or see differently from those who are laughed at. The danger of laughter, for example, when it is directed against Malvolio in *Twelfth Night*, is that the one against whom it is directed may become permanently alienated from the community that laughs. If the laughter is generous and its object pliable, however, the result may be a release from rigidity and an incorporation of the one who was formerly excluded from the community into a new and larger social order.

Writing independently of Bergson, FREUD in 1905 published *Jokes and Their Relation to the Unconscious*. An important function of jokes, he argued, lies in their power to overcome a person's defenses against the content of a witicism, a content that a person might ordinarily resist if it were presented in another form. In this sense, form becomes a verbal or artistic equivalent of a psychological defense structure by making what was threatening tolerable.

In 1948 Northrop FRYE published his highly influential essay "The argument of comedy," which he later expanded into a full comic theory in *Anatomy of Criticism*. Frye noted that there are two fundamentally different kinds of comedy: one which descends from the "old comedy" of Aristophanes and the other from the "new comedy" of Plautus and Terence. The basic assumption in the old comedy is that the structures of society are immutable and that aberrations can only be held up to ridicule. After a brief period of festive holiday, life returns to normal and conformity reasserts itself, or the deviant and defiant are banished. But in the new comedy, which had a profound influence on Shakespeare, the basic assumption is that social structures can be reshaped. Thus, what may begin as a rigidly alienating social order, as at the beginning of *A Midsummer Night's Dream* or *As You Like It*, can itself be transformed and made to conform to individual human needs or desires. Such plots often require a temporary escape from a rigid order of law or custom, a sojourn into a natural place, and then a return to a regenerated social world. (Here the pattern is strikingly similar to that outlined in the Bible in Isaiah 35–6.) Frye's account of old and new comedy historicizes the tensions that Bergson and Freud detected in laughter and jokes.

A common element in plots that include the creation or regeneration of a vital social order is that they depict or elicit a kind of ecstasy, literally a coming out of the self for the sake of participation in a RITUAL of artistic communion that parallels or derives its power from religious celebration.

Reading
Bergson, Henri 1900 (*1980*): "Laughter."
Freud, Sigmund 1905 (*1960*): *Jokes and Their Relation to the Unconscious.*
Frye, Northrop 1957: *Anatomy of Criticism.*
MICHAEL PAYNE

comics   A series of sequential images that convey a story. Some comics are published in magazine forms called comic books. The word "comic" is a misnomer because, although many are humorous, most comic books today relate exciting adventure stories and drama. Despite the efforts of many publishers and critics alike to change the genre's appellation to "sequential art" or "graphic novels," the term "comic" appears to have stuck.

Comics have been praised as one of the few uniquely American art forms. Although comic art dates back to ancient times, such as cave drawings, Egyptian hieroglyphics, and Greek vases, the idea of putting words and pictures together did not gain popularity until the 1700s. In 1754 Benjamin Franklin urged the American colonies to unite in his cartoon, "Join, or Die," depicting a segmented snake that represented the disjointed colonies.

During the 1800s many American artists created political cartoons, using such artforms as prints, woodcuts, and lithographs. *Harper's Weekly* regularly featured the extremely influential work of Thomas Nast. In 1832 the French artist, Honoré Daumier (known as the father of modern cartooning) served six months in prison for drawing a caricature of King Louis Philippe entitled *Gargantua*. It would not be the last time the comic artform would suffer such undue response.

In February 1896 the *New York World* newspaper tested its new yellow ink by printing it on the main character in Richard F. Outcault's comic, "Hogan's Alley." It increased circulation to such an extent that the future of the comic strip was assured.

The basic idea of reprinting existing comic strips into a tabloid did not originate until the early 1900s. That brainstorm can be attributed to the famous journalist and publisher, William Randolph Hearst, who gathered Outcault's "funnies" into a short-lived publication called the *Yellow Kid Magazine*. It took more than three decades before someone thought about collecting new stories into the comic book form.

In 1933 Max Gaines published the first original comic book, which was entitled *Funnies on Parade*. Two years later Walt Disney entered the industry, and the comics boom was under way. By the end of the decade, many publishers who had dealt with pulp fiction made the move to the comics industry. The advent of these adventure-oriented creators led to the birth of the pivotal force that would define the future of comic books for good or ill – the super hero. This super hero was, of course, Superman, created by two Cleveland college students, Jerry Siegel and Joe Shuster. A year later, costumed characters such as Batman, Captain America, the Sub-Mariner and Captain Marvel proliferated in the printed page of most comic magazines.

The 1939–45 war prompted the need for patriotic super heroes. Subtle propaganda for the war effort depicted these heroes battling against the villainy of the Third Reich. Several nonsuper hero concepts emerged during this period, most notably Archie in 1942.

After the war the popularity of the super hero slowly declined, to be replaced with a growing interest in humor, romance, science fiction, war, and westerns. In 1950 William Gaines pioneered several series of horror comics under the imprint of Entertaining Comics (EC). Four years later, however, a book entitled *Seduction of the Innocent* was published by Dr Frederic Wertham, a longtime vociferous critic of comic books. Its accusations led to public hearings by the US Senate Subcommittee to Investigate Juvenile Delinquency on the allegedly ill effects upon children of reading comic books. These hearings led to the institution of the self-regulatory Comics Code Authority, which spelled the end for EC's horror line. Within a year, all EC books except *Mad* were discontinued.

DC Comics, the publishers of Superman and Batman, dominated the super hero market, or what was left of it, for the next few years. Then the creative team of Stan Lee and Jack Kirby at Marvel Comics introduced *The Fantastic Four* in 1961, followed by *The Hulk* and *The Amazing SpiderMan*. Unlike their predecessors, these characters were not perfect or godlike. They had real human problems to which their audience could relate.

Meanwhile, in 1967, the first "underground comic," *Zap*, was created by Robert Crumb. Underground comics reflected the new freedom of the late 1960s. They explored themes such as sex, drugs, and the COUNTERCULTURE movement through unique visual images.

The 1970s was a period of slight decline that was turned around in the 1980s by the direct distribution market catering for comic book specialty shops. This system nurtured the development of the independent market, which introduced titles such as Dave Sim's *Cerebus the Aardvark*, a modern satire in which stinging parodistic dialogue is combined with impeccable timing and storytelling.

The major comic book publishers, such as Marvel and DC, developed higher-quality formats which showcased the artistic merit of the medium. However, these publishers were still primarily interested in super hero fare skewed toward the younger reader. That is not to say that there were no super hero comics that adults could not sink their teeth into. Frank Miller's *The Dark Knight Returns* (1986) portrays a middle-aged Bruce Wayne coming out of retirement to visit his wrath upon Gotham City's criminal element once again as the Batman. But his obsession with criminals begins to spill over into psychosis. Miller's Batman becomes a violent SYMBOL of American dissolution and idealism.

Frank Miller and artist Bill Sienkiewicz reintroduced a sophisticated version of a character already familiar to Marvel fans in *Elektra: Assassin* (1986), a story of savage political satire mixed with psychodrama, surrealism, and stream of consciousness storytelling.

Perhaps the best new series of 1986 was DC's *Watchmen*, by Alan Moore and Dave Gibbons. This richly textured story explores what super heroes would be like in the real world. Gibbons's collaboration with Moore redefined the relationship between image and word in the comic book. There is a subtle interplay between the two that is the goal and the challenge of the medium.

Nevertheless, many critics feel that creators like Miller and Moore are only leading audiences of arrested adolescents into a childlike adultishness, ignoring the possibilities that exist within the medium. Europe and Asia have typically embraced comics as reading matter suitable for adults, therefore their results have been a more sophisticated product, both visually and thematically, than the super hero comics in the United States. Recognizing an audience other than adolescent boys prompted European and Asian publishers to realize the need for other topicality. Only recently have those foreign concepts begun to influence the English-speaking world of comics.

With the advent of Art Spiegelman's best-selling and critically acclaimed *Maus: A Survivor's Tale* (Pantheon, 1988) and the second volume, subtitled *And Here My Troubles Began* (Pantheon, 1991) a large number of general readers are for the first time experiencing a new kind of adult-oriented graphic storytelling. *Maus* has enjoyed phenomenal success, including a long run on the *New York Times* best-seller list and a well-deserved Pulitzer Prize. It dispenses with the narrow conventions and existential confines dictated by its comic predecessors.

At its most basic level, *Maus* is the story of Vladek Spiegelman, a survivor of Auschwitz, as told to his son, Artie. Spiegelman substitutes animals for different types of humans. Jews are portrayed as mice, Nazis as cats, and Americans as dogs. This narrative device ironically casts the human condition in a more harrowing light. Spiegelman is acutely aware of the comic medium's power to make things very immediate, pushing them into your mind in ways other media do not.

Unfortunately, most of the comics published in the English-speaking world are still genre-bound. This shortcoming is due to the fact that most of the comic creators are those who grew up reading comics. Thus it becomes a self-selecting group. Until that mindset is challenged, comic books, including ones like *Maus*, will continue to be relegated to the juvenile section of your local book store.

Reading

Benton, Mike 1989: *The Comic Book in America.*
Daniels, Les 1991: *Marvel: Five Fabulous Decades of the World's Greatest Comics.*
Eisner, Will 1985: *Comics & Sequential Art.*
Fox, Martin, ed. 1988: *Print.*
Levin, Bob 1988: "Comics."
McCloud, Scott 1993: *Understanding Comics.*

GLENN A. HERDLING

communication, phatic *See* PHATIC COMMUNICATION

Communicative action   Communicative action is central to HABERMAS's claim that interpersonal understanding is dependent on norms of truth, sincerity, justice, and freedom. Whether acknowledged or not, uncoerced agreement requires that dialog partners have equal chances to deploy SPEECH ACTS, and utterances are comprehensible, true, appropriate, and sincerely spoken. Communicative action is illocutionary speech where validity claims are open to public scrutiny, making possible an ideal consensus based solely on the force of better argument. This emacipatory dimension of language, however, is counterfactual – it is recovered through philosophical critique rather than empirical observation. Hence it is also known as the "ideal speech situation."

Reading

Habermas, J. 1981 (*1987*): *Theory of Communicative Action.*

LAURENCE J. RAY

communitarian ethics   A currently influential movement of thought in Anglo–American ethical and political philosophy, it holds that our best – indeed our only – source of wisdom and guidance in these matters is the appeal to what counts as good, humane, responsible, or civilized conduct according to the standards and values that prevail within our own cultural community. This means rejecting any "formalist" (for example, Kantian) idea of ethical judgment as based on abstract principles – or universal maxims – which must then be somehow applied to particular cases through the exercise of a faculty ("practical reason") that supposedly transcends all localized differences of interest, custom, peer-group loyalty, religious affiliation, political culture, etc. It is simply not possible, these thinkers maintain, to adopt such a standpoint above or beyond all the values, beliefs, and social obligations that constitute a shared way of life for the agents concerned.

Alasdair MacIntyre's controversial book *After Virtue* (1980) provides the most elaborate statement of this communitarian position in ethics and political theory. According to MacIntyre we live in a world of fragmented beliefs and value systems which – as he describes them in the book's arresting first paragraph – resemble the wreckage from some natural or manmade catastrophe, some event that has left us with just bits and pieces from which to reconstruct the science, the technology, and the entire lost CULTURE of Western civilization. In ethical terms the catastrophe has occurred through the loss of those organic values – that sustaining sense of communal participation and purpose – which once enabled a philosopher like Aristotle to link the private with the public virtues, or the conduct of a rich and fulfilling individual life with the conduct of one's affairs in the wider (civic or sociopolitical) sphere. Thus the history of Western post-Hellenic ethical thought is the history of a long – indeed epochal – decline into various forms of morally debilitating dualism. Chief among these are the public/private dichotomy, the split between "rational" and "emotive" or "evaluative" orders of judgment, and – equally disastrous in MacIntyre's view – the KANTian elevation of pure moral will into an abstract (universal) set of maxims and imperatives. This produces the idea of morality as a law whose very nature is to thwart all the pleasures of a life lived in accordance with our best (most humanly satisfying) forms of personal and collective endeavor.

Hence the predominantly somber cast of MacIntyre's historical reflections. What we have lost, perhaps beyond recall, is that eudaimonic (Aristotelian) conception of the virtues that saw no need for any such conflict between moral obligation and the natural desire to make the best use of our innate dispositions, talents, and practical skills. This was a conception that equated the good with a full and unimpeded exercise of whatever activities conduced to our all-round wellbeing as citizens, thinkers, artists, soldiers, politicians, or creatures whose happiness is at every point bound up with our role as members of a flourishing cultural community. It also included a certain narrative element, that is, a capacity to view our own life-projects as contributing to a story whose meaning and significance derived from its enactment within that same context of communally sanctioned purposes, values, and beliefs. But again we have lived on, as MacIntyre argues, into an epoch of splintered value-spheres which set up a false dichotomy between what is good for us as private individuals in quest of personal fulfillment and what is good for "society" (or the public interest) conceived as imposing a stern moral check upon our "lower," self-seeking, unregenerate instincts and desires. On occasion MacIntyre appears to be suggesting that we might yet come up with some replacement narrative, some revived sense of communal meaning and purpose that would mend this chronically disabling condition of divided moral identity. Elsewhere he writes more in the gloomily diagnostic mode of one who believes that the sickness is so far advanced that no such salvation is any longer possible.

MacIntyre's arguments are open to various criticisms. One is that his ethical and political values are deeply conservative, not only in their backward-looking attachment to ancient Greek notions of social virtue but also in their failure to register – and criticize – the massive (indeed structural) injustices that went along with the Greek way of life. Thus he, like Aristotle, appears oddly blind to the flagrant partiality (not to say hypocrisy) of an ethics that on the one hand cherishes this human need for enhanced self-fulfillment through the exercise of everyone's innate gifts and talents, while on the other condoning the existence of a slave and female population defined (in effect) as subhuman and hence proscribed from exerting any claim to possession of those same gifts and talents. Another, more generalized version of this criticism has to do with the incapacity of communitarian ethics to explain (or justify) the dissident stance of those who on principle – or in good conscience – feel obliged to reject the prevailing beliefs, customs, values, or social mores of their own cultural community. According to MacIntyre there is just no way that such justification can be had, requiring as it does an appeal to alternative (extra-communal) grounds, reasons, or principles which signal the lapse into yet another version of those baneful Kantian antinomies.

This is not to suggest that all thinkers of a communitarian persuasion adopt so deeply conservative a view of the goods that we have lost through our agelong slide into a medley of diverse, competing ethical values. Some others – Michael Walzer among them – adopt a pluralist outlook which appears far removed from MacIntyre's position. Thus Walzer takes it as the chief virtue of our present way of life in the Western LIBERAL democracies that they are able to support such a range of diverse creeds, ideologies, and lifestyles without giving rise to fundamental conflicts that would tear society apart. However, this pluralism turns out to have certain limits, namely those defined by our belonging to a given cultural community within which some (and not other) modes of speech, thought, and conduct are deemed meaningful or worth a hearing by members of our communal peer group. So there is still the question – as posed by MacIntyre – of what could then count as an adequate reason or ethical justification for opposing policies adopted in the name of "liberal democracy" but serving to promote (say) the interests of US global HEGEMONY or those of one particular well-placed socioeconomic group. Hence the very different senses of the word "liberal" espoused on the one hand by egalitarian thinkers like John Rawls, and on the other by conservative defenders of a classical free-market LIBERALISM such as Robert Nozick. From Walzer's communitarian standpoint one would have to conclude simply that each way of thinking had its place among the range of currently available options, and therefore that any judgment between them could only be a matter of private inclination or group loyalty.

This argument draws on various sources in philosophy and CULTURAL THEORY. HEGEL was the first to criticize KANT for his abstract conception of morality and his failure to reckon with the range of diverse value-commitments – political, social, civic, and familial – that made up the realm of Hegelian ethical *Sittlichkeit*. From the later work of WITTGENSTEIN it takes the idea that we can go no further in explaining or justifying certain "language games" or "forms of life" than simply to remark that they make good sense – and have no need of such justification – when viewed in the context of our cultural traditions, linguistic practices, and so forth. There is also a marked elective affinity between communitarian ethics and certain strains of postmodernist thinking, not least on account of their shared antipathy toward the truth claims and values of ENLIGHTENMENT critique. This kinship emerges most clearly in the narrative turn – or the appeal to "first-order natural pragmatic" story-telling modes – which Jean-François LYOTARD offers as a postmodern substitute for those old (now defunct) "meta-narrative" absolutes of freedom, progress, justice, truth-at-the-end-of-inquiry, etc. It is also evident in Richard RORTY's neopragmatist idea that truth is nothing more than what is (currently and contingently) "good in the way of belief." On this view philosophy is best employed in devising new narratives, metaphors, styles of creative self-description, etc., by which to promote the ongoing cultural "conversation of mankind." Some critics – myself included – hold that this amounts to nothing more than a handy pretext for postmodern attitudes of uncritical acquiescence in the current self-images of the age.

See also CIVIL SOCIETY; END OF PHILOSOPHY, ETHICS, INTERPRETATIVE COMMUNITIES; NUSSBAUM, MARTHA, POLITICAL PHILOSOPHY; WILLIAMS, BERNARD.

Reading
Benhabib, Seyla M. 1992: *Situating the Self: Gender, Community and Postmodernism in Contemporary Ethics.*
MacIntyre, Alasdair 1980: *After Virtue: A Study in Moral Theory.*
——1988: *Whose Justice? Which Rationality?*
Nussbaum, Martha C. 1980: *Love's Knowledge: Essays on Philosophy and Literature.*
Rorty, Richard 1989: *Contingency, Irony, and Solidarity.*
Sandel, Michael 1982: *Liberalism and the Limits of Justice.*
Walzer, Michael 1983: *Spheres of Justice: A Defence of Pluralism and Equality.*
——1987: *Interpretation and Social Criticism.*
Williams, Bernard 1985: *Ethics and the Limits of Philosophy.*
CHRISTOPHER NORRIS

communities, interpretative *See* INTERPRETATIVE COMMUNITIES

comparative literature The study of literatures across frontiers. Originally coined in the early nineteenth century, the term became highly controversial in the twentieth century owing to differing usages and interpretations. Some scholars have seen it as essentially literary history, following Goethe's concept of *Weltliteratur*; some have seen it as a field of study comparing the "soul" or "spirit" of different CULTURES; others have sought to demonstrate the certainty or otherwise of "influence" between writers. The so-called French school promoted binary study between two authors or literary SYSTEMS, in contrast to the American school which argued for wide cross-disciplinary comparison. These two approaches were often reflected in a terminological distinction that sought to demonstrate

a difference between "comparative" and "general" literature. Emphasis on the relationship between literature and national culture in the nineteenth century led to reaction in the twentieth century when comparative literature came under the dominance of FORMALISM, and the focus was on belief in the myth of the universal civilizing power of literature regardless of cultural context.

Since the 1970s comparative literature has moved away from the debates on what or how to compare that had so concerned formalist scholars. There has also been a move away from the earlier focus on canonical TEXTS and prioritization of European and North American literature in favour of a much broader systemic approach that compares and contrasts means of literary production, changing cultural contexts, and the role of literary texts in different national traditions. It is possible to argue that a great deal of exciting, innovative work in comparative literature today is taking place in programs defined variously as gender studies, POSTCOLONIAL STUDIES, intercultural studies. This tendency reflects the abandonment of attempts to demonstrate that comparative literature is a discipline in its own right in favor of an approach that sees comparative literature as it was originally conceived in the 1820s, that is, as a methodology.

Comparative literature today is a term used to describe programs of study that cross national or linguistic boundaries (for example, European studies, African studies, CARIBBEAN STUDIES) and to describe research that considers the transmission of texts across cultures. It draws upon comparative anthropology, DISCOURSE theory, reception theory, TRANSLATION STUDIES, CULTURAL MATERIALISM, and a range of other approaches. In Europe and North America it is primarily a term used to describe an approach to literary study that is not restricted to a single system and is in the process of shaking off its formalist legacy. In other parts of the world it is a term used to discuss the relationship between national literature and other literary SYSTEMS and is therefore an intensely politicized form of literary study.

There is an international comparative literature association and a large number of separate national associations, many of which publish their own journals and hold interdisciplinary seminars and conferences.

Reading
Bassnett, Susan 1993: *Comparative Literature: A Critical Introduction.*

Eagleton, Terry 1983: *Literary Theory: An Introduction.*
Koelb, Clayton, and Noakes, Susan, eds 1988: *The Comparative Perspective on Literature. Approaches to Theory and Practice.*
Lefeveré, André 1992: *Translation, Rewriting and the Manipulation of Literary Fame.*
Levin, Harry 1972: *Refractions. Essays in Comparative Literature.*
Majumdar, Swapan 1987: *Comparative Literature, Indian Dimensions.*
Prawer, Siegbert 1973: *Comparative Literary Studies: An Introduction.*
Schultz, H.J. and Rhein, P.H., eds 1973: *Comparative Literature, The Early Years.*
Warren, Austin, and Wellek, René 1968: *Theory of Literature.*
Weisstein, Ulrich 1974: *Comparative Literature and Literary Theory.*
Wellek, René 1970: *Discriminations: Further Concepts of Criticism.*

SUSAN BASSNETT

competence   A term introduced into linguistics by Noam CHOMSKY (1965, p. 3) to refer to the knowledge that a native speaker has of a language. The term was contrasted with *performance*, the actual use of language in concrete situations.

The distinction between competence and performance has been bitterly criticized, but the criticisms are groundless, since the distinction underlies virtually all work in linguistics, Chomskyan or otherwise.

Recent work such as Chomsky (1986) uses other terms such as "SYSTEM of knowledge" or "I-language" instead of competence. A wider notion of *communicative competence*, proposed by Dell Hymes (1972), has been influential in applied linguistics. *See also* CHOMSKY, NOAM; GENERATIVE GRAMMAR.

Reading
Chomsky, N. 1965: *Aspects of the Theory of Syntax.*
——1986: *Knowledge of Language.*

RAPHAEL SALKIE

competence, literary   *See* LITERARY COMPETENCE

complex, Oedipus   *See* OEDIPUS COMPLEX

complexity   Complexity, with its attendant contradictions, is what Robert VENTURI likes in architecture, what he sees as inherent to the medium and the program of architecture, and what he finds is suppressed by the unbending geometry of orthodox modern architecture. Specific features of complexity, such as double- and multi-functioning elements, contrasts between the inside and the outside, dramatic visual juxtapositions, and redundancies of design statement are what, for Venturi, make architecture responsive to human experience, and give both validity and vitality.

Reading
Venturi, Robert 1966: *Complexity and Contradiction in Architecture.*

GERALD EAGER

condensation/displacement   Essential aspects of the workings of unconscious processes, and especially of symptoms and the DREAM-WORK, as analyzed by FREUD (1900). Thanks to the mechanism of condensation, a single unconscious idea can express the content of several chains of association; the mechanism comes into play at the nodal point at which they intersect. Condensation explains the apparently laconic nature of the MANIFEST CONTENT of the dream, as compared with the richness of the LATENT CONTENT. The term displacement refers to the process whereby the emphasis or intensity of an unconscious idea is detached from that idea and transferred to a second and less intense idea to which it is linked by chains of association. The effect or emotional charge attached to a highly sexualized idea may, for instance, be displaced on to a more neutral image or idea. In such cases displacement is an effect of censorship.

Condensation and displacement are likened by LACAN (1957), for whom the UNCONSCIOUS is structured like a language, to the rhetorical figures of METAPHOR AND METONYMY.

Reading
Freud, Sigmund 1900: *The Interpretation of Dreams.*
Lacan, Jacques 1957: "The agency of the letter in the unconscious or Reason since Freud."

DAVID MACEY

conjuring   The system of magic and medicine that forms part of the black folk religion of vodun, which was practiced in black slave communities across the DIASPORA and which continued to flourish well into the twentieth century. Often regarded as a descendant of the African priest or healer, the conjurer performed various social functions for the black community, including fortune-telling, avenging wrongs, curing psychological and physical ailments, and interpreting natural and supernatural SIGNS. A practice largely discredited as superstitious in the West, conjuring has been celebrated by numerous black writers as a system of alternative folk knowledge that has enabled an oppressed group to exercise psychological control over an unjust social environment. The term "conjuring" has recently acquired an increased metaphorical currency in black feminist criticism, with the publication of Marjorie Pryse's essay, "Zora Neale Hurston, Alice Walker, and the 'ancient power' of black women" (1985), which claims that the black women's fictional tradition derives its unique literary authority from its recovery of black folk cultural practices such as conjuring.

Reading

Hurston, Zora Neale 1935 (*1978*): *Mules and Men*, Part II.

Levine, Lawrence W. 1977: *Black Culture and Black Consciousness: Afro-American Folk Thought from Slavery to Freedom.*

Pryse, Marjorie 1985: "Zora Neale Hurston, Alice Walker, and the 'ancient power' of black women."

MADHU DUBEY

connotation/denotation The denotation of a word is its literal meaning or "dictionary definition." Its connotations are the additional meanings, such as implications or associations, which it takes on when used in specific contexts. The word "pig" denotes a particular kind of animal, but if used as an insult it has a connotation of greediness.

The distinction took on a special role in modern criticism, first in I.A. RICHARDS and C.K. Ogden's *The Meaning of Meaning* (1923), and later in NEW CRITICISM. More recent, poststructuralist criticism, by contrast, "contests the hierarchy of denotated and connotated" and refuses to "privilege" denotation as the primary meaning (BARTHES, 1973).

Reading

Barthes, Roland 1973a: *S/Z*.

Garza Cuaron, Beatriz 1991: *Connotation and Meaning*.

IAIN WRIGHT

consumer culture A rather loose term which began to be used by revisionist Marxists in the 1980s to signal their new approach to the marketplace. They wanted to rethink consumers' previously assumed "irrationality," whether this irrationality was defined in terms of MARX's concept of commodity fetishism or in the psychoanalytically inflected approach of the FRANKFURT SCHOOL. Consumption, in Martyn Lee's words, was still taken to be the moment when economic activity and cultural practice combined, but it was now argued (in the pages of the British Communist Party magazine, *Marxism Today*, for example) that as a cultural practice it could not be understood as entirely determined either by the circulation of capital or by individual psychopathology. Consuming is, rather, a social practice, which has two theoretical implications. First, consumer culture can only be understood by reference to the *institutions* of consumption, to shops and shopping malls, consumer magazines, and advertisements. The pleasures of consumption are, in fact, social pleasures. This was particularly important for feminists, who could thus rescue the woman's activity of shopping – and window shopping – from the condescension of cultural theorists, and for SUBCULTURE theorists, who argued that consumption was the site on which the "active" consumer transformed a commodity into a SYMBOL of "resistance." This related to the second argument: as culture, consumption is a symbolic practice; it has to be interpreted. Its aesthetic value is not, as Frankfurt scholars would have it (see W.F. Haug, 1986) simply the effect of a manipulative advertising industry, but also depends on consumers' ability to read and *enjoy* aesthetic SIGNS. For consumer culture, the form, the packaging, is as meaningful as the content, what is packaged.

This argument reflected the influence of POSTMODERNISM and, in particular, Jean BAUDRILLARD's critique of the Marxist theory of use value, and marked, in political terms, a shift of focus from the social relations of production to the social relations of consumption. This is turn reflected the impact of the NEW RIGHT on the theoretical agenda. The implication of the term "consumer culture" was the social identity articulated in the marketplace, in the organization of taste, and not, as Marx had argued, in the workplace, in the organization of labor. "Consumer culture" was thus an attempt to conceptualize from the left the new social map being drawn by advertisers and market researchers in terms of demographics and "lifestyle." People are what they eat, and the critical task was to understand consumption. "Consumer culture" turned out, however, to be more useful as a rhetorical than an analytical device. To use the term was to gesture slyly at one's own joy in shopping (and to signal one's agreement that "CLASS" was a limited concept); it was not, though, a concept that was properly tested in research, and by the end of the 1980s it seemed as dated an idea as an old Levi's 501 advertisement.

Reading
Baudrillard, Jean 1972: *For a Critique of the Political Economy of the Sign.*
Haug, W.F. 1986: *Critique of Commodity Aesthetics.*
Lee, Martyn J. 1993: *Consumer Culture Reborn: The Cultural Politics of Consumption.*

SIMON FRITH

contemporary Indian historiography *See* SUBALTERN STUDIES

content analysis Content analysis was developed as a research tool by early sociologists of the mass media, primarily for comparative purposes – its first use seems to have been in pre-1914 American studies of newspaper coverage of foreign affairs. It is a quantitative methodology which depends on two problematic assumptions: first, that one can readily distinguish verbal (or other) SIGNS in a TEXT from the reading "context"; second, that such content can be measured "objectively" – that different readers faced with the same text would "measure" the same content. That said, media "content" may take a variety of forms, and content analysis was influentially used, for example, in FRANKFURT SCHOOL studies of American popular songs and magazines (see Peatman and Lowenthal, 1942–3). While this quantitative approach has been discredited (cultural theorists are now much more attuned to the *active* and *subjective* interpretation of pop texts) the underlying assumption about standardization has not, and content analysis is still employed in most arguments about media bias and media effects (see, for example, the work of the Glasgow University Media Group or the debate on television violence).

Reading
Docherty, David 1990: *Violence in Television Fiction.*
Glasgow University Media Group 1976: *Bad News.*
Lowenthal, Leo 1942–3: "Biographies in popular magazines."
Peatman, J.G. 1942–3: "Radio and popular music."

SIMON FRITH

content, manifest/latent *See* MANIFEST/LATENT CONTENT

contradiction Two types of contradiction may be distinguished: (i) formal, *logical contradiction*, or the simultaneous assertion and negation of any proposition; (ii) *dialectical contradiction*, variously conceived within the Hegelian and Marxist traditions – such as inclusive real oppositions (for example, between the forces and relations of production). The compatibility of (ii) with (i) has been endlessly debated.
See also HEGELIANISM; MARXISM.

Reading
Bhaskar, R. 1993: *Dialectic: The Pulse of Freedom.*
Colletti, L. 1975: "Marxism and the dialectic."
Lukács, G. 1923 (*1971b*): *History and Class Consciousness.*

GREGORY ELLIOTT

counterculture A term developed in the 1960s (see Roszak, 1970) to make sense of the spectacular new youth and student subcultures and, in particular, the American hippie. The term, as Musgrove (1974) points out, had two uses. On the one hand, it described what Richard Neville (1970) called "play power," a set of ideas, beliefs, and values that opposed the dominant culture (which, in this context, meant capitalism, protestantism, and militarism); counterculturalists valued the spiritual over the material, hedonism over prudence, tolerance over prejudice. "Counterculture" referred, on the other hand, to a group of people, those people who because of their different ideas refused to live in "straight" society and "dropped out" of it. The counterculture thus described both new social practices – drug use, "free" sex, nondirective education, etc. – and the institutions that supported these practices – communes, alternative newspapers and magazines, free schools, "underground" festivals, etc. The counterculture is usually thought to have dissolved in the 1970s, the victim of its own contradictory attitudes (to technology and materialism), its internal differences (about sexual politics or drug (ab)use, for instance), and systematic legal harassment. Nevertheless, its values and, to some extent, its "alternative" institutions live on, whether in the symbolic form of a Grateful Dead concert or in the activities of the New Age Travelers.

Reading
Musgrove, Frank 1974: *Ecstasy and Holiness. Counter Culture and the Open Society.*
Neville, Richard 1970: *Play Power.*

Roszak, Theodore 1968 (*1971*): *The Making of a Counter Culture*.

SIMON FRITH

countertransference   *See* TRANSFERENCE (COUNTER)

Critical Inquiry   In 1974 Sheldon Sacks founded *Critical Inquiry*, a quarterly publication from the University of Chicago Press, and gave it the subtitle: "a voice for reasoned inquiry into significant creations of the human spirit." Later issues omit this subtitle, but the journal's goal remains the same; *Critical Inquiry* is a pluralistic journal concerned with CRITICAL THEORIES of vastly diverse range and origin. As the current editor W.J.T. Mitchell wrote in 1982, *Critical Inquiry* should not be considered "aimless eclecticism;" the journal blends its own brand of pluralism in an attempt to provoke and mediate arguments in numerous areas of critical thought. Mitchell labels the practice "dialectical pluralism," which "insists on pushing divergent theories and practices toward confrontation and dialogue." The goal, by Mitchell's admission, is idealistic and never actually realized. In practice, however, *Critical Inquiry* provides the next best alternative: an intriguing sequence of debates among distinguished scholars. Its one downfall is that the writing is often distractingly intellectual and plagued with academic jargon.

Every issue contains essays by internationally known writers: Frank KERMODE, Jacques DERRIDA, Stanley FISH, and Michel FOUCAULT appear alongside M.H. Abrams, Donald DAVIDSON, and Catherine Stimpson. While the editors of *Critical Inquiry* are always pleased to discover unknown, younger contributors, ultimately the journal reflects the current work of its elite contributors. In his 1982 piece on critical inquiry and the state of criticism, Mitchell offers a "confession:" "because we regard their work as barometric, we sometimes print essays by famous writers which do not come up to our normal standards." In other words, in an attempt to accurately convey the current scene of criticism, the editors often print articles by well-known writers, "even when we do not think that they are up to much good."

Critical Inquiry has responded to the evolution of critical theory by devoting issues, either in part or in full, to PSYCHOANALYSIS, feminism, and the politics of interpretation (to name a few) and by printing papers from conferences on metaphor and narrative. Occasionally the editors publish a group of articles under a common heading; for example, Seamus Heaney and Joyce Carol Oates have contributed to the "Artists on Art" sections of separate issues. In 1986 Mitchell added a section called "Books of Critical Interest." Perhaps the most interesting section of the journal is one labeled "Critical Response," which appears in nearly every issue. Here writers respond to previous articles, and the resulting debates can span several issues. But dialogue between critics is not restricted to this section. One of the long-running debates began in the Summer 1982 issue with Steven Knapp and Walter Benn Michael's article "Against theory" and ended in March 1985 with a special section (three articles) on "Pragmatism and literary theory;" the entire dialog has been collected and published in a book, *Against Theory: Literary Studies and the New Pragmatism*.

Now part its twentieth anniversary, *Critical Inquiry* continues its distinguished reputation for its attention to critical thought.

TARA G. GILLIGAN

critical theory   In the strict sense, critical theory is the interdisciplinary project announced by Max HORKHEIMER and practiced by members of the FRANKFURT SCHOOL and their successors, whereby the ENLIGHTENMENT ideal of a CIVIL SOCIETY might be achieved by bringing scientific research to bear on MARX's theory of social change. In a looser sense, critical theory is now a more general term, under which research projects in the social sciences and/or humanities attempt to bring truth and political engagement into alignment. In both senses, critical theory is an offspring of the Kantian tradition of thought that prizes self-knowledge (see KANT and NEO-KANTIANISM).

The most useful, succinct elaboration of these definitions of critical theory has been proposed by Raymond Geuss (1981, pp. 1–2):

1. Critical theories have special standing as guides for human action in that:
    (a) they are aimed at producing enlightenment in the agents who hold them, i.e. at enabling those agents to determine what their true interests are;
    (b) they are inherently emancipatory, i.e. they free agents from a kind of

coercion which is at least partly self-imposed. . . .

2. Critical theories have cognitive content, i.e. they are forms of knowledge.
3. Critical theories differ epistemologically in essential ways from theories in the natural sciences. Theories in natural science are objectifying; critical theories are reflective.

Critical theory bravely, but perhaps quixotically, persists in confronting a recurring chain of skeptical epistemological questions: Do truth and goodness relate to each other and if so how? Do the fruits of knowledge embody a desire for moral action or a temptation to ethical and legal violation? If knowledge of the good does not lead to the good, what good, then, is knowledge?

A tempting, facile escape from these perennial questions is simply to bracket them and set them aside by claiming that a particular research project is not designed to deal with the ethical and/or political implications of its results. However uncertain and tentative its achievements, critical theory, nevertheless, gives the highest importance to self-criticism; to marking the ethical/political position from which one works in order that such a position can be available for examination by critical readers or other reflective audiences; to the recognition that knowledge constitutes power; and to the conviction that the supposedly amoral and apolitical position is also *a position* that requires critical reflection. Geuss's definition of critical theory, outlined above, recognizes that not all forms of knowledge assume this self-reflexive responsibility.

Reading
Geuss, Raymond 1981: *The Idea of a Critical Theory: Habermas & the Frankfurt School.*
Hoy, David Couzens, and McCarthy, Thomas 1994: *Critical Theory.*
Norris, Christopher 1991: *Spinoza and the Origins of Modern Critical Theory.*

MICHAEL PAYNE

criticism, bolekaja *See* BOLEKAJA CRITICISM

criticism, feminist *See* FEMINIST CRITICISM

criticism, linguistic *See* LINGUISTIC CRITICISM

criticism, literary *See* LITERARY CRITICISM

criticism, Marxist *See* MARXISM AND MARXIST CRITICISM

criticism, moral *See* MORAL CRITICISM

Criticism, New *See* NEW CRITICISM

criticism, nuclear *See* NUCLEAR CRITICISM

criticism, patristic *See* PATRISTIC CRITICISM

criticism, practical *See* PRACTICAL CRITICISM

criticism, psychoanalytic *See* PSYCHOANALYSIS AND PSYCHOANALYTIC CRITICISM

criticism, reader-response *See* READER-RESPONSE CRITICISM

Culler, Jonathan (1944–) American commentator on STRUCTURALISM and its relations with DECONSTRUCTION and POSTSTRUCTURALISM. His work on these movements stems from his own engagement with the condition of literary scholarship in the late twentieth century. He utilizes structuralism and what follows it as a means of revitalizing literary critical practice, which he sees as a discipline in and of itself. Structuralism provides him with the means to do so, since it is concerned with the exposition of fundamental meanings.

Reading
Culler, Jonathan 1973: "The linguistic basis of structuralism."
—— 1975 (*1989*): *Structuralist Poetics.*

PAUL INNES

cultural anthropology Although the following generalization will be modified further on, at the outset one can say that cultural anthropology is that branch of anthropology devoted to the study of CULTURE. What is culture? Although there are legions of definitions (as a beginning, see Kroeber and Kluckhohn, 1950), culture is what makes, for example, Navajos similar to each other and different from Cherokees. We humans are not the only species that engages in cultural behavior, but ours is the only species that has come to depend on culture as the principal means by which we adapt to our environment, get along with each other, and survive.

All species other than humans base their adaptation on a genetic inheritance of programmed behavior and capabilities. Although the human capability for culture is also biologically founded, humans pass down their lifeways – strategies for collective survival – not through the genes, but through teaching each new generation of children the lifeway of parents. Is it important that humans have chosen a system based on teaching rather than genes for adaptation? Yes. Culture is the reason why our single species occupies more niches – from tundra to the tropics, the forest to the desert, the mountains to the plains – than any other species. (There is an exception to this: certain species, such as fleas and body lice have made the human body their habitat. Where we go, they go, so their geographic distribution is as extensive as ours.) The reason why the same species that lives in sweltering heat can also live in subzero climates is that humans in cold climates have cultures that teach them how to make warm clothes and tightly sealed, well-insulated houses. Simply put, culture has been, for humans, an adaptational breakthrough of unparalleled magnitude. It is the most successful means of biological adaptation the earth has ever witnessed; it is why humans put other species in zoos, aquaria, and conservatories and not the other way around.

The basis of cultural anthropolgy is a question that has very likely intrigued every human society, past and present: why do peoples behave differently from one group to another? To the observing group, the cultural ways of alien peoples look at least strange, and perhaps illogical, perhaps primitive, perhaps morally wrong. In the mid-nineteenth century the confluence of POSITIVISM, the spreading belief that the natural world is the product of orderly, discoverable forces, and the emergence of systematic investigative methods became the preconditions on which an anthropology could be invented.

In order to answer this question (why do peoples behave differently) a concept was needed which could serve as a tool for thinking about these behavioral differences. The concept was culture, which came together in a workable form around 1860 (see Lowie, 1937). Three critical aspects of culture were identified: (i) that culture was manifested in behaviors – customs – that are patterned and shared, (ii) that cultural behaviors are learned from society, not biologically inherited, and (iii) that cultural behaviors are arranged into what E.B. Tylor called "a complex whole." A fourth feature, adopted more slowly, is that culture consists of "shared ideas"; thus, behaviors and artifacts are not culture themselves, but are reflections and products of those shared ideas. Cultural anthropology emerged as the enterprise for studying culture, conducted by professionals who identify themselves and each other as anthropologists, who maintain ways to communicate and debate, and who are conversant with a common toolkit of concepts, terms, and methods.

By 1900, especially under the influence of Franz BOAS, anthropology in the United States had adopted the view that culture could be best researched by approaching it within four general subfields, only one of which was cultural anthropology, archaeology, and linguistics. In Europe cultural anthropology comprises the direct field study of living societies and the analysis of the data gathered in those field studies. There it is usually called "social anthropology" and maintains little contact with the other subfields, seeing itself as more akin to sociology. In the United States, however, four-field collaboration achieved a kind of orthodoxy that dominated the enterprise until about 1960 and still enjoys substantial loyalty today.

The specific subject matter of cultural anthropology seems to be as diverse as human behavior and interest. Specialized groups, often with their own publications and computer networks, cover such widely focused cultural domains as kinship, EDUCATION, medicine, psychological issues, economics, work, ECOLOGY, language, feminist studies, innumerable regional and cultural zones, computers, tourism, migration, herding societies, fishing societies, human rights, indigenous knowledge, and on and on. There is too a family of efforts focused on how indigenous societies classify and organize domains of knowledge, such as botanical resources ("ethnobotany"), medicinal remedies ("ethnomedicine"), and astronomical phenomena ("ethnoastronomy").

Cultural Anthropology as a Science Cultural anthropology has, since the time of BOAS, understood itself as a would-be science. Thus the stated goals of cultural anthropologists were to gather and rely on primary data collected in a rigorous and systematic manner, to test hypotheses against the data, to assume that cultural behavior was the product of discoverable cause and effect relationships, and to seek reliable, nonobvious predictions about culture. Yet a fully scientific study of culture has never been achieved. Mainly this is due to the intangible nature of culture, the ethical framework that constrains experimentation with a people's lives, and the fact that cultures are, to a significant degree, one of a kind.

Further realities constrain the goal as a science. Field research in cultural anthropology relies heavily on what can be called "the rapport bridge." Quality data on much of culture has to come from the people who practice it. That information is only made available when trusting relationships exist between them and the ethnographer. Usually this takes the form of mutual friendship. In any other science, personal relationships interposed between investigator and data are anathema, casting doubt on the objectivity of the data obtained. The "double-blind" experimental technique that is insisted upon in much research physiology and psychology illustrates the efforts made to eliminate the personal linkage. In cultural anthropology, however, eliminating personal relationships blocks access to the data.

Another unusual feature of cultural anthropology has been the conviction that a culture can most thoroughly be understood when the anthropologist sees the society not only as an outside observer, but also from the "inside" – through the world view of a native. These two viewpoints are commonly referred to as the "emic" (external) and "etic" (inside) systems. In this author's view, how one explains epistemologically the need for the emic view has always been somewhat vague. Perhaps it is because most cultural behaviors make little sense until one know the (emic) meaning to the participants. Just why the chicken is killed is not very clear until one has heard the people doing the killing, and, moreover, understood the way in which the chicken and the killing look within their larger scheme of things. This seems to be true even when you conclude that although people say the chicken dies to obey the gods, you find it is because there are too many chickens.

Thus the discipline's claim to be a science is compromised. Cultural anthropologists do not design

experiments, most field researches cannot be replicated elsewhere, each culture as a unit of study is substantially unique, one consciously seeks to build a personal, value-laden relationship between the investigator and the data, and the emic, inside view is usually sought. Mostly these divergences are necessary entailments for the study of culture, but they also mean that cultural anthropology's claim to be a science falls somewhat short.

Nonscience Models Cultural anthropology's self-image as a science has, in recent decades, come to be joined by alternative self-images. For example, the humanist anthropologists have argued that there is no way to be certain that the anthropologist's rendition of a culture depicts something objectively real. Consequently the humanists appear to argue that culture is better experienced than analyzed. Sociobiology, MATERIALISM, STRUCTURALISM, feminism, and other bounded frameworks also tend to modify in their own ways an exclusively scientific model of cultural anthropology.

The association of anthropology with the humanities has always been important. The study of cultural symbolism and its expression in RITUAL and ART has a lineage that moves from Frazer's *Golden Bough* to LÉVI-STRAUSS's *Raw and the Cooked*, to Turner's *Anthropology of Performance*. The common ground with the humanities lies not only with the narrative and performance, but also with the essentially introspective mode of discovery that characterizes much of both endeavors.

Another, newer variety of cultural anthropology responds to a widening change in the anthropologist's relationship to indigenous societies, where much of the fieldwork is done. With the flourishing of ethnic pride, these societies typically insist on having a deciding and often managerial role in what information will be gathered and what will be done with it. Advancing a science of culture is not usually high on their agenda. Cultural anthropologists find that the indigenous society is now a full partner in the venture. In these circumstances the criterion for research is not theory testing, but its usefulness to the host society. As a result, primary fieldwork among today's indigenous societies is increasingly a collaborative matter, and the old division between "pure" and "applied" cultural anthropology is no longer clear.

It is important not to leave the impression that all cultural anthropology entails a field study of an indigenous society. That is false. Particularly since the 1930s, cultural anthropologists have studied a steadily widening range of societies and social groupings, including peasant villages, towns, cities, factories, schools, hospitals, work groups, impoverished urbanites, comfortable suburbanites, and countless others. On the whole, groups remain as accessible as ever. Thus cultural theory testing will have ample research sites, though interpretation is more difficult when only a part of a larger culture is in view.

In addition, a major part of cultural anthropology's work does not depend on new field data. Much analysis is done using cultural examples already in hand. Over the past 130 years anthropologists have documented to a large extent perhaps 3,000 cultural cases whose information lies in library volumes, data bases, and other sorts of reports. The analysis of cultural principles using multiple cases simultaneously is called ethnology, and given the accumulation of cultural data already in hand, ethnology would have a long future even were no further data gathered.

Findings   Those seeking to look at specific findings and questions being pursued by cultural and other types of anthropologists may find the well-indexed *Annual Review of Anthropology*, now in its twenty-third year, a rewarding place to start. Periodicals, such as the British journal, *Man*, the French journal, *L'Homme*, the Swiss journal, *Anthropos*, the Mexican journal, *America Indigena*, and the American journals, *American Anthropologist* and *American Ethnologist*, will be found to be sources of current cultural research and debate, and entry-points to the vastly larger intellectual endeavor called cultural anthropology.

After some 130 years of professional work, anthropologists have found that the cultural concept remains a central anchorage to the discipline. The working definitions of culture continue to be diverse and not always mutually compatible, reflecting the intrinsic difficulty which human social behavior poses for those who would explain and predict it. Some anthropologists eschew the concept altogether. Yet the question that founded the discipline (why do peoples behave differently?) remains as relevant today as it did in the discipline's infancy, and culture remains the most productive concept for answering it. Beyond that question, culture is important in its own right: it remains the singular attribute that has accorded our species an unrivaled success among the earth's biological populace. Culture also presents us with unique dangers, giving our species

the capability to destroy each other at genocidal levels, to inflict cruelty with satisfaction, and to limit the life chances of vast numbers of our fellow humans. Culture remains arguably the most important aspect for us to know more about. Central to that investigation is cultural anthropology.

Reading

Fox, Richard G. 1991: *Recapturing Anthropology*.
Honigmann, John J. 1973: *Handbook of Social and Cultural Anthropology*.
Kroeber, Alfred L. and Kluckhohn, Clyde 1952 (*1963*): *Culture: A Critical Review of Concepts and Definitions*.
Lowie, Robert H. 1937: *The History of Ethnological Theory*.
Turner, Victor W. 1986: *The Anthropology of Performance*.

THOMAS C. GREAVES

cultural materialism   A critical approach which developed in Britain during the late 1970s and 1980s, cultural materialism is difficult to pin down as a theoretical and analytical concept. This is partly because it is often used in a polemical or descriptive rather than conceptual way. There is clearly a link between "cultural," "dialectical," and "historical" materialism, and "cultural materialism" is allied to MARXISM, although often implicitly rather than explicitly. It is also hard to define because the concept itself depends on both the tension between and the breakdown of its constituent terms – "culture" and "materialism," or rather, material forces – in ways which change the meanings of both. Thus the concept is materialist in that it suggests that cultural artifacts, institutions, and practices are in some sense determined by "material" processes; culturalist in its insistence that there is no crude material reality beyond culture – that culture is itself a material practice. To a certain extent, then, cultural materialism hangs on a PARADOX: culture is itself material, yet there is always a further, shadowy, material reality that lies beyond it, and from which it derives its meaning. In this way cultural materialism runs the risk of mimicking the very idealism it seeks to repudiate. Moreover, as Raymond Williams pointed out in "Problems of materialism" (repr. in Williams, 1980), "materialism" is itself an implicitly metaphysical abstraction, and the concept of "the material" itself is constantly shifting. In its repudiation of mysticism and idealism, materialism has tended to be connected with radical political projects, but it is not inherently radical and there are clearly dangers in linking "frozen material laws" with particular political strategies.

Cultural materialism was first developed as a description of his own method as much as a critical term by Raymond Williams, who clearly placed his work within a Marxist political and intellectual tradition in his later writings, although wishing to avoid the rigid and formulaic concepts of materialism mentioned above. Cultural materialism develops out of historical materialism, but, like other critiques of "classic" Marxism, is critical of its economic determinism, and in particular of the hierarchical division between "BASE" and "SUPERSTRUCTURE," whereby political institutions, cultural forms, and social practices are seen as reflecting and being ultimately governed by economic forces and relationships. In his essay "Base and superstructure in Marxist cultural theory" (repr. in Williams, 1980), Williams emphasized the need to see the "base" as much as the "superstructure" as a process embodying different kinds of relationships rather than as an unchanging structure. He stressed the importance of developing a theory of power and IDEOLOGY that can encompass a range of forms of production and reproduction. Why, he suggests, should the pianist be seen as less productive than the piano maker?

Cultural materialism maintains that any theory of culture (not only Marxist) that presumes a distinction between "art" and "society" or "literature" and "background" is denying that culture – its methods of production, its forms, institutions, and kinds of consumption – is central to society. Cultural forms should never be seen as isolated texts but as embedded within the historical and material relationships and processes which formed them, and within which they play an essential part. Williams's argument, that means of communication are themselves means of production rather than subordinate to some more "real" primary process, is crucial to this analysis. Human communication (whether it be "natural" forms such as speech, song, dance, drama, or the technological media) is itself socially productive as much as re-productive; moreover, it parallels other kinds of productive processes. These technologies of cultural production play a crucial part in shaping cultural forms and institutions, but do not determine them. A more nuanced and intricate theory of power is necessary to understand the ways in which dominant meanings and identities are produced, by state institutions, religious beliefs, education, and the media, and how they are contested or assimilated by subordinate and appositional groups. Williams

developed his analysis of both the selective tradition and DOMINANT, RESIDUAL, and EMERGENT cultures to encompass this.

Cultural materialist analysis developing from Williams's work has tended to elaborate the latter aspects of his theories, and to emphasize processes of institutional cultural power in the shaping of identities rather than focusing on material production in the narrower sense, drawing on ALTHUSSER's theory of IDEOLOGY, GRAMSCI's conception of HEGEMONY, and FOUCAULT's definition of power. It has, moreover, tended to move again toward interpretation of specific TEXTS, concentrating on the role they play in forming an English literary tradition and a dominant English national identity. This is partly because of the institutional conditions within which this work is taking place – within English literature departments of universities. Cultural materialism has recently been self-consciously developed in Britain to denote a more "political" counterpoint to NEW HISTORICISM in the United States, both tendencies focusing on Shakespeare and the Renaissance. In fact there is a considerable degree of overlap between the two tendencies, and although they have been developed in distinct institutional conditions, it is artificial to draw too firm a line between them. During the late 1980s and early 1990s a spate of debates on "the Shakespeare industry" appeared in British journals and more widely in the press, exploring the role that "Shakespeare" played not as an individual but as a cultural institution, continually produced and reproduced from a CANONICAL selective tradition as the centerpiece of the English literary heritage and in the light of contemporary notions of political legitimacy. Critics of this work complained that its account of cultural power was too monolithic, that it did not adequately address the contradictions in Shakespeare, but saw his plays as the passive bearers of the dominant ideology.

In fact most cultural materialist criticism has stressed the ways in which TEXTS contain the seeds of opposition to the dominant structures they embody; they certainly do not see all canonical texts as straightforwardly complicit with the powers of the state, then or now. The analysis of cultural power depends on acknowledging its potency, its ability to speak to audiences in different historical situations, though not in a timeless way. Many of Shakespeare's plays, particularly those set in historical and Roman times, have been reframed in various specific situations to legitimize the exercise of state violence. However this does not mean that the inherent meaning of all his work is to condone such violence or that it cannot form a part of very different agendas or inspire oppositional and alternative meanings: the British trade union leader Tom Mann was much given to quoting *Henry V*. Indeed, as Jonathan Dollimore, Alan Sinfield, Catherine Belsey, and Kathleen McCluskie have maintained, the stress has increasingly been on the subversive and dissident power of oppositional and marginal groups to reread and remake texts, shifting the emphasis from WRITING and production in the original situation to reproduction and reading and the ideological contexts in which this takes place now.

Although many of the most explicit examples of cultural materialist criticism have been in RENAISSANCE STUDIES, there is also a substantial body of work on eighteenth and nineteenth-century writing which develops a much longer history of Marxist and materialist criticism of the novel: the work of Georg LUKÁCS, Ralph Fox, and Arnold Kettle, as well as Raymond WILLIAMS and contemporary literary theory. Ian Watt's important work on the rise of the novel has been developed by critics such as Michael McKeon and Terry Lovell, while John Goode and Peter Widdowson have analyzed the ways in which Thomas Hardy and George Gissing were both situated in and contesting late nineteenth-century ideologies and forms of LITERARY PRODUCTION. FEMINIST CRITICISM, too, has taken up and expanded Virginia WOOLF's argument in *A Room of One's Own* (1926) that it is material conditions which enable women to write, and that the development of the novel is dependent on this gendered material and ideological possibilities and constraints.

See also DOMINANT/RESIDUAL/EMERGENT; NEW HISTORICISM; WILLIAMS, RAYMOND.

Reading

Belsey, Catherine 1985: *The Subject of Tragedy: Identity and Difference in Renaissance Drama.*
Dollimore, Jonathan, and Sinfield, Alan, eds 1985: *Political Shakespeare.*
Drakakis, John, ed. 1985: *Alternative Shakespeares.*
Lovell, Terry 1985: *Consuming Fiction.*
Sinfield, Alan 1992: *Faultlines: Cultural Materialism and the Politics of Dissident Reading.*
Williams, Raymond 1961: *The Long Revolution.*
——1980: *Problems in Materialism and Culture.*
——1981: *Culture.*

JENNY BOURNE TAYLOR

cultural studies   A diverse body of work from different locations concerned with the critical analysis of cultural forms and processes in contemporary and near-contemporary societies.

There is no stable or single version of "cultural studies," any more than there is of "English" or the other familiar self-proclaimed academic "subjects." Instead the provenance and purposes of work in cultural studies have in important ways been various and context-specific. Currently, work is being initiated and carried forward in disparate locations and academic circumstances despite the increased visibility of work grouped together as cultural studies in globalized academic publishing. Consequently any narrative of the "development" of cultural studies (particularly if it stresses founding "fathers" or places) tends to be misleadingly overcoherent, though since new ventures require myths of origins, references to, for example, a "Birmingham school" have acquired their own momentum and significance. In fact, despite the plethora of such narratives (which this version will not escape), self-questioning about intellectual and political purposes and appropriate academic (or extra-academic) locations for the work have been among the few consistent features of analyses now widely recognized for their intellectual vitality and their questioning of existing frames – even though the term "cultural studies" itself was first used only in the 1960s. Of the various attempts to regroup intellectual fields since then (WOMEN's, black and peace STUDIES are other examples), cultural studies, drawing on the polysemy attached to "CULTURE" itself, has been a notable survivor, attractive for many and perhaps contradictory reasons.

One set of circumstances for work later called cultural studies arose in Britain and some other countries during the 1950s and after. They included the personal experiences of various people whose own lifetimes and education entailed migrations across different cultural borders and worlds; developments in postwar societies resulting in considerable cultural change and innovation; and the inadequacy of existing academic disciplines to take account of either. Little work was being done on marked and visible cultural differences which (despite predictions of "embourgoisement") included class and regional differences, new forms of POPULAR CULTURE, youth cultures, "COUNTERCULTURE"; little either on the pervasive newer forms of media, advertising, and music put into circulation through the "cultural" or "consciousness" industries. Sociology in its prevailing British and North American versions was typically policy-led, quantitative and positivist. The study of literatures and languages was engaged with the close reading of particular TEXTS but little with work outside the "CANON," with what later became known as "theory," or with contemporary developments. Wider intellectual engagements were unusual so that MARXISM, for example, was known only in easily devalued "economistic" terms.

New intellectual interests were thus marked out with difficulty. A generation of quite different writers (compare for instance BARTHES in France with HOGGART in England) had to discover a new way of working as they moved, unevenly and in stages, away from the hostile and despairing treatment of contemporary culture found in the ahistorical work of American NEW CRITICISM, in the comprehensive but later embittered questioning of F.R. LEAVIS, or in the only partly known and rigorously bleak work of the FRANKFURT SCHOOL. Raymond WILLIAMS produced in a variety of articles, books, and journalism wide-ranging analyses of culture and cultural history, which were guardedly optimistic about new forms of media, while making astute political connections from his position as a founder of the New Left and self-described Welsh European socialist. Richard Hoggart wrote about the threatened strengths of working-class culture in Yorkshire and established at Birmingham the CENTRE FOR CONTEMPORARY CULTURAL STUDIES, whose members, including Stuart HALL and many others, began to publish on youth culture, media, education, and on theories and methods in the new areas. By the 1980s much energy, in difficult conditions, had produced a body of material which in Britain, and increasingly in some former countries of the Commonwealth and the USA, could be seen to have marked out a distinctive space and way of working for cultural studies.

The phrase "culture is ordinary" used by Williams in 1958 (see Gray and McGuigan, 1993) made a political claim against the exclusions of "selective traditions" of culture. His writing suggested that culture understood as meanings in negotiation is found in all kinds of "texts," across different sites and institutions and throughout everyday life. If ADORNO and others had observed the fractures between HIGH and POPULAR CULTURE (Schoenberg and Hollywood film as the "torn halves of an integral freedom" to which they did not add

up), Williams recalled that culture could mean cultivation and growth, and argued for the democratic extension of culture as a shared work and common space. The agenda set for the study of culture thus became extremely wide, challenging the restrictions implicit in the divisions of academic organization and knowledge production. It also became contentious in both questioning judgments of cultural quality and its political engagement. By the end of the 1960s many different political events and movements led to a view of culture not as outside politics, nor as part of an organic (LEAVIS) or functionalist (Parsons) view of society, but as a site of conflict and struggle. Contemporary initiatives (for example, from the black and women's movements) in "cultural politics" claimed political possibilities in cultural activity in ways unrecognized by the labor movement and either the social democratic or communist left. Because cultural analysis would include social and political dimensions, making connections across academic boundaries, the way was quickly opened for challenges offered by rediscovered traditions of Marxist thought.

The impulses behind cultural analysis were thus and have remained a mixture of the intellectual, the personal, and the political. Typical work (for example, Williams (1961), Hall et al. (1978), Coward (1984), Gilroy (1987)) was exploratory and eclectic, addressing new objects of study and creating new kinds of analyses. While very different sites of culture were examined (from working-class or youth culture to political DISCOURSES, from the cultures of schools and workplaces to those of shopping and consumerism, from versions of the national culture to "ENTERPRISE CULTURE," from the cultural forms of DIASPORA to those of lesbian sexuality), their analysis has often been explicitly committed, with distinctively personal, autobiographical, evaluative, and political dimensions, rather than laying claim to canons of science or objectivity. Studies have also unevenly combined various drawings or raids upon disparate bodies of theoretical work with a grounded, concrete attention to particular cultural forms and situations.

If any one theme can be distinguished in the first phase of cultural studies, it is that of culture as the site of negotiation, conflict, innovation, and resistance within the social relations of societies dominated by power and fractured by divisions of GENDER, CLASS, and "RACE." Though specific analyses gave different weight to moments of domination or subordination, cultural forms and processes were seen as dynamic forces and not as secondary to or predictable from institutional forms or political and economic organization and decisions. Close study of cultural forms went alongside and contributed decisively to a larger account of contemporary societies, informed by social theories any by the perceptions of a political stance. Various forms of Marxism, with a particular stress on class divisions, the state, domination, and the workings of IDEOLOGY, underpinned much important work (for example, that of Stuart Hall). However, since Marxism, though concerned with struggle, typically did not recognize a category of culture (beyond that of class consciousness) the work of later Marxists, VOLOSHINOV for his theory of language, semiotic struggle, and "multiaccentuality," and GRAMSCI for his account of HEGEMONY, have been highly influential.

Later work from the women's movement delivered a critique of the gender-blindness of Marxism, forcefully establishing the centrality of PATRIARCHY and gender divisions within cultural analysis (see, for example, Franklin et al. (1991)). By the 1980s, in both Britain and North America, questions of racism and anti-racism, migration and diaspora were also profoundly important politically and in the political analysis of culture (CCCS (1982). At present a heightened attention to issues arising from globalization, reinforced by POSTMODERNISM, further extends an already complex social analysis whose key terms (ideology, the state, gender, class, "race") have to be both thought and used alongside each other and carefully questioned.

Cultural forms have themselves been studied within a giddying acceleration of theoretical and "methodological" PARADIGMS. While some semiological work has seemed to remain text-bound and perhaps spuriously scientific, it has drawn attention to languages and procedures of representation. That meaning is constructed through language is illuminated powerfully both in work on discourse in critical linguistics and in FOUCAULT's work on forms of knowledge and power. Quite other dimensions of culture such as subjectivity, fantasy, and sexuality have been broached through the difficult terrain of psychoanalytic thought. Even so, there are other areas of culture where an adequate language of analysis is still to be found (for example, music) or where work has hardly begun (for example, religion).

The characteristic object of cultural studies is,

however, neither a theoretical commentary strengthened by cultural references nor a particular form of culture, but a cultural process or moment, analyzed for particular purposes and in a specific place and time. Culture is located neither in texts, nor as the outcome of its production, nor only in the cultural resources, appropriations, and innovations of lived everyday worlds, but in different forms of sense making, within various settings, in societies incessantly marked by change and conflict. Culture is neither institutions nor genres nor behavior but complex interactions between all of these. It has been the decisive contribution to cultural studies of ethnographies, participant observation, interviewing, and the study of lived worlds to show, for example, that however sophisticated may be the cultural study of a text, a policy, an ideology, or discourse, a form is used, reworked, and transformed by different groups in ways unpredictable from formal analysis. This is true of how media are taken up, selectively used, and explained (see ENCODING/DECODING), the ways in which school pupils or a workforce construct their experiences, the selective appropriations or innovations which people make of discourses, ideologies, and various cultural forms in their daily lives. In this important area work has differed in both approach and interpretation. There are various kinds of subtle and theoretically informed textual analysis, and other studies dealing with the complexities and challenges of observation and interviews. By either route, stress has been laid differently upon, say, the degree of closure brought about through ideologies disseminated through dominant forces of production or upon the potentiality of spaces for creativity and resistance (itself a problematic but important term in cultural studies work). The work of Willis, Radway, and Fiske typifies a divergence of empirical focus, the theoretical working of material, and in the complex mix of resources brought to bear on what is done and how it is written, including questions about the intended audience or constituencies for such work.

There issues are inextricably linked with the locations in and from which cultural studies can be carried out. The new work necessarily sustained a critique of the "disciplines" whose limits brought the exploration and innovation into being. If the now professionalized disciplines of higher education valuably included a concentration upon distinctive objects of knowleddge, core concepts and productive ways of working, they also erected hierarchies and boundaries. Issues may be first considered from a disciplinary background but their pursuit may lead elsewhere. One model for this work has been that of collaboration between those trained in different disciplines, producing (as in the Birmingham Centre) group work and joint authorship which proved to be supportive, valuable in its outcomes, and a challenge to the competitive individualism of some parts of the academy. Some of the best-known texts in this field have resulted from joint work, and in future this may include collaboration between teaching and research staff and students working in different parts of the world. There has also been some debate and ambivalence about whether universities are the only or best place in which to pursue cultural studies. Williams saw the work as rooted in the adult education wing of the labor movement, others have tried to develop networks, alliances, and dialogs with other groups. While 30 years ago academics were sometimes found commenting and writing in the media, there has now been some lessening of the possibilities in the West for debates in a public sphere. All this forms part of a contradiction, of which those working in cultural studies are aware, between the development of a critical space, open as wide as possible, and the necessity to work somewhere in the university while developing connections and dialogues elsewhere as circumstances permit.

The characteristic divide between humanities and social sciences is particularly obstructive to cultural studies, which seeks to understand meanings as they are made, exchanged, and developed within wider social relations. Cultural studies within literature departments, instead of questioning the whole disciplinary formation, run some danger of being appropriated within schools of "theory" or, perversely, of being confined to "popular" and extracanonical WRITING. Opportunities seem to be wider in the study of foreign cultures, or in area studies (including American and Russian studies, while the British Council appears to see cultural studies in Britain as part of "British" studies) where the restrictions of literature, language, and institutions may be remapped in cultural studies. Meanwhile in the social sciences it has always been clear that cultural studies are wider and other than media studies, but there are important moves in both media and communication studies towards a dialog with more qualitative work in which media cannot be separated from many other social and cultural developments. Sociology too shows signs of giving cultural issues greater weight, sometimes confined to a subspecialism called "the sociology of culture" and sometimes with greater or lesser unease about the credentials of a newcomer. Elsewhere cultural studies forms the basis for analytical work and debates within such practice-based subjects as fine art, textiles, photography, and music.

At one level all this is part of a debate about whether cultural studies (and much other recent work) are of necessity cross-disciplinary, interdisciplinary or (Clarke) "undisciplined," or is part of a shift into a "postdisciplinary" period in academic work, perhaps linked to other postmodern developments. New convergences arise with work in geography or critical linguistics. Cultural studies in many parts of the world offered a third way between empiricisms and the abstractions of neo-Marxist (for example, HABERMAS) and other forms of theory, and also a space in which to deal with urgent contemporary and political questions running across existing divisions of intellectual labor. That space has to be found and developed, although its location and form will vary from one setting to another, at times within (and questioning) a discipline, at others a program across departments or a shared arena with different memberships. These are equally issues about the construction of a course or curriculum in cultural studies, and ways of working, learning, and teaching most appropriate to students bringing their own agendas and for whom equally the personal, political, and intellectual are present at once.

Thus there can be no single agenda or best place for cultural studies if proper account is taken of changing and also particular circumstances. That is why work so far exemplifies Gramsci's comment on culture itself, that it represents an infinity of traces without an inventory, given the impact of divergent paradigms, formations, and political movements and situations. However, while this account has concentrated on the "First World," it seems likely that interests in cultural studies from many other parts of the world, combined with the heightened speed of globalization and awareness of its implications, may serve to decenter the West in cultural studies in the future. Postmodernist PARADIGMS are active in cultural studies as everywhere else, but postcolonial approaches may question them in significant ways. There will be a more informed awareness of international movements, cross-cultural issues, cultural migrations, and hybridities. Characteristic models of cultural domination and subordination will need to become more complex, and no longer exclude more mainstream cultural forms – say the cultures of the suburbs. The study of cultural policy and the application of cultural studies to policy issues, or to take a different instance the cultural study of science or religion, have scarcely begun.

The current situation is, as before, paradoxical. "Cultural studies" has become a widely recognized and referenced body of work, of interest to many kinds of students but at times also outside education, characterized by a rich (and not yet absorbed) diversity of approaches and interests and also by a degree of (possibly cherished) marginality. There are few working in this area and with few resources. A space has been made, with difficulty, for the registration of important issues outside the existing educational agenda, but the previous disciplines are changing (deceptively fracturing) while cultural studies now has its own languages and institutional presence, not always conducive to participation in a wider and public debate. Work in cultural studies is likely to remain volatile, self-reflexive, and alert to new questions, but may need now to help contribute toward more of a common agenda with attached priorities, across the specialist interests of the humanities and social sciences, and to respond to a new period in which the hegemony of the New Right, and also of the West, is fast breaking up.

Reading

Adorno, T.W. 1991: *The Culture Industry: Selected Essays on Mass Culture.*
Agger, B. 1992: *Cultural Studies as Critical Theory.*
Blundell, V., Shepherd, J., and Taylor, I., eds 1993: *Relocating Cultural Studies.*
Centre for Contemporary Cultural Studies 1982: *The Empire Strikes Back.*
Clarke, J. 1991: *New Times and Old Enemies: Essays on Cultural Studies and America.*
Coward, R. 1984: *Female Desire: Women's Sexuality Today.*
During, S., ed. 1993: *The Cultural Studies Reader.*
Fiske, J. 1989: *Understanding Popular Culture.*
Franklin, S., Lury, C., and Stacey, J. 1991: *Off-Centre: Feminism and Cultural Studies.*
Gilroy, P. 1987: *There Ain't No Black in the Union Jack: The Cultural Politics of Race and Nation.*
Gray, A., and McGuigan, J. 1993: *Studying Culture: An Introductory Reader.*
Green, M., ed. 1987: *Broadening the Context: English and Cultural Studies.*
Hall, S., Critcher, C., Jefferson, T., Clarke, J., and Roberts, B. 1978: *Policing the Crisis: Mugging, the State and Law and Order.*
Hardt, H. 1992: *Critical Communication Studies: Communications, History and Theory in America.*

Journal of the MidWest Modern Language Association 1991: "Cultural studies and New Historicism."
McRobbie, A. 1994: *Postmodernism and Popular Culture.*
Radway, J. 1984 (*1987*): *Reading the Romance.*
Williams, R. 1961: *The Long Revolution.*
Willis, P. 1979: *Learning to Labour.*

MICHAEL GREEN

cultural theory *See* INTRODUCTION

culture   A term of virtually limitless application, which initially may be understood to refer to everything that is produced by human beings as distinct from all that is a part of nature. However, it has often been observed that since nature is itself a human abstraction, it too has a history, which in turn means that it is part of culture. In his efforts to deal with the apparently universal occurrence of incest prohibitions in human societies, Claude LÉVI-STRAUSS candidly admits that the distinction between culture and nature is an instance of theoretical BRICOLAGE, in the sense that the distinction is simultaneously inadequate and indispensable. Two extreme attempts to limit the meaning of the term can be found in its technical use by North American anthropologists to refer to the primary data of anthropology, and in its honorific use, from the seventeenth to the nineteenth century (for example, by Matthew ARNOLD) to refer to the finest products of civilization. In a bold effort to avoid these extremes, Clifford Geertz defines culture by way of SEMIOTICS as the "webs of significance" spun by human beings (1973, p. 5). Yet even such an open definition as this presupposes an extraordinarily powerful (but perhaps justifiable) role for the semiotic in human life.

Raymond WILLIAMS begins his famous essay on "culture" by admitting that it is "one of the two or three most complicated words in the English language" (1983, p. 87). The complexity, however, is not just a matter of the utility of a term or the efficacy of a concept. For those who confront the living reality of cultural conflict, the issue may be one of having –or not having – oneself or one's relations recognized by another culture's definition of the human. Homi Bhabha, accordingly, concludes that "there can be no ethically or epistemologically commensurate subject of culture." If it is not possible to identify a transcendent humanity that is not itself based on a particular culture's sense of value, then all that is left is what Bhabha calls "culture's archaic undecidability" (1994, p. 135). If one ethnic or national group can define another as nonhuman or subhuman, then culture becomes suddenly and tribally specific and exclusive. The definition itself is an act of violence and an invitation to potential if not actualized genocide. When one culture eliminates what it considers not human, it identifies itself, according to its own definition, as human. Cultural identification in such a context takes on ultimate power.

Although some of the initial violence of cultural definition has been recognized as an instance of ORIENTALISM, or a Western effort to define and specify Asian culture as the alien – or idealized – other, more recent politically active efforts have been exerted to draw cultural definitions within what were once unified nation states in Eastern Europe or Africa. Just as Nazi definitions of the human required efforts to exclude Jews and just as southern American definitions of humanity once excluded blacks, so now in South Asia, Africa, and elsewhere in the world cultural definitions are instruments of the political power of identity exclusion. To define "culture" is to define the human; to be excluded from the definition can have an ultimate cost.

Since the middle of the nineteenth century, culture has been subjected to a range of definitions that extend from Arnold's all-embracing sense of the possibility of human perfection to Pierre Bourdieu's systems of symbolic violence. In *Culture and Anarchy* (1869) Arnold thought of culture as a redemptive pursuit through a principally literary education of the best that human beings had thought and said. In his view, culture in this sense has the potential of harmoniously unifying all of human society. In part transmitted by T.S. ELIOT, this mission for literary culture has been very influential in Britain and the United States. Not surprisingly, the intellectual revolutions brought about by the thought of Charles Darwin, Karl MARX, Friedrich ENGELS, Friedrich NIETZSCHE. and Sigmund FREUD have had profound effects on post-Arnoldian theories of culture. In a perverse version of Darwin's theory of evolution, the American anthropologist Lewis Henry Morgan in 1877, despite his humanitarianism and efforts on behalf of native American culture (See NATIVE AMERICAN STUDIES), developed a system for hierarchically classifying cultures according to evolutionary stages. Other early cultural evolutionists included Edward Burnett Tylor (1832–1917), who founded the British school of

social anthropology. ENGELS too had an evolutionary (or perhaps de-evolutionary) view of culture, most clearly expressed in his *Origin of the Family, Private Property and the State*, where he sees the emergence of civilization as not only magnifying previously existing systems of labor but also creating the merchant class, "a class that makes itself the indispensable intermediary between any two producers and exploits them both" (Marx and Engels, 1968, p. 548). While suspicious of progressivist ideas and uses of history, Nietzsche (1983, p. 123) thought he saw "*true* culture" emerging from a recovery of the "*moral* nature" of the classical Greeks in repudiation of the legacy of Rome. For Freud, especially in *Civilization and Its Discontents* (1930), culture provides not only a bulwark against nature but also as such an unrelenting source of opposition to instinct, which leads in turn to a continuous discontent by human beings with that structure of defense that they have created out of their always divided subjectivity.

Reading
Bhabha, Homi K. 1994: *The Location of Culture*.
Bourdieu, Pierre 1993: *The Field of Cultural Production*.
Jenks, Chris 1993: *Culture*.
Kroeber, A.L., and Kluckhohn, C. 1952: *Culture: A Critical Review of Concepts and Definitions*.
                                                    MICHAEL PAYNE

culture, consumer   *See* CONSUMER CULTURE

culture, counter   *See* COUNTERCULTURE

culture, enterprise   *See* ENTERPRISE CULTURE

culture, folk   *See* FOLK CULTURE

culture, high   *See* HIGH CULTURE

culture industries   Culture industries can be defined, simply enough, as those industries which produce cultural goods. Or, to put it the other way round:

Generally speaking, a cultural industry is held to exist when cultural goods and services are produced and reproduced, stored and distributed on industrial and commercial lines, that is to say on a large scale and in accordance with a strategy based on economic considerations rather than any concern for cultural development. (UNESCO, 1982)

This definition applies both to cultural forms which depend on "craft production" and "mass reproduction" (as in the publishing industry and, to some extent, the music business) and to media which depend on large-scale capital investment and collective technological production with an elaborate division of labor (such as the film and television industries). There is by now, indeed, a large body of sociological and business studies literature on "the production of culture," studies which examine in detail the industrial "value-adding" process through which songs, novels, television programmes, films, etc. must these days pass (see, for example, Peterson, 1976).

The use of the term "culture" in such descriptions means, however, that the analysis of the culture industries is never, in fact, a simple matter of economics or management theory. To describe the film, music, publishing, or television industries as culture industries (rather than as, say, ENTERTAINMENT INDUSTRIES) is to imply critical questions about both their creative practices and social effects.

The first systematic, analytic use of the term "culture industry" can thus be found in the FRANKFURT SCHOOL critique of mass culture (see, for example, Horkheimer and Adorno, 1947 (*1972*) and Adorno, 1991). For HORKHEIMER and his German colleagues, the point of the term "culture *industry*" was its implication that the Marxist critique of commodity production in general could (and should) be applied to the production of symbolic goods in particular, to the production of goods whose "use value" was aesthetic, diverting, and ideological. The culture industries were thus like any other capitalist industry: they used "alienated" labor; they pursued profit; they looked to technology – to machinery – to provide a competitive edge; they were primarily in the business of producing "consumers."

The implications of this approach to mass culture are familiar: the mode of cultural production determines cultural value; the formal qualities of mass cultural goods are an effect of production techniques and the management of competition; the "pleasures" of mass culture are essentially irrational, the effect of the efficient commercial manipulation

of desire. Ironically, the first argument (given a Romantic gloss) became commonplace within the cultural industries themselves, where a distinction came to be made between cultural goods produced for "commercial" and "artistic" reasons (this was the basis of the late 1960s distinction between "rock" and "pop" music, for example). And if, in practice, it is difficult to find any form of contemporary culture that is not, somewhere along the line, implicated in the process of industrial production (even Schoenberg's music is primarily heard on record), the Frankfurt argument was now turned on its head: to assign a cultural commodity aesthetic value is to imply that it is, somehow, produced "autonomously" (for "artistic purposes"). And this is, in turn, indicated by its challenge to or denial of the usual technical conventions and sales formulas of mass cultural production. It is claimed, in other words, that some goods (some films, some records, some books) really are different, individual, or unique; this is not just the appearance of "difference" within that *standardization* of the mass cultural product which was, for ADORNO, the essence of the industrial process. The distinction can then be drawn, similarly, between serious appreciation (of the songs of Bob Dylan, the films of Martin Scorsese, the books of Stephen King) and mindless consumption (of Kylie Minogue records, Elvis Presley movies, and Jeffrey Archer bestsellers). Even within the DISCOURSE of the cultural industries themselves, in short, a distinction is drawn between goods produced (and consumed) for purely "commercial reasons" (and thus worthless) and goods which exist for "artistic reasons," which cannot therefore really be understood as part of the industrial process at all!

For the Frankfurt scholars, though (Adorno found this sort of argument – about jazz, for instance – ludicrous), the analytic significance of the term "culture industry" was that it described a production *system*, a system in which cultural forms were determined by the logic of capital accumulation and not by any particular creative or political decisions taken by any particular artists or entrepreneurs. Detailed textual analysis or comparison was unnecessary; all that mattered was to understand the basic production process (Adorno wrote about "popular music," not about specific songs), and so, whatever radical or critical claims they may make, the effect of cultural commodities is always the same: the *manipulation* of desire in the pursuit of profit.

The Frankfurt school, in other words, treated cultural consumption as pathological, as something to be explained in psychological and psychoanalytic terms (there was, significantly, a clear overlap in its thinking here with that of the advertising business, which was, of course, precisely interested in the problems of consumer control), and, in the end, Horkheimer and Adorno used the term "culture industry" very broadly, to describe the way in which a capitalist economy depends on the production not of goods but of needs:

> The stronger the position of the culture industry, the more summarily it can deal with consumers' needs, producing them, controlling them, disciplining them, and even withdrawing amusement; no limits are set to cultural progress of this kind. (Adorno and Horkheimer, *1972*, p. 144)

From this critical perspective, entertainment ("amusement") is crucial to social reproduction, and Frankfurt studies in the 1930s and 1940s tended to focus on the culture of entertainment, on music, film, radio, and magazines (and besides, as Adorno pointed out, fascism was a particularly "entertaining" form of mass political mobilization, preoccupied with symbol and style and the use of the unconscious).

Critical British and American cultural theorists have customarily approached the mass media from a different position, and for them the term "culture industry" has therefore had a different significance and focused different concerns (see Williams, 1961). Here the political questions are about ownership and control; the issue is the ownership of knowledge and the control of information (and the key culture industries are thus taken to be the press and broadcasting rather than, say, pop music and the cinema). From this perspective, the specific policies of specific individuals do matter; texts (newspapers, magazines, television programs) can be compared and studied – they reveal the effects of different owners, producers, and organizations.

This is to raise the question of whether or not a culture industry is necessarily a capitalist form, whether its practices are inevitably the effect of commercial logic: can the state not influence or control or regulate cultural production? These questions have been addressed, in particular, to broadcasting, and answered through the concept of public service: "public service broadcasting" is thus defined as an alternative to "commercial broadcasting," a way of funding program production and organizing radio and television audiences which is determined by neither market forces nor advertiser needs. Public service broadcasting (and, in principle, other culture industries could be organized along similar lines), is thus financed by taxes or license fees and is not subject to the ideological or political views of any particular property owner – its problem is, rather, to negotiate the tricky relationship between state and government, between political and professional control. Similarly, public service broadcasters are answerable to the needs of the "public" rather than to those of advertisers or sponsors or shareholders, and the "public" in this context is a composite, made up of numerous "minorities." A public service broadcaster like the BBC is, in short, expected to present news and information in an "unbiased" and "balanced" way, but also to pay attention to all citizens' interests, to assemble audiences rather than to service markets.

In the context of analysis of the culture industries, though, the important point about public service broadcasting is the evidence it provides that the organization of cultural production is an effect of state policies and legislative frameworks and not just of market forces; in broadcasting practice, therefore, the question is not *either* public service *or* commerce, but rather the state *regulation*, more or less detailed, of the cultural marketplace. Regulation here is not just an economic matter (a question of ownership and control) but an ideological and a moral issue. Libel, secrecy, and obscenity laws, for example, have an effect on both what is (or is not) produced and on who may consume it.

In the 1980s, partly as a result of technological changes that meant that the nation was no longer the "natural" market boundary for cultural goods (as satellite and cable operators began to compete with broadcasters, so television became, like the cinema, records, and print, an essentially international medium), and partly as an effect of the political emphasis on the use of market rather than state forces to determine investment and production decisions, there was across North America and Western (and then Eastern) Europe a general "deregulation" which had a marked impact on the culture industries. The decline of public service broadcasting in particular meant, at least in the short run, new opportunities for "independent" program makers and producers (and technological changes, particularly digitalization, made possible the decentralization of even high-quality audiovisual production in all sectors of the mass media). This was the context for a new use of the term "culture industries," with reference to their contribution (in comparison with other industries) to wealth creation and employment. This was, to begin with, a national response to the globalization of cultural production. Governments began to ask themselves a question that was simultaneously economic and political: does a country need a television industry? A music industry? A sports industry? (Any more than it needs a car industry? A computer industry?) What was the balance of economic and political profit and loss in cultural investment?

These questions had a different resonance at the local level. Regions and cities which were facing economic decline as a result of the collapse of the old heavy industries (steel, coal, shipbuilding, etc.) looked to the "service sector," to culture industries, as a possible source of new investment, new jobs, a new municipal profile. In the United States Baltimore was the influential pioneer of this economic strategy, which meant, among other things, repackaging the now dead industries as culture, as "heritage," as an attraction for tourists. In Britain "cultural industries policy" was first developed at the end of the 1970s by the left-wing Greater London Council, and although its strategy reflected London's importance as a media and culture centre, the GLC's treatment of the cultural sector as an industrial sector was taken up by most large Labour-controlled municipal councils in Britain in the 1980s.

There are clearly contradictions between these various accounts of culture as industry (even though they all derive in one way or another from a socialist critique of liberal economics) and they have rather different political implications (Adorno, for example, and Raymond Williams too, would surely find it bizarre that a left-wing socialist council should invest in, say, a video promotion studio). When they originally used the term "culture industry," Horkheimer and Adorno were deliberately creating

a little *frisson*, putting together two terms that were meant to be kept apart: "culture" was usually seen as quite independent of the economy. And even now, when we are much more accustomed to the argument that the market is the best guarantor of quality and choice in this economic sector as in any other, there remains a residual belief that the production of culture is not quite like (or should not be quite like) the production of other goods, that it has an ideological and ethical significance that cannot be entrusted to market forces. It is striking, for example, that the politicians most committed in the 1970s and 1980s to the deregulation of the media in ownership terms (Thatcher and Reagan, for example) were also committed to increased regulation in moral terms (with reference to "video nasties," the "promotion" of homosexuality, etc.).

In short, culture industries are both like and unlike other industries; and they are always therefore going to be the subject of intense political and theoretical debate. Culture is too important for the life and meaning of a nation for its production to be left to private enterprise; and culture is too valuable as a source of power and profit for private entepreneurs to leave it alone.

Reading
Adorno, T.W. 1991: *The Culture Industry: Selected Essays in Mass Culture.*
——and Horkheimer, Max 1947 (*1972*): *Dialectics of Enlightenment.*
Peterson, R.A. 1976: *The Production of Culture.*
UNESCO 1982: *Cultural Industries. A Challenge for the Future of Culture.*
Williams, Raymond 1961: *The Long Revolution.*
                                                    SIMON FRITH

culture, musicology and   *See* MUSICOLOGY AND CULTURE

culture, urban   *See* URBAN CULTURE

D

Daly, Mary (1928–) US radical lesbian feminist philosopher. Daly's first major books, *The Church and the Second Sex* (1968) and *Beyond God the Father* (1973), criticized misogyny in the Christian churches and argued that men's spiritual authority over women is a major component of PATRIARCHY and must be rejected. Her third and most controversial book, *Gyn/Ecology* (1978), initiated new formal and thematic directions in Daly's work. Arguing that patriarchy constructs reality primarily through language, Daly deconstructs patriarchal TEXTS as she seeks a new language with which to realize radical feminist consciousness and spirituality. *Gyn/Ecology*, while excitedly praised, was also criticized in an "Open letter" by Audre Lorde as racist in its rhetorical strategies, falsely universalizing, and exclusive. Although Daly never responded to Lorde in print, the subsequent debate among feminists productively clarified arguments for and against radical feminism, ESSENTIALISM, and separatism. Academic feminists in the United States rarely cite Daly's later work, including *Pure Lust* (1984), *Webster's First New Intergalactic Wickedary of the English Language* (1987), and *Outercourse* (1992), but Daly remains popular and influential among radicals, especially those influenced by French feminism, who value Daly's increasingly bold experimentation with language.

See also ESSENTIALISM; LESBIAN FEMINISM; PATRIARCHY.

Reading
Daly, Mary 1978: *Gyn/Ecology: The Metaethics of Radical Feminism.*
——1984: *Pure Lust.*
——1992: *Outercourse: The Be-Dazzling Voyage: Containing Recollections from my Logbook of a Radical Feminist Philosopher (Be-ing an account).*
Lorde, Audre 1980 (*1981*): "An open letter to Mary Daly."
GLYNIS CARR

dasein Departing from the ordinary German use of the word, the German philosopher Martin HEIDEGGER used it to stand for the mode of being of man, as distinguished from the mode of being of tools and that of things. Dasein is characterized by being-in-the-world, and the latter is characterized by the fundamental "moods" of care and anxiety. Dasein is also essentially temporal, it is oriented towards the future and is being-towards-death. With this concept of Dasein, Heidegger rejects the understanding of the nature of man in traditional metaphysics and religion.

Reading
Heidegger, M. 1927 (*1980*): *Being and Time.*
J.N. MOHANTY

Davidson, Donald (1917–) One of the most influential of contemporary American philosophers, Davidson is best known for his work in the theory of meaning. The key problem here is the "creativity" of language, the ability of speakers to understand a potential infinity of sentences on the basis of a finite stock of words and constructions. Davidson takes his cue from the logician Tarski, who showed how to devise a semantics for an artificial language, enabling the determination of the truth conditions for each of the language's sentences. In "Truth and meaning" (Davidson, 1984b, Essay 2), Davidson indicates how this may be done for natural languages and, crucially, claims that such a theory of truth is also a theory of meaning. Roughly, to understand a language is to grasp how its elements contribute to the truth conditions of the sentences in which they occur.

This approach has interesting results for CULTURAL and CRITICAL THEORY. First, it rules out any cultural relativism according to which peoples differ radically as to how the world is. This is because translation of a foreign language presupposes not only our ability to recognize the conditions under which its speakers hold their sentences to be true, but also the "charitable" assumption that they succeed, by and large, in holding to be true what actually *is* (by our own lights) true (Davidson, 1984b,

Essay 9). Second, because the meaning (that is, truth-conditions) of a sentence is independent of individual uses of it, there is no such thing as non-literal meaning, since metaphors etc. are phenomena of use. A metaphorical utterance of "X" differs from a literal one, not in meaning, but in its aim of, say, evoking images (Davidson, 1984b, Essay 17).

Recently ("A nice derangement of epitaphs," in LePore, 1986) Davidson has rejected the common assumption that communication requires *shared conventions* among speakers. It proceeds, rather, by speakers making *ad hoc* adjustments in their individual theories of meaning so as to match them temporarily and to the degree required by the particular verbal exchange.

See also LANGUAGE THEORIES; METAPHOR AND METONYMY.

Reading

Davidson, Donald 1980: *Essays on Actions and Events.*
——1984b: *Inquiries into Truth and Interpretation.*
LePore, Ernest, ed. 1986: *Truth and Interpretation: Perspectives on the Philosophy of Donald Davidson.*
Ramberg, Bjorn T. 1989: *Donald Davidson's Philosophy of Language: An Introduction.*

DAVID E. COOPER

De Man, Paul (1919–83) American deconstructionist. Born in Antwerp, de Man was educated in Belgian universities in the years leading up to the Nazi occupation. He began his writing career in an anti-Nazi journal, *Les Cahiers du Libre Examen*, which he edited for a short while. Unable to escape into France during the Belgian occupation, de Man obtained a job through the offices of his uncle, Hendrik de Man, in a French journal, *Le Soir*. He also wrote at this time for the Flemish journal *Het Vlaamsche Land*. De Man's pieces in these journals were discovered after his death by the Belgian scholar Ortwin de Graef. At least some of the pieces were deemed to be antisemitic even by de Man's followers. An essay singled out for attention is entitled "Jews in contemporary literature" (1941), where de Man focused on the contribution of Jews to the European intellectual tradition. De Man suggested that the isolation of the Jewish race from the European intellectual mainstream would not adversely affect European culture. Though this may be charitably understood as staving off vulgar antisemitism, the matter gets more complicated when de Man suggests that Jews could be resettled in an "island colony." It should, however, be stated in de Man's defence that he quit his job with *Le Soir* in late 1942 when the true extent of the Nazi persecution of Belgian Jews began to come to light.

De Man's early writings can be retrospectively understood as offering us a valuable clue to his lifelong suspicion of aesthetic IDEOLOGY and his insistence on the ethical necessity of its DECONSTRUCTION. De Man was not the only European intellectual to be bewitched by the lure of the nationalist aesthetic, as is evident from the history of modernism. The disenchantment with LIBERAL democracy was a widespread problem in Europe during the interwar years. The call for decisive action over endless bouts of rationalism in political theory afflicted the political climate with an intensity that is difficult for a postwar intelligentsia to appreciate. In the choice between cosmopolitanism and nationalism, the latter seemed to offer something more concrete than the by now empty universal ideals of the ENLIGHTENMENT. Leading socialists like Hendrik de Man began to believe that National Socialism, by effecting change, might lead to a better alternative than the slow pace of reform in a liberal democracy; hence the temptation to collaborate. The Nazi aestheticization of the nation-state also seemed to offer a solution to the age-old problem of ALIENATION. Cultural despair gave way to the politics of soil, race, and blood. The Nazis encouraged the belief that European nations could piggyback their way into nationhood on Germany. De Man went along with this idea. He began to write in praise of the German nation and its aesthetic ideals. With this went a devalorization of French literature: whereas the Germanic spirit manifested itself in a penchant for organization, the French were trapped in the endless analysis of the self. De Man also appears to have been a historicist at this time. The Third Reich promoted a teleological vision of history; in de Man this is translated into the question of an unconscious aesthetic determinism as it manifests itself in literary history. Of course, there was not a perfect alignment between his aesthetic and political ideology, but the interimplication of these two theoretical categories was to dominate his later work as a deconstructionist.

De Man's skepticism about the efficacy of political action, in his later career, can then be understood as a response to the naive enchantment and subsequent despair of his early journalistic career. Again and again he would announce programmatically that the problems of language (reading) had made it impossible to attend to the questions of history. The preface to his *magnum opus*, *Allegories of Reading* (1979), begins with the famous words: "I began to read Rousseau seriously in preparation for a historical reflection on Romanticism and found myself unable to progress beyond local difficulties of interpretation." De Man's interest in the "local difficulties of interpretation" was forged initially by his encounter with the new criticism of Reuben Brower, his mentor at Harvard, where he earned a doctorate in the 1950s. After an early stint at Harvard, de Man went on to teach at Cornell, Zurich, Johns Hopkins, and finally at Yale, where he became, in Frank Lentricchia's words, the Godfather of the "Yale Mafia." As the head of the so-called Yale school of deconstruction, de Man became the most influential literary theorist in America. His best-known books, *Blindness and Insight* (1971) and *Allegories of Reading* (1979), were fruits of that period. De Man's influence over a whole generation of theorists resulted from a rare combination of pedagogical, philological, and philosophical skills. His originality lay in discovering the "method" of reading that was to shake up academia under the rubric "deconstruction" independently of the French philosopher, Jacques DERRIDA. De Man is also credited by the literary historian Frank Lentricchia with having anticipated the central theoretical insights of Harold BLOOM, Geoffrey Hartman, and J. Hillis Miller. De Man's tenure as the *eminence grise* of deconstruction at Yale also saw the advent of Derrida's annual summer sessions there in the 1970s.

Since the success of the Yale "school" is often diagnosed as a shrewd mixture of American NEW CRITICISM with continental esoterica, it will be important to ask what exactly de Man borrowed from the New Critics. The primary virtue of the New Critics was a willingness to read closely without being distracted by grandiose schemes of thought. The promotion of its favourite TROPES, IRONY and PARADOX, was at least based on a willingness to read the TEXT "literally." But this does not mean that de Man was willing to buy all the theoretical claims of the new criticism. An important exception was the question of symbolism. Both romanticism and the New Criticism had bought into the mythical therapeutics of the SYMBOL. T.S. ELIOT had famously referred to the dangers of the "dissociation of sensibility" that resulted from the poet's inability to find an "objective correlative." This disjunction between imagination and reason

was understood to be the result of a historical rupture, viz., the English Civil War. This historical myth had its political counterpart in the ideology of the AESTHETIC. De Man's problematization of the symbol and its deconstruction into allegory marks a decisive shift in the fortunes of what a political criticism informed by deconstruction might be. The literary equivalent of this is the deconstruction of METAPHOR into METONYMY, nature into CULTURE, etc. It is at this point that de Man's work resonates with Derrida's more systematic questioning of the binarization of modes of consciousness in the Western metaphysical tradition.

Reading
De Man, Paul 1971 (*1989*): *Blindness and Insight: Essays in the Rhetoric of Contemporary Criticism*.
—— 1979: *Allegories of Reading: Figural Language in Rousseau, Nietzsche, Rilke, and Proust*.
—— 1984: *The Rhetoric of Romanticism*.
Lentricchia, Frank 1980: *After the New Criticism*.
Norris, Christopher 1988: *Paul de Man: Deconstruction and the Critique of Aesthetic Ideology*.
Waters, Lindsay and Godzich, Wlad, eds 1989: *Reading De Man Reading*.

SHIVA KUMAR SRINIVASAN

death of author   *See* AUTHOR, DEATH OF

decentered structure   A category introduced by ALTHUSSER to distinguish between the Marxist and Hegelian concepts of totality (see MARXISM and HEGELIANISM). According to him, the Hegelian totality was an "expressive totality," whose parts were so many appearances of an original essence which is the demiurge of history. Transposed to historical MATERIALISM, this conception generated an economic ESSENTIALISM which abolished the RELATIVE AUTONOMY and "specific effectivity" of the superstructural levels of the SOCIAL FORMATION.

By contrast, the Marxist concept of totality was a complex one, to which neither "expressive" nor "mechanical" models did justice. The Marxist whole was inseparable from the parts or elements of which it was constituted. It was characterized by irreducible states of OVERDETERMINATION, since each social practice or contradiction formed the "conditions of existence" of the others. Accordingly, it contained no essence to be expressed, or center to be reflected: it was a "decentered structure." Nevertheless, it was a "structure in dominance," unified by a dominant structure and by economic "determination in the last instance."

In his Lacanian-influenced work on IDEOLOGY, Althusser likewise maintained that the human subject was "decentered," for it was "constituted by a structure which has no 'center' either, except in the imaginary misrecognition of the 'ego'" (1964, pp. 170–1).

Reading

Althusser, L. 1964 (*1971*): "Freud and Lacan."
——and Balibar, E. 1968 (*1990*): *Reading Capital.*
Geras, N. 1972 (*1986*): "Althusser's Marxism: an account and assessment."

GREGORY ELLIOTT

decoding   *See* ENCODING/DECODING

deconstruction   School of philosophy and literary criticism forged in the writings of the French philosopher Jacques DERRIDA and the Belgian/North American literary critic Paul DE MAN.

Deconstruction can perhaps best be described as a theory of reading which aims to undermine the logic of opposition within TEXTS (see BINARY OPPOSITION). For Derrida this requires a scrutiny of the essential distinctions and conceptual orderings which have been constructed by the dominant tradition of Western philosophy. In a series of engagements with thinkers as diverse as Plato, HEGEL, ROUSSEAU, KANT, HUSSERL, AUSTIN, and LÉVI-STRAUSS, Derrida adopts a strategy of reading which questions the assumptions and limitations of textual meaning by revealing how the polarities and certainties a text has proposed have actually been constructed through a series of preferences and repressions which have privileged certain ideas, values, and arguments above others. Derrida's point is that what has been presented as a dichotomy in Western thought, such as man/woman, is in fact merely a difference which has been manipulated into a hierarchy. However, contrary to some literary and postmodern appropriations of his writings, Derrida's thought does not aim at the dissolution of analytic distinctions altogether, nor is he concerned with a simple reversal of hierarchical oppositions. As Derrida and some of his more subtle acolytes are well aware, positing difference against identity succeeds only in falling back within the very logic of binary opposition their deconstructive enterprise tries to resist. Instead Derrida works to

displace and reinscribe concepts into larger and more encompassing contexts. His typical practice includes applying the meaning and potential of a concept against the limits within which it has been constructed. Hence his questioning of the "structurality of STRUCTURE," the cause of the cause, or the context of the context attempts to prise open the metaphysical closures of Western philosophy.

At its best, Derridean deconstruction lays bare the logic, presuppositions, and structures which constitute the dominant tradition of Western thought. As Barbara Johnson observes, deconstruction is a form of immanent critique which situates itself inside a text in order to tease out the "Warring forces of signification within the text" (Johnson, 1984, p. 5). Deconstructive criticism does not claim to resolve such textual conflicts and contradictions in some ideal Hegelian synthesis. Rather, it believes there to be something intrinsic to the structure of language (for Derrida – writing) which complicates any attempted textual unity. Derrida's terms "differance" and "dissemination" articulate both the possibility and the impossibility of pinning down a coherent, unproblematic meaning of a text (see WRITING).

Derrida's modified concept of writing functions as a metaphor for the absence of both a unitary subject and a stable referent in any text, whether spoken or written. Such absences (he claims) are the unavoidable consequence of using SIGNS to make and communicate meaning. The intervention of the linguistic sign divides the subject and the referent from themselves, and it is these divisions and absences which open up the possibility of textual misinterpretations and misunderstandings. It is the search for these systematic contradictions and uncontrollable ambiguities in meaning which perhaps best characterizes deconstructive criticism.

Derrida's deconstructionist method entails highlighting a pair of oppositions with a text and then demonstrating, via a close attention to the logical contradictions, repressions, and limitations of the argument, how the opposition ceases to hold up under analytic critique. For example, in *Speech and Phenomena* (1967c) Derrida deconstructs the "essential distinction" Husserl makes between expressive and indicative signs. Derrida places under scrutiny the possibility of maintaining a pure realm of expressive signs which transmit the voice of consciousness independently of their articulation in an indicative language. This quest for an unmediated expressive consciousness breaks down (Derrida maintains) at those points where Husserl must recognize the necessity of language and the indicative as being inseparable from the very possibility of any expression. An immanent expressive consciousness would remain imprisoned in the subject's head without the conditional intervention of indicative signs. The very necessity of such an intervention renders consciousness nonself-identical, opening it out into the realm of the social, historical, and conventional.

By a curious reversal of logic, Derrida shows how what has been relegated to a secondary status in Husserl's argument (indicative signs) actually conditions any conscious expression. Derrida's critique aims not at a reversal of the opposition, but rather an articulation of the PARADOXES, AMBIGUITIES, and CONTRADICTIONS which destabilize the initial opposition. So, in the case of Husserl, Derrida exposes how what has been posited as the source of meaning (expressive consciousness) remains dependent on, and therefore affected by, what has been constructed as of secondary importance, therefore deconstructing the initial opposition.

Deconstruction not only scrutinizes the primary texts of Western culture, it also reflects on the readings and interpretations which have produced the status of these dominant works. Deconstruction is therefore a reflection on the act of reading, examining how interpretations have been produced, and what these interpretations have marginalized, presupposed, or ignored. Derrida's readings require a meticulous attention to textual evidence and logical contradiction where the movement of writing may subvert the interpreter's quest for a unified meaning. This search for incoherences and points of resistance marks Derrida's poststructuralist break with the unifying and systematizing methodologies of theoretical STRUCTURALISM.

Derrida's critique of conceptual oppositions is often facilitated by his focus on what has been relegated to the margins of a text's argument. His typical practice often demonstrates how footnotes, metaphors, elisions, and other details an author has deemed to be of little importance to the task at hand, actually condition the explicit argument of a text. It is this always implicit subtext which Derrida attempts to reveal as a determining force, a textual unconscious which can always be read against the grain of what a text intends to say. Importantly, Derrida's critique of intentionality does not simply abandon it in favor of a limitless textual freeplay of interpretation. Rather, it explores the structural

constraints which always render explicitly stated intentions liable to deconstruction. Such a deconstruction often proceeds by illustrating how authorial arguments undermine themselves by falling victim to the very ideologies or methodological procedures they have diagnosed as deficient or outdated in other theorists' work, or by demonstrating how the metaphysical aspects of a thinker's philosophy may actually be undone by some of his most radical theoretical notions. This point is evident in Derrida's reading of SAUSSURE in *Of Grammatology* (1967a) where Derrida reveals how Saussure's most radical principles (the arbitrariness of the SIGN and meaning through difference) undo his metaphysical belief in the existence of a "natural bond" between spoken words and true meaning.

What Derrida seeks to elucidate in his readings of Western philosophy is the necessary "logic of supplementarity" which is inscribed in every pretence towards clear-cut conceptual distinctions. For Derrida, there is always something which eludes the grasp of conceptual self-identity. There is a necessary lack present in every identifying moment, a lack which is inherent in the very STRUCTURE of language which must be used to define and articulate concepts. Importantly, the supplement is not simply the result of an error or slip on the part of the author. Rather, it is something systematic which can be most easily identified in the texts of those thinkers who are most rigorous in their conceptual work.

In a manner strikingly similar to the strategy of NEGATIVE DIALECTICS developed by the German philosopher Theodor ADORNO, Derrida attempts to include within thought all that has been considered heterogeneous to it. The supplement is always there as the nonidentity within identity which undermines the distinction between the two. Like Adorno's, Derrida's thought is anti-foundationalist in its belief that any first principle, or privileged starting point for a coherent philosophical system, is already split by the differential and supplementary structure of language (see SAUSSURE). To understand concepts, origins, and centers as "always already" different from themselves in their very inception in language is to question the whole practice of constructing stable identities between terms. Once it is acknowledged that concepts do not exist in their own solitary space with a clear, unambiguous, unitary meaning attached to them, any opposition based on identity becomes difficult to sustain. Deconstruction elucidates both the differences within and the differences between supposedly stable identities.

Deconstruction has had an impact on numerous disciplines within cultural criticism, the humanities, and the social sciences. In sociology, Anthony Giddens has integrated Derrida's insights into a theory of structuration which attempts to articulate the at once constraining and enabling dialectic of structure and SUBJECT, while in historical scholarship New Historicists and cultural materialists have utilized deconstructive arguments in order to uncouple classical oppositions between cause and effect, text and context, and primary and secondary sources.

Despite Derrida's academic training in philosophy, his writings have exerted their greatest influence in literature departments, particularly in the United States, where critics such as J. Hillis Miller, Geoffrey Hartman, and Allan Bloom have assimilated Derrida's insights in order to break with many of the traditional assumptions of literary criticism.

Perhaps the most articulate of the North American deconstructors was Paul DE MAN. For de Man, deconstruction required a thorough reading of a text's rhetorical constitution. De Man's usual deconstructive maneuvers focus on those moments in a text where the logic of an argument becomes complicated and undermined by the figural language of the text. For de Man this conflict of meaning between the literal and the figural is a persistent occurrence in the texts of Western philosophy. His readings of the central texts of Western CULTURE demonstrate how philosophy cannot escape the dimension of figural language, no matter how far it presses its claims to communicate clear and distinct conceptual meanings. De Man maintains that the task of theory (that is, deconstruction) is not to impose itself upon a text but rather to follow through the literal and figural textual logic in order to spot the places where a text self-deconstructs and resists theoretical reduction, by slipping away from its own stated intentions as well as the critic's best attempts to explain it. For a de Manian there is something inevitable about a text's deconstruction and it is the responsibility of the astute critic to elucidate these moments.

The direct challenge posed to the philosophical tradition by deconstructionists such as de Man and Derrida has led to many Anglo-American philosophers adopting a position of cautionary skepticism toward the value of deconstruction's claims. Clearly, any theory which appears so radically to

challenge many of the cherished beliefs of philosophers will be treated with due caution. However, the reaction of many philosophers to the project of deconstruction has often been based on summary readings of Derrida (for example, HABERMAS) or, even worse, the rhetoric of some of Derrida's less philosophically responsible literary acolytes. The important point to grasp is that deconstruction, at least that form of critique practiced by Derrida and de Man, aims less to turn the tables on philosophy, by privileging rhetoric above reason or fiction above truth, and more to developing a philosophically accountable theory of the workings of rhetoric, METAPHOR, and language.

As Derrida explains in his essay "White mythology," which appears in his book *Margins of Philosophy* (1972b), concepts may indeed be regarded as sublimated metaphors, lacking any secure referential gound in their functioning as substitutes for other words; however, at the same time the notion of metaphor itself can only be understood and developed by the resources of philosophy which conceptualizes metaphor, rhetoric, and figuration. Hence Derrida's point is not that deconstruction enables a reversal of the opposition between philosophy and literature, concepts and metaphors, but rather it allows a rethinking of the conditions of possibility of both philosophy and literature, and how the two may in fact be articulated together. Deconstruction's strongest claim is that the two must be thought together if theorists are to produce the most rigorous account of both philosophy and literature.

The alleged political radicalism of deconstruction has been challenged by Marxist critics (see MARXISM). Pointing to deconstruction's lack of explicit political commitment and its neglect of social and economic reference, these critics, Terry EAGLETON (1981) and Peter Dews (1987) most prominent among them, argue that undermining political and institutional antagonisms cannot be reduced to an exposé of textual conflicts. Other critics have been less keen to close off the political potential of deconstruction. Marxists, feminists, and postcolonial critics such as Michael Ryan (1982), Barbara Johnson (1990), and Gayatri Spivak (1994) have all harnessed deconstructive methods to challenge many of the ideological and institutional structures of Western culture. To affirm a politics of deconstruction would perhaps be premature, but its potential may reside in its persistent questioning of the ideologies, dogmatisms, and hierarchies of existing political thought. This impulse may not spark a revolution, but it might ensure a democratic vigilance towards postrevolutionary complacencies. *See also* DE MAN, PAUL; DERRIDA, JACQUES; POST-STRUCTURALISM.

Reading

Culler, J. 1982: *On Deconstruction: Theory and Criticism after Structuralism.*
De Man, P. 1979: *Allegories of Reading: Figural Language in Rousseau, Nietzsche, Rilke, Proust.*
——1986: *The Resistance to Theory.*
Derrida, J. 1967a (*1976*): *Of Grammatology.*
——1967c (*1973*): *Speech and Phenomena and Other Essays on Husserl's Theory of Signs.*
——1972 (*1982*): *Margins of Philosophy.*
Hartman, G., ed. 1979: *Deconstruction and Criticism.*
——1981: *Saving the Text: Literature/Derrida/Philosophy.*
Johnson, B. 1984: *The Critical Difference: Essays in the Contemporary Rhetoric of Reading.*
——1990: *A World of Difference.*
Norris, C. 1989: *Deconstruction and the Interests of Theory.*
——1991: *Deconstruction: Theory and Practice.*
Ryan, M. 1982: *Marxism and Deconstruction: A Critical Articulation.*
Spivak, G. 1994: *Outside in the Teaching Machine.*

PAUL NORCROSS

defamiliarization (also "baring the device") A term used mainly by formalist literary critics, among them Viktor Schklovski, Roman JAKOBSON, and other members of the Soviet and Czech formalist circles of the 1920s and 1930s. In their view the chief function of poetic language was to defamiliarize our normal (everyday or prosaic) modes of perception. This it achieved by deploying a wide range of linguistically "deviant" devices – METAPHOR AND METONYMY, SYMBOLism, rhyme, rhythm, meter, complex patternings of sound and sense – in order to focus our attention more sharply on those devices themselves and also on the new-found possibilities of experience which they serve to evoke. The idea is captured most precisely in the Russian word *ostranenie* (or "making strange"). Shelley had advanced a similar claim when he spoke of POETRY's power to create the world anew by stripping away the "veil of familiarity" – the routine, automatized habits of response – which exert such a deadening effect upon our minds and sensibilities. For Schklovski this idea had ethical as well as aesthetic or literary implications. The familiar was that which consumed and destroyed all our most vital experiences, from the reading of poems and novels to our food, clothing, friendships, marriages, political involvements, and indeed the very sense of ourselves – and others – as living particulars not to be subsumed under general (custom-made) categories. Poetry could help to resist this process by "baring the device," that is to say, through its capacity to FOREGROUND and renovate the resources of a language worn smooth by conventional usage.

There is a parallel here with the ALIENATION EFFECT (*Verfremdungseffekt*) which the dramatist Bertolt Brecht proposed as a means of jolting theatre audiences out of their passive, complacent, or "bourgeois" habits of mind. It also finds a close – if less fashionable – analogue in the work of an overtly moralizing critic like F.R. LEAVIS. For in his essays on poetry – especially on Shakespeare, Donne, and Keats – Leavis constantly stresses the link between language in its "creative–exploratory" aspect and those modes of heightened or revivified perception that constitute an adequate ("mature" and "sensitive") response. That Leavis rejected literary theory as a pernicious distraction from the critic's proper business may offer one clue as to why some theorists – Paul DE MAN among them – for their part regard this whole way of thinking as a species of naïve mimetic delusion or wholesale "aesthetic ideology."
See also FORMALISM.

Reading

Bann, Stephen, and Bowlt, John E., eds 1973: *Russian Formalism.*
Lemon, Lee T., and Reis, Marion J., eds 1965: *Russian Formalist Criticism: Four Essays.*
Matejka, Ladislav, and Pomorska, Krystyna, eds 1980: *Readings in Russian Poetics: Formalist and Structuralist Views.*

CHRISTOPHER NORRIS

deictics *See* SHIFTERS/DEICTICS

Deleuze, Gilles (1925–95) and **Guattari, Félix** (1936–92) French philosopher and French psychoanalyst respectively. Much of modern European thought, especially in France since the 1939–45 war, has actively been in search of a means to bring philosophy and psychoanalysis – particularly MARX and FREUD – into fruitful contact with each other. The extraordinary partnership of Deleuze and Guattari had been more successful than any other such attempt to achieve this contact. In the final book they wrote together – *What* *is Philosophy?* (1991) – they arrived at an elegant summary of their common project, which had been previously launched in *The Anti-Oedipus* (1972). The question asked in the title of their last book is promptly answered. Philosophy, they say, is "the art of forming, inventing, and fabricating concepts" (Deleuze and Guattari, 1991 (*1994*), p. 2). Realizing, however, the incompleteness of this answer, they proceed to supply an agent who forms, invents, and fabricates. Philosophy requires "conceptual personae" who are friends. Here the gap that Aristotle opened up between himself and Plato, the divide he marked between truth and friendship, is brought to closure. "With the creation of philosophy, the Greeks violently force the friend into a relationship that is no longer a relationship with an other but one with an Entity" (p. 3). Although they do not name this an Aristotelian violence, Deleuze and Guattari quickly move to subdue it and to reaffirm friendship and agency. While acknowledging that two friends inevitably assume positions of "claimant and rival," they proceed, nevertheless, to affirm that "the philosopher is the concept's friend" in the sense that he is the "potentiality of the concept." They thus want to embrace NIETZSCHE's claim that concepts do not wait, like heavenly bodies, but they must be invented with "their creator's signature." What should not be missed here, however, is their unique combination of a rigorous conceptual sense with a specifically human grounding for philosophy. That is likely to remain the distinctive feature of their collaboration, and their final book will doubtless establish itself as one of the most elegant answers to philosophy's most persistent question. Deleuze has also written extensively, not only on the major TEXTs of philosophy, but also on FILM STUDIES.

Reading
Deleuze, Gilles, and Guattari, Félix 1991 (*1994*): *What is Philosophy?*
Descombes, Vincent 1979 (*1980*): *Modern French Philosophy.*
Hardt, Michael 1993: *Gilles Deleuze: An Apprenticeship in Philosophy.*

                                        MICHAEL PAYNE

Della Volpe, Galvano (1895–1968) Marxist theorist. Included in the empirical or neo-Kantian school of Western Marxism, Della Volpe's central aim is to rescue MARXISM from the humanists, such as LUKÁCS and Korsch, who reject the materialism

of the natural sciences, and to reestablish Marxism as a materialist sociology. In his TEXT *Logic as a Positive Science* (1950), Della Volpe draws out the positivist themes inherent in Marxism, as he discusses Marx's revision of the circle of the HEGELian dialectic from Abstract–Concrete–Abstract (A–C–A) to Concrete–Abstract–Concrete (C–A–C), or the circle of materialist epistemology. What has become known as the Della Volpean reconstruction is an attempt to prove the scientificity of Marxism. Della Volpe argues that the reconstruction of the Hegelian dialectic effects a transition from "*a priori* assertions to experimental forecasts" (Della Volpe, 1980, p. 198). Critics of the Della Volpean school, most notably one of the theorist's own pupils Lucio Colletti, argue that his hypernaturalistic approach to MARX ignores the themes of REIFICATION and ALIENATION.

Though Della Volpe joined the Italian Communist Party (PCI) relatively late in 1944, he exercised a formative influence on an emerging group of theorists which included – apart from Coletti – Pietranera, Rossi, and Cerroni, who pursued the scientific and deterministic implications of his work in analyzing Italian society.

Reading
Anderson, P. 1976 (*1989*): *Considerations on Western Marxism.*
Jay, M. 1984a: *Marxism and Totality.*
                                        MARY ELLEN BRAY

denotation   *See* CONNOTATION/DENOTATION

Derrida, Jacques (1930–) French philosopher. Educated at the Ecole Normale Supérieure, Paris, Derrida is best known in the anglophone world for forging the critical practice of DECONSTRUCTION. His earliest philosophical influences came from the tradition of PHENOMENOLOGY as represented by HEGEL, HUSSERL, and HEIDEGGER, with a book-length introduction to Husserl's *Origin of Geometry* (1962) marking Derrida's first published work.

Derrida's broad defense of Husserlian phenomenology in his earliest writing placed him outside the dominant theoretical STRUCTURALISM which hegemonized French intellectual CULTURE during the 1960s. However, the first glimmerings of Derrida's deconstructive method and structuralist sympathies, later to accord him widespread acclaim, are evident in his reading of Husserl's philosophical idealism. Derrida's critique of Husserl demonstrates how any notion of an immanent consciousness, able to glean an objective knowledge of ideal objects, breaks down at those points in Husserl's argument where language and WRITING are recognized as unavoidable means of communication and knowledge. The ideal of a pure and immanent perception becomes problematized when the tools of such a consciousness must come from a social, historical, and conventional language produced independently of both the object and the SUBJECT. The intervention of the structural sign as a necessary medium of representation, dividing and deferring the possibility of a pure self-consciousness, is a persistent theme in Derrida's readings of the dominant tradition in Western philosophy.

Critical attention to Derrida's work increased during the mid-1960s, particularly in the United States, where in 1966 Derrida delivered his seminal paper, "Structure, sign and play in the discourse of the human sciences," at Johns Hopkins University (later to be published in *Writing and Difference* (1967b)). The occasion, a conference celebrating structuralism, saw Derrida scrutinizing the very history and theoretical constitution of the concept of structure via a detailed exposé of the presuppositions and limitations of LÉVI-STRAUSS's structural anthropology. Focusing on the metaphorical construction of the notion of structure and its privileging of central explanatory terms, Derrida sought to provoke a questioning of the "structurality of structure": a reflection on the constructedness of what have been presumed in structuralist DISCOURSE as unconditioned centers and origins which supposedly provide grounds for objective accounts of diverse phenomena. These foundations (Derrida claims) are assumed to have a fixed meaning, a "transcendental signified," which functions as an unmovable limit on the "play" of structure, thereby closing off the possibilities of structural instability and change.

Derrida's argument did not aim to transcend structuralism. Rather, it turned structuralist arguments against their own limits and presuppositions. His acute observation that the supposition of stable structures depends on the privileging of a fixed center or given origin, posited independently of structural determination, enabled him to become more rigorously structuralist than the structuralists themselves. The poststructuralist moment Derrida's arguments were supposed to initiate refers less to a break with structuralism and more to an expansion of structuralism to its logical self-

undermining conclusions (see POSTSTRUCTURALISM). By drawing predominantly on the resources of structural linguistics (see SAUSSURE), Derrida attempted to show how any ground for a structuralist science is "always already" divided from itself via its constitution in the differential structure of language. First principles and master concepts (on this account) tend less to be naturally important explanatory tools and more to be arbitrary constructs designed to privilege a certain way of thinking and reasoning above other possibilities.

The year 1967 was to prove the most important in terms of Derrida's publishing and reception history. Three major books: *Writing and Difference, Speech and Phenomena*, and *Of Grammatology* witnessed Derrida following NIETZSCHE and Heidegger in elaborating a critique of "Western metaphysics." Western thought, Derrida claimed, had been structured in terms of hierarchical oppositions where one of the terms had been given a qualitative and/ or temporal priority over a supposedly derivative, inferior, or undesirable OTHER (see BINARY OPPOSITION). For Derrida such dichotomies tend to privilege identity, immediacy, and presence over difference, deferral, and absence.

Many of Derrida's encounters with the tradition of Western thought attempt to reveal and undermine what he sees as the fundamental binarism which betrays this "Western metaphysics of presence," that of speech over writing. Western philosophy from Plato onwards (Derrida says) has classed writing as a parasitic and imperfect representation of the pure ideas contained in the living voice of speech. This hierarchy, he argues, is produced by a logocentric culture which privileges the thinking, speaking subject who knows his own mind, says what he means, and means what he says. In opposition, Derrida's critique attempts to subvert the belief in the "voice of consciousness" – that is speech seemingly dependent on a subject's pure spontaneity of thought; an expression of ideas freely independent and undetermined by any supplementary structures, CODES, and conventions taken from the world outside the mind.

In opposition to this, Derrida proposes that speech is in fact a form of writing, where the speaker's meanings and intentions are always deferred. The very structural possibility of spoken words being transcribed into a written form reveals speech to have the same general characteristics as writing, and the consequence of this recognition (Derrida maintains) is that speech should not be regarded as an unambiguous transmission of clear and intended meaning from person to person, but must instead be studied as a form of writing, a dissemination, where meaning is continually being reinscribed and reinterpeted in different contexts. By writing, Derrida does not mean merely the inscriptional mark of the signifier; rather he means the system of spatial distinctions and temporal deferrals which are inscribed in any system of SIGNS.

Derrida destabilizes the dichotomy between speech and writing with his notion of a general or "arche-writing," at once reversing the opposition and reassessing the respective elements by placing the identities given them by metaphysical discourse into question.

Similarly, Derrida's deconstruction of AUSTIN's speech-act theory proceeds by highlighting a pair of oppositions, in this case between serious and nonserious SPEECH ACTS, and then demonstrating how the distinctions Austin constructs fail to stand up to close textual scrutiny. The features Austin assigns to supposedly parasitic, nonserious speech acts (such as citations and textual graftings) also permeate so-called "serious" speech acts, which can only function owing to the repetition inscribed in every meaningful sign. Derrida's deconstruction of the opposition entails at once a reversal and displacement of its component parts under a general covering concept, this time a "general citationality." Any representation, any SIGNIFYING element, whether phonic or graphic, must presuppose a structure of repetition, what Derrida calls "iterability," which undermines any pretence towards self-present and context-free meaning. The very possibility of a word being repeated and interpreted in a potentially infinite range of situations and contexts undermines its metaphysical claims to self-identity.

However, in his reading of Austin, Derrida is not merely replacing a metaphysics of the sign with a metaphysics of context. The potential limitlessness of context (Derrida claims) and the impossibility of securing an immanent, self-present context closes off the possibility of some pure contextual determination of meaning that is not always already reinscribed in a different context. What results in Derrida's writing is a radical contextualization and historicization of meaning which attempts to endlessly defer any final suppression of the process of reinscription and recontextualization.

For Derrida there is always a "logic of the supplement" inscribed in any pretense toward clear conceptual identity. There is always something which escapes and subverts the logic of binary opposition and it is these excesses and resistances which Derrida turns against metaphysical thinking. By immersing himself within the very structure of a text's argument, Derrida attempts an immanent critique which would expose its CONTRADICTIONS, limitations, and presuppositions. It is not that a text can be deconstructed because of a weakness or flaw in a thinker's argument, which can then be remedied. It is rather that there is something structural in the very nature of writing which necessitates contradiction and interdependence. It is this structural logic which Derrida attempts to articulate.

By seizing on authorial repressions, footnotes, and other seemingly incidental details, often confined to the margins of a text, Derrida tries to demonstrate by a reversal of traditional logic how what has been posited as central, primary, or originary remains affected by, and therefore dependent upon, what has been constructed as secondary, marginal, or derivative. What Derrida calls APORIAS are those moments where oppositions are held in mutual suspension, neither term of which can be granted structuring primacy or qualitative superiority. Derridean logic therefore replaces the logic of either/ or with a logic of both/and (and/or) neither/nor. Hence on the speculative question of which came first at the origin of language, the social structure or the individual utterance, the answer is both and neither, an indeterminancy which has led to some criticisms of Derrida from the followers of the tradition of analytic philosophy, who point to his dissolution of conceptual distinctions into a general field of textuality and indeterminancy. This is a criticism invited by many postmodern appropriations of Derrida's work (see POSTMODERNISM), but a criticism less powerful when faced with the analytic power of many of Derrida's own most analytically rigorous essays (for example, in his volume *Margins of Philosophy*, 1972b).

Contrary to many appropriations of his work, Derrida maintains a complex notion of authorial intentionality, a commitment particularly evident in his readings of Saussure, ROUSSEAU, FOUCAULT, and Austin. Derrida regularly shows how authorial intent monitors and is modified by structural constraints. Indeed, his readings often register their effect by contrasting the intentions of an author with what he is constrained to mean. Derrida's typical use of the notion of intentionality focuses on what an author may have considered to be an irrelevant or insignificant detail; or a theoretical model an author has claimed to transcend; and then he shows how the author remains imprisoned within the very conceptual structures he seeks to undermine or dispense with. As Derrida comments in his critique of Foucault's history of unreason: how can a history of madness be written "from within the very language of classical reason itself, utilizing the concepts that were the historical instruments of the capture of madness" (*Writing and Difference*, 1967b (*1978*) p. 34)?

Derrida himself accepts the impossibility of completely escaping metaphysics. His prose often parades the sweat and strain which comes from the recognition that in order to subvert metaphysics he must occupy its very intellectual constraints. Derrida's solution to this dilemma takes the form of his strategic deployment of double-edged concepts which unhinge the logic of binary opposition. A supplement can be both an addition and a substitute; a pharmacon both poison and cure; and hymen both consummation and virginity. Such a doubleness is the characteristic feature of Derrida's thought and serves in differing contexts as a substitution for the double movement of writing (differance) as at once the condition of possibility and impossibility of meaning.

The reception of Derrida's work has been a site of conflict and controversy, with philosophers tending to dismiss his work with all the fervor with which literary critics have embraced it. Derrida's biggest institutional impact has perhaps been in North American literature departments. Critics such as Geoffrey Hartman, J. Hillis Miller, and Allan Bloom have assimilated and developed Derrida's insights in all manner of creative ways in order to subvert the traditional assumptions of LITERARY CRITICISM. Such a reception of Derrida's work among literary acolytes has prompted the suspicions of ENLIGHTENMENT philosophers, for example, Jürgen HABERMAS (*1987*), who dismisses Derrida's thought (on the basis of an inadequate acquaintance with his work) as a species of irrationalist postmodern theorizing. However, postmodern thinkers like Richard Rorty (1982) have heralded Derrida as a postphilosophical literary stylist, a latter-day sophist, who is at his best when he reveals philosophy as little more than a collage of METAPHORS, rhetorical devices, and unanchored language games. Derrida, Rorty claims, undermines the pretensions of philosophy by revealing it for what it is: simply a form of WRITING with no privileged access to meaning and truth.

Such postmodern readings of Derrida are encouraged on the evidence of some of his more exuberant texts, such as *Glas* (1974), where Derrida puns and wordplays his ways between the boundaries of philosophy and literature as represented by Hegel and Genet in juxtaposed columns of print. Similarly Derrida's response to SEARLE in "Limited Inc abc" (1977) accords little respect to analytic distinctions as well as the copyright laws, as he employs a variety of textual graftings in order to turn Searle's text inside out.

However, other commentators have defended Derrida's philosophical merits with a particular stress on his earlier work as providing the "hard labor" of his philosophical enterprise. These critics, Christopher NORRIS (1987) and Radolphe Gasche (1986) most prominent among them, maintain that Derrida's work pays the utmost attention to matters of argumentative detail and philosophical accountability, often producing readings that are more philosophically rigorous than much analytic philosophy. In an attempt to wrest Derrida's work away from a neo-Nietzschean postmodern skepticism, these critics argue that Derrida's style of thought can best be situated within the broad tradition of post-Kantian critical reason.

Certainly the appearance of Derrida's long-deferred book-length engagement with the Marxist tradition, *Spectres of Marx* (*1994*) seems to confirm the analysis of the likes of Norris. This book finds Derrida going clean against the grain of much of the postmodernist wisdom which proclaims the demise of MARXISM as an intellectual and political activity. Arguing strongly against modern variations of the "end of history" and "end of Marxism" theme, and acknowledging his own intellectual debt to the Marxist problematic, Derrida calls for the continual reading and rereading of the texts of Marxism, and the urgent contemporaneity of Marxism as a political practice. This most recent work underlines what is perhaps Derrida's greatest achievement: his persistent questioning and rethinking of what have become taken-for-granted intellectual complacencies.

See also DECONSTRUCTION; POSTSTRUCTURALISM; STRUCTURALISM.

Reading
Derrida, J. 1962 (*1978*): *Edmund Husserl's "Origin of Geometry:" An Introduction.*

——1967a (*1976*): *Of Grammatology*.
——1967b (*1978*): *Writing and Difference*.
——1967c (*1973*): *"Speech and Phenomena" and Other Essays on Husserl's Theory of Signs*.
——1972a (*1981*): *Positions*.
——1972b (*1982*): *Margins of Philosophy*.
——1974 (*1986*): *Glas*.
——1977: "Limited Inc abc."
——1993 (*1994*): *Spectres of Marx: The State of the Debt, the Work of Mourning, and the New International*.
Norris, C. 1987: *Derrida*.
Wood, D., ed. 1991: *Derrida: A Critical Reader*.

PAUL NORCROSS

determinacy   First used by the scientist Hermann von Helmholtz, the term "determinacy" or "determinateness" has a broad application. The condition of being determinate can imply a certain constraint upon contingency, effected by assigning definite qualities to an entity or process. HEGEL, for example, distinguishes between "being," which is abstract, and "determinate being," which possesses qualities. But, in Marxist theory and sociology, "determinacy" (more usually "determinateness") has often been linked with a prior process of determination (not to be confused with predetermination). Understood in this sense, determinateness has figured centrally in the works of structuralist Marxists such as ALTHUSSER, who have stressed the "scientific" and deterministic thrust of MARX's CANON rather than the elements which emphasize human agency in historical transformation. Althusser uses the concept of OVERDETERMINATION (taken over from FREUD) to express the specificity of the Marxist notion of CONTRADICTION and in particular its divergence from Hegel's dialectic. Whereas Hegel's formulation of CONTRADICTION as the causal site of historical change is "simple," embodying a process of cumulative internalization of previous forms of consciousness and history, Marx's notion of contradiction is "overdetermined": it is determined not uniformly but by a variety of levels and instances of the SOCIAL FORMATION it animates.

Althusser's views have generated much debate, made possible by the dialectical and flexible approach of Marx and ENGELS themselves to the degree of determinacy possible in historical predictability and inevitability. While they stress the ultimately determinative power of the economic substructure, they suggest that what makes this power determinate is its location within a peculiar complex of circumstances; they also allow for some autonomy and influence of superstructural elements themselves.

Reading
Althusser, L. 1965b (*1970*): *For Marx*.
Engels, F. 1968: "Letter to J. Bloch."

M.A.R. HABIB

diachrony   *See* SYNCHRONY/DIACHRONY

dialectics, negative   *See* NEGATIVE DIALECTICS

diaspora   A term traditionally associated with the Jewish exile, but now used in CULTURAL THEORY to cover a range of territorial displacements, either forced, such as indenture and slavery, or voluntary emigration. Recent formulations have stressed not only the complex ties of memory, nostalgia, and politics that bind the exile to an original homeland, but also sought to illuminate the lateral axes that link diasporic communities across national boundaries with the multiple other communities of the dispersed population. Paul Gilroy's (1993) image of the "Black Atlantic," for instance, evokes an imagined geography of the African diaspora, a space not reducible to an original source, but where divergent local experiences of widely dispersed communities interact with shared histories of crossing, migration, exile, travel, and exploration, spawning hybrid CULTURES. Much of the current work on borders, transnational networks, and global public culture draws on this concept of the diaspora to understand the spectrum of displacements, revivals, and reconfigurations of identities and traditions that characterize the contemporary global cultural landscape.
See also HALL, STUART; HYBRIDITY.

Reading
Appadurai, Arjun 1990: "Disjuncture and Difference in the Global Cultural Economy."
Gilroy, Paul 1993: *The Black Atlantic: Modernity and Double Consciousness*.
Hall, Stuart 1990: "Cultural identity and diaspora."

RADHIKA SUBRAMANIAM

discourse   In its broadest, least technical sense, "discourse" means simply "talk" or "conversation," sometimes with the hint of a didactic purpose (thus "sermon," "treatise," or "lengthy address to some particular topic"). This latter development seems rather at odds with the word's etymology, going back to the Latin verb *discurrere*, "to run about," "range widely," "wander off course," etc. And indeed there is something of the same ambiguity – or tendency to pull in opposite directions – when the word is taken up (as it has been often of late) into the usage of various specialized disciplines. I shall therefore look at some of the issues it raises for philosophy, linguistics, and the human sciences in general.

The linguist Emile BENVENISTE was among the most influential thinkers in this field. According to him, "discourse" has to do with those aspects of language that can only be interpreted with reference to the speaker, to his or her spatiotemporal location, or to other such variables which serve to specify the localized context of utterance. It thus lays claim to a distinctive and well-defined area of study, one that includes the personal pronouns (especially "I" and "you"), DEICTICS of place ("here," "there," etc.) and temporal markers ("now," "today," "next week,") in the absence of which the utterance in question would lack determinate sense. Structural linguistics – following SAUSSURE – treats language (*la langue*) as a transindividual network or economy of SIGNIFYING elements, conceived in ideal abstraction from the individual speech act. Benveniste on the contrary sets out to analyze the various subject positions ("enunciative modalities") that constitute the realm of discourse, PAROLE, or language in its social-communicative aspect. Nevertheless, what he shares with Saussure's poststructuralist disciples is the working premise that subjectivity is constructed in and through language, since quite simply there is nothing (no possible appeal to the Kantian transcendental SUBJECT, to *a priori* concepts, self-evident truths, primordial intuitions, facts of experience, or whatever) that would offer a secure vantage point beyond the play of discursive representations. Clearly there are large philosophical implications bound up with this idea of language (or discourse) as the absolute horizon of intelligibility for thought and knowledge in general.

This is also what sets Benveniste's work apart from J.L. AUSTIN's otherwise similar concern with the kinds of performative or SPEECH-ACT modality exhibited by various instances of everyday discourse. It may well be the case – as argued by poststructuralist adepts like Shoshana FELMAN – that Austin's theory is itself subject to all manner of performative

slips, "misfires," and returns of the linguistic unconscious repressed. However, these anomalies require much ingenious coaxing from the style of down-to-earth, commonsense talk that goes with Austin's suasive appeal to the wisdom enshrined in "ordinary language." Benveniste writes out of a very different intellectual culture, one that has traditionally laid most stress on the Cartesian virtues of system, method, and lucid self-knowledge. All the more provocative, therefore, is the way that his work seems to open a cleft – a moment of slippage or dehiscence – between the self-possessed subject posited by Descartes' *cogito, ergo sum* and the SUBJECT as construed in discourse-theoretical terms, that is to say, a pronominal "position" caught up in the endless passage from signifier to signifier.

Such at least is the reading of Benveniste propounded by poststructuralists eager to dissolve all the certitudes (or "foundationalist" truth claims) of philosophy from Descartes to the present. On this account it is the merest of illusions – albeit an illusion deeply bound up with the entire project of "Western metaphysics" – to imagine that thinking could ever attain the kind of punctual, transparent, self-present grasp envisaged by "logocentric" reason. In Benveniste's terms the error can be diagnosed as a failure to distinguish between two levels of discourse, those pertaining respectively to the "SUBJECT OF THE ENOUNCED" and the "SUBJECT OF THE ENUNCIATION." Thus when Descartes offers the *cogito* as an indubitable ground of knowledge – a last refuge against all the threats of epistemological doubt – he can do so only by performing what amounts to a rhetorical sleight of hand, an utterance that seeks to collapse this distinction between the "I" who thinks and the "I" that is constituted as the subject–object of its own reflection. In that case, poststructuralists would argue, the Cartesian project necessarily miscarries, since it generates linguistic APORIAS beyond its power to contain or control. And the same applies to those subsequent philosophies – from KANT to Husserl – which invoke some version of the transcendental subject as locus and arbiter of truth.

Hence the recent spate of speculative work – mostly by literary theorists – on the margin between philosophy and PSYCHOANALYSIS, the latter having taken its own poststructuralist turn through the teachings of the eminent (if maverick) practitioner Jacques LACAN. To this way of thinking – "French FREUD" in colloquial parlance – there is no means of access to the unconscious save through the discourse between analyst and patient, a discourse whose transferential character is marked by all manner of linguistic swerves, substitutions, and displacements. Moreover, we can best read Freud by attending to those symptomatic moments in his work where the "agency of the letter" (or the deviant "logic" of the signifier) emerges to disrupt and complicate his own project. If the UNCONSCIOUS is indeed "structured like a language," as Lacan claims, then the insights of linguistics – especially those derived from the work of structuralist thinkers like Saussure and JAKOBSON – are simply indispensable for any reading that would respect the exigencies of the Freudian text and not fall prey to various kinds of naive or mystified account. This may require some degree of terminological latitude, as when Lacan suggests that terms like "CONDENSA-TION" and "DISPLACEMENT" were adopted by Freud (*faute de mieux*) from the mechanistic discourse current in his time, but that now – after Jakobson – we should reader the one as "METAPHOR" and the other as "METONYMY," thus restoring the unconscious to its proper dimension as a field of tropological drives and exchanges. Metaphor then becomes that aspect of the dreamwork – or the process of secondary revision – whereby one signifier substitutes for another, or where numerous meanings condense into a single image or symptom (OVERDETERMINATION). And metonymy stands in not only for "displacement" – the endless passage from signifier to signifer – but also for *desire* in so far as it connotes a kind of structural nonfulfillment, an ineluctable lack which he equates with the Saussurian "bar" between signifier and signified. For desire is distinguished from straightforward (instinctual or physical) need by its entanglement in precisely those structures of discourse – of transference and deferred meaning – which prevent it from ever coinciding with its object in a moment of achieved equilibrium.

We are therefore (Lacan argues) hopelessly mistaken if we hold psychoanalysis accountable to standards of enlightened truth-seeking thought. It is the sheer *opacity* of the Freudian text – its resistance to any kind of lucid expository treatment – which Lacan views as the purveyor of truth, albeit a "truth" that can scarcely be expressed in conceptual or rational-discursive terms. This is also (though some would consider it a charitable reading) why Lacan's own texts go out of their way to create syntactic and stylistic obstacles for anyone who looks to them in hope of discovering an easy

route of access to the Freudian corpus. On the contrary, such access is everywhere denied by a style that raises difficulty into a high point of principle, or which (less kindly) takes bafflement as a guard against the requirements of plain good sense. Again it is Descartes who figures most often as the thinker who first set philosophy out on its delusory quest for "clear and distinct ideas." But PSYCHO-ANALYSIS has traveled the same path, Lacan argues, in so far as it has embraced the imaginary ideal of a pure, unimpeded self-knowledge, an end point to the therapeutic process when all such resistances would fall away and the subject accede to a full understanding of her/his (hitherto repressed or sublimated) motives and desires. It is against this heresy – which he associates chiefly with American ego psychology – that Lacan directs both his fiercest polemics and his practice of a style that makes no concessions to the Cartesian "tyranny of lucidity."

Some philosophers – Jürgen HABERMAS among them – have rejected not only this Lacanian reading of Freud but also the entire poststructuralist project of which it formed a prominent part. In his early book *Knowledge and Human Interests* (1968) Habermas set out to defend psychoanalysis against the charge of "irrationalism" that has so often been leveled against it. Freud is, on the contrary, a thinker who belongs very firmly to the ENLIGHTENMENT tradition, or in the company of those – from Kant to Husserl – who have sought to sustain the "philosophic discourse of MODERNITY" in the face of various threats from skeptics and opponents like NIETZSCHE. At this time Habermas had not yet adopted his stance of overt antagonism toward POST-STRUCTURALISM and allied strains of counterenlightenment thought. However, it is clear enough already that he interprets Freud's cardinal maxim – "Where *Id* was, there shall *Ego* be" – in a manner diametrically opposed to Lacan's teaching. On this account the phrase is best construed as a version of the Kantian motto *Sapere aude!* ("Have the courage to think for yourself!"), that is to say, as an appeal to the values of reason and emancipatory knowledge in the private as well as the public–political sphere. Thus for Habermas the task of psychoanalysis is to bring the subject to a conscious (reflective) awareness of those repressed or sublimated memories, motives, and desires that would otherwise stand in its way. In so far as Freud's theories can claim any kind of intellectual validity or therapeutic power, they must be seen as deriving from that same tradition of enlightened *Ideologiekritik*, a tradition whose resources Habermas equates with the interests of a genuine participant democracy premised on the values of open dialogical exchange.

Nothing could be further from Lacan's response to the question that Freud famously posed in the title of his late essay "Analysis terminable or interminable?" From a Lacanian standpoint there is simply no end to the detours of the unconscious signifier, the way that language – or the discourse of desire – is forever caught up in a metonymic chain whereby truth becomes purely a figment of the IMAGINARY, a function whose value cannot be assigned except in relation to this or that transient subject position, like the purloined letter in the story by Edgar Allan Poe which Lacan took as a kind of allegorical *mise-en-scène* for the psychoanalytic encounter. Such are the complexities of TRANSFERENCE and counter transference – the two-way exchange of SYMBOLic roles between patient and analyst – that nobody can occupy the privileged position envisaged by the ego psychologists and other perverters of the Freudian truth. Like Descartes (as Lacan reads him), they are the victims of a specular misrecognition whose effect is precisely to bolster the ego's deluded hopes of making reason master in its own house. Small wonder that Habermas, in his later writings, has targeted this whole poststructuralist discourse as a species of latter-day Nietzschean irrationalism allied to a deeply conservative turn against the truth claims of enlightened critique. To this the Lacanians respond – predictably enough – by deploring his attachment to an outworn discourse of reason, enlightenment, and truth, a discourse (so it is argued) whose liberal rhetoric conceals a tyrannizing will-to-power over language, desire, and whatever eludes its self-assured rational grasp.

It is hard to imagine any possible *rapprochement* between those (like Habermas) who would uphold the values of critical-emancipatory thought and those others (postmodernists and poststructuralists among them) who regard such values as possessing no more than an illusory or long since obsolete appeal within the philosophic discourse of modernity. And this despite the fact – very evident in his recent writings – that Habermas has himself travelled a long way toward acknowledging the force of certain anti-foundationalist arguments, thus abandoning at least some areas of the Kantian high ground staked out in a work like *Knowledge and Human Interests*. What this amounts to is a version of the currently widespread "linguistic turn," the invocation of language as an ultimate horizon of intelligibility, or the denial that we can ever attain any knowledge save that vouchsafed through discourses, language games, SIGNIFYING SYSTEMS, structures of representation, etc. Habermas has taken full measure of these arguments, redefining his project in terms that derive from speech-act philosophy and the theory of COMMUNICATIVE ACTION, as distinct from those epistemological concerns that characterized his earlier work. However, he rejects the postmodern-pragmatist idea that discourse – so to speak – goes all the way down, that rhetoric (not reason) is what finally counts, since the only criterion for a valid or persuasive argument is the extent to which it happens to fit in with some existing language game or cultural "form of life." Such doctrines are philosophically bankrupt, expressing as they do a vote of no confidence in the capacity of thought to criticize false beliefs, to distinguish valid from invalid truth claims, and to analyze the causes – psychological or social – that produce various kinds of prejudice, self-ignorance, or "commonsense" dogmatism. Moreover, they are politically and ethically harmful in so far as they promote a conservative agenda of inert consensus-based values and attitudes, an "end-of-ideology" creed which equates truth with what is (currently and contingently) "good in the way of belief."

This is why Habermas describes his project as a "transcendental pragmatics," one that makes room for a critique of those existing values from the standpoint of an "ideal speech-situation," a regulative idea (in the Kantian sense) of what we can and should aspire to as participating members of a free and open democratic society. For it is clearly the case that any current (*de facto*) consensus may always be subject to a range of distorting pressures and influences, as for instance through the workings of state censorship, press manipulation, media bias, educational underprivilege, inequalities of access to the relevant information sources, etc. What Habermas therefore seeks to conserve – and what sets him decidedly at odds with the current postmodern-pragmatist wisdom – is a critical sense of those factors that conspire to thwart or frustrate the shared aspiration to a public sphere of openly communicable reasons, motives, interests, and values. Nor are these issues confined to the realm of abstruse philosophical debate. For it can readily happen – as with recent variations on the post-ideological/"new world order" theme – that some existing currency of consensus belief in, for example, the virtues of "LIBERAL democracy," US style, is taken at face value without any question being raised about the sheer gulf that exists between rhetoric and reality, or the actual effects of US policy in the domestic and geopolitical spheres. Only by keeping such distinctions in view can philosophy live up to its social and ethical task, that is to say, its commitment to a critique of consensus values wherever these serve as a refuge or smokescreen for other, less humanly accountable interests. To this extent – and despite his concessions to the anti-foundationalist case – Habermas still keeps faith with the discourse of enlightened or critical-emancipatory thought, a project whose central (Kantian) tenet is the exercise of reason against the more beguiling self-images and rhetorics of the age. *See also* BAKHTIN, MIKHAIL; CODES; CRITICAL THEORY; DISCURSIVE PRACTICES; EPISTEME; LANGUAGE, PHILOSOPHY OF; LANGUAGE THEORIES; LANGUE/PAROLE; METALANGUAGE; POST-MODERNISM; STRUCTURALISM.

Reading
Benveniste, Emile 1971: *Problems in General Linguistics.*
Coulthard, M. 1977: *An Introduction to Discourse Analysis.*
Coupland, Nikolas, ed. 1987: *Styles of Discourse.*
Foucault, Michel 1972: *The Archaeology of Knowledge.*
Habermas, Jürgen 1971: *Knowledge and Human Interests.*
——1979: *Communication and the Evolution of Society.*
——1987: *The Philosophical Discourse of Modernity.*
Halliday, M.A.K. 1978: *Language as Social Semiotic.*
Lacan, Jacques 1977: *Ecrits: A Selection.*
——1978: *The Language of the Self: The Function of Language in Psychoanalysis.*
MacDonell, D. 1986: *Theories of Discourse: An Introduction.*
van Dijk, T.A. 1985: *Handbook of Discourse Analysis.*
CHRISTOPHER NORRIS

discursive practices   One of a series of related terms – others being discursive formations, objects, relations, regularities, and strategies – introduced by Michel FOUCAULT (1974). Discursive practices are characterized by groups of rules that define their respective specificities. In contrast to the analysis of DISCOURSES as SYSTEMS of SIGNS, Foucault treats discourses as "practices that systematically form the objects of which they speak."
See also ARCHAEOLOGY OF KNOWLEDGE; ARCHIVE.

Reading
Foucault, M. 1971: "Orders of discourse."
——1974: *The Archaeology of Knowledge.*
BARRY SMART

displacement   *See* CONDENSATION/DISPLACEMENT

dissociation of sensibility   The supposed rupture between thought and feeling in the seventeenth century. T.S. ELIOT coined the term in his essay on "The metaphysical poets" in 1921, describing it as "something which happened to the mind of England between the time of Donne . . . and the time of Tennyson" so that sensibility ceased to be "unified" and poets "thought and felt by fits, unbalanced." Eliot later noted that it "had a success in the world astonishing to its author," and it in fact became the foundation of an entire revisionist literary history, especially in the work of F.R. LEAVIS and the New Critics. Later critics have shown that it is extremely doubtful whether any such historical event actually took place.
See also BROOKS, CLEANTH; ELIOT, T.S.; LEAVIS, F.R.; NEW CRITICISM; TATE, ALLEN

Reading
Bateson, F.W. 1951: "Contributions to a dictionary of critical terms. II: Dissociation of sensibility."
Eliot, T.S. 1921 (*1975*): "The metaphysical poets."
Kermode, Frank 1957: *The Romantic Image.*
IAIN WRIGHT

dominant / residual / emergent   Raymond Williams defined and discussed these concepts explicitly in *Marxism and Literature* (1977), though similar ideas about cultural power relationships and the processes of change can be traced back to *Culture and Society* (1958). His argument that a culture is composed of a set of relations between dominant, residual, and emergent forms is a way of emphasizing the uneven and dynamic quality of any particular moment. It represents a shift away from more monumental epochal analyses of history in the manner of HEGEL and LUKÁCS, where periods or stages of history succeed one another and each epoch is characterized by a dominant mode or spirit of the times. Williams argued that it is possible to make general distinctions between different periods of history based on modes of production between "feudal" and "bourgeois," for example, or "capitalist" and "late capitalist." However, he pointed out that these dominant formations are in themselves too broad and need to be further broken down into differentiated moments. Moreover, each epoch not only consists of different variations and stages, but at every point is also composed of a process of dynamic, contradictory relationships in the interplay of dominant, residual, and emergent forms. This opens up a space to analyze the role that subversive and oppositional identities and movements play within the dominant culture, and how effective they might be in shifting it.

Neither residual nor emergent forms simply exist within or alongside the dominant culture. They operate in a process of continual tension, which can take the form of both incorporation and opposition within it. Residual forms are different from archaic ones in that they are still alive, they have use and relevance within contemporary culture. They represent a previous institution or tradition which is still active as a memory in the present, and thus can both bolster the dominant culture or provide the resources for an alternative or opposition to it. In Britain the monarchy could be seen as a residual institution that is gradually being perceived as archaic within popular discourse as it loses its cultural legitimacy. Conversely, the current ethnic and nationalist conflicts in the former Yugoslavia and Soviet Republics can be seen as an example of residual identities challenging and overturning former dominant ones, though not in progressive ways. The rise of religious extremism in various parts of the world is another instance of residual forms challenging the HEGEMONY of liberal Western capitalism. Indeed, it could be argued that all ethnic and religious identities are constructed through the process of keeping residual forms alive, expressing STRUCTURES OF FEELING which the dominant culture denies or represses.

Emergent cultures also develop in relation to dominant formations, and in practice it can be difficult to draw a clear line between residual and emergent forms, for both often consist of private or marginalized spheres of experience which the dominant culture initially fails to acknowledge or recognize. For example, new social forces in contemporary Western society – feminism, the peace movement, and green politics – challenge both the dominant culture and residual oppositional forms such as the "traditional" labour movement, yet may themselves base their identities on selective traditions, or on residual notions of nature. Williams stresses that the dominant culture is itself dependent on incorporating aspects of emergent forms to maintain its legitimacy and hegemony, and that it is often difficult to distinguish between what is genuinely emergent and what is merely novel. The assimilation of subcultural and subversive styles and fashions into mainstream culture is one example of such incorporation. Another is the way in which critical movements, such as poststructuralism, initially an emergent trend in opposition to a residual/dominant literary CANON, have now become a new dominant literary institution.

See also STRUCTURE OF FEELING; WILLIAMS, RAYMOND.

Reading
Williams, Raymond 1961: *The Long Revolution*.
——1977: *Marxism and Literature*.
——1979: "Base and superstructure in Marxist cultural theory."

JENNY BOURNE TAYLOR

double-consciousness   A term central to BLACK CULTURAL STUDIES, which was first articulated by W.E.B. Dubois in *The Souls of Black Folk* (1903). Expressing the acute disenchantment of black intellectuals with post-Reconstruction American society, DuBois argued that all black Americans suffer from a sense of double-consciousness, or conflict between their black and American cultural identities. Caused by the enforced exclusion of blacks from mainstream American society at the turn of the century, this self-division obstructs the development of authentic self-consciousness, for it compels black Americans to regard and evaluate their black identities through the lens of the dominant white culture. Although DuBois's formulation of this dilemma has been criticized (for reflecting a sense of cultural ALIENATION produced by DuBois's intellectual training at elite American educational institutions), the concept of double-consciousness has continued to resonate and exert considerable analytical power in contemporary discussions of the mixed cultural identity of Afro-Americans.

Reading
DuBois, W.E.B. 1903 (*1969*): *The Souls of Black Folk*.
MADHU DUBEY

Douglas, Mary Tew   (1921–) British social anthropologist. She is known for her studies of religion and symbolism, pollution and moral order, her ethnography of the Lele of the Kasai, and for GROUP/GRID analysis. She was one of the leaders of neostructuralism in British anthropology in the 1960s, along with Edmund Leach, Rodney Needham, and Victor Turner. This PARADIGM meant a shift away from the previous focus on norms and actions to an interest in symbolic systems. Mary Douglas derived her interest in the sociology of religion from her education at the Sacred Heart Convent in Roehampton. She subsequently studied philosophy, politics, and economics at Oxford, and then developed an interest in Africa and in anthropology during her job in the Colonial Office 1943–6. She took a BSc in anthropology in Oxford in 1948, where she studied with Evans-Pritchard. She did fieldwork in Zaire (then the Belgian Congo) 1949–50 and again in 1953, and received her PhD in 1951. Her dissertation, published as *The Lele of the Kasai*, has become a classic of ethnography.

In the course of a distinguished academic career, she has authored many books and articles, and coauthored or edited others. She taught for many years at the University of London, retiring with a full professorship in 1978. In 1977 she moved to the United States, serving as resident scholar and director at the Russell Sage Foundation, then teaching at Northwestern University till 1985, and at Princeton till 1988.

Douglas's studies of pollution brought her original fame. In *Purity and Danger* she investigates rituals of purity and impurity, analyzes the significance of dirt and cleanliness in daily life, and examines the social basis for pollution beliefs. She is interested in looking at boundaries and their ritual affirmation. In *Natural Symbols* and some of her other writings, she links CULTURE and society and relates social organization to cosmology. In her symbolic analysis, she focuses less on the meaning of SYMBOLS than on their patterns and STRUCTURES and the relations between them. Her investigations of the nature of classification systems have led to other concerns, such as the study of food as the means to decode systems of social information. She shows that the choices people make about what they eat and how they prepare and present food reflect the organization of social life. Menus can be looked at in terms of categories and opposites: meals contrast with drinks, solids with liquids. In this way the structure of meals can be likened to the structure of myths.

She is also known for her methodology of GROUP/GRID analysis for classifying social relations in order to compare different cultures and their social organization. Her more recent work moves to a broader examination of contemporary society, contrasting modern culture with its predecessors and discussing its evolution. Among her coauthored books, *The World of Goods* investigates the communicative role of economic goods, and the ways individuals reaffirm status through consumption. Another investigates pollution in American industrial society and the growth of the environmental protection movement.

See also GROUP/GRID.

Reading
Douglas, Mary T. 1963: *The Lele of the Kasai*.
—— 1966 (*1985*): *Purity and Danger*.
—— 1970 (*1973*): *Natural Symbols*.
—— and Isherwood, B. 1979: *The World of Goods*.
JANET MACGAFFEY

dream-work A generic term in psychoanalysis referring to all those operations which transform the raw materials of a dream (classically defined as a form of wish fulfillment) into its MANIFEST CONTENT. The raw material of a dream may include dream-thoughts, physical stimuli, childhood memories, allusions to the TRANSFERENCE situation and the day's residues, or in other words, elements from the waking life of the previous day that appear in the dream. The principal operations of the dream-work are CONDENSATION/DISPLACEMENT and secondary revision; it is also governed by conditions of representability. Secondary revision rearranges the dream in such a way as to generate a relatively consistent and coherent scenario; conditions of representability govern the selection and transformation of dream-thoughts into visual images. The overall effect of the dream-work is distortion: although the manifest content is relatively coherent, it is difficult to recognize the latent elements contained within it. The latent content of a dream can be recovered only through interpretation. Freud (1900; 1901) stresses that the dream-work is not a creative process, but one which merely transforms material. It is the dream-work and not the LATENT CONTENT that is the essence of the dream.

Reading
Freud, Sigmund 1900: *The Intepretation of Dreams*.
—— 1901b: "On dreams."
DAVID MACEY

Durkheim, Emile (1858–1917) French social theorist. Recently a friend and I were hiking along a well-established trail in a state park. At the trailhead a sign announced that the trail was restricted to hikers and that no bicycles were allowed. Further on we encountered a couple of youngsters tearing along on bicycles. My friend shouted out that bicycles were not allowed. The cyclists looked sheepish and rode on. My friend's protest nicely illustrates the collective consciousness, a central concept around which Emile Durkheim built much of his theory of society.

Emile Durkheim clearly ranks among the foremost social theorists of all time for both sociology and anthropology. Writing and teaching at the end of the nineteenth century and the beginning of the twentieth, Durkheim succeeded in focusing both fields centrally on group-level social phenomena – social institutions and culture respectively – and in providing both fields with a firm self-identity as a science with practical applications. These ideas had occurred to earlier writers, but Durkheim had global influence owing to the elegance of his analysis, the brilliance of his writing and lecturing, the breadth of his scholarship, and his lifelong commitment to reshaping social investigation into a new scholarly enterprise.

Son of a long line of Jewish rabbis, Durkheim himself initially planned to study for the rabbinate. These expectations were put aside, however, as his studies moved to philosophy, metaphysics, and other subjects. He sought admission to the prestigious Ecole Normale Supérieure, preparing for a career as a teacher, and was admitted. There he was influenced particularly by the philosopher Boutroux, noted for his critiques of scientific argumentation, and by the historian Foustel de Coulanges, whose focus on the development of social forms became his own. The writing of Comte and Spencer provided much of the specific body of social thought upon which Durkheim was to construct his own sociology. While he disagreed with Comte's view in many respects, Durkheim took from Comte the proposition that society could be analyzed by the methods of science (Comte proposed the term "sociology" for this), and that the conclusions could be used to construct an improved society. He was also to disagree sharply with Spencer, but he adopted Spencer's general evolutionary scheme for social progress, and Spencer's assumption that societies were organized as social SYSTEMS.

Durkheim proposed a new conception of the relationship between individuals and their society. Here he disagreed with Comte, who, with many others, assumed that social consensus and loyalty were the summation of the sentiments of the member individuals and that society as an aggregation derived from individuals. This necessarily led to the conclusion that social norms have to be taken into account as a reflection of interests individuals have in common. Psychological, biological, and economic incentives were among the sources examined for laws, customs, and values held in common. Durkheim argued, on the other hand, that society constituted a separate level of reality. Societies were social systems that had their own imperatives, especially to maintain a working whole. To a large extent, the attitudes and interests of individuals stem from the society in which they live. Thus social patterns can be analyzed quite apart from the psychological, economic, and personal characteristics of individuals.

To analyze social systems Durkheim proposed two conceptual tools. The first was the "social fact." Durkheim did not argue that social facts were empirical objects, as he is sometimes misread, but an intellectual device allowing scientific methods of investigation to be applied to social phenomena. The key criterion of a social fact was that it had "coercive effect" over individuals. Where that was true, Durkheim argued, analysis could proceed as thought it were a real object.

When my friend admonished the cyclists, she illustrated the second of Durkheim's conceptual tools, collective conscience. Durkheim proposed that the social identity of individuals transcends the aggregate of individual interests and psychologies. Comprising both intellectual and moral dimensions, the collective conscience links individuals to the social systems, shapes their desires, conforms their behavior to the common good, and follows its own path of development.

Durkheim invested much effort in studying societies of different types, a cross-cultural enterprise that brought his work to the attention of anthropologists. He discerned that the solidarity of a social system was differently constituted for small, traditional societies compared with large, complex ones. In small societies individuals shared similar bodies of information and interests, and performed similar roles in society. Sanctions in these societies were geared to ensuring conformity. Using a term that has confused readers for generations, Durkheim called this form of solidarity "mechanical solidarity." When populations grew larger and societies more densely settled, a necessary division of labor developed and the social system was integrated around complementary roles for individuals. Using an organismic model, Durkheim termed the basis of these systems "organic solidarity," where groups of individuals would have different interests and sectors of the system would function in complementary ways. Law in these societies was "restitutive," functioning to ensure that the interdependencies of distinct sectors remained viable.

Among his many published writings, three books are central. In *Division of Labor* (1893) he set out most of his analysis of society. In *Suicide* (1897) he shows that what seems to be an entirely individual-based event is demonstrably a predictable response to social, systematic factors. In *Elementary Forms of the Religion Life* (1912) Durkheim points to the focal place that religion plays in maintaining the social system and solidarity of individuals. This book, situated in a case analysis of Australian TOTEMISM, is the culmination of Durkheim's life-long analytical enterprise and his most complex analysis. Taken together, his works strongly influenced many who succeeded him. Among those who developed major bodies of theory upon a foundation of Durkheim's work are, notably, Talcott Parsons in sociology, A.R. Radcliffe-Brown and Claude LÉVI-STRAUSS in anthropology, and Marcel MAUSS who straddled both fields.

Emile Durkheim has been accused of blocking the proper exploration of psychological, historical, and economic factors, and the role of the individual in shaping society. In truth, however, social science is built around an interplay of system-level analysis and individual, external factors. For both sociology and anthropology Durkheim is the anchor point for system-based explanations and the classic statement of the concomitants of that approach.

Reading

Durkheim, Emile (1893) (*1984*): *The Division of Labor in Society*.
——(1895) (*1938*): *Rules of Sociological Method*.
——(1897) (*1951*): *Suicide*.
——(1912) (*1968*): *The Elementary Forms of the Religious Life*.
Harris, Marvin 1968: *The Rise of Anthropological Theory*.
Lowie, Robert H. 1937: *The History of Ethnological Theory*.
Thompson, Kenneth 1982: *Emile Durkheim*.

THOMAS C. GREAVES

E

Eagleton, Terry (1943–) British critic, novelist, and playwright. Terry Eagleton is doubtless the most widely read Marxist critic now writing in English. He appears to have systematically and successfully defied the usual social and professional British class boundaries in a way that has contributed to his work. Eagleton is now Thomas Warton Professor of English Literature at Oxford. His many publications include a number of small pamphlet-size books – such as *Criticism and Ideology* (1976), *Marxism and Literary Criticism* (1976), *The Function of Criticism* (1984), and *The Significance of Theory* (1990) – which have all reached a wide audience. But he has also written several more detailed books for what is still a substantial readership. These include *Walter Benjamin* (1981), *Literary Theory: An Introduction* (1983), and *Ideology of the Aesthetic* (1990). In his inaugural lecture as Warton Professor, Eagleton (1993, p. 19) repeated a note that he has sounded throughout all of his recent criticism:

> If . . . everything just goes on as it is, English studies can abandon an illusion that they have anything of significance to say to those outside the charmed circle of academia. And if this comes about, then it will represent a profound betrayal of their own finest traditions. For all the greatest moments of English criticism . . . have been points at which, in speaking of the literary work, criticism has found itself unavoidably speaking of more than it – found itself, indeed, mapping the deep structures and central directions of an entire culture.

His commitment is clearly to the transformative powers of critical literary study.

Reading
Eagleton, Terry 1983: *Literary Theory: An Introduction.*
——1993: *The Crisis of Contemporary Culture.*
                                              MICHAEL PAYNE

ecology   The term "ecology" is rooted in the Greek word *oikos*. In pre-Socratic thought this term is defined as "the whole house," that is, the unity of nature and the sciences. Nature was understood to be permeated by the mind and was, therefore, thought to be alive, intelligent, and rational. Moreover, nature (animals, plants, etc.) was held to participate in the intellectual development of the world. Humans were a part of this nature and had no intention to dominate or control. Nature was in a state of totality, developing in a cycle in which all things were related to and dependent on each other. Despite the constant challenge by theology, this totality of nature formed and remained the basic economic and social structure for all agrarian societies throughout the Middle Ages. The ALIENATION of humankind from nature first entered a critical stage during the age of European bourgeois ENLIGHTENMENT in the eighteenth century. The result was the advancement of the principles of the market economy and technology, both theoretically based on "objective-scientific" methodology.

Bourgeois liberation from feudal suppression began in England and France as early as the late seventeenth century. These developments were based partly on a positive view of nature in which the bourgeoisie saw itself as the dynamic class, capable of changing society. This evolutionary process also led to the recognition of the Great Chain of Being, which should never be broken, as Alexander Pope wrote in his *Essay on Man* (1735). Such ecological insights were reflected in two major changes after 1750 which were based on the slogan of the impending French Revolution: "liberty, equality, fraternity." Baroque garden concepts were replaced with principles based on the ideal of nature, and a first attempt was made to establish animal rights.

Gardens and garden concepts must be understood as a reaction to the massive clearcutting of forests in France in the latter part of the eighteenth century. The attempt to redefine the relation between nature, CULTURE, and society invoked the hope for the possibility of humans recognizing themselves as a part of the order in nature. Humans should find their place in nature as in a garden, as Jean-Jacques ROUSSEAU and others stressed in their writings. The garden was understood to be an ideal landscape in which interventions into nature and its suppression by humans should not be visible; the landscape reflected the multiplicity, the simplicity, and thus the totality of nature. Based on such concepts, gardens were thought to convey the meaning of liberty, thereby enabling humans to place themselves within the quietness and the harmony of nature. In addition, revolutionaries such as Jean-Jacques Rousseau and Morelly combined the economic use of forests with political freedom from an ecological perspective.

Liberty trees were special SYMBOLS at public celebrations of the revolution. These trees represented the cycle of nature and were to function as a guide for a society within nature. A very special liberty tree was the oak tree, which mirrored the overcoming of societal resistance by nature. Accordingly, all local trees were seen as symbolizing the principle of equality, while exotic trees illustrated the principle of brotherhood. In order to move such ideal concepts into a more practical realm, newly wedded couples were first to plant 100 trees and thereby prove their responsibility for the future of society.

In addition, programs for the reforestation of large areas were also supposed to contribute to the welfare of the public and to correct the destructive forces of clearcutting. The goal of all these activities and plans was to overcome the contrasts between the CITY and the countryside and change France into a big garden city. On the one hand this city was to reflect valuable artwork within the concepts of revolutionary art determined by its usefulness; on the other hand the beauty of the garden city was to be enhanced by landscaping and parks. Such architectural concepts, as well as the lifestyle that was to be realized in this city, were seen as ecological. Furthermore, it was hoped that such concepts would spread revolutionary goals to the countryside.

In the same manner that revolutionaries rejected aristocratic luxury parks as parasitic, antisocial, and destructive; they also argued for the equality of all animals. In order to regain the liberty and dignity of animals caged in by the ruling class, the notion of usefulness was stressed again. Since animals experienced the same pain and the same suffering as humans, animals had to become their true partners. The general admiration for animals culminated in the demand that animals were to be kept in open-air enclosures. In England liberal voices were raised postulating equal rights not only for pets but for all animals, for example, in *On the Duty of Mercy and Sin of Cruelty to Brute Animals* (1761) by Humphrey Primatt and *The Cry of Nature, or An Appeal to Mercy and Justice on Behalf of the Persecuted Animals* (1797) by John Oswald. Some even went so far as to regard the hunting, slaughtering, and eating of animals as cannibalism.

However, these ecological concepts failed. Instead, the principles of a "free market economy" described by Adam Smith in his book *Enquiry on the Nature and the Causes of the Wealth of Nations* (1776) prospered. Thus ecological concepts moved to the background at the beginning of the nineteenth century, when the bourgeoisie saw liberation into capitalism as its primary goal. ENLIGHTENMENT concepts in regard to nature were still found in works by Alexander von Humboldt, Ralph Waldo EMERSON, and Henry David Thoreau. In *Views of Nature* (1808) Humboldt vividly described the unity of nature on the American continent, commenting on the abundance of animals and plants in their geographical, geological, and biological variety, and stressing the pristine character of nature still untouched by economic developments. Despite the obvious religious implications in such works, nature was presented in the form of an ecological totality, which would enable humankind to return to a primordial state.

Such descriptions, however insightful, had no impact on overall economic developments. More successful were animal rights activists, including writers and philosophers such as Percy Bysshe Shelley, Jean-Antoine Gleizès, and Arthur Schopenhauer. Several "vegetarian societies" were founded in England and France in the early nineteenth century and several laws were passed prohibiting cruelty to animals. These attempts finally reached a broader public toward the end of the nineteenth century when such well-known individuals as John Ruskin, Robert Browning, Mark Twain, George Bernard Shaw, Richard Wagner, Charles Darwin, Henry S. Salt, and H.G. Wells protested against vivisection or wrote books and essays in which they embraced vegetarianism.

Within the political and economic development of the bourgeoisie a renewed interest in ecological concepts unfolded in Germany, England, and the

United States around 1850. Such perceptions were noted in the works of Wilhelm Heinrich Riehl (*Natural History of the German People*, 1851–69), Charles Darwin (*On the Origin of Species by Means of Natural Selection, or the Preservation of Favoured Races in the Struggle for Life*, 1859), and George Perkins Marsh (*Man and Nature*, 1864). While Riehl hoped to stop the process of industrialization and urbanization by recommending a return to an agrarian-feudalist society, March, noting the degree of pollution and destruction of the East Coast of the United States, argued for a government-organized, rational approach to natural resources. Darwin, on the other hand, was hoping for a predominance of altruism over egotistic desires. His book, however, was understood mostly and especially by social Darwinists as an interpretation of the principles of market economy, competition, and progress. Equally well known were the concepts of monism, based on both Darwin's evolutionism and a romantic pantheism. The German monist intellectual Ernst Haeckel became world famous and in his *General Morphology of Organisms* (1866) was the first to define ecology as the various relations of animals and plants to one another and to the outer world.

Industrialization and urbanization in the nineteenth century in Europe and North America similarly led to ecological insights among the theoreticians of socialism. While Karl MARX had praised capitalism as the only revolutionary force within modern developments in the 1840s, he later had doubts about the capitalist means of production when he noticed the economic and social conditions in England in the 1850s and 1860s. In *Capital* (1867) he wrote that capitalism constituted the overexploitation not only of the worker but also of natural resources. Consequently, he saw the circulation of matter between the soil and humans as the only possibility for a lasting fertility of the soil and nature in general. In his opinion, capitalist production developed the technology and the combination of a variety of social processes only to exploit all original sources of wealth: the soil and the laborer. Along the same lines, Friedrich ENGELS wrote in his *Dialectics of Nature* (1871 (*1973*)) that every victory over nature at the same time meant a loss with unforeseeable and unknown consequences. While Marx and Engels did not speculate about the future of socialism, other artists and writers such as Peter Kropotkin and William Morris did. Kropotkin's *Fields, Factories and Workshops*

Tomorrow (1899) was based on the notion of anarchism to establish an ecological future, and served as a practical model for North American and European communists and anarcho-syndicalists such as Gustav Landauer, Bertrand RUSSELL, and Heinrich Vogeler well into the 1920s. Morris, on the other hand, in his novel *News from Nowhere* (1890), designed a blueprint of an ideal socialist society free of all class differences as well as all forms of exploitation. Morris's concept of ecology was most striking in his definition of beauty, which he understood as the most powerful and most positive tool against the ugliness of planned obsolescence in consumer society.

In the United States, which by the early 1880s after a period of unleashed economic growth had replaced England as the largest industrial power, individuals such as John Muir noted the effects of economic "progress" on nature. In his most popular book, *Our National Parks* (1901), in which he paid tribute to Emerson, Thoreau, and Charles Sprague Sargent, he wrote that, while the beauty of nature still existed, it was also extremely endangered by industrialization, urbanization, and farming. To overcome the devastation caused by the utilitarian forces of the industry, Muir argued for a government-organized administration of the forests, as well as for the preservation of nature within the National Park System, which had been established in 1872. However, Muir's strong religious worshipping of nature prevented the public from understanding the political implications of his recommendations.

While William Morris, like many utopian thinkers around 1900, saw socialism as the only political force which would enable the coherence of social interchange prescribed by the natural laws of life, the German petty bourgeois *Heimatschutz* ("protection of homeland") movement must be understood as a reaction against both socialism and capitalism. Between 1880 and 1914 teachers, authors, and civil servants published a large number of essays and books that described vividly the consequences of rapid industrialization and urbanization in Germany: widespread pollution of water and air, the clearcutting of forests, and the devastation caused by tourism and billboards. When the *Heimatschutz* organization was founded in 1904 it demanded the institutionalization of a national park system modelled after that of the United States. Moreover, its goals included the protection of the German homeland in its natural and historical environment, the preservation of flora and fauna, as well as local architecture. However, *Heimatschutz* activists hoped that the polluting and exploitative system could be overcome simply by "good intentions." Despite their outreach, which led to international conferences in Paris (1909) and Stuttgart (1912) in which almost all European countries and Japan participated, their fight remained ineffective.

The examination of ecological concepts during the era of European fascism, and especially National Socialism in Germany, is somewhat problematic. While coalitions of fascist parties with bourgeois governments were the rule in almost all European countries in the 1920s and 1930s, it was only the Nazis who seem to have expressed certain environmental concerns. Indeed, the Nazis adopted some ideas of the petty bourgeois *Heimatschutz* movement, the life reform movements from around 1900, and the settlers movement from the 1920s, all of which they regarded as precursors to volkish IDEOLOGY. The leading theoretician was Richard Walter Darré, who became Minister for Agriculture in 1933. His goal was to develop Germany into a healthy peasant state, built on a biologically dynamic agriculture. Supporters of such ideas believed they had a strong ally in Adolf Hitler, who was well known for his love of animals, his vegetarianism, and his rejection of vivisection. Such inclinations, however, soon turned out to be false, since Hitler's true goals were the creation of jobs and the development of a strong military industry. The results were renewed industrialization, massive migrations from the land to the cities, and thus large-scale environmental degradation. Even several laws which were passed between 1934 and 1936 to protect German "art, culture, and nature" were purely of a propagandistic character. More and more, National Socialism revealed itself as an ideologically incoherent system ruled by the dictatorship of the gaining and maintaining of power. Such power struggles, along with the politics of military armament and economic autarky, were diametrically opposed to any ecological concepts. None the less, the display of hypocritical laws and their vegetarianism based on Buddhist occultism severely corrupted all sincere concepts of ecology and vegetarianism in Germany.

After 1945 the United States emerged as the leading economic and political power of the West. Thus it is no surprise that the interest in ecological concepts after the end of the 1939–45 war emerged first in that country. The analyses were based mostly on different experiences, namely the dust storms of the 1930s resulting from soil erosion, clearcutting and overgrazing, as well as the development of biological, chemical, and atomic weapons during the war. Scientists such as Fairfield Osborn (*Our Plundered Planet*, 1948) and Aldo Leopold (*Sand County Almanack*, 1949) were among the first to warn of diminishing natural resources and the growing world population and to outline ecological alternatives. The first book to become a bestseller was Rachel Carson's *Silent Spring* (1962), listed in the *New York Times* for 31 weeks. Carson outlined the negative effects of the use of pesticides, which contaminated the earth's surface and would soon endanger all forms of life on the planet. In addition, books such as Barry Commoner's *Science and Survival* (1963), Gary Snyder's *Earth Household* (1963), Paul Ehrlich's *The Population Bomb* (1968), Theodore ROSZAK's *The Making of a Counter Culture* (1968), and Barry Commoner's *The Closing Circle: Nature, Man, and Technology* (1970) drew more and more attention to the pollution of soil, water, and air, population growth, and the merciless eradication of wild animals and plants. The slogan "biology or death" reached widespread popularity when the mass media repeatedly reported on chemical warfare in Vietnam and publicized environmental catastrophes such as the oil spills caused by the tanker *Torrey Canyon* off the British coast in 1967 and the blowout of the oil platform off the coast of Santa Barbara, California, in 1969. Among the first to adopt the term "ecology" were the hippies, who popularized slogans such as "solar energy," "water power," "turning on to nature," or "survival with grace" in magazines such as *The Mother Earth News*. In referring to "the great refusal," a term coined by Herbert MARCUSE, the hippies did not want to participate in the destruction of nature and instead embraced the idea of the simple life.

All these publications and protests contributed to the environmental campaign which Gaylord Nelson from Wisconsin started in the US Senate, leading to the establishing of the semi-official "Earth Day" in 1970 and the founding of the Environmental Protection Agency (EPA). More than 500,000 people participated in the first "Earth Day" activities, building either on the EPA's "ecotactics" or on recycling, a more sparing use of resources as well as the activities of the individual. It was hoped that these measures would soon allow a return to normalcy.

But the doomsday shock was further reinforced by a study conducted by European industrialists and scientists, developed at the Massachusetts Institute of Technology in Boston, fostered by the "Club of Rome," and published in 1971 under the title *The Limits to Growth*. The goal of this analysis was to determine the timeframe for the collapse of the economic system due to the oppositional state of diminishing natural resources and the growth of the world population. Among the recommendations were a drastic limitation on population growth, a sparing use of resources, and a radical reduction in consumerism. Since the book was translated immediately into almost all languages, it can be seen as the beginning of an unprecedented, worldwide, environmental awareness, as well as the onset of the theoretical DISCOURSE on ecology. Moreover, the study indirectly reinforced the understanding that, in terms of pollution and exploitation of natural resources, there was little difference between a privately organized economy and an economy run by the state.

The large number of publications concerning "environmental protection" caused a number of developments, starting in the 1970s. Among the first was the founding of international organizations such as *Greenpeace* in 1971, which protested against atomic testing, air and water pollution, as well as the killing of animals. Owing to intense media coverage, this protest reached an increasingly concerned public around the globe. In order to resist the process of constant industrialization, ecologists such as E.F. Schumacher and Murray Bookchin prescribed the concept "small is beautiful," which aimed at a comprehensible world view within a locally defined economy, thus displaying the ecological slogan "Think globally, act locally." A typical example for this concept was Ernest Callenbach's novel *Ecotopia* (1975), a blueprint for a peaceful and ecological society that has abandoned the devastation and exploitation of nature. In his novel, *Ecotopia Emerging* (1981), Callenbach even described how a growing ecological consciousness led to concrete politics that resulted in the separation of the states of Oregon, Washington, and Northern California from the rest of the United States. Such books reflected realistically events in North America and Europe during the 1970s, namely the formation of "green" movements.

Moreover, the oil crisis which marked the beginning of the 1970s also led to a search for different energy sources. Consequently, atomic power was hailed as a savior from all energy problems. Protests against the construction of atomic power stations were waged across Western Europe throughout the 1970s, leading to a well-organized peace movement by 1980. In the United States the No-Nukes movement expressed similar goals and received widespread support, particularly after the "accident" at the Pennsylvania atomic power plant on Three Mile Island in March 1978 became public knowledge.

The first "green" party to gain worldwide attention was the West German Greens (*Die Grünen*), which was founded in 1980 and at that time consisted of a variety of protest groups, including leftists, feminists, anarchists, pacifists, and conservative farmers. Prominent members of this anti-party party, as they called themselves, were the feminist Petra K. Kelly (*Fighting for Hope*, 1983) and the Marxist Rudolf Bahro. Similarly, East German Marxists such as Wolfgang Harich (*Kommunismus ohne Wachstum?/ Communism without Growth?* 1975) and Robert Havemann (*Morgen. Die Industriegesellschaft am Scheideweg/ Tomorrow. Industrial Society at the Crossroads*, 1980) critiqued the report by the "Club of Rome," offering ecosocialism as a possible solution. Such ecological and political alternatives were indirectly supported by the study *Global 2000* (1980), initiated by US President Jimmy Carter. This analysis predicted a world population of 6.3 billion by the year 2000, growing desertification, rapid diminishing of natural resources, increase in the devastation of ecosystems, etc. However, the growing number of right-wing governments in the early 1980s in the "First World" and their promises for more economic "progress" quickly dismissed such warnings as apocalyptic and unfounded.

The promises for "growth" were partly related to the decision of NATO in 1979 to station more strategic weapons in Western Europe. Despite massive protests by the peace movement supported by the Greens, especially in Germany, the deployment of Cruise missiles and Pershings was begun in 1982. This resulted in widespread anger and fear, and found its artistic expression in literature and films thematizing "the death of nature" as well as scenarios of an impending atomic apocalypse. Moreover, theories defining the present time in terms of "postmodernity" and *posthistoire* were popularized in the United States and Europe, thereby adding to a growing fragmentation of environmental politics. Nevertheless, such developments did not stop ecological parties and movements worldwide from becoming the most popular political force in the 1980s. Their peaceful and ecological politics were reinforced by disasters such as Chernobyl (1986) and Bhopal (1989), the long-term ecological consequences of which will remain unknown for many years.

The 1971 report *The Limits to Growth* had also made obvious that the wealth of the "First World" was entirely dependent on the exploitation of the "Third World." Political activism of the 1960s against the war in Vietnam and for the liberation of the peoples in the "Third World" increasingly grew into protests against the devastation of the "Third World" during the 1970s and 1980s. Protests raged against the clearcutting of the rainforest, the plundering of resources in Antarctica, the killing of whales for "scientific research," the overfishing of the world's oceans, the dumping of atomic and chemical waste into the oceans, etc. These activities were often led by international organizations such as *Greenpeace* and supported by local ecological organizations and parties.

The period of unleashed economic "growth" in the industrialized counties which lasted throughout most of the 1980s added to the feeling of powerlessness, hopelessness, and apathy among many people, leading to a withdrawal from political action. Such individuals and groups generally welcomed the arrival of New Age philosophy of which the physicist Fritjof Capra (*The Turning Point*, 1982) was probably the most prominent figure. Not unlike the followers of "deep ecology," their dream was to regain the unity of humankind and nature, based on the ideas of anthropocentric spirituality and biocentric equality. Moreover, such individualistic prophecies were mostly guided by the understanding that the coming of the "new age" cannot be stopped, despite the ongoing devastation and exploitation of nature. This fragmentation enabled heavy attacks worldwide on organizations such as *Greenpeace* by the industry and mass media. According to such accusations the only difference between *Greenpeace* and multinational corporations was that their "profits" were based on "selling" an ecological ideology which was untimely, unnecessary, and just as exploitative. Thus the "Earth Summit," orchestrated by the industrialized nations in Rio de Janeiro in the summer of 1992, did not lead to any results, since the criticism of world trade and its devastating impact on the world's ecosystem was systematically excluded from the discussion.

There can be no doubt that the concepts of ecological movements and individuals so far have failed to gain influence on the ideology of "growth" and "development." In the wake of the political changes in the Eastern bloc countries, "free market economy" again has become the dominating principle by which the exploitation of natural resources and the "Third World" is legitimized. On the other hand, the large number of publications, ranging from a "red–green" left (for example, the periodical *Capitalism, Nature, Socialism*) to scientific treatises such as Donella and Dennis Meadows's and Jørgen Randers's *Beyond the Limits: Confronting Global Collapse, Envisioning a Sustainable Future* (1992) and the "World scientists' warning to humanity" (1992), signed by 1,575 scientists from 69 countries, as well as liberalist politicians examining the future of the planet in their books, is proof that the debate about the survival of humankind has entered a crucial stage. However, such liberalists tend to fail in their analysis of the relation between the exploitation of natural resources, consumer ideology, and population growth. Such an analysis is vital, considering the projected population growth and the impending "irreversibility" in the devastation of nature before the middle of the twenty-first century. Obviously, radical changes of this course, which has been described aptly as suicidal, are necessary. Political and economic programs based on ecological insights such as solidarity, brother- and sisterhood, and guided by the concept "fewer people, less consumption" are needed in order to avoid a relapse into the Stone Age. Similarly, a new ETHICS in respect of nature, culture, material needs, and life in general, along with an educational system built on respect, tolerance, and peacefulness, is essential. The decentralization of political and economic power is a first step in order to return responsibilities to regions and local businesses, producing high-quality and long-lasting goods made by individuals who can be proud of their achievements. Similarly, alternative energy sources need to be developed, mass tourism has to be reduced drastically, and rare resources must be recycled. Overall, the industrialized countries have to move away from a society run by high-tech computers and instead have to find programs for the integration of nature and technology on a local level. Of course, such activities require much planning as well as a challenge to the right to the unlimited exploitation of nature.

Reading
Bassin, Mark 1992: "Geographical determinism in fin-de-siècle Marxism: Georgii Plekhanov and the environmental basis of Russian history."

Bookchin, Murray 1980 (*1991*): *Toward an Ecological Society*.

Bramwell, Anna 1989: *Ecology in the 20th Century. A History*.

Collingwood, R.G. 1945 (*1972*): *The Idea of Nature*.

Eckersley, Robyn 1992: *Environmentalism and Political Theory. Toward an Ecocentric Approach*.

Grimm, Reinhold, and Hermand, Jost, eds 1989: *From the Greeks to the Greens. Images of the Simple Life*.

Grundmann, Rainer 1991: *Marxism and Ecology*.

Harten, Hans-Christian, and Harten, Elke 1989: *Die Versöhnung mit der Natur. Gärten, Freiheitsbäume, republikanische Wälder, heilige Berge und Tugendparks in der Französischen Revolution*.

Hermand, Jost 1991: *Grüne Utopien in Deutschland. Zur Geschichte des ökologischen Bewusstseins*.

Illich, Ivan 1973: *Tools for Conviviality*.

Levins, Richard, and Lewontin, Richard 1985: *The Dialectical Biologist*.

McCormick, John 1989: *Reclaiming Paradise. The Global Environmental Movement*.

Pepper, David 1993: *Eco-Socialism. From Deep Ecology to Social Justice*.

Tokar, Brian 1987 (*1992*): *The Green Alternative. Creating an Ecological Future*.

PETER MORRIS-KEITEL

education The issues of cultural representation, selection, and production in education are exemplified at their sharpest by the debates on the school curriculum. Three approaches to discussions of CULTURE and school curricula can be characterized: (i) the derivation of curricula from analyses of culture (the cultural representation model); (ii) the critique of cultural reproduction through school curricula (the IDEOLOGY–critical model); (iii) the generation of curricula to further social justice (the cultural production and empowerment model). These approaches reinterpret a Weberian analysis of the links between culture, social status, the economic order, and the distribution of power in society (see Weber's analysis of society in terms of CLASS, status, and power (1922)).

During this century several attempts have been made to derive curricula from an analysis of culture. Some of these reveal the intertwining of culture and social CLASS. T.S. ELIOT's *Notes Towards the Definition of Culture* (1948) argues for the preservation of a "HIGH CULTURE" classical and academic curriculum (for example, the arts, philosophy, manners, the accumulated wisdom of the past) which is taught to a social elite and which helps to preserve an elitist society. Culture, in this definition, is a social accomplishment, a locater of class. In the United Kingdom this was echoed in Bantock's *Towards a Theory of Popular Education* (1975) in which a "high culture" curriculum was to be the preserve of a social elite while a "folk curriculum," rather than an academically "watered down" curriculum, was to be made available to the working classes, comprising recreations and pastimes, dance, media studies, family life, affective/artistic/physical (as opposed to cognitive/intellectual) curricula, design, and craftwork. The social divisiveness of such curriculum proposals was parallelled by Midwinter's (1972) work in which working-class children were to study curricula which deemphasized literacy and numeracy and which placed great store on the study of the immediate physical environment, "warts and all," and community education. Differential access to differential curricula was seen to reproduce the societal status quo.

Attempts to break the nexus of social class and school curricula have been made through moves to ensure equality of access to a common culture curriculum. Such moves adopt an anthropological rather than elitist interpretation of culture, defining it as everything that is created by humans and which is shared and transmitted by members of social groups. Cultural analysis here adopts a more neutral, descriptive approach than those designed to perpetuate class divisions. The *Core Curriculum for Australian Schools* (Curriculum Development Centre, 1980) comprised elements of a common multiculture – seeking a form of cultural integration which emphasized interaction between diverse groups – and an identification of core learning processes, learning experiences, and knowledge, an entitlement to which was the right of all children.

In the United Kingdom Lawton's *Education, Culture and the National Curriculum* (1989) provides a fuller example of a curriculum which addresses specific features of a culture. He identifies "cultural invariants" (for example, the economic system, sociopolitical system, technology system) and characterizes these in the context of contemporary England (for example, dense population, urbanized, industrialized, multicultural, secular), moving to a series of prescriptions for curricula which represent key elements of English culture (for example, studying urbanization, economic systems, multicultural education, political education, tolerance). Lawton's work on cultural analysis over two decades, however, has been criticized for being superficial, neglectful of critique, silent on issues of power and conflict, value-laden, under-researched, consensus-seeking, and selective (Whitty, 1985). Nevertheless Lawton, in stating that the curriculum is necessarily a selection from culture, sets the ground for a fuller analysis of the problems that this selection brings. These include the problem of cultural inclusion and exclusion, the legitimacy of decision makers, and the interests which are served by such inclusion and exclusion, in short a sociology and ideology critique of school knowledge.

An ideology critique of school knowledge questions the functions of school knowledge in its relationship to the wider society. Young (1971) argued that school curricula celebrated an academic culture, focusing on mental rather than manual aspects of education, being literary, individualized, abstract, and unrelated to everyday life. In the same volume BERNSTEIN linked this to forms of social control, arguing that according high status to academic knowledge reproduced existing class and power differentials in society. Poulantzas (1975) extended this analysis by arguing that schools reproduce the mental/manual social divide in the qualifications that they award, essentially rewarding mental activity and disqualifying (not certificating) manual labor, a view that was given empirical support in Willis's *Learning to Labour* (1977). That the school curriculum is tenaciously resistant to the abandonment of an academic tradition and its cultural links with state-endorsed social reproduction can be seen in Hargreaves's references to the "hegemonic academic curriculum" (1989).

Nor does simply equalizing access to an academic curriculum guarantee that the socially and culturally reproductive effects of schooling will be upset easily. BOURDIEU's powerful analysis of the school as a conservative force (1976) argues that students' success at school is a function of their possession of "cultural capital" and "habitus" (Bourdieu, 1977) (for example, dispositions, attitudes, and motivations to learning; parental support for education; social advantage; ease in dealing with authority figures; linguistic ability; high culture). Students with the cultural capital and habitus that correspond with those in schools can maximize their uptake of the school curriculum, for they can engage with it easily and comfortably; for those students with limited cultural capital or different habitus the school curriculum represents an alien culture such that their uptake of it is correspondingly limited. The same curriculum, offered equally to all, produces differential outcomes which, in turn, perpetuate the societal status quo. The curriculum, therefore, performs an ideological function in reproducing cultural and social inequality under the guise of equality of opportunity, suggesting that it is natural ability rather than structural inequality which causes differential outcomes, focusing attention away from the socially reproductive effects of academic curricula.

Bourdieu's analysis resonates with ALTHUSSER's (1972) structuralist account of education as an IDEO-LOGICAL STATE APPARATUS which functions to prepare students in terms of ideology and knowledge to fulfill differing economic demands of capitalism. This theme is extended in Bowles's and Gintis's (1976) account of the operation of the "hidden curriculum" of developing personality traits which prepare future factory workers in America (1976), in a study of differential teacher expectations and interactions by social class in New Jersey schools by Anyon (1980), and in Delpit's (1988) analysis of how "cultures of power" are reproduced in classrooms. In all of these accounts there is little opportunity for teachers and students to escape from the mechanism.

In contrast to these watertight and deterministic systems, Giroux (1983) argues that schools are "relatively autonomous" institutions, that teachers are not "cultural dopes" or puppets of the state. Teachers and students can exert their agency. Recognizing this, however, renders the problems of cultural imperialism in curricula no less soluble. Cultural analysis has to engage issues of power and legitimacy in curricula and their relationship to the wider society; it requires a political analysis of the school curriculum.

Giroux argues that cultural domination is as pervasive as it is insidious, and therefore teachers and students will need to seize any opportunity for resistance; they will need to look for "chinks in the armour." This enterprise will entail a critical interrogation of curricula to question whose cultures are "named" (confirmed) and whose are "silenced" (disconfirmed) in them (Fine, 1987), be they in terms of RACE, CLASS, GENDER, or subcultural membership. This endorses the message of Freire's *Pedagogy of the Oppressed* (1972), which advocates the empowerment of currently disempowered social groups by developing literacy programs which are rooted in the concrete experiences of different cultural groups of Brazilian society.

Decisions on curriculum content reflect and reinforce the power structures of society. Anyon's (1981) analysis of American social studies textbooks found that they omitted and delegitimized (i) conflict and alternatives to capitalist economies;

(ii) inequalities of power by race, class, and gender; (iii) inequalities of political and economic power. In the United Kingdom the contentious nature of the cultural content of curricula was evidenced in the debate over proposals for a history curriculum, which was seen to celebrate white, supremacist, and imperialist cultures. Apple (1993) argues that the imposition of a national curriculum in American schools disregards cultural diversity in favor of a putative, identifiable, mainstream culture. The effects of this, however, are to reproduce existing power differentials in society and to serve a wider conservative political culture of consumerism, acquisitiveness, competitiveness, and privatization which perpetuates the power of the already empowered and the disempowering of the already disempowered. Echoing Giroux, Apple argues that the proposal for a national curriculum issues from a dominant and dominating culture and is ideological in that, under the guise of serving individual freedoms, the agenda for the curriculum given by the dominant political power is not called into question. Rather, he argues, it is the conditions for cultural diversity in the school curriculum that should be guaranteed in proposals for a national curriculum.

The ideology critique of Giroux's works owes much to the CRITICAL THEORY of the FRANKFURT SCHOOL, particularly the work of ADORNO, HORKHEIMER, and MARCUSE. More recent analyses of the curriculum are informed by aspects of the work of Jürgen HABERMAS. Habermas's threefold schema of knowledge–constitutive interests can be used to identify the interests at work in the curriculum and to suggest an agenda for cultural empowerment (for example, Grundy (1987) and Smyth (1991)). A curriculum which is premised on Habermas's technical interest is culturally controlled and controlling, that is, it is culturally and socially reproductive. A curriculum which is premised on Habermas's HERMENEUTIC interest is culturally reproductive in its effects (rather than necessarily its intentions) in that its concern for understanding overlooks questions of legitimacy and ideology critique. Habermas's emancipatory interest suggests a curriculum which, through active and experiential pedagogies, interrogates the legitimacy of social and cultural determinants of school knowledge and promotes the collective empowerment of diverse cultures and subcultures in society (Morrison (1994a). The link between critique and empowerment recharges and politically radicalizes Dewey's progressivism for the promotion of democracy

(Morrison, 1989). In this view the school curriculum becomes socially transformative rather than reproductive. It furthers social justice and the realization of collective existential futures, equalizing and redistributing power in society.

Further, Habermas's appeal to COMMUNICATIVE ACTION (1984; 1987) can be seen as a means of breaking the "suppression of generalizable interests" of scientific rationality. Communicative rationality, in which interests, powers, and cultural empowerment are rendered transparent and judged by their capacity to realize the "ideal speech situation" and constraint-free communication, celebrates the cultural specificity of school curricula. In Habermasian terms, the lifeworlds of teachers and students can be "recoupled" to structural elements of society through curricula which work on and with the cultural fabric of specific societies and groups. This argues for a cultural problematization of school curricula (both formal and hidden) and the espousal of pedagogies which derive from the "ideal speech situation," for example: cooperative and collaborative work; discussion-based teaching; activities which critically interrogate curriculum content; autonomous and experiential learning; negotiated learning; community-related activities; problem-solving activities (Morrison, 1994b).

Arguing for culturally diverse curricula suggests that power to take decisions on curriculum content is diffuse and decentered. While this accords with Foucauldian notions of multiple sites and channels of power (FOUCAULT, 1980), while it breaks with Marxist conceptions of the limited locus of power (see MARXISM), and while it recognizes that education is an "essentially contested" concept, this view sits uncomfortably with the experience of many nations across the world where decisions on curriculum content are taken by increasingly interventionist and *dirigiste* governments. However, the cultural problematics of school curricula will not go away; struggles over cultural representation, cultural diversity, and the empowerment of cultural groups in curricula continue to reflect the coupling of power and ideology in society and continue to treat the school curriculum as a "contested terrain" (Giroux, 1983). The case against cultural diversity in the curriculum argues for a central cultural spine in society to counter the perceived threats to the existing social and moral order which are posed when diversity slips into relativism; the case for diversity argues that anything else is either ideological or socially reproductive.

Reading

Althusser, L. 1972: "Ideology and ideological state apparatuses."

Anyon, J. 1980: "Social class and the hidden curriculum of work."

——1981: "Schools as agencies of social legitimation."

Apple, M. 1993: *Official Knowledge: Democratic Education in a Conservative Age.*

Bantock, G. 1975: "Towards a theory of popular education."

Bourdieu, P. 1976: "The school as a conservative force: scholastic and cultural inequalities."

——1977: *Outline of a Theory of Practice.*

Bowles, S., and Gintis, H. 1976: *Schooling in Capitalist America.*

Curriculum Development Centre 1980: *Core Curriculum for Australian Schools.*

Delpit, L.D. 1988: "The silenced dialogue: power and pedagogy in educating other people's children."

Eliot, T.S. 1948: *Notes Towards the Definition of Culture.*

Fine, M. 1987: "Silencing in public schools."

Foucault, M. 1980b: *Power/Knowledge: Selected Interviews and Other Writings 1972–77.*

Freire, P. 1972: *Pedagogy of the Oppressed.*

Giroux, H. 1983: *Theory and Resistance in Education.*

Grundy, S. 1987: *Curriculum: Product or Praxis.*

Habermas, J. 1984: *The Theory of Communicative Action. Vol. I: Reason and the Rationalization of Society.*

——1987: *The Theory of Communicative Action, Vol. II: Lifeworld and System.*

Hargreaves, A. 1989: *Curriculum and Assessment Reform.*

Lawton, D. 1989: *Education, Culture and the National Curriculum.*

Midwinter, E. 1975: "Curriculum and the EPA community school."

Morrison, K.R.B. 1989: "Bringing progressivism into a critical theory of education."

——1994a: *Implementing Cross-Curricular Themes.*

——1994b: "Habermas, pedagogy and the school curriculum."

Poulantzas, N. 1975: *Classes in Contemporary Capitalism.*

Smyth, J. 1991: *Teachers as Collaborative Learners.*

Weber, M. 1922a (*1948*): "Wirtschaft und Gesellschaft."

Whitty, G. 1985: *Sociology and School Knowledge.*

Willis, P. 1977: *Learning to Labour.*

Young, M.F.D., ed. 1971: *Knowledge and Control.*

KEITH MORRISON

eighteenth-century studies   There is more than one eighteenth century, just as there is more than one form of CRITICAL and CULTURAL THEORY. The English literature, history, and culture of the period 1660–1798, variously known as "Augustan," "neoclassical," "ENLIGHTENMENT," and simply "eighteenth-century" – a period consciously and consistently interested in its relations with the Greek and Roman classical past as well as with its own recent civil and political history – has not received the kind of striking and transforming attention

from contemporary theoretical readings as have Renaissance, Romantic, and modern literature. One reason for this relative lack of interest in eighteenth-century literature by critical theorists lies in what is taken to be the recalcitrance of the material itself. Eighteenth-century thought has commonly been perceived as absolutist, positivist, rational, and logocentric – philosophical and literary properties that DECONSTRUCTION, DISCOURSE theory, Lacanianism, feminism, NEW HISTORICISM, and other forms of cultural theory have sought to challenge since the 1960s. John Bender (1992), for example, sees the conservative nature and the linguistic and political unawareness of traditional eighteenth-century studies as rooted in its similarities to the postulates of eighteenth-century thought itself, a historical and epistemological situation that has enforced the confidence and unreflexiveness of that traditional scholarship, but which has also obviated the possibility of real critical knowledge that only comes, according to Bender who cites Anthony Giddens (1990), when the inquirer stands *outside* the framework of reference occupied by the object of study. This not only challenges traditional positivist historical scholarship, which has assumed that critical truth depended on seeing the past in *its own terms*, but it *also* implies that the recent advent of CRITICAL THEORY in eighteenth-century studies challenges the ideals and frame of reference of the eighteenth century itself.

It is precisely this apparent subversiveness of critical theory with regard to meaning, truth, and historical continuity – values that have been central to the ideological study of the period – that eighteenth-century scholars have deplored. An implicit debate has continued between those who see historical understanding as reading works of the century "on and within their own terms," and those who see it as necessarily entailing a reading from the perspective of later developments. The best recent critical work, including some of the books in the reading list below, is able to incorporate both perspectives, while the least stimulating believes in the self-sufficiency of one or the other perspective.

However, the act of distinguishing between what is "of the past" and what is "of the present" is problematic, because, as Hayden White, Stephen Greenblatt, Michel FOUCAULT, and other cultural historiographers (not to mention postcolonial critics) have argued, historical understanding and the language in which it is encoded are influenced by the

IDEOLOGY of our present position. This situation cuts both ways, delimiting the parameters of *both* traditional and theoretical approaches to the eighteenth century. On the one hand, the eighteenth century is understood as deeply empirical, referential, and ordered, and therefore the ahistoricity and skepticism of Derridean and DE MANian deconstruction suggest values and procedures hostile to the notions of evidence, history, and truth that have underpinned eighteenth-century scholarship. On the other hand, the assumption that critical and cultural theory has developed textual and philosophical apparatuses that *exceed* the techniques and capacities of Dryden, Rochester, Pope, Swift, Fielding, Richardson, Johnson, Boswell, Gibbon, and Burke – to mention only a few canonical male writers of the period – effectively not only keeps the eighteenth century fixed in a hegemonic mode in our minds, but also reveals the historical and critical naivety of contemporary theory.

This situation raises an acutely important point about the nature of historical knowledge and the grounds of evidence for historical understanding that pertains to contemporary literary studies in general. The question of whether "history" is real or textual has haunted every debate about the value of critical theory. Indeed, one might argue that the importance of the question of historical consciousness and historical knowledge in eighteenth-century literature and eighteenth-century studies is an indication of the centrality of the eighteenth century in literary history rather than its marginality. But the exemplariness of eighteenth-century thought in this respect is exactly the opposite of what Bender takes it to be in the article cited above. For the resistance that canonical eighteenth-century literature has shown to critical theory is highly revealing of two factors that are seldom if ever taken into consideration by "specialists." It tells us as much about the point of view from which eighteenth-century works are *read* as it does about the works themselves; and it exemplifies a mode of historical consciousness and historical *production* that POSTMODERNISM has only recently discovered and articulated in its reading of NIETZSCHE, FOUCAULT, and BAKHTIN. It is precisely the understanding of the self-consuming artifacts of the human mind and the relativity of language that make a writer like Johnson develop a skeptical prose in his essays that constantly questions and undercuts its *own* most serious statements, and builds into itself a *resistance to* sameness and homogeneity. Like

de Man, Derrida, and Lacan, Johnson's sensitivity to the APORIA of language, to the darkness of the human heart underlying the bright civility of civilized linguistic constructions, postulates and embodies the irreducible importance of the human nature whose site witnesses these enactments. Here is the recognition that knowledge, history, and meaning exist not in the realm of the divinely guaranteed, but in the material *relationships* between people, between mind and world, between signifier and signified – and between the human being and God.

While Johnson's *Dictionary* is still taken as the embodiment of conservative, linguistic logocentrism, a careful reading of the "Preface" to that work reveals the extraordinary degree to which Johnson yields to the historicity of language, and to his extensive understanding of the SEMIOTIC nature of language. Likewise, Johnson's *Lives of the Poets*, testifies to an awareness of the textuality of civilized structures, memory, and personal and poetic identity, even while the work enacts a linguistic activity that gives the reader access to general human experience for which the word "truth" is not an inappropriate designation. However, while the paradoxical textuality of "truth" is unproblematic for Johnson, traditional eighteenth-century scholars operate as if it is pretextual and absolute, and critical theorists devote their energies to eliminating it altogether as a meaningful concept and experience.

These Johnsonian phenomena, shared to a lesser extent by other eighteenth-century writers (for example, Dryden, Swift, Hume, Gibbon) are unusual in their capacity to hold together creatively experiences of change and permanence. The *resistance* generated between them is integral to the historical knowledge of Johnson's texts. This historical knowledge – akin to Foucault's "genealogy" (1984c) and different in kind from the positivism which equates history with the referential depiction of *a priori* "fact" – is at the center of postmodern debates about history, authority, textuality, self, and the concept of the author. Certain works of metafiction by Peter Ackroyd, Jeanette Winterson, Graham Swift, J.M. Coetzee, and Italo Calvino already exemplify various ways in which postmodern culture is continuous with, though different from, eighteenth-century culture. The translational relationship between these and other postmodern novelists and the eighteenth centuries that they ventriloquize will become increasingly important and influential in the general rethinking of the continuities and discontinuities between the present and the past of which critical and cultural theory are part. This is also the perspective from which history is recognized as the product of the present moment's continuing negotiation with and invention of the past, and that power and authority (as Bender notes) become political realities shaped by historical discourse of one kind or another. My sense, however, is that the eighteenth century is more self-reflexive than Bender suggests about discursive power and contingencies.

The period's particular political awareness may well be seen in the sociological and anthropological elements in eighteenth-century historiography rather than in the political and constitutional history that has until recently been the focus of political readings of the period (see, for example, J.C.D. Clark, Howard Erskine-Hill, and Howard D. Weinbrot). While eighteenth-century scholarship has as yet resisted the appropriation of fully developed semiotic, linguistic, and deconstructive methods—such as we find, for example, in de Man on Shelley, Hartman on Wordsworth, and Derrida on Mallarmé, Joyce, and ROUSSEAU – it has effectively assimilated a variety of cultural and new historical methodologies that subtend political discursiveness. In fact, the work of Foucault, Bakhtin, Blanchot, and other theorists has facilitated an expansion of the eighteenth-century CANON to an extent unmatched in other literary "periods," as may be seen in the works by Bender, Landry, Castle, De Bolla, EAGLETON, McKeon, and NUSSBAUM listed below.

Scholarly works on eighteenth-century topics now, as a matter of course, discuss the various subjective and artistic experiences of women, the sick and insane, and various forms of social, political, legal, and sexual marginality. The curricular and critical success of Roger Lonsdale's *Eighteenth-Century Women Poets: An Oxford Anthology* (1989) is one indication of the extent to which women's work has become part of the central stream of eighteenth-century culture. Recent work in the field has become increasingly interdisciplinary. In the United States this movement has been supported by the American Society for Eighteenth-Century Studies (ASECS), its annual conference, its journal, *Eighteenth-Century Studies*, and other important journals in the field, such as *The Eighteenth Century: Theory and Interpretation*. The movement toward interdisciplinarity and pluralism – for all of its methodological problems (see Fish, 1989b) – has had a democratizing effect on eighteenth-century studies

in the Unites States. In the United Kingdom the politics of European union, and the traditional insularity and EMPIRICISM of the English, have complicated the process of internationalization in this field, although not in other areas (such as CULTURAL STUDIES *per se*), but it must be noted that the *British Journal for Eighteenth-Century Studies* has published work on British, American, and European cultural history since its inception in 1971, though with a lower theoretical profile. Most notable is the advent of new professional societies for the study of the eighteenth century, such as the South African Society for Eighteenth-Century Studies. Its first conference and conference proceedings (see Leighton, 1992) were organized around the theme of the rights of humankind, and revealed the critical and philosophical application of Enlightenment concepts to the contemporary political and cultural situation in South Africa in a very eighteenth-century spirit.

Both the United Kingdom and the United States have witnessed to some extent the breaking down of the barriers between the traditional GENRES, such as the epic, formal verse satire, and the lyric, and have seen a cross-fertilization with formerly "minor" genres such as diaries, letters, journalism, travelogues, and legal and historical texts of different kinds. In fact, the notions of "literature" and "English" have come under scrutiny in eighteenth-century studies over the last ten years with a deliberateness that belies the still popular notion of the eighteenth century as a conservative period. The greatest beneficiary of this shake-up has been the novel, now the subject of major American critical studies that have effectively established it as having the kind of centrality to eighteenth-century culture as the epic and verse satire had 20 years ago.

In conclusion, eighteenth-century studies is a rich, many-sided, paradoxical field of investigation which turns out to be most open to theoretical inquiry even at the moment that it appears to be most closed. It is striking that Derrida, Deleuze, Foucault, BARTHES, BACHELARD, LÉVI-STRAUSS, Lacan, and LYOTARD have all found eighteenth-century texts central to their work in theory.

See also APORIA; CANON; DECONSTRUCTION; EMPIRICISM; ENLIGHTENMENT; FOUCAULT; GENEALOGY; IDEOLOGY; NEW HISTORICISM; POSITIVISM; POSTMODERNISM; SEMIOTICS; SIGN; TRADITION.

Reading
Ballaster, Ros 1992: *Seductive Forms: Women's Amatory Fiction from 1684 to 1740*.

Bender, John 1987: *Imagining the Penitentiary: Fiction and Architecture of Mind in Eighteenth-Century England.*

Castle, Terry 1986: *Masquerade and Civilization in Eighteenth-Century English Culture and Fiction.*

Clingham, Greg (forthcoming): *Writing Memory: Textuality, Authority, and Johnson's "Lives of the Poets."*

Crawford, Robert 1992: *Devolving English Literature.*

Damrosch, Leo, ed. 1992: *The Profession of Eighteenth-Century Literature: Reflections on an Institution.*

De Bolla, Peter 1989: *The Discourse of the Sublime: Readings in History, Aesthetics, and the Subject.*

Eagleton, Terry 1982: *The Rape of Clarissa.*

The Eighteenth Century: Theory and Interpretation. Vol. 28, 1987.

Landry, Donna 1990: *Muses of Resistance: Laboring-Class Women's Poetry in Britain, 1739–1796.*

McKeon, Michael 1987: *Origins of the English Novel, 1660–1740.*

Nussbaum, Felicity 1989: *The Autobiographical Subject: Gender and Ideology in Eighteenth-Century England.*

——and Brown, Laura, eds 1987: *The New Eighteenth Century: Theory, Politics, English Literature.*

Rousseau, G.S., and Porter, Roy, eds 1988: *Sexual Underworlds of the Enlightenment.*

Schwartz, Richard B., ed. 1990: *Theory and Tradition in Eighteenth-Century Studies.*

GREG CLINGHAM

Eisenstein, Sergei (1898–1948) One of the greatest film directors of all times, a pioneer of the Russian revolutionary cinema, whose film *Battleship Potemkin* has been honored as the greatest film ever made. However, almost from the very beginning of his career, Eisenstein was criticized by official Soviet critics for the excessive intellectualism of his films, especially *The Ten Days That Shook the World* (1928) and *The Old and the New* (1929). In the early 1930s Eisenstein took an extensive trip to Europe and America, entertaining a thought of staying in the West. After an unsuccessful attempt at making the movie *Que Viva Mexico* and problems with Hollywood producers, Eisenstein was forced to return to the Soviet Union, where he experienced several disciplinary setbacks, the most publicized of which was the shelving of his film *Bezhin Meadow* (1935) because of its pronounced religious symbolism. During the prewar years and the entire 1939–45 war, Eisenstein finally achieved official recognition and silenced his critics. He produced a patriotic film *Alexander Nevsky* (1938) as a warning to Nazi Germany, and the first part of the unfinished trilogy *Ivan the Terrible* (1945). *Alexander Nevsky* was Eisenstein's first sound film. In it he experimented with the principles of "vertical montage," which meant the correlation between visual imagery and sound (the score for the film

was written by A. Prokofiev). Stalin personally liked the lavishly produced Part I of *Ivan the Terrible*, which depicted Ivan as a strong ruler fighting government corruption and intrigue, and Eisenstein was awarded a Stalin Prize for his film. However, Part II, which was completed in 1946 and showed the Tsar as a paranoiac despot surrounded by ruthless henchmen bearing an unmistakable resemblance to Stalin's secret police, was condemned and shown only in 1958, five years after Stalin's death. The director died in 1948 before he had time to complete his trilogy.

In their praise for Eisenstein's cinematic achievements, critics often overlook his contribution to the development of the poetics of cinema and the general theory of SEMIOTICS. Eisenstein's theoretical works are inextricably connected with his practice, and his arguments grow directly out of the analysis of his cinematic experiments, like the films *Strike* (1925) and *Battleship Potemkin* (1926) which were based on the main discovery of Eisenstein, the principles of *montage*. In his essay, "Synchronization of Senses," Eisenstein defines montage as the following: "Piece A, derived from the elements of the theme being developed, and piece B, derived from the same source, in juxtaposition give birth to the image in which the thematic matter is most clearly embodied." In other words, montage appears as a connection in a sintagmatic sequence of two pictorial signs, each of which can correspond to a concrete object (the denotation of this SIGN). These two signs in the combination with one another become a complex, abstract SYMBOL which correlates to a new concept and not to those denotations.

Eisenstein turns the syntax of a work of art into a means for the studies of semantics. From the very beginning of his career Eisenstein treats cinematic works in semiotic terms. In his first published theoretic work *Montage of Attractions* (LEF in 1923), based on the analysis of his own constructivist production of A. Ostrovsky's play *Enough Simplicity in Every Wise Man*, Eisenstein considers the Attraction, by which he means "every aggressive moment in [an art work], i.e., every element of it that brings to light in the spectator those senses or that psychology which influences his experience – every element that can be verified and mathematically calculated to produce certain emotional shocks in a proper order within the totality," as a semantic sign in the general system of the analyzed production: "I establish attraction as normally being an independent and primary element in the construction of a theatrical production – a molecular (i.e., compound) unity of the *efficiency* of the theater and of *theater in general.*" His concept of a shot as a cell of montage is connected with a more general idea of reflection of the macrostructure of an art work, derived from the work's theme, in every detail and the entire structure of that art work. Montage becomes the mechanism for the activation of signs and thus generates the meaning of the second order. "*Representation* A and *representation* B must be so selected from all the possible features within the theme that is being developed, must be so sought for, that their *juxta-position* . . . shall evoke in the perception and feelings of the spectator the most complete *image of the theme itself*" (p. 69). By breaking down the static progression of logical action, montage of arbitrary selection and independent actions advances the representation to a new semantic plane.

Eisenstein pays special attention to the notion of structure, which he treats as an interconnection of elements which allows for the creation of complex, semantically charged, spatial oppositions. Thus developing visual semantics in *Battleship Potemkin*, Eisenstein proceeds from the eastern Yang–Yin symbol of the two counterbalancing tendencies of evolution and involution and the dynamic dual distribution of forces, comprising the active or masculine principle (Yang) and the passive or feminine principle (Yin). He adds to the Yang–Yin opposition the traditional Slavic odd and even count and gives it a visual representation, for example, in the scene where boats, the sails of which resemble both birds' wings and the helicoidal symbol of Yang–Yin, bring food (and therefore life) to the sailors of *Potemkin*. He develops this notion further in his articles, essays, and lectures of the 1930s and establishes in them the principles of development of a theme in the entire structure of an art work. From the 1930s Eisenstein attempts a scientific description and conscientious assimilation of "emotional thinking," the process which was very close to the findings of the Russian psychologist L. Vygotsky in the area of prelogical thinking and its reflection in contemporary ART. The originality of Eisenstein's approach consists of the fact that his studies of the syntax of situations in cinema produce not simply an analysis of fixed symbols but an active structure of basic situations which reveals certain primary archaic significance of these situations.

Eisenstein's ethnological and semiotic sketches still remain unpublished, but, according to V. Ivanov's statement in his book *Sketches on the History of Semiotics in the USSR*, they are extremely interesting, not only because they anticipate the later semiotic theories, but also because they reveal a new, unexplored layer of Eisenstein's artistic experiments.

Reading
Aumont, Jacques 1983a: "Montage Eisenstein, I: Eisensteinian concepts."
——1983b: "Montage Eisenstein, II: Eisenstein taken at his word."
Bordwell, David 1993: *The Cinema of Eisenstein*.
Eisenstein, Sergei 1942: *The Film Sense*.
——1949: *Film Form*.
——1982: *The Nonindifferent Nature*.
Kleberg, Lars, and Lovgren, H., eds 1987: *Eisenstein Revisited: A Collection of Essays*.
Machado, Arlindo 1981: "Eisenstein: a radical dialogism."
Salvaggio, Jerry L. 1979: "Between formalism and semiotics: Eisenstein's film language."
Thompson, Kristin 1981: "Eisenstein's *Ivan the Terrible*: a neoformalist analysis."
Whittock, Trevor 1980: "Eisenstein on montage metaphor."
SLAVA I. YASTREMSKI

Eliot, Thomas Stearns (1888–1965) American (later British) critic. By far the most influential critic writing in English in the twentieth century, Eliot in effect set the terms and created the CANON for criticism for 50 years, from the end of the 1914–18 war until the "turn to theory" in the early 1970s. The dominant critical positions – Leavisism in England and NEW CRITICISM in the United States – were essentially elaborations of the key pages of his earlier essays, collected together in *The Sacred Wood* (1920).

Eliot never wrote a full-length critical work, saying that he had "no general theory," and claimed to be surprised at how influential his occasional essays had become, describing them as merely "a by-product of my private poetry workshop." However, taken together they in fact constitute a comprehensive literary theory, a new map of English literature, and, underpinning both, a potent and idiosyncratic philosophy of history. All three reflect a single vision, a vision of order and disorder: the disorder of the modern mind and modern history ("the immense panorama of futility and anarchy" as Eliot called it), and the longing for a world of imaginary order we have lost. The pivot of the whole enterprise was his enormously influential notion of the DISSOCIATION OF SENSIBILITY, the fatal split between thought and feeling supposed to have occurred in the early seventeenth century with the growth of science and skepticism, which resulted in later poets (and, by implication, CULTURE as a whole) being one-sided, either overintellectual (the eighteenth century) or overemotional (the Romantics and Victorians). This picture, filled out in Eliot's many essays on individual writers, changed the taste of his time and, worked out more comprehensively by admirers such as LEAVIS and EMPSON in England and the New Critics in America, created an entirely new canon. The great English writers were now seen as the "school of Donne,"while Milton, the eighteenth century, and Romantic and Victorian poetry were downgraded.

Eliot's governing ideal of the "unified sensibility," the middle way between the excesses of rationalism and the excesses of emotionalism, clearly had deep roots in his own psyche as well as in his early work as a philosopher, and it generated all his other key concepts. He urged a return to what he called "classicism" – self-discipline by submission to external authority (initially a humanist authority but later identified with religious orthodoxy) as opposed to the emotional egotism of Romanticism and LIBERALISM, the followers of the "inner voice." True poetic originality was to be gained by submission to "tradition" (increasingly, "*the* tradition"), by impersonality ("Poetry is not a turning loose of emotion, but an escape from emotion; it is not the expression of personality, but an escape from personality"), and by the creation of an objective correlative, an adequate externalization of the author's private feelings.

These were powerful critical tools. However, they were too controversial to remain unchallenged. It became increasingly clear that Eliot's picture of literary history was not very historical and was basically the projection of his own preoccupations, the "by-product" of the imagination that created *The Waste Land*. They led to quirky readings of individual texts (*Hamlet* was seen as a failure, Milton's style a disaster, Donne a kind of symbolist) and, more generally, to an oversimplified and monolithic picture of "the tradition" and to an idealist view of history "a pattern of timeless moments." This no longer seems a very useful way of understanding history or a useful basis for a literary HERMENEUTICS. While Eliot's essays remain striking and stimulating, it now seems best to read them, not (as his admirers did) as the keystone of a general literary theory and historiography, but as the "workshop criticism" of a highly idiosyncratic poet whose deep fear of the "disorder" of MODERNITY, science, liberalism, and HUMANISM we need not endorse.

See also DISSOCIATION OF SENSIBILITY; NEW CRITICISM.

Reading
Ellmann, Maud 1987: *The Poetics of Impersonality: T.S. Eliot and Ezra Pound.*
Gray, Piers 1982: *T.S. Eliot's Intellectual and Poetic Development, 1909–1922.*
McCallum, Pamela 1983: *Literature and Method: Towards a Critique of I.A. Richards, T.S. Eliot and F.R. Leavis.*
Wellek, René 1986d: "T.S. Eliot."

IAIN WRIGHT

Ellmann, Mary (1921–) US feminist literary critic. Ellmann's *Thinking About Women* (1968) is a classic feminist TEXT, reminiscent of Woolf's *A Room of One's Own* (1928), with which it shares both thematic concerns and narrative and rhetorical strategies. Ellmann's major thesis is that while "sexual exigency" – the perceived need for men to be physically "strong" and women to be nurturing mothers – has become redundant and obsolete in the twentieth century, Western thought still proceeds mainly by "sexual analogy": that is, our language for expressing thought classifies nearly all experience and phenomena in terms of sexual difference. Through the mid-1980s, before the synthesis of American and French feminist approaches, *Thinking About Women* was widely read by both camps. Ellmann's chapters on "Feminine stereotypes" and women writers' "Responses" inaugurated the feminist analysis of "images of women" and inspired GYNOCRITICS, while French feminists praised Ellmann's verbal playfulness, use of irony, and attention to contradictions in sexual discourse ("I am most interested in women as words – as the words they pull out of mouths," p. xv).

See also GYNOCRITICS.

Reading
Ellmann, Mary 1968: *Thinking About Women.*
Moi, Toril 1985: *Sexual/Textual Politics. Feminist Literary Theory.*

GLYNIS CARR

emergent *See* DOMINANT/RESIDUAL/EMERGENT

Emerson, Ralph Waldo (1803–82) American essayist, poet, and philosopher. Although his work as a poet and orator has usually eclipsed his importance as a thinker, Emerson was one of the first American philosophers of international stature. He was deeply interested in NIETZSCHE, who translated some of his writings and often quoted from them. In 1833 Emerson travelled to England, where he met several writers of note, including Wordsworth, Coleridge, and Carlyle. In the 1990s he was the controversial focal point of efforts to bridge the gap between Anglo-American and European philosophy and literature, social criticism, and philosophy, for example, in the writings of Stanley CAVELL, Harold BLOOM, Richard Poirier, and Irving Howe.

MICHAEL PAYNE

empiricism Empiricism is an epistemology – a theory of the source, nature, and scope of knowledge. Conforming to, and formative of, modern "common sense," empiricism asserts that knowledge of "matters of fact and real existence" (Hume, 1748, IV (i)) originates in – hence is founded upon – experience gained through the senses, and must be vindicated by reference back to it. Since the source of the ideas which furnish the materials of knowledge is "sense impressions," empiricists (for example, Bacon, Locke, and Hume) reject the *a priori* doctrines of rationalism, which maintain that the human mind is provided with innate ideas from which knowledge can be derived independently of experience. As Locke (1690) famously declared, at birth the mind is a *tabula rasa* – "white paper, void of all characters" – upon which the truths of experience are subsequently inscribed. Whereas rationalism takes mathematics as its PARADIGM of knowledge, empiricism models it upon experimental natural science, assuming its results to have been established by induction from (or reference to) what were later called "observation statements." Science can treat only of observable entities – the given "facts" – immediately available to sense perception, and should discard all untestable abstractions and speculation (those of metaphysics, for example) as "nothing but sophistry and illusion" (Hume, 1748, XII (iii)).

The contention between empiricism and rationalism is as old as philosophy itself, and has survived KANT's attempt to reconcile the competing claims of experience and reason with his transcendental idealism. However, despite the slide towards subjectivism and skepticism generated by arguments from experience, empiricism, codified by John Stuart Mill in his *System of Logic* (1843), can be said to have dominated the PHILOSOPHY OF SCIENCE well into the twentieth century. It attained its most systematic expression in the LOGICAL POSITIVISM of the Vienna Circle (see Ayer, 1936), which sought to discredit any propositions about the world which were unamenable to verification by observation, dismissing ETHICS and AESTHETICS, along with theology, as neither true nor false, but simply devoid of meaning. The task of science – the only practice that could legitimately claim to provide knowledge – was the pursuit of explanation by the construction of general laws which stated the causal relations between observable phenomena. Controlled experimentation or observation, confronting any theory with the discrete, theory-neutral facts, would then demonstrate its (in)compatibility with the relevant evidence. Such procedures were equally applicable in – indeed, mandatory for – social theory if it was to be credited with scientific status.

POSITIVISM – a doctrine of the methodological unity of the sciences subscribed to by the pioneers of sociology (Comte and DURKHEIM) – came under sustained attack from HERMENEUTICS, which postulated the peculiarity of the cultural sphere, and hence the specificity of any "human science" aspiring to an understanding (*Verstehen*) of it. Insisting upon the distinction between the *Geisteswissenschaften* and the *Naturwissenschaften*, Dilthey and his successors did not, however, contest the adequacy of empiricism as an epistemological account of the natural sciences. That challenge emerged, in a variety of forms, from philosophers and historians of natural science itself. In the Anglo-American tradition, it is associated with the work of KUHN and FEYERABEND (Chalmers, 1978); and in France, with that of BACHELARD and ALTHUSSER (Lecourt, 1975).

POPPER (1934) had offered an internal critique of logical positivism, substituting "falsifiability" for "verifiability" as the criterion for the demarcation between science and non-science, on the grounds that even an infinite number of empirical corroborations could not logically confirm a proposition, whereas falsification would serve to disprove it. Conceiving science as a process of "conjecture and refutation" – the equally indispensable moments of theory construction and empirical testing – Popper nevertheless continued to accord a decisive role to the latter as "the impartial arbiter" *within* and *between* theories, and upheld a nonlinear notion of scientific progress as the gradual accumulation of knowledge by empirical trial and error. The "sophisticated falsificationism" advanced by his follower Lakatos (1974) sought to secure the notion of science as provisional, fallible knowledge in the light of ensuing critiques.

In Anglophone philosophy the most corrosive of these came from Kuhn (1962). Partially converging with the French epistemological tradition of "rational materialism" – the Bachelardian-Althusserian prioritization of theoretical "problematics" over experience and experimentation – Kuhn argued that the empirical indeterminacy and radical mutability of scientific theory were attested by the actual – discontinuous – history of the sciences. Theories were not subject to empirical acid tests on the basis of atomistic facts. There was no such thing as theory-neutral observation/observation statements; the "facts" were themselves theory-dependent, and thus could not function as the indubitable foundation of knowledge. The "correspondence theory of truth" – truth as agreement between a statement about an empirical state of affairs and the "way things actually are" – was untenable. Observation and experimentation were structured by a PARADIGM – the particular conceptual framework governing "normal science" at any particular time by virtue of a consensus among the scientific community. The evaluative criteria posited by different paradigms were "incommensurable." Therefore – at least on a widespread reading of Kuhn – there could be no *rational* adjudication between competing theories, and scientific change did not amount to scientific progress.

Radicalized in the "epistemological anarchism" of Feyerabend (1975), the category of "incommensurability" was subsequently generalized from rival *scientific* theories to the relationship between scientific and *non*scientific DISCOURSES. If all "knowledge" was a *historically* and *culturally specific* product, articulated in an irreducibly *conceptual* – and hence wholly or partly untranslatable – language, no *neutral* arbitration between the truth claims of different discourses was available.

Crossed with allied themes – whether from (POST)STRUCTURALISM, invoking the linguistics of SAUSSURE and the genealogy of NIETZSCHE, WITTGENSTEINIAN PHILOSOPHY OF LANGUAGE (for example, the notion of language games), or "anti-foundationalist" pragmatism, in the work of Rorty – a hybrid critique of empiricism resonates widely in CULTURAL and CRITICAL THEORY today. In the

shorthand form of the "discursive construction of reality," it is frequently taken to vindicate epistemological perspectivism – the doctrine that the world is to be interpreted through a plurality of conceptual SYSTEMS, none of which possesses greater cognitive validity than any other – and ethical/aesthetic relativism – the view that there are, and can be, no universal standards of good and bad. (Such a critique dissolves the fact/value dichotomy of empiricism by relativizing the first as well as the second term. But reason remains a Humean slave, albeit now of Nietzschean passions.) Thus far, it has resisted countercritiques from anti-empiricist and anti-positivist realisms, which seek to distinguish between the anti-empiric*ist* and the anti-empiric*al*, and to reconcile the social relativity with the cognitive objectivity of knowledge.

Contemporary anti-empiricism has profound implications for the character and status of cultural and LITERARY CRITICISM; for any AESTHETICS which seeks to defend ART (whether formally "realist" or not) as a mode of knowledge (see Lovell, 1980); and for questions of aesthetic value.

Reading
Ayer, A.J. 1936 (*1987*): *Language, Truth and Logic*.
Bhaskar, R. 1975: *A Realist Theory of Science*.
Chalmers, A. 1978 (*1987*): *What is This Thing Called Science?*
Feyerabend, P. 1975 (*1993*): *Against Method: Outline of an Anarchistic Theory of Knowledge*.
Hume, D. 1748 (*1987*): *An Enquiry Concerning Human Understanding*.
Kuhn, T.S. 1962 (*1970*): *The Structure of Scientific Revolutions*.
Lakatos, I. 1974: "Falsification and the methodology of scientific research programmes."
Lecourt, D. 1975: *Marxism and Epistemology*.
Locke, J. 1690 (*1988*): *An Essay Concerning Human Understanding*.
Lovell, T. 1980: *Pictures of Reality*.
Macherey, P. 1966 (*1978*): *A Theory of Literary Production*.
Popper, K. 1934 (*1987*): *The Logic of Scientific Discovery*.
GREGORY ELLIOTT

Empson, Sir William (1906–84) English critic. Empson was the most brilliant, entertaining, and eccentric representative of the new style of "close reading" that emerged in the English-speaking world in the 1920s and 1930s, and his *Seven Types of Ambiguity* (1930) was its PARADIGMATIC work. Empson never systematically developed a theoretical position, but he has been an enormous influence and a continuing one, as the poststructuralists' recent rediscovery of him demonstrates.

Seven Types is a defense of "the analytical mode of approach" and shows the strong influence of I.A. RICHARDS. Like Richards, Empson sought to replace the loosely emotive and "appreciative" criticism of his day with rigorous and reasoned argument: "the reasons that make a line of verse likely to give pleasure, I believe, are like the reasons for anything else; one can reason about them." For Empson that reasoning entailed a minute dissection of the multiple interdependence – which he calls "AMBIGUITY" – of different forms of meaning in poetry. Richards had written, "the all-important fact for the study of literature . . . is that there are several kinds of meaning," and Empson pursued the implications of this to their limit, unpicking a Shakespearean sonnet, for example, to reveal "a general sense of compacted intellectual wealth, of an elaborate balance of variously associated feeling."

Empson's essay is closely focused on individual TEXTS, and often on tiny parts of those texts, but implicit in it is an entire revisionist history of English literature, similar to that of Richards and T.S. ELIOT, and centered like theirs on an admiration for Renaissance POETRY and a critique of Romanticism. Implicit in it too, and also powerfully influential on the way criticism was to develop, is a pessimistic view of the state of the English language which "needs nursing by the analyst very badly indeed" in order to "give back something of the Elizabethan energy to what is at present a rather exhausted language."

Empson's second book, *Some Versions of Pastoral* (1935), carried the program further and represented a striking extension of his range. *Seven Types* had been essentially a random collection of texts chosen to show off a particular analytic method: the method was not systematized and the texts were rarely related to one another or to their contexts. Now Empson outlined the social history of a whole ambiguous GENRE, and implicitly offered that genre as central to English literary culture. Pastoral (the idealizing of the relationship between rich and poor) had been identified in passing in *Seven Types* as one example of the "clash between different modes of feeling," but it was now placed center stage and scanned for its "latent political ideas." The result is what later Marxist critics would call an "ideological reading," but one that carefully resists *reducing* literature to IDEOLOGY. Gray's *Elegy*,

for example, is seen both as an expression of "bourgeois ideology" (since "by comparing the social arrangement to Nature he makes it seem inevitable, which it was not, and gives it a dignity which was undeserved") and as the expression of a "permanent truth" about the wastefulness of human life. Shakespeare's sonnets are analyzed not only to reveal an underlying "ironical acceptance of aristocracy" but also as intensely private works.

In Empson's third book, *The Structure of Complex Words* (1951), he was still working away at ambiguity, and the model of emotional–intellectual interaction which he had inherited from Richards. By 1951, however, he had become more skeptical of Richards's legacy, particularly as institutionalized in American NEW CRITICISM. Although the book is offered as a sketch for "a new kind of dictionary," its underlying concern is with the semantic status of emotion in literature and to attack Richards's peculiar and historically damaging doctrine that "the Emotions given by words in poetry are independent of their Sense." By minute semantic and historical analysis, Empson shows the extraordinary richness of the interplay between multiple senses and multiple emotions in the simplest words – "honest" in *Othello*, for example, "sense" in *The Prelude*.

Empson spent most of the 1930s and 1940s in the Far East, and was alarmed on his return to England to find that under the ever-increasing influence of Eliot, the "neo-Christians" had taken over in the English departments. Much of his later criticism is designed as a counterattack, notably in *Milton's God* (1961), a lively and controversial polemic against "the torture-horror and sex-horror" of Christianity in the guise of an analysis of the CONTRADICTIONS of the theology of *Paradise Lost*.

Several collections of Empson's essays were published in his later years and posthumously, and show him at his polemical best, especially when up against the neo-Christians, making angry attempts to rescue Donne's skepticism from Dame Helen Gardner or Joyce's socialism and anti-clericalism from Hugh Kenner. All of them, like his entire life's work, are wonderfully vigorous, irreverent, often wildly idiosyncratic attempts to save LITERARY CRITICISM from "the habitual mean-mindedness of modern academic criticism, its moral emptiness combined with incessant moral nagging, its scrubbed prison-like isolation," into which he felt that the influence of Eliot, LEAVIS and the more preachifying New Critics had brought it.

See also AMBIGUITY; RICHARDS, I.A.

Reading
Gill, Roma, ed. 1974: *William Empson: the Man and his Work*.
Norris, Christopher 1978: *William Empson and the Philosophy of Literary Criticism*.
—— and Mapp, Nigel, eds 1993: *William Empson: The Critical Achievement*.
Wellek, René 1986e: "William Empson."
                                                CHRISTOPHER NORRIS

enactment/realization   Terms used in F.R. LEAVIS's LITERARY CRITICISM for the active functions of literary language, by contrast with inert verbal forms. Rather than merely representing or "reflecting" some exterior state or process, genuinely literary language actually performs or revives it in its own form, texture, rhythm, or figures.

Reading
Casey, John 1966: *The Language of Criticism*.
                                                CHRIS BALDICK

encoding/decoding   A model for analyzing processes of communication, explored particularly in television research. Drawing on SEMIOLOGY and on the writing of BARTHES, the approach suggests that meanings arise from a work of signification through CODES, of which audiences make sense in ways which may differ. The model emphasizes power and conflict in the construction of representations, and tensions between media organizations and their publics, so that "preferred" meanings may be accepted, negotiated or opposed in ways linked to not only CLASS, GENDER, and "ethnicity" but also to positions in DISCOURSE and to viewing/reading contexts. Such analyses are difficult and contested (it is argued that the "codes" are hard to distinguish and that audience "resistance" has been exaggerated). However, in stressing attempts to secure "dominant" meanings and even more, the activity of media users has stimulated empirical and theoretical work, raising important issues.

Reading
Corner, J. 1980 (*1986*): "Codes and cultural analysis."
Hall, S. 1980a: "Encoding/decoding."
Lewis, J. 1985: "Decoding television news."
Morley, D. 1992: *Television, Audiences and Cultural Studies*.
                                                MICHAEL GREEN

end of philosophy   Fashionable theme pursued by various thinkers who urge that "philosophy" as hitherto conceived (say from Socrates to Descartes,

KANT, and the modern Anglo–American analytic tradition) no longer has anything valid, relevant, or interesting to say. Sources include NIETZSCHE and FOUCAULT (on the GENEALOGY of values and power/knowledge); HEIDEGGER's reading of "Western metaphysics" as an epoch whose closure (or limiting horizon) supposedly emerges through a depth-ontological account of that same exhausted tradition; holistic theories of meaning and truth as advanced by "postanalytical" philosophers like W.V. QUINE and (arguably) Donald DAVIDSON; cultural relativism in its manifold forms, among them Thomas KUHN's PHILOSOPHY OF SCIENCE and the so-called strong program in SOCIOLOGY OF KNOWLEDGE; the idea of "weak thinking" (*pensiero debole*) aptly thus described by its proponent Gianni VATTIMO; and again – subsuming all these – the widely heralded linguistic (or HERMENEUTIC) "turn" in philosophy and other disciplines inspired by thinkers such as WITTGENSTEIN, GADAMER, and Rorty. The work of Jacques DERRIDA is often invoked in this context, despite his frequent declarations to the contrary, that is, his insistence that to DECONSTRUCT the TEXTS of philosophy means to read them *differently* – with greater attentiveness and rigor – but not to indulge in futile gestures of "postphilosophical" abandon. A case can be made (albeit unconvincingly) that Kant was the first to declare such an "end of philosophy" with his argument that certain kinds of speculative metaphysics exceeded the bounds of rational inquiry and were therefore to be counted illegitimate. But this current way of thinking is in general characterized by its downright rejection of all such critical ENLIGHTENMENT values (see POSTMODERNISM).

Reading
Baynes, K., Bohman, J., and McCarthy, T., eds 1987: *After Philosophy: End or Transformation?*
Rajchmann, J., and West, C., eds 1985: *Post Analytic Philosophy*.
Redner, Harry 1986: *The Ends of Philosophy*.
Rorty, Richard 1980: *Philosophy and the Mirror of Nature*.
Vattimo, Gianni 1985 (*1988*): *The End of Modernity*.
                                                CHRISTOPHER NORRIS

Engels, Friedrich   (1820–95)   Political economist, activist, and philosopher. Engels's importance lies in his collaboration with Karl MARX to produce a critique of capitalist society based on a materialistic conception of history, his attempt to formulate a "scientific" basis for socialism, his explorations of the connections between dialectics and natural science, his analyses of working-class conditions, as well as the development of the family and the state. The initial dissemination, clarification, and popularization of Marxist ideas owed more to Engels than to the endeavors of Marx himself.

Born in Barmen, Prussia as the son of a textile manufacturer, Engels commenced training in 1838 for a business career. But, pursuing his philosophical and political reading, and moving to Berlin in 1841, he quickly became influenced by the thought of HEGEL, the dominant figure in German philosophy. For a while Engels associated with Bruno Bauer and the Young Hegelians. The following year was to prove equally decisive in the formation of Engels's thought: settling in Manchester, England, he started work at a factory in which his father was a shareholder. He saw at first hand the miserable conditions suffered by British workers, his research into these conditions being published as *The Conditions of the Working Class in England* in 1845. Here, Engels argued that the degraded conditions of the English proletariat, generated by its industrial exploitation, would eventually mold it into a revolutionary political force.

At this time English labor interests were particularly active and pressing for reform. Chartism was a widespread movement and the Welsh utopian social reformer Robert Owen had gained a following, as had his counterpart Charles Fourier in France. It was in this agitative climate that Engels became a socialist. He had already started to correspond with Marx, whom he had met in 1844 in Paris. Here, from his own reading of the French socialists as well as Feuerbach, Marx also had turned to socialism. In early 1844 Engels had published an article "Outlines of a critique of political economy" in the *Deutsch–Französische Jahrbüher* to which Marx had also contributed two essays. Engels' argments, charging that private property and accumulation of capital increased the degradation of the workers and therefore the class struggle, had alerted Marx to the importance of economics in historical analysis.

Engels and Marx produced in the same year a joint book, *The Holy Family*, expressing their now common antagonism against the "Holy Family" of the brothers Edgar and Bruno Bauer and their Young Hegelian circle. In an incisive critique, Marx and Engels undermined from every aspect the views of this circle: its renunciation of radicalism and espousal of a moderate LIBERAL philanthropy; its

speculative idealism which substituted a Hegelian self-consciousness for real people, with its implication that thought could somehow generate change; its apriorism and the sheer inaccuracy of its empirical knowledge of the working classes; and its self-entrapment in the "mire" of Christian-Germanic nationalism. Marx and Engels argued that the proletariat or masses, so derided by the "absolute criticism" of Bauer and company, were actually the real agents of historical change. The difference between Marx's and Engels's materialist approach and the idealism they attacked was crystalized in Engels's pithy statement: "*History* does *nothing*, it 'possesses *no* immense wealth', it 'wages *no* battles'. It is *man*, real, living man who does all that . . . history is *nothing but* the activity of man pursuing his aims" (Marx and Engels, 1956, p. 116).

Engels and Marx further collaborated to produce *The German Ideology* (1846) which marked their break with Feuerbach's MATERIALISM and expressed their own materialistic conception of history, characterized by a number of features:

(i)   it is the activity and conditions of material production, not mere ideas, which determine the structure of society and the nature of individuals; law, ART, religion, and morality are an efflux of these material relations;

(ii) the evolution of division of labor issues in the concentration of private property, a conflict between individual and communal interests (the latter assuming the status of an independent power as the state), and estrangement or ALIENATION of social activity;

(iii) all struggles within the state are euphemisms for the real struggle between classes; it is this struggle which generates social change;

(iv) once technologically assisted capitalist accumulation, concentration, and world expansion have led to a world of sharply contrasting wealth and poverty, and working classes become conscious of their historical role, capitalism itself will yield to a communism which will do away with private property and base itself on human need rather than the greed of a minority for increasing profit.

Between 1845 and 1847 Engels lived in Brussels and Paris where he and Marx, attempting to forge international working-class cooperation, were commissioned by the German Communist League to set forth the main tenets of Communism. The result was *The Communist Manifesto* of 1848. This astonishingly compressed book described the victorious revolution of the bourgeoisie against feudalism, the principles of capitalist society, centered on private property, the need for expansion of markets, and the reduction of all human relations, including family and GENDER relations, to commercial relations. It expressed also the aims of the Communists: to abolish not only private property but also the other foundational institutions of capitalism such as nation, state, and CLASS itself.

In 1848 revolutions broke out in France and elsewhere in Europe. Both Engels and Marx returned to Prussia where their democratic journal was eventually suppressed. Marx was deported and Engels took part in the armed popular struggle against the reactionary and victorious counter-revolution. Both soon returned to England, Engels settling as a clerk in Manchester until 1870 while Marx lived in London. Their collaboration continued, however, Engels also providing his friend with financial support. Engels pursued his interest in the natural sciences from a historical materialist standpoint, his observations eventually being published in the 1920s as *Dialectics of Nature*. (Engels, 1939) The themes of these essays include development of the natural sciences in both inorganic and organic realms, the historical connections between science and religion, spiritualism, and the poverty of naive EMPIRICISM. Engels traces the development of the scientific "revolution" to the period of the Reformation and Renaissance, where thinkers had universal interests, not being in thrall to the modern bourgeois division of labor. At that time, says Engels, science was revolutionary, especially in emancipating itself from theology. However, by the first half of the eighteenth century, science offered a conservative vision of nature as eternal and immutable rather than historical. In this domain advances were made by French materialism and in particular by KANT, who attempted to explain the solar system as a process, possessing a history, rather than as something created by God. Through such figures as Laplace and Herschel, science eventually accommodated Kant's insights. It was through Darwin and his contemporaries that nature was shown to be in eternal flux; hence modern thought returned to the outlook of the great Greek philosophers. Only with man, says Engels, do we enter history in so far as this is self-created through material production. Yet the modern technologized bourgeois subjugation of nature has produced increasing misery of the masses, the much-lauded free competition between human beings actually being the normal state of the animal kingdom as described by Darwin.

Engels effectively places man within a materialist cosmology: the cycle of matter is eternal and indestructible, thinking humanity being but one of its changing faces. He views nature as proving the truth of dialectics: it does not merely revolve in a recurring circle but also undergoes genuine change (see MATERIALISM). Engels's views here arguably reflect the limitations of nineteenth-century science, a point stressed by those such as LUKÁCS, who have charged him with POSITIVISM. Engels's work on science and dialectics in general has generated much controversy, especially some of his comments on the scientific status of Marx's economic "laws" and the inevitability of their operation. These have helped inspire deterministic readings of MARXISM.

Retiring in 1870 to London where Marx was suffering from ill health, Engels continued alone as leader of the First International, founded by Marx in 1864 to unite workers' movements of all countries. He produced *Anti-Dühring* (Engels, 1939), a polemical tract directed against Eugen Dühring of Berlin University, who in propounding his own socialist theory had attacked Marx. In the course of expounding his own and Marx's socialist principles (extending through natural science, morality, and political economy), Engels attacked the socialist state envisaged by Dühring, which would effectively replicate the *gendarmerie* of the existing Prussian state. According to Engels, Dühring's insistence that religion should be prohibited in his future state represented a naive misunderstanding of the dialectical nature of economic forces and the fact that religion was but one form of ALIENATION which would die a natural death. In primitive societies, suggests Engels, men had externalized forces of nature, which were reflections of their own mentalities. In more developed societies, social forces emerge as equally alien. In bourgeois society God is "the alien domination of the capitalist mode of production." Dühring does not understand that it is not knowledge but social action, namely the repossession of the means of production, which will bring social forces under the domination of society rather than appearing as something foreign and transcendent. An abridged version of Engels's book appeared in 1880 under the title *Socialism: Utopian and Scientific* (Engels, 1975). Translated into at least ten languages, this enjoyed a wider circulation among working-class movements than even the *Communist Manifesto*.

In the year after Marx's death in 1883, Engels wrote *The Origin of the Family, Private Property and the State* (Engels, 1972), a text widely regarded as the pivotal Marxist document for feminist theory since it alone, among the works of Marx and Engels, offers a comprehensive attempt to explain the origins of PATRIARCHY. Lewis H. Morgan's *Ancient Society* (1877), from its research into prehistoric Native American SYSTEMS of kinship, had arrived at similar conclusions to Marx's in his critique of a society based on commodity production. Drawing on this book and Marx's own detailed notes on it, Engels traced the rise of patriarchy through increasingly sophisticated economic and social configurations, from primitive communal systems to a class society based on private property.

Following Morgan's schematization, Engels describes three main forms of marriage, conforming to three stages of human development: "for the period of savagery, group marriage; for barbarism, pairing marriage; for civilization, monogamy supplemented by adultery and prostitution" (Engels, 1972, p. 105). In the tribe, descent and inheritance occurred through the female line. However, as wealth increased, the man acquired a more important status in the family than the woman, and this "mother right" was eventually overthrown in what Engels sees as a momentous revolution in prehistory: "The overthrow of mother right was the *world historical defeat of the female sex*" (Engels, 1972, p. 87). Engels says that, with the predominance of private property over common property, father right and monogamy gained ascendancy, marriage becoming increasingly dependent on economic considerations. Because of the economic dependence of the woman on the man in bourgeois society, the husband "is the bourgeois, and the wife represents the proletariat" (Engels, 1972, p. 105). Engels suggests that the first premise for the emancipation of women is the reintroduction of the entire female sex into public industry, and that when the means of production become common property, the individual family will cease to be the economic unit of society. The economic foundations of monogamy as it presently exists will vanish, along with the institutions of the state which preserved them.

In 1886 Engels wrote *Ludwig Feuerbach and the End of Classical German Philosophy*, in which he attempted to broach once again a subject only sporadically addressed during his 40 years of collaboration with Marx since *The German Ideology*: the relation of historical materialism to Hegel. Engels's treatment is comprehensive, elucidating the Hegelian dialectic and its historical division into conservative and radical factions, a dichotomy inhering in its revolutionary form and reactionary content. He also addresses more fully the limitations of Feuerbach's MATERIALISM and morality which are "cut exactly to the pattern of modern capitalist society." He offers acute analyses of ideological developments, especially in religion and law; as for philosophy in Germany, it is at the end of its tether, the 1848 revolution marking the eclipse of idealist theory by revolutionary practice: "The German working class movement is the inheritor of German classical philosophy" (Marx and Engels, 1968, p. 622).

At this late stage of his life Engels was active in the formation of the Second International. He undertook the additional labor of editing and publishing the second and third volumes of Marx's *Capital* in 1885 and 1884 respectively. He began work on the fourth volume, uncompleted, however, because of his death, and eventually published as *Theories of Surplus Value*. All in all, despite his modesty, Engels exerted considerable influence on Marx's thought and life. In his speech at Marx's graveside, Engels had emphasized Marx's combination of intellectual gifts with practical commitment: he was not only "the greatest living thinker" but "before all else a revolutionist." In his own clarity of moral vision, intellectual subtlety, and political daring, Engels was not far behind.

See also MARX.

Reading

Carver, T. 1990: *Friedrich Engels: His Life and Thought*.
Engels, F. 1939 (*1970*): *Herr Eugen Dühring's Revolution in Science (Anti-Dühring)*.
——— 1975: *Socialism: Utopian and Scientific*.
——— 1940 (*1973*): *Dialectics of Nature*.
——— 1972 (*1985*): *The Origin of the Family, Private Property and the State*.
Lenin, V.I. 1987: *Introduction to Marx, Engels, Marxism*.
Levine, N. 1975: *The Tragic Deception: Marx Contra Engels*.
McLellan, D. 1977 (*1978*): *Engels*.
Rigby, S.H. 1992: *Engels and the Formation of Marxism*.

M.A.R. HABIB

Enlightenment   An eighteenth-century cultural movement which attacked the authority of tradition, especially in matters of church and state, in the name of the public use of reason. KANT famously defined the Enlightenment as "man's emergence from his self-imposed immaturity," and gave its motto as *sapere aude*! – "Dare to understand!" The Enlightenment was a Europe-wide phenomenon, associated with the decline of feudalism, the growth of printing, and the increasing economic and social power of the bourgeois classes. It is important to note the national differences between its forms, in particular, the MATERIALISM of the French *Encyclopedists* (d'Alembert, Diderot, Helvetius, Holbach), the Scottish interest in political economy (Fergerson, Hume, Smith, Stuart), and the more cultural and historical concerns of the Germans (Goethe, Herder, Lessing, Schiller).

In the period since the 1939–45 war, the idea of the Enlightenment has increasingly become the battleground for disputes over the concept of reason and the progressive or oppressive character of the heritage of European CULTURE. More recently, it has provided the focus for debates between the followers of FOUCAULT and HABERMAS, in which both sides understand the Enlightenment as the project of MODERNITY.

Reading
Cassirer, Ernst 1932 (*1951*): *The Philosophy of the Enlightenment*.
Foucault, Michel 1986a: "What is Enlightenment?"
Gay, Peter 1967: *The Enlightenment: An Interpretation*.
Habermas, Jürgen 1985 (*1987*): *The Philosophical Discourse of Modernity*.

PETER OSBORNE

enterprise culture   Ideological term developed in 1980s political debate, particularly in Britain (where "enterprise culture") was often taken to describe American culture). The term was used in two ways. On the one hand, it referred to the social conditions necessary to promote "enterprise," defined here in straight capitalist terms as the willingness to take a financial risk. It was argued (by Margaret Thatcher, for example) that enterprise was not just a response to market incentives but also depended on an *attitude*, an attitude embodying self-sufficiency, an identification of one's family with one's property (and vice versa), and a hostility to socialism, to all forms of state dependency, and indeed, to the very idea of "society." And this fed into the second use of the term: "enterprise culture" also described the CULTURE of the new,

1980s entrepreneurs, the culture of competitive, hard-working, self-driven, anti-establishment greed depicted in the film *Wall Street* and given the popular label of "yuppie."

SIMON FRITH

entertainment industry   A concept in economics (not much used in CULTURAL THEORY but the preferred descriptive term in the entertainment business itself) which refers to those industries which make their money from people's leisure or "play" activities. The entertainment industry is therefore usually taken to include the film industry, the music business, broadcasting, the provision of cable and satellite services, the manufacture of toys and games, gaming and betting, sport, the performing arts, and amusement and theme parks. The use of the term "entertainment industry" usually precludes any discussion of such industries' ideological activities or cultural effects, and implies, rather, an interest in management structure and business practice (compare the term CULTURE INDUSTRIES).

Reading
Vogel, Harold L. 1986 (*1990*): *Entertainment Industry Economics*.

SIMON FRITH

enunciation/enounced, subject of the   *See* SUBJECT OF THE ENUNCIATION/ENOUNCED

episteme   A term central to FOUCAULT's archaeology of the human sciences (1973) which describes transformations in the configuration of knowledge from the classical to the modern age. The concept of the episteme refers to the cluster of relations through which DISCURSIVE PRACTICES achieve a form of unity as "epistemological figures, sciences, and possibly formalized systems" (Foucault, 1974, p. 191).
See also ARCHAEOLOGY OF KNOWLEDGE.

Reading
Foucault, M. 1973: *The Order of Things: An Archaeology of the Human Sciences*.
——1974: *The Archaeology of Knowledge*.
——1989c: "An historian of culture."
Smart, B. 1985: *Michel Foucault*.

BARRY SMART

Erikson, Erik Homberger (1902–) German-American psychoanalyst and psychiatrist. Erikson was trained by and worked with Anna Freud, and was one of the few men to work in the field of child analysis in its early days. Erikson's work adopts a developmental perspective and centers upon the concepts of identity and ego strength, used to connote the ability to unify extremes. Development is viewed not as a simply linear process but as proceeding from a series of struggles, each focusing upon new life problems.

Reading
Erikson, E.H. 1950: *Childhood and Society.*
——1959: *Identity and the Life Cycle.*

DAVID MACEY

essentialism Minimally, the doctrine that particular things necessarily possess essences or fixed natures in virtue of which they are what they are: particular things of determinate kinds. The idea is that nothing can remain one and the same, validly reidentifiable as such, if its assignable nature is lost or altered (as when a tree, cut down for lumber, loses its specific nature, being-a-tree, though it retains its generic nature as wood). There is no single version of essentialism universally acknowledged to be true. Plato, for example, appears to have held that the things of the inconstant natural world lack all fixity, hence lack essences; nevertheless, their intelligibility presupposes and depends upon our grasping, through *doxa* (opinion), the changeless forms that natural things imperfectly "imitate." Aristotle, who is generally conceded to be the author (particularly in *Metaphysics*) of the classic form of essentialism, holds that real particulars, things, *ousiai*, necessarily have fixed natures. Unlike Plato, Aristotle appears to believe that these "natures" or essences do not exist apart, but are manifested only in the changing or changeless things of the real world. Humans, Aristotle says, possess an intuitive theorizing power of reason (*nous*) for directly discerning the essences of things: this, in effect, is the necessary condition of Aristotelian science. In contemporary theories of science, notably in the view of Karl POPPER, the thesis that natural events and phenomena are governed by exceptionless universal laws of nature *and* that human investigators are capable of discerning such laws is said to be tantamount to essentialism. Hence doubts about the realist interpretation of the laws of nature

(as by Bas van Fraassen (1941–)) are, effectively, doubts about certain forms of essentialism.

In Aristotle, therefore, essentialism concerns both the reality of a thing and its intelligibility. Aristotle is not inflexibly insistent on the thesis in all domains of inquiry. For instance, in the biological sciences he appears to be more concessive (than in the purely physical sciences) regarding the provisionality of assigned essences; and in the arts and practical life, though practical reason as well as theoretical reason is in some not always entirely clear sense tethered to essences, human activity may actually proceed without invoking the powers of demonstrative science (hence, without essences). In the seventeenth and eighteenth centuries, the rise of modern nominalism (associated with British EMPIRICISM) challenged, as in the work of Thomas Hobbes (1588–1679) and John Locke (1632–1704) the twin tenets of essentialism: first, by insisting that essences concern the names of things, not their "natures" (Hobbes); second, by insisting that in so far as things have real essences, their essences are unknown, and that the "nominal" essences by which we guide ourselves are verbal and sufficient for our scientific inquiries (Locke).

Furthermore, the question arises, particularly among the medievals, of whether universals, the generic structures – whether apart from particular things or manifested in or only in particular things or imposed by the mind on aggregated things or identified merely in the general use of names (what have come to be variously called the doctrines of realism, conceptualism, and nominalism regarding universals) – themselves exist. The plausibility of choosing among these alternatives seems enhanced by admitting a supreme Creator. Nevertheless, in modern times, *predicables* as opposed to *particulars* (or things) are, for instance, in the apt distinction developed by Charles Sanders PEIRCE, *real* but not *existent*. We should now say that if they obtain in the world, predicables (as real) answer to predicates (which are then their names), whereas proper names ("Sir Walter Scott"), definite descriptions ("the author of *Waverley*") and indexicals ("this," "that") denote particulars or individual things (actual or existent or, more disputably, fictional or imaginary). On Peirce's view, therefore, predicables are *real* but do not *exist*. What exists, Peirce says, manifests secondness, that is, resists us or other existing things, as by the actual weight of a heavy table that one attempts to move; whereas what is real is what, as we judge, may be found in the world independently of our particular existence and mode of understanding, even if only by our inquiry. These are said by Peirce to exhibit thirdness. On this view, there *are* (exist) no universals, though there *are* "real generals." Hence essentialism can survive the rejection of universals.

The deeper question regarding essences (or essential predicables) concerns: (i) whether there *are* real generals, whether generality is real and in what way real; and (ii) whether essences, even real generals, are necessary to the existence of real particulars (that is, what exists is said to be real, but what is real need not exist). Now then, the discussion of what exists (in the modern sense), particularly regarding individuation, numerical identity, and reidentification under conditions of change does not appear to have been adequately pursued until comparatively late in the history of philosophy: first, with the clarification of the meaning of "exists" (as in Immanuel KANT's (1724–1804) opposition to the famous Ontological Proof of God's existence and, much later, in the development of modern notions of a predicative calculus, with Gottlob FREGE (1848–1925)). Kant's work supports a very strong disjunction between contingent claims of existence and sheer intelligibility; and Frege's pioneer work in formalizing logic draws attention to the important difference between purely syntactic and semantic issues, even where they prove inseparable (as in Frege's famous discussion of identities: "$a = a$" and "$a = b$").

Aristotle formulated (in *Metaphysics* Book Gamma) the strongest form of essentialism, arguing that what is real is changeless; that particular things subject to change (*ousiai*) are real (that is, exist) in virtue of their possessing invariant natures (or essences); and that the denial of the second condition necessarily leads to CONTRADICTION or incoherence. *That* claim is easily demonstrated to be false, that is, the *modal* claim that essences are necessary to what is real and that the denial is self-contradictory. *If* nominalism or conceptualism or, less radically, doctrines like those attributed to Plato, Hobbes, and Locke (above) may be admitted, then Aristotle's thesis fails. One may in fact say that a large part of the history of Western philosophy has been occupied with testing the coherence of denying both strong and weak versions of essentialism.

There are, in effect, two very large strategies that challenge the necessity – and beyond that, the plausibility – of essentialism. One concerns the analysis of real predicables (general attributes); the other concerns the analysis of entities and phenomena belonging to the artifactual world of human CULTURE, hence perhaps also extending to the "natural" world to the extent that it too is, in some measure, an "artifact" or "construction" of human culture. The first addresses the deep problem that the theory of universals ultimately ignored, namely how precisely we justify extending a predicate term to new instances beyond the PARADIGMs by which what they designate is first introduced. In a post-Kantian world, that is, in a world in which there is no principled disjunction between the conditions of our understanding the way the world is structured and the way the world is actually structured, general predicates and predicables are, in some ineluctable way, artifactual, but not for that reason arbitrary. Furthermore, if the conditions of human understanding are themselves historicized, so that the concepts and categories by means of which we understand the world are artifacts of our changing history, then it begins to appear plausible (arguably, even ineluctable) that DISCOURSE may behave coherently without adhering to essentialism. And if, with regard to the second strategy, whatever belongs to the world of human culture – persons, artworks, actions, institutions, language, and the like – are themselves historicized artifacts, then certainly the original modal thesis (that essentialism favors) cannot be shown to hold. Roughly speaking, the treatment of both of these strategies at the end of the twentieth century is at the very least hospitable to the coherence of denying essentialism.

A specimen alternative will be helpful here. It may be fairly argued that on Ludwig WITTGENSTEIN's (1889–1951) "later" view, the defensible extension of general terms to new cases depends upon and is a function of the social practices (of language and institutionalized life) that Wittgenstein collects as *Lebensformen*. That is, whether, say, a color term or a term designating a style of painting or the recognizable interests of political parties or the like is correctly or justifiably extended to *new* cases cannot be determined except consensually (but *not*, for that reason, criterially) in accordance with what a functioning society is able and willing to tolerate as a valid extension. Furthermore, if this general *lebensformlich* account is historicized in some way that belongs to the themes of post-French Revolutionary thought – as in accordance, say, with Karl MARX, or Hans-Georg GADAMER, or Michel FOUCAULT, or others, then the range of consensual tolerance will itself vary from society to society and from one time to another within the same society. Under such circumstances, essentialism will fail. For present purposes, it is enough to see that the option is coherent and perhaps even descriptively true of known societies. In effect, what this means is that the particulars that we identify in discourse can be assigned properties (predicables) without being assigned fixed natures or essences, and that as long as such "natures" can be managed consensually in historically changing ways (as just noted, speaking of predication), without invoking essences, then essentialism (in its modal form) is demonstrably false and (in its descriptive nonmodal form) decidedly implausible.

JOSEPH MARGOLIS

estrangement This term has undergone a considerable history of attempted clarification, conducted especially with a view to distinguishing it from ALIENATION, its habitual synonym. Although the concept is present in earlier writers such as ROUSSEAU, it first acquires a central status in the WRITINGS of HEGEL and MARX. The German word used by Hegel in *The Phenomenology of Spirit* to denote "estrangement" overlaps in its meaning with the terms used to designate "externalization" and "objectification." All of these notions belong to the second stage of Hegel's dialectic: an entity which in the first stage is apprehended as merely given and self-identical is viewed in the second stage as "self-estranged" or "externalized", its identity being comprised by the totality of relations into which it enters. The third stage abrogates this estrangement and restores identity, in a larger, mediated, and universal sense.

In his *Economic and Philosophical Manuscripts of 1844* (1959 (*1981*)), Marx praises this dialectic for recognizing that human beings create the objective world through labor, but criticizes it for its purely speculative supersession of estrangement; Marx makes a crucial distinction between mere objectification or externalization and estrangement or alienation. The latter is a specific social condition associated with the bourgeois world, and especially private property: the individual experiences the products of his own labor, and the entire "objective" world, including the state, as alien to him. This estrangement, says Marx, can be abolished only "practically," by revolution. The concept of estrangement has also had a wide currency in socio-

logy, psychology, and certain areas of philosophy such as EXISTENTIALISM.

See also ALIENATION.

Reading
Torrance, J. 1977: *Estrangement, Alienation, and Exploitation: A Sociological Approach.*
Walliman, I. 1981: *Estrangement: Marx's Concept of Human Nature and the Division of Labor.*

M.A.R. HABIB

ethics Ethics is the branch of philosophy which studies the nature and criteria of right and wrong action, obligation, value and the good life, and related principles. Throughout its history it has been a normative and critical discipline, concerned with not only the analysis of concepts but also justifications and principles of how life should be lived. Usually without seeking to supply advice about immediate particularities (in the manner of preachers or agony columns), it has always retained a relevance to practical principles, whether at the level of individual action or political policy. Thus principles of ethics necessarily underlie social and political philosophy, disciplines concerned ultimately with the ethics of power and the ethics of SOCIAL FORMATIONS and practices.

More colloquially, "ethics" is used of the morals of various societies or the moral standards implicit in their behavior. In this sense, ethics is as various as humanity. Importantly, ethics (in this sense) is perennially open to appraisal by ethics (in the sense defined above).

History of Ethics Ethics cannot be understood independently of its historical development. The connections between ethics, society, and politics were recognized in the ancient world by Plato and Aristotle. Seeking to reply to the relativism and skepticism of the Sophists, Plato argued that instances of goodness participate in the universal Form of the Good, instances of justice in the Form of the Just, etc., and that these Forms are among the proper objects of human knowledge. The Forms exist independently of governments and the gods, which may thus be appraised (and found wanting) by thinkers who study the Forms.

Aristotle was another objectivist, but unlike Plato held that the Forms exist only in particular instances. He taught that the virtues are learnable dispositions to choose the reasonable mean between extremes of feeling and behavior. The good life entails developing the distinctive function of the human soul, that is, reason, and this requires the development of practical wisdom, and therewith the virtues, and ideally of theoretical wisdom (that is, metaphysics). Aristotle's works concerning *Ethics* and *Politics* form a sequence, the *Politics* concerning the kind of political arrangements appropriate for the development of the virtues as analyzed in the *Ethics*.

When Aristotle's *Ethics* was rediscovered in the Middle Ages, the Christian philosopher Thomas Aquinas found his teleological approach congenial, but adapted his account of virtue and the good life, such that the Christian virtues of faith, hope, and charity were included alongside the cardinal virtues of courage, prudence, temperance, and justice. The highest form of the good life now involved the contemplation of God.

Early modern philosophers, however, responded differently to ancient influences. Thomas Hobbes (1588–1679) inferred from his reading of the Greek historian Thucydides that self-preservation is the universal motive, and (influenced by Euclid) held that moral principles are to be deduced from axioms such as the sole desirability of one's own good. The rational course is to enter a contract consisting of common principles if others will do the same. One principle is that individuals contract to obey (with minimal qualifications) a sovereign authority for the sake of common security (Hobbes, 1651). *Contractarianism* has recently been revived (in more liberal guise) by John Rawls (1971).

In the following century the ancient philosophy of Epicureanism (which held that pleasure and the absence of pain is the only good) was revised as *utilitarianism*, the doctrine that the criterion of right action (or rules governing right action) is the production of the greatest available balance of pleasure over pain. Like Epicureanism (which was often employed to criticize the ethics taught by official religions in the ancient world), utilitarianism was deployed (by philosophers like Jeremy Bentham (1748–1832) and John Stuart Mill (1806–1873)) to conduct rational critiques of the established order.

Meanwhile Immanuel KANT (1724–1804), influenced rather by the stress of the ancient Stoics on humanity's capacity for rationality and on the rightness of the rational, taught that rightness is unrelated to the consequences of action. Only those acts are right whose maxim could desirably become a universal law, that is, which could be adopted universally. Expressed like this, the "categorical imperative" has been charged with contentless FORMALISM, but this charge does not apply to Kant's alternative formulation, which enjoins agents to treat humanity as an end and never as a means only. This particular approach attracted widespread support during the twentieth century.

Among Continental philosophers of the nineteenth century, Friedrich NIETZSCHE's advocacy of a transvaluation of values remains influential. In the twentieth century, existentialists such as Jean-Paul SARTRE castigated the bad faith of accepting others' judgments (what Kant would call "heteronomy"), urging an authenticity which recognizes no preexisting principles; all values are created anew in acts of choice. While both these approaches presuppose unacknowledged values, their impact has often enlivened much of the philosophy of more analytic traditions.

Issues in Contemporary Ethics   Twentieth-century ethics focused for several decades on *metaethics*, that is questions concerning the objectivity and status of moral and valuational DISCOURSE, and this debate continues. *Cognitivists* hold that the language of morality and values admits of truth and (sometimes) knowledge. One kind of cognitivism is *naturalism*, which maintains that at least some ethical terms are translatable into factual language, whether empirical or metaphysical. This view, however, is widely held to include the "naturalistic fallacy" (G.E. Moore, 1903), roughly the "fallacy" of defining language which is indefinable and has a peculiar meaning of its own.

Cognitivists (including G.E. Moore), believing that naturalism is fallacious, adopted *nonnaturalism*, the belief that at least some moral properties are neither complex and analyzable properties, nor natural (for example empirical), but simple and irreducible. Moore's account of how the presence of goodness, construed as a simple, unanalyzable quality, can be apprehended, is that this is achieved by acts of intuition. Philosophers unconvinced by this moral epistemology have often concluded that nonnatural properties belonging to a kind of their own are not properties at all, and have resorted to *noncognitivism*.

In one of its forms, *emotivism*, noncognitivism claimed that there are no truths in moral discourse, and thus no propositions either; moral discourse rather serves to express the feelings of the utterer and generate similar feelings in hearers. While factual claims are presupposed, this discourse has more in common with utterances like "hurrah" and "boo" than with a search for truth, and similarly it typically employs persuasive definitions in the attempt to exercise partisan influence. This kind of position, however, came widely to be seen as incapable of providing for the scope of reason in moral discourse or the requirement that one's judgments be consistent.

By widespread consent an improved form of noncognitivism was *prescriptivism*, as put forward by R.M. Hare (1981). For Hare the primary meaning of moral discourse consists in guiding action, in the strong sense of prescribing, whether for others or for oneself, which actions (etc.) are to be done. Moral language must satisfy the requirement that like cases be judged alike, but as long as appraisers judge (and act) alike about their own cases, their prescriptions about others count as moral ones. Further, since SUBJECTS of judgments can be expected to put themselves in the positions (in turn) of all affected parties, and since no one would prescribe that their own interests (as expressed in their preferences) be ignored, the only rational prescriptions are those which take into account all interests on an equal footing, or (in other words) utilitarian ones. Thus Hare maintains that prescriptivism generates preference utilitarianism.

While noncognitivists have increasingly been recognizing rationality in moral discourse, other philosophers have been reconstructing naturalism, with its stress on objectivity and reason. While few have supplied reductionist definitions of ethical terms, many have maintained that naturalist definitions cannot be known to be fallacious beforehand, and that there is often a reasonable route from naturalistic premises (about wants, needs, or interests) to moral conclusions. Others (such as Philippa Foot, 1978) have stressed that acceptance of particular evaluations cannot be construed as optional; there are certain virtues which everyone needs, and the very concept of morality itself supplies limits to the grounds which may be adduced in moral discourse. Accordingly there can be a basis for truth claims in ethics after all.

Yet others have contended that it is only within moral traditions or moral practices that moral reasoning is valid, that these traditions are what gives life its meaning, and that to step outside them is to forgo the kind of context in which moral discourse makes sense. Sometimes this *communitarian* position is allied to an Aristotelian account of ethics in terms of the virtues proper to the various traditions or practices, as in the recent work of A.C. MacINTYRE (1988). Other defenders of an Aristotelian emphasis on the virtues maintain that there is enough in common between the experiences of life of all human communities for at least some of the virtues to be universal, and defend them on a nonrelative basis (Nussbaum, 1993).

Normative Ethics Where first-order principles of obligation and right action are concerned, the approach based on rights should be mentioned alongside the utilitarian, contractarian, and KANTIAN approaches. While all approaches recognize various (derivative) rights, this approach makes rights fundamental, whether as presocial human rights, grounded in an individual's humanity, as natural rights, bestowed by God or nature, or as self-evident rights, presupposed in people's widespread discomfort at any overriding of individual needs or interests. Adherents of this *rights-as-premises* approach have included John Locke in the seventeenth century and Robert Nozick in the twentieth. Problems of this approach include the resolution of disagreements concerning the identity of such fundamental rights, and the contradictions arising when the fundamental rights of different individuals conflict.

Contractarian approaches, as in Rawls (1971), have the advantage of supplying a decision procedure by appeal to contract-making situations. However, they encounter the problems that the interests of non-rational parties are apt to be omitted, and that representatives of future generations cannot be included in the contract, since the contract determines how many such generations there will be. Also their attempt to derive moral principles from the preferences of self-interested agents has been widely criticized for their implausibly abstract and deracinated concept of the self.

In stressing that humanity should never be treated solely as a means, the *Kantian* approach evokes widespread sympathy, despite the obscurity of the notion of treating humanity as an end. This position gains strength by requiring that individuals be given moral consideration as opposed to inviolability; *rule consequentialism*, however, can also require this. Its weakness lies in its disregard for at least some of the avoidable consequences of action; for in cogent accounts of responsibility these consequences are included.

Consequentialism is at its most defensible when

it incorporates rules which enshrine and ground rights and justice, and when premised on a defensible value theory. The value theory of utilitarianism is usually regarded as too narrow, since not everything can turn on either the happiness of sentient creatures or the satisfaction of preferences. For a plausible theory, other values – suggestions include autonomy (Glover, 1977) and the development of characteristic human powers (Hurka, 1993) – must be included. Equally, provision must be made for prioritizing the satisfaction of basic needs, and for weighing this plurality of values in some nonarbitrary manner (Attfield, 1995).

Applied Ethics   In recent decades philosophers have rediscovered the applicability of ethical reasoning to important public issues in areas such as biomedical ethics, environmental ethics, and the ethics of development, population, and war. The application of ethics in these areas was commonplace from earliest times to the ENLIGHTENMENT, but was marginalized as not the proper concern of philosophy in the analytic philosophy of the first six decades of the twentieth century.

In environmental ethics, principles have been elaborated for taking into account the well-being of future generations and nonhuman species or their members. Its debates promise to enhance the adequacy of traditional theories concerning the scope of moral standing, intrinsic value, and obligation. Development ethics studies the concept of development and issues surrounding the related priorities, and promises to modify received accounts of the good life. Population ethics covers concepts such as overpopulation and the relations of quantity and quality of worthwhile life (see Parfit, 1984). The ethics of war refines and appraises the Just War doctrine of Aquinas, applying concepts such as proportionality to the unprecedented circumstances of modern warfare. Thus some of the most penetrating work in ethical theory is to be found, paradoxically, in practical applications of ethics to the modern world.

Biomedical ethics exemplifies this further, concerned as it is with the ethical problems arising in medicine and related disciplines. The field is dominated by deontological theories on the one hand – usually rights-based or Kantian – and consequentialist theories on the other – usually some form of utilitarianism. Thus the principle of informed consent, based on a Kantian principle of respect for autonomy or self-determination, is taken to be central to the practice of medicine, particularly in a clinical setting. At the same time a recently developed and widely debated approach to resource allocation is based on maximizing quality-adjusted life years (QALYs), and is to that extent an application of utilitarianism.

However, although a few ethicists believe in a "theory down" approach, whereby the philosopher provides the moral theory, which is then strictly applied to provide a final resolution of the problem in hand, most take a dialectical approach, whereby the details of particular cases inform the formulation of a moral framework, which may be more or less complex but is by no means definitive.

The attempts by some philosophers to provide absolute rulings, conspicuously contrasting with their apparent inability to do so satisfactorily, have led some to a radical rejection of the role of the philosopher in medical ethics. It has been claimed that the philosopher has no distinctive expertise that cannot be shared by the informed layperson. However, it is clear that philosophy does share some central concerns with medical ethics. In attempting to determine the status of the human fetus or the criteria of death, for example, it is necessary to appeal to not only moral theory, but also theories of personal identity and the nature and status of the human mind.

Thus some who accept the criticisms leveled against mainstream medical ethics have responded not by rejecting the possibility of a specifically philosophical contribution, but by searching for different, more enlightened approaches, most remaining within the analytic tradition, but some beginning to venture beyond it.

Feminist Ethics   Feminist ethics has been particularly active on this front. For example, the work of moral psychologist Carol Gilligan (1993) has inspired the development of an ethics of care. Traditional moral theories – or at least those which are currently most popular – are based on formal, abstract reasoning; fundamental rules are discovered and applied by an autonomous moral agent who is able to abstract from the particularities of a situation. Both deontological and utilitarian theories fit this model. Gilligan, however, claims to have discovered a "different voice" in moral reasoning: women who conceive of moral problems in such a way that "the moral problem . . . requires for its resolution a mode of thinking that is contextual and narrative rather than formal and abstract" (p. 19). Thus, far from moral decision-making demanding that certain details of a situation, such as the relationships between the individuals concerned, be disregarded in order to reach a universal or impartial judgment, the ethics of care demands a responsiveness to those details, in order that care is provided and relationships are maintained.

Although much of the debate operates on a theoretical level, drawing, for example, on feminist epistemology and the claim that there is a masculine bias in traditional models of rationality, the relevance of these insights for applied ethics, and especially medical ethics, is clear. First, the ethics of care begins with the moral agent as situated within a particular, unique set of circumstances and is therefore embedded in practical examples. Second, feminist ethicists, including many of those not affiliated to the ethics of care, share some of the central concerns of medical ethicists. Most notable, perhaps, is the concern with reproductive technology. Here feminists have been particularly vocal in pointing to not only the special interest that women have in the debate and the different perspectives that they can offer, but also to the fact that any discussion of reproductive self-determination or reproductive choice (in terms of which the debate is often couched) must be contextualized to take in all the relevant details of the positions from which women make their choices.

While skepticism regarding the claims of mainstream moral theory has generated an interest in contextual approaches such as the ethics of care, some recent philosophers maintain that the *postmodern* rejection of the subject, and therewith of the duality of subjects and objects, makes many of the above issues outmoded, such as the debate between objectivism and subjectivism, and the problem of the status of intrinsic value (Norton, 1991). Some of these theorists appeal to the supposed interdependence of observers and objects which they detect in the Copenhagen interpretation of quantum physics, and develop in consequence an observer-dependent account of value and thus of ethics. But standardly they presuppose the very distinctions which they seek to elide, and generate a form of radical skepticism which forfeits the capacity to appraise injustice and exploitation. Faced by such disastrous skepticism, it is crucial that ethics retains the capacity to supply countercritiques, and refuses to abandon its perennially critical character.

Reading

Aman, Kenneth, ed. 1991: *Ethical Principles for Development: Needs, Capacities or Rights?*
Attfield, Robin 1995: *Value, Obligation and Meta-ethics.*
Held, Virginia, ed. 1993: *Feminist Morality.*
Lee, Keekok 1989: *Social Philosophy and Ecological Scarcity.*
MacIntyre, Alasdair 1967: *A Short History of Ethics.*
——1981: *After Virtue: A Study in Moral Theory.*
Midgley, Mary 1979: *Beast and Man: The Roots of Human Nature.*
Rolston, Holmes III 1988: *Environmental Ethics: Duties and Values in the Natural World.*
Singer, Peter 1979: *Practical Ethics.*
——ed. 1986: *Applied Ethics.*
Williams, Bernard 1985: *Ethics and the Limits of Philosophy.*
Winkler, Earl R., and Coombs, Jerrold R., eds 1993: *Applied Ethics: A Reader.*

ROBERT ATTFIELD AND SUSANNE GIBSON

ethics, communitarian   *See* COMMUNITARIAN ETHICS

ethnicity   The awareness sensed by a group of its cultural distinctiveness in contrast to other groups. Even the most remote societies observe and compare themselves with contrasting, neighboring societies; consequently, ethnicity is fundamentally a political phenomenon based on perceived differences between groups. Further, ethnic difference is almost always critically evaluated; one's own variety is usually seen as superior, an attitude termed ethnocentric.

Since the advent of empires in the fifteenth century, it has been increasingly likely that societies will be incorporated into larger political entities. Though assimilation into the CULTURE of the dominant group has often occurred, it appears much more frequent that groups are absorbed politically but not culturally. The result is ethnic groups occupying the position of a minority (or majority) within a larger, multiethnic political STRUCTURE. In these multiethnic states, egalitarianism is uncommon. Ethnocentrism and its biological variant, RACISM, are the rule; stable power sharing is not.

Ethnic awareness focuses on the group's customs, conceptualized by social scientists as culture. Anthropologists describe in comprehensive terms the breadth of a group's culture, but since ethnicity is self-awareness, how members of a society define their distinctiveness will differ from what the anthropologist describes. Indeed, it may be politically expedient to exaggerate the actual degree of distinctiveness, as in the tragic case of Bosnia.

Factors which build ethnic solidarity include origin myths, oral tradition, pride in the achievements of heroes, distinctive foods and dress, a separate religious history, a strong identification with a homeland, sacred sites and localities of past events, artistic and musical styles, and language. These factors may be conserved from the past, embellished, or fabricated anew to support the desire for group solidarity.

Ethnic pride, a common associate of ethnic self-awareness, has risen sharply in recent years, contributing powerfully to wars, massive population displacements, and separatist movements. Meanwhile, enclave ethnic groups have since the 1960s escalated their quest for home rule, constitutional recognition as a group apart, territorial demarcation, and often some form of sovereignty.

The cultures of all peoples change, though usually in ways that maintain an underlying cultural core. Thus Native Americans in the United States choose leaders through balloting, use fax machines to lobby Congress, and operate gambling casinos. Skeptics argue that they are thus no longer owners of a distinctive tradition and deserve no special consideration or recognition as a group. These politically convenient attitudes fail to accord to these societies the same option to change that the skeptics would vigorously demand for their own society, and also deny the likelihood that such groups are preserving their anchor values and ideas.

Ethnic distinctiveness appears to have been a feature of our species since humans became cultural animals. Today, while borrowing cultural ideas has never been easier or more widespread, ethnicity seems certain to remain a fundamental principle of contrast, divisiveness, and unity among human communities.

Reading
Foster, George 1960: *Culture and Conquest.*
van den Berghe, Pierre L. 1973: "Pluralism."

THOMAS C. GREAVES

ethnophilosophy Ethnophilosophy designates a practice alongside the discipline of African philosophy, but one which has earned the strong disapproval of authoritative figures among African philosophers. The designation indicates its critics' perceptions that ethnophilosophy, which its practitioners represent as legitimate philosophy, blurs the distinctions between true philosophy and ethnography, and that it is in fact ethnology with philosophical pretensions. The typical and seminal ethnophilosophical text is Placide Tempels's *La Philosophie bantou* (1945), translated into English as *Bantu Philosophy* (1969), in which the author undertook to demonstrate the existence of a Bantu ontological system and a Bantu philosophy which had hitherto not been synthesized or systematized in any explicit fashion. Tempels, a Belgian Catholic missionary priest who worked for many years in the Congo, believed that by virtue of being human, the Bantu, like all human societies, had a philosophy, and also that, even though they might be unaware of their ontology or their philosophy, and consequently might be unable to articulate it, they none the less lived intuitively by it. He believed furthermore that an outsider trained in such matters could accurately·synthesize the ontology by studying the thoughts, beliefs, and practices of the people. Following Tempels's lead, some African scholars undertook to distill other examples of African philosophy from ethnological data. Alexis Kagame in *La Philosophie bantu-rwandaise de l'être* (Bantu–Rwandan Philosophy of Being, 1956) and *La Philosophie bantu comparée* (Comparative Bantu Philosophy, 1976), unveiled what he described as a collective system of thought among the Bantu, a system that was profound and implicit, one lived rather than deliberated upon, and which, being unanimist, was also superior to systems ascribable to individual thinkers, such as characterized the West. He claimed further that this philosophy, though implicit and collective, was nevertheless amenable to Aristotelian analysis. In anglophone Africa the figure most associated with ethnophilosophy is John Mbiti, author of *African Religions and Philosophy* (1969).

The objections to ethnophilosophy come from African philosophers who are products of European universities and are consequently steeped in the Western tradition of philosophy. Sometimes referred to as academic philosophers because of their customary affiliation with the philosophy departments of African universities, they are predominantly from francophone Africa, and leftist in their ideological orientation. They take issue, for example, with, among other aspects of the practice, precisely the one Kagame cites as its claim to superiority over Western philosophies – its unanimism. In the view of the academic philosophers, chief among whom is the Beninois Paulin Hountondji, the very suggestion of unanimism (attested to by such formulations as "bantu philosophy," "African philosophy," "*La Philosophie bantou–rwandaise*," and so forth) is contrary to the nature of true philosophy. Philosophy, for them, is an individual activity, an individual's intellectual engagement with experience. Far from being unanimist, therefore, it is pluralistic, and, in the words of Paulin Hountondji, the chief campaigner against ethnophilosophy, characterized by an "irreducible polysemy of discourse" (Hountondji, 1983, p. 179). Also, inasmuch as they regard philosophy as a conscious and rigorous intellectual activity, the opponents of ethnophilosophy reject the notion of an implicit philosophy, one *lived* by adherents who remain unaware of its existence. Also unacceptable to them is the ethnophilosophers' methodology, which seems to accord equal value to all members of a society as reliable informants on ethnological matters. Other prominent anti-ethnophilosophers are Stanislaus Adotevi and Marcien Towa.

Rejecting Tempels's contention that all human beings possess a philosophy, these academic philosophers argue that philosophy is a science preoccupied with analyses of written TEXTS. Science cannot exist without WRITING, and since traditional African societies were illiterate, and therefore ignorant of science, they could not have had philosophy. They deflect Tempels's charge that denial of philosophy to any group of humans is tantamount to denying its humanity by conceding that African thinkers of the past must have reflected on the issues that are central to Western philosophy, in other words, that they must have philosophized; but they insist that, since we have no record of their reflections or their findings, we do not have their philosophy or any evidence of it. Hence the intriguing concept of philosophers without philosophy.

Although the debate about ethnophilosophy is primarily a contest concerning the integrity of philosophy as a discipline, its critics are also animated by a preoccupation with progress. They perceive ethnophilosophy and its claims as both symbolizing and valorizing the features of traditional African thought and habits that were responsible for the misfortunes the continent and its people had experienced, from enslavement through colonization and eventual (or consequent) underdevelopment. For example, the Ghanaian Kwasi Wiredu points out that unanimism and implicitness reflect the authoritarianism of the traditional system, which requires people to live by timeless

CODES established by remote ancestors, and the youth to defer unconditionally to the old who are held to be incontrovertible custodians of wisdom. The resulting stifling of initiative, he argues, militates against initiative and the development of the mind.

Some of the academic philosophers, while accepting the need to clearly distinguish ethnology from philosophy, are uneasy about the insistence by Hountondji and his colleagues that no philosophy is uncompromisingly a science, and that the Western practice is normative. They also balk at the suggestion (by Towa especially) that Africa's future lies in Africans assimilating the spirit of Europe. In something of a compromise between the forces of philosophy and ethnophilosophy, H. Odera Oruka proposes what he describes as "sage philosophy," defined as "the expressed thoughts of wise men and women in any given community," which can be in writing, saying, or arguments (1990, p. 51). He recognizes the thoughts of Ogotemmeli as expressed to Marcel Griaule as an example. Another example would be the thoughts of Yoruba sages which Barry Hallen and J.O. Sodipo discuss in *Knowledge, Belief and Witchcraft: Analytic Experiments in African Philosophy* (1986).

Reading

Griaule, M. 1965: *Conversations with Ogotemmeli: An Introduction to Dogon Religious Ideas.*
Hallen, Barry, and J.O. Sodipo 1986: *Knowledge, Belief & Witchcraft: Analytic Experiments in African Philosophy.*
Hountondji, Paulin 1983: *African Philosophy: Myth and Reality.*
Kagame, Alexis 1956: *La Philosophie bantou–rwandaise de l'être.*
Mbiti, John S. 1969: *African Religions and Philosophy.*
Mudimbe, V.Y. 1988: *The Invention of Africa: Gnosis, Philosophy, and the Order of Knowledge.*
Oruka, H. Odera 1990a: *Trends in Contemporary African Philosophy.*
Tempels, Placide 1969: *Bantu Philosophy.*
Wiredu, Kwasi 1980: *Philosophy and an African Culture.*

OYEKAN OWOMOYELA

European cultural studies in Western Europe

The phrase "CULTURAL STUDIES" – used in the original English – has become current among scholars in university departments of English in Western continental Europe. It joins other terms with longer histories: the French *civilisation* and the German *Landeskunde*, and in Scandinavia the English *civilization*. Through the French and German terms there are links with scholarship in other languages and other university departments with their own traditions and interpretations of what shall be the context for the teaching of a foreign language at higher and, by extension, secondary education levels. It is a particular characteristic of cultural studies in these situations that it is inseparable, at least with respect to teaching if not research, from the issues of language learning and the fact that most students will become schoolteachers. Despite the advanced levels of language mastery of many students in higher education in mainland Europe – particularly in English – the fact that the language and CULTURE are foreign is significant for the development of cultural studies. This then also means that in methods of teaching and researching, cultural studies includes comparison with and reflection on the culture and cultural identities of the learners and the society in which they live.

The German term *Landeskunde* has a complex history, reflecting a high degree of pedagogical interest in relating language to contexts other than literary, and also encapsulating the relationship of foreign language learning in higher and secondary education to historical events. In the 1920s and 1930s *Kulturkunde*, as part of the teaching of English, was a means of encouraging the appreciation of German culture by contrasting it with that of English-speaking countries. This approach then facilitated the process of *Gleichschaltung* in 1935 of foreign language teaching in Nazi Germany. After the defeat of Nazism, the first response in West Germany was to attempt to make *Landeskunde* value-free by emphasizing its subordination to the aim of acquiring the skills of communication. *Landeskunde* should provide the necessary information to facilitate communication and a positive – and often false – image of "Merry Old England" as a means of creating enthusiasm, motivation, and a readiness for contact among learners. In the case of American studies, the development was influenced by notions of reeducation and democracy, and the study of politics and contemporary history was introduced earlier than in English studies. A parallel development to include contemporary politics and history also took place in departments of Romance studies, more familiar with the concept *civilisation* (see below). None the less, at university level *Landeskunde* remained the marginal province of nonprofessorial teachers and researchers, with traditional literature studies dominating the high ground. In the German Democratic Republic,

the dominance of Marxist–Leninist theory provided a critique of *Kulturkunde* up to 1945 and a basis for "a systematic, transferable knowledge of the foreign culture(s) . . . but these suggestions were, at least in part, impaired by the fact that they presented *one* instead of a variety of competing views of the foreign culture(s) under discussion" (Kramer, 1994, p. 28).

Dissatisfaction with the attempt to replace *Kulturkunde* with a neutral *Landeskunde* led in West Germany, in the 1980s, to the introduction of the work of Raymond WILLIAMS, Stuart HALL, and the Birmingham Centre for Contemporary Cultural Studies. Dieter Buttjes (1981) and Jürgen Kramer (1983) were particularly influential in making cultural studies accessible to a wider audience and the eventual instigation in 1990 of an annual meeting on cultural studies – using the English term – outside the existing institutional structures which were still resistant to challenges to traditional forms of literature teaching. Coincidence with the unification of Germany ensured the participation of researchers from the former GDR – the second conference being held in Jena – and a broader methodological and content focus than cultural studies in the British tradition.

The French term *civilisation* has a much longer and more general history than *Landeskunde*, and, rather than referring to a discipline associated with language teaching, designates the "object" of study itself. Within the academy, however, the term is used to refer to an area of teaching and research, *l'étude de la civilisation*, which is "a pretty close equivalent to what comes to be known in Britain and elsewhere as 'cultural studies', provided the term 'cultural' is taken to mean the mechanism, practice and institutions through which the world is interpreted, meanings are conveyed, internalised in people's minds and recycled . . . a quest for a total interpretation" (Révauger, 1993a, p. 26). *Civilisation* shares with *Landeskunde* a hitherto marginal role in university English departments in France and a consequent desire on the part of some proponents to define the area of study in terms of a discipline, while acknowledging the advantages of standing at the crossroads of pluridisciplinarity, where innovations are more likely to take place.

Links are none the less made with existing disciplines within English departments, and with broader traditions in French education, through the methodology of textual commentary or documentary analysis and the concept of *explication de texte*. This detailed practical skill of explaining TEXT and its relationship to context also requires knowledge of a culture or *civilisation*, and is not unlike the detailed analysis of texts within their broad sociohistorical context practiced in some versions of cultural studies.

Though the English term "civilization" is perhaps avoided in British and American institutions because of its "complicated and much disputed relation with the modern social sense of *culture*" (Williams, 1983, p. 59), it is not entirely shunned in Scandinavian departments of English. In Norway, the deliberate introduction of *civilization* was part of the familiar problem of establishing a teaching and research base, and credibility as a discipline (Oakland, 1993, p. 34). Disciplinary bases hitherto included sociology, history, and political science, as well as the methods of textual analysis.

Common to the situations discussed so far is the problem of establishing an institutional base against the resistance of other areas of study, particularly literary studies. Protagonists in the debate seem to be undecided whether they should take their strength from pluridisciplinarity or establish a clearly demarcated new discipline. Though the former promises innovation, the latter is more acceptable to institutions. Furthermore, although some proponents of cultural studies are specialists in American studies, many focus their research on Britain, and a further factor in institutional struggles is the introduction of the concept of British studies and, in Germany, a *Journal for the Study of British Cultures*, which will no doubt support the professionalization of specialists on Britain.

A similar kind of support for teachers and researchers in the *civilisation* of France is offered by a survey of the teaching of *civilisation* in the French departments of European universities (Campos et al., 1988). Here we find the by now familiar debates about the scope and nature of the subject, together with detailed accounts of the courses offered and discussion of institutional and professional problems similar to those of English departments. If we accept the general comparability of cultural studies, *Landeskunde*, and *civilisation*, it is clear there are many people concerned, in many kinds of foreign language departments, including those in Britain. It is, however, also evident from this survey that *civilisation* remains "the poor relation" to study of language and literature, lacking space in the curriculum, status in the eyes of most professional staff, and an explicit

theoretical and disciplinary base (Campos et al., 1988, p. 103).

The fact that cultural studies as part of foreign language teaching introduces students to a society and culture other than their own has several significant dimensions. First, on a geopolitical level, the relationships between the countries studied need to be acknowledged as part of the teaching and research. The provision of material and financial support for the study of its culture by country A in the universities and schools of country B is doubtless part of its political agenda. The critical study of country C by researchers in country D who are also teachers of future mediators between the two countries – economists, business people, teachers, politicians – has undefined but real influences on international relationships.

Such geopolitical considerations should lead to a comparative methodology in teaching and research, the significance of which is only beginning to be recognized among the many other debates about the nature of cultural studies and institutionalization. Where the students are from several countries, comparative methods become inevitable (Husemann, 1994), but are no less important in homogeneous classes. The effects are not only a better understanding of the geopolitical relationships between countries (Sevaldsen, 1993) and the images of other cultures in our own society, but also a reflexive understanding of one's own culture and cultural identities. This helps not only the definition of self – at national, regional, and individual levels – but also serves others in their self-understanding through critical analysis from an outsider perspective.

The practical significance of this juxtaposition of interpretations of others and self becomes evident for students in their contacts with members of the culture and society in question. This is, however, not merely the provision in *Landeskunde* of the background information necessary in intercultural meetings. As social actors engaged with other cultural identities, their own identities are inseparable from interaction and communication, as is their critical awareness of the relationship between self and otherness. It is in the verbal and nonverbal, the explicit and implicit meanings exchanged through the foreign language, that students practice their cultural studies.

Yet there is little recognition of the needs of students of cultural studies as language learners, whose grasp of the language and culture will inevitably remain incomplete and different in kind from that of a native speaker. The pedagogy and learning theory of cultural studies for foreign language learners is not considered or, at best, is imported inappropriately from cultural studies for native speakers. Furthermore, some of these language-and-culture learners will themselves become teachers of a foreign language-and-culture and, in the French and German traditions at least, the issues of *Landeskunde* and *civilisation* in higher education cannot be divorced from teaching in secondary education, usually at more elementary levels of language learning where issues of pedagogy cannot be so easily ignored. It is not surprising, therefore, that in Germany in particular, the development of theory of *Landeskunde* and cultural studies has been prosecuted by *Didaktiker*, university teachers and researchers responsible for the training in methods of teaching of future secondary school teachers.

A rare exception is offered by Campos et al. who discuss the relationship between school-level and university-level teaching of *civilisation* in terms of three levels of learning. They argue (1988, p. 122) that whereas at an elementary level learners need information about the meanings of words, at intermediate and advanced levels the teaching of *civilisation* can be separate from language teaching. Furthermore, it is only at university level that a critical dimension is appropriate. Such a view does not, however, adequately recognize the complexity of language learning, the interrelationships of acquisition of linguistic skill and knowledge with affective as well as cognitive development in experience of another culture – in the classroom and more particularly in a foreign country – at all levels of learning. This kind of argument betrays the lack of an adequate learning theory for all levels, the absence of a pedagogy of comparative methods, and, in particular, the need to develop a pedagogy of experiential learning for students at all levels who in increasing numbers spend substantial periods of residence and learning in another country. These are the glaring needs of cultural studies in continental Europe and beyond, when cultural studies is taught and researched in contexts of foreign language learning.

Reading
Buttjes, D., and Byram M., eds 1991: *Mediating Languages and Cultures.*
——1989: "Landeskunde-Didaktik und Landeskundliches Curriculum."

Byram, M., ed. 1994: *Culture and Language Learning in Higher Education.*
Cain, A., ed. 1991: *Enseignement/Apprentissage de la civilisation en cours de langue.*
Campos, C., Higman, F., Mendelson, D., and Nagy, G. 1988: *L'Enseignement de la civilisation française dans les universités d'Europe.*
Kramer, J. 1990: *Cultural and Intercultural Studies.*
Porcher, L. 1986: *La Civilisation.*
Puren, C. 1988: *Histoire des méthodologies.*
Révauger, J-P., ed. 1993b: *Civilization: Theory and Practice.*
Zarate, G. 1993: *Représentations de l'etranger et didactique des langues.*

MICHAEL BYRAM

exchange In combination with reciprocity, the essence of all social interaction. Following Polanyi, exchange is of three types: reciprocal (for example, gift giving), redistributive (tax and expend), and market (barter and sales). Social relationships are at issue with the first, authority with the second, and, mainly, the distribution of goods with the third.

Reading
Polanyi, Karl 1957: "Economy as instituted process."

THOMAS C. GREAVES

existentialism A philosophical position associated with two main theses: first, that humans have a special sort of existence that always points beyond itself and which cannot be assimilated to the mode of existence of nonhuman things; second, that it is possible to overcome the error of conceiving of ourselves as fundamentally alienated or estranged from the world by revealing the dependence of a significant world upon human meaning-bestowing practices.

Such a characterization of existentialism is not uncontentious, especially when compared with the received popular view. Existentialism is often popularly portrayed as advocating a form of nihilism and a consequent flight into irrationality: the world as a whole is without meaning or value and actions are groundless and arbitrary; the lack of any necessity for the existence or order of the world leads to a sense of despair and *Angst* in the face of actions and a life that is free but, if we are honest, seen as irredeemably and utterly groundless and futile; the individual can at best act only in response to his "true self," knowing no external standards exist against which to check his values.

That such a view of existentialism is mistaken

can be gleaned from an examination of the two most important existentialists, HEIDEGGER and SARTRE. That the misconception has arisen is traceable partly to the inclusion of just about anyone from the history of human thought who has emphasized our ALIENATION from a world that seems to provide no justification for, and is unresponsive to, any SYSTEM of values, often with the added complication of the "death of God" as external arbiter and law giver. Such a view is found in the writing of Albert Camus. There is also a confusion between existentialism as a systematic philosophical position and existentialism as a historical movement associated with its hangers-on who adopted the term to justify, in the apparent absence of anything but gratuitous and arbitrary guides to action, an egoistical, nihilistic, and sometimes hedonistic lifestyle tending towards self-destruction.

Apart from those already mentioned, important thinkers for the understanding of existentialism are Kierkegaard, JASPERS, MERLEAU-PONTY, Ortega y Gasset, and Simone de BEAUVOIR. More controversially, NIETZSCHE is sometimes added to this list.

Far from embracing our supposed alienation from the world, existentialism seeks to overcome it. It does so by rejecting the fruit of Cartesian philosophy which in one sense culminates in the PHENOMENOLOGY of Husserl. While existentialism accepts Husserl's view that the distinctive nature of human consciousness is its intentionality – that in any conscious act there is always a pointing to an object of attention – it rejects the Cartesian-inspired project of a significant world emerging from a process whereby all the contingencies of the human perspective are stripped from our conception of the world to reveal it as it is in itself: a view from nowhere. It is the world thus characterized, supposedly the true objective view of it, which is revealed by the nonperspectival disinterested standpoint of the detached ego or soul, that inevitably leads to a fundamental rift with and our alienation from the world. The first step in undermining this view comes from making phenomenology existential, holding that not only is all consciousness intentional, but that also it must in its conscious acts point to something that is not-consciousness. This undercuts the idealism latent in Husserl's pure phenomenology. Existentialism attempts to overcome world alienation by arguing for the logical primacy of the world significances that arise from our concrete encounter with the world as actors with distinctively human needs and

purposes. Without such concrete being-in-the-world in a manner distinctive of human conscious existence (see Heidegger's term DASEIN) – as opposed to as a detached transcendental ego – no world of any significance would emerge at all, and without such significances there is no mechanism for referring to the world. There can be no *a priori* apprehension of pure meanings. We are beings "thrown" *in* the world, and it is only in grappling or dealing with it as a problem in human actions and projects, encountered as an "obstacle," that a world of significance appears at all. In this sense there is no question of one's being alienated from the world, for we have recaptured the primacy of a world that is suffused with human values, that is, the concrete everyday world essential to human survival and action, which is not one made flat by neutral disinterest, but one highlighted and given shape by human concerns. It must be emphasized that such a human world, one of significances-for-human-beings, is not inferior to the world of scientific or metaphysical speculation, or one that is merely "subjective," to be transcended by a truer "objective" view, for such a disinterested view, if possible at all, is in fact parasitic upon the world arising from our being-in-the-world: the world as it is for human beings. The whole tendency of existentialism is to erase the subjective–objective dichotomy, since the basis for its articulation is misconceived.

The distinctive mode of human existence is in Sartre's phrase that it is what it is not, and is not what it is. Consciousness, being-for-itself, stands out from the mode of existence of things, being-in-itself. Unlike a nonhuman thing which simply is, human conscious existence has no predetermined essence fixing its nature; rather, it makes itself in its acts and is constantly becoming, pointing beyond itself to future projects. Human existence is characterized by the process of becoming, and only by including in its description what it is not yet can a description be adequate. Indeed, only in death can some kind of assessment of what kind of person one was be legitimately made. The interdependence of the existence of consciousness (as not-a-thing which emerges only in its separation from the nonconscious object of its conscious act) and the existence of the world (which is intelligibly referred to, has significance and meaning, only as an object for consciousness) dissolves the mind–body dualism that leads to the problem of the knowledge of the existence of the external world and our alienation from it. In the same way our knowledge of other minds is grounded in some aspects of our self-awareness which presuppose that we view ourselves as an object for others.

Existentialism emphasizes our freedom by arguing that in the human mode of being existence precedes essence. We first are, then become what we are. Existentialism argues thus not to support the view that human action must be arbitrary, capricious, and irrational, based perhaps on gut instincts or an adherence to being "true to oneself" – there is in fact no self other than that created in acts – but rather to emphasize that the responsibility for one's life rests only with oneself. It does not entail that moral choice is merely one of invention. To deny this freedom is to act in "bad faith." To live in full knowledge of our freedom, that we are responsible for our life and cannot pass such responsibility to an external authority – we would in any case have to choose – is to live with authenticity. To live capriciously and inconsistently with disregard for the consequences of one's decisions, and without commitment, would be to live inauthentically.

Reading
Blackham, H.J. 1961: *Six Existentialist Thinkers: Kierkegaard, Nietzsche, Jaspers, Marcel, Heidegger, Sartre.*
Cooper, David E. 1990: *Existentialism.*
Solomon, Robert C. 1972: *From Rationalism to Existentialism.*
——1988: *Continental Philosophy Since 1750.*
Warnock, Mary 1970: *Existentialism.*

JOHN SHAND

F

fallacy, affective *See* AFFECTIVE FALLACY

fallacy, intentional *See* INTENTIONAL FALLACY

Fanon, Frantz (1925–61) Martinican psychiatrist and revolutionary. After finishing his medical studies, Fanon published *Black Skin, White Masks* (1952), an existentialist psychological and socioeconomic analysis of the effects of colonization in Martinique, where European CULTURE had imposed "an existential deviation" (p. 16) on blacks. In that work, Fanon studied the processes of "epidermalization" and "lactification" – the interiorization of an inferiority complex based on socioeconomic iniquities, and the desire to "whiten the race" (p. 47) respectively. By analyzing these phenomena, Fanon meant to liberate "the man of color from himself" (p. 10), to achieve "the effective disalienation of the black man" (p. 12). In the opening chapter of *Black Skin, White Masks*, "The negro and language," Fanon exposed the acculturating power of language in the colonial context. Asserting that "to speak is to exist absolutely for the other," (p. 17) Fanon critiqued the inferior status attributed to Creole in favor of French as the language of "civilization" in the Antilles and demonstrated that the denigration of the local language as "inferior" was a key to understanding the dehumanization of colonization. Asserting that every colonized people "finds itself face to face with the language of the civilizing nation . . . the culture of the mother country," Fanon observed that to speak the language of the colonizer was to carry the (imposed) weight of an entire civilization, and to bury one's own traditions and history. In chapter 5 of *Black Skin, White Masks*, "The fact of blackness," Fanon examined the benefits and shortcomings of the negritude movement. While he concluded that negritude was limited by its positing of a universal black essence, Fanon criticized Jean-Paul SARTRE's statement (in *Black Orpheus*) that negritude was

merely the negative term in a dialectical progression where concerns of race would be absorbed by an international proletariat.

From 1953 to 1956 Fanon practiced medicine at the psychiatric hospital at Blida-Joinville in Algeria. In 1956 he resigned from his position, protesting at the inhumane treatment of Algerian patients by French doctors. In 1957 he was expelled from Algeria, and went to Tunisia to work for the Algerian nationalist National Liberation Front (FLN). From Tunisia, he contributed to the underground newspaper *el Moudjahid*. *A Dying Colonialism* is an account of his involvement in the Algerian war of independence (1954–62). In *The Wretched of the Earth* (1961), Fanon analyzed political development in the Third World, especially in Algeria and Africa, and elaborated a theory of liberation rooted in violent action. Arguing that force subtended the entire colonial enterprise, Fanon believed that decolonization could succeed only after the colonized had liberated themselves from the colonial heritage of inferiority and submission by the use of force. In *The Wretched of the Earth* Fanon wrote: "At the level of individuals, violence is a cleansing force. It frees the native from his inferiority complex and from his despair and inaction; it makes him fearless and restores his self-respect" (p. 73). Critics of this position have pointed out the lack of "illumination" that violence has in fact produced in the postcolonial period, while others credit the "mythic" power of Fanon's message. *See also* EXISTENTIALISM; SARTRE.

Reading
Fanon, Frantz 1952 (*1989*): *Black Skin, White Masks*.
——1959 (*1988*): *A Dying Colonialism*.
——1961 (*1988*): *The Wretched of the Earth*.
——1964 (*1988*): *Toward the African Revolution*.
Gendzier, Irene L. (1973): *Frantz Fanon: A Critical Study*.
Senghor, Léopold Sédar, ed. 1948: *Anthologie de la nouvelle poésie nègre et malgache*.

JEANNE GARANE

father, name of *See* NAME OF THE FATHER

feeling, structure of   *See* STRUCTURE OF FEELING

Felman, Shoshona   American literary theorist, heavily influenced by LACAN. In an important essay, she closely examines Henry James's *The Turn of the Screw*, reading it as an exploration of TRANSFERENCE (Felman, 1977). Later essays (Felman, 1987) continue to explore Lacan's theory of transference, with particular reference to pedagogical institutions and the manner in which the teacher is constructed as a "subject presumed to know."

Reading
Felman, Shoshona 1977: "Turning the screw of interpretation."
——1987: *Jacques Lacan and the Adventure of Insight: Psychoanalysis in Contemporary Culture.*
DAVID MACEY

femininity   A term with a dual meaning, "femininity" refers first to the ensemble of cultural forms, meanings, and values conventionally associated with women. Thus certain forms of adornment (dress and makeup) or personal qualities (passivity, mystery, sexual allure) have functioned traditionally as cultural markers of femininity. Secondly, "femininity" refers to gender identity, to the sense of self that enables social subjects to say "I" as a woman.

It is common in many areas of biological and medical science to root distinctions between women and men in biological differences. In this account, femininity appears as a natural essence which is both tied exclusively to women (thus so-called effeminate men appear abnormal or deviant), and whose influence is felt directly in all areas of social life (thus women are deemed "biologically" unsuited to certain types of work, artistic activity, etc.; Gunew, 1990, p. 207). This biological ESSENTIALISM has been a focus of debate in numerous disciplines, from social science to philosophy and LITERARY CRITICISM. The main impulse for a critique of essentialist versions of femininity has come, however, from feminism. Here, the argument that a woman's biology is her destiny is seen as a source of women's subordination; for if women are "naturally" (anatomically, genetically, hormonally) inferior, then feminist demands for women's equality, or for the cultural validation of femininity, are null and void.

In theorizing the cultural acquisition of femininity, critics have engaged cultural-theoretical debates on the question of the human SUBJECT and its philosophical status. Since the eighteenth century, the dominant source of conceptions of subjectivity has been ENLIGHTENMENT HUMANISM, which assumes the human individual as a pregiven entity, and ascribes to her/him a status as the source of all action and meaning. The subject of humanism is, importantly, ungendered; both women and men may theoretically realize their full potential as self-defining individuals.

In practice, however, women have regularly been excluded from or marginalized within CULTURE and history. Feminist critics of humanism have looked therefore to theoretical traditions which enable an understanding of sexual difference and inequality, and thus relativize the supposedly universal category of the human individual. Various theories have been influential in dislodging the humanist subject from the center stage of history. MARXISM has offered an understanding of subjectivity as the product of socioeconomic determinants; thus femininity appears in Marxist-feminist accounts as socially produced, centrally via the sexual division of labor which assigns to women the "feminine" labor of care and nurturance (Barrett, *1988*). STRUCTURALISM, POSTSTRUCTURALISM, and SEMIOTICS have sought – albeit in very different ways – to understand sociosexual identities as the products of language and cultural systems, of DISCOURSES, to use poststructuralist parlance, which are structured outside of the human individual. Here femininity becomes a position in or an effect of culture, rather than a pregiven essence bequeathed to women by nature.

Psychoanalysis, finally, is similarly anti-humanist in its conception of subjectivity as split between conscious and UNCONSCIOUS psychic domains. Importantly, PSYCHOANALYSIS is also centrally concerned with sexual identity and its cultural formation. FREUD's account of sexual identity as produced in the hitherto unsexed infant during its passage through the OEDIPUS COMPLEX has been especially influential (though it has not gone uncontested within psychoanalysis itself; see, for instance, Chasseguet-Smirguel, 1981). LACAN's appropriation of Freud, with its emphasis on the role of language in shaping sexual identity, has also been formative, particularly within so-called French feminism: thus the work of Julia KRISTEVA, Luce IRIGARAY, and Hélène CIXOUS turns precisely on the issue that most preoccupied Lacan, that of the part played by language in producing sexual difference at the psychic level.

In psychoanalysis, then, femininity appears as the result of a complex process of psychic development in infancy, a process which, moreover, is never fully achieved, since, as Jacqueline Rose puts it, "the unconscious never ceases to challenge our apparent identity as subjects" (Mitchell and Rose, 1982).

See also GENDER and MASCULINITY.

Reading

Barrett, M. 1980 (*1988*): *Women's Oppression Today*.
Chasseguet-Smirguel, J. (*1981*): *Female Sexuality: New Psychoanalytic Views*.
Freud, S. 1925 (*1977*): "Some psychical consequences of the anatomical distinction between the sexes."
——1931: "Female sexuality."
Gunew, S., ed. (*1990*): *Feminist Knowledge. Critique and Construct*.
Mitchell, J. 1974 (*1979*): *Psychoanalysis and Feminism*.
——and Rose, J., eds. (*1982*): *Feminine Sexuality. Jacques Lacan and the Ecole Freudienne*.
Moi, T. (*1985*): *Sexual/Textual Politics*.

ERICA CARTER

feminism, lesbian   *See* LESBIAN FEMINISM

feminist criticism   Feminist criticism has grown mainly out of the modern feminist movement of the 1960s and 1970s, although it found inspiration in earlier works such as Simone de BEAUVOIR's *The Second Sex* (1949) and Virginia WOOLF's *A Room of One's Own* (1928). Women of many nationalities have developed its techniques and analyses but the main activity has occurred in the United States and in France. The two early works of de Beauvoir and Woolf exemplify the difference between French- and English-language strands: the French book philosophizes and universalizes, drawing back from narrative, whereas the English one is a literary work which turns often to specific and personal story.

Early American feminist criticism of the later 1960s and early 1970s recognized no authority and so is not associated with any one woman or group of women. Nevertheless, it has achieved considerable authority itself by working largely within the universities and, many have charged, colluding with the critical establishment. In its first phase it was flamboyantly engaged and disputed any notion of neutrality in criticism; insisting on yoking personal and political, it often turned the consumption of literature into a kind of therapy, with criticism the account of a personal awakening. Such critics as Kate Millett found much CANONICAL literature overtly misogynist and implicated it in woman's political and psychological oppression, while discovering in undervalued works such as Charlotte Brontë's *Villette* feminist messages hitherto concealed from readers. Revising concepts of themselves, learning to understand, for example, the libertine oppressive nature of what had seemed the libertarian sexual philosophies of the 1960s, feminist criticism noted the stereotypes literature had foisted on women, such as the *femme fatale*, the whore, the angel in the house, and the moral guardian of man, and it tied these representations to the degradation of women in life. Literary analysis, largely in the hands of men, should be used by women to control and influence meaning and to show that gender is a fundamental determinant in literature and life. American LITERARY CRITICISM, which had elevated those TEXTS most demeaning to women, was especially attacked by such critics as Annette Kolodny and Judith Fetterley, who revealed the cultural betrayal of women. It was also argued that male literary history had systematically downgraded the genres in which women chose to write; for example, women's domination of the nineteenth-century American popular novel had become simply a matter of regret in most literary histories. This exclusion suggested that a major task of feminist criticism was the reinscribing of women writers in history. This became the agenda of the mid-1970s.

Opinions differed on whether women excluded from the dominant tradition could be integrated into a tradition that was constructed on the basis of their exclusion or whether women could ever be thought to constitute a separate tradition. Some critics such as Ellen Moers seemed to suggest the creating of a separate women's tradition, whereas Elaine SHOWALTER insisted that women writers formed a subculture, not a culture; because of the interrupted nature of women's literary history, the transience of female fame and the self-hatred that alienated women from a sense of collective identity, it was impossible to speak of a women's tradition or movement. The culmination of the effort of the mid-1970s to create a general sense of women writers was Sandra GILBERT and Susan GUBAR's *The Madwoman in the Attic* (1979), which found in the already canonized writers an essential pattern of repetition – the suppressed female. The authors agreed that women writers responded to sociocultural constraints by creating SYMBOLIC narratives that expressed common feelings of constriction, exclusion, and dispossession, and they connected textuality and sexuality, genre, and GENDER, psychosexual identity and cultural authority. Together with most of the early critics, Gilbert and Gubar concerned themselves primarily with women writers of the nineteenth and twentieth centuries, and there was little sense that their generalizations were time- or CULTURE-specific. The concentration on women writers was connected with the contemporary emphasis on distinctive female experience such as motherhood, celebrated along with female bonding and creativity by the poet critic Adrienne RICH. Some critics took inspiration from Nancy CHODOROW's revision of traditional FREUDian psychology to celebrate the maternal principle, and from Mary Daly, who envisaged the femaleness of deity and a transformation of personality through language.

By the late 1970s American feminist criticism was feeling the tug of theory, and a split occurred between those who felt that feminist criticism should develop a theory or utilize a male one and those who saw any theory as the authoritarian voice of PATRIARCHY. The latter wanted to continue the construction of a female framework for analyzing women's writing and the development of models based on the study of female experience; they worried that theory would separate feminist criticism from feminism as a political cause. Whether pro- or anti-theory, most critics became extremely self-aware and labels were given to various aspects of study, for example, Showalter's gynocritics for the study of women writers and the feminist critique for the study of the representation of women. After a flirtation with the American forms of DE-CONSTRUCTION, the theoretically inclined turned excitedly towards French women theorists, despite the fact that most of these wished to avoid the label "feminist," regarding feminism as deeply implicated in the masculine systems of thought. Through French theory, Freud, scorned by Kate Millett and early feminist critics, entered feminist criticism as a force. French theory was attractive to many women because it concentrated on inner life, not public history, provided a ready-made language for discussing gender, and delivered academic status and glamour through its intellectual difficulty. Others felt profoundly ambivalent toward all bodies of theory as male and feared the replacement of the concept of the woman writer with the concept of the feminine in writing.

The French writers most influential in the English-speaking world were Julia KRISTEVA, Hélène CIXOUS, and Luce IRIGARAY. Despite great differences, each came from an idealist philosophical tradition. They opposed those intellectual modes that posited an empirical reality as deeply flawed and Anglo-Saxon, and they tended like Simone de BEAUVOIR to universalize rather than historicize. They used techniques popularized by Jacques DERRIDA, who denied the validity of traditional rational thought, arguing that all meaning of an event was temporary and relative, and located in a relation of difference from all other linguistic events. They were even more heavily influenced by the psychoanalytical theories of the Freudian revisionist Jaques LACAN, who also argued for an absence at the center of language, but from unconscious desire rather than linguistic difference. The child has the illusion that the language fulfills desires, since it exists in what was called the symbolic order, the area of law, order, the phallus, and the father. The girl coming to consciousness in language where gender identity was composed was offered a series of subject positions only through submission to the phallic symbolic order. Taking the outlines of this Lacanian analysis, the French women theorists argued that, if symbolic DISCOURSE demanded submission to the phallocentric and if women were indeed alienated from linguistic cultural structures at the profoundest level, then they might turn to a nonsymbolic discourse and so escape the dominance of reason and logic. Irigaray and Cixous posited a feminine writing, *écriture féminine*, which was a utopian projection of femininity, a writing from the body which came from a pre-Oedipal, prelinguistic space anterior to the symbolic. The WRITING escaped the symbolic order and its illusory fulfillment of desire, and was connected with the rhythms, secretions, and sexual organs of women; it became disruptive, punning, and private. *Écriture féminine* operated outside patriarchal structures on the edge of culture. While partly viewing it as a biological possession of women deriving from the mother, Cixous argued that it might be produced by men or women; but Irigaray, the most influential theorist on American feminist criticism of the late 1970s, denied this, insisting that it was a fluid and creative writing from the female body. From a different perspective Julia Kristeva posited a space called the SEMIOTIC, separate from the symbolic; a space which, grounded on the mother, was the place of semiotic flow, the source of anarchy, disorder, ambivalence, and silence. The space could function as the locus of disruption, displacing the symbolic order where the binary categories of male and female fell into place, and it could express femaleness before acculturation. The use of semiotic seemed a more voluntary mode to Irigaray and Cixous than the use of *écriture féminine*; it was open to either gender and available within the symbolic order to challenge the combination of MASCULINITY and law. Kristeva, Irigaray, and Cixous all made much of the unrepresentability of woman, defining "Woman" as what could not be said, what was beyond ideologies and nomenclatures. Such views made the empirical enterprise of American feminist criticism seem absurd, since women writers of the past whom it was trying to rescue had written from within their experience, and experience in the French view simply reinscribed the symbolic. Only psychoanalysis with its desconstructing of the difference that experience reiterated could help women move forward. Ordinary discourse had to be deconstructed and reinvented, and women had to learn to speak outside the phallocentric and logocentric structures.

The view of the French women theoreticians had considerable influence on feminist criticism, initially through departments of French. Some critics began to use sophisticated verbal and philosophical desconstructions of Lacan and Derrida with the intention of destabilizing the notion of gender positions in texts; the works of Alice Jardine, Gayatri Spivak, and Mary Jacobus were examples, though none was as visionary as Cixous or Irigaray. The Scandanavian theorist Toril Moi used some of the analysis to attack the naivety of American feminist criticism, while others such as Elaine Showalter and Janet Todd defended its historical, political, and general feminist aims against what seemed a mystifying and simultaneously reductive analysis. Many women took issue with the ideas of anatomy as textuality and of a revolutionary break with patriarchal language, and they noted the French women's reliance on privileged male texts, however deconstructed and desecrated, as well as their retreat from political activism. At the same time other women, such as Juliet MITCHELL and Jacqueline Rose in England and Jane Gallop in the United States, used some of the techniques of DECONSTRUCTION to criticize or develop the legacy of PSYCHOANALYSIS.

In the later 1980s the use of techniques deriving from Lacan and Derrida and influenced by French women theorists intersected with the ideas of Michel FOUCAULT and NEW HISTORICISM to effect a change in the understanding of literary and cultural history. Women such as Margaret Homans, Ellen Pollak, and Terry Castle showed the past dominance of male discourse and described the strategies women used to avoid it; Catherine Gallagher and Nancy Armstrong read literary texts in relation to other sorts of literature to examine ways in which the structuring of gender relations informed relations to class; others revealed how fear of women influenced the development of scientific or philosophical systems or movements, such as the ENLIGHTENMENT or modernism. While these developments were undoubtedly exciting, some critics, such as Judith Newton, noted that many concepts ascribed even by feminists to New Historicism, such as the construction of subjectivity and sexuality, seemed to have been anticipated within feminism, and she concluded that once again the discourse of the less powerful did not escape the conditions of its own production. In addition, such analyses sometimes tended to bring together too forcefully the physical and metaphysical and rely too heavily on the pun and linguistic trick. Simultaneously with these developments, many more empirically inclined critics, seeing the passing of the heroic universalizing of American feminist criticism and noting the institutionalization of women's studies in the United States and to a far smaller extent in European countries, realized that much historical spadework remained to be done. Consequently there was a movement backwards in the study of English literature from the Victorian and modern periods, which had been the dominant concern of earlier critics, into periods such as the Middle Ages and the eighteenth century, and there was much closer study of specific groups of women, such as diarists or Civil War pamphleteers, study which helped toward the breakdown of hierarchial genres and literary periodization.

While feminist criticism has not greatly influence traditional male scholarship, a few men such as Terry EAGLETON and Stephen Heath have engaged with its findings, although their efforts have been regarded as too mastering by Showalter and Spivak. Many have raised the subject of masculinity; gay male critics in particular have used some of the techniques of feminist criticism to study the homophobia inscribed in literature and culture. Occasionally there has been fruitful work using the perspectives of women and gay studies, but sometimes there has been acrimony between feminists and gay men jostling for status as primary victims of the dominant culture.

From early on, feminist criticism was accused of being middle-class, heterosexual, and white; in the late 1960s and early 1970s Lillian Robinson frequently chided it for ignoring class. This was more a subject for British feminists, who usually expressed a socialist allegiance, but the Marxist and socialist character of the movement there made women wary of elitism, university feminism, and of engaging in a feminist criticism not immediately part of a wider feminist cultural critique. The results were that not a great deal of critical work was done in the 1970s on canonical writers, even by the MARXIST-FEMINIST LITERATURE COLLECTIVE, and the emphasis was on popular culture and a feminist analysis of Marxist literary theory. The Marxist work which developed in the 1980s in Britain and the United States tended to be heavily ALTHUSSER-ian, drawing on psychoanalytical theory as well as MARXISM. De Beauvoir and Cixous had brought together oppressions of RACE and gender but they tended to use race as a metaphor for gender. In the United States Alice Walker found the term "femin-ism" racist and coined "womanist" to refer to black women's writing practice and criticism; critics such as Barbara Christian and Barbara Smith were in-sistent that gender was not a unitary term nor was experience universal, as early American feminists seemed to have implied, and that race made a rad-ical difference to any analysis. Lesbian critics also felt marginalized by feminist criticism. Such women as Monique WITTIG in France and Adrienne Rich in the United States noted differences in reading and writing strategies and raised the issue of whether there was a lesbian aesthetic distinct from a femin-ist one. In the late 1980s Third World women, especially those such as Spivak working in the United States, focused attention on colonialism and gender, so attacking again the universalizing tend-ency of earlier feminist criticism.

Reading

Cixous, Hélène 1975 (*1981*): "The laugh of the Medusa."
Beauvoir, Simone de 1949 (*1984*): *The Second Sex*.
Christian, Barbara, ed. 1985: *Black Feminist Criticism*.
Gilbert, Sandra M., and Gubar, Susan 1979: *The Mad-woman in the Attic*.
Irigaray, Luce 1974 (*1985*): *Speculum of the Other Woman*.
Jardine, Alice 1985: *Gynesis: Configurations of Woman and Modernity*.
Kristeva, Julia 1980 (*1984*): *Desire in Language: A Semi-otic Approach to Literature and Art*.
Millett, Kate 1970 (*1971*): *Sexual Politics*.
Mitchell, Juliet, and Rose, Jacqueline, eds. 1982: *Femin-ine Sexuality: Jacques Lacan and the École Freudienne*.
Moers, Ellen 1976: *Literary Women: The Great Writers*.
Moi, Toril 1985: *Sexual/Textual Politics: Feminist Literary Theory*.
Showalter, Elaine 1977: *A Literature of Their Own: British Women Novelists from Brontë to Lessing*.

JANET TODD

Feyerabend, Paul (1924–94) Austro-American philosopher, who with KUHN and Imre Lakatos (1922–74) was one of the main post-Popperian philosophers of science. Following war service in the German army and studies in Vienna, Feyer-abend spent time in Britain working with Karl POPPER before moving in 1958 to California, where he was a professor at Berkeley. After early papers on the philosophy of quantum physics, Feyerabend wrote some highly influential papers critical of em-piricist PHILOSOPHY OF SCIENCE. However, as the title of one paper – "How to be a good empiricist" – suggests, Feyerabend was not totally repudiating the empiricist approach, but was criticizing the narrowness of the dominant conception of science.

In its place he argued for theoretical prolifera-tion, claiming that scientists should work not with one theory to the exclusion of all rivals, but with a range of incompatible theories, each of which could suggest fruitful ways forward, while all could be sources of empirical criticism. In this way the pro-duction of both theories and empirical tests could be maximized, and science would benefit. Feyer-abend also rejected traditional claims that scientific development is cumulative, and, like Kuhn, used the idea of incommensurability.

By the time he wrote *Against Method* Feyerabend was developing his ideas in opposition to those of Lakatos, whose "methodology of scientific research programmes" he saw as a beneficial but still insuf-ficiently radical adjustment of Popper's methodo-logy. The book was to have been a joint venture with Lakatos, but his early death frustrated this project. So Feyerabend's part of the book appeared alone and, with its slogan that in science "any-thing goes," caused much contumely to be heaped upon the head of its author. This anarchist (or in Feyerabend's preferred term, "Dadaist") theory of knowledge resulted from his claim that any notion of a fixed scientific method is untenable on histor-ical, philosophical, and political grounds. Feyer-abend's apparent irrationality in refusing to expel such things as propaganda and voodoo from science did not recommend the book to the intellectual establishment.

It is not clear what sort of reputation Feyerabend will leave. Much of his work on physics and meth-odology will continue to be influential, while his later books could become resources for those who want to challenge complacency in ideas, for eventually he generalized his notion of proliferation, suggesting that science should take its place alongside religion,

ART, myth, etc., none having any exclusivity but each offering some potentially liberating view of the world. His overall self-assessment was that he was a social philosopher, concerned with the perennial philosophical quest for the good life. In fact Feyerabend's social philosophy is the weakest part of his writings, veering somewhat unstably between an extreme individualism, in which everything (including one's scientific allegiances) is a matter of personal taste, to an extreme democracy, in which everything (including scientific theories) is put to the popular vote. Perhaps this shows what happens when the exceedingly fertile seeds of a central European education in physics and philosophy, history and drama are allowed to germinate under the Californian sun.

See also SCIENCE, PHILOSOPHY OF.

Reading

Couvalis, George 1989: *Feyerabend's Critique of Foundationalism.*

Feyerabend, Paul 1975: *Against Method: Outline of an Anarchistic Theory of Knowledge.*

——1981a: *Realism, Rationalism and Scientific Method (Philosophical Papers, Volume 1).*

——1981b: *Problems of Empiricism (Philosophical Papers, Volume 2).*

——1991: *Three Dialogues on Knowledge.*

Stove, David C. 1982: *Popper and After: Four Modern Irrationalists.*

ANDREW BELSEY

film studies Film studies is not an arcane subject, but it may very well be a nonsubject, in so far as there is no coherent body of work that can be adduced, and, although there is plenty of dogmatism in discussing film, there is no party line to hew to or rebel against. The term suggests that there is such a body of work, made up of serious theoreticians. But who are they? The Soviets, Kracauer, Bazin, Cavell, DELEUZE, perhaps, all decidedly different in their views of film. The crucial fact is that it has been the best of the film makers who have been the best students of film. Although there have been some valuable thinkers about the art, considered below, the truest studies in film have come from its practitioners, the directors. They developed, broadened, revised, and disturbed film making, and the best of them knew exactly what they were doing.

Hence "film studies" should be an essay on films, how directors created them with very clear intentions, not on writing about films. When Miklos

Jansco made *Winter Sirocco* (1969), using only 13 shots in fewer than 100 minutes, he was a theoretician as well as a director, for what he did was radical, a test of how far one could push an idea: could audiences follow the choreography of actors and a mobile camera for such lengths of time? To write about the "theory" of that film would be pointless; it had been done. And the best directors, perhaps a dozen or so, have been both makers *and* critics of the art. The proper analogy is John Keats and his sensitivity and understanding of "negative capability." His sparrow in the gravel is eloquent.

Oddly, film as a medium first and then as an art, from its beginnings in the late nineteenth century, evoked very little reflection for the first 30 years of its existence. In the early days it was the work of practitioners, part of an industry seeking profits. That they were to develop it into an art was inevitable. D.W. Griffith, the greatest of those early directors, because he was adept in finding new ways of telling a story, by understanding how time was flexible and how space could be a toy in a director's hand by cutting, and by the use of close-ups and other devices, sounds like Joseph Conrad (perhaps echoing him?) when he said, "I just want to make you see," but that is the remark of an artist, not a student of film.

The first film studies of any value, however, do come from directors, the Russians EISENSTEIN and Pudovkin, developing from Kuleshov, one of those who had watched, over and over again, a bad print of Griffith's *Intolerance*, which had somehow made its way to Moscow after the Bolshevik Revolution. Their thinking came directly from their own work in creating what is now called "Soviet montage," which, important as it is, will sadly be found in only a half-dozen years of the 1920s. Their concepts of montage were diverse, Eisenstein believing (and that he could create) in "collision," while Pudovkin saw it in terms of "linkage." Nevertheless, for the first time there were thoughtful ways in which to consider the new art. Each certainly believed that the films he made (in the 1920s) manifested his theory, but it would take a very long essay to attempt to show that *Potemkin* (Eisenstein) differed theoretically in montage from *The End of St Petersburg* (Pudovkin). Both, however, saw correctly and said in a joint manifesto that sound films would "destroy the culture of montage" (1928). And, in a cruel irony, the simultaneously tightening grip of Stalinism began to make it impossible for either to create the films he envisaged, conceivably adapting already established montage. Further, one may suspect that neither director would have *written* about film theory had he been able to produce freely.

In the 1930s everyone went to the movies, it seemed, but only Walter Benjamin gave them some thought. His essay of 1935 introduced the concept of "the aura," the uniqueness of an object or person, which could not now, on film, be mechanically reproduced: "man has to operate with his whole living person, yet forgoing the aura. For aura is tied to his presence, there can be no replica of it." It is an appealingly cross-grained idea in a period of dazzling, perhaps worshipped, "movie stars." Benjamin was writing in exile, as Europe was drawing toward the 1939–45 war, and his essay's anti-fascism and socialism can still speak to us.

It was in the 1940s that film studies began to appear. Siegfried Kracauer's *Theory of Film* (1947) reflects some very basic thoughts about film and "the nature of reality." "Films alienate our environment in exposing it." On film, a leaf in a breeze or a bit of river in motion, not to speak of the gesture of a woman's hand or the mobility of a crowd, show familiar things in a way that transforms them. In one sense Kracauer merely states the obvious, but it is an obvious fact that needed to be presented in his careful, well-organized fashion.

In a similar way Bela Balazs (1945) confronts his readers with the close-up, especially a face on the screen. "Facing an isolated face takes us out of space, our consciousness of space is cut out and we find ourselves in another dimension." And further, "it is much easier to lie with words than with the face," which film consistently proves. Balazs's pages on Dreyer's *Jeanne d'Arc* (1928), the last great silent film, should be recognized for their simple brilliance. The examination of Jeanne is a long scene of faces, Falconetti as the Maid ultimately overpowering all the male faces of her inquisitors with her genuine conviction, in close-up. It is one of the magisterial passages in all the years of cinema, one that all students should revere and see again and again. We are witnessing the unsayable, the knowledge of which is what WITTGENSTEIN means by physiognomy.

It was throughout the 1930s and 1940s that a few directors, notably Renoir, Welles, and Rossellini, advanced the art of film making, and their theorist, André Bazin, editor of *Cahiers de Cinéma*, followed them shortly. For this writer, Bazin remains the most valuable of thinkers about film, although he died in 1958. Jean Renoir, probably the greatest of film directors, even suggested, in his preface to volume I of Bazin's collected essays, *What Is Cinema?*, that film itself might die, the hundreds of millions of feet of celluloid decayed in their cans, but that people would still be reading Bazin, reconstructing that lost world from his words.

Bazin, of course, understood the necessity and value of montage, although he was very alert to the limitations of the Soviet method and how, in a number of different ways, it had filtered into French and American movie making. What Bazin saw, especially first in Renoir and Welles, was how the deep focus shot, used with the very long take and mobile camera (in Renoir's masterpiece, *Rules of the Game*, 1939, there are only 337 shots in 110 minutes, an outstandingly low ratio), made for a new, richer kind of film making. The heart of Bazin's thinking lies in his essay "The evolution of the language of cinema":

(1) depth of focus brings the spectator into a relation with the image closer to that which he enjoys with reality. Therefore . . . independently of the contents of the image, its structure is more realistic;

(2) that . . . implies, consequently, both a more active mental attitude on the part of the spectator and a more positive contribution on his part to the action in progress. While analytical montage only calls for him to follow his guide . . . here he is called upon to exercise at least a minimum of personal choice. It is from his attention and his will that the meaning of the image in part derives.

(3) From the two preceding propositions, which belong to the realm of psychology, there follows a third which may be described as metaphysical, montage . . . by its very nature rules out ambiguity of expression. . . . On the other hand, depth of focus reintroduced ambiguity into the structure of the image if not of necessity . . . at least as a possibility. (*What Is Cinema?* vol. I, 35–6)

Bazin went on to show how the Italian neorealists (their own term was *verismo*, indicating a slight difference that matters), chiefly Rossellini and de Sica, were concerned to preserve the ambiguity of reality, seeking to transfer to the screen its continuum, often in the close-up of the face of a child.

Jean Renoir, though, is properly the hero of Bazin's seminal essay.

> [Renoir] alone in his searchings as a director prior to *Rules of the Game* forced himself to look back beyond the resources provided by montage and so uncovered the secret of a film form that would permit everything to be said without chopping the world up into little fragments, that would reveal the hidden meanings in people and things without disturbing the unity natural to them.

Bazin's book on Renoir, edited by François Truffaut, is essential, for he discusses or notes most of the films in Renoir's long career. Truffaut put it together from reviews and memoranda, so it is necessarily somewhat scrappy. Nevertheless, it contains, in his sharp, sure way, much of what went into Bazin's thesis, still unsurpassed, of how Renoir changed the way films can be made and how we view them. Only shortly after Bazin's untimely death the *nouvelle vague*, made up of directors who had first been critics for *Cahiers de Cinéma*, were creating film after film of a vast variety of kinds that can be seen as stemming from their work with and understanding of Bazin. This was contemporaneous with Fellini's masterpiece, $8\frac{1}{2}$, moving beyond his earlier neorealistic work. One wants to ask: Does the shade of Bazin feel fulfilled?

For film study, there has been little in English to engage one's attention. A few critics have written brilliantly about particular films, but they are workers in the field, none of them ready to posit an aesthetic. Even Susan SONTAG, whose essays on Bergman and Godard (*Styles of Radical Will*, 1969) open up some new possibilities for thinking about film, has never put forward a coherent theory concerning film, as she did about photography. To pick up an earlier concept, is this because she herself has been a film maker and continues to write fiction? First of all, she is an artist.

The other writer in English worth listening to is Stanley CAVELL, a man who could talk about Hawks's *Bringing Up Baby* for many days: he loves film. For him, to study films is by remembering them, like dreams, which is true for everyone, although, as with Kracauer and others, an obvious fact not put into print before. He is gifted at telling us what we already know: "The ontological conditions of the motion picture reveal it as inherently pornographic" – Bazin's keyhole, the *voyeur*

of many others. Cavell, more than any other writer, makes the experience of watching a film a *bodily* one, kinetic. He knows where he is, connected to the strange fact of the thrust of light across an auditorium and images on a flat screen pretending to be three-dimensional, and how he physically reacts to all of that, another obvious but most important fact. However, he will be larger, of course, asking: "How could film be art, since all the major arts arise in some way out of religion?. . . . Because movies arise out of magic; from *below* the world" (Cavell, 1971).

Stepping forward, the only recent writer on film who makes one reconsider chiefly the films of the mid-twentieth century – sadly, perhaps, the peak of film making – is Gilles DELEUZE, whose two volumes of *Cinema* (1986; English translation 1989) develop the thesis that "the movement-image of the classical cinema gave way, in the post-war period, to a direct time-image." This break happens because of the devastation of European cities in the war, causing "situations which we no longer know how to react to, in spaces we no longer know how to describe." Rossellini's trilogy speaks eloquently to him here:

> Situations could be extreme, or . . . those of everyday banality . . . what tends to collapse, or at least to lose its position, is the sensory-motor schema which constituted the action-image of the old cinema. And thanks to this loosening of the sensory-motor linkage, it is time . . . which rises up to the surface of the screen. Time ceases to be derived from the movement, it appears in itself and itself gives rise to *false movements*. Hence the importance of *false continuity* in modern cinema: the images are no longer linked by rational cuts and continuity, but are relinked by means of false continuity and irrational cuts. (Deleuze, 1989, vol. 2, p. xi)

Admirably fresh thinking by another man who loves film, one who can be usefully downright and concrete: "Renoir has sometimes been criticized for his taste for the makeshift and improvisation. . . . This is in fact a creative virtue, linked to the substitution of the scene for the shot" (Deleuze, 1989, vol. 2, p. 86). The latter may be obvious, like so much written about film, but only if one thinks about it, which so few do. "Film studies," then, is dry ground, not much has grown there, and the best students invariably point out the obvious, for which all concerned should be grateful; too few see the egg on the plate.

So the film directors have been the bast students of film. All learned from their daily practice and from seeing in the films of others some of the mysteries of the art. François Truffaut, a fine director, was also the critic who, controversially, introduced the theory of "*la politique des auteurs*," arguing that the director making his films, one after the other, like a poet or a novelist, will be a recognizable "author." The *auteur* theory redeemed *style*, which was easy to see in Griffith, Chaplin, Keaton, and the Soviets, but not clear at all for film makers working with sound from the 1930s to the 1960s. For example, Howard Hawks, considered an *auteur*, made comedies, westerns, historical epics, and adventure films over many years in Hollywood, but they all manifest the Hawks style. Truffaut, basically a film maker, gave the art a new critical concept. That is the way "film studies" have been, for the most part.

Reading

Balazs, Bela 1945 (*1990*): *Theory of the Film*.
Bazin, André 1967 (*1971*): *What Is Cinema?* 2 vols.
——1971: *Jean Renoir*.
Benjamin, Walter 1935 (*1968*): "The work of art in the age of mechanical reproduction."
Cavell, Stanley 1971: *The World Viewed: Reflections on the Ontology of Film*.
Deleuze, Gilles 1991: *Cinema*, 2 vols.
Eisenstein, S.M. 1949 (*1957*): *Film Form & Film Sense*.
Kracauer, Siegfried 1947 (*1960*): *Theory of Film: The Redemption of Physical Reality*.
Mast, Gerald, Cohen, Marshall, and Braudy, Leo, eds 1974 (*1992*): *Film Theory and Criticism*.
Pudovkin, V.I. 1933: *Film Technique*.
Sontag, Susan 1966: *Styles of Radical Will*.
Truffaut, François 1978 (*1994*): *The Films in My Life*.

KARL PATTEN

Fish, Stanley (1938–) Literary critic, professor of English and law at Duke University. Originally a Renaissance scholar and New Critic, Fish has become the founding father and one of the leading exponents of American reader-oriented criticism.

In the 1960s, during the heyday of STRUCTURALISM, Fish published his *Surprised by Sin: The Reader in Paradise Lost* (1967), which today is considered the first book working within the framework of the now surging field of READER-RESPONSE CRITICISM.

For Fish, the issue "is simply the rigorous and disinterested asking of the question, what does this word, phrase, sentence, paragraph, chapter, novel, play, poem, *do?*" (1980, pp. 26–7) as opposed to the – more conventional – question, what does a literary TEXT *mean?*

Fish's reader-oriented theory is programmatically called "affective stylistics," because Fish challenges the New Critics' warning against the AFFECTIVE and the INTENTIONAL FALLACY by turning it against itself. Whereas the New Critics argue that meaning resides in the formal features of a poem, rather than in the reader's emotion or the author's intention (see NEW CRITICISM), Fish holds that both formal features and authorial intention are only ever affected by the conventions the readers bring to bear on the TEXT. They do not exist outside the "informed" readers' experience. The readers' experience, in turn, is socially constructed: the readers' responses are not controlled by the text they read – a text, Fish argues, can mean anything – but by the INTERPRETIVE COMMUNITY they belong to. In Fish's theory, reading becomes the product of a set of shared community assumptions.

While being clearly indebted to both Wolfgang ISER's theory of aesthetic response and Jacques DERRIDA's poststructuralist philosophy of DISCOURSE, Fish's stance is at once less comprehensive than Iser's and less radical than Derrida's.

Reading

Fish, S. 1967: *Surprised by Sin: The Reader in Paradise Lost*.
——1980: *Is There a Text in this Class? The Authority of Interpretive Communities*.
Freund, E. 1987a: "Literature in the reader: Stanley Fish and affective poetics."

EVELYNE KEITEL

flâneur French term for a city stroller, popularized by BENJAMIN in his work on Baudelaire and nineteenth-century Paris. The *flâneur* is the cultural consumer as modern hero, moving anonymously through the crowd, experiencing CITY life as a succession of compelling but instantaneous impressions.

PETER OSBORNE

folk culture "Folk culture" is a term which only make conceptual sense by reference to a particular interpretation of "industrial culture." As Shiach (1989) shows, the idea of the "folk" was developed in the context of industrialization, and can only be understood by reference to the critique of industrial society developed by Romanticism. Folk culture described the culture of preindustrial (premarket, precommodity) communities, and was therefore taken to be organized around a number of characteristics: the oral transmission of songs, tales, and history; aesthetic authorization by tradition; the integration of nature and CULTURE, body and mind; expression through RITUAL, in the collective deployment of SYMBOLS. There are obvious similarities between such descriptions of European folk cultures and anthropological accounts of communities in Africa and Asia, but "folk" is not an anthropological term. It is an ideological construct; it necessarily includes a critique of "modern" societies.

The idea of folk culture has in fact served a number of different political and cultural ends (see Harker, 1985). As an aspect of nationalist IDEOLOGY, folk culture is taken to be expressive of the true spirit of a nation, of its underlying beliefs and values, as articulated in specific forms of dress, speech, music, story telling, cookery, design, etc. Thus folk music – and folk music collecting – became an essential part of the construction of European national identities in the nineteenth century (and folk songs and dances were a feature of the "national" compositions of such composers as Dvořák, Vaughan Williams, and Bartok).

However, the idea of folk culture was also taken up by MARXISTS, in the construction of working-class consciousness ("the folk," it should be noted, describes only serfs and peasants; members of any ruling class are, by definition, excluded). On the one hand, "the folk" defined the continuity of proletarian culture (as people moved from the countryside to the city); on the other hand, folk culture could be presented as the "pure" form of working-class culture, untouched by the seductions of commerce (or amplification). These arguments were developed by the Communist Party in both the United States and Britain in the 1930s (as part of the Popular Front strategy), and continued to be influential in the IDEOLOGY of folk music in the postwar period (they had a strong influence on the ideology of rock, for instance).

The most common use of the idea of folk culture today is almost certainly as a tourist attraction, a way of signaling what makes a country or locale *different*. In this sense, "folk culture" now describes ways of singing, dancing, dressing, and, indeed, of making things, which are artificially preserved by the state as a kind of domesticated exotica (and as the basis of a business in souvenirs).

Reading

Harker, Dave 1985: *Fakesong: The Manufacture of British Folksong, 1700 to the Present Day.*
Shiach, Morag 1989b: *Discourse on Popular Culture.*

SIMON FRITH

foregrounding A term that originated in Russian FORMALISM, where it was used to indicate an interdependence between SUBJECTS and objects. The formalists maintained that while perceiving an object or an artifact, the subject "foregrounds" some of its properties and "suppresses" others. This concept was later developed in Czech STRUCTURALISM by Mukarovsky and JAKOBSON. Mukarovsky saw "maximum foregrounding of the utterance" as one of the most important functions of poetic language. Jakobson (1990b) took the idea of "foregrounding utterance" a step further in his "Linguistic and poetics" where he argues that the structural aspect of literary expression can easily be accommodated within the SEMIOTIC concept of encoded communication.

Reading

Dry, Helen 1992: "Foregrounding: an assessment."
Short, M. 1973: "Some thoughts on foregrounding and interpretation."
Weber, Jean Jacques 1983: "The foreground–background distinction: a survey of its definitions and applications."

SLAVA I. YASTREMSKI

formalism An aesthetic tendency characterized by the separation of form and content in works of ART and literature in which the predominant significance is given to formal aspects. Although, as a tendency, formalism was always a part of world art and literature, its emergence as a definite trend is usually dated to the end of the nineteenth century, when formalism receives its theoretical foundation in the musicology of E. Hanslick and the art criticism of Heinrich Wölfflin. It achieves its classic form and acquires its name in the "Formal school" of Russian literary criticism during the 1920s. Hanslick maintained that music has no content apart from its medium. The focus of Wölfflin's investigation was the detection of the visual laws of organization of artistic form. He based his formalist typological method on the notion of the development of the art of painting as an evolution of visual forms. The next step in the early development of formalism was taken by Oskar Walzel in his comparative studies of works of painting, music, and literature. Walzel based his approach on studies of the inner laws of art works. The ideas of early formalism found their practical implementation in the works of European Symbolists, based on the principles of ALIENATION of ART from reality ("Art is Free, Life is Paralyzed" proclaimed members of the Russian World of Art movement) and of art for art's sake. The philosophical foundations of the formalism of the symbolists were built on the ideas of subjective idealism (NEO-KANTIANS, NIETZSCHE, Bergson). From the point of view of the adherents of formalism, the goal of art is to represent reality as a perception or a vision and not as a recognition or an understanding. The cognitive aspect of art was minimized and the subjective factor became predominant. As one of the members of Russian formalism, B. Engelgardt, wrote in his book *Formal Method in the History of Literature* (Leningrad, 1927), the unique language of individual form transmits the subjective, often subconscious emotions which cannot be described through conventional forms. Therefore the SYSTEM of the expressive means predetermines the selection and organization of the transmitted meaning.

Formalism receives even more consistent and complete realization in futurism. Futurists maintained that the main goal of an artist was the creation, through experiments with verbal material, of an artistic form which contained the immanent semantic meaning of the resulting artwork. For example, Russian cubo-futurists, whose works served as analytical material for the Russian formalists of OPOYAZ and the Moscow Linguistic Circle, tried to find the semantics of poetic language by discovering the inner structure of words and, by the analysis of new words, the meaning, consisting of the sum total of meanings of the word's individual components ("self-sufficient word"). Additionally, these formalist discoveries resulted in the development of a new language consisting of self-sufficient words called "beyondsense" or "transrational" language. We can say that, starting with futurism, formalism becomes associated with modernism, sharing the inextricable characteristics of the modernist literature: the desire to overthrow the past and rejection of old literature combined with invention of a new form for the sake of invention itself.

Receiving further theoretical support in the structuralist linguistics of Baudouin de Courtenay and F. de SAUSSURE, formalism continued its life in the semantic analysis of I.A. Richards, which combined "deep psychology" in the spirit of Freud with abstract formal analysis. From the mid-1930s, the NEW CRITICISM in England and the United States generated a new interest in Russian formalism, from which it borrowed the ideas of an absolute autonomy of creative process and the independence of an artist and his/her work from the social historical surroundings.

See also FORMALISM; NEW CRITICISM.

Reading
Lehman, David 1990: "The not-so-new formalism."
Liu, Alan 1989: "The power of formalism: the New Historicism."
McManmon, John 1990: "Formalism, structuralism, poststructuralism, and text."
Nichols, Bill 1989: "Form wars: the political unconscious of formalist theory."
Wellek, René 1963: "Concepts of form and structure in twentieth-century criticism."
Willingham, John 1989: "The New Criticism then and now."

SLAVA I. YASTREMSKI

formalism, Russian   *See* RUSSIAN FORMALISM

formation, social   *See* SOCIAL FORMATION

fort-da game   The game played by an eighteen-month-old boy, as described by FREUD (1920). The child repeatedly throws a wooden reel out of his cot and then retrieves it by means of the attached piece of string, accompanying his action with the interjections *ooo* (interpreted by Freud as meaning *fort*, the German word for "gone") and *da* ("there"). The game staged the disappearance and reappearance of objects within the child's reach, and SYMBOLized his triumphal achievement in allowing his mother to go away without protesting. In the Lacanian perspective (Lacan, 1953), the alternating *Fort! Da!* are interpreted in linguistic terms as differential phonemes; their manipulation by the child therefore prefigures the use of a diacritical linguistic system.

Reading
Freud, Sigmund 1920: *Beyond the Pleasure Principle.*
Lacan, Jacques 1953 (*1977*): "The function and field of speech and language in psychoanalysis."

DAVID MACEY

Foucault, Michel (1926–84) French philosopher, historian, social analyst. Influences include the philosophical works of NIETZSCHE and HEIDEGGER, the writings of BATAILLE and Blanchot, the example of Dumézil, Canguilhem, and Hyppolite, and more generally the tradition of critical thought which runs from the work of HEGEL through to the analyses of the Frankfurt school (Foucault, 1971; 1977; 1986). Foucault's wide-ranging analyses do not fit easily into existing disciplinary categories. His ideas and investigations have had a significant impact on a number of different fields of inquiry, ranging from philosophy, history, sociology, and political science to literary and CULTURAL STUDIES.

Foucault's several analyses are clustered around three sets of concerns, namely (i) the formation and transformation of SYSTEMS of knowledge, and the constitution of regimes of truth; (ii) technologies of the self, and (iii) the constitution of forms of subjectivity. The analyses conducted by Foucault range over a series of topics, including mental illness/madness (*Mental Illness and Psychology* and *Madness and Civilization*); medical perception (*The Birth of The Clinic*); the formation of the modern human sciences and the analysis of systems of knowledge (*The Order of Things* and *The Archaeology of Knowledge*); discipline, punishment, and the prison (*Discipline and Punish*); and sexuality and subjectivity (*The History of Sexuality*, 1976). In addition to the studies identified above, there are numerous papers and interviews on related themes, as well as other essays on literature, including a monograph on the work of Raymond Roussel, *Death and the Labyrinth*, of which Foucault remarked, "I would go so far as to say that it doesn't have a place in the sequence of my books. . . . No one has paid much attention to this book, and I'm glad" (1987, p. 185). Coming from the analyst who has approached the question of the " 'author' as a function of discourse" (Foucault, 1977, p. 124), such a remark constitutes a virtual provocation, an incitement to pay attention to the TEXT in question.

Foucault was a member of a generation of postwar French students who found the existing parameters of intellectual inquiry, namely MARXISM, PHENOMENOLOGY, and EXISTENTIALISM, limited and inappropriate for the subjects in which he was interested. His various studies of formations of domains of knowledge and their consequences; relations of power and techniques of government exercised over individuals; and modes of relation to the self, represent a break with and constitute a challenge to approaches derived from Marxism, phenomenology, and existentialism (Smart, 1983).

Situating Foucault's work is not easy; it crosses and challenges disciplinary territories and it does not readily fit into conventional analytical categories. Foucault's analyses clearly cannot be accommodated within the perspectives of Marxism, phenomenology, or existentialism, but identifying a positive location for the various analyses is more difficult. The work has been described as beyond both HERMENEUTICS and STRUCTURALISM, and more positively, by virtue of a complex and changing combination of archaeological and genealogical approaches, as exemplifying an "interpretive analytics" (Dreyfus and Rabinow, 1982). Other analysts have located Foucault's work within an opaque constellation of approaches known as "POST-STRUCTURALISM" (Dews, 1987). Finally, some have identified Foucault as an exponent of what has come to be known as "POSTMODERNISM" (Hoy, 1988). The classification of Foucault's work as "poststructuralist" and/or "postmodern" remains controversial, for the terms in question do not have a well-defined referent. As Foucault once remarked in an interview, "I do not understand what kind of problem is common to the people we call postmodern or post-structuralist" (Raulet, 1983, p. 205).

Less controversial is the evidence of a relative shift of emphasis in Foucault's work away from the archaeological form of inquiry exemplified by the earlier studies of reason and unreason, the medical gaze and formation of the clinic, and the emergence of the modern epistemological configuration and with it the human sciences, to the genealogical investigations of the later works on power–knowledge relations, governmental technologies, sexuality, and subjectivity. The implication here is not of a methodological break, but rather of a displacement of archaeological analysis. Archaeology did not disappear from Foucault's work when emphasis began to be placed on relations of power and knowledge; it continued to serve as an appropriate methodology for the analysis of "local discursivities" in a manner complementary to genealogy (Foucault, 1980).

In the course of his intellectual practices Foucault sought to generate a very different conception of the role of the intellectual, one that contrasts starkly with the universalizing, legislative pretensions of the conventional modern intellectual. For Foucault the aim of intellectual activity was not to answer the question, "What is to be done?" The function of the intellectual and of knowledge in general was not considered to be "to tell us what is good," but rather to provide an analysis of an event or situation "in its various complexities, with the goal of allowing refusal, and curiosity, and innovation" (Foucault, 1988a, p. 13). To that extent Foucault offers a different model of the intellectual as a critical interpreter, and his work presents a radically different critical history of thought.

To those accustomed to turning to the WRITINGS of intellectuals for solutions, Foucault represents an enigma. In Foucault's work it is not solutions or advice that one finds but "how and why certain things (behaviour, phenomena, processes) became a *problem*" (Foucault, 1988b, p. 16). The emphasis is placed on how and why particular forms of behavior came to be characterized, classified, analyzed, and treated – in short, problematized – as, for example, "madness," "crime," "sexuality," and so on. In this way Foucault (1988c) sought to question and erode "self-evidentnesses and common-places," to contribute to the transformation of "ways of perceiving and doing things," and to draw attention to the possibility of new forms of subjectivity.

Two remarks, one from a friend and colleague, the other from his principal intellectual adversary, provide a measure of Foucault's significance. The French historian Paul Veyne, a friend and colleague, commented shortly after Foucault's death: "[his] work seems to me to be the most important event of thought in our century" (quoted in Eribon, 1922, p. 328). From a radically different and, for the most part, critical perspective, the German sociologist Jürgen Habermas remarked: "Within the circle of philosophers of my generation who diagnose our time, Foucault has most lastingly influenced the *Zeitgeist*" (1986, p. 107). Without doubt Michel Foucault is one of the major figures in twentieth-century thought, and his work will continue to exert a profound and beneficial influence across a number of disciplines and fields of inquiry. *See also* ARCHAEOLOGY OF KNOWLEDGE; GENEALOGY.

Reading
Bouchard, D.F., ed. 1977: *Language, Counter-Memory, Practice: Selected Essays and Interviews by Michel Foucault.*
Dews, P. 1987: *Logics of Disintegration: Post-Structuralist Thought and The Claims of Critical Theory.*
Dreyfus, H.L. and Rabinow, P. 1982: *Michel Foucault: Beyond Structuralism and Hermeneutics.*
Eribon, D. 1992: *Michel Foucault.*
Foucault, M. 1971: "Orders of discourse."
——1969 (*1986*): "What is an author."
——1980a: "Two lectures."
——1986b: "Kant on enlightenment and revolution."
——1987: *Death and the Labyrinth: The World of Raymond Roussel.*
——1988a: "Power, moral values, and the intellectual: an interview."
——1988b: "On problematization."
——1988c: "Question of method: an interview with Michel Foucault."
Habermas, J. 1986: "Taking aim at the heart of the present."
Hoy, D.C. 1988: "Foucault: modern or postmodern?"
Raulet, G. 1983: "Structuralism and post-structuralism: an interview with Michel Foucault."
Smart, B. 1983: *Foucault, Marxism and Critique.*

BARRY SMART

Fowler, Roger (1938–)   British linguist. Since 1979, Fowler has been professor of English and linguistics at the University of East Anglia, Norwich, where he has taught since 1964. Fowler's main influence has been in the field of "critical linguistics," which he and a group of colleagues pioneered during the 1970s. Critical linguists maintain that neither a TEXT nor an analyst can be sociopolitically neutral, but that analysis of the language of any text can reveal its underlying IDEOLOGY. *See also* LINGUISTIC CRITICISM.

Reading
Chilton, P., ed. 1985: *Language and the Nuclear Arms Debate: Nukespeak Today.*
Fowler, R. 1991: *Language in the News.*
——Hodge, R., Kress, G., and Trew, T. 1979: *Language and Control.*

KIRSTEN MALMKJÆR

Frank, Manfred (1945–)   German philosopher and literary critic; professor of philosophy at the University of Tübingen. Frank's extensive writings, which address topics ranging from the AESTHETICS and philosophy of early German Romanticism to the contemporary debate between HERMENEUTICS and (post)STRUCTURALISM, are unified by a common thread: the attempt to vindicate the notion of the human SUBJECT by appealing to the hermeneutic conception of selfhood developed in early Romantic philosophy and poetry.

Frank seeks to vindicate the notion of the subject by showing that it need not be conceived in terms of autonomous self-grounding and pure self-reflexivity, as it had been conceived by thinkers like KANT. Instead, Frank demonstrates, already in early Romanticism philosophy and POETRY had conceived and concretized the subject as a continuing process of interpretive individuation. This is the occasion for Frank's intensive focus on the Romantic era and its distinctive notion of temporality. Frank argues that a consistent conception of temporality underlies both philosophy and poetry in early German Romanticism, and through an appeal to specific authors of the period he shows how philosophy seized upon this notion and how poetry concretized it through language. Frank exhibits the idea of the temporality of self-consciousness through an examination of the philosophies of Schlegel, Solger, and Novalis, and he demonstrates that these thinkers share a concept of temporality which anticipates Henry James's notion of "stream of consciousness" as well as the reflections on internal time consciousness conducted by Bergson and Husserl. The problem of ultimate grounding in German idealism leads back not to substantiality or pure self-reflection, but rather to an idea of temporal flux in which the present is forged out of "remembrance" oriented on the past and "longing" oriented on the future; the subject is conceived not as self-grounding, but rather as grounded in an experience of something beyond itself. To this extent Frank shows early Romanticism to be incompatible with the idealist Fichte's attempt to invoke a transcendental self-grounding of the subject as the fundamental principle of all philosophizing. Frank invokes Schlegel's notion of time as "longing for the infinite" and Novalis's conception of human reality as an insubstantial "not-being-something," conceptions which challenge the conventional wisdom that modern German philosophy is without exception based on presence. Frank draws an essential link in this connection between Novalis and the thought of Schlegel, Solger, and Hardenberg; and he argues that this philosophical conception of selfhood as a cipher finds poetic expression in early Romanticism, above all in Ludwig Tieck's early poetry as well as in his theoretical treatises.

Frank develops this conception of the self by turning to Schleiermacher's HERMENEUTICS as a crucial if forgotten set of reflections on the notion of the subject, reflections which promise to help overcome the "conflict of interpretations" which RICOEUR sees between structuralism and hermeneutics. Rather than taking the subject as a fixed starting point, Schleiermacher takes it as a focal point for questioning and self-reflection; Frank believes that, by proceeding from such a conception, it should be possible to balance the seemingly antagonistic poles of individuality and universality in the process of interpretation. This appeal to Schleiermacher's hermeneutics, Frank contends, can overcome the conflict between two methodological claims: the claim of structuralism to undermine the determinacy of meaning and the subject by arguing for the primacy of systems of signification; and the claim of hermeneutics to be able to transcend the (structural) conditions of meaning production toward increasingly adequate self-understanding.

Through this appeal to Schleiermacher, Frank seeks to overcome the commitment of DECONSTRUCTION to the death of the subject, by rethinking the notions of subject and individual in a hermeneutically enlightened manner. Frank turns to the domain of prereflective experience as the basis for explaining consciousness and meaning, and he rightly sees that the notion of individual, prereflective "acquaintance of consciousness with itself" is irretrievably lost in both structuralism and the poststructuralism of thinkers like Derrida. Frank's conception of individuality acknowledges the limits of self-consciousness while promising to elucidate both the struggle of individual human beings to relate to one another and the struggle of individual interpreters to appreciate the stylistic uniqueness of individual literary TEXTS. The individual is neither its own author nor the source of structure or order; instead, as a constant threat to orderings, the individual plays an irreducible role in the constitution of meaning. What Frank ultimately seeks is a hermeneutic model of subjectivity as individuality, in which structuralist SEMIOTICS is employed to inform hermeneutics so that hermeneutics need not fall prey to the anti-rationalism of HEIDEGGER'S EXISTENTIALISM.

One aim here is to accommodate semiotic and deconstructive interpretations of texts within an essentially hermeneutic model, in effect rejecting the poststructuralists' radical claim that meaning is ultimately undecidable. Frank's hermeneutic approach invokes Heidegger's notion of ek-static projection and GADAMER'S hermeneutic notion of dialogue with tradition, though Frank's defense of subjectivity is ultimately stronger than Gadamer's. Frank refers to this hermeneutic modification of poststructuralism as "neostructuralism:" the constitution of meaning requires both "differance" or "differentiality" *and* subjectivity conceived as individuality. Without the individuality-pole of this relation, Frank argues, there can be no meaning-events.

One application of this modification is Frank's passing critique of the political implications of post-structuralism, which amount to indifference masquerading as the quest for liberation from oppressive structures. In particular, Frank exhibits unanticipated, potentially tragic connections between extreme poststructuralist positions and fascism.

Reading
Frank, Manfred 1972: *Das Problem "Zeit" in der deutschen Romantik. Zeitbewußtsein und Bewußtsein von Zeitlichkeit in der frühromantischen Philosophie und in Tiecks Dichtung.*
—— 1977: *Das Individuelle-Allgemeine. Textstrukturierung und -interpretation nach Schleiermacher.*
—— 1979 (*1980*): "The infinite text."
—— 1987 (*1992*): "Is self-consciousness a case of 'présence à soi'? Towards a meta-critique of the recent French critique of metaphysics."
—— 1990: *Das Sagbare und das Unsagbare. Studien zur deutsch-französischen Hermeneutik und Texttheorie.*
—— 1991: *Selbstbewusstsein und Selbsterkenntnis: Aufsätze zur analytischen Philosophie der Subjektivitat.*
—— 1986: *Die Unhintergehbarkeit von Individualität. Reflexionen über Subjekt, Person, and Individuum aus Anlass ihrer "postmodernen" Toterklarung.*
—— 1984 (*1989*): *What is Neostructuralism?*
GARY STEINER

Frankfurt school   What is now known as the Frankfurt school of CRITICAL THEORY began in 1930 with Max HORKHEIMER's directorship of the Frankfurt Institute of Social Research, to which he gave a new and specific direction. In his inaugural address (Horkheimer, 1968) he announced the importance of launching a systematic, interdisciplinary program in critical theory that would combine methods of scientific research with a Marxist theory of society. As this program developed during the next decade with Horkheimer's collaboration with Herbert MARCUSE, Theodor W. ADORNO, and Erich Fromm, two important revisions of MARX resulted. First, critical theory reached out to embrace new developments in PSYCHOANALYSIS, as Marcuse and Fromm especially labored to produce a synthesis of Marx and FREUD. Second, Horkheimer and Marcuse became convinced that the proletariat had become so much a part of the capitalist system that it had lost its potential for revolutionary social change. By the end of the decade, however, with the rise of fascism and Stalinism, their confidence that intellectual reflection could become an effective, progressive substitute for proletarian revolution began to wane and to be replaced by NEGATIVE DIALECTICS, which questioned the ENLIGHTENMENT ideal of political change brought about by rational processes. Horkheimer and Adorno's *The Dialectic of Enlightenment* (1947), a complex text that was largely written during the early 1940s, is an important statement of this disillusioned position, especially in its skepticism about the possibility of social change resulting from scientific research. As an institution, the Frankfurt school, as it was during its first phase, began to break up soon after it began. Adorno left Germany in 1934, and throughout the 1940s the school was in exile in New York, where new and alternative theories were developed. The school reopened in Frankfurt in 1950, and Adorno became its director in 1958. Jürgen HABERMAS's critique of *The Dialectic of Enlightenment* (Habermas, 1985) and the development of his theory of COMMUNICATIVE ACTION have opened up important new directions for critical theory.

Reading
Arato, A., and Gebhardt, E., eds 1978: *The Essential Frankfurt School Reader.*
Geuss, Raymond 1981: *The Idea of a Critical Theory: Habermas & the Frankfurt School.*
Honneth, Axel 1985: *Critique of Power: Stages of Reflection of a Critical Theory of Society.*
Horkheimer, Max 1972: *Die gegenwartige Lage der Sozialphilosophie und die Aufgaben eines Instituts für Sozialforschung.*
Horkheimer, Max, and Adorno, Theodor W. 1947 (*1972*): *The Dialectic of Enlightenment.*
Jay, Martin 1973: *The Dialectical Imagination: A History of the Frankfurt School and the Institute of Social Research 1923–50.*
MICHAEL PAYNE

Frege, Gottlob (1848–1925)   German philosopher of logic, mathematics, and language, known chiefly for his work in refining and extending the scope of SYMBOLIC logic with the introduction of quantifiers and other technical devices. Frege's contribution in this field is esteemed by some – Michael Dummett prominent among them – as the greatest since Aristotle and the source of all the most important developments in recent analytic philosophy. Less successful was Frege's early attempt to establish the foundations of mathematics on a purely logical basis, an enterprise that foundered (as he came to believe) on certain intractable paradoxes in set theory discovered and brought to his attention by Bertrand Russell.

Most important for critical and cultural theorists is Frege's cardinal distinction between "sense" and "reference." These are the standard – though not altogether satisfactory – translations of the German words *Sinn* and *Bedeutung*. The "sense" of a term is its meaning as defined by the role it plays, or the semantic attributes it possesses, in some given natural language. The "referent" of that term is the object which it designates or the real-world entity which it serves to pick out when properly deployed. Thus there exist some names of (for example) fictive or hypothetical objects, characters or events which may be said to possess *sense* but not *reference*. That is, we can assert a great many things about the persons encountered – or the actions narrated – in fictional TEXTS since those texts themselves provide all the relevant information. But we are not thereby committed to the belief that, in order for our statements to be meaningful, they must have reference to some actually existing (or historically attested) entity of which they can then be determinately true or false.

This was how Frege sought to resolve certain longstanding problems in the area of logic, meaning, and truth. His argument finds a close parallel in Russell's "theory of descriptions," likewise intended to remove the anomaly of sentences – such as "the present King of France is bald" – which would appear to be neither true nor false since they lack any object (any real-world referent) to which those values might apply. Russell's solution was to analyze the sentence into its underlying logical (as opposed to its surface and misleading grammatical) form. It would then read: "there is one and only one person reigning over France, and there is no one reigning over France who is not bald." In this case the sentence would be manifestly false in respect of its initial premise.

Another main purpose of Frege's sense/reference distinction was to explain how certain seemingly redundant or tautologous sentences – such as "the Morning Star is [identical to] the Evening Star" – may none the less serve to communicate items of factual or informative knowledge. On the face of it this is a purely *analytic* proposition, that is, one in which the subject and predicate refer to the same item (the planet Venus), and whose truth is therefore a matter of logical necessity devoid of material or substantive content. But, as Frege points out, we could in fact learn something from the above sentence if we happened not to know already that those two expressions ("the Morning Star" and "the Evening Star") referred to the same celestial body. What we learn is that they both designate the same referent even though their senses

– the meanings they possessed within our previous descriptive language – appeared to pick out different objects. Frege also offers the example of two explorers approaching a mountain from opposite sides – and from different linguistic communities – only to discover that they had each been applying their own name to what they *thought* were separate features of the landscape, but what in fact turned out to be the selfsame mountain (or referent) under two distinct senses or descriptions.

These cases may appear somewhat strained or artificial. Nevertheless, it is worth noting that discoveries and truth claims in science very often take the form of propositions that are now (once securely established) on the face of it tautologous but which at first conveyed a novel and informative truth about the structure of physical reality. Thus for instance: "water is H_2O," "heat is the mean kinetic energy of molecules," "$e=mc^2$," "blueness is the property of reflecting light of wavelength 4400A," etc. These would all have to be seen as strictly tautologous (noninformative) statements were it not for our grasp of the sense/reference distinction, that is, the fact that although each pair of terms designates an identical *referent*, it does so through the conjunction of two distinct *senses* which serve to communicate a genuine (nonself-evident) item of scientific knowledge. Again, Russell arrives at a similar conclusion by applying his "theory of descriptions." A case in point would be the sentence "Scott was the author of *Waverley*," a fact which apparently came as news to King George IV.

Such arguments have played a large part in Anglo-American analytic philosophy since the early years of this century. They operate on the premise that everyday (natural) language may often give rise to error – or to "systematically misleading" forms of expression – owing to its failure to articulate logical distinctions with sufficient clarity or rigor. This idea was rejected by J.L. AUSTIN and exponents of the "ordinary language" approach that dominated Oxford philosophy during the 1950s and 1960s. In their view – also much influenced by WITTGENSTEIN – it was altogether wrong to suppose that language stood in need of such logical regimentation, or that mere "analysis" could somehow uncover truths more important than the great stock of wisdom enshrined in the nuances, distinctions, and subtleties of usage to be gleaned from our everyday habits of talk. Hence what Richard RORTY and others have noted as an emergent split or parting of the ways within the broad camp of so-called linguistic philosophy.

POSTSTRUCTURALISM is another (albeit very different) school of thought which has pursued its own path to some highly dubious doctrines – for example, the "arbitrary" nature of the sign, the infinitized "freeplay" of meaning, the linguistic (or discursive) construction of reality, etc. – without paying heed to Frege's sense/reference distinction. Had it done so then we might have been spared much confusion, especially with regard to SAUSSURE's idea of the two-term relation between signifier and signified. This is taken by poststructuralists to entail nothing less than a wholesale ban – a proscriptive veto – on any appeal to the referent as the third term in the SEMIOTIC triangle. In fact this approach was adopted by Saussure as a purely heuristic or methodological convenience for analyzing language in its structural–synchronic aspect. He never once claimed – and indeed quite expressly denied – that language could communicate or its workings be adequately explained in the absence of the referential function. Nothing could more clearly illustrate the misunderstandings that have come about through poststructuralism's stance of self-imposed isolation from other, more cogent and philosophically informed traditions of thought. *See also* LANGUAGE, PHILOSOPHY OF; LOGICAL POSITIVISM.

Reading
Dummett, Michael 1973: *Frege's Philosophy of Language*.
Frege, Gottlob 1952: "On sense and reference."
——1977: *Logical Investigations*.
Rorty, Richard, ed. 1970: *The Linguistic Turn*.
                                    CHRISTOPHER NORRIS

Freud, Sigmund (1856–1939) The founder of psychoanalysis was born in Freiberg (Moravia) into a rather poor Jewish family. In 1860 the family moved to Vienna, which was to be Freud's home until 1938, when the Nazi invasion of Austria forced him into exile in London.

Ambitious and successful at school, Freud entered medical school in 1873 but did not graduate as a doctor of medicine until 1881. Freud's initial research and publications were on anatomy and physiology, and the significant turning point came in 1885–6 when a travel bursary allowed him to study under Charcot at the Salpêtrière in Paris. He was particularly struck by the evidence for the existence of hysteria in men as well as in women,

and by the manner in which Charcot could reproduce his patients' hysterical symptoms by posthypnotic suggestion. On his return to Vienna, Freud set up in private practice as a specialist in nervous diseases. From this point onwards, his biography is synonymous with the history of PSYCHOANALYSIS.

Between 1887 and 1904 Freud corresponded at length with Wilhelm Fliess, a German ear, nose, and throat specialist who was preoccupied with establishing the existence of a male sexual periodicity analogous to the menstrual cycle and with a hypothetical nasal reflex neurosis predicated upon a link between the nose and the genitals. Despite the bizarre nature of his theories, Fliess served as a sounding board for Freud, who began to elaborate his own theories and, although not intended for publication, the letters provide a unique account of the origins of psychoanalysis (Freud, 1985). The correspondence also represents the beginning of a characteristic pattern. The lengthy relationship with a male colleague gave way to a period of estrangement in which theoretical and personal differences overlapped, and eventually to hostility. Freud's relationships with Breuer, with whom he collaborated on a series of studies of hysteria in female patients (Breuer and Freud, 1893–5), and subsequently with JUNG, were to follow the same pattern (see Freud, 1974).

It was during the period of the correspondence with Fliess and in his collaborative work with Breuer that Freud began to develop his theory concerning the origins of hysteria. According to the so-called seduction theory, hysteria is a form of neurosis that results from a repressed memory of a sexual trauma (rape, sexual abuse) in childhood. The memory of the trauma is repressed, but is then reactivated, with pathological effects, at puberty. Freud (1896) was convinced that all cases of hysteria could be traced back to such an event. This first scenario implied the traumatic irruption of adult sexuality into the life of a passive and asexual child. Puzzled by the improbably high incidence of incest in accounts given by patients, Freud was finally forced to admit to Fliess that he no longer believed in his own theory of the etiology of hysteria (1985, p. 264).

The seduction theory was gradually replaced with other theories generated by the discovery of a spontaneous infantile sexuality, which indicated that no external stimulus is necessary for the child to develop sexual theories and fantasies. The final outcome was the theory of the OEDIPUS COMPLEX, according to which the scene of seduction results from the incestuous wishes of the child rather than the aggression of the parent. Freud's rejection of the seduction theory has occasioned much controversy and even the accusation that he abandoned a "true" theory in order to silence women and children (Masson, 1984). The claim is exaggerated, and Freud did not lose sight of the reality of the sexual abuse of children. In his last unfinished exposition of psychoanalytic theory, he refers to it as being common enough and does not deny that it has traumatic effects (Freud, 1938). Its incidence is not, however, enough to explain the universal existence of Oedipal ambivalence.

Throughout the period of his correspondence with Fliess and his collaboration with Breuer, Freud suffered from a variety of psychosomatic complaints which he sought to remedy through a difficult process of self-analysis. The self-analysis is never described by Freud in any detail, but it is the subject of many passing allusions, notably in *The Interpretation of Dreams* (Freud, 1900; see Anzieu, 1975). Freud's early experience of working with neurosis and his own self-analysis were the factors that led to the slow emergence of the classic form of a therapeutic method designed, in Freud's words, to transform "hysterical misery into common unhappiness" (Breuer and Freud, 1893–5, p. 305).

Inspired by Charcot, Freud initially used hypnosis as a means of removing repression, but soon abandoned that method in favor of what he described as the cathartic method. Suggestion replaced full hynosis; the pressure of the analyst's hand on the forehead of the patient proved sufficient to convince the latter that the traumatic memory could be recovered. The patient was encouraged to evoke and relive the traumatic event and to "abreact" it in a kind of verbal purgation. The cathartic method was in its turn abandoned in favor of free association, which has since become the basis of all psychoanalytic treatment. The analysand is required to say what he or she thinks or feels, selecting nothing and omitting nothing. A similar fundamental rule applies to the analyst, who must listen with poised or evenly suspended attention, giving no importance to any particular aspect of what is being said so as to allow his own unconscious to work. Significantly, Freud did not take notes for fear of allowing his attention to be either distracted or too concentrated. The analytic setting is the locus for the emergence of the all-important phenomenon of TRANSFERENCE.

Freud's first great work was *The Interpretation of Dreams* (Freud, 1900), which provides perhaps the most lucid, and certainly the most attractively readable introduction to his theory of the UNCONSCIOUS and to its workings (see DREAM-WORK; CONDENSATION/DISPLACEMENT). It and the closely related *Psychopathology of Everyday Life* (1901) provide the evidence that neurotic behavior, in attenuated form, is observable in all human beings and that its manifestations indicate the universality of the unconscious. On the basis of these investigations and his case studies, Freud elaborated his first topography or model for the understanding of the psyche. This model centers upon the topographical distinction between the unconscious and preconscious–conscious systems.

The psychoanalytic discovery of the unconscious was complemented in the early 1900s by the elaboration of a theory of sexual development (Freud, 1905). Elements of such a theory can be found in the correspondence with Fliess, in early papers, and in the studies of hysteria. However, Freud's first coherent account of psychosexual development is to be found in the three essays of 1905, which underwent constant revision and expansion until the third and final edition of 1926 (Freud, 1905). Although the essays do have something in common with the work of sexologists like Kraft-Ebbing and Havelock Ellis, they also offer a full account of human development, and establish that perversion is part of a continuum with normal behavior and not evidence of depravity or degeneracy. One of the striking features of the three essays is Freud's ability to combine a high degree of nonjudgmental tolerance in his discussions of perversion with the belief that genital heterosexuality is the final goal of healthy sexual development.

Sexuality itself is no longer equated with genitality and is extended to include all activities and pleasures which are not explicable in terms of biological or functional need. The relationship between the two is exemplified in Freud's exploration of infantile sexuality and particularly the oral stage. Thumb sucking and related forms of auto-erotism represent a recovery of the pleasure of sucking at the breast, with the desire for sexual pleasure gradually becoming separated from the satisfaction of the biological need for nutrition.

More generally, Freud proposes a series of stages in psychosexual development, each typified by the primacy of a specific erotic zone and by characteristic forms of OBJECT-RELATIONS. The primacy of the genital zone is not pregiven and is only established by the organization of the libido or sexual instinct; libido is distinguished from the self-preservation instincts predicated upon the biological needs. The earliest stage is described as being oral: the experience of pleasure is bound up with the lips and with the act of sucking, and the very young child relates to its object (primarily the mother) in terms of eating and being eaten. The emergence of the anal stage represents a major advance in both motor control and intellectual development. Feces, for instance, can be given a SYMBOLIC meaning and become a gift to be offered or retained. In the final genital stage, the sexual instinct becomes subordinate to reproductive functions and all other zones are subordinated to the genital zone.

The child who figures in Freud's account is invariably a boy, and it is clear that he has difficulty in supplying a comparable account of the development of girls (see in particular the chapter on "Femininity" in Freud, 1933). Its introduction required the introduction of a phallic stage, a key development in Freud's theorization of the Oedipus complex, and the thesis that both boys and girls believe that sexual difference results from castration. Notoriously, female sexuality itself remained a "dark continent" (Freud, 1926, p. 212), and the relationship between psychoanalysis and feminism has therefore always been a fraught one (see FEMININITY; LACAN, JACQUES; MITCHELL, JULIET; PHALLUS).

Freud's first topography remained almost unaltered until 1920, when he modified it considerably by introducing the notion of a death drive (Freud, 1920). Its introduction was in part an attempt on Freud's part to explain the existence of phenomena such as repetition and the conservative nature of instinctual life, which cannot be explained in terms of a search for libidinal satisfaction. The pleasure principle itself refers to the psyche's need to reduce levels of TENSION or excitation, pleasure itself being the release of tension. Freud now began to speculate about a desire to reduce tension to zero, to return to an inorganic state. The existence of something beyond the pleasure principle could, in Freud's view, explain sadistic phenomena and the PARADOX whereby death can be described as the goal of life. The death drive is part of a dualistic theory, and the opposite pole to the life instincts; the two poles are often referred to as Thanatos and Eros respectively. The death drive is perhaps the most cotroversial aspect of Freudian theory; it is really only KLEIN who takes it on board in its full implications.

At the same time, Freud was also revising the very foundations of his work by introducing a second or structural topography which differentiates between the three agencies of id, ego, and superego (Freud, 1923). The id represents the instinctual pole of the personality, and its contents are the expression of the activity of the drives. The superego acts as a censor or judge supervising the ego and originates from the internalization of parental prohibitions and images of authority. The ego itself is the most difficult of the agencies to describe. The term (*Ich*) has a philosophical ancestry and is used in some of Freud's earliest WRITINGS. Although it can be described as the "surface" of the psyche, the ego is not entirely synonymous with conscious subjectivity, and some of its elements are held to be unconscious. It is, on the other hand, the agency responsible for rational thought, reality testing, defenses against instinctual demands, and the object of prohibitions fom the superego (see the article entitled "Ego" in Laplanche and Pontalis, 1967).

After 1925 no further major theoretical innovations were made and the last period of Freud's life was largely devoted to the writing of the wide-ranging and speculative essays on art and civilization (see PSYCHOANALYSIS AND PSYCHOANALYTIC CRITICISM), which undertake psychoanalytic investigations into the origins of religion and morality (Freud, 1930), culminating in the final study of Moses (Freud, 1939). The essays are generally pessimistic, seeing civilization as based upon repression and constantly threatened by the instinctual.

Reading

Anzieu, Didier 1975: *Freud's Self Analysis.*
Breuer, Joseph, and Freud, Sigmund 1893–5: *Studies on Hysteria.*
Freud, Sigmund 1896 (*1974*): "The aetiology of hysteria."
—— 1900: *The Interpretation of Dreams.*
—— 1901a: *The Psychopathology of Everyday Life.*
—— 1905a: *Three Essays on the Theory of Sexuality.*
—— 1920: *Beyond the Pleasure Principle.*
—— 1923a: *The Ego and the Id.*
—— 1926: "The question of lay analysis."
—— 1930: *Civilization and its Discontents.*
—— 1933: *New Introductory Lectures in Psychoanalysis.*
—— 1938: "An outline of psychoanalysis."
—— 1974: *The Freud/Jung Letters.*
—— 1985: *The Complete Letters of Sigmund Freud to Wilhelm Fliess 1887–1904.*
Gay, Peter 1988: *Freud: A Life for Our Time.*
Laplanche, Jean, and Pontalis, J.B. 1967 (*1973*): *The Language of Psychoanalysis.*

Masson, Jeffrey Moussaieff 1984: *The Assault on Truth: Freud's Suppression of the Seduction Theory.*

DAVID MACEY

Friedan, Betty (1921–) US feminist writer. Betty Friedan published *The Feminine Mystique* in 1963 and founded the National Organization for Women (NOW) in 1966, two events that galvanized the white women's liberation movement of the 1960s. Friedan's articulation of LIBERAL feminism (which she calls "mainstream feminism") is widely and (usually) uncritically accepted. For a thorough critique, see Eisenstein (1981).

Reading
Eisenstein, Zillah 1981: *The Radical Future of Liberal Feminism.*
Friedan, Betty 1963: *The Feminine Mystique.*
——1981: *The Second Stage.*

GLYNIS CARR

Friedman, Milton (1912–) Leading monetarist, exponent of positive economics of the Chicago school, Nobel Prize winner, and doyen of the liberal NEW RIGHT. He challenged the postwar Keynesian orthodoxy by (i) explaining the 1930s depression in the United States in terms of government failure – an inappropriate reduction in the quantity of money in circulation between 1919 and 1933; and (ii) denying the supposed trade-off between inflation and unemployment. Inflation was explained in terms of the quantity of money in circulation; unemployment in terms of impediments to the market. He is an advocate of the retrenchment of government activity and the dispersal of its power, who believes that "competitive capitalism" is "a necessary condition for political freedom."

Reading
Friedman, M., ed. 1956: *Studies in the Quantity Theory of Money.*
——1962: *Capitalism and Freedom.*
——and Friedman, R. 1980: *Free to Choose.*

JOHN CALLAGHAN

Frye, Northrop (1912–91) Canadian critic and literary theorist. Frye graduated from Victoria College, University of Toronto, and Merton College, Oxford. For most of his professional life he taught at Victoria College. One of the most influential literary theorists of the twentieth century, Frye has been most often associated with myth or archetypal criticism, although he disliked labels and denied having founded a school.

His first book, *Fearful Symmetry: A Study of William Blake* (1947), revolutionized Blake studies and demonstrated, for the first time, Frye's synoptic approach to literature. The book constituted a challenge to those critics who had neglected or despised Blake's long prophetic works in favor of the more comprehensible and frequently anthologized *Songs.* Frye sought to demonstrate the total coherence of Blake's work, often standing back from the details of the poems in order to reveal the underlying STRUCTURE or myth that makes sense of the whole.

Such a critical practice was a direct challenge to NEW CRITICISM, and Frye's next book, *Anatomy of Criticism: Four Essays* (1957), extended the methodology to the whole tradition of Western literature and LITERARY CRITICISM. This ambitious undertaking, carried out with encyclopedic virtuosity, established Frye as one of the most exciting critics of his generation. Deploring the lack of theoretical rigor and appropriate vocabulary in the profession, Frye sets out to provide a technical vocabulary and a synoptic view of the whole of criticism (and by implication of the whole of literature) that will establish a scientific basis for literary studies. He assumes that "just as there is an order of nature behind the natural sciences, so literature is not a piled aggregate of 'works,' but an order of words" (Frye, 1957). He perceives that order operating at four different levels of criticism: (i) historical, a theory of modes, derived in large part from Aristotle; (ii) ethical, a theory of SYMBOLS in four phases (literal, formal, mythical, and anagogic); (iii) archetypal, a theory of myths; and (iv) rhetorical, a theory of genres. The most influential has been his theory of myths, or archetypal criticism. Whereas FORMALISM had assumed a total form for the individual literary work, archetypal criticism assumes a total form for literature as a whole, which moves from the apocalyptic at one extreme to the demonic at the other, from heaven to hell. Further classification reveals four structuring myths or pregeneric categories, corresponding to the four seasons: COMEDY (the mythos of spring); romance (the mythos of summer); TRAGEDY (the mythos of autumn); and IRONY or satire (the mythos of winter). Moreover, within each mythos Frye recognizes six phases. These theories were developed and applied in studies on an extraordinary range of writers and works, including Shakespeare, Milton, English

Romanticism, T.S. ELIOT, Canadian literature, and the Bible.

Frye's work has provoked extreme reactions, ranging from adulation to hostility. He combines encyclopedic scholarship with daring theoretical speculation; an Aristotelian passion for classification with a Blakean vision; wit and humor with deep seriousness. He is a humanist critic in the line of Matthew ARNOLD, but he revived and renovated the biblical exegesis of the medieval schoolmen. Paradoxical and polemical, he is assured of a permanent place in the history of literary theory.

Reading
Balfour, Ian 1988: *Northrop Frye.*
Bates, Ronald 1971: *Northrop Frye.*
Cook, David 1985: *Northrop Frye: A Vision of the New World.*
Denham, Robert D. 1978: *Northrop Frye and Critical Method.*
——1987: *Northrop Frye: An Annotated Bibliography of Primary and Secondary Sources.*
Hamilton, A.C. 1990: *Northrop Frye: Anatomy of his Criticism.*
Kogan, Pauline 1969: *Northrop Frye: High Priest of Clerical Obscurantism.*

PAULINE FLETCHER

Fugitives A group of American poets and critics. The group was based at Vanderbilt University in Nashville, Tennessee, and published *The Fugitive*, a bimonthly magazine of poetry and critical essays, from 1922 until 1925. John Crowe RANSOM was the dominant figure and the Fugitives' positions are epitomized in his "Thoughts on the poetic discontent" (1925), an attack on Romanticism and a defense of "the wisdom of irony" which prefigures the central preoccupations of NEW CRITICISM. The Fugitives were bitterly opposed to the scientific and technological tendencies of modern civilization, and (as their name suggests) pictured themselves as fighting a lonely defensive struggle against it. After the Scopes Monkey Trial of 1925, when a schoolteacher was convicted of teaching Darwinism in a Tennessee school, the Fugitives turned more and more to a political and cultural defense of the values of the Old South. The group broke up in the mid-1920s as its leaders became more and more preoccupied with economic and political issues, and was subsumed into the SOUTHERN AGRARIANS.

See also NEW CRITICISM; RANSOM, JOHN CROWE; SOUTHERN AGRARIANS; TATE, ALLEN.

Reading
Conkin, P.K. 1988: *The Southern Agrarians.*
Fekete, John 1977: *The Critical Twilight.*
Young, T.D. 1985: "The Fugitives: Ransom, Davidson, Tate."

IAIN WRIGHT

functionalism The practical and artistic are interwined in the creation of architecture, but the belief about architecture promoted in functionalism is that the practical (how well a building is constructed and works) takes precedence over the artistic (how beautiful or delightful to experience a building is). Functionalism appears in two overlapping phases in the late nineteenth century: the first holds simply that the artistic is secondary to the practical, and the second – a more extreme position – denies that the artistic is important at all. In the first phase it is argued that if a building is responsive to structural requirements and the needs of its occupants, its artistic character will emerge on its own. This is the view that is suggested by Louis Sullivan's statement, "form follows function." In the second phase, the sole measure of a structure is how fit it is to fulfill its use. This view is captured in LE CORBUSIER's statement: "a house is a machine to live in." In the first phase of functionalism architecture is aligned with the useful arts, and its architects are inspired by buildings of vernacular traditions, such as barns and farmhouses; in the second phase architecture is understood as a science, and its architects seek out the work of engineers for ideas, such as bridges and factories. Both phases of functionalism, then, look to utilitarian structures, and both find there an absence of unnecessary decoration. So functionalists also strive in their work for a clean, uncluttered appearance, and they sometimes create buildings in which the order and clarity of the artistic statement seems to take precedence over the practical.
See also INTERNATIONAL STYLE; MIES VAN DER ROHE, LUDWIG.

Reading
Kostof, Spiro 1985 (*1995*): *A History of Architecture: Settings and Rituals.*

GERALD EAGER

G

Gadamer, Hans-Georg (1900–) German philosopher. He was a pupil and friend of Heidegger. His project is known as *philosophical* HERMENEUTICS, which, following HEIDEGGER's theme of the interpretative character of DASEIN, shows that the mode of our whole human experience in the world is hermeneutic, always occupied with interpretation and understanding. Language receives a prominent position not only as underlying all understanding, but also as providing the fundamental dimension of hermeneutics, the infinite *dialog* we are. Philosophical hermeneutics, enhanced with the Aristotelian conception of practical wisdom, can inform our daily praxis, and thus serve as practical (moral) philosophy.

Although Gadamer has been a leading philosopher in Germany, his influence and popularity in the English-speaking countries have only recently become apparent, mainly owing to the extensive attention paid to his major work *Truth and Method*, published in 1960. His hermeneutics has shown itself to be closely related to almost every other discipline in the humanities, the social and historical sciences, LITERARY CRITICISM, and aesthetic theory, where the notions of interpretation and understanding are constantly at stake.

Gadamer, in his *Truth and Method*, pursued the recovery of "truth" and knowledge in areas beyond the control of scientific method. In the experience of ART, philosophy, and literature, truth is communicated that cannot be verified or approached by the methodical means available to the (natural) sciences. The human sciences (social, political, historical disciplines, including economics, psychology, archaeology, etc.) can also mediate truth, if properly attained by overcoming their naive methodical approaches. Based on the experience of retrieving truth embedded in history and CULTURE, Gadamer structures a new notion of understanding. In accordance with Heidegger, understanding is shown to be a universal mode of existence ascribed to the human agent. It establishes our ontological disposition in the world as interpretative beings.

Nevertheless, truth in art is not easily accessible. It is blocked by the ALIENATION of our aesthetic consciousness. When we view a work of art, by considering it as an object of aesthetic judgment, we usually fail to listen to its immediate claim. This is more obvious with historical works of art, such as the religious creations of the Greeks, where the divine was experienced in artistic works related to gods. Assessing these works as objects of our aesthetic judgment, the world of their experience is lost. For Gadamer, this practice shows an alienation, especially when it stops the authentic experience and the immediate truth claim of art. The task then becomes the recovery of truth as artistic knowledge, different of course from scientific knowledge.

A similar alienation dominates the historical consciousness as it develops in the human sciences. Historical science, for example, attends to only one part of our contact with historical tradition. It confronts tradition as an object of study, thus not allowing tradition to "speak to us." The scientific practice which does not permit listening to its truths shows, in Gadamerian thought, an enormous alienation. Our hermeneutic consciousness (the awareness of our hermeneutic experience) also betrays alienation. In our effort to understand another person, if we simply decipher the other's statements, based on the "I" and "thou" division, we are unable to listen to what the other person says from within her horizon.

There are two universal aspects of our understanding that Gadamer brings to light: its *historicality* (HISTORICITY), that is, its immersion in history and tradition, and the *linguisticality* of understanding, which shows its entanglement within language. In order to unearth the historical dimensions of our understanding, he proceeds to the human sciences (thus concretizing the historical situation of DASEIN, a theme not developed by Heidegger).

According to Gadamer we never understand without *prejudices* (preconceptions). Even the most familiar case of textual understanding indicates how we begin with certain preconceptions, eventually retained or changed in the course of reading, which itself proceeds by further projections and anticipation of meaning (seen here as the HERMENEUTIC circle, which in previous hermeneutic tradition was considered as the interplay between parts and whole, and now between prejudices and projections). Gadamer sees prejudices to be necessary starting points to any understanding, and he undertakes the rehabilitation of the term, which sounds negative as a result of its treatment in the ENLIGHTENMENT. The latter believed in knowledge free from any prejudice. According to Gadamer, the interpreter in a reflective engagement must become aware of his own prejudices, which are historically produced and part of any attempt in interpreting and understanding meaning. Thus he can avoid gross misunderstandings.

Philosophical hermeneutics does not supply a method of understanding; it only clarifies the conditions which accompany any act of understanding. One of these is "temporal distance," which indicates the temporal gap separating us, as interpreters, from a historical event or a past TEXT. Temporal distance illustrates the historicality of our attempt to understand, also making us aware of our prejudices. It works as a filter to separate and retain the productive prejudices, while rejecting those which are limited, unproductive, or erroneous.

In historical studies, we cannot simply place ourselves opposite the past text and treat it as an object of study which bears no relation to us (HISTORICISM). In the historical gap between ourselves and the text, the latter has released its "effects" in history. Preunderstandings and shared knowledge usually characterize our approach. They are the products of these effects on us. For example, all opinions of, historical research into, and evaluations of Homer's *Iliad* form its effects. The power of "effective history" is always at work, and serious deformation of knowledge can result if we ignore it.

One of the most productive Gadamerian metaphors is the notion of "horizon." This includes what surrounds us from our particular position in history and language. We belong to the horizon of our tradition. However, considering the horizon of the text, as a past alien horizon, the text cannot speak to us. The same occurs in conversation if we do not include our own horizon. We cannot validate the other person's claims, since we cannot listen to him/her. Instead, we must overcome the particularity of our own horizon and reach a higher common ground that can sustain both positions. This describes the *fusion of horizons*. In it the meeting of the present with the past occurs, although we are aware of the tension of the two.

Two further points underline Gadamer's theory of understanding. First, the horizon of the present cannot be formed without the past, thus displaying the necessity of knowing tradition. Second, belonging always to a tradition, we move along with it. Therefore any act of understanding, accepting its own historicality, must appreciate tradition. Such fusion of horizons, of the present and the past, is part of our hermeneutical experience of the world.

The fusion of horizons is further detailed by the need to render the sayings of the text to our particular situation. We must *apply* the horizon of the text to ourselves, and not interpret it arbitrarily. The prime example here is legal hermeneutics, where the judge *applies* (interprets) the law to suit specific legal cases.

Moving to the domain of language, Gadamer's main thesis is that "all understanding is interpretation." This claim is crucial for his hermeneutical theory. If true, whatever the discipline, literature, social, or natural sciences, our understanding proceeds on interpretational steps. Translation from one language to another gives a good example of how interpretation is achieved as highlighting. In conversation, similarly, one tries to understand what the other person says. An imperceptible translation takes place, as each participant attempts to understand the other's views from his/her point. Conversation entails translation in a *common* language.

Gadamer's demands on interpretation reach their climax, and also they become more problematic, when he makes the strong claim that linguistic interpretation is the form of all interpretation. This appears to be so when understanding the text or the words of another person. However, what about understanding a musical performance or someone's gestures? Although our experience of understanding in such cases appears immediate or intuitive, Gadamer believes that linguistically shaped previous experience and knowledge accounts for our ability to understand. A soloist interpreting a piece of music does so from previous experience, from teaching, reflection, tradition, comparison, all linguistically achieved. Language underlies the ability to highlight (interpret) or distinguish what is essential. The basic assumption here is that all of our experiences are linguistic in nature. Without language we would never have the experience we receive and which we can communicate. Language *constitutes* the world we know.

By introducing language as the background of any act of understanding, Gadamer shifts his accounts of the hermeneutical act to be informed by a philosophical view of language. As a result, a further picture of the human position and the world in language emerges.

Language becomes the fundamental mode of operation in our-being-in-the-world. It becomes the necessary condition for the world's existence as we know it. Unlike animals living in a habitat, "we have world" (*Welt haben*), upon which we can reflect and, with our "projective" ability, *free* ourselves from it. This ontological position concerning freedom arises from the fact of having language. But is language a prison? Gadamer's answer is that, since all understanding is linguistic in nature, and since language indicates the presence of reason, then from the fusion of one's horizon with the horizon of other traditions, or of other persons, reason moves beyond the boundaries of any particular language.

Important conclusions follow upon his theoretical positions on language. Our ontological placement in language and historical tradition entails that *there is no privileged perspective*. Also, each historical time we interpret tradition, we interpret it *differently*. Although these views define an anti-foundationalist philosophical position, do they invite a strong relativism? Gadamer insists that his position does not result in absolute relativism. The interpretations we achieve are "objective" in the specific historical time they are produced.

Central to his approach is the notion of truth. Truths are transmitted in culture and history, which our hermeneutic experience can grasp. By the notion of truth, Gadamer does not have in mind propositional statements which can be verified or validated. Truth appears to coincide with insight that has been handed down to us by past cultures. Furthermore, as in art, a play has an impact upon its audience, so truth, when noticed, "makes a claim upon us." Its presence grasps us. The whole notion of truth (close to the Heideggerian notion of truth as disclosure) is impregnated with further qualifications: it reveals aspects of Being.

There is, however, another aspect of language which displays its ontological significance and role beyond just a means of communication. Being presents itself in language. The way things present themselves in language is part of their being. We expand our views within language, but they are all aspects of the world. The world is not different from the views in which it present itself (Gadamer, 1960). Language is the place where the "I" meets the world. Although it is a difficult view to follow, since it contradicts (objectivist) common sense, it nevertheless portrays a very intimate relation between language and the world. Such an approach presents a claim beyond any other PHILOSOPHY OF LANGUAGE.

Looking at the position of the human agent in language, further implications are stressed. The example of conversation becomes central in Gadamer's development of the notion of understanding. Conversation includes the specific practice of *question* and *answer*. Every assertion (in text or in speech) can be considered an answer to a question. This process throws light on our hermeneutical experience. To start a conversation, we need also to reach "agreement," not sharing the same ideas on the subject matter, but establishing a common ground for the two different positions that are heard. Conversation here portrays vividly the exchange shaping the dialogic relationship between ourselves, but also the text which can be thought of as a partner in discussion. The other person and the text also must be allowed to pose their questions to us.

It is our presence in *dialogue*, where Gadamer's conception leads. "The dialogue we are," as he says, shows all the dimensions of our communal life. His conception of dialogue is shaped upon the familiar examples of Platonic dialogues. Dialogue is thought of as overcoming alienation and bringing people together. No one remains the same in it, but one changes with questioning and appropriating what is other. Partners in dialogue realize some solidarity emerging (Ricoeur and Gadamer, 1982).

The picture of philosophical hermeneutics would be incomplete without the humanist notion of *Bildung* (self-formation, cultivation). The primacy of the self-formation of the individual is prior to any other ideal of knowledge, especially knowledge as technologically exploitable. Together with common sense, judgment, and taste, all can be acquired (taught) from education and culture.

In his debate with HABERMAS, Gadamer was able to defend the "universal claim of hermeneutics" that all understanding is interpretation, but failed to show how his hermeneutics can be critical of tradition and its authority. However, some critical abilities of philosophical hermeneutics could be detected in the process of self-reflection. One needs to become aware of one's prejudices by putting them "at risk," in the effort to understand others, the text, or tradition. While Gadamer's hermeneutics was conceived as "a corrective" against the methodical alienation of the sciences, such a pursuit could inform a critical attitude.

His theory of language lies in the area of speech (PAROLE), and Gadamer stresses the fact that he is not interested in the function of language or propositional statements. He is concerned with what the text, or the other person, says. What makes understanding possible is the forgetfulness of language, that is, of its formal elements. He charges DERRIDA for one-sided attention to the concept of SIGN, rather than listening to the word as it is employed in conversation. The (Derridian) "difference" should be found in the spoken word, not in the sign (Gadamer, 1989).

Gadamer has produced a number of works on art since *Truth and Method*, attempting to move away from the subordination of art to the theme of truth in the human sciences (Bernasconi, in Gadamer, 1986). His views are based on Heidegger's conception of art, although he wishes to expand it beyond "great art" and include a larger number of art forms. As in earlier works, Gadamer introduces the concept of *mimesis*, through which we can understand modern art. If this is so, artistic changes have not resulted in discontinuities, and contemporary art can still be approached through tradition.

Situating us in language and historical tradition, Gadamer has registered our concrete finitude as interpretative but also dialogical beings, entering communication and "agreement." His enlarged conception of truth gives life to the Heideggerian "language is the house of Being."

Underlining his achievements, we can confidently say that, besides the task of revealing methodical alienation and pointing to truths from tradition, he has brought to light the universal dimensions of our hermeneutical experience. He has accomplished this, first, by presenting a historicized ontology of Dasein, second, by providing us with an insightful and dynamic (yet undeveloped) theory of language, and third, by evoking an ontological picture of Being (what it means to be, how the world *is*), in which language itself becomes the horizon of Being.

There are a number of difficult and unclear parts in his presentation. Proper articulation of how the world is presented in language (avoiding Platonic associations) has yet to be achieved. The need for further clarity on his notion of truth has already become a pole of attraction for current research. The work of Gadamer, created in a long and productive life engagement, offers vast areas of insight and subjects for further elaboration. Although not his main target, he inescapably provides an account of "reading the text," an issue at the heart of contemporary literary criticism. The social, political, and historical sciences, with their interpretative (*verstehenden*) approaches belong also to the immediate sphere of the influence of his teachings. Our experience of finitude through the inexhaustibility of the experience of meaning, his writings on the authenticity of literary text (Gadamer, 1989), participation in the original phenomenon of language as dialog, indicate just a few moments of his thought.

Paul RICOEUR has called Gadamer's attempt a *recollection of tradition*, which leaves aside the "hermeneutics of suspicion" (NIETZSCHE, MARX, FREUD) (Ricoeur and Gadamer, 1982). Notwithstanding Gadamer's intention to awaken our "hermeneutic consciousness" and also pay attention to our "historical consciousness" which is filled with "the multiplicity of the voices that echo the past," one may observe the following in connection with Ricoeur's remark. "The dialogue we are" might appear illuminating for conceptualizing the existential position of the human being. But what kind of dialog is it? Is it in the singular? Instead of overcoming alienation and communally being brought together, we find ourselves participating in fragmented dialogs (of ruptured multicultural traditions and divided communities). Rather than the Platonic dialog, we experience the presence of forces and power imposing DISCOURSES. More often, individuals, groups, classes, sexes, nations, seem to have been denied participation in dialog. The metaphor of the dialog may hide and exclude areas of nondialog. In order for it to become a convincing overall picture of human existence, it is in need of further historicization and ability to include that which it has left unattended.

See also HEIDEGGER.

Reading
Gadamer, H.-G. 1960 (*1993*): *Truth and Method*.
——1976: *Philosophical Hermeneutics*.
——1981: *Reason in the Age of Science*.

—— 1986: *The Relevance of the Beautiful and Other Essays.*
—— 1989: "Text and interpretation."
Ricoeur, P., and Gadamer, H.-G. 1982 (*1991*): "The conflict of interpretations: debate with Hans-Georg Gadamer."
Silverman, H.J., ed. 1991: *Gadamer and Hermeneutics.*
Teigas, D. 1995: *Knowledge and Hermeneutic Understanding: A Study of the Habermas–Gadamer Debate.*
Wachterhauser, B.R., ed. 1994: *Hermeneutics and Truth.*
Warnke, G. 1987: *Gadamer: Hermeneutics, Tradition and Reason.*
Weinsheimer, J.C. 1985: *Gadamer's Hermeneutics: A Reading of Truth and Method.*

DEMETRIUS TEIGAS

gay politics Emancipatory politics for gays was one of the most prominent civil rights movements to develop in the United States, Canada, Australia, and Europe during the late 1960s. Its inspiration came, in large part, from aspects of the Women's Liberation Movement, sometimes called the "second wave" of modern feminism. In addition, calls for gay pride among gays took their lead from Afro-Americans championing the empowering ideal of black pride. The label "gay" was adopted by members of this sexual SUBCULTURE as a positive form of self-definition to replace the term "homosexual," a word that had negative connotations, particularly in its clinical context.

The founding moment of Gay Liberation is generally taken to be June 27, 1969. On that night, large crowds in the Stonewall Inn in Greenwich Village, New York City, gathered to mourn the death of Judy Garland, whose public persona and private sufferings had proved to be an important point of identification for many gay men. A police raid on this club backfired when lesbians, gay men, and cross-dressed men and women fought back so hard that the police had to barricade themselves against attack. Rioting against the police continued for the next five days. Within a matter of months, national political organizations had been established in countries in the industrialized West. The first meeting of the British Gay Liberation Front, for example, took place at the London School of Economics on November 13, 1970, and had its basis in student politics.

Gay Liberation was truly revolutionary in its earliest days. Opposed to patriarchal domination, the structure of the nuclear family, and self-oppression, Gay Liberation insisted that lesbians and gay men should "come out" of their "closets," meaning that they should make a public declaration of their sexual identity so that political change could be achieved with the strength of a developed gay community. Reformist groups, such as the British Committee for Homosexual Equality and the American Mattachine Society, frequently found it difficult in the 1970s to coordinate their efforts with the confrontational campaigning tactics of "gay libbers." Public demonstrations of Gay Pride began in the early 1970s. The first annual British Gay Pride march took place in London on April 1, 1972. It has, for over 20 years, attracted many thousands of men and women who wish to celebrate their sexual liberation. In the United States, the level of political organization has from the outset been very high indeed. The lesbian and gay lobby was among the top fund raisers for President Clinton's electoral campaign in 1992.

It is true to say that in Britain both Gay Liberation and the Committee for Gay Equality and equivalent American groups did not provide equal access for lesbians, and this meant that many women chose to put their energies into feminist campaigns or into separatist LESBIAN FEMINISM. Although the Gay Liberation Front lost much of its revolutionary fervor by the early 1980s, it none the less did much to persuade public opinion that lesbian and gay relationships were as valid as heterosexual ones.

New life was injected into the movement, if by a cruel IRONY, by the discovery of gay men either infected with HIV or living with AIDS in the early 1980s, leading to the formation of successful direct action groups such as ACT UP (AIDS Coalition to Unleash Power) on both sides of the Atlantic. There are continuing campaigns in Britain to lower the age of consent for male same-sex relationships, and for the decriminalization of lesbians and gay men serving in the armed forces.

In the early 1990s a younger generation of lesbian and gay political activists developed the highly imaginative forms of campaigning against the HOMOPHOBIA aroused by fears of HIV and AIDS in the name of a liberatory "queer" politics. Queer activism promised to be more inclusive in terms of GENDERS, sexualities, and ethnic identities than had previously been achieved by Gay Liberation. Bisexuals, for example, began to organize separately in the mid-1980s because of lesbian and gay hostility towards men and women who enjoyed both same-sex and other-sex relationships. The idea of deploying "queer" as an empowering political term when the word still stood as an insult hurled at lesbians and gay men was the subject of considerable controversy. Its usage emerged in part through forms of thinking about sexual identity developed by Michel FOUCAULT, whose work has helped to shape emergent lesbian and gay studies within the academy.

Reading
Bristow, Joseph, and Wilson, Angie, eds 1993: *Activating Theory: Lesbian, Gay, Bisexual Politics.*
Fuss, Diana, ed. 1991: *Inside/Out: Lesbian Theories, Gay Theories.*
Gay Left Collective, eds 1980: *Homosexuality: Power and Politics.*
Hutchins, Loraine, and Kaahumanu, Lani, eds 1991: *Bi Any Other Name: Bisexual People Speak Out.*
Watney, Simon 1987: *Policing Desire: Pornography, AIDS, and the Media.*
Weeks, Jeffrey 1977 (*1990*): *Coming Out: Gay Politics in Britain from the Nineteenth Century to the Present.*
JOSEPH BRISTOW

gaze One of Jacques LACAN's four fundamental concepts of psychoanalysis, which he defines as follows: "in the scopic field, the gaze is outside[;] I am looked at[;] that is to say, I am a picture" (Lacan, 1977, p. 106). In keeping with his theory of the MIRROR-STAGE, Lacan thought of such paintings as Holbein's *The Ambassadors* as a lure or means of captivating the viewer. The gaze, then, is what emanates from the painting itself, capturing the viewer. In her account of the gaze, Julia KRISTEVA at first implies a reversal of the Lacanian process. Her Holbein example, *The Body of the Dead Christ in the Tomb*, which seems at first merely to invite the gaze of the viewer, eventually captivates it: "Our gaze follows the slightest physical detail, it is, as it were, nailed, crucified, and is riveted to the hand placed at the center of the composition" (Kristeva, 1989, p. 114). For both Lacan and Kristeva, then, the viewer is not a free observer but rather the captive of the painting which does the gazing, thus turning the viewer into a picture in the ordinary sense of the object of viewing.

Reading
Kristeva, Julia 1989: *Black Sun.*
Lacan, Jacques 1973 (*1977*): *The Four Fundamental Concepts of Psychoanalysis.*
Payne, Michael 1993: *Reading Theory: An Introduction to Lacan, Derrida, and Kristeva.*
MICHAEL PAYNE

gender A term denoting the attributes culturally ascribed to women and men. Distinctions are conventionally drawn between gender and sex, the latter being understood as the sum of the physical characteristics that make us biologically "women" and "men." More recently, however, the sex/gender opposition has begun to be questioned by theorists who argue that our perceptions of biology, nature, or indeed sex, are formed only within language and CULTURE. Here, notions of sex as beyond CULTURE and gender as within it are refused, since the concept of an innate biological sex is itself the product of, and thus "inside" culture and history.

Though gender has been a focus of attention across the human sciences, the main impetus for gender *critique* (as opposed to its supposed disinterested study) has come in the second half of the twentieth century from feminism. Feminists have argued for an understanding of FEMININITY and MASCULINITY as cultural constructs since, if gender is culturally acquired, it becomes open to change. Debate on the relations between culture, power and gender has been dogged, however, by (often fierce) disagreements, which relate in turn to theoretical and methodological conflicts within feminism itself. In an effort to historicize gender analysis, many European feminists turned first, for instance, to MARXISM – a tradition valued for its insistence on the historically constructed nature of *all* social and cultural relations. Yet classical Marxist models of *economic* determinism (see BASE AND SUPERSTRUCTURE) proved inadequate to the *cultural* analysis of gender; thus debate has centered more recently on structuralist, poststructuralist, and psychoanalytic theories that illuminate the specifically cultural dimensions of gendered identity.

There are clear differences among these three theoretical traditions. Writers influenced by STRUCTURALISM have seen gender as the product of universal cultural laws and conventions, of the "grammar," as it were, that frames linguistic and cultural expression. Thus – to take just one instance – structuralist accounts of gender and narrative might focus on the conventional positioning of the male hero as active SUBJECT and the heroine as passive object of narrative action. In POSTSTRUCTURALISM, by contrast, the notion of universal cultural laws is jettisoned, and replaced with a vision of meanings and identities as the result of perpetual processes of linguistic and cultural production. Thus, for instance, in Judith Butler's Foucaultian account (see Michel FOUCAULT and Butler, 1990), the emphasis shifts from gender as a given SYMBOLIC entity, to gender*ing* as a *practice* that is historically productive of gender identities. The emphasis here on the fluidity of gender is mirrored, finally, in much psychoanalytic theory. Here, gender is seen first as the result of development in early infancy, centrally of the OEDIPUS COMPLEX, through which boys are said to acquire an active (masculine) and girls a passive (feminine) subjectivity. At the same time, many theorists (for example, Mitchell and Rose, 1985) take from psychoanalytic accounts of the unconscious as a disruptive psychic force a notion of the impossibility of fully stabilized gender identity. Thus in PSYCHOANALYSIS, as in poststructuralism, gender identity appears historically unstable, and therefore – so the argument goes – open to political change.

If there are disagreements over the theory and indeed the politics of gender, there is at least some consensus on the issues at stake in gender critique. Criticism of modern gender forms has centered on three areas. First, gendered systems of BINARY OPPOSITION are censured for their division of sexual identity into two opposing camps. Against this binarism, it is argued both that there is no necessary link between gender and biological sex – women may espouse elements of masculinity and *vice versa*, and, more radically, that femininity and masculinity themselves are coercive categories, imposing as they do a rigid dualism on potentially plural meanings and identities.

Second, critical attention has focused on the hierarchy implicit in gender binarism, on the assumption, that is, of masculine authority and feminine subservience. Cultural theorists and critics have contributed to this political dimension of gender debates by studying the role of cultural practices and forms in consolidating – or disrupting – gender hierarchies and norms.

A third and final dimension of the cultural critique of gender concerns the relationship between gender dualism, sexuality, and sexual orientation. We have seen that many critics contest notions of the biological "naturalness" of gender. Historians of sexuality, particularly since Foucault, have made the parallel argument that sexuality is the product of cultural processes: we are not born, but we become bisexual or "straight," gay or lesbian. Sexual object choice is not, however, straightforward. Under the prevailing Western system of "compulsory heterosexuality" (Rich, 1980), a distinction is drawn between legitimate and illegitimate (lesbian, gay, bisexual) sexual practices, and heterosexuality

is established as the social norm. Importantly, the demarcation line between heterosexuality and its opposites enforces an equally rigid division between the genders, for the only socially legitimized expression of sexual desire is that between "women" and "men." Thus in this account, gender and sexuality are interdependent, and gender transformation becomes contingent on the disruption of heterosexual norms.

Reading
Barrett, M. 1980 (*1988*): *Women's Oppression Today*.
Beauvoir, S. de 1949 (*1984*): *The Second Sex*.
Butler, J. (*1990*): *Gender Trouble. Feminism and the Subversion of Identity*.
Mitchell, J., and Rose, J., eds (*1985*): *Feminine Sexuality: Jacques Lacan and the Ecole Freudienne*.
Rich, A. 1980: "Compulsory heterosexuality and lesbian existence."

ERICA CARTER

genealogy A term which achieves prominence in Michel FOUCAULT's post-ARCHAEOLOGY OF KNOWLEDGE analyses of relations of power and knowledge. Genealogy represents a radically different conception of historical analysis, one that is influenced to a degree by the work of NIETZSCHE (Foucault, 1977). In contrast to traditional forms of historical analysis which place emphasis on stable forms and uninterrupted continuities, genealogy emphasizes the complexity, fragility, and contingency associated with historical events. Genealogy draws attention to "local, discontinuous, illegitimate knowledges" and challenges "the centralizing powers which are linked to . . . organized scientific DISCOURSE within a society such as ours" (Foucault, 1980, pp. 83–4). Genealogy affirms the perspectivity of knowledge. The publication of *Discipline and Punish: The Birth of the Prison* (1977) served notice of a relative shift of emphasis in Foucault's work from archaeological analyses of discursive formations to genealogical analyses of power-knowledge relations.

Reading
Foucault, M. 1971 (*1977*): "Nietzsche, genealogy, history."
——1980a: "Two lectures."
——1988c: "Questions of method: an interview with Michel Foucault."

BARRY SMART

generative grammar A term sometimes misleadingly used to refer to Noam Chomsky's approach to linguistics as a whole, though in fact it forms only one part of his research program (see CHOMSKY, Noam). A generative grammar of a language is an explicit, formal grammar which does not assume any prior linguistic knowledge. The term *generate* is a technical one from mathematics: an instruction such as "Start with 2 and add 3 four times" is said to generate the set {2, 5, 8, 11, 14,}. In linguistics, a rule such as "put adjectives before nouns" generates the set of expressions which includes *hot summer, red balloon*, and so on.

A generative grammar is a model of what a speaker of a language knows. It is not intended to model the way a speaker actually produces stretches of language, as an uninformed understanding of "generate" might suggest. A generative grammar is a system of knowledge that is put to use, along with other psychological and physical mechanisms (such as recall from memory or the operations of the ear) in producing and understanding language.

For Chomsky a generative grammar is only a step on the road to universal grammar (UG). Recent work, sometimes given the name "government and binding theory" after some of its principal theoretical concepts, has accordingly put more emphasis on general *principles* of grammar than on particular *rules* of grammar. A good example is the notion of "transformational rule" (see TRANS-FORMATION). In early work a special transformation was proposed for each type of construction. Passive constructions had a passive transformation which changed (i) into (ii); questions had a question transformation which changed (iii) into (iv), and so on:

(i)   The French colonized most of North Africa.
(ii) Most of North Africa was colonized by the French.

(iii) Ruby can operate an electric drill.
(iv) Can Ruby operate an electric drill?

The main thing that these transformations do is move words and phrases about, and recent work replaces these construction-specific rules by a general rule, usually called "Move-alpha," which means "Move anything anywhere." This rule obviously generates many impossible sentences (like *Most of North was colonized Africa by the French*) as well as good ones. The impossible ones are ruled out, however, by a small set of general principles which apply to *all* sentences.

One proposed principle states that only constituents can move, where a constituent is a word and all the words that modify it. In example (i), *most of North Africa* is a constituent, consisting of the noun *Africa* with the other words modifying the noun. Thus we can move *most of North Africa* to the front of the sentence in (ii). To compose the impossible sentence, though, we would have to move *most of North*, which is not a constituent, to the front. That is why this example is impossible.

This principle and other more complex ones are claimed to be part of UG by Chomsky and his fellow researchers. It is unlikely that a linguist who simply wanted to analyze the facts of English would have come up with this kind of approach to grammar. The focus on principles, rather than rules, results from Chomsky's basic interest in UG.

Reading
Chomsky, N. 1991b: *Knowledge of Language*.
Haegeman, L. 1991: *Introduction to Government and Binding Theory*.
Radford, A. 1988: *Transformational Grammar*.
Salkie, R. 1990: *The Chomsky Update: Linguistics and Politics*.

RAPHAEL SALKIE

genetic structuralism   A term adopted by GOLDMANN to describe his method of cultural analysis. Although Goldman coined the phrase, he believed the basic method had been elaborated by HEGEL, MARX, FREUD, PIAGET, and the young LUKÁCS. Goldmann's method is a STRUCTURALISM because, in considering cultural phenomena, it concerns itself not with immediate appearances or content, but with significant mental structures. Such structures are totalities in which the component parts are dependent on the whole. But unlike BARTHES, LÉVI-STRAUSS, or ALTHUSSER, Goldmann stresses that such structures must be understood in terms of their origin in the historical process. Any given totality can be inserted into a larger totality; thus a literary TEXT could be seen as a totality with its own structure, or as a component of a whole epoch of social history.

In particular Goldmann develops the concept of a "world view," the set of aspirations, ideas, and feelings elaborated by a whole social CLASS at a stage in its history. Such a world view is produced by a collective SUBJECT, but may find its most coherent expression in a major literary or philosophical text. Goldmann gives the most concrete exposition of the method in *The Hidden God* (Goldmann, 1956). In strengthening the state machine, Louis XIV of France undermined the power of one section of the nobility, the *noblesse de robe*, leaving it with no historical future or hope in the world; hence many of its members turned to Jansenism, a variety of Catholicism stressing human inability to achieve salvation without divine grace. Goldmann establishes a HOMOLOGY between the situation of this class and the "tragic vision" presented in the theology of Pascal and the plays of Racine. Although Goldmann has been accused of downplaying the role of the individual artist or thinker, his stress on the collective roots of cultural creation remains an important contribution to CULTURAL THEORY.

Reading
Goldmann, L. 1956 (*1964*): *The Hidden God.*

IAN H. BIRCHALL

Genette, Gérard (1930–) A foremost French practitioner and theorist of NARRATOLOGY. His work on Mareel Proust's *A la Recherche du temps perdu* (1913–27) in his book *Narrative Discourse: An Essay on Method* (1980) is usually considered to be a model of narratological technique.

Genette's theory of exactly what it is that constitutes the concerns of narratology is most fully expressed in *Figures of Literary Discourse* (1982). Although he acknowledges the relationship between STRUCTURALISM and NARRATOLOGY, that structuralism is the foundation for narratology, he specifies that he uses structuralism without becoming subservient to it. His theorizing of narratology therefore consists of a movement beyond the initial structuralist impulse. This movement takes its most concrete form in his problematizing of the relations between the literary TEXT on the one hand, and the historical moments of its production and its reception by the reader on the other. This leads him to remark not only that critical DISCOURSE is the obverse of literary discourse, but also that the distinction between the two is somewhat blurred. This potential contradiction is the source of much of his work.

One of Genette's basic principles is that there is a fundamental difference between real, that is poetic, language, and ordinary language. Literary language occupies the space in between these two extremes. To some extent he therefore privileges the poetic over the literary, although he does

attempt to deal with this problem by referring to generic categories. Thus, for example, for Genette one of the main indicators of generic difference between POETRY and prose is STYLE. A writer has no control over his or her style, just as with the language itself. However, the writer is responsible for the methods of writing which indicate his or her classification as a novelist, a realist, and so on. Genette does not specify exactly what constitutes style in this context, since it is not a method of writing. Such problems mark his text with a concern for the internal boundaries of narrative fiction, leading him to state that he sees structuralism as resistant to external ideological pressures. Despite this reference to structuralism's claim to be an objective science, he continually returns to problems posed for structuralism by change. Every time he does so, he reduces the problem to one of internal relations; the link between the reader and the author is one of enmeshment; literary references are simple transtextual repetitions; the literary text is simply a METONYMY for the literary tradition. In this formulation, it is the critic who invests the text with IDEOLOGY; the text itself is already outside the play of history. His theory is a totalizing construct.

Nevertheless, he is aware that such a procedure is ultimately reductive, noting that structuralism is able to deal best with texts which are most easily accessible to this kind of reading. A realization that other methods are also available lies behind this admission, and he states that the structuralist approach is unable to attend to the relations between literature and social life as a whole.

Reading
Genette, Gérard 1980: *Narrative Discourse: An Essay on Method.*
——1982a: *Figures of Literary Discourse.*

PAUL INNES

Geneva school Name given to a diverse group of twentieth-century literary critics with varying ties to Geneva; they have in common friendship and a phenomenological approach that reconstitutes an implied world view from the language of the TEXT. Marcel RAYMOND (1897–) is the first Geneva school figure, the teacher of Jean Rousset (1910–) and Jean Starobinski (1920–), and the author of various works that influenced Albert Béguin (1901–57), Georges POULET (1902–91) and, through

Poulet, Jean-Pierre RICHARD (1922–). Poulet's influence on J. Hillis Miller (1928–) drew the latter into the Geneva circle until the American critic turned to DECONSTRUCTION.

Geneva critics reject objective formalist criticism as overly mechanical, and devise various analytic strategies to recuperate the forms of individual consciousness exhibited in literary language. They select evidence, usually without regard to context, from an author's complete writings instead of considering separate (that is, formally defined) works. They look for an authorial consciousness existing at a prereflexive level where SUBJECT and object are fused; an individual *cogito* (after Descartes) expressing that consciousness; descriptions of space and time in the text as analytic keys for reconstituting the picture of consciousness; and the author's projection of different versions of reality as an evolving effort to find harmony by reconciling daily experience with the underlying *cogito*. Avoiding aesthetic judgment, they often seek larger perspectives in patterns of historical consciousness, in existential "authenticity," or, later, in a psychoanalytic framework.

See also PHENOMENOLOGY.

Reading
Lawall, Sarah N. 1968a: "Marcel Raymond."
Miller, J. Hillis 1966 (*1991*): "The Geneva school."
Poulet, Georges 1969: "Phenomenology of reading."

SARAH N. LAWALL

genre analysis In his justly celebrated *Anatomy of Criticism* (1957) Northrop FRYE elegantly distinguished what he called the four "pregeneric forms" on the basis of the sense that forms of literary art relate to human and natural phenomena, such as the movement from birth to maturation and on to old age and death; to the sequence of the cycles of the seasons; and to the alternation of day and night. Thus he proposed a pregeneric cycle as an analogy to the four seasons, as though charted on an undrawn circular diagram. If a line were drawn through the center of the circle and the lower area shaded, then a movement within the upper half might correspond to day or summer, the lower half to night or winter, a movement up from dark to light as spring, and a movement down from light to dark as fall. If one were to superimpose on these natural forms the pregenres of romance (for summer), IRONY (for winter), COMEDY (for spring)

and TRAGEDY (for fall), then a correspondence of observed nature with the forms of literary art might be determined. But when Frye turned to the more daunting task of accounting for all of the various literary forms – sonnets, odes, lyrics, autobiographies, masques, etc. – he was unable to match the profound simplicity of his pregeneric forms.

Paul Hernadi (1972), however, in a supplement to Frye, has suggested that overlapping Frye's seasonal forms are the imitative genres of lyric, dramatic, and epic, each of which imitates a portion of what lies beyond it. According to this scheme, lyric is an imitation of thought that moves from an ostensible topic inward to the consciousness of the thinker. The dramatic is a kinetic, rather than a concentric mode, which brings together two or more minds in communion or agon, leading to action. The epic, which may look back to encompass lyrical, meditative thought and dramatic kinesis, sets out to embrace ecumenically the sense of a whole world, leaving nothing outside. Thus the three principal genres move from thought to action to world, each encompassing what comes before, and all unstable in reference to the others.

Reading
Frye, Northrop 1957: *Anatomy of Criticism*.
Hernadi, Paul 1972: *Beyond Genre: New Directions in Literary Classification*.

MICHAEL PAYNE

Gilbert, Sandra (1936–) and **Gubar, Susan** (1944–) US feminist literary critics. Although each member of this pair is an accomplished critic in her own right, it is as a team that Gilbert and Gubar have made the most significant impact on FEMINIST CRITICISM in the United States. Their monumental study of nineteenth-century British and American women writers, *The Madwoman in the Attic* (1979), in some sense represents the apex of American feminist work in the 1970s on women's literary tradition and the female imagination. In a lively, yet densely informative style, Gilbert and Gubar analyzed the response of women writers to severe cultural restraints, especially to gendered ideologies of literary and cultural authority that denied women's agency and creativity. Revising Harold BLOOM's theory of the ANXIETY OF INFLUENCE, Gilbert and Gubar showed how women's texts come to share a specific, coherent set of themes, images, TROPES, SYMBOLS, formal structures, and

narrative strategies that, however guarded or disguised, express women's rage at cultural dispossession, their madness and fragmentation within
patriarchy, and rebellion against it. *Madwoman*,
which was runner-up for a Pulitzer Prize in 1980,
was enthusiastically received as brilliant proof of
the existence of a separate female literary tradition,
and further, as proof that women's writings must
be evaluated on their own aesthetic terms. Still,
some feminists criticized the book for its reductive
approach to women's ART, its suggestion that all
women's TEXTS ultimately signify the same thing
(repressed female anger), and its tendency to valorize the experience of white, middle-class, English-
speaking women, to generalize in a way that implied
the existence of a single women's CULTURE and
universal female AESTHETIC. In 1985 Gilbert and
Gubar's *Norton Anthology of Literature by Women*
was similarly received: gratefully, as a SYMBOL of
the new legitimacy of feminist critical approaches
to women writers, and nervously, as a premature
effort to create a CANON of women writers in English that would surely harden notions of literary
history and patterns of inclusion and exclusion that
feminist critics had yet thoroughly to understand,
let alone come to consensus about. In 1988 Gilbert
and Gubar extended the argument of *Madwoman*
to twentieth-century women writers in their gar-
gantuan, two-volume *No Man's Land*. As coeditors,
they have produced two volumes of feminist essays
on POETRY and poetics: *Shakespeare's Sisters* in 1979
and *The Female Imagination and the Modernist Aesthetic* in 1986. Gilbert and Gubar's work is not
only required reading for specialists in women's
literature, but their collaboration itself has played
a role in the history of WOMEN'S STUDIES. It has
sparked an important discussion about the value
and significance of collaboration in feminist methodology, as opposed to patriarchal practices of intellectual hierarchy, competition, and individual
ownership of ideas.
See also ANXIETY OF INFLUENCE; FEMINIST CRITICISM.

Reading
Gilbert, Sandra M., and Gubar, Susan 1979: *The Madwoman in the Attic: The Woman Writer and the Nineteenth-Century Literary Imagination.*
——1988: *No Man's Land: The Place of the Woman
Writer in the Twentieth Century.*
——eds 1979: *Shakespeare's Sisters: Feminist Essays on
Women Poets.*
——eds 1985a: *The Norton Anthology of Literature by
Women: The Tradition in English.*

——eds 1986: *The Female Imagination and the Modernist
Aesthetic.*

GLYNIS CARR

Girard, René (1923–) French literary theorist.
Girard has spent most of his career in the United
States. He has taught at various universities including SUNY-Buffalo, Johns Hopkins University, and
Stanford University, where he is currently professor
of French language, literature, and civilization.
Girard is best known for a theory of mimesis, which
argues that all human desire is imitative and not
innate. Mimetic desire is triangular in structure
and encompasses a relation between a SUBJECT, an
object, and a mediator. Mediation can be either
internal or external. Internal mediation requires a
mediator who is historically accessible to the subject
like a friend or a rival. External mediation requires
a mediator who is not immediately available like,
say, Napoleon, FREUD, etc. It is mediation and not
intrinsic properties that make objects desirable. If
desire is mediated, then desire becomes the desire
to be the other. Girard introduces the resonant
phrase "ontological sickness" to describe this phenomenon. What is sought in the other is the promise
of being. Girard's theory of mimetic desire was
first worked out in *Deceit, Desire, and the Novel*
(1966).

Girard has derived a new theory of psychology
from his notion of mimetic desire. His critique of
Freudian PSYCHOANALYSIS revolves around the
two key psychoanalytic myths, namely those of
Oedipus and Narcissus. Girard rejects both the
importance of sexuality and the libidinal quest for
objects in the Freudian model, for they do not
incorporate mimetic desire. In the Oedipal model
Freud seems to imply that the child's desire for
the mother is originary; this overlooks the mimetic
structure of Oedipal desire. It is in imitating the
father that the child acquires a desire for the mother.
In Girard's words "[t]he mimetic process detaches
desire from any predetermined object, whereas
the OEDIPUS COMPLEX fixes desire on the maternal
object." Girard denies that narcissism exists in the
way Freud implies that it does. Freud's prototype
of the narcissitic subject, the so-called narcissistic
woman, does not really have a sufficient sense of
being; she merely pretends to have this aura of
being as a ruse to catch the desire of others. Girard's
theory of mimetic desire also implies a new account
of other psychoanalytic concepts like masochism,

sadism, and homosexuality. The masochist is a subject who is unwilling to recognize lack in the mediator of desire. He would rather hold on to the illusion that being exists in someone else even if it is denied to him. Masochism then consists of the choice of mediators who will forbid access to the object(s) of desire. In sadism there is a reversal of structure. The sadist convinces himself that he has in fact attained to a sufficiency of being and can therefore be the mediator for another subject who will be denied his object(s) of desire. Homosexuality can also be understood as a perversion of mimesis. Here desire is transferred from the object to the mediator. If all desire is mimetic, then Girard will need to address the origin of this desire and seek to understand its function in the SYMBOLIC. This he seeks to do with the concept of the scapegoat.

Mimetic desire can lead to conflict and violence. In *Violence and the Sacred* (1977) Girard emphasizes the fact the violence is often visited on a surrogate victim. This victim can decrease the intensity of violence generated in a social context by functioning as a scapegoat. Scapegoating tends to be communal. Once the scapegoat has been killed, it ironically takes on the aura of a savior. It is revered for having restored harmony in the community. Girard has read Greek tragedy and other literary TEXTS as evidentiary of scapegoating. Girard's interest in myth also stems from their connection to the problematic of scapegoating. He argues that myths are not pieces of fiction but have roots in the real. The thematics of myths reveal a transition from a structure of undifferentiation to a differentiation that is achieved by the death of the victim. In *The Scapegoat* (1986) Girard moves from myth to the TEXTS of persecution. He argues that scapegoating no longer works to insure social harmony in the Judeo-Christian world as it once did. He credits this to the Bible's portrayal of the victim's perspective. In recent years Girard has produced "nonsacrificial" readings of biblical myths, most notably in *Job: The Victim of His People* (1987) and *Things Hidden since the Foundation of the World* (1987).

Reading
Girard, René 1977: *Violence and the Sacred*.
—— 1966 (*1984*): *Deceit, Desire, and the Novel: Self and Other in Literary Structure*.
—— 1986: *The Scapegoat*.
—— 1987: *Job: The Victim of His People*.
—— 1987: *Things Hidden Since the Foundation of the World*.

Goslan, Richard 1993: *René Girard and Myth: An Introduction*.

SHIVA KUMAR SRINIVASAN

Glissant, Edouard (1928–) Martinican poet and novelist. In *Caribbean Discourse: Selected Essays* (1981), Glissant reaffirms the cultural and historical specificity of Martinique within the "series of multiple relationships" that compose Caribbean diversity, and elaborates upon the notion of *métissage* (hybridity). Asserting that "no people has been spared the cross-cultural process," Glissant deconstructs the category of "unique" origins and proposes a "cross-cultural poetics" where a Self/Other dichotomy would yield to an exchange between the Self and An/other (*autrui*).
See also RACE AND RACISM.

Reading
Dash, J. Michael 1989: "Introduction" to *Caribbean Discourse: Selected Essays*.
Glissant, Edouard 1981 (*1989*): *Caribbean Discourse: Selected Essays*.

JEANNE GARANE

Glyph A journal of textual studies with a brief but interesting history, which can best be explained in two distinct phases, as a publication first of the Johns Hopkins University Press and later of the University of Minnesota Press.

Samuel Weber, associate professor of comparative literature at Johns Hopkins when he founded *Glyph* in 1977, announced the journal's program: to encourage intellectual discourse on methods of representation and textuality. The goal of the journal was to challenge the boundaries of what Weber called the "crisis of representation" and the "practice of textuality." Among the more pressing issues, as Weber saw it, was the "problematization of the representational framework of Western metaphysics," especially in the work of NIETZSCHE, MARX, FREUD, HEIDEGGER, and DERRIDA.

The Statement to Contributors printed in each issue welcomed papers concerned with "the confrontation between American and Continental critical scenes," a topic which remained a vital concern during the initial years of the journal's publication. During this time, and in the second phase as well, *Glyph* published papers by an impressive group of contributors. The editorial board, too, was prominent in the table of contents. The first issue of

Glyph included articles by Weber and his coeditor Henry Sussman, three articles by board members, and one each by Paul de Man ("The purloined ribbon") and Jacques Derrida ("Signature event context").

The first phase of *Glyph*, a semi-annual publication, ended with volume 8 in 1981. In his closing remarks, a dejected Weber traced dwindling circulation patterns and noted that the journal had strayed from its original intentions, suggesting also that the journal had been associated too closely with Derrida's *Of Grammatology* and DECONSTRUCTION, a concept which was hinted at but never explicitly mentioned in the opening program. *Glyph*'s second phase, Weber explained here, included a move to the University of Minnesota – where, incidentally, Weber himself moved – and a switch to a yearly publication schedule. These technical changes, according to Weber, required a "redefinition of the situation and character of our work, deriving from the experiences accumulated during our first four years of publication." The new series, not published until 1986, only lasted several years, during which time it was edited by Weber, Sussman, and Wlad Godzich, who established in their preface the journal's shift in focus from a concern with problems of representation to an emphasis on a "greater currency of concerns" arising from contemporary criticism. As part of this shift, each volume was to revolve around a central issue; *Demarcating the Disciplines*, the title of the 1986 publication, is a prime example.

TARA G. GILLIGAN

Goldmann, Lucien (1913–70) Romanian–French cultural theorist. After youthful clandestine activity in a Marxist organization, Goldmann left his native Romania and went in 1934 to France, where he spent most of the rest of his life. A committed Marxist, Goldmann was profoundly hostile to Stalinism, and thus rather isolated among French left intellectuals before 1968. An advocate of "revolutionary reformism" in the 1960s, his revolutionary commitment revived in 1968.

For Goldmann, philosophy, literature, and ART are all rooted in the daily life of human beings in specific societies, and are to be seen as means of responding to the fundamental human problems which arise in these societies. Goldmann applied his methodological approach of GENETIC STRUCTURALISM to a wide range of fields; the philosophy

of KANT; Jansenism in seventeenth-century France; a critique of EMPIRICISM in sociology; REIFICATION in the twentieth-century novel; and the theater of Jean Genet. Goldmann's isolation from political practice led him to defend MARXISM purely as a method of interpretation, and after 1968 his work was often neglected in favour of apparently more militant versions of Marxism. Nevertheless, aspects of his work had a significant influence, notably on the later work of Raymond WILLIAMS and the early Julia KRISTEVA.

Reading
Evans, M. 1981: *Lucien Goldmann*.
Goldmann, L. 1956 (*1964*): *The Hidden God*.
——1967 (*1970*): "The sociology of literature: status and problems of method."
Naïr, S. and Lowy, M. 1973: *Goldmann*.

IAN H. BIRCHALL

Gombrich, Ernst (1909–) Austrian-born British art historian. The story of Sir Ernst Gombrich's life as an art historian is told by Gombrich himself in two places: in "An Autobiographical Sketch" from *Topics Of Our Time: Twentieth-Century Issues in Learning and Art* (1991) and in the dialogue between Didier Eribon and himself from *Looking for Answers: Conversations on Art and Science* (1993). The first illustration in the *Conversations* book is a photograph of Gombrich, aged about 4, holding up an earthworm for the camera. While this photograph does not have the technical mastery that Gombrich finds in the work of Henri Cartier-Bresson, discussed in the last essay in the *Topics* book (the head and face, and the earthworm, are somewhat out of focus, while the embroidery on the shirt and the shiny belt are vividly recorded and preserved), it does have the look of the selection of the "right moment" that is consistent in the experience of Cartier-Bresson's work and occasionally can be found in the lucky snapshot. Perhaps in this photograph of a youthful Gombrich can be seen the art historian who is eager to share and takes pleasure in sharing his discoveries, and who, like Leonardo da Vinci (whom he admires above all), puts nature before art.

That he was born in Vienna was important to Gombrich because it was a place where, at that time, psychology and music could enter his life. Upon entering Vienna University, he chose to read art history with Julius van Schosser, "a wise teacher of doubts," rather than with Josef Strzygowski, who was known for the polemic approach of his lectures.

Gombrich's PhD thesis on Giulio Romano's Palazzo del Te showed that Mannerism could be better understood as a search for surprising and dramatic effects to suit the tastes of the Gonzaga court of Mantua, rather than as the result of a psychological crisis during the age. At this time he was invited by Ernst Kris to work with him in applying Freud's ideas about wit to the visual arts through a study of caricature. It was through Kris that Gombrich was recommended to Fritz Saxl of the Warburg Institute, which had recently moved from Hamburg to London.

During the war years in England Gombrich was one of the group that monitored radio broadcasts from Germany. From this unpromising task Gombrich learned a useful lesson about perception by the need to fill in the sometimes meaningless sounds of the broadcasts with words that were suggested to him by his knowledge of the language and the context of the message. After the war Gombrich returned to art history, writing about the mythologies of Botticelli. This paper is one of those collected in the volume, *Symbolic Images: Studies in the Art of the Renaissance* (1972), which is one of four volumes of Gombrich's collected essays in Renaissance art and culture. Earlier, while still in Vienna, Gombrich had written what had become a successful world history book for children. As a companion volume, the publisher suggested that Gombrich write a history of art for children. From that idea came *The Story of Art*, first published in 1950, and now in its sixteenth English edition (1995). This popular commentary on the history of art led to the double life that Gombrich says he has, being known by some only as the author of *The Story of Art* and by others only as the author of scholarly papers. Rather, this makes clear what is a special strength of Gombrich's work: that it brings together the broad insights of the generalist with the sharp focus of the specialist.

The idea of the play between knowing and seeing in the experience of pictures around which *The Story of Art* is structured was further developed by Gombrich in the light of the psychology of perception in the influential *Art and Illusion: A Study in the Psychology of Pictorial Representation* (1960). In this study, Gombrich explains that changes in representational art occur when an artist modifies the schematic conventions of image-making by examining the schema against the observation of nature. The idea of the process of making and matching proceeding through schema

and correction is also generally the subject of the papers collected in *The Image and the Eye: Further Studies in the Psychology of Pictorial Representation* (1982). Norman BRYSON turns a critical GAZE on this idea, arguing that a description of the image as a surface for perceiving rather than for producing meaning supresses the reality of the image as SIGN, and makes the viewer as a historical as the physiology of sight. *The Sense of Order: A Study in the Psychology of Decorative Art* (1979) was written, Gombrich said, partly as an antidote to the criticism of *Art and Illusion* that he was concerned only with representation in ART. This thematic study of decoration in light of information theory examines the play between expectation and surprise which shapes messages conveyed in words, music, and decorative motifs. The choice of this topic itself was for Gombrich an application of this theory, in that by choosing the neglected SUBJECT of decoration and approaching a more general problem in the discipline, Gombrich was interrupting the pattern of sameness and narrowness that he generally sees in the literature of art history.

Gombrich finds that, while the current study of art history examines questions of interest, such as women, blacks, and the art market, it does not concern itself enough with art. In the Epilogue of *Conversations*, Gombrich says that he sees the art historian as fighting for values. Then when asked what values he is fighting for, he answers, "I think I can say this is very simply: the traditional civilization of Western Europe." In this time of emphasis in the discipline on diversity, MULTICULTURALISM, and interdisciplinary approaches, Gombrich is a staunch defender of traditional art history. Perhaps this Gombrich also can be seen in the snapshot of the four-year-old with the earthworm, who insists that we view the object of his interest that he steadfastly holds up to the camera for display.

See also ART; AVANT-GARDE; RENAISSANCE STUDIES.

Reading
Gombrich, Ernst 1950 (*1995*): *The Story of Art*.
——1960 (*1969*): *Art and Illusion: A Study in the Psychology of Pictorial Representation*.
——1963 (*1971*): *Meditations on a Hobby Horse and Other Essays on the Theory of Art*.
——1966 (*1978*): *Norm and Form: Studies in the Art of Renaissance I*.
——1972 (*1978*): *Symbolic Images: Studies in the Art of Renaissance II*.
——1979: *The Sense of Order: A Study in the Psychology of Decorative Art*.

——1982: *The Image and the Eye: Further Studies in the Psychology of Pictorial Representation.*
——1991: *Topics of Our Time, Twentieth-Century Issues in Learning and in Art.*
——and Eribon, Didier 1993: *Looking for Answers: Conversations on Art and Science.*

GERALD EAGER

Goodman, Paul (1911–72) American writer and intellectual. A radical liberal and man of letters, Goodman's extensive output included novels, poetry, and political pamphlets as well as works of social criticism. In *Growing Up Absurd* (1960) he condemned American society for failing its youth and hence became something of a hero to both the beatniks and the counterculturalists of the 1960s. He also founded the Gestalt school of PSYCHOANALYSIS. His intellectual position has been variously described as anarchist, utopian, communitarian, and progressive. In fact he represents the non-Marxist strain in Western radicalism, with a personal and basically pragmatic vision which combined elements from utopian, anarchist, and FREUDian schools of thought.
See also COUNTERCULTURE.

Reading
Goodman, P., Perls, F., and Hefferline, R. 1951: *Gestalt Therapy.*
——1960 (*1966*): *Growing Up Absurd.*
King, R. 1973: "Paul Goodman."

COLIN CAMPBELL

grammar, generative *See* GENERATIVE GRAMMAR

grammatology The study of WRITING. When they have not been concerned with specific problems of deciphering, studies of writing have been paradoxically historical undertakings (Ducrot and Todorov, 1972). For this reason the efforts of grammatologists to uncover the historical origins of writing have been impossible, since they necessarily rely on written records, which obviously do not extend into preliteracy. Nevertheless, grammatology sets out to counter the disparaging treatment of writing in linguistics that goes back to JAKOBSON, SAUSSURE, ROUSSEAU, and beyond. In the history of philosophy the scandal of writing is as old as Plato's *Phaedrus*. For Saussure, writing is a monstrous and pathological imposition on speech, which for Rousseau was the "natural" condition of

language. DERRIDA, however, in his *Of Grammatology* (1967) set out to expose not only the Platonic and Rousseauist use of writing to privilege speech, but also the related misconception that spoken language makes the objects of signification present, and the reliance of Western theology and metaphysics on these maneuvers. Grammatology thus reaches deeply into the recesses of PHILOSOPHY OF LANGUAGE and CULTURE.

Reading
Derrida, Jacques 1967a: *Of Grammatology.*
Ducrot, Oswald, and Todorov, Tsvetan 1972 (*1979*): *Encyclopedic Dictionary of the Sciences of Language.*
Gelb, I.J. 1963: *A Study of Writing: The Foundations of Grammatology.*

MICHAEL PAYNE

Gramsci, Antonio (1891–1937) Marxist theorist and political activist. Gramsci's main contribution to MARXISM is widely thought to lie in his elaboration of the notion of HEGEMONY. Gramsci was born in Sardinia, and from the age of 11 was obliged to work to augment the income of his impoverished family. Despite difficulties of both finance and health, Gramsci won a scholarship in 1910 at Turin University where he specialized in linguistics and philology, falling under the influence of the idealist philosophers Benedetto Croce and Francesco De Sanctis. But Gramsci was already a socialist and moved in a circle of like-minded companions including Palmiro Togliatti and Angelo Tasca. Gramsci eventually forsook his brilliant studies for an active life in politics.

In Turin Gramsci became involved in the working-class movement which, partly as a result of the 1914–18 war, was on a rising wave of militancy. He joined the Italian Socialist Party (PSI) in 1913 and by 1917 had been elected Secretary of the Socialist Section in Turin. By the end of the war, Gramsci's study of MARX, Engels, and Lenin had impelled him to reject philosophical idealism. In 1919 he founded the newspaper *Ordine Nuovo* (New Order), an organ of the Factory Councils' movement in Turin which aimed to reach out to the Italian proletariat, articulating its real problems and goals. The focus of Gramsci's theory and practice was the means whereby the workers' movement could gain power (Gramsci, 1977, p. 133), this being one of the broad ramifications of his later concept of political hegemony. In preparation for the Russian Revolution of 1917, Lenin and Trotsky had sought to displace state capitalist trusts by administrative councils called "soviets," democratic organs of working-class power reminiscent of the Paris Commune. These councils, comprising deputies from factory workers to whom they were answerable, had organized political strikes and demonstrations and had armed the workers. They had been perceived by Trotsky as an embryonic form of a workers' government.

Seeking to extend the historical role of such councils beyond their Russian context, Gramsci looked to the Italian Factory Councils to assume a similar function (Gramsci, 1957, p. 22). Gramsci stated that *Ordine Nuovo* was built around the hypothesis of "autonomous revolutionary action" by the working class; as such he resisted the idea of his old comrade Tasca that the Factory Committees should align themselves with the Trade Unions and federations; these, Gramsci insisted, rested on merely private and contractual obligations, whereas the Councils were a public institution.

Such autonomous revolutionary potential on the part of the proletariat could only be realized, argued Gramsci, through political *and* intellectual autonomy. A mass movement alone was insufficient: its unity needed to embrace both northern and southern Italy, as can be gleaned from Gramsci's preoccupying argument in his later essay "The southern question," but also, initiated through a vanguard with working-class roots and sympathies, this class "must train and educate itself in the management of society," acquiring both the culture and psychology of a dominant class through its own channels: "meetings, congresses, discussions, mutual education." Moreover, the "laws of the workers' State need to be executed by the workers themselves" (Gramsci, 1977, p. 171). Only then will political compromise in all its guises be forestalled. *Ordine Nuovo* had aimed precisely to install itself as a platform for focusing such preparatory activities: to convince workers and peasants to arrive at their own conception of the world through workmen's circles and youth groups as well as to develop "new forms of intellectualism" grounded in the practical experience of working-class life (Gramsci, 1957, pp. 21, 122).

Working-class solidarity showed itself in a confrontation with Turin industrialists and a general strike which, though unsuccessful, further galvanized the movement. However, disillusioned over the Socialist Party's failure to impress its image on the course of events, Gramsci and others formed the Italian Communist Party (PCI) in 1921. Faced with a consolidation of the Fascist regime, Gramsci strategically reneged on his earlier sectarianism, calling for the Communists to align themselves with all forms of opposition to fascism, by now the only realistic hope. Visiting Moscow in 1922, he returned in 1924 to assume leadership of the Party, and founded its journal *Unità* (*Ordine Nuovo* having been coerced into closing down). In the Parliamentary elections of April, 19 Communist candidates, including Gramsci, were elected, notwithstanding the oppressive climate of intimidation by Fascist squads. But the Fascists won an overwhelming victory and in 1925 Mussolini announced his own dictatorship. Gramsci was arrested in 1926 and sentenced to 20 years' imprisonment. After 11 years of maltreatment and confinement, during which he never once saw his Russian wife Giulia Schucht or his two small children, Gramsci died in 1937.

Gramsci wrote some 34 notebooks while in prison, ranging from literary topics such as Dante and Pirandello to philosophical and political themes. These were not published until after Mussolini's downfall. Gramsci's LITERARY CRITICISM insisted on understanding literary production within its historical and political context (as against Croce's ahistorical view of ART as autonomous) and, following De Sanctis, viewed the critic's task as one of harmonizing with the general cultural and political struggle towards a socialist order. The most persistent theme of the notebooks straddled both philosophical and political domains: the link between the intelligentsia and revolutionary practice, which forms a continuous thread running through Gramsci's thought both prior to and after his incarceration.

In an essay on the formation of intellectuals, Gramsci argued that every class aspiring toward power and entering an economically dominant role in the theater of history creates a group of intellectuals, organically united with its economic imperatives. These "organic" intellectuals confer upon the class homogeneity, consciousness of its function, as well as organizing society so as to facilitate the expansion of this class. However, the class must also assimilate and conquer a portion of the "traditional" intellectuals, those bound to the previous order; this will help to veil even the most radical upheavals under the mantle of historical continuity. The relation between intellectuals and the means of production itself is of course indirect, mediated by a complex superstructure of which intellectuals are the "officials."

There are, says Gramsci, two "floors" or bases of superstructure: civil society, consisting of private organizations, and political society which is the state. It is within the former sphere that intellectuals exert their function of social HEGEMONY, encouraging a "spontaneous consent" on the part of the populace to ruling-class ideas and ambitions. In contrast, the state legally insures discipline through direct rule and coercion. Gramsci's use of "intellectual" here is broad, covering the hierarchy from original thinkers and scientists at the apex to administrators and propagators of received class wisdom at the bottom. Gramsci points out that the mass formation of intellectuals in modern society has led to their sharing the standardized features of other masses: competition, unemployment, (scholarly) overproduction, and emigration.

From a revolutionary standpoint, this mass of intellectuals is precisely what is required. In "The southern question" Gramsci urges that this mass intellectual formation must endure a break, part of it arising as a left-wing tendency oriented towards the revolutionary proletariat (Gramsci, 1957, p. 51). In "The modern prince" Gramsci's starting point is Machiavelli's "revolutionary" inquiry into what the prince must be in order to lead the people to the foundation of a new state. The modern prince, Gramsci explains, can no longer be an individual but an organism: the political party which aims to found a new type of state. This transformation to a socialist state cannot be successful without the proletariat's own organic intellectuals forging an alternative hegemony.

Underlying Gramsci's notion of hegemony are certain fundamental readings of Marx and Marxism. Above all, he views Marxism as an integrated scheme, encompassing not only philosophy, history, and politics, but also the grounding of these in economic life. This emerges, for example, in a review where he chastises Bukharin for his mechanical separation of the various tendencies of Marx's work. Gramsci's view acts as a broad preface to the notion of hegemony which is effectively a metonymic affirmation of the dialectical connection between economic and superstructural spheres, stressing the transformative role of human agency rather than relying on the "inevitability" of economic determinism. Moreover, Gramsci regards Marx's most fundamental innovation in political science as his insistence that human nature is historically determined, rather than being abstract, fixed, and immutable (Gramsci, 1957, p. 140). It is

this which endows with a wealth of philosophical and political coherence Gramsci's characterization of the state which presides enablingly over the propriety of his view of hegemony: "the State must be seen as an 'educator' in that it aims precisely to create a new type and level of civilisation" as well as a certain type of citizen (Gramsci, 1957, p. 187). It is because civil society and the state educate or mold human nature into a vehicle of consent and conformity that, given a broad democratic educational base, the organic intellectuals can initiate the process whereby the proletariat remolds its own humanity.

Gramsci's view of hegemony is also perhaps an attempt to answer what he sees as a deficiency in the history of Marxism. In "Marxism and modern culture" he suggests that two crucial tasks have confronted Marxist theory and practice: to combat modern ideologies in their most refined form, thereby attracting and creating its own independent core of intellectuals; and to educate the masses. The second task, says Gramsci, has absorbed Marxism at the expense of the first. The dissemination of Marxism at a populist cultural level, while imperative, is utterly inadequate for overcoming the IDEOLOGY of the educated classes. Gramsci views Marxism as still in its popularizing stage, but adds that it contains within itself the dialectical principle for overcoming this. It must now enter the long process of developing a core of intellectuals; in this light, Gramsci's notion of hegemony might be viewed as an interesting attempt to extend Marxist theory in general on the basis of a practice whose theorizing was rooted in the particular exigencies of an Italian context. On account of the political and practical shrewdness underlying Gramsci's theories, he is widely regarded as one of the foremost contributors to the Marxist cause.

Reading

Bellamy, R., and Schecter, D. 1993: *Gramsci and the Italian State.*

Fontana, B. 1993: *Hegemony and Power.*

Gill, S., ed. 1993: *Gramsci, Historical Materialism and International Relations.*

Jay, Martin 1984: "The two holisms of Antonio Gramsci."
M.A.R. HABIB

Greenberg, Clement (1909–) American art critic, considered by Michael Fried to be "the foremost critic of new painting and sculpture of our time." Grounded in KANT's self-critical method (his use of logic to examine the limits of logic) and nourished by the MARXIST view of capitalist culture, the two basic components of Greenberg's criticism appear in "AVANT-GARDE and Kitsch" (1939): that ART is about its own craft, specifically that painting is about the forms inherent to it, and that new art is a revolt against materialist tradition. These components are used by Greenberg to seek an understanding of the modernist art with which his criticism is most readily associated, namely abstract expressionism, which he later preferred to call painterly abstraction (and which Harold ROSENBERG characterized as action painting). The essentials of this art, described in "American-type painting" (1955), include first, an emphasis on surface (for example, the pulsating flatness of Marc Rothko), second, a de-emphasis of value contrasts (that is, the pulverization of light/dark contrast by Pollock), and third, a large format to make up for the loss of the illusion of space resulting from the first two. Also essential to this art was that it emerged as a major art by assimilating the major art of preceding periods. This is emphasized in the essay "Modernist painting" (1961), where the fundamental effect of flatness that painting sought, as self-criticism of painting eliminated the effect of any other medium from itself, was traced backed from Mondrian, through cubism and impressionism, to the suppression of sculptural effects in sixteenth-century Venetian painting. Greenberg's *Post Painterly Abstraction* (1964) equates the work of the Color Field painters (that is Morris Louis and Kenneth Noland) with Impressionism, and sees its essential form – openness – as a reaction to the closed, centralized images of abstract expressionism. Criticism of Greenberg's criticism centers for some critics (T.J. CLARK) on its formalism – the belief that painting is primarily about its medium as form rather than its medium as meaning, and for others (Rosalind KRAUSS) on its HISTORICISM – the belief that painting has a universal meaning inherent to it alone, and that the meaning of the work of art is a condition of the path it has traveled through history. Perhaps the most vivid criticism of Greenberg's FORMALISM and historicism is to be seen in the 1966 event by the British conceptual artist John Latham: Greenberg's book *Art and Culture* was checked out of St Martin's School of Art library, some pages from it were selected to be chewed, others to be chemically treated, and together fermented with yeast and bottled – and then a year later the book was returned to the library in this form. This event has entered the history of art as Latham's *Art and Culture*, 1966-9 (MOMA, New York), an assemblage of bottles and documentation in an attaché case.

Reading
Greenberg, Clement 1961 (*1968*): *Art and Culture.*
——1964: *Post Painterly Abstraction.*
——1986: *The Collected Essays and Criticism.*

GERALD EAGER

Greer, Germaine (1939-) Australian cultural critic. A prolific writer and editor, Germaine Greer's unorthodox work, which is difficult to categorize, treats subjects as diverse as feminism, fascism, menopause, fertility, women artists and poets, and Shakespeare. Her first book, *The Female Eunuch* (1970), is an early feminist classic in which Greer, influenced by EXISTENTIALISM, urges women to free themselves by refusing to stifle their own originality and intelligence. Her essay on the Tulsa Center for the Study of Women's Literature is an important manifesto for feminists engaged in the recovery of women's literature and history.
See also FEMINIST CRITICISM.

Reading
Greer, Germaine 1970: *The Female Eunuch.*
——1979: *The Obstacle Race: The Fortunes of Women Painters and Their Work.*
——1984: *Sex and Destiny: The Politics of Human Fertility.*
——1982: "Tulsa Center for the Study of Women's Literature – What we are doing and why we are doing it."
——ed. 1988: *Kissing the Rod: An Anthology of Seventeenth-Century Women's Verse.*

GLYNIS CARR

Greimas, Algirdas Julien (1948-) Lithuanian theorist of SEMIOTICS who lives in France. His work on structural semantics has had some influence upon NARRATOLOGY.

Greimas's work is a movement toward a linguistic theory that will deal with all the ways in which meaning is produced in literary language, from sentences, through discursive passages, to the full significance of a TEXT and its relations with other texts. He begins from a basic structuralist premise: that there is a commonality of language which constitutes a sort of set of all that it is possible to say or write (see LANGUE/PAROLE), and which is composed of BINARY OPPOSITIONS. However, he develops this theory in order to try to account for changes in the meanings of specific lexical elements as they are utilized in different sentences. He does so by invoking the structuralist account of meaning being produced as an operation of difference (see Ferdinand de SAUSSURE). For Greimas the different uses of a lexical item in different contexts produces a network of differential meanings which is set up by the repetition of the item. Thus the use of the same word in two different sentences throws up a double set of binary oppositions: one for the meanings produced in each sentence in and of itself (see ACTANT), and another for the relation between the two sentences. This formulation is known as the semiotic rectangle, a figure which performs a unifying operation between the two sentences. This figure accounts for the meanings produced by the relationship between the two sentences. As one moves from sentence to sentence, a coherent picture of meaning for the text as a whole is gradually produced from the individual sentences and their relations with one another. Layers of meaning accumulate harmoniously and coherently in such a way that every layer complements the others. In this formulation, every level should shed light on the features of every other level, so that a construction of unitary meaning is objectively achieved.

Greimas is, however, aware that his theory is problematical, given that the identification of these kinds of correspondences can vary radically from reader to reader. Cultural context impinges upon his attempt to produce, in a classic structuralist move, an objective science of reading. He attempts to resolve this problem by reference to a form of LITERARY COMPETENCE. Analysis of the various levels of meaning, from a single word up to relations between texts, is organized in strata of classification which are always subject to the reader recognizing the meanings. The repetition of elements of the levels of classification is at the heart of the production of meaning in this schema. However, this operation may not always be successful if a reader does not have access to the cultural baggage which might be assumed to be necessary for a full reading of the sort proposed by Greimas. His theory represents an important attempt to produce a comprehensive theory of narrative, but it cannot deal with the problem faced by STRUCTURALISM in general: how to deal with cultural change.

Reading
Greimas, A.J. 1966: *Semantique Structurale*.
——1970: *Du Sens*.

——1987: *On Meaning: Selected Writings in Semiotic Theory*.

PAUL INNES

Grice, Paul (1913–88) Until moving to America, Grice was a distinguished figure in postwar Oxford philosophy, whose main influence has been on the theories of meaning and conversation/communication. In his "Meaning" (Grice, 1989, essay 14), he crucially distinguished between two general kinds of meaning, "natural" and "nonnatural," illustrated respectively by "Those spots mean measles" and "That remark, 'He's a pig,' means that John is greedy." The second kind, which is the main concern of linguists and philosophers, is analyzed in terms of intention. Roughly, a speaker means that *P* by his remark if he openly intends his audience to believe that *P*, and on the basis of their recognition of that intention. (This is elaborated in Grice, 1989; essays 5–6.) A controversial consequence of this approach is that the meanings of sentences are functions of the intentions which speakers would generally have in uttering them.

Grice often stresses that utterances typically "implicate" (for example, intimate, suggest) something other than what they strictly say. His theory of conversation (Grice, 1989, essays 2–3) is designed to explain this. Conversation standardly proceeds on the assumption that the speakers are obeying various "maxims" (for example, "Be relevant," "Speak the truth." An important issue is whether these "maxims" are, as Grice seems to hold, cultural universals.) Hearers identify what is "implicated," typically by working out what speakers must be intending to convey, given that they are, despite appearances, obeying the "maxims." This suggests an interesting way of accounting for the identification of metaphorical and ironical meanings. Much recent work in pragmatics takes its lead from Grice's theory of conversation (for example, Sperber and Wilson, 1986). *See also* LANGUAGE, PHILOSOPHY OF; METAPHOR.

Reading
Grandy, R., and Warner, R. 1986: *Philosophical Grounds of Rationality*.
Grice, Paul 1989: *Studies in the Ways of Words*.
Sperber, D., and Wilson, D. 1986: *Relevance: Communication and Cognition*.

DAVID E. COOPER

group/grid Anthropologist Mary DOUGLAS's formula for classifying social relations. She is interested in how individuals are controlled by society. *Group* refers to a bounded social unit, whereas *grid* refers to the rules by which people relate to one another on an ego–centered basis. Strong grid consists of insulations between individuals which prevent free interaction. As insulation weakens, individuals have more freedom to relate to each other as they wish. She creates a fourfold table: strong grid, strong group; strong grid, weak group; weak group, weak grid; weak grid, strong group; then uses the various combinations for comparative analysis of CULTURES.

Reading
Douglas, Mary, T. 1970 (*1973*): *Natural Symbols: Explorations in Cosmology.*
——and Isherwood, B. 1979: *The World of Goods.*
JANET MACGAFFEY

Guattari, Félix *See* DELEUZE, GILLES, AND GUATTARI, FELIX

Gubar, Susan *See* GILBERT, SANDRA, AND GUBAR, SUSAN

gynocritics A term coined by Elaine SHOWALTER to refer to the study of women's writings in order to construct women's literary history and explore questions of literary influence, tradition, INTERTEXTUALITY, and the processes by which significance is produced both generally and particularly in subjugated female communities. Because gynocritics is committed to a method that is sociohistorical and materialist, but not necessarily Marxist, it makes extensive use of scholarship in women's history, psychology, and sociology, and has aggressively expanded the definition of literature to include diaries, journals, and other previously neglected but culturally important forms of writing. Early gynocritical manifestos and discussions of method are collected in Showalter (1985), and one of the fullest realizations of gynocritical theory remains Showalter's *A Literature of Their Own* (1977). In the 1970s, scholars working on women of color criticized gynocritics' racial biases, exclusions, and faulty generalizations, but through the 1970s and 1980s, most work on women writers of color can also be classified as gynocritical. One of gynocritics'

earliest projects (which remains ongoing) has been the recovery and reevaluation of a vast number of female-authored texts. Combined with similar projects in black and ethnic studies, this work has forced an extensive reconfiguration of the literary CANON since the mid-1970s. Gynocritics has produced numerous studies of individual authors, as well as literary histories for women writers of virtually every period; such studies often emphasize the relation between genre and GENDER, and increasingly, between genre, gender, RACE, CLASS, and nationality. Without always acknowledging it, earlier gynocritical work relied on a particular theory of mimesis: women writers apprehend objective reality and describe it directly in their TEXTS, rendering texts authentic mirrors of female subjectivity and records of female experience. Reading was generally construed as a transaction between women writers and readers united in the discovery of individual and collective female identity. For this, French feminists and other poststructuralists until the mid-1980s dismissed gynocritics as theoretically naive, criticizing gynocritics' failure to question the apparent transparency of language as a medium of representation (Moi, 1985). While gynocritics might have launched a more forceful defense of the humanist project (the fulfillment of which, after all, would entail revolutionary social change), since the late 1980s there has been extensive work synthesizing American and French feminist approaches, as well as eloquent defenses of the heterogeneity of feminist discourse, which have allowed feminist scholars to move beyond this acrimonious debate. Today, gynocritics tends to incorporate poststructural insights, and remains one of the most exciting and productive modes of scholarship.
See also FEMINIST CRITICISM; INTERTEXTUALITY; SHOWALTER, ELAINE.

Reading
Moi, Toril 1985: *Sexual/Textual Politics.*
Showalter, Elaine 1989: "A criticism of our own: autonomy and assimilation in Afro-American and feminist literary theory."
——1977: *A Literature of Their Own: British Women Novelists from Brontë to Lessing.*
——1933: "American gynocriticism."
——ed. 1985: *The New Feminist Criticism: Essays on Women, Literature, and Theory.*
Todd, Janet 1988: *Feminist Literary History.*
GLYNIS CARR

H

Habermas, Jürgen (1929–) German philosopher, sociologist, and critical thinker. He has been the most influential philosopher in Germany since the 1960s with frequent interventions as a social and political critic. In the 1990s his influence extended rapidly not only on the Continent, but also in the Anglo-Saxon academic world.

He has been a member of the FRANKFURT SCHOOL for Social Research and shares with it HEGELian and MARXist views of history, society, and its evolution. His CRITICAL THEORY is rooted in the spirit of the critical theory of the Frankfurt school, although it has been transformed and directed to the SYMBOLic forms of social interaction (language and communication). His early attempts to formulate a "critical social theory with practical intent," that is, a critical theory of modern capitalist society, initially focused on the critique of "scientism" (the positivist belief of sciences in themselves as the only category of possible knowledge) and the associated "technocratic consciousness" which imposes technocratic ideals on practical life.

Habermas never accepted the pessimism of the Frankfurt school's conception of "instrumental reason" (reason used entirely as an instrument within a "means–ends" rationality) prevailing in capitalist societies. He believed that reason had not been eclipsed in modern societies, but that it was still available in the form of an emancipatory interest. The critique of scientism could free his critical theory from positivist beliefs in pure theory and allow for a solution to the problem of connecting theory and its practical implementation, away from the instrumental solutions provided by the expert.

The search for epistemological foundations for his critical theory was pursued in *Knowledge and Human Interests* (1968). In it (drawing from PEIRCE, Dilthey, and FREUD), Habermas linked "knowledge" to three (a priori) cognitive interests: technical, practical, and emancipatory, corresponding respectively to the natural sciences, social sciences, and the critical science of PSYCHOANALYSIS. Psychoanalytic science (with its depth-hermeneutical

analysis and its ability for self-reflection) was considered to be an exemplary existing model of critique and emancipation, which could eventually provide the basic features for his critical social theory.

As in psychoanalysis, the idea of "distorted speech" is transported to societal forms in order to comprehend IDEOLOGY as "systematically distorted communication." Although Habermas never demarcated convincingly what could count as normal speech situation, the concept of ideology was removed and studied beyond its classical definition as false knowledge. He also contended that society could now be analyzed in terms of language, labor, and power (overcoming Marx's limitations, who had reduced the self-formation of the species exclusively to the category of labor). In order to locate distorted communication, he incorporated some areas of HERMENEUTICS into his critical theory. In a lengthy debate with GADAMER he defended his use of hermeneutics as a critical force in his theory, but he also gained invaluable insights for adopting hermeneutics in his later writings on social theory and communicative actions.

Criticizing the ideological mechanisms producing distorted communication in modern societies, Habermas proposed the concept of "ideal speech situation" (as an ideal of free and unconstrained communication) which could play the role of a normative conception.

The notion of "reconstructive sciences" was employed to indicate those scientific projects which employ a KANTian notion of reflection (by asking, for example, what are the necessary conditions for a specific human competence). In the 1970s he continued his reconstructive attempts in the linguistic field in order to provide a "universal pragmatics," that is, a theory of the universal features of human linguistic competences (basic structures and fundamental rules), which could clarify his notion of communication and the deviant case of systematically distorted communication. At the same time he worked on a theory of social evolution (in affinity to his Marxist–Hegelian heritage), as a "reconstruction of historical materialism." In this attempt social evolution can be understood as the development of learning capacities of the species as both development of moral insight and empirical knowledge referring to technological advances and mastery of nature.

In 1981, with the publication of his *Theory of Communicative Action*, Habermas moves further away from the PARADIGM of consciousness-centered reason to the paradigm of language (as speech). This shift is designed to provide his critical theory of society with new normative foundations, instead of the a priori postulations of his earlier work. In communication, by entering speech, where at least one speaker and one hearer are present, we do not simply utter sentences but we also simultaneously *relate* to the objective world, to other members in society, and to our inner private thoughts, feelings, and desires, by making claims in these three dimensions. In actual life we use language at a performative level. The validity of such claims (which Habermas distinguishes correspondingly between truth claims, claims of normative rightness, and claims to sincere expressions) can be decided upon the reasons and insights provided by the participants. Claims of this kind are open to criticism and validation. Disputed claims are treated in argumentation, and *agreement* can be reached without resorting to force.

According to Habermas, "communicative rationality" refers to our experience of unconstrained argumentative speech and its unifying consensus. This perspective originates in the function of language for social integration or the coordination of plans of different actors in social interaction. Communicative rationality ensures that our efforts are oriented toward intersubjective *understanding* and *agreement* without the use of force. As long as communicative rationality (aiming at consensual agreement) increases within a "communication community" we observe the expansion of unconstrained coordination of action and consensual resolution of conflicts (provided they are not beyond the bounds of cognitive approach). The rationality of everyday communicative practice uses argumentation as a "court of appeal." It continually excludes direct or strategic use of force.

His main hypothesis is that we live in a lifeworld in which we coordinate our actions through communication. It is with this coordination that the species maintains itself. Although modern societies are penetrated by cognitive–purposive rationality,

which results in *teleological actions*, the basic core which underlies all forms of community is communicative rationality. In this way Habermas is able to advance the claims of his social theory by providing a *universalistic* and thus *objective* bond as the foundation of every society. The strength of his paradigm of communicative rationality, as he agrees, depends upon the fruitfulness of research programs which are based on it.

The lifeworld guarantees the unity of the objective world and the intersubjectivity between its members (for action coordination), thus promoting the process of understanding and consensus. The lifeworld always shapes the background and remains implicit and precritical. The lifeworld carries with it cultural tradition and is essential for the socialization of the individual. Opposite to it operate social SYSTEMS, such as the economy and state administration. While the lifeworld is reproduced in terms of communicative rationality, instrumental action prevails in the systems. The imperatives of the system penetrate the lifeworld and, conversely, the systems depend on the accomplishments of the lifeworld (individual skills, mass loyalty). While MARX had held a very linear view between BASE AND SUPERSTRUCTURE, Habermas shows the interactive relation of lifeworld and social system. He calls "colonization of the lifeworld" the case when the intervention of the systems produces disturbances to lifeworld's reproduction. They are seen as *pathologies* and are manifested as loss of meaning, anomie, and personality disorder.

But who are the agents and the forms of protest in areas of social conflict today? According to Habermas, all protest movements issue from the colonization of the lifeworld, whenever it has been ruptured or is endangered by external systemic forces. All protest groups can be characterized as resistances to the tendencies of colonization of the lifeworld, and an emancipatory potential is visible in those which pursue new forms of social life in cooperation and community. The *decolonization* of the lifeworld does not dictate its isolation from all modernization. The more communicatively rationalized the lifeworld, the better the chance for developing institutionalized resistances which can limit the destructive function of systemic forces. The public sphere is the central place for agreements to be reached discursively.

Drawing from Weber, Habermas delineates a theory of MODERNITY (Habermas, 1981; English translation 1984). Modern society can be viewed as the outcome of the rationalization of the lifeworld and differentiation of social systems. Nevertheless, modernization of the lifeworld has resulted in its splitting into three value spheres (science, morality, and art). Habermas explains the "dark side" of modernity as the outcome of one-sided and distorted rationalizations. In modern societies the sphere of science has been given a privileged position, as scientific–technological rationality, over the spheres of art and morality. He believes that the "unfinished project of modernity" requires a new cultural tradition based on the reintegration of all these three spheres of life (Habermas, 1983b).

Concerning HERMENEUTICS, as in earlier projects, it plays a vital role in Habermas's approach. Communicative action is bound to interpretation. In the model of speaker/hearer which Habermas provides for the performative function of language, both participants stand in an interpretative relation. The need for hermeneutics extends into everyday life since its most ordinary features have become strange. Hermeneutic employment in the social sciences is the normal case. However, the use of hermeneutics should not be permitted to lead to any sort of relativism. The social sciences should be both *objective* and *theoretical*. This condition, Habermas believes, can be achieved by a "negotiated impartiality" gained from the interpreter's position.

In the sphere of ETHICS Habermas proposes his theory of DISCOURSE ethics which intends to replace the Kantian categorical imperative. He takes moral argumentation to be distinct from other forms of argumentation in the sense that it is not about the validity of truth claims; instead it aims at establishing whether human actions and the norms governing them are right.

The basic idea behind discourse ethics (which Habermas calls principle (D)) is that norms are valid only when they meet or could meet with the approval of all affected in their role as participants in a practical discourse. This principle indicates the procedural character of solving moral problems within argumentative boundaries.

However, the whole idea of a discourse ethics (especially the condition that a norm must be met with general approval) is not arbitrary, neither should it be taken simply as a suggestive gesture. It relies upon a more profound and universal principle (which Habermas borrows from MEAD). According to this principle, every *valid* norm must fulfill a certain condition: all affected by it can accept *freely* the *consequences* and its *side effects* which

can be anticipated to occur in its implementation for the satisfaction of everyone's interest. Habermas proposes this principle as a *rule of argumentation* (principle (U)), which strengthens and explicates his terms of discourse ethics.

He argues that principle (U) does not resemble the Kantian a priori fashioned categorical imperative; instead it is a transcendental-pragmatic consideration of universal and necessary presupposition of argumentation. That is, if we are bound to argumentation and its communicative dimensions for reaching agreement and understanding, then there is no other identifiable alternative to sustain such argumentation, except for principle (U). He believes that principle (U) offers a *universally* valid ethics, and does not depend on the reflections and intuitions of a particular CULTURE and epoch. On the other hand, his ethical theory does not provide solutions to moral issues; it only indicates the *procedural* steps for substantive matters to be resolved. Concrete moral dilemmas and moral conflicts should be solved within argumentation which participants enter freely and in an equal cooperative relationship for the search of truth. The only recognizable force here is "the force of better argument."

The historicity and high relativism of solutions of moral issues are evident if Habermas's propositions remain at this level. For him discourse ethics is basically a reconstructive science which, in anthropological terms, views the human agent equipped with moral competences, and morality as a safety device for the vulnerability of the individual in sociocultural forms of life. Such vulnerability arises from the tension which develops between the growth of the personal identity of the individual, and his simultaneous exposure and dependence upon interpersonal relations and social ties. Moralities are formed to protect both the individual (his dignity), and the web of intersubjective relations necessary for survival within the community. Thus the conceptions of *justice* (equal rights and respect for the individual) and *solidarity* (addressed to the well-being of the community) are formed.

Following Lawrence Kohlberg's theory of the development of moral consciousness, Habermas not only seeks confirmation for the scientific reconstruction of the moral competences of the individual, but he also envisages the (ambitious) program of the phylogenetic moral development of the species. In this course of construction, it could be shown that *universal* forms of moral judgment prevail, and that the structural differences between moralities could be attributed to different stages of moral capacity, thus avoiding cultural and historical relativism.

Using Kohlberg's theory of moral competences as background, Habermas suggests that entering discourse on the validity of a norm is similar to that of validating truth claims. Social norms are transformed into possibilities of regulation of life forms and can be accepted as valid or refuted as invalid. The upshot of his moral theory is that Habermas abandons the idea of moral truths as values, and reinstates them as learned knowledge and competences acquired in the social evolution of the species.

Undoubtedly, the breadth of Habermas's projects since the 1960s is enormous. His voice of critical resistance has been strongly anchored to the premise of communicative rationality. Not everyone, though, shares the same convictions. Those who believe that the employment of (unified) reason in social life (as the completion of the MODERNITY project) is the prime task today will find in Habermas's proposals a potent ally. Those who are skeptical and have observed the narratives of modernity fading away will find in Habermas a powerful opponent to test the strength of their arguments.

It is true that the weight of his hope lies with the social sciences, which can undertake the task of objective knowledge in reconstructive research programs. Philosophy has been seen to collaborate with the sciences, undertaking the task of developing a more advanced theory of rationality. For these reasons his theses are certain to be discussed by sociological, anthropological, and political disciplines, and partly in social and political philosophy. However, his theses on communicative rationality and particularly his latest attempts on discourse ethics are bound to attract considerable discussion in traditional departments of philosophy, as well as in literary and CULTURAL STUDIES.

It is also fair to him to mention the following. In his discourse ethics an uneasy tension of a twofold dichotomy develops. The reformulated Kantian categorical imperative (taken as a rule for entering argumentation) underlines the formalism of his theory. On the other hand, *substantive* issues cannot be met by his theory and are left to be solved by the (hopefully developed) cognitive moral capacities of the participants in argumentation. The balance here is critical and we may ask whether we are in a better position to solve substantive moral issues than before.

Habermas continually attempts to retain together the historical (contingent) and the universal (as is the case with his reconstructive sciences). He is caught in an unresolved contradictory position, although it has also become his motor for further reformulations and research projects.

Modernity is presented as a *unique* historical project for the human species, since further rationalization of the lifeworld based on communicative rationality can guarantee the promise of ENLIGHTENMENT: a life informed by reason. According to Habermas there is no other clear alternative. The Hegelian inbuilt teleology of this model is apparent. One can appreciate the context of LYOTARD's criticism against a unified goal of history and a totalizing subject (integrating the three spheres of life) inherent in Habermas's project (see Lyotard, 1979).

His model of communicative action juxtaposing speaker and bearer in conversation appears as an "innocent" exchange of statements, underlined by the aim of agreement and understanding. In such a discourse, no forces, no power relations, no antagonisms enter, and, to many, this basic hypothesis for a reconstructive science of communicative action would appear as a non-pragmatic conception, but rather as an ideal, deontological, and attractive proposition.

Habermas's conception of human life, although successfully embedded in the lifeworld, is dictated by sociological, scientific, universal principles. This conception cannot exhaust the function of language (for example, metaphoric speech, poetic language), rich cultural histories, or reconstruct the history of the human species based solely on cognitive processes and developmental stages of learned capacities. His views (notwithstanding their dynamic explanatory force and ability to guide research programs) register as a *restricted* view of human history. A reflective acquaintance with literature, philosophy, and cultural studies could easily show that life forms are many times richer, yet intrinsically more dominated, than the premises of Habermas's theory would allow.

See also COMMUNICATIVE ACTION; CRITICAL THEORY.

Reading
Bernstein, R.J., ed. 1985: *Habermas and Modernity.*
Dews, P., ed. 1986: *Autonomy and Solidarity: Interviews with Jürgen Habermas.*
Habermas, J. 1962 (*1989*): *The Structural Transformation of the Public Sphere: An Inquiry into a Category of Bourgeois Society.*
——1981 (*1987*): *The Theory of Communicative Action.*

——1983a (*1992*): *Moral Consciousness and Communicative Rationality*.
Holub, R.C. 1991: *Jürgen Habermas: Critic in the Public Sphere*.
McCarthy, T. 1984: *The Critical Theory of Jürgen Habermas*.
Rassmussen, D.M. 1990: *Reading Habermas*.
Roderick, R. 1986: *Habermas and the Foundations of Critical Theory*.
Teigas, D. 1995: *Knowledge and Hermeneutic Understanding: A Study of the Habermas–Gadamer Debate*.

DEMETRIUS TEIGAS

Hall, Stuart (1932–) British sociologist/cultural theorist. Hall's contribution to the field of British cultural studies is far-reaching and intertwined with the histories of the CENTRE FOR CONTEMPORARY CULTURAL STUDIES at the University of Birmingham (where he was the director during the 1970s, as well as being an editor of the *New Left Review* from 1957 to 1961), and the trajectory of the NEW LEFT in Britain. One genealogy of CULTURAL STUDIES locates itself in the debate between the socialist HUMANISM of WILLIAMS, HOGGART, and THOMPSON and traditional Marxist approaches to contemporary cultural politics. British cultural studies emerges as a dialogue between humanistic MARXISM, which Hall call "culturalism," and the antihumanism of ALTHUSSER'S structural Marxism through a new reading of Antonio GRAMSCI (see Grossberg, 1989, p. 119).

As one of the leading black intellectuals in postwar Britain, Hall's extensive writings have emerged out of a political and intellectual commitment of Marxism to offer a materialist theory of IDEOLOGY and DISCOURSE that draws upon PSYCHOANALYSIS and DECONSTRUCTION. As a major theorist of the politics of contemporary British CULTURE and society, Hall's collaborations with different groups as well as his own contributions have produced some of the most influential theories of the nature of cultural and historical specificity. While there were numerous influences, political struggles, questions, and forms of collective work that shaped and extended Hall's writings beyond the confines of traditional left inquiry, his own work reflects the complex ways in which RACE intersects with GENDER and CLASS relations in the larger intellectual formation of British Marxism.

Focusing on the ideological functions of mass media, POPULAR CULTURE, consumption, and visual pleasure within various SUBCULTURES as well as within dominant structures of power during the 1970s and 1980s, Hall's work opened different avenues of inquiry into violence, terror, the nature of SUBJECT formation, concepts such as Eurocentrism and the West, and the limits of rationalist ideology in Margaret Thatcher's Britain (Hall et al., 1978). Hall's writings about political processes, identity politics, and the problems of the subject have been very influential for contemporary cultural studies, film theory, theories of spectatorship, and black theory.

See also BLACK CULTURAL STUDIES; DIASPORA; HYBRIDITY.

Reading
Centre for Contemporary Cultural Studies, 1982: *The Empire Strikes Back*.
Grossberg, L. 1989: "The formation(s) of cultural studies."
Hall, S. 1980c: "Cultural studies: two paradigms."
——1981: "Notes on deconstructing the popular."
——1982: "The rediscovery of ideology: return of the repressed in media studies."
——1985a: "Signification, representation, ideology: Althusser and the post-structuralist debates."
——1985b: "The toad in the garden: Thatcherism amongst the theorists."
——et al. 1978: *Policing the Crisis*.
——Hobson, D., Lowe, A., and Willis, P., eds 1980: *Culture, Media, Language*.
——and Jefferson, T., eds 1976: *Resistance through Rituals*.

MAY JOSEPH

Harris, Zellig (1915–92) American linguist. Based at the University of Pennsylvania, though he spent much of his time in Israel, Harris is usually cited nowadays for three things. First, his 1951 book *Methods in Structural Linguistics* is seen as the brilliant swan song of American structuralist linguistics (see LANGUAGE THEORIES). Second, he introduced Chomsky to linguistics (see CHOMSKY, Noam), and his use of the term TRANSFORMATION prefigured its use in Chomsky's work. Third, he coined the term "DISCOURSE analysis", and attempted to extend structuralist techniques to longer stretches of language (Harris, 1952).

Harris is often dismissed as being of historical interest. Structuralist linguistics is taken as dead and buried, Chomsky now rules OK, and discourse analysis uses completely different methods from those pioneered by Harris. In fact, Harris continued to produce important and original work until quite recently (cf. Harris, 1982). Unfortunately, his work ignores virtually everything in the field except research by himself and his close colleagues.

The unfamiliar assumptions and terminology in his work have in turn meant that everyone else in the field has tended to ignore Harris. Anyone who does not think this is a pity should read Harris's masterly paper on Sapir (Harris, 1972), clearly the work of an outstanding mind (see SAPIR, Edward).

Reading
Harris, Z. 1951: *Methods in structural linguistics.*
——1951 *(1972)*: "Review of *Selected Writings* by Edward Sapir."
——1952: "Discourse analysis."
——1982: *A Grammar of English on Mathematical Principles.*
RAPHAEL SALKIE

Hassan, Ihab (1925–) Ihab Hassan is among the most important of the critics who announced and promoted the emergence of POSTMODERNISM in literature. The first significant work of this kind was his *The Dismemberment of Orpheus: Toward a Postmodern Literature* (1971) *(1982)*, in which he argued that literary postmodernism is a continuation and intensification of the "will to unmaking" to be found in modernist artists and writers. Later works such as *Paracriticisms* (1975) and *The Right Promethean Fire* (1980) engage with more general issues in contemporary CULTURE, such as the role of science in a postmodern age, and, drawing eclectically on a wide range of disciplines and authorities, attempt to forge a "multivocal" style of critical writing, employing dialogue, collage, and typographical invention to match the postmodernist condition that is their subject. His *The Postmodern Turn* (1987) gathers together essays on postmodernism written from 1967 to 1987.

Reading
Connor, Steven 1989: *Postmodernist Culture: An Introduction to Theories of the Contemporary.*
Hassan, Ihab 1971 *(1982)*: *The Dismemberment of Orpheus: Toward a Postmodern Literature.*
——1975: *Paracriticisms: Seven Speculations of the Times.*
——1980: *The Right Promethean Fire: Imagination, Science, and Cultural Change.*
——1987: *The Postmodern Turn: Essays in Postmodern Theory and Culture.*
Klinkowitz, Jerome 1988: *Rosenberg, Barthes, Hassan: The Postmodern Habit of Thought.*
STEVEN CONNOR

Hegel, Georg Wilhelm Friedrich (1770–1831) German philosopher. In 1818 Hegel was called to a chair in philosophy in Berlin in order to quell the revolutionary spirits of students inspired by the French Revolution. In one of the ironies of history, which Hegel made it his life work to discern, a more "revolutionary" philosopher could hardly have been found to quash a revolution. It is not at all implausible to claim that Hegel was the most influential philosopher in world history. If nothing else, his great critic, Karl MARX, created an IDEOLOGY from HEGELIANISM that convulsed the entire world for more than a century.

Hegel was the first philosopher to write a work entitled "philosophy of history" and the core of his genius lies in the discovery of history as a category for philosophical thought. The "discovery" of history constituted a radical break with virtually the whole of the Western philosophical tradition. Not only has philosophy never been quite the same since, but also Hegel's historical "method" deeply influenced everything from theology to basic conceptions of political and social life.

Philosophy – and almost all other intellectual efforts prior to Hegel – was based on the model of natural science. True knowledge has traditionally been associated with "the universal." In biology, the investigator is not interested in the particular individual at hand, but in the universal character of the species. In moral philosophy, one is interested in "the nature of humanity," not John Smith (or Pocahontas) as a universal standard for ethical behavior. Hegel insisted that the real was historical; the supposed universal truth asserted, the general nature discovered, was a function of some specific historical CULTURE.

By emphasizing the historical character of truth, Hegel became the spiritual father of such modern movements as EXISTENTIALISM and DECONSTRUCTION. Existentialism with its insistence that "existence precedes essence" (SARTRE) asserts that morality must be "created" from the particular life of the historical individual since there is no moral essence which intervenes. Deconstruction revels in what Jacques DERRIDA calls the "dance of innumerable choreographies," the historically rooted nature of various beliefs and values.

Hegel's notion of history is in the long run opposed to the use made of it by the aforementioned contemporary philosophies. For Hegel, history is not just a lively dance of particulars; it is somehow a connected and "progressive" story. History (and thought) moves by a "dialectic" through a series of accomplishments, ALIENATIONS, and higher-level reconciliations: thesis, antithesis, and synthesis in his technical terminology. MARX seized upon the dialectic and proclaimed that world history was moving inevitably through this process of alienation and reconciliation toward a communist society.

An example of simplified Marxist dialectic may illustrate the process. The initial period of human artifice is in "manufacture," literally *hand*-making (*Communist Manifesto*, I). At that stage of production, the worker and his work are one. The hand-made object reflects the special skill and character of the worker. With the advent of the machine – which increases the productivity of the worker – the worker is "alienated" from his product. The machine-made product does not reflect the worker's person. The worker does not master the product, the product rushing down the assembly line masters the worker. Thus in an effort to increase the power of the worker through the use of mechanism, we have in fact lessened the "power" of the worker by enslaving him to the machine. We unknowingly create the antithesis of the original thesis, the alienation of the original accomplishment.

Analysis of "alienation" *à la* Hegelian dialectic is widely practiced, for example, by "pop" psychological and sociological critics, without recognizing the patrimony of the concept. It is the ultimate step in the dialectic that has been the most controversial: the reconciliation or synthesis of thesis and antithesis "on a higher level." In the Marxist interpretation, this would be the reconciliation of the worker with the product when the workers own the (machine) means of production. While critics of modern society have been all too conscious of a variety of alienations, most solutions have been "regressive," not "progressive". In the *Communist Manifesto*, Marx and Engels excoriated various romantic utopians of the day who wished to return to Gothic visions, the life of simple artisans and sturdy yeoman farmers. History moves forward inexorably and one cannot return to earlier and simpler stages of life.

The French Revolution was yet another attempt to solve the alienation of human history – an alienation which Hegel sees as the origin and engine of historical existence. The revolution did not seek to regress in history, but to transcend history altogether. It was a revolution based on reason and the rights of man, but, for Hegel, human society cannot be based on a universalist concept of humanity discovered by some transcending scientific reason. Hegel's view that one cannot "hurry history" made him the obvious choice for a chair

in "counterrevolutionary" philosophy. At the same time, however, his allegiance to historical dialectic projects human history as a series of radical reversals: the secret alienation within every reconciliation drives societies to dissolution and revolt.

While Hegel's sense of dynamic history seems everywhere evident in the intellectual methods of the contemporary world, his ultimate "solution" appears everywhere rejected. Hegel envisioned an "end of history," some final synthesis not subject to further radical reversal. The history of Hegelianism can be divided more or less along the lines of those who accepted the solution and denied the method or accepted the method and denied the solution. In the nineteenth century, British idealists, as represented by F.H. Bradley, bypassed the historical development but accepted the "logical" structure of the dialectic. Experience was deeply conflicted, mere appearance; reality, in contrast, lies on the other side of human conception. Hegel's work on "logic" was their fundamental text. With the rejection of idealism at the beginning of the twentieth century as EMPIRICISM and the reality of experience were reasserted, it seemed as if Hegelianism was thoroughly discredited and abandoned. The French – notably Jean Hyppolite, who learned German by translating the *Phenomenology of Mind*! – seized on the earlier works of Hegel in order to emphasize the historical struggle embedded in the master's convoluted description of the human mind (*Geist*, spirit). The historical Hegel reemerged and became the subject of extensive study.

Finally, "phenomenological" method became a watchword among German philosophers like Husserl and HEIDEGGER, but without the dialectical "progress" characteristic of Hegel's original formulation. Husserl's phenomenology relates more to the epistemological tradition of Descartes, while Heidegger's "quest for being" has a meditative and "static" quality incommensurate with the revolutionary *agon* embedded in Hegel's struggle of the human spirit.

Despite the apparent rejection of the Marxist "end-of-history" scenario, there have been put forward deep arguments that Hegel was fundamentally correct: history has in some sense come to an end. (Alexandre Kojève is the most penetrating of the commentators on this issue. His American translators and "disciples," Alan Bloom and Leo Straus, removed residual MARXISM from Kojève and gave currency to "end-of-history" analysis for American readers.) For Hegel, history is a special form of human consciousness. Not all periods of the past have used historical thinking to understand their world. History emerges only when individuals come to a realization of their basic freedom. Only free individuals can make (or think) history. The social conditions under which a recognition of freedom first came forward were, however, politically oppressive. In the modern world there appears to be a universal recognition of individual freedom (the rise of "democracies"). At that point, social change continues but the categories of change are no longer historical. The basic struggle to recognize individuals is now finished, so whatever oppositions and conflicts occur, they are the working out of a historical reality already achieved.

Reading
Hyppolite, J. 1974: *Genesis and Structure of Hegel's Phenomenology of Spirit.*
Kojève, A. 1947 (*1977*): *Introduction to the Reading of Hegel.*
O'Brien, G.D. 1975: *Hegel on Reason and History.*
Taylor, C. 1975: *Hegel.*

G. DENNIS O'BRIEN

Hegelianism Broadly defines various movements influenced by the philosopher HEGEL. Traditionally Hegelianism was split between the so-called "right" and "left" Hegelians. Right Hegelians affirmed the anti-transcendent direction of Hegel's work: the notion that one must wait out historical development and not attempt to impose some rational utopia on human society. Left Hegelians, on the other hand, were impressed with the radical ALIENATIONS and disruptions which marked Hegel's view of history; they postulated inevitable revolutions, perhaps a final revolution which would solve the conflicts of human society.

G. DENNIS O'BRIEN

hegemony Derived from the Greek word *hegemōn* (leader, commander, guide, ruler), hegemony has generally been used (by both Marxist and non-Marxist thinkers) to refer to either political domination or leadership. It acquires a more specific import in the work of Antonio GRAMSCI, who, developing MARX's own insights, argues that the economic and political ascendancy of a given CLASS is organically connected with a preparatory achievement of cultural and intellectual hegemony. The

intellectuals sympathetic to this class have an organizational function: to articulate the world view of the class, thereby giving it a unity and consciousness of its aims; to help structure social institutions in accordance with these aims; and to foster an environment of *consent* to the ideas of the class. Taking cognizance of this, a socialist revolution must have its path prepared by its own core of intellectuals who, by galvanizing the working masses into a politically self-conscious agency and working toward institutional and individual acceptance of its ideas, develop an alternative hegemony (rather than relying on coercion by the state). The notion of hegemony thus embodies a more dialectical connection between superstructure and economic base than that allowed by a deterministic reading of Marx, which sees historical change and revolution as generated necessarily by developments at the economic level.

See also ALTHUSSER, LOUIS; GRAMSCI, ANTONIO; MARX, KARL.

Reading
Femia, J.V. 1981: *Gramsci's Political Thought: Hegemony, Consciousness and the Revolutionary Process.*
Fontana, B. 1993: *Hegemony and Power.*
Gramsci, A. 1971: *Selections from Prison Notebooks.*

M.A.R. HABIB

Heidegger, Martin (1889–1976) A student of Husserl's, whose chair at Freiburg he was to inherit, Heidegger is increasingly perceived, with WITTGENSTEIN, as one of the two most influential philosophers of the twentieth century. Most movements in European thought since – EXISTENTIALISM, HERMENEUTICS, POSTSTRUCTURALISM, for instance – bear the mark of his thinking, as do much contemporary theology, environmental philosophy, and "deconstructionist" LITERARY CRITICISM.

As with Wittgenstein, it is necessary to distinguish between an "early" and a "later" Heidegger, before and after his so-called turn (*Kehre*) during the 1930s. Heidegger's contribution, and the effect of his "turn," are best understood through three related themes which, despite radical modulation, remain constant throughout his voluminous writings and lectures. Much of Heidegger's power stems from the intriguing interweaving, within these themes, of philosophical abstraction and concrete critique of the modern condition.

The first theme is that, despite its usual suppression, the central philosophy issue is "the question of being." Being is neither the sum total of particular beings, nor their common property, nor a special kind of being (God, say), but that through which all beings are made possible. In the early *Being and Time* of 1927, Heidegger claims that we are brought to a sense of being through, ironically, those "moods" like *Angst* when particular beings fade into insignificance or "nothingness." Heidegger's approach is to delineate various modes of being through phenomenological reflection on the experiences of those creatures, ourselves, whose own being is an "issue" for them. But the task of moving from this to a characterization of being as such was left uncompleted, the later explanation being that the approach had been too anthropocentric, too "humanistic" (1978, *V*). Indeed, Heidegger comes to see the history of Western metaphysics – of Western civilization, in fact – as the story of a "forgetfulness of being" due to the hubristic, though pardonable, attempt to represent and measure reality through human constructs. The final, "nihilistic" chapter of the story is NIETZSCHE's denial of being in favor of a "becoming," identified with the strivings of an anthropomorphically conceived "will to power." Hubris reaches its apogee in the *Übermensch*. What makes the "forgetfulness of being" pardonable is that responsibility for it rests with being itself. Heidegger now portrays being as a "presencing" which lurks concealed behind the beings which it has allowed to become present for us, and which we then submit to our representational schemes.

The second persistent theme is the uniqueness of human existence, *Dasein* ("being-there"). A main target in *Being and Time* are those scientific and philosophical views, like those of Descartes, in which humans are treated as objects alongside other physical objects, distinguished primarily by their also being SUBJECTS of perception. This view, argues Heidegger, misconstrues both *Dasein* and the character of things in the world. These latter are not, in the first instance, encountered as mere perceptual objects or material substance, but as "equipment" and "ready-to-hand": that is, as items which owe their identities to the places they occupy within such human activities as farming. Regarding a plough, or indeed a tree, as a physical substance is a secondary, derivative way of encountering things. *Dasein*, meanwhile, is no "ego–object," like Descartes's *cogito*, but intentional activity, a "project." Always "ahead of itself," it is intelligible only through its future oriented engagement with the world, not

through some set of intrinsic causal properties. Since the world is intelligible only through this human engagement or "care" (*Sorge*), it follows that the relation between world and *Dasein* is not contingent and causal. Neither is even thinkable without the other. In the later writings, the rather Promethean emphasis on man as an activity diminishes, his uniqueness now being due to a special "destiny" as the "shepherd of Being." "Being-there" is no longer being "out there," engaged in the world, but being the "there," the "clearing," where being "presences." Being still requires man, no longer because things only have their "equipmental" identities within the field of human "care," but because, to realize its essence as presencing, there must be an audience for what is made present. (In some very late articles, Being and man are depicted as the mutually dependent dispensations of a mysterious "Event" (*Ereignis*, 1972)).

The final theme is that human existence, at least in modernity, is "out of tune" with its true essence. In *Being and Time*, *Dasein* is said to live, for the most part, "inauthentically." Absorbed in particular objects and pursuits, "tranquilized" in the conventional ways of the anonymous "Them" (*Das Man*), reiterating the clichés of the day in "idle chatter," people rarely, if ever, summon themselves to that "resoluteness" which would authentically register their status as individual sources of meaning and "care." Authentic individuality, nevertheless, is possible only for people infused with the traditions of a genuine community. Heidegger's belief that National Socialism would realize an ideal of tradition and community helps explain his temporary allegiance to the NSDAP. (The Party facilitated his election as Rector of Freiburg University in 1923.)

Another reason for the Nazi affiliation was what Heidegger saw as the movement's agrarian resistance to industrialization and technology, for his own hostility toward these tendencies was soon to inform most of his later work. The technological attitude, indeed, now becomes for Heidegger the primary manifestation of man's ALIENATION from his true nature. Man's essential "destiny" is to "shepherd" being, to "let being be." However, technology, as the will to power in action, is the culmination of the "forgetfulness of being." It orders the world to human material requirements, putting everything "on tap" as "standing reserve" (*Bestand*), without regard for the intrinsic natures of rivers, fields, animals, or whatever (1978, *VII*).

For "salvation" from the technological stance, Heidegger turns increasingly toward ART. A painting, like Van Gogh's of the peasant's shoes, brings out and recalls us to the integrity of things, displaying their proper place in relation to the earth, to ourselves, and even to the gods (1978, *IV*). But, above all, it is the poets, like Hölderlin and Trakl, who can reinaugurate our atrophied sense of being. Poetic language is the "house of being." By patiently "listening to the call of being," the poet may then give human voice to what is intimated; and we, in our turn, listening to the poet, may then accommodate to the "command of Being" and fulfill our "destiny" as "shepherds" (1971). (Few will demur from George Steiner's remark that Heidegger reads poetry like no one else (Steiner, 1979).)

The mystical tone in these later writings is unmistakable. (Reading a book on Zen, Heidegger apparently remarked that here was what he had been striving to express for years.) Admirers of *Being and Time* may, like Sartre, find this tone unappealing. Those to whom it does appeal may endorse Heidegger's own opinion of *Being and Time* as a work still in thrall to a metaphysical tradition whose overthrow would, quite literally, be our salvation in this "destitute age."
See also EXISTENTIALISM; PHENOMENOLOGY.

Reading
Guignon, G., ed. 1993: *The Cambridge Companion to Heidegger.*
Heidegger, Martin 1927 (*1980*): *Being and Time.*
——1971: *Poetry, Language, Thought.*
——1972: *On Time and Being.*
——1978: *Basic Writings.*
Marx, Werner 1971: *Heidegger and the Tradition.*
Murray, M., ed. 1978: *Heidegger and Modern Philosophy.*
Steiner, George 1960 (*1977*): *Heidegger.*
DAVID E. COOPER

hermeneutics The art or technique of interpretation. The history of hermeneutics goes back to the ancient Greeks. The name was (via a probably false etymology) thought of as deriving from that of the messenger god Hermes. The development of a defined area of modern theory termed hermeneutics out of the practice of scriptural interpretation was predominantly the work of Friedrich Schleiermacher (1768–1834), Wilhelm Dilthey (1833–1911), Martin HEIDEGGER (1889–1976), and Hans-Georg GADAMER (1900–). In recent theory hermeneutics has often been regarded as an ap-

proach to TEXTS that is no longer methodologically defensible. Poststructuralism sees itself as renouncing hermeneutics' metaphysical goal of finding the text's original meaning. Jacques DERRIDA contrasts "two interpretations of interpretation": one – hermeneutics – "seeks to decipher, dreams of deciphering a truth or an origin that escapes the play and the order of the sign, and lives the necessity of interpretation like an exile"; the other – a deconstructive conception informed by NIETZSCHE's claim that truth is the repressive reduction of the infinite diversity of particular intuitions to forms of identity – "affirms play and tries to go beyond man and humanism" (Derrida, 1967b, p. 427). Meaning for Derrida is not a stable origin prior to the signifier, or a goal beyond it, but is dependent upon the inherently unstable signifier. However, this polemical contrast of hermeneutics and DECONSTRUCTION obscures the complexity of the question of interpretation in the history of modern hermeneutics.

Hermeneutics has nearly always involved a tension between the idea that the interpreting SUBJECT should surrender to the transformative power of the text and the idea that the meaning of a TEXT can only emerge via the creative initiatives of its interpreters. The former notion has a long history in various traditions of theology. The latter notion emerges most clearly in the Romantic movement, where it derives from Fichte's radicalization of KANT's insight into the role of the spontaneity of the subject in the constitution of a knowable world (see Bowie, 1990, chapter 3). Many of the debates over hermeneutics can be seen as playing out some version of this tension, which is also fundamental to twentieth-century philosophy. Gottlob FREGE and the tradition of analytical philosophy that develops from his work see meaning, for example, as determined by the medium of communication rather than by the consciousness of the individual subject. Recent directions in literary theory and European philosophy see the role of the subject in the understanding of texts as subverted by the subject's failure to be present to itself, because of the incursion of language, in the form of "tradition" (Gadamer), *différance* (Derrida), or the "symbolic order" (LACAN), into the very structure of subjectivity. Does meaning, then, derive from the text or from its reception? Is the interpreter subject to language or master of it? Such questions go to the heart of modern philosophy.

Kant's problems with the question of judgment are central to the development of modern hermeneutics. In the *Critique of Pure Reason* (1781) Kant saw judgment as the "capacity to subsume under rules." He realizes, though, that there cannot be rules for the application of the rule to the particular case, for this would lead to an infinite regress. Judgment must therefore depend upon the prior "schematizing" capacity of the understanding, which gives an initial coherence to experience before it can be subsumed into judgments (see Bell, 1987). Kant distinguishes in the *Critique of Judgment* between judgments of particulars based on a preexisting general rule ("determinant judgments") and those based on trying to establish a rule in relation to the particular ("reflective judgments"). This distinction points to Friedrich Ast's idea of the "hermeneutic circle" (1808), in which the parts of the text to be understood depend on the understanding of the whole, and vice versa. The fact that Kant's distinction cannot ultimately be sustained is at the root of the development of both Schleiermacher's and subsequent hermeneutics. Schleiermacher shows that even in the case of a determinant judgment the application depends upon a prior contextual understanding which cannot be derived from a rule. The resistance of interpretation to any codification in the form of rules is essential to the varying versions of modern hermeneutics, and had, until the advent of W.V. QUINE's, Donald DAVIDSON's, and Hilary PUTNAM's "holism", most clearly distinguished hermeneutic accounts of meaning from accounts of semantics in analytical philosophy.

According to Gadamer's history of hermeneutics, however, Schleiermacher and then Dilthey reinforce the subjectivist aspect brought into philosophy by Kant's epistemology and AESTHETICS. This subjectivism is supposedly evident in the notion of *Einfühlung*, "empathy" with the producer of the text by its interpreter. Schleiermacher himself, though, never uses the word *Einfühlung*, and what he means by "divination," the word he does use, is what children do when they learn language on the basis of having no prior rules, and what we do in making judgments despite the lack of determining rules of application (see Frank, 1977; Bowie, 1990, chapter 6). Gadamer's argument also ignores the role of J.G. Hamann's linguistic critique of Kant in 1784 in the development of Romantic thought (see Bowie, 1990, chapter 6).

The most influential aspect of the work of Dilthey is really his distinction between understanding, *Verstehen*, which is characteristic of the human sciences, and explanation, *Erklären*, which defines the natural sciences. The questioning of this distinction in this century has led to the revaluation of hermeneutics in contemporary theory. The defensive attitude evident in Dilthey's attempt to raise the historical claims of the human sciences to the level of positive knowledge of the natural sciences was already potentially undermined by Nietzsche's doctrine of "perspectivism" in his work in the 1880s. For Nietzsche "interpretation" becomes the fundamental manner in which the "will to power" functions, and is therefore the basis of all forms in the manifest world: "The will to power *interprets*: in the constitution of an organ it is a question of an interpretation" (Nietzsche, 1980, vol. 12, p. 139). The will to power's "self-interpretation" in the form of determinate manifestations, from inanimate objects, to organisms, to signifiers, is actually a version of the Romantic notion, present in the work of Schleiermacher, Friedrich Schlegel, and Novalis, and developed in aspects of the Schelling's critique of HEGEL, that the absolute cannot be grasped from within the world of articulable knowledge (see Frank, 1984, (*1989*); Bowie, 1990, chapter 8). In Nietzsche's version of this position, the "will to power" becomes the self-interpreting ground of the finite manifest world. This ground can never appear as itself (which means, of course, that even giving it a name like the "will to power" is a problem) and must constantly interpret itself by becoming finite, thereby failing to be present as itself.

It is from conceptions of this nature, which reject the idea of truth in language as correspondence to reality, that the reformulation of the "hermeneutic circle" in the work of Heidegger develops. Given the structural impossibility of thought ever being able to encompass its own relationship to its ground, Heidegger regards the circularity of self-interpretation as inescapable. Interpretation is fundamental to being *in* the world, and cannot be understood from an extramundane position. Any interpretation, including explanation in the natural sciences, depends upon the fact that what is interpreted must *already* be understood or "disclosed" for it to be put into question at all. As such: "The decisive factor is not to get out of the circle but to get into it in the right way (Heidegger, 1927 (*1980*), p. 153). As opposed to being a transcendental SUBJECT confronted with a world of alien objects that it must interpret, *Dasein* is always already situated in an interpreted world. This world is constituted by the hermeneutic "as-structure of understanding" that precedes the "apophantic 'as' of the proposition" (ibid., p. 158). Heidegger's early writings thus echo the stress on prepredicative understanding present in Schleiermacher's appropriation of Kant's "schema," as well as carrying on the refusal in German idealism and Romanticism to conceive of the subject as separate from the object world.

For Heidegger *Dasein* is that being that can relate to its own being. As such it "ex-ists" in a way that other beings (*Seiendes*) do not. Heidegger's reformulation of hermeneutics is part of his attempted "destruction" of ontology in the tradition of Western metaphysics. "Being" (*Sein*) for Heidegger cannot be understood as objective existence in relation to the knowing subject. The notion of the presence of the object to the subject's direct intuition differs from the affirmation or negation of an (already interpreted) state of affairs in a proposition. The ontological difference of beings (*Seiendes*) and being (*Sein*) can best be understood as the difference between the merely contingent (and uncommunicable) existence of objects for individual consciousness and the truth about the world of interpreted states of affairs that is revealed in the moving structure of understanding something *as* something that is articulated in language (see Manfred Frank in Wood, 1992, pp. 218–34, and Tugendhat, 1992, pp. 57–65 and 108–35). The question of being for Heidegger is, then, inseparable from language. Heidegger's major contribution to hermeneutics is his identification of a tension between a hermeneutic conception of truth as the happening of "world disclosure" that we experience, for example, when art reveals the world in ways that cannot be propositionally stated, and the notion of truth as warranted assertability in propositions. The effects of such a tension can be seen in the new developments in the history of science associated with Thomas KUHN, Michel FOUCAULT, and others, as well as in the work of "postanalytical" philosophers like Richard RORTY and, in his recent work, Hilary Putnam, where the role of hermeneutic experience even in the natural sciences is seen as vital.

The most influential development of Heidegger's ideas has been the work of his pupil Gadamer. In *Truth and Method* Gadamer investigates the tension between a hermeneutic understanding of truth as "disclosure," which he sees in the continuing relevance of the great works of Western art, and the "method" of the natural sciences. In line with both Nietzsche's and Heidegger's anti-subjectivism, as well as with the Lutheran notion of the transformative power of the text, Gadamer insists on the fact that the subject is always already located in language and tradition: "Being that can be understood is language" (Gadamer, 1975, p. 450). Language itself is *ichlos* ("self-less"); understanding is the movement of the individual into the happening of intersubjective "tradition." The power of Gadamer's position lies in its valorization of the open encounter with the "OTHER," whether simply as other people, great ART, or other CULTURES, which is able to transform the subject who engages with that other. He sees the alternative to this open encounter as the objectification of what is to be understood in the manner of the objectifications of natural science. The power of his position is, however, itself bought at the expense of a series of REIFICATIONS of the kind suggested in the later Heidegger's notion that "Language speaks. Man speaks to the extent to which he corresponds to language" (Heidegger, 1959, pp. 32–3), or in Derrida's assertion that the subject is an "effect" of the "general text" (Derrida, 1972a, p. 122). Gadamer's position is questionable because new revelations and understandings of being are effectively seen as the work of language itself, rather than of its individual speakers. While the acceptance of new revelations must take place via linguistic agreement, this is no explanation of the genesis of such new revelation, which cannot derive from language itself.

It is against this tendency to reification in the hermeneutic tradition deriving from Heidegger, as well as in poststructuralism and analytical philosophy, that the work of Manfred Frank is directed. For Frank the reification characteristic of so much twentieth-century theory of language is a result of taking one approach to subjectivity in Western philosophy as the only possible approach. Following the German Romantics and SARTRE, Frank does not see the subject as master of language, but avoids the reification of locating meaning in the code rather than in those who understand and articulate via the code. The critique of the Cartesian "PARADIGM of subjectivity," in which an isolated subject tries to cross the gap between self and not-self, is common to thinkers as diverse as Heidegger, Ryle, and HABERMAS. Such a subject must necessarily fail to cross the gap between the self and its other. However, the question remains, as Frank suggests, as to whether a paradigm in which this gap is always already crossed via the intersubjective medium of language does not repress the irreducible individuality of each language user, which Schleiermacher saw as the root of the need for the art of interpretation. Joel Weinsheimer exemplifies the reification that Frank opposes when he claims of Gadamer's view of interpretation: "To understand is to interpret, to *say* what one understands, or more precisely, to participate in the event in which the understood interprets itself in language" (Weinsheimer, 1991, p. 119). Gadamer suggests: "Every word makes the whole of the language to which it belongs resonate, and makes the whole world view that it is based on appear" (Gadamer, 1975, p. 434). As such Gadamer retains an essentially Hegelian conception of a world which reflects itself in language, in the form of the "self-interpretation of being." This makes language into an equivalent of Hegel's *Geist*, in that the individual subject only makes sense to the extent that its meanings are part of an overall process, in which the part is a self-reflection of the whole. How, though, can this be *known*? Who is seeing the relationship between reflecter and reflected, language and being? Without an external third viewpoint one has no right to make assertions about the identity of language and being that eliminate the individual subject from that identity. Gadamer's putting hermeneutics on the agenda of both European and analytical philosophy is, then, a major achievement, but the future of hermeneutics will depend upon finding ways of restoring a chastened but still active subject to the process of interpretation.

Reading

Bleicher, Joseph 1980: *Contemporary Hermeneutics: Hermeneutics as Method, Philosophy, and Critique.*
Bruns, Gerald 1992: *Hermeneutics Ancient and Modern.*
Dilthey, Wilhelm 1976: *Selected Writings.*
Frank, Manfred 1984 (*1989*): *What Is Neo-Structuralism?*
——1989b: *Das Sagbare und das Unsagbare.*
——1992: *Stil in der Philosophie.*
Gadamer, Hans-Georg 1986: *Hermeneutik II. Wahrheit und Methode 2.*
Hörisch, Jochen 1988: *Die Wut des Verstehens.*
Kant, Immanuel 1790 (*1988*): *Critique of Judgement.*
Müller-Vollmer, Kurt 1986: *The Hermeneutics Reader.*
Ormiston, Gayle L., and Schrift, Alan D., eds 1990: *The Hermeneutic Tradition: From Ast to Ricoeur.*
Palmer, Richard 1969: *Hermeneutics: Interpretation Theory in Schleiermacher, Dilthey, Heidegger, and Gadamer.*
Ricoeur, P. 1969 (*1974*): *The Conflict of Interpretations.*
Schleiermacher, Friedrich 1977: *Hermeneutik und Kritik.*

ANDREW BOWIE

heteroglossia A term introduced by the Soviet semiotician and cultural theorist Mikhail BAKHTIN. It is derived from the two Greek words for "other" and "language," thus yielding the sense: "that within DISCOURSE which cannot be reduced to the order of any single, self-authorized voice or code." Bakhtin developed a sociological poetics which rejected both the formalist emphasis on static (ahistorical) structures and stylistic devices and also those modes of social-realist criticism that stressed the importance of historical context but ignored the specificity of literary language. He sought to steer a path between and beyond these opposed temptations by devising a typology of discourse genres that would link the distinctive formal features of various kinds of TEXT to their conditions of cultural production and reception.

Thus it is Bakhtin's view that no SIGN SYSTEM is entirely self-enclosed, since each and every utterance takes rise from a heteroglossic multitude of meanings, values, social discourses, cultural CODES, etc. In some genres – for instance, lyric poetry or autobiography – there is a countervailing stress on "private" (first-person) expression, and hence a clearly marked generic drive to contain or restrict this centrifugal movement. The same may apply to prose writing during periods of authoritarian rule when language is subject to a strict policing of its otherwise subversive potential. However, sometimes this produces just the opposite effect, as Bakhtin brings out in his study of Dostoevsky. For the novel is of all genres the most irrepressibly prone to generate a range of polyphonic meanings, voices, or subject positions whose sheer multiplicity cannot be reduced to any single omniscient narrative viewpoint. It belongs to a tradition – or counter-tradition – of anarchic and irreverent humor whose origins Bakhtin discovers in a certain (noncanonical) reading of the Socratic dialogues, and also, more directly, in the late Roman genre of Mennippian satire. Thereafter it emerges at irregular intervals, mostly during periods when a strong (highly centralized) system of state or church control coexists with a folk-based culture wherein those dominant values are held up to mockery through forms of parodic inversion. Such is the carnivalesque mode of WRITING – the topsy-turvy realm of meanings, priorities, social distinctions, religious and secular power structures, etc. – as Bakhtin presents it in his best-known work, *Rabelais and His World*. Heteroglossia is one name for this vision of a language everywhere traversed by the energies of popular protest and instinctual desire.

Reading
Bakhtin, Mikhail 1965 (*1984*): *Rabelais and His World.*
—— 1975 (*1981*): *The Dialogic Imagination: Four Essays.*
—— 1929 (*1984*): *Problems of Dostoevsky's Poetics.*
—— 1979 (*1986*): *Speech Genres and Other Late Essays.*
CHRISTOPHER NORRIS

high culture   A term which (according to the *Oxford English Dictionary (OED)*) began to be used in the middle of the nineteenth century to make two sorts of distinction: in class terms, between the CULTURE of the elite and that of the "low;" and in aesthetic terms, between "serious," autonomously produced, "true" ART and trivial, commercially produced, "mass" art. In 1849 George Eliot, the *OED*'s first source, thus symptomatically contrasts "high culture" with "feminine culture." In the twentieth century the CANON was implicated with commerce anyway, and preservation of the high cultural ideal became the particular task of the academy, departments of literature, music, and art.
SIMON FRITH

historians, *Annales*   See ANNALES HISTORIANS

historicism   The theory and practice which privileges historical explanation on the grounds that ideas, values, and practices – indeed all things human – are discrete products of particular CULTURES rather than transhistorical manifestations of essential, universal features of human identity and society. The precise meaning of historicism has been sufficiently contested, by both historicists and their critics, that John Cannon has recently suggested that this "confused and confusing word . . . should be abandoned" (1988, p. 192). Indeed, "historicism" is already untenable, Cannon claims, because it has become an exclusively pejorative synonym for determinism, cultural relativism, and the abdication of objectivity (pp. 193–4). However, this negative definition neither constitutes a genuine critique of historicism nor effectively signals its obsolescence. While critics have sometimes attacked historicism as deterministic (Popper, 1945a, pp. 76–83), many early historicists explicitly articulated historicism as a critique of absolutist conceptions

of value and knowledge. Moreover, cultural and epistemological relativism are the very aspects of the "old historicism" that recent new historicisms in both literary and historical studies have revived and radicalized.

Early twentieth-century German historicism, which emerged from an inchoate nineteenth-century historicism (Iggers, 1973, pp. 456–60), rejected the positivistic assimilation of the past to general laws. Ernst Troeltsch (1923) sought instead to recover past cultures as "always-new and always-peculiar individualisations" (p. 14). Friedrich Meinecke defined historicism as "a process of *individualising* observation" (1936, p. lv); and, because it admits of the "endless variety" of cultures, historicism and "relativism . . . belong together" (p. 486). Karl Mannheim's historicist sociology incorporated historicism's *cultural relativism* and elaborated its *epistemological relationism*: "all historical knowledge is relational knowledge, and can only be formulated with reference to the position of the observer" (1929, p. 71). Historicism necessarily undermines "objective historical knowledge": because all human endeavors are historically contingent, any historian's account of the past must reflect a particular cultural perspective. Cultural and epistemological relativism – Mannheim's distinction between relativism and relationism notwithstanding – constituted a "crisis of historicism" for some historicists (for example, Troeltsch), but historicism – despite challenges from STRUCTURALISM (Lévi-Strauss, 1962), MARXISM (Althusser, 1965a), and quantitative history – has been vital in Europe since the 1930s.

By contrast, historicism has remained well outside the objectivist mainstream of the Anglo-American historical profession, despite its early influence on Charles Beard and Carl Becker (LaCapra, 1985, pp. 20–32; Novick, 1988, pp. 28–31, 155–8). Since 1970, however, a distinctly poststructuralist historicism has emerged. For example, scholars of women's, minority, and gay and lesbian history have opened a historical front of the poststructuralist critique of "the transcendent SUBJECT." Following Michel FOUCAULT's claim that "nothing in man – not even his body" escapes "the influence of history" (1971a, p. 153), historians and critics have argued that aspects of identity previously assumed to be *natural* and *essential* – for example, GENDER (Davis, 1976; Scott, 1988), RACE (Appiah, 1985; Gates, 1985 and 1990), and sexuality (Foucault, 1976; Boswell, 1982; Halperin, 1989) – are in fact historically *constructed*. In literary studies, Stephen Greenblatt's study of the "construction of identity" (1980, p. 7) in Renaissance England introduced the NEW HISTORICISM's critique of a "timeless, cultureless, universal human essence" (p. 4).

The historicist fracturing of the category of "the subject" was precipitated by the recuperation of women, minorities, and marginal culture as historical subjects – a project pioneered by historians such as W.E.B. DuBois (1935), Gerda Lerner (1971), Emmanuel Le Roy Ladurie (1975), and Natalie Zemon Davis (1975). Recently, Joan Scott has undertaken a historicist pluralizing of historical agency: traditional histories, she claims, efface the historical "particularity and specificity of all human subjects" by figuring the elite white male as a "universal representative for the diverse populations of [a] culture" (1983, p. 25; cf. Huggins, 1986). The new historicisms thus share poststructuralism's emphasis on difference and its "suspicion of closed systems, totalities, and universals" (Montrose, 1992, p. 393). By recovering not only differences *between* cultures but differences *within* particular cultures, the new historicisms diverge from the old Rankean historicism's impulse to discover in any culture a totalizing *Weltanschauung* (Jay, 1984a, p. 74). Thus the New Historicism, for example, treats a literary TEXT not as an embodiment of the "spirit of the age" but as a particular representation shaped within a heterogeneous culture (Greenblatt, 1982; Dollimore, 1985).

The new historicisms critically reshape the universal subject and *Zeitgeist* as "the elite subject" and "hegemonic ideology." Oppositionalist historians have long remarked the way traditional history reproduces hegemonic culture's effacement of marginalized agents and discourses. (Gates (1990) and others have critiqued the same phenomenon in literary history and CANON formation.) In early studies of racism and slavery, Afro-American historians historicized orthodox history as a function of contemporary racist politics (see DuBois, 1935 and Franklin, 1957), but they believed a corrective, activist objectivism could recover the "truth" of the past and achieve "justice in history" (Franklin, 1957, p. 47). By contrast, Thomas Holt (1986) rethinks racist history as an epistemological problem: "the biases that left slaves, as people, out of the history of slavery were not simply racial. They more often had to do with. . . . how knowledge, or fact itself, was defined" (p. 7). Yet knowledge, Holt claims, is "a function of where we stand" and "where we stand

is a function of our political and social relations" (p. 7). Thus, for the poststructuralist historicist, epistemological relativism and politics intersect.

Nevertheless, history writing is political not only because it is shaped by present politics but also because the "dissemination of new histories is political action with historical consequences" (Holt, 1986, p. 1). Poststructuralist historicism conceives history as action rather than epistemology (see Hunt, 1991) because it claims that historians *produce* knowledge about the past rather than *recover* the past's "truth" (see Scott, 1988, p. 9). History, Scott argues, "is not purely referential but is rather constructed by the historian" (1989, p. 681). Thus conceived, history is powerful – rather than accurate or inaccurate – because knowledge about the past helps to construct knowledge in and for the present (Scott, 1988, p. 2), and knowledge, according to Foucault, is power (1977a). Scott thus argues that because the historian's "representations of the past help construct gender for the present" (p. 2), critical analyses of gender in the "past and present [are] a continuous operation" (p. 6). Contemporary objectivists find in such claims an indulgent imposition of the historian's "reality" at the expense of the "reality of the past" (Elton, 1991, p. 11; cf. Himmelfarb, 1989). However, perhaps poststructuralist notions – especially versions of Derrida's claim that there is nothing, not even a "real" past, outside the text – pose a new crisis internal to historicism because they seem to undermine its defining emphasis on the difference between present and past. For most historicists, however, the acknowledgement of the textuality of the past and the historian's embeddedness does not lead to an erasure of the past (see, however, Hayden White) but rather to the historicizing of the present.

See also NEW HISTORICISM.

Reading
Althusser, Louis 1965a (*1979*): "Marxism is not a historicism."
Foucault, Michel 1971 (*1977*): "Nietzsche, genealogy, history."
Greenblatt, Stephen 1990: "Resonance and wonder."
Jameson, Fredric 1979 (*1988*): "Marxism and historicism."
Mannheim, Karl 1924 (*1972*): "Historicism."
Meinecke, Friedrich 1936 (*1972*): *Historicism: The Rise of a New Historical Outlook.*
Scott, Joan Wallach 1988: *Gender and the Politics of History.*
White, Hayden 1975 (*1986*): "Historicism, history, and the figurative imagination."

OLIVER ARNOLD

historicism, New *See* NEW HISTORICISM

historicity A fundamental feature of human existence, according to HEIDEGGER. One should, however, distinguish between "history," "historicality," and "historicity." Historicality is the property of being *in* history. Historicity is the condition of the possibility of history. One can distinguish between three levels of historicity (see HUSSERL, DERRIDA): historicity of human existence, historicity of *a* culture; and historicity of scientific thinking and, in the long run, philosophy. A mere fact (*Tatsche*) or an event does not have historicity. Only an ideal meaning, as Derrida insists in his work on *Husserl*, can have it.

J.N. MOHANTY

Hjelmslev, Louis (1899–1965) Danish linguist. Hjelmslev is best known for his systematic elaboration of the work of Ferdinand de SAUSSURE and for developing a glossematic theory of language in *Prolegomena to a Theory of Language* (1943), which is his best-known work. Like Saussure, he aspired not only to develop linguistics into an exact science but also to establish it as the paradigmatic human science. Hjelmslev's theory of glossematics rests on distinctions between form and substance, expression and content. Although his analysis of the forms of language employs mathematical models, Hjelmslev was also determined not to neglect the human subject who uses language, which led him to an interest in psychology and PSYCHOANALYSIS. Although they are not uncritical of his work, both Jacques DERRIDA and Julia KRISTEVA have been markedly influenced by Hjelmslev.

Reading
Derrida, Jacques 1967a (*1976*): *Of Grammatology.*
Hjelmslev, Louis 1943 (*1961*): *Prolegomena to a Theory of Language.*
Kristeva, Julia 1974a (*1984*): *Revolution in Poetic Language.*
MICHAEL PAYNE

Hoggart, Richard (1918–) English writer on cultural and social change, literature, media, and education. He taught in the armed services and adult education, publishing a study of W.H. Auden (1951) and then *The Uses of Literacy* (1957). Vividly written and unorthodox in construction, this was at once influential, reaching a broad public through successive paperback editions. The book drew partly upon personal experiences in studying changes within the working-class culture of the north of England, discussing everyday life, media, and POPULAR CULTURE, and also the trajectory through education of "scholarship boys." Closely observed details, warning against nostalgia, were set against the influence, skeptically observed in the shadow of F.R. LEAVIS, of American cultural trends. Running over existing disciplinary boundaries while celebrating the strengths of working-class life, the book attracted criticism but also enormous attention. Its author soon became a regular commentator on cultural issues, for instance, as a defense witness in the D.H. Lawrence censorship trial (1960) and as a key member of a committee on the quality of British broadcasting (Pilkington Report, 1962). At Birmingham University he founded the CENTRE FOR CONTEMPORARY CULTURAL STUDIES, as whose first director he inaugurated with Stuart HALL its extensive and pioneering activities, before moving to work in a senior position for UNESCO, with the Arts Council of Great Britain, and as Warden of Goldsmiths' College, London. He has published prolifically on a wide range of issues and his responses to different social and cultural worlds, distinctive voice, and moral concern are well articulated in the several books of his autobiography.

Reading
Hoggart, R. 1957 (*1958*): *The Uses of Literacy.*
——1970: *Speaking to Each Other.*
——1988: *Life and Times.*
MICHAEL GREEN

homology A term used by GOLDMANN in the context of his GENETIC STRUCTURALISM. It indicates a similarity of structure between social and cultural phenomena of different orders, despite outward appearances. Thus Goldmann suggests homology between a fairy tale and the experience of a social group, or between the novel and a society based on exchange value.

IAN H. BIRCHALL

homophobia Pathological hatred of lesbians and gay men. GAY POLITICS has taken homophobia as one of its main targets. The roots of this phobia probably lie in dominant cultural understandings of GENDER, particularly masculinity. Same-sex desire can be threatening to those institutions of power, such as the family and the state, that assume that heterosexuality is a natural, as opposed to a cultural phenomenon.

Reading
Dollimore, Jonathan 1986: "Homophobia and sexual difference."

JOSEPH BRISTOW

hooks, bell – also Gloria Watkins Black feminist theorist. Hooks uses her combined position as a marginalized black woman and privileged intellectual to generate critiques of racism and sexism within feminism, civil rights, and contemporary CULTURE. Theoretical meditations on concepts such as "homeplace," "postmodern blackness," and "revolutionary pedagogy" exemplify her intellectual commitment to personal experience, to anti-essentialist understandings of identity, and to maintaining an activist agenda in writing, teaching, and everyday life. Her scholarship targets a diverse array of alternative and mainstream cultural practices – from representations of RACE and GENDER in popular media and black women's autobiography to institutionalized oppression on the street and in the academy.

Reading
hooks, bell 1984: *Feminist Theory: From Margin to Center.*
——1989: *Talking Back: Thinking Feminist/ Thinking Black.*
——1990: *Yearning: Race, Gender, and Cultural Politics.*
——1992: *Black Looks: Race and Representation.*

SHANNON JACKSON

Horkheimer, Max (1895–1973) German philosopher. From 1930 he was Director of the Institute of Social Research in Frankfurt, home of the FRANKFURT SCHOOL. Horkheimer was initially a strong advocate of a philosophically reflective empirical social science, aiming at the comprehension of the social process as a whole through the development of a new interdisciplinarity. (He originally studied psychology before turning to philosophy as his specialism.) Such knowledge was to be instrumental to political action – in particular, the establishment of a planned economy. However, as his thought progressed during the period of fascism in Germany, Horkheimer's conception of this project became increasingly philosophical and anti-scientistic.

By the late 1940s, during his exile in the United States, he had come to see philosophy as the last bulwark of critical thought against the degeneration of science into a narrowly technological POSITIVISM (Horkheimer, 1947). Such technological rationality was viewed as the essence of an authoritarian state form common to advanced capitalist and communist societies alike. To begin with, this account was accompanied by the utopian prospect of a new, nonrepressive relationship to nature which would provide the basis of social freedom. In his later years, Horkheimer tended towards a Schopenhauerian pessimism (and a *rapprochement* with religion) which distanced him intellectually from other members of the Frankfurt school (Horkheimer, 1962).

Horkheimer is best known for his essay "Traditional and critical theory" (1937), which is widely held to define the Frankfurt school's project of an open, critical MARXISM insulated from the historical contingencies of political practice. The essay generalizes MARX's critique of political economy on the basis of a broadly HEGELian conception of reason to produce an essentially philosophical model of critical thought. Such thought, it is claimed, places itself in opposition to reality and in solidarity with the struggle for freedom by viewing all social practices from the standpoint of "reason and will." The wider historical conditions underlying the perceived break between theory and politics are outlined in Horkheimer's important joint work with ADORNO, *Dialectic of Enlightenment* (1944).

The continuity of Horkheimer's writings lies less in their relationship to Marxism than in the critique of a narrowly instrumental reason for which truth is defined by the dictates of *self-preservation* – a theme first treated in the early work on Machiavelli, Hobbes, and Vico (1930). It is this idea, reread through NIETZSCHE, that forms the core of Adorno's and Horkheimer's account of a dialectic of ENLIGHTENMENT, whereby freedom from nature is won only at the cost of the repression of "inner nature" in the formation of rational subjectivity.

Apart from his work on the philosophical foundations of CRITICAL THEORY, Horkheimer produced numerous essay on politics and culture. He also coordinated and contributed to the Institute's ambitious collective projects such as *Studies on Authority and the Family* (Institute for Social Research, 1936). His early work was the inspiration behind HABERMAS's attempt to reformulate the project of critical theory in the 1960s, in order to escape the impasse of Adorno's negativism.

Reading

Dubiel, Helmut 1978 (*1985*): *Theory and Politics: Studies in the Development of Critical Theory.*
Held, David, 1980 (*1989*): *Introduction to Critical Theory: Horkheimer to Habermas.*
Horkheimer, Max 1938 (*1972*): *Critical Theory: Selected Essays.*

PETER OSBORNE

humanism   Generically, humanism refers to any SYSTEM which accords paramountcy to human interests and possibilities. Paramountcy has gradually become exclusivity and humanism now colloquially denotes rejection of the belief in an omnipotent and omniscient God. In postwar intellectual controversies, however, it is distinguished not from theism, but from "theoretical anti-humanism." It is indicative of the latter's influence upon CRITICAL and CULTURAL THEORY that humanism currently invariably has connotations of ESSENTIALISM – anthropocentrism, ethnocentrism, etc. – in sharp contrast to its formerly positive – secular and humanitarian – resonance (humanity as the "measure of all things").

Debates over humanism frequently conflate issues which, although related, require to be distinguished:

(i)   whether there is such a thing as a common *human nature*;

(ii)   if so, whether it consists of the capacities of "rationality," "consciousness," "moral agency" traditionally attributed to the constitutive *human subject*;

(iii)   whether human nature is a basic *explanatory* concept of social theory, and, more broadly, whether *human agency* possesses explanatory primacy in accounting for sociohistorical phenomena;

(iv)   if so – if the human individual has a role in "making history" – whether history is an anthropological process with a purpose;

(v)   whether humanism grounds *humanitarianism*, providing foundations for a *normative critique*, as well as an explanation of social conditions.

Contrary to what is often implied, answers to these questions are not mutually exclusive. It is, for example, possible to affirm (i), while denying (ii), (iii), (iv), and (v); similarly, (i), (ii), (iii), and (v) may be affirmed, while (iv) is denied. More generally, theoretical anti-humanism is perfectly consistent with practical humanism.

Crudely periodized and categorized, the modern humanist controversy began in France as a difference between Heideggerian PHENOMENOLOGY and Sartrean EXISTENTIALISM, gradually escalated into a European contest between STRUCTURALISM and phenomenology and humanist MARXISM, and has persisted as an item in the global contention between POSTSTRUCTURALISM, in its NIETZSCHEan/ Heideggerian inflections, and its diverse opponents, conservative, LIBERAL, and Marxist.

In his "Letter on humanism" (1947) HEIDEGGER objected to SARTRE's identification of the Cartesian *cogito* as the starting point of existentialism and the basis for a humanism (cf. Sartre, 1946). Renouncing any conception of "man" as *imago Dei*, Heidegger argued that "every humanism is either grounded in a metaphysics or is itself made to be the ground of one" (1947, p. 225). Humanism did not do justice to man's humanity: "Man is not the lord of beings. Man is the shepherd of Being" (p. 245).

In the 1950s Heideggerian pastoralism seemed more appropriate to someone rusticated to the Black Forest than those domiciled in the Latin Quarter. But Heidegger's assimilation of humanism to metaphysics anticipated the philosophical repertoire of subsequent years. From the outset this possessed a directly political charge. De BEAUVOIR (1949) pioneered feminist scrutiny of the credentials of humanism, inadvertently revealing the "masculinism" of her companion's existentialism. Above all, opposition to France's colonial war in Algeria (1954– 62) led intellectuals to denounce the hypocrisies of "classic humanism" (BARTHES, 1957, p. 101); for Sartre it stood exposed as "racist" (1961, p. 22). Such criticisms tended, however, to counterpose a "genuine" humanism to the inadequacies or iniquities of the received doctrine.

Theoretical anti-humanism proper was the banner of professed or presumed structuralists: LÉVI-STRAUSS, LACAN, FOUCAULT, and ALTHUSSER. Lévi-Strauss's *The Savage Mind* (1962), with its assault upon Sartre's *Critique of Dialectical Reason* (1960), sounded the leitmotifs. Humanism consisted of a subject-centered epistemology, inevitably replicating the Cartesian circle, and a subject-constituted history, spuriously universalizing historically and culturally specific (Western) assumptions. It was therefore an IDEOLOGY or philosophical anthropology. A scientific anthropology would, by definition, be a "structural" one – anti-empiricist, anti-historicist, and anti-humanist. "The ultimate goal of the human sciences," Lévi-Strauss announced, "is not to constitute man but to dissolve him" (1962c, p. 247) – a declaration that would be adopted and radicalized at the close of Foucault's *Order of Things* (1966).

The late 1950s and early 1960s had witnessed a renaissance of humanist Marxism – not only Sartre, but also LUKÁCS, GOLDMANN, and Lefebvre – which appealed to the Feuerbachian writings of the young Marx (1975), with his ethical philosophy of history as the (dis)alienation of man, the "supreme being." "Socialist humanism" aspired to offer a "third way" between consumer capitalism, whose ideology of liberal humanism mystified the oppressive realities of ALIENATION and REIFICATION, and Stalinism, at whose hands Marxism had been converted into a repressive *raison d'état*. But STRUCTURALISM received Marxist reinforcement from Althusser's convergent reconstruction of historical MATERIALISM. Motivated by the conviction that humanism could not supply the basis for a theoretical or practical "de-Stalinization," Althusser pointed to the increasing adoption of socialist humanism as the official ideology of Communism.

For Althusser, as his collaborator MACHEREY put it (1966, pp. 66–7), with mocking reference to Feuerbach's humanism, "anthropology is merely an impoverished and inverted theology." The "myth of man" was therefore to be expelled from Marxism, and the putative science of history rescued from guilt by association with it, by conceiving history as a "process without a SUBJECT or telos" (for example, Althusser, 1976, pp. 94–9). History was neither the unfolding of an immanent purpose, nor the product of creative human agency: *contra* Marx, "men" were *not* "both the authors and the actors of their own drama." Human beings were subjects *in* history, rather than the subjects *of* it. Provoking E.P. THOMPSON's socialist-humanist counterblast (1978), Althusser maintained that the predicates attached to the subject by humanism – consciousness, experience, agency, beliefs, values – were constituted in and by society (more especially, ideology).

After 1968 structuralist "objectivism" was superseded by poststructuralism, in its deconstructionist and genealogical forms, with DERRIDA joining Foucault in Nietzschean opposition to humanism. According to the latter's genealogy of modern morals (1975), "power-knowledge" (for example, penology) operated via a subjectification of persons. There were no grounds, however, for theoretical critique of such DISCOURSES as ideologies, or for normative critique of them as repressive. For science and ethics were equally implicated in the regimes and politics of truth. No metadiscourse eluded the ubiquitous will to power/knowledge. Under the umbrella of POSTMODERNISM, and the slogan of difference, these and cognate themes are common currency today, albeit that they are challenged by representatives of the FRANKFURT SCHOOL (for example, HABERMAS, 1985). Without any pretense to settle some intractable disputes, a few concluding reflections may be offered.

First, under the spur of the environmental crisis, there has recently been a revival of philosophical and ethical naturalism, introducing a "nonanthropocentric" concept of human nature whereby *Homo sapiens* is placed on a continuum with other animal species. Second, while the critique of humanist "moralism" – any discourse that abstracts from the factual states that culturally condition moral values – is cogent, it does not entail ethical relativism. Third, any anti-humanism that subscribes to epistemological perspectivism subverts its intention to provide a more adequate account of social relations than humanism; similarly, if it adheres to ethical relativism, it encounters insurmountable problems in sustaining the normative claims it advances against the oppressive homogenizations of humanism. Fourth, while the notion that history is the enactment of a collective human purpose has been discredited, denial of a constitutive role in history to human beings is a fallacious deduction from a correct premise. Fifth, the human agency/social structure dichotomy appears misconceived, both because there is no plausible trans-historical answer to the question it poses, and because it is difficult to envisage its terms as anything other than *interdependent* in the reproduction and transformation of societies. In this and other respects, the polemical themes of "humanism" and "anti-humanism" are arguably part of the problem, not part of the solution.

Reading

Althusser, L. 1976a: *Essays in Self-Criticism.*
Barthes, R. 1957 (*1982*): *Mythologies.*
Beauvoir, S. de 1949 (*1987*): *The Second Sex.*
Habermas, J. 1985 (*1987*): *The Philosophical Discourse of Modernity.*
Heidegger, M. 1947 (*1993*): "A letter on humanism."
Lévi-Strauss, C. 1962c (*1981*): *The Savage Mind.*
Macherey, P. 1966 (*1978*): *A Theory of Literary Production.*
Marx, K. 1975: *Early Writings.*
Sartre, J.-P. 1946 (*1990*): *Existentialism and Humanism.*

———1961 (*1967*): "Preface to Frantz Fanon, *The Wretched of the Earth*."
Soper, K. 1986: *Humanism and Anti-Humanism.*
Thompson, E.P. 1978: *The Poverty of Theory and Other Essays.*

GREGORY ELLIOTT

Husserl, Edmund (1859–1938) German philosopher, founder of PHENOMENOLOGY, and major influence on such thinkers as GADAMER, HEIDEGGER, MERLEAU-PONTY, RICOEUR, and SARTRE. Husserl was a prolific writer, whose work is being collected in a series of volumes under the general title *Husserliana*. His most important publications are *Ideas: General Introduction to Pure Phenomenology, Experience and Judgment: Investigations in Genealogy of Logic, The Paris Lectures, The Idea of Phenomenology, Cartesian Meditations: An Introduction to Phenomenology, Formal and Transcendental Logic, The Crisis of European Sciences and Transcendental Phenomenology: An Introduction to Phenomenological Philosophy,* and *Phenomenological Psychology.* His "Origin of Geometry" ("Die Frage nach dem Ursprung der Geometrie") has been reissued with an important commentary by Jacques DERRIDA.

Especially in *Ideas* and *Formal and Transcendental Logic,* Husserl developed a theory of the structures of consciousness and an account of how the mind works, based on a series of overlapping distinctions, including sensuous "hyletic data" in contrast to intentional "noeses." Hyletic data are sensory materials passively received by the mind and are without meaning or conceptual articulation. They are thus literally the given (the datum) of experience. Noetic elements, in contrast, are those that, by virtue of their intentionality, bestow sense on the otherwise inert hyletic data. The noetic relies on the assumption of the stable, transcendental ego. Thus Husserlian phenomenology assumes a naïve ego psychology as its base, perhaps because Husserl was writing simultaneously with Freud (*Ideas* was first published in 1913). Although Julia KRISTEVA relies heavily on Husserl's theory of language, nonetheless she is severely critical of his concept of the transcendental ego (Kristeva, 1974, p. 166.)

Husserl's project was to advance a science of beginnings, or a first philosophy. In order to provide philosophy with such a scientific beginning, he attempted to remain aloof from all theories or anticipatory ideas. To this end he asserted his "General Thesis of the Natural Standpoint," which holds that there is a "fact-world" existing "out there," that it always exists, and that it may at certain points appear "other" than it was supposed (Husserl, 1913, p. 97.)

Reading
Bell, David 1990: *Husserl.*
Husserl, Edmund 1913 (*1962*): *Ideas: General Introduction to Pure Phenomenology.*
Kristeva, Julia 1974: *Revolution in Poetic Language.*

MICHAEL PAYNE

hybridity   A concept in LATIN AMERICAN, CARIBBEAN, US minority, and POSTCOLONIAL STUDIES. The term "hybrid" is commonly assumed to be anything of mixed origin, of unlike parts. While the word "hybrid" has various genealogies – such as linguistic and horticultural – in literary and CULTURAL STUDIES it refers to the idea of occupying in-between spaces; that is, of being of many, composite, or syncretic entities, new formations, creole or intermixed peoples, mestizaje, dingo. Proponents of theories of hybridity include Edouard GLISSANT, W.E.B. DuBois, Gloria Anzaldua, Homi Bhabha, Guillermo Gomez-Pena, Stuart HALL, George Lamming, E. Kamau Braithwaite, Michelle Cliff, Roberto Ratamar.
See also BLACK CULTURAL STUDIES; DIASPORA; HALL, STUART.

MAY JOSEPH

I

ideological state apparatus A category introduced by ALTHUSSER, whose distinction between
the repressive state apparatus (RSA) and ideological state apparatuses (ISAs) is related to
GRAMSCI's differentiation between coercion and
consent. Whereas the RSA operates by force, the
ISAs – the family, schools, the mass media, etc. –
function to reproduce existing relations of production by subjecting social classes to the dominant
IDEOLOGY.

Reading
Althusser, L. 1970 (*1993*): "Ideology and ideological state
  apparatuses."
——1976b (*1983*): "Note on the ISAs."
Gane, M. 1983: "On the ISAs episode."
                                          GREGORY ELLIOTT

ideology According to a recent survey (McLellan,
1986, p. 1), ideology is "the most elusive concept
in the whole of social science" and "an essentially
contested concept." Its elusiveness is aggravated by
the fact that the term scarcely figures in the work
of thinkers who have influenced twentieth-century
constructions of the concept (for example, DURK-
HEIM, FREUD, SAUSSURE); while oeuvres in which
it looms large (including that of its eighteenth-
century progenitor, Antoine Destutt de Tracy) have
little or no resonance today.

  The terms of contestation include the *epistemological status*, the *sociological salience* and *function*,
the *political inflection* and *implications*, and the *sub-
jective/psychological* or *objective/social character* of
ideology. This has permitted a bewildering variety
of conceptual permutations within both MARXISM
– the tradition with which the term is principally
associated – and rival doctrines (for example, the
SOCIOLOGY OF KNOWLEDGE or LIBERALISM).

  Drastically oversimplifying, conceptions of ideology, whether Marxist or non-Marxist, can be
specified according to four broad and nonexclusive
parameters:

(i) the epistemologically *negative* – ideology as a
    type of distorted, false thought (for example,
    the "consciousness" of human subjects in capi-
    talist society);
(ii) the socially *relative* – ideology as any set of
    opinions, beliefs, attitudes (for example, the
    "world view" of a social group or class);
(iii) the *restricted* – "theoretical ideology" (a more
    or less conscious system of ideas);
(iv) the *expanded* – "practical ideology" (the more
    or less unconscious medium of habitual
    behavior).

(i) is characteristic of the main accounts offered by
MARX and Engels; (ii), while present in Marx's
1859 Preface, may be regarded as substantially an
innovation after Marx, featuring in LUKÁCS's
Hegelian Marxism and in Mannheim's critique
of the *parti pris* of historical MATERIALISM. (iii)
encompasses (i) and (ii), and predominated in
philosophico-political controversies up to the 1960s;
whereas (iv), initiated by Marx, developed by
GRAMSCI, and elaborated by ALTHUSSER, supplied
the received definition – and site of critical debate
– in much CULTURAL THEORY thereafter. Indeed, it
may be said that the "problematization" of
Althusserian and related endeavors to retrieve the
concept of ideology from the perceived discredit
into which it had fallen by association with (i) and
(ii) has induced a pervasive contemporary disaffection with it.

  Positive and pejorative connotations have accompanied "ideology" since it was coined in 1797
by de Tracy to denote the "science of ideas," bearing upon both substantives in that formula. De
Tracy conceived his project as an intellectual "mechanics" which would complement the social "physics" hankered after by the ENLIGHTENMENT. Armed
with EMPIRICISM, a "Newton of the science of
thought" could identify – and correct – the erroneous reasoning which impeded progress (above
all, the "prejudices" instilled by "tyrants and
priests"). For the *idéologues*, as for the *philosophes*

generally, the requisite antidote to religious and other obscurantisms was secular education, dispensed by the suitably enlightened. Napoleon's subsequent denigration of "ideologists" as "nebulous metaphysicians," whose rationalist schemas neglected "knowledge of the human heart and of the lessons of history," pioneered a derogatory theme which became a *topos* of Cold War anti-Marxism. Paradoxically, however, not dissimilar accents echoed in Marx's original treatment of the subject in the mid-1840s.

In *The German Ideology* (1932, part 1), Marx and Engels interrogated Feuerbach's critique of religion as the PARADIGM of human ALIENATION, criticizing it as an ideological critique of ideology. The left-Hegelians had imparted an illusory autonomy to ideas, rooting both the subject/predicate "inversions" of theology (God/Man) *and* their correction (Man/God) in thought. In place of such "idealism," Marx and Engels urged a "historical materialism," according to which "social being" determined "social consciousness." The matrix of ideological "mystification" was the "material base" of society – the "actual life-process" of "real individuals" which governed the (re)production of ideas in any historical conjuncture. Deployed in a negative and critical sense, ideology was understood as the distorted thought which derived from, and in turn served to mask, the social contradictions inherent in CLASS society, thereby directly or indirectly legitimating a structure of domination. As with any instance of the phenomenon, the particularity of abstract "German ideology" was explicable by the peculiarities of concrete German reality. Moreover, it could be vanquished only by a revolutionary political practice that would transform the social conditions which had engendered it.

Often incorrectly classified as a theory of "false consciousness," in which ideology is merely an epiphenomenal illusion to be dispelled by positive science, Marx and Engels's account of the ideological mechanism is vulnerable to criticism on the grounds of the sensationalism of its central *camera obscura* metaphor, which implies that the human mind spontaneously misrepresents the external objects presented to sense experience.

Analogous problems beset the analysis of capitalist ideology in *Capital* (1867, vol. 1, ch. 1), which revolves around the notion of commodity fetishism (and the alienation it constitutes). Here "social being" *tout court* is not inverted in "social consciousness," because social being itself is divided.

Ideological inversions reflect actual inversions in a stratified reality. Ideology is not the failure to perceive reality, for reality is ideological, comprising a realm of objective appearances – the "phenomenal forms" of the sphere of commodity circulation – which conceal by inversion the "essential relations" of the capitalist mode of production, in the interests of the dominant, exploiting class. Ideology transcribes liberal-capitalist appearances – that "very Eden of the innate rights of man [wherein] alone rule Freedom, Equality, Property and Bentham." Science, by contrast, is *counterphenomenal*, explaining how the "enchanted world" of capitalism comprises surface phenomena which travesty its underlying modality. It is therefore indispensable to the exposure of the dehistoricizing effects of "NATURALIZATION" and "universalization," typical of bourgeois ideology – a necessary, but insufficient, condition of "changing the world."

If in *The German Ideology* the source of ideology is idealism, in *Capital* it is the capitalist economy. The misperception/misrepresentation of reality is inscribed in reality, which generates a false knowledge of itself. Social agents passively assimilate and articulate the deceptive "phenomenal forms" perceptible from their structural location as "supports" of capitalist relations of production.

The economic ESSENTIALISM of this determinate nexus between social position, cognitive deficiency, and class interest was, if anything, accentuated in Lukács's subsequent reaction against the "mechanical materialism" of the orthodox Marxism of the Second International. Taking its cue from a letter of Engels to Mehring, and moulding historical materialism to the Procrustean bed of the BASE AND SUPERSTRUCTURE topography, it had diffused the notion of "false consciousness." Lenin, basing himself upon the 1859 *Preface*, had already advanced an alternative – neutral or even positive – conception of ideology (for example, "scientific socialism" as proletarian ideology), but it was Lukács who offered the most systematic account of it. In *History and Class Consciousness* (1923), he fused the category of commodity fetishism with the Weberian analysis of "rationalization" in a theory of REIFICATION. On this construction bourgeois ideology was indeed "false consciousness," but not so much because it was ideology as because it was bourgeois. The social genesis of ideas determined their cognitive status. The (in)validity of an ideology was dependent upon the historical "class situation" of the collective subject whose expression it was. Thus, whereas the antinomies of bourgeois ideology transposed reified capitalist actuality, it was the unique privilege of the proletariat, as the "identical subject–object of history," to possess in Marxism the "proletarian science" of the (mis)adventures of the occluded social totality.

Notoriously, however, this represented the "imputed" (true) class consciousness of the proletariat – as opposed to its "psychological" (false) consciousness which, until and unless rectified, remained in thrall to the reifying logic of capitalism. Accordingly, over and above its dubious valorization of the "reform of consciousness" in the revolutionary process, Lukácsian HISTORICISM is condemned to a vicious, self-subversive, epistemological circle. In making the truth relative to the ascribed consciousness of the historically most progressive class, it presumes what it must demonstrate: the cognitive superiority of the proletarian standpoint.

Lukács's deduction of the falsity of bourgeois ideology from its capitalist origins prompted Mannheim's historicist critique of the truth claims of Marxism. Sponsoring an objection which enjoyed a prosperous (if rarely attributed) posterity, in *Ideology and Utopia* (1929) he contended that Marxism postulated the social determination – and hence cultural limitation – of all ideas, yet exempted itself from the historical critique this logically entailed, and to which it subjected all other *Weltanschauungen*, claiming a monopoly on knowledge when it was merely one partial viewpoint among a myriad others. As with contemporary perspectivism, this posed the dilemma of epistemological relativism for Mannheim – a conclusion he sought (unsuccessfully) to avoid via his "relationism."

Lukács had inaugurated the Western Marxist preoccupation with ideology as a central mechanism in the maintenance of capitalism, in defiance of socialist expectations after the 1914–18 war and the Bolshevik Revolution (Anderson, 1976). And his legacy was to be resumed, not only in the GENETIC STRUCTURALISM of GOLDMANN, but also – in pessimistic form – by the FRANKFURT SCHOOL – whether in ADORNO's critique of ideology as "identity thinking," which suppresses "difference," or in MARCUSE's diagnosis of the psychonormality (that is, psychopathology) of everyday life in advanced industrial societies (*One-Dimensional Man*, 1964). Lukács had made the equation between natural science and bourgeois ideology. For Marcuse

science was "instrumental reason" which had been absorbed into the routine reality of consumer capitalism, constituting a vehicle of human alienation that could be undone neither by an impotent "CRITICAL THEORY" nor by the traditional – now incorporated – working class. If "high" art alone held out *une promesse de bonheur* against the omnipotent, quasi-totalitarian logic of capital (including commodified mass culture), residual rebellious impulses were confined to the marginalized and excluded subjects of the First World.

An analogous scenario, albeit with antithetical political implications, was projected contemporaneously by transatlantic, liberal-democratic heralds of "the end of ideology" in welfare capitalism (see Bell, 1960 (*1979*)). Ideology was conceived as the opposite of empirical science – a specific kind of system of thought at once suffused with fanatical irrationalism and purblind rationalism. And Marxism was an exemplary instance of it: a "totalizing" theory whose practical correlate was "totalitarian" politics.

The liberal empiricism of this position was doubtless facilitated by the fact that it has been the United States' "fate as a nation not to have ideologies but to be one" (Richard Hofstadter, quoted in McLellan, 1986, p. 82). Its obituary of ideology proved premature, however. In a political conjuncture marked by the global crisis of the postwar settlement, historical materialism and, with it, the concept of ideology experienced a remarkable renaissance.

Two Marxist initiatives were of especial significance here. The first – Gramsci's brilliant reflections on the political and cultural specificity of the West in his *Prison Notebooks* (1929–35) – introduced the effective distinction between theoretical and practical ideology into Marxism. Recasting Machiavelli's contrast between "force" and "fraud" as distinct, though combined, modes of class domination – viz., coercion and consent – Gramsci, like Lukács, advanced a positive conception of ideology. "Organic ideologies," the world views of fundamental social classes, were indissolubly theoretical and practical, running the gamut of cultural phenomena from abstract philosophy to "common sense." According to a widespread interpretation of Gramsci, class domination in Western societies was not solely – or even predominantly – attributable to the repressive deployment (or deterrent threat) of force in "political society," but the achievement and exercise of HEGEMONY (including, crucially, ideological direction) in CIVIL SOCIETY. The proletariat possessed a dual consciousness – that, beholden to the capitalist class, imposed in the institutions of civil society, and that derived from its daily experience of the world. The "progressive" aspects of the latter required fostering by the "collective intellectual" of the Communist Party, if the revolutionary potential it harbored for a new hegemony was to be realized. As promoted by organic intellectuals of the proletariat, the "philosophy of *praxis*" – Gramsci's designation for Marxism – was the unity of theory and practice, a revolutionary "conception of the world" capable of cementing a counterhegemonic social bloc.

Gramsci's historicist affinities with Lukács are the most problematic aspect of his immensely influential propositions. Adapting elements of Gramscian Marxism, Althusserianism aimed to surmount this problem by dispensing with its HISTORICISM and pragmatism, and insisting upon the cognitive autonomy of historical materialism.

Althusser's theory of ideology, which might be categorized as a negative but nonpejorative conception of it as essentially "practico-social," arguably owed more to the Durkheimian notion of "collective representations" and the Freudian account of civilized "illusions" than to Marx. It dissented from its rivals on three main grounds:

(i) Rejecting economic determinism, Althusser allotted ideology RELATIVE AUTONOMY as an objective domain of social reality;
(ii) affirming its "materiality," he expanded its definition from ideas to "lived relations," and from conscious to unconscious dimensions of social experience; and
(iii) repudiating HUMANISM, he depicted it as the mechanism of the formation of human subjects endowed with the necessary illusion of autonomy (such that they considered themselves the unacknowledged legislators of their own world).

For Althusser, ideology was distinct from – but not the antithesis of – science, since it comprised a quite different, "incommensurable . . . register of being" (Eagleton, 1991, p. 139): the ideo-affective, "imaginary" realm of "lived experience." In his seminal essay of 1970, "Ideology and ideological state apparatuses," Althusser sought to integrate a general theory, influenced by LACAN's rereading of Freud, of the ideological INTERPELLATION of the individual as a subject, with a specific political theory, indebted to Gramsci, of the functioning of IDEOLOGICAL STATE APPARATUSES in the reproduction of capitalist relations of production. In the process, he conjoined sociological and epistemological premises for his controversial deduction, contrary to Marx, that there would be no "end of ideology" under Communism. Ideology would persist, both because of the ineliminable opacity of the deep structures of any conceivable SOCIAL FORMATION and because human beings were not the rational animals of pre-Freudian liberal humanism. (The subject was not the substratum of conscious agency, but the illusory ego of the psychic apparatus.)

Althusser's ingenious proposals were met with three principal reservations, concerning their supposed economic FUNCTIONALISM, political pessimism, and epistemological dogmatism. But before attending to these, we should register the remarkable range of work produced under the separate or joint auspices of Gramsci and Althusser from the 1960s onwards. Coinciding with cognate structuralist and semiotic analyses of myth as the "imaginary resolution of real contradictions" (LÉVI-STRAUSS) or the "naturalization" of history (BARTHES), a "triple alliance" was established in France between Althusserian Marxism, Lacanian psychoanalysis, and Saussurean linguistics. In the work of PÊCHEUX, for example, it led to a resumption of "discourse analysis", pioneered by V.N. Voloshinov (*Marxism and the Philosophy of Language*, 1929), which examined ideology as a matter of DISCOURSE, or the inscriptions of social power in language. In figures associated with TEL QUEL, it spawned a notion of ideology as the arbitrary, but motivated, "closure" of the infinite productivity of language, inclining KRISTEVA and others to a preference for the polysemic texts of high modernism over those of classical realism. In Britain the *Tel Quel* option was pursued by the editors of SCREEN (for example, Heath and Mulvey); while a version of Althussero-Lacanianism was appropriated by MITCHELL for the feminist explanation of "woman's estate" in patriarchal capitalism. However, the Gramscian stimulus was equally pronounced – whether in the reinterpretation of British CULTURE and society advanced by ANDERSON and his colleagues in the *NEW LEFT REVIEW*; or in the investigations of HALL and Co. at the CENTRE FOR CONTEMPORARY CULTURAL STUDIES, which abandoned the traditional aestheticist disdain for POPULAR CULTURE and broadened the social optic of Marxism to encompass nonclass identities.

Such was the proliferation of ideology critique, and such was the explicit or implicit significance accorded it, that a predictable reaction set in. Abercrombie et al. (1980) challenged the putative "dominant ideology thesis" featuring in much *marxisant* discussion of the topic, on theoretical and empirical grounds (above all, for underestimation of what Marx dubbed the "dull compulsion of economic relations"). This did not, however, serve to inhibit the prevalent "culturalism" or "ideologism" (for example, in the analyses of "Thatcherism" advocated by *Marxism Today* in the 1980s). Of greater moment in the discrediting of the concept as an analytical tool, however, was a series of converging critiques of historical materialism from varieties of POSTSTRUCTURALISM. In hybrid forms they constitute the consensual position in mainstream contemporary theory.

Seeded by the GENEALOGY of NIETZSCHE, FOUCAULT's replacement of the ideology/science dichotomy with the power–knowledge couplet has proved particularly attractive to critics of the alleged "scientism" and "reductionism" of the Marxist tradition. As popularized, Foucauldian and similar counterconstructions partially replicated the objection in Mannheim's sociology of knowledge to the self-assigned "privileged" status of Marxism; they might be encapsulated in Carlyle's inimitable (ideological) maxim: "Orthodoxy is my doxy, heterodoxy is thy doxy." Yet they are far more radical, comprising: (i) epistemological antirealism (rejection of the category of "representation" as intrinsically empiricist); (ii) a consequent cognitive perspectivism and evaluative relativism or pragmatism; and (iii) a suspicion of reason as, if not a Humean slave of the passions, then a Nietzschean accomplice of power (Eagleton, 1991, pp. xi–xii).

Perhaps the most salient anglophone versions of the case have issued from the self-consuming enterprises of "post-Althusserianism" (for example, Hirst, 1979) and "post-Marxism" (Laclau and Mouffe, 1985). The Althusserian postulate of the ubiquity of ideology, rendering it coterminous with culture, posed the problem of how it could be known, let alone transformed. The canonical answer – science – inspired skepticism on the grounds that it conferred an unwarrantable "privilege" upon Marxist metadiscourse. According to

Hirst and his fellow thinkers, for example, the project of epistemology was inherently "rationalist" and correspondingly "dogmatic." Its Althusserian-Marxist variant was no exception, remaining ensnared in a pre-Saussurean account of signification (the mistaken belief that the signified preexisted the signifier, conflated with the different claim that the linguistic SIGN possesses an extralinguistic referent). Recycling this imposture, Marxism pretended to supply a true account of real causal relations. It did not. Conforming to the condition of any social theory, it did not represent (that is, reflect) some extradiscursive reality, but constituted its objects in discourse, discursively constructing a social totality governed by economic determination. This was a theoretical demerit with deleterious political consequences ("essentialism," "classism," "workerism," etc.). And if the possibility of social science was unfounded, then its traditional "other" – ideology – should be abandoned as an irredeemably epistemological category.

There are good reasons to believe that such critiques of epistemological dogmatism exhibit a dogmatism all of their own. On the one hand, historical materialism neither declines to justify its knowledge claims nor does it purport, in Cartesian or Hegelian fashion, to afford certain and absolute knowledge of social phenomena. By contrast, conventionalism, and the pragmatism with which it is often conjugated, appears to assert a knowledge of the modalities of discourse, and to immunize its own constructions by invoking the impossibility of any objective validation. Kindred considerations underlie HABERMAS's enduring commitment to "emancipatory critique" as a form of legitimately "interested" rationality; or EAGLETON's reanimation of a critical notion of ideology as "false or deceptive beliefs . . . arising not from the interests of a dominant social class but from the material structure of society as a whole" (1991, p. 30).

This conception returns us to a negative definition of ideology, while preserving something of the expanded understanding of it. Above all, without repudiating theoretical explanation, it emphasizes the indispensability of the political transformation of the social structures that engender ideological misrepresentations. And it regards the current reedition of the "end of ideology," in which avant-garde theory coalesces with the liberal pluralism of RORTY's "North Atlantic postmodern bourgeois liberal democracy," as the narcissistic self-image of a quintessentially ideological age.

Reading

Abercrombie, N., Hill, S., and Turner, B.S. 1980: *The Dominant Ideology Thesis*.
Althusser, L. 1984 (*1993*): *Essays on Ideology*.
Anderson, P. 1976 (*1989*): *Considerations on Western Marxism*.
Eagleton, T. 1991: *Ideology: An Introduction*.
——ed. 1994: *Ideology*.
Gramsci, A. 1929–35 (*1971*): *Selections from the Prison Notebooks*.
Hirst, P. 1976 (*1979*): *On Law and Ideology*.
Laclau, E., and Mouffe, C. 1985: *Hegemony and Socialist Strategy: Towards A Radical Democratic Politics*.
Larrain, J. 1979: *The Concept of Ideology*.
Lukács, G. 1923 (*1971b*): *History and Class Consciousness*.
McLellan, D. 1986: *Ideology*.
Mannheim, K. 1929 (*1960*): *Ideology and Utopia: An Introduction to the Sociology of Knowledge*.
Marx, K., and Engels, F. 1932 (*1976*): *The German Ideology*.

GREGORY ELLIOTT

imaginary/symbolic/real The three orders of the intersubjective world, as theorized by LACAN. The concept of the imaginary, which owes a great deal to SARTRE (1940), refers to both the capacity to form images and the alienating effect of identification with them, as in the MIRROR-STAGE (Lacan, 1949). The symbolic is primarily the order of CULTURE and language; this is the order into which the SUBJECT is inserted or inscribed thanks to the Oedipus complex and submission to the NAME OF THE FATHER (Lacan, 1953). The Real is not synonymous with external or empirical reality, but refers to that which lies outside the Symbolic and that which returns to haunt the subject in disorders like psychosis (Lacan, 1958).

Reading

Lacan, Jacques 1949 (*1977*): "The mirror stage as formative of the function of the I as revealed in psychoanalytic experience."

implied reader Wolfgang ISER's term for a response-inviting structure in a literary TEXT. The implied reader consists of a network of strategies, schemata, patterns, blanks, indeterminacies, and points of view that both trigger and, to a certain extent, delimit the reader's response.

EVELYNE KEITEL

industries, culture *See* CULTURE INDUSTRIES

industry, entertainment *See* ENTERTAINMENT INDUSTRY

industry, record *See* RECORD INDUSTRY

influence, anxiety of *See* ANXIETY OF INFLUENCE

intentional fallacy A term central to NEW CRITICISM, which derives from the title of an essay by W.K. Wimsatt and Monroe C. Beardsley, "The intentional fallacy" (1946). The essay seeks to detach the judgment of a literary TEXT from an understanding of the author's intention in writing it. A poem (the New Critics tend to privilege POETRY in their works, but the concept is equally applicable to other genres) "goes about the world beyond [the author's] power to intend about it or control it"; it should be understood in terms of the "dramatic *speaker*" of the text, not the author, and be judged only by whether it works or not. The notion of the "autonomous," self-validating "text itself," which assumes its meaning and value solely in the form of its independent verbal structure, and which alone is the proper study of LITERARY CRITICISM, lies at the heart of New Criticism.

The intentional fallacy has been subjected to rigorous critical commentary since its first exposition. Nevertheless, the issues raised by the concept are still at the centre of debates around the author/text/reader nexus. Ironically, new impetus for these has stemmed from the contradictory but significant relations between New Criticism and DECONSTRUCTION. The latter's decentering of the author and authority and its emphasis on textuality seem to imply a kinship with the intentional fallacy; however, deconstruction's premise of a text's continual reproduction in the reading of it runs entirely counter to the literary IDEOLOGY of New Criticism – which has taken the determinate "text itself" as the ultimate arbiter of its own meaning.

Reading

Cioffi, Frank 1963: "Intention and interpretation in criticism."
Eagleton, Terry 1983 (*1992*): *Literary Theory*.
Lentricchia, Frank 1980: *After the New Criticism*.
Watson, George 1962: "The mid-century scene."
Wimsatt, W.K., and Beardsley, Monroe C. 1946 (*1954*): "The intentional fallacy."

PETER WIDDOWSON

international style The name given by Henry-Russell Hitchcock and Philip Johnson, in the catalog of the 1932 architecture exhibition at the Museum of Modern Art, to a group of buildings (particularly those by Walter Gropius, LE CORBUSIER, Ludwig MIES VAN DER ROHE, and J.J.P. Oud), designed between the end of the 1914–18 war and 1931. Generally, the design of these buildings is described as stressing the handling of function, but in which FUNCTIONALISM is subordinated to the aesthetic element in architecture. Specifically, the basic artistic conventions that shape the style of these buildings are described as placing emphasis on volume rather than mass, on regularity rather than symmetry, and on ordering of detail rather than application of ornament – and, added later by Hitchcock, emphasis on the articulation of structure.

Reading
Hitchcock, Henry-Russell, and Johnson, Philip 1932 (*1966*): *The International Style.*

GERALD EAGER

interpellation   A category introduced by ALTHUSSER (1970, pp. 44–57) to designate the imaginary mechanism of mutual recognition by which IDEOLOGY operates to constitute concrete individuals as human subjects. Denying the constitutive role of the human SUBJECT, Althusser argues that subjects of experience are ideologically produced and thereby equipped to perform the roles to which they are allocated in the social division of labor.

Althusser's account of subject formation has been widely criticized for the circularity of its argument – its presupposition of a subject with the capacity to recognize, and respond to, its interpellation – and the fatalism of its politics – its effective equation of "subjectification" and "subjection."

Reading
Althusser, L. 1970 (*1993*): "Ideology and ideological state apparatuses."
Barrett, M. 1993: "Althusser's Marx, Althusser's Lacan."
Hirst, P. 1976 (*1979*): "Althusser and the theory of ideology."
Therborn, G. 1980: *The Ideology of Power and the Power of Ideology.*

GREGORY ELLIOTT

interpretive communities   A term pertaining to Stanley FISH's reader-oriented theory of literature (see READER-RESPONSE CRITICISM). Interpretive communities consist of a group of "informed readers" (Fish) who possess both linguistic competence by having internalized the syntactic and semantic knowledge required for reading, and LITERARY COMPETENCE by being familiar with our literary conventions.

By way of introducing the concept of interpretive communities, Fish argues that the informed reader's interpretive perceptions and aesthetic judgments are not idiosyncratic but socially constructed; they depend heavily on the assumptions shared by the social group or groups to which the reader belongs. Interpretive communities adopt particular kinds of reading strategies which will, in due course, determine the entire reading process, the stylistic peculiarities of a literary TEXT as well as the experience of assimilating them.

If Fish's categories were to be taken seriously, reader-response criticism would cease to be riddled with questions concerning either the mode of existence of the literary work or the AESTHETICS of perception (the active and creative process a reader engages in when reading a text): both would collapse into a set of assumptions and conventions shared among a socially defined community of readers.

Reading
Culler, J. 1981a: "Stanley Fish and the righting of the reader."
Fish, S. 1980: *Is There a Text in this Class? The Authority of Interpretive Communities.*

EVELYNE KEITEL

intertextuality   A term proposed by Julia KRISTEVA, drawing on Mikhail BAKHTIN's notion of dialogism ("the necessary relation of any utterance to other utterances") to indicate a TEXT's construction *from texts*: a work is not a self-contained, individually authored whole, but the absorption and transformation of other texts, "a mosaic of quotations" (Kristeva, 1967). This is a matter not of influence (from one author or work to another), but of the multifarious and historically variable relations between works as heterogeneous textual productions ("influence" is simply one limited and limiting figure of intertextuality). Kristeva developed this perception in a generic study of "the text of the novel" as resulting from the combination or transposition of several different SIGN systems (Kristeva, 1970), while Roland BARTHES analyzed a single Balzac story as a tissue of "voices," redeploying and recasting fragments from a range of discourses on which it depends for its intelligibility (Barthes, 1970). Such an approach through intertexuality situates literary structure within social structure as itself textual. Nothing is given other than constituted within DISCOURSE and a text is not the reflection of some nontextual "exterior" but a practice of writing that inscribes – and is inscribed in – the social as just such an intertextual field, a mesh of textual systems.

In a move characteristic of POSTSTRUCTURALISM, intertextuality displaces intersubjectivity: the reading of a text is seen not as a subject-to-subject exchange between author-source and reader-receiver, but as the performance by author *and reader* of a multitude of writings that cross and interact on the site of the text. A text is thus never finished, written once and for all; it exists in the continuing time of its intertextual production, which includes the texts of its future (those that will be brought to its reading) – as intertext it has, in Barthes's words, "no law but the infinitude of its recurrences." Though the condition of all texts, intertextuality may also be used evaluatively, distinguishing texts which attempt to cover up their intertextual nature from those which acknowledge and display it. Where Balzac refers his novels to the truth – the depiction – of an externally grounded reality, Joyce, self-described as "a scissors-and-paste man," offers *Finnegans Wake* as "stolentelling," an accumulation of bits and pieces of writing from the world as infinite text. Modernism in this distinction marks exactly the break from which the problem of intertextuality is posed *as such*.

Michael Riffaterre, defining intertextuality as the reader's perception of the relations between a text and all the other texts that have preceded or followed it, is concerned to allow both for *aleatory* intertextuality (the reader brings the text into play with his or her familiar texts) and *obligatory* intertextuality (the "hypogram" or core intertext that is a work's matrix, presupposed in its reading) (Riffaterre, 1979). Gérard GENETTE proposes five types of *transtextuality*, his overall term for the relations a text may hold with others; with intertextuality limited to the specific relation of *copresence*, the effective presence of one text in another through quotation, plagiarism, or allusion (Genette, 1982). A particular intertextual history is provided in Henry Louis Gates's account of the Afro-American literary tradition as characterized by SIGNIFYIN(G): texts talking to and from

other texts in a self-reflexive process of repetition and revision that seeks to make representational space for "the so called Black Experience" (Gates, 1988).

Reading
Barthes, Roland 1970 (*1975*): *S/Z*.
Genette, Gérard 1982b: *Palimpscstes: la littérature au second degré*.
Kristeva, Julia 1967: "Word, dialogue and novel."
Riffaterre, Michael 1979 (*1983*): *Text Production*.
STEPHEN HEATH

Irigaray, Luce (1932–) French feminist philosopher, linguist, and psychoanalyst. Irigaray is perhaps the most influential of the three major French feminists (see CIXOUS; KRISTEVA). Her first major work, *Speculum of the Other Woman* (1974) with its critique of psychoanalysis, led to her marginalization by the Lacanians and the Freudian school, but has continued to provoke debate among feminists.

Irigaray's work starts from the premise that established (male) SYSTEMS of thought fail to represent or take account of the feminine and its desire. This assertion is derived, in part, from her analysis of Plato's philosophy in *Speculum* (1974), where the impulse to impose order on the formless nondifferentiation of the cave (*hystera*, hence matrix or womb) results in the repression of the cave as origin. The exclusion of what cannot be accounted for in this imposed order or "economy of the same," means that what is outside remains unidentified, indistinct, and unarticulated. This model is explained by Irigaray in terms of the specular. The idea of the speculum in Irigaray's work draws on its use as a mirror, and as an instrument used to view women's sexual organs; thus the speculum looks into the other – the feminine – but finds there only a reflection of itself/the viewer. This system is used to provide a critique of FREUD, where the specularity of thought serves to erase female sexuality, as her "sex" (used by Irigaray to refer to the genitalia) presents no visible sign (that is, phallus) to view. Freud is seen to contribute to the "economy of the same" by articulating his psychoanalytic system around the primacy of the PHALLUS, against which the female sex is defined by lack and the desire for what it cannot possess. In this system, Irigaray argues, Freud's emphasis on the superior activity of the male results in the designation of woman as a "receptacle" to hold the male "product" (1977).

Freud's insistence on the need for the girl child to make the transition from clitoral to vaginal pleasure marks the male need for woman to fulfill her role as "a hole-envelope that serves to sheathe and massage the penis" (1977, p. 23). This results in the erasure of woman's pleasure, exiled beyond the parameters of male discourses and institutions.

In *This Sex Which Is Not One* (1977), a response to readers' questions raised by *Speculum* (1974), Irigaray expounds and expands her critique of Freud and LACAN, and attempts an explanation of what constitutes the OTHER, the feminine. Woman's pleasure lies not in looking (the mirroring and replication of the same) but in touching. This touching, in the first instance, is located in the woman's sex, where the lips of her vagina endlessly touch: "her genitals are formed of two lips in continuous contact. Within herself, she is already two – but not divisible into one(s) – that caress each other" (1977, p. 24). Her sex then is double, in contradistinction to male sexuality, located in the singularity of the phallus. In this way her sex is always plural, in excess of what is defined for her, and her relationship to the other is fundamentally different, as the other lies within herself. Irigaray argues that women thus have an increased capacity for alterity, and access to an economy based upon proximity rather than upon ownership and property. The female body is thus the site of an alternative SYMBOL, for the touch allows a desire which cannot be contained within the economy of the gaze, where woman is the passive object.

Language is vital in the perpetuation of these systems as well as being, for Irigaray, the site of the potential to subvert them. The inclusion of the other within woman renders her language incomprehensible to male DISCOURSE because her speech is "always not identical to what she means" (1977, p. 29), at the same time as language cannot articulate the "feminine." It is precisely this position of alterity which Irigaray suggests will serve to change the existing structures. In the initial stage, it is mimicry which will serve to introduce women into the systems of male discourse: "One must assume the feminine role deliberately. Which means already to convert a force of subordination into an affirmation, and thus begin to thwart it" (1977, p. 76). This means demanding to speak as a (masculine) "subject," while making visible by "playful repetition" what was supposed to remain invisible. The project is not to assert woman as either subject or object, but to "[jam] the theoretical machinery itself," and to enact a "*disruptive excess*" in order to undo the language structures which maintain the submission and exploitation of the "feminine." (1977, p. 78). Such a practice is discernible in Irigaray's own writing, as she undermines meaning and syntax by a series of puns and wordplays, and unsettles the linearity and teleology, not only of the texts she reads, but also of the texts she writes.

Although Irigaray's theories are complex, challenging, and frequently misread, her work provides a revolutionary counter to the empiricist criticism of Anglo-American feminism, by stressing that it is experience itself which has to be questioned.

Reading
Gallop, Jane 1988: *Thinking Through the Body*.
Grosz, Elizabeth 1989: *Sexual Subversions: Three French Feminists*.
Irigaray, Luce 1974 (*1985*): *Speculum of the Other Woman*.
——— 1977b (*1985*): *This Sex which is Not One*.
Moi, Toril 1985: *Sexual/Textual Politics: Feminist Literary Theory*.
Sellers, Susan 1991: *Language and Sexual Difference: Feminist Writing in France*.
Whitford, Margaret 1991: *Luce Irigaray: Philosophy in the Feminine*.

DANIELLE CLARKE

Irish studies Irish studies is the critical examination of the cultural, social, economic, and political practices of the peoples of Ireland, often including the Irish diaspora in Canada, the United States, and Australia as well. Perhaps because Irish culture seems so inextricably related to the political, ethnic, and religious conflicts that have dominated Irish history, organizations such as the International Association for the Study of Anglo-Irish Literature (IASAIL) and the American Conference for Irish Studies (ACIS) have taken an interdisciplinary approach to Irish studies for many years, embracing scholarship in history, anthropology, sociology, linguistics, literary studies, and other disciplines. Fredric Jameson's injunction to "Always historicize" may seem an unnecessary reminder in regard to modern Irish studies, in which history has most often been seen as an inevitable backdrop for the understanding of CULTURE. Hundreds of years of English colonialism in Ireland have created a culture that is at once European and postcolonial (as is always the case in discussing contemporary Ireland, one must distinguish between the Republic of Ireland, which gained its independence in 1921, and the six counties of Northern Ireland, which still struggle daily with the effects of colonialism). As a result of this history of conflict, Irish cultural and political rhetoric during the nineteenth and twentieth centuries has been characterized by long-standing and powerful binary oppositions between Celt and Anglo-Saxon, Catholic and Protestant, Irish language and English, rural and urban, and so on.

Nationalism and identity politics are central areas of concern in Irish CULTURAL STUDIES. A variety of cultural and political positions founded upon political affiliation and ethnic, religious, and linguistic allegiances makes the identification or establishment of one Irish character or of one form of "Irishness" highly problematic. At the same time, as Seamus Deane and others have argued, much of the force of Irish cultural production since the end of the eighteenth century has come from the urge to create or identify and/or to disrupt some variety of essential Irishness, some sense of a stable Irish national identity, whether that identity is based on a nationalist vision of Irishness, a unionist or loyalist desire to assert Britishness over Irishness, or a more cosmopolitan and European vision of Ireland. According to Deane and others, the shattered and scattered heritage of a colonized culture such as Ireland demands – like Humpty Dumpty – to be put back together again, but every reconstruction of history and national identity is at the same time an interpretation or even a fictionalization of history, and is always a political act. Much contemporary scholarship in Irish studies revolves in one way or another around the study of these various attempts at consolidating or disrupting versions of Irishness and Irish history that serve to reify or consolidate one political position or another. The title of Seamus Deane's *Celtic Revivals* (1985) indicates this sense of a series of competing attempts to define and redefine Irishness or Celticity, from W.B. Yeats's "indomitable" Anglo-Irish aristocracy allied with an idealized Celtic peasantry, to Daniel Corkery's nationalist vision of a "hidden Ireland" of Gaelic traditions, to the destabilized or absurd Irelands of James Joyce, Samuel Beckett, or Flann O'Brien.

Recent Irish cultural studies scholarship tends to focus on the ideological and semiotic constitution of Irish culture – especially nationalist culture – by exploring and articulating the "mythologies" (in Roland BARTHES's sense of the word) that

undergird that culture. Thus recent studies have concerned themselves with "The literary myths of the revival" (Deane, 1985), "Myth and martyrdom" in Irish republicanism (Kearney, 1988), "The myth of the motherland" (Kearney in Field Day, 1986), and the mythological and literary backgrounds of the Easter Rising of 1916. Contemporary writers are casting a critical look back at nineteenth-century ethnology, linguistics, political theory, and literary history to better understand the ways in which culture served as a battleground for competing ideologies in Ireland. Nineteenth-century attempts to fashion one sort of Ireland or another were echoed by twentieth-century versions of Ireland and Irishness constructed by varieties of Irish nationalism, the Irish Literary Revival at the turn of the century, and the government of the Republic of Ireland after independence. David Cairns and Shaun Richards (1988), Seamus Deane (1985), Richard Kearney (1988), and many others have investigated these various efforts to "write" Ireland.

The role of POPULAR CULTURE in Ireland has also received an increasing amount of interest in its relation to nationalism and to literature, music, and ART. Cheryl Herr's study of the influence of Irish popular culture on the works of James Joyce in *Joyce's Anatomy of Culture* (1986) is one particularly notable example, demonstrating Joyce's interest in the discourses of Irish newspapers, the popular stage, and sermons. In fact, the analysis of highly influential Irish modernist writers such as Joyce and Samuel Beckett forms an important part of Irish studies, and much discussion has been devoted to debating the questions of Beckett's Irishness and Joyce's status as a nationalist writer. Other recent studies have set new directions in Irish studies by focusing on the impact of multinational investment on Irish culture and the ways in which an ideal Ireland has been constructed by advertising to attract international investment and tourism (Herr, 1994; Gibbons, 1988).

One particularly influential source for much of contemporary Irish cultural studies was the journal *The Crane Bag*, edited by Mark Hederman and Richard Kearney, and published from 1977 to 1985. This periodical provided a forum in which many of the most important voices in Irish cultural studies were able to debate recent CRITICAL THEORY and Irish cultural issues, and it introduced ideas related to poststructuralism into many of the theoretical debates concerning Irish culture. The term "the fifth province" was first used in *The Crane Bag* to denominate a theoretical space outside the four provinces of Ireland – Connacht, Leinster, Munster, and Ulster – in which the myths and rhetoric of Irish culture – particularly of nationalism and unionism, the two dominant political discourses in Northern Ireland – could be questioned, exposed, and reworked.

The most important cultural studies project of recent years in Ireland is the Field Day Theatre Company. Field Day was established in the city of Derry in 1980, 12 years after the beginning of the political crisis that began in Northern Ireland in 1968. Field Day began as a group of Northern Irish intellectuals and artists from both the Protestant and Catholic communities, including Brian Friel, Stephen Rea, Tom Paulin, David Hammond, Seamus Deane, Thomas Kilroy, and Seamus Heaney. In the plays and pamphlets it sponsored, Field Day sought to examine the rhetoric of both unionism and nationalism, highlighting the intricate relationships between language, fiction, history, and power. Field Day hoped to encourage new forms of cultural expression that would acknowledge the multicultural traditions that compose Irish culture and create new ways of seeing and speaking about old problems.

Field Day has produced some of the best recent drama in Ireland, beginning with Brian Friel's *Translations* in 1980, and has published a number of important pamphlets by its own members and other Irish cultural critics such as Richard Kearney, Declan Kiberd, and Terence Brown. Field Day pamphlets have addressed the myths and stereotypes underlying various Irish identities, the creation of competing notions of "Ireland," the Protestant idea of liberty, and many other topics. The most recent collection of essays attempted to broaden Field Day's perspective (and perhaps its audience as well) by presenting three essays by the international cultural theorists Terry EAGLETON, Fredric Jameson, and Edward SAID, whose critical perspectives allied the Field Day position more closely with MARXIST CRITICISM and POSTCOLONIAL STUDIES.

The publication of the much-heralded collection *The Field Day Anthology of Irish Writing* (Deane, 1991) was an important moment in Irish studies, bringing together a great amount of literary, historical, and political writing within a cultural studies framework that emphasized relations between different types of DISCOURSE – between popular and elite discourses, between colonizer and colonized, and so on. This anthology is a remarkable attempt to provide both primary texts and detailed commentary on Irish writing from the earliest Irish epics to contemporary Irish writing, a self-conscious effort to identify and discuss a tradition of Irish writing that is in fact multicultural, deriving itself from the various communities that make up Irish cultural history. *The Field Day Anthology* stresses the colonial and postcolonial nature of Irish culture and includes a wide range of writing from a variety of historical and political points of view: traditionally recognized high ART, philosophical WRITING, political prose and speeches, letters, popular songs, as well as writing in the Irish language. The three-volume anthology presents not only the largest available selection of Irish writing, but also insightful essays (many by authors already mentioned in this essay) introducing the various sections of the anthology. This project also demonstrates many of the complexities and difficulties of Irish cultural studies, however, for while *The Field Day Anthology* broke new ground in establishing a sense of the traditions of Irish writing, it also exposed a traditional failing in the study of Irish culture. The anthology's much-noted and most significant flaw was its tendency to omit important contributions by women, in both its selection of Irish writing and its selection of section editors (all of whom are male). This omission and the vocal reaction to it underscore the importance of women's contributions in CULTURAL STUDIES and THEORY in Ireland today, and a fourth volume of the *Field Day Anthology* devoted to the writing of Irish women is under way.

Two of the principal critics of the *Field Day Anthology*'s omission of women's writing – Eavan Boland and Edna Longley – serve as good examples of the ways in which WOMEN'S STUDIES have made a vital contribution to Irish cultural studies. Eavan Boland is a poet and essayist from the Republic of Ireland whose poetry highlights the role of myth in constructing the position of women in Ireland. In her important essay *A Kind of Scar: The Woman Poet in a National Tradition* (1989), she examined the ways in which nationalism has created a mythic association of Ireland and woman in mythical figures such as Mother Ireland, Cathleen ni Houlihan, and the Dark Rosaleen – all representations of a beleaguered nation – an association that has in turn created stereotypes that govern the behavior and social roles of women.

The relationship between nationalism and gender politics has been a subject of much debate among Irish feminists, in tandem with practical and theoretical discussions of the social and political status of women, in both the Republic of Ireland and Northern Ireland. Edna Longley has written many essays on Irish cultural matters; her pamphlet *From Cathleen to Anorexia: The Breakdown of Irelands* (1990), written partly as a response to Boland's essay, goes farther than Boland in criticizing the discourses of both unionism and nationalism, advocating a cosmopolitan, European sense of Irish identity. Women's writing and women's studies are arguably the most active and exciting areas of Irish studies at present, and women are playing prominent roles in Irish writing, art, film, and cultural studies. One notable contribution in film is Anne Crilly's documentary *Mother Ireland* (1989), which allows a variety of Irish women to speak to the effects of the equation of nation and woman in the nationalist tradition.

Irish studies is a thriving field of cultural studies. As Ireland enters the European community more fully in coming years and as the political situation in Northern Ireland continues to demand new and imaginative solutions, cultural studies will remain a crucial and controversial area of inquiry in Ireland. Central questions about national identity, the effects of colonialism, the political effects of cultural discourse, the role of POPULAR CULTURE, and the position of women within Irish culture will continue to provide subjects for debate in Irish studies for years to come.

See also CULTURAL STUDIES; HISTORICISM; IDEOLOGY; POPULAR CULTURE; POSTCOLONIAL STUDIES; WOMEN'S STUDIES.

Reading
Bartlett, Thomas, et al., eds 1988: *Irish Studies: A General Introduction.*
Boland, Eavan 1989: *A Kind of Scar: The Woman Poet in a National Tradition.*
Cairns, David, and Richards, Shaun 1988: *Writing Ireland: Colonialism, Nationalism and Culture.*
Crilly, Anne, dir. 1989: *Mother Ireland.*
Deane, Seamus 1985: *Celtic Revivals.*
——gen. ed. 1991: *The Field Day Anthology of Irish Writing.*
Eagleton, Terry, Jameson, Fredric, and Said, Edward W. 1990: *Nationalism, Colonialism, and Literature.*
Field Day Theatre Company 1986: *Ireland's Field Day.*
Gibbons, Luke 1988: "Coming out of hibernation? The myth of modernity in Irish culture."
Hederman, Mark, and Kearney, Richard, eds 1982 and 1987: *The Crane Bag Book of Irish Studies.*

Herr, Cheryl 1986: *Joyce's Anatomy of Culture.*
——1994: "A state o' chassis: mobile capital, Ireland, and the question of postmodernity."
Kearney, Richard 1988: *Transitions: Narratives in Modern Irish Culture.*
Lloyd, David 1993: *Anomalous States: Irish Writing and the Post-Colonial Moment.*
Longley, Edna 1990: *From Cathleen to Anorexia: The Breakdown of Irelands.*

JOHN S. RICKARD

irony   A term which has several related but distinct meanings. In its broadest sense, it describes a situation in which appearance and reality are in conflict. A specific literary form of such "situational" irony is dramatic or tragic irony where, for example, the significance of a situation is hidden from a character but known to the audience. The most celebrated example is Sophocles' *Oedipus Rex*. whose hero relentlessly pursues the murderer of his father without realizing that he is himself the murderer.

Irony, in a narrower verbal sense, is a figure of speech in which the intended meaning of an utterance differs from (usually directly contradicting) its apparent meaning. One of the most famous literary examples is Antony's speech in *Julius Caesar* in which he convinces his audience that Caesar was noble and his assassins dishonorable while apparently arguing the opposite. In its most emphatic form, as in this speech, verbal irony becomes sarcasm.

Although irony has been a major element in Western literature since its origins in Greek tragedy, it became centrally important in twentieth-century criticism. Following I.A. Richards's proposal that "irony might provide a kind of test of the quality of poetry," the New Critics used it as a general term of praise for the "complexity" and "maturity" of attitude which they looked for in the best poetry.

Reading
Booth, Wayne 1974: *A Rhetoric of Irony.*
Muecke, D.C. 1970: *Irony.*

IAIN WRIGHT

Iser, Wolfgang   (1926–)   German literary critic and professor of English literature at the University of Konstanz, Germany, and the University of California at Irvine. Together with his colleague at the University of Konstanz, Hans Robert Jauss,

Iser founded the so-called Konstanz school in the early 1970s, a strand of reader-oriented LITERARY CRITICISM steeped in the German philosophical tradition.

Iser's *Wirkungsästhetik* or theory of aesthetic response (not to be confounded with Jauss's *Rezeptionsästhetik* or reception theory), centers on the structure of the reading process, on the inter-subjectively comparable and dynamic interactions between a literary TEXT and its reader. Iser calls this structure, which is inscribed in the text and can therefore be analyzed as part of the text, the IMPLIED READER.

In Iser's model of the reading process, meaning is neither arbitrary nor static, but only ever consti-tuted in the acts of decoding and assimilating a literary text, through the convergence of text and reader. Text and reader are seen as two separate poles of a relationship, one of them artistic (the author's creation), the other aesthetic (the reader's "concretization"). Iser draws on Edmund Husserl's PHENOMENOLOGY as well as on Roman Ingarden's phenomenological AESTHETICS to account for the mode of existence of the literary work. He makes use of Hans-Georg GADAMER's HERMENEUTICS to conceptualize the reader's acts of processing a text, and he calls on Gestalt psychology to sketch out the dynamic interactions between text and reader.

Ingarden's notion of a literary text contains a concept of stratification; he holds that any text consists of several textual layers, each comprising a series of schemata, patterns, and strategies. Ingarden's view of literature is indebted to the classical concept of ART as a symbolic represen-tation of ORGANIC UNITY. Thus the function he ascribes to the various strata in the text is to or-chestrate a "polyphonic harmony," which means that the different strata must be processed in such a way that they can chime with one another. Lively interactions between text and reader are hardly possible here; the text dominates the reader, and processing the disparate layers is an activity subor-dinated to the guidance of the text. Iser incorpo-rates Ingarden's concept of stratification into his own theory, but turns it upside down by empha-sizing those very features Ingarden neglects: the breaks, gaps, and blanks between the various lay-ers and segments of the text. In Iser's theory, con-toured "points of indeterminacy" instigate, contain, and, to a certain degree, delimit the reading pro-cess. These textual features stimulate the reader to produce meanings which could not otherwise

come into existence, meanings with a dimension of virtuality. The reader is brought to formulate the as yet unformulated, as Iser has it. By introducing the concepts of textual indeterminacy and the vir-tual dimension of literary meaning, Iser has brought two new and stimulating notions to the study of literature.

Iser defines the pole of the reader, the indi-vidual acts of processing the text, by drawing on hermeneutics. Each sentence that is read opens up a horizon of perception which will in due course be confirmed, challenged, or undermined. The information gained on one page will fade out on the next, or be called upon and modified. Using data provided by what he or she has already read and making assumptions about what is still to come, the reader tries to wrest meaning from the text, to grasp it through a series of ever-changing view-points and horizons.

Iser uses some of the theoretical propositions of Gestalt psychology to conceptualize the dynamic interactions between text and reader. Gestalt psy-chology holds that the human mind does not per-ceive things as unrelated bits and pieces but only ever as meaningful and organized wholes. Gestalt psychology explores the ontology (structure, form, unity, configuration) of such *Gestalten* as "figures" standing out against a "ground." According to Iser, the interactions between text and reader consist of a highly complex process in which, on the one hand, the reader endeavors to convert open, and thus inherently unstable *Gestalten* into closed, sta-ble ones, while, on the other hand, the text with its contradictions, negations, and points of indeter-minacy tries to undermine that very attempt: that is to say, many of the *Gestalten*, well formed as they may at first appear to the reader, will have to be undone again in the course of the reading pro-cess with its ever fluctuating horizons, they will have to be broken up, revised, reconstructed, and maybe abandoned altogether. In his attempt to make sense of the text, the reader will select certain tex-tual elements and assemble them into seemingly consistent wholes. He will exclude some elements and foreground others. He will try to hold differ-ent perspectives or move from one perspective to the next. Iser does not leave the reader entirely free to impose meaning on the text, nor does he let the text dominate the reader, but sees their inter-action as a fairly even game (see READER-RESPONSE CRITICISM).

Iser's ultimate interest lies in the realm of

anthropology. Reading, for Iser, constitutes an encounter with the yet unknown and results in a continuous testing of our capacities and boundaries, an enlarging and refining of our cognitive faculties. In short, reading is seen as a uniquely valuable consciousness-raising activity.

By being indebted to hermeneutics, which stresses the centrality of consciousness in all our acts of understanding, and to phenomenology, which studies the essence of phenomena as they sift into and subsequently form sediments in our consciousness, Iser's theory also overemphasizes our cognitive interaction with a literary text. The fact that our unconscious, our emotions, and or our GENDER may play an important role in how we interact with the world and process literary texts is hardly ever reflected in his work.

Nevertheless, Iser's theory of aesthetic response, being well grounded in German philosophy, is cogent, coherent, and comprehensive. Even more important, it is amenable to practical literary criticism. It continues to exert an ever-growing influence on the development of reader-response criticism.

Reading
Freund, E. 1987b: "The peripatetic reader: Wolfgang Iser and the aesthetics of reception."
Iser, W. 1974: *The Implied Reader: Patterns of Communication in Prose Fiction from Bunyan to Beckett.*
—— 1978: *The Act of Reading: A Theory of Aesthetic Response.*
—— 1980: "Interaction between text and reader."
—— 1980: "The reading process: a phenomenological approach."
Kuenzli, R.E. 1980: "The intersubjective structure of the reading process: a communication-oriented theory of literature."
Riquelme, J.P. 1980: "The ambivalence of reading."
EVELYNE KEITEL

Islamic studies Given the vast scope of Islamic studies, in terms of subject matter, history, and geography, this brief account will limit itself to indicating certain crucial developments and suggesting the ways in which major modern theories have begun to make incursions into analyses of Islam. Traditionally, Islamic scholarship has occupied a number of areas: translating, editing, and interpreting the *Qur'an*, revered by Muslims as the Word of God revealed to the Prophet Muhammad; compiling and assessing the authenticity of the *Hadith* or sayings of the Prophet; producing increasingly accurate biographies of the Prophet; rediscovering, editing, and translating works of Islamic literature and philosophy; and analyzing the historically complex connections between Islamic and European CULTURE.

Islam (meaning "submission" to the will of God) is characterized primarily by its uncompromising monotheism, its absolute insistence that God is One, and that the Prophet Muhammad was His final messenger to humankind. It sees itself as continuing what is true in Judaism and Christianity and reveres the Hebrew prophets, including Christ. Its main prescriptions and tenets include the profession of faith, prayer, fasting, pilgrimage, charity to the poor, humility, honesty in trade, personal cleanliness, and the absolute spiritual equality of all human beings before God. Islam is officially dated back to 622 AD, the year of the *Hijra* or the Prophet's flight from Mecca (the town in Arabia where he was born) to Medina to escape persecution by the Meccan traders, whose lifestyle and profit were threatened by the new religion. It was in 610 AD that Muhammad experienced his first Divine revelation in the cave of Hira outside of Mecca. This and subsequent revelations were compiled, shortly after the Prophet's death, into the *Qur'an*, which literally means "recitation." This book, whose Arabic text has survived unchanged for over 14 centuries, is the primary source of authority in Islam, complemented, sometimes problematically, by the *Hadith* and the historically developed CANONS of Islamic law or *Shari'a*.

The long traditions of Islamic theology and philosophy, flourishing from the eighth to the thirteenth centuries and stagnating somewhat thereafter, were highly eclectic, drawing on Greek, Persian, and Christian thought. Their concerns overlapped considerably with those of Christian theology: free will, predestination, anthropomorphism, the nature of the Divinity, the connections between human and Divine law, and the reconciliation of reason and revelation. Many of the thinkers prominent in these traditions have long been known through their influence on Western thought: the Neoplatonists al-Farabi (Alfarabius) (870–950) and Ibn Sina (Avicenna) (980–1037); the sharply nonconformist al-Razi (Rhazes) (d. 923?); al-Ghazali (1058–1111) who attempted to reconcile orthodox Islamic doctrine with the mystical insights of Sufism; and the Aristotelian Ibn Rushd (Averroes) (1126–98).

There has also existed a vast body of exegesis of

the *Qur'an*, ranging from the early commentary of Ibn Jarir al-Tabari (838–922) to the unfinished work of the Egyptian modernist Muhammad 'Abduh (1849–1905) and the interpretations of Abul Kalam Azad (1888–1958) and Kenneth Cragg. The problems – of historical contextualization, etymology, and law – occupying these commentators have overlapped to some extent with those confronted by translators of the *Qur'an*. Characteristic problems have included: the abrogation of certain earlier verses by subsequent revelations; the chronology and coherence of the whole; the historical departure of some Arabic words from their original meaning in the *Qur'an*; and the semantic comprehensiveness or distinctness of certain Arabic words, equally resistant to translation.

On a broader level, the history of translation of the *Qur'an* reveals that the study of Islam has been a phenomenon of Western politics, scholarship, and thought as much as it has been a governing imperative of the Islamic political, cultural, and legal world. Modern critical approaches in particular have been conducted largely by Western scholars, especially by Muslims trained in Western as well as Eastern traditions. The first Western translation of the *Qur'an* was completed in 1143 by the English scholar Robertus Retenensis, under direction from Peter the Venerable, Abbot of Cluny. Motivated by hostile intentions, this version was profoundly inaccurate yet served as the basis for early European translations. Equally distinguished by its inaccuracies was Alexander Ross's English rendering of the 1647 French translation published by André du Ryer. Ross offered no claim to scholarly impartiality, urging in his preface that the *Qur'an* was a repository of follies which would confirm the "health" of Christianity. In 1649 the Arabic text of the *Qur'an* was published in Hamburg; availing himself of this as well as a new Latin version (1698) by Ludovico Maracci, George Sale produced a more accurate English version in 1734. Again, Sale's endeavors were polemical regarding both Islam and Catholicism: he viewed the exposure of the "imposture" of Islam and its overthrow as a "glory" reserved for Protestants. Sale's was the standard text for English readers until the late nineteenth century; it was the version which stood behind Edward Gibbon's ambivalent assessment of Muhammad.

The methods of the Higher Criticism, applied to the Christian Gospels in the nineteenth century, eventually made their impact on Qur'anic

translation and exegesis: J.M. Rodwell's translation changed the order of the *Suras* or Qur'anic chapters and his assessment of Muhammad as inspired by a sincere monotheism was certainly more impartial and "scientific" than that of his predecessors. Other notable translations have included those by Henry Edward Palmer (1880) and Marmaduke Pickthall (1930), an English convert to Islam. A.J. Arberry's version (1955) attempts to recapture the rhetorical and rhythmical patterns which lie behind the splendor of the original. Since then, numerous other renderings have appeared, some by Muslim scholars such as Abdullah Yousuf Ali. These have attempted to grapple with the problems enumerated above in the light of increasingly sophisticated historical and philological research, as well as the need to translate the spirit of the *Qur'an* into idioms of relevance to the twentieth century.

In general, Western studies of Islam progressed from viewing it in the twelfth century as a Christian heresy or a false religion to more systematic and disciplined approaches in the late sixteenth and seventeenth centuries. The following account of these trends is indebted in part to Albert Hourani's splendid book *Islam in European Thought* (1991). From 1587 Arabic was taught at the Collège de France in Paris. Chairs of Arabic were established at the Universities of Leiden (1613), Cambridge (1632), and Oxford (1634). Eventually, clearer pictures of the Prophet of Islam emerged, acknowledging at least his inspired message and the historical role of his reaffirmation of Divine unity. Such assessments were offered in Simon Ockley's *The History of the Saracens* (1718) and F.D. Maurice's *The Religions of the World and Their Relations with Christianity* (1847). However, portrayals of Islam as a dangerous threat to Christianity have persisted into the twentieth century: William Muir's *The Life of Muhammed* (1912) remained a standard text for many years.

Until the nineteenth century, accounts of Islam were generally based on the *Qur'an*, the Prophet's life, and the view that Islam was spread by the sword. Some of the first attempts to see Islam in the broader context of world history were made by J.G. Herder (1744–1803) and G.W.F. Hegel (1770–1831). Hegel saw Islam's assertion of an utterly transcendent Divinity as an essential stage of world history but one which had to be sublated by a more dialectical connection of immanence and transcendence between human and Divine (Hegel, 1956, pp. 356–7). Also in the nineteenth century arose the "science" of comparative philology: the close study of languages and their meanings in their mutual connections. Prominent figures in this development were Franz Bopp (1791–1876) and especially Ernest Renan (1823–92) who believed that particular languages embodied given possibilities of cultural development. He saw Islam as a "closed" religion, locked in an abstract perception of divine unity and impervious to refinement or development through science, philosophy, or ART. Like Hegel, he saw Europe as bearing the burden of future world-historical progress. Renan's *Life of Jesus* (1863) developed the Higher Critical techniques embodied in David Strauss's *Life of Jesus* (1835). Both works attempted to examine the Gospels in their historical context, with attention to questions of their coherence and veracity. These methods were brought into the study of Islam by Julius Wellhausen (1844–1918), Silvestre de Sacy (1758–1838), Ignaz Goldziher (1850–1921), and Louis Massignon (1883–1962). Renan had refused to view the life of Christ as a series of isolated incidents generating a completely new religion; rather, he placed that life in a broader historical development from Hebrew traditions (Renan, 1955, pp. 388–93). Likewise, these analysts placed the *Qur'an*, the *Hadith*, and the life of the Prophet in a more comprehensive cultural context, examining, for example, the connections between Islam and pre-Islamic Arabia in their actual complex continuity rather than viewing Islam as a complete break from the past. In England, the tradition of Islamic studies acquired strength only in the nineteenth century from figures such as W. Wright (1830–89), R.A. Nicholson (1868–1945), D.S. Margoliouth (1858–1940), and H.A.R. Gibb (1895–1971).

While these scholars continued to apply the methods of philological and cultural analysis, the more recent generations of scholars, social scientists, and anthropologists have begun to apply Marxist, sociological, feminist, modernist, and even deconstructive and psychoanalytical methods to the study of all aspects of Islam. These newer approaches have entailed a questioning of the motives and methods of Orientalism as well as the use of "Islam" as an explanatory category. Clifford Geertz addresses the dilemma of the unity and identity of Islam in his *Islam Observed* (1968). André Raymond's work refers historical developments in Egypt to economic conditions rather than to "Islam." Max Weber's theses concerning both

Christianity and Islam have generated some important Marxist and sociological analyses of Islam. In *The Protestant Ethic and the Spirit of Capitalism*, Weber had correlated the rise of capitalism to a large extent with the rationalism and "this-worldliness" of Calvinism and Lutheranism (Weber, 1978, pp. 174–6); this position had contradicted MARX's and ENGELS's materialist explanation of capitalist development which, however, had been very incompletely extended to Islamic societies. Maxime Rodinson's *Islam and Capitalism* (1978) rejects the idea that capitalism failed to develop in Islamic societies as a result of Qur'anic injunctions or proscriptions in the *Hadith* or *Shari'a*. He argues, rather, that capitalist development was stunted by the state's domination of trade relations, the self-sufficiency of local village economies, and nomadic invasions. Other important studies in this vein include Bryan S. Turner's *Weber and Islam* (1974) which, arguing for the convergence of Marx's and Weber's views on Asiatic society, sees secularization to the extent that it has occurred in Islamic societies as essentially mimetic of Western capitalist secularization. Perry ANDERSON has an illuminating section on the political development of Islam in his *Lineages of the Absolutist State* (1974). Rodinson's materialist principles of explanation are carried into his biography *Muhammad* (1980). Attempting to give an impartial and humanistic account of the life of the Prophet, Rodinson examines Islam as an ideological movement. While he accepts that the Islamic community has possessed a distinct identity, he argues that religious IDEOLOGY did not overwhelmingly transform Arab societies: many factors of economic life and the vicissitudes of political power were impervious to religious adherence or the norms of Islam (Rodinson, 1980, pp. xiv, xxxiv–xxxix). Marshall Hodgson's *The Venture of Islam* (1974) is an ambitious attempt to rethink the role of Islam in world history, attributing to it a cultural predominance and independence lasting into the nineteenth century.

What might loosely be called "modernistic" interpretations of Islam, which attempt to reconcile Islamic teachings with modern thought, date back to the late nineteenth century. Prominent in the development of such endeavors were Jamal al-Din Afghani (1839–97) and his especially renowned disciple Muhammad 'Abduh (1849–1905), who attempted a reinterpretation of the *Qur'an* in the light of reason, arguing that Islam is a tolerant and humane religion. In India, Sir Sayyed Ahmed

Khan (1817–98) advocated a modern approach to education and helped found Aligarh University with a view to providing access to Western thought within an Islamic context. The Egyptian statesman, scholar, and writer Taha Hussein (b. 1889) applied modern exegetical methods to classical Arabic TEXTS, arousing fierce opposition from traditional scholars. Sayyed Amir 'Ali urged fresh readings of the *Qur'an* freed from the closed readings of the *'Ulama* or religious elite. He argued, for example, that polygamy was implicitly condemned by the *Qur'an*.

A major figure in Islamic modernism was Sir Muhammad Iqbal (1876–1938), the greatest Urdu poet of the twentieth century, who also wrote in Persian. His lectures entitled *The Reconstruction of Religious Thought in Islam* (1934) represent an important attempt to recast Islamic doctrine in the light of modern Western thought. Drawing on NIETZSCHE, Bergson, and the Persian mystical poet Rumi, Iqbal reacts against what he perceives as the fatalism and asceticism which have come to dominate Islamic thought: he affirms the reality of the creative self which aspires towards the highest individuality, that of God (Iqbal, 1978, pp. xvii–xix; 1934, p. 181). Recent modernistic discussions of Islam have included Fazlur Rahman's *Islam and Modernity* (1982), which argues for a holistic critical and rational rereading of the *Qur'an* and *Hadith* in the light of their fundamental intentions, rather than elevating to an unauthentic authority particular statements abstracted from their historical and cultural contexts. Iqbal had already rejected the trite oppositions, such as that between religion and science, which had pervaded so much of nineteenth-century Western as well as Islamic debate. The language of literary and CULTURAL THEORY, also spurning such oppositions, has begun to permeate recent discussions of Islam. Akbar S. Ahmed's *Postmodernism and Islam* (1992) explores the connections between Western modernism, POSTMODERNISM, and Islam, stressing especially the role of the media – and of some Muslim extremists – in offering distorted and essentialist images of Islam. Ahmed offers a fascinating overview of current ideological conflicts underpinning the study of Islam (Ahmed, 1992, pp. 154–91).

In fact, the history of image construction of Islam has furnished the subject matter for recent critiques of the Orientalist tradition. The best-known work in this mode is Edward W. SAID's *Orientalism* (1978) which attempts to expose the categories and methods of Orientalist scholarship as not only lacking the impartiality they claim, but also as being part of a broader Western project to define and effectively construct the "Orient" for its own political, economic, and ideological purposes. Said carries this venture into the contemporary political scene in his *Covering Islam* (1981).

Aziz Al-Azmeh's more recent *Islams and Modernities* (1993) might be called deconstructive: it rejects "Islam" as a unifying category of historical or cultural explanation. Such a category is based on an essentialist DISCOURSE of identity and irreducible difference which has both led to the study of Islam through transcendental essences such as "Shi'ism" and generated notions of changeless Oriental properties. Culturally specific differences have thereby been reduced to binary structures, assigning the Islamic world qualities such as irrationality, servitude, and stagnation, which are opposed to the inclusive European categories generated by the ENLIGHTENMENT: reason, freedom, and perfectibility (Al-Azmeh, 1993, pp. 18–24). Moreover, such POSITIVISM and ESSENTIALISM have infected the very heart of Islamic studies: philology. These strategies have been instrumental in constructing images of Islam, ranging historically from those of heresy and the Anti-Christ to more modern portrayals of Islam as anachronistic. They have also fostered a genetic and enumerative scholarship, obsessed with the explanatory power of origins and proceeding merely by the addition of further detail. Al-Azmeh argues that Islam as a category of Orientalist discourse must be dissolved and the notion of objectivity reexamined in the light of modern theoretical techniques (Al-Azmeh, 1993, pp. 141–3). Islamists, stresses Al-Azmeh, have been equally guilty of promoting an essentialist discourse: they overlook the fact that Islamic law has never been a rigid code, that it is not grounded in the actual experience of Muslims, and that it has historically enjoyed a wide latitude, being shaped in consonance with the requirements of Islamic ideology (Al-Azmeh, 1993, pp. 8–12).

The flexibility of Islamic law has lain at the heart of one of the most stubbornly controversial issues concerning Islam, the status of women. Many commentators have held that Islam vastly improved the conditions of women in medieval Arabia, restricting polygamy, abolishing female infanticide, granting women free will in marriage and the ability to initiate divorce, giving them rights of property and inheritance (though not equal to those of men), and even permitting women to assume political government. This argument rests on the view that in pre-Islamic Arabia women had virtually no rights and were treated as chattels, comprising part of the estates of their husbands and fathers. Even Islam's allowing men to take four wives has been justified by the fact that polygamy was to some extent a solution to the number of excess women who were in need of support. Modern scholars tend to view the nature of the changes between pre-Islamic and Islamic eras as somewhat more complex, claiming, for example, that before Islam, women performed certain crucial functions as priestesses, prophets, and warriors and that Islam narrowed this range of roles.

Certainly, some of the important early women of Islam played a vital part in the growth of the religion. The Prophet's first wife Khadija, a prominent businesswoman, was the first convert to Islam and undoubtedly her social status aided Muhammad in that initial decisive period. Muhammad's final and youngest wife 'Aisha, who survived him by many years, was acknowledged as a source of authority regarding the authenticity of the *Hadith* and was regularly consulted on matters of religious law and custom. She played a decisive part in the first civil war in Islam over the succession to the Caliphate (the official governership of Islam), which generated the schism between *Sunni* Muslims (followers of the *Sunnah* or "way" of the Prophet) and *Shi'ahs* or *Shi'ites* ("followers" of 'Ali, the first cousin of Muhammad, whose succession they advocated). Other notable women in Islam have included the Sufi mystic Rabi'a al-'Adawiyya (d. 801) of Basra, and the distinguished scholars Umm Hani (d. 1466) and Hajar (b. 1388). The male mystical philosopher Ibn al-Arabi (1165–1240) stressed the complementary nature of the sexes as well as the feminine dimension of the Divine.

In modern times, especially from the late nineteenth century onwards, some male modernists such as Muhammad 'Abduh included among their modernizing proposals calls for the reform of women's education and laws concerning marriage and divorce. A feminist landmark in Arab society was Qassim Amin's *Tahrir al-Mar'a* (*The Liberation of Woman*) (1899) which generated heated dispute. Feminists of the early twentieth century included Huda Sha'rawi, a founder of the *Intellectual Association of Egyptian Women* (1914), who espoused a Westernized feminism, and Malak Hifni Nassef whose feminism shunned "Western" imperatives such as unveiling. Prominent women writers in the Islamic world have included the Indian-born novelist Qurratulain Haider; the Iranian poet Forugh Farrokhzad (1935–67); and Iraqi-born Nazik Al-Mala'ika (b. 1923), a seminal figure in modern Arab poetry. More recently, the novelist Nawal El-Saadawi has attempted to expose the psychological and physical abuse of women; the Pakistani poets Fahmida Riaz and Kishwar Naheed have explored sensual themes and the psychology of male–female relationships; the Bangladeshi writer Taslima Nasreen is currently facing fierce public and governmental antagonism for her outspoken feminism and atheism. Writers such as Rana Kabbani have pleaded, on the basis of their experience of Western and Islamic cultures, for a dialog between the values enshrined in each.

Prominent among recent feminist studies of Islam are Fatima Mernissi's *The Veil and the Male Elite* (1991) and Leila Ahmed's *Women and Gender in Islam* (1992). Situating Islam's prescriptions concerning women in a historical context, Mernissi's stimulating book argues that the spirit of Islam's intentions was to procure equality for women. Ahmed's treatment of the subject, to which part of the foregoing account is indebted, is also historical. She traces the varying status of women from pre-Islamic times in the Middle East through the GENDER configurations of successive periods of Islam to the present. At the core of her argument is that while Islam secluded women from a range of activities, it has embraced a tension between its "stubbornly egalitarian" ethical vision and the hierarchical structures of marriage pragmatically instituted in Islamic societies. She points out that the *Qur'an* is remarkable among religious texts in that it is addressed to women as well as men, and traces in detail the developments outlined above, such as the crucial role of women in constructing the verbal texts of Islam and the growth of feminism in the Arab world. She also argues insightfully against a Western-style feminism which uncritically inscribes itself into the old imperialist narratives: Western women assume that they can pursue feminist goals by redefining their cultural heritage, but Muslim women, it is implied, can seek such goals only by rejecting their own culture for Western ideals. She also observes the historical linkage of feminism and imperialism: in the late nineteenth century some male imperialists, such as Lord

Cromer, the British Consul General in Egypt, led the attack abroad against Muslim "degradation" of women while being staunchly resistant to feminism at home. Equally, however, Ahmed criticizes the stagnant assumption of Islamists that the meaning of gender in the initiatory Islamic society was somehow unambiguous; this meaning, states Ahmed, was contested from the beginning. What we need, she asserts, is a feminism which is informed and vigilantly self-aware. Ahmed's arguments call for a sensitivity to the cultural construction of values and images, for example, the veil, a symbol in the West for downright oppression in Islam, has a very different range of significance – including that of resistance to oppression – in the Arab World.

In general, the excellent work of Mernissi, Ahmed, Said, Al-Azmeh, and others serves as a salutary reminder that modern critical approaches still have much to cover in the vast field of "Islam." It remains a sad fact that, with the arguable exception of Muhammad Iqbal, the Islamic world has not produced a major modern philosopher.

Reading

Ahmed, Leila 1992: *Women and Gender in Islam.*
Ali, A. Yusuf 1934 (*1983*): *The Holy Qur'an: Text, Translation and Commentary.*
Arberry, A.J. 1950: *Sufism: An Account of the Mystics of Islam.*
——1955: *The Koran Interpreted: A Translation.*
Azami, M.M. 1978: *Studies in Early Hadith Literature.*
Cragg, Kenneth 1984: *Muhammad and the Christian.*
——1988: *Readings in the Qur'an.*
——1985: *The Call of the Minaret.*
Gabrielli, Francesco 1957 (*1984*): *Arab Historians of the Crusades.*
Guillaume, Alfred 1954 (*1977*): *Islam.*
Hourani, Albert 1991: *Islam in European Thought.*
Kandiyoti, Deniz, ed. 1991: *Women, Islam and the State.*
Lings, Martin 1983: *Muhammad: His Life Based on the Earliest Sources.*
Myers, Eugene A. 1964: *Arabic Thought and the Western World.*
Rahman, Fazlur 1982: *Islam and Modernity.*
Rodinson, Maxime 1961 (*1980*): *Muhammad.*
——1966 (*1978*): *Islam and Capitalism.*
Spiegelman, J., Khan, P.V.I., and Fernandez, T. 1991: *Sufism, Islam and Jungian Pschology.*
Watt, W. Montgomery 1962 (*1987*): *Islamic Philosophy and Theology.*

M.A.R. HABIB

J

Jakobson, Roman (1896–1982) Russian structural linguist and, from 1926, a member of the PRAGUE LINGUISTIC CIRCLE. He began his career as president of the Moscow Linguistic Circle, and so was at the heart of Russian FORMALISM. He and his colleagues were interested in the relative autonomy of literary works, especially in terms of exactly what it is that distinguishes them from nonliterary language. His own concern was with the internal relations which he saw as the main feature of literature, such as elements of linguistic patterning and phonological correspondence. A major figure in the development of STRUCTURALISM, Jakobson links Russian formalism with later developments in structuralism as a whole. He integrated Russian formalist thought with an overall framework derived from the linguistics of Ferdinand de SAUSSURE. He is therefore linked with the emergence of SEMIOTICS, and was instrumental in the production of theories of DEFAMILIARIZATION and METAPHOR AND METONYMY. His interest in Saussure was, however, not one of simple acceptance. His relationship with Saussurean linguistics was one of dialog; he tended to take what he could use without simply reproducing Saussure's theory. In this respect he developed structural linguistics out of a meeting of formalism and structuralism. Jakobson found Saussure's antinomies to be too inflexible for his own needs, especially with regard to the study of parole (see LANGUE/PAROLE), which Saussure had shunned. This gave Jakobson a way to deal with linguistic change, something which was not possible for Saussure.

From his work on the integration of the two movements, Jakobson elaborated a theory which claimed that meaning and form are in fact inseparable, so that, for semantic analysis, grammatical forms are fundamentally bound up with their meanings. He therefore replicated in his theories some of the crucial concepts which have come to be associated with structuralism, especially the importance accorded to BINARY OPPOSITIONS. In this context, for Jakobson, all forms of communication were constituted by the interplay between six fundamental elements, each of which correlates to a general typology: addressor (emotive); addressee (conative); a message passed (poetic); the mutual code which renders intelligibility possible (metalinguistic); the means of COMMUNICATION (PHATIC); and a situation to which the message relates (contextual reference). Any element may predominate, so that, for example, in the case of POETRY, the message itself is the focus of attention. Accordingly, Jakobson considered poetics to be an element of linguistics, a type of relatively self-conscious linguistic practice. Poetry draws attention to itself in addition to its communicative function. In attempting to apply structural linguistics to poetic analysis, Jakobson produced several readings which are considered to be classic examples of structuralist literary criticism.

In his criticism Jakobson attempted to show that structuralist techniques can reveal the patterns which structure any given TEXT. An objective critical science was therefore a possibility (but see also BINARY OPPOSITION and STRUCTURALISM for further discussion of this kind of structuralist claim). Jakobson put his theory into practice by dividing the poems he read into groups of stanzas. These groups were organized around binary oppositions such as outer/inner. He then paid very close attention to elements of symmetry between the groups, for example, the uses of pronominal forms or patterns of adjectival variants. He also paid a great deal of attention to phonological patternings and correspondences, something which was always one of his main interests. His theoretical position in respect to this area was that sounds are structured by a SYSTEM of relations by difference, just as language is. The sound system of a poem is part of the functional system which comprises the poem as a whole: the term he used for the basic element of this system was the "phoneme." As with the linguistic SIGN, the phoneme exists in relation to other phonemes in the system of which they are a part, and he made great efforts to identify the various correspondences which made up the system. He applied this research to the problem of sound change in language development as well as to his readings of poetic texts.

In effect, Jakobson's analytical method was to enumerate instances of symmetry, producing lists of syntactically similar features which structure the poem as a whole. A problem with this approach, of course, is that it privileges simple numerical preponderance. Another and much more crucial problem is that it assumes that a repetition of internal elements is all that matters in the exposition of a text. The possibility of an almost endless reading of patterns would imply that the scientific method which Jakobson sought to achieve may not be possible. Thus his claim that his method simply and objectively found in the text patterns (and hence meanings) which were already there precludes the observation that such a reading can always find what it is looking for. The reading can in fact be seen to produce the patterns, so that the relationship of the reader to the text is much more problematical than Jakobson assumed (see also STRUCTURALISM for more discussion of this topic).

To some extent Jakobson anticipated these difficulties. He tried to explain the functions performed by each of the patterns which he discerned, especially in the case of the relation between phonological correspondences and semantic ones, so that the two became of equivalent relevance in the reading process. He made reference to a relationship between these correspondences and the reader's own experience. The act of reading a poem was supposed to awaken the reader's experience, and so the patterns which exist in poetry are somehow equivalent to the reader's perceptions. In fact, these immanent structures do not have to be perceived by the conscious reading mind: in this theory syntactic patterns will always echo thought patterns, even if the reader is not fully aware of them. Jakobson therefore assumed that his structural linguistics was objectively correct.

Reading

Jakobson, Roman 1971: "On realism in art."
——1990a: *On Language.*
——1962–90b: *Selected Writings.*
——and Jones, Lawrence G. 1970: *Shakespeare's Verbal Art in th'Expence of Spirit.*

PAUL INNES

James, C.L.R. (1901–89) Caribbean man of letters. Cyril Lionel Robert James was born in Trinidad, January 4, 1901, one year after the historic Pan-African Congress in London – an organization in which he would play an active part subsequently. James, along with the other great Pan-Africanist from Trinidad, George Padmore, formed the International Friends of Ethiopia, in response to Mussolini's invasion of Ethiopia in 1935. James edited the monthly journal *International African Opinion*. In the emerging struggle for decolonization in various parts of the African diaspora, it was James who in *A History of Negro Revolt*, drew attention to the historical antecedents of the political struggles of the time.

Known simply by his initials, and to his close associates as "Nello," he became one of the Caribbean's great men of letters. A philosopher, James was an astute Marxist and Hegelian dialectician. He was also a social and cultural critic, sports writer, novelist, playwright, political activist, and labor organizer.

James published *La Divina Pastora* in 1927. This was one of his earlier pieces of fiction. He also published *Triumph* (1929) in the literary journal *Trinidad*. During this period James also completed his only full-length work of fiction, *Minty Alley*, which was published in England in 1936. C.L.R. James left the Caribbean in 1932 for the United Kingdom. He had taken with him a completed manuscript – a biography of the Trinidadian trade union leader Captain Cipriani. *The Life of Captain Cipriani: An Account of British Government in the West Indies* was published in 1932. Immediately upon his arrival in England, he became politically active, joining the British Labour Party but finding himself "to the left of the Labour party." His leftist militancy led him to join the Trotskyists in London. Interviewed in 1987 James noted, "I came to London and in a few months I was a Trotskyist."

From England C.L.R. James moved to the United States in 1938, where he remained until 1952, when he was deported in the throes of the McCarthyite communist witch hunts. As with his arrival in England, James wasted no time in establishing contact with the Trotskyists in the United States. He became a member of the Socialist Workers Party (SWP). James initially broke with the Trotskyists in 1940 on ideological and tactical grounds. He was highly critical of the SWP's defense of Soviet orthodoxy. James, who used the pseudonym "J.R. Johnson," and Raya Dunayevskaya (a close comrade of James) whose pseudonym was "Feddie Forest," were the main critics of this orthodoxy within the SWP. This faction became known as the Johnson–Forest Tendency and later rejoined the Trotskyists, only to leave again in 1950.

Along with his political activity during this period James's intellectual contribution was marked by the publication of his seminal work on the overthrow of slavery and the establishment of the first black independent nation in the western hemisphere. This account of the Haitian Revolution of 1791–1803 was published in 1938 as *Black Jacobins: Toussaint L'Ouverture and the San Domingo Revolution*, and has become a classic. James also published in 1937 *World Revolution 1917–1936: The Rise and Fall of the Communist International*, and coauthored *State Capitalism and World Revolution* (1950).

At the heart of C.L.R. James's world view was a notion contained in a letter to Constance Webb, written in 1944, "to develop the consciousness, the independence, the sense of destiny, the sense of responsibility, among the masses of people." James valued this ideal very dearly. His was a life of intellectual rigor and popular practice and engagement. James was as comfortable being a colleague of Jomo Kenyatta, a mentor to the former Prime Minister of Trinidad and Tobago, Eric Williams, or advisor to Kwame Nkrumah, as he was organizing workers, or politically mobilizing them into his Workers and Farmers Party in Trinidad in 1966. His interests were wide and divergent, some may even say contradictory. It was this intellectual perspicacity and fecundity which drove him to write about the social, cultural, and historical forces at work in the game of cricket in his now famous *Beyond a Boundary* (1963), and it was his deep love and interest in literature which resulted in his examination of Herman Melville as a critic of bureaucratic capitalism and authoritarianism in his *Mariners, Renegades and Castaways: The Story of Herman Melville and the World We Live In* (1953).

If *Notes On Dialectics: Hegel, Marx, Lenin* (1948) signaled the evolution of James's political thinking, then his *Party Politics in the West Indies* (1962) articulated his attempt to interpret and apply MARXISM creatively to the specific cultural milieu. Controversies over the privileging of his cultural work over his political work (see Cudjoe, 1992), or the neglect of his writing on the Hispanic Caribbean (see López Springfield, 1992), or his admiration of European intellectual traditions over other types of tradition, or how his emphasis on class analysis at times marginalized importantant considerations of race (see Martin, 1972, and Worcester, 1992), are testimony to the remarkably complex legacy that James has left the world. C.L.R. James died in London in 1989 and was buried in Trinidad in May of the same year. Since his death, his intellectual contribution has become even more celebrated in the recent publication of several journal articles, two biographies, two major collections of his work, and three anthologies dedicated to various dimensions of the Jamesian oeuvre. These publications, along with those still in press, in addition to his own published work, will secure James's intellectual contribution for posterity.

Reading
Cudjoe, Selwyn 1992: "C.L.R. James misbound."
James, C.L.R. 1936 (*1971*): *Minty Alley.*
—— 1937 (*1973*): *World Revolution 1917–1936: The Rise and Fall of the Communist International.*
—— 1938: *The Black Jacobins: Toussaint L'Ouverture and the San Domingo Revolution.*
—— 1948 (*1980*): *Notes on Dialectics : Hegel, Marx, Lenin.*
—— 1953 (*1986*): *Mariners, Renegades and Castaways: The Story of Herman Melville and the World We Live In.*
—— 1962 (*1984*): *Party Politics in the West Indies.*
—— 1963 (*1983*): *Beyond a Boundary.*
——Dunayevskaya, Raya, and Boggs, Grace 1950 (*1986*): *State Capitalism and World Revolution.*
Martin, Tony 1972: "C.L.R. James and the race/class question."
Worcester, Kent 1992: "A Victorian with the rebel seed: C.L.R. James and the politics of intellectual engagement."

LINDEN LEWIS

Japanese studies Although many of the most important Western texts in CULTURAL and CRITICAL THEORY have been translated into Japanese, Japanese studies are not generally well known in Western countries. A large number of books by members of the FRANKFURT SCHOOL, from ADORNO and HORKHEIMER to HABERMAS, are available in Japanese translations, along with most of the works of BENJAMIN and FROMM. Texts by such French structuralists as SAUSSURE, LÉVI-STRAUSS, LACAN, ALTHUSSER, and FOUCAULT can be read in Japanese, as well as the most important studies in semiology (SEMIOTICS) by BARTHES, BAUDRILLARD, KRISTEVA, HJELMSLEV, BAKHTIN, JAKOBSON, PEIRCE, and Norris. Poststructuralists, such as DERRIDA, Deleuze, and LYOTARD, are also well represented in Japanese translation. There is also great interest in British cultural studies in Japan. The major texts of HOGGART and Raymond WILLIAMS have been translated; and the writings of HALL and David Morley are often referred to and discussed by Japanese scholars, although no translations of their work have yet appeared. Both HEIDEGGER and Jacques Derrida took great interest in the problems of translating their work into Japanese and wrote detailed, open letters to their translators.

In addition to these translations and a countless number of introductions and reviews, Japanese scholars have uniquely interpreted and developed Western theories, especially in the terrain of SEMIOTICS. Saussure's theories have exerted a very strong influence over Japanese linguists. *Course in General Linguistics* (1916) was translated into Japanese in 1928, approximately 30 years earlier than the first English version. It was the first translation of this seminal work to appear anywhere in the world. Keizaburo Maruyama (1981) has concentrated his study of Saussure on manuscript transcriptions and student notes that were found in the 1950s and emphasizes that the *Course* as published does not necessarily represent Saussure's theory. He rejects the idea of *langue* as statically grasped and transcendentally located over a speaker's *parole*, which has been attributed to the author of the *Course*. Maryuama focuses on the arbitrariness or artificiality of SIGNS and the linguistic system itself, which have the power to define or generate human perceptions. *Language* as the capacity of symbolization or categorization occupies the pivotal point in his study. The artificiality or unnaturalness of signs is the root of a "fetishism of culture" (1984), because the unperceived arbitrariness of signs makes the artificiality of CULTURE look natural. From this perspective, he develops a semiology of culture, which includes important psychoanalytic themes (1987). Maruyama has a strong interest in Saussure not simply as a linguist, but as a profound thinker. Yoshiro Takeuchi, another eminent cultural semiologist, shares some important theoretical assumptions with Maruyama, but criticizes him for attaching too great an importance to literary language, and thus his tendency to neglect the languages of daily life (Takeuchi and Maruyama, 1982).

Yoshihiko Ikegami is one of the leading linguists and semiologists in Japan and has written in both Japanese and English. One of his major concerns is not so much rule-governed linguistic behavior as rule-changing or rule-creating. For him poetics, rather than linguistics, is the ultimate theoretical

model for semiology (1982; 1983; 1991). Ikegami has developed a detailed comparison of linguistic representation in Japanese and English. For example, in describing an event, English tends to single out the human being as the acting agent, while Japanese is inclined to focus on the event as a whole; consequently, the human being taking part in the event is often submerged in the whole. There is a marked tendency in Japanese to represent the occurrence of an event as caused by some power or "nature" that transcends the human being as agent. In tending to weaken or even efface the agency of the individual, Japanese fuses and emphasizes transition and development. Ikegami calls this "becoming," and characterizes Japanese as a "becoming-language" in sharp contrast with English as a "doing-language." Not only, according to his theory, is the human merged with nature, but the individual is often incorporated into the group. Such a synecdochic relationship applies further to TEXT and context: In Japanese, Ikegami argues, the former is not clearly articulated in contrast to the latter and tends to merge homologously with it.

Roland Barthes visited Japan in the 1960s and wrote *The Empire of Signs* (1970), comparing his passion for Japan with Stendhal's for Italy. Koichiro Shinoda claims that this book aims to present ideological criticism of French or Western society by analyzing a completely different linguistic structure and semiotics. Among a number of introductions and interpretations written about Barthes and his works, Shinoda's (1989) is outstanding. Shinoda points out that Barthes resisted any adjective (such as "structuralist") being assigned to him, since his thinking continued to change all through his life. Shinoda tries to comprehend his thought in this way, by concentrating on Barthes's many changes in theoretical position. Chronological description and analysis are therefore important to his purpose. Asking why Barthes changed his standpoint incessantly, Shinoda concludes that he was a new type of thinker who feared that, in the age of highly technologized civilization, every thought would otherwise be forced into a stereotype.

The late Motoki Tokieda was a renowned "anti-Saussurean," who developed an original theory and entered into academic controversies with Japanese Saussureans that extended from the 1940s to the 1950s. But from the point of view of contemporary Saussurean studies, as exemplified by Maruyama's works, Tokieda does share important points of agreement with Saussure. Tokieda sharply opposes a static or transcendental view of language, that is, he claims to be able to comprehend language only in relation to the individual act of expression and understanding. The object of linguistics is then, for him, the specific linguistic acts of associated individuals. His theory has deep implications not only for Saussurean studies but for communication studies as well.

Tokieda's basic position implies the rejection of methodological individualism in favor of a dialogical perspective. From a monological standpoint, the meaning of a message is likely to be determined solely by an account of the speaker's psychic state, including his or her perceptions, emotions, and intentions. Tokieda's dialogism denies the monopoly of meaning by the speaker. It is the hearer who adds the final meaning, which is not necessarily the same as the speaker's. Tokieda's theory further implies not merely dialogism but also interactionism. By interaction or "cooperation" is meant the mutual adjustment of actions. For instance, one can imagine two doctors cooperating to perform an operation on a patient. "Speaker" and "hearer" are not appropriate terms for such cooperating doctors. "Actor A" and "actor B" are more to the point. Although he admitted that formerly he "used to observe linguistic structures themselves abstractly by separating languages from the whole of human acts," Tokieda came to advocate locating linguistics in the process of mutual adjustment of actors. "We cannot really understand languages if we observe communications alone," separated from interactions of which communications are part (Tokieda, 1955). In this respect Tokieda's perspective is unique among Japanese linguists and semiologists and is comparable to the later work of Raymond Williams.

If, as Tokieda argues, communications are located indissolubly in cooperations or connected activities, the primary or indispensable function of language is the evocation of the act of the OTHER, because without the other, connected activities, or the mutual adjustment of actions between or among actors cannot proceed. Although the descriptive function of language has long been, explicitly or implicitly, a presupposition of linguists and philosophers, WITTGENSTEIN in his later works and AUSTIN in his SPEECH ACT theory began a criticism of this descriptivistic prejudice. The descriptivistic view of language is static and monological, as well as methodologically individualistic. While sharing this criticism with Wittgenstein and Austin, Tokieda's interactionism cannot fully overlap with their theories. As Keiichi Noe has shown (1985), despite the terms "illocutionary act" and "perlocutionary act," Austin's speech-act theory is not fully interactionistic. Tokieda's work approaches the terrain of social psychology. As a linguistic theory, it is unique and critical. Indeed, Tokieda confesses that his experiences during and after the 1941–5 war made it possible to construct his theory. Probably his observation of ordinary people cooperating enabled him to understand the fundamental function of language.

Among Western social psychologists, George Herbert Mead is quite pertinent to Tokieda's view of linguistic cooperation. Mead attaches special importance to interaction and cooperation. Tokieda criticizes the "enclosure" of meaning within *langue* or the speaker's intentional message. Instead, the hearer's attachment of meaning is basic; and finally, incited or evoked action or response of the other occupies the critical locus in his theory of meaning. Mead anticipated much of this theory: "We want to approach language not from the standpoint of inner meanings to be expressed, but in its larger context of co-operation in the group taking place by means of signals and gestures. Meaning appears within that process" (Mead, 1934). Although meaning is most often considered in terms of language, Mead presents the radical perspective that meaning is not first a matter of language but rather a process of interaction and cooperation. Toshihiko Aida (1991) discusses this idea and argues that only from the perspective of interactionism can the origin of meaning in language and the consciousness of meaning in human beings be explicated. Consciousness of meaning cannot be separated from intelligence, mind, and consciousness in general or from self-consciousness in particular, all of which also have their origins in interacion. That interaction comes theoretically first is crucial to his theory, although it has often been overlooked by American interactionists. Meadean interactionism plays a cardinal role for Habermas in establishing the concept of "communicative action" (Habermas, 1981). As Hideki Maeda has pointed out (Maruyama, ed. 1985), Tokieda's works will continue to be of importance for Saussurean studies, and (it should now be added) for linguistics, semiology, and communication studies as well.

Reading
Barthes, R. 1970 (*1982*): *The Empire of Signs.*
Ikegami, Y. 1981: *Linguistics of DOING and BECOMING.*

——1991: *The Empire of Signs: Semiotic Essays on Japanese Culture.*
Maruyama, K. 1981: *The Thought of Saussure.*
——1984: *The Fetishism of Culture.*
Saussure, F. de 1916 (*1959*): *Course in General Linguistics.*
Shinoda, K. 1989: *Roland Barthes.*
Takeuchi, Y. 1981: *The Theory of Culture.*
Tokieda, M. 1941: *The Principle of the Study of the Japanese Language 1.*
——1955: *The Principle of the Study of the Japanese Language 2.*

TOSHIHIKO AIDA

Jaspers, Karl (1883–1969) Trained as a doctor and psychiatrist, Jaspers turned to philosophy during the 1914–18 war, publishing in 1919 his *Psychology of World Views*, which he later called the first truly existentialist book. Despite his influence on contemporaries in Germany and France, the bulk, repetitiveness, and turgid style of his writings have made Jaspers unattractive to later generations.

It is two themes from KANT which inspire Jaspers's thinking. First, the limits of empirical and scientific understanding, which render it incapable of grasping reality as a unitary whole and of elucidating the nature of the self. Second, and relatedly, the "ambiguous" or "antinomical" character of human beings, at once denizens of the natural world and enjoying *Existenz*, a spontaneous freedom and responsibility for determining the course and significance of their lives.

It is the insistence on *Existenz*, and the ways we experience it through the *Grenzsituationen* ("boundary situations") of mortality, guilt, and sheer contingency, which warrant Jaspers's classification as an existentialist. But it is misleading to follow SARTRE and label him a "Christian existentialist." While Jaspers thought that our sense of reality's wholeness and freedom as a "gift" were "ciphers" pointing to a transcendent order, the "Encompassing," he denied that this order could be explained in familiar religious terms – or indeed in any terms: "Whatever we think we know about the deity is superstition."

Perhaps Jaspers's most persistent motif is the "paradox" that human beings must occupy standpoints, moral ones included, for which no validation is feasible. Instead of trying to resolve the "paradox" we must cultivate a "philosophic faith" which respects the freedom to occupy different standpoints, resists the reduction of men to items of nature (as Jaspers thought FREUD and MARX were attempting), and encourages an openness to the intimations of the transcendent. In his emphases on indeterminacy, eclecticism, and openness, Jaspers presages some current "postmodernist" attitudes.

See also EXISTENTIALISM.

Reading
Jaspers, Karl 1950: *The Perennial Scope of Philosophy.*
——1951: *The Way to Wisdom.*
——1969–71: *Philosophy.*
Schilpp, P.A., ed. 1957: *The Philosophy of Karl Jaspers.*
Wallraff, Charles F. 1970: *Karl Jaspers: An Introduction to his Philosophy.*

DAVID E. COOPER

jokes Jokes are, according to Freud's analysis (Freud, 1905), characterized by many of the same features as dreams and the DREAM-WORK, namely CONDENSATION/DISPLACEMENT. They afford a release of intellectual tension, while the uncovering of unconscious material (much of it sexual) in the conscious system strikes us as comic. Jokes also allow a recovery of the infantile pleasure in nonsense and in the almost physical handling of words. Freud's study of jokes is regarded by LACAN (1957) as one of the CANONical texts on the UNCONSCIOUS and as evidence that the unconscious is structured like a language.

Reading
Freud, Sigmund 1905 (*1960*): *Jokes and their Relation to the Unconscious.*
Lacan, Jacques 1957 (*1977*): "The agency of the letter in the unconscious, or reason since Freud."

DAVID MACEY

jouissance A French word with a range of senses of "enjoyment," including that of sexual orgasm. It was given critical currency by Roland BARTHES whose *Le Plaisir du Texte* distinguished between textual pleasure (*plaisir*) and textual *jouissance*. The former means comfort in reading, delight in a mastery of given forms; the latter is unsettling, an abrupt loss of subject identity and cultural grounds. The distinction draws on the psychoanalytic work of Jacques LACAN, for whom *jouissance* names the experience of a tension beyond any satisfaction in pleasure and which bears on the very limits of subjectivity, on the radical effects of the human SUBJECT's constitutive division in language.

Reading
Barthes, Roland 1973b (*1976*): *The Pleasure of the Text*.
Lacan, Jacques 1960 (*1977*): "Subversion of the subject
and dialectic of desire."
Žižek, Slavoj 1989: *The Sublime Object of Ideology*.
                                                    STEPHEN HEATH

judgment   This is a prominent concept in modern
philosophy, which since Descartes has been concerned with establishing the legitimacy of theoretical, practical, and aesthetic judgments. Descartes's
Discourse on Method (1637) is dedicated to the establishment of "correct judgment," and the principle
task of Antoine Arnauld's Cartesian *Logic or the
Art of Thinking* (Port Royal Logic) (1662) is that of
"training the judgment, making it as exact as we
can." The Enlightenment concern with the justification of the legitimacy of judgments is exemplified by KANT's critical philosophy. Kant describes
all thinking as judgment, and in each of his three
critiques attempts to establish the limits and legitimacy of theoretical, practical, and aesthetic judgments.
The critiques may be read as dissections of the
faculty of judgment in the course of which Kant
discovers an irresolvable tension between its two
distinct but related modes. The first mode of judgment is discriminative, and its exercise consists of
the discernment of differences; the second is subsumptive, and consists of the subsumption of a
particular case under a universal law. Kant shows
that the relationship between the two modes of
judgment is undecidable: discriminative judgment
assumes a law by which to make its discriminations,
while subsumptive judgment assumes a discrimination between particulars before it may apply a
universal.
   Since Kant the issue of judgment has been upper-
most in both the theory and practice of criticism.
Attempts to prefer discriminative judgment have
been met by the criticism that it covertly assumes
a law or principle, while subsumptive judgments
made according to CANONical criteria are accused
of ignoring or suppressing differences. The recent
focus of CRITICAL THEORY on the problem of judgment itself should, however, contribute to sharpen-
ing critical sensitivity to the undecidability or
"APORIA" of judgment.

Reading
Benjamin, Andrew, ed. 1992: *Judging Lyotard*.
Caygill, Howard 1989: *Art of Judgement*.
Lyotard, François, et al. 1985: *La Faculté de Juger*.
                                                    HOWARD CAYGILL

Jung, Carl Gustav   (1875–1961)   Swiss psychiatrist, depth psychologist, founder of the school of
thought termed "analytical psychology." It was in
1907 that Jung and Sigmund Freud first met in
Vienna, and Jung became interested in Freud's
work in PSYCHOANALYSIS. By 1909, however, the
two men had experienced a rupture after an extended residence together at Clark University in
Massachusetts, and by 1913 they had broken definitively following the publication of Jung's *Transformation and Symbols of the Libido* (renamed
Symbols of Transformation). There were three fundamental reasons for the split. First, Jung was unable
to accept Freud's concept of *libido* as being limited
to *sexual energy*, believing instead in an energizing
theory based on a *principle of opposites* (1969a, pp.
18ff.). Jung conceived of the psyche as a dynamic,
self-regulating system whose energy (or libido)
grows out of a tension that flows between two opposing poles; to discover what something means,
one must constantly attend to its obverse or opposite. The second major point of contention between
Freud and Jung concerned the way the UNCON-
SCIOUS content was to be interpreted symbolically,
whether as the sole reflection of a *personal* conflict,
or as the manifestation of a *collective* aspect of the
individual psyche whose contents are repeated
through myriad universal myths. Freud could not
formally embrace this view, mostly because he saw
in it an implicit admission of inherited racial experiences. Jung, however, did not mean to imply that
experience as such is inherited. Rather, he fathomed
a deeper structure of the unconscious than the
personal unconscious, the dwelling place of instinctive impulses to actions shaped and influenced by
the experiences of (wo)mankind, but which can become manifest only through individual experience
and so appear as individual acquisitions. Finally,
disagreements that occurred during the mutual
analysis of dreams brought an end to the relationship between Freud and Jung.
   Jung made the unconscious comprehensible in
terms of the spiritual quest of (wo)mankind; for
him its "depths" are not always dark and negative
as they are to Freud. Although the unconscious
extends into the lower layers of one's animal nature,
Jung believes that it also reaches up, out, and beyond
to a higher dimension of being. It is not merely the
repository of everything objectionable, infantile –
even animal – in ourselves, but the ever-creative
principle in a person's life (1970, p. 15). Jung initially wanted to call his own school of thought

"complex psychology" before he named it "analytical psychology," demonstrating the importance he attributed to this aspect of the psyche. He defined *complexes* as "psychic entities which are outside the control of the conscious mind. They have split from consciousness and lead a separate existence in the dark realm of the unconscious, being at all times ready to *hinder or reinforce* conscious functioning" (1953; italics mine). Complexes, then, are two-faced: they can produce totally opposite effects, be evil or good, destructive or constructive. The aspect they show depends largely on the conscious attitude and how they affect a person's capacity for understanding and moral evaluation.

Jung uses the term *individuation* to refer to the gradual, lifelong process of balancing and harmonizing the individual psyche so that consciousness and the unconscious ultimately come to complement and compensate one another. The vehicle of individuation can be a dream or any fantasized image which the individual is asked to describe or elaborate in any number of ways, "dramatic, dialectic, visual, acoustic, or in the form of dancing, painting, drawing, or modelling" (1969a, p. 202) Individuation, which develops most noticeably in the second half of life, can also been construed as a quest of "self-realization," an *archetypal* (collective) psychic process that enables the individual to experience his or her spiritual life; as such it is a key to the interpretation of world religions, myths, and philosophies. Jung sees a similarity between the inner transformations in individuation and religious conversion.

Individuation is sometimes described as a psychological journey toward self-discovery that cannot occur without suffering. It can at times seem to take a circuitous path and lead in circles or, more accurately, in spirals. The process begins with a wounding of the conscious personality, when a person first has an inkling that there exists a *shadow* complex, or the dark, negative, and inferior side of the personality, the sum of all those unpleasant qualities usually hidden and the "other side" of behaviors that have been cultivated within consciousness (1969b, part II, pp. 8–9). One must learn to live with this often terrifying aspect of oneself, for there is no psychic wholeness without a recognition and assimilation of opposites. The confrontation with the shadow perforce entails a dissolution of the *persona* or the conscious ideal of the personality, the mask worn in one's daily intercourse in society. The "journeyer" will also meet

with the ARCHETYPES of the unconscious and face the danger of succumbing to the peculiar fascination of these primordial factors, "uniform and regularly recurring modes of apprehension" (1969a, p. 137). In particular, he or she will encounter, respectively, the *anima* or *animus* archetype, the complementary feminine element contained in the unconscious of a man or the masculine element found in the unconscious of a woman. These principles of "femaleness" and "maleness" are not to be confused with FEMININITY or MASCULINITY inherently characterizing women or men, but should be construed instead as SYMBOLIC images associated, for example, with the ancient Chinese concepts of *yin* and *yang* or with the modern Jungian constructs of *eros* and *logos*. Eros, for Jung, is associated with the connective quality of relationship, while Logos goes with that of discrimination and cognition (1969b, part II, p. 14).

After the anima and animus, the two archetypes that are likely to exert influence on a man's or woman's life are the *old wise man* and the *great mother*. These can appear in various other forms – in a man, for instance, as a king or hero, medicine man or savior, trickster or mighty man (for example, magician or devil); and in a woman as an earth mother or a primordial mother (for example, witch). When these archetypes are awakened, a man or a woman may come to believe that he or she really possesses the *mana*, or the seemingly magical power and wisdom they hold. Jung terms possession by these archetypes *inflation*, which "involves an extension of the personality beyond individual limits, in other words, a state of being puffed up" (1953, p. 143). Nevertheless, the feeling of omnipotence that comes through inflation is an illusion and can compel a person to overestimate his or her strength and capacity. One does not really possess the supposed wisdom of a superhuman god or spirit or demon (in the case of a man) or of an overprotective or tyrannical mother figure (in the case of a woman); both manifestations are in fact voices from the unconscious that need to be consciously apprehended and understood for their true value to become accessible. Because of the danger of possession and of inflation, Jung says that one of the fundamental aims of individuation is "to divest the self . . . of the suggestive power of primordial images" (1953, p. 174).

Ideally, in the end, if they are fortunate, a man or woman will succeed in reconciling opposing elements in their beings, and such integration can be formulated as the finding of the "God within," or as the apprehension of the archetype of wholeness, the *self* (1953, p. 238). Phrases such as totality, the center of personality, and wholeness capture the essence of "selfhood." During crucial stages of the individuation, Jung observes, there is often an important association between an inner thought, vision, dream, or premonition and an outer event that may pass unnoticed because, "considering the psychic relativity of space and time, such a connection is not even conceivable" (1969a, p. 526). More to the point, the individual has not yet learned to be aware of the uncanny type of meaningful coincidence and to make the necessary connections. The term *synchronicity* is used to describe the existence of a significant relationship between inner and outer events that are not themselves causally linked, but whose apprehension, in the final analysis, enables a woman or man to be most fully interrelated and interconnected as a human being and to experience the mysterious ecstasy of selfhood in its most transcendent form.

See also ARCHETYPES; COLLECTIVE UNCONSCIOUS; FREUD, SIGMUND.

Reading

Fordham, Frieda 1953 (*1970*): *An Introduction to Jung's Psychology*.

Johnson, Robert 1983: *We: Understanding the Psychology of Romantic Love*.

Jung, C.G. 1963: *Memories, Dreams, Reflections*.

Progoff, Ira 1973: *Jung, Synchronicity and Human Destiny*.

Singer, June 1972: *Boundaries of the Soul: The Practice of Jung's Psychology*.

Ulanov, Ann 1971: *The Feminine in Jungian Psychology and in Christian Theology*.

Von Franz, Marie-Louise 1973: *Interpretation of Fairy Tales*.

Whitmont, Edward 1969: *The Symbolic Quest – Basic Concepts of Analytical Psychology*.

SUSAN L. FISCHER

K

Kant, Immanuel (1724–1804) German Enlightenment philosopher. Kant spent his entire life in the East Prussian city of Königsberg (now Kaliningrad), where he studied and taught philosophy at the university. In spite of this unpromising provincial background, he produced a body of philosophical writings which have had an incalculable influence upon modern philosophy and CRITICAL THEORY. His work is conventionally divided into "precritical" and "critical" periods. In the writings of the first period between 1747 and 1780, including *Observations on the Feeling of the Beautiful and Sublime* (1764) and *On the Form and Principles of the Sensible and Intelligible World* (1770), Kant developed an essayistic and unsystematic critique of the rationalism of the early German Enlightenment. In the second, "critical" period Kant systematized this critique in the critical trilogy *Critique of Pure Reason* (1781, second edition 1787), *Critique of Practical Reason* (1788), and *Critique of Judgement* (1790) on which his reputation now rests.

In the "critical philosophy" Kant attempted to establish the sources and limits of legitimate theoretical, practical, and aesthetic JUDGMENTS. In doing so he criticized existing claims to legitimate judgments, describing his work as a contribution to "the age of criticism." For him nothing was exempt from criticism or "the test of free and open examination"; neither religion nor the state "may exempt themselves from it," and especially not the intellectual disciplines and institutions supported by, and supportive of, these institutions. His procedure of rigorously scrutinizing critical judgments for their presuppositions and exclusions still implicitly governs the enterprise of "criticism" and "critical theory."

In the first critique, *Critique of Pure Reason*, Kant critically examines the claims to theoretical knowledge made by the "pure reason" of metaphysics. The first part of the book, on "transcendental aesthetic" and "transcendental analytic," was envisaged by Kant as the critical replacement for traditional ontology, and determines the limits of legitimate judgments about the world of objects. Legitimate knowledge is restricted to appearances in space and time which are organized according to the framework of the 12 categories of the understanding. Kant regarded any attempt to extend judgments beyond these limits to objects such as God, the SUBJECT, and the world as leading inevitably to the illusions unmasked in the second section of the critique on the "Transcendental Dialectic." In this part of the critique, Kant shows in detail how the attempts to make judgments concerning the "unitary subject" yield to the illusory inferences or "paralogisms" of psychology, those concerning the "world" to the consistent but contradictory conclusions of the "antinomies" of cosmology, and those of God to the impossible and specious proofs of theology.

The first critique illustrates the constructive and destructive aspects of the critical philosophy: by first establishing the limits of legitimate knowledge, it is then possible to detect and criticize illegitimate claims, regardless of their institutional and political dignity. This project is continued in the second and third critiques. In the *Critique of Practical Reason* Kant criticizes existing principles of practical judgment for covertly including unjustifiable empirical elements which severely qualify human freedom and autonomy. He proposes instead a "categorical imperative" – "Act only according to that maxim whereby you can at the same time will that it should become a universal law" – which would guard against such qualifications of freedom. In the *Critique of Judgement*, the founding text of modern AESTHETICS, Kant criticizes accounts of aesthetic judgment which rest on either a sense of the agreeable (for him, eighteenth-century theories of taste) or an intuition of perfection (German aesthetic theory). In place of these "heteronomous" principles he proposes extremely severe conditions for a valid aesthetic judgment of taste: it must be disinterested, of universal validity but not conceptual, end-directed but without reference to an end, and necessary. In seeking a basis for these conditions

Kant turned increasingly to an account of a public, critical common sense or "CULTURE." The work also contains an extensive analysis of the experience of the sublime and a critical analysis of teleological judgment.

The ambiguity in Kantian criticism between the "constructive" establishment of criteria of legitimate judgment and the "destructive" critique of all claims to spurious legitimacy has haunted the reception of his work. Critics from HEGEL and NIETZSCHE, to HORKHEIMER, ADORNO, DERRIDA, and LYOTARD regard Kant as having, in Nietzsche's words, "broken open the cage" only to creep back into it. Consequently, twentieth-century critical theory has been characterized by the radical extension of criticism to reason and the human subject itself, not stopping at the limits established by Kant, but criticizing those limits themselves. Some critics such as HABERMAS regard this development as "irrationalist" and "anti-Enlightenment"; however, in its "free and open" examination of reason itself, such radical critique closely conforms to Kant's own definition of the critical Enlightenment as the "free and open examination" to which "everything must submit."

See also AESTHETICS.

Reading
Guyer, Paul 1979: *Kant and the Claims of Taste.*
Heidegger, Martin 1967: *What is a Thing?.*
O'Neill, Onora 1989: *Coustructions of Reason.*

HOWARD CAYGILL

Kermode, Frank (1919–) British literary critic. Frank Kermode is one of the most versatile literary critics of this century. His early work (1947–67) included influential critical essays and books on Shakespeare, Spenser, Donne, Milton, and Marvell, as well as on a wide range of modern writers, including W.B. Yeats, T.S. Eliot, Wallace Stevens, and (later) D.H. Lawrence. A continuing concern in this work was an effort to determine the constituent features of classicism, Romanticism, and modernism. In retrospect, such publications as his introduction to the Arden edition of Shakespeare's *The Tempest* (1954) and *The Romantic Image* (1957) can be read as subtly theoretical texts. With the publication of the highly influential *The Sense of an Ending* (1967), however, Kermode's writing became more explicitly theoretical, although his work as a critic and reviewer has continued unabated.

During his tenure as Lord Northcliffe Professor at University College London, Kermode organized a series of seminars on literary theory, which introduced many important European theorists to Britain and – along with the Modern Masters series that he edited for Fontana – influenced a generation of scholars, students, and general readers. A rare glimpse of Kermode's teaching activities is also available in *English Renaissance Literature: Introductory Lectures* (1974). His innovative critical scholarship and teaching continued when he assumed the position of King Edward VII Professor at Cambridge, a post he resigned after a much publicized incident concerning a junior colleague whose tenure decision was publicly associated (perhaps mistakenly) with a referendum on poststructuralism (see Kermode, 1990b, p. 80).

The implicitly biblical interests of *The Sense of an Ending* became more overt in Kermode's *The Genesis of Secrecy* (1979) and in his contributions to *The Literary Guide to the Bible* (1987). In these books Kermode addressed such perennial questions as the limits of interpretation, the determination of the CANON (sacred and secular), and the relationship between criticism and narrative, which were productively conflated in the Judeo–Christian tradition of midrash (see Kermode, 1979). Three recurring themes in Kermode's more recent theoretical work have been the processes of interpretively accommodating classic TEXTS under varying historical circumstances (1975; 1985), the historical contingencies of value (1988), and the indispensable role of the aesthetic appetite in dealing with works of ART (1990a). As well as being an extraordinarily accommodating and cooperative scholar, often working as a coauthor and coeditor, Kermode's criticism has also been theoretically ecumenical. He has, however, consistently warned against the loss of the critical vocation in the wake of current theoretical activity.

Reading
Kermode, Frank 1967: *The Sense of an Ending: Studies in the Theory of Fiction.*
——1975: *The Classic.*
——1979: *The Genesis of Secrecy: On the Interpretation of Narrative.*
——1985: *Forms of Attention.*
——1988: *History and Value.*
——1990a: *An Appetite for Poetry.*
——1990b: *Poetry, Narrative History.*
——Fenden, S., and Palmer, K. 1974: *English Renaissance Literature: Introductory Lectures.*

MICHAEL PAYNE

Klein, Melanie (1882–1960) Austrian-born psychoanalyst and pioneer of psychoanalysis of children. Born in Vienna, Klein apparently first came into contact with psychoanalytic literature in Berlin in 1914–15, at which point she went into analysis with Sandor Ferenczi; her earliest papers, written in 1921–3 (and now included in Klein, 1975a) are based upon the direct observation and analysis of her own children. After a move to Berlin, where a further analysis with Karl Abraham was truncated by his death, she began to work with young children and to develop her distinctive play technique. Contacts with English analysts subsequently led to an invitation to London, where Klein settled and lived until her death and where she immediately found a much more sympathetic audience than in Berlin. Increasingly she found herself in demand as both a child analyst and a training analyst. Klein's work is the single most important influence on the OBJECT-RELATIONS school. Always a controversial figure, her differences with Anna Freud over both theory and technique almost led to splits within the British Psychoanalytic Society; an actual schism was avoided by the establishment of Kleinian, FREUDian, and "Middle" groups within the same society. The Kleinian group is currently the largest.

Klein's play technique was born of the impossibility of analyzing young children on the couch and the realization that play is a form of work and therefore a possible means of communication. Play permits a representation of fantasies, wishes, and experiences, and free play is an equivalent of free association in adults. Children were allowed to play with collections of very small toys kept in special lockers, and with water, paper, and paste. Klein observed, discussed the games, and joined in as required. Her approach to games was based on a strict analytic orthodoxy. Play was a matter of manipulating and interpreting unconscious symbols and had no pedagogic content or goal. The technique resulted from the conviction that thought is, from the outset, a matter of how objects – both imaginary and real – are positioned in relation to one another and the SUBJECT. As a result, Klein was able to work with children aged as young as 3 years. Virtually all her theoretical contributions to PSYCHOANALYSIS emerge from her use of the play technique. It is a measure of Klein's success that a notion which seemed so controversial when it was first introduced now looks so commonplace.

Klein's work on the early OEDIPUS COMPLEX – which, she claimed, was observable at the beginning of the second year of life; FREUD himself held that truly Oedipal feelings emerged between the ages of 3 and 5 – convinced her of the importance of the part-object, in her view an object for the child rather than for the instinct, as in Freud's original formulation. The breast, for instance, is ascribed properties on the basis of both the child's experience of its mother and the projection of its own fantasies. Thus the oral gratification afforded by the breast makes it "good"; its withdrawal or denial makes it "bad." At the same time, the child projects its love on to the gratifying breast and its hate or aggressiveness on to the bad breast. The object is thus "split." One of the key features of successful child development is the integration of split objects into more realistic forms of discrimination.

Klein's concentration on object-relations leads to a departure from Freud's emphasis on libidinal and developmental stages and to a new emphasis on positions, which are not clear-cut structures but rather characteristic postures adopted by the ego with regard to its objects. Splitting and the associated ambivalence toward the object are characteristic of the paranoid–schizoid position, possibly the earliest mode of object-relations. This position is further characterized by the mechanism of projective identification: the child has sadistic fantasies of attacking the mother's body from within and invading it. As the infant begins to integrate the good and bad part-objects into a perception of a whole object, it begins to experience anxiety at the possibility of losing or destroying its object. This is referred to as the depressive position, and is regarded by Klein as resulting originally from the feeling of guilt aroused by ambivalence to the object. The depressive position gives rise to a desire to make reparation to the object and is overcome through a further process of integration, but may be reactivated in mourning or depression.

Klein's relationship with classic Freudian theory is not an easy one to describe. She is often criticized by more orthodox Freudians for her assumption that an intellectually immature child can perform such complex mental operations, and the sometimes mechanical quality of her readiness to interpret a train as the child's penis and the station as the mother's body. On the other hand, she is one of the rare post-Freudian analysts to take the notion of a death drive and innate aggression so seriously, and it is certainly this which gives her work its undoubted emotional power. The emphasis on the mother, which is a characteristic feature of object-relations theory in general, represents a departure from Freud's patriarchal emphasis, though it would be difficult indeed to describe Klein as a feminist.

Reading
Grosskurth, Phyllis 1986: *Melanie Klein.*
Hinshelwood, R.D. 1989: *A Dictionary of Kleinian Thought.*
Klein, Melanie 1975a: *Guilt and Reparation and Other Works 1921–1945.*
——1975b: *Envy and Gratitude and Other Works 1946–1963.*
——1975c: *The Psychoanalysis of Children.*
——1975d: *Narrative of a Child Analysis.*
Segal, Hanna 1979: *Klein.*

DAVID MACEY

knowledge, archaeology of *See* ARCHAEOLOGY OF KNOWLEDGE

knowledge, sociology of *See* SOCIOLOGY OF KNOWLEDGE

Kojève, Alexandre (1902–68) The best-known interpreter of HEGEL. He was a Russian *émigré* who settled in Paris where he taught his famous Hegel seminar at the Ecole Pratique des Hautes Etudes from 1933 to 1939. After the 1939–45 war and until his death in 1968, Kojève worked in the French Ministry of Economic Affairs, where he was one of the earliest architects of the European community and the GATT (General Agreement on Tariffs and Trade) talks.

Kojève's seminar on Hegel exerted a remarkable influence on a whole generation of French intellectuals including Raymond Queneau, Georges BATAILLE, Maurice MERLEAU-PONTY, André Breton, Jacques LACAN, Raymond Aron, and Jean-Paul SARTRE. Leading figures of POSTMODERNISM such as Michel FOUCAULT and Jacques DERRIDA also pay tribute to him and are deeply indebted to his reading of Hegel. And thanks to his lifelong friendship with Leo STRAUSS, his influence on American Straussians such as Allan Bloom and Francis Fukuyama is unmistakable.

Kojève read Hegel through the eyes of MARX and HEIDEGGER simultaneously. For Kojève, history begins with the relationship between master and slave and ends with a "universal and homogeneous state" in which men and women live in conditions of equality, prosperity, and mutual recognition, free of war. According to Kojève, history ends with Capitalism, not Communism. Marx could not have anticipated the fact that twentieth-century capitalism would overcome all of its internal contradictions. Capitalism has succeeded in disseminating its wealth throughout the mass of the population, and in so doing, it has rendered the socialist revolution impossible or irrelevant because it has deprived it of its object – ending the impoverishment of the masses.

Kojève maintained that the age of revolution is past and that the end of history is already here. The capitalist imperative has destroyed national boundaries and created an efficient, rational, technological, and homogenized world. In so doing, it has destroyed the ideological grounds for war – when everyone watches the same television shows, hums the same tunes, loves the same fast food, and has the same conception of the good life, what is there to fight about? Global peace will prevail. The universalistic dream of the ENLIGHTENMENT has finally become a reality. The ideals of freedom, equality, and prosperity have become the global ends of politics. All that is left is to work out the technicalities. Civil servants like Kojève are the order of the day. Despite his apparent optimism, Kojève did not romanticize the end of history too much. He assumed that there would be some obstinate and irrational people who would pit themselves against the real and the rational. This is why the End-State will need a Universal Tyrant. Long before the end of the Cold War, Kojève anticipated that America would be the heart of the universal and homogeneous empire and the model of the new world order.

No sooner did Kojève confer finality on the rational order of the world than he became nostalgic for the excitements of the Hegelian dialectic. The end of history seemed drab, passive, even animalistic. Scholars describe this as a "turn" in his thinking, but I believe that his disenchantment is the logical result of his premises. Kojève offers us a fascistic reading of Hegel's dialectic which glorifies negativity, death, terror, and mastery. Then he posited an end of history in which these great and glorious attributes have vanished. The upshot of the matter is that Kojève transforms Marx's conception of the end of history as the "realm of freedom" into Heidegger's "night of the world."

Kojève's portrayal of the end of history as a tyranny of an arid, technological rationalism has contributed a great deal to the postmodern disenchantment with Enlightenment. It explains the postmodern repudiation of reason as a sham which conceals a thirst for global despotism.

Against the Kojèvean vision it may be objected that the earth cannot sustain a prosperous technological existence for humankind on a global scale and that the prosperity of some will always be purchased at the expense of others. Even if the technological miracle were possible, Kojève need not have feared that the excitement of war would become a thing of the past. Far from pacifying the world, the homogenization of the globe has fueled tribal sentiments. All over the globe bloody wars are being fought, not for concrete ends, but as a quest for identity and difference in a supposedly homogeneous world.

Reading

Auffret, Dominique 1991: *Alexandre Kojève: La Philosophie, l'état, la fin de l'histoire.*
Drury, Shadia B. *Alexandre Kojève: The Roots of Postmodern Politics.*
Fukuyama, Francis 1992: *The End of History and the Last Man.*
Kojève, Alexandre 1947: *Introduction to the Reading of Hegel: Lectures on the Phenomenology of the Mind.*
Strauss, Leo 1963 *(1991)*: *On Tyranny.*

SHADIA B. DRURY

Krauss, Rosalind E. (1940–) American art critic, historian, and OCTOBER founder and editor who, responding to postmodern ART, crusades against myths about viewing the art object (for example, that it can be seen as a logical and organic whole within which can be found a meaning that matches one intended by the artist) preserved by formalist art criticism and traditional art history. A device used by Krauss to call attention to her structuralist and poststructuralist strategy is to blend the voices of literature and criticism in her WRITING, as she does in *The Optical Unconscious.*
See also AVANT-GARDE; FORMALISM; GREENBERG, CLEMENT; POSTMODERNISM; STRUCTURALISM.

Reading

Krauss, Rosalind 1985: *The Originality of the Avant-Garde and Other Modernist Myths.*
——— 1993: *The Optical Unconscious.*

GERALD EAGER

Kristeva, Julia (1941–) Of Bulgarian origin, Julia Kristeva is a literary theorist, linguist and, since 1979, a practicing psychoanalyst.

Kristeva came to Paris on a research scholarship in 1966 and rapidly became associated with Todorov, BARTHES, and the TEL QUEL group of novelists and theorists. She was influential in popularizing the work of BAKHTIN and Russian FORMALISM, and in elaborating the important concept of INTERTEXTUALITY. Kristeva's earlier work (1969) is heavily influenced by the scientific ambitions of SAUSSURE's linguistics and by MARXISM, and concentrates on elaborating a theory of the emergence of subjectivity within language. In common with other members of the *Tel Quel* group, she tends to emphasize the role of the aesthetic, and especially the avant-garde exemplified by writers like Mallarmé, as a harbinger or even an agent of revolutionary social change (Kristeva, 1974a).

As the reference to PSYCHOANALYSIS begins to become a dominant theme, Kristeva draws on and extends LACAN's notion of the SYMBOLIC to elaborate her own notion of the SEMIOTIC, which describes the circulation of presignifying drives in and through the body of the pre-Oedipal child. The role of the OEDIPUS COMPLEX is to organize and harness the semiotic and to make it serve the symbolic. To support her views on the semiotic, Kristeva appropriates the term *chora* from Plato; it refers to the undifferentiated bodily space occupied by mother and child. The *chora* itself remains effectively unknowable, but is glimpsed through the cracks in the symbolic opened up by avant-garde poetic practices. Given that the *chora* and the semiotic are primarily maternal – or at least nonpatriarchal – writers like Mallarmé and Céline, who are held to be working with the semiotic, can be regarded as quasi-female figures regardless of their actual GENDER. Kristeva's later theoretical works concentrate upon images of the maternal and invoke FREUD's brief study of the UNCANNY to elaborate a notion of the abject (Kristeva, 1980a).

As a result of essays like that on women's time (Kristeva, 1979), Kristeva has often been associated with the "new French feminisms" of CIXOUS and IRIGARAY, but she has always been hesitant about identifying herself as a feminist and has expressed doubts about the pertinence of the gender category of "woman" (see Atack, 1986).

In political terms, Kristeva's evolution has taken her from a temporary enthusiasm for China, celebrated in an account (1974b) of a brief visit to that country, to an enthusiasm for the United States (1977), and latterly to a return to a defense of a very traditional view of the French Enlightenment as productive of universal values (Kristeva, 1990a). Her first novel (1990b) was a rather disappointing and thinly disguised exercise in autobiography.

Reading
Atack, Margaret 1986: "The other: feminist."
Kristeva, Julia 1969: *Sémiotiké. Recherches pour une sémanalyse.*
——1974a: *Revolution in Poetic Language.*
——1974b: *About Chinese Women.*
——1977: "Why the United States?"
——1979: "Women's time."
——1982: *Powers of Horror.*
——1990a: *Lettre ouverte à Harlem Désir.*
——1990b: *Les Samuraïs.*
Moi, Toril, ed. 1986: *The Kristeva Reader.*

DAVID MACEY

Kroeber, Alfred Louis (1876–1960) North American anthropologist. Kroeber received an MA in English literature in 1897 and a PhD in anthropology under Franz Boas at Columbia University in 1901. From then, almost until his death, he taught anthropology and was museum curator (later director) at the University of California at Berkeley. Kroeber conducted fieldwork in the Philippines and Peru, although he is better known for his work among Native American groups in California and the southwestern United States, especially his work with the cultural informant he called Ishi, reputedly the last survivor of the traditional Yahi Indians of northern California.

Influenced by the historical particularism of BOAS, Kroeber avoided scientific explanation and the formulation of universal laws of CULTURE (nomothetic approach) in favor of description and the tracing of cultural patterns in time and location (ideographic approach) as a primary purpose of his (and anthropology's) efforts. Kroeber stressed the humanistic rather than the scientific side of anthropology and CULTURAL STUDIES, but the question of how cultural customs and styles arise, spread, and decline dominated his work. He stressed multiple causality in explaining cultural phenomena, and he argued against all forms of reductionist explanations, affirming instead that "the immediate causes of cultural phenomena are other cultural phenomena." This led him to formulate the concept of the "superorganic" – that some areas of culture develop quite independently of other areas more linked to biological

needs and environmental constraints – for which he was criticized. A skillful writer, teacher, and organizer of information, Kroeber produced over 500 works, including some of massive scope in the history of cultural studies.

See also CULTURAL STUDIES; NATIVE AMERICAN STUDIES.

Reading
Driver, Harold E. 1962: *The Contribution of A.L. Kroeber to Culture Area Theory and Practice.*
Kroeber, A.L. 1923 (*1948*): *Anthropology.*
——1944: *Configurations of Culture Growth.*
——1952: *The Nature of Culture.*
——1957 (*1963*): *Style and Civilization.*
Kroeber, Theodora 1970: *Alfred Kroeber: A Personal Configuration.*
Steward, Julian H. 1973: *Alfred Kroeber.*

JAMES PHILLIPS

Kuhn, Thomas S. (1922–) American historian and philosopher of science. After producing a number of historical studies, Kuhn published *The Structure of Scientific Revolutions* (1962), a historiographical study of science which has had an impact far exceeding that expected – or even desired – by its author. Although Kuhn has published further works, it is *The Structure* which has remained centerstage to become one of the most influential texts of recent decades. Its force grew from its challenge to the traditional historical picture of science as continuous and progressive development. Instead, Kuhn offered an account in which the history of science is constituted by stable, almost dogmatic periods of research ("normal science") separated by radical discontinuities ("scientific revolutions").

For Kuhn the fundamental unit of analysis is the scientific community. Its members are bound together by their professional education, which in turn is based on previous scientific achievements. A particular scientific community, concerned with some scientific specialism, will look to the achievement that founded that specialism as the basis for its continuing research. Such an achievement is what Kuhn calls a PARADIGM, and research based on a paradigm is what he calls "normal science."

A paradigm, which is constituted by a shared commitment to a constellation of laws, theories, techniques, and standards, will have had some success in solving scientific problems, and will therefore constitute a way of thinking about further problems, the idea being to extend the existing success of the paradigm into new areas. A paradigm must therefore be open-ended as well as successful, but its further development is essentially self-limiting: it cannot challenge its own foundations. This is why normal science is "puzzle-solving," seeking further articulation of the paradigm but eschewing major novelties. As Kuhn puts it, normal scientific research is "a strenuous and devoted effort to force nature into conceptual boxes supplied by professional education" (1970, p. 5).

While the paradigm continues to solve puzzles, its success will be cumulative, but never total. Although there will be many failures accompanying the successes, one of Kuhn's major claims is that such failures are not falsifying counterinstances, as POPPER claimed, but are merely regarded as anomalies, or are even not regarded at all. It is only when anomalies pile up, or when the members of a scientific community begin to feel insecure about them, that they play a significant role in science. When anomalies become too numerous or too serious they will precipitate a crisis for the community, a realization that the paradigm is no longer serving its purpose as the basis for normal research. The response will be a proliferation of ideas and theories from which a new paradigm will eventually emerge. Then a scientific revolution will have taken place.

For Kuhn a scientific revolution is a noncumulative event, a discontinuity or radical break that changes everything. In sociological terms, two paradigms represent "incompatible modes of community life" (1970, p. 94). Paradigms are incommensurable – literally cannot be measured against each other – because they have no internal standards in common and do not acknowledge external standards. It follows from this account that science cannot be progressive in the traditionally accepted way, for there is no basis for saying that a new paradigm is better than the one it superseded; yet Kuhn does want to retain a vestige of progressivism in science, claiming that its development through revolutions is like irreversible evolution from primitive beginnings.

One major criticism of Kuhn is that his account of scientific revolutions brings irrationality into science, for there is no good reason for paradigm choice, and Kuhn's use of terms like "*Gestalt*-switch" and "conversion experience" simply fuels the critics' ire. Yet it is clear that a new paradigm must succeed in restarting the puzzle solving which broke down with the crisis in the previous paradigm, even though this process has, at it were, shifted to a new basis. Whether this is compatible with genuine incommensurability must, however, remain questionable.

A second major problem for Kuhn is the ambiguous use of the term "paradigm," which includes major changes like the one from the Ptolemaic to the Copernican world view, with all its religious, social, and ideological consequences, and changes such as the development of the oxygen theory of combustion, of interest only to specialists. This led Kuhn to distinguish the broader commitments of a scientific community (the "disciplinary matrix") from the particular achievements ("exemplars") which were the basis of normal science, and to claim that it was the latter that were the subjects of his account of paradigms.

However, this attempt at terminological restriction has not been very successful, and neither has Kuhn's more general attempt to limit the use of his ideas. Kuhn stated that his account of paradigms and revolutions was specific to the natural sciences, and that no other area exhibits the requisite maturity or discipline in its structure to be susceptible to his analysis. But very little attention has been paid to this ruling, and paradigms in the broad, ambiguous sense have continued to populate the writings of psychologists, sociologists, economists, historians, philosophers, literary theorists, and cultural analysts of all sorts.

This is just as it should be, for no author has the right to limit the uses to which his or her ideas are put, and no TEXT can prescribe the limits of its own reception. Yet Kuhn's work was fundamentally misunderstood from the start. Appearing in the 1960s, *The Structure* was bound to be assimilated to the revolutionary spirit of the times, and even to be appropriated by the anti-scientific skepticism of the following decades. But far from being a radical tract for its times, it is in fact a highly conservative defense of natural science and the procedures followed by its practitioners. It is a defense based on history and sociology, an attempt to move away from any philosophical or value-based account of science, and to present an account of scientific development in purely factual terms. But, rightly, the origin of Kuhn's project has failed to restrict its influence.

See also SCIENCE, PHILOSOPHY OF.

Reading

Barnes, Barry, 1982: *T.S. Kuhn and Social Science.*

Gutting, Gary, ed. 1980: *Paradigms and Revolutions: Appraisals and Applications of Thomas Kuhn's Philosophy of Science.*

Hacking, Ian, ed. 1981: *Scientific Revolutions.*

Kuhn, Thomas S. 1957: *The Copernican Revolution: Planetary Astronomy in the Development of Western Thought.*

——1962 (*1970*): *The Structure of Scientific Revolutions.*

——1977: *The Essential Tension: Selected Studies in Scientific Tradition and Change.*

Lakatos, Imre, and Musgrave, Alan, eds 1970: *Criticism and the Growth of Knowledge.*

Radnitzky, Gerard, and Andersson, Gunnar, eds 1978: *Progress and Rationality in Science.*

ANDREW BELSEY

L

Lacan, Jacques (1901–81) French psychoanalyst. Lacan was without doubt the most controversial psychoanalyst since FREUD. He was also one of the most authoritative and had considerable impact both inside and outside the psychoanalytic community, influencing developments in LITERARY CRITICISM, philosophy, feminism, and film theory.

Lacan's career was a stormy one. Elected to the Institut Psychanalytique de Paris in 1934, he and others resigned from it in 1953 to found the Société Psychanalytique de Paris. Their departure resulted in the withdrawal of recognition by the International Psychoanalytic Association. The issues leading to the resignation were complex, consisting of a great deal of internal politics and a number of personality clashes, although centered on Lacan's use of variable or short sessions in his training analyses and refusal to adhere to the convention of the analytic hour. In 1963 the same issue resulted in splits within the SPP (which was never recognized by the IPA) and in the founding of Lacan's Ecole Freudienne de Paris. Lacan regarded his treatment at the hand of the IPA as an excommunication and likened it (1973, pp. 3–4) to the *kherem* and the later *chammata* that expelled Spinoza from the synagogue. The EFP was a flourishing, if perpetually crisis-ridden organization, but was unilaterally dissolved by Lacan in 1980. A number of rival organizations now claim to be the legitimate heirs to Lacan's thought; the most important is the Ecole du Champ Freudien, directed by Lacan's son-in-law and literary executor Jacques-Alain Miller (see Roudinesco, 1986).

Lacan's only "real" book is his doctoral thesis, which discusses the relationship between paranoid psychoses and personality (Lacan, 1932). His reputation rests primarily on the papers which he reluctantly collected as *Ecrits* (1966). Prior to their publication, the main channel for the transmission of Lacan's teachings was the seminar which began as a private study group reading the "Dora" case (Freud, 1905a) in 1951, and which gradually developed into a public forum and one of the more notorious spectacles of Parisian intellectual life. The seminar is in the course of publication; three volumes are currently available in English translation (Lacan, 1973; 1975; 1978).

Lacan originally trained as a doctor of medicine and a psychiatrist before entering analysis with Rudolph Lowenstein in 1934, and soon gained a reputation as a clinician and diagnostician of outstanding acumen. His earliest publications were in medical journals and deal with paranoid psychoses; they owe a great deal more to French psychiatric traditions and particularly to his teacher Clérambault than to Freud. In the doctoral thesis, for example, the pre-Freudian categories of mental automatism and erotomania are invoked to explain the origins of paranoia. During the 1930s Lacan was close to the surrealists; his early attempts to find a parallel between literary forms and pathology are definitely related to their artistic practices and to both Salvador Dali's critical paranoia and Breton's promotion of automatic writing. The association with the surrealists is not surprising; to his chagrin, Freud was given a much warmer reception by the surrealists than by the French medical and psychiatric establishments (see Macey, 1988) and it was in the same milieu that Lacan's thesis found its most avid readers. Surrealism was to remain an important influence; many of the literary allusions that abound in Lacan's writings are to surrealist authors and his very style owes something to their work.

Lacan's first major contribution to psychoanalytic theory is his description of the MIRROR-STAGE. His account of this crucial phase in development is strongly marked by the HEGELIANISM of Kojève (see the OTHER), and the same influence is also apparent in the related paper in which TRANSFERENCE is recast as a dialectical series of identifications (Lacan, 1951). Despite the sophistication of Lacan's wide-ranging philosophical references and his incorporation of elements of HEIDEGGER, Kojève's reading of HEGEL provides the most solid philosophical underpinnings for his theories.

It was the manifesto-like paper read to the 1953 Conference of the SPP and known as the Rome DISCOURSE that truly announced Lacan's return to FREUD (Lacan, 1953, in 1966 and 1977). The slogan had two primary meanings. On the one hand, Lacan was calling for a return to a close reading of Freud's TEXT, for a literal reading of Freud, rather than the accumulated secondary literature. The accomplishment of that reading was the constant goal of the seminar. The slogan also expressed a bitter hostility to ego psychology, seen as a dominant IDEOLOGY and a form of behaviorism which obscures Freud's inspiration and even the discovery of the unconscious. For Lacan, ego psychology represented the adaptation of the individual to an environment and a suppression of the Freudian discovery that, as the mirror-stage demonstrated, the ego was the product of alienating identification, was not coterminous with the SUBJECT and could therefore not be master in its own house.

Lacan takes quite literally Anna O's definition of PSYCHOANALYSIS as a talking cure (see Breuer and Freud, 1893–5). Speech is the sole medium of the analysis, and the function and field of speech and language must be central to both psychoanalytic clinical practice and the training of psychoanalysts. In his 1953 paper Lacan does not invoke any specific linguistic theory, but refers to a general concept of speech and language which draws upon sources as diverse as Heidegger and LÉVI-STRAUSS (1949). Heidegger supplies the dichotomy between empty and full speech, referring respectively to the stereotypical DISCOURSE in which the analysand is alienated and the effective and therapeutic use of a speech which can take account of the other. Lévi-Strauss is used by Lacan to outline the all-important theory of language as a SYMBOLIC system. Language is the element which defines subjectivity because its use always implies a reference to the other. The symbolic is an order superimposed upon the domain of nature, in which there are no lines of descent or systems of kinship. Freud's theory of the OEDIPUS COMPLEX can now be reformulated in terms of the subject's inscription within a symbolic system which prohibits incest as the subject submits to the law that is pronounced in the NAME OF THE FATHER.

The symbolic is one of the three interconnected orders that structure intersubjective existence (see IMAGINARY/SYMBOLIC/REAL). A similarly triadic structure, which may contain a reference to Freud's triad of id, ego, and super-ego, appears in the triple structure of need, demand, and desire, which, like the theory of the symbolic, relates to the transition from nature to CULTURE. Need refers quite simply to a biological level and the need for nutrition. Demand describes the expression of need in language: the subject is obliged to express or translate biological need in symbolic terms. The residue, or the incompatibility between need and demand, is referred to by Lacan as desire, which rapidly becomes the central theme. Whereas Freud's patients were driven by wishes and impulses, Lacan's subjects are driven by desire, and he can therefore claim that the psychoanalytic equivalent to Descartes's *cogito* is *desidero*. Elements of the theory of desire can be seen in the theorization of the mirror-stage, and it is clear that Lacan's debt to Kojève is still enormous in the 1960 paper on the dialectic of desire and the subversion of the subject (1960, in 1966 and 1977) and in the argument that man's desire is the desire of the other. Ultimately, desire is always a desire for recognition. Like Freud before him, Lacan frequently claims not to be a philosopher, but his theorization of desire relies heavily upon themes that ultimately derive from Hegel.

It is really only in the 1957 paper on the "Agency of the letter" (1957, in Lacan, 1966 and 1977) that linguistics begins to be appropriated by Lacan. The linguistics in question is that of SAUSSURE, though Lacan also makes much use of the work of JAKOBSON's work on phonemes and on METAPHOR AND METONYMY. Following Saussure, language is seen as a synchronic system of discrete units, and meaning is seen as emerging from their interaction. As Lacan puts it, meaning insists in and through a chain of signifiers; it does not consist of any one element. It is the primacy accorded to the signifier that signals Lacan's departure from Saussurean orthodoxy. Whereas the linguist stressed the meaningful unity of signifier and signified within the SIGN, the psychoanalyst divorces the two and stresses that there is no final correspondence between the two poles. Signifier and signified will never coincide in any absolute sense, and it is only the privileged signifier known as the PHALLUS that guarantees an element of stability by putting an end to the otherwise interminable sliding of the signifier. Lacan's appropriation of elements of Saussure allows him to argue that the UNCONSCIOUS is structured like a language, a claim further supported by the perceived similarity between the formations of the unconscious (symptoms,

DREAM-WORK) and the rhetorical figures of META-PHOR AND METONYMY, which are held, following Jakobson, to represent the two poles of the workings of language.

Lacan's claim that the unconscious is structured like a language has always been controversial. To some analysts, it represents an intellectualization of psychoanalysis which effectively avoids the entire issue of effect and emotion (Green, 1986), while it has often been pointed out that Lacan's reliance on early Freudian texts like *The Interpretation of the Dreams* (Freud, 1900) and *Jokes and Their Relation to the Unconscious* (Freud, 1905b), which lend themselves much more easily to a linguistic reading than, say, *The Ego and the Id* (Freud, 1923), means that his return to Freud is based upon a highly selective reading.

Although Lacan saw his primary work as the formation of analysts and the defense of the return to Freud, his work has found varied applications and has effectively become part of a general cultural field in which psychoanalysis is an element in broader elaborations. In the 1960s that field seemed to promise an articulation between MARXISM and psychoanalysis which could provide a materialist account of how subjects were constituted in and by IDEOLOGY (Althusser, 1964). Lacan thus became part of a triple alliance with ALTHUSSER and FOUCAULT, the common denominator being their theoretical anti-humanism. That alliance paved the way for an initial appropriation by feminism (Mitchell, 1974), though the Marxist component was soon lost. The appeal for feminists was that Lacan appeared to offer a way around the more problematic pronouncements of Freud on femininity and that the theory of the phallus avoided Freud's residual biologism by theorizing the symbolic or even formal constitution of GENDER identities. Not all feminists accept that argument and the question of Lacan's relevance to feminism remains highly controversial (see Irigaray, 1977). The importance ascribed to the figure of the phallus exposes Lacan to the serious charge of PHALLO-GOCENTRISM, while the primacy he accords to language and the signifier exposes him to the criticism that he has in fact reproduced the theological theory that "in the beginning was the Word."

Reading

Althusser, Louis 1964: "Freud and Lacan."
Bowie, Malcolm 1991: *Lacan.*
Breuer, Joseph, and Freud, Sigmund 1893–5: *Studies on Hysteria.*

Freud, Sigmund 1900: *The Interpretation of Dreams.*
——1905b: "Fragment of an analysis of a case of hysteria."
——1905c: *Jokes and their Relation to the Unconscious.*
——1923a: *The Ego and the Id.*
Green, André 1986: *On Private Madness.*
Irigaray, Luce 1977a: "The poverty of psychoanalysis."
Lacan, Jacques 1932: *De la Psychose Paranoïaque dans ses Rapports avec la Personalité.*
——1951: "Intervention on transference."
——1966: *Ecrits.*
——1973: *The Four Fundamental Concepts of Psycho-analysis.*
——1975: *The Seminar of Jacques Lacan. Book 1, Freud's Papers on Technique 1953–54.*
——1977: *Ecrits: A Selection.*
——1978: *The Seminar of Jacques Lacan. Book 2, The Ego in Freud's Theory and in the Technique of Psycho-analysis.*
Lévi-Strauss, Claude 1949: *The Elementary Structures of Kinship.*
Macey, David 1988: *Lacan in Contexts.*
Mitchell, Juliet 1974: *Psychoanalysis and Feminism.*
Roudinesco, Elisabeth 1986: *Jacques Lacan & Co.: A History of Psychoanalysis in France 1925–1985.*

DAVID MACEY

Lacoue-Labarthe, Philippe (1940–) French philosopher and literary theorist, much influenced by the work of HEIDEGGER, DERRIDA, and LYOTARD. He has written mainly about topics in the history of French and German post-Romantic thought, including the intensely problematical relationship between ART, representation, ETHICS, and politics. Lacoue-Labarthe traces this relationship back to its origins in Plato's ambivalent doctrine of *mimesis*, and thence forward, via KANT, to its latterday emergence in those forms of highly charged aesthetic IDEOLOGY – from NIETZSCHE to (at least certain aspects of) Heidegger's thinking – which raise such values into a touchstone of revealed historic and political truth. This project is pursued with great subtlety, range of scholarship, and critical rigor in *The Literary Absolute* (coauthored with Jean-Luc Nancy) and in *Typography*, a series of interlinked essays on the theme of mimetic desire, rivalry, and the politics of representation. Lacoue-Labarthe is at his weakest – like so many commentators – when attempting to make out a case for Heidegger as the deepest thinker of these and related issues.

Reading

Lacoue-Labarthe, Philippe 1989: *Typography: Mimesis, Philosophy, Politics.*
——1990: *Heidegger, Art and Politics: The Fiction of the Political.*

CHRISTOPHER NORRIS

language, philosophy of Despite obvious interconnections, philosophy of language should be distinguished from (i) linguistic philosophy, (ii) philosophy of linguistics, and (iii) semantics (in the "professional" sense). The first of these is a method, applicable in all areas of philosophy, marked by close attention to the use of words. The second is a branch of PHILOSOPHY OF SCIENCE, concerned with the specialist vocabulary and methodology of linguistics. The third is a program for assigning objects, classes, etc. to words so as to yield specifications of the truth conditions of sentences.

Philosophy of language is the attempt, primarily, to provide an integrated and illuminating general account of the relations between language and speakers, and language and the world. (A language, after all, is both used *by* and *between* people, and *about* the world.) In the one area belong such various issues as the innateness of linguistic knowledge alleged by CHOMSKY, and the proper taxonomy of the speech acts whereby we "do things with words." In the second belong issues like the parallelism (or lack of it) between structures of language and reality, and the nature of referential expressions. The two areas come together in the theory of meaning. No account of meaning can be adequate which does not explain both how people understand words and how words relate to the world. A common criticism of the view that meanings are "ideas" in the head is that this leaves unclarified how words "get a grip" on reality. Equally, "realist" theories – in terms, for instance, of the objective truth conditions of sentences – are sometimes criticized for leaving unclarified how words manage to be grasped by speaker/hearers.

A striking feature of twentieth-century philosophy is the central place occupied by philosophy of language. Several factors have contributed to this "linguistic turn." First, developments in logic not only provided new tools for the analysis of language (for example, quantifiers), but also revealed apparent gaps between a grammatical "surface" and the underlying logic which, many philosophers held, language must possess. This perception inspires the attempt – variously undertaken by, say, FREGE, Russell, CHOMSKY, and DAVIDSON – to analyze everyday language into its logical structures.

Second, there has been the growing sense, partly inspired by psychology and anthropology, of the intimate connection between thought and language. Here we need to distinguish two themes, both prominent in the later work of WITTGENSTEIN. One is that the very criteria for identifying thoughts are necessarily linguistic. One cannot ascribe this or that thought or concept to a creature without its capacity to manifest it verbally. The other is that the general ways in which a society of CULTURE thinks and conceives of reality is inextricably bound up with the language it happens to speak. Both philosophical psychology and philosophical anthropology, therefore, require a philosophy of language.

Finally, it is apparent that doctrines about language and meaning can have profound and disturbing implications for philosophy at large. A striking example was the logical positivists' verificationist theory of meaning. If only empirically verifiable sentences (and those of logic) are meaningful, then the pronouncements of theology, ETHICS, and philosophy itself must be a kind of nonsense. More recently, the "disappearance of the self" and "DEATH OF THE AUTHOR" conclusions of "poststructuralist" writers in France are drawn from the idea that a person is, so to speak, a fly caught in a free-floating web of unstable meanings over which he or she has no autonomous control or grip.

See also AUSTIN; CHOMSKY; DAVIDSON; DERRIDA; FREGE; GRICE; HEIDEGGER; LOGICAL POSITIVISM; QUINE; SPEECH ACTS; WITTGENSTEIN.

Reading
Cooper, D.E. 1987: *Philosophy and the Nature of Language.*
Devitt, M., and Sterelny, K. 1987: *Language and Reality: An Introduction to the Philosophy of Language.*
Hacking, I. 1975: *Why Language Matters to Philosophy.*
Harrison, B. 1979: *An Introduction to the Philosophy of Language.*
Martinich, A., ed. 1990: *The Philosophy of Language.*
DAVID E. COOPER

language theories There are many different ways of studying language. In any field certain kinds of issues tend to dominate research at a given time, and certain kinds of theories are proposed in response to them. If one theory is dominant for a time and is then replaced with another, there are usually historical forces at work which it makes sense to try and identify. The relationship between a theory and its historical context can be straightforward or complex, and clarifying this relationship can be the best way to grasp what theories set out to do.

The development of language theories can usefully be surveyed as follows. For each phase we can identify the historical background, what the key issues were taken to be, and the main theories that were formulated. And we can say how the main scholars of each period would have answered the questions: "What is language?" and "What is theory?"

The first coherent theories of language in modern times were developed in the early nineteenth century as a result of changes in European colonialism. Earlier colonialists had been happy to wipe out the original inhabitants of the lands they seized, or to use them for slave labor in agriculture. Industrialization made it necessary to develop a larger administrative and managerial elite in the colonies, and the colonial powers therefore reluctantly decided to educate at least some of the "natives." Part of the process was a drive to convert them to Christianity. Administrators and missionaries began to study the languages of their colonial subjects.

It soon became clear that some of these "exotic" languages were not so exotic after all: Sanskrit, the language of the ancient Hindu scriptures, was found to have striking similarities to classical Latin and Greek; and living tongues like Persian, Sinhalese, and Hindi were similar to many of the languages of Europe. The obvious question was: How come? The field of comparative philology emerged as scholars attempted to solve this puzzle. The theory that prevailed was that all these languages were descendents of one language, dubbed Indo-European, which was spoken in Eastern Europe and Asia Minor in prehistoric times (cf. Lehman, 1967; Thieme, 1955).

This theory rested on two crucial foundations. First, scholars had to develop precise tools for analyzing the most concrete features of different languages, namely their sounds and their word structure. The relevant fields, phonetics and morphology respectively, therefore made huge strides. Second, it was necessary to have a general theory of how and why languages changed to prevent the kind of wild speculation that had flourished in some previous attempts to map the origins of words. A rigorous theory of language change duly emerged. In the early part of the century a key figure like Franz Bopp (1791–1867) would have said that language was an organism which had decayed and been simplified since the glories of classical times. Asked about theory, he would have mentioned analytical rigor and the importance of general patterns. Later scholars such as Karl Brugmann (1849–1919)

would have disagreed with the word "decay" in the first answer, but accepted the second answer, stressing the word "general."

By the early part of the twentieth century a new puzzle began to come to the fore. Technological progress meant that even more "natives" had to be educated and made literate. Once again it was the missionaries who led the way, setting up mission schools in the colonies and translating the Bible into the local languages. Whereas in the previous period the focus had been on dead languages, and hence on writing rather than speech, the central questions now were how to describe living languages accurately, particularly spoken language, and how to design writing systems for those (the majority) which did not have one.

Solving the first question was the major impulse behind the structuralist theories of language that were developed in Europe and America during this period. These theories made the structure of languages (sounds, words, syntax) their central concern, marginalizing or ignoring questions of the meaning and use of language. There were two reasons for the emphasis on structure. First, it was thought that meaning and use were not amenable to rigorous scientific investigation. Second, scholars wanted to describe each language in its own terms, rather than carrying over the analytical terminology used for European languages, a practice that had had adverse consequences when modern languages were described in school grammars using concepts from Latin and Greek grammar. The structuralist linguistics of this period aimed to provide a set of automatic procedures by which a linguist could extract the structures of any language from a moderate amount of data (see Zellig HARRIS).

The second issue, creating writing systems, led to further refinements in studying the sound systems of different languages, the field of phonology. The concept of the phoneme – a class of sounds in a language which do not contrast with each other – was central here. In English, for instance, the "l" sounds in *feel* and *leaf* are different; but one always appears at the beginning of a word while the other appears at the end: they are members of the same phoneme and can therefore be represented in writing by the same letter. This type of reasoning was important in devising efficient writing systems. Writing systems also raised social and political problems, however. The African language Shona is a good example. Far from being one language, Shona is a cluster of dialects which differ in their pronunciation, grammar, and vocabulary. One dialect, called Zezuru, was used as the basis for the writing system (and the dictionaries and grammars) of "standard Shona." Zezuru was used because it happened to be the dialect of Harare (then called Salisbury), where most Europeans settled.

The period of STRUCTURALISM coincided with the growth of organized nationalist resistance to colonialism in many colonies. Treating each language in its own terms as a complex structure fitted in well with the emphasis on taking pride in traditional languages and CULTURES that was promoted by these nationalist movements (and supported by many linguists). Recording indigenous languages for posterity was also important because many of them were dying out as a result of the earlier genocidal colonialism mentioned above, which still persisted in certain parts of the world.

The main figures of this period were Ferdinand de SAUSSURE (1857–1913) in Europe, and Leonard Bloomfield (1887–1949) in America (cf. Saussure, 1913; Bloomfield, 1933). A language for Bloomfield was considered to be all the utterances produced by a speech community. Asked about theory, he would have talked about a reliable method for collecting, analyzing, and organizing these utterances.

The next major change is linked with the 1939–45 war. Expertise in languages such as German, Russian, or Japanese became an important strategic asset for the allied powers during and after the war, and the armed forces needed quick and efficient ways of learning these and other languages. After the war, languages that had not been widely studied in Europe and America, such as Arabic, Chinese, and Malay, became important. Many of the structuralist linguists were drafted in to design language teaching materials, and the field of "applied linguistics" made its appearance as the question of how best to learn and teach new languages became the central one. Repetitive structural drills were the favored solution, resulting from the emphasis on structure in linguistics and from the influence of behaviorism (a set of techniques for rewarding desired behaviors and penalizing unwanted ones) in psychology. Key figures were Earl Stevick and Robert Lado (cf. Lado, 1964). Asked to define language, early applied linguists would have talked of a set of habits learned from experience. A theory for them was a set of practical techniques that reliably produced a desired outcome.

At the end of the war the United States had by far the most powerful economy in the world, and embarked on what people later wistfully remembered as the postwar boom, fueled in large part by massive military spending and armed intervention anywhere that the strategic interests of the country and its allies were threatened. The relative freedom from economic pressures in some sections of the population enabled scholars to look beyond the urgent practical questions of the previous two periods. Technology made huge strides, and the invention of the computer in particular was indirectly responsible for the emergence of the next set of puzzles, since it led to a new branch of mathematics called formal language theory, one of whose practitioners was Noam CHOMSKY.

Chomsky takes the view that language – more accurately, the grammar of a language – can only be seen coherently if we regard it as a system of knowledge in the mind of a person who speaks that language. He goes on to argue that many properties of language are innate in humans: each of us, he says, has abstract grammatical rules and principles encoded in our genes – programmed into our brains, if you prefer. The grammar of a particular language emerges when certain limited choices allowed by the genetic program are made by the young person acquiring language, on the basis of simple data available to any child. What Chomsky developed, then, is a *biological* theory of language. Asked to define language, Chomsky would say that it is not a useful concept: the interesting concept is grammar, seen as a biological system. A theory for Chomsky is an attempt to explain why some part of the world is the way it is (cf. Chomsky, 1988; Salkie, 1990).

Some remarks are needed to complete this picture. First, the four phases were not as discrete as I have portrayed them. For instance, both Saussure and Bloomfield did important work in historical linguistics; indeed, Bloomfield's classic 1933 book contains some excellent discussion of how the meanings of words change over time, as well as the better-known claim that the study of meaning is not a part of scientific linguistics. Furthermore, each phase influenced the next: the tools developed and the results achieved in one period laid the groundwork for the next (see Robins, 1967, for a more complete picture).

Second, relating each period to its historical background should not be taken as denigrating the achievements of the scholars concerned. The reconstruction of Indo-European, for instance, in the complete absence of supporting historical or archaeological evidence, must rank among the great intellectual achievements in history. Analyzing previously unrecorded languages, teaching languages, and making proposals about genetic properties of languages – these all demand intensive thought and hard work. In general, developing novel ideas is difficult – certainly much more difficult than seeing in hindsight why it happened.

Third, the theories surveyed here have always been built by a small minority of scholars concerned with language. Most of those who work with language are interested in description rather than theory, in learning or teaching languages, or helping people with language problems, more than with intellectual structures. This is not surprising: there are more car mechanics in the world than theoretical physicists for the same reason. Both have their part to play in the scheme of things.

Reading
Bloomfield, L. 1933: *Language.*
Chomsky, N. 1988: *Language and Problems of Knowledge.*
Lado, R. 1964: *Language Teaching.*
Lehman, W., ed. 1967: *A Reader in Nineteenth-Century Indo-European Historical Linguistics.*
Robins, R. 1967 (*1990*): *A Short History of Linguistics.*
Salkie, R. 1990: *The Chomsky Update: Linguistics and Politics.*
Saussure, F. de 1916 (*1959*): *A Course in General Linguistics.*
Thieme, P. 1957 (*1982*): "The Indo-European language."
RAPHAEL SALKIE

langue/parole A fundamental dichotomy in STRUCTURALISM derived from the work of Ferdinand de SAUSSURE. *Langue* is the abstract totality of language available to a linguistic community; *parole* is the concrete use made of this totality in individual utterance. For Saussure, *langue* is the proper subject for linguistic analysis.

Reading
Jakobson, Roman 1990: *On Language.*
Saussure, Ferdinand de 1990 (*1972*): *A Course in General Linguistics.*
PAUL INNES

latent content *See* MANIFEST/LATENT CONTENT

Latin American studies Latin American studies is an interdisciplinary field of research relating to the people, cultures, and natural environment of the Americas to the south of the United States, including the islands of the Caribbean. The field incorporates as well studies relating to people of Latin American descent living in the United States or Canada.

The area of Latin American studies embraces a wide variety of disciplines, including art, archaeology, film, history, linguistics, literature, and music in the humanities, anthropology, economics, geography, political science, and sociology in the social sciences, and biology and environmental research in the natural sciences. In keeping with the scope of this dictionary, the current entry will emphasize CULTURAL and CRITICAL THEORY in Latin American studies during the twentieth century.

The term "Latin America" is generally accepted by scholars in the Americas and throughout the world. Scholars are quick to qualify the overarching conceptual unity the term suggests, however, by calling attention to the diversity of nationalities, ethnic groups, languages, histories, and geographical conditions that exist in the huge expanse between Tierra del Fuego and the United States–Mexico border. This entry will reflect the emphasis placed on Spanish America (the 18 nations in which Spanish is an official language, as well as Puerto Rico) within Latin American studies. For studies dealing specifically with the Caribbean, see CARIBBEAN STUDIES.

Latin American intellectuals have engaged primarily in theories about Latin American or national literatures, arts, and cultures and their place in the world, rather than theorizing about culture, literature, and art in a universal sense. Much of the critical and cultural theory from Latin America in the twentieth century has dealt with the question of a national or a Latin American cultural identity. At the same time, if identity may be considered the warp of Latin American literary and cultural studies in the twenetieth century, then the concern for justice in the social and political arenas on both national and international levels constitutes the weft.

At the beginning of the twentieth century the molding of a Latin American consciousness is supported by the cosmopolitan spirit of the Spanish American modernists (*modernistas*) and Brazilian Parnassians, on the one hand, coupled with a concern about the aggressive stance of the United States in the western hemisphere on the other. The Cuban writer José Martí plays an important role in the creation of this transnational spirit, with his call for Latin Americans to realize, in a spiritual rather than a political sense, Simón Bolívar's vision of a unified America. Martí also reiterates Andrés Bello's urging that Latin Americans relate to their environment in an original way without imitating European models. While favoring progress for Latin America, Martí opposes nineteenth-century Argentine writer Domingo Faustino Sarmiento's position that the cultural imperative in Latin America was for "civilization," identified with Europe and urban life, to triumph over "barbarism," associated with the often violent forces of nature and the harshness of rural life. Uruguayan writer José Enrique Rodó takes up the standard of pan-Latin American consciousness in *Ariel* (1900), an essay based on a theme and characters from Shakespeare's *The Tempest*. Rodó places Latin America, identified with the figure of Ariel and representing humanistic and spiritual values, in opposition to the United States as Calibán, the symbol of base materialism.

The cosmopolitan spirit of the modernist essayists is manifested in the poetic genre as well, especially in the work of Rubén Darío. In *Prosas Profanas (Profane Proses)* (1896) Darío celebrates a refined sensibility and select aesthetic values that he traces from nineteenth-century French symbolism and Parnassianism to the French eighteenth century, Mandarin China, the European Middle Ages, and ancient Greek philosophy and mythology. Darío's appropriation of distant times and places for a Latin American aesthetic consciousness avoids problematizing the relationship of Latin America to Europe in particular, and claims a place in the world for Latin American writers and artists. Darío's subsequent exploration of the spiritual as well as aesthetic values of a Hispanic humanist tradition in *Cantos de vida y esperanza* (1905) (*Songs of Life and Hope*) and in his later works offers a counterpoint to his earlier aesthetic views, while announcing his solidarity with Spanish America, in particular, against the perceived threat of Anglo-Saxon America's imperialism. Both *modernismo* and the *postmodernismo* of such figures as Gabriela Mistral, Ramón López Velarde, and the young César Vallejo are based on AESTHETICS that become intertwined with ethical and moral values.

The Spanish American modernist and Brazilian Parnassian poets' pursuit of purist aesthetic values and the essayists' concern for ethical and spiritual values must be understood as part of a growing opposition to the philosophy of POSITIVISM, the dominant intellectual force in Latin America in the second half of the nineteenth century. Positivism, with its veneration of empiricist knowledge, comes increasingly under fire from intellectuals for its view of technology as a means of mastering nature, as well as for its objectification of human beings and creations. In reaction to this philosophy, much of the intellectual activity of philosophers, artists, and writers in the twentieth century is devoted to the exploration of nonempirical and often non-rational thinking. The philosophy of humanism offers an attractive alternative to positivism for many Latin Americn intellectuals. Benedetto Croce's idea of creative or artistic thinking as a valid form of knowledge and his idea of the fusion of intuition and artistic or literary expression are well received in Latin America, especially in Argentina. Henri Bergson's theory of vitalism and his interest in subjective experience are also popular among intellectuals seeking alternatives to positivism. It is from the perspective of humanism that the Dominican writer Pedro Henríquez Ureña affirms that Latin American literature, from its beginnings at the end of the fifteenth century, has formed part of the Western tradition. In his *Seis ensayos en busca de nuestra expresión* (*Six Essays in Search of Our Expression*) (1928), Henríquez Ureña calls on Latin American intellectuals to explore, both creatively and critically, their national and pan-American literary traditions.

In contrast with the aesthetic values of the previous generation, writers of the 1910s and 1920s prefer to focus on national concerns and tend to seek the elements of a Latin American identity in rural or provincial life. In Spanish America, novelists, in particular, associate the national identity with rural America, as in Ricardo Güiraldes's *Don Segundo Sombra* (1926) (*Don Segundo Sombra*, 1935) and Rómulo Gallegos' *Doña Bárbara* (1929) (*Doña Barbara*). Gallegos' novel, like *La Vorágine* (1924) (*The Vortex*, 1935) by José Eustasio Rivera, portrays a potentially violent American nature capable of resisting or even destroying civilization. In Brazil, the movement signalling a new awakening of a nationalist consciousness is initiated around 1922 under the banner of *modernismo*. It combines literary and artistic experimentation, much like that of the European avant-garde, a will to forge a national character that includes Afro-Americans and indigenous peoples, and a concern for social justice.

In countries with large Native American and mestizo populations, the "indigenist" novel is taken up with renewed vigor. For the most part these novels, such as Jorge Icaza's *Huasipungo* (1934), Ciro Alegría's *El mundo es ancho y ajeno* (1941) (*Broad and Alien Is the World*, 1941) and José María Arguedas's *Los Ríos Profundos* (1958) (*Deep Rivers*, 1978), are designed to provide insight into the world of Native Americans and to indict their treatment at the hands of *criollos* and mestizos alike. In Mexico the concern for a national identity comes on the heels of the Mexican Revolution. The institutional and social reforms it produces reflect a broader definition of the national culture which emphasizes the contribution of indigenous and mestizo peoples to Mexican culture. Literary works dealing with the revolution, primarily narrative works, such as Mariano Azuela's *Los de Abajo* (1916) (*The Underdogs*, 1962), portray the uprising of indigenous peoples and the dispossessed in a favorable light. While much of Mexican intellectuals' attention is directed inward, the philosopher and Minister of Education José Vasconcelos theorizes in *La raza Cósmica* (1925) (*The Cosmic Race*, 1979) that Mexico is in the vanguard of a universal process that will create a new and superior race produced by the fusion of Native Americans with people of European ancestry. In Haiti the Indigenist movement begins in 1928 as a reaction against the United States' occupation of the country. One of the best-known works associated with this movement is Jacques Roumain's novel *Gouverneurs de la rosée* (1944) (*Masters of the Dew*, 1947).

From the 1920s through the 1970s two broadly based intellectual currents, the humanist and the Marxist, provide sometimes competing and at times complementary perspectives on the central questions of identity and justice in Latin America. Focusing on Latin American history and culture, they both attempt to inscribe the Latin American experience into a larger circle of meaning.

José Ortega y Gasset's application of phenomenological analysis to literature and culture in the 1910s and his philosophical perspective on history and culture in the 1920s are influential in Latin America, primarily in Argentina and Mexico. Ortega's insistence that a philosophy of "man" must consider the individual in terms of the particular time and place in which he or she lives dovetails with the concern of many Latin American intellectuals for a national or Latin American philosophy. The line of thinking espoused by Ortega is continued in Mexico by José Gaos and then by Leopoldo Zea in *En torno a una filosofía americana* (1945)

(*Regarding an American Philosophy*). Indeed, the humanistic vein in twentieth-century Latin America is translated into an "anthropological" current from the emergence of culture as an object of philosophical investigation, following a course charted by Giambattista Vico in the eighteenth century and Wilhelm Dilthey in the nineteenth century. Max Scheler's work in philosophical anthropology, which addresses the place of the human being in the cosmos, is instrumental in focusing critical attention on the study of culture from the perspective of philosophy in Latin America. Samuel Ramos' *Perfil del hombre y la cultura en México* (1934) (*Profile of Man and Culture in Mexico*) and Francisco Romero's *Teoría del hombre* (1952) (*Theory of Man*), as well as that of Miguel Reale's *Filosofía do direito* (1953) (*Philosophy of Law*) all relate to philosophical anthropology. Ramos, in particular, perceives the latter philosophical current as a humanistic undertaking in his *Hacia un nuevo humanismo. Programa de una antropología filosófica* (1940) (*Toward a New Humanism. Program of a Philosophical Anthropology*).

MARXISM reorients the concern for a Latin American cultural identity toward an analysis of the capitalist and imperialist domination of Latin America and the struggle by oppressed peoples for social, economic, and political justice in the region. The Peruvian writer José Carlos Mariátegui grounds his study of the problems facing his country, particularly that of the marginalization of the large indigenous population, in Marxist theory. In *Siete ensayos sobre la realidad peruana* (1928) (*Seven Essays on Peruvian Reality*, 1971) Mariátegui describes the similarity between the "communist" society of the ancient Incas and the Communism championed by the newly formed Soviet Union. The murals of the Mexican artists Diego Rivera and Emilio Orozco affirm the dignity of the indigenous peoples of America and celebrate Mexico's peasant and worker classes. The identification of the pre-Columbian indigenous peoples of the Americas with peasant or worker classes and that of the Spanish with the capitalist elite is developed extensively in Pablo Neruda's poetic work, *Canto General* (1950) (*General Song*).

The philosophies of existence provide a bridge between the humanist and Marxist lines of investigation in the 1940s and 1950s. Martin HEIDEGGER's *Being and Time*, published in Spanish in 1951, is read by some intellectuals from the perspective of the ethical and political implications of EXISTENTIALISM. Jean-Paul SARTRE's theory of existence, and especially his later argument that writers and artists must commit themselves to social and political change, are also influential in Latin America. While such writers as Octavio Paz, José Lezama Lima, and the young Julio Cortázar pursue radical change primarily within the literary or aesthetic realm, others like Neruda, Alejo Carpentier, Ernesto Cardenal, Jorge Amado, and the young Mario Vargas Llosa affirm the need to foment societal change through their work.

Under the influence of existentialism, the question of identity is treated primarily on an individual level. Octavio Paz, in *El laberinto de la soledad* (1950) (*The Labyrinth of Solitude*, 1961), analyzes the individual Mexican's crisis of identity, incorporating elements of philosophy, primarily phenomenological and existential, as well as aspects of PSYCHOANALYSIS into his essay. He presents the Mexican as "the OTHER" and theorizes that the Mexican's very ALIENATION and marginalization from the center of Western civilization makes him representative of contemporary Western man. Julio Cortázar's *Rayuela* (1963) (*Hopscotch*, 1966) portrays the existential search for meaning by an Argentine intellectual living in Paris. Cortázar treats the theme of "the other" in *Rayuela* and several of his short stories, a theme also explored by Octavio Paz in his poetry and essays. Jorge Luis Borges also manifests a concern for personal identity and for "the other" in his mature work, as the title of one of his works, *El otro, el Mismo* (1969) (*The Other, the Same*), indicates. Borges's much documented skepticism, often linked to that of Spinoza, contributes to the philosphical resonance of the literature of the mid-twentieth century.

The twentieth-century search for liberating alternatives to chronological and historical time, undertaken by such Latin American poets as Vicente Huidobro, César Vallejo, and Pablo Neruda in the first half of the twentieth century, becomes prominent in Latin American narrative in the 1950s. Latin American writers are the beneficiaries of these poets' avant-garde models of experimentation with time, as well as the innovative narrative styles of James Joyce, Marcel Proust, and William Faulkner. In addition, Latin American narrative writers inherit Heidegger's idea of being as inextricably tied to the experience of time. The theoretical investigation of mythic and ritual views of time by Ernst Cassirer and anthropological studies of "primitive" peoples by scholars such as Claude Lévi-Strauss suggest that Latin American cultures may be closer to liberating experiences of time than those of Europe or North America. Experimentation with time in the narrative structure and theorizing about models of time are central elements of the works associated with the "boom" of the Latin American novel: Alejo Carpentier's *Los pasos perdidos* 1953 (*The Lost Steps*, 1956) and *El reino de este mundo* (1949) (*The Kingdom of This World*, 1957), Cortázar's *Rayuela*, Juan Rulfo's *Pedro Páramo* (1955) (*Pedro Páramo*, 1959), *La región más transparente* (1958) (*Where the Air is Clear*, 1960), by Carlos Fuentes and Gabriel García Marquez's *Cien años de soledad* (1967) (*One Hundred Years of Solitude*, 1970).

Carpentier's idea of "lo real maravilloso" (the marvelous-real) and García Marquez's formulation of "realismo mágico" (magical realism) combine the Renaissance and utopian views of America as a "New World" with a more contemporary desire for a nature unsubjugated to human will and a time and space that have not been reduced to an order by rational consciousness. Carpentier, in particular, presents Native American culture in *Los pasos perdidos* and Afro-American culture in *El reino de este mundo* in opposition to European models of consciousness. Octavio Paz's poetic exploration of Asian cultures and regions in *Ladera este* (1969) (*East Side*) and other works suggests an alternative to the Western cultural tradition as well. Carpentier and Lezame Lima theorize that the aesthetic best representing an authentic Latin American mode of expression is the baroque. They describe a contemporary style of literature, particularly POETRY and novels, as neobaroque, exemplified by Carpentier's *Concierto Barroco* (1974) (*Baroque Concert*), Lezama's *Paradiso* (1966) (*Paradiso*, 1974), and Fuentes' *Terra Nostra* (1975) (*Terra Nostra*, 1976). In various ways all of these works affirm the value of imagination and tend to circumscribe the role of reason and logic in human actions and creations.

In the 1960s and 1970s some Latin American theorists and creative writers seek to break down the boundaries dividing disciplines, particularly those separating the humanities from the social sciences. Uruguayan critic Angel Rama emphasizes the need to study literature from the perspective of social and political theories and concerns. Peruvian philosopher Augusto Salazar Bondy affirms his belief that a Latin American philosophy must come to terms with the fact of the region's continued existence as a colony of more developed nations. Salazar Bondy also expresses concern at Latin American philosophers' and intellectuals' elite status and their isolation from the majority of the population. The Argentine philosopher Arturo Andrés Roig, among others, reinterprets Rodó's identification of Calibán with barbarism. Roig suggests that Calibán represents, in effect, the Native American, Afro-American, and mestizo majority of Latin America. In the religious realm, exponents of the Catholic theology of liberation, such as Gustavo Gutiérrez, Juan Luis Segundo, and Leonardo Boff proclaim that the church must work to make social justice for poor and marginalized people a reality.

Also in the 1960s and 1970s, writers and other creative artists attempt to remove the barriers between the literary/artistic world and that of ordinary people, especially the underprivileged classes. Perhaps more than other genres, the theater in Latin America challenges the audience with the dramatic experience to confront social and political problems. Bertolt Brecht's ideas on the political relevance of theater combine with the ideology of social and political revolution. Dramatists such as Griselda Gambaro, Jorge Diás, Osvaldo Dragún, Jose Triana, and Egon Wolff incorporate theories and staging techniques from the theater of the absurd and Artaud's theater of cruelty as a means of effecting changes in the audience's consciousness. In theater, as well as in poetry, there are attempts to move beyond an elite or middle-class audience to address working-class and and rural audiences. Michel Foucault's discovery of the carnavalesque as a traditional means of undermining authority coincides with dramatists' exploration of Iberian and Catholic cultural traditions and rituals, as well as those of Native Americans and Afro-Americans.

Attempts are made in the 1960s and 1970s to have previously marginalized and disenfranchised groups become creators of literature and art. Poetry and drama workshops aimed at working-class people, peasants, Native and Afro-Americans appear in a number of countries, among them Cuba, Nicaragua, Argentina, Mexico, and in Hispanic communities in the United States. In narrative, the growth of testimonial literature during the 1970s and 1980s creates a vehicle for people who have been victims of political repression, such as Rigoberta Menchú of Guatemala, to denounce their oppressors. An "Indianist" movement, in which Native Americans express their concerns in their own voices

(in contrast to the "Indigenist" movement of the 1920s and 1930s), mobilizes to protest the celebratory conmemoration of the 500 years since the first European encounter with Native American peoples.

Women's writing renews the Latin American search for identity from a feminist perspective in the 1970s and 1980s, while FEMINIST CRITICISM addresses the general omission of women in both humanist and Marxist critical analysis. Simone de Beauvoir's *The Second Sex* (1949) is the theoretical work most credited with raising feminist consciousness in Latin America. Women writers such as Rosario Castellanos, Elena Poniatowska, and Rosario Ferré publish novels, in particular, that feature female protagonists and narration from a feminist perspective. Castellanos undertakes a rewriting of Mexican cultural history in the theatrical work *El eterno femenino* (1975) (*The Eternal Feminine*). Her humorous tone is adopted by Rosario Ferré in *Colloquio de las perras* (1990) (*The Colloquy of the Bitches*), in which Ferré criticizes the lack of verisimilitude in primarily male writers' depiction of women in Latin American literature. In this work Ferré assumes a humanist perspective, placing her voice within a broader Hispanic tradition, with her adaptation of Cervantes's *Coloquio de los perros* (*Colloquy of the Dogs*). Lucía Guerra's middle-class protagonist in *Más alla de las máscaras* (1984) (*Beyond the Masks*) embarks on a search for personal identity that leads to the realization that liberation for her as a woman must be pursued in conjunction with the struggles for justice of all oppressed groups. Feminist criticism has resulted in new interest in Latin American women writers and artists of previous generations or periods, such as María Luisa Bombal, Clarisse Lispector, Victoria Ocampo, Frida Kahlo, and Sor Juana Inés de la Cruz. Other women writers, such as Luisa Valenzuela and Isabel Allende, remain more aloof from feminist theorizing. Valenzuela cultivates a critical novel that may include political analysis and psychoanalytical insights. Allende's work, at times manifesting qualities associated with magical realism, as in *Eva Luna* (1987) (*Eva Luna*, 1988) explores the motives of the heart, along the lines of Pascal or Scheler, in contrast with the highly intellectual search of such "boom" writers as Cortázar and Carpentier.

European and North American critical theory has had a considerable impact on the analysis of Latin American literature and culture. Russian FORMALISM appears in the southern cone, in particular, in the first half of the twentieth century and gives way to STRUCTURALISM in the 1950s. Both critical studies stemming from Marxist theory, under the influence of the FRANKFURT SCHOOL, and phenomenological studies, in particular from the GENEVA SCHOOL, are carried out in the 1950s and 1960s. SEMIOTICS is the most pervasive critical theory in Latin America in the 1970s. FOUCAULT is, perhaps, the most frequently invoked poststructuralist critic, in part because his readings of literature and culture correspond to anthropological and historicist tendencies in Latin American critical theory. Since the 1980s much of Latin American critical writing has been devoted to feminist criticism, neohistoricism, and postcolonial theory.

See also CARIBBEAN STUDIES.

Reading
Castillo, Debra A. 1992: Talking Back. Toward a Latin American Feminist Literary Criticism.
Echevarría, R.G., and Pupo-Walker, E., eds 1995: The Cambridge History of Latin America.
Fernandez Moreno, C., and Ortega, J. 1980: Latin America in its Literature.
Foster, D.W., ed. 1992: Handbook of Latin American Literature.
Fuentes, Carlos 1992: The Buried Mirror. Reflections on Spain and the New World.
Gracia, Jorge J.E., ed. 1986: Latin American Philosophy in the Twentieth Century. Man, Values, and the Search for Philosophical Identity.
Jackson, Richard L. 1988: Black Literature and Humanism in Latin America.
Mitchell, Cristopher, ed. 1988: Changing Perspectives in Latin American Studies: Insights from Six Disciplines.
Paz, Octavio 1985: One Earth, Four or Five Worlds. Reflections on Contemporary History.
Rama, Angel 1985: La crítica de la cultura en América Latina.
Solé, Carlos A., ed. 1989: Latin American Writers.
Yúdice, George, Franco, Jean, and Flores, Juan, eds 1992: On Edge. The Crisis of Contemporary Latin American Culture.
Zavala, Iris 1992: Colonialism and Culture. Hispanic Modernism and the Social Imaginary.
Zea, Leopoldo, ed. 1986: América Latina en sus ideas.
ALICE J. POUST

law, philosophy of   Currently an area of active interdisciplinary exchange between theorists of jurisprudence and literary critics (Stanley FISH most prominent among them) who raise questions of legal interpretation from a broadly HERMENEUTIC, neopragmatist, or COMMUNITARIAN standpoint. There is also a more heterodox school of thought by the name of Critical Legal Studies, which draws many of its ideas from the work of French thinkers like Jacques DERRIDA and Michel FOUCAULT. These approaches differ widely in their political bearing and the extent to which they take issue with the dominant (broadly liberal) tradition of modern Anglo-American jurisprudence. What they all have in common is a turn toward language (or to DISCOURSE, rhetoric, and narrative) as a means of questioning received priorities and methodological ground rules. In the following brief survey I shall attempt to summarize the main lines of argument and their relation to other, more conventional forms of legal doctrine and reasoning.

From the received viewpoint jurisprudence is chiefly concerned with establishing adequate grounds or procedures for the adjudication of particular cases with reference to existing statutes, principles, legal provisions, or case law precedents. For the most part – it is assumed – this process will be fairly straightforward. That is to say, a direct appeal is made to some relevant or appropriate item of law which can be shown to fit the case in hand, or to provide for such cases by virtue of its scope as a generalized or covering principle. Of course there is still room for disagreement over just how those principles or precedents apply, and also – more controversially – over whether there exists a neutral adjudicative standpoint for determining their relevance or applicability in any given instance. Traditionally, legal theorists have drawn a distinction between, on the one hand, clear-cut cases for which there exists some adequate statutory provision, or which can readily be brought under some prior ruling, and on the other hand those "hard cases" where problems arise – and where judges may find themselves creating legal precedent – for lack of any firm or explicit procedural guidelines.

A similar distinction is held to obtain between the realms of statute law and case law. Thus the former has at least the appearance of being couched in plain, unambiguous terms, or of providing in advance all the necessary means – precepts, principles, statements of intent, limiting clauses, and so forth – by which to determine their legitimate scope and precise meaning in this or that context. Case law, conversely, always has an interpretative element, a point at which judgment must be exercised with regard to the relevance of past proceedings, their import for the case in hand, and the extent to which they offer guidance in arriving at a just and equitable verdict. Here it cannot be a matter of adopting some generalized covering-law precept (or match between case and case), such that the result would follow directly from a (quasi)-algorithmic application or a straightforward decision-procedure. Rather, it requires that each instance be interpreted in light of the manifold details, circumstances, motives, and other individuating features which complicate the comparison between them.

Both of these distinctions have lately come under attack from theorists in the Critical Legal Studies camp and from others who seek to deconstruct or challenge the instituted order of juridical discourse. Thus it is argued that statute law (no less than case law) always entails a large measure of interpretative license; that its scope and provisions cannot be simply read off from the sacrosanct "words on the page"; and hence that any talk of due process, the separation of powers between executive and judicial branches, of neutral (unbiased) application, and so forth, is merely a disguise for some covert political agenda that dares not speak its name. And in case law, so it is argued, we should likewise be suspicious of the distinction between "easy" (or straightforward) and "hard" cases, since this also very often obscures the extent to which seemingly self-evident, rule-governed, or "commonsense" modes of judgment may conceal all manner of ideological prejudice. Such ideas have a longer prehistory of active debate in the US than in the British legal system.

These questions were first raised in a programmatic way by the American legal realist school of the 1930s and 1940s. Their thinking was much influenced by Marxist and left-sociological analyses, as well as by wider demographic factors and the sense of a looming crisis in domestic and world economic and political affairs. Where the current theorists differ is chiefly in their looking to a range of alternative sources – POSTSTRUCTURALISM, POSTMODERNISM, DECONSTRUCTION, DISCOURSE theory, Foucauldian "GENEALOGY," etc. – as a substitute for those older, unfashionable modes of sociopolitical critique. Thus the talk is now more often of law as the site of conflicting TEXTual or narrative strategies, of multiple and heterogeneous "subject positions" within language, or of the way that legal discourse secures its authority by assuming a "meta-linguistic" stance supposedly above and beyond the level of first-order natural narrative pragmatics. (See the entry on Jean-François LYOTARD for one influential source of this line of argument.) Such has been the widespread "linguistic turn" across various present-day disciplines, jurisprudence latterly among them. Its effect is most visible in the oft-repeated claim that "reality" is itself a discursive construct, a purely notional ground of appeal which will always be contested – like the "facts" or the "evidence" in any given case – from a range of competing (incommensurable) viewpoints. Hence Lyotard's postmodernist idea of justice as a matter of maximizing narrative differentials, judging so far as possible "without criteria," and refusing to privilege any one "phrase genre" (for example, the cognitive) above all the rest. For otherwise, he argues, we risk the kind of "totalitarian" gesture that will seek to suppress the narrative "differend" between various phrases-in-dispute, and will thereby commit a juridical wrong against one or other (or maybe both) parties.

This argument is pursued to various, more or less radical ends, according to the theorist's political persuasion and the degree of his or her avowed disenchantment with the discourse of mainstream (whether "conservative" or "liberal") jurisprudence. For some – for example, the liberal communitarians – what is most important is to keep open the ongoing pluralist cultural conversation, and prevent any abstract creeds, theories, or principles from seeking to monopolize the moral high ground. In their view jurisprudence can best promote this common good by acknowledging the range of its own (past and present) social applications, and the impossibility of rising above them to some vantage point of absolute justice or truth. Thus Ronald Dworkin argues for a narrative conception of legal and judicial history wherein judges, lawyers, students, theorists, concerned lay-persons, and others can view themselves on the analogy with a "chain novelist," one who takes up the story at a certain point in its development and continues it with the aim of both conserving narrative coherence and responding creatively to new and unforeseen challenges. This would be a principled but also (in the good sense) a pragmatic endeavor. It would seek to promote the flourishing of social-democratic institutions and the enlargement of a genuine participant public sphere.

For others on the left-libertarian wing of Critical Legal Studies such arguments amount to nothing more than a species of high-toned apologetic pleading for the current status quo. To their way of thinking this "liberal" discourse is shot through with various contradictions, APORIAS, and instances of sheer hypocrisy or bad faith which can best be exposed by a sedulous attention to its blind spots of ingrained prejudice. In short, there is no alternative but to question every last method, precept, and principle of what is nowadays regarded – on a broad consensus of qualified legal opinion – as just or equitable practice. In its cruder, more reductive variant this doctrine amounts to an exercise of wholesale "trashing," that is, taking the pronouncements of various legal or judicial authorities and showing how they *always* self-deconstruct into forms of manifest *non sequitur*, performative contradiction, illicit passages from fact to value, concealed judgmental priorities, etc. Although deriving avowedly from the work of deconstructionists like Jacques DERRIDA and Paul DE MAN, these writings all too often display nothing like the same degree of closely forcused exegetical rigor or alertness to localized complexities of logic, grammar, and rhetoric. They are also prone to undermine their own case – in the familiar relativist fashion – by blocking any recourse to normative values or principles (of justice, equity, due process, etc.), against which to measure existing abuses of juridical authority. As with Foucault, there comes a point at which skepticism leans over into a downright cynical conviction that *all* claims-to-truth or statements of principle partake of a ubiquitous will-to-power that can only be resisted by opting for a strain of hard-boiled, blanket, antinomian rhetoric.

Elsewhere the critical insights of deconstruction are deployed to much subtler effect. Thus, for instance, it may be shown how contract law gives rise to aporias – or moments of undecidability – when it attempts to articulate a working distinction between the public and private domains. Or again, it may be argued with reference to the statute/case law dichotomy that this rests on an implicit axiomatics of language, one which in turn presupposes the existence of a clear-cut demarcation between constative and performative orders of utterance, and which thus runs up against those problems analyzed in Derrida's deconstructive reading of speech-act philosophy. Similar arguments have been advanced with regard to issues of corporate responsibility, of positive discrimination in various (for example, professional or academic) contexts, and of free speech *vis-à-vis* the interests of public peace or anti-racist legislation. Some of the most interesting work in this field deals with issues of contract law and the extent to which contractual obligations remain legally (or morally) binding when due account is taken of the different contexts – or

the range of circumstantial factors – that bear upon the parties concerned. In each of these cases, and others besides, the aim is not merely to "trash" legal precedent in a spirit of iconoclastic zeal, but also to bring out those stress points where the discourse of law contravenes its own principles or generates specific conflicts of motive and intent.

Indeed, this question of "framer's intention" – or the "spirit" as opposed to the "letter" of the text – is one that has given rise to much debate, especially as regards the founding articles of US constitutional law. Commentators divide sharply on the issue of how far it is possible to define or respect those intentions, given all the far-reaching social, political, and cultural changes that have occurred since the articles in question were first set down. Thus for some it appears quite pointless to raise such questions, since (i) there is no means of knowing for sure what the framers had in mind, apart from what they actually (and often ambiguously) wrote; and (ii) they were of course in no position to anticipate what kinds of construction might in future be placed upon their words by judges, legislators, or social policy makers with very different evaluative priorities. After all, one consequence of "respecting" their (presumed) original intentions would be to uphold the institution of slavery, or to treat slaves (and women) as falling outside the otherwise "universal" realm of human democratic rights and freedoms. Such a viewpoint would nowadays find few advocates even among the most conservative commentators. Nevertheless, there still remains the question of just what kinds or degree of hermeneutic license may be warranted by the appeal to contemporary ideas of social and political justice. And here – once again – there is much scope for disagreement between, on the one hand, those who would recommend that we abandon all thought of respecting the framers' intent, and on the other hand those who defend such an attitude so long as it carries the saving clause: "what the framers *would have meant* by their chosen form of words had they been living at the present time and cherished the same (broadly democratic) aims, values, and ideals."

This "constructivist" position does seem to capture the best, most intuitively adequate sense of what is required in the constant process of adjustment between the letter of a written constitution and its "spirit" as construed in light of present-day values and concerns. It also has much in common with Dworkin's liberal conception of law as an ongoing chain narrative – or open-ended dialogue – where issues of principle are closely bound up with the shared aspirations and communal self-images of the age. However, this leaves room for the skeptic to ask why certain principles (and not others) are deemed worthy of admission to the dialogue, or again, why the liberal consensus – thus defined – should exclude certain voices as beyond the pale of civilized juridical discourse. This liberal-pluralist ethos may always turn out to have sharp limits of tolerance when confronted with a challenge – like that of the Critical Legal Studies movement – which declines to play by the current (consensus-based) rules of the game. And indeed it is hard to see how the skeptic's charge could be answered from a liberal-communitarian standpoint, or in terms of the appeal to currently prevailing values and beliefs as the ultimate criteria of what should count as a legitimate contribution to debate.

It is the same problem that often crops up with those forms of anti-foundationalist doctrine – in epistemology and ETHICS alike – which deny all recourse to grounds or principles beyond the currency of in-place consensus belief. This opens the way to a relativist outlook that can offer no reasoned argument (apart from local custom, pragmatic inclination, or ingrained cultural habit) for regarding some beliefs as well founded or just and others as lacking any such claim to good faith and rational assent. Therefore it follows that the skeptic will always win in debate with the liberal communitarian, since the latter can provide nothing more convincing by way of principled justification than a conventionalist (for example, WITTGENSTEINian) appeal to language games, narratives, cultural "forms of life," or the way we just happen to do things in our cultural neck of the woods. And then it is plain sailing for the skeptic to protest – by a simple *tu quoque* riposte – that her or his viewpoint is unrepresented in this cosy pluralist orthodoxy.

Nobody has exploited this rhetorical turn to more ingenious knock-down effect than the literary critic Stanley Fish. Indeed "literary critic" is really a misnomer in Fish's case since he has lately moved out from that narrow disciplinary base into various other fields, among them jurisprudence, ethics, philosophy of mind and language, cultural history, and sociology of knowledge. That Fish currently holds a joint appointment in English and law at Duke University is one indication of his wish to break down those traditional (and, in his view, quite arbitrary or culture-specific) divisions

of intellectual labor. His argument, briefly summarized, is that all these disciplines (or pseudo-disciplines) in the end come down to what is currently and contingently "good in the way of belief" That is to say, it is only with reference to some given "INTERPRETIVE COMMUNITY" – whether cultural, linguistic, professional, academic, or whatever – that we can offer some account of their rising or declining fortunes. Truth *just is* what it is taken to be according to the values that happen to prevail within some such (more or less broadly defined) "community" of like-minded thinkers. And the same goes for all those other purely honorific terms – "reason," "principle," "justice," "equality," "progress," "democracy," and so forth – which may occupy the high ground of cultural debate at some given time. Not that one can pick and choose at random among them, or choose to deploy some wholly different rhetoric without the least regard for existing conventions. This would be to place oneself outside that relevant community, and thus pass up any chance of gaining a respectful or serious hearing. Nevertheless, Fish argues, they should still be seen at bottom as just rhetorical gambits, designed to win credence among those whose opinions count, and who thus constitute the target "community" for those who hope (say) to influence the course of debate, to gain academic tenure, or to persuade a judge or jury to their way of thinking. Beyond that, there is nothing more substantive at issue – nothing deeper, more "principled," or consequential – than the choice between this or that rhetoric or language game on wholly pragmatic grounds.

These arguments of Fish have been taken up by a school of neopragmatist literary and legal theorists who (in a somewhat pyrrhic gesture) declare themselves intransigently "against theory." Their point, once again, is that nothing is affected by the move to a high-toned discourse of "reason" or "principle" (or, for that matter, a critical discourse of "ideology," "contradiction," "aporia," etc.), since these terms merely serve to signal the user's allegiance to some existing – whether mainstream or dissident – interpretative community. Thus on the one hand there are "positive" theorists, among them liberals like Dworkin, who adopt a rhetoric of "law as principle" in the mistaken conviction that such talk can provide a philosophical or ethical backup for their preexistent habits of belief. On the other there are those – "negative" thinkers of various stripe, among them deconstructors, feminists, advocates of the law-and-society approach, or the Critical Legal Studies movement – who, whatever their differences of "theory" or "principle," subscribe to the same delusory idea that beliefs can be changed (in this case subverted) by an exercise of independent or critical thought. On the issue of "framer's intention" likewise there is nothing to choose (bar the rhetoric) between theorists who bring up all manner of arguments in defense of a "strong" constructivist position and skeptical debunkers who subject such claims to all the standard anti-intentionalist lines of attack.

In Fish's view it is a similar (and equally futile) debate that divides literary critics. Thus the issue is joined between defenders of a conservative approach, such as E.D. Hirsch, who think to establish adequate grounds (as well as an ethical imperative) in support of their case for respecting the author's intention, and opponents who declare that such a project is neither feasible nor (indeed) desirable. However, according to Fish and his disciples in the "against-theory" camp, both parties are equally naive in supposing that it makes any difference what they happen to think as a matter of theory or principle. It is simply the case that when we read a text – or construe an article of law – we are always (necessarily) imputing some intention which allows us to treat it as meaningful discourse, rather than a jumble of letters (or marks) quite devoid of intelligible sense. Not that this should give any comfort to Hirsch or the advocates of framers' intent. On the contrary, it denies that we could ever have grounds – theoretical or principled grounds – for choosing between rival "intentionalist" accounts, or coming up with some method, hermeneutic theory, decision procedure or whatever to point understanding in the right direction. For there is just no way that theory ("positive" or "negative") can affect such issues of interpretative choice. Rather, it is always a question of adopting any theory – or, in Fish's preferred idiom, any line of available "theory talk" – which happens to suit our present argumentative purposes or our sense of what will work best in terms of suasive strategy.

Thus theorizing is a wholly *inconsequential* activity, one that can never effect the least change in our own (or other people's) existing habits of belief. Of course there are uses (rhetorical uses) for "theory talk," for instance, when one seeks to impress colleagues, to be published in the right journals, or produce some clincher in seminar or conference debate. Nevertheless, to the extent that such strategies work, one will always be addressing an "interpretative community," at least some of whose members already subscribe to one's own theoretical line, and all of whom will share enough points of reference – professional, academic, cultural, etc. – to prevent any breakdown of communication. In short, one will either be preaching to the (wholly or halfway) converted, or, in the exceptional case, saying something so radically new and strange that one's theory talk will fall upon deaf ears and thus fail in its purpose. From which Fish concludes:

(i) that such talk is just a species of suasive rhetoric;

(ii) that "theory" drops out in all but name;

(iii) that belief goes "all the way down" and cannot be dislodged except by some other (rhetorically more efficacious) belief; and

(iv) that such shifts come about only in response to a change in the prevailing climate of opinion as registered by a given (broad-based or specialized) "interpretative community." Moreover

(v) this is nothing to worry about since we can perfectly well carry on arguing, disagreeing, criticizing, giving "reasons," adopting a "principled" stance and so forth in just the same way as before, but now, thanks to Fish, with no illusions concerning the truth of our beliefs or their justice as defined by some absolute (non-culture-specific) set of criteria.

If theory is an inconsequential activity then so is its abandonment or our ceasing to place any credence in its stronger (that is, consequentialist) claims. And in any case, as Fish mock-ruefully concedes, it is unlikely that any mere argument "against theory" will have the least effect on our habits of theory talk so long as such talk continues to enjoy some measure of communal esteem. Nor should it, indeed, given Fish's own belief that quite simply *nothing follows*, in theory or in practice, from our accepting or rejecting his case against theory.

All the same, it is clear that his argument does have some large (and disabling) consequences for those various disciplines – jurisprudence among them – which continue to invoke just the kinds of distinction that Fish would dismiss out of hand. If he is right (whatever that could mean), then we should have to conclude that their practitioners had always been laboring under a massive delusion whenever they thought to find reason or justification for rejecting some ideas as erroneous, misguided, unprincipled, or ethically repugnant, and endorsing others *despite and against* the currency of established values and beliefs. Such an interpretation would apply right across the disciplinary board, from philosophy of science to epistemology, ethics, political theory, social anthropology, and (of course) literary criticism. This is where Fish started out and where relativist doctrines – in a range of geared-up (postmodern or poststructuralist) forms – have pretty much conquered the field. Hence, as I have said, the frequent allusions to literary theory that have become almost *de rigueur* for legal theorists with an eye to the high ground of cultural and intellectual fashion. Hence also the ease with which an adept like Fish can run rings around those "positive" or "negative" theorists, liberal communitarians or dissidents in the Critical Legal Studies camp, who adopt a halfway relativist stance, one that stops short at their own favored range of values and beliefs.

However, I should not want to suggest that nothing useful or progressive has emerged from these recent developments in philosophy of law. Nor is it true that Critical Legal Studies can justifiably be treated as a school or movement subscribing to any fixed (however heterodox) set of doctrines. If the "trashing" approach falls plump into Fish's sights as an instance of unwitting rhetorical self-subversion, then there are many other examples, some of which I have mentioned above, where these theorists offer a meticulous deconstructive close-reading of statute law or case law texts with profound implications for the conduct of juridical debate. That the issues have become so sharply polarized in the United States is no doubt owing to a number of distinctive historical and cultural factors. These include the existence of a founding charter whose articles are open to varied (for example, "conservative" and "liberal") constructions; the role played by judicial review as a matter of widespread public concern; and the power exercised by Supreme Court justices to overturn even the most seemingly well-entrenched programs of state legislature. In Britain these debates enjoy nothing like the same degree of public visibility. This is perhaps one reason why the work produced by critical legal scholars in this country, Peter Goodrich among them, has adopted a rather different focus. Thus Goodrich addresses himself on the one hand to rather specialized issues in rhetorical theory *vis-à-vis* the discourse of law, and on the other to particular (well-documented) cases of judicial bias, abuse of corporate power, antiunion legislation, and pretenses of neutral adjudicative treatment in issues of (for example) private capital venture versus state welfare or local authority provision.

His work seems to me a model of its kind in both these respects. That is, it rejects the kind of leveling or all-purpose deconstructive gambit, the treatment of law as *nothing more* than a species of rhetorical imposture, which will always be open to Fish's line of shrewdly debunking the *tu quoque* response. Goodrich follows de Man and Derrida in locating those specific aporias (or tensions between logic, grammar, and rhetoric) that mark the stress points in legal discourse. These in turn give a hold for some cogent criticism of the interests, economic and sociopolitical, that often emerge at just those points to disturb the appearance of a neutral, even-handed dispensation of justice. However, such arguments can have no force if applied in a blanket (quasi-deconstructive) manner which takes for granted the collapse of all operative distinctions between truth and falsehood, principle and prejudice, or the values of communal justice and those of some partisan "interpretative community." This has been especially so at times like the 1990s when the British legal system has been subject to some 15 years of steadily increasing right-wing political pressure and miscarriages of justice at every level, from police frame-ups to rigged appeal-court procedures and judicial connivance at government malpractice. Indeed this situation has all the makings of a full-scale legitimation crisis, were it not for the prevailing cynical wisdom that expects nothing better and on balance prefers to stick with the devil it knows.

It is the same attitude, in inverted form, which responds by "trashing" legal institutions or by rejecting all talk of reason, justice, and principle as so much naive or self-serving liberal rhetoric. However, this is just one (albeit rather prominent) example of the current interdisciplinary exchange between philosophy of law and what has come to be known – mainly in departments of literature – under the capacious cover-term "theory." That these developments have another, more critical and progressive aspect may be judged from the virulent attacks heaped upon them by conservative defenders of old corruption in the name of tradition or "commonsense" values. Here at least jurisprudence has something to learn from the intensive theorizing among literary and cultural critics since the mid-1970s. One lesson is precisely to avoid that path toward a simplified leveling of genre distinctions, among them the distinction between law and literature, which ends up (like Fish) by assimilating every kind of discourse to the realm of rhetoric, fiction, or what is currently "good in the way of belief."

See also COMMUNITARIAN ETHICS; DETERMINACY; DISCOURSE; DISCURSIVE PRACTICES.

Reading

Derrida, Jacques 1992: "Force of law: the mystical foundation of authority."
Dworkin, Ronald 1986: *Law's Empire*.
——ed. 1977: *The Philosophy of Law*.
Fish, Stanley 1989a: *Doing What Comes Naturally: Change, Rhetoric and the Practice of Theory in Literary and Legal Studies*.
Fitzpatrick, Peter, and Hunt, Alan, eds 1987: *Critical Legal Studies*.
Gibbons, John, ed. 1994: *Language and the Law*.
Goodrich, Peter 1986: *Reading the Law: A Critical Introduction to Legal Method and Techniques*.
——1987: *Legal Discourse: Studies in Linguistics, Rhetoric and Legal Analysis*.
Hart, H.L.A. 1983: *Essays in Jurisprudence and Philosophy*.
Kelman, Mark 1986 (*1992*): *A Guide to Critical Legal Studies*.
Leyh, Gregory, ed. 1992: *Legal Hermeneutics: History, Theory and Practice*.
Marmor, Andrei 1992: *Interpretation and Legal Theory*.
Sarat, Austin, and Kearns, Thomas R., eds 1991: *The Fate of Law*.
Unger, Roberto Mangabeira 1986: *The Critical Legal Studies Movement*.
White, James Boyd 1985: *Heracles' Bow: Essays on the Rhetoric and Poetics of the Law*.

CHRISTOPHER NORRIS

Le Corbusier (Charles-Edouard Jeanneret) (1887–1965) Swiss-born French architect. Le Corbusier and Ludwig MIES VAN DER ROHE are almost exact contemporaries, and the architecture of Le Corbusier and that of Mies follow closely related paths to meet at a very similar stylistic point at almost exactly the same time. Both Le Corbusier's Villa Savoie, Poissey, 1929–31, and Mies's German Pavilion for the International Exposition, Barcelona, 1929, have become indispensable examples of the design and aesthetic which emphasizes technical perfection and which has come to be called the INTERNATIONAL STYLE. After this momentary meeting in the history of architecture, their work moves on in contrary directions to arrive in the 1950s in very different places. Mies's Seagram Building, New York, 1958, shares the same concerns with precise proportioning and the subtle play of color and texture as his Pavilion, but Le Corbusier's Notre Dame du Haut, Ronchamp, 1950–5, with its thick and rough textured walls, irregular size and placement of openings, the Brancusiesque roof, seems very unlike his Villa. Seeing the architectural distance that comes to separate Mies's corporate office tower from Le Corbusier's chapel, and then looking back on the Villa Savoie and the German Pavilion, the two separate directions Mies's and Le Corbusier's work will take after 1930 appear to be already charted. Mies's impeccable Pavilion seems turned inward to be found in concentrated form in the fine detailing of the "Barcelona" furniture of its interior; Le Corbusier's elevated Villa turns outward and upward to reach a climax in the freeform sculptural windscreen on the rooftop solarium. The path followed by Mies is like the narrow one seen in the paintings of Mondrian – the continued refinement and condensation of a purist vocabulary; the path taken by Le Corbusier is more like the broad one found in the work of Picasso – the continuing exploration and expression of a personal vision. While Mies seems at his best creating the isolated monument for a single individual (for example, the Farnsworth House, Plano, Illinois, 1946–50), Le Corbusier embraces the challenge of designing building complexes for large numbers of people (for example, ideal cities like the Ville Radieuse, 1930–9, high-density housing such as Unité d'Habitation, Marseilles, 1947–52, and the new capital at Chandigarh, India, 1951–6). The different paths taken by Mies and Le Corbusier may be summarized in the following two images: first, Mies measuring with calipers the spaces between the travertine blocks in the terrace of the Farnsworth House to make sure they are perfectly placed; and second, Le Corbusier surveying Rio de Janeiro from an airplane and envisaging a viaduct megastructure built in a line along the coast between the ocean and the mountains. It may be that the two different lines of sight these images represent are similar in one respect, that is, because Mies was too close, concentrating on the rightness of the smallest detail of design, and because Le Corbusier was too distant, striving to solve vast civic problems, they both sometimes lost sight of the people whose lives their art was meant to serve.

Reading
Le Corbusier 1929 (*1971*): *The City of Tomorrow and its Planning (Urbanisme)*.
———1960: *Creation is a Patient Search*.

GERALD EAGER

Leavis, Frank Raymond   (1895–1978)   British literary critic. In his teaching at Cambridge and in the journal *Scrutiny* (1932–53), Leavis was a major participant in English debates on CULTURE, defending a high literary model of the cultural "center" against threats from science and mass culture. He revised, and severely restricted, the CANON of English literature in *Revaluation* (1936) and *The Great Tradition* (1948), employing a strong form of MORAL CRITICISM partly inherited from ARNOLD. His general cultural criticism lamented the destruction of the English rural "organic community," whose values survived only in the literary tradition. Despite affiliations with the modernism of Eliot, he continued the Romantic anti-capitalist line of cultural critique from Carlyle and Ruskin and mediated through Lawrence, showing relentless Protestant hostility to cultural bureaucracies and institutions (the BBC, Oxford University, the London literary journals), and a zealous belief in literature's "life-enhancing" value. Drawing on the work of his wife Q.D. Leavis (1906–81) in her *Fiction and the Reading Public* (1932), and on Eliot's DISSOCIATION OF SENSIBILITY thesis, Leavis outlined a historical sociology of English culture as decline and disintegration, in *Mass Civilization and Minority Culture* (1933) and later works. In this model, the shared national culture and vibrant language of Shakespeare's time has broken down, under pressures from popular education and journalism, into a sterile "high" culture (for example, Joyce, Woolf, Auden) and a mindless "low" culture of cinema and pulp fiction. Leavis's disciples ("Leavisites") were an influential force in British education in the 1950s and 1960s, and some introduced the (morally dismissive) study of advertising into their classrooms. Since the critiques of his nostalgic conservatism by Raymond Williams and others, Leavis is now regarded (despite his anti-establishment polemics) as a reactionary force in English literary studies, usually because of his anti-theoretical stance and his defense of a tightly exclusive canon.
See also SCRUTINY.

Reading
Baldick, Chris 1983: *The Social Mission of English Criticism 1848–1932*.
Mulhern, Francis 1979: *The Moment of "Scrutiny"*.
Samson, Anne 1992: *F.R. Leavis*.

CHRIS BALDICK

Left, New   *See* NEW LEFT

legitimation   A central term of Max Weber's political sociology, denoting the process of claiming legitimacy: a recognition on the part of the governed of the right of those who govern to rule over them (Weber, 1922b). States may be classified according to the different principles of legitimacy to which they lay claim. As a description of the role of ideas in the acquisition and maintenance of political power, the idea of legitimation may be compared to the Marxist concept of IDEOLOGY, although it attributes greater independence to the normative dimension of political life. It was integrated into a neo-Marxist theory of the state by HABERMAS (1975). The concept gained preeminence in the late 1970s in the course of a debate over whether or not the NEW RIGHT attack on welfare provision would delegitimize the liberal capitalist state.

Reading
Beetham, David 1991: *The Legitimation of Power*.
Connolly, William, ed. 1984: *Legitimacy and the State*.
Habermas, Jürgen 1975: *Legitimation Crisis*.

PETER OSBORNE

lesbian feminism   A social movement whose aim is the elimination of social and cultural practices that oppress women for whom sexual and emotional relationships with other women are primary. The starting point for the history of lesbian feminism is the reorganization of GENDER IDEOLOGY at the turn of the twentieth century that simultaneously created and demonized lesbianism as a sexual identity. Before that reorganization certain sexual practices were considered gay, but anyone might engage in them; today gays are considered a class of persons and homosexuality a sexual identity.

The beginning of the gay liberation movement is usually marked by the Stonewall riot of 1968, when gays refused to be arrested by New York City police during a raid on a gay bar, but numerous homophile organizations of the 1950s, such as the Daughters of Bilitis, provided a grass-roots organization of lesbians from which the lesbian feminism of the 1960s emerged. After Stonewall, a flood of openly self-identified lesbians joined feminist organizations such as the National Organization of Women, founded in 1966, forcing feminist theory and political practice far beyond its liberal roots toward a radical reinterpretation of heterosexuality as the bulwark of PATRIARCHY. Lesbians such as Charlotte Bunch, Ti-Grace Atkinson, and Adrienne Rich theorized that heterosexuality was not merely a sexual "identity" – and certainly not the only "natural" or "normal" one – but a compulsory social system, an institution as well as an ideology that oppressed all women. The radicals' slogan was "feminism is the theory – lesbianism is the practice."

By 1971 the lesbian feminist presence in hitherto liberal feminist organizations became so vocal as to alarm the heterosexual constituency. Betty FRIEDAN's was a prominent voice arguing that although lesbians were welcome in feminist organizations, they should remain "closeted" so as not to provoke a vilification that would undermine the movement. In the "gay/straight split" that ensued, lesbian feminists entered a separatist stage; throughout the 1970s they would work to create alternative communities and social structures in which the power of "woman-identified women" could be released. The AIDS crisis beginning in the 1980s inspired a resurgence of homophobia in the dominant culture so mighty that when the Moral Majority called for the incarceration and execution of gays there was little if any public outcry. In response, many lesbian feminists joined efforts with gay men, reactivating the old homophile alliance between gay men and lesbian women eschewed in the separatist 1970s.

Now lesbian feminists are widely distributed throughout the political spectrum: they work in all factions of the feminist movement, which has generally repudiated its homophobic position of the early 1970s, in separatist communities and organizations, and in organizations working for gays' rights generally. By the 1990s there was considerable academic attention to every aspect of gay and lesbian history and experience. *The Lesbian and Gay Studies Reader* (Abelove et al., 1993) not only collects an extensive number of important essays in gay and lesbian cultural studies, but provides extensive "Suggestions for Further Reading" on all aspects of this topic.

Reading
Abelove, Henry, Barale, Michele Aina, and Halperin, David M., eds 1993: *The Lesbian and Gay Studies Reader.*

GLYNIS CARR

Lévi-Strauss, Claude (1908–) French anthropologist. It is not often that an anthropologist achieves such stature that he is described as a hero. Claude Lévi-Strauss has done so (viz. *Claude Lévi-Strauss: The Anthropologist as Hero*, edited by E. and T. Hayes, 1970). Lévi-Strauss, whose writings span the half century following the 1939–45 war, is the central anchorage of what is known as structural anthropology or French STRUCTURALISM. The approach is distinctive, complex, fruitful, has many practitioners, and achieves in all respects the status of a school of thought. Remarkably, Lévi-Strauss's writings not only originated the school, but, 50 years later, were still at its cutting edge.

Lévi-Strauss identifies his most important intellectual forebear as Jean-Jacques Rousseau. In Rousseau's writings he found the central tenet of his own work: that accounting for the transition from animal to human, from a state of nature to a state of CULTURE, was the central problem in the study of human beings. Other major mentors for Lévi-Strauss are Emile DURKHEIM and his student Marcel MAUSS. From Durkheim Lévi-Strauss takes several propositions. He is anti-reductionist: social behavior cannot be reduced to psychology or physics or biology. Social behavior originates in coherent, logical systems whose configurations are elusive, but discoverable with meticulous comparative work. An individual's own volition is inconsequential; individuals are modeled on the social systems in which they live; to explain behavior, look to the social system. With Mauss he shares the conviction that the study of small, traditional societies will provide a rich harvest of comparative cases, avoiding the complexities and distortions that come with civilizations. Further, the foundation of being human is reciprocity, the sense of obligation that comes from giving and receiving. Reciprocity underlies all human society, distinguishes it from all animal interaction, and creates a social system based on exchange. Finally, Lévi-Strauss embraces the notion from both Durkheim and Mauss that some domains of human custom are "total"; that is, they conjoin several subsystems of the whole at once. These domains are priority targets of investigation if one seeks to discern the underlying system that organizes a society. The two cultural domains with which Lévi-Strauss has mostly worked, kinships and mythologies, have this "total" quality.

To these propositions Lévi-Strauss adds his own. Lévi-Strauss argues that the structure of a social system is unconscious to all participants and is never plainly in view. The key to discovering it is to be found in the science of linguistics, and this is because, Lévi-Strauss argues, both language and cultural systems are built on the same principles. There is a reason for this: both are lodged in the human brain and necessarily reflect its neurological organization. Thus both language and culture use a quite small number of components which, with the application of limited number of principles, generate the vast richness of language and culture respectively.

In language the basal components are phonemes, the smallest standardized sounds that convey meaning. The way linguists identify phonemes is by a technique known as contrastive pairs. Thus in English "pin" and "bin" convey different meanings, and yet the only difference in the sound units is between the "p" sound and the "b" sound. Because substituting one for the other changes the meaning, the "p" and "b" are two English phonemes. The technique succeeds because phonemes are organized in contrastive, paired relationships called BINARY OPPOSITIONS. They have to be, says Lévi-Strauss, because the neurology of the human brain operates in binary pairs.

For Lévi-Strauss cultural systems too are built on a fairly small number of meaning units – SYMBOLS – that can be identified by using the contrastive pair technique. The complication is that the meaning of symbols is often disguised. Symbols can be reversed (TRANSFORMATIONS) or otherwise changed in a number of ways. Unraveling them requires the extremely meticulous examination of ethnographic data, much of which will not be what it seems. Success yields an inverted pyramid that begins with the surface ethnography and proceeds downward through a series of decoded contrastive pairs representing symbolic expressions of oppositional choices around which the cultural system is built. As with language, cultural systems are means of transmitting and receiving.

The two major domains to which Lévi-Strauss has devoted most of his efforts are kinship and myth. Within kinship he focuses on marriage rules, and in an elegant analysis of a widespread but puzzling custom, the preference that spouses should be first cousins, he concludes that, owing to these rules, male-administered kin groups (clans) are locked into reciprocal relationships. What is transmitted between them are women; clans give away daughters and receive wives in return. The second domain is mythology. In a four-volume series that will probably be his *magnum opus, Mythologies* (1964; 1966; 1968; 1973), Lévi-Strauss examines hundreds of indigenous myths, leading the reader through oppositional analyses to reveal their underlying systems.

The empiricist traditions in anthropology, especially in Britain and the United States, have resisted French structuralism. The criticisms chiefly target the impossibility of independently verifying the decoded structure. Lévi-Strauss energetically rejoinders that Empiricism itself is a matter of successive approximations, of dialectical debate and replacement, and that structuralist findings are only similar (see Sholte, 1973, pp. 683–7 for further discussion).

Claude Lévi-Strauss is one of the giants of contemporary thought. The above is no more than an extract from the vast corpus of sophisticated, erudite scholarship and commentary that he has produced over more than half a century. His analysis and findings have stimulated and guided scholars in many fields, especially philosophy and the literary humanities. French structuralism achieved its greatest saliency in the 1960s and the 1970s. Outside France it has since receded in the face of new scholarly enthusiasms. None the less, in accounting for mythic symbolism, no new approach has yet displaced French structuralism concerning underlying symbolic meanings or the systemic relationship they may bear to each other.

Reading
de Waal Malefijt, Annemarie 1974: *Images of Man: A History of Anthropological Thought.*
Lévi-Strauss, Claude 1955 (*1973*): *Tristes Tropiques.*
——1966: *The Savage Mind.*
——1949 (*1969*): *The Elementary Structure of Kinship.*
Scholte, Bob 1973: "The structural anthropology of Claude Lévi-Strauss."

TOM C. GREAVES

liberal The author of the article on liberalism in the *Encyclopedia Britannica* (1993) traces liberal values back to the pre-Socratic philosophers and the Bible, where are found "a sense of the importance of human individuality, a liberation of the individual from complete subservience to the group, and a relaxation of the tight hold of custom, law, and authority" (p. 422). Richard Hofstadter (1955) describes the liberal tradition in the United States as "popular, democratic, progressive" (p. 13).

The following principles derive from a credo put forward by David Spitz and based upon the perspective of John Stuart Mill's *On Liberty*:

(i) Liberty. Because freedom of inquiry and discussion is essential to the correction of unjust inequalities, and because people disagree over the nature of justice, freedom possesses greater value than equality or justice.

(ii) Privacy is necessary to thought for inquiry and discussion and for discovering one's individuality.

(iii) Property. People precede and transcend property in value, but property has a positive role in promoting human well-being by empowering individuals against government, corporations, and majority opinion.

(iv) However, in so far as the sovereignty of property is employed contrary to the public good, it must be contained.

(v) Utility. The test is social utility, for rights adhere to human beings, not institutions.

(vi) Power. Because power tends to corrupt, surrounding its possessor with toadies who fill him or her with illusions of self-importance and inhibit alternative ideas and actions, we should distrust power and authority.

(vii) Toleration. Because only the gods know with certainty, acknowledgement of one's limitations implies acceptance of the limitations of others, which leads to open discussion for discovering truth and remedying social ills.

(viii) Democracy. The advantages of individual liberty suggest the beneficence of democratic polity, since free discussion and examination of evidence and provision for error are more likely to yield value than any form of absolutism.

(ix) Truth and Rationality. Individual liberty, democracy, and informed debate are the foundations of the rational pursuit of truth.

(x) Change and Reform. Because everything changes, rational people are prepared to accept change, to understand it, and to direct it slowly for the benefit of society. Reform conduces to individual freedom in a democratic process of dealing with change.

(xi) Revolution. In contrast, the violence of revolution disrupts inquiry and debate so essential to individuality and democracy and leads to aggrandizing power and authority.

However, this set of beliefs obscures the changes in meaning of the liberal ideal over time (see LIBERALISM). As every aspect of society in England and the United States changed in the early decades of the twentieth century, for example, as the Great Depression produced the Wagner Act and Social Security in the United States, curbing private property and giving birth to the welfare state, the Millian libertarian ideal was increasingly joined with ideas of equality and justice, or at least security (for racial segregation and women's subordination went untouched), carried out in the name of preserving individual opportunity within a more humane capitalism.

Reading
Hofstadter, Richard 1955: *The Age of Reform: From Bryan to F.D.R.*
The New Encyclopedia Britannica 1993: "Modern socio-economic doctrines and reform movements" – "Liberalism."
Spitz, David 1982: *The Real World of Liberalism.*
JAMES R. BENNETT

liberalism   A creed and a history. Louis Hartz perceives a liberal history of US political thought based essentially upon John Locke, the "Lockian creed" of individual liberty enshrined in the Constitution and enacted by the Supreme Court. The American way of life is the practical application of that creed with two exceptions (which explain why the United States contrasts so distinctly from Europe): feudalism and therefore socialism. He distinguishes two conflicting strands of US liberalism: the "Whigs" (capitalist, wealthy, big property owners) and *petit bourgeois* democrats. The element of "Algerism" (the drive to forge ahead with luck and pluck) further energizes the values of liberalism. Paradoxically, the addition of nationalism and patriotism transforms liberalism into its totalitarian, McCarthyite opposite.

The view from Europe differs because of its feudal past and the ensuing conflictual rise of socialism. Bullock and Shock, for example, reveal the apparently incoherent but historically evolutionary history of the Tory, Whig, Liberal, and Socialist parties in England. English aristocratic

Whig liberalism was born out of the seventeenth-century struggle (the principles of 1688) for freedom of conscience and the resistance of Parliament to the arbitrary authority of the king, out of which developed "the principles of civil and religious liberty, the rule of law and the freedom of the press, the institutions of parliamentary government, limited monarchy and an independent judiciary" (p. xx).

This liberal tradition was challenged by new growth in trade, industry, population, and the middle class – a new class of manufacturers, merchants, bankers, and businessmen – and by newly authoritative utilitarian ideas. Two groups of often linked thinkers provided new directions for liberalism: one, the political economists (Adam Smith, Malthus, Ricardo, James Mill, McCulloch, Nassau William Senior, and J.S. Mill); the other, the Benthamites or philosophical radicals (Bentham, James Mill, Grote, Romilly, Place, Bowring, Molesworth, and Joseph Hume). They were intensely individualist. All progress derived from the unhampered initiative of self-interested individuals; minimal government – *laissez-faire* – should be the rule, since natural economic laws operate invisibly for the general good. Especially should the state avoid meddling with foreign trade: free trade was the doctrine of economists and philosophical radicals. Related to this belief in noninterference in economics were political ideas. In foreign policy they opposed colonies and imperialism and supported national liberation movements as in Greece; in domestic policy they opposed governmental abuse of power and supported civil liberties. The Whigs had opposed the abusive powers of the monarchy; the political economists and radicals opposed the abusive powers of the monarchy and aristocracy by advocating the extension of electoral democracy. Underlying all was a commitment to the rationalist principle of reform through utility and the liberation of natural forces in society. Between 1830 and 1870 these ideas exerted great influence in England. The logic of 1688 gradually worked itself out in the Reform Bill of 1832, extending the suffrage to the middle class and later to the laboring class and women.

Nevertheless, they were not the sole direction England was taking, for they were under attack as early as the movement for state regulation of the brutalities of the workplace, as in the Ten Hours Bill. Experience and sympathy with people struggling to be free taught liberals that the gross inequalities bred by *laissez-faire* capitalism necessitated

state intervention. From the point of view of oppressed wage slaves or Radical reformers, Tories and Whigs were scarcely distinguishable. Eventually support for state mediation in economics and other aspects of society and the drive to extend political democracy produced the Liberal Party out of the Whigs in the 1860s.

From the Free Trade Anti-Corn Law League of the 1840s, to the struggle over Irish independence and sympathy with Italian liberty, to the second Reform Act of 1867 as the next great step in the extension of the franchise and the constituency of the Liberal Party, under the leadership of Palmerston and Gladstone the Liberal Party changed the nature of British politics. From 1859 to 1874 Gladstone carried out a series of Liberal reforms in free trade initiatives; the disestablishment of the Irish Church; the Education Act of 1870; the opening of the universities to Nonconformists, and the Civil Service to competitive examination; neutrality in the Franco-Prussian War; and many more. When he returned to politics in 1874 he supported intervention in various international problems by the Concert of Europe, by the European Powers engaged not separately in imperialist pursuits but jointly to ensure justice against aggression, as in the Balkans. All peoples should enjoy freedom and all nations should enjoy equality of rights, he believed: Liberal views leading eventually to the League of Nations and the United Nations. The Liberal, utilitarian belief in the necessity of freedom for the development of individuals and nations is perhaps most dramatically seen in Gladstone's struggle for Irish Home Rule, the Irish as much deserving of freedom as the Italians, Greeks, and Bulgars. However, this position split the Liberal Party.

Gradually the old Liberal commitment to *laissez-faire* gave way to a new Liberalism based upon the concept of liberty of opportunity backed by the state. Less and less were the individual and the state seen as separate and opposed; the task of the state was more and more seen to be the creation of conditions in which people could exercise their faculties freely. The Reform Acts of 1867 and 1884, extending the franchise to almost universal male suffrage, markedly qualified the electoral monopoly which the middle and upper classes had enjoyed since 1832, and, combined with the depressions of the 1870s and 1880s, opened the industrialized nation's problems of poverty and exploitation to more radical reforms. An early manifestation of the new power of a working-class electorate was the municipal socialism in Birmingham in the 1870s, where Liberal Radicals established public ownership and social welfare programs. However, these changes took their toll on the party by the transfer of allegiance of manufacturing, commercial, and Whig constituencies to the Tories. And Gladstone's determination to carry Irish Home Rule drove Radicals out of the party. Although the party won in 1906 under Lloyd George, that year also marked the foundation of the Labour Party. Reforms continued under Lloyd George's leadership of the Liberal Party, such as the Parliament Act of 1911 which further extended political democracy, and the Insurance Act, but increasingly the working classes demanded fundamental changes in the economic and social system. After the 1914–18 war the party steadily lost votes to the Labour Party, which gradually replaced it as instrument for those who sought radical solutions to social problems. Nevertheless, the Liberal Party as the party of reform based upon the idea of individual liberty continued, and was revitalized by the theories of Geoffrey Keynes in the 1920s and 1930s, which rejected the antithesis of socialism and capitalism.

Continental European Liberals shared the same goals: parliamentarianism; free market economics; and freedom of speech, expression, and worship (Salvadori, 1972). Liberty is the fundamental value, the liberty of individual autonomy, the capacity for choice. This capacity (and here is a second key value) is based on reason. Liberty and reason are inseparable, and together they enable the growth of other central values – open-mindedness, moderation, and toleration. These values oppose the unreason of revelatory authoritarianism and dogmatism. Implied in these values is an emphasis upon self-government and therefore the parliamentary process; laws derived from the consent of all and equal for all; the value of private property as a guarantee of individual autonomy; and education for individual development and a prerequisite to self-government. Liberals believe that this creative freedom has produced the progress of increased knowledge, better standards of living, and more efficient governments.

Its origins are the advocates of religious tolerance in the sixteenth century; the self-governing United Provinces in 1579; the English Bill of Rights of 1689; the French Declaration of the Rights of Man and Citizens of 1789, and the Constitution of 1791. It became a clearly defined movement embodied in parties and programs. "In countless Continental revolutions between 1820 and 1876, Liberals played an important, at times dominant, role" (Salvador, 1972, p. 3): southern Europe in 1820–1; the Polish insurrection against Russia in 1830; the Swiss civil war in 1847, Germany in 1848–9; and Italy in 1859–61. Liberalism was delayed by Bourbon absolutism, Prussian militarism and Lutheranism, the armies of Austria and Louis-Napoleon, and by the Vatican in Italy, but the liberal attack on authoritarianism was heard everywhere – Kossuth in Hungary, Mazzini in Italy, Thorbecke in the Netherlands (and Bolivar in South America). Thanks to Liberals, Switzerland, Scandinavia, and the Lowlands became the most advanced nations in continental Europe. During the first quarter of the twentieth century, Liberal governments were headed by Caillaux and Herriot in France, Stresemann in Germany, Giolitti in Italy, Canalejas in Spain, Tisza in Hungary, Venizelos in Greece, and in other countries too. Liberals persuaded the Russian czar to replace autocracy with limited constitutionalism, and Liberals (Lvov, Miliukov, Shingarev) were leaders of the first provisional government in 1917.

The enemies of Liberalism range from right to left. Naziism and Stalinism suppressed Liberal values and institutions. And some critics of Liberalism detect hypocrisy in the discrepancies between ideals and practice. For example, to some the US banner of "freedom" seems only a facade for power. When real freedom, not merely formal freedom, has been energetically pursued (trade unions, suffragettes, the poor, blacks), the people have been met by repressive laws, courts, police, and the army. "'Liberalism' is not a descriptive phrase for the experience with civil liberties and rights in America, but an ideological mystification to hinder it" (Kolko, 1984, p. 280).

The Liberalism of today has shed the exuberant optimism of a Condorcet, who averred that human perfectibility is indefinite, or of a Helvetius, who believed human happiness awaited only a perfected education. The mass killings and torture that continue with the increasing improvement of weapons, the increasing mass malnutrition, hunger, and starvation, the eradication of forests and species, the destruction of atmospheric ozone and the creation of global warming, and other global disasters have sobered Liberal hopes. Perhaps this realism will inspire more effective reforms, or at least better defensive rearguard actions.

See also ENLIGHTENMENT; GAY POLITICS; HETERO-
GLOSSIA; HUMANISM; IDEOLOGY; WOLLSTONECRAFT,
MARY.

Reading
Bullock, Alan, and Maurice Shock, eds 1957: *The Liberal
Tradition: From Fox to Keynes.*
Hartz, Louis 1955: *The Liberal Tradition in America: An
Interpretation of American Political Thought Since the
Revolution.*
Kolko, Gabriel 1984: *Main Currents in Modern American
History.*
Salvadori, Massimo, ed. 1972: *European Liberalism.*
JAMES R. BENNETT

liminality The defining quality of a RITUAL of
transition (van Gennep, 1908) when a novitiate is
in neither the former nor the subsequent social
category. Turner's work on the liminal period has
stimulated intense social, psychological, and cultural research. The term has also spread to literature and other disciplines, labeling circumstances
when social conventions are suspended.

Reading
Gennep, Arnold van 1908 (*1960*): *The Rites of Passage.*
Turner, Victor 1982: "Liminal to liminoid, in play, flow,
and ritual."
TOM C. GREAVES

linguistic criticism Linguistic criticism is TEXT
analysis which concentrates on the connections between language choices and the social world. It is
the distinctive contribution made by Roger FOWLER,
with Robert Hodge, Gunter Kress, Tony Trew,
and Gareth Jones, to linguistic theory and the sociology of language.

Linguistic critics hold that, far from having
unmediated access to the world, the members of
any (sub)CULTURE subscribe to particular belief
systems or ideologies which largely determine their
conception of reality. The world is a social construct, and a major part of the structuration takes
place through language. Therefore systematic analysis of the language of the texts through which members of a society interact – its social DISCOURSES –
can lay bare the processes through which language
users attempt to uphold or oppose any given status
quo.

Although in principle eclectic, linguistic critics
rely mainly on concepts and methods derived from
systemic-functional linguistics (Halliday, 1978;
1985), a theory which shares their basic assumptions

about language and reality, and incorporates a grammar based on the principle that situational (social)
features are instrumental in determining language
choices.

Any text type is open to linguistic criticism, but
a major interest of linguistic critics remains the
linguistic analysis of literary texts; in fact, the term
is intended to recall and contrast with "literary
criticism" (Fowler, 1981, p. 24).

In contrast with the objectivist assumptions of
many literary critics of the 1960s and 1970s (see
NEW CRITICISM), linguistic critics hold that, although
literary texts are accorded special value, there is
nothing intrinsic to their language that distinguishes
them from other text types. Furthermore, literary
texts "mean" only within a certain cultural context, to readers/analysts who have their own ideological position. No reading of any kind of text is
ever objective, so no text can have any objective
meaning.

Fowler is equally critical of structuralist linguists'
efforts to carry out linguistic analysis of (literary)
texts. He objects in particular to the assumption
that the analysis should treat every linguistic aspect as equally significant. What makes linguistic
analysis into linguistic *criticism* is that the selection
of features for the analysis to focus on is informed
by the analyst's awareness that extratextual factors
influence linguistic choices. Such extratextual factors are traditionally studied by scholars in other
disciplines such as sociology, philosophy, and history, but linguistic criticism and literary criticism
must take account of these disciplines, and of each
other.

Another text genre favoured by linguistic critics
because of its high social visibility is newspaper
reportage (see Fowler, 1991).

Most linguistic criticism is not only politically
aware, but avowedly politically motivated, its proponents typically falling on the left of the political
spectrum. For this reason, the discipline is often
perceived as threatening or dismissed as propagandist. This charge is unfounded, for the method
can be employed by analysts of any political persuasion to examine any text type. It is more difficult to dismiss some of the objections raised by
theorists favourably disposed toward the aims of
linguistic critics. For example, Thompson (1984,
p. 126) criticizes their identification of "belief
systems" with "ideologies," their failure to define
either term, and the absence from their work of
a clearly defined theory of society.

Reading
Fowler, R. 1981: *Literature as Social Discourse: The Practice of Linguistic Criticism.*
———1986: *Linguistic Criticism.*
———1991: *Language in the News.*
———Hodge, R., Kress, G., and Trew, T. 1979: *Language and Control.*

KIRSTEN MALMKJÆR

literacy   The term "literacy" is used, in descriptions of individuals or whole social formations, to indicate the possession of skills in reading and writing. Much argument in CULTURAL THEORY has been concerned, however, with exactly what level of skills constitutes "literacy," either now or in earlier historical periods; and debate has also focused on how literacy (which always exists in a mix with oral channels of communication and representation, and is unevenly distributed across any given society) affects individual psychology, social organization, or cultural reproduction. Frequently the term is used metaphorically, to indicate other interpretative or decoding skills, as in "TV literacy," "computer literacy," or "political literacy." *See also* ORALITY.

Reading
Levine, Kenneth 1986: *The Social Context of Literacy.*
Ong, Walter J. 1982: *Orality and Literacy: the Technologizing of the Word.*

ALAN DURANT

literary competence   A term used in STRUCTURALISM for the basic reading ability needed to relate a TEXT to the greater collectivity of language which is assumed to lie behind the individual text or utterance. It encompasses cultural and literary references as part of the process of the production of meanings.

Reading
Culler, Jonathan 1975 (*1989*): *Structuralist Poetics.*
Eagleton, Terry 1983 (*1985*): *Literary Theory: An Introduction.*

PAUL INNES

literary criticism   Before the advent of CRITICAL THEORY, literary criticism was commonly regarded as the formulation and defense of value judgments about works of literature by people widely read in both literature and criticism. Their institutional location was often universities and colleges, and like literary journalists (but unlike critical theorists) they tended to see their work as "secondary" to the "primary" TEXTs of literature. However much it might be despised by writers, literary criticism could be perceived as the socially useful application of quality controls to literary production by experts whose job is to ensure that the highest standards are maintained.

This construction of literary criticism rests on two assumptions. First, that "literature" is an identifiable commodity, easily distinguishable not only from "nonliterature" but also from inferior versions of itself, such as "popular literature" and "subliterature." And second, that "literary value" can be defined in such generally acceptable terms that it can be appealed to by literary critics as a criterion for distinguishing good writing from bad. Both assumptions have undergone radical critiques since Northrop FRYE ridiculed in his *Anatomy of Criticism* (1957) the promotional and demotional games played by literary critics with literary texts.

Earlier theories of literature are "essentialist" in their contention that a literary work has distinctive features which mark its "literariness" and enable us to distinguish literature from nonliterature. These specificities are identified with varying degrees of precision. Sometimes ingredient x is as vague as "wit" in discussions of seventeenth-century poetry, or "the sublime" in the eighteenth century, or ORGANIC UNITY in the nineteenth and twentieth centuries. At other times, however, it can be highly specific, as when Russian FORMALISM claims that what distinguishes "poetic" from nonpoetic uses of language is that poetry manifests a "making strange" (*ostranenie*) or "defamiliarization" of ordinary language. Once identified, distinctive features can be taken as normative, upgraded to criteria of value, and applied prescriptively as touchstones for promoting some texts and demoting others. Every influential school of criticism has privileged a particular type of text, and treated the characteristics of such texts as normative in order to discredit other modes of criticism grounded on other types of text.

Consequently, texts can go in and out of fashion with the changing of the critical guard. Edmund Spenser's *The Faerie Queene* (1596) will rank highly whenever "copiousness of invention" is a criterion of excellence (as it was in sixteenth-century rhetorical criticism); but when the principal criterion is "stylistic economy," Spenser's poem will be judged too prolix for literary tastes stimulated by heroic couplets in the eighteenth century or imagist poems in the twentieth. Other cornucopian texts – such as the plays of William Shakespeare or the novels of James Joyce – survive different styles of criticism by offering a wide diversity of "characteristics," and by appealing to different critics for different reasons create the illusion of transhistorical permanence.

Such phenomena lend credence to the rival "constitutivist" theory that "assertions of value refer primarily not to the structural properties of texts, but to their performance as literary texts" (Ellis, 1974, p. 102). A text is recognized as literary not because of what it is (the essentialist claim), but by being read as if it were literature, just as Marcel Duchamp obliged people to view a men's urinal as if it were art when he exhibited one in an art gallery. "Literature" is accordingly not an essence but a category of writing, into and out of which texts can be moved, as when the Bible comes to be read "as literature," or Stephen Crane's novel *The Red Badge of Courage* (1895) as an eyewitness account of the American Civil War. "Literature" is whatever a community elects to call by that name and read in "literary" ways. It becomes institutionalized by a pedagogical system which determines and then promulgates a CANON of literary texts for study and oversees the interpretation of its constituent texts.

Once secured by either essentialist or constitutivist practices, literary texts are duly processed by the literary-critical machine. "Corrected" by textual editors and annotated by scholars, they are susceptible to three main types of critical inquiry. An author-centered criticism will use them as biographical or psychobiographical evidence and judge the writer by the work, thus committing what text-centered critics call the biographical fallacy. In the twentieth century text-centered critics have been guided by T.S. ELIOT's modernist contention that great literature is impersonal, and accordingly have bypassed biography to focus on "the text itself." Examples include British PRACTICAL CRITICISM as pioneered by I.A. RICHARDS and taught by William EMPSON and F.R. LEAVIS; American NEW CRITICISM as practiced and popularized by Cleanth BROOKS; and the DECONSTRUCTIONist criticism of J. Hillis Miller and Paul DE MAN.

New Criticism scorned as the AFFECTIVE FALLACY the proposition that literary critics ought to concern themselves with how readers respond to literary texts. Given the fact that there are only three sites on which any kind of literary criticism

can establish itself – the author (producer), the text (product), and the reader (reception) – it was perhaps inevitable that the HEGEMONY of New criticism was broken not by returning to author-based criticism (against which text-based critics had defined themselves, most notably in the theory of the INTENTIONAL FALLACY), but by focusing on the part played by readers in the construction of literary meaning and literary value. For if (as constitutivists claim) literary texts are not "given" to us by authors but constituted as such by reading practices, it follows that literary texts are not the sources of literary value but the sites on which literary values are produced (cf. Bennett, 1979, p. 174). Literary criticism thus mutates into the kind of reception studies undertaken by Hans Robert Jauss and the READER-RESPONSE CRITICISM of Wolfgang ISER and Stanley FISH.

Those mindful of the etymological derivation of the word "critic" from the Greek *krites* ("judge") usually favor the prescriptive view that "evaluation" is the *raison d'être* of literary criticism. Text-centered critics consider that judgments should be based not on such "extrinsic" factors as the writer's "ideas" or "reputation," but arrived at inductively by a responsive attentiveness to that most "intrinsic" phenomenon of all, the words on the page of the text in itself. "Everything worth saying in criticism of verse and prose," F.R. Leavis declared, "can be related to judgments concerning particular arrangements of words on the page" (Leavis, 1948, p. 120). In these terms, although the stockpiling of information about literary texts (bibliographical, lexicographical, historical, explicatory, etc.) may be a legitimate activity in the broad field of literary studies, it does not constitute literary criticism, and may well be a way of avoiding the difficult task of judging whether the text in question is any good or not.

Developments in both the theory of language and the theory of value have weakened the prescriptivist view that literary criticism must be evaluative to justify its name. In the early twentieth century a revolutionary shift of emphasis in LANGUAGE THEORIES away from prescriptive grammar (how to speak and write correctly) to descriptive linguistics (how we actually speak) helped make "description" a more authentic mode of inquiry in the humanities than "prescription." It enabled us to see that the purpose of a dictionary, for instance, is not to enshrine the preferred "meanings" of words but to record shifts in their "usage": "correctness" here becomes a relative term, measured by the appropriateness of a particular word or expression in the context in which it is used. The definition of literary criticism as evaluative thus becomes merely one usage among many of a term which, in the opinion of a scholar who has probably read more criticism than anybody else, cannot be defined more narrowly than "any DISCOURSE on literature" (Wellek, 1986, p. xvii).

In its evaluative form, literary criticism is preoccupied with VALUE IN LITERATURE, which is seen as being intrinsic to literary works and distinguishable from those extrinsic values by which we live. The point of *aestheticizing* literary texts in this way is to protect them against the kind of "irrelevant" criticism which resulted in D.H. Lawrence's *Lady Chatterley's Lover* (1928) being banned by moralists for its obscenity and castigated by feminists for its sexism. Such problems can be obviated if the text is treated as an autonomous world of words whose formal excellences can be appreciated and faults rebuked without reference to such considerations as whether it has "a tendency to deprave and corrupt" (the legal definition of obscenity) or perpetuates the oppression of women by offering demeaning representations of them. It so happened that *Lady Chatterley's Lover* was deemed on literary criteria to be not a very good novel, and so the business of matching intrinsic with extrinsic evaluations is much less problematic here than in the case of *The Rainbow* (1915), which offended contemporary moralists but is highly esteemed by nonfeminist critics as a modernist classic. This is a recurrent problem for advocates of literary value. If you admire the formal experimentalism of Ezra Pound's *Cantos* (1930–64), can you – should you even try? – to ignore their fascist politics if you yourself happen to be anti-fascist? Can religious beliefs (or one's lack of them) be kept apart from a literary evaluation of T.S. Eliot's *Four Quartets* (1944)?

To those who think such distinctions are neither possible nor desirable, the category of literary value is obstructionist in distracting attention from the social responsibilities of writers and the social consequences of what they write. For such readers, literary texts should not be depoliticized by aestheticizing practices, but *politicized*. This is to be done not by "introducing" politics into allegedly apolitical literary works, but by drawing attention to the politics which is there already (notably in the ways it represents its subject matter), and

by asking whose interests are served by a critical practice which overlooks such problems in the course of attending to the text's "purely" literary features.

As literary value becomes indistinguishable from social value when literary texts come to be politicized, value itself ceases to be thought of as a transhistorical absolute and comes to be seen instead as a variable construct, subject to historical contingencies and deeply fissured along the fault lines of RACE, CLASS, and GENDER. Value is treated as a front for various kinds of hidden politics, each of which can be exposed and opposed by the dominant styles of politicized criticism. Should the crypto-politics of literary criticism be deemed to be social class, for instance, MARXIST CRITICISM will demonstrate that the literary texts most favored by those middle-class people who historically have constituted the readership for literature embody middle-class values, no matter how successfully they may be thought of as having transcended the specificities of class by their insights into a common and classless humanity. When gender is the crypto-politics targeted, various types of FEMINIST CRITICISM will demonstrate that the dominant literary culture is masculinist, and promote literary texts which embody alternative and gynocentric values. And when literary value is perceived as an ideological apparatus for demoting texts produced by non-Europeans, the consequences of its concealed and Eurocentric racism will be critiqued by readers located in BLACK CULTURAL STUDIES and SUBALTERN STUDIES. Each of these politicizing styles of criticism comes to be further fissured by differences within it: feminist criticism, for example, recognizing its own heterosexual bias, generated lesbian feminist criticism, and its critique of gender helped articulate a GAY POLITICS, whose institutionalization as gay studies was in turn critiqued by queer theory.

Critical theory has not, as is sometimes claimed, destroyed literary criticism, but taught it to define its subject positions and procedures with increased ideological awareness.

Reading
Bennett, Tony 1979: *Formalism and Marxism.*
Eagleton, Terry 1983: *Literary Theory: An Introduction.*
Ellis, John 1974: *The Theory of Literary Criticism.*
Leavis, F.R. 1943 (*1948*): *Education and the University.*
Ruthven, K.K. 1979: *Critical Assumptions.*
——1984: *Feminist Literary Studies: An Introduction.*
Wellek, René 1986a: *English Criticism 1900–1950.*
                                           K.K. RUTHVEN

literary production   MARX and ENGELS affirmed
that, since human beings produce themselves and
the objective world by labor, ART is one aspect of
production in general. This means that literature
is produced not only as an element of superstructure by agents working within given social, intellectual, and literary traditions, but also enters into
the relations of production which comprise the
economic infrastructure of society. As the "final
product" of a labor process which works on raw
materials, literature is part of the dialectic of connections between production and consumption.
Hence the meanings of literary TEXTS are conditioned by their status as commodities. These insights
have been developed by Marxist thinkers such as
Lenin, Walter BENJAMIN, Bertolt BRECHT and Pierre
MACHEREY, who have attempted to displace the
Romantic view of literature as "creation" by accounting for it in terms of social practice, relations
between artist and audience, and the possible revolutionary transformation of the forces of artistic
production by the artists themselves. Non-Marxist
theories which have explored literature as production include PSYCHOANALYSIS, FEMINIST CRITICISM
and NEW HISTORICISM.

Reading
Benjamin, W. 1973: "The author as producer."
Eagleton, T. 1976: *Marxism and Literary Criticism.*
Macherey, P. 1978: *A Theory of Literary Production.*
                                                    M.A.R. HABIB

literature, comparative   *See* COMPARATIVE
LITERATURE

literature, value in   *See* VALUE IN LITERATURE

logical positivism   A movement of thought that
originated in Vienna during the 1920s, exerting a
strong (albeit short-lived) influence on epistemology and PHILOSOPHY OF SCIENCE, mainly in the
English and German-speaking countries. Its central tenet was the "verification principle," intended
to clear away vast tracts of meaningless "metaphysical" talk, or at least to declare them out of
bounds for the purposes of rigorous analytic inquiry. This doctrine held (i) that the meaning of a
sentence, proposition, or statement is given by its
truth conditions; and (ii) that such truth must

either be determined by empirical observation –
that is, through direct knowledge-by-acquaintance
or the results of scientific experiment – *or* derive
solely from the logical (analytic) form of the statement in question, as with the truths of mathematics, geometry, and strict deductive (syllogistic)
reasoning. The latter would be purely tautologous
– that is, quite devoid of factual or informative
content – in so far as their predicate contained
nothing more than was given in their subject.
(Thus for instance: "all bachelors are unmarried
men.")

The upshot of this program, rigorously applied,
was such as to render nonsensical most – if not all
– of our everyday speech acts and unregimented
habits of talk, along with the "truths" (or pseudo-
truths) of ETHICS, AESTHETICS, theology, sociology,
psychology, and other such merely "emotive," "subjective," or "evaluative" modes of utterance. All
the same, there were those, including some ethical
philosophers and the literary critic I.A. RICHARDS,
who were so impressed by the seeming force of the
logical-positivist case that they adopted precisely
such a face-saving rhetoric to characterize their
own endeavors. For Richards, this entailed a complete severance between the realm of poetic meaning and that of propositional truth. Thus poems
possessed "emotive" value in their use of "pseudo-
statements" – or make-believe (non-truth-func-
tional) orders of utterance – to evoke certain rich
and complex states of mind in the receptive reader.
This anti-cognitivist bias in literary theory has remained a constant factor during manifold changes
of doctrine and fashion, from the American NEW
CRITICISM of the 1940s to recent POSTSTRUCTURAL-
ISM. The same reactive pattern may be seen in
Roland BARTHES's early polemic *Critique et verité*,
directed against the supposed value-neutrality of
traditional (positivist) French literary scholarship.

One notable exception to this rule is William
EMPSON's fine but neglected book *The Structure of
Complex Words* (1951). Here he takes issue not only
with Richards but also – in a lengthy Appendix –
with proponents of the emotivist view in ethics,
anthropology, and PHILOSOPHY OF LANGUAGE. For
Empson, this amounts to a vote of no confidence
in human reason, allied to a taste for certain forms
of paradoxical mystery-mongering which leave judgment open to the "active false logic" of irrationalist creeds and doctrines. His response is to elaborate
a theory of logico-semantic implication which applies just as much to literary as to other (scientific

or "everyday") uses of language, and which thus comes out in firm opposition to any idea of poetry as somehow exempt from the standards of plain-prose rational accountability. Empson is quite clear about the limits of the logical-positivist program, its incapacity to deal with the greater part of what we (rightly) take as meaningful statements with a fair claim to assertoric warrant and truth-telling status. Nevertheless, he also sees the need, unlike Richards, to extend and refine the resources of logical analysis to a point where it becomes adequate to account for those complex orders of meaning (too easily treated as "emotive") that characterize poetic language. That his book has received so little serious attention from subsequent literary theorists is a measure of both its profound originality and their lingering suspicious attitude toward logical positivism in its full-fledged, hardline, or reductive variants.

In fact, that program turned out to harbor deep-laid difficulties, even for its most committed supporters. After all, as was quickly remarked, the verification principle failed to make sense on its own terms, since it was neither analytically (self-evidently) true by virtue of its logical form, nor susceptible to proof from direct observation or empirical test procedures. Under pressure from skeptical philosophers like QUINE – notably in his essay "Two dogmas of empiricism" – the positivist program gave way by degrees to a holistic (or contextualist) theory of meaning which rejected the analytic/synthetic distinction, maintained that all statements (whether logical or factual) were open to radical reinterpretation under different "ontological schemes," and thus – in Quine's famous metaphor – relativized truth to the entire existing "web" or "fabric" of beliefs held true at any given time. Whence it followed that belief in centaurs or in Homer's gods was ontologically on a par with belief in the axioms of Euclidean geometry, the ground rules of logic, or the existence of brick houses on Elm Street, just so long as one's scheme was adjusted here and there (or subject to wholesale revision) in such a way as to accommodate those items. And so it came about, ironically enough, that these developments in "postanalytic" philosophy could be drawn (by shrewdly eclectic commentators such as Richard RORTY) into a kind of loose-knit tactical alliance with HERMENEUTIC, POST-MODERN, and poststructuralist strains of CULTURAL and LITERARY THEORY. Nothing could be further from what the logical positivists envisaged when

they first set out to place philosophy of science on a firm methodological footing.

See also LANGUAGE, PHILOSOPHY OF; SCIENCE, PHILOSOPHY OF.

Reading
Ayer, A.J. 1936: *Language, Truth and Logic.*
——ed. 1959: *Logical Positivism.*
Empson, William 1951: *The Structure of Complex Words.*
Parkinson, G.H.R., ed. 1968: *The Theory of Meaning.*
Quine, W.V.O. 1953a (*1980*): "Two dogmas of empiricism."
Russell, Bertrand 1956: *Logic and Knowledge.*

CHRISTOPHER NORRIS

Lovejoy, Arthur O. (1873–1961) Philosopher and intellectual historian. Author of *The Revolt Against Dualism* and *The Great Chain of Being*, Lovejoy was a central figure in American philosophical debates of the first half of the twentieth century.

The product of a childhood marked by the death of his mother in his infancy and the influence of a strongly evangelical father, Lovejoy's early intellectual development centered upon a reaction to the uncertainty of the emotions and intense religious experience by postulating the clarity and efficacy of reason. He broke through the somewhat rigid mores of the American philosophical academy by becoming, in effect, a "historian of ideas" whose objective was to construct a philosophy which made the experienced universe intelligible.

Within Lovejoy's investigations only epistemological and psychological dualism could allow the coexistence of a real sensory world and a world of ideas. His search for a vindication for the efficacy of ideas led to his widely read interdisciplinary work *The Great Chain of Being*, in which he followed the ideas of plenitude, continuity, and gradation from their Aristotelian origins through the Romantic period of the early nineteenth century. Building upon earlier work on the creation of what he referred to as a "rational theology," Lovejoy's philosophical perspective was essentially psychological, dwelling upon origins of human motivation and behavior – linking his method of inquiry to Smith's *Theory of Moral Sentiments* as a systematic approach to creating a new, comprehensive history of human intellectual development.

Lovejoy was also known for his groundbreaking work in establishing and defending standards and conventions (*vis-à-vis* the necessity of open exchange of ideas) for academic freedom within the American academy.

Reading
Lovejoy, Arthur O. 1936: *The Great Chain of Being: A Study of the History of an Idea.*
——1960: *The Revolt Against Dualism: An Inquiry Concerning the Existence of Ideas.*
——1961: *Reflections on Human Nature.*
Wilson, Daniel J. 1980: *Arthur O. Lovejoy and the Quest for Intelligibility.*

JAMES P. RICE

Lukács, Gyorgy (Georg) (1885–1971) Hungarian philosopher, politician, aesthetician. Born into a wealthy Jewish family in Budapest, Lukács was to launch on an intellectual and political journey which, though fraught with antagonism, compromise, and reversals, left him the highest star in the constellation of twentieth-century Marxist aestheticians. His doctorate, conducted under George Simmel's supervision in Berlin, was in sociology, and his initial interest in MARX was as a sociologist. He subsequently moved in an interdisciplinary circle of acquaintances which included Ernst BLOCH and Max Weber. As well as falling under the influence of these figures, he was indebted to Kierkegaard, HEIDEGGER, Georges Sorel, Rosa Luxemburg, KANT, and especially HEGEL. A general orientation toward philosophical idealism is evident in his major works of this period: *Soul and Form* (1911), *History of the Development of Modern Drama* (1911), and *The Theory of the Novel* (1916). The last of these advances Lukács's renowned thesis that the novel is the epic of the modern world, attempting to reconstitute formally a unity (of abstract and concrete, universal and particular) belonging to the world of the epic but long since shattered by subsequent historical configurations (Lukács, 1916 (*1971a*), pp. 56–69).

Returning to Budapest in 1917, Lukács joined the Hungarian Communist Party in 1918, his decision inspired largely by the Russian Revolution but also representing a culmination of his lifelong hatred of capitalism. Thereafter, his aesthetic concerns were eclipsed by political imperatives. He became Commissar of Education in the short-lived Communist government of 1919 under Bela Kun, after whose overthrow he escaped to Austria, traveling thence to Germany and Russia. His *History and Class Consciousness* (1923) suffered a hostile reception from the Communist movement, on a number of accounts: it overlooked the centrality

of labor to Marxist analysis; it offered an idealistic concept of revolutionary praxis; and above all, it attempted to reinstate the Hegelian category of totality at the center of the Marxist system, drawing a direct line of descent from the Hegelian dialectic to historical materialism, relegating the intermediary role of Feuerbach to the background. It also defined orthodoxy in MARXISM as exclusively a question of methodology rather than content, and conducted an unwelcome polemic against ENGELS.

Lukács was later to admit that in some ways his book had effectively attempted to "out-Hegel Hegel" (1923 (*1971b*), p. xxiii). The book was denounced with particular vehemence by Bela Kun whose political sectarianism Lukács had strategically and bitterly opposed. However, its analysis of class consciousness, and particularly of ALIENATION as central to the critique of capitalist society, exerted a profound influence on not only Marxist theory but also other areas such as French EXISTENTIALISM. It stands in a sense at the centre of Lukács's CANON, as the final synthesis of his development since 1918 and marking the turning toward his subsequent economically grounded vision of Hegel's dialectic. Lukács's strategic publication of a self-criticism and his monograph, *Lenin: A Study on the Unity of His Thought* (1924) a more orthodox study, went some way toward reconciling him with the Party. He regarded such a strategy as his "entry-ticket" into history, since Communism appeared to furnish the only effective forum for meaningful resistance to emerging fascism.

In 1928, as the Hungarian Communist Party prepared for its Second Congress, Lukács was asked to draft its political theses. The resulting "Blum Theses," urging the Party to work toward an independent rather than soviet republic, were regarded as regressive, since Hungary had already been allied as a soviet republic in 1919. Notwithstanding Lukács's publication of a self-criticism, the climate of fierce antagonism to his proposals obliged him to withdraw from politics in 1929. This initiated his more or less exclusive devotion to Marxist theory and AESTHETICS. In 1930–1 he took up a research post at the Marx–Engels Institute in Moscow, where his reading of Marx's recently deciphered *Economic and Philosophical Manuscripts of 1844* (Marx, 1959 (*1981*)) struck him with the force of a revelation. He saw this text as confirming his insistence, in *History*, on the importance of alienation in Marxist theory and as underlining that book's essential failure to view alienation as only one specific instance of what Hegel had called objectification or externalization. In an earlier review, Lukács had insisted, as against Bukharin (at the time second only to Stalin in the leadership of the Russian Communist Party) that economic forces are the determinants, not the products, of technological development. Lukács's work on Lassalle and Moses Hess also impelled him to define more closely the connection between economics and dialectics, culminating in his massive and brilliantly intricate *The Young Hegel* (1938 (*1975*)). An imposing feature of this work is its articulate attempt to distinguish between Marxist integrations of Hegel and distorted bourgeois versions which assimilate Hegel into either Romantic or irrational thought, which Lukács viewed as a slippery incline toward despotic and imperialist apologetics (1975, pp. 3–16).

After a two-year stay in Berlin, Lukács was forced to flee in 1933 to the Soviet Union, where he stayed until 1944. His study of the connections between dialectics and economics and the ontology of social being generated an attempt to construct a Marxist aesthetics. His literary studies during this period also assumed a coded anti-Stalinist role while exhibiting a surface continuity with the official SOCIALIST REALISM promulgated especially by Stalin's overseer of "IDEOLOGY," A.A. Zhdanov. These studies included *The Historical Novel* (1937) and essays later collected under the titles *Goethe and His Age* (1947), *Studies in European Realism* (1948), and *Essays on Thomas Mann* (1949). In these works Lukács correlates the rise of genres such as the historical novel with a bourgeois growth of historical consciousness, itself grounded in economic transformations. Sir Walter Scott, Balzac, and Tolstoi are viewed as the great exemplars of "realism" in the sense advocated by Lukács.

At the centre of Lukács's concept of realism is precisely the category of totality expressed in *History*, based on Hegel's notion of the concrete universal whereby the universal is not separate from but immanent in its particular expressions. Hence Lukács advocates a theory of reflection whereby ART expresses a totality of historical forces rather than mechanically documenting accidentally related surface details of the world. He views Balzac as the greatest realist, his characters embodying historically typical traits in the very texture of their individuality. Regarding realism in drama, Lukács sees Shakespeare as concentrating typical human relations around historical collisions "with a force

unparalleled before and after him." Lukács's aesthetics at this stage might be summarized by his comment of 1931 that the portrayal of human character is a question of applying dialectics in the field of literature (1980, p. 26). Lukács views the mere photographic reproduction of reality by art as naturalism, a category whose derogated status embraces much literature written under the banner of Zhdanovism, as well as many of Balzac's realist successors such as Flaubert (1937 (1962), pp. 193–9).

Lukács also arrays his notions of realism against the ideology and literary forms of modernism which he sees as a descendant of naturalism. In his view, the ontological image of the human being offered by modernists such as Joyce, Beckett, and Kafka is asocial, alienated, fragmented, and pathologically inept as a political agent. Lukács rejects the power of this image to act as a critique of capitalism because it is not only ahistorical but also elevates alienation to a seemingly eternal *condition humaine*. He had in fact been embroiled in the 1930s in a controversy with Bertolt Brecht, whose own "ALIENATION EFFECT" was in Lukács's eyes part of a formalist procedure. However, their notions of realism actually overlapped in crucial imperatives, such as that to capture the "typical" or "historically significant," a fact overridden in the perhaps politically motivated mutual opposition of these writers.

After the 1939–45 war Lukács was appointed professor of aesthetics and philosophy at the University of Budapest. His works of philosophical and aesthetic synthesis in this period included *The Destruction of Reason* (1954) and *The Meaning of Contemporary Realism*, written in 1956. After the popular uprising against Communism in the same year, Lukács became Minister of Culture in Imre Nagy's coalition, whose government was terminated abruptly by Soviet tanks. The first of these works displays Lukács's continuing preoccupation, in the context of German thought and literature, with the struggle between rationalistic humanism and barbaric irrationalism. In *The Specific Nature of the Aesthetic* (1962) Lukács confronts the enormous task of constructing a Marxist aesthetic, a project which includes:

(i)   viewing the aesthetic contextually as one mode of reflecting reality among others and elaborating the specific traits of the aesthetic mode as expressing objectivity conjoined with peculiarity of subjective conditions and genesis;

(ii) understanding art as another form of humans making themselves through their work; the articulation of a genuinely dialectical and historical method as well as the historical nature of objective reality itself;

(iii) stressing the connections between Marxism and other traditions of thought (Lukács draws upon Aristotelian mimesis as well as ideas from Goethe, Lessing, and others); and

(iv) clarifying the opposition between idealist and materialist aesthetics as well as the historical and ideological relations between immanence and transcendence.

In 1971 Lukács produced *Towards an Ontology of Social Being* and had planned a study of ETHICS which was still in its initial stages at the time of his death. Whatever unity can be claimed by Lukács's work as a whole rests on his persistent return to Hegel and his sustained endeavor to understand and clarify Marx and the Marxist tradition through the logical and historical schematic avenues opened up by the Hegelian dialectic. His ideas, in particular his analyses of ALIENATION, class consciousness, and the dialectical character of Marxism, have had far-reaching reverberations for those who have opposed the Hegelian orientation of his work as well as those who have developed it. He is arguably the profoundest philosopher that Marxism has produced.

See also MARXISM AND MARXIST CRITICISM.

Reading
Gluck, M. 1985: *Georg Lukács and His Generation.*
Goldmann, L. 1977: *Lukács and Heidegger: Towards a New Philosophy.*
Jameson, F. 1971 (*1974*): *Marxism and Form.*
Kadarkay, A. 1991: *Georg Lukács: Life, Thought, and Politics.*
Lukács, G. 1916 (*1971a*): *The Theory of the Novel.*
——— 1923 (*1971b*): *History and Class Consciousness.*
——— 1937, 1962 (*1983*): *The Historical Novel.*
——— 1975: *The Young Hegel.*
——— 1980: *Essays on Realism.*
Rockmore, T. 1992: *Irrationalism: Lukács and the Marxist View of Reason.*

M.A.R. HABIB

Lyotard, Jean-François (1925–) Jean-François Lyotard first became widely known and discussed in the English-speaking world with the publication of the English translation of his book *The Postmodern Condition* in 1984, and indeed remains most influential as an analyst and proponent of POSTMODERNISM. But he also has to his credit a very considerable body of philosophical, political, and aesthetic writings, which are now beginning to be more widely known and understood. He was connected from 1954 to 1964 with the Marxist group Socialism or Barbarism, a loose affiliation of workers, militants, and intellectuals, and was particularly active in his support for the revolutionary insurrection in Algeria, and critical of the French military response. During the late 1960s he became a leading figure in attempts to transform the institution where he held his own post as teacher of philosophy, the University of Paris at Nanterre, and in the notorious *événements* of May 1968 which proceeded from this. Lyotard's suspicion of institutionalized knowledge and bureaucratized control of thought is to be seen in his denunciation at the time of "the inevitable subordination of both the 'contents' of culture and the pedagogical relation to the sole operative categories of capital: production and consumption" (Lyotard, 1993, p. 48). Like many other French intellectuals taking part in the 1968 uprising, Lyotard turned away in its defeated aftermath more and more emphatically from the institutions of politics themselves, especially those associated with the Communist Party and bureaucratic state Marxism. In an essay written in 1989, Lyotard construes the principles of the Socialism or Barbarism group in terms which in fact anticipate the preoccupations in his own work which led to his distancing from the group:

> The idea that guided Socialism or Barbarism was ultimately . . . the idea that there is something within a system that it cannot, in principle, *deal with* . . . something intractable is hidden and remains lodged at the secret heart of everything that fits into the system, something that cannot fail to make things happen in it. (Lyotard, 1993, pp. 166–7)

Much of the rest of Lyotard's work is concerned with defining the nature of such unspeakable, unsystematic, but politically potent "events" within formal political or philosophical systems. As he puts it in his more recent philosophical idiom, it is a matter of finding ways of acknowledging and respecting "the has-it-happened-yet . . . that *thing* that the event is even before signification" (Van Reijen and Veerman, 1988, p. 301). His *Discours, Figure*, which appeared in 1971 (and remains untranslated), and *Libidinal Economy* (1974, trans.

1993) draw on psychoanalysis to articulate a radical politics centered on the mobile intensity of drives and bodily pulsations, rather than on the formal orderings and channelings of such intensity, for example, by language, that Freud called the secondary processes. *Discours, Figure* distinguishes the realm of "figure," or primary psychic process, from the realm of "discourse," or secondary process, which mediates and contains the eruptive force of the figural. As in the contemporary work of Gilles DELEUZE, Félix GUATTARI, and Julia KRISTEVA, the force and experience of the aesthetic are central to Lyotard's politics of intensity.

By the late 1970s and early 1980s Lyotard had become more than ever disillusioned with the presumptuous universalism of formal MARXISM. At the same time his work began to show a concern with questions of morality, justice, and legitimacy which had not been conspicuous in the extravagant and volatile ultra-leftism of his writing in the 1970s. It appears, for example, in his work *La Condition Postmoderne* (1979, trans. 1984). This book argues that the modern period since the late eighteenth century has been governed by the power of certain universalizing "metanarratives" in philosophy and politics, notably the HEGELian narrative of the emancipation of self-conscious spirit through history, and, linked to this, the Marxist narrative of progressive universal political emancipation. Lyotard argues that the power exercised by such narratives, either to assimilate or to exclude all other identities, histories, and temporalities, is totalitarian, and leads inexorably to horrors such as the Holocaust. The postmodern condition is one of "incredulity" toward metanarratives. In place of the dominative and self-legitimating "we" of the universal humanity presupposed and sustained by such metanarratives, Lyotard imagines with optimism a world of multiple, small-scale collectivities, none of which has the legitimacy to subordinate others. Central to this analysis is the concept of "language games" which Lyotard borrows from the later WITTGENSTEIN. A language game may be defined as the form of shared SYMBOLic action constituted by every act of communication. Language games include such actions as describing, promising, prescribing, and exhorting. In his later work *The Differend* (1984, trans. 1988), Lyotard extends this analysis. Central to this work, as it is to *Just Gaming* (Lyotard and Théhaud, 1979, trans. 1985), a series of discussions about the nature of justice which reads like an informal preparation for *The*

Differend, is the sense of the fundamental injustice that is done whenever one language game is subordinated to or interpreted in the light of another. Lyotard proposes that justice consists in remaining attentive to the conditions of "differend," or absolute incommensurability, which obtain between utterances or language games that conflict without there being any third language game in which to mediate them. It is the role above all of ART, especially the postmodernist art that Lyotard has promoted since the late 1970s, to preserve and bear witness to the incommensurability of languages and the multiplicity of ways of being. Central to this concern with the ethical responsibility of art is Lyotard's rereading of Immanuel KANT's philosophy of the sublime in his *Critique of Judgement* (1790, trans. 1952). Kant described the experience of the sublime as the dizzying sense of a failure of correspondence between an experience or idea, and the conceptual structures we have available to understand it. For Lyotard, the principle of the sublime is not so much that of inconceivable largeness, as it was for Romantic aesthetic philosophy, as the unencompassable complexity of human relations and events (Lyotard, 1991, trans. 1994). Lyotard's promotion of a postmodernist art of the sublime is intended to preserve that paradoxical representation of the fact of unrepresentability. In his most recent work, a collection of essays entitled *The Inhuman* (1988, trans. 1991), Lyotard has refocused some of these questions in terms of the transformed experience of time in the postmodern world, arguing for an art and philosophy that will resist the desire for the absolute domination of time, based as it is on the violent forgetting of the inevitable lack or irresolution of being that temporal existence creates.

Reading
Benjamin, Andrew, ed. 1989: *The Lyotard Reader*.
Lyotard, Jean-François 1971: *Discours, Figure*.
—— 1974 *(1993)*: *Libidinal Economy*.
—— 1979 *(1984)*: *The Postmodern Condition: A Report on Knowledge*.
—— 1984 *(1988)*: *The Differend: Phrases in Dispute*.
—— 1986 (1993): *The Postmodern Explained to Children: Correspondence, 1982–1985*.
—— 1988 *(1991)*: *The Inhuman: Reflections on Time*.
—— 1991 *(1994)*: *Lessons on the Analytic of the Sublime: Kant's Critique of Judgement Sections 23–29*.
—— 1993: *Political Writings*.
—— and Thébaud, Jean-Loup 1979 *(1985)*: *Just Gaming*.
STEVEN CONNOR

M

Macherey, Pierre (1938–) French Marxist theoretician, former pupil and collaborator of Louis ALTHUSSER, and senior lecturer in philosophy at the University of Paris (Sorbonne). Macherey's work has focused on three main areas: (i) elaboration and rectification of a Marxist theory of literature; (ii) elucidation of the philosophical singularity of Spinoza as a critic, *avant la lettre*, of HEGELIANISM and its Marxist reprises; (iii) investigations of modern French philosophy (in particular, the development of the tradition of "historical epistemology" by Georges Canguilhem and Michel FOUCAULT).

A year after his contribution to the collective Althusserian rereading of MARX's *Capital* (1965), Macherey's 1966 book, on which his reputation in the anglophone world is based, appeared in Althusser's *Théorie* series. More tentative in self-conception than its English title suggests, *Pour une théorie de la production littéraire* employed BACHELARDian–Althusserian categories to initiate a theory of the *differentia specifica* of literary DISCOURSE, in its complex interrelations with IDEOLOGY and science. Insisting upon the *autonomy*, as opposed to the *independence*, of literary TEXTS, Macherey sought to displace non-Marxist FORMALISM (literature as the aesthetic transcendence of ideology) and vulgar Marxist reductionism (literature as the aesthetic transcription of ideology). Against the then dominant CANONS of MARXIST CRITICISM – especially the realism of Georg LUKÁCS – Macherey rejected any conception of literary works as creation ("HUMANISM"); as the expression of a CLASS subject ("HISTORICISM"); as the translation of ideology ("reductionism"); or as the reflection/representation of reality ("EMPIRICISM").

In accordance with Althusser's concept of practice, the literary text was conceived by Macherey as the end product of a labor of artistic transformation of ideological and linguistic raw materials. A scientific criticism would eschew evaluation and interpretation, both of which effectively replaced the object of analysis, and instead attend to the text as a determinate material practice in and on ideology (understood, in Althusserian fashion, as the unconscious medium of human existence). The effect of literary form was to fissure the unity of the text and "produce" ideology in such a way as to expose its relations with its sociohistorical conditions of existence. "[T]he analogy of a knowledge and a caricature of customary ideology" (1966, p. 59), the literary text furnished an "implicit critique" of ideology, whose modalities could by grasped via a SYMPTOMATIC READING of the text's "UNCONSCIOUS."

Foreseeing the cooperation of a range of disciplines (historical MATERIALISM, FREUDian PSYCHOANALYSIS, and SAUSSUREan linguistics) in a *sui generis* but non-autarkic Marxist criticism, Macherey's ingenious proposals were widely adopted and adapted in the 1970s (for example, by Terry EAGLETON in England). However, although advancing a powerful critique of the prior Marxist inheritance, they were in turn subjected to telling criticism – for example, for postulating an invariant literature–ideology relationship and assigning a privileged status to the literary aesthetic (see Bennett, 1979). In response (for example, Macherey and Balibar, 1974), Macherey drew upon the linguistic research of Renée BALIBAR and Althusser's notion of the educational IDEOLOGICAL STATE APPARATUS to sketch a theory of literary *reproduction*, which was not, however, readily exportable from France. Macherey's subsequent work has been more strictly philosophical in character for the most part (for example, his reading of Spinoza (1979) as anti-Hegel and anti-Descartes). However, in a recent collection (1990) his principal interests have converged in studies of French "literary philosophy."

Reading
Bennett, Tony 1979: *Formalism and Marxism*.
Jameson, Fredric 1981 (*1989*): *The Political Unconscious*.
Macherey, Pierre 1965: "A propos du processus d'exposition du *Capital*."
—— 1966 (*1978*): *A Theory of Literary Production*.
—— 1979: *Hegel ou Spinoza*.

—— 1989: *Comte: La philosophie et les sciences*.
—— 1990 (*1995*): *The Object of Literature*.
—— and Balibar, Etienne 1974 (*1993*): "On literature as an ideological form."

GREGORY ELLIOTT

MacIntyre, Alasdair (1929–) American philosopher. Although he had already written a history of ETHICS and several other books, it was not until the publication of *After Virtue: A Study in Moral Theory* in 1981 that MacIntyre became a central figure in contemporary ethical theory. His work has generated wide interest in three main areas: the importance of virtue- rather than rule-based ethical theories; the ethical importance of narrative; and "communitarian" attacks on LIBERALISM.

After Virtue's central historical-philosophical thesis is that the failures of ENLIGHTENMENT ethical theories (like those of KANT and the utilitarians) as well as those of their twentieth-century heirs (like Hare and Rawls) leave us with the choice: Aristotle or NIETZSCHE? Aristotle's teleological ethics was precisely what Enlightenment theories rejected, and so they failed to contextualize their moral rules within a structure including the contrast between "human-nature-as-it-happens-to-be" and "human-nature-as-it-could-be-if-it-realized-its-*telos*." By rejecting the notion of a human *telos* Kant and the utilitarians left no genuine function for their moral rules to play (MacIntyre, 1981 (*1984*), chapter 5). This then led to "emotivist" critiques of those theories (critiques based on the notion that morality is nothing but an expression of personal preference or feeling). Though emotivism fails on philosophical grounds – moral expressions, unlike expressions of feeling, at least purport to objectivity – morality in the twentieth century is deployed as if emotivism were true, as we engage in ethical "debates" we know to be rationally interminable. Nietzsche saw more clearly than others the nature of the Enlightenment's failure and tried to articulate, according to MacIntyre, a kind of honest emotivism, one which no longer masked its desire for power.

By contrast MacIntyre develops a neo-Aristotelian account of the virtues which contains at least three crucial features (MacIntyre, 1981 (1984), chapters 14 and 15):

(i) Certain coherent, complex, cooperative, and socially established human activities ("practices") produce a contrast between "internal" and "external" goods – goods which can come only from within the performance of an activity as opposed to goods attainable in all sorts of ways, like wealth or prestige. The virtues are those human qualities which allow us to attain *internal goods* and without which we cannot attain them.

(ii) Rather than the democratized, fragmented self of twentieth-century emotivism, MacIntyre develops a *"narrative concept of selfhood:"* our actions and selves are intelligible only because of the stories we tell. (A human being is, as he puts it, "essentially a story-telling animal.") Human life has the unity of a quest – a quest for the good human life – and so the virtues are those qualities which sustain that quest and the narratives required for it.

(iii) Narratives and the achievement of internal goods are not simply the work of isolated individuals, but instead require a historical context. *Traditions* provide that context and the virtues thus require traditions to sustain them.

In *After Virtue* MacIntyre refuses to give up the notions of moral truth and rationality, and his subsequent works attempt to develop these notions more fully even as they expand and modify MacIntyre's historical tale. Exploring conflicts between several philosophical traditions, including the tradition of political liberalism, *Whose Justice? Which Rationality?* (1988) develops an account of truth which attempts to go between the horns of the absolutist–relativist dilemma: the "rationality of traditions." Only traditions which allow themselves to be called into question can be deemed rational, and MacIntyre suggests that liberalism may fall short on this score. *Three Rival Versions of Moral Enquiry* (1990) offers a fairly detailed account of the history of the university as part of an argument against the Enlightenment project, here understood as the encyclopedia tradition, and against Nietzsche's heirs, for example, Michel FOUCAULT. The former are criticized for their understanding of "progress," while the latter are examined regarding a possible genealogy of their own genealogies.

Though MacIntyre's wide-ranging historical work is central to his philosophical approach, he also has a Socratic sense for the criterion of living one's thought. Perhaps above all else his attempts to criticize opponents *from the inside* bespeak a commitment to philosophical dialectic that is rarer than it should be.

Reading

Gaita, R. 1983: "Virtues, human good, and the unity of a life."

MacIntyre, A. 1981 (*1984*): *After Virtue: A Study in Moral Theory*.

—— 1988: *Whose Justice? Which Rationality?*

—— 1990: *Three Rival Versions of Moral Enquiry: Encyclopedia, Genealogy, and Tradition*.

Stout, J. 1984: "Virtue among the ruins: an essay on MacIntyre."

JEFFREY S. TURNER

MacKinnon, Catharine (1946–) US feminist legal scholar and activist. Catharine MacKinnon's controversial analysis of sexual violence provided the theoretical foundation for the feminist anti-pornography movement launched in the 1980s in the United States and Canada. All of MacKinnon's work, beginning with her first book, *Sexual Harassment of Working Women* (1979), proceeds from the axiom that male supremacy informs every aspect of women's lives: from the segregation, stratification (devaluation), and sexualization of women's work to the construction of feminine personality, sexuality, and even quite literally, the construction of women's very *bodies* as small, weak, and vulnerable. Unlike French feminist theories, MacKinnon's does not posit the existence of a natural, or essential, female body: women's sexuality, in fact sex itself, is redefined as the eroticized and sexualized subordination of women to men. Because male supremacy can be maintained only by the coercion of women, what passes as sexuality in PATRIARCHY is always infused with violence against women. MacKinnon's critique of the laws relating to sexual violence therefore emphasizes the impossibility of distinguishing between "sex" and "violence," between "normal" and "criminal" sexual activity. In a collection of engaging public speeches, *Feminism Unmodified* (1987), MacKinnon defends her definition of pornography as "the sexually explicit subordination of women through pictures or words that also includes women presented dehumanized as sexual objects who enjoy pain, humiliation, or rape; women bound, mutilated, dismembered, or tortured; women in postures of servility or submission or display; [or] women being penetrated by objects or animals." This definition represents a significant discursive shift, for the DISCOURSE of pornography had been structured historically by concepts of obscenity and free speech. The anti-pornography laws based on her work thoroughly break with legal tradition: they are civil rights laws allowing victims of coercion, force, assault, and trafficking to sue civilly for reparation of harm inflicted on them by users of pornography.

MacKinnon's theory of women's relationship to the state, articulated in *Toward a Feminist Theory of the State* (1989), begins with the observation that men dominate women without the support of positive law and that male supremacy is inscribed in and legitimated by legal discourse such that women's pursuits of remedies for sexual oppression rarely succeed in the courts. She concludes by redefining key legal concepts such as consent, privacy, and especially equality. MacKinnon argues that legal reasoning is governed by male supremacist epistemologies, which have particular difficulty imagining the possibility that "difference" and "equality" might coexist. In such a context, the claims of women and racial minorities for "equality" have been continually thwarted; the law functions to ensure white male supremacy, reifying dominance as "difference" and legitimating coercion so that it looks like "consent." Here, as in *Feminism Unmodified*, MacKinnon carefully distinguishes her own project from both Marxist and liberal ones.

In her most recent work, *Only Words* (1993), MacKinnon carefully scrutinizes the "collision course" of legal and other discourses concerning equality and free speech, recommending, first, a thorough critique of the way the First Amendment has been used to valorize the speech of ruling classes while silencing subjugated ones and, second, a reinterpretation of the Fourteenth Amendment in positive terms concerned less with prohibiting violations than with "chartering legal intervention for social change" (p. 73). In plain terms, MacKinnon argues that, because the freedom of the powerful constitutes the inequality of the powerless, their speech must be constrained in order to liberate the silenced speech of those whom they oppress. Finally, her argument critiques both SPEECH ACT theory and DECONSTRUCTION as she examines the material conditions under which words are construed either formalistically as "only words" or as acts themselves. Anyone interested in the scholarly debates concerning the materiality of discourse would want to consider her insistent argument that the pornographer's *text* was once a woman's *life*.

MacKinnon has been severely criticized by the right as well as the LIBERAL left, including feminists, some of whom are concerned that the radical feminist premises of her work would be recuperated by the state and used to censor other feminists, particularly lesbians and other unpopular sexual minorities. An extremely vocal constituency of poststructural critics, including Donna Haraway (1985), objects to MacKinnon's "version of radical feminism [as] a caricature of the appropriating, incorporating, totalizing tendencies of Western theories of identity grounding action" (p. 200). In this view, MacKinnon's argument is one that not only polices and suppresses difference among women, but also produces a narrow and authoritarian doctrine of women's experience: if male dominance and desire defines both "woman" and "sex," then woman is a nonbeing whose only experience is that of sexual violation. More recently, Teresa Ebert (1993) defended MacKinnon from these charges while arguing that what she calls "ludic feminism" is insufficient for the feminist project of transforming gender relations of inequality.

See also PATRIARCHY.

Reading
Ebert, Teresa 1993: "Ludic feminism, the body, performance, and labor: Bringing *materialism* back into feminist cultural studies."
Haraway, Donna 1985 (*1990*): "A Manifesto for cyborgs: Science, technology, and socialist feminism in the 1980s."
MacKinnon, Catharine 1979: *Sexual Harassment of Working Women: A Case of Sex Discrimination.*
——1987: *Feminism Unmodified: Discourses on Life and Law.*
——1989: *Toward a Feminist Theory of the State.*
——1993: *Only Words.*

GLYNIS CARR

Man, Paul de   *See* DE MAN, PAUL

manifest/latent content   Key terms in the psychoanalytic theory of dreams. A product of the DREAM-WORK, the manifest content is the dream as recounted by the patient and prior to any interpretation. The latent content is revealed by the analysis of the manifest content and by the interpretation of associations. The relationship between the manifest and latent content of a dream, or of other formations of the UNCONSCIOUS, is often likened to that between versions of the same subject matter written in two different languages.

Reading
Freud, Sigmund 1990: *The Interpretation of Dreams.*

DAVID MACEY

Marcuse, Herbert   (1898–1979)   German philosopher. A central figure in the FRANKFURT SCHOOL of critical theorists. Marcuse remained in the United States after HORKHEIMER and ADORNO returned to Germany in the early 1950s. He later became a prominent spokesman of the NEW LEFT. He is best known for his application and development of the perspective of Frankfurt CRITICAL THEORY to the task of rethinking the politics of self-emancipation. His consistent commitment to politics, and a preoccupation with the practical fate of the Marxist enterprise, set Marcuse apart from other members of the Frankfurt school and enabled him to find a wider audience for their ideas during the heady days of the late 1960s and early 1970s.

Marcuse was among the first of an older generation of Marxists to look "outside" the working classes of advanced capitalized societies for sources of anti-capitalist revolt in the oppression of women and blacks, in the utopian aspirations of students, and in the exploitation of the peoples of the Third World. Yet he viewed these contributions to political struggle as an enrichment of the classical concept of socialism, rather than its refutation. He constantly sought to rework the philosophical foundations of socialism in response to changing historical conditions.

His writings are unified by a concern with philosophical anthropology and the emancipatory resources of the aesthetic dimension of human existence. His best-known essay, "The affirmative character of culture" (1937), warns of the dangers of CULTURE becoming a substitute for true happiness, and an accomplice to the mystification of the present, once it is separated from the struggles of everyday life.

His life work may be divided into four main periods:

1928–32   the attempt to utilize HEIDEGGER's *Being and Time* (1927) as the phenomenological basis for a Marxist philosophy of revolution: the project for a "concrete philosophy" (Marcuse, 1928);

1932–41   the replacement of Heidegger's EXISTENTIALISM as the philosophical basis for a reformed MARXISM with the HUMANISM of MARX's newly discovered *Economic and Philosophical Manuscripts* of 1844, and the development of a general model of dialectical criticism out of a rereading of HEGEL (Marcuse, 1941);

1952-8 a radical interpretation of FREUD's theory of instincts which was to provide theoretical inspiration for the sexual politics of the 1960s (Marcuse, 1955);

1958-78 the analysis of industrial societies in terms of the dominance of a narrowly technological (and ultimately irrational) reason, the repression of sensuality, and a consequent transformation in the social bases of revolt (Marcuse, 1964; 1969; 1972).

Marcuse's contribution to critical theory lies primarily in the series of concepts produced by his Marxist reading of Freud - *surplus repression*, the *performance principle*, and *repressive desublimation* - and their application to the analysis of the commodified cultural forms of US capitalism. His later writings are increasingly concerned with the transformation of humanity's relationship to nature and the role of a "new sensibility" in nurturing the instinctual bases of revolt. In this respect they provide a crucial link between classical MARXISM, PSYCHOANALYSIS, and the ecological and women's liberation movements of the 1960s and 1970s. His final work was a forthright affirmation of the continuing critical potential of autonomous artistic expression: *The Permanence of Art* (translated into English in 1977).

Reading

Geoghagen, Vincent 1981: *Reason and Eros: The Social Theory of Herbert Marcuse*.
Katz, Barry 1982: *Herbert Marcuse and the Art of Liberation*.
Kellner, Douglas 1984: *Herbert Marcuse and the Crisis of Marxism*.
Herbert Marcuse, 1937 (*1968*): "The affirmative character of culture."
——1955 (*1966*): *Eros and Civilisation: A Philosophical Inquiry into Freud*.
——1964: *One-Dimensional Man: Studies in the Ideology of Advanced Industrial Society*.
——1969: *An Essay on Liberation*.

PETER OSBORNE

Marx, Karl Heinrich (1818–83) German political, economic, philosophical theorist and revolutionist. The influence of Marx's materialistic conception of history, according to which capitalism will preside over its own decline and open the way for socialism, has been vast. Until the collapse in 1991 of the Communist systems of the USSR and Eastern Europe, a third of the world's population had been living under political administrations claiming descent from Marx's ideas. His impact on the world of thought has been equally extensive, embracing sociology, philosophy, economics, and CULTURAL THEORY.

Marx's thinking can be approached in terms of philosophical, economic, and political strata. As a philosopher, his development has its roots in his early life. Born into a Jewish family where his father had imbibed ENLIGHTENMENT rationalist principles, Marx was exposed to the ideas of Voltaire, Lessing, and Racine. He studied law at the University of Bonn and then Berlin. However, much of his time was spent in literary composition, and for a while he was enamoured of the Romanticism then in vogue. While these influences were never fully to recede, they were superseded by Marx's seminal encounter with the work of G.W.F. HEGEL, whose dialectic shaped the form of Marx's earlier and arguably his later thought. The dialectic did not comprise the commonly cited triad of thesis, antithesis, and synthesis: Hegel cited this formula only twice in his entire work and Marx never used it. In Hegel's hands, the dialectic had both logical and historical dimensions. Logically, it was a unifying method of thought designed to overcome the gulf between the human self and the world, between subject and object, created cumulatively by the hitherto developed social configurations of which philosophy was the rational expression. The three-stage dialectic formalized into a principle the imperative that thought was a *process* rather than a mechanical tool, as it had been in the hands of previous one-sided attempts to understand the world, such as MATERIALISM or EMPIRICISM. In the first stage an object was apprehended in its sensuous immediacy; the second stage adopted a broadened perspective which saw the object as "externalized," as having no independent identity but constituted by its manifold relations with its context. The third stage, from a still wider standpoint, viewed the object as a "mediated" unity, its true identity now perceived as a principle of unity between universal and particular, between essence and appearance. In this way, "plant" could be viewed as the unifying principle of its own developing stages, bud, blossom, and fruit. Historically, Hegel sees societies, from the Oriental world through the Greek and Roman to the modern German world, developing through successive stages of the dialectic; this is a movement through increasing self-conscious awareness that the external world is a construction out of human subjectivity as well as a movement toward freedom, whereby society's laws become more and more rational while the individual sees in the law an expression of his own free will. Hegel sees this as a movement of Absolute Spirit from its initial imprisonment in pure immediacy to its self-realization as universal.

The importance of the dialectic for Marx stems from his awareness that the "freedom" Hegel speaks of is the freedom of the then revolutionary bourgeois class to bring down the economic and political edifice of feudalism whose social hierarchy rested on irrational theology and superstition: society could now be organized on rational principles, a freer market economy, and a human subject who saw his individual interests enshrined in the general law. Hence the dialectic provided a powerful political tool, one which could negate a given state of affairs. It also furnished Marx with a model of history not only driven by political and ideological conflict but also where earlier phases were "sublated," both preserved and transcended, in their negation by subsequent phases. For a while Marx associated with the "Young Hegelians," who attempted to exploit the negative power of the dialectic in political analysis. But Marx's reading of French socialists such as Proudhon, his concern with immediate political issues, his exposure to Feuerbach's materialism, and his encounter with Frederick ENGELS's analyses of capitalism impelled him to view the dialectic of history as motivated by material forces. Hegel had correlated the historical period of the French Revolution, the period marking a bourgeois rise toward hegemony, with the second phase of the dialectic, the phase of externalization or estrangement.

In the *Economic and Philosophical Manuscripts of 1844* (1959; 1981), Marx's essential argument against Hegel is that this estrangement or ALIENATION in bourgeois society cannot be overcome by mere thought: existence and essence can only be harmonized "in a practical way, by means of a revolution." While Marx praises Hegel's dialectic inasmuch as it grasps the importance of labor, by which man creates himself, he views it as abstract because it is a "divine process," first negating religion and then restoring it. Marx effectively equates the retention of religion by Hegel's dialectic with its retention of the ideal of private property. Hence Marx views Hegel's standpoint as "that of modern political economy," by which he means the bourgeois economists Smith, Say, and Ricardo. So Marx, following Feuerbach, opposes the third stage of the dialectic, the negation of the negation, which restores and justifies the state of alienation. In religious and economic spheres Marx advocates two kinds of HUMANISM: "atheism, being the supersession of God, is the advent of theoretical humanism, and communism, as the supersession of private property, is . . . the advent of practical humanism." Hence for Marx the third stage of the dialectic is practical, not something which can be resolved in theory (Marx, 1959, pp. 127–43). Marx's striking equation of religion and private property as expressions of alienation had been hinted at in an earlier article on Hegel, where Marx regarded religion as having an ideologically apologetic and politically refractive function: "Religion is the sigh of the oppressed creature, the heart of a heartless world . . . It is the *opium* of the people" (Marx and Engels, 1957, p. 39).

This central insistence on the unity of theory and practice lies at the core of Marx's politics and is summarized in his "Theses on Feuerbach" (1845): "The philosophers have only *interpreted* the world, in various ways; the point, however, is to *change* it" (Marx and Engels, 1973, p. 95). While Marx's political views occur throughout his writings, often occasioned by immediate political events, their pivotal notions of CIVIL SOCIETY, state, and CLASS are succinctly expressed in *The German Ideology* in 1846 (Marx and Engels, 1970) and the *Communist Manifesto* in 1848 (Marx and Engels, 1952). In the former, Marx further develops his critique of Hegel's dialectic into what he calls the materialistic conception of history, which is the broad foundation on which he analyzes these political notions. The initial premise of this conception is that man's first historical act is the production of means to satisfy his material needs; the fulfillment of these leads to the production of new needs. The family, at first the only social relation, is eventually unable to accommodate these increased needs, which arise from increased population. The production of life, from both labor and procreation, is thus both natural and social: a given mode of production is combined with a given stage of social cooperation. Only after passing through these historical moments, says Marx, can we speak of human beings possessing "consciousness," itself a "social product." Hence the realms of IDEOLOGY, politics, law, morality, religion, and ART are not independent, but are an efflux of a people's material behavior: "Life is not determined by consciousness, but consciousness by life" (Marx and Engels, 1970, pp. 47–51).

This model of superstructure and economic base furnishes the form of Marx's analyses of state, class, and ideology. The foundational context of these analyses is the history of the division of labor. Marx traces various stages of this history, affirming that they are effectively different forms of ownership. At first the division of labor takes an elementary form in tribal ownership, where the social structure is limited to an extended family. Ancient communal and state ownership sees the union of tribes into a city; as immovable private property evolves and its concentration begins in early Rome, the division of labor becomes more developed, generating a conflict of interests between town and country. Class relations between citizens and slaves are now completely developed. In feudalism, the directly producing class is not the slaves but the enserfed peasantry. The urban counterpart of feudal landownership is corporative property and organization of trades. The need for bourgeois association against the nobility and for communal markets led to the formation of guilds, while the accumulated capital and stable numbers of craftsmen generated the relation of journeyman and apprentice, which yielded an urban hierarchy similar to that in the country. In general terms, Marx argues that division of labor is an index of the development of production. It leads to the separation of industrial and commercial from agricultural labor, hence a conflict of interests between town and country. It then effects a separation of individual and community interests (Marx and Engels, 1970, pp. 43–6). Moreover, the division of labor which first manifested itself in the sexual act appears eventually in its true shape as a division of material and mental labor; this is the point at which "pure" theory becomes possible, a point which Marx acknowledges, however, with some qualification.

Marx cites three crucial consequences of the social division of labour, first, the unequal distribution of labor and its products, and hence private property. The latent slavery in the family, says Marx, is the first property. He goes so far as to equate division of labor and private property, under the relation of product and activity. The second consequence is the state. The division of labor implying a contradiction between individual or family and communal interest, the latter assumes an independent form as the state, as an "illusory communal life" divorced from the real interests of both individual and community. It is based especially on classes, one of which dominates the others.

It follows that all struggles within the state are disguised versions of the struggle between classes. As Marx later declaims in The Communist Manifesto in 1848: "The history of all hitherto existing society is the history of class struggles" (Marx and Engels, 1952, p. 40). The class which is struggling for mastery must gain political power in order to represent its interest as the general interest (Marx and Engels, 1952, 52–3). Here is the germ of Marx's concept of ideology: the class which is the ruling material force in society is also the ruling intellectual force. Having at its disposal the means of production, it is empowered to disseminate its ideas in the realms of law, morality, religion, and art, as possessing universal verity. Dominant ideas of the aristocracy such as honor and loyalty were replaced after bourgeois ascendancy with ideas of freedom and equality, whose infrastructure comprised class economic imperatives (Marx and Engels, 1970, pp. 64–5). As Marx states in The Communist Manifesto, the bourgeoisie "creates a world after its own image." The modern state, then, "is but a committee for managing the common affairs of the whole bourgeoisie" (Marx and Engels, 1952, pp. 45–7).

This conception of the state in part embodies Marx's rejection of Hegel's view of the connection between civil society and the state. Hegel had characterized civil society as the sphere of personal and economic relations between men, as opposed to the political institutions which formalize these relations. Civil society is effectively a stage of mutual competition between private interests. Hegel had argued that such conflicting interests would be transcended and harmonized by the state. Marx disagrees: in his articles "On the Jewish question" and "Contribution to the critique of Hegel's philosophy of right," he employs Feuerbach's characterization of man as a "species-being," while stressing nevertheless the social basis of humanity to argue that mere political emancipation, represented by publicly institutionalizing individuals' private interests in the state, "leaves intact the world of private interest" and must give way to human emancipation, which is not directed by class but universal interests. The proletariat can redeem itself only by a total redemption of humanity: "This dissolution of society, as a particular class, is the proletariat." Hence, for Marx, civil society is the basis of the state, not vice versa; the latter, representing merely particular class interests, cannot overcome the conflictual nature of the former without abolishing itself (Marx, 1963, pp. 58, 16).

The third consequence of the division of labor is what Marx calls "estrangement" or "alienation" of social activity. Not only does division of labor force upon each person a particular sphere of activity whereby his "own deed becomes an alien power opposed to him," but also the social power or "multiplied productive force" as determined by division of labour appears to individuals, because their cooperation is forced, as "an alien force existing outside them" which develops independently of their will. "How otherwise," asks Marx, "does it happen that trade . . . rules the whole world through the relation of supply and demand . . . ?" (Marx and Engels, 1970, pp. 54–5).

This question, far from rhetorical, yields a broad avenue into Marx's economics, which can receive only cursory treatment here. As with his philosophy and politics, Marx's economic views, worked out largely in the *Grundrisse*, a huge manuscript unpublished in his lifetime, and expressed in volume I of *Capital* (1867), derive in one sense from his inversion of Hegel's dialectic, expressed by Marx in his statement that with Hegel the dialectic "is standing on its head. It must be turned right side up again, if you would discover the rational kernel within the mystical shell" (Marx, 1954, p. 29). Implied here is an insistence on labor as the foundation of economic life. The bourgeois economists Smith and Ricardo had expressed the labor theory of value, whereby an object's value was measured by the amount of labor it incarnated. Developing their distinction between use value and exchange value, Marx insisted that a commodity needed to be of use in order to command the power of exchange with other commodities or money; this power, however, was not a reflection of use value but rather of market conditions (Marx, 1954, pp. 43–8). The contradiction between these two types of value emerges in the commodification of labor power itself, which generates the class conflict between labor and capital. Also instrumental in this conflict is what Marx called surplus value, whereby labor power as embodied in production is incompletely compensated: the worker, putting in eight hours daily, might be paid for the value of the products generated by only four hours' work.

Marx saw such economic exploitation as underlying the ultimate downfall of capitalism: his various chapters in the first volume of *Capital* describe the "greed" on the part of the capitalists for surplus labor, their attempts to intensify labor and profit by both technology and control of resources by imperial expansion, as well as increasingly to centralize capital in the hands of fewer and fewer owners. In an apocalyptic passage, he states:

> along with the constantly diminishing number of the magnates of capital . . . grows the mass of misery, oppression, slavery, degradation, exploitation; but with this too grows the revolt of the working-class, a class always increasing in numbers, and disciplined, united, organised by the very mechanism of the process of capitalist production itself. The monopoly of capital becomes a fetter upon the mode of production, which has sprung up and flourished along with, and under it. Centralisation of the means of production and socialisation of labour at last reach a point where they become incompatible with their capitalist integument. This integument is burst asunder. The knell of capitalist private property sounds. The expropriators are expropriated.

Significantly, Marx sees this as part of a dialectical process moving from feudalism through capitalism to the final stage of communism, whose essential feature is common ownership of land and the means of production: "capitalist production begets, with the inexorability of a law of Nature, its own negation. It is the negation of negation" (Marx, 1954, p. 715). Hence the capitalist world represents the second phase of the dialectic, negating feudalism. Communism is the "negation of the negation," whereby the contradiction between private property and socialized production is resolved by the establishment of socialized property. Equally, the contradictions within the self, hitherto alienated from its own labor, as well as those between individual and communal interests, are abolished.

In his "Preface to *A Contribution to the Critique of Political Economy*," Marx had expressed this economic dialectic by saying that it was when "the material productive forces of society" came into conflict with "the existing relations of production" that historical upheavals resulted (Marx, 1976, p. 3). In *The German Ideology* Marx suggests that the estrangement which governs the second phase of the dialectic, the phase of bourgeois domination, can be abolished by revolution, given two practical premises: it must have rendered most men propertyless and also have produced, in contrast, an existing world of wealth and culture (Marx and Engels, 1970, p. 56). However, he also emphasizes the universality or world-historical nature of this conflict: such revolution presupposes not only highly developed productive capacities, but also that individuals have become enslaved under a power alien to them – the world market. Marx accepted that the struggle between classes might begin in specific nations but must inevitably be conducted as an international struggle, given that the bourgeois mode of production dictated constant expansion of markets and the coercion of all nations, "on pain of extinction," into the bourgeois economic mold (Marx and Engels, 1952, p. 47).

In the realm of literature and ART, Marx's views are somewhat piecemeal and inconclusive, generating a rich variety of attempts by Marxist critics to assemble his insights into coherent theories. A nucleus of elements can be distinguished as the common starting point of most Marxist theories. First, art is a commodity and like other commodities can be understood only in the fullness of its connections with ideology, historical class conflict, and economic substructure. Second, art is one aspect of man's self-creation through labor. It is part of the process whereby an "objective" world is created out of a collective human subjectivity. Third, language is not a self-enclosed system of relations but must be understood as social practice, as deeply rooted in material conditions as any other practice (Marx and Engels, 1970, p. 51). Having said this, both Marx and Engels appear to have granted a relative autonomy to art, acknowledging that there was not a relation of simple reflection between art and its material substructure (Marx, 1977, p. 359). See MARXISM AND MARXIST CRITICISM.

Is Marx dead? Can we, finally, consign his work to historical and political obsolescence? After all, have not socialism and Communism failed? Has Marxism not proven its inability to be realized in practice? Have not the remaining socialist states in the world been forced to initiate capitalist enterprise so as to jolt into life their barren economies? Have not economic and personal freedom, not to mention democracy, won the day? It is surely time for Marxism to acknowledge that it speaks from beyond the grave.

Perhaps the greatest irony in all this triumphalism is that the collapse of Communism can best be explained in Marxist terms: this entails partly the recognition that most of what has passed for "communism" has had but remote connections with the doctrines of Marx or his followers. Moreover,

Marx's critique of capitalism was dialectical. He regarded capitalist society as an unprecedented historical advance from centuries of benighted feudalism. The bourgeois emphasis on reason, practicality, on technological enterprise in mastering the world, on ideals of rational law and justice, individual freedom, and democracy were all hailed by Marx as historical progress. His point was not that communism would somehow displace capitalism in its entirety but that it would grow out of capitalism and *realize* its ideals of freedom and democracy. For example, Marx shrewdly points out that the "individual" in capitalist society is effectively the bourgeois owner of property; individual freedom is merely economic freedom, the freedom to buy and sell. The constitution and the laws are entirely weighted in favor of large business interests and owners of property. Private property, Marx points out, is already abolished for the nine-tenths of the population in capitalist society who do not possess it. The labor of this vast majority, being commodified, is as subject to the vicissitudes of the market as any other commodity.

One of the main sins of capitalism, according to Marx, is that it reduces all human relations to commercial relations. Even the family cannot escape such commodification: Marx states that, for the bourgeois man, the wife is reduced to a mere instrument of production. Moreover, once the exploitation of the laborer by the manufacturer has finished, then he is set upon, says Marx, by other segments of the bourgeoisie: the landlord, the shopkeeper, the pawnbroker. In bourgeois society "capital is independent and has individuality, while the living person is dependent and has no individuality" (Marx and Engels, 1952, pp. 51, 53, 65–70). As an internal critique of the tendencies of capitalism and its crises, Marxism is uniquely incisive. Without the influence of Marxism as a body of thought, the claims of the law to be eternal, of the bourgeoisie to represent the interests of the entire nation, and of individuality and freedom to be universal, would have encountered little more than academic challenge. The idea of the present as a historical phase, with roots in the past and branches in the future, would be confined to books rather than being a matter of long-term political practice. Moreover, the vocabulary and concepts of Marxism have exercised a decisive and formative influence on other modern theories, both radical and reactionary: feminism, DECONSTRUCTION, STRUCTURALISM, EXISTENTIALISM, and NEW HISTORICISM all owe some debt to Marxist thought and have striven to develop a dialogue with it.

Even after the collapse of the so-called Communist bloc, many of Marx's ideas can still be seen to be operative: that capitalism would be driven to engulf the entire world, penalizing nations which resisted; and that, despite the protests of conservative sociologists to the contrary, societies everywhere have indeed become polarized in terms of capital and labor. It is rapidly becoming a cliché, with no grounding in truth, that most of the population in Western capitalist nations is now middle class: Marx said that even those owning land and property could belong to the proletariat, since their mortgage liability meant that they were not truly owners of either. Moreover, to equate the success of capitalism with the failure of socialism is to misconceive their relation as one of outright opposition rather than as a blooming of humanity from a self-exhausting machine. Marxism serves as a perpetual reminder that poverty, illiteracy, crime, political oppression, and the stifling of mass human potential are neither to be accepted as inevitable nor to be remedied by individual or group acts of good will. They are structural phenomena with roots in a given economic system and must be addressed as such. Given the political climate of the world at present, it may be that the arguments of Marx and Engels must enter into sustained dialogue and possible compromise with both the apologists of this economic system and those espousing humanitarian causes within it. Nevertheless, as long as human poverty, immiseration, and oppression exist, whether under the banner of liberalism, communism or religious fundamentalism, the arguments of Marx will retain their motivational foundation and their relevance in human affairs.

See also ENGELS; MATERIALISM.

Reading
Carver, T., ed. 1991: The Cambridge Companion to Marx.
Lefebvre, H. 1982: The Sociology of Marx.
Lenin, V.I. 1987: Introduction to Marx, Engels, Marxism.
McLellan, D. 1975: Karl Marx.
——1973 (1977): Karl Marx: His Life and Thought.
Melotti, U. 1977: Marx and the Third World.
Meynell, H.A. 1981: Freud, Marx, and Morals.
Moore, S.W. 1993: Marx Versus Markets.
Norman, R. 1980: Hegel, Marx and Dialectic.
Russell, B. 1934: The Meaning of Marx: A Symposium.
Seigel, J.E. 1993: Marx's Fate: The Shape of a Life.
Wiley, N., ed. 1987: The Marx–Weber Debate.

M.A.R. HABIB

Marxism and Marxist criticism   Founded by Karl MARX and Friedrich ENGELS, in a complex synthesis/supersession of German philosophy, English political economy, and French utopian socialism, Marxism comprises:

(i)   a general theory of human history, postulating the ultimately determinant role therein of successive "economic formations" or modes of production; and

(ii) a particular theory of the development, reproduction, and transformation of the capitalist mode of production, identifying one of its principal antagonistic social classes – the proletariat – as the potential historical agency of a transition to communism.

From the early 1850s Marx devoted himself to the elaboration of (ii), expounded in the three volumes of the unfinished *Capital* (1867–95). The closest approximation to a systematic account by him of (i) appears in the enormously influential 1859 Preface to *A Contribution to the Critique of Political Economy*, with its celebrated BASE AND SUPERSTRUCTURE topography. In it the "base" – the "economic structure of society" – is accorded explanatory primacy over the "legal and political superstructure," and the "forms of social consciousness" or "ideological forms" (aesthetic included) said to "correspond" to it, in any SOCIAL FORMATION.

An account of cultural practices was thus inscribed in principle in the "materialist conception of history," as a subset of the theory of "ideological forms"; it was not, however, developed in the work of the founders, who nevertheless ventured some relevant *obiter dicta* on the subject. Seeking to refute mechanistic constructions and applications of historical materialism, which converted the base/superstructure model into a Procrustean bed, in a late series of letters Engels argued that the explanatory claims of the theory were compatible with evidence for the autonomy of ideological forms. Although the product of historically specific material and social conditions, literary works, for example, were thus not the mere passive reflection in artistic form of some real content, which explained them as a cause does its effects. At the same time, in their specifically aesthetic judgments Marx and Engels indicated a pronounced affinity with literary realism, encapsulated by Engels as "the truthful rendering of typical characters under typical circumstances," and exemplified, notwithstanding his reactionary political allegiances, by the fiction of Balzac.

These propositions set the terms and constitute the enduring, interrelated cruces, of aesthetic controversy within Marxism and against it: the base/superstructure nexus, and the attendant perils of mechanical determinism and economic reductionism; the *differentia specifica* (if any) of art *vis-à-vis* IDEOLOGY (for example, art as the transcendence or the transcription of ideology); realism and anti-realism; literature and politics (the themes of "partisanship" or "commitment"); the question of literary value ("eternal," as in Marx's Hellenism, or mutable?).

Following Mulhern (1992, pp. 2–17), the intellectual history of Marxism and Marxist criticism can be conveniently divided into three overlapping phases:

(i) Classical Marxism – the "scientific" *Weltanschauung* systematized by Engels in the late 1870s and 1880s, extended by the leading thinkers of the Second (Social-Democratic) International (for example, Kautsky and Plekhanov) and the Third (Communist) International (for example, Lenin and Trotsky), and then debased into the orthodox doctrine of global Communism down to its implosion a century later;

(ii) Western Marxism – the philosophical revolt against the POSITIVISM of (i), pioneered by Korsch and LUKÁCS in the early 1920s and continued, in a rich diversity of forms, by GRAMSCI in Italy, BENJAMIN and the FRANKFURT SCHOOL in Germany, Lefebvre, SARTRE, and GOLDMANN in France, and arguably WILLIAMS in Britain, into the 1960s;

(iii) "critical classicism" – a "materialist" reaction against the declared or alleged HEGELIANISM of (ii), associated with the schools of DELLA VOLPE and especially ALTHUSSER, which climaxed in the 1970s, whereafter, in a reversal of critical alliances, certain of its polemical themes converged with POSTSTRUCTURALISM in a critique of historical materialism which commands widespread assent today.

Given Marx's abstention, the task of producing a general philosophical statement of Marxism as a conception of history fell to Engels. His *Anti-Dühring* of 1878 (Engels, 1939), sanctioned by Marx and received as the *summa* of their "world outlook,"

subsumed it under the metaphilosophy of "modern materialism," the putative "science of the general laws of motion and development of nature, human society and thought." A typical late nineteenth-century enterprise and a hybrid, despite itself, of Hegelianism and positivism, "dialectical materialism" as it became known aspired "to devise a scheme of knowledge unified in method and integrated in its results, capable of mastering the evolutionary and structural ascent from protein to poetry in a single cognitive operation" (Mulhern, 1992, p. 6). Under this rubric, the succeeding generation of theorists – whether Mehring in *The Lessing Legend* (1893) or Plekhanov in *Art and Social Life* (1912) – modestly began the extension of Marxism to the aesthetic domain, initiating a variant of the sociology of literature.

In 1908 the poet Blok had warned the Russian intelligentsia, "History, that same history which, they say, can be reduced simply to political economy, has placed a real bomb on the table." Nine years later, amid the convulsions of the 1914–18 war, it exploded in Petrograd. Subsequent Marxist thought about CULTURE and ART was fundamentally inflected by the vicissitudes of revolutionary construction and retrenchment in the Soviet Union. Lenin's prior defense of the "classical heritage" found itself under challenge from the voluntarism of the Proletkult, intent upon making a *tabula rasa* of the prerevolutionary past. Repudiating any such nihilistic prospectus, Trotsky's *Literature and Revolution* (1923) simultaneously rejected the CANONS of RUSSIAN FORMALISM – the most original critical enterprise of these turbulent years, seeded by linguistics and futurist poetics, which theorized literature as the signification and DEFAMILIARIZATION (rather than the imitation or reflection) of social reality. *Contra* Plekhanov's conception of literature as "the mirror of social life," Trotsky characterized it as "a deflection, a changing and a transformation of reality, in accordance with the peculiar laws of art." But for him SHKLOVSKY, Eichenbaum, TYNYANOV, JAKOBSON and co. were, in their exclusive exploration of generic literariness, "followers of St John" and "underlabourers of the device."

Formalism achieved a belated, remarkably productive *rapprochement* with Marxism towards the end of the 1920s, in the postformalist current represented by BAKHTIN. The fate of his classic work on Rabelais – written in 1940, but not published until 1965 – symbolizes its brutal interruption. For by now the consolidation of Stalinism, the lethal political instrumentalization of Marxism – as decidedly illiterate as it was determinedly autarkic – and the intensification of cultural controls in the Soviet state and international Communist movement alike, spelt the doom of intellectual experimentation. SOCIALIST REALISM was promulgated by Zhdanov in 1934 as the official aesthetic doctrine of the USSR. A noxious blend of cultural traditionalism and political voluntarism, assigning artists the role of "engineers of the human soul," its prescriptions – *partinost'* (partisanship), *narodnost'* (popularity), *klassovost'* (class character of art), etc. – mandated a line of unrelieved crudity, the Stalinist bugbear of most Marxist criticism of note thereafter.

As Mulhern (1992, p. 9) has observed, "[t]he long reign of party dogmatism, through the decades of Stalinism proper and beyond, was also a golden age of Marxist aesthetics." Formed, and scarred, by the defeat of revolution in the West and its degeneration in the East, the heterodox, minority currents of Western Marxism took varying degrees of distance from the bureaucratic breviary of "dialectical and historical materialism" (see Jameson, 1971). However otherwise heterogeneous, they were united in two fundamental respects: by a philosophical critique of the "scientism" of orthodox Marxism, initiated in Lukács's *History and Class Consciousness* (1923), and resumed in Gramsci's *Prison Notebooks*, via a revindication of HISTORICISM and HUMANISM; and by an overwhelming preoccupation with cultural analysis, especially of literature and art, attested by the culmination of Lukács's career in his *Aesthetik* (1963), ADORNO's in *Aesthetic Theory* (1970a), and Sartre's in a three-volume study of Flaubert, *The Family Idiot* (1971–2).

Paradoxically, perhaps, the founder of Western Marxism – the loyal Communist, Lukács – became the main philosophical ornament of the protocols of socialist realism for the duration of anti-fascist Popular Frontism (1935–9), when dictatorial vice paid cultural homage to bourgeois–democratic virtue. Lukács's dogmatic advocacy of literary realism, against modernism and naturalism alike, incited a series of complex, multilateral exchanges – between BLOCH and BRECHT, BENJAMIN and ADORNO, covering the full range of perennial and conjunctural issues – which forms one of the central debates in modern AESTHETICS (Bloch et al., 1977).

Despite his political conformism, and notwithstanding his exaggerated stance in the 1930s – the equation of modernism with irrationalism; the identification of the latter with fascism – Lukács's

aesthetic options remained consistent throughout his career, from the pre-Marxist *Theory of the Novel* (1916), via *The Historical Novel* (1937) and *Studies in European Realism* (1950), to *The Meaning of Contemporary Realism* (1958), with its characteristic antithesis between Mann and Kafka. His exclusive sponsorship of realism in fiction, its paradigmatic instances and classical models furnished by Balzac and Tolstoy, was rooted in an evolutionist and expressivist literary history. This plotted the decline of the novel after 1848 into the twin *bêtes noires* of naturalism (for example, Zola), taxed with "objectivism," and FORMALISM (for example, Musil), indicted for "subjectivism," against the European bourgeoisie's renunciation of its revolutionary class vocation. The Lukacsian conception of the novel as an "intensive totality," reproducing the "extensive totality" of society and thereby constituting a "reflection of objective reality" (1958, p. 101), presupposed epistemological realism (more specifically, a correspondence theory of truth in which narrative DISCOURSE was the transparent signifier of the essential reality disclosed by historical materialism).

The divergent countercritiques elicited by this doctrine of literary realism shared common ground with it: namely subscription to a *cognitivist* theory of art as a means of understanding historical reality. For Adorno, as for Lukács, specific forms of art possessed this privileged capacity intrinsically; and he was thus prompted to emulate his opponent's project of elaborating a Marxist version of a non-Marxist ideology of the aesthetic (albeit a modernist rather than realist one). For Brecht, by contrast, intervening in the controversy as a "producer," adjudging Lukács and his cothinkers "enemies of production" and accusing them of "formalism" for their valorization of the conventions of the nineteenth-century novel, realism was a *political* goal whose *formal* means were historically variable. Authentic realism was apprised of the fact that "[r]eality changes; in order to represent it, modes of representation must also change" (Bloch et al., 1977, p. 82). His own "epic theatre," memorably vindicated by his friend Benjamin (1966), centrally entailed "unmasking the prevailing view of things," to be achieved by anti-naturalist devices which produced the requisite ALIENATION EFFECT in the audience (compare the Russian Formalists' notion of ESTRANGEMENT).

Articulating a Marxist *Kulturkritik* of mass/POPULAR CULTURE, Adorno had as little time for Brecht's poetics as he did for Lukács's politics.

Suffused with the "instrumental rationality" of the natural sciences, and sustained by the "mass deception" of the CULTURE INDUSTRY, the advanced liberal capitalism depicted in Adorno and HORKHEIMER's *Dialectic of Enlightenment* (1944) was a quasi-totalitarian "administered universe" for which the velleities of aesthetic realism and political commitment held no terrors. Modernist art, in which Lukács, wedded to "reflection" theory, could discern only a decadent caricature of actuality, secreted "the negative knowledge of the actual world" (Bloch et al., 1977, p. 160). The last imperiled refuge of "negation," its images embodied a contradiction and critique of the abstract exchange value which had invaded every sphere of the totality, staging a refusal of reconciliation with a degraded social reality. The value of works of art precisely consisted of their constitutive, irreducible formality. If not offering *une promesse de bonheur*, "As eminently constructed and produced objects, [they] point to a practice from which they abstain: the creation of a just life" (Bloch et al., 1977, p. 194). Reproving Sartre's 1948 manifesto, *What is literature?* Adorno insisted, "This is not a time for political art, but politics has migrated into autonomous art."

The postwar florescence of CRITICAL THEORY, not only in Germany, but also in America where MARCUSE remained after 1945, relaying its distinctive concerns in *One-Dimensional Man* (1964) and completing *The Aesthetic Dimension* (1977) shortly before his death, renders it the dominant tradition within Western Marxism. In France, meanwhile, the presiding theorists were Sartre, engaged with DE BEAUVOIR and others in the ambitious synthesis of historical materialism and EXISTENTIALISM which issued in the *Critique of Dialectical Reason* (1960); and GOLDMANN, whose GENETIC STRUCTURALISM, unveiled in *The Hidden God* (1956), reclaimed the writings of the early Lukács and employed the epistemology of the psychologist PIAGET. Eschewing the former's dogmatism, he did not avoid his schematism in a theory of literary texts as the artistic transposition of the "world view" of the social class or group to which their authors belonged.

This was the Marxist philosophical setting in which Althusser, against the grain of post-Stalin Communism, advanced an "anti-humanist" and "anti-historicist" recasting of the substance of historical materialism. Antithetical to the putative Hegelianism of Western Marxism, charged with ESSENTIALISM, Althusserianism was simultaneously hostile to the "economism" of orthodox Soviet Marxism. Displacing the base/superstructure topography, in *For Marx* (Althusser, 1965b) and *Reading "Capital"* (Althusser and Balibar, 1965) Althusser and his collaborators (for example, BALIBAR) reconceptualized the social totality as a complex, DECENTERED STRUCTURE of irreducible "practices," entering into processes of OVERDETERMINATION, while enjoying RELATIVE AUTONOMY and "specific effectivity," determined only in the "last instance" by the economy (Althusser, 1965, pp. 87–127). To execute this comprehensive reconstruction they turned, under the banner of a "return to Marx," to Freudian PSYCHOANALYSIS à la LACAN and the linguistics of SAUSSURE, sealing a *de facto* "triple alliance" between them and Marxism for the Parisian season of STRUCTURALISM. Accordingly Althusser, while adamantly reasserting the scientific status of Marxism, implicitly retracted its pretension to constitute an autarkic world view.

Althusser's own pronouncements on art, including some arresting reflections on Brechtian dramaturgy (1965, 129–51), accorded a signal cognitive privilege to it, alongside science, *via-à-vis* an otherwise ubiquitous ideology, which was theorized as "imaginary relations" and rendered coterminous with "lived experience." His pupil MACHEREY systematized these proposals in his sketch *"for* a theory of literary production" (1966). Insisting upon the autonomy of literary texts, Macherey conceived them as the product of a labor of artistic transformation upon ideological raw materials, a determinate material practice in and on ideology. The effect of literary form was to "produce" ideology in such a way as to disclose its relations with its real conditions of existence and thereby supply an "implicit critique" of it. The specificity of literature lay, then, in its subversion of the "necessary illusions" of ideology. And the task of its analyst, renouncing evaluation and interpretation, was to provide a knowledge of its peculiar modalities.

As it affected both the substance and the status of historical materialism, Althusserianism had an enormous impact upon Marxist CULTURAL and critical THEORY, largely defining the terms of debate for a decade or more. In the anglophone world, where it was received concurrently with the schools of Western Marxism (largely via the *NEW LEFT REVIEW*), it inspired the ambitious programme of EAGLETON (1976). Directed against the local humanist canons of both LEAVIS and WILLIAMS, Eagleton's analysis nevertheless queried the existence of an invariably subversive text/ideology relationship and ventured a "transitive" theory of differential literary value. Rejecting, like the later Macherey, the received question of philosophical aesthetics – what is literature? – Eagleton drafted a new agenda: a theory of literary *re*production/consumption.

Where classical Marxism after Marx had generally subscribed to scientific positivism and artistic realism, and much Western Marxism to anti-scientism and anti-realism, this broadly Althusserian phase witnessed a distinctive conjunction of science and modernism. The synthesis of historical materialism, psychoanalysis, and SEMIOTICS attempted by the *maoisant* TEL QUEL (KRISTEVA et al.) involved a recovery of prewar Russian and German figures and debates. Its cross-Channel transfer to SCREEN (Heath and co.) issued in a single-minded avant-gardism, affixing ideological valences to aesthetic forms – crudely, modernist/open/oppositional versus realist/closed/dominant (see Coward and Ellis, 1977). Such inversion of Lukacsian filiations, widely diffused after 1968, consummated the rupture with realist modes of artistic representation which, in generating the illusion of a transcription of social reality, supposedly reproduced the fixed subject-positions of the dominant ideologies of capitalism and PATRIARCHY.

The confluence of conventionalist epistemology, inferred from Saussurean linguistics, and aesthetic modernism, identified with Joyce in fiction, Brecht in drama, or Godard in cinema, effected not only a generalized displacement of epistemological realism, but a counterposition of avant-garde to popular culture. Elsewhere, in the developing CULTURAL MATERIALISM of Williams (1977), the research of the CENTRE FOR CONTEMPORARY CULTURAL STUDIES, directed by HALL, and a richly varied FEMINIST CRITICISM (cf. MITCHELL), different kinds of problematization of the received object ("literature") and discipline ("criticism") were conducted. Challenging the traditional CANON, these both expanded and equalized the corpus, while diversifying the modes of its analysis.

Under the combined impact of intrinsic theoretical difficulties and extrinsic political histories, the ecumenical alliance between historical materialism and "structuralism" broke down towards the end of the 1970s. Variously drawing upon the GENEALOGY of FOUCAULT, the DECONSTRUCTION of DERRIDA, or the POSTMODERNISM proper of LYOTARD and BAUDRILLARD, and mediated, for example, by the discourse theory of LACLAU, varieties of

"post-Marxism" (compare Bennett, 1990) emerged in its wake. These subjected Althusserian Marxism to concerted criticism for its alleged epistemological dogmatism, rejecting the science/ideology distinction as a repressive ruse of POWER; and class reductionism, repudiating the category of the totality in the name of difference. Under the rubric of CULTURAL STUDIES, and deflecting the slogans of "materialism" and "anti-humanism" against Althusser, there crystallized "a new canon of subversion, the counterenlightenment thematics of 'post-structuralism' " (Mulhern, 1992, pp. 15–16), of which NIETZSCHE, following the death of strange gods, was the tutelary deity.

Preaching (if scarcely practicing) a euphoric nescience, this postlapsarian critical formation is, by virtue of its very perspectivism and relativism, politically progressive in self-conception. Ironically, however, its populist culturalism reverses the evaluative signs, but reproduces the problematic, of *Kulturkritik*, subordinating the narrowly political to the expansively cultural. As deployed in much colonial discourse theory, its strategies, implemented in an indiscriminate running polemic against Marxism and the "metaphysics," essentialism, ethnocentrism, etc., to which it is assimilated, have recently provoked a confident countercritique (Ahmad, 1992). But pending the next revolution of the wheel of fashion in academic "theory," it represents the dominant consensus of contemporary anglophone "radical" criticism; while Marxism, experiencing the gravest crisis in its crisis-ridden history, is generally perceived as discredited. Whether this amounts to just arbitration of respective reputations is another matter. Certainly, Anglo-American "post-Marxism" has produced no *oeuvre* of comparable range and power to that of a Williams, from *Culture and Society* (1958) to *The Politics of Modernism* (1989), or a Jameson, from *Marxism and Form* (1971) to *Postmodernism* (1991). And it is probably safe to conclude, in the words of Freud, that "a contradiction is not a refutation; an innovation not necessarily an advance."

Reading
Ahmad, Aijaz 1992: *In Theory: Classes, Nations, Literatures.*
Althusser, Louis 1965b (*1990*): *For Marx.*
Benjamin, Walter 1966 (*1983*): *Understanding Brecht.*
Bennett, Tony 1990: *Outside Literature.*
Bloch, Ernst, et al. 1977 (*1980*): *Aesthetics and Politics.*
Coward, Rosalind, and Ellis, John 1977: *Language and Materialism.*
Craig, David 1975: *Marxists on Literature: An Anthology.*

Eagleton, Terry 1976 (*1978*): *Criticism and Ideology*.
Jameson, Fredric 1971: *Marxism and Form*.
Lukács, Georg 1958 (*1963*): *The Meaning of Contemporary Realism*.
Macherey, Pierre 1966 (*1978*): *A Theory of Literary Production*.
Mulhern, Francis, ed. 1992: *Contemporary Marxist Literary Criticism*.
Williams, Raymond 1977: *Marxism and Literature*.
GREGORY ELLIOTT

Marxist-Feminist Literature Collective

(1975–77) An informal network of women students and teachers in adult and higher education, which met regularly in London from 1975 to late 1977. The MFLC was a reading group focusing on classic Marxist writings on literature as well as the new French theories (often distributed freshly translated, in typescript, to members): from Marx, Saussure, and Macherey to Lacan, Kristeva, and Irigaray.

For the Sociology of Literature Conference at the University of Essex in 1977 the collective wrote a collaborative paper entitled "Women's Writing: *Jane Eyre, Shirley, Villette, Aurora Leigh*," and read it, polyphonically, in a line of nine women across the lecture room. The paper has been reprinted and cited frequently, and is seen as a key document in early British socialist-feminist LITERARY CRITICISM. The collective met for a short time after the Essex Conference; its members have since stayed in contact and have gone on to publish FEMINIST CRITICISM in Britain and the United States.

See also FEMINIST CRITICISM.

Reading
Kaplan, C. 1986: "The feminist politics of literary theory."
HELEN TAYLOR

masculinity The GENDER that is culturally constructed upon an anatomically male BODY. Masculinity defines identifiable sets of behavior, forms of speech, and styles of bodily comportment that serve to keep men dominant in a patriarchal society. In most cultures, masculinity is the dominant term in a BINARY OPPOSITION which subordinates FEMININITY. Theorists of CULTURE and society insist that masculinity cannot be discussed with any measure of success without specifying it as a phenomenon in relation to CLASS, "RACE," generation, region, and sexuality. In the late 1980s and early 1990s, a large number of academic studies of masculinity appeared, many of which were authored by heterosexual men who wished to undermine male domination. Their project in part shared the aims of FEMINIST CRITICISM and GAY POLITICS. Several of these men named themselves male feminists, although some of their female critics claimed that feminist identity and politics were the preserve of women alone.

Reading
Connell, R.W. 1987: *Gender and Power: Society, the Person and Sexual Politics*.
Jardine, Alice, and Smith, Paul, eds 1987: *Men in Feminism*.
JOSEPH BRISTOW

materialism Materialism has occupied a wide range of forms, common to which is the central assertion of the primacy of matter over mind or spirit in any explanation of the world. Strong materialism holds that reality consists exclusively of material things and their varying combinations. Weaker forms of materialism acknowledge the importance, albeit secondary, of mental operations. Given this insistence on interpreting reality in material terms, the history of materialism has exhibited both an affiliation with the natural sciences and a persistent antagonism toward explanation of events in terms of spiritual or supernatural agency.

Though its roots stretch back through the sixth and fifth centuries BC to Thales and Parmenides, materialism proper begins with the fifth-century thinker Democritus (on whom Marx was to write his doctoral dissertation) and his teacher Leucippus. They viewed the world as consisting exclusively of an infinite number of material atoms whose interaction unceasingly yielded new combinations. King Lear's warning to Cordelia that "Nothing will come of nothing" derives from this materialist philosophy, which holds equally that nothing can be destroyed. Hence the notions of a created world and supernatural agency are precluded. In the same century Empedocles attempted a materialistic explanation of organic life, constructing the influential theory of the four elements, earth, air, fire, and water. He believed that the universe evolved cyclically through the harmony and discord of these elements.

The anti-religious motivation of materialism resurged strongly in the philosophy of Epicurus (342–270 BC) who, notwithstanding his vulgarized reputation, preached an ETHICS based on material reality and freedom from superstition. The Roman poet Lucretius (c. 100–c. 55 BC) saw Epicurus as the precursory champion of his own cause in *De*

Rerum Natura which began from the tenet: "Nothing can ever be created by divine power out of nothing" (Lucretius, 1951, p. 31). Lucretius attempted a "scientific" materialistic explanation of sensation, mental life, society, and cosmology, denying both human immortality and the existence of the soul.

Apart from its sporadic and partial emergence in figures such as the scholastic Duns Scotus (c. 1266–1308), materialism was largely held in abeyance from Classical times through the Middle Ages by the Church-sanctioned domination of the theology of Augustine and the Aristotelian–Christian synthesis of Aquinas. While the French materialist Pierre Gassendi (1592–1655) sought to displace Aristotle with Epicurus in this synthesis, he was still working within a Christian providential framework. It was in the work of Thomas Hobbes (1588–1679) that materialism found a genuine rebirth. Hobbes applied the assumptions of seventeenth-century science – in particular those of Galileo and Newton – to all areas of inquiry. His view of the universe as corporeal and in motion also encompassed man, who was effectively a machine in movement. Elevated to paramount importance in Hobbes's materialism was the operation of causality; while he accepted the Final Causality of the "Supreme Being", his conception of God as corporeal was a far cry from the God of Christianity. It was on a materialist as opposed to the prevailing theological basis that Hobbes constructed his political theory. Hobbes's "pure" materialism was motivated in part by his rejection of Descartes's dualism between mind and body.

French materialism appeared on the world historical stage during the epoch of ENLIGHTENMENT, articulated by such figures as Denis Diderot (1713–84), Julien de La Mettrie (1709–51), and Paul Heinrich Dietrich d'Holbach, whose prototypical work *Système de la nature* appeared in 1770. While Diderot's eventual materialistic and atheistic outlook was the result of his intellectual journey through deism and immanent pantheism, La Mettrie and d'Holbach were less equivocal in grounding explanations of nature, including human behavior, in physical causes and undermining the theological paraphernalia of the immortal soul and spiritual agency. The increasing definition of physics, chemistry, and biology as empirical sciences in the eighteenth and nineteenth centuries, as well as as the historical success of Darwinism, gave materialistic explanations of the world an increasingly authoritative basis to which their claims could be referred.

Even thinkers not strictly classifiable as materialist, such as Voltaire, Locke, and Hume, owed the possibility of their respective emphases on reason, sensation, impressions, and ideas to the same emerging intellectual HEGEMONY of science. Indeed, KANT's idealism, premised on his distinction between phenomena (things as conditioned by human sensibility and understanding) and noumena (things as they might be if presented purely to thought, apart from sensibility) was informed by a historically unavoidable respect for science. In Kant's phenomenal world, causality is as universally operative as in the world of the materialists.

Ironically, materialism found sophisticated treatment in HEGEL, the father of modern absolute idealism, as well as in MARX and ENGELS, whose title to materialism is fraught with qualification. Hegel did not reject materialism outright; he saw it, rather, as one-sided, merely a stage in the dialectical apprehension of reality. Like EMPIRICISM, of which it is the systematic expression, it divides the world by analysis into discrete material entities but fails to see the unity underlying these, a unity not inhering in the entities themselves. This philosophical attitude, says Hegel in his *Logic*, remains in bondage to the world as immediately given, whereas reality is not a random collection of entities but a rational, historically interrelated system. Moreover, "matter" is an abstraction, which is never itself perceived or given. What are perceived are its particular manifestations (Hegel, 1873, pp. 62–4). Hegel also historically situates materialism, along with empiricism, rationalism, and utilitarianism, as one of the forms of bourgeois thought.

These insights crucially molded the materialism of both Marx and Engels. It was Engels who coined the phrase "historical materialism" and the Russian Marxist Plekhanov who termed the Marxist philosophy "dialectical materialism." Both terms cover the same materialist disposition peculiar to MARXISM, the former stressing materialism as the basis of historical development, while the latter indicates a methodological emphasis in the apprehension of reality. The dialectical method views reality not as a conglomerate of fixed entities but as a changing totality of related parts at whose core is a dynamic interaction between human labor and the natural world. Marx's own reflections on materialism, both traditional and dialectical, are focused primarily in his writings of 1844–6 (see also MARX). In the *Economic and Philosophical Manuscripts of 1844* (1959), Marx views Feuerbach as the "true conqueror" of the Hegelian idealist philosophy and praises his achievement in establishing "true materialism" and "real science" by making the social relation of "man to man" the principle of his theory. Marx stresses that his own analysis of political economy is "wholly empirical." Viewing the entire discipline of "pure" philosophy as the latest expression of an alienated religious consciousness which ultimately justifies social injustice, Marx correlates atheism (the abolition of religion) as the advent of theoretical HUMANISM with communism (abolition of private property), which signals the advent of practical humanism. Marx suggests that his own doctrine of naturalism or humanism, which combines theory and practice, is the "unifying truth" of both idealism and materialism (Marx, 1959, pp. 14, 127–136, 142). What is encapsulated in these statements is Marx's two-sided polemic against both idealism and previous forms of materialism, a polemic which works toward the dialectical harmony of their one-sided truths.

This procedure receives further clarification in *The Holy Family* (first published in 1844), where Marx sees eighteenth-century French materialism as engaged in a two-pronged onslaught: against contemporary religion and theology and against the seventeenth-century metaphysics of Descartes, Malebranche, Spinoza, and Leibniz. Marx thus identifies two broad strands of French materialism. The latter is what interests Marx more since it leads to socialism and communism: with its roots ultimately in Democritus and Epicurus, its modern development is heralded by Gassendi and Bayle and runs through Bacon, Hobbes, Locke, Condillac, and Helvetius, Bentham and the socialists Robert Owen, Dezamy, and Gay. What links this second line of materialism with Marx's own thought is the recognition that, if knowledge is indeed derived from sensation and experience, the empirical world must be rearranged so that man experiences what is truly human in it. Moreover, as stressed by some of these thinkers, man's nature is not to be found in individuals but in their social relations (Marx and Engels, 1956, pp. 154–66).

In *The German Ideology* (first published in 1845), Marx expresses his materialistic conception of history, the premise of which is the empirically verifiable set of conditions determining man's production of his material life. It is this material economic activity, as embodied in productive forces and social relations, which determines the nature of individuals, society, and historical development. Hence

consciousness, ideas, morality, and religion have no independent existence or history, but are dialectically (as opposed to one-sidedly) dependent upon the economic substructure. This means that consciousness itself is a social product and that the "individual" of bourgeois society is a result, not the starting point, of history. Hence Marx decries (i) the materialism of Feuerbach, who fails to see the sensuous world as a historical product; (ii) traditional empiricism which views history as a collection of dead facts; and (iii) idealism which reduces history to an "imagined activity" (Marx and Engels, 1970, pp. 25, 42–7, 58–61).

Marx's "Theses on Feuerbach" of 1845 offer a more focused expression of his materialism: the highest point reached by previous materialism, says Marx, is "the contemplation of single individuals in 'civil society.'" For Marx, however, reality is not an inert collection of material entities to be grasped by detached contemplation, but an interaction between a collective historical human subjectivity and the material world it generates through its material activity or labor. Truth is hence not a theoretical but a practical question and human nature is never fixed but is "the ensemble of social relations." Finally, historical materialism represents the point at which philosophy reestablishes its connections with practice: "The philosophers have only *interpreted* the world, in various ways; the point, however, is to *change* it" (Marx and Engels, 1973, pp. 92–5).

Engels perpetuated Marx's insistence that materialism must be dialectical, particularly in his *Anti-Dühring* of 1878, where he defended the Hegelian aspects of Marxism against attacks from Eugen Dühring. Drawing upon Hegel's *Philosophy of Nature*, he formulated certain dialectical laws of nature: the law that quantitative changes abruptly become qualitative (which Engels also saw happening in terms of economic and political history); the law of interpenetration of opposites, whose tension generates change; and the law of the negation of the negation, which Engels held to apply not only through nature but also in history and philosophy. Marx had already viewed socialism as the negation of capitalist society, which itself had negated feudalism. But, even more than Marx himself, Engels stressed the importance of an organic connection between the natural sciences and philosophy. Hence, in his manuscripts posthumously published as *Dialectics of Nature* in 1925, he saw Hegel as anticipating the development of the nineteenth-century sciences which viewed things as part of a larger process of change and evolution rather than as static and isolated atoms (Engels, 1940b).

In "Ludwig Feuerbach and the End of Classical German Philosophy" (first published in 1886), Engels criticized the vulgar, "metaphysical," and ahistorical materialism of Buchner, Vogt, and Moleschott, who based their thought upon eighteenth-century mechanistic models of natural science which investigated both dead and living things as finished objects. Engels saw the nineteenth-century development of the natural sciences as increasingly confirming the dialectical method and the dialectical operation of nature. He drew particular attention to "three great discoveries": the cell as the basic unit of development; the transformation of energy which showed that forces in nature were mutually transforming manifestations of universal motion; and the Darwinian view of man as the result of a long process of evolution. All of these pointed to the dialectical character of the interconnections of nature, which was also true, on a conscious level, of the history of human society (Marx and Engels, 1968, pp. 597–9, 610–12). While Engels accepted that mind's ultimate origin was matter, he was far from holding that it was reducible to matter. And while he stated that the influences of the external world are reflected in the human brain as feelings, thoughts and volitions, he refers to these as "ideal tendencies" (p. 600), and his writings generally suggest a mutual interaction between the mind and the world.

Engels's ambivalent treatment of Hegel's dialectic is of the utmost importance here: he views Hegel's system as "a materialism idealistically turned upside down," one which regards nature as expressing merely the ALIENATION of the absolute idea, which advances beyond crude materialism in seeking causes wider than individual motives as the driving forces of history but seeking these causes in philosophy rather than in history itself (pp. 596, 613). Historical materialism identifies the actual motives of entire peoples and classes. However, Engels vehemently denies that Hegel can be discarded; rather, his dialectic must be transformed into a materially based science of "the general laws of motion," of both the external world and human thought (pp. 593, 609). Engels does indeed view the materialistic conception of history as scientific; nevertheless, it should be recalled that he is implying a conception of science itself as flexible and dialectical.

In the twentieth century Lenin further developed dialectical materialism to include the notion of *partinost* or partisanship. Developing Marx's and Engels's view that "detached" philosophical speculation was an illusion, Lenin affirmed that socialist commitment was part of the definition of genuine materialism, which was essentially a philosophy of action. In *Materialism and Empirio-Criticism* (1909), designed to counter the spread of "dangerous" idealistic views, Lenin adopted Engels's "theory" of reflection and attacked phenomenalism, which reduced physical entities to complexes of sensation, insisting that science revealed matter as ontologically prior to mind. However, Lenin drew a distinction between his own "philosophical" materialism, which held matter to be independent, and "scientific materialism," whose definition varied according to scientific development. Despite his earlier onslaught against idealism, Lenin's revaluations of Hegel in his *Philosophical Notebooks* (1933) perhaps come nearer to the heart of the German thinker than the analyses of Marx and Engels themselves. Lenin saw, for example, that idealism itself was a reductive category as applied to Hegel. Marxist thinkers have continued to expound and extend Marx's materialism, some in the tradition of LUKÁCS, emphasizing its dialectical nature, while others such as ALTHUSSER have stressed its scientific claims.

The continued success and prestige of the natural sciences in the twentieth century have led to a proliferation of non-Marxist forms of materialism. The attack on theology and metaphysics was continued by logical POSITIVISM, initially centered on the "Vienna Circle" including Moritz Schlick, Otto Neurath, and Rudolf Carnap. Also numbered among its adherents are the early Russell and early WITTGENSTEIN. Working in the tradition of Hume and Comte, these new positivists sought to reshape empiricism in the light of modern logic and mathematics, adopting a criterion of empirical verifiability and thereby dismissing "metaphysical" claims as meaningless. The philosopher's prime concern, so they claimed, was to clarify the meanings of statements.

This concern for linguistic clarity centrally motivated Wittgenstein's friend Gilbert Ryle, who explored analytical behaviorism which was materialistic inasmuch as it displaced analysis from psychology itself to the behavior expressing it. Some commentators have viewed Wittgenstein also as a behaviorist. But perhaps what lies at the core of his "materialism," if indeed the term is applicable, is the idea that language itself is social and material, and while its relation with the world is determined by convention rather than any absolute correspondence, skepticism toward the reality of the external world is preempted by the unavoidably social character of the language which must articulate it.

Even FREUD's work might be placed in a materialist tradition in so far as it excludes metaphysical explanations of the mind and world, seeking instead to account for psychological traits by tracing their causes to material conditions. The materialism of much modern literary and CULTURAL THEORY has in fact been initiated from Freudian and Marxist insights: a unifying characteristic of the varieties of FEMINIST CRITICISM is their insistence on the material conditions of GENDER relations, including the treatment of the female body itself, as explanatory vehicles. Jacques DERRIDA, the initiator of DECONSTRUCTION, has centralized the Hegelian notion of difference in his critique of Western metaphysics: to the extent that he attempts to expose the reduction of "difference" by various forms of transcendentalism, Derrida might be viewed as a materialist. The so-called NEW HISTORICISM, stemming partly from FOUCAULT, also attempts to view given texts as participants of a broader cultural history. The long history of materialism suggests the breadth of its application. In general it might be viewed as a series of attempts to harmonize with the findings of contemporary science, to reject transcendent explanations of the world, to view language as a social practice, and to paint a moral, political, and cosmological picture which contains humanity's observable practice and the world's observable features at its center.

Reading
Descartes, R. 1951 (*1960*): *Meditations.*
Engels, F. 1940a: *On Historical Materialism.*
Hobbes, T. 1991: *Leviathan.*
Lange, F.A. 1974: *The History of Materialism.*
Locke, J. 1964 (*1975*): *An Essay Concerning Human Understanding.*
Lucretius 1951 (*1986*): *On the Nature of the Universe.*
Russell, B. 1946: *Is Materialism Bankrupt? Mind and Matter in Modern Science.*
Wittgenstein, L. 1958 (*1969*): *Philosophical Investigations.*
M.A.R. HABIB

materialism, cultural   *See* CULTURAL MATERIALISM

Mauss, Marcel   (1872–1950)   French sociologist and anthropologist. He was the nephew and close supporter of the great sociologist Emile DURKHEIM, and, like him, born into a rabbinic family. Nevertheless, he was not religious. He studied under his uncle at the University of Bordeaux and did brilliantly. Subsequently he went to Paris to study ancient languages and anthropology. In 1901 he was Director of Studies at the Ecole Pratique des Hautes Etudes in the history of religion of indigenous people, and in 1925 he helped to found and became joint director of the Institut d'Ethnologie at the University of Paris. He was professor at the Collège de France from 1931 to 1939 and retired in 1940.

Durkheim was the leader of a gifted group of scholars that included Mauss. The primary organ for their writing was the *Année Sociologique*, a journal begun by Durkheim in 1898. The group was decimated by the 1914–18 war and Durkheim died in 1917. Mauss was his literary executor and the leadership of the school also fell to him. He twice tried to revive the *Année Sociologique* in the 1920s and again in the 1930s, without any great success. He suffered during the Nazi occupation of Paris and survived, but the experience left him unable to work.

Mauss influenced not only ethnographers but also linguists, psychologists, historians of religion, and others in the social and human sciences. His writings are fragmented and scattered; none appeared as a book until the publication of a collection of essays and lectures in 1950. His early works were mostly done in collaboration with Durkheim or others. His influence came less from his published works than from the mediation of colleagues and followers. His research brought together ethnology and psychology, holding that the latter was dependent on and limited by cultural factors. He pioneered some of the concerns of American anthropologists such as Ruth Benedict and Margaret MEAD on the effects of cultural differences in child rearing, and opened up the new field of the cross-cultural study of body techniques to show that behavior is hardly ever innate but learned and determined by social norms.

Mauss based his theories on detailed comparative analysis of existing anthropological data, since he never did fieldwork. His most famous and influential publication, *The Gift*, is generally held to be the founding work of economic anthropology, profoundly influencing not only economic anthropologists but also LÉVI-STRAUSS and the structuralist school. It introduced the notion of the *total social fact* rather than the institution as the subject for investigation in sociology. Mauss saw the gift as a total social phenomenon with legal, economic, political, religious, and other dimensions. He strove to dispel the idea current in his time that small-scale economies produced only for subsistence rather than for exchange, showing that surplus is everywhere produced, though the motives for exchange may be different from those in our own society. He showed that in what he termed "gift economies" exchange was motivated by the obligation to give, to accept gifts, and to return them.

Reading
Lévi-Strauss, Claude 1950 (*1987*): *Introduction to the Work of Marcel Mauss.*
Mauss, Marcel, and Hubert, H. 1902–3 (*1972*): *A General Theory of Magic.*
——1923–4 (*1990*): *The Gift: The Form and Reason for Exchange in Archaic Societies.*
——1924 (*1979*): *Sociology and Psychology.*
JANET MACGAFFEY

Mead, Margaret (1901–76) North American anthropologist. Mead studied psychology at Barnard College, then began graduate studies in anthropology at Columbia University in 1923 under Franz Boas. In the 1920s she conducted fieldwork in Samoa and New Guinea to learn about "the kind of social arrangements that make easy transition to adulthood possible." In 1928 she was appointed assistant curator of ethnology at the American Museum of Natural History in New York, which remained her base for most of her professional life. In the 1930s her study (with Gregory Bateson) of the cultural context of schizophrenia in Bali helped to introduce the extensive use of film and photographic techniques in ethnography. During the 1939–45 war Mead used anthropology to assist the Allied war effort in various ways. In 1947 Mead joined the anthropology department at Columbia University, and became an increasingly popular public lecturer. In the late 1950s she assisted international agencies and the United Nations in dealing with issues of racism and postcolonial transition, and during the 1960s she began writing and lecturing about the cultural causes of unrest among youth, and about GENDER and the role of women in North American society.

A founder of culture and personality studies, Mead argued that cultural traditions and customs, especially in socialization, are a central force in shaping both individual and group personality and behavior, and that human improvement means understanding and changing the cultural context in which people live. Perhaps more than any other intellectual in the twentieth century, she influenced the popular understanding of the importance of the cultural context in issues such as RACE, sexuality/gender, and aggression.

See also BOAS, FRANZ.

Reading
Bateson, Mary Catherine 1984 (*1988*): *With a Daughter's Eye: A Memoir of Margaret Mead and Gregory Bateson.*
Mead, Margaret 1928: *Coming of Age in Samoa: A Psychological Study of Primitive Youth for Western Civilization.*
——1930: *Growing Up in New Guinea: A Comparative Study of Primitive Education.*
——1935: *Sex and Temperament in Three Primitive Societies.*
——1949: *Male and Female: A Study of the Sexes in a Changing World.*
——1964: *Anthropology, a Human Science: Selected Papers, 1939–1960.*
——1970: *Culture and Commitment: A Study of the Generation Gap.*
——1972 (*1975*): *Blackberry Winter: My Early Years.*
——1977: *Letters from the Field: 1925–1975.*
JAMES PHILLIPS

mediation A key term of dialectical logic, denoting the process by which things come to be what they are through their relations to other things, the logical expression of the universal interconnectedness of phenomena. According to HEGEL, all knowledge is a movement from the immediate to the mediate, culminating in the "absolute" knowledge of the philosophical system in which the STRUCTURE of reality is expounded as a whole.

PETER OSBORNE

Merleau-Ponty, Maurice (1908–61) French philosopher and man of letters. Merleau-Ponty studied at the Ecole Normale Supérieure in Paris, and subsequently taught at various *lycées*, the Ecole Normale, the Sorbonne, and the Collège de France. Following the 1939–45 war he served as an editor, together with Jean-Paul SARTRE and Simone de BEAUVOIR, of *Les Temps Modernes*.

Throughout his philosophical writings, Merleau-Ponty worked to critique and provide an alternative to the Cartesian presuppositions of philosophical idealism. According to Merleau-Ponty, by treating the world as a complex object of knowledge which is exhaustively reducible to a set of correlates of acts of conceptualization, critical idealism presents us with a model of reality which is logically systematic but which fails to acknowledge the underlying discontinuities between consciousness and the world. Against Descartes, who had argued that the mind is capable of establishing absolute certainty about its own nature as well as about the essential nature of the material world, Merleau-Ponty seeks to underscore the fundamental ambiguities and discontinuities of existence where the spirit of Cartesianism had sought to transcend them. Where Descartes and idealism argued for a theory of consciousness in terms of a detached, disembodied, contemplative knower, Merleau-Ponty argues for a notion of "flesh," according to which consciousness is inelectuably incarnate in the midst of the world. For Merleau-Ponty the Cartesian presupposition that the individual self is independent and self-sufficient fundamentally distorts the phenomena of relating oneself to others and to the world. In this respect Merleau-Ponty's thought owes a significant debt to the early HEIDEGGER's view of human existence as always already situated in the midst of a social world; but Merleau-Ponty goes unmistakably beyond Heidegger in insisting that consciousness must be thought as embodied.

Fundamental to Merleau-Ponty's rethinking of human experience is his dual appropriation of empirical psychology and PHENOMENOLOGY. In each case the appropriation entails a critique of the tradition. In the case of empirical psychology, Merleau-Ponty criticizes the stimulus–response model of perception for assuming that things and events in the world have an objective reality in virtue of which they can affect us and in virtue of which they can be recognized to be distinct from us as well as from one another. Instead he opts for a version of Gestalt theory, invoking its figure-ground conception of perceptual wholes while rejecting the naturalistic assumption of thinkers like Wolfgang Köhler that perceptual complexes are determined by biological states. In addition, Merleau-Ponty contributes to Gestalt theory the threefold distinction between "syncretic," "amovable," and "symbolic" forms, which correspond roughly to instinctive behavior which is not the product of learning, changeable forms which are independent of the objects and are learnable (for example, learning that a given object can be used in different ways), and cultural objects whose meaning is variable and goes beyond use-relations. In addition, he treats language itself

as a Gestalt which interacts with our other bodily fields or horizons in constituting a coherent experience of the world.

The phenomenological orientation of Merleau-Ponty's transformation of Gestalt theory is evident in his rejection of the objective characterization of space in rationalism (for example, Descartes's *res extensa*) and his insistence that we must conceive of space as "lived," that is, that theorizing about space (and *mutatis mutandis*, for phenomena like time) must be guided by the concrete phenomena of actual spatial comportment. Merleau-Ponty's critique of the phenomenological tradition is most evident in his critique of Husserl's commitment to the primacy of the individual knower (or transcendental ego) and the primacy of intentionality as the basic form of this ego's experience; it is also evident in his rethinking of Heideggerian DASEIN in terms of the lived body.

In rejecting traditional accounts of experience in favor of a Gestalt-based approach, Merleau-Ponty seeks to reassess the fundamental interrelationship between self and world. Where the tradition seeks to analyze the self as a being which is independent of the world and whose most fundamental mode of relating to the world is detached cognition, Merleau-Ponty's phenomenological orientation leads him to take lived experience as the starting point in characterizing self and world. Whereas in the traditional Cartesian view the body is considered to be a subordinate and inessential dimension of human existence, for Merleau-Ponty the body is neither inessential nor a mere object; for him the body is an irreducible lived perceptual horizon which is absolutely fundamental to our encounter with the world. Much of Merleau-Ponty's work is devoted to a detailed characterization of this perceptual encounter with the world, which stands in stark contrast to traditional attempts to proceed from sense data or essences. Where for Cartesian thinkers the problem of experience is one of establishing a connection between an autonomous self and an objective world, for Merleau-Ponty the problem is one of analyzing the primordial encounter between the two; for Merleau-Ponty this primordial encounter is the necessary foundation upon which traditional conceptual abstractions like "self," "world," "essence," and "sense datum" can be made in the first place.

This reversal of traditional dualistic accounts of experience leads Merleau-Ponty to recognize a fundamental relationship between the ways in which the world is disclosed in perception and in ART. In his writings on art, Merleau-Ponty focuses primarily on painting and argues for a reversal of the traditional concept of art as mimesis. Where the tradition, following Plato, seeks to characterize art as imitation of a precedent and independent natural world, Merleau-Ponty argues that self and world mutually condition each other in such a way that nature can be said to imitate art. In "Eye and mind" (1964a) he approvingly cites the sculptor Giacometti's statement that authentic art works have the power to influence fundamentally the ways in which we see and experience the world: in this regard Merleau-Ponty's assessment of the place of art in human experience shares basic affinities with Heidegger's position in "The origin of the work of art."

In his political writings Merleau-Ponty develops an ambivalent form of MARXISM which seeks to inscribe human subjectivity into history. In *Humanism and Terror* (1947) he acknowledges the power of concrete material relations to shape and condition human consciousness, and he criticizes Soviet Marxism for its tendencies toward terror and deception, arguing for a distinction between revolution and terror as acceptable and unacceptable forms of violence respectively. Later, in *Adventures of the Dialectic* (1955), Merleau-Ponty continues to endorse a version of Marxist historicism and dialectic; but he rejects Marxism's claim to exclusivity as the agent of historically legitimate social change, and he advances the idea of a "noncommunist left" as the proper vehicle for revolution.

Reading
Heidsieck, François 1971: *L'Ontologie de Merleau-Ponty.*
Hyppolite, Jean 1963: *Sens et existence dans la philosophie de Maurice Merleau-Ponty.*
Merleau-Ponty, Maurice 1955 (1973): *Adventures of the Dialectic.*
—— 1964a (*1964*): "Eye and mind."
—— 1947 (*1969*): *Humanism and Terror.*
—— 1942 (*1962*): *The Phenomenology of Perception.*
—— 1942 (*1963*): *The Structure of Behavior.*
—— 1964 (*1968*): *The Visible and the Invisible.*
Waelhense, Alphonse de 1951: *Une Philosophie de l'ambiguité: L'existentialisme de Maurice Merleau-Ponty.*
GARY STEINER

metalanguage Language about language: a technical term in linguistics for a "second order" terminology which describes a "first order" language. Although the "first order" language being discussed

may use the same national language as the "second order" metalanguage, the difference between the two is defined by the way in which the metalanguage uses specific concepts. Accordingly, a metalanguage will include certain terms. An example would be the way in which structural linguistics uses expressions such as "structure," "oppositions," and so on. In structuralist theories, especially that of Roman JAKOBSON, metalanguage is a critical language which constitutes a scientifically objective analytical method. In addition, he sees it as a fundamental part of the process of language acquisition. Thus, when learning its first language, a child begins by making noises which have no function other than to suggest an intention to communicate: the sounds carry no lexical items that are recognizably meaningful. As the child grows, the metalinguistic operation continues to be of utmost importance, since it guides how the child thinks about language. Jakobson defines aphasia as the loss of this basic metalinguistic operation. Jakobson's theory therefore concentrates on the way in which metalinguistic operations are carried out in relation to the "first order" language. He extends his analysis to the metalinguistics of paraphrase and synonymy, and then to translations between languages, and even the relations between different SIGN systems.

However, Roland BARTHES notes that it is possible for a metalanguage to have a metalanguage of its own, in a potentially infinite series. Thus a critic may use a metalanguage to write about a literary TEXT, and another critic may comment on the first critic, and so on. It is in this sense, as in others, that Barthes can be seen to be moving into POSTSTRUCTURALISM.

Metalanguage becomes a term used in SEMIOTICS in a shift similar to that employed by Barthes. In semiotic theory, a metalanguage is itself a sign system which refers to another sign system: the technical term for this referential relationship is "denotation." This is a development of the structuralist use of metalanguage, with the crucial distinction being that a metalanguage itself constitutes a sign system. Thus critical DISCOURSE is metalinguistic in its relation to literary texts, but the two constitute separate sign systems. Moreover, it is the relation between the two which produces the "meaning" of the text, rather than some inherent qualities in the text in and of itself. The use of a metalanguage by a semiotician therefore opens a text up to elements which structuralism would refuse to consider by denoting them as being outside the text. The implication of this theoretical position is that it should be possible for critical metalanguage to uncover the ways in which the text relates to other sign systems. In this way semiotics attempts to deal with topics such as context and the moments of historical production and later reading, which were very problematical for STRUCTURALISM.

Reading
Culler, Jonathan 1975 (*1989*): *Structuralist Poetics*.
Hawkes, Terence 1977: *Structuralism and Semiotics*.
Jakobson, Roman 1990a: *On Language*.
Lotman, Yury 1977: *Analysis of the Poetic Text*.

PAUL INNES

metaphor and metonymy Metaphor substitutes one term for another: metonymy substitutes an element of a term for the term itself. Following the work of Ferdinand de SAUSSURE, Roman JAKOBSON theorized that a relation of BINARY OPPOSITION between the two underpins the production of literary language. Beginning with an essay on aphasia, he concluded that metaphor was based upon similarity, metonymy upon contiguity. He went on to state that metaphor is the fundamental figure used in POETRY, while metonymy is crucial to the operations of prose, although the tension between the two does produce instances of the use of the opposing element. He reached the position that they are in fact the primary functions underlying the operation of language.

Theories of the relation between metaphor and metonymy have also been produced in PSYCHO-ANALYSIS AND PSYCHOANALYTICAL CRITICISM. The crucial terms "condensation" and "displacement" as they are used in psychoanalytical theory are the equivalent of Jakobson's binary opposition. The continual condensation and displacement of images in dreams accord metaphor and metonymy a similar importance. Jacques LACAN picks up on this equivalence, theorizing that since the UNCONSCIOUS operates in accordance with the relations between metaphor and metonymy, it is in fact structured like a language.

Reading
Jakobson, Roman 1990a: *On Language*.
Lacan, Jacques 1968: *The Language of the Self: The Function of Language in Psychoanalysis*.

PAUL INNES

Mies van der Rohe, Ludwig (1886–1969) German/American architect. Many of the factors that contribute to the development of modern architecture converge in the work of Mies – including, for example, the prairie-style houses of Frank Lloyd Wright, the "neoclassical" factories of Peter Behrens, the naked brick buildings of Hendrick Petrus Berlage, and the building techniques believed to be appropriate to and expressive of the new materials of reinforced concrete, steel, and glass – and are distilled by the mind and imagination of Mies into the most pure, and most imitated, form of the INTERNATIONAL STYLE of modern architecture. Mies's project for an office building, Friedrichstrasse, Berlin, 1921, which is the earliest proposed example of a skyscraper enclosed entirely in glass, exhibits the "skin-and-bones" construction and aspect that is a fundamental aspect of Mies's work. The German Pavilion for the International Exposition, Barcelona, Spain, 1929, reveals the simple elegance (the "less is more") of Mies's architecture, which is expressed also in Mies's flawless "Barcelona" chair that is integrated into the space of the Pavilion like a fine piece of minimal sculpture.

In 1938, after realizing (perhaps belatedly) that his apolitical attitude about architecture did not fit into the politics of Nazi Germany, Mies emigrated to the United States to become the director, and architect of the new campus, of the Illinois Institute of Technology in Chicago. In the Farnsworth House, Plano, Illinois, 1946–50, Mies made even more out of less, enriching and condensing the enclosing space of this small house into a refined rectangular temple reduced to a pristine statement of floor plate, supporting columns, roof plane, and glass curtain walls. Mies's Seagram building, New York, 1958, is the projected Berlin glass skyscraper project of nearly three decades earlier brought into existence, its crisp and bold structure and surface now seeming to symbolize corporate efficacy and authority. Philip Johnson, who contributed to the design of the Seagram building, is the most unabashed admirer of Mies. Johnson's own house, the so-called Glass House, New Canaan, Connecticut, 1949, is a frank homage to the German Pavilion and the Farnsworth House, and a glass display case for enshrining Mies's "Barcelona" furniture.

Johnson's admiration for Mies's work is offset by Robert VENTURI's understanding of the Miesian aesthetic – where Johnson sees the exquisite clarity of the architecture of Mies, Venturi finds forced simplicity. For Venturi, the reductive and exclusionary character of Mies's work results in an architecture which ignores the clutter that is a necessary part of human experience. So while the spaces made by Mies may be ideally proportioned, to Venturi they are unyielding and unable to "survive the cigarette machine." The essence of Mies's poetic vision of architecture is expressed in his phrase "less is more"; Venturi's view of Mies, and his pragmatic approach to architecture, is summarized in his comment that "more is not less"; both are more or less correct.

Reading
Johnson, Philip 1947 (*1978*): *Mies van der Rohe.*
Venturi, Robert 1966: *Complexity and Contradiction in Architecture.*

GERALD EAGER

Millett, Kate (1934–) US feminist literary critic. Kate Millett's controversial study of literary misogyny, *Sexual Politics* (1970), earns her a prominent place in the history of FEMINIST CRITICISM. *Sexual Politics* was the first major American study of sexism in literature; it inaugurated that mode of inquiry that would later be named "the feminist critique": the identification and analysis of derogatory and stereotyped representations of women in male-authored TEXTS, and the scrutiny of those processes by which sexist HEGEMONY is created in academia (notably, the exclusion of female-authored texts from the CANON of literary studies and the valorization of sexist interpretative strategies). Although Toril Moi has emphasized that Millett's work is not theoretically rigorous in any sense of the term recognizable today, it does share several important assumptions with the new CULTURAL STUDIES: that a continuity exists between literary and nonliterary texts (such as pornography and televised texts), and that literature is a crucial site for the production of IDEOLOGY. Millett examined the intimate relationships between "images of women" in literature, ideologies of GENDER, and the real lives of women, particularly such phenomena as the daily rape, sexual harassment, and abuse of women. *Sexual Politics* launched a forceful denunciation of FREUDian psychology as it was then commonly applied to literature in the United States. Although defenders of the status quo used Millett's bisexuality, bitter sarcasm, and angry tone to discredit her, D.H. Lawrence, Henry Miller, Norman Mailer, and Jean Genet will never be read in quite the same way; indeed, only Lawrence's reputation as a "great" artist has survived in the

wake of Millett's rereading. Feminist critics can generally be faulted for neglecting to preserve their own early history: few appreciative recent critical studies of *Sexual Politics* exist (notable exceptions are Humm and Tong). A serious, collective reevaluation of the first decade of feminist criticism, including *Sexual Politics*, is long overdue.

Reading
Humm, Maggie 1986: *Feminist Criticism: Women as Contemporary Critics.*
Millett, Kate 1970: *Sexual Politics.*
Moi, Toril 1985: *Sexual/Textual Politics: Feminist Literary Theory.*
Tong, Rosemarie 1989: *Feminist Thought: A Comprehensive Introduction.*

GLYNIS CARR

mirror-stage   The theory of the mirror-stage was the first major contribution to psychoanalytic thought to be made by Jacques LACAN, and it remains the cornerstone of his account of the construction of subjectivity, as well as his opposition to ego psychology. The mirror-stage was originally described in a paper read to the Marienbad Conference of the International Psychoanalytic Association in 1936, but Lacan's findings were not published until after the 1939–45 war (Lacan, 1948 and 1949). Lacan's description of the mirror-stage draws on two main sources: the psychological description of a child's reactions when faced with its reflection in a mirror, supplied by Henri Wallon in his work on the origins of character (see Wallon, 1984), and the contrasting findings of primate ethology, which demonstrates that young chimpanzees, unlike children, are indifferent to the sight of their mirror-reflection.

This crucial stage in human development occurs between the ages of 6 and 18 months. At this age, the child is still virtually helpless and has yet to coordinate its motor functions. Lacan attributes this to the prematurity of birth in human beings. The reflection seen in the mirror (or equivalent) gives the child an image of the physical and motor unity it will achieve, and is therefore greeted with jubilation. The young child intellectually anticipates and identifies with the image of what it will become, and the basis is thus laid for later identifications. Identification is to be understood in the psychoanalytic sense of the internal transformation that occurs when the subject assumes an image.

Although the mirror-stage is a crucial developmental stage, it also represents a profound AL-IENATION as the child identifies with something that is, by definition, IMAGINARY and OTHER. It thus implies a process of simultaneous recognition and misrecognition. From the outset, the child identifies with an ideal image which provides the matrix for the ego, viewed by Lacan as an imaginary construct in which the SUBJECT is alienated. The ego is always an alter ego marked by an aggressive relativity and therefore cannot be equated with the subject. The mirror-stage is responsible for the subsequent appearance of the threatening and regressive fantasy of what Lacan calls the "body-in-pieces," in which anxiety about fragmentation or disintegration comes to the fore.

The mirror-stage and its dialectic of recognition and misrecognition have specific effects at the interpersonal level, which dominate the child's behavior in the presence of other children. Lacan uses the term transitivism to describe the characteristic combination of identification and aggression. The child who strikes another claims to have been struck; the child who sees another fall bursts into tears. The foundations are thus laid for the identification of slave with master, of seducer with seduced.

Reading
Lacan, Jacques 1948: "Aggressivity in psychoanalysis."
——1949: "The mirror-stage as formative of the function of the I."
Wallon, Henri 1984: *The World of Henri Wallon.*

DAVID MACEY

misreading A term in literary theory, used especially by Harold BLOOM to refer to the primary object of reading, which is not a TEXT but the relationship between texts. Because "the interpretation of a poem necessarily is always interpretation of that poem's interpretation of other poems" (Bloom, 1975, p. 75), one of the first tasks of reading is to determine how the poem being read responds to its precursor(s). If the poem is itself the product of a strong reading, the poet will have succeeded in managing the ANXIETY OF INFLUENCE produced by reading other strong poets. In order to open imaginative free space for themselves in which to make new poems, poets deal with their precursors by acts of interpretative reduction, willful misprision, or productive misreading. In *Kabbalah and Criticism* Bloom acknowledges the precursor of his theory of misreading, which is Gershom

Scholem's work on Kabbalah, a gnostic tradition of reading that is now belatedly recoverable only by antithetical criticism. Misreading is not simply misunderstanding a poem. It is rather the consequence of responding fully to its intimidating power.

Reading
Bloom, Harold 1973: *The Anxiety of Influence: A Theory of Poetry.*
——1975: *Kabbalah and Criticism.*
de Bolla, Peter 1988: *Harold Bloom: Towards Historical Rhetorics.*

MICHAEL PAYNE

Mitchell, Juliet (1940–) British psychoanalyst. *Psychoanalysis and Feminism* (1974) attempted to refute the feminist critique of FREUD (see de BEAUVOIR, FRIEDAN, and GREER), claiming that Freud provided an analysis *of*, rather than a blueprint *for*, patriarchal society. In particular, Mitchell defends Freud from the charge of biological determinism, arguing that he was concerned with the transformation between mental life and biology as it is influenced by CULTURE and institutions. For Mitchell, PSYCHOANALYSIS "established the framework within which the whole question of female sexuality can be understood" (1966, p. 252) as it traces the relations between generality and particularity; not describing what a woman is, but how she comes into being. She thus connects an understanding of the laws of the UNCONSCIOUS with an understanding of the political and economic ideologies which oppress women.

Reading
Mitchell, Juliet 1966 (*1984*): *The Longest Revolution: On Feminism, Literature, and Psychoanalysis.*
——1974: *Psychoanalysis and Feminism.*

DANIELLE CLARKE

modernity The quality, experience, or period of the "modern." The idea of modernity highlights the novelty of the present as a break or rupture with the past, opening out into a rapidly approaching and uncertain future. In its broadest sense, it is associated with the ideas of *innovation*, *progress*, and *fashion*, and counterposed to the ideas of *antiquity*, the *classical*, and tradition. As a way of differentiating the most "up-to-date" elements of the present from those which establish a continuity with the past, modernity has been attributed as many properties over the years as there have been competing definitions of the historical present. In its most general form, it is best understood as a structure of historical time consciousness.

The term "modernity" (*modernité*) can be traced back to Baudelaire's essay on the French painter Constantin Guys, "The painter of modern life" (Baudelaire, 1845). It was introduced there to refer to "whatever contemporary fashion may contain of poetry within history," and defined as "the ephemeral, the fugitive, the contingent," a "distillation of the eternal from the transitory." This nicely captures the Janus face of modernity as a particular experience of change, the intensity of which pushes it to the point of reversal. In Walter BENJAMIN's terms (Benjamin, 1938/9), once it is abstracted from any particular content, "the new" is "always-ever-the-same." As such, modernity may be said to repress duration (the experience of temporal continuity) in favor of a series of more or less instantaneous "shocks," fragmenting subjectivity and producing a crisis in narrative forms of representation.

"Modernity" is at base a category of AESTHETICS, in the most general sense of denoting a particular experience of time. Yet its historical dimension – the fact that this way of experiencing time emerges only at a particular historical moment, within particular kinds of society – ties it closely to the sociological study of cultural forms.

As a sociological concept, modernity is primarily associated with industrialization, secularization, bureaucracy, and the CITY. Different theorists offer competing interpretations of which social processes are most important to the experience of "the modern," but as a discipline, sociology is unified by the restriction of its subject matter to what it defines as "modern" societies. ("Premodern" societies fall under the aegis of either anthropology or history.)

For DURKHEIM it is the move from "mechanical" to "organic" forms of solidarity, consequent upon the increasing division of labor, which is the sociological key to modern life. In Tonnies this is conceived as a move from the interpersonal ties of community (*Gemeinschaft*) to the anonymous individuality of "society" (*Gesellschaft*). In Max WEBER it appears as a generalized process of rationalization and disenchantment, whereas in Simmel it is the objectified form of modern CULTURE, exemplified by money, which lies at the heart of the alienated subjectivity of modern life. For MARX on the other hand, modernity, with its constant renewal of the impulse toward change, is an effect of the

dynamics of capital accumulation. Marx distinguishes himself from the mainstream of academic sociology by periodizing history according to "modes of production," rather than in terms of a simple modern/premodern binary.

The difficulty with the "modern" as a category of historical periodization is that its meaning changes relative to the time (and place) of the classification. We may distinguish five main stages in the development of the idea since its emergence within Western culture at around the time of the collapse of the Roman Empire in the fifth century AD.

1. To begin with, the Latin term *modernus* (derived from *modo*, meaning recently) was used to replace the cyclical opposition of "old and new" characteristic of pagan antiquity with a sense of the present as an irreversible break with the past. It was this sense of the present as "new" which was the basis for the conflicts between ancients and moderns which punctuated the Middle Ages from the second half of the twelfth century to the beginnings of the Renaissance.

2. The first major semantic shift took place with the development of the consciousness of a new age in Europe in the course of the fifteenth century. This was initially registered by the emergence of the terms "Renaissance" and "Reformation" denoting the threshold of a new (unnamed) period; by the designation of the preceding epoch, now taken to be definitively over, as the "Middle Ages"; and by the fixing of the term Antiquity to denote the pagan culture of ancient Greece and Rome. In the process, a new relationship between the ancient and the modern was established at the expense of the Middle Ages, since the Renaissance gave precedence to the ancient over all other cultures. At this stage the modern was opposed to the medieval, rather than to the ancient, and it had a right to preference only in so far as it imitated the ancient.

3. In a third stage, running through the sixteenth to the end of the seventeenth century, the terms Renaissance and Reformation became descriptive of now completed historical periods. This called for a term denoting the new period as a whole which followed the Middle Ages. It was at this point that the connotation of novelty in the term *modernus*, meaning "of today" as opposed to "of yesterday" – what is over, finished, or historically surpassed – was revived. The Renaissance had attempted to replace the

authority of the Church with the authority of the ancients. It was the ancients themselves who now came under attack from the standpoint of the present in the famous Quarrel of the Ancients and the Moderns, or the "Battle of the Books" as it came to be known.

4. It was during a fourth phase, the ENLIGHTEN-MENT and its aftermath, that this sense of a qualitative newness about the times, of their being completely other and better than what had gone before, was consolidated. Two things made this possible: a reorientation towards the future consequent upon Christian eschatology's shedding of its expectation of the imminent arrival of doomsday, and the opening up of new horizons of expectation by the advance of the sciences, and the growing consciousness of the "New World" and its peoples. The abstract temporality of "the new" took on an epochal significance, since it could now be extrapolated into an otherwise empty future, without end, and hence without limit. The distinctive structure of modernity as a form of historical time consciousness may thus be seen to derive from a combination of the Christian conception of time as irreversible with criticism of its corresponding concept of eternity.

These developments culminated at the end of the eighteenth century, in the context of the acceleration of historical experience precipitated by the Industrial and French Revolutions, in the transformation of a series of historical terms. "Revolution," "progress," "development," "crisis," *Zeitgeist*, "epoch," and "history" itself all acquired new temporal determinations at this time. As Koselleck (1979) puts it: "Time is no longer the medium in which all histories take place; it gains an historical quality . . . history no longer occurs in, but through, time. Time becomes a dynamic and historical force in its own right." It is because of the qualitative transformation in the temporal matrix of historical terms which occurs at this time that "modernity" in the full historical sense of the term is generally taken to begin here. The modern is no longer simply opposed to either the ancient or the medieval periods, but more generally to "tradition."

It is this full sense of modernity, opening up a new period by virtue of the quality of its temporality, which is registered in the mid-nineteenth century in Baudelaire's definition,

cited above. The logic of the new, fashion, and aesthetic modernism may thus be understood as the result of an aestheticization of "modernity" as a form of historical consciousness and its transformation into a general model of social experience.

5. Finally, to take us up to the present, we must add a fifth stage in which the peculiar and paradoxical abstractness of the temporality of modernity is at once problematized and affirmed. This is the stage after the 1939–45 war, during which, as Raymond Williams (1989) has put it, "'modern' shifts its reference from 'now' to 'just now' or even 'then,' and for some time has been a designation always going into the past with which 'contemporary' may be contrasted for its presentness." "Modernity," fixed now as a discrete historical period within its own temporal scheme, hardens into a name and is left stranded in the past. The Quarrel of the Ancients and the Moderns is replaced with a Quarrel of the Moderns and the Contemporaries. The Contemporaries become Postmoderns.

To become postmodern, however, in this sense at least, is simply to remain modern, to keep in step with the times. "What, then, is the postmodern?" Lyotard (1982) asks. "Undoubtedly part of the modern. A work can [*now*] only be modern if it is first postmodern. Postmodernism . . . is not modernism at its end but in the nascent state, and this state is constant."

"Modernity" thus plays a dual role as a category of historical periodization: it designates the contemporaneity of an epoch to the time of its classification, but it registers this contemporaneity in terms of a qualitatively new, self-transcending temporality which has the simultaneous effect of distancing the present from even that most recent past with which it is thus identified. It is this paradoxical doubling or inherently dialectical quality which makes "modernity" both so irresistible and so problematic a category. It is achieved by the abstraction of the logical structure of the process of change from its concrete historical determinants.

The temporal matrix thus produced has three main characteristics:

(i)   exclusive valorization of the historical present over the past as its negation and transcendence, and the standpoint from which to periodize and understand history as a whole;

(ii) openness toward an indeterminate future characterized only by its prospective transcendence of the historical present and its relegation of this present to a future past;

(iii) a tendential elimination of the historical present itself as the vanishing point of a perpetual transition between a constantly changing past and an as yet indeterminate future.

"Modernity," then, has no fixed, objective referent: "It has only a subject, of which it is full" (Meschonnic, 1992). It is the product, in the instance of each utterance, of an act of historical self-definition through identification and projection which transcends the order of chronology in the construction of a meaningful present. It is this sense of modernity as a ceaselessly renewed act of historical self-definition and projection which underlies HABERMAS's reformulation of the idea of modernity as an "incomplete project" (Habermas, 1980). However, whereas the content of such acts of self-definition is always relative to the historical location and projects of the actors concerned, both Habermas and his "postmodern" opponents tend to fix the meaning of "modernity" through its historical association with the Enlightenment. For them, "modernity" is equivalent to the incomplete project of enlightenment.

This has the merit of focusing debate onto a specific social project, but it obscures the structure of the concept of modernity, repressing its fluidity, formality, and paradoxical dynamics. In this respect, it reflects the wider historical process of colonialism during which a specific (European) present was imposed as the measure of social progress on a global scale. It is within the framework of this kind of definition of the "modern" that the term "*modernization*" came to be used in the United States after the 1939–45 war to refer to a form of social and economic "development" in Third World countries, modeled on a particular version of the history of capitalism in the West. Similarly restricted definitions of "modernity" can be seen at work in economic debates about the future of Eastern Europe after the fall of Communism, and in cultural debates about religious "fundamentalism."

What these debates illustrate is, first, that the concept of modernity remains the privileged site for the articulation of competing views about the relationship of past, present, and future; and second, that it is bound up, inextricably, with the contradictory cultural legacy of European colonialism. For if modernity is primarily a *temporal* concept, it none the less became possible in its fully developed form only on the basis of certain *spatial* preconditions: namely the unification of the globe through colonial navigation (allowing for the thought of "history" as a whole) and the hierarchical distinction of European from non-European cultures (in which a historical differential could be introduced *within* the present).

As the cultural constitution of Western societies is transformed (especially by immigration) and their economic HEGEMONY is challenged – throwing the very concept of "the West" into crisis – the prospect is opened up of new and more "hybrid" definitions of modernity within the terms of its PARADIGMatic temporal form: "postcolonial contra-modernities" (Bhabha, 1991) and "countercultures of modernity" (Gilroy, 1993), bearing the promise of a new historicity.

Reading
Berman, Marshall 1982 (*1983*): *All That is Solid Melts Into Air: The Experience of Modernity.*
Blumenberg, Hans 1983: *The Legitimacy of the Modern Age.*
Calinescu, Matei 1987: *Five Faces of Modernity: Modernism, Avant-Garde, Decadence, Kitsch, Postmodernism.*
Frisby, David 1985: *Fragments of Modernity: Theories of Modernity in the Work of Simmel, Kracauer and Benjamin.*
Gilroy, Paul 1993: *The Black Atlantic: Modernity and Double Consciousness.*
Habermas, Jürgen 1980 (*1985*): "Modernity – an incomplete project."
——1985 (*1987*): *The Philosophical Discourse of Modernity.*
Hall, Stuart, ed. 1992: *Understanding Modern Societies: An Introduction.*
PETER OSBORNE

moral criticism The term "moral criticism" has sometimes been applied to a tendency in modern anglophone LITERARY CRITICISM since ARNOLD, and particularly to the positions of such critics as F.R. LEAVIS and Lionel TRILLING. Distinguishing these critical positions from various kinds of FORMALISM, it indicates the prominence of moral and ethical vocabularies in their terms of judgment: maturity, sincerity, honesty, sensitivity, or courage become important criteria in the valuation of literary and other works. From a strict formalist standpoint, such terminology betrays habits of reading that are imperfectly emancipated from the INTENTIONAL FALLACY in their apparent confounding of textual with authorial characteristics. And although moral criticism is rarely as theoretically naive as its opponents claim, it encounters genuine problems of this kind in its attempts to read through the TEXT to the originating "quality of mind" that has produced it.

Moral criticism should by no means by confused with a merely censorious or moralistic attitude to CULTURE. A secularized puritanism is seldom absent from its DISCOURSE (notably in the critical writings of Leavis and D.H. Lawrence), but an important gulf lies between its judgments and those, for example, of Plato in his proscription of poets from the ideal republic, or of Victorian reviewers who would condemn a novel for its failure to mete out appropriate punishment to an adulterous character. In fact the tradition of moral criticism arises from various defensive strategies designed to deflect or repel just such attempted suppressions of artistic liberty: the tradition of the "defense of poetry" is, at least in its Romantic phase, one in which the author claims a higher moral vision and thus the prophetic license to ignore the petty legalistic prohibitions of a transient moral code. Such claims are implicit in Wordsworth's 1800 and 1802 Prefaces to Lyrical Ballads, and explicit in Shelley's posthumously published A Defence of Poetry (1840), in which the essentially beneficial moral effect of poetry is discovered in its power to awaken the imaginative sympathies of its readers.

In the later nineteenth century, Shelleyan principles provided foundations for two lines of moral criticism. In the first, Matthew Arnold placed an enormous responsibility on poetry as the replacement for failing religious creeds, and accordingly demanded from it the qualities of nobility, serenity, and "high seriousness." In the second, Shelley's argument about the extension of moral sympathies became an important resource in the defense of the realistic novel – the form by now central to debates about literature's moral influence. For George Eliot, W.D. Howells, and others, the novel's ability to develop our sympathies with other kinds of people made it a great force for moral understanding and against bigotry. This general plea had to be upheld against a more narrowly moralistic disapproval of French fiction, with its major theme of seduction and adultery: for the mainly Protestant cultures of Britain and the United States, the French novel was dangerously sex-obsessed. The anglophone tradition of moral criticism defined itself largely within the context of a century-long contest

between sexual censorship and the novel (from the Madame Bovary scandal of 1857 to the Lady Chatterley trial of 1960), generally upholding the moral value of imaginative sympathy in the sensitive realistic treatment of adult relationships, while often repudiating the "excesses" of French sensationalism. Along the way it evolved the modern conception of the novel as an art, distinct from the seedier realms of pornography or journalism.

The compromise thus effected in this emergent moral criticism between the prophetic privilege of the writer and the guardians of public decency was endangered by the simultaneous emergence of a forthright aestheticism which flatly denied the relevance of moral discourse to art. Most boldly – and to moral critics, most unhelpfully, in the light of his subsequent disgrace – Oscar Wilde declared in his Preface to The Picture of Dorian Gray (1891) that "There is no such thing as a moral or an immoral book. Books are well written, or badly written. That is all." Twentieth-century moral criticism had thus to fend off not only philistine meddling but also this kind of aestheticist defiance, which in detaching art completely from moral questions thereby destroyed its chief claim to beneficial social influence. A revised formula emerged, which still insisted on the crucial moral value of the literary work, but which removed it from the discussion of overt ethical lessons, placing it instead at the level of the writer's basic apprehension of the world – or the quality of the artist's "sensibility." In these terms Henry James, in his 1908 Preface to The Portrait of a Lady, wrote of "the perfect dependence of the 'moral' sense of a work of art on the amount of felt life concerned in producing it" (James, 1987, p. 484). This formula, along with similar declarations by D.H. Lawrence in his scattered essays on the life-enhancing capacities of the novel, provided the basis for much of the moral criticism of F.R. Leavis, notably in its identification of moral value in literature with realistic perception of "life." Realism was to become an important component of Trilling's moral criticism, too: for him the great value of the novel as an agent of moral education lay in its exploration of reality as more complex than our received notions of righteousness.

The fortunes of moral criticism in this tradition reached their height in the 1950s, in the influence enjoyed by Trilling's The Liberal Imagination (1950) and by Leavis's The Great Tradition (1948). For both critics, judgments about literature were emphatically judgments about life and its relative values.

In Leavis's case especially, the relentless insistence on moral seriousness and maturity, however, and the vitalistic vagueness of the much-invoked "life," provoked numerous objections to the restrictive tendencies of this form of criticism. The rise of high theory in the 1970s all but removed problems of literature's moral status from the critical agenda, and the discourses of "POSTMODERNISM" scarcely deign even to recognize them; but in more political forms they resurface in both FEMINIST CRITICISM and the British Marxist tradition of WILLIAMS and EAGLETON.

Reading
Buckley, Vincent 1959: *Poetry and Morality: Studies in the Criticism of Matthew Arnold, T.S. Eliot and F.R. Leavis*.
French, Philip 1980: *Three Honest Men: Edmund Wilson, F.R. Leavis, Lionel Trilling*.
James, Henry 1987: *The Critical Muse: Selected Literary Criticism*.
Lawrence, D.H. 1985: *A Study of Thomas Hardy and Other Essays*.
Leavis, F.R. 1948 (*1972*): *The Great Tradition: George Eliot, Henry James, Joseph Conrad*.
——1986: *Valuation in Criticism and Other Essays*.
Trilling, Lionel 1950 (*1979*): *The Liberal Imagination*.
——1956 (*1978*): *A Gathering of Fugitives*.

CHRIS BALDICK

Mudimbe, V.Y. (1941–) V.Y. Mudimbe's contribution as an intellectual, writer, anthropologist, philosopher, critic, and theologian has been considerable. As part of the postcolonial intelligentsia writing in both French and English, Mudimbe's works have raised some of the most fundamental and difficult questions about the nature of knowledge, the conditions of knowing, the deeper problems inherent within the critical and methodological tools available, and the limits within which contemporary theories and philosophy both produce what has come to be known as Africa and are produced by it. Mudimbe poses Africa as a series of philosophical inquiries in which he explores DISCOURSES about, by, and on Africa.

Reading
Mudimbe, V.Y. 1973: *Entretailles*.
——1974: *L'autre face du royaume*.
——1976: *Before the Birth of the Moon*.
——1982: *L'Odeur du père*.
——1988: *The Invention of Africa: Gnosis, Philosophy, and the Order of Knowledge*.
——1991: *Parables and Fables*.

MAY JOSEPH

Mukarovsky, Jan (1891–1975) Czech philologist, literary critic, and theoretician of literature. In the late 1920s and throughout the 1930s, Mukarovsky was the leading representative of the Prague Linguistic Circle and one of the pioneers of STRUCTURALISM.

Mukarovsky's early work bears an unmistakable influence of RUSSIAN FORMALISM and at the same time introduces elements of structuralism into the analysis of Czech poetry and prose, further developing theory and TYNYANOV's concept of SYSTEM of systems. In particular, Mukarovsky proposed the analysis of artistic work as a dialectical unity formed by the work's dynamic structure. As is evident from his book *Aesthetic Function, Norm, and Value*, the concept of the aesthetic function lies at the core of Mukarovsky's poetics. On the basis of the theory of an Austrian psychologist K. Büller, who singled out three basic elements of verbal communication – the author, the addressee, and the subject of communication – the Czech scholar distinguishes three main functions of language: expressive, appellative, and communicative, which he calls practical functions. To these three functions, which are directed toward nonverbal goals lying beyond the borders of a verbal SIGN, Mukarovsky adds an aesthetic function, which makes the structure of the verbal sign the center of critical investigation. In his essay "Two studies of poetic designation," Mukarovsky maintains that the "orientation of the aesthetic function toward the sign itself is the direct result of the autonomy peculiar to aesthetic phenomena." The focus for Mukarovsky is on transmitting information. The signs are used only as a means that can be dismissed once the content of the information is communicated. Language, "the most highly developed and complete system of signs," is always communicative in a wider sense, including its use of aesthetic function. In this particular function the focus shifts toward the construction of the "sign made out of signs." Mukarovsky admits that the boundary separating the aesthetic function from practical functions is not always distinct and that practical functions cannot be "entirely suppressed in a purely autonomous artistic expression; consequently, every poetic work is . . . simultaneously a presentation, an expression, and an appeal." However, the aesthetic function is present in every practical activity and dominates the communicative function. Owing to its domination over the communicative function, the aesthetic function changes the very nature of the communication.

Therefore Mukarovsky can say that the aesthetic function "dialectically negates" the information-transmitting orientation of the communicative function of the signs without denying either their communicative character or their ability to transmit verbal messages.

Mukarovsky, together with other members of the Prague Linguistic Circle, rejects both the early Russian formalists' view of literature as an autonomous reality and the sociological approach to literature characteristic of the socialist realist critics. As Mukarovsky states in his *Studies in Aesthetics*:

> Without a semiological direction the theorist will always tend to consider the work of art as a purely formal construction, or as a direct reflection of the psychological or even physiological disposition of the author, either in the distinct reality expressed by the work, or in the ideological, economic, social or cultural situations of a given environment. This will lead the theorist to treat the developmental process of art as a sequence of formal transformations or to ignore the developmental process (as do some schools of psychological aesthetics), or to conceive it as a passive reflection of a process external to art.

Instead, Mukarovsky points out that poetry and literature in general develop through a series of structures (political, economic, ideological, literary), which change in time, not separately from one another but by forming a structure of higher order, a structure of structures with its own hierarchy based on its dominant elements. This structure of structures differs from Tynyanov's system of systems in that, by means of the general theory of signs, Mukarovsky supplies an explanation of the mechanism that makes the interaction among different cultural systems possible. As Jurij Striedter writes in his *Literary Structure, Evolution, and Value*, Mukarovsky

> offers a vision of a literary work not as a series of linguistic signs fixed for the purpose of artistic communication but as a fabric of meanings concretized by the receiver on the basis of this artifact and with the aid of conventionalized codes. Only this fabric of meanings is capable of becoming the actual object of aesthetic contemplation and valuation (in Czech structuralist terminology, the "aesthetic object"). (Striedter, 1989, p. 93)

As if anticipating future semiotic theories, Mukarovsky offers a mechanism for the investigation of literary work: "Only the semiological point of view will allow theoreticians to recognize the autonomous existence and the essential dynamism of the structure of art and to understand its evolution as an immanent movement, but in a relationship in constant dialectic with the evolution of other fields of culture." The key element of this mechanism is the notion of the dynamic dominant presented in Mukarovsky's "Standard language and poetic language" (1932):

> The dominant gives a poetic work its unity. However, this is a kind of unity which has been characterized in aesthetic as "unity in diversity," a dynamic unity in which one can sense at the same time both harmony and lack of harmony, rather like convergence and divergence. Convergence is determined by striving towards the dominant, divergence by a resistance to the striving which can be seen in the static background of non-actualized components.

The discovery of the dominant enables a literary critic to determine the value of a literary work. Mukarovsky, unlike Marxist critics for whom the value of a literary work consists of the ideologically correct representation of a social environment, saw the value of a literary work in its ability, based on its innovative deviation from literary tradition and convention, to challenge the total view of society. *See also* PRAGUE LINGUISTIC CIRCLE.

Reading
Dolezel, Lubomir 1982: "Mukarovsky and the idea of poetic truth."
Gandelman, Claude 1988: "The dialectic functioning of Mukarovsky's semiotic model."
Moked, G. 1988: "Objective features of text-analysis according to Mukarovsky: a brief survey and some critical remarks."
Mukarovsky, Jan 1977: *The Word and Verbal Art. Selected Essays by Jan Mukarovsky.*
——— 1978: *Structure, Sign, and Function. Selected Essays by Jan Mukarovsky.*
Schwartz, W. 1989: "Some remarks on the development, poetic range and operational disposition of Mukarovsky's term 'semantic gesture.'"
Striedter, Jurij 1989: *Literary Structure, Evolution, and Value. Russian Formalism and Czech Structuralism.*
Winner, Thomas 1987: "Text and context in the aesthetic theories of Jan Mukarovsky."

SLAVA I. YASTREMSKI

multiculturalism A term, says Henry Louis Gates, Jr (1993), whose "boundaries are not easy to establish," though it has pointed generally since the 1960s to "the messy affairs of cultural variegation." In that regard it connotes either some mode of transnational interrelationships between the CULTURES of two or more countries, or it suggests in a more circumscribed manner the broader dimensions of multiple cultural identities within the boundaries of a single nation.

Although the world can be viewed as "fissured by nationality, ethnicity, RACE and GENDER," it is none the less inherently "multicultural already" as indicated by its easily discernible "mixing and hybridity" (Gates). Thus the word "multiculturalism" can be seen as having referentiality, however ambitious or ambiguous, to transnational associations between the cultures of two or more nations. The use of the term in this sense has focused usually, but not entirely, on the evidence of literary culture. Books such as Stuart Hirschberg's *One World, Many Cultures* (1992) and Barbara Salomon's *Other Voices Other Vistas: Short Stories from Africa, China, India, Japan and Latin America* (1992) clearly embody this concept.

Within the twentieth-century context of the evolution of world history as evidenced by the intercontinental exploding populations and the general public recognition of the increasing number of nation-states, the underlying assumption of the intrinsic superiority of "Western tradition" has been necessarily called into question and revaluated in order to acknowledge and incorporate "the heritage of a variety of peoples and cultures" (Dasenbrock, 1992). Thus the foci of this newer interest have been global, international, and inclusive, thereby compelling a reconsideration of intellectual, political, economic, and social perspectives so as to be aware of and to respect both perceived differences and commonalities among peoples and cultures. The principal SYMBOL on the world stage for the cognizance of this new reality in the half-century since the 1939–45 war (1945–95) is preeminently the organization of the United Nations in its General Assembly and Security Council, and in the several structures by which that institution manifests its global presence and operations: United Nations Educational, Scientific and Cultural Organization (UNESCO); World Health Organization (WHO); Food and Agriculture Organization (FAO), and others. The charter for the United Nations bears witness to this latter-day phenomenon

of global pluralism in the stating of its purposes as the maintenance of international peace and security, the development of friendly relations among the states, and the achievement of cooperation in solving international economic, social, cultural, and humanitarian problems. Other factors also contribute to the impact of global pluralism, for example, the burgeoning trend toward a global economy as a powerful catalyst generating the need for enlargement of perspective about the paradox of a shrinking world geopolitically.

This international and inclusive effort has not been without its detractors, however, in reacting to what has been characterized as the demise of the "traditional Western CANON of knowledge" and values and hence the demise of the very *raison d'être* for Western nations and culture. Allan Bloom has argued this case vigorously in *The Closing of the American Mind* (1987) by observing what he calls "the decomposition of the university" (a symbol for culture) due to the general lack of "solidarity in defence of the pursuit of truth" either in the natural sciences, the social sciences, or the humanities: "gone is the time when there was the expectation of a universal theory of man that would unite the university and contribute to progress, harnessing Europe's intellectual depth and heritage with our vitality." What remains for the students in the society, according to Bloom, is a belief that all truth is relative, buttressed by a feeling of allegiance to some vacuous concept of equality; therefore higher education both fails democracy and impoverishes the souls of its citizens. In a somewhat less dogmatic view Dinesh D'Souza in *Illiberal Education* (1992) does not oppose outright the inclusion of the cultural works of non-Western nations, but cautions against the imposition of ideological tenets as factors in the selection and study of such works, as well as in the uncritical distortions of non-Western cultures in the guise of prejudiced prescriptions. To counter the implications of such views as illustrated in the reputed dictum of Saul Bellow: "I will read the Zulus when they have produced a Tolstoy," perhaps what is needed is the attitude espoused by David Aronson in *Teaching Tolerance* (1994) as "the central and defining value" for social and cultural relations; for

if tolerance requires at a minimum that we respect each other's freedom, it also suggests a substantive vision of the good life. A life of personal growth, wealth of experience, dedication to the struggles of others, spontaneity, joy, and wholehearted opposition to ignorance and fear-mongering; this is what we wish for children and for ourselves. We are here only once, and it would be narrow and incurious not to look around.

However cogent the foregoing meaning of the term "multicultural" may appear, that definition has been rivaled if not overshadowed by a second principal focus of concern in the emerging widespread recent usage of this term. Indeed the term has been prominently used in the United States with what appears to be a more circumscribed significance that has evoked intense controversy. In fact "multiculturalism" has become what Carlos Cortes calls "the omnipresent, often-celebrated, often-excoriated 'M' word" (1994). E.D. Hirsch's book *Cultural Literacy: What Every American Needs to Know* (1987) contained only a passing allusion to "multicultural education" and no definition. Six years later the second edition of the *Dictionary of Cultural Literacy* (1994) explicitly defined the term "multicultural" as "the view that the various cultures in a society merit equal respect and scholarly interest" and specified its locus as the United States in the 1970s, 1980s, and 1990s. Hence the term's second usage has been basically an outgrowth of certain segments of American academic and educational interests in order to provide a kind of umbrella credibility for the study of ethnic diversity and pluralism by such varied groups as Afro-Americans, Chicanos and Chicanas, Asian-Americans, Hispanics, Native Americans, and gays and lesbians, and for the expression of concern about the representation to the majority society of the cultural identities of RACE, GENDER, ETHNICITY, and sex, both currently and historically.

Taken seriously, the pursuit of this broader knowledge within an increasingly culturally diverse society results inevitably in a profound reconsideration of the notion of an indispensable dominant cultural tradition existing in the society and the means whereby that assumed validity of dominance has been perpetuated by history, education, language, politics, CLASS, and values. Within American society a continuing tacit assumption (with obvious resultant practices) up to the 1939–45 war and just after centered upon the idea that, although American culture had been geographically and historically viewed in relation to regions, nevertheless the most important values and influences inherent in that culture were generated from New England and the upper Eastern seaboard, or as expressed by Simonson and Walker (1988): "a particular white, male, academic, eastern U.S., Eurocentric bias" was present in the "concept of American culture." Just as the defining image of "the melting pot" had been applied to the manner in which diverse groups of immigrants were supposed to be assimilated into a new nation and to develop a new identity of commonality, so also in culture, especially literary, a counterpart description became evident in the use of the word "mainstream" – an image which "has long haunted the study of American culture," says Paul Lauter in referring to "The literatures of America" (1990). The image immediately signals the marginalizing of individuals, groups, and works as stated in phrases such as "writers of color," "most women writers," and "regional or ethnic writers." Indeed, in the 1930s, 1940s, and 1950s a popular textbook used in colleges and universities for the study of literary culture was *Major American Writers*; 40 male authors and 2 female authors were included in the 2,000 pages because "they constitute the core of the national letters" or the "mainstream." This contrasts with an increasingly popular textbook of the 1990s, *The Heath Anthology of American Literature*. It consists of two volumes totaling 6,000 pages containing selections from several hundred authors representing "as fully as possible the varied culture of the United States" from the earliest era to the most recent, including "a large number of lost, forgotten or suppressed literary texts," and "works of literary accomplishment" based on the principle of "how a text engages concerns central to the period in which it was written as well as the overall development of American culture." The book illustrates more recent images than "mainstream" as seen in the use of "mosaic" and "quilt," implying both the reality of the specific parts as well as the whole portrayal they constitute.

The intensity of the controversy elicited by this second usage of the word "multiculturalism" is clearly evident in the extent to which the newer emphasis has been attacked intellectually as a dilution of core knowledge and values, for example, by Arthur Schelesinger in *The Disuniting of America* (1991). That usage is also manifested in the practical steps that have been taken officially to forestall the implications of the concept, for example, by the Lake County, Florida, school board which adopted in 1994 a policy requiring its public school teachers to "instill in our students an appreciation of our American heritage and culture such as our republican form of government, capitalism, a free enterprise system, patriotism, strong family values, freedom of religion and other basic values that are superior to other foreign or historic cultures" (Jacobs, 1994). It is not surprising, then, as Gates pointed out, that "multiculturalism" becomes "a sweet or bitter mouthful, depending on your sympathies."

See also CULTURAL STUDIES.

Reading

Brenkman, John 1993: "Multiculturalism and criticism."
Erickson, Peter 1991: "What multiculturalism means."
Franklin, Phyllis, ed. 1993: "Multiculturalism: the task of literary representation in the twenty-first century."
Graff, Gerald, and Robbins, Bruce 1992: "Cultural criticism."
Kaetz, James P., ed. 1994: "Multiculturalism and diversity."
Leitch, Vincent B. 1994: "Cultural studies."
Lynch, James 1993: *Multicultural Education in a Global Society.*
Simonson, Rick, and Walker, Scott, eds 1988: *Multicultural Literacy.*

FRED L. STANDLEY

musicology and culture Musicology is dated by the *Oxford English Dictionary* as a term first recognized in 1919. The *OED* offers an etymology from the French *musicologie*, but the concept certainly derives from the German *Musikwissenschaft*, most notably from a widely influential German journal article published by Guido Adler in 1885, entitled (in translation) "The scope, method and aim of musicology" (Bujić, 1988). Adler laid down a distinction between historical and systematic musicology, the one concerning what might be called, for convenience, "facts" (Adler calls this "history"), the other concerning structures of music itself, aesthetic approaches, pedagogy, and ethnographics (Adler wrote of the "dominating principles in the individual branches of music"). In defining the term, the *OED* opts for exclusion: musicology is the study of music "other than technique of performance or composition." Most of those who are not musicians will assume that technique of performance or composition is the vital area of the study of music, and that musicology must therefore be peripheral and perhaps self-gratifying. On the contrary, from PSYCHOANALYSIS to GENDER studies it has been almost a weather gauge of critical thought. Not without reason did Umberto Eco observe in *A Theory of Semiotics* (1979) that SEMIOTICS, and, it might be added, STRUCTURALISM in general, pick up on ways of thinking and theorizing that have been familiar in musicology for centuries.

Obviously the twentieth century was a time of acute personal introspection among intellectuals in response to the fragmentation of CULTURE against the persistent backdrop of our cultural heritage. In musical styles these overlaps have happened before. In the early seventeenth century there was bitter dispute between entrenched traditionalism in musical composition and a visionary modernism that failed to lay down the sorts of precedent it foresaw. In the late eighteenth century "enlightened" modernists (nowadays we remember Haydn and Mozart above all others) simply wrote Baroque practice, including Bach and Handel, out of the script in the cultured public mind, as the musicology of the time reflects. By and large people lost interest in old music, and the thirst for the new was at its height. The twentieth century was different again. We have to take stock of the fact that there were two cultures in play for an astonishingly long time – those who listened to Schoenberg, and those who listened to Rachmaninov, to put it in an emblematic way, almost as one might place abstract and representational visual art side by side. Yet that is to look only at the musical "high art" of the century, and only at the product. What we also have to take stock of is the impact of technology, which brings in the question of who "uses" the music of which musicology is the study, and how it is produced (by composers and performers) and managed, which is surely also a part of modern musicology, the *OED* notwithstanding.

Fools rush in to easy analogies between the arts, but there is no harm in logging how closely the trends of twentieth-century culture in general were reflected in and, it could be claimed, sometimes driven by, the music of the age: expressionism, futurism, dada, minimalism – these and the similar great themes of early modern, modern, and postmodern artistic expression are concepts as familiar in musicology as in any other field of cultural history. Indeed, one of the fascinating aspects of the age of fragmentation, founded on what Christopher Butler (1994) calls a "withdrawal from consensual languages," is how each new creative wave has swept as a unifying force through the different arts. Of course some well-known, towering alliances of actual people (Schoenberg/Kandinsky) or of influence and adaptation (Joyce/Berio) are one clear sign of this. To those interested in CULTURAL THEORY, however, what is even more striking is the consensus of critical terminology and conceptual aspirations. The modern musicologist can read the history and theory of, say, postmodern architecture and have no difficulty in understanding the general points at issue, the attitudes struck, the underlying aspirations.

Before comment on the general trends of musicology, three important subsidiary matters need to be aired. First, musicology in the sense of "pure" music history will figure here in contention rather than as a central consideration. Musicology in this sense emerged from a fairly amateurish obscurity in the English language into a surge of music-historical inquiry, principally in America, in the 1930s and 1940s, establishing a tradition that continues to this day. Lang's *Music in Western Civilization* (1941), for example, was a momentous step, and part of a community of interest among such as Austin, Bukofzer, Grout, Reese, Sachs, and Strunk. What these and other scholars, including many of European extraction, took pride in was a scientific approach to music-history writing, addressing basic topics – origins, analogy, periodization, continuities, the "great-man" theory (a gendered theory if ever there was one), theories of progress, growth, development, revolution, evolution (Allen, 1962). The accumulation of what has become classic historical musicology is immense. Witness the progression from a small-format fifth edition of *Grove's Dictionary of Music and Musicians* in 1954 to 1980 and the 20-volume, large-format *New Grove*. Not only in music-history writing, but also in the editing and publication of old music from the medieval period onwards, has the information explosion broken musicological ground. This fine, progressive movement, the modern musical mind rediscovering what have become libraries full of compositions from earlier ages, was taken for granted, by and large, until voices of protest began to appear in the 1970s and 1980s (Kerman, 1985). What is the point, it was asked, of producing reams of printed music, yielded by thousands of postgraduate and professional careers, that hardly anyone is likely ever to sing, play, or hear? Music theorists, given the premium they place upon the close (time-consuming, and musically and intellectually challenging) study of musical structure and effect, and their natural tendency to be interested mainly in recent and contemporary music, in "living" art, naturally joined

in the questioning chorus. During this recent period "historical musicologist" and "theorist" have become in some quarters terms of mutual abuse, though nowadays, as is observed below, new antinomies are emerging. It is fair to say that at least some of the work of what may be called "pure" musicology can be carried out by those who possess little or no skill in actually composing, performing, or contributing to the critical understanding of music itself. Thus it is not a petty debate but an artistic one, and it is not surprising that historical musicology in these aspects has been put on the defensive.

Second, if introversively one may rehearse the Schoenberg/Rachmaninov divide, extroversively the real divide appeared in the 1960s (with its roots after the 1914–18 war in the development of musical recording and broadcasting) when popular music became a mass product and, as with FILM STUDIES (see KRISTEVA), began to develop its own canon of scholarship and critical thought. From the Beatles to Madonna a new phenomenon swept the world, vastly exceeding the impact of jazz, swing bands, crooners, Hollywood film music, and the other foretastes of a music that is truly of the people. There were two Western musics in the twentieth century, and the terms popular and classical come so easily to us that the revolution they represent is easily missed; a few centuries ago, the (vague) equivalent would have been "secular" and "liturgical," terms for which a modern dictionary would find essentially no current use. What the great majority of people around the world think of as "their" music is something for which musicology finds little place, even if for the specialist there are many fascinating crossovers.

Third, and following on from what I have called the "real divide" within Western music, it was in the late twentieth century that musicology spread its net throughout non-Western cultures. One has the impression from many sources that ethnomusicology, part of "systematic musicology," was virtually invented and remains indebted to one man (Pete Seeger); yet in an era of mass democratization, communication, travel, and migration it was inevitable that anthropology would burgeon in the groves of academe, and within anthropology, ethnomusicology. Here too the predictable antinomy, rather like that between historical musicology and theory, arose between a contextual camp, more sociologically and methodologically orientated, and the structurally orientated research of the music of "other" cultures. The debate continues; and a constant factor is intrusion. It is one thing to study the influence of Balinese music on Debussy. It is quite another (see CANON) to study, say, the largely uncharted world of mid-century black American revivalist musical preaching in the 1930s, where the white researcher, depending to an exceptional extent on "oral history," will find most doors firmly closed.

Within musicology, it is particularly in music theory that interdisciplinary impact has been tested. Behaviorism brought, in 1956, its standard textbook of the musicological appropriation of information science (Meyer, 1956). Mentalism (see CHOMSKY) inspired a new popularization of the idea of music as a hierarchical "language" (Bernstein, 1976); and the semiology of music (see SEMIOTICS) was developed throughout the 1970s and 1980s into a global musicological theory, based on Molino's tripartitional sociological model of a "poietic" pole (all facets of production), an "esthesic" pole (all facets of reception), and a "neutral" pole which provisionally inscribes immanent structures (Nattiez, 1990). Without doubt, however, the two dominating music-analytical theories of recent times have been manifestations of structuralism (Dunsby and Whittall, 1988). On the one hand there is musico-structural analysis based on the theories and techniques of Heinrich Schenker, whose ideas were forged in the "DURKHEIM–FREUD–SAUSSURE" ethos of the early twentieth century, although it was to Goethe and post-Kantian idealist philosophy that Schenker pointed for authority. Schenkerian notation has become a lingua franca of music-critical research. Looked at through the wrong end of a telescope, it is roughly analagous to a Chomskian tree structure, and that the two – grammatico-semantic analogues of music and language – could be taken for distant relatives is no accident (see JAKOBSON). On the other hand, new music in the twentieth century created new challenges, which were met conspicuously by Allen Forte, whose textbook on pitch structure dominated the field from 1973 onwards. Forte developed procedures called "pitch-class analysis" by adapting aspects of set-theory mathematics to the problems of understanding harmonic structure in early twentieth-century "atonal" composition, and indeed other repertories. Within musicology, there is no denying the mighty conceptual gulf between projects such as *The New Grove* and Forte's Yale project of the 1970s and 1980s in building up a substantial body of research based on set theory. They have one obvious feature

in common, however: without computers, neither could have happened as they did.

These trends have engendered new movements, which present themselves as reactions, indeed complaints, but which may turn out to be developments, however subversively. First, musicology remained until rather late in the day what used to be thought of as a gender-free zone, that is, male-dominated. Starting with the impatience one expects from a theorist rather than a historical musicologist, Susan McClary set the whole issue ablaze:

> Musicology fastidiously declares issues of musical signification to be off-limits to those engaged in legitimate scholarship. It has seized disciplinary control over the study of music and has prohibited the asking of even the most fundamental questions concerning meaning . . . It is finally feminism that has allowed me to understand both why the discipline wishes these to be nonissues, and also why they need to be moved to the very center of inquiries about music. (McClary, 1991)

This is noted not as a record of the ephemeral: cultural historians of the future will surely know about *Feminine Endings* as they wade through the masses of citations, articles, and already books devoted to McClary's ideas, or arguments from the same climate (Citron, 1993). Like most writers of her generation and on her subject McClary is overtly indebted to well-established, even old-fashioned feminist literary studies, rather than to musicology (see FEMINIST CRITICISM). This musicological issue is not or is not only an issue of exclusion, that women's music has not been played or studied, and that women scholars have been inconspicuous (in the large publication *Companion to Contemporary Musical Thought* 57 experts contributed learned articles, and it appears that only four female experts were to be found, or found suitable – see Paynter et al., 1992). The nub of the argument, it seems, is that were these imbalances rectified, and whatever the means of rectification, the whole PARADIGM of musicology would alter, not necessarily for the better, but for a different paradigm that would represent justice and cultural richness. *The New Grove Dictionary of Women Composers* is of course a record of cultural failure that is not its protagonists' fault, which seems quite a pointless enterprise; it is perhaps typical of modern musicology of this kind, fortunately a minority activity despite establishment hype, to have serenely ignored the lessons of critical theory that it appears never to have studied.

Second, as to new movements, this sociological debate is being conducted in a shifting musicological environment that has led to the appearance in recent literature of the term New Musicology. The theory boom that began to elbow the historical musicology establishment into retreat between roughly 1960 and 1985, and which, as has been indicated, was at root a structuralist enterprise, was always a potential victim of anti-formalism (see FORMALISM). Our musical legacy, it would be claimed, needed to be interpreted in context, not through the grid of some cold, contemporaneous critical methodology, but as part of the cultural world in which it arose (for example, Kramer, 1990). This ingredient, a call for "humanistic criticism" that one can now see was a sustained and growing campaign in the 1980s, mainly in America, has of course a distinguished pedigree in cultural theory. Another ingredient, the increasing interest in musical "narrative," may seem to be more in line with the study of structure (see NARRATOLOGY), but its main manifestations so far, notably in the work of Carolyn Abbate (1991), seem to authorize a loose, impressionistic approach to criticism that has been called "intoxicating" and "dazzling" but lacking "rigor." These ingredients may well amount to a recipe for the renewal of modern musicology, perhaps in the sense of a new "structuration" (see Giddens, 1973). In other words, the PARADIGM shift called for by McClary and Citron is imbricated with one, more fundamental, that has already been diagnosed (see ADORNO) and is being monitored, in which tradition figures large.

Reading

Abbate, C. 1991: *Unsung Voices: Opera and Musical Narrative in the Nineteenth Century.*

Bernstein, L. 1976: *The Unanswered Question: Six Talks at Harvard.*

Bujić, B., ed. 1988: *Music in European Thought, 1851–1912.*

Butler, C. 1994: *Early Modernism: Literature, Music, and Painting in Europe, 1900–1916.*

Citron, M.J. 1993: *Gender and the Musical Canon.*

Dunsby, J., and Whittall, A. 1988: *Music Analysis in Theory and Practice.*

Kerman, J. 1985: *Musicology.*

Kramer, L. 1990: *Music as Cultural Practice 1800–1900.*

Lang, P.H. 1941: *Music in Western Civilization.*

McClary, S. 1991: *Feminine Endings: Music, Gender, and Sexuality.*

Meyer, L.B. 1956: *Emotion and Meaning in Music.*

Nattiez, J.-J. 1990: *Music and Discourse: Toward a Semiology of Music.*

Paynter, J. et al., eds 1992: *Companion to Contemporary Musical Thought.*

JONATHAN DUNSBY

N

name of the father   In Lacanian psychoanalysis, the paternal metaphor which founds the SYMBOLIC, and the agency of the symbolic law. The symbolic law is negative and privative, and it is the invocation of the name of the father that maintains the incest taboo and abolishes the child's primal and immediate relationship with the mother through the agency of the OEDIPUS COMPLEX. The foreclosure or suppression of this basic signifier results in a gap in the symbolic universe and is, in Lacan's view, the factor that triggers psychosis.

Reading
Lacan, Jacques 1958: "On a question preliminary to any possible treatment of psychosis."
——1981: *Le Séminaire de Jacques Lacan. Livre Trois: Les Psychoses 1955–1956.*

DAVID MACEY

narratology   A theory of narrative based on premises provided by STRUCTURALISM, especially the work of the French structural anthropologist Claude LÉVI-STRAUSS on myth. For Lévi-Strauss all myths are versions of basic themes, and the narrative structures of individual myths relate to a universal STRUCTURE which underpins all of them. A myth is an instance of the operation of this universal structure, a relationship which is analogous to the distinction between LANGUE/PAROLE advanced by Ferdinand de SAUSSURE. In this scheme, a "mytheme" is an element of the universal structure which can appear in different mythic narratives. Lévi-Strauss reads myths in reference to one another in order to uncover the relations which structure their narrative. He develops from this operation a theory of the collective existence of certain elements, which he then posits as being somehow prior to the mythic narratives themselves, in a form of collective consciousness.

Another figure crucial to the development of narratology is Vladimir PROPP, an exponent of RUSSIAN FORMALISM. He attempted to define the narrative elements common to all folk tales in a manner similar to that employed by Lévi-Strauss. Claude BREMOND is a later narratologist who most closely follows Propp, although he attempts to account for moments of choice in the narrative, moments which are structured by a relation of difference to the discarded choices.

However, the search for a theory which has universal applications becomes most problematical for those who follow Lévi-Strauss and Propp. A.J. GREIMAS does attempt to achieve a universal grammar of narrative by means of a type of semantic analysis of sentence structure (see also ACTANT). From this starting position, he produces an analysis of characterization in the novel. According to Greimas, characterization as a whole is achieved by cumulative memorization. The elements memorized are the various figurations attached to the name of the character at different points in the TEXT. He attempts to move from this psychological operation performed by the reader to an identification of the discursive figurations which function to constitute the character. He therefore concentrates on the production of an analysis of the text in which the actant plays the role of the character. His method is, essentially, to read character as the product of a thematic relationship between the grammatical subject position on the one hand, and the thematic roles which qualify it on the other. It is important to note that in his theory there is a very specific relationship between the individual occurrences of these thematic elements and the discursive recognition of a character. Greimas states that the movement from a narrative structure to a discursive structure takes place by means of this very relationship. This happens when actantial roles take control of thematic roles. His introduction of the latter phrase has considerable consequences for the development of narratology as a whole. It implies that there is not only a multiplicity of levels in any given literary TEXT, but that the relations between these levels are subject to one set of binding rules. DISCOURSE is, for Greimas, the potentiality out of which certain specific thematic roles are produced, and the rules which govern this process are equivalent to the relationship of *langue/parole*. His concept of the textual actor functions to unite the specific problematics of actant, actantial role, and thematic role. This provides overall discursive recognitions such as the meanings associated with a given character. The actor is a controlling nexus because it functions in an actantial role and a thematic role at the same time. By analyzing the actor, the critic is therefore able to perform an analysis of the relational structure which spans the various textual levels. Greimas describes this operation as a "transforming doing." It provides for the possibility of movement from one state, or textual level, to another. This theory provides narratology with a concept for dealing with the relations between narrative structure and linguistic structure. Many further developments in the field have taken place in terms of an expansion of Greimas's theory in this respect. He has also had some effect on SEMIOTICS, especially since his production of a science of narratology corresponds to the semiotic concept of METALANGUAGE as constituting a SIGN system in itself. Nevertheless, one problem still exists for this kind of theory, and that is the role played by the reader. Greimas seems to assume that the position of the reader is a simple unitary one, but this problem becomes much more acute for other narratologists.

In this way, for example, the Bulgarian theorist Tzvetan Todorov reads *Les Liaisons dangereuses* in accordance with the Greimas model by utilizing the three sets of actants as the fundamental relations between characters in any given narrative. Thus the combinations produced by desire, communication, and participation determine the "rules of action" used in the novel. For example, if a person loves someone, then the interests of the first person will be focused upon making the second person return the love. But Todorov is nevertheless aware of the problem of how to guarantee objectivity in the production of such a schematic. This results in a movement in his later work away from this position, although his intention is still the production of some sort of universal grammar of narrative operations. He attempts to produce a metalanguage which gives objectively verifiable descriptions. This would neatly sidestep the tendency of the critic to force a text to produce the desired meanings, which are then announced to have been present in the text all the time. This metalanguage consists of three "primary categories." The first,

"proper names," is comprised of grammatical subjects, but without internal properties. The second, "adjectives," is subdivided into states, properties, and conditions. The last, "verbs," is a category which is capable of three actions: the modification of a situation; the commitment of a crime; and the punishing of a criminal. These three fundamental categories weave the text in and through a set of five modes which are based upon the linguistic classification of "mood." The five modes are the "indicative" (events or actions which actually occurred); the "obligatory" (the legal obligations elaborated by society); the "optative" (the character's wishes); the "conditional" (if one character performs a certain action, a second will then perform another action); and the "predictive" (at a certain moment in the narrative a specific event shall occur). The meanings the reader associates with certain characters are the result of the syntactical conjunction of their grammatical subject position with various predicates as the text moves through the formulations posited by Todorov. Thus the total effect of "character" is gained by the associations produced by the relationship between the subject position associated with a certain character on the one hand, and the variations in the plot modes on the other. He constructs this entire metalanguage in the hope that the insights gained by his theory of narrative structure can be interrelated with an investigation of linguistic structure. The result should be a complete understanding of the operation of narration itself. As with many such basically structuralist theories of narrative, however, no attempt is made to theorize the relationship between reader and text: Todorov's theory simply assumes that the reader will be competent in uncovering the structures.

Another theorist who attempts to develop a science of narratology from the basic structuralist premise is Gérard GENETTE. He theorizes narrative in terms of the relations between *récit*, the order of events as they are represented in a given narrative; *histoire*, the chronological order in which the events occurred; and *narration*, the narrative act itself. He pays minute attention to categories of analysis such as the narrator and the kind of voice or viewpoint he or she uses, and the relationship of narrator to narratee. For Genette, narrative is the result of the relations between these various elements. He utilizes five basic areas in which these elements interact: the narrative's ordering of time; the varying lengths of time accorded to plot events by the narrative; the frequency with which an event is narrated as well as the frequency with which it actually occurred; the narrative techniques used and the viewpoint of the narrative persona; and the act of narration *per se*. Genette refers to the fact that other categories can exist, but his scheme at least enables the essential difference between narration and narrative to be grasped.

Narratology, however, is also an area of structuralism which intersects most closely with POSTSTRUCTURALISM. The works of Roland BARTHES examplify the way in which structuralism is problematized by what follows. In *S/Z* he attempts a narratological analysis which does not treat the literary text as the object of a disinterested scientific inquiry, thus marking a radical break with the claims of structuralism. In this book the function of the reader is the production of meaning: the reader engages in a diacritical process with the literary. This leads to Barthes's later work, in which exactly what it is that constitutes the literary itself is left undefined. For Barthes there is no original idea, there is only intertextual repetition. It is with regard to this most problematical area that Barthes's contribution to narratology is in fact only a stage in his own development into a poststructuralist figure.

A further development in narrative theory is the work of Fredric Jameson in *The Political Unconscious: Narrative as a Socially Symbolic Act*. While not specifically a narratological work in that it is more explicitly hostile to structuralism in general, it takes some of the theories of narratology as its starting point. Greimas's attempt to produce a homogeneous theory of levels is one of the main starting points of Jameson's project, which is no less than the construction of a Marxist theory of narrative. Jameson focuses specifically on Greimas's concept of the semiotic rectangle, reappropriating Greimas's homological scheme for his own purposes. In effect, he sees the static nature of the concept, organized as it is around BINARY OPPOSITIONS, as a very precise model for the operation of ideological closure. He therefore utilizes the semiotic rectangle in a critical practice which analyzes the closure of meaning in the literary text. Thus Jameson rejects the structuralist impulse toward the perception of objective elements which is inherent in Greimas's work. Jameson states that this kind of theorizing of closure permits an interrogation of the ideological system, one which will lay bare terms which have been repressed by the

closure performed by the narrative. The reconstruction of these repressed therms takes place in and through the concept of the "political unconscious," which has the added advantage for Jameson of politicizing psychoanalytical theories of the UNCONSCIOUS. Jameson criticizes Greimas's theory for its inability to deal with the character, despite all of its attempts to do so. He analyzes this inability as an incapacity to theorize the SUBJECT. He sees Greimas's problem in this respect as the result of an ahistorical imposition of the bourgeois subject upon narrative forms which predate the emergence of the elements needed in the composition of this subject: the Cartesian ego, the construction of a differential relation between private and public, the emergence of a canonical "literature," and so on. Jameson utilizes Greimas's theory at precisely the points at which it breaks down, that is, when the narrative text deviates from Greimas's assumptions. This is especially important for characters which are seen by Jameson to operate as two actants. In this way he produces a rigorous methodology for the production of meanings against the grain of ideological closure itself. This operation of closure draws his attention to the existence of the fundamental structuralist concept of binary opposition as it is used by Greimas. Jameson rereads binary opposition as the very model of social contradiction, and it is this which is managed by the literary text. Jameson utilizes narratological theory in order to change it into something else. His theory marks one point at which narratology intersects with MARXISM AND MARXIST CRITICISM. Narratology must therefore be seen in relation to developments in critical and cultural theory other than structuralism.

Reading
Barthes, Roland 1973a (*1990*): *S/Z*.
Bremond, Claude 1973: *Logique du Récit*.
Genette, Gérard 1980: *Narrative Discourse: An Essay in Method*.
——1982a: *Figures of Literary Discourse*.
Greimas, A.J. 1966: *Semantique Structurale*.
——1970: *Du Sens*.
——1987: *On Meaning: Selected Writings in Semiotic Theory*.
Jameson, Fredric 1981 (*1989*): *The Political Unconscious: Narrative as a Socially Symbolic Act*.
Lévi-Strauss, Claude 1971 (*1981*): *The Naked Man*.
Propp, Vladimir 1958 (*1968*): *Morphology of the Folktale*.
Todorov, Tzvetan 1967: *Littérature et Signification*.
——1971: *Poétique de la Prose*.

PAUL INNES

nationalism, black *See* BLACK NATIONALISM

Native American studies The literatures of American Indian peoples represent an integral part of Native American studies. Creation and emergence myths, etiological myths, ceremonial chants and prayers, legends, and historical narratives embodied in various oral traditions have provided traditional listeners with the collective cultural wisdom that maintains order and control in the universe, and they afford the non-Indian listeners/readers insight into the respective tribe's world view. These oral TEXTS reveal the people's moral and aesthetic values, relation to the natural world and spiritual powers, views of the landscape as a numinous and living entity, methods of controlling evil and disease, and, perhaps most important, they provide the community with a sense of identity by making the past a viable part of the present by affirming the mythic and historic links to a sacred tribal geography.

Oral literatures are not only an important field of study in their own right, but essential for the student of Native American literature written in English. One of the many accomplishments of contemporary Indian writers such as N. Scott Momaday (Kiowa), Louise Erdrich (Ojibwa), and Leslie Marmon Silko (Laguna Pueblo) is the conscious continuation of the oral tradition in their fictions. This requires readers to be not only aware of the oral quality of their writings and the sacred role of language in oral CULTURES, but also to employ a broadly interdisciplinary approach to their texts by drawing on relevant materials from anthropology, tribal mythology, religion, and history. Reading Momaday's *House Made of Dawn*, for instance, requires an understanding of the curative function of the Navajo Night Chant, from which the novel takes its title, insight into the Bear Maiden myth's relation to the novel's plot, knowledge of the ritual function of Pueblo ceremonial races, and careful, culture-specific readings of such symbols as the moon and the dawn, which are essential for an accurate interpretation of the novel's conclusion. If Momaday's works invite research into their Navajo, Kiowa, and Jemez Pueblo backgrounds, the critics of Leslie Silko's writing must explore Navajo and Laguna Pueblo cultures. To appreciate fully the complexity of *Ceremony*, one must delineate the parallels between the Laguna emergence story and the protagonist's mythic quest. Anthropological and ethnographic studies help crit-

ics recognize the roles of Spiderwoman and katchina figures in Laguna mythology and the significance of directional and color symbolism within the Laguna sacred geography. Moreover, this novel is perhaps the best example in contemporary Native American literature of how the oral tradition provides a mythical matrix which determines individual lives and events across generations. In *Tracks*, Louise Erdrich draws heavily on Ojibwa myth in her portrayal of Nanapush as the modern incarnation of the traditional trickster figure, as well as in her linkage of the lake monster, the Misshepeshu, to Fleur's, the female protagonist's, supernatural powers. These examples illustrate that readers of Native American literatures must accept the challenge of crossing cultural boundaries and immerse themselves in the study of culture-specific background materials. This will lead not only to insights into other cultures' modes of knowledge, but also create a fruitful distance from which one's own cultural assumptions can be critically reevaluated.

It must be noted, however, that the approach to Native American texts outlined above has come under attack by postmodern critics, most notably by Gerald Vizenor and Arnold Krupat. Vizenor, a widely published Ojibwa novelist and critic, contends that critics in the past have relied too heavily on STRUCTURALISM and other social science theories in their interpretations of Native American literary TEXTS (Vizenor, 1989). In the following statement he articulates his objections to these critical strategies and calls for new approaches to American Indian texts:

> Native American Indian literatures are unstudied landscapes, wild and comic rather than tragic and representational, storied with narrative wisps and tribal discourse. Social science theories constrain tribal landscapes to institutional values, representationalism and the politics of academic determination. The narrow teleologies deduced from social science monologues and the ideologies that arise from structuralism have reduced tribal literatures to an "objective" collection of consumable artifacts. Postmodernism liberates imagination and widens the audience for tribal literatures; this new criticism rouses a comic world view, narrative discourse and language games on the past. (1989)

Arnold Krupat, in his Preface to *For Those Who Come After: A Study of Native American Autobiography*, faults postmodern critics for concentrating on established canonical texts, "thus miss[ing] out on some extraordinary opportunities to test and apply their ideas" to Native American literatures (1985). He is more blunt in his judgment of conventional critics, or "literary pragmatists," as he calls them, whom he accuses of allowing themselves "to carry on at some virtually pretechnological level of critical naiveté; the amount of unself-conscious twaddle about plots and characters and the poetry of place that goes on at the literary end of Native American studies would never be tolerated in the study of, say, Faulkner or William Carlos Williams, of Emily Dickinson or Thoreau" (1985). Despite such harsh words, Krupat's purpose is finally to encourage Native Americanists and theorists to join forces.

Krupat's own study of Native American autobiography, *For Those Who Come After*, is an excellent example of how modern theory can enhance our understanding of Native American writing. His opening chapter, "An approach to Native American texts," is indispensable reading. However, his "The dialogic of Silko's *storyteller*," which is included in Gerald Vizenor's *Narrative Chance: Postmodern Discourse on Native American Indian Literatures* (1989), reveals some of the problems of privileging theory at the expense of close textual analysis. In this article, Arnold Krupat offers a BAKHTINian reading of Silko's text which he treats as autobiographical writing. While Bakhtin's views of language as "heteroglossic" and "polyvocal" are helpful in describing Silko's use of multiple voices and story variants, the fluidity of the storytelling, and the dialogic character of her discourse, one may ask whether the application of Bakhtinian theory truly reveals anything that Silko, who carefully instructs the reader in the nature of oral DIS-COURSE, does not already convey without the ballast of technical jargon, and whether this kind of reading does not overburden the primary text unnecessarily. Perhaps Krupat's own comment that Native American literatures offer postmodern critics opportunities "to test and apply their ideas" (1985) is a hint that his approach remains focused primarily on the theory itself, rather than on the illumination of the primary text by the application of theory.

Krupat's treatment of Silko's title story, "Storyteller," is a useful example of how a careful structuralist analysis can render the theoretical approach more fruitful. Even if Krupat considered an exhaustive reading beyond the scope of the article, the story's centrality, not only to *Storyteller* as a whole but also to his Bakhtinian perspective, surely would have warranted more than the brief observation that "The storyteller of the title is the protagonist's grandfather, a rather less benign figure than the old storyteller of Silko's biographical experience; nonetheless, the stories he tells are of the traditional, mythic type" (Krupat, 1989). Indeed, "Storyteller" offers an opportunity to integrate theory and "pragmatic," in this case mythic and SYMBOLIC analysis.

As I noted in "What other story?: mythic subtexts in Leslie Silko's 'Storyteller,'" the old man (Krupat mistakenly assumes he is the young woman's grandfather) is by no means the only storyteller – the grandmother, the female protagonist, and the omniscient narrative voice that has mysteriously survived the story's final glacial cataclysm are others – nor is his bear narrative the dominating discourse in the story. Silko explicitly contrasts the old man's storytelling with another story with which the female protagonist must acquaint herself to understand her role fully. These features of the story fit precisely Bakhtin's notion of the heteroglossic and polyvocal nature of language as well as his idea that "All there is to know about the world is not exhausted by a particular discourse about it" (quoted in Krupat, 1989). In fact, at the heart of "Storyteller" are the conflicting claims of the old man's story, which anticipates the final winter for the white exploiters only, and those of the mythic subtexts, which foretell the end of humankind as punishment for the global destruction they have wrought.

The analysis of the story's references to traditional Eskimo doomsday myths and a close reading of its apocalyptic symbolism reveal that the overt theme of CULTURE clash is secondary to Silko's ecological concerns, lending support to Krupat's claim that one of Native American literature's central premises is "that a global, ecosystemic perspective is the necessary condition of human survival and that such a perspective prohibits anthropocentrism" (1985).

The many fine contributions to Gerald Vizenor's *Narrative Chance* offer ample evidence that modern critical approaches have already shed new light on Native American literature. However, as my brief discussion of "Storyteller" shows, theory is no substitute for close textual analysis, nor is it helpful to assert the supremacy of advanced literary theory over more traditional approaches if Krupat's goal of a "*rapprochement* between the two separate camps of theorists and Native Americanists" (1985), with all its potential for the future study of Native American literature, is to be realized.

Reading

Allen, Paula Gunn, ed. 1983: *Studies in Native American Literature: Critical Essays and Course Designs.*
Indian Voices: The First Convocation of American Indian Scholars: 1967.
Krupat, Arnold 1985: *For Those Who Come After: A Study of Native American Autobiography.*
Layton, Robert, ed. 1989: *Conflict in the Archaeology of Living Traditions.*
McGuire, Randall H. 1992: "Archaeology and the first Americans."
Owen, Louis 1993: *Other Destinies: Understanding the American Indian Novel.*
Owen, Roger C. 1967: *The North American Indian: A Source Book.*
Roemer, Kenneth 1983: *Native American Renaissance.*
Ruoff, A. LaVonne Brown 1990: *American Indian Literatures; An Introduction, Bibliographic Review, and Selected Bibliography.*
Swann, Brian, ed. 1983: *Smoothing the Ground: Essays on Native American Oral Literature.*
Vizenor, Gerald, ed. 1989 (*1993*): *Narrative Chance: Postmodern Discourse on Native American Indian Literatures.*
Wiget, Andrew 1985: *Native American Literature.*

JAMES PHILLIPS AND MATTHIAS SCHUBNELL

naturalization (vraisemblance) A method of interpretation by which the work is related to the cultural order as a whole: a term utilized often in STRUCTURALISM. With regard to the literary TEXT, this operation can be viewed as the domestication of a potentially disruptive text by a dominant literary order, or as the process of assimilation by which the great literary tradition renews itself. When the process is compete, the text seems "naturally" to display meanings which accord with the tradition as a whole. Structuralist critics tend to see the process of naturalization as an inherent operation of the human mind.

Reading

Culler, Jonathan 1975 (*1989*): *Structuralist Poetics.*
Hawkes, Terence 1977: *Structuralism and Semiotics.*

PAUL INNES

negative dialectics A phrase popularized by ADORNO (1966), referring to a contradictory process of reflection between thought and its object which is never finally resolved into the identity of a true knowledge. It was originally used to describe the structure of Plato's early "Socratic" dialogs. These function to draw attention to the ignorance of all the participants, rather than to show the superiority of any particular point of view. Adorno uses it to describe a materialist version of KANT's dialectic, in which it is the *limits* to knowledge which are at issue, rather than a Socratic skepticism about knowledge as such.

Reading

Adorno, Theodor W. 1966 (*1973*): *Negative Dialectics.*

PETER OSBORNE

neo-Kantianism This was the dominant current in German philosophy at the turn of the twentieth century and was influential across the humanities and social sciences. It originated in a "return to Kant" in the mid-nineteenth century, following a period of HEGELian and neo-Fichtean HEGEMONY over the intellectual direction and institutions of German philosophy. The neo-Kantians may be divided into the "Marburg" and "Heidelberg schools," each of which pursued a distinct interpretation of KANT. The Marburg school represented by Hermann Cohen emphasized the theme of validity, what it was that made judgments valid, while the Heidelberg school represented by Rickert and Lask focused upon the creation of value: the former may be described as an "objective," the latter as a "subjective" idealism.

The main impact of neo-Kantianism on CULTURAL THEORY was in the areas of the sociology, the history of ART, and the history of ideas. The sociologists of art influenced by this current of thought were Georg Simmel, Max Weber, and Georg Lukács. They all inclined toward the subjective idealism of the Heidelberg school, although Weber combined aspects of both traditions. Simmel's work in the sociology of art included studies of Rembrandt, Rodin, and other contemporary artists, and emphasized the tension between the active creation of meaning or "life" and its presentation in "form." Weber's study of the sociology of music is ostensibly less indebted to the metaphysical side of neo-Kantianism, and was dedicated to tracing the impact of the rationalization of the form and content of social life on the organization and technology of music. Lukács's pre-Marxist neo-Kantian period prior to the 1914–18 war was represented in his *Heidelberg Aesthetics.* This attempted to answer the pseudo-Kantian question, "We have works of art, how are they possible?" by reference to a "pure doctrine of validity" which was neither "metaphysical" nor "psychologistic," but which pointed toward a sociology of art.

Most of the neo–Kantian-inspired sociology of art from the early twentieth century is now largely of antiquarian or specialist interest, in contrast to the continuing significance of the debates it inspired in art history. The Heidelberg school was represented in art history by the work of Wilhelm Worringer in *Abstraction and Empathy* (1907) and *Form in Gothic* (1912), works influenced above all by Georg Simmel. Worringer presented the theoretical bases of his historical analysis in strictly neo–Kantian terms, considering "form" as the synthetic construction of a subjective "artistic will" striving to express itself. As opposed to the subjective idealism of the Heidelberg school manifest in Worringer, the emphasis of the Marburg school on objective idealism, or the validity of form beyond the accidents of history and culture, is embodied in the work of Heinrich Wölfflin. Wölfflin's art history concentrated on the formal similarities manifest in a genre or the work of an artist, for example, in his study *The Art of Albrecht Dürer* (1905) which rests on the general "Kantian" claim that each artist possesses a particular categorical structure of perception, and the more specific claim that the structure of perception possessed by Dürer consisted of the transposition of natural phenomena into line. The study traces this transposition, or act of formal synthesis, through selected works of the artist. This formalist approach to art history, shorn of any explicit reference to its philosophical basis in neo–Kantianism, continues to exert a significant influence on the discipline.

One of the most enduringly influential examples of Marburg neo–Kantianism is in the approach to the history of ideas developed by Ernst Cassirer. His works on the Renaissance and the ENLIGHTENMENT have had considerable influence on the emergence of the discipline of the history of ideas in the United States. His writings evince a fascinating tension between the neo–Kantian formalist impulse and the necessary confusion of historical source materials. When successful, the result is an extremely stimulating and coherent presentation of historical evidence; but when unsuccessful, the presentation becomes formally schematic and the citation of historical evidence somewhat aimless.

The main contribution of neo–Kantianism lies less in its own logical and metaphysical investigations of validity and values than in the influence it exerted upon surrounding disciplines. Its analysis of form provided an important principle for the construction of historical narratives in sociology, art history, and the history of ideas. However, the use of this formal principle for the organization of historical materials brought with it the threat of a reversion to its neo–Kantian origins as a subjective or objective idealism. For this reason a great deal of recent work in CULTURAL STUDIES has self-consciously distanced itself from "FORMALISM" and "idealism" without, however, engaging theoretically with their shared neo–Kantian origins.

Reading
Köhnke, Klaus Christian 1991: *The Rise of Neo-Kantianism*.
Rose, Gillian 1981: *Hegel Contra Sociology*.
Willey, Thomas E. 1978: *Back to Kant: The Revival of Kantianism in German Social and Historical Thought*.
                                                        HOWARD CAYGILL

The New Criterion   Made distraught by the state of intellectual discourse, a group of neo–Conservatives established *The New Criterion* in 1982. In their opening pages the editors set the pace for what continues today to be a dissenting voice in LITERARY and art CRITICISM; they painted a dismal picture of the academic world, accusing journals and institutions of deliberately failing to uphold certain standards of quality in academic and critical work and of being influenced by prevailing left-wing political attitudes. They wrote: "Today, more often than not, the prevailing modes of criticism have not only failed to come to grips with such tasks, they have actually come to constitute an obstacle to their pursuit." The founding editors saw it as their task to challenge the "sheer trendiness" of radical theorists, and so in September 1982 they established a journal "to apply a new criterion to the discussion of our our cultural life – a criterion of truth."

The journal espouses a conservative, traditional outlook on art and literature; the articles which appear monthly in *The New Criterion* typically challenge what the editors see as a dangerous "new wave of thought," sometimes with hostile attacks on other journals. The 1982 opening remarks touched on the editors' criticism of *Art History* for being "programmatic"; even later, Roger Kimball, who joined the editorial board as managing editor in November 1989, lambasted *OCTOBER*, a journal founded in 1976 on the belief that economic and social concerns set the context for art and criticism, for "combining fashionable academic jargon with radical political ideology." Other *New Criterion* articles have presented critical examinations of aspects of the art world, art movements, and museums. In 1984 an entire issue of the journal was devoted to the reopening of the Museum of Modern Art in New York. The journal also prints articles on literary and cultural criticism; Kimball, a prolific contributor, has submitted articles ranging from a discussion of Terry Eagleton to one entitled "Debating the humanities at Yale." In September 1989, the editors added a section called "Notes & Comments." In each issue, they present in this section a short discussion of current issues. The topic of the first "Notes & comments" was Mapplethorpe and the NEA; they argued for "rethinking of the proper purposes of federal support for culture and the proper mission of the NEA."

TARA G. GILLIGAN

New Criticism An American critical movement. Originating in the 1920s in the early work of T.S. ELIOT, I.A. RICHARDS, and John Crowe RANSOM, New Criticism became a self-conscious campaign at the end of the 1930s, and the dominant form of American academic criticism in the 1940s and 1950s. It is a notoriously slippery and contested term, but there is general agreement that Ransom, Allen TATE, and Cleanth BROOKS (see individual entries) were its leading figures and that New Criticism's distinguishing feature was a style of close verbal analysis in which each TEXT was treated as a self-contained or "autotelic" structure. The New Critics called this "intrinsic" analysis, and it turned out to be extremely problematic, even self-contradictory, both as a concept and in their practice and influence. A truly "intrinsic" criticism would be an extreme FORMALISM and, although that was what it degenerated into when New Criticism became an institutionalized orthodoxy, its founding fathers were anything but formalists. They were motivated by a deep concern with the world beyond the text, passionate ARNOLDian crusaders for CULTURE against anarchy. Hence the paradox that their adversaries have attacked them both for teaching students artificially to isolate texts from history and, simultaneously, for preaching a pessimistic and nostalgic vision of history to those same students. Both charges have some validity. The New Critics could never decide whether they wanted literature to be a sanctuary from history, a closed model of order, or combatively *engagé*.

The roots of this paradox lie in the movement's own history. Like several other influential critical schools, notably that of F.R. LEAVIS in England, New Criticism's story is that of a failed political movement which, checked in its wider ambitions, retreated to the academy and textual analysis. The founding fathers were part of the "Southern Renaissance" and had been members first of the FUGITIVES and then of the SOUTHERN AGRARIANS, promoting an idealized vision of the rural Old South as an alternative to the industrial North and all the forces of dehumanizing modern science and technology which it represented. When their "back to the land" campaign was unsuccessful, they returned to their literature departments and transformed their cultural politics into LITERARY CRITICISM. Ransom, the New Critics' chief guru, was perfectly explicit about this. In launching their campaign, he told Allen Tate, "our cue would be to stick to literature entirely. There's no consistent, decent group writing in politics . . . in the severe field of letters there is vocation enough for us." The only way of returning to the order of the past was now "formally," through art and literature, and after the "red fury" of agrarianism had died away, he and his comrades in arms retreated for this purpose to a "minority pocket of the culture," that is, to "educational institutions, with pockets of 'humanities,' whose interest has identified itself increasingly with ours." This was not a retreat to the individual contemplative life and the monastic cell, however. One form of organized propaganda campaign was simply exchanged for another. In his influential essay "Criticism, Inc.," Ransom called belligerently for "a new order of studies: the speculative or critical ones" as opposed to the ruling orthodoxy of historical scholarship: "now it is the Age of Criticism." As with the Leavisites in England, this was to be a war of the critics against the scholars, and it was fought with great determination and institutional effectiveness, starting with Ransom's founding of *The Kenyon Review* in 1939 (soon followed by the revamped *Southern Review*, *The Sewanee Review*, and *The Hudson Review*), and backed up with numerous undergraduate workbooks (Brooks's *Understanding Poetry* has probably been the best-selling critical work of the century), revisionist histories such as Brooks's *Modern Poetry and the Tradition*, the Kenyon Review Fellowships and especially with the Kenyon School of English and the Gauss Seminars at Princeton, summer schools whose purpose was to train the new critical cadres to throw into the frontline against the scholars. The aim was to take over English studies in America and they were brilliantly successful.

The aesthetic effects of this history were marked. Just as F.R. Leavis explicitly offered his style of criticism as a substitute for a vanished "organic community," so Ransom argued, "The little world [poetry] sets up is a little version of our natural world in its original dignity, not the laborious world of affairs. Indeed, the little world is the imitation of our ancient Paradise, when we inhabited it in innocence," and on this logic it followed inevitably that criticism too should be postlapsarian and backward-looking, offering the poem as a microcosm of and a compensation for a lost Edenic order.

The agrarians' political terminology had to be aestheticized in the process, but that was not difficult to achieve: organicist metaphors could be easily shifted from the Old South to lyric poems if you did not think too hard about them or the category confusions that were likely to result, and in any case they did not have to invent a new vocabulary. One was already to hand in the work not only of Ransom himself but also in that of T.S. Eliot and I.A. Richards, the patron saints of the movement. Eliot in particular had already prepared the way in his early essays, which slid continually between close textual criticism and grand synoptic historical generalizations, and many of the New Critics' central statements were reworkings of the most notorious instance of this elision, Eliot's theory of the DISSOCIATION OF SENSIBILITY, in which he extrapolated from close verbal analysis of Donne's poetry to a generalization about "something that happened to the mind of England" in the seventeenth century, when, under the pressure of the new science and religious skepticism, the unified medieval culture was finally lost. The New Critics seized eagerly on the analogy between Eliot's imaginary Renaissance moment and their own. Allen Tate suggested that the Southern Renaissance was like, "on an infinitesimal scale, the outburst of poetic genius at the end of the sixteenth century, when commercial England had begun to crush feudal England." The two Fall myths could be amalgamated.

I.A. Richards', influence reinforced Eliot's. In his work the New Critics found another meditation on order and its loss, another attempt to counter the "chaos" of the modern world with literary models of equilibrium and unified sensibility, and they appropriated many of his terms. Richards had, for instance, offered IRONY as one of the highest forms of harmonious integration and proposed that it "might provide a kind of test of the value of poetry," while Ransom went even further to define irony as "the ultimate mode of the great minds . . . the rarest of the states of mind, because it is the most inclusive," and the term became a New Critical keyword. Richards had praised the harmonious interactions of multiple levels of meaning in the best poetry; his insights were developed in his pupil William EMPSON's concept of AMBIGUITY, and this too became a *sine qua non* of the best poetry. One student trained at the Kenyon School of English recalled, "Vigorously, we 'explicated' in and out of class . . . and where we couldn't find an ambiguity we made one." A whole lexicon of cognate terms, such as Brooks's "PARADOX" and Tate's "TENSION," followed.

The typical New Critical "intrinsic reading" thus made no pretense to be value-free, a kind of neutral empirical technique. It was highly a-prioristic. It attempted to demonstrate the qualities of ironic or paradoxical "wit" in the poetry it admired (and it found these mainly in poetry; it was notably unsuccessful in dealing with drama or prose fiction) and to deplore their absence from those it did not. On the basis of these value judgments, a complete and highly distinctive history of English literature was then constructed, the story of the "tradition of wit," how this tradition came to be broken in the seventeenth century, how it persisted intermittently or in underground forms in apparently unwitty poets like Wordsworth; how it was reborn in T.S. Eliot and Anglo-American modernism.

The main reason for New Criticism's puzzling insistence on treating each poem as a closed and autonomous object is thus clear. Since the poem was the vestige of and the surrogate for the irretrievably lost "old society – the directed and hierarchical one" (Ransom) – and since it was thus simultaneously the pattern for an ideal form of knowledge, an anti-scientific knowledge which "treats an order of existence, a grade of objectivity, which cannot be treated in scientific discourse" (Ransom), it had to be inviolable. Anything like the current postmodernist picture of texts (as in the deliberately anti-New Critical version known as NEW HISTORICISM) as unstable force fields, fractured and breached by all the shockwaves of history, would destroy the whole enterprise. The New Critics needed an ideal text like Keats's Grecian Urn (an image they frequently invoked), a still unravish'd bride of quietness.

Yet New Criticism's one-sided fixation on the virtues of "intrinsic" reading and the illegitimacy of various extrinsic "heresies" (as they insisted on calling them) nevertheless still seems excessive. Why should critics with so strong a sense of the pressure of history repeatedly have dismissed historical readings as "extrinsic?" The answer is to be found in the second, postagrarian phase of the movement's own history, the war of the critics against the scholars. The traditional literary historians counterattacked very strongly; indeed the upstarts who, according to the Modern Language Association's 1948 presidential address, did nothing but fetishize complexity and ambiguity, were undermining 2,500 years of the humanist tradition. "History" therefore became the enemy, the epitome (along with Marxist criticism, the New Critics' other main *bête noire*) of reductive "extrinsic" readings. Understandably, since they themselves were often caricatured, the New Critics used caricature as their chief weapon against the scholar foe. "Almost every English professor is diligently devoting himself to discovering 'what porridge had John Keats,'" according to Cleanth Brooks. "This is our typical research: the backgrounds of English literature. And we hopefully fill our survey textbooks with biographical notes." If this were true, resistance was clearly needed, but this is a trivial notion of what the historical approach might be, and too much energy was expended in knocking the stuffing out of straw men instead of looking for better ways of marrying historical research and close reading. Even the best of the New Critics, let alone the many simplistic imitators of their "intrinsic" method, did not seem able to make a distinction between the historical approach *per se* and the particular reductive notions of history as "background" practiced by their opponents, and their arguments were often confused as a result. A prime example is Wimsatt and Beardsley's "The intentional fallacy," perhaps the most influential of all New Critical manifestos or fallacy denunciations. What Wimsatt and Beardsley set out to argue was the unexceptionable case that the success of a poem should not be judged solely in terms of its author's intentions. But their rambling and defensive polemic rapidly slid, once again, into assertions of the superiority of "internal" to "external" analysis, a peculiar dismissal of "background" information about Donne's knowledge of astronomy as irrelevant to the interpretation of his poetry, and generalized ridiculing of "the historical approach." The

effect of the piece was that generations of students were taught that externally derived information about an author's intentions (and by extension all other forms of "extrinsic" information about a text's historical context) was somehow inadmissible evidence, not only a distraction from but also an actual threat to the internally ordered meaning system that was the poem itself.

In retrospect it is now clear that, on this central issue of how to use external evidence in interpretation, New Criticism simply became muddled by its own partisan and overpolarized terminology. Cleanth Brooks, also out to extirpate intentionalist heretics, wrote, for example, "even where we know a great deal about the author's personality and ideas, we rarely know as much as the poem itself can tell us about itself." This is to face the interpreter with an unnecessary either/or choice between biography and criticism, but the main objection to it lies in the naivety of Brooks's concept of "the poem itself." That was the keystone of the whole New Critical enterprise and unhappily it was a nonexistent object.

However unintended their anti-historical bias was, however understandable in the heat of the moment and in the midst of the institutional polemics of the 1940s, the result was that the New Critics simply did not much interest themselves in either historical issues or the general problems of historical interpretation, and this had a damaging long-term effect on criticism which is only now, in a more recent "turn to history," beginning to be overcome.

What had started off as a liberating new emphasis on close rigorous reading, a welcome corrective to both vaguely impressionistic criticism and the more stultified and pedantic forms of historical scholarship, itself became narrow and stultified. It polemicized itself into an impossible corner, both philosophically (for no text *is* an island) and pedagogically (for students often do want to know about history), and expired there.

See also AMBIGUITY; BROOKS, CLEANTH; DISSOCIATION OF SENSIBILITY; ELIOT, T.S.; EMPSON, SIR WILLIAM; FUGITIVES; IRONY; ORGANIC UNITY; PARADOX; PRACTICAL CRITICISM; RANSOM, JOHN CROWE; RICHARDS, I.A.; TATE, ALLEN; TENSION.

Reading
Culler, Jonathan 1988: *Framing the Sign: Criticism and Its Institutions.*
Fekete, John 1978: *The Critical Twilight.*

Foster, Richard 1962: *The New Romantics: A Reappraisal of the New Criticism.*

Graff, Gerald 1979: "What was New Criticism?"

———1987: *Professing Literature: An Institutional History.*

Lentricchia, Frank 1980: *After the New Criticism.*

Ohmann, Richard 1976: *English in America: A Radical View of the Profession.*

Stewart, John Lincoln 1965: *The Burden of Time: The Fugitives and Agrarians.*

Webster, Grant 1979: *The Republic of Letters.*

Wellek, René 1986f: "New Criticism."

IAIN WRIGHT

New Historicism A form of textual analysis which developed in the United States during the 1980s and has now become firmly established in many English literature departments there and in journals such as *Representations, New Literary History, English Literary History,* and *English Literary Renaissance.* It cannot, however, be described as a unified approach or position, more a cluster of concerns which have been developed and elaborated in diverse ways – indeed the reluctance to adopt an overarching narrative of its own methodology has become one of its features. Like CULTURAL MATERIALISM (which is often described as its "British" counterpart) New Historicism sees itself as a radical approach, growing out of critical engagement with both MARXISM and POSTSTRUCTURALISM. Like cultural materialism too, it has been particularly elaborated in work on the Renaissance, especially that of Stephen Greenblatt, Jonathan Goldberg, Jean E. Howard, Karen Newman, and Louis Montrose, although it has also permeated work in other periods: Catherine Gallagher, Nancy Armstrong, and D.A. Miller's work are examples of New Historicist analysis of nineteenth-century CULTURE. However, the claims of the *newness* of this "turn to history" (which seems strange to British readers) needs to be situated itself within the context of American academic institutions and traditions.

New Historicism was first clearly defined as a critical tendency by Stephen Greenblatt in 1982 in his introduction to the collection of essays *The Forms of Power and The Power of Forms in the English Renaissance.* Here he contrasted the approaches expanded in these essays with the hitherto dominant procedures in American critical practice: "traditional literary history" and New Criticism. The former approach, Greenblatt maintained, exemplified in the writing of J. Dover

Wilson, sought to impose an artificial unity on Renaissance TEXTS, making them internally coherent and reflective of an equally organic world view, both of which tended to legitimize dominant modes of power. The latter focused exclusively on a dehistoricized text, repressing its political meanings. The new method, he argued, emphasized the contradictions within the cultural formation of each historical moment, indeed made these contradictions their subject. Following Raymond WILLIAMS, this New Historicism eschewed distinctions between literature and the cultural and social context within which it was produced, instead seeing modes of representation as constituting rather than simply reflecting social reality. New Historicism aimed to produce a "poetics of culture"; reading CANONical texts within, and as part of, multiple forms of WRITING, cutting across the distinction between fiction and nonfiction in exploring the formation of specific DISCOURSES and institutions.

New Historicism, then, represents a turn to history, but is often coy about what implied notion of historical change and social process is being invoked. Its theoretical reference points are diverse, and include Raymond Williams, Clifford Geertz, Michel FOUCAULT, Louis ALTHUSSER, Mikhail BAKHTIN, and Michel de Certeau. In some respects it places itself in a skeptical relationship to a historical materialist tradition, invoking a set of social relations and productive forces within which texts are embedded, while being critical of the hierarchical division between a determining base and a determined superstructure. Taking this point further and drawing on Foucault's work, New Historicism shares with poststructuralism a distrust of totalizing social theories and "grand narratives," continually problematizing the standpoint from which specific perceptions and theories are formed, though often in the process reinforcing the secure institutional base from which such deconstructing assertions are made.

New Historicism stresses the interdependent nature of cultural forms and institutions, and reads all traces of the past as texts, narratives to be interpreted. In refusing to give precedence to any particular story, it runs the risk of falling into complete relativism, in which history becomes an infinitely repetitive and regressing set of reflections. Stephen Greenblatt's work in particular is sensitive to these problems. In *Marvellous Possessions: The Wonder of the New World* (1991) for example, he argues that his emphasis on anecdote rather than totalizing explanatory stories mirrors the perceptions of the European encounter with America which he is analyzing. Nevertheless, he also points out that purely local knowledge is simply the underside of the totalization of which he is critical. He acknowledges that in foregrounding some of these anecdotes as representative stories, as somehow metaphoric, he is pointing to more generalized structures of power, though these often remain implied. In doing so, however, he runs the risk of reproducing the kind of "world view" that New Historicism claims to avoid.

Thus new historicist criticism, as Louis Montrose claims, emphasizes the "historicity of texts and the textuality of history." But these two projects may entail distinct, even contradictory methodologies and notions of history itself. The "HISTORICITY of texts" suggests that writings are produced within specific social, cultural, and economic conditions, and that at some level they are determined by those conditions, even as they contribute to their formation. The "textuality of history" emphasizes that history itself can be apprehended only as a collection of representations, open to multiple mediations, renarrations, and interpretations. However, both approaches recognize the problem of *how* to read historically – how to acknowledge one's own situatedness, yet make the conceptual leap necessary to apprehend the radical difference of the past. As modern readers we continually run the danger of reading texts anachronistically, seeing them as mirrors or projections of our own concerns rather than attempting to excavate the complex meanings they may have had when they were written.

The emphasis on the "textuality of history" draws on both Foucault and de Certeau's writing in seeing history itself as a set of archaeological traces and as narratives whose meaning is compounded by the narrative of history writing itself. To some extent these approaches could be seen as epochal rather than historical, marginalizing issues of social change and determination by concentrating on particular historical moments as EPISTEMES – self-contained structures of knowledge which do not necessarily tally with our own. Another starting point which shares this "flattening" perspective is CULTURAL ANTHROPOLOGY, particularly the writings of Clifford Geertz. Geertz's work on cultures radically different from his own entailed reading the symbolic structures of these societies as stories which their inhabitants tell about themselves. "The culture of a people is an ensemble of texts,"

he wrote, "themselves ensembles which the anthropologist strains to read over the shoulders of those to whom they properly belong" ("Deep play: note on the Balinese cock fight" in *Myth, Symbol and Culture*, 1974, p. 29). Much new historicist work too wishes to "read over the shoulder" of moments in the past, aiming at "thick description" of the processes at work within them by close reading of specific works.

For all the stress on decentering the text, however, much New Historicist work still privileges literary over other forms of discourse, though it might expand its definition. In the first place, as many of its critics have pointed out, it does often seem to return to canonical writing and to extrapolate an entire social dynamic from the close reading of a specific work or TROPE. Second, literary, and specifically dramatic forms of playing and performance are seen as key metaphors for the society as a whole. For example, Greenblatt's *Shakespearian Negotiations* (1988) reads the Elizabethan stage as a central economic, political, and psychic institution. Elizabethan society was organized around theatricality, he argued; the notion of performance was central to both the shaping of individual subjectivity and the power relationships permeating society as a whole, manifested by pageant, public ceremony, and display. Renaissance drama does not simply reflect this theatricality – it produces, reproduces, and negotiates it in a much more complicated way, and thus it is impossible to draw a distinction between aesthetic and other kinds of social energy and discourse.

This stress on negotiation and renegotiation, in which dramatic forms actively shape the power relationships of their society, continually subverting yet also ultimately contained by dominant forms of state ideological power, has led some critics of New Historicism to argue that it has become mesmerized by the notion of "ideological entrapment," on which it relies. Alan Sinfield, for example, argues in *Faultlines: Cultural Materialism and the Politics of Dissident Reading* (1992) that the approach does not realize its own political potential, too easily falling into the relativism and FORMALISM of poststructuralist rhetoric, and failing to consider how dissident reading strategies might be developed. Some feminists have also argued that New Historicism runs the risk of reinforcing the marginality of oppressed groups, though others have developed its methods to focus on the power play of GENDER. It has, some claim, simply become another professional approach, quickly engulfed and incorporated by an insatiable American literary institution. *See also* CULTURAL MATERIALISM; WILLIAMS, RAYMOND.

Reading
Dollimore, Jonathan 1990: "Shakespeare, cultural materialism, feminism and Marxist humanism."
Ferguson, Margaret W., Quilligan, Maureen, and Vickers, Nancy J., eds 1985: *Rewriting the Renaissance: The Discourses of Sexual Difference in Early Modern Europe.*
Geertz, Clifford 1973 (*1993*): *The Interpretation of Cultures.*
Goldberg, Jonathan 1983: *James I and the Politics of Literature: Jonson, Shakespeare. Donne and their Contemporaries.*
Greenblatt, Stephen 1988: *Shakespearean Negotiations.*
—— 1991: *Marvellous Possessions: The Wonder of the New World.*
Healy, Thomas 1992: *New Latitudes: Theory and English Renaissance Studies.*
Howard, Jean E., and Connor, Marion F., eds 1987: *Shakespeare Reproduced: The Text in History and Ideology.*
Montrose, Louis 1986: "Renaissance literary studies and the subject of history."
Newman, Karen 1991: *Fashioning Femininity and English Renaissance Drama.*
Nicholls, Peter 1989: "Old problems and New Historicism."
Veeser, H. Aram, ed. 1989: *The New Historicism.*

JENNY BOURNE TAYLOR

New Left In general, *left*, often with an initial capital, refers to LIBERAL or radical views in politics that evolved during the 1950s, 1960s, and 1970s. Ideologically and globally, according to Cranston (1971), the New Left may be partly defined (for there are national differences) in contrast to the Old Left by their relationship to Karl MARX. The Old Left made capitalism and the rights of labor its central concerns, adhered to party lines, and envisaged the industrial working classes becoming the universal revolutionary class. In contrast, representatives of the New Left are independent and individualistic, emphasizing not the economist Marx of *Capital* (1954), but the sociologist and humanist of The *Economic and Philosophical Manuscripts of 1844* (1959), and look to the proletariat of the impoverished peasants of the Third World, the blacks in the ghettoes, and alienated bourgeoisie and intellectuals for change.

Nigel Young identifies a "core identity" for the NL, composed at first (late 1950s and early 1960s) of nonviolent direct action, civil disobedience, antimilitarism, utopian pacifism, and decentralized participatory democracy to create an alternative community opposed to the established injustice and insanity of RACISM and nuclear war. These beliefs were expressed, for example, by the antinuclear Committee of 100/Aldermaston marches and the Campaign for Nuclear Disarmament (CND) in England, the Southern US Montgomery bus boycott (1955) that brought Martin Luther King, Jr, to prominence, the sit-ins, and the Mississippi Freedom Summers of the broadening Civil Rights Moment, the Berkeley Free Speech Movement of 1964 (and similar activities at Columbia University, Berlin, Nanterre, the London School of Economics). The nuclear peace movement added a transnational element (the CND's positive neutralism, A.J. Muste's Third Camp ideas) that linked NL movements internationally. During the late 1960s the NL became more violent in tactics and attitude – in the United States the increasing influence of Black Power and Progressive Labor at home and advocacy of anti-imperialist, military liberation abroad; in Europe the the Red Brigades in Italy, the Red Army Faction (Baader-Meinhof) in Germany, the Angry Brigade in Britain, Action Directe in France. Nonviolent influence waned under police violence and violent response, the deaths of Muste, King, and Paul Goodman in the United States, and other pressures.

The year 1968 was the climax of the NL's struggle for a reconstituted world (Caute, 1988). Rebellions swept the industrial West, composed of the offspring, especially students, of the more privileged citizens. Only in America did blacks provide an element of both the alienated and exploited. The moral protest against media manipulation, consumerism, racism, and imperialism found common focus, particularly in the Vietnam War. In the United States President Johnson abandoned a run for a second term; King was murdered; draft evasion was widespread; the Democratic National Convention was a battleground; Columbia University, San Francisco State College, and other colleges experienced insurrection; in Europe, Germany's most influential student leader was shot and rioting spread across the country; France was temporarily paralyzed by its worst revolt since 1871; Czechoslovakia witnessed its brief Prague Spring of parliamentary liberalization (until the Soviet invasion and repression in August); student demonstrations were met with army bullets in Mexico City; students went on the rampage in Madrid; massive student protests struck universities in Japan.

Although by the 1970s the Western democracies had returned to business as usual, there were achievements. In the United States the South was substantially desegregated, the rule of the Ku Klux Klan generally broken, the electoral situation transformed, a war challenged though not ended. Globally a vision of a world undivided by rulers and ruled, rich and poor, RACE, CLASS, OR GENDER, has been sustained, at least on local levels. Although Third World idealism has disappeared, anti-imperialist and anti-apartheid demonstrations continue. The women's movement, though it rejected the male-dominated NL, was a product of it.

See also ALTHUSSER, LOUIS; CANON; EAGLETON, TERRY; ENGELS, FRIEDRICH; FANON, FRANTZ; FRANKFURT SCHOOL; GRAMSCI, ANTONIO; MARCUSE, HERBERT; MARXIST-FEMINIST LITERATURE COLLECTIVE; NEW LEFT REVIEW; SAID, EDWARD; SARTRE, JEAN-PAUL; THOMPSON, EDWARD; WILLIAMS, RAYMOND.

Reading
Bacciocco, Edward, Jr 1974: *The New Left in America: Reform to Revolution 1956–1970.*
Caute, David 1988: *The Year of the Barricades: A Journey Through 1968.*
Cranston, Maurice 1971: *The New Left: Six Critical Essays on Che Guevara, Jean-Paul Sartre, Herbert Marcuse, Frantz Fanon, Black Power, R.D. Laing.*
Diggins, Patrick 1992: *The Rise and Fall of the American Left.*
Young, Nigel 1977: *An Infantile Disorder? The Crisis and Decline of the New Left.*

JAMES R. BENNETT

New Left Review Journal of the British New Left, founded in 1960, initially edited by Stuart HALL, and including among its contributors E.P. THOMPSON and Raymond WILLIAMS. From 1962 *NLR* came under the iconoclastic direction of a younger cohort, which reoriented it towards the traditions of Western Marxism (for example, GRAMSCI and ALTHUSSER) and then, after 1968, revolutionary socialism (Leninism and Trotskyism). Under the editorship of Perry ANDERSON, *NLR* and its publishing imprint, New Left Books/Verso, exercised a decisive, controversial influence upon the growth of anglophone Marxist culture in the 1960s and 1970s. By adopting a more ecumenical editorial policy, *NLR* has survived the contemporary crisis of socialism and remains a major international journal of socialist theory.

GREGORY ELLIOTT

New Right The term used to denote a broad range of LIBERAL and conservative ideas which came to prominence in Britain, France, and the United States during the 1970s in opposition to social democratic/New Deal ideologies, practices, and institutions. By then various forms of state intervention adopted since the 1930s in the name of economic growth, social justice, and political stability had become associated with persistent inflation, economic stagnation, and the corrosion of government authority. In this context a revival of interest in both economic LIBERALISM and the conditions for social order and government authority was translated into at least the rhetoric – and to some extent the practice – of British and American government in the 1980s.

Monetary stability, according to economic liberals such as Milton FRIEDMAN, could be achieved by strict government control of the quantity of money in circulation, while economic efficiency and growth could be obtained by disengaging the state from economic activity – on the assumption that individuals responding to price signals in markets provide the best mechanism to achieve these goals. Interventionist government, in this view, distorts the price mechanism and spawns coercion, bureaucracy, uniformity, and the dominance of producers' interests rather than those of the consumer. Friedrich von Hayek's social epistemology was influential in supporting these contentions with the argument that only decentralized markets could sift the complex, dispersed knowledge of human needs which collectivist politics is condemned to guess. Nevertheless, agreement about the superiority of markets and of the need for sound money has not prevented considerable disagreement among economic liberals over means and policy priorities. In rejecting the moral case for income redistribution, for example, some have gone so far as to classify all forms of taxation as illegitimate infringements of individual rights and thus argued for the privatization of all state responsibilities – even the military. The minimal state, as preferred by libertarians such as Robert Nozick, is thus in some ways close to anarchism.

This points to an even bigger Tension between the liberal and conservative components of the New Right. Though their opposition to "big government" and mutual regard for private property provide obvious points of overlap, the conservative preoccupation with order, hierarchy, and government authority – not to mention the idea that society can be likened to an organism with "personality and will" – is at odds with the liberal contention that a society is nothing more than the collection of individuals who comprise it. As SCRUTON has shown, the value of individual liberty is, for a conservative, "subject to another and higher value, the authority of established government" and this can be menaced as much "by mercantile enthusiasm," the language of individual rights, and the "disease" of democracy as by the socialist quest for social justice and egalitarianism. The institutions that sustain economic competition and enterprise are, in this conservative view, only a component of the desirable social order, not synonymous with it. This explains why such people have shown much more concern than the economic liberals with the many and diverse threats to social cohesion which they perceive in social change and reform – whether these forces are thought to undermine family, educational standards, national identity, the established church, public order, monarchy, or individual morality. Here, then, is a big program for strong, obtrusive government. But again – as with the economic liberals – a range of emphases and policy prescriptions can be derived from this conservative defense of the "organic," hierarchic social order including, to take just one instance, a broadly based battle for the defense of "national culture" which at one extreme becomes the overt racism of an Alain de Benoist in France.

Reading
Barry, N. 1987: *The New Right.*
Levitas, R. 1986: *The Ideology of the New Right.*
Durham, M. 1992: *Sex and Politics: The Family and Morality in the Thatcher Years.*
Gamble, A. 1988: *The Free Economy and the Strong State.*
JOHN CALLAGHAN

Nietzsche, Friedrich Wilhelm (1844–1900) Born in Röcken, Germany, Nietzsche studied classical philology at the Universities of Bonn and Leipzig (1864–5). He became professor of classical philology at the University of Basel, Switzerland in 1869 at the age of 24, but resigned from this post ten years later owing to ill health, having been granted a pension. Nietzsche's creative life spanned from the publication of *The Birth of Tragedy* in 1872 to the production of *Twilight of the Idols* and *The Antichrist* (a vehemently polemical attack on Christian belief) in late 1888. In January 1889

Nietzsche suffered a mental collapse from which he never recovered. He was cared for by his mother, and subsequently by his sister, until his death in 1900. The apparent ease with which it is possible to read Nietzsche's books is deceptive. Stylistically, he is one of the most approachable of philosophers, but the complexity of his ideas and their development defies simple exegesis. What follows merely selects some of the more influential aspects of his thought and places them in the context of their effect upon recent philosophy and CRITICAL THEORY.

Nietzsche's writings have had a significant impact on philosophy, literature, critical theory, and even theology. Figures as diverse as Sigmund FREUD, Martin HEIDEGGER (who views Nietzsche primarily in the context of his own critique of western metaphysical thought), Jean-Paul SARTRE, D.H. Lawrence, Thomas Mann, Georg LUKÁCS, Theodor ADORNO, Jacques DERRIDA, and Jean-François LYOTARD have all been subject in one way or another to his influence. In the twentieth century Nietzsche's name has had a chequered history: it has been associated by various critics of the times with the German militarism of the 1914–18 war and the Nazism of the 1939–45 war – an association primarily caused in the latter case by the unscrupulous exegetical attitudes of Nazi "intellectuals," and by his sister's own Nazi sympathies. In the English-speaking world Nietzsche's postwar rehabilitation was in large part due to Walter Kaufmann's classic study, *Nietzsche: Philosopher, Psychologist, Antichrist* (1950; fourth revised edition 1974) which challenged many widely held misconceptions about his philosophy.

Nietzsche was initially influenced by the thought of Schopenhauer, and also by his association with the composer Richard Wagner, and his early writings (principally *The Birth of Tragedy* (1872) and two of the four *Untimely Meditations*, "Schopenhauer as Educator" and "Richard Wagner in Bayreuth," published in 1874 and 1876 respectively) pay homage to these figures. *The Birth of Tragedy* is a remarkable text which attempts to reinterpret the significance of Greek tragedy by understanding it as a sublimated expression of the inherent violence of ancient Greek CULTURE. Nietzsche's analysis introduces the aesthetic categories "Apollinian" and "Dionysian" as a means of decoding the meaning of Greek tragedy. The Apollinian represents the formal constraints and structures necessary for artistic expression: "the

form-giving force, which reached its consummation in Greek culture" (Kaufmann, 1974, p. 128).
The Dionysian, on the other hand, embodies violent and chaotic forces of becoming. These forces,
Nietzsche argues, were harnessed and sublimated
by the Apollinian element to make possible the
production of the classical Greek cultural legacy.
Wagner's music is presented in *The Birth of Tragedy* as a means for attaining a rejuvenated contemporary German national culture akin to that
achieved by the Greeks. By the time he wrote
Human, All Too Human (1878), however, Nietzsche
had turned away from Wagner, seeing him not so
much as a source of hope for the future of culture
as a symptom of contemporary decline. Likewise,
Nietzsche came to view Schopenhauer's pessimistic philosophy in a more critical light, while his
attitude toward nationalism steadily hardened (a
tendency already hinted at in the first *Untimely
Meditation*, devoted to attacking the "cultural
philistinism" exemplified by David Strauss's *The
Old and the New Faith*).

Nietzsche's books spanning 1878–82 mark what
some scholars have termed his "positivistic" period (Habermas, *1981*). Whether or not such a
term can adequately serve to define the approaches
Nietzsche experimented with in *Human, All Too
Human, Daybreak* (1881), and *The Gay Science* (published in 1882, with Book V added in 1885), many
of the themes and concerns which are taken up in
his later works receive their preliminary airings in
these books – for example, an increasing epistemological skepticism, a growing interest in psychology and physiology, the development of a power
theory, the famous announcement of the "death of
God," and the recasting of ethical issues in terms
of these ideas. Equally, *Human, All Too Human*
marks a turn to the aphoristic style of expression
which Nietzsche was to adopt in most of his later
works.

The production of *Thus Spoke Zarathustra* (parts
I and II, 1883; part III, 1884; and part IV 1885)
marks the beginning of Nietzsche's most productive period. An often rhapsodic text, *Zarathustra*
takes the form of a philosophically oriented biblical parody. Most significantly, it announces
the need for the "overman" (*Übermensch*) as the
supreme goal of human activity. The overman represents for Nietzsche the highest expression of
human potential, a creative being able to give
meaning to a universe which can no longer be
adequately explained in terms of the outmoded

metaphysical postulates and religious beliefs of
Christian ontology.

In his mature thought Nietzsche developed a
holistic view of the cosmos in which all identities
are the product of relations of force (*The Will to
Power, 1968*, section 1067). This notion forms
the basis for his contention that life itself can be
comprehended in terms of an interplay of power
relations: "power" as such does not exist, but
"power-relationships between two or more forces"
do (ibid., 631). All living beings are an expression
of this network of contending forces. All life,
Nietzsche holds, seeks to enhance its own feeling
of power, which is none other than an expression
of its "will to power." The pursuit of power can
have many forms of expression, ranging from the
tyrannical desire to control others to the ascetic's
will to self-denial and self-discipline, which enhances his or her feeling of power by subjugating
the demands of the body.

The emphasis on power in Nietzsche's thinking
forms the basis for his critique of conventionally
accepted moral codes, and forms the core of *On the
Genealogy of Morals* (1887; *1968*). Ethical systems,
according to Nietzsche, can be divided into two
different camps representing contending interests,
"master morality" and "slave morality." Master
morality evaluates the world from the perspective
of attained domination and power. In consequence,
Nietzsche argues, master morality is primarily affirmative in character since it emanates from the
standpoint of a dominant social grouping which
first affirms itself as "good," and only after that
conceptualizes those of a lower rank as "bad." Slave
morality, on the other hand, is generated from the
perspective of the oppressed. The slave feels him-
or herself to be the helpless victim of a superior
force and, unable to take practical action to rectify
the situation, labels that force "evil." The slave's
conception of "good" is a secondary, "reactive"
(Deleuze, 1983) consequence of this negative judgment. In Nietzsche's terms, Christian culture is a
prime example of slave morality, while ancient
Roman culture exemplifies master morality. Mo-
DERNITY finds itself caught between the two ethical
forms: "today there is perhaps no more decisive
mark of a '*higher nature*' . . . than that of being a
genuine battleground of these opposed values"
(Nietzsche, 1968, part I, p. 16). Nietzsche's concern with modernity, that is, with what he came to
see as the nihilistic heritage of a Christian tradition
which had reached the point of self-destruction,

marks him out in the eyes of many critics as the progenitor of POSTMODERNISM. According to Gianni Vattimo, for example, "It could be legitimately argued that philosophical post-modernity is born with Nietzsche's work" (Vattimo, 1988, p. 164).

During the postwar period Nietzsche's thought exerted a marked influence upon philosophers and theorists in a variety of ways. Within the Frankfurt school, the neo-Marxist tendencies which epitomize the approaches of Max HORKHEIMER, Theodor ADORNO, Herbert MARCUSE, and Walter BENJAMIN are frequently tempered by elements of Nietzschean skepticism. For example, the force of Nietzsche's critique of rationalist principles contributes a significant element to Adorno and Horkheimer's *Dialectic of Enlightenment* (1944), which charts the development of the enlightenment in terms of a struggle for power which, in its attempt to banish prescientific mythologies, recoils into creating a new mythological structure of rationalist tenets to replace them. Adorno's later development – especially in *Minima Moralia* (1951), which uses the aphoristic style favoured by Nietzsche, and *Against Epistemology* (1956) – frequently exhibits a Nietzschean turn of thought, whereby the foundational principles of critical reason are consistently revealed as having an all too human, and hence questionable, basis.

Among those thinkers within the structuralist and poststructuralist traditions, Nietzsche's impact is most obviously evident in the work of Michel FOUCAULT, Gilles DELEUZE, Paul DE MAN, Jacques DERRIDA, and Jean-François LYOTARD. Foucault's attempt at elucidating a "genealogical" model of history self-consciously draws upon Nietzsche's analysis of power and his critique of the "subject" in a way which seeks to overturn both liberal and Marxist presuppositions about knowledge and politics. For Foucault, as for Nietzsche, knowledge is not composed of an autonomous body of abstract theorems that exist independently of prevailing social forces. On the contrary, the striving for knowledge is in fact a striving for mastery over reality; hence "knowledge" is in fact a term which can be thought of as being synonymous with "power."

For Gilles Deleuze, Nietzsche is a thinker worthy of close and careful interpretation (see Deleuze's *Nietzsche and Philosophy*, first published in 1962) and the source of a number of key terms in his own philosophical vocabulary. Deleuze sees Nietzsche as a "nomadic" thinker who spurns the dualistic institutional and state structures which dominate modern life in favour of a monistic and yet polymorphous philosophy of becoming. Perhaps the most interesting example of Nietzsche's influence on Deleuze is to be found in *A Thousand Plateaus* (Deleuze and Guatarri, 1980), which draws upon Nietzsche's psychological and physiological accounts of power relations in its formulation of a highly problematic critique of authoritarian discourse, replete with an essentialism consisting of "nomadic essences."

Nietzsche also casts his distinctive shadow over the deconstructive work of both Paul de Man and Jacques Derrida. For de Man (1979), Nietzsche's texts are PARADIGM cases of self-deconstructing arguments which destabilize their own structure. Derrida too sees Nietzsche as a precursor of the deconstructive techniques which he himself has used to criticize the "logocentric" tendencies of the Western tradition. However, Nietzsche is also a much more problematic figure for Derrida than he is for Deleuze. For example, Derrida's analysis of the "left" and "right" tendencies of Nietzschean DISCOURSE in *The Ear of the Other* (1982) demonstrates a critical concern with the "destinational" structures of justification supplied by Nietzsche's own writings, and their subsequent appropriation by seemingly opposed positions. Jean-François Lyotard's postmodern discourse is marked by a cross-fertilization of Nietzschean and KANTIAN influences in its advocacy of both an agonistic view of human relations and the role of an aesthetically oriented AVANT-GARDE (see *The Postmodern Condition*, 1979). Lyotard's position, however, has been modified by his reading of philosophers from the analytic tradition (principally Kripke and WITTGENSTEIN). In *The Differend* (1983) he constructs a formalistic philosophy of language in which the term postmodern is rendered a potentially problematic manifestation of Nietzschean discourse: "a goal for a certain humanity . . . (A bad parody of Nietzsche. Why?)" (section 182).

Reading

Adorno, T.W. 1951 (*1974*): *Minima Moralia. Reflections from Damaged Life*.
——1956 (*1982*): *Against Epistemology*.
——and Horkheimer, M. 1944 (*1973*): *Dialectic of Enlightenment*.
Ansell-Pearson, Keith 1991: *Nietzsche contra Rousseau: A Study of Nietzsche's Moral and Political Thought*.
Bridgwater, Patrick 1972: *Nietzsche in Anglosaxony*.
de Man, Paul 1979: *Allegories of Reading: Figural Language in Rousseau, Nietzsche, Rilke, and Proust*.

Deleuze, Gilles 1962 (*1983*): *Nietzsche and Philosophy.*
——and Guatarri, Félix 1980 (*1988*): *A Thousand Plateaus.*
Derrida, Jacques 1978b (*1979*): *Spurs: Nietzsche's Styles.*
——1982b (*1988*): *The Ear of the Other.*
Foucault, Michel 1977: "Nietzsche, genealogy, history."
Habermas, Jürgen 1968 (*1981*): *Knowledge and Human Interests.*
Hollingdale, R.J. 1973: *Nietzsche.*
Kaufmann, Walter 1950 (*1974*): *Nietzsche: Philosopher, Psychologist, Antichrist.*
Lampert, Laurence 1993: *Nietzsche and Modern Times: A Study of Bacon, Descartes and Nietzsche.*
Lyotard, Jean-François 1979 (*1989*): *The Postmodern Condition.*
——1983 (*1988*): *The Differend: Phrases in Dispute.*
Nietzsche, Friedrich 1872 (*1968*): *The Birth of Tragedy.*
——1873–6 (*1983*): *Untimely Meditations.*
——1878–80 (*1986*): *Human, All Too Human.*
——1881 (*1982*): *Daybreak.*
——1882/7 (*1974*): *The Gay Science.*
——1883–5/92 (*1976*): *Thus Spoke Zarathustra.*
——1886 (*1968*): *Beyond Good and Evil.*
——1887 (*1968*): *On the Genealogy of Morals.*
——1888/1895 (*1976*): *The Antichrist.*
——1901 (*1968*): *The Will to Power.*
Vattimo, Gianni 1985 (*1988*): *The End of Modernity.*

PETER J. SEDGWICK

Norris, Christopher (1948–) British critical theorist. Although many of his early publications dealt with music and musicians, Norris began to attract a wide readership with his lucid commentaries on literary and CRITICAL THEORY, especially in such books as *Deconstruction: Theory and Practice* (1982), *The Deconstructive Turn* (1983), *The Contest of Faculties* (1985), *Jacques Derrida* (1987), *Paul de Man* (1988), and *Deconstruction and the Interests of Theory* (1989). Although he has readily admitted that occasionally the ludic writing of DERRIDA and other theorists has invited a misreading of their work, he has nevertheless strongly emphasized the importance of truth claims and the search for a philosophical grounding of ethical and political responsibility in the discourses of contemporary literary and critical theory. When he finds an abandonment of these ENLIGHTENMENT commitments – as in the writings of LYOTARD, BAUDRILLARD, FISH, and RORTY, for example – his criticism can be scathing (see Norris, 1990; 1991; 1992; 1993). The range and depth of his reading and the power of his critique, which continues to be inspired by the thought of William EMPSON, have earned him a unique credibility that enables him to instruct both literary theorists on their often shallow knowledge of philosophy and traditional philosophers on

the superficiality of their dismissals of literary theory.

Reading
Norris, Christopher 1982: *Deconstruction: Theory and Practice.*
——1983: *The Deconstructive Turn: Essays in the Rhetoric of Philosophy.*
——1985: *The Contest of Faculties: Philosophy and Theory after Deconstruction.*
——1987: *Jacques Derrida.*
——1988: *Paul de Man: Deconstruction and the Critique of Aesthetic Ideology.*
——1989: *Deconstruction and the Interests of Theory.*
——1990: *What's Wrong with Postmodernism: Critical Theory and the Ends of Philosophy.*
——1991: *Spinoza and the Origins of Modern Critical Theory.*
——1992: *Uncritical Theory: Postmodernism, Intellectuals and the Gulf War.*
——1993: *The Truth about Postmodernism.*

MICHAEL PAYNE

nuclear criticism   A focus of intense though rather short-lived interest among (mainly) deconstructionist literary critics during the early to mid-1980s. The most influential source text was Jacques DERRIDA's essay "No apocalypse, not now (seven missiles, seven missives)," first delivered at a Cornell University conference in 1984 and then published – along with other contributions – in a special number of the journal *Diacritics.* This debate examined further a number of themes that were already prominent in the discourse of AVANT-GARDE literary theory. It coincided with a tense period in US–Soviet relations when the right-wing Reagan administration seemed about to abandon the hitherto prevailing doctrine of Mutual Assured Destruction, that is, the so-called "balance of terror" which (according to nuclear strategists) had so far prevented the outbreak of global war. Thus Reagan took to speaking casually of the Soviet Union as the "evil empire," while hawkish policy makers such as Caspar Weinberger discussed the prospect of a "limited" (tactical) nuclear exchange which could somehow be contained short of an all-out, annihilating confrontation. In this context it appeared to many that the choice was between two competing forms of lunacy, the one caught up in an escalating "logic" of bluff and counterbluff whose outcome was beyond rational calculation, while the other – in the name of a "new realism" – looked set to provoke nuclear catastrophe by adopting a yet more aggressive rhetorical stance.

Thus Derrida raises the following questions with regard to "nuclear criticism":

(i) What authority do its practitioners possess vis-à-vis those other, more established disciplines or fields of specialized knowledge (scientific, technological, diplomatic, militaro-strategic, etc.), whose competence in such matters is standardly taken for granted?

(ii) What can this presumptive "competence" amount to when the stakes are so unthinkably high – and the issues so far beyond "rational" comprehension – as to offer no hold for anything that resembles those familiar (expertly accredited) forms of knowledge? For is it not the case

(iii) that in this domain there exist no reliable protocols, no criteria of adequate method or valid inference, no appeal to patterns of predictive reasoning, of well-founded conjecture by analogy with past experience, and so forth, that would serve to determine the truth or falsehood of any given claim? For, as Derrida writes, "[a]ll of them [the putative 'experts'] are in the position of inventing, inaugurating, improvising procedures and giving orders where no model . . . can help them at all" (Derrida, 1984, p. 22). On which grounds

(iv) might it not be argued that "competence" in this matter belongs just as much to those – literary critics, rhetoricians, deconstructionists, speech-act theorists, and others – whose concern is precisely with interpretative issues that exceed the parameters of logical discourse or rational decidability? "We can therefore consider ourselves competent," Derrida suggests, "because the sophistication of the nuclear strategy can never do without a sophistry of belief and the rhetorical simulation of a text" (p. 26). Whence the further question

(v) as to the status of the so-called nuclear referent, that to which all these discourses (supposedly) allude in their various modes of description, analysis, strategic calculation, threat and counterthreat, simulated (war game) scenarios, and so forth. This referent cannot be equated with the weapons themselves – with their number, accuracy, degree of technological advancement, speed, range, "first-strike" capacity, or whatever – since these factors only count in so far as they partake of an escalating rhetoric (that of nuclear "deterrence") whose

stakes are defined entirely in performative as opposed to constative or factual-descriptive terms.

Thus: "If there are wars and a nuclear threat, it is because 'deterrence' has neither 'original meaning' nor measure. Its 'logic' is the logic of deviation and transgression, it is rhetorical-strategic escalation or nothing at all" (Derrida, 1984, p. 29). Then again, one might construe the nuclear "referent" as that of global war or the "unthinkable" happening – the end game catastrophe – toward which all these discourses gesture. Such debate is presumably conducted either with the purpose of preventing its occurrence (as in the case of "classical" deterrence theory), or with a view to planning the event and securing the best possible chance of victory and survival for one side only should war eventually break out. The latter was the line of argument adopted by those soidisant new "realists" of the early 1980s – Weinberger among them – who envisaged the United States "prevailing" in a limited (tactical) nuclear exchange. In their view hostilities would somehow stop short of wholesale destruction by allowing the belligerents time to pull back and avoid firing their entire arsenal of intercontinental ballistic missiles.

Of course (as its critics were quick to point out), this doctrine introduced a new and dangerous destabilizing element into a field – that of US–Soviet nuclear diplomacy – whose precarious balance depended on the threat of precisely such an all-out war of mutual annihilation. It was thus likely to provoke the Soviets into an early use of their own first-strike capacity, since after all they would have nothing to lose thereby if the US strategists were thinking in similar terms. It also ignored what they (the Soviets) had adopted as a matter of "realist" policy, that is, the assumption – hitherto shared with their US counterparts in the deterrence theory camp – that a nuclear exchange could not in fact be confined to the deployment of "limited" (tactical or battlefield) weapons, but would rapidly and inevitably escalate to the catastrophic point of no return. In this case (again) the strategic imperative on both sides would be to launch as many as possible of one's own warheads at the first opportunity and thus save them from preemptive destruction by the first wave of incoming enemy missiles.

Such are the APORIAS of nuclear discourse, deterrence doctrine, and its various supposed alternatives. Their effect – as Derrida sees it – is to delegitimize any form of knowledge which stakes its authority on the existence of a given nuclear "referent," or on the presupposed capacity of human reason to figure out ways and means of coping with the nuclear threat. In this field "there is a multiplicity of dissociated, heterogeneous competencies," such that "any knowledge is neither coherent nor totalizable" (Derrida, 1984, p. 22). And again:

> The dividing line between *doxa* and *episteme* [i.e. between "mere opinion" and "knowledge"] begins to blur as soon as there is no longer any such thing as an absolutely legitimizable competence for a phenonomenon which is no longer strictly techno-scientific but techno-militaro-politico-diplomatic through and through, and which brings into play the *doxa* or incompetence even in its calculations. (p. 24)

This is the weak or negative justification for nuclear criticism. Since the self-appointed "experts" are so manifestly out of their depth in confronting such a range of intractable problems, aporias, or wholly unforeseeable turns of event, therefore (so it is argued) the field is wide open for others, literary theorists among them, to discuss these issues with an equal claim to competence. More specifically, they – and deconstructionists in particular – may well have something useful to contribute on this question of undecidability, or the way in which nuclear discourse problematizes the relation between truth and falsehood, fact and fiction, constative and performative speech-act genres, or reality and its various orders of textual or rhetorical simulation.

However, there is a further intriguing suggestion in Derrida's essay – the "strong" thesis, as it might be called – which became the main focus for subsequent debate on the topic of nuclear criticism. This is the claim that DECONSTRUCTION has a special affinity with the discourse on nuclear war since it belongs to an epoch that has confronted the prospect of an absolute, remainderless catastrophe, one that would leave no trace of a civilization – or a written archive – by which to assess, represent, or commemorate the strictly unthinkable event. Derrida broaches this theme with a series of cryptic allusions to Mallarmé, Kafka, Beckett, and others, whose TEXTS may be read as gesturing toward that silence on the far side of

everything that has comprised our history and cultural tradition to date. It is a topos that has also been taken up – for the most part by literary theorists – with reference to the Kantian sublime. For here also there is the obscure intimation of a thinking that would somehow transcend the limits of everyday phenomenal cognition, that mode of understanding which (as KANT describes it) brings sensuous intuitions under adequate concepts, and thereby affords us veridical knowledge of the world. This discourse on the sublime is analogous with nuclear criticism in so far as they both have to proceed in the absence of any known or (indeed) any knowable referent; that is to say, in so far as they both take rise from a moment of anticipatory trauma which lacks an adequate (commensurable) object in the domain of past or present experience. Such is at any rate the best, most intelligible construction that I am able to place upon these often obscure and riddling statements with regard to the nuclear sublime.

Thus, in Derrida's words:

> the historicity of literature is contemporaneous through and through, or rather structurally indissociable, from something like a nuclear *epoch* (by nuclear "epoch", I mean also the *épochē*; suspending judgment before the ultimate decision). The nuclear age is not *an* epoch, it is the absolute *épochē*; it is not absolute knowledge and the end of history, it is the *épochē* of absolute knowledge. (p. 30)

The reference here is to Edmund HUSSERL and the project of transcendental PHENOMENOLOGY, a topic to which Derrida devoted two early books and whose formative influence on his own thinking – however critical his treatment of it – is everywhere manifest in his later work. Thus "nuclear criticism" is somehow to be thought of as a radicalization – a pressing to the limit – of those issues posed by a deconstructive reading of the Western "logocentric" tradition of thought in which Husserl stands (in Derrida's view) as the last and most rigorous exponent. In that case – the strong thesis again – deconstruction would inhabit that critical zone where thought comes up against the absolute limits of truth, knowledge, reason, logic, or adequate representation. This is on account of its peculiar expertise (or "competence") in a range of strictly undecidable issues, among them "the relations between knowing and acting, between constative and performative speech-acts, between the invention that finds what was already there and the one that produces new mechanisms or new spaces" (Derrida, 1984, p. 23).

One could venture various explanations for the fact that nuclear criticism enjoyed only a brief period of high visibility in the pages of *Diacritics* and other such organs of advanced CULTURAL and literary THEORY. One is the lessening of tension that has occurred with the breakup of the Soviet empire, the decommissioning of (at least some) nuclear weapons, and the advent – supposedly – of a "new world order" in which there no longer appears to be any imminent threat of global catastrophe. Nevertheless, these are scarcely reasons for unqualified optimism, as Ken Ruthven reminds us in his sombre epilogue to the only book-length study to date on the topic of nuclear criticism. After all, there remain vast stockpiles of warheads and delivery systems, some of them now unaccounted for and most likely under the control – such as it is – of forces in the warring ex-Soviet republics and other violently unstable regions. From this point of view the situation is perhaps more dangerous (or less amenable to "expert" forms of strategic thinking, rational calculation, crisis management, etc.) than at the time when Derrida delivered his lecture at Cornell. What has changed is that highly specific conjuncture – of rhetorical "escalation" to the point of aporia or absolute "undecidability" – from which this movement first took rise and in which it discovered a short-lived pretext for some fairly arcane and wire-drawn argumentation.

At its best nuclear criticism offered a focus (albeit, at times, an oddly angled one) for exposing the sheer illogicality of deterrence theory and alternative strategic doctrines. To this extent it made common cause with other approaches – for instance, by philosophers in the broadly analytic (or Anglo-American) camp – which addressed similar issues in a different, less apocalyptic style. (See, for example, Blake and Pole, 1983 and 1984.) Even so, the suspicion still hangs over many of these texts – Derrida's included – that by thus raising the rhetorical stakes they are indulging a form of runaway doomsday paranoia which itself partakes of that same pseudo-logic, that escalating language of crisis and terminal catastrophe whose effects they purport to analyze. In this context more than most, it is important that certain distinctions should not be blurred. These include the boundaries be-

tween fact and fiction, reason and unreason, or reality and its various counterfeit guises – wargame scenarios etc. – where any such confusion is likely to generate real-world crises and catastrophes of the kind so vividly prefigured in the 1960s film *Dr Strangelove*. Which is also to say, *pace* Derrida, that theorists should not make light of the distinction between constative and performative speech-act genres, whatever their seeming "undecidability" when encountered in certain (surely aberrant) forms of nuclear strategic discourse. Nor should they devise sophistical pretexts for distracting attention from the nuclear "referent," whether this be construed in terms of an all too real nuclear arsenal or in cognizance of the all too present and future possibility that those weapons will actually be used. What is required is a level-headed analysis which underestimates neither the capacities of critical reason nor the forces ranged against it in the name of "deterrence," "realism," "containment," "first-strike potential," "damage-limitation," etc. Otherwise – to adapt Karl Krauss's famous remark about psychoanalysis – there is a risk that nuclear criticism will become just one more symptom of the selfsame disease for which it purports to offer a cure.

See also DISCOURSE.

Reading
Blake, Nigel, and Pole, Kay, eds 1983 (*1984*): *Dangers of Deterrence* and *Objections to Nuclear Defence*.
Derrida, Jacques 1984: "No apocalypse, not now (seven missiles, seven missives)."
Diacritics vol. 14, no. 2 (*1984*): Special number on the topic of nuclear criticism.
Ferguson, Frances 1984: "The nuclear sublime."
Jervis, Robert 1984: *The Illogic of American Nuclear Strategy*.
Klein, Richard 1990: "The future of nuclear criticism."
Ruthven, Ken 1993: *Nuclear Criticism*.
Solomon, J. Fisher 1988: *Discourse and Reference in the Nuclear Age*.

CHRISTOPHER NORRIS

Nussbaum, Martha (1947–) American philosopher and classicist. Nussbaum's first book was a critical edition of, and set of commentaries on, Aristotle's *De Motu Animalium*, at the time a rather neglected part of his corpus. Her more recent works branch out from these Aristotelian origins and offer reflections on Greek and Hellenistic thought, ETHICS, rhetoric, the nature of human action, and the connections between philosophy and literature.

Part of the inspiration for the basic idea of *The Fragility of Goodness: Luck and Ethics in Greek Tragedy and Philosophy* (Nussbaum, 1986) comes from Bernard WILLIAMS's work on "moral luck." Nussbaum tests Williams's skepticism about the existence of a moral value immune to luck by working through the embodiment of this claim in certain ancient Greek texts, as well as the way these texts construct and consider an ethics of rational self-sufficiency which would be immune to luck. Thus readings of parts of tragedies by Aeschylus, Sophocles, and Euripides show an acknowledgement of the role luck plays in our moral lives, and the perils of the attempt to make oneself rationally self-sufficient. Plato's works, on the other hand – at least parts of the *Protagoras*, *Phaedo*, *Republic*, and *Symposium* – are read as an attempt to escape the realm of luck. The Platonic philosopher strives to make values commensurable, thereby attempting to avoid conflicts of value, and to limit exposure to those things which might make value vulnerable, such as the effects of the passions and strong, enduring commitments to others. Parts of Aristotle's corpus finally offer a complex account of human beings that acknowledges the roles contingency and the body must play in the lives we actually lead. Both Aristotle's method of "saving the appearances" and his accounts of the relations between reason and desire, for example, complement tragedy's insight into the limitations of human self-sufficiency.

The basic themes of this work are also gathered together in *Love's Knowledge: Essays on Philosophy and Literature* (1990), which offers reflections on novels by Henry James, Charles Dickens, Marcel Proust, and others, as well as further thoughts on Plato and Aristotle. For Nussbaum, the novels in question deserve philosophical attention in part because they offer answers to the question, "How should one live?" – answers which are based on four claims: (i) the incommensurability of values; (ii) the priority of the particular and hence of perception, rather than Kantian or Platonic reason; (iii) the ethical value of emotions; (iv) the ethical value of "uncontrolled happenings" (Nussbaum, 1990, chapter 1, section E). These essentially Aristotelian answers are communicated in a form which matches this content perfectly, for the novels both embody these claims and call for their readers to respond in terms of them (Nussbaum, 1990, chapter 1, section A).

Not surprisingly, Nussbaum's readings of the works of tragedians, novelists, and philosophers have been called into question. One example is her treatment of Plato: his works, when read as dialogues rather than as proto-treatises, embody many of the features Nussbaum most admires in philosophical literature, while challenging some of her most prized substantive philosophical theses. Her tradition-bound readings of Plato's texts seem to keep her from confronting both an embodiment of some of her formal claims and a challenge to her substantive claims about incommensurability, particularity, and luck – and thus perhaps also from confronting a challenge to her views about the interpenetration of form and content.

Reading
Eldridge, R. 1992: "'Reading for Life:' Martha C. Nussbaum on philosophy and literature."

Nussbaum, M. 1986: *The Fragility of Goodness: Luck and Ethics in Greek Tragedy and Philosophy.*

—— 1990: *Love's Knowledge: Essays on Philosophy and Literature.*

—— 1992: "Reply to Richard Eldridge."

—— 1994: *The Therapy of Desire: Theory and Practice in Hellenistic Ethics.*

JEFFREY S. TURNER

O

Oakeshott, Michael (1901–90) Conservative political philosopher. He argued (1962) that "almost all politics today have become Rationalist or near-Rationalist" in the sense that improvement, even perfection, is promised from the application of abstract ideas. Claimed that the conservative disposition – skeptical, averse to change, and valuing highly "every appearance of continuity" – would insist that the office of government is "merely to rule" on the basis of contingency and experience, not to impose other beliefs and activities upon its "subjects." The proper role of government is thus that of the umpire, not the Babelian "pursuit of perfection as the crow flies." Conservatives are unable to agree whether the Thatcher governments of the 1980s embodied the Rationalism Oakeshott opposed or merely worked for the elimination of its past accretions – a controversy symptomatic of the confused identity of the NEW RIGHT itself.

Reading
Greenleaf, W.H. 1965: *Oakeshott's Philosophical Politics*.
Oakeshott, M. 1962 (*1991*): *Rationalism in Politics*.
——— 1975: *On Human Conduct*.

JOHN CALLAGHAN

object-relations A widely used term in PSYCHOANALYSIS, originally referring to the SUBJECT's mode of relating to the world. More specifically, it designates that branch of post-Freudian psychoanalysis which concentrates upon the early relationship between mother and child. Heavily influenced by KLEIN and further elaborated by authors like Fairbairn (1952) and WINNICOTT, object-relations theory represents a major current in British psychoanalysis. The concentration on the mother–child relationship implies a move away from the more patriarchal theories of Freud.

The term "object" is used by Freud in his discussion of the psychology of drives (Freud, 1905). He distinguishes between the drive's source, object, and aim (the act toward which the drive tends), using "object" in the sense in which one speaks of "the object of one's affections." It is on this basis that Klein constructs her theory of the good and bad object, the prototype being the breast, alternatively seen as a source of nourishment and a persecuting object, as the child projects on to the mother its ambivalent love and hate, themselves the outcome of the duality between life and death instincts.

Reading
Fairbairn, W.R.D. 1952: *An Object Relations Theory of the Personality*.
Freud, Sigmund 1905a: *Three Essays on the Theory of Sexuality*.

DAVID MACEY

October Inspired by Russian constructivism and by the belief that economic and social concerns set the context for ART and criticism, three art critics – Rosalind KRAUSS, Annette Michelson, and Jeremy Gilbert-Rolfe – founded *October* in the spring of 1976. The quarterly journal, as they presented it in their opening editorial, was to stand apart from other "overspecialized reviews" such as *Artforum* and *Film Culture*, and to provide a forum for intertextual critical dialogue. The founding editors identified the need for a journal which could support an intense examination of structural and social influences on art. "Art begins and ends with a recognition of its conventions," they wrote.

The aim of *October* is to publish theoretical and critical essays on visual arts, film, performance, and music; the editors, according to their manifesto, will publish pieces on literature which bear a significant relation to these first four categories. All of the articles published in *October* are grounded in MATERIALISM or idealism. Since its origin, *October* has placed a strong emphasis on contemporary art practices, and many of the articles contained in its pages explore the influence of past artists on current work. As the title suggests, the founding editors were inspired by the 1917 revolution in Russia and by the film *October* which Sergei EISENSTEIN was commissioned to produce in 1927. The second is-sue of *October* includes a translation of notes by Eisenstein on his film *Capital*. *October* has also produced a succession of articles written by im-portant theorists, beginning with Michel FOUCAULT, who wrote the lead article, an essay on Magritte's "Ceci n'est pas une pipe," for *October*'s first issue.

October has never been without enemies. Its opponents, especially the neo-conservatives who comprise the editorial board of THE NEW CRITE-RION, a right-wing journal founded in 1982, envis-age it as the epitome of a degenerate academic world and condemn it for its highly intellectual, exclusive tone. "The entire (dare I say it?) super-structure of 'scholarship' erected in these essays is intended not to further knowledge but to dazzle the reader," Roger Kimball wrote in *The New Criter-ion*. The journal, he claims, is "often opaque and unintellectual." Such criticism, while not surpris-ing for a radical publication, contrasts with the intent of *October*'s founders, who, in fact, presented their journal as an alternative to what they saw as superficial enterprises in art criticism, and as a retreat from both the cliché-driven publications and the "pictorial journalism which deflects and compromises critical effort."

TARA G. GILLIGAN

Oedipus complex   An essential concept in PSYCHOANALYSIS, which helps to explain the young child's incestuous desire for the parent of the oppo-site sex and jealousy of the parent of the same sex. The concept derives from the Greek myth of Oedi-pus, who murdered his father and married his mother. In structural terms, the Oedipus complex describes the child's difficult transition from the dual mother–child relationship to a triangular situ-ation in which the role and authority of the father can be recognized. Failure to negotiate that transi-tion is the primary psychoanalytic explanation for the existence of psychopathological conditions. Freudians usually date the Oedipus complex to the ages 3 to 5 years; followers of Melanie KLEIN claim that it develops much earlier.

In his early correspondence with Fliess, FREUD (1985, p. 272) refers to his own experience of "being in love with my mother and jealous of my father" and to his conviction that this is "a universal event in early childhood." It is not, however, until 1910 that he employs the canonical expression "the Oedipus complex" (1910, p. 171). References to

Oedipus Rex, often associated with *Hamlet*, occur throughout Freud, but no one TEXT is devoted to a detailed account of the Oedipus complex itself.

Initially, the notion of an Oedipus complex is outlined in terms which directly recall the original myth; the child perceives his mother as an object of sexual desire, and his father as the rival who prevents him fom realizing that desire (Freud, 1910). It is significant that at this stage Freud's "child" is a boy. The full elaboration of the Oed-ipus complex and its extension to include girls requires the incorporation of the castration com-plex and the phallic stage into Freud's theory. The phallic stage of development is found in both sexes and is characterized by the "childhood theory of sexuality" which explains sexual difference by as-suming that all human beings were originally en-dowed with a penis and that anatomical difference is only the result of castration (Freud, 1908). At this stage, only maleness exists for the child; femaleness does not exist and the alternative is between having a male genital and being castrated (Freud, 1923). The Oedipal boy typically sees castration as a punishment inflicted by the jealous father; in the case of the girl matters are less clear, as she may feel that she has been deprived of a male genital by her mother. The Oedipus com-plex is described as being gradually "dissolved" for the boy by the threat of castration. Its dissolu-tion inaugurates a latency period characterized by a desexualization which will last until the onset of puberty. For the girl, the dissolution of the Oed-ipus complex implies the adoption of a feminine attitude towards her father and the use of a "sym-bolic equation" to displace her wish for a penis onto a desire for a baby (Freud, 1924).
See also LACAN; PHALLUS.

Reading
Freud, Sigmund 1908a: "On the sexual theories of children."
—— 1910b: "A special type of choice of object made by men."
—— 1923b: "The infantile genital organization: an inter-polation into the theory of sexuality."
—— 1924: "The dissolution of the Oedipus complex."
—— 1985: *The Complete Letters of Sigmud Freud to Wilhelm Fliess 1887–1904*.

DAVID MACEY

ontological relativity   A doctrine associated chiefly with the American philosopher W.V.O. QUINE, and subject to intensive discussion since the 1950s. The argument may be summarized briefly as follows.

(i) There is no single "ontological scheme" – no ultimate framework for dividing up the world into objects, processes, events, or the causal relations between them – that could claim to correspond uniquely to the way things stand "in reality."

(ii) On the contrary, there is a vast (perhaps infinite) number of possible alternative schemes, each with its own ontological commitments, its preferred range of constituent objects or physical *realia*.

(iii) What we take as facts or truths – items of veridical belief – are always, in principle, subject to revision under pressure from conflicting (or "recalcitrant") evidence.

This argument applies even to our firmest, most deeply entrenched habits of belief. That is to say, its scope extends from empirical observations (which in Quine's view are always to some extent "theory laden") to the so-called logical laws of thought – like the laws of excluded middle or noncontradiction – which we tend to regard as fixed and immutable. Here also their truth is not a matter of strict, *a priori* validity but the result of their having worked quite well so far and their still hanging together with the rest of what we take as factual, self-evident, or rational belief.

Hence Quine's well-known metaphor of the entirety of our beliefs at any given time as comprising an overall "fabric" or "web," with empirical truths-of-observation occupying a region near the periphery, and at the center those (for us) indubitable truths of logic that appear self-evident to reason. According to him there is no such absolute distinction to be drawn between "synthetic" and "analytic" propositions, between factual and logical truth claims, or other variants on this binary model proposed by philosophers from Leibniz through KANT to FREGE. It is always possible that some new development in the physical sciences – such as relativity theory or quantum mechanics – may force all manner of drastic revisions, not only at the periphery but also at the heart of our existing ontological scheme. Thus in certain instances it may turn out, contrary to usual expectations, that the most economical (least disruptive) way of maintaining overall coherence is to make some adjustment to the logical ground rules rather than strive to interpret new data in accordance with hitherto "unassailable" laws such as noncontradiction or excluded middle. What this means – simply put –

is a kind of pragmatic tradeoff, a redistribution of truth predicates over the total system of beliefs, so as to maximize consistency and minimize conflicts at every point.

From all of this it follows that there is ultimately no deciding the issue between rival ontological schemes, differing ideas of what should count as real-world, physically existent objects and the "laws of nature" (or causal relations) that constitute an adequate descriptive or explanatory framework. Every scheme will have its own strictly immanent, framework-relative criteria for deciding where exactly – or where roughly – the line should be drawn between real and other (for example, fictive, imaginary, hypothetical, or mythic) entities. Thus "[p]hysical objects are conceptually imported into the situation as convenient intermediaries – not by definition in terms of experience, but simply as irreducible posits comparable, epistemologically, with Homer's gods." Not that Quine is in the least disposed to give up his trust in the natural sciences as our best current source of knowledge and advocate a return to belief in Homer's gods or suchlike (to us) improbable fictions. "The myth of physical objects is epistemologically superior to most in that it has proved more efficacious than other myths as a device for working a manageable structure into the flux of experience." Still there is no reason, as Quine sees it, to consider this anything more than just a product of our own (scientifically informed) world view, our current idea of what should properly count as an item of veridical belief. "In point of epistemological footing the physical objects and the gods differ only in degree and not in kind."

Quine's example of quantum mechanics has been taken up by others – Hilary PUTNAM among them – as a test case for the claim that discoveries in science may force us to abandon (or radically revise) the most "elementary" precepts of logical thought. In Putnam's view the problems of interpretation encountered in the microphysical domain are such as to require the development of a "quantum logic" whose principles would admit – that is to say, would not exclude *a priori* – the various paradoxical results reached by scientific experiment. These include the uncertainty principle, complementarity, the wave/particle dualism, the impossibility of assigning precise (simultaneous) values to a particle's location and momentum, and the so-called collapse of the wave packet – that is, into wave or particle form – at the moment of attempted measurement. Until recently most of these findings belonged to

the realm of hypothetical thought experiment, conducted – like Einstein's famous series of debates
with Niels Bohr – in the absence of equipment or
available technology for determining their physical
outcome. (See bibliographical entries for Brown,
1991; Fine, 1986; and Gibbins, 1987, below.) But
they were none the less taken as offering strong
evidence for or against the various conjectures
advanced in the course of that debate. That is,
both parties were agreed upon this much at least:
that what held as a matter of proven necessity in
the speculative (thought experimental) domain must
also hold for any physical situation – any real-
world context or achieved laboratory setup –
wherein that experiment might actually be carried
out. Otherwise there could be no point in advancing such hypotheses and counterhypotheses with
a view to testing their validity claims under specified (albeit as yet physically unrealizable) conditions. To this extent quantum theory – on whatever
construal – presupposed both a degree of realist
commitment and the application of certain logical
criteria (including the principle of noncontradiction)
in order to decide what followed from the thought
experiment in question.

This squared well enough with Einstein's conviction that there were indeed objective truths to
be known, even as regards quantum phenomena,
and hence that any uncertainties had to do with
the limits of present-day knowledge, the inadequacy
of existing measurement techniques, or the incompleteness of the theory itself. Thus there might
turn out to be "hidden variables" so far unaccounted
for – perhaps a wide range of yet more elementary
particles – whose discovery would resolve these
problems and avoid such a highly unsatisfactory
state of affairs. In Bohr's view, conversely, quantum phenomena could never *in principle* be fully
described, let alone explained, in a language (that
of classical physics) which inevitably imposed its
own framework of causal, logical, and spatiotemporal
categories. On the other hand physicists had no
alternative but to conceive their experiments and
formulate the results in a language comprehensible
to themselves and others. John Honner puts the
case as follows in his fine recent study of Bohr and
the philosophical implications of quantum theory.

Unambiguous reports on atomic observations
require the use of ordinary everyday concepts,
drawn from a Newtonian world of space–time
and causality, a world of discrete, identifiable

objects. Hence we are caught in the position of
having to use terms from one view of nature to
report on a quite contrary vision, in which sharp
subject–object separation and continuity of observation are no longer tenable. What is observed
as a wave is also observed as a particle, and
the application of mutually exclusive concepts
is justified once the framework of complementarity is substituted for that of continuity and
univocity.

Honner thinks that these paradoxes are best understood, if not resolved, by interpreting Bohr as a
TRANSCENDENTAL realist in something like the
Kantian sense of these terms. That is, we can have
no direct knowledge of quantum mechanical events,
as distinct from our representations of them as
given in the language of "classical" physics. Such
knowledge is strictly impossible, as Kant argued,
since it claims access to a noumenal realm – a
realm of things-in-themselves – and ignores the *a
priori* constitutive role of human perceptions, concepts, categories, and forms of representation.
However, this is no reason for adopting an attitude
of outright epistemological skepticism. In Kant's
view – and likewise in Bohr's, as Honner interprets it – we can still offer arguments in the transcendental ("conditions of possibility") mode for
supposing *both* that those conditions apply to all
possible forms of human experience and knowledge, *and*, moreover, that they cannot be drastically at variance with the way things stand in reality.
Thus, according to Honner, "Bohr's position is
not a subjectivist one, in which it might be claimed
that reality does not exist unless the observer is
engaged with it." On the contrary, "his entire argument is aimed at providing a framework for
applying our limited observation-language to real
events lying at the boundary of the univocal application of such concepts."

Still it may be argued – as by more critical commentators, Karl POPPER among them – that Bohr's
interpretation of quantum phenomena was anti-
realist (and indeed subjectivist) in so far as it placed
an unbridgeable gulf between those "real events"
and the "observation language" perforce used to
describe them. This "great quantum muddle" was
compounded, Popper thinks, by a habit of projecting interpretative problems into the notional object
domain. Hence the idea that any anomalies encountered in the act of observation or measurement must
somehow pertain *to the object itself* – to the quantal

system and its (supposed) indeterminate properties – rather than figuring in a statistical or probabilistic account of how that object might be expected to behave. Only then will it appear an inescapable conclusion that quantum phenomena have no "objective" reality since their showing up in whatever form – as waves, particles, or (hypothetically) as "wave packets" – is always the result of some observer intervention which decisively affects the given outcome. Popper sees this as an error much akin to that of interpreting demographic statistics – the distribution figures for age, income, voting behavior, the incidence of certain work-related illnesses, etc. – as if they pertained *to some particular individual* whose attributes could therefore be assigned only a certain probability value. "Unfortunately," Popper writes,

> many people, including physicists, talk as if the distribution function (or its mathematical form) were a property of the *elements* of the population under consideration. They do not discriminate between utterly different categories or types of things, and rely on the very unsafe assumption that "my" probability of living in the South of England is, like "my" age, one of "my" properties – perhaps one of my physical properties. (1982)

It is a version of this same category mistake, according to Popper, which has led theoretical physicists and philosophers of science to speak of "a duality of particle and wave" or of "wavicles." It has also given rise – quite against Bohr's intent – to the idea that "objective reality has evaporated," and that uncertainty prevails in the macrophysical as well as the microphysical domain. This is to mistake the whole point of Bohr's argument for the complementarity principle, that is, his argument that, when thinking about quantum mechanical phenomena, we may often be required to make use of multiple (sometimes "logically" conflicting) viewpoints, languages, conceptual schemes, ontological frameworks, etc. Such phenomena cannot be described in the language of "classical" physics precisely *because* that language offers, at least for most practical purposes, an adequate account of conditions obtaining at the macrophysical (Newtonian as well as "everyday" or "commonsense") level.

So there is clearly no warrant for the kinds of abusive extrapolation, or loosely analogical thinking, which appeal to quantum physics (along with

chaos theory, Gödel's incompleteness theorem, and other such currently fashionable *topoi*) as notional support for the idea that science has moved into a "postmodern" phase where values such as truth, logic, and reason have become pretty much obsolete. (See the entry on Jean-François LYOTARD for a fairly representative example.) However, this is not so much a downright caricature of Bohr's position as a selective emphasis on those anti-realist (or ontological-relativist) aspects of it which Popper singles out for criticism. That is to say, Bohr's argument does quite explicitly drive a wedge between quantum physical "reality" and whatever can be known, observed, or said about it in any language (any logico-semantic framework or system of representation) available to the natural sciences. And there is a deep problem here, as noted above, if one considers the extent to which thought experiments – even those purporting to exceed the very limits of "classical" explanation – still require some recourse (whether overt or tacit) to those same values of truth, logic, and objective reality. In other words the thesis of ontological relativity cannot be propounded, or cannot advance any arguments in its own support, without at some point calling that thesis into question, or adducing evidence at odds with its own more extreme formulations.

We can now perhaps return to Quine's "Two dogmas" essay with a better understanding of the issues it raises, for that essay has been influential across a range of disciplines, from PHILOSOPHY OF SCIENCE to epistemology, sociology, cultural criticism, HERMENEUTICS, and literary theory. Very often it is espoused as a *fait accompli* – scarcely in need of further argument – that realist ontologies have now been discredited (or relativized to some local and contingent belief system taken as a whole); that there is no longer any workable distinction between matters of fact (or empirical evidence) and matters of logical necessity; that *all* truth claims, the latter sort included, are in principle subject to revision; and therefore that logic and epistemology should henceforth be "naturalized" to the point where they best fit in with the currently prevailing state of consensus belief. These arguments have received an unqualified endorsement from, among others, neopragmatist thinkers such as Richard RORTY and Stanley FISH, who regard them as signaling a welcome end to the grandiose delusions of mainstream (for example, Kantian or modern analytical) philosophy. They have also struck a responsive chord with postmodernists like Lyotard and, more directly, with skeptical philosophers and historiographers of science (for example, Thomas KUHN and Paul FEYERABEND), whose work draws heavily on Quine's doctrines of meaning holism and ontological relativity. Nor has it been lost upon disciples of Michel FOUCAULT how close is the resemblance between Quine's metaphor of the total "web" or "fabric" of belief and Foucault's idea of discursive formations as determining the limits of authorized (veridical or "scientific") utterance from one such DISCOURSE, PARADIGM, or EPISTEME to the next. In each case it follows – or is taken to follow – that there exist no criteria for comparing, contrasting, or translating between such paradigms since any attempt to do so would *de facto* ignore their strictly incommensurable character. Moreover, it would always end by imposing its own (paradigm-specific) criteria for what should count as an adequate, logical, or consistent set of standards for judging between them.

However, such contentions are open to criticism on a number of grounds. One, as we have seen, is the fact that quantum physics – a favored example of ontological relativity for Quine and other commentators – neither entails nor (arguably) offers strong support for that doctrine in its wholesale form. Popper again puts this case most forcefully: "the denial that we can understand quantum theory has had the most appalling repercussions, both on the teaching and on the real understanding of the theory." It may be that Popper has misinterpreted Bohr and that Honner is justified in his counterclaim to the effect that Bohr was both a "moderate realist" – at least with regard to objects and events in the macrophysical domain – and a thinker who deployed transcendental (conditions-of-possibility) arguments for establishing the truth of quantum theoretical conjectures. If so, then Quine is demonstrably wide of the mark when he invokes quantum theory as bearing out his case for an across-the-board doctrine of ontological relativity which would treat the "myth" of physical objects as ultimately "on a footing" with the myth of Homer's gods, centaurs, and suchlike imaginary referents. This amounts to a manifest confusion of realms between the micro (subatomic) order of events, where such a doctrine may, at least conceivably, be justified, and the macro realm of "physical objects" (like Quine's "brick houses on Elm Street"), where its adoption leads to all manner of palpable absurdities.

This is not just a question of interpretative dispute about what Bohr may have meant by certain – often obscure and cryptic – passages in his writing. Nor is it confined to what philosophers, literary theorists, and others have made of these analogies with quantum theory at its present (more developed but still highly speculative) stage of advancement. Rather, it has to do with with some far-reaching issues about the nature, capacities, and limits of human understanding, issues that have come very much to the fore in recent philosophic debate. One influential line of argument against the more extreme varieties of ontological-relativist doctrine is that put forward by Donald DAVIDSON in his much-discussed essay "On the very idea of a conceptual scheme." Davidson sets out to refute the whole cluster of theories – summarized above – which assert some version of the argument for radical meaning variance across and between language games, paradigms, discourses, interpretative frameworks, etc. The effect of such theories is to foster an attitude of deep-laid cognitive or epistemological skepticism, one that in principle puts up barriers to the prospect of interlinguistic or transcultural understanding. His response takes the form (once again) of a transcendental argument from the conditions of possibility for language and communicative utterance in general. That is to say, these conditions are *necessarily* presupposed by anyone, including the self-professed skeptic, who expects that her or his views on the subject will at least make sense (if not be endorsed) according to certain shared criteria.

Davidson's recommendation, in brief, is that we stop thinking of "truth" as relative to (or "constructed in") this or that language, ontology, conceptual scheme, structure of semantic representations, or whatever. This is to move the matter backward, according to Davidson. Rather, it is the notion of truth – or the attitude of holding true – that must be taken as basic to all language and therefore provides at least a minimal starting point for figuring out what speakers mean in otherwise (to us) quite opaque contexts of utterance. Davidson's chief target here is the Quinean idea of "radical translation," that is, the famous thought experiment in which an anthropologist attempts to compile a translation manual for some remote (hitherto "undiscovered") language and culture. Quine's point is that, even with the best-willed "native informant" – and even where the context seemed wholly unambiguous, as, for instance, if he or she gestured toward a rabbit and produced the utterance "gavagai!" –

still the anthropologist could not be sure that "gavagai = rabbit" as a matter of straightforward definitional equivalence. They might have been saying a whole range of other, less directly informative things, such as "nice fluffy creature," "good to eat," "saw one like it yesterday," or (Quine's own exotic instance to emphasize his point about ontological relativity) "undetached rabbit-part." In other words – a point also made by WITTGENSTEIN – there is no *a priori* reason to suppose that the act of ostensive definition (that is, pointing at an object and uttering its name) either functions in the same way from one culture to the next or provides any sure criterion for picking out intended objects of reference.

Davidson's response to all this is quite simple. In order to find such possible breakdowns in communication we have to start out from the basic assumption that the native informant must at least hold certain things true. From this it follows that his or her language must possess the means of distinguishing valid from invalid modes of reference, predication, logical inference, evidential warrant, and so forth. That is why syntax, in Davidson's laconic phrase, is so much more "sociable" than semantics. It is a shared feature of various present-day relativist doctrines – whether Quinean, Kuhnian, Foucauldian, poststructuralist, or derived from the ethno-liguistic speculations of a thinker like Benjamin Lee WHORF – that they all move straight from a semantics-based conception of language to a doctrine of full-scale meaning holism which is taken to exclude (or radically to problematize) the possibility of translating with any degree of assurance between one and another language, discourse, paradigm, conceptual scheme, or whatever. But the picture changes quite decisively, so Davidson would urge, when we switch attention to the "syntax" – to the logical connectives, quantifiers, relative pronouns, predicative functions, devices for cross-reference, etc. – in the absence of which no language could communicate adequately. What then becomes clear is that skeptics or relativists like Quine, Foucault, Whorf, and company are tacitly relying on those same interlingual resources even as they seek to conjure up the specter of "radical translation" as a strictly impossible enterprise.

Thus Whorf, while arguing that Hopi Indian and English cannot be "calibrated," still purports to offer an English translation of sample Hopi sentences and – what is more – to describe some of the salient differences between their mental universe (ontology or world view) and our own. There is a similar problem with Kuhnian talk about the radical "incommensurability" of scientific paradigms. In fact Kuhn manages to explain quite convincingly – even with respect to "revolutionary" periods of crisis and paradigm change – how these shifts came about and what effect they had on the operative meaning of terms like "mass," "gravity," "light," or "combustion." In Quine's case likewise, it is hard to reconcile his express doctrines of wholesale meaning variance and ontological relativity with his forthright commitment to various theses regarding the scope and limits of knowledge in general. Such, briefly stated, is Davidson's argument for rejecting any form of meaning holism that relativizes "truth" to some particular language game, paradigm, ontology, semantic framework, or conceptual scheme. Thus philosophers are wrong – "get the matter backward," once again – if they regard convention (defined in these various ways) as the precondition for language, and language in turn as the precondition for whatever counts as "true" by the lights of some particular (linguistic, cultural, or INTERPRETIVE) COMMUNITY. On the contrary, Davidson asserts, truth (or the attitude of holding true) is a logically primitive notion, one that is presupposed in every act of understanding, whether within or between such communities.

There is much disagreement and uncertainty, not least in Davidson's own later writings, on the question of what follows from this argument as stated in the formal or transcendental mode. Thus Davidson appears to vacillate between the claim that it does have substantive (nontrivial) implications and the claim that it offers a generalized theory – an abstract (since universally applicable) account of truth – which must therefore be neutral as between differing epistemological viewpoints. (See POSTANALYTIC PHILOSOPHY for further discussion of this issue.) However, we are not obliged to accept either Davidson's scaled-down version of the argument or the conclusion drawn by neo-pragmatist commentators like Richard Rorty, that is, that his (Davidson's) failure to resolve the issue either way is itself presumptive evidence that no stronger theory is viable. For there is still the possibility of combining that argument with other, more developed or substantive accounts of meaning, reference, and truth. Among the most promising resources here are those offered by recent work in philosophy of science and by the causal-realist theory of naming and necessity advanced by philosophers like Saul Kripke. What they share with Davidson's approach is a rejection of the *descriptivist* idea (dominant in analytical philosophy since Frege and Russell) that the act of reference – of picking out an object – is a matter of applying the appropriate criteria as given by some current conceptual scheme or system of intralinguistic representation. On this account we are able to perform or interpret such acts only in virtue of our first having grasped the *sense* of the referring expression, that is, the various descriptions, properties, or identifying attributes standardly imputed to the referent in question. As applied by Frege and Russell, this doctrine was taken to be fully compatible with a realist epistemology and a strong commitment to truth values reached by the logical analysis of language in its various (referential and other) uses. However, it left a way open for more skeptical ideas of the relation between language and truth – products of the postanalytic, neopragmatist, or linguistic "turn" – which rejected that prescriptive order of priority and saw no reason to privilege any one such (culture-specific) ontological scheme.

So it was that the descriptivist theory gave rise to a chapter of developments increasingly at odds with its own original program. Kripke's proposal is to halt that drift by treating *reference* (not sense) as the primary term and thereby securing a stable – or at any rate logically accountable – order of relationship between word and object. In this view the paradigm case of linguistic meaning is one in which a name (a "proper name" in Kripke's technical, nonstandard usage of that term) becomes firmly attached to an object or through an act of stipulative reference. Thereafter the sense may undergo various refinements, for instance when "gold" – originally identified as a yellow, ductile metal with the property of dissolving in *aqua regia* – is subject to further scientific scrutiny and defined in terms of (say) its atomic valence or microphysical structure. Nevertheless, these later specifications still refer to *gold* as the primary *designatum*, that to which the subsequent "chain" of senses leads back as its originating source and anchor point. It is only with reference to that first act of naming – what Kripke calls the initial "baptism" – that we are able to pick out the substance in question and trace the process whereby it acquired a more complex, detailed, or adequate range of descriptive criteria.

Here again, as with quantum physics, the point is often argued through thought experiments devised,

in this case, to establish the priority of reference over sense and the paradoxes (or counter-intuitive results) that result from working on the opposite assumption. Kripke's examples are mostly concerned with modal or "possible worlds" logic, that is, they entail asking what would be the case if the senses, meanings, or attributes that we standardly take as attaching to certain natural kinds or proper names (for example, "gold," "water," "Aristotle," "Julius Caesar") turned out to be false or misapplied. Thus, for instance, what if there existed another "possible world" in which gold and water had different molecular constitutions? And again, what if it transpired that Aristotle had *not* been the pupil of Plato, tutor of Alexander, "last great philosopher of antiquity," author of the *Poetics, Posterior Analytics* (etc., etc.)? Or that Caesar had never in fact crossed the Rubicon but decided to turn back at the last moment? Clearly, Kripke argues, we should not then be driven to conclude – on pain of manifest absurdity – that "gold" was not gold, "water" not water, "Aristotle" not Aristotle, and "Caesar" not Caesar. Rather, we should say (in the case of "gold" or "water") that these terms still denoted the identical substances for the necessary reason that "we as part of a community of speakers had a certain connection between ourselves and a certain kind of thing." In the case of Aristotle or Caesar we should likewise want to say that these names still referred to the same two persons – that is, their real-world historical bearers – despite our having been mistaken up to now as regards their descriptive (or identifying) criteria.

Such is Kripke's idea of proper names or natural kind terms as "rigid designators," that is, expressions whose referent is fixed across all "possible worlds." Only thus, he argues, can we avoid those patent absurdities – like holding that Shakespeare was *not* in fact Shakespeare if he should turn out eventually not to have written the plays – which result from a purely descriptivist theory of sense and reference. No matter what the details of their subsequent career or life history, these persons – Aristotle, Caesar, and Shakespeare – are picked out uniquely as the once-living individuals who bore those names and whose identity was fixed (so Kripke maintains) at the moment of conception. The argument also has far-reaching implications for issues in epistemology, ontology, and philosophy of science. It has led to a widespread revival of interest in the topic of natural kinds, one which figured centrally in discussion of these matters from

Aristotle down, but which fell into disrepute – for reasons we have seen – with the advent of the modern (analytical-descriptivist) approach. Connected with this is Kripke's argument for the existence of *a posteriori* necessary truths. Such truths are on the one hand a result of empirical inquiry, of attaining knowledge from scientific experiment or from the acquisition of better, more advanced or adequate observational techniques. They are also – once arrived at – *necessarily* a part of our informed knowledge of the world. Thus they are neither analytic (self-evident to reason and hence incapable of conveying any newly discovered truths about the world) nor *a priori* in the purebred rationalist sense of being somehow presupposed in each and every act of human understanding. Nor again can they be classified – after Kant – as belonging to the order of synthetic *a priori* judgments, those whose necessity is *both* a matter of empirical warrant *and* of some grounding intuition in the very nature of thought and experience. Rather, they are the kinds of truth that emerge from an investigative treatment of the way things stand in reality, and which then take on their necessary character in virtue of the knowledge thus acquired.

It is this sort of knowledge – so Kripke maintains – which is passed down through the "chain" of transmission that leads from the inaugural act of naming to its later refinements and modifications. In which case "the natural intuition that the names of ordinary language are rigid designators can in fact be upheld." The skeptic (or descriptivist) may urge on the contrary that "something's having intuitive content is very inconclusive evidence in favour of it." But then, Kripke counters, "what more conclusive evidence can one have about anything, ultimately speaking?" This should not be taken as a face-saving retreat into some kind of feeble or unargued "commonsense" EMPIRICISM. Kripke's position is one that finds powerful support from current thinking in philosophy of science, notably the causal-realist and critical-realist approaches of Wesley Salmon and Roy Bhaskar. (See reading list below.) Simply put, it is the argument that we find out more about the nature and structure of the physical world from a process of inquiry that identifies ("fixes") certain natural kinds for investigative treatment, and which then goes on to establish, for instance, their chemical properties, molecular structures, or causal dispositions. Thus, for instance, it is a matter of *necessary* truth, borne out by adequate research, that certain (nowadays) well-known properties, "being characteristic of gold and not of iron pyrites, show that the fool's gold is not in fact gold."

Of course such knowledge cannot be possessed by everyone, least of all in those specialized areas of science where only a few have the needful expertise to actually *know*, in a firsthand, authoritative way, what the rest of us are obliged to take very largely on trust. However, in Kripke's account this situation is provided for by the fact that these items of received knowledge will ultimately point back to their source in a context of original discovery and thence, through various later refinements, to our present (no doubt unequally shared) acquaintance with the relevant facts. Putnam has made this point more explicit by referring to the cognitive and linguistic "division of labor" that allows for the increased specialization of expert domains while permitting nonexperts (an informed lay community) to claim at least a tolerable working grasp of the issues concerned. (See the entry on Jürgen HABERMAS for a different but compatible line of approach to these questions.) At any rate it seems fair to conclude, on the strength of both Davidson's and Kripke's arguments, that the case for full-scale ontological relativity has not so much been proven as taken on board, across a range of present-day disciplines, without adequate critical scrutiny.

See also DETERMINACY; EMPIRICISM; ESSENTIALISM; LANGUAGE, PHILOSOPHY OF; LOGICAL POSITIVISM; METALANGUAGE; PARADIGM.

Reading

Bohr, Niels 1934: *Atomic Theory and the Description of Nature.*

Bhaskar, Roy 1989: *Reclaiming Reality: A Critical Introduction to Contemporary Philosophy.*

Brown, James Robert 1991: *The Laboratory of the Mind: Thought Experiments in the Natural Sciences.*

—— 1994: *Smoke and Mirrors: How Science Reflects Reality.*

Davidson, Donald 1984b: "On the very idea of a conceptual scheme."

Fine, Arthur 1986: *The Shaky Game: Einstein, Realism, and Quantum Theory.*

Gibbins, Peter 1987: *Particles and Paradoxes: The Limits of Quantum Logic.*

Heisenberg, Werner 1958: *Physics and Philosophy: The Revolution in Modern Science.*

Hollis, Martin, and Lukes, Steven, eds 1982: *Rationality and Relativism.*

Honner, John 1987: *The Description of Nature: Niels Bohr and the Philosophy of Quantum Physics.*

Kripke, Saul 1980: *Naming and Necessity.*

Kuhn, Thomas S. 1970: *The Structure of Scientific Revolutions.*

Lyotard, Jean-François 1986: *The Postmodern Condition: A Report on Knowledge.*

Popper, Karl 1982: *Quantum Theory and the Schism in Physics.*

Putnam, Hilary 1983b: *Realism and Reason.*

Quine, W.V.O. 1953a: "Two dogmas of empiricism."

——1969: *"Ontological relativity" and Other Essays.*

Rorty, Richard 1980: *Philosophy and the Mirror of Nature.*

——1991: "Texts and lumps."

Salmon, Wesley C. 1984: *Scientific Explanation and the Causal Structure of the World.*

Schwartz, Steven, ed. 1977: *Naming, Necessity, and Natural Kinds.*

Whorf, Benjamin Lee 1956: *Language, Thought and Reality: Selected Writings.*

CHRISTOPHER NORRIS

opposition, binary   *See* BINARY OPPOSITION

orality   The term "orality" describes a condition of society in which speaking and listening form the only or principal channel through which linguistic communication takes place. By far the majority of languages in the history of the world, and most languages in use today, are used primarily "orally" in this sense. (It has been estimated, for example, that only about 3 percent of all extant languages have "literatures," in even the most general sense.) Orality is of special interest in literary and CULTURAL THEORY because of the suggestive contrasts it offers with the practices and cultural horizons of modern, industrialized, literate societies.

The differing conditions of orality and LITERACY result from what Jack Goody and Ian Watt have called two distinct "technologies of the intellect": speech and writing (Goody and Watt, 1968). Stylistically, for example, communications in speech and communications in writing typically have different characteristics. Spoken texts are likely to display less syntactic embedding, less use of explicit connectives, greater dependence on nonverbal contextual clues and more use of fillers and repetition than written texts. Speech and writing are also acquired differently. Except in pathological cases, orality is the result of a universal process of language acquisition in humans which requires (at least as regards a first language) little or no formal instruction – though it can be trained towards specialized, conventional capabilities in oral societies, such as memorization and formulaic narration. Literacy, on the other hand, is acquired only by the deliberate process of learning to read and write, usually in formal, educational situations; and this dependence of literacy on education has

given rise to complex historical and policy arguments regarding how much skill in reading and writing someone needs to have in order to be judged "literate."

Major cultural consequences have been taken to follow from the distinction between orality and literacy. Extrapolating from contrasts between speech and writing to speculate about the psychodynamics of members of cultures with access to only spoken traditions, some commentators have suggested that the orality/literacy distinction should replace earlier cultural "great divide" distinctions such as those between primitive and civilized, or prelogical and logical societies. Goody and Watt, for example, point out that writing (unlike speech) can be kept stable for scrutiny on the page, and scanned forwards and backwards – so facilitating large-scale argument and discussion, including complex logical derivations such as sequences of syllogisms (hence a special significance in the emergence of logic in Greece roughly coincidentally with the earliest use of a fully phonetic-alphabetic script). However, whereas literacy facilitates a new degree of abstraction and objectivity – as well as greater historical accuracy than oral histories and genealogies, which place less emphasis on historical record than on current relevance – orality retains and foregrounds magic or ritualistic properties of language, as well as maintaining a sense of communal identity. On the basis of these and similar arguments, Goody and Watt propose that the oral/literate distinction should mark the boundary between anthropology (which would study oral societies) and sociology (which would study literate societies). Literacy is in this framework assumed to create a new relationship between the individual and language, and in important ways to determine modes of thought and social organization (so displacing a common tendency in earlier, more evidently ethno-centric anthropology, to attribute cognitive differences to innate differences between ethnic groups).

Perplexing arguments about the psychologically and socially determining capacities of literacy, however, is a divergence between two viewpoints: an "autonomous" and an "ideological" view of literacy. The "autonomous" view (see Goody and Watt, 1968) describes literacy as a complex of skills which do not carry any particular ideological load and which are isolable from political structures and social formations, actively *causing* kinds of social change. The "ideological" view (see Street, 1984) suggests that the skills and applications of literacy always exist within a particular social matrix of goals, ideologies, and distributions of social roles, such that "literacy" itself is only ever an instrument of other determining social and political forces, never itself an autonomous agent. Developing – in both theory and practice – a particularly influential version of an "ideological" view of literacy, the Brazilian educationalist Paolo Freire rejects any distinction in a given social situation between communicative means (reading and writing) and the content or material that is to be read or written, choosing instead to connect reading the word with reading the world in programs directed toward what he calls "emancipatory literacy" (see Freire, 1972).

As regards twentieth-century industrialized societies, arguments over orality and literacy take on an added importance, as a result of massive extensions in the use of modern communications media. Walter Ong, for example (in Ong, 1982, and elsewhere), has proposed the term "secondary orality" – by contrast with his "primary orality" – to describe skills needed to cope with such transition. "Secondary orality" is a new social condition which involves, in a changing mix with established literate modes, specialized understanding of the adapted, "oral" systems used in radio, telephones, audio recording, TV, and film. The large-scale social consequences of such a transition into "secondary oral" societies have been widely discussed not only by Ong but also, earlier, by Marshall McLuhan (for example, McLuhan, 1964).

From the perspective of literate societies, literate forms (as well as literate people) are often assumed to be of higher cultural status and special importance is often attached to a CANON of religious, legal, and/or constitutional documents. This social prestige contrasts interestingly with privileges which, Jacques DERRIDA points out (Derrida, 1976) are attributed in philosophically problematic ways to speech, creating what he calls "phonocentrism": a condition of speech which allows it to appear somehow closer to thought and to immediate self-presence; or, since writing is a largely secondary system modeled on speech, to be considered the proper subject of modern linguistic investigation.

For modern CRITICAL and cultural THEORY, a cluster of important issues emerge from the discussion of orality and literacy. Interesting questions can be posed, for instance, about the medium in which literary TEXTS exist. While literature is usually taken to mean books, this notion is problematized by the concept of "oral literature," given the meaning of "oral" (relating to that which is spoken) and the etymology of "literature" in *litterae* (Latin: "letters"). Moreover, since many constituent elements of literature feature prominently in contemporary cultural forms in media other than "letters" (for example, narrative occurs in film and television; lyricism is found in pop song lyrics, etc.), many of literature's apparently defining properties can be seen to exist outside "writing." Such apparent anomalies undermine literature's generally assumed defining connections with "literate" forms and "literate" cultures.

Issues also arise concerning ideas of authors and authorship. In oral societies – not only those which have what are typically considered oral "literatures," but also (according to work by Milman Parry and Albert Lord (see Lord, 1968) the classical Greek culture of Homer – the notion of an author does not exist in anything like the form which gives it its importance in most traditional literary criticism. Rather, "authorship" exists in such societies, if at all, within conventions of communal improvisation and formulaic composition; it is only with a transition to a literate society – especially one possessing the institutions of print literacy – that the modern category of an author fully emerges.

Finally, questions surround notions of audiences or readerships (notice the medium-specific resonances of these two terms). Reading is not simply a matter of interpretation drawing on a routine physical and cognitive process, but a socially formed, and very unevenly distributed, set of skills and conventions. Limits on the historically constituted readerships for literature – crucial for any socially based theory of reception or READER–RESPONSE CRITICISM – are set by social patterns of literacy, which differ massively between societies and periods; in this way issues of orality and literacy are central to a culture's defining conditions of production and reception.

See also LITERACY.

Reading

Derrida, Jacques (*1976*): *Of Grammatology.*
Finnegan, Ruth 1977: *Oral Poetry: Its Nature, Significance, and Social Context.*
Freire, Paolo 1972: *Pedagogy of the Oppressed.*
Goody, Jack 1987: *The Interface between the Written and the Oral.*
——and Watt, Ian 1968: "The consequences of literacy."

Graff, Harvey 1982: *Literacy and Social Development in the West: A Reader.*
Levine, Kenneth 1986: *The Social Context of Literacy.*
Lord, Albert 1968: *The Singer of Tales.*
McLuhan, Marshall 1964: *Understanding Media: The Extensions of Man.*
Ong, Walter J. 1982: *Orality and Literacy: the Technologizing of the Word.*
Parry, Milman 1971: *The Making of Homeric Verse.*
Street, Brian 1984: *Literacy in Theory and Practice.*

ALAN DURANT

organic unity If a literary work is said to have organic unity it is pictured as being structured like a living body, animal or (more usually) vegetable, rather than, say, like a machine or some other manmade or inert object.

The image has a long history, beginning with Plato and then developed fully by Aristotle. It was given a new lease of life in German Romanticism, where it played a central role, and was brought into the English tradition by Coleridge, paraphrasing Schlegel. It was revived again by the NEW CRITICS in North America, and by the school of LEAVIS in England, both of whom based their praise of organic unity in literature on an analogy with and a nostalgia for "the organic community" (an imaginary antebellum South for the Americans, an imaginary Old England for the Leavisites). By this time, however, the metaphor was beginning to seem worn out, partly because of its intrinsic inadequacies – a poem evidently is not actually much like a plant – and partly because its political connotations became more and more apparent and disturbing in the mid-twentieth century, especially in the "blood and soil" organicism of the Nazis. The consensus now seems to be that "organic unity" is no more than a vaguely honorific term, rather than a useful analytic tool.

Reading
Abrams, M.H. 1953: *The Mirror and the Lamp.*
Rousseau, George, ed. 1972: *Organic Form: The Life of an Idea.*
Ruthven, K.K. 1979: *Critical Assumptions.*

IAIN WRIGHT

orientalism A term for the European invention or idea of the Orient, associated with the thought of Edward SAID. The Orient is not simply an originating place of European languages and CULTURE; it is also, in Said's view, an indispensable European image of the OTHER, which has made it possible for Europe to define itself. Furthermore, as a construct of European ideological DISCOURSE, orientalism has made it possible for the West to dominate, colonize, and restructure the Orient. Although Said (1978, p. 3) has often acknowledged the importance of FOUCAULT's theories of discourse and epistemological power, orientalism also carries traces of DERRIDA's theory of "European hallucination" (1967, p. 80). As Western scholars began to translate Asian languages, Derrida argues, they began to construct an ideal image or Chinese fantasy of a perfectly complete linguistic and cultural presence that was not afflicted by European incompleteness and absence. However, such an idealized, hallucinated Other was simply created to fulfill a European need. Orientalism and the European hallucination are in this sense complementary forms of ETHNOCENTRISM.

Reading
Derrida, Jacques 1967a (*1976*): *Of Grammatology.*
Said, Edward 1978 (*1979*): *Orientalism.*

MICHAEL PAYNE

other, the A highly ambiguous term referring, in Lacanian usage, to one pole of a subject–object dialectic, to alterity in general and, usually when capitalized, to the symbolic and the UNCONSCIOUS. The origins of the concept of the other are HEGELian, and can be traced specifically to the enormously influential reading of *The Phenomenology of Mind* undertaken by by Alexandre Kojève in the 1930s (Kojève, 1947). Lacan was a regular attender at the seminar at which this reading was presented, and while Kojève's name does not figure in the *Ecrits*, his influence is palpable throughout. Kojève inscribes the subject–other (master–slave) relationship within a field of conflict dominated by a mutual desire for recognition. Man's desire can thus be said to be the desire of the other. The formula is often used by Lacan, but it is far from uncommon in the work of postwar Hegelians in France. In this usage, the other is also the specular image perceived and identified with in the MIRROR-STAGE. The symbolic Other tends, in contrast, to refer to the autonomous and effectively anonymous structures of language and the symbolic, as well as to the unconscious, in so far as they organize the very existence of individual subjects.

Reading
Kojève, Alexandre 1947: *Introduction to Hegel. Lecture on "The Phenomenology of Mind."*
Lacan, Jacques 1960: "Subversion of the subject and dialectic of desire."

DAVID MACEY

overdetermination   Originally a FREUDian category, referring to the fact that formations of the unconscious result from a plurality of causes and/or that they are related to a multiplicity of unconscious elements. The interpretation of dreams, for example, discloses the work of CONDENSATION and DISPLACEMENT. In the former, a number of dream thoughts are represented in a single image; in the latter, a significant thought is represented in a seemingly trivial image.

The notion was adapted from Lacanian PSYCHOANALYSIS by ALTHUSSER in "Contradiction and overdetermination" (1965, pp. 87–128). It was deployed by him to conceptualize a "structural" (or "metonymic") causality distinct from the "expressivism" of HEGELian Marxism, and the "mechanism" of orthodox MARXISM, for which all social contradictions were manifestations of an underlying economic contradiction. Althusser's endeavor went beyond the causal pluralism to which it is reduced when "overdetermination" is read as codetermination by the superstructural levels. His ambition was an alternative configuration of the SOCIAL FORMATION as a complex but unified totality, and hence of the presence of the social whole in its parts. Any contradiction was marked by the other contradictions that constituted its conditions of existence within the totality, defining the pattern of dominance and antagonism in a given historical conjuncture.

Reading
Althusser, L. 1965 (*1990*): *For Marx.*
Laplanche, J., and Pontalis, J.-B. 1967 (*1973*): *The Language of Psycho-Analysis.*

GREGORY ELLIOTT

P

paradigm A term introduced by Thomas KUHN into the PHILOSOPHY OF SCIENCE, where it stood for the shared commitment by the members of a scientific community to a particular form of scientific practice. Against Kuhn's advice, the term has been generalized to apply to almost any theoretical, philosophical, or ideological commitment.

Reading
Kuhn, Thomas S. 1962 (*1970*): *The Structure of Scientific Revolutions*.
Lakatos, Imre, and Musgrave, Alan, eds 1970: *Criticism and the Growth of Knowledge*.

ANDREW BELSEY

paradigmatic *See* SYNTAGMATIC/PARADIGMATIC

paradox An apparently self-contradictory statement which, on examination, reveals an important truth, as when Donne writes of love that "to enter in these bonds is to be free" and Wordsworth that "The Child is father of the Man."

Paradox has been a strong element in Western literature from its beginnings, but was an especially common device in early seventeenth-century "metaphysical" POETRY, and thus, like IRONY and AMBIGUITY, it became a central term for NEW CRITICISM, whose theories were based on an attempt to use the metaphysicals as a model for all good poetry. Cleanth BROOKS went so far as to argue that "paradox is the language appropriate and inevitable to poetry."
See also AMBIGUITY; BROOKS, CLEANTH; IRONY; NEW CRITICISM.

Reading
Brooks, Cleanth 1947 (*1968*): *The Well-Wrought Urn*.

IAIN WRIGHT

parapraxis In psychoanalytic theory, an act, such as a slip of the tongue, whose goal is not achieved and which is replaced with another. Like symptoms, parapraxes are demonstrated by FREUD (Freud, 1901) to be compromise formations resulting from the conflict between conscious intentions and repressed feelings or impulses.

Reading
Freud, Sigmund 1901a: *The Psychopathology of Everyday Life*.

DAVID MACEY

parole See LANGUE/PAROLE

patriarchy Literally, "patriarchy" means "rule of the father." In academia, the term first gained theoretical currency among anthropologists, who used it to describe any society in which an elder male (the "father") holds absolute power over all others in that society, including younger and subordinate males unrelated by blood. By the early 1970s "patriarchy" had become one of the key terms of feminist theory. Feminists, however, tended to use the term not to indicate a certain type of society, but to signal the concept that male dominance is a universal organizing principle of all societies.

Although patriarchy is manifested in an endless variety of historically and culturally specific forms, all human societies are patriarchal in that they are segregated and stratified by sex such that women are oppressed in social and political institutions; they divide productive and reproductive labor by sex and discriminate against women economically; they privilege men over women generally, guaranteeing men greater and nonreciprocal access to women's material and immaterial resources; they value men and MASCULINITY more highly than women and FEMININITY; and their discursive and SYMBOLIC SYSTEMS centralize, standardize, and normalize male subjectivity and points of view while casting woman as the objectified "OTHER."

Patriarchy is the universal system of male dominance that feminists aim to abolish. Not only has the term "patriarchy" been extremely useful in articulating relationships between seemingly disparate sexist practices, but contests over the meaning of the term have clarified differences among feminist positions and been a crucial vehicle for advancing feminist theory.

An early feminist problematic concerned the question of patriarchy's origin, especially whether the transhistorical, cross-culturally universal fact of male dominance could be explained in terms other than those provided by biological determinism. Is male dominance, in other words, natural and therefore inevitable, or is it the consequence of some historical development in CULTURE and therefore subject to intervention and transformation?

Some feminists such as Shulamith Firestone (1970) accepted the premises that "biology itself – procreation – is at the origin of the dualism" between male and female and that male dominance is both natural and inevitable, but only under certain material conditions, such as lack of reliable birth control. Changes in those material conditions, such as the development of new reproductive technologies in the twentieth century that severed women from their biological role as mothers, made possible a feminist revolution.

Other feminists took a psychological approach to the problem of origins, finding that once the biological processes of paternity became known and fatherhood became a meaningful social fact, patriarchal kinship systems evolved in response to incest taboos: men subordinated women in order to regulate their own homosocial relationships while simultaneously guaranteeing sexual access to females (Mitchell, 1974).

Still others examined the archaeological record for evidence of nonpatriarchal societies, finding that a prehistoric, goddess-worshipping matriarchy was brutally and forcefully overthrown by dispossessed males (Stone, 1976). Although interest in goddess religions continues to inform the social practices of some feminist communities and even figures prominently in theories of ecofeminism, by the 1980s academic interest in prepatriarchy had decidedly waned as anti-foundationalist POSTSTRUCTURALISMS cast doubt on the epistemological status of so-called master narratives and generally foreclosed questions about origins of any kind. It survived only among post-Lacanian psychoanalytical critics, especially proponents of *écriture féminine*, who rearticulated prepatriarchy as an individual psychological state associated with the pre-Oedipal period, before the insertion of the SUBJECT into language and CULTURE, the "law of the father."

Yet another early problematic included questions of whether patriarchy, understood as an overarching category of male dominance, was analytically separable from other forms of dominance, such as racial oppression, and other modes of production, such as capitalism, and if so, whether it was the primary mode of women's oppression. Radical feminists, such as Kate MILLETT (1970), argued that sexism is not only analytically independent, but primary, the original political division in society and the model for all other divisions, including those based on RACE and CLASS. Marxist feminists generally argued against the biologizing tendencies of radical feminist theories of patriarchy, claiming instead that, although male dominance is autonomous and therefore analytically separable, it is not independent from analysis of class formation and struggle. Patriarchal exploitation cuts across class lines but GENDER relations and women's experiences of sexism are mediated by their specific positions in the economic mode of production (Barrett, 1980).

Marxists disagreed about whether male dominance was primary: some argued that some form of male dominance existed in all modes of economic production; others claimed that the general equality of men and women within economic classes in precapitalist Europe signaled the primacy of class instead. Black feminists and other women of color criticized the term "patriarchy" for its implication that all women form a single, unified sex class and are identically and equally oppressed by men. White-authored theories of patriarchy efface differences among women and the transection of sexual categories by racial and ethnic ones such that some women have considerable power over some men and are formidable agents in the oppression of other women (Carby, 1987). By the late 1980s these critics were joined by postcolonial theorists such as Gayatri SPIVAK (1987), who argued that nationality is as important an axis of difference as race, class, and ETHNICITY.

At the same time, both left and right-wing articulations of poststructural theory also exerted pressure on feminists to question whether systemic understandings of the social, such as those inscribed in the term "patriarchy," are legitimate or illegitimate, useful or derelict. Is patriarchy an overarching totality that exists in reality or is the social more accurately and usefully understood only in more localized terms? As early as the 1970s some feminists had already objected to the large scale implied by theories of patriarchy. Gayle Rubin (1975) suggested that to avoid analytic confusion between "patriarchy" and sex–gender systems in general, feminists must retain the earlier, more specific anthropological definition. Barrett argued that certain ideological constructions of relationships "predicated on the PARADIGM . . . of a father–daughter relationship [such as] the pathological attempts of bourgeois fathers to insist on their daughters' dependence . . . also represent a legitimate use of the term" (1980, p. 15). In the 1980s feminists influenced by FOUCAULT rejected the inscription in the term "patriarchy" of a notion of power as centralized and primarily repressive and juridical in its operations, finding it more useful instead to understand the social as a matrix of localized relationships infused with power, "innumerable points of confrontation [and] focuses of instability, each of which has its own risks of conflict, or struggles" (Foucault, *Power/Knowledge*).

Through the 1980s Foucauldian feminist theories argued that feminist practice is only possible at the microlevels of society where power actually circulates; the question of large-scale social STRUCTURE was put off. Such articulations of POSTMODERNISM, especially those also informed by DECONSTRUCTION, tended to emphasize the textuality of the social world, the processes by which human subjects and identities are discursively produced. Consequently, they advanced a political agenda in which the top priority was to destabilize, through subversive WRITING practices, normative and totalizing relationships between signifier and signified, between human subjects and their identities. By the late 1980s the distance between academic feminist theorists and their grass-roots constituencies was wider than it had ever been before; not only did most activists find academic theoretical writing inaccessible, but also many of the political practices celebrated by academics, such as miming, parody, or pastiche, seemed absurd and irrelevant; indeed, "ludic postmodernism" (the term is Teresa Ebert's) seemed to dismantle "politics" and "feminism" altogether.

In the late 1980s and early 1990s an exciting group of feminist theorists, including Teresa Ebert, Norma Alarcon, Evelyn Brooks-Higgenbotham, Donna Haraway, and Chandra Sandoval, have attempted to move beyond this impasse by rewriting postmodern theories, both in accessible terms and in terms that once more permit analysis of large-scale social structures, global "totalities" like patriarchy, RACISM, and capitalism. The "resistance postmodernism" that has resulted from their efforts does not derogate deconstruction, seeing it as a necessary intervention in patriarchal cultural politics but insufficient in itself to achieve the emancipatory project of feminism. Instead, the great tasks of the 1990s are to rearticulate the insights of ludic postmodernism in a theory of language that assumes that significance is the product of social struggle and to theorize the highly differentiated positioning of "women," especially as that positioning informs such social practices as the increasingly specialized division of labor in multinational capitalism, racial formation, and the formation of colonial and postcolonial states.

See also DECONSTRUCTION; ESSENTIALISM; FEMINIST CRITICISM; FOUCAULT, MICHEL; POSTSTRUCTURALISM.

Reading
Barrett, Michèle 1980: *Women's Oppression Today: Problems in Marxist Feminist Analysis.*
Carby, Hazel 1987: *Reconstructing Womanhood: The Emergence of the Afro-American Woman Novelist.*
Ebert, Teresa 1991: "The 'difference' of postmodern feminism."
—— 1993: "Ludic feminism, the body, performance, and labor: Bringing *materialism* back into feminist cultural studies."
Firestone, Shulamith 1970 (*1971*): *The Dialectic of Sex.*
Millett, Kate 1970: *Sexual Politics.*
Mitchell, Juliet 1974: *Psychoanalysis and Feminism.*
Rubin, Gayle 1975: "The traffic in women."
Spivak, Gayatri 1987a: *In Other Worlds: Essays in Cultural Politics.*
Stone, Merlin 1976: *When God Was a Woman.*
GLYNIS CARR

patristic criticism   The term "patristic" refers to the Fathers of the early Christian Church – St Ambrose (c. 339–97), St Jerome (c. 347–419/420), St Augustine (354–430), and Gregory the Great (c. 540–604) in the Latin Church; Basil the Great (c. 330–c. 379), Gregory of Nazianzus (c. 329–c. 390), Athanasius (c. 293–373), and John Chrysostom (347–407) in the Eastern Church – and their theological commentary, as well as the work of other ecclesiastics who lived from about the second to the seventh or eighth century. This period saw seven general councils of the one universal Catholic Church; the development of an ecclesiastical orthodoxy; and a vast scope of patristic literature in support of Christian orthodoxy in Western culture. Excellent critical editions of this commentary, including that of patristic ecclesiastics who wrote from the eighth to the early sixteenth century, are published in the voluminous *Corpus Scriptorum Ecclesiasticorum Latinorum* (*CSEL*) and *Corpus Christianorum, Series Latina* (*CCSL*) and *Series Graeca* (*CCSG*).

During the years after Christ's death, St Paul actually inaugurated the typological and allegorical modes of interpreting the Gospels, when he reconciled in his Epistles Jewish traditions and Old Testament materials with the New Testament scripture. In Paul's figural or typological method, important individuals and events of the Old Testament were identified as "types" prefiguring New Testament persons and actions. Adam was held to prefigure, to be a "type" of Christ: as Adam introduced sin into the world, and all men who followed him were born sinners, so Christ introduced grace and salvation into the lives of all men (Romans 5: 12–21). An apt example of his allegorial method occurs when Paul reconciles the relationship between the Old Testament covenant of law and the New Testament covenant of spiritual redemption when he comments upon the birth of Abraham's two sons, Ishmael and Isaac – the first by the slave Hagar and the second by his wife Sarah (Galatians 4: 21–31). Paul says that Hagar represents "Sinai, a mountain in Arabia [which] corresponds to the present Jerusalem for she is in slavery [under Roman rule] along with her children"; but Sarah represents the heavenly New Jerusalem and God's promise of spiritual liberation from sin which comes from Isaac and his descendants through subsequent Old Testament books to be realized in the Gospels of Jesus Christ. The Old Testament was understood by Paul (and exegetes to follow) to be a divinely inspired book which often in prophecies cloaked elements of God's eternal plan for mankind; and its truths and promise were fulfilled in the life and teachings of Jesus in the New Testament.

It was to the early commentators of the church to develop patristic analysis and bring the method to a more comprehensive, detailed explication of biblical materials. The eastern Christian scholar, Origen (c. 185–c. 254), following contemporary practice in Alexandrian schools of interpreting the Greek myths and Homeric works allegorically, accepted to an extent the literal sense of scriptural writings, but argued that more profound meanings were to be found in discovering their moral and spiritual senses. The allegorical method was adopted and further developed by Ambrose, Bishop of Milan, and Augustine, Bishop of Hippo. The importance of patristic commentary was enormous in its own era and tremendously influential in the centuries to follow. By the twelfth century the method had been refined and reached its most characteristic expression in "the fourfold sense of interpreting sacred scripture"; and it was employed by St Thomas Aquinas (1225–74) and many others of his time when writing on matters of theology, philosophy, and moral conduct.

The first of the fourfold senses, the literal or historical meaning, was for Thomas a fit object for scientific study; the *litterae* were held to be the "vessels" which preserved the other three, essentially important spiritual senses. The literal was distinguished by its historical or "carnal" meanings, that is a TEXT's worldly or earthly, not holy or sanctified meanings. The other three senses conveyed spiritual implications: the moral (through which proper ethical conduct is inferred); the allegorical, typological, or figural; and the anagogical (in which biblical references relate to Christian eschatology, the events to come in the days of the Last Judgment or in the afterlife of individual souls). A classic, nonbiblical literary use of this method was set forth by Dante (1265–1321) in his letter to Can Grande della Scalla (c. 1318); here the poet explicitly describes how the fourfold scriptural meanings should be employed to interpret his *Divina Commedia* (c. 1307–21).

Through the patristic and medieval periods and into the early sixteenth century, this HERMENEUTIC, or method of biblical interpretation, often was varied to accommodate the interest of the commentator who offered the exegesis (the interpretation). Of course, some exegetes emphasized one or another of the four levels of meaning at the expense of others, while many employed two or more levels simultaneously. Inasmuch as the Bible has been regarded as a sacred book, there were those who argued that commentary in its literal sense was the most (or only) legitimate interpretation since the Scriptures were inspired by God who through them speaks to mankind, always saying what is intended. None the less, the vast body of scriptural interpretation which developed and has come to be associated with patristic exegesis followed the method of differentiating and commenting upon the *littera*, or obvious meaning of the text, and its *sententia*, or spiritual and doctrinal meanings.

The writings of the exegetical tradition have over the centuries been of great interest to scholars in history, theology, and philosophy in attempting to research and understand the thinking and beliefs which permeated the early Christian world and so influenced the entire medieval period that followed. The strength of the continuing patristic influence upon Western thought can also be seen in the use of typological and allegorical elements in the work of such post-Middle Ages writers as George Herbert, Edmund Spenser, William Blake, and Nathaniel Hawthorne. Over the centuries work by some textual critics, philologists, biblical scholars, and art historians has often included study of and research into patristic texts.

However, a new direction in patristic commentary was inaugurated during the early 1950s by several literary critics, like the American scholar D.W. Robertson, when they proposed that much secular POETRY of the medieval period was written against the background of patristic thought, and that it had to be taken into account when attempting an analysis of medieval literary texts. Strenuous objections were raised to this approach by other critics, such as E. Talbot Donaldson, who argued that at least two questionable assumptions lay behind the method: (i) that orthodox belief did not change from the time of the patristic Fathers to Aquinas; and (ii) that patristic interpretations and references were available to secular writers and had a good chance of being understood by their audiences.

None the less, Robertson and others argued with much success that obvious bibilical allusions and citations carried a recognizable tradition of thought from the patristic period into the medieval, and the patristic exegetical tradition itself offered a vast index of commentary and provided excellent background for understanding bibilical associations and motifs of medieval secular literature. Chaucer and other contemporary secular authors were not to be read as exegetes solemnly interpreting the Vulgate Bible, but as artists who used biblical references and elements of Christian tradition in evocative, novel ways. Moreover, to be understood by their audiences, which were largely aristocratic and educated, these writers need not have a systematized, exhaustive knowledge of the vast exegetical writings of patristic thought, only an understanding of tenets and significant interpretations, biblical tales, and SYMBOLic images that had permeated medieval social thought. Some authors like Chaucer, none the less, were obviously well read in early ecclesiatical writers such as Boethius (470/5–525).

The element of love appearing in secular medieval literature, specifically the *cupiditas* dominant in courtly love – for example in Geoffrey Chaucer's *Troilus and Cressida* or Chrétien de Troyes's *Percival* – was set in satiric relief against (at times even reconciled with) the church's teachings about Christian love, *caritas*. Absolon's frustrated lust and misadventures when pursuing Alison in Chaucer's "The miller's tale" is artfully explicated in this manner by Robert Kaske (see Bethurum, 1961, pp. 52–60). Kaske demonstrates how a knowledge of commentary by patristic exegetes of the *Song of Solomon* enhances the comedy of Chaucer's tale by contrasting the carnal love of Absolon and Alison with that found by exegetes in the relationship between the lovers in the *Song of Solomon*.

During the 1950s and 1960s the work of literary critics like Robertson, Kaske, and Bernard Huppe in explicating texts through study of patristic commentary received considerable favorable attention among scholars, and has had an ongoing impact on the teaching of medieval literature in schools today. However, with the advent of postmodern criticism during the late 1960s and 1970s, patristic analysis (based as it is upon the assumption of divinely inspired bibilical truth) has been edged from a place of prominence in literary scholarship.

See also BIBLICAL STUDIES; HERMENEUTICS.

Reading

Auerbach, Erich 1959: "Figura."
Bethurum, Dorothy, ed. 1961: "Patristic exegesis in the criticism of medieval literature."
Lampe, G.W.H., ed. 1969: *The Cambridge History of the Bible*. Volume II. *The West from the Fathers to the Reformation*.
Lubac, Henri de 1959–64: *Exegese mediéval; Les quatre sens de l'écriture*.
Smalley, Beryl 1984. *The Study of the Bible in the Middle Ages*.

JOHN J. JOYCE

Pêcheux, Michel (1938–83) French philosopher and linguist. A pupil of ALTHUSSER, Pêcheux's research was conducted under the SIGN of the "triple alliance" (1975, p. 211) between Althusserian MARXISM, Lacanian PSYCHOANALYSIS, and Saussurean linguistics. Pêcheux criticized existing linguistic models (especially that of CHOMSKY) and argued for the analysis of language as a social practice, or DISCOURSE, imbricated with IDEOLOGY. Seeking to surmount difficulties in Althusserian theory, Pêcheux proposed three mechanisms by which

SUBJECTS may be constructed: "identification," "counteridentification," and "disidentification."

Reading
MacCabe, C. 1979: "On discourse."
MacDonell, D. 1986: *Theories of Discourse.*
Pêcheux, M. 1975 (*1982*): *Language, Semantics and Ideology.*
Woods, R. 1977: "Discourse analysis: the work of Michel Pêcheux."

GREGORY ELLIOTT

Peirce, Charles Sanders (1839–1914) American philosopher. As a cofounder of both SEMIOTICS and pragmatism, Peirce is justly considered one of the most important and most innovative of American philosophers. He is, however, also one of the most neglected, which may in part be the result of his inability to resolve the rival demands of popular and professional authorship. His technical language and rigorous arguments lost him the kind of informed general audience that Emerson, James, and Dewey were able to attract; but his failure to publish a major book – despite his many brilliant if scattered papers, lectures, letters, and essays – deprived him of the appropriate professional recognition as well. In a footnote to his seminal pragmatist essay "How to make our ideas clear," Peirce wrote: "Consider what effects, that might conceivably have practical bearings, we conceive the object of our conception to have. Then, our conception of these effects is the whole of our conception of the object" (Peirce, 1958, p. 181). If this cardinal principle of pragmatism were applied to Peirce's own work, it would appear fitting that he is celebrated for the effects of his ideas on other thinkers. Peirce's writings, none the less, range widely over topics that remain crucial for contemporary philosophy: the foundational role of logic, the history and PHILOSOPHY OF SCIENCE, pragmatism, semiotics, and epistemology. His pioneering work in semiotics, however, has the greatest continuing importance for CULTURAL and CRITICAL THEORY. Indeed, Clifford Geertz (1973, p. 5) has argued that CULTURE is principally a semiotic concept.

Peirce's "Some consequences of four incapacities" sets forth the essence of his theory of the SIGN. Although everything that appears to consciousness, he argues, is a "phenomenal manifestation of ourselves," that does not preclude the possibility of there being a phenomenon of something without us. At the moment when we think, we appear to ourselves as a sign. A sign has three references: (i) to some thought that interprets it; (ii) *for* some object that it is thought to be equivalent; (iii) *in* some respect that connects it with its object. However, since a sign is not identical with what it signifies, it must have some characteristics unique to itself. These are, first, the representative function which makes it a *representation*; second, the pure denotative application, or real connection, which brings one thought into *relation* with another; and third, the material quality, or how it feels, which gives thought its *quality* (Peirce, 1868, p. 56). It is typical of Peirce that his most lucid elaboration of this semiotic theory appears in his letter, dated 12 October 1904 (Peirce, 1958, pp. 381–93) to Lady Viola Welby, the author of *What Is Meaning?* It may not be accidental – or costly to his reputation – that Peirce had important connections with early developments of FEMINISM in America through his first wife, whom he divorced. Peirce was always a prototypical intellectual in that he was an exile even in the midst of the New England academic world into which he was born. He died in poverty, and his widow sold his papers – most of them at that time unpublished – to Harvard University for $500, after President Eliot and the trustees of the University had ignored even William James's pleas on his behalf. The year after Peirce's death a version of SAUSSURE's *Cours de Linguistique générale* was published, which has continued to eclipse the American philosopher's unique contribution to semiotics.

Reading
Eco, Umberto 1979: *A Theory of Semiotics.*
Hawkes, Terence 1977 (*1989*): *Structuralism and Semiotics.*
Hookway, Christopher 1985: *Peirce.*
Peirce, Charles S. 1868 (*1958*): "Some consequences of four incapacities."
——— 1958: *Selected Writings.*

MICHAEL PAYNE

phallogocentrism A condensation of "phallocentrism" and "logocentrism," originally coined by DERRIDA (1967; 1980) and given wider currency by deconstructionist critiques of the privileging of the logos as the site of truth, and by feminist critiques of PATRIARCHY, and especially of the primacy ascribed to the PHALLUS by LACAN.

Reading
Derrida, Jacques 1967a: *Of Grammatology.*
——— 1980: *The Post Card; From Socrates to Freud and Beyond.*

DAVID MACEY

phallus The term is rarely used by FREUD, who normally employed it to refer to the ancient symbol of sovereign power (Freud, 1910, p. 125; 1918, p. 204). The adjective "phallic" is common in Freud, but the noun form is usually (Freud, 1923) simply synonymous with penis. Although Freud consistently refers (1905) to a phallic stage in development in which sexual difference is held by the child to be predicated on a castrated (female)/noncastrated (male) distinction, he does not elaborate any concept of the phallus as such. In LACANian PSYCHOANALYSIS, "phallus" is used to emphasize the SYMBOLIC value taken on by the biological organ in intersubjective relations and in the course of accession to the symbolic. For some feminists the theory of the phallus offers a means of escaping Freud's residual biologism and constructing a theory of sexual difference which places more emphais on cultural and symbolic factors (Mitchell, 1974).

Lacan's concept of the phallus was elaborated primarily in his writings of the 1950s. In the 1956 seminar on the psychoses (Lacan, 1981) the phallus is held to be the mediating element in the castration complex, an imaginary object which the child finally accepts as being in the father's possession. It is in the important paper on the meaning of the phallus (Lacan, 1958) that Lacan begins to speak of the phallus as a privileged signifier which marks the articulation of desire and the logos. From this new perspective, the phallus is the object of the mother's desire and the child attempts to identify with that object in order to satisfy both the mother's desire and its own desire for the mother. The phallus is, however, a signifier or symbol (there is some confusion over this in both Lacan and the work of his followers) and the child cannot be that signifier. It is the child's entry into the symbolic that will allow it to accept that the phallus is not the attribute of an individual, but the signifier of sexual difference itself. It is this articulation of desire, lack, and language which exposes Lacan to the accusation of PHALLOGOCENTRISM.

One of the more disturbing features of arguments about the status of the phallus is that, while Lacan and his followers insist that the phallus–penis distinction is to be found in Freud, they often rely upon French translations which introduce a distinction that does not exist in either the German or the English TEXT. Attempts to locate the phallus–penis distinction in Freud should therefore be viewed with some suspicion.

Reading
Freud, Sigmund 1905a: "Three essays on the theory of sexuality."
——1910c: *Leonardo da Vinci and a Memory of His Childhood.*
——1918: "The taboo of virginity."
——1923b: "The infantile genital organization: an interpolation into the theory of sexuality."
Lacan, Jacques 1958: "The meaning of the phallus."
Mitchell, Juliet 1974: *Psychoanalysis and Feminism.*
DAVID MACEY

phatic communication A type of verbal communication which implies a willingness to converse; a term coined by Roman JAKOBSON. A phatic utterance needs convey no meaning in and of itself, but can consist of culturally acceptable phrases which simply signal friendliness, such as talking about the weather in some countries.

Reading
Eagleton, Terry 1983 (*1985*): *Literary Theory: An Introduction.*
Hawkes, Terence 1977: *Structuralism and Semiotics.*
PAUL INNES

phenomenological reduction Phenomenological reduction is another name for the method of "bracketing" applied by Husserl in his phenomenological philosophy. The name is used to stand for three different procedures: in each case, something is "bracketed" and something is the "residue." First, there is the *eidetic* reduction: in this case one "brackets" the existence as well as the variable features of a class of things, the purpose being to let the invariant features or the eidos stand out as the residue. Second, "phenomenological–psychological reduction": in this case, one "brackets" the question of existence or nonexistence of the object in an intentional act (such as perceiving or believing) the residue is the object-as-intended (that is, as believed or as perceived) as the correlate of the intentional act, or what is technically called the noema–noesis correlation. Third, the transcendental reduction (or, *ēpochē*): one brackets the basic belief-in-the-world, so that consciousness (with its noesis–noema structure) is exhibited as the transcendental, meaning-conferring, and world-constituting source.
J.N. MOHANTY

phenomenology A twentieth-century philosophical movement distinguished by a concentration on descriptions of experience which reveal the "meanings" things have for human beings prior to theoretical interpretation. Phenomenology has exerted an immense influence on both cultural and LITERARY CRITICISM.

The term "phenomenology," which derives from a Greek word for "appearance," was first coined in the eighteenth century to refer to the "theory of illusion," but its meaning was soon widened. For KANT, phenomenology was the study of phenomena, by which he meant actual and possible objects of experience (real or illusory), as distinct from unknowable "things-in-themselves" or noumena. For HEGEL, it was the study of the various forms which consciousness has taken in history on the way to the mind's absolute knowledge of itself. During the nineteenth century it came to mean, for the most part, little more than the descriptive study of any given subject matter (see Schmitt, 1967).

It is with the work of the German philosopher Edmund HUSSERL and his collaborators, in the first decades of the twentieth century, that the term becomes the name of a distinctive philosophical tendency. Several of Husserl's definitions of "phenomenology" presuppose the truth of his own controversial claims, with the unwelcome consequence that, for someone who does not accept those claims, there can be no such discipline. For example, if it is defined as "the theory of the essential nature of the transcendentally purified consciousness" (Husserl, 1962, p. 161), then the possibility of phenomenology depends on the (disputed) existence of such a consciousness. So it is better to understand "phenomenology" as referring to both Husserl's own philosophical position (at least, from about 1910 onwards) *and* any other which is sufficiently similar to this. How similar is similar? It is unfortunate to impose such strict criteria that Martin HEIDEGGER, Maurice MERLEAU-PONTY, and Jean-Paul SARTRE are denied the label. For one thing, they all called themselves "phenomenologists"; for another, Husserl's own thinking, during his final years, was moving in the directions taken by these writers. Most important, however, there are a number of Husserlian themes to which, despite important modulations, these philosophers also subscribe. I shall follow the familiar practice of describing Husserl's phenomenology as "pure" and that of the later writers as "existential."

After listing the common themes to which all phenomenologists, in their different ways, subscribe, I outline Husserl's "pure" position and then the criticisms leveled against this by his "existential" successors. Finally, I consider some ramifications of phenomenology in the fields of cultural and LITERARY CRITICISM.

Common Themes The first theme is that of the primacy of "fundamental description." This reflects the traditional conception of philosophy as a "basic" inquiry which refuses to take for granted the assumptions made – reasonably enough for their own purposes – by other disciplines. The ambitions of these other disciplines, notably the natural sciences, are typically those of analysis, explanation, justification (of beliefs and theories), and prediction. However, these ambitions presuppose a level at which what is analyzed, explained, etc. is properly described and identified. Such descriptions must, moreover, be fundamental in the sense that they do not covertly contain the results of analyses and theories. Otherwise, we would not have reached the "basic" level. These "fundamental descriptions" at which philosophy aims must, therefore, be of things as they are "for us," as encountered in ordinary, untutored experience. For any description of things – in terms, say, of their molecular composition – which was disjoint with such experience could only be the product of "tutored" theorizing. It is this return to a level of "fundamental description" of things which is enjoined by the favorite slogan of phenomenology, *Zu den Sachen* ("Back to the things themselves"). (See, for example, Husserl, 1962, p. 74f; Heidegger, 1980, p. 50.)

Unfortunately, this return to "the things themselves" is remarkably difficult, since even our everyday thinking is imbued with theoretical assumptions and "prejudices." Hence – the second common theme – the need for an operation of "abstaining from" or "bracketing" such assumptions and "prejudices." (Husserl uses the Greek word *epochē* for this operation). The point is less to call such assumptions into doubt than simply "to put them out of play," so that they do not infect our "fundamental descriptions." A phenomenological description of colors, for example, will have "bracketed" scientific considerations about light waves and the like. The example indicates a third theme, what Merleau-Ponty calls the "foreswearing of science" (1981, p. viii). It is not simply that, along with all other theoretical assumptions, those of the sciences must be "bracketed" – though, given the immense prestige of the sciences and the pretension of some scientists to be offering the only correct account of things, this "bracketing" is especially urgent. Two further points are being made. First, the accounts of the world and ourselves offered by the sciences are necessarily parasitic on a more "primordial" one which they cannot therefore overturn. Second, the sciences typically have excessive explanatory ambitions, particularly in the field of human consciousness and behavior. What "fundamental description" will reveal is that our experiences and actions are not of the right kind to lend themselves to the causal explanations of science.

Of what kind are they, then? The answer is contained in the fourth theme, the doctrine of intentionality. This notion is variously interpreted within the phenomenological movement, but on two central points there is agreement. First, many of our mental states and actions are irreducibly "directed toward" or "about" objects. To hope or to search is to hope or to search *for* something. Any adequate description of such a state or action must therefore make reference to its object, and cannot consist simply in an account of, say, certain "sense data" or bodily movements which are occurring. Second, it is a crucial feature of these "intentional" states and actions that their objects do not have actually to exist. The child hopes for Santa Claus's arrival; the Spaniards searched for El Dorado; the drunkard keeps seeing pink rats. Hence the relation between an "intentional" state and its object cannot be a *causal* one. Rather it is one of "meaning." What makes it possible for a linguistic expression to be "about" something, even when (like "Santa Claus") it refers to nothing in reality, is its possession of a meaning or sense. Similarly, an "intentional" state or action has a "meaning" which may or may not be satisfied by an actual object or goal. The central focus of phenomenological description is therefore upon the meanings through which we are related to our world. Since possession of meaning is essential to our experiences and actions, and since meanings are not the kind of thing susceptible to the causal explanations of the sciences, the fundamental examination of experience and action cannot be a natural scientific one.

As the example of hope indicates, it is not only "cognitive" mental states which relate us to the world through a network of meanings. "Affective" states – moods, emotions, and so on – are also "directed" and possess significance, so that the examination of these can yield important results for our understanding of ourselves and the world.

This is the last of the common themes: the insistence on the philosophical importance of "affective" intentionality. A good example is provided by the phenomenon of *Angst* which Heidegger, Sartre, and Merleau-Ponty, in their different ways, all regard as revelatory of crucial dimensions of our relationship to the world. Certainly it is not to be treated as a mere "inner stirring" or discomfort. (See, for example, Sartre, 1957, pp. 27ff, where it is argued that *Angst* is an experience of oneself as totally free to decide one's actions.)

I have stated these common themes in terms sufficiently broad for most phenomenologists to subscribe to. However, much of the interest yielded by the literature of this movement resides in the more detailed – and contentious – ways in which different philosophers have developed and modulated the themes. I begin with the "pure" position of Husserl.

"Pure" or Transcendental Phenomenology   For Husserl, phenomenological descriptions of objects and our experiences of them aspire to be "fundamental," not only in the sense of being free from "prejudices," but in being *a priori* and "apodictic." That is, they must be necessarily, indubitably, and self-evidently true. This is the point of his defining phenomenology as a "rigorous science" which "aims exclusively at establishing 'knowledge of essences'" (1962, p. 40). It is to be achieved, in part, by what Husserl calls "eidetic reduction." For an object of my experience to count as a tree, I must "intuit" it to have those features which remain invariable as a I "freely imagine" the object altering all its other features, while remaining a tree. These invariable features constitute its essence or eidos.

However, a more radical "reduction" is required if we are to exclude irrelevant matters from our descriptions. Since the actual existence of objects is contingent and dubitable, we must "bracket" the "natural attitude" which takes such existence for granted. Although the world "goes on appearing as it appeared before . . . the natural believing in [its] existence" is suspended (1977, p. 20). Now, among the "objects" whose existence is thus "bracketed" are *ourselves*, considered as embodied persons or "empirical"/"natural" egos. With this "reduction," "there exists no 'I' . . . the natural human ego . . . is reduced to the transcendental ego" (1975, p. 10). This latter is not an object of experience – not a denizen of the world, if such exists – but the "pure" SUBJECT or "spectator" which remains after everything else has been "bracketed."

Unlike some other philosophers, such as Descartes, who – if only for methodological reasons – have "reduced" the world to the operations of a conscious subject, Husserl is insistent that our mental states must generally be understood as directed toward objects. But since these objects of consciousness are "intentional" ones, the non-existence of their "correlates" in reality, like Santa Claus, is no obstacle. Description of these states contains two components, which Husserl calls the "noetic" and "noematic." A noetic description of seeing a tree focuses on what makes the act one of seeing rather than, say, touching or remembering the tree. Its noematic description is of the "meaning" of such acts. This, crudely put, is an account of the conditions which would have to be met for the object of the acts actually to exist. Thus the act of seeing a tree creates expectations of further experiences I must be able to obtain by way of confirming that I was indeed seeing a tree. This has an important implication for "the nature of reality." In one sense Husserl is not denying the real existence of things, since we sometimes do obtain the anticipated experiences which confirm such judgments as "I am seeing a tree." On the other hand, no sense can be made of the idea of a world existing independently of consciousness. This is because the very sense of "The tree exists" can only be given in terms of the "fulfilling," by further experiences, of the conditions contained in the noetic content – the "meaning" – of conscious acts. For this reason, Husserl describes his philosophy as a form of "transcendental idealism."

Husserl himself wrote relatively little on the "meanings" of emotional and affective mental states, concentrating primarily on perceptual acts. Nevertheless, some of his associates did address these areas, a good example being Max Scheler's account of moral experience (1954). It is, Scheler argues, totally unfaithful to such experience to regard moral evaluation as the mere expression of a "subjective" mood or personal preference. A moral evaluation is necessarily experienced by its subjects as directed toward objective features, values. (It is interesting to note that some recent anti-objectivists in analytic moral philosophy concede that their position flies in the face of the "feel" that moral judgments have for us. See, for example, Mackie, 1978, pp. 48f.)

"Existential" Phenomenology The shift from "pure" to "existential" phenomenology occurs with Heidegger's insistence that "[human] existence is

more than mere cognition in the usual spectator sense," for this "presupposes existence" (1982, p. 276). The source of understanding and meaning, therefore, is not Husserl's "disinterested spectator of [the] worldly ego and its life," but the thoroughly "worldly" human agent in his living engagement with the world. With this shift, the distinctive claims of "pure" phenomenology must be either abandoned or radically revised.

To begin with, it no longer makes sense totally to suspend "the natural attitude," to "bracket" the whole of empirical reality. That would require, impossibly, that we could entirely detach ourselves from that very engagement with the world which is presupposed by "mere cognition." Nor can it be a sensible ambition to offer a complete description of our experience, for any description is made by people from the viewpoint of a "situation" which they cannot, at the same time, submit to detached examination. My very adaption to the world in a certain way, says Sartre, means that I cannot completely "decipher" it (1957, p. 200).

It follows next that, if I cannot "reduce" the whole of empirical reality, there is no such entity as the "pure" or "transcendental" ego – for that was supposed to be what was left over after such a "reduction." The notion of "pure" egos is problematic on other grounds. Stripped of all physical and other empirical features, how could they be individuated? Why suppose, with Husserl, that there are many such egos and not, say, just one "branching" ego? If we must speak of the self at all, says Heidegger, this can only be "the factual self, the concrete person" (1962, p. 602).

Most important of all, perhaps, the central notion of intentionality must be rethought. By "bracketing" the world and encapsulating the objects of experience *within* the conscious subject, Husserl perverts that notion, whose importance, surely, is to stress that experience is intelligible only as directed towards what is "outside." Intentional experience is not the cognition of "meanings" or "essences" which may or may not be "fulfilled" by things in a real world, but, first and foremost, the understanding which permeates our intelligent, purposive dealings with the world. Meanings are not timeless "essences" to grasp through intuition, but the purposes which inform our actions and the "significations" which things assume for us in the light of those purposes. The "meaning" of a hammer is not a noema or schema which some objects might fit, but the role the hammer plays in relation to other objects and to our own projects. For this reason, Merleau-Ponty argues that the human BODY, far from being just one more "bracketable" item in the world, is itself a crucial source of meaning. It is through the body that there is "imposition of meaning" (1981, p. 147).

"Existential" phenomenology retains the thought that in a sense the world is dependent on human beings. But this sense is not Husserl's. The point is no longer that the world can only be understood as that which would "fulfill" the expectations implicit in acts of perception. It is, rather, that the world is a totality of significant objects, each of which only obtains its significance – its identity, indeed – through the place it occupies in a network of human activities and purposes.

Culture and Literature Analytic philosophers have, for the most part, regarded the philosophical enterprise as a relatively modest and self-contained one. Phenomenologists, on the other hand, took themselves to be addressing, in the most fundamental way, what Husserl and Heidegger respectively called "the crisis of European existence" and "our destitute age." The modern crisis, as they saw it, was rooted in underlying attitudes for which phenomenology could provide a cure.

None was more messianic than Husserl himself during his final writings of the 1930s. Europe, he argued, had fallen victim to a "barbarian hatred of spirit," reflected in a new "tribalism" and nationalism, in a return to myth, and in moral nihilism or relativism – in short, in a rejection of rationality. Since, for Husserl, the distinctive glory of "Western man" was the pursuit and exercise of universal reason, this was a tragedy. His main point, however, was that this loss of faith in reason was an understandable reaction against the perverted notion of rationality which had become increasingly dominant since the Renaissance. "The European crisis has its roots in a mistaken rationalism . . . its exteriorization, its absorption in 'naturalism' and 'objectivism'" (Husserl, 1965, pp. 179 and 191).

There are two main aspects to this "mistaken rationalism." First, the "mathematicization of the world" by the natural sciences: the pretense, that is, that the world of experience – including the meanings and values there encountered – is a merely subjective illusion behind which lies the only real world, that of the measurable entities of the sciences. (Heidegger was to make a similar point in his critique of technology.) Second, the reduction

of mind or spirit – which, in truth, is the source of all meaning, including that attaching to the statements of science – to something merely "objective" (the brain, perhaps, or a mechanical "mental substance" distinguished only by the "stuff" of which it is composed). It was inevitable, Husserl argues, that there should be an "irrationalist" revulsion against a rationality which so reduced the world and ourselves, thereby debarring itself from even discussing the moral and spiritual issues which are the most vital concerns of human beings. The solution, of course, is to recapture an earlier ideal of rationality, not yet infected with "objectivism": an ideal now kept alive in the ambitions of transcendental phenomenology.

The relegation to the sphere of what is "merely subjective" of anything not encompassed in the "objective" world of the sciences was also a target for criticism by phenomenologists writing on culture in the narrower sense of the arts and literature. A central figure here was the Polish philosopher, Roman Ingarden. Much of his work consisted in drawing careful distinctions between genuinely aesthetic and nonaesthetic attitudes to works of art, and between the very different "objects" often confused under the heading of "work of art." For example, we must distinguish between the novel as a work of art proper, its physical or "existential substrate," and the "aesthetic object" which emerges when the reader "concretizes" the work by imaginatively reconstructing what is left indeterminate by the author (a character's face, say). However, a constant target of Ingarden is the familiar idea that ascriptions of value to a work of art merely register the subjective pleasures of the audience. For one thing, it is impossible to specify the relevant pleasures except as those ensuing on the recognition of the work's own value. For another, "if these pleasures constituted the sole value . . . it would not be possible to attribute value to the work itself," but only to our own states (Ingarden, 1979, p. 43). This would contradict the undeniable phenomenological fact that it is the work itself to which value is ascribed.

Another "classic" in the phenomenology of literature is Sartre's distinction between two kinds of writing – mischievously labeled "prose" and "POETRY." In the former, words are used to present and talk about things; in the latter, the words are themselves the things presented. Hence the criteria for judging "prose" and "poetry" are quite different. Only in the former case, for example, is the author's political and moral "commitment" relevant (Sartre, 1983, ch. I).

See also BRACKETING; EXISTENTIALISM; PHENOMENOLOGICAL REDUCTION; TRANSCENDENTAL PHILOSOPHY.

Reading
Bell, D. 1990: *Husserl*.
Cooper, D.E. 1990: *Existentialism: A Reconstruction*.
Dreyfus, H.L., ed. 1982: *Husserl, Intentionality, and Cognitive Science*.
Hammond, M., Howarth, J., and Keat, R. 1991: *Understanding Phenomenology*.
Husserl, E. 1900–1 (*1970*): *Logical Investigations*.
——1936 (*1970*): *The Crisis of European Sciences and Transcendental Phenomenology*.
Ingarden, R. 1931 (*1973*): *The Literary Work of Art*.
Kockelmans, J., ed. *Phenomenology: The Philosophy of Edmund Husserl and its Interpretations*.
Mohanty, J.N. 1989: *Transcendental Phenomenology*.
Sartre, J.-P. 1937 (*1957*): *The Transcendence Of The Ego*.
Spiegelberg, H. 1960 (*1982*): *The Phenomenological Movement*.

DAVID E. COOPER

philosophy, African *See* AFRICAN PHILOSOPHY

philosophy, end of *See* END OF PHILOSOPHY

philosophy of language *See* LANGUAGE, PHILOSOPHY OF

philosophy of law *See* LAW, PHILOSOPHY OF

philosophy of science *See* SCIENCE, PHILOSOPHY OF

philosophy, postanalytic *See* POSTANALYTIC PHILOSOPHY

philosophy, transcendental *See* TRANSCENDENTAL PHILOSOPHY

photography Critical thought on photography in the twentieth century has encompassed arguments in the early part of the century for its acceptance as an ART form, writings on the impact of photography upon more traditional art media, the development of a history of the medium, and recent work by writers and artists to develop a theory for the medium. Much recent work in photography draws from various currents in postmodern thought in an attempt to deconstruct modernism in art, to replace the master narratives of high FORMALISM with "the discourse of others" (Foster, 1983), and to lead to the recognition of the art object (image) as a contingent entity. For those writers and artists who have produced this recent work, POSTMODERNISM can best be defined as a crisis in Western representation in which photography has played a central critical role. The influence of CRITICAL THEORY on the work of these artists and writers is crucial to understanding their projects, and many of the relevant theorists focus upon photography because of its interdisciplinary nature. The adaptability of the medium is perhaps its only governing characteristic. This is evident in the diverse uses of the medium in CULTURE, art being only a small portion of its "use." The basis for many of the questions arising in the prominent art of the 1980s drew from philosophical and interdisciplinary resources, such as PHENOMENOLOGY, LITERARY CRITICISM, SEMIOTICS, MARXISM, feminism, and PSYCHOANALYSIS. Primary to these projects were questions of audience and institutional constraints placed upon meaning evident in high modernist art. The influence on the art world of these theories has meant a dissolving of boundaries between disciplines and between theory and practice. A pertinent example of the latter is feminist art, which relies on critical intervention as a "tactical necessity" (Foster, 1983). The blurring of boundaries mirrors similar occurrences in other more traditional academic disciplines. The crossing of theory and practice is also evident in the increasing number of practicing artists who are also critical writers on photography.

To better understand the postmodern project and photography's role in it, it is first necessary to examine the development of photography as a modernist medium.

The first comprehensive history of the medium was written by Beaumont Newhall (1937). Originally conceived as a catalog for the Museum of Modern Art exhibition "Photography: 1839–1937," Newhall's *History of Photography* became the book which was crucial to photography's being accepted as a legitimate art form. The study of photography as a distinct discipline gained acceptance through the development of its official history; and Newhall's book, which has been revised and expanded several times, continues to serve as an important text on photographic history. Newhall places particular emphasis upon the "purist" version of the medium's history, neglecting to cover the varied cultural contexts in which photographs operate. This version of the medium was carried in exhibitions at the Museum of Modern Art in New York for decades, beginning with the curatorial visions of photographer Edward Steichen and later with John Szarkowski.

A group of like-minded photographers in the first 20 years of the century, loosely associated under the term "purism," sought to establish photography as an art form by the identification of characteristics and qualities inherent to the medium. Modernism in photography, and likewise in painting, sought to establish a "universal" photographic form, the depoliticization of art, and an emphasis upon the purity and autonomy of the medium as an art form. Among those characteristics considered as solely "photographic" were sharpness of focus with highly rendered detail and an unmanipulated approach to subject matter. Photographers influenced by this aesthetic formed a group, referred to as the "f-64 group," named for the smallest aperture on a large format lens producing the sharpest of detail.

One of the chief proponents of the purist aesthetic was a practitioner, Alfred Steiglitz. Steiglitz led the way to having photography accepted as an art form with his many activities, including his 291 Gallery and the journal *Camerawork*, which controlled not only the production but also the promotion of his own work and the work of others he supported. Steiglitz wanted to elevate photography to the status of painting, POETRY, and sculpture; and he was instrumental in developing photography as a modernist medium.

Ironically, early in his career, Steiglitz was associated with pictorialism, whose aesthetic ran directly counter to the desires of the purists. The pictorialist aesthetic was characterized by highly contrived tableaux similar to period paintings. Pictorialism was later criticized by the purists for excessive sentimentality and for being too closely derived from painting. It soon became equated with popular "low art" and its aesthetic was disregarded. A.D. Coleman in his 1976 essay "The directorial mode" believed that histories of the medium neglected this area and focused almost solely on the purists' ideals for the medium.

In order to develop the medium as an art form, the purists reconciled form with self-expression through abstraction in ways similar to the painting of that day. In his 1975 essay "On the invention of photographic meaning," an essay highly influenced by the writing of Roland BARTHES, Allan Sekula cited Steiglitz's own description of how his most famous image "The steerage" occurred, in order to highlight the desire of modernist photography to deny the representational status of the photograph. In the 1920s Steiglitz produced a series of images of clouds he called "Equivalents," where the narrative is completely dropped out of the photograph. Steiglitz saw these images as equivalent to feelings and emotions. Purist ideals in the work of other photographers, such as Paul Strand, Edward Weston, Imogene Cunningham, and Ansel Adams likewise emphasized individual expression, abstract form, and an apolitical approach to subject matter.

Photographic purism in Europe was led by Lazlo Moholy-Nagy and the Bauhaus school aesthetic of "form following function." The Bauhaus, influenced by the Russian constructivists, called for a revitalized art, a more democratic art form which emphasized experimentation with an objective scientific eye. Photography fitted into their new vision well, for it represented not only an art form accessible to the masses but also one which utilized the latest of scientific technologies. The European brand of modernism had a political base, while the American version was apolitical, emphasizing individual expression and genius. In America the Bauhaus aesthetic found its way to the Institute of Design in Chicago through Moholy-Nagy, who founded the school as the New Bauhaus School of Design in 1937. Aaron Siskind and Harry Callahan later formed one of the first graduate programs there and influenced a generation of photographers. Siskind's work merged sensibilities from both schools of thought – his close-up, flattened views of painted signs and decaying walls resemble the abstract expressionist paintings of Franz Kline, while remaining within the spirit of experimentation. Man Ray, an American who was first influenced by Steiglitz's purist vision, made his career primarily in Paris, working closely with Marcel Duchamp and the dadaists. For Man Ray, photography was but one of many media available for use: the idea was of primary importance over the actual art object.

In America a split was formed in the early part of the twentieth century between photography that utilized the social character of the medium and work that fitted into the purist conception of "art" photography. Socially conscious photographers, such as Lewis Hine, Walker Evans, and much later Robert Frank, believed the "art" of photography lay in its ability to document the everyday world. In the case of Hine, who was trained as a sociologist, the original context for his work reveals the political nature of these images. His work frequently illustrated pamphlets for liberal social reform and was part of such projects as exposing the horrors of child labor. Sekula described the split between art photography and documentary photography as "symbolist folk-myth vs. a realist folk-myth" (Sekula, 1975). In the work of the purists the photographer is a seer, art being the expression of inner truth. In documentary the photographer is a witness, and the photograph is a reportage of empirical truth.

Hine and Evans, along with other photographers such as Dorothea Lange and Ben Shahn, were employed by the United States government in the 1930s as part of the Farm Security Administration (FSA) Project headed by Roy Stryker. The FSA Project aimed to document the rural poor to appeal to the sensibilities of middle-class urbanites. Historian James Curtis exposed the IDEOLOGY behind this project. He found images not officially released by the project, which reveal an explicit political agenda behind the choice, and in many cases manipulation of the subject matter by the photographers to fit into the ideological and aesthetic needs of both the artist and Stryker. Evans, for example, frequently moved or removed elements in composing his images of rural workers' homes to fit his purist aesthetic sensibilities. Lange, when photographing her most famous image, *Migrant Mother*, took several shots until she had composed her subjects to resemble a Madonna with child image, one where the woman's plight would appeal to the sensibilities of educated urban viewers of the image. By the time Robert Frank began *The Americans*, his documentary of the United States published in 1959, he acknowledged personal expression as part of his project.

In Europe the socially concerned photography of Eugene Atget, August Sander, and Bill Brandt was grounded in class realism. Susan SONTAG, in her book of 1973 *On Photography*, identifies a difference between American and European documentary photography. Sander, whose project was to document the German people before the 1939–45

war according to their professions, treated all his subjects in the same cool way. His project was thus vastly different from the FSA Project. In her book, Sontag comments on the photography of other artists, as well as on aspects of the medium outside of the art world, such as tourist photography, family photography, police records, billboards, and advertising. Sontag positions the medium as a broad cultural phenomenon whose influence on seeing and knowledge is far-reaching.

One of the first theorists to write on photography within a political context was Walter BENJAMIN. Benjamin wrote of the impact of technology on several branches of art, and in his essay "The work of art in the age of mechanical reproduction" (1936) Benjamin identified the issue of AUTHENTICITY and art as beginning with the trade of art objects. With mechanical reproduction possible with photography, the authority of the art object, or what Benjamin terms its unique "aura," is eroded. A plurality of copies now replaces the unique existence of the original. Perhaps one of the most profound ramifications of mechanical reproduction for art addressed in the essay is the notion that art is no longer based on ritual but instead on politics. The basis for this notion resides in the reduced distance between viewer and art object afforded by reproductions of works of art formerly not available for viewing to a wide audience. The "cult value" of a work of art decreases as its accessibility increases. Benjamin cites Stone Age cave drawings and medieval cathedral statues not visible from ground level as examples of work made for magical and spiritual purposes, as opposed to being produced to "be on view." This emancipation from ritual provided a new function for art, which he terms the "artistic function."

John Berger in the early 1970s wrote an extension of Benjamin's thoughts into the interpretation of advertising imagery. He cites a connection between the strategies of oil painting and those of advertising photography, by capitalization on desire. Berger's treatment of advertising photography predates later work of artists and writers, primarily in the 1980s, who critique the strategies of advertising practices.

The beginnings of postmodern thought in art can be traced to STRUCTURALISM and POSTSTRUCTURALISM, particularly in the writings of Barthes, DERRIDA, FOUCAULT, and LÉVI-STRAUSS. These writers think of CULTURE as a corpus of CODES or myths. The writings of Roland Barthes are of particular importance to photography and to the development of a "theory of photography." In his 1961 essay "The photographic message," Barthes examined a particular "type" photograph, the press photograph. Barthes first identified a concept crucial to understanding photography as a cultural product. The source of meaning in all photographs is based upon its "use," upon its context. He emphasized that his project was one which was an analysis of CODES vs. signifieds, an examination of the cultural vs. the literal message of the press photograph. It is in this essay, and in "Rhetoric of the image," that Barthes identified "the photographic paradox," which he described as the coexistence of two messages, one neutral (natural, "denoted") and the other invested (cultural, "connoted") (see CONNOTATION/DENOTATION). Barthes also applied his literary notion of INTERTEXTUALITY to images, identifying images as "polysemous" entities that have underlying them a "floating chain of signifieds" (Barthes, 1961).

Barthes concluded that "pure denotation" in the photograph could only exist on the level of the traumatic image. In line with notions of the trauma in FREUDian, and later, LACANian PSYCHOANALYSIS, Barthes described the trauma as a suspension or blockage of meaning. Twenty years later, in *Camera Lucida* (1980), Barthes retained the idea of the traumatic image, while transforming his earlier terms "denotation" and "connotation" into the terms "punctum" and "studium." In this, his last book, Barthes dispensed with the methodologies of psychoanalysis and instead utilized ideas drawn from PHENOMENOLOGY, a move which Victor Burgin, in his 1986 essay "Re-reading *Camera Lucida*," described as having severe consequences for the development of photography theory. Heavily influenced by the writings of Barthes, but with an eye towards further developing a link to Lacanian psychoanalytic theory, Burgin in this essay located the persistent operation of the unconscious in Barthes's discussions of the "punctum" in connection with particular photographs. The "punctum," formerly the denotative, now aligned with the Lacanian real, the unsymbolizable, the "plenitude which is effaced in the very moment it is experienced" (Burgin, 1986).

Rosalind KRAUSS was also highly influential in developing a theory for the medium. Krauss, like Burgin, utilized Lacanian theories of the unconscious in several books and essays on photography and art that appeared in the journal *OCTOBER*. In her reexamination of surrealism and photography's place in it, she positioned photography as a radical critique of representation. Like Barthes, Krauss examined the photograph as a contingent message, although Krauss's focus was primarily on art photography. In attempting to find a discourse proper to the medium, Krauss concluded, in "A note on photography and the simulacral," which refers to ideas drawn from both Benjamin and Foucault, that photography itself was a project of DECONSTRUCTION in which art was distanced and separated from itself (Krauss, 1984).

New currents in the art world in the late 1970s placed photography at the center of critiques of representation. Andy Grundberg in his essays on interactions between art and photography located the source of the increased appearance of photography in the mainstream art world in conceptual art, where the idea is of primary importance in a work of art. This turn to photography by conceptual artists in the late 1960s and 1970s sprang from the quintessential modernist desire to produce art that subverted traditional notions of what art was. Artists such as Bruce Nauman and Douglas Huebler initially turned to photography as a means of documenting their performances. John Baldessari and Robert Cumming dismantled the "truth" effect of the photograph in their exploration of notions about perception by creating explicitly false illusions for the camera. A precursor for this use of the photography was Yves Klein's "The Leap" of 1960, a photograph of the artist diving out of a second-storey window. The photograph was a fake and yet it presented the event as if it were real.

Hans Haacke used photography specifically for its objectivity in a series of works which sought to undermine the separation of the art world from political realities by exposing the connections between the art world, wealth, and social inequities. His work and the work of other conceptual artists sought to dematerialize art and to subvert its consumption. The use of the infinitely reproducible photograph fitted into this aim. The conceptualist influence also reached more traditional areas of art photography, influencing the work of many artists, including Duane Michals, Lewis Baltz, and Lucas Samaras. In John Pfahl's "Altered landscapes," the artist overtly manipulated traditionally sublime landscape views, questioning the veracity of the photograph as a document while poking fun at the work of such modern masters as Ansel Adams. Robert Heinecken's contact-printed magazine pages produced a series of multilayered, tonally reversed images. Much of this work had an implicit feminist message, for it utilized advertising photography, saturated as it is with stereotypical images of women.

These new currents in the use of photography reveal a fundamental shift in the medium's identity. While photography reached its goal of being accepted as a modernist art form, the terms of this goal, the purity and autonomy of photography as a medium, were no longer relevant concerns in the art world. Ironically, all the increased attention to the medium has in turn increased its market value in the art world. Photography's centrality has meant it is no longer the "outsider" of the art world that it was once thought to be.

In the 1980s the art world increasingly turned toward photography as a way to reaccess the social and in turn as a means to reinvigorate art. Photography in most of this work serves as a vehicle for critique. This is evident in the work of such artists as Barbara Kruger, Louise Lawler, and Victor Burgin. The early work of Cindy Sherman accessed the look of Hollywood film stills as a means to expose the ideology which operated in them. In her "Untitled film stills," the artists poses herself in stereotypical passive rolls, questioning at once conventions of *film noir*, sexual identity, and the "self-portrait." Richard Prince in a sense realized the end of the modernist project in a refusal to make art. His work as an artist comprised mostly the choosing, arranging, and rephotographing of magazine photographs, utilizing the already "full" world of images as his source. As a result, his work unmasks the syntax of editorial and advertising photography. Sherrie Levine, too, drew upon already existing images, although she turned to the world of modernist photography itself as a source for her rephotographed "masterpieces." In rephotographing and presenting as her own such works as Weston's famous *Torso of Neil*, she drew attention to the imaginary boundary between high art photography and other diverse uses of the medium, as well as undermining notions of authenticity and authorship. However, postmodernism in art as a critical enterprise is itself problematic, for although much of this work takes a critical stance towards the marketplace, it attempts its critique within that same marketplace.

Richard Bolton, in the introduction to his anthology *The Contest of Meaning*, called for a stronger alliance between the production of art and its theory; in particular he called for a radical repoliticization of photography and art. The project addressed in this collection of essays, including writing by both historians and practitioners, such as Douglas Crimp, Deborah Bright, Martha Rosler, and Abigail Solomon-Godeau, is the rewriting of a history of the medium that recognizes its social embeddedness in cultural productions of many types besides art.

In the 1990s Johnathon Crary developed a new PARADIGM for thinking about photography in the context of Western perspectivalism, in rejecting the linear narrative of technical progression that leads from the CAMERA OBSCURA to photography. Crary located a theoretical rupture in the early nineteenth century, which shifted from a geometrical optics to a physiological account of vision. Former historical accounts of photography have consistently placed the camera obscura as the model for the present-day camera, but Crary's arguments dismantled this line of thinking. This new paradigm is important for theorizing the newest shift in the medium toward digital technologies.

Reading
Barthes, Roland 1961: "The photographic message."
——— 1977 (*1991*): *Image, Music, Text.*
——— 1980 (*1981*): *Camera Lucida.*
Benjamin, Walter 1936: "Art in the age of mechanical reproduction."
——— 1970 (*1992*): *Illuminations.*
Bolton, Richard, ed. 1989 (*1992*): *The Contest of Meaning: Critical Histories of Photography.*
Burgin, Victor 1986: "Re-Reading *Camera Lucida.*"
——— 1986 (*1990*): *The End of Art Theory: Criticism and Postmodernity.*
Coleman, A.D. 1976: "The directorial mode: notes towards a definition."
Crary, Johnathon 1990 (*1992*): *Techniques of the Observer: On Vision and Modernity in the 19th Century.*
Curtis, James 1989: *Mind's Eye, Mind's Truth: FSA Photography Reconsidered.*
Foster, Hal, ed. 1983 (*1991*): *The Anti-Aesthetic: Essays on Postmodern Culture.*
Gauss, Kathleen McCarthy, and Grundberg, Andy 1987: *Photography and Art: Interactions Since 1946.*
Goldberg, Vicki, ed. 1981 (*1988*): *Photography in Print.*
Krauss, Rosalind 1985 (*1993*): *The Originality of the Avant-Garde and Other Modernist Myths.*
——— 1984: "A note on photography and the simulacral."
Newhall, Beaumont 1937 (*1982*): *The History of Photography.*
Sekula, Allen 1975: "On the invention of photographic meaning."
Sontag, Susan 1973 (*1977*): *On Photography.*

LYNN CAZABON

Piaget, Jean (1896–1980) Major Swiss structuralist thinker in the fields of psychology and epistemology. From the outset of his career, he was interested in studying how intellectual structures are established in the human being. This was to be his key to the way in which knowledge is acquired. The result was that he spent a great deal of his time on the development of intelligence during childhood.

For Piaget, human beings construct solutions which, if they work, are necessarily linked structurally with the laws of the human mind and, ultimately, natural laws. On a broader scale, he moves from this position to a theorizing of the growth of an individual's reasoning faculties in relation to a progression of human understanding in general. Since the individual's intelligence and the intelligence of the human race in general are ultimately derived from one and the same structure, that of the biological human being, the relation between the two is one of mutually verifiable complicity. This theory is the root of his concern with psychology, and links it with his concern with epistemology. For Piaget, the relation between the two is of such importance that he cannot simply study one or the other; he must pay attention to both, in tandem.

In keeping with his structuralist method, Piaget concentrated on the relations between elements. Thus he looked at the growth of individual reasoning in and through its relationship with the world exterior to the individual. In order to do this, he developed a METALANGUAGE based upon slightly modified vocabulary and symbolic logic. For example, the term "schema" is his term for an organized set of actions, such that if a child learns to reach for one thing, it can apply that experience to reaching for another. The child may do this without being able to explain how it arrived at its conclusion, and this is where intuition plays a part. However, this intuition is not a mysterious phenomenon: it is the result of the very structure of learning rooted in the human brain. Ultimately, the development of adult intelligence is the result of a move from such purely physical actions to an ability to solve problems by thought alone. Thus, for Piaget, thoughts were once actions, and it is this theoretical position which underpins his developmental psychology. It is the way that the biological organism is structured which permits the individual's adaptive intelligence to develop. The stages of this development, however, are problematical, since the way in which the intellect is structured varies depending on the age of the child. The way in which the move from one stage to the next is managed

is not clear, and Piaget's term for this gap is "décalage."

It is clear that for Piaget the development of reasoning is structured as a relation of differences between one stage and the others, and this is what marks him as a major exponent of STRUCTURALISM. Moreover, he uses a version of structural linguistics similar to that of Ferdinand de SAUSSURE as the basis for his theory of the child's realization of the operation of signification. For Piaget, there is a fundamental difference between the signifier and the significate (his equivalent of Saussure's signified), and this difference is predicated upon the essential structure of representation as it is present in the human mind. As it develops, the child changes the mode of its signifying operation from SYMBOL to the sociably shared SIGN.

Accordingly, Piaget's developmental psychology provides him with a basis for attempting to deal with the wider issues of signification and epistemology. In effect, he sees the emergence of the intellect as a natural operation which, although influenced by language and CULTURE, is in fact separate from them. For Piaget, this operation is the fundamental process of signification and epistemology itself, whether mathematical, logical, or psychological. All are rooted ultimately in the structure of the human mind. When he attempts to deal with the problem of the contribution of unconscious impulses to creativity, he derives from his theory the concept of a relational distinction between unconscious and conscious work, rather than an absolute one. By paying attention to the structure of learning itself, he sidesteps the problem of the relative inaccessibility of the UNCONSCIOUS. His position that the intellect is structured in the way he describes allows him to invoke that structure as somehow prior even to the unconscious, a maneuver familiar from other structuralist usages of a kind of "deep structure." The neurological structure of the human brain overdetermines the development of the intellect, and thus is also what lies behind the movements in epistemology. For Piaget, therefore, the history of epistemology is a single huge developmental process. This recalls similar claims on the part of structuralist literary critics such as Gérard GENETTE and other proponents of NARRATOLOGY for a literary tradition. It also raises similar problems, because it entails the production of a monological structure which is an attempt to account for all human activity in the field. It marginalizes the possibility of positions which challenge the integrity of the overall conception. In Piaget's theory, the movement from developmental psychology to epistemology is therefore the direct equivalent of the process of NATURALIZATION which takes place in structuralist literary studies. Any interrogation of the order he produces can be recuperated by recourse to the inherent biologism of his model. Ultimately, any powerful challenge to his theory would require an interrogation of the way he reduces intellect to the human neurological network, as a kind of biological humanism similar to that employed by Claude LÉVI-STRAUSS in his work on myths. It is, however, possible to avoid even this necessity, by concentrating on the historically precise characteristics of different epistemologies. Thus Michel FOUCAULT utilizes the concept of the epistemological break to call into question any straightforward narrative of epistemology along the lines assumed by Piaget. A radically historicizing maneuver of this kind would pay more attention to the possibilities opened up by Piaget to the discontinuities he uncovered in the child's development, as they apply to epistemology itself in his model.

Reading
Boyle, D.G. 1969: *A Student's Guide to Piaget.*
Piaget, Jean 1950: *The Psychology of Intelligence.*
——1953a: *Logic and Psychology.*
——1953b: *The Origin of intelligence in the Child.*
——1959: *The Language and Thought of the Child.*
PAUL INNES

play A term used by DERRIDA to indicate both a certain looseness or movement, which can always be found within structures and processes of signification, and the sort of amusement associated with playfulness. In French *le jeu* conveys this ambiguity much as it does in English. Play in both senses invites those processes of internal or self-reflexive critique that Derrida has practiced as DECONSTRUCTION and FOUCAULT as GENEALOGY. It has been observed by Christopher NORRIS, among others, that when Derrida's writing becomes too playful he has (perhaps unwittingly) invited the mistaken judgment that he has abandoned entirely the seriousness of truth and political engagement.

Reading
Derrida, Jacques 1967b (*1978*): *Writing and Difference.*
MICHAEL PAYNE

plot *See* STORY/PLOT

poetry Various authors, having attempted to define poetry, have admitted that such an enterprise is "dangerous," "impossible," or "meaningless," given the wide and loose range of the application of the term. Northrop FRYE opens his essay "Approaching the lyric" with the warning: "Some people believe that literary terms can be defined." It would be wise therefore to consider the term in its most differentiated, traditional genres, its narrative, dramatic, or lyrical forms. However, these genres too fall into subgenres, traditions, schools, and hierarchies, and these in turn become over time indistinct or interchangeable. Thus David Lindley concludes in his excellent and lengthy definition of the term "lyric": "if it is difficult to demarcate the lyric as a genre or cluster of sub-genres, then to make sense of the applications of the modal term 'lyrical' is, in the end, virtually impossible."

Roger Fowler and Allen Rodway, in *A Dictionary of Modern Critical Terms*, rightly lead us back from such impossibility, as do most explicators of the term, to the etymology of the word, pointing out that in the original Greek, poetry refers simply to "something made," whether in verse or not. One may value such an activity of "making" as either inferior, as Plato did, or superior, as the Romantics did, to a given reality. Implicit in such a polarity are the two major poetic theories: poetry as imitation (mimesis), which gave rise mainly but not exclusively to epic and dramatic poetry and which remained unchallenged through the eighteenth century; and poetry as expression, which brought the lyrical poem to unprecedented significance. Before the Romantic revolution poetry as mimesis was mainly employed to interpret a given reality and, as Horace and later Sir Philip Sidney and Samuel Johnson had demanded, to delight and instruct the audience. However, as M.H. Abrams has noted, Aristotle's unprecedented minute attention to the forms of poetry, independent from its mimetic reference, implies that poetry, even in Aristotle's mimetic theory, acquired an implicit aesthetic autonomy with no other criteria than its own form and internal structure. For Aristotle the historian "describes the thing that has been," whereas the poet imagines "a kind of thing that might be. Hence poetry," he continues, "is something more philosophic and of graver import than history, since its statements are of the nature rather of universals." Such a privileging of poetry over history, and of AESTHETICS over nature, is reflected also in Aristotle's *Physics*, where he points out, "art in some cases completes what nature cannot bring to a finish." Thus Sidney's notion that "poetry does not depend on nature but creates a second nature of its own" is not a radical departure from Aristotle. Referring to Aristotle's distinction between the poet and the historian, Sidney sees in the "peerless poet" on the other hand an ideal mixture of the philosopher and the historian: "he coupleth the general notion with the particular example." Such a definition of the poet permits Sidney not only to call into question the authority of philosophic and historical DISCOURSE, but also to liberate poetry from the philosopher's and the historian's alleged rhetorical self-deceptions and to bestow upon the poet an unprecedented authority, the authority of self-conscious fictionality: "though he recount things not true, yet because he telleth them not for true, he lieth not."

The controversy over the nature of poetic truth presupposes of course, as it does in Sidney's *Defense*, a mimetic standard. Once that standard was abandoned in the mid-nineteenth century, as Christopher Clausen has pointed out, Wordsworth's "great truths" eventually become Frost's "clarification of life – not necessarily a great clarification such as sects and cults are founded on, but . . . a momentary stay against confusion." Poetic truth thus becomes "dramatic truth" (Cleanth BROOKS), poetic statements become "pseudo statements" (I.A. RICHARDS) and finally, in Archibald MacLeish's phrase: "A poem should not mean / But be."

Such maxims have their beginnings in the Romantic movement. When Wordsworth in his Preface to the *Lyrical Ballads* (1800) declared that poetry was "the spontaneous overflow of powerful feelings," the authority of poetry shifted to an unverifiable inward subjectivity. "The paramount cause of poetry," as M.H. Abrams usefully sums up, "is not, as in Aristotle, a formal cause, determined primarily by the human actions and qualities imitated; nor as in neoclassical criticism, a final cause, the effect intended upon an audience; but instead an efficient cause – the impulse within the poet of feelings and desires seeking expression, or the compulsion of the 'creative' imagination." The rise of the lyric initiated by the Romantic movement thus generated such debatable notions as "genius," "originality," "immediacy," "presence," "transcendence." Although the lyrical poem is by no means an invention of the Romantics (Spenser, Shakespeare, and Milton were great lyric poets as

well), it became thereafter the vehicle for expressions of an existential situation markedly different from the social experiences hitherto rendered by satires, epics, odes, ballads, or pastorals. While there a theme or SUBJECT was given and mimetically transformed into a particular verse form, often for public performance, the lyric was by comparison a solitary monologue, allegorized by Shelley, who defined the poet as "a nightingale who sits in darkness and sings to cheer its own solitude with sweet sounds; his auditors are as men entranced by the melody of an unseen musician." Such a definition of the poet as solitary singer has survived, with important shifts of emphasis, in the examples of the French symbolists and their various successors, the modernists, the confessional poets, or the deep imagists. Generally, lyric poetry is "overheard," as Northrop Frye suggests. It is an "art of language," Lewis Turco writes when he defines, significantly, the larger term poetry. For by poetry today we customarily mean lyric poetry, even if the lyric mode may well, particularly in the nineteenth and twentieth centuries, have absorbed some other more elaborate or public forms, such as the ode, the elegy, or the ballad.

Since the lyric is by definition brief, intense, and concentrated, as Poe announced in his "Philosophy of composition," it alone could justify the term poetry. Through Poe's influence on the French symbolists, the lyric became a self-referential order of words, or mental correspondences, *un forêt des symboles*, as Rimbaud called it, in which one might lose one's way. When Eliot wrote in "Little Gidding," "prayer is more / than an order of words," it is likely that he sought a way to transcend the solipsistic aestheticism and enigmatic inwardness of the symbolist poem. The notion, particularly of the autonomous lyrical poem, goes back to KANT's aesthetic, which assigns the work of art no cognitive value but (merely) a purposeful purposelessness. Thus Auden could say (about Yeats's poetry): "poetry makes nothing happen," even if it is precisely this nonutilitarian, ahistoric, atemporal quality that assures poetry that "it survives / In the valley of its making where executives / Would never want to tamper." Auden's expulsion of the executives from the valley of poetry responds wittily to Plato's expulsion of the poets from his republic, where Plato had darkly warned that poetry "endangers the whole system."

Plato's warning is of course not a warning against harmless illusions, but perhaps against the kinds of implications inherent in the political autonomy of art, indeed in the self-absorbed intensity of such poetic tableaux as Frost's "Stopping by woods on a snowy evening" (1923). The traveler of Frost's poem appears to be initially undertaking the same journey that Northrop Frye thinks of when he defines poetry as a ritual turning away "from our ordinary continuous experience in space and time, or . . . from the verbal mimesis of it." Examples to illustrate this, as Frye points out, may extend beyond the subjective lyric to such varied forms of poetry as the meditative Old Testament Psalms, to the dramatic monologues of Byron's *Childe Harold*, or the lyrical narrative of Wordsworth's *Prelude*. The short, intense, subjective lyric, however, Frye claims, "superimposes a different kind of experience" on the narrative rhythms of time and life. The implications of a definition of poetry as opposing the constructions of meaning through narrative, intimates therefore the radical otherness of poetry, its structurally, aesthetically, even politically disruptive qualities. The French symbolist poets and their modernist successors, both European and American, thus demand that the poem refuse to translate into the terms of prose and paraphrase, or what these terms signify, into the narrative of historical existence. The symbolist, the modernist, or the aesthetic tradition that has given rise to and derived from these forms of poetry, would thus find, as Denis Donoghue has proposed, the purest expression of poetry in a "release" of language "from the office of representation into the mercy of fictiveness." We find such fortunate instances, as Donoghue points out, in images "of pure presentation." Such images demand of the reader consequently disinterested acts of pure perception, although one may wonder if such acts, since they are utopias in poetry, are possible in criticism.

Even if poetry is nothing but an order of words, it is like all artistic creation necessarily occasioned by psychological and historical realities. "Mad Ireland," as Auden writes, "hurt [Yeats] into poetry." Baudelaire's *Fleurs du mal* grew out of social ills and personal suffering. If the Romantic conception of the poem is that of the SYMBOL, defined by Coleridge as "partak[ing] of the Reality which it renders intelligible," more recent theories have stressed the impossibility, and necessary self-mystifications attending such aesthetic transcendence of time and history (see Paul DE MAN). From a demystified perspective (if that perspective does not itself claim an aesthetic disinterestedness) one

would allow poetry an aesthetic respite from the world "if and only if one is attempting to follow an imperative not to stop there," as Barbara Johnson puts it. Her imperative takes its authority from a rejection of an aesthetic solipsism, a stopping by woods on snowy evenings or upon Westminster Bridges, because these inward forms of otherness permit an idealization and neutralization of an intrinsic otherness that would amount to a synthesis of what always remains, and should remain, Johnson implies, an unbridgeable difference within. Such an irreparable difference, by which every poem remains self-divided rather than homogeneous, duplicitous rather than self-identical, has led to a preference of allegory over symbol. If Coleridge dismissed allegory as "empty echoes which the fancy arbitrarily associates with the apparitions of matter," Paul de Man inverts Coleridge's preference for the symbol over allegory:

Whereas the symbol postulates the possibility of an identity or identification, allegory designates primarily a distance in relation to its own origin, and, renouncing the nostalgia and the desire to coincide, it establishes its language in the void of this temporal difference. In so doing it prevents the self from an illusory identification with the non-self, which is now fully, though painfully, recognized as the non-self.

Such a theory, echoing as it does the existentialist's fear of bad faith, is lastly indebted to a materialist or historicist mode of thinking, one that prohibits any transcendence of material circumstances through symbol, METAPHOR, or ART. It demands that we remain aliens in the world.

Virgina Woolf has reminded us that fiction is "like a spider's web, attached ever so lightly perhaps, but still attached to life at all four corners." Nevertheless, in poetry, one might insist, these attachments would have to be established in other, perhaps more tenuous ways: first, perhaps in the allowance that the poem may indeed refuse to be attached at all, with all the attendant political and religious implications; and second, in the admission of the necessity, nevertheless, of such attachments. Unlike music, words are inevitably referential, taking their meanings, rebellious or not, from the daily conventions of language, and that may account for the tensions within which poetry must define itself. Unlike music, which needs no apology, the history of poetry is therefore also the history of its defenses, and thus the history of criticism and literary theory. Intersecting with its endless critiques and defenses in theory and criticism, and while yet standing on the brink of silence and music, poetry seeks manifold interdisciplinary connections, but withholds, it seems, any assent to forms of appropriation.

Reading
Abrams, M.H. 1953: *The Mirror and The Lamp.*
——1993: *A Glossary of Literary Terms.*
Donoghue, Denis 1976: *The Sovereign Ghost: Studies in Imagination.*
Hollander, John 1981: *Rhyme's Reason.*
Hosek, Chavia, and Parker, Patricia, eds 1985: *Lyric Poetry: Beyond New Criticism.*
Howard, Richard 1980: *Alone With America: Essays on the Art of Poetry in the United States since 1950.*
Lindley, David 1985: *Lyric.*
Miller, J. Hillis 1965: *Poets of Reality.*
Milosz, Czeslaw 1983: *The Witness of Poetry.*
Perloff, Marjorie 1990: *Poetic License: Essays on Modernist and Postmodernist Lyric.*
Rajan, Tilottama 1980: *Dark Interpreter: The Discourse of Romanticism.*
Scholes, Robert 1969: *Elements of Poetry.*
Vendler, Helen 1988: *The Music of What Happens: Poems, Poets, Critics.*
Williamson, Allan 1984: *Introspection and Contemporary Poetry.*

HAROLD SCHWEIZER

politics, gay   *See* GAY POLITICS

pop art   "Pop art" was a term apparently first used by the British art critic Lawrence Alloway during a series of seminars organized by the Independent Group at the Institute of Contemporary Arts in London in the early 1950s. In its original British meaning (most fully explored by the artist and teacher, Richard Hamilton), "pop art" drew attention to the aesthetic value of American mass-produced goods – cars, clothes, domestic appliances, magazines, comics, etc. In particular, the Independent Group argued that these "pop" works were at the leading edge of the artistic exploration of new technical means of visual production and communication, and they thus challenged the conventional distinction between high and low CULTURE, between "pure" and "applied" ART. If this was initially a theoretical or pedagogical point, and simply meant framing commodities and advertisements as art works for study, for formal analysis, Hamilton soon began to incorporate pop objects and images into his own work, and his biggest influence

on students like Peter Blake and British pop artists of the 1961 Young Contemporaries exhibition was his collage *Just what is it that makes today's homes so different, so appealing?* in the 1956 Independent Group show, "This is tomorrow." "Pop art" thus came to describe gallery art that "borrowed" mass cultural imagery, and this was certainly true in the United States where the label "pop art" was applied to such painters as Jasper Johns (originally a commercial artist) who began to show his painting series of banal objects in 1958; Claes Oldenburg who opened "The Store" (selling painted plaster replicas of food and food containers) in 1961; Roy Lichtenstein, whose first blown-up comic strips were shown in 1962; and Andy WARHOL. There were marked differences in aesthetic strategy between British and American pop artists (the former more romantic in their use of pop material, the latter more concerned with technique and realism) and also, just as important, between their respective art worlds. What was more obvious in New York than London was that pop art was not just an aesthetic movement, but also carried its own commercial implications (most enthusiastically and brilliantly seized on by Warhol), as the use of icons turned paintings into advertisements for themselves, as pop art imagery was deployed as pop imagery, and as artists were marketed as stars.

Reading
Hamilton, Richard 1982: *Collected Words 1953–1982.*
Lippard, Lucy R. 1970: *Pop Art.*
Livingstone, Marco, ed. 1991: *Pop Art.*

SIMON FRITH

Popper, Karl   (1902–94)   British philosopher of science. Though born in Vienna, Austria, Popper lived in England from 1946. He began his career as a critic of the LOGICAL POSITIVISM of the Vienna Circle. His first major publication was *Logik der Forschung* (1934). Rightly fearing a Nazi takeover of his country, Popper left Austria for New Zealand in 1937. He taught at Canterbury College of the University of New Zealand until 1945. Here he wrote his seminal work on political theory, *The Open Society and Its Enemies* (1945). This catapulted him into an international career in philosophy. Popper went on to teach philosophy at the London School of Economics and Political Science for over two decades. He retired as Professor of Logic and Scientific Method. Popper was knighted in 1965, and died in 1994.

Popper's influence on the PHILOSOPHY OF SCIENCE has been phenomenal. Best known for introducing the "falsification" criterion, Popper argued that scientific laws cannot be conclusively proved: they can only be falsified. By this Popper meant that no amount of verification of a scientific law would guarantee its truth value. It has been known since the time of the philosopher David Hume that no number of observation sentences of the form "X causes Y" can lead to a provable generalization – a counterinstance to a scientific law cannot be logically ruled out. Induction is a habit of mind; it is not a logical necessity. This makes all scientific knowledge provisional. Popper's achievement lies in shifting the philosophical emphasis from the truth value of a theory to the rationale for theory choice.

Reading

Ackerman, Robert John 1976: *The Philosophy of Karl Popper*.
Magee, Bryan 1973 (*1982*): *Karl Popper*.
O'Hear, Anthony (*1980*): *Karl Popper*.
Popper, Karl 1934 (*1980*): *The Logic of Scientific Discovery*.
——— 1945 (*1966*): *The Open Society and Its Enemies*.
                                    SHIVA KUMAR SRINIVASAN

popular culture   "Popular culture" is a term which in both everyday and academic usage quickly slips free from its ties to any firm theoretical account of either CULTURE or the popular. It is obviously a concept that only makes sense as a comparative, although the implied contrast is not obvious at all: "unpopular culture" is not a commonly used descriptive term (and its meaning would anyway be unclear), and the more usual comparisons are, in fact HIGH CULTURE, FOLK CULTURE, and mass culture. A further problem is that "popular culture" is used, often interchangeably and somewhat confusingly, to refer to both specific cultural and symbolic objects and to "a whole way of life."

In analytical practice there seems to have been, then, three overlapping ways in which the term "popular culture" has been used. First, popular culture is defined as that culture which is produced *for* the people. The "people" in this approach are thus taken to be a sector of the market, a body of consumers, and "popular culture" describes certain commodities. This is the context in which popular culture is distinguished from folk culture by reference to its industrial means of production. However, the term is also used in distinction from mass cul-

ture by reference to an argument about consumption. "Popular culture" implies a culture rooted in particular (usually class-based) social processes, relations, and values; "the people" are not the anonymous "masses." In short, in this commercial context, "popular culture" is both a quantitative and qualitative concept; it refers to audience size – to be popular a record or film or fiction must sell or be viewed in relatively large numbers (relative to the sales and viewing figures for high cultural or elite goods); it also refers to the quality of these consumers and viewers, to their attitudes to and uses of cultural goods – to be "popular" a record or film or fiction must be consumed in certain ways (ways clearly differentiated from those in which cultural elites consume their goods). In the end, in fact, the qualitative measure is more important than the quantitative measure in this context. Although many "popular" songs, films, and television shows have smaller sales and viewing figures than successful classical records, art movies, and high-quality TV programs, the distinguishing label "popular" still seems appropriate.

In this respect, the marketplace approach overlaps with another definition of popular culture as the culture *of* the people, as those symbolic objects and practices which somehow express or give shape to popular beliefs, values, and traditions. This definition is continuous with (rather than opposed to) the concept of folk culture (though now applied to industrial peoples), and implies that what makes a commodity "popular" is not for whom (or for how many people) it is produced (the market definition) but how it is interpreted. The cultural meaning of a commodity, in other words, is determined in the social processes of consumption (even if such processes inevitably include forms of recognition and appreciation of what is taken to be "in" the cultural community at issue). This approach depends, then, on a definition of the "people" as a specific social group, with delineated social ties and values. In British CULTURAL STUDIES the people were thus originally defined in CLASS terms: popular culture meant working-class culture (see Hoggart, 1959), although such groups may now be defined along other social fissures – in terms of black popular culture, Scottish popular culture, women's popular culture, and so on.

Two features of this approach to popular culture need stressing. First, it refers to the *history* of the popular, to the ways in which past values and devices are embedded in cultural TEXTS such that they represent people's sense of their own historical identity. Second, an important purpose of popular culture from this perspective is to mark off a social group from other social groups, to establish the terms of *cultural difference*. Culture is thus a discursive practice, and the critical theorist must be able to read the signs; popular culture can, in this respect, be defined in *formal* terms (and there may be a more or less tight "homology" drawn between cultural form and group values). Popular culture, in short, is that culture which expresses the aesthetic, ideological, hedonistic, spiritual, and symbolic values of a particular group of people; we can read those values in popular practices, TEXTS, and objects. From this analytic perspective, in other words, we will describe, say, a TV show as "popular television" not because of its viewing figures, nor because of its producers' marketing tactics, but because of its formal qualities, its aesthetic strategies, its organization of pleasure.

Though this approach thus becomes text-based (with institutions and practices read as texts, as in Hoggart's work), it clearly overlaps with a third definition: popular culture as the culture produced *by* the people. The reference point here is not amateur production, do-it-yourself craft, domestic versions of the professional arts, but people's ways of life. Popular culture is defined here in anthropological terms, by reference to processes as well as objects, to relationships as well as images. Popular culture thus becomes "everyday life", what "the people" *do*, ways of talking, eating, dressing, playing, working, worshipping. . . . Such activities can be treated in detached, descriptive terms, in a kind of obsessive mapping of cultural idiosyncrasy (as familiar, for example, in so-called "popular studies" in the United States), or in more political, conflictual terms, by drawing attention to the ways in which groups wrest and exercise symbolic power for themselves (see, for example, Paul Willis's concept of "common culture" in Willis, 1990). Either way, academic analysts occupy an ambiguous relationship to the object of study, to a culture which is both strange and familiar, part of their own everyday lives yet foreign to them, and the application of such anthropological methods as ethnography to one's own culture (which became increasingly common in popular cultural studies in the 1980s) is fraught with difficulty, not least the temptation to define "popular culture" as the "other" of academic culture, thus assigning to "the people" the solutions to intellectuals' own cultural and ideological dilemmas.

The problem here (and it is a problem for the academic analysis of popular culture whatever definition is initially adopted) is how to define "the people." The implicit argument (reflecting the history of CULTURAL STUDIES) is that the people are working-class people, that popular culture is working-class culture. However, this equation becomes problematic if theorists are not, in fact, drawing on Marxist social theory, and it becomes particularly problematic when applied to contemporary media culture – the "working class" is not necessarily the primary market for "popular" books or films or records, for top-rating television programs or even tabloid newspapers. One solution to this problem is to refine references to social class, to focus on different cultural categories, always qualifying "popular culture" with another adjective – black popular culture, teenage popular culture, rural popular culture, etc.

Another strategy is to change tack altogether, and to see the very term "popular," the very idea of "a people," as itself the cultural issue one should be investigating. "Popular culture" can then be used to describe those commodities, those activities, those symbolic institutions which *produce* the people, which produce, that is to say, a particular form of collective identity, a particular set of attitudes and values, a particular sort of recognition, a particular sense of belonging. Popular culture in this sense has obvious implications for and effects upon the social categories of nation and RACE, GENDER and CLASS, age and taste.

The focus here shifts back to texts (texts as activities as well as objects), but now in terms of their popular cultural work – their modes of address, their construction of audiences, their symbolizing power. The questions this approach raises concern the relationship between the "popular" and "the public," and the definition of popular culture thus becomes a political issue, related to the political problem of mobilizing the people (as in different forms of democratic and populist movement). The "popular," to put this another way, defines the site of a particular sort of struggle for political and ideological power (for this argument see Open University, 1989).

The importance of the Open University approach to popular culture was not its theoretical sophistication, nor its attempt to apply a range of analytic methods to a complex, multifaceted issue, but its understanding that the essence of popular culture is its conceptual slipperiness, its fluidity, and lack of clear definition. Any critical analysis of popular culture must, therefore, be concerned to open up the concept rather than to close it down. This became clear in the 1980s, when cultural studies took a populist turn (partly as an effect of its increasing success as a teaching and textbook subject, partly in its response to the influence of populism in broader debates about state and market and cultural value). It became commonplace, for example, to equate "popular" with the commercially successful (begging the question of the relationship between a commercial transaction and a cultural investment; we do not necessarily *like* the films we go to or the programs we watch) and, simultaneously, with the working class, the economically "powerless" (begging the question of how class is constituted by culture). The result was a position (see Fiske, 1989, for example) in which "popular culture" describes both commercially successful commodities (by one definition) and "resistant" practices (by another), but in which it is not therefore seen to be essentially contradictory. Rather, the implication seems to be that the consumption of popular performers (Madonna, say) or texts (*Married with Children*, for example) is, in itself, a political act. This is not an argument that is likely to be sustained in the 1990s – popular culture is too tricky an idea to be pinned down by such a neat gesture.

Reading
Fiske, John 1989: *Understanding Popular Culture.*
Hoggart, Richard 1959: *The Uses of Literacy.*
Open University 1989: *Popular Culture.*
Willis, Paul 1940: *Common Culture.*
SIMON FRITH

positivism A philosophical theory or doctrine which combines a number of theses about the nature of knowledge and reality. As with all philosophical theories there is much debate about its own nature although the following indicate its major theses: (i) What really exists is what can be experienced by the senses or what is susceptible to experimental manipulation. (ii) This reality is the subject matter of science. (iii) Only scientific knowledge is genuine knowledge. (iv) Nonscientific cognitive claims, such as those of myth, religion, and metaphysics, are idle and spurious.

Although these theses have older origins, it is Auguste Comte (1798–1857) who is regarded as the founder of positivism as a doctrine. He put forward a historical theory, according to which human thought evolves through theological and metaphysical stages until it reaches the positive or scientific stage, in which science consists of descriptive laws of phenomena able to be experienced, rejecting "explanations" in terms of "causes" or any other hidden essences or mysterious entities.

Positivism took a somewhat different direction in the twentieth century, when LOGICAL POSITIVISM became the official outlook of the philosophers and scientists of the Vienna Circle, who were able to benefit from the much more sophisticated methods of philosophical and logical analysis supplied by FREGE, Russell, and WITTGENSTEIN. The logical positivists developed a demarcation principle to separate science from nonscience; this stated that only scientific statements were open to verification by empirical procedures. This was combined with the "verification principle," which linked the meaning of a statement with its method of empirical verification. Since nonscientific statements had *no* method of empirical verification, they were literally nonsense! Thus the logical positivists believed that they had eliminated from philosophy all its traditional religious and metaphysical aspects, leaving only logic and a scientifically pristine theory of knowledge.

The overall aim of positivism was to boost the claims of science as the one and only true approach to understanding the world, including the social world. Although this aim is still widely held, the details of positivist philosophy have been heavily attacked by critics such as QUINE, POPPER, KUHN, FEYERABEND, and many others, and the positivist movement has all but disappeared. Nevertheless, positivism has had a highly positive impact on late twentieth-century thought, and it does not deserve its fate of having degenerated to such an extent that the term is now largely used negatively to denounce any view which is too narrow, too empiricist, or which predates POSTMODERNISM.
See also EMPIRICISM; SCIENCE, PHILOSOPHY OF.

Reading
Achinstein, Peter, and Barker, Stephen, eds 1969: *The Legacy of Logical Positivism.*
Ayer, A.J., ed. 1959: *Logical Positivism.*
Hanfling, Oswald 1981: *Logical Positivism.*
Kolakowski, Leszek 1972: *Positivist Philosophy: From Hume to the Vienna Circle.*
ANDREW BELSEY

positivism, logical *See* LOGICAL POSITIVISM

postanalytic philosophy A movement of thought that rejects many tenets of the mainstream ("analytical") tradition dominant in Anglo-American philosophy since the 1920s. This tradition was characterized chiefly by the premise that everyday (natural) language may often give rise to error – or to "systematically misleading" forms of expression – by its failure to articulate logical distinctions with sufficient clarity or rigor. Hence (for instance) Gottlob FREGE's canonical distinction between *sense* and *reference*, designed to explain how seemingly tautologous or pleonastic statements (like "the Evening Star is identical with the Morning Star") may in fact possess informative content by virtue of our ability to grasp precisely that distinction. Bertrand Russell's "theory of descriptions" – as applied to the analysis of empty (nonreferring) expressions like "the present King of France" – was another paradigmatic example of this attempt to get beyond the surface confusions of everyday or ordinary language, and thereby reveal a more perspicuous order of logico-semantic form.

The label "postanalytic" is one that is nowadays attached to so many diverse, loosely affiliated schools of thought that it might seem to lack any adequate definitional criteria. It is perhaps best described as a reactive movement, one that rejects any version of the drive to regiment language on a basis of clear-cut logical terms and distinctions. Its earliest showing was the argument brought against LOGICAL POSITIVISM by critics who remarked that a central plank in that program – the so-called verification principle – was incapable of coherent formulation. This program held that the class of meaningful statements was that class whose members were exclusively restricted to (i) factual or empirical propositions, the truth of which could be cashed out in terms of observational warrant; and (ii) analytic (or self-evidently valid) statements – like "all bachelors are unmarried men" – whose truth was a function of their logical form, that is, whose predicates were "contained in" their subjects and which were therefore true by definition while conveying no factual or informative content. All other expressions must henceforth be treated as meaningless or merely "metaphysical." The latter ranged from our everyday (unregimented) statements of veridical belief to the languages of ETHICS, AESTHETICS, LITERARY CRITICISM, and suchlike "emotive" habits of talk.

For a while this argument seemed to carry great force, even among literary theorists like I.A.

RICHARDS. Thus Richards felt himself driven to concede that the "truth" of poetry was a matter of its purely emotive benefits, its capacity to evoke certain moods – or certain complex states of attitudinal response in the reader – which had nothing to do with its truth as construed in propositional or referential terms. A similar strategy characterized the American NEW CRITICISM of the 1940s and 1950s. These thinkers took issue doctrinally with Richards's psychologistic approach, since they wanted criticism to be "objective" in the sense that it located meaning (or structures of complex verbal interaction) strictly within the "words on the page" as construed through techniques of rhetorical close reading, quite apart from all the vagaries of individual reader response. Nevertheless, they sought to avoid any confrontation with the claims of LOGICAL POSITIVISM by treating POETRY as a privileged realm of "ambiguity," "irony," "paradox," "plurisignification," etc., thereby cutting it off at a stroke from any dealing with language in its other (cognitive, veridical, or referential) aspect. This movement of retreat is visible not only in Anglo-American criticism, where the impact of logical positivist thinking was felt at an early stage. It is also very marked in French STRUCTURALISM and POSTSTRUCTURALISM, as can be seen in a work like Roland BARTHES's *Critique et vérité*. Barthes was reacting against an older and (as he saw it) a thoroughly hidebound tradition of positivist scholarship dominant in French academic thought since the time of Auguste Comte. However, his response – like that of Richards though pushed to a more paradoxical and provocative extreme – was again to drive a wedge between "truth" and criticism, and thus to equate literature (*écriture*) with whatever exceeded, contested, or subverted the grim paternal law of method and system.

This brief background history may help to explain why so many thinkers of otherwise diverse persuasion have come to be grouped under the rubric "postanalytic." They include both downright rejectionists and cautious revisionists, literary theorists with no time for "philosophy," and philosophers of a broadly HERMENEUTIC (or "continental") bent with a good deal of time for literary theory. In the latter camp also are neopragmatists like Richard RORTY who wish to have done with "philosophy" in the old (constructive, analytic, or problem-solving) mode, but who think that we should keep the conversation going for the sake of its pluralist or democratic ethos; thinkers of a

COMMUNITARIAN persuasion who reject "founda-tionalist" (truth-based) arguments in favor of an appeal to consensus-based notions of the ethical and social good; and – among the "cautious revisionists" – philosophers who have criticized the analytic program from within (so to speak) by remarking on the various problems it inherits from logical positivism. As these critics have often pointed out, that program self-evidently failed to meet its own stipulative requirements. That is to say, the verification principle could be justified *neither* by empirical proof *nor* in virtue of its logical form, its standing to reason as a matter of purely analytic (tautological) truth. Later on, this criticism was extended to the various proposed substitute doctrines (such as logical EMPIRICISM), which attempted to save some version of the analytic PARADIGM – the commitment to principles of logical consistency, conceptual rigor, and empirical truth – while abandoning the verification principle in its original (self-refuting) form. What I shall seek to do in the remainder of this essay is trace the often tangled skein of alliances – whether overtly acknowledged or not – which makes up the postanalytic "turn" in present-day philosophical debate.

On one possible version the account would go back to J.L. AUSTIN and exponents of the "ordinary language" approach that dominated Oxford philosophy during the 1950s and 1960s. In their view – also much influenced by the later WITTGENSTEIN – it was altogether wrong to suppose that language stood in need of logical regimentation, or that mere "analysis" could somehow uncover truths more important than the great stock of wisdom enshrined in the nuances, distinctions, and subtleties of usage to be gleaned from our everyday habits of talk. Thus Wittgenstein came to think that most philosophical problems were the result of language "going on holiday," or of philosophers becoming lost in abstruse and pointless puzzles of their own artificial devising. All that was required, by way of curative influence, was to redirect attention to the range and multiplicity of our everyday communal "language games" and, beyond these, to the various cultural "forms of life" which provided their only needful legitimizing context. Then again there were those, Gilbert Ryle among them, who adopted a kind of midway position, maintaining an attitude of qualified respect for the sanctions of customary usage while also remarking the various sorts of error – or "category-mistake" – which resulted from folk-psychological beliefs like the notion of mind

and BODY as existing in separate (though somehow connected) ontological realms. Clearly there is a tension between Ryle's approach and the Austin–Wittgenstein line since "ordinary language" is itself shot through with numerous relics of Cartesian dualism, relics that Ryle summarily dismissed as the myth of the "ghost in the machine." Hence what Richard Rorty and others have noted as an emergent split or parting of the ways within the broad camp of so-called linguistic philosophy.

That the term "postanalytic" has sometimes been applied to philosophers like W.V.O. QUINE is largely the result of their adopting a holistic theory of meaning and truth which rejects any version of the Frege/Russell argument. Such is the upshot of Quine's celebrated attack, in his essay "Two dogmas of empiricism," on the idea of a clear-cut distinction between analytic and synthetic orders of judgment, or those that are self-evidently true in virtue of their logical form (that is, whose predicate is wholly contained within their subject) and those that include some element of empirical or real-world knowledge by acquaintance. In Quine's view this distinction has to go, along with various other items of otiose *a priori* conceptual baggage, among them the dualism of "content" and "scheme" and the Fregean idea of propositions as bearing determinate values of truth and falsehood, since these alone give a hold for analysis in terms of the distinction between sense and reference. Thus Quine sees no point in halting the contextualist movement which started out by treating the proposition (rather than the word) as its minimal unit of significance, and which must surely end, so he argues, by extending this holist principle to the entire "fabric" or "web" of beliefs taken as true at any given time in any given community of knowledge. From this it follows (again *contra* Frege and Russell) that our current ontological commitments must be viewed as contingent or culture-specific, and not as possessing some privileged status – some ultimate claim to truth – such that they could never be subject to revision as a result of changes in our overall structure of beliefs.

What is more, this relativity extends all the way from what we take as empirical truths of fact (those belonging to the "periphery" of the web where observation statements supposedly match with reality) to propositions at the "analytic' core, which we think of as embodying "laws of thought," or as including principles (like noncontradiction or excluded middle) which cannot be revised without falling into manifest nonsense or illogicality. Quine sees absolutely no reason to maintain this distinction. According to him, we can always redistribute predicates across the whole fabric of accepted belief so as to preserve some particular favored item, even if – as occurs (arguably) in certain interpretations of quantum mechanics – this means abandoning the ground rules of logical thought. "Any statement can be held true come what may, if we make drastic enough adjustments elsewhere in the system" (Quine, p. 44). Thus there is ultimately no deciding, in point of ontological status, between centaurs, Homer's gods, numbers, set-theoretical classes, and brick houses on Elm Street.

That he himself has some fairly strong preferences in this regard – for example, for brick houses over centaurs and set theory over Homer's gods – is nothing more than a product of his own (albeit firmly held) commitment to a given ontological scheme, namely that of the present-day physical sciences. "For my part," he concedes, "I do, *qua* lay physicist, believe in physical objects and not in Homer's gods; and I consider it a scientific error to believe otherwise" (Quine, p. 44). Nevertheless, as regards their epistemological status, "the physical objects and the gods differ only in degree and not in kind," for "both sorts of entities enter our conception only as cultural posits." No doubt there comes a point where we must choose between them, if only to avoid cluttering our schemes with all manner of redundant or otiose items. Thus "the myth of physical objects is epistemologically superior to most in that it has proved more efficacious than other myths as a device for working a manageable structure into the flux of experience" (p. 44). However, these distinctions are again "only a matter of degree," of what Quine calls the "vaguely pragmatic inclination to adjust one strand of the fabric of science rather than another in accommodating some particular recalcitrant experience" (p. 46). That is to say, we are mistaken – still attached to one or other residual dogma of EMPIRICISM – if we take such choices to embody something more than a preferential means of adjusting the fabric with least disturbance to our current habits of belief.

I have taken this rather lengthy excursus via Quine in order to point up some of the resemblances between his position and other present-day versions of the argument from or to ontological relativity. What they all have in common is the break with any form of truth-functional or proposition-based analysis, that is, any theory – like those of Frege or Russell – that would seek to define the logical structure of well-formed referring expressions. What they put in its place is a doctrine of meaning-holism which relativizes truth and reference to the *entire existing set* of beliefs, truth claims, or attitudinal dispositions which happens to prevail within some given community of knowledge. This doctrine received its most detailed critical review in the book by Fodor and Lepore, *Holism: A Shopper's Guide* (1991). Their conclusion, briefly stated, is that there exist, as yet, no compelling or decisive reasons for adopting this view, and that on balance the problems outweigh the benefits when applied to issues in epistemology, ontology, PHILOSOPHY OF SCIENCE, cognitive psychology, and other fields. One such problem, clearly visible in Quine, is that of radical meaning-variance between ontological schemes. This is the doctrine that terms (whether referring expressions or logical connectives) may undergo drastic revision in the passage from one scheme to another, with the result that nothing could ultimately count as an instance of adequate translation or cross-paradigm understanding.

It is the same line of argument that has been taken up by skeptical or relativist philosophers of science, among them Thomas KUHN and, more egregiously, Paul FEYERABEND. According to them, the process of paradigm change is such as to prevent any possible assurance that we possess transtheoretical criteria of meaning or reference for terms like "mass," "gravity," "combustion," "atom," "electron," and so forth. It follows from the Quinean thesis of meaning-holism that these terms can be construed only in relation to the various frameworks of belief – or favored ontological schemes – wherein they have played a role from one such paradigm to the next. Moreover, it happens on occasion, according to Kuhn, that science undergoes a period of radical ("revolutionary") change when even its most basic presuppositions are called into doubt, thus creating a likewise wholesale shift in the operative sense (or definitional criteria) attached to certain crucial concepts. Such were, for instance, the transitional periods of crisis that occurred at the turning point between Ptolomeic and Copernican conceptions of the solar system; in the passage from Newtonian (absolute) ideas of gravity, space, and time to their reinterpretation as special cases within Einstein's more encompassing general theory of relativity; and – most recently – with the emergence of quantum mechanics as a theory that has forced some radical rethinking of the very nature of scientific explanation *vis-à-vis* the putative ground rules of classical logic. In each case, so it is argued, the shift is such as to reconfigure the entire domain of objects, events, physical laws, and the modes of understanding best fitted to cope with recalcitrant or anomalous data.

Thus Quine takes quantum mechanics as his chief exhibit in pressing the strong revisionist claim that there is absolutely nothing – even the supposed *a priori* "laws" of logical thought – that might not be subject to some measure of pragmatic "adjustment" under pressure from the evidence of new observations thrown up by the physical sciences. And Feyerabend goes one better than Kuhn – "better' by his own lights as a self-professed "anarchist" in epistemological matters – when he urges that we sink the difference between 'normal" and "revolutionary" periods of scientific thought. In his view science can become more creative (as well as more socially responsible) by dropping its old, objectivist pretense of disciplined inquiry, protocols of method, established research procedures, etc., and acknowledging the open-ended range of possibilities – of alternative redescriptions – that results from this conversion to a thesis of wholesale ontological relativity. These arguments have not been lost on "postanalytical" philosophers like Richard RORTY, anxious to bid farewell to philosophy as a rational, constructive, truth-seeking discipline. What should now take its place, in Rorty's view, is the idea of an ongoing "cultural conversation" where philosophy – or the DISCOURSE still bearing that name for want of any handy alternative – gives up on its old self-deluding (for instance, epistemological or ethical) pretensions. It can then offer various novel metaphors, vocabularies, narratives, or modes of inventive self-description which serve an "edifying" (as opposed to a constructive or a problem-solving) purpose, and which thereby resist the encroachment of other – state-sponsored or quasi-universalist – limits on our private freedom.

My point here is that Rorty arrives at this extreme version of the dichotomy between private and public realms by way of a doctrine of meaning-holism that derives from both "postanalytical" thinkers like Quine and Kuhn and philosophers in the broadly hermeneutic ("continental") tradition such as HEIDEGGER, GADAMER, and – more questionably – DERRIDA. For indeed Rorty is nothing if not eclectic. Other sources include Wilfred Sellars (on the "myth of the given"), the later Wittgenstein

for his problem-dissolving talk of "language games" or cultural "forms of life," and Michel FOUCAULT – whether as "archaeologist" or Nietzschean "genealogist" of knowledge – for his holistic leveling of the natural and the human sciences to so many shifting configurations in the omnipresent order of "discourse," analyzed on principle without the least regard to issues of validity or truth. What these all have in common, despite their manifest differences of styles and approaches, is the idea (again *contra* Frege and Russell) that propositions should enjoy no privileged status as bearers of determinate truth or falsehood values, since the "unit of meaning" (in Quinean parlance) is the entirety of language, discourse, or beliefs held true at any given time. This comes out most clearly in Rorty's habit of jumping clean across from talk of "vocabularies" to equally vague talk of the "language game" or "cultural conversation," in which those vocabularies somehow find their place. Nowhere are we offered any adequate explanation of just what role (scientific, critical, historical, ethical, etc.) those vocabularies are supposed to play, of the specific truth claims or validity conditions that apply to different orders of discourse, or of just why one such language game should at length – and for reasons other than mere boredom with the old way of talking – give way to a preferred alternative. For Rorty, as indeed for Foucault, it appears to be a process of random cultural drift, with the minimal difference that Foucault speaks dramatically of seismic disruptions and "epistemological breaks," where Rorty adopts a more laid-back idiom of periodic changes in the "cultural conversation."

It seems to me that little of value can emerge from the current, much-heralded *rapprochement* between "postanalytic" and continental philosophy so long as it pursues this line of least resistance premised on doctrines of meaning-holism and full-scale ontological relativity. Such arguments have taken a variety of forms, depending on the candidates put up for election to the new cross-party alliance. Thus Rorty greets Foucault as a sympathetic spirit in so far as he can plausibly be read as a "private ironist," one who is content to pursue his own project of aesthetic "self-fashioning" – or come up with new "vocabularies" to describe that project – while not straying into the public domain of politics, social theory, or ethics in the wider (non-self-preoccupied) sense. That Foucault's later thoughts on the "care of the self" are at times open to such a reading is one result of his espousing a version of this present-day linguistic turn, this holistic dispersal of meaning and truth across the range of "discourses" that somehow both constitute the subject and provide his or her only means of private self-cultivation. How there could possibly be a self to cultivate – given his (and Rorty's) attitude of wholesale skepticism toward any "deep further fact" about the self and its modes of understanding, reflective self-knowledge, ethical judgment, etc. – is, to say the least, something of a puzzle. This puzzle is directly related to their holistic (or all-out contextualist) view of "truth" as just a product of the way that beliefs hang together in the various language games, discourses, or "final vocabularies" that happen to prevail, for no particular reason, at this or that given time. It then becomes simply impossible to conceive how ethics might be founded on an exercise of responsible judgment in respect of what is known (to the best of our critical capacity) from the exercise of truth-seeking thought.

There is the same problem about current attempts to establish an alliance between postanalytic philosophy and hermeneutics in the Heideggerian or depth-ontological mode. Rorty has made a number of essay-length overtures in this direction, though his promised book on Heidegger has never materialized, perhaps on account of precisely this difficulty. Other commentators – Mark Okrent among them – have all the same pressed ahead with Rorty's project to the point of claiming Heidegger as a kind of honorary pragmatist *malgré lui*, one who can be coaxed back into the fold by stressing his talk of situated being-in-the-world and tactfully downplaying his other, more *echt*-ontological themes and concerns. (Hubert Dreyfus's commentary on *Being and Time* accords them a somewhat more respectful hearing.) What these approaches share is a sense that analytic philosophy has arrived at a stage, with its turn toward holistic or contextualist paradigms, where any talk of "truth" is in danger of becoming largely redundant. That is to say, it either drops out altogether (as in Rorty's neopragmatist appeal to what is "good in the way of belief") or else figures merely as a product of formal definition. Such is the "disquotational" theory – devised by Alfred Tarski and taken up by Donald Davidson – where "true" has the role of a metalinguistic predicate that applies to every veridical statement in a given language, but which then cancels out, for all practical purposes, so as to leave those first-order statements quite unaltered. Thus for instance: "'snow is white' is true in language L iff [that is if and only if] snow is white." By means of this formal notation, so the argument runs, one can generate a corresponding "T-sentence" for every sentence in the object language, and thus recursively generate a theory of truth which matches those sentences point for point in respect of their extension (that is, their reference) to items of veridical belief.

However, the problem with this whole line of thought is that it offers nothing more than a purely circular definition of "truth," one that satisfies the formal requirements for such a theory while failing to provide any more specific or substantive set of criteria. So one can see why many commentators – Rorty, Dreyfus, and Okrent among then – have sought a way beyond what they perceive as this dead-end predicament. Such is at least one sense of the term "postanalytic philosophy": the quest for an alternative to that entire tradition of thought, starting from logical positivism, whose upshot, after so much critical scrutiny, seems to be *either* a formalized (semantic or metalinguistic) theory of truth devoid of explanatory content, *or* on the other hand a pragmatist conception that reduces truth to the currency of in-place consensus belief. For each of the above thinkers it is clear that this alternative must come from outside the analytical mainstream, and moreover, that it needs a Heideggerian (or depth-ontological) approach to questions of meaning and truth. As I have said, they differ quite considerably in the extent of their commitment to Heidegger's project, that is, their willingness to value his thought at its own "epochal" or world-transformative estimate, rather than treating it – like Rorty – as a source of new language games, "final vocabularies, or optional metaphors we can live by." In fact one could argue that it is a mark of the "postanalytic" appropriation of Heidegger – as distinct from the work of *echt*-Heideggerian commentators – that the former sorts of commentary always entail some degree of doctrinal nonattachment, some drawing back at the point of endorsing his more "ontological" pronouncements. Rorty is the most explicit about this, since according to him what is useful in Heidegger (as likewise in Hegel, Nietzsche, Dewey, Foucault, Derrida et al.) is simply his offering a novel set of terms for the ongoing "cultural conversation," and thereby helping to wean us away from old (for example, Kantian or "analytic") styles of talk. Dreyfus and Okrent are perhaps best seen as halfway converts with a strong pragmatist leaning and with at least sufficient analytical awareness not to be drawn entirely into the realm of Heidegger's depth-ontological talk.

So there is reason to think, without undue skepticism, that "postanalytic" philosophy is at present just one of those modish terms (along with "postmodernism" and the like) which serve to cover a multitude of otherwise fissile and disparate trends. Certainly the prefix "post" is misleading if taken (as it is very often among cultural and literary theorists) to suggest that there is no longer any place for the virtues of clear and precise analytical thought. Perhaps the main cause of this confusion is the way in which the term "analytic" has been annexed to the Anglo-American (as distinct from the "continental") tradition of philosophic thought, thus implying that its fortunes are exclusively bound up with episodes within that tradition. However, we might do better to abandon these crudely reductive categorizations and the prejudicial habits of thought which tend to go along with them. After all, there are numerous shared concerns, a genealogy that becomes more complex (or less clearcut) the further one traces it back, and – most important – a common point of departure in those issues (like the analytic/synthetic dichotomy) which Kant was the first to articulate in their distinctively modern form. Where on the map should we place figures like Frege, Husserl, and (more ambiguously) Wittgenstein, whose work surely answers to no such tidy parcelling out of geophilosophical domains? And again, what reason can there be – ingrained prejudice aside – for withholding the descriptor "analytic" from work of such subtlety, rigor, and intelligence as Derrida's at its best? Given these problems there seems little point in defining "postanalytic" philosophy beyond its present function as a label of convenience, a catch-all term for whatever slips through the standard doxographical net.

See also COMMUNITARIAN ETHICS; DAVIDSON, DONALD; END OF PHILOSOPHY; HERMENEUTICS; LOGICAL POSITIVISM; METALANGUAGE; LANGUAGE, PHILOSOPHY OF; POST-MODERNISM; RORTY, RICHARD; SCIENCE, PHILOSOPHY OF.

Reading

Apel, Karl-Otto 1980: *Toward a Transformation of Philosophy*.
Baynes, Kenneth, Bohman, James, and McCarthy, Thomas, eds 1987: *After Philosophy: End or Transformation?*
Bernstein, Richard 1983: *Beyond Objectivism and Relativism*.
Davidson, Donald 1984a: *Inquiries into Truth and Interpretation*.
Dreyfus, Hubert L. 1991: *Being-in-the-World: A Commentary on Heidegger's "Being and Time," Division I*.
Fodor, Jerry, and LePore, Ernest 1991: *Holism: A Shopper's Guide*.
Goodman, Nelson 1978: *Ways of Worldmaking*.
Okrent, Mark 1988: *Heidegger's Pragmatism: Understanding, Being, and the Critique of Metaphysics*.
Putnam, Hilary 1983b: *Realism and Reason*.
—— 1992: *Renewing Philosophy*.
Quine, W.V.O. 1953a: "Two dogmas of empiricism."
Rorty, Richard, ed. 1971: *The Linguistic Turn*.
—— 1989: *Contingency, Irony, and Solidarity*.
West, Cornel, and Rajchman John, eds 1985: *Post-Analytical Philosophy*.

CHRISTOPHER NORRIS

postcolonial studies   Unqualified, the term "postcolonial studies" would incorporate the study of all the effects of European colonization in the majority of the CULTURES of the world, and include all the academic disciplines in use in institutions of learning across the globe. Clearly, it is only from a great distance, for instance, that of the Western academy, that so vast a formation can be assumed to have coherence. Consequently, it is only from the narrowed perspective of the Western academy that the term "postcolonial studies" appears feasible. This entry will perforce share such a perspective, focusing on primarily anglophone postcolonial CULTURAL STUDIES as it has developed in the Western academy, though this development has of course had to take note of the work being done elsewhere in the Third World.

Yet even from this narrowed perspective, the rubric "postcolonial" has caused anxiety, based in part on the confusion surrounding the prefix "post," and in part on the staggering geographical, temporal, and theoretical sweep of the term. Cultural critics who read "postcolonial" to mean "the end of colonialism" are troubled by its implication that so-called decolonizations in the Third World effected a clean break from colonial exploitation. Others, more alert to the necessary ambiguity of the prefix "post," do not take it as a synonym for "de" or "ex," and are consequently able to read "postcolonial" to mean "since colonialism began." For them, the term covers a vast terrain of decolonized/neocolonized cultures that may have witnessed the end of one phase of Western imperialism – the formal dismantling of colonial political/administrative machinery – only to enter the next phase, with Western imperialism now organizing them in the interests of its late capitalist economies.

A second objection to the rubric is that, in its present Western institutional usage, it effectively elides an array of differences: for instance, between a vast number of nations and cultures in Africa, Asia, and the Caribbean; between internally colonized European communities, such as the Irish, and Third World postcolonial nations; and, finally, between recently postcolonial Third World nations, and the European-settled ex-colonies of Australia, New Zealand, and North America, in which any surviving indigenous non-European populations are now reduced to minority status. Structured as it is on the ground of difference, postcolonial studies is always under the obligation, outlined by Gayatri C. Spivak and other theorists, to persistently examine the relationship between various postcolonial formations – and to do so without assuming either their a priori coincidence (so that one can be made to represent another in the academy) or their a priori radical discontinuity (so that the difference between them need be theorized).

Some have also questioned the rubric "postcolonial" on the grounds that it delineates Third World nations in terms of their relation to postcolonizing powers rather than their internal concerns or their relation to each other. A related argument is that postcoloniality offers an inappropriate context for cultural practices that emerged under (post)colonialism but were not primarily concerned with this context. These arguments, based loosely on the feeling that the rubric "postcolonial" overemphasizes the power and role of imperialism, come surprisingly often from the same critics who found the term objectionable because it underestimated the exploitative scope of imperialism as well as its continuing strength (see Ahmad, 1992). The counterargument for retaining "postcolonial" is that, if it defines Third World nations according to their relation to European imperial centers rather than according to their relation to each other, it does so in a descriptive rather than prescriptive effort to keep in sight the material homogenization that came in the wake of past and present imperial control, and that will not simply disappear if left unnamed. Indeed, if the common designation "postcolonial" obligates cultural theorists from various Third World nations to reflect on their relation to each other, that is something to be welcomed, not dreaded. Finally, the criticism that postcoloniality is a misleading context for Third World cultural practices that do not directly engage with it is often met with the rejoinder that TEXTS produced within a larger political context can be read in its terms, whether or not the texts anticipate such a reading or, more generally, such a positioning of themselves.

As these debates should make clear, the rapid institutionalization of postcolonial studies has resulted in an ongoing and close scrutiny of its scope and method. For postcolonial studies to retain its oppositional charge, it will be necessary that the ambiguity of the prefix "post" be kept in sight; that specific differences within its rubric be actively mobilized and understood not just in terms of national origins but also of CLASS, GENDER, RACE, sexual and ethnic orientations; and finally, that increasingly complex and rigorous ways be found to read cultural practices in their political contexts.

An older but recurring debate within postcolonial studies is over Third World discourses of pan-nationalism, nationalism, and diaspora. Each offers one way for Third World communities to construct cultural and political identities in opposition to Western imperial prescriptions. Pan-nationalisms, which arose in the early phases of some anti-imperial struggles, were short-lived but powerful movements that added a great impetus to cultural production. An example is *Negritude*, which called on people of African descent across Africa, Europe, and the Americas to forge a collective identity beyond national boundaries, recognize their shared history of oppression and resistance, and celebrate and preserve a common culture rooted in Africa. Although *Negritude* attracted prominent literary and political figures such as Leopold Senghor (Senegal) and Aimé CÉSAIRE (Martinique), it was also, from its inception, criticized from other revolutionary perspectives, for instance, that of Frantz FANON (Martinique). Although he was drawn to the affirmatory politics and creative energies of *Negritude*, Fanon found its oppositional political stance to be a mere reversal rather than a fundamental displacement of Western ethnocentrism; as such, it remained locked in the essentialist terms dictated by that ethnocentrism. Marxists such as Fanon believed that anti-imperial struggles would necessarily be organized on the model of the nation-state; if a cross-continental resistance had to be chosen, it would need to be based on class rather than race.

Pan-nationalisms generated a vast literary and cultural archive, much of it committed to reviving "authentic" and "classic" precolonial indigenous practices, often in direct challenge to imperial/ colonial pronouncements on the cultural impoverishment of the colonized. While appreciating the energy of this cultural project, critics such as Fanon questioned its nativist rhetoric of authenticity, and its petrification of culture into static, essentialized, and classicized forms outside the reach of the masses. The debate over authenticity has often been revived in postcolonial studies, for instance, with the incorporation of Western CRITICAL THEORY (see Appiah, 1984; Bhabha, 1994; and Ngugi, 1986).

The majority of anti-imperialist struggles, especially in the twentieth century, have been organized not on pan-nationalisms but the model of the nation-state. Recent discussions of nationalism have historicized this model as something not ordained in nature but produced in response to specific needs of European economies during their industrial phase. Critics of nationalism argue that the nation-state model, held out to Third World cultures as their only entry into the global economy after decolonization, did not necessarily address their specific needs. Further, nationalist movements were led by middle-class Western-trained leaders who, in their efforts to present a united front to colonialism, often curbed the more radical demands of feminists and subalterns, and were thus unable fundamentally to transform the oppressive political structures they inherited from colonialism.

Like pan-nationalisms, nationalist struggles and DISCOURSES have been immensely productive in the cultural sphere, although their own rhetoric of authenticity has also raised some questions from Third World feminist and subaltern critics. In their efforts to preserve an untainted, classic, precolonial, and indigenous tradition, these discourses sought to ward off the influence of living and POPULAR CULTURES. As is frequently the case, they called on women to assume the role of the keepers of tradition, thus reimmersing them in the rhetoric of purity and sanctity, and assigning them the most passive, secondary, and privatized spaces in the official narrative of nationalisms (see Jayawardena, 1986; Mohanty, 1991).

The critique of these discourses from the viewpoint of those excluded by it, such as subalterns and women, is an increasingly powerful strain within postcolonial studies. This criticism is sometimes misrepresented as a nostalgia for colonial IDEOLOGY and institutions, and sometimes reduced to a tradition versus MODERNITY debate, with indigenous practices being seen as traditional and therefore oppressive for women and the subaltern, and the Western as modern and more emancipatory. In fact, however, few Third World subaltern and/ or feminist critics of nationalism are apologists for Western imperialism, and few endorse its claims of having eradicated oppressive feudal and patriarchal indigenous practices. Instead, scholars such as the subaltern collective in Indian, Ngugi wa Thiong'o in Kenya, and Rey Chow in China have read imperialism as not only actively suppressing the more feminist and egalitarian of indigenous institutions and cultural practices, but also as driving indigenous PATRIARCHY to increasingly reactionary excesses against women and subalterns in an effort to maintain its strength *vis-à-vis* the colonizers. Third World feminist and subaltern histories/cultural studies have thus been engaged in a dual task: close analyses of colonial *and* indigenous patriarchal power, and crucial archival work to recover lost/neglected female and subaltern cultural texts and resistances. This work has been tremendously effective in opening up the closed, official narratives of nationalism, and clearing the space for a study of popular cultural practices, including film and music; street and creolized languages; oratures (or oral literatures); and politicized and agitprop genres such as testimony, prison memoirs, and street theater.

Contemporary discussions of nationalism have also had to address the question of postcolonial DIASPORAS. Earlier colonial institutions of slavery, indenture, and forced migration, and more contemporary divisions of labor between the Third and First Worlds have scattered large groups of the colonized across the globe. Left to negotiate new ethnic identities for themselves *vis-à-vis* both the European-descended majority populations and groups of non-European displaced and disenfranchised people, various diasporas from Africa, Asia, and the Caribbean have given rise to questions about multiple-rooted ethnic identities and languages. Diaspora theorists such as Homi Bhabha, Rey Chow, Stuart HALL, Wilson Harris, and Trinh T. Minh ha focus on cultural production within communities almost exclusively populated by displaced Third World populations, such as the Caribbean, as well as on Third World immigrant cultures within the First World, such as the black British. From a variety of theoretical perspectives, these critics have proposed that identity and language be read not as closed, static, and imbued with essences, but rather as performative, "hybrid," "creolized," and existing "on the borders" of various interpellating systems. The focus on diaspora has also led feminists such as Chandra Mohanty to call for a dialogue between theorists of gendered subalternity in the Third World and First World women of color. The concept of diaspora has emphasized the need for postcolonial studies to enter a sustained dialogue with Afro-American or native American studies, again without presupposing an entire coincidence or a complete discontinuity of interests. Unfortunately, however, such efforts have often been thwarted in the academy by the phenomenon of various marginalized studies being made to compete for resources.

In diaspora communities, the question of language of course takes a very different form from that of the indigenous cultures of Africa or Asia. In the latter, activists and theorists such as Ngugi, who himself turned from writing in English to writing in Gikuyu, have called for postcolonial writers to return to indigenous languages. While acknowledging that postcolonial writing in European languages has subverted these languages with oral and written indigenous traditions, and thus displaced colonial literary PARADIGMS and genres, Ngugi argues that the most scrupulous and innovative efforts to Africanize the English language will still not make that language accessible to the majority of Africans. Further, if writers continue to work within colonial languages and structures in an effort to subvert them, they will run the risk of being recuperated as minor strains and SUBCULTURES within European cultural traditions. In a similar vein, SUBALTERN STUDIES in India have focused not on the history and cultural production of a Western-trained middle class writing in English or classicized indigenous languages, but of disenfranchised Indian masses working in the vernacular. However, in the context of Caribbean or black British diasporas, where the language of the majority is a European one, there is clearly less impetus for returning to the original language of one's culture than for creolizing European languages. This difference notwithstanding, diaspora theorists and theorists of subalternity in the Third World share the common goal of studying the languages not of high culture, but of the people.

Underlying the debates over the rubric of postcoloniality and over nationalism, pan-nationalism, and diaspora are various theories of identity and the production of culture. A central impetus in postcolonial studies has been the resistant reading of power – in its complex colonial, neocolonial, patriarchal, discursive, and material manifestations – so as to unsettle its epistemology, its claims to truth, and its strategies of representation. An attentiveness to the ways in which meanings are produced and value-coded in language has always marked postcolonial studies, exemplified in landmark works such as Edward Said's *Orientalism* (1978). Although formalist-universalist claims that culture and language are produced autonomously of the political context have sometimes been internalized by Third World writers and critics, especially when postcolonial scholarship was organized under the rubric of "commonwealth studies," these claims have been contested from their inception. As a result, the theorizing of language and culture has been central to postcolonial studies, notwithstanding vast differences between various theoretical perspectives.

The role of Western(ized) theories in postcolonial studies has been the first subject of debate. With the proviso that postcolonial cultural texts have always themselves theorized meanings and values, critics such as Barbara Christian have attacked the inaccessible languages of Western theories; their refusal or inability to speak to the situation of the Third World; and their institutional effect of distracting postcolonial studies from crucial archival work and political praxis. Those opposed to this view maintain that Western theories, which themselves criticize the closures of Western systems of thought from their margins, can be disengaged from any leanings towards patriarchal or imperial ideology and thus made useful for postcolonial studies. Such postcolonial theorists question the residual nativism beind the blanket rejection of Western theories, and argue against the polarization of theory and praxis, or theoretical and empiricist scholarship, urging that while one kind of work cannot replace the other, each must be used productively, in Spivak's words, to "interrupt" the other and bring it to crisis.

A variety of theoretical approaches characterizes postcolonial studies at present, of which the three most prominent, the Marxist, the psychoanalytic, and the deconstructive will be briefly described below. Third World feminisms have intervened powerfully in each approach, insisting that it address the concepts of gender, sexuality, and varied discourses of patriarchy not merely as secondary issues within the larger inquiry, but rather as questions that could transform the terms of the inquiry.

Marxist and feminist-Marxist critics have asked persistent questions about the institutional apparatuses through which postcolonial cultural texts are produced and circulated; about the HEGEMONY of high literary AESTHETICS over popular culture; about the vanguardist and "native informant" roles postcolonial intellectuals sometimes assume vis-à-vis the masses; and, following the intervention of Marxist-feminists, about the role of gender and sexuality in the production of culture. Although Western Marxists such as MARX, Mikhail BAKHTIN, Antonio GRAMSCI, and Louis ALTHUSSER have strongly influenced postcolonial studies, for instance, the work of FANON, Spivak, Ngugi, Hall, Chow, and the subaltern studies collective, some Western Marxists have also been criticized for their minimal engagement of postcoloniality, and for their periodization, which positions the Third World in a time lag in relation to the First, reading it as the historical past of the First World present (see, for instance, Fanon's critique of Jean Paul SARTRE; Said's critique of Marx; and Madhava Prasad's critique of Jameson).

Aspects of psychoanalytic theory have also powerfully influenced theorists such as Fanon and Homi Bhabha, feminists such as Trinh T. Minh ha and Rey Chow, and postcolonial Althusserians, who have used PSYCHOANALYSIS to complicate Marxist teleological narratives of power and resistance. Such critics are drawn to psychoanalysis for its ability to position power and resistance in the contexts of desire, psychic investments, and the processes through which identities are constructed in language. Psychoanalytic critics approach identity as not given or static, but as performative and staged within language. By mobilizing FREUDian and LACANian concepts such as "fetish" and "mimicry" in the context of postcoloniality, theorists such as Bhabha have drawn attention to the ambivalences within colonial stereotypes and within various subject positions occupied by any one "consciousness." While Third World psychoanalytic feminists share these interests, they have also criticized some of the male approaches, including Fanon's, for their inability or refusal to address questions of gender, sexuality, and sexual orientation, and to go beyond the patriarchal subtexts of thinkers such as Freud. Psychoanalysis continues to have a strong appeal for Third World feminists such as Trinh and Chow because of its sustained interest in questions of sexuality, and its narrativization of sexed and gendered identity.

However, like Western Marxisms, Western psychoanalysis has not been embraced uncritically. The larger Marxist critique of the psychoanalytic approaches is that they have not theorized beyond individuated psychic resistances to collective action. An early instance of the unease generated by the more ahistoricized forms of psychoanalysis is Fanon's critique of O. Mannoni, who isolated such static PARADIGMS as the "dependency complex" of the colonized with little reference to the systemic material exploitation of colonialism. Third World Marxist-feminists such as Spivak have pointed to the ORIENTALISM, ahistoricism, and even antifeminism of Freud as well as of some contemporary French feminists such as KRISTEVA, while still suggesting that French feminism can be usefully extended to a postcolonial context.

Finally, Derridean DECONSTRUCTION (rather than its US version) has strongly influenced the work of Spivak and translation theorists such as Tejaswini Niranjana. The appeal of deconstruction for political resistant readings is precisely its persistent questioning of the kind of originary and foundational thinking that has characterized Western universalist, humanist, and colonial discourses. Spivak also describes deconstruction as a reading strategy that consistently questions the objectivity and innocence of the reader, and is thus of immense use to postcolonial readers as a reminder of their own complicity in the structures of thought that they critique.
See also CARIBBEAN STUDIES; DECONSTRUCTION; FANON, FRANTZ; FEMINIST CRITICISM; ORIENTALISM; PSYCHOANALYSIS; SAID, EDWARD; SUBALTERN STUDIES.

Reading
Ashcroft, Bill, et al., eds 1989: The Empire Writes Back: Theory and Practice in Postcolonial Literatures.
Bhabha, Homi 1994: The Location of Culture.
Center for Contemporary Cultural Studies 1982: The Empire Strikes Back.
Chow, Rey 1993: Writing Diaspora: Tactics of Intervention in Contemporary Cultural Studies.
Fanon, Frantz 1961 (1982): The Wretched of the Earth.
——1967: Black Skin/White Masks.
Guha, Ranajit, and Spivak, Gayatri C., eds 1988: Selected Subaltern Studies.
Harlow, Barbara 1987: Resistance Literature.
Harris, Wilson 1983: The Womb of Space: The Cross Cultural Imagination.
Jayawardena, Kumari 1986: Feminism and Nationalism in the Third World.
Mohanty, Chandra Talpade, et al., eds 1991: Third World Women and the Politics of Feminism.
Ngugi wa Thiong'o 1986: Decolonising the Mind: The Politics of Language in African Literature.
Pines, Jim, and Willeman, Paul, eds 1989: Questions of Third Cinema.
Said, Edward 1978: Orientalism.
——1993: Culture and Imperialism.

Spivak, Gayatri Chakravorty 1987: *In Other Worlds: Essays in Cultural Politics.*
——1994: *Outside in the Teaching Machine.*
Trinh T. Minh ha 1989: *Woman, Native, Other: Writing Postcoloniality and Feminism.*

APARAJITA SAGAR

postmodernism Postmodernism names many different kinds of cultural object and phenomenon in many different ways. Among these, perhaps three different applications of the term may broadly be distinguished. First, postmodernism designates a number of developments in the arts and CULTURE in the second half of the twentieth century. The reference point and point of departure for this form of postmodernism are the various forms of modernism that flourished in the arts and culture in Europe in the first half of the century. Second, it describes the emergence of new forms of social and economic organization, again roughly since the end of the 1939–45 war. As such, its reference point and point of departure is the movement of modernization which characterized the early years of the century, with the growth of industry, the rise of the mass market, and the accelerations in automation, travel, and mass communication. Third, it signals a particular kind of theoretical WRITING and reflection, usually, though not exclusively, writing and reflection which takes the first or second area as its object. It may be useful to distinguish these three areas of application with the terms *postmodernism*; *postmodernity*; and *the postmodern*. (It should be said that this division is a convenience adopted for present purposes alone, and does not correspond regularly to usages of these three variants in critical writing.)

Diagnoses of postmodernism have extended to nearly every artistic form and area of cultural practice, but the argument about the emergence of a postmodernist reaction to an earlier modernist movement has tended to take its clearest and strongest form in those areas in which modernism had previously been most clearly and visibly defined, for example, architecture, the visual arts, and literature. Central to the influential claims on behalf of postmodernism articulated by writers such as the architectural critic Charles Jencks and the literary critic Ihab HASSAN was a sense that the challenge or revolutionary energy of earlier forms of modernism had hardened over the twentieth century into conventional artistic procedures and respectable institutional forms. There two writers offer markedly

different accounts of the ways in which postmodernism emerges out of and surpasses this now institutionalized modernism. For Jencks (1991) what is at stake is the loosening of the authoritarian style and sensibility of international modernism and the opening up of architecture to a new diversity of STYLES and functions. Thus the ideal of a building that would be austerely and nakedly *itself*, announcing and performing its function without ornament or excess, is to yield to an ideal of a building that would variously embrace, mimic, and converse with its architectural and nonarchitectural contexts. Such an architecture is typically not pure or self-consistent but hybrid, in terms of its blending of different styles drawn from past and present. For Hassan (1987) the postmodernist impulse is to be found not in a clear break with modernist styles in literary writing so much as in a return to some of the more fractious and uncontrollable forms of AVANT-GARDE practice that had characterized literary and artistic modernism at its outset: the consuming fury of Alfred Jarry's "pataphysics," the playful iconoclasm of dadaism, the embrace of dynamism in vorticism and futurism. Hassan finds support for this view of postmodernism as a renewal rather than a surpassing of modernism in the work of Jean-François LYOTARD, for whom, paradoxically, postmodernism may be said to come *before* rather than *after* modernism. "A work can become modern only if it is first modern," Lyotard declares. "Postmodernism thus understood is not modernism at its end but in the nascent state" (Lyotard, 1984, p. 79).

Central to many definitions of artistic postmodernism is a refusal of the value of aesthetic autonomy. For many modernist artists and writers, the value of ART was to be defined purely on its own terms. In criticism of the visual arts especially, the justification of modernist technique was that it fulfilled Immanuel KANT's proposal in his *Critique of Judgement* (1790) that aesthetic feelings were or should be wholly disinterested, which is to say independent of the desires, interests, and conflicts of ordinary life. The value and purpose of art thus came to be defined in terms of a number of refusals and negations: a refusal of personality; a refusal of expressive intention; a refusal of any ambition to represent the real world, or represent it realistically; a refusal of social norms and conventions, especially the conventions of communication itself.

Artistic postmodernism may be defined largely as a refusal of this refusal – a negation of the ideal of art's autonomy and separateness from the world. For some commentators, this means a returning sense of the necessary connections between art and the social and political realm from which modernism had abstracted it. Where the ideal of aesthetic autonomy was concentrated for modernism is the idea that the work of art ought to be seen as a perfected and self-sufficient object, for example, a contrary impulse reveals itself in the dissolution of the artistic object and the fascination with temporal process characteristic of certain forms of postmodernism, such as the conceptual and performance art of the 1960s and beyond. Thus one may summarize the shift in attitudes toward the work of art from modernism to postmodernism as a new preference for complexity over purity, plurality over stylistic integrity, and contingency or connectedness over autonomy.

Postmodernity signifies the breakdown or radical transformation of the modes of social, economic, and political modernity that had been dominant in most Western industrial nations from the mid-nineteenth to the mid-twentieth century. As with artistic postmodernism, opinions differ as to whether this constitutes a simple passage beyond or an intensification of the capitalist forces expressed in modernity.

One of the earliest and most developed narratives of the emergence of postmodernity was provided by Daniel Bell in his book *The Cultural Contradictions of Capitalism*, first published in 1976. Bell suggests that advanced capitalism has moved from being an economic and cultural system based upon the disciplines necessary for production to one centered on the pleasures of consumption. This in turn changes the status of art and culture. Artistic modernism had been produced, Bell argues, out of a fierce antagonism between the puritan ethic of work and conformity and the hedonist cult of self-expression and self-enlargement characteristic of modernist writers and thinkers such as NIETZSCHE, Lawrence, WOOLF, and others. A postmodern condition is reached when these modernist values, which had previously been the preserve of a small and dissident artistic minority, become generalized in a consumer society. Bell is only one of a number of writers who see the defining condition of postmodernity as a certain aestheticization of economic conditions: "The autonomy of culture, achieved in art, now begins to pass over into the arena of life. The post-modernist temper demands that what was previously played out in fantasy and imagination

must be acted out in life as well. There is no distinction between art and life. Anything permitted in art is permitted in life as well" (Bell, 1979, pp. 53–4).

A similar claim is advanced by Jean BAUDRILLARD, who, in a series of books produced from the late 1960s onwards, had been criticizing those economistic theories such as MARXISM, which made the function of the economy the determining factor in social life and saw the forms and forces of production as the central principle of every economy. In his early work, Baudrillard argued that culture and the processes of representation and reproduction more generally had gained a primacy over the economic "base" from which Marxist theory held them to be a secondary emanation. Social analysis must learn, he argued, to understand the primary role of social SIGNS, CODES, and languages in contemporary society. His later work extends this analysis remarkably to argue that the explosion in the technological means of simulation and reproduction has brought about a priority of signs over the real. The postmodern world (though Baudrillard rarely uses the term) is one in which experience and reality are codified and mediated to such a point as to have become irretrievable in themselves. Where previous eras can be characterized by the different kinds of relationship obtaining in them between reality and the socially produced images of reality, our contemporary world has seen the domination of the self-sufficient "simulacrum," the image that "bears no relationship to any reality whatsoever . . . [and] is its own pure simulacrum" (Baudrillard, 1983, p. 170). Such a condition accompanies and is in some ways determined by the move from a production economy to an economy based on consumption, in which goods are not produced to supply already existing needs, but rather as a secondary response to needs which are themselves conjured "in the first place" by advertising and marketing strategies.

David Harvey's account of the condition of postmodernity proceeds along lines similar in some respects to those of Bell and Baudrillard, though with a very different focus and political attitude. In his *The Condition of Postmodernity* (1989) Harvey sees postmodernity as the result of an intensification of the very energies of transformation and dissolution which had been associated with modern capitalism, energies which, in assimilating more and more areas of life to the logic of the marketplace, had caused a radical undermining of previously stable values, beliefs, and economic forms. Post-modernity, according to Harvey's report, brings about an undermining of the very forms of social and political organization which had supplanted traditional forms in MODERNITY. In place of the clear division of economic interests between the owners of capital and those who sell their labor, along with the clear patterns of social antagonism and identification, and even spatial-geographical forms brought about by these divisions, the global economy of postmodernity is characterized by im-permanence of interests, volatility of economic conditions, insecurity in patterns of employment, and plurality of class and political identification. Harvey focuses in particular upon the "space–time compression" brought about by accelerations in travel and telecommunications. In a world in which distance no longer represents any kind of material constraint upon economic activity, such that space is measured in the shorter and shorter intervals of time required to traverse it, space, so to speak, dissolves into time. Under these conditions, profit is not measured in terms of material increase, but as a gain in turnover time, or an increase in the rate of consumption. Where the domination of modern capitalism had come about partly by means of the rationalizing science and technology that allowed space to be controlled at a distance, the furious pace of transformation in postmodernity creates a sense of place that is paradoxical and evanescent. Nevertheless, Harvey insists that these economic and cultural transformations are exten-sions of, rather than fundamental breaks in "the invariant elements and relations that Marx defined as fundamental to any capitalist mode of produc-tion" (Harvey, 1989, p. 187). As such he does not, as Baudrillard so obviously does, abandon the aspir-ation to provide progressive political understand-ing of the present.

For Harvey, as for others such as Scott Lash and John Urry (1987) and Alan Lipietz (1987), social and economic postmodernity may be mea-sured conveniently in terms of the dissolution of the form of organized capitalism represented by the Ford motor corporation in the middle years of the twentieth century. Ford typified a mode of production which depended upon large, rationalized factories, dedicated to the mass production of a minimally varied single item. Such a form of organ-ization is centralized, concentrated upon production, and driven by economies of scale. It tends to de-mand and provide stable and continuous patterns of employment. A "post-Fordist" pattern of eco-nomic organization, by contrast, is much more de-centralized; today a motor car will not be assembled in one factory in one location, but in a variety of locations and by a number of different workforces, both of which are subject to sudden and unpre-dictable variation, in the pursuit of efficiency or for political reasons. The dispersal and mobility of production in past-Fordism is matched to the sense of the diverse and shifting patterns of demand in a mass market that is no longer perceived either as passive or homogeneous. Economies of scale, based upon the savings in the cost of production brought about by minimizing variation in the product, give way in post-Fordism to economies of scope, in which the mobility of taste and fashion is met by increased differentiation of the product. Thus the largest and most powerful economic corporations are not producers of single, identifying products, but conglomerates, aggregating a set of different and constantly changing interests and involvements which traverse the boundaries of nation-states with ease.

These developments cooperate with the other principal defining condition of social and economic postmodernity, namely the shift from an economy based upon goods to one based upon the supply of information and services. In a regime of this kind, images and life-styles are as much the subject of economic marketing and exploitation as the goods which accompany them, and indeed, an ever-increasing proportion of economic activity as a whole is centered on the generation and circulation of signs and reproductions: news, TEXTS, films, images, music, software. Capitalist modernity nursed the fear that the assimilative hunger of the market might end up annihilating culture altogether; Fredric Jameson points to the surprisingly inverse effect brought about by postmodernity, namely the "pro-digious expansion of culture throughout the social realm, to the point at which everything in our social life – from economic value and state power to practices and to the very structure of the psyche itself – can be said to have become 'cultural'" (Jameson, 184, p. 87). Such developments lead to a move away from the clarity and permanence of affiliations and values in the sphere of political belief and practice, as a politics based upon class antagonism gives way to an "identity politics" based upon a more complex and dispersed sense of affili-ation and power, and an uneven configuration of sexuality, age, GENDER, and ethnic identity.

There are a number of ways in which post-modernism in the arts is held to reflect or bear out these changes is the social and economic sphere. Many writers stress the parallels between the playful multiplication of styles and mixing of media characteristic of postmodernist art and literature and the move from centralization to decentralization, the sense of accelerated relativity of values, and the dissolution of stable norms and identities in social and political life generally. In a similar way, an art that pushes self-consciousness to the extreme, acknowledging and reveling in its status as fiction or image, seems appropriate to a world that seems to be more and more preoccupied with the fashioning and contemplation of images of itself. Perhaps the most influential account of the relation between postmodernism and postmodernity is that of Jean-François Lyotard in *The Postmodern Condition* (1984). Lyotard suggests in that book that modernity comes into being with the replacement of divine or providential narratives of human destiny with more secular but no less universal narratives, or "metanarratives," which impart a sense of the irresistible linear progress of human history toward some singular destination – the achievement of fully self-conscious "spirit" in HEGELian philosophy, the universal emancipation of human beings in Marxism. The postmodern condition comes about with the collapse of or extreme skepticism toward these universalizing metanarratives. In place of a single narrative of the unfolding of an essential humanity, Lyotard proposes a multiplicity of different histories and local narratives that is incapable of being summarized or unified in one all-encompassing story. Postmodernist art and culture assist this multiplication of identities and ways of speaking by resisting every kind of formalization, and attesting to the sublime complexity and incommensurability of human worlds.

For others, however, the very condition of postmodernity is one in which the relations between the separate realms of social and economic life on the one hand and art and culture on the other have undergone a more fundamental transformation. If it is true that there are powerful parallels between the innovative energies of artistic modernism and the social and political turbulence of modernity, it is also true that artistic modernism is often characterized by its sense of implacable opposition to the modern world which it inhabits. Seen in this way, the very smoothness of the interchangeability

between postmodernist art and social and economic postmodernity may seem less like a vital affinity and more like a collapse of the distance and differentiation necessary for art and literature to claim any serious or transforming function. For proponents of this view, such as Terry Eagleton (1986), the striking correspondences between postmodernity and postmodernism are a sign of the numb and inert compliance of postmodernist art with the forces of commodification.

If one of the important characteristics of the postmodern condition is the rise of a generalized self-consciousness in cultural life, then it may seem fitting that one of the most striking evidences of the condition is the emergence of "the postmodern" as a style or sensibility within critical writing itself, such that certain forms of writing *about* postmodernism, whether in philosophy, social theory, CULTURAL STUDIES, or LITERARY CRITICISM, come to perform and even consciously to promote the values or qualities that are its object. The ambiguity of the phrase "postmodern theory," which does not allow the senses of "theory *of* the postmodern" and "theory *as* the postmodern" to be easily distinguished, is therefore appropriate as well as confusing. If the postmodern condition is one in which previously separated or opposed areas or forms begin to merge, then one might indeed expect postmodern theory to come to resemble its object. Much postmodern writing in philosophy, cultural studies, and WOMEN'S STUDIES deliberately compromises the clarity of the distinction between fiction, art, and criticism (just as postmodernist art often entails highly theoretical reflection upon its own nature and purpose). Such writing may refuse to adopt the neutral voice and distanced perspective that are still conventional in academic writing, forcing acknowledgement of the situated character of every utterance. It may offer forms of dialog between cooperating and competing voices as a polyphonic filling out of the authoritative closure of the single voice. It may, as in certain texts by Roland BARTHES, such as his *A Lover's Discourse* (1977, trans. 1978) or Jacques DERRIDA, such as his *Glas* (1974, trans. 1986) or "Living on: borderlines" (1979), adopt some of the techniques of the modernist avant-garde, such as collage and typographical experimentation, to pluralize and complicate the experience of the reading. Some feminist writers such as Luce IRIGARAY, in her *Speculum of the Other Woman* (1974, trans. 1984), have sought in a similar way to generate forms of critical and theoretical writing that would delegitimize academic authority. Such writing perhaps attempts to put itself in the place of the postmodernist avant-garde as defined by Jean-François Lyotard, "working without rules in order to formulate the rules of what *will have been done*" (Lyotard, 1984, p. 81).

Reading

Barthes, Roland 1977 (*1978*): *A Lover's Discourse: Fragments.*
Baudrillard, Jean 1988: *Selected Writings.*
Bell, Daniel 1976 (*1979*): *The Cultural Contradictions of Capitalism.*
Connor, Steven 1989: *Postmodernist Culture: An Introduction to Theories of the Contemporary.*
Derrida, Jacques 1974 (*1986*): *Glas.*
——— 1979: "Living on: borderlines."
Docherty, Thomas, ed. 1993: *Postmodernism: A Reader.*
Eagleton, Terry 1986: "Capitalism, modernism and postmodernism."
Harvey, David 1989: *The Condition of Postmodernity: An Enquiry into The Origins of Social Change.*
Hassan, Ihab 1987: *The Postmodern Turn: Essays in Postmodern Theory and Culture.*
Irigaray, Luce 1974 (*1985*): *Speculum of the Other Woman.*
Jameson, Fredric 1984: "Postmodernism, or the cultural logic of late capitalism."
Jencks, Charles 1991: *The Language of Post-Modern Architecture.*
Kant, Immanuel 1790 (*1952*): *Kritik der Urteilskraft.*
Lash, Scott, and Urry, John 1987: *The End of Organized Capitalism.*
Lipietz, Alan 1987: *Mirages and Miracles: The Crisis of Global Fordism.*
Lyotard, Jean-François 1979 (*1984*): *The Postmodern Condition: A Report on Knowledge.*

STEVEN CONNOR

post-Soviet studies   A term that describes a new approach to literature and CULTURE in Russia after the collapse of the Soviet system and the disintegration of the Soviet Union in the fall of 1991. However, it must be recognized that post-Soviet studies originated in the late 1980s, as they grew directly out of the policy of *perestroyka* (restructuring) and *glasnost* (openness), which was introduced in 1986 by the former Soviet premier Mikhail Gorbachev, incorporating the dissident and unofficial literature and criticism of the Soviet era. The artists and critics who were opposed to the Soviet system, and who therefore were persecuted by it, then formed the mainstream of post-Soviet studies. The distinction between studies done at home in the conditions of constant oppression in opposition to the official directions of Soviet literature and culture, and studies of Russian and Soviet literature and culture conducted abroad, where scholars and critics were generally free to express their opinions, has since lost its significance. There is currently no separation between official and unofficial ART and criticism.

The first sign of this change was the publication of previously inaccessible archival materials and works of authors, critics, and philosophers suppressed under the Soviet regime. For example, in 1986 the magazine *Ogonyok* published a selection of POETRY and a short biographical essay on the poet Nikolai Gumilev, who was executed in 1921 on charges of participation in a counterrevolutionary conspiracy. Gumilev was the first victim of the Soviet regime among Russian artists. His works were not published in the Soviet Union, and there had been no attempt at an analysis of his poetry since the time of his death. The Gumilev publication opened the floodgates of publishing activities. At the present time there are no authors who are banned in Russia. Works by everyone – from the suppressed Soviet writers of the 1920s and 1930s like Bulgakov and Platonov, to old émigré writers like Nabokov and Merezhkovsky, the third-wave émigré writers like Aksyonov and Brodsky, the dissidents Solzhenitzyn and Sinyavsky, Western writers labeled "modernist" like Proust, Joyce, Kafka, and SARTRE, or those who were considered politically incorrect like Orwell, Musil, and Henry Miller – are now available.

The publication of previously suppressed materials is coupled with the task of reassessing past values. Soviet IDEOLOGY and the method of the SOCIALIST REALISM as a dominating form of LITERARY and cultural CRITICISM are firmly rejected in post-Soviet studies. Having discarded ideological and methodological baggage, contemporary critics and scholars have undertaken a broad (if rather chaotic) search for new criteria of evaluation. They see a need to provide a new interpretation of Russian and Western classical literature, utilizing new approaches in critical analysis – from poststructuralism and deconstruction to culturological and mystical philosophical approaches, which are marked by extreme pluralism in the opinions of the post-Soviet critics. This pluralism has replaced the semantic duality that was one of the most important aspects of Soviet literature and culture before the fall of Communism in Russia. Unable to express their views and opinions openly and forced at the same time to exist within the Soviet system, those artists, critics, and scholars who considered themselves honest and progressive invented a special Aesopean language to convey their messages to the reading public. This language determined a careful selection of verbal material and presupposed a special attitude toward the written word, on the part of both the writer and his/her reader who knew how to read not what was written, but what was implied in the TEXT. Even the period of *glasnost* was marked by the duality of thought, by both the dual system of evaluation and a dual time scale (the wretched, vulgar, present Soviet time vs. the expected, genuine, final time associated and identified with the free, Western world of science, art, and creative life) and a dual perception of artists and critics themselves. On the one hand, they were prophets of the coming new world of freedom, but on the other hand, the victims of this world in which they now had to stop solving the problems of culture and country and to earn their daily bread. In spite of this duality, both the official and unofficial criticisms were monolithic. The orthodox Soviet critics were united by the Marxist-Leninist ideology; the opposition critics were united by the principle that if something did not fit the Procrustean bed of the official Soviet literature or the method of social realism, it must be good. This principle in its reverse form is carried out today: everything which was created within the framework of the official Soviet culture is now considered bad.

This typically Russian, indiscriminate rejection of the entire Soviet culture gives rise to serious concern on the part of some critics. The refusal to reevaluate the art of socialist realism is regrettable, not only because its analysis could reveal most fully the mechanism of totalitarian culture, but also because it makes impossible any analysis of the unofficial Soviet literature that was created during that period by "comparing" it with the official literature.

The liberation from the totalitarian culture of socialist realism was initially perceived as the freedom of the word and the spirit, not simply in the sense of basic human rights but as "a re-creation of the world" and "a reinterpretation of destinations" (Aitmatov, 1993, p. 11). However, with the disintegration of the totalitarian regime, "the conflict between the spirit and power," which constituted the most important theme of the Soviet epoch and had almost universal significance for the Soviet creative world, disappeared as well. Artists had to take the freedom test; and many failed it, being unable to write *for* and not *against* something.

The collapse of the state system of control and support of the arts has been another factor that contributes to the crisis keenly felt in post-Soviet culture. The physical state of post-Soviet studies is extremely difficult. Many critical literary journals have closed, owing to the lack of funds and the decline of interest on the part of the general public. Furthermore, there are neither new institutions nor other mechanisms of support for the humanities and the arts. The critics who grew accustomed to existing contrary to and at the same time within the limits of the Soviet socialist structure of culture are now forced to compete with commercial publications in a struggle that they feel they are losing. Critics exist mostly by publishing their works in a handful of the remaining thick journals, such as *Novy Mir* (*New World*), which have Western sponsors, or by finding a way to travel and teach in Western universities. Genuine literature is inexorably losing its position, giving way to a surrogate of cheap books and mass culture, particularly of American exports. Very much in the spirit of Western LIBERALISM, in place of the faith in the might of the word comes *repressive tolerance* (Kagarlitsky, 1993, p. 132).

Post-Soviet studies are also marked by a radical change in relationships between the artist or critic and his/her reader, and in the perception of the artist by the Russian public. In Russia historically, literature and literary criticism had always been more than just a form of art. For centuries they were a forum for discussion of "life and death questions," and the Russian reading public always looked to literature for answers, viewing writers and critics as teachers of life. Now in the conditions of absolute freedom, "the writer and belle lettres have lost their formerly sacrosanct status, that certain halo of the righteous" (Aitmatov, 1993, p. 14) as the public begins to view literature purely as entertainment. As Marietta Chudakova (1991, p. 5) correctly pointed out in her article in *Literary Gazette*, "for the first time in nearly two centuries, our society is ceasing to be literature-centric." An event taking place in one sphere of culture is no longer perceived as having a universal significance; the unity of the common intellectual reading has disappeared; the very notion of the intellectual significance that used to give rhythm to the existence of the entire class of Soviet intelligentsia is not there any more. There is no longer a culture-centered reader, as new classes of readers have appeared. For example, women have emerged as the main readers of popular literature, and they have brought with them new tastes and themes: sex, love, eroticism, forcing the writers and critics to make necessary adjustments. Post-Soviet literature and criticism explore themes that were unthinkable before the fall of Communism in Russia: from religion and New Age mysticism to eroticism and sex, and from ethnogenesis and metaphysics to the absurd and grotesque.

Some critics look in desperation at the present state of Russian culture, feeling that "the word itself is dying and losing its old passion and strength; the great Word of literature, which traditionally has been an organic part of the spiritual life, has been that life itself" (Selivanova, 1993, p. 44). The leading dissident writer of the 1960s and 1970s, Alexander Solzhenitsyn, sees the contemporary state of Russian culture as a catastrophe which, in his opinion, has resulted from the amorphousness of Russian national consciousness, from the indifference towards one's own nationality. Salvation can be found only in developing the feeling of patriotism, which Solzhenitsyn defines as follows: "Patriotism is a whole and persistent feeling of love towards your homeland and your nation combined with your service for her" (Solzhenitsyn, 1994, p. 174). The writer, V. Rasputin, also sees the only solution to the present spiritual bankruptcy to be the revival of the sense of nationalism based on religious faith. Many scholars entering post-Soviet studies from previous decades lament the general decline and impoverishment of humanistic culture in Russia; the reason for which they see in the interruption of cultural traditions and traditions of "Holy Russia" in particular. As the only panacea for national spiritual revival, they suggest the return to teaching Scripture and Russian Orthodox ETHICS. Scholars, like the academician Likhachev, call for the Russian people to confront their own history, which is perceived as an equivalent to personal national repentance. Critics of this inclination see in this striving towards historical knowledge of the recent past a solution to the national tragedy.

Unfortunately, they do not realize that the new generation of Russian intellectuals perceive Scripture, religion, and cultural traditions quite differently. The Scriptures, which were used and studied in secret under the Soviet regime, have now become the source of remaking and sacrilege. The unrepentant society and especially its intellectual elite have chosen alternative paths in finding the "national myth," which would explain the historical

concreteness of their actions. Instead of restoring ties to traditional Russian religious culture, contemporary writers and critics throw a bridge to the lost traditions of modernism. They substitute for the sacred, historical, cultural space (Likhachev, 1994) a nonexistent one that reflects the predominant theme of the post-Soviet culture – the conviction that in contemporary Russian society people live in a country where nothing has meaning for anyone.

We must remember that with the end of socialist realist art, modernism, which was the alternative to the official culture in Russia, ended as well. It has been replaced with POSTMODERNISM, which forms the first of the two major divisions of post-Soviet studies. Today's creators of postmodernist literature are yesterday's Soviet underground. While they were underground, the artists and critics believed they were composing a literature of truth to offset the programmed official lie. That underground has now surfaced and has collided with a reality which is so complex and contradictory and, moreover, changing with such speed, that the constant battle with socialist realism has turned out to be simply absurd. Postmodernist literature and criticism reflect a deep intellectual crisis. They recreate a deconstructed, paradoxical world which contradicts normal moral instincts and from which the primary human subject has disappeared. In an attempt to think in universal categories, post-Soviet criticism in the form of postmodernism has entered an abstract, speculative, utopian space where humans with their character, will, and motives are turned into an abstraction.

The perception of contemporary reality in Russian postmodernism can be defined by the title of Milan Kundera's novel, *The Unbearable Lightness of Being*, which leads to perceiving as "unbearably light" all old absolutes and authorities (both ideological and ontological, universal and personal) which were previously unshakable. Postmodernism expresses the tragic state of the world, which is perceived as an escape from the turn of history, and itself can be called "the end of history," beyond which one could expect the return and rebirth of the human soul in the forgotten, lost, universal history of personality. The mission of postmodernism in Russia could be defined as that of Charon transporting the "dear shadows" into the land of the dead.

The best manifestation of postmodernism in Russia is conceptualism. Originating in the linguistic experiments of futurists, conceptualists have arrived at a totally different vision, although perfectly fitting the contemporary life; instead of the futurists' "beyonsense" language of higher reality, we encounter the deliberate misarticulation and linguistic ALIENATION of the conceptualists. As Mikhail Epstein correctly points out: "The conceptual treatment of language leaves us in a space of tense silence, of the decay and decrepitude of all existing or possible words – in a kind of nirvana of discarded sign systems and absolute, extrasubjective, extralinguistic meaning-conjecture" (Epstein, 1993, p. 265). Such an approach to the representation of reality is charged with a final eschatological meaning. Conceptualism separates signifiers from the signified and demonstrates the transparency and illusory quality of the latter (Epstein, p. 265).

An alternative to conceptualism is a new realism or more properly, postrealism. Postrealism is characterized, on the one hand, by the belief on the part of its creators in real existence of higher spiritual entities and by the desire to attract the reader to them; and, on the other hand, by an attempt at a synthesis of the traditional, ideological view of the world and the subjective, personal, individual sphere.

Postrealism is a method based on the principle of relativity understood in universal terms, according to which the constantly changing world is perceived dialogically through the total openness of an author's position toward the universe. Thus postrealism becomes an "existential realism," since it is based on "the faith without a faith." Mikhail BAKHTIN is perceived as a founder of the AESTHETICS of postrealism, the relative aesthetics that proposes a view of the world as an eternally changing, liquid entity in which there are no distinctions between top and bottom, eternal and transient, existence and nonexistence. "Meta-realism is a poetics of homogeneous, indivisible unfolding of a multifaceted reality, where, for the sake of observing a theocentric world structure, the lyrical 'I' gives way to lyrical 'it'" (Epstein, p. 263). The search for the meaning of life is transferred into "The life of insects" (the title of Viktor Pelevin's story), and hope for the future is realized through the discussion of suicide (M. Butov's story "In memory of the suicide Seva"). As a critic, Irina Rodnyanskaya writes that the paradox of the contemporary literary situation consists of the fact that "the most humanistic prose is from the life of in-

sects, and the most optimistic is about 'unmotivated' suicide" (Rodnyanskaya, 1993, p. 227).

Postrealism returns to the traditional Russian perception of literature as a teacher of life. The pronouncements of some post-Soviet critics and writers by inertia go far beyond the strictly literary analysis and often acquire a "prophetic urgency." Thus an analysis of an individual literary work grows into a meditation on the present state or the future path of Russian society. For example, in a recent essay entitled "The third path, or the priceless gift of Atlantis. An attempt at the newest philosophical-polyclinical studies," postrealist critic A. Andreev analyzes "the word well-known to all strata of population which defines . . . the male life-giving organ." Proceeding from the fact that this word in Russian is composed of three letters, which came to the Russian language from the Greek "x," "y," and "twice rotated in the three-dimensional space Latin 'z'" and which, according to the author, constitutes the gift of Atlantis to the Russian civilization, he, in absolute seriousness, deduces that this triad represents "the three axes, three coordinates, three vectors" which determine the structure of the universe. Thus the word consisting of these three letters becomes the universal logos, which explains the special mentality of the Russian people, their innate attraction to the eternal. In his conclusion, the author defines the messianic idea of Russia and her people. According to him, it consists not of "some special political, economic or social structures," but of the fact that the Russian people possess this gift of Atlantis, the universal logos consisting of three letters. By penetrating into the depths of this universal logos, Russia will be able to accomplish the true coup in human history: to leave the technocratic path of the development of civilization, the path designed for satisfaction of immediate, transient needs, and to enter the logocratic path, the path of exploring inner, essential, constant values. Russia's task is to follow this path and to lead all humanity along it.

In the post-Soviet reality, postrealism fulfills the cosmogonical function of creation of a new myth. To offset the frightening chaos of modernism, socialist realism established its totalitarian cosmos, which did not allow any deviations from the CANON and in which there was no freedom of thought, no pathos of discoveries; but it provided the fatalistic optimism that guaranteed happiness in the end. Postmodernism, asserting that culture is chaos, established complex cultural poetics in which a living person with his/her pains and destinies turns out to be replaced by a bunch of mutually exclusive associations. Postrealism completes the culturological work of postmodernism. It attempts to comprehend chaos through a person and for the sake of a person, and thus to find a teleological connection, which may become the purpose and justification of a singular human life surrounded on all sides by the attributes of chaos. Out of chaos postrealism restores the cosmos, which rediscovers the wholeness of the world in its discreteness, the unity and stability in the repulsion of opposites, the balance in the very process of endless movement, and creates a dialogue of the opposing elements which does not reconcile cosmos and chaos but harmonizes chaos (Leiderman and Lipovetsky, 1993, p. 238).

See also POSTMODERNISM; SOCIALIST REALISM.

Reading

Aitmatov, Chingiz 1993: "The intellectual crisis, the demise of totalitarism, and the fate of literature."

Aksyonov, Vassily 1993: "Distrophy of the 'thick' and *bespredel* of the 'thin' (literary notes)."

Andreev, A. 1993: "Trety put', ili Bestsennyi dar Atlantidy. (Opyt noveishego filosofsko-poliklinicheskogo issledovaniya.)"

Arkhangel'sky, A. 1993: "Proza mira"

Epstein, Mikhail 1993: "After the future: on the new consciousness in literature."

Gudkov, L., and Dubin, B. 1993: "Bez napryazheniya . . . Zametki o kul'ture perekhodnogo perioda."

Kagarlitsky, Boris 1993: "A step to the left, a step to the right."

Kustanovich, Konstantin 1993: "Erotic glasnost: sexuality in recent Russian literature."

Latynina, Yuliya 1993: "Dedal i Gerkules, ili Neskol'ko rassuzhdenii o pol'ze literatury."

Leiderman, N., and Lipovetsky, M. 1993: "Zhizn posle smerti, ili Novye svedeniya o realizme."

Likhachev, D. 1993: "O russkoi intelligentsii."

——1994: "Kul'tura kak tselostnaya sreda."

Popov, Yevgeny 1993: "The silhouette of truth."

Rasputin, Valentin 1993: "'Motherland' is not an abstract notion."

Rodnyanskaya, Irina 1993: "Gipsovyi veter. O filisofskoi intoksikatsii v tekushchei slovesnosti."

Selivanova, Svetlana 1993: "From the seventies to the nineties."

Semenov, Oleg 1993: "Iskusstvo li – iskusstvo nashego stoletiya?"

Shreider, Yu 1993: "Mezhdu molokhom i mamonoi."

——1994: "Tsennosti, kotorye my vybiraem."

Shusharin, D. 1994: "Vozvrashchenie v kontekst."

Solzhenitsyn, A. 1994: "'Russkii vopros' k kontsu XX veka."

SLAVA I. YASTREMSKI

poststructuralism A general term in the history of late twentieth-century thought that is used to designate, often dismissively, a wide range of discrete thinkers, including BARTHES, DELEUZE, DE MAN, DERRIDA, FOUCAULT, GIRARD, and SAID. The word was coined to refer to the intellectual movements that emerged from the International Colloquium on Critical Languages and the Sciences of Man, which was held at Johns Hopkins University in 1966. Perhaps the most influential paper delivered at that conference was Derrida's "Structure, sign, and play in the discourse of the human sciences," which was subsequently published in the proceedings of the conference (*The Structuralist Controversy*) and as a chapter in *Writing and Difference*, with an important epigraph from Mallarmé's *Un Coup de dés* that anticipates poststructuralism.

Although Derrida does not use the word "poststructuralism," his essay offers the best opening into the concept. An important event has taken place in the concept of structure, he announces, (see STRUCTURALISM). Acknowledging that it may seem strange to use the word "event" in relation to STRUCTURE he nevertheless proceeds to show that a rupture has occurred in this concept and in its history. Structure, as word and concept, is as old as Western science and philosophy. Indeed, it is so much a part of the root network of ordinary language and thought that it is easy to forget its metaphorical character. In this forgetfulness bred of excessive familiarity, "the structurality of structure" (Derrida, *1978*, p. 278) has been neutralized; and it has been allowed to assume a center point of presence, and fixed origin in language and thought. This has been done to limit the PLAY of structure. Structure, especially the center of a structure, keeps play within limits, however. The center operates as a metaphor within the metaphor of structure. It works to close off play and does not allow for substitution, permutation, or transformation. The center is that which is unique in a given structure. Although center governs structure, it is not structured in turn. The center is a still presence from which the attempt may be made to conceive of structure itself as "a full presence which is beyond play" (p. 279). The entire history of the concept of structure, however, manifests the substitutions of one center for another or the assignment of different forms or names to the center, such as "the Word" for "God." To think through the structurality of structure in this way – to recognize *center* and *presence* as metaphors – is not to do violence to the structure of language or the structure of a given text. On the contrary, it is to be aware of what structure is and has been; it is to reflect on "a central presence which has never been itself, has always already been exiled from itself into its own substitute" (p. 280). At such moments of critical reflection as this, language ceases to be a transparent medium of reflection or the undifferentiated substance of thought; it now becomes part of the universal problematic. Poststructuralism therefore is not an abandonment of structure but rather a critical reflection upon its dynamics. It neither brings philosophy to an end (see END OF PHILOSOPHY) nor attempts to work outside of philosophy.

While systematically opposing rigid, oppressive, and monolithic structure, poststructuralism is not an invitation to irresponsible formlessness. Instead, poststructuralist critique celebrates the liberating potential within human forms and accepts the responsibility of reflecting upon them. In this respect it is a kind of critical reading that champions WRITING, although its procedures can be extended, at least by analogy, to all human activities.

Poststructuralism is often loosely and misleadingly equated with POSTMODERNISM or identified exclusively with DECONSTRUCTION in support of the erroneous claim that poststructuralists are unified enemies of meaning and truth. The most ambitious effort of this sort is Manfred FRANK's *What Is Neostructuralism?* which attempts to reduce French poststructuralism to antirationalism and to oppose it to German rationalism. The publication of *Textual Strategies: Perspectives in Post-Structuralist Criticism* (1979) made poststructuralist thought widely available to American and British readers, while serving as an important correction to the assumption that there is a single definition or essence that constitutes poststructuralist practice.

Reading

Derrida, Jacques 1967 (*1978*): *Writing and Difference*.
Frank, Manfred 1984 (*1989*): *What Is Neostructuralism?*
Harari, Josué V., ed. 1979: *Textual Strategies: Perspectives in Post-Structuralist Criticism*.
Macksey, Richard, and Donato, Eugenio, eds 1970: *The Structuralist Controversy*.
Payne, Michael 1993: *Reading Theory: An Introduction to Lacan, Derrida, and Kristeva*.

Sturrock, John, ed. 1979: *Structuralism and Since: From Lévi-Strauss to Derrida*.

MICHAEL PAYNE

Poulet, Georges (1902–91)   Critic of the GENEVA SCHOOL. Born in Belgium, influenced by Marcel RAYMOND, Arthur LOVEJOY, and Gaston BACHELARD, Poulet taught in Edinburgh, Baltimore, Zürich, and Nice, while developing an analytic approach that emphasizes categories of space and time as keys to understanding literary TEXTS, and the coordination of these categories to reconstruct an implied author's identity or *cogito*, that is, the Cartesian "I think" that represents an individual act of consciousness. Poulet's brilliantly seductive LITERARY CRITICISM has also been controversial because it marshals evidence from an author's complete writings without recognizing either context or the unity of individual works. Rejecting formal structures and critical objectivity, he correlates key words to define a characteristic organizing consciousness that persists throughout each writer's entire work. His *Studies in Human Time* (1949–68) describe the spiritual careers of authors from the Renaissance to the twentieth century, prefacing them with a larger "history of human consciousness" that outlines, century by century, the evolution of concepts of existence. Later books consider individual authors (*Proustian Space*, 1963) and literary critics (*The Critical Consciousness*, 1971). Key phrases are "interior distance," the mental universe projected by the TEXT; *foyer*, a generating core or starting point unique to each author's experience; and "criticism of consciousness" or "criticism of identification," the critical attempt to reproduce in oneself the author's mode of experience. Poulet's approach is the obverse of DECONSTRUCTION: he emphasizes *cogito*, not PAROLE; person, not language; and manifold constructions of presence, not traceries of deferral and absence.
See also RICHARD, JEAN-PIERRE.

Reading

De Man, Paul 1971: "The literary self as origin: the work of Georges Poulet."
Lawall, Sarah N. 1968: "Georges Poulet."
Miller, J. Hillis 1971 (*1991*): "Geneva or Paris: Georges Poulet's 'criticism of identification.'"
——1982: "Hommage à Georges Poulet."
Poulet, Georges 1949–68 (*1956*): *Studies in Human Time*.
——1949–68 (*1959*): *The Interior Distance*.

—— 1969: "Phenomenology of reading."
—— 1963 (*1977*): *Proustian Space.*

SARAH N. LAWALL

practical criticism The critical method originating from I.A. RICHARDS's *Practical Criticism* (1929), a work recording a teaching experiment at Cambridge in which students were asked to analyze unidentified TEXTS.

In its broad sense, practical criticism is thus synonymous with "close reading" or the French *explication de texte*. But, historically, it came to mean something much more specific and contentious, the New Critical doctrine of "intrinsic" analysis which encouraged students to read a text (usually a short poem) as an isolated object, exploring its internal STRUCTURE and functioning without reference to, say, its author's biography or its historical context. In its pure form this would mean asking the reader to interpret Milton's "When I consider how my light is spent" without knowing that he was blind, or Blake's "Tyger" without knowing that the tiger was a contemporary metaphor for the French Revolution.

Practical criticism has been widely criticized not only for being unhistorical, and for depending on an indefensible ideal of the autonomous text, but also for focusing too exclusively on the purely verbal aspects of literature and neglecting other elements, such as patterns of action in drama or PLOTS in novels, which also determine meaning.

See also EMPSON, WILLIAM; NEW CRITICISM; RICHARDS, I.A.

Reading
Crane, R.S. 1953: *The Languages of Criticism and the Structure of Poetry.*
Richards, I.A. 1929 (*1964*): *Practical Criticism.*

IAIN WRIGHT

practices, discursive *See* DISCURSIVE PRACTICES

Prague Linguistic Circle For two decades the Prague Linguistic Circle charted the course of modern linguistic and literary studies. The morphological and phonological theories of current generative linguistics as well as the central notions of modern SEMIOTICS are direct legacies of the circle.

The first meeting of the Prague Circle was held in the office of Vilém Mathesius at Charles Uni-

versity on October 6, 1926 to discuss a paper read earlier that day by Henrik Becker. In addition to Becker and Mathesius, that initial gathering included the anglicist Bohumil Trnka, the slavists Roman JAKOBSON and Bohuslav Havránek, and the orientalist Jan Rypka. The meeting ended on a general note of agreement that the group should meet regularly to develop a new agenda of language study. Although Mathesius is considered the founder of the Prague Circle, Jakobson, a former member of the Moscow Linguistic Circle, shaped it and steered its course for nearly two decades.

While SAUSSURE was a major influence on the research program of the Prague Circle, the brand of STRUCTURALISM which emerged from the Prague Circle was distinct from that of the GENEVA SCHOOL set afoot by Saussure. In his first address to the circle, Jakobson argued against Saussure's position that language studies completely divorce synchronic and diachronic analyses since synchronic phonology can be fully explained only in terms of diachronic processes currently under way in a given language. Jakobson and his colleagues were also attracted by the new concepts of the "phoneme" (smallest distinctive linguistic element of sound) and "morpheme" (smallest meaningful linguistic element), introduced by Baudouin de Courtenay and Nikolai Kruszewski. Before arriving in Prague, Jakobson was convinced that studying individual sounds in isolation was pointless; rather, individual sounds (phonemes) must be studied in terms of the patterns they form within a given language. This led him to his notion of "contrast." Linguistic sounds constitute morphemes (stems and affixes) whose function is to convey distinctive meanings. To accomplish this, morphemes and ultimately phonemes must contrast with one another. If two phonemes do not contrast, say, as /t/ and /d/ do in English, they cannot discriminate meaningful elements, as /t/ and /d/ (alone) distinguish the two words *tip* and *dip*. The system of contrasts, based on distinctive properties like vocal vibration, position of the tongue, and nasality, form the patterns of sounds in languages.

Jakobson and Nikolai Trubetzkoy, who joined the group in 1928, also developed the distinction between purely phonological rules, conditioned by phonological (sound) phenomena alone, and morpho(pho)phonological rules, which are sound variations conditioned by morphological phenomena. This distinction with all its implications remains fundamental to the all contemporary theories of linguistics. Trubetzkoy's monograph on the subject, published posthumously in 1939, laid the foundation for that distinction as well as Jakobson's later work on distinctive phonological features.

That new linguistic agenda was presented to the First International Congress of Linguists which convened in The Hague in April of 1928. The circle's *Phonological Theses* were signed by Jakobson, Trubetzkoy, and Sergei Karcevskij and published in the proceedings of the Congress along with the *Program of Linguistics Analysis*, signed by Jakobson, Mathesius, and Trubetzkoy, as well as the editors of Saussure's *Cours générale linguistique*, Charles Bally and Albert Séchehaye. The initial meeting of the Congress thus served as the catalyst of the European structuralist school of linguistics, since it was the Prague Circle and the Geneva school, later joined by the Linguistic Circle of Copenhagen, which defined the basic program of structuralism, the precursor of modern generative linguistic theory.

The following year the first International Congress of Slavists convened in Prague and the circle was actively engaged in its preparations. By this time its members had developed a rounded program of language study, which it presented to the Congress as another set of theses. These theses cast a totally new light on the issues of phonology, the newly delineated area of morphophonology, morphology, syntax, and lexicography. They also addressed questions of linguistic geography and language standardization. The first two issues of the circle's journal, *Travaux du Cercle Linguistique de Prague*, were also presented to the Congress. It would continue to have an enormous impact on linguistics and poetics until its demise in 1939.

The early ties with the Moscow Circle were underscored in 1928 when two of its outstanding members, Boris Tomashevsky and Yuri Tynyanov, spoke before the Prague Circle. The Moscow Circle was closely associated with FORMALISM and its notion that the study of ART be restricted to the inner laws of the work alone without reference to external facts. The idea that a literary work could be understood in isolation from its milieu, ignoring its historical legacy, was as foreign to the thinking of the Prague Circle as the notion that linguistic sounds could be analyzed in isolation. Jan Mukařovský played the cardinal role in developing the literary positions of the circle, although Jakobson and, later, René Wellek contributed handsomely. These three and their colleagues accorded structure a central position in their theories of art but a richer endowment than had the formalists. Mukařovský felt that structure was hierarchical and extended far beyond individual works. Beyond the structure of any single work of art was the structure of that genre of art itself, and beyond that, the structure of art itself. Literary theory and, ultimately, all aesthetic theory, must take a work of art in the context of all the internal and external relations within this hierarchy.

The Prague Circle saw linguistic and poetic structuralism cut from the same bolt. Since language turns on the classic linguistic sign, an indissoluble association of SYMBOL and meaning, in the 1930s the Prague school began to interpret all art in terms of signs. This notion provided further proof that form could not be studied aside from content and led Mukařovský and Jakobson to the works of the Russian philosopher Mikhail BAKHTIN and Charles S. PIERCE. The combination of these various threads of thought led to the semiotic theories of the Prague Circle, which directly molded the Eastern and Western Europe schools of semiotics.

The activity of the circle diminished rapidly after the sudden rise of the Communist Party to power in Czechoslovakia in 1948. By that time Jakobson and Wellek had moved on to the United States and Mathesius and Trubetzkoy had both passed away. Attempts in the 1950s and 1980s to revive the circle never achieved the intellectual heights of the original organization.

See also BAKHTIN, MIKHAIL; JAKOBSON, ROMAN; MUKAROVSKY, JAN; PEIRCE, C.S.; RUSSIAN FORMALISM; SAUSSURE, FERDINAND DE; SEMIOTICS; STRUCTURALISM.

Reading

Dirven, R., and Fried, V., eds 1987: *Functionalism in Linguistics.*

Matejka, L., and Titunik, I.R., eds 1976: *Semiotics of Art; Prague School Contributions.*

Matejka, L., ed. 1978: *Sounds, Sign and Meaning. Quinquagenary of the Prague Linguistic Circle.*

Steiner, P., ed. 1982: *The Prague School: Selected Writings, 1929–1946.*

Tobin, Y., ed. 1988: *The Prague School and its Legacy, in Linguistics, Literature, Semiotics, Folklore, and the Arts.*

Vachek, J., and Duskova, L., eds 1983: *Praguiana, Some Basic and Less Known Aspects of the Prague Linguistic School.*

Vachek, J. 1966: *The Linguistic School of Prague: An Introduction to its Theory and Practice.*

Wellek, R. 1969: *The Literary Theory and Aesthetics of the Prague School.*

ROBERT BEARD

preunderstanding That understanding is never without any presupposition, but is always on the basis of a prior "fore-structure" or preunderstanding, was first pointed out by Martin HEIDEGGER. This fore-structure consists of fore-having, fore-sight, and fore-conception; together they make up the "hermeneutic situation" (Heidegger, 1927). The idea was implicit in what Husserl called predelineation (*Vorzeichnung*).

J.N. MOHANTY

primitive classification The phrase derives from an essay on the subject authored by French social theorist Emile DURKHEIM and Marcel MAUSS, appearing in *Année Sociologique* of 1903. The authors asked: how and why do human beings classify their social and physical world? Their answer, exhaustively critiqued by Needham in his introduction to the 1963 English translation, is mainly of historical interest. In the years since, however, the analysis of indigenous classification systems has blossomed: how societies classify such domains as kinsmen, flora and fauna, medicines and illness, supernatural entities, and the color spectrum, and what principles underlie those classifications, have stimulated elegant and fruitful analyses.

Reading
Berlin, Brent, and Kay, Paul 1969: *Basic Color Terms: Their Universality and Evolution.*
Durkheim, E., and Mauss, M. 1903 (*1963*): *Primitive Classification.*

THOMAS C. GREAVES

production, literary *See* LITERARY PRODUCTION

Propp, Vladimir (1895–1970) A Russian formalist most famous for his structural analysis of the Russian folk tale (1968), Propp can be considered an important influence on the development of NARRATOLOGY, especially with regard to work on plot composition.

The impetus behind Propp's work was similar to that of STRUCTURALISM. He was interested in finding the rules which were fundamental to the folk tale. His work on plot was based upon that of Veselovsky, who saw plots as subdivided into "motifs." Propp expanded this formulation, analyzing them in terms of "roles" which constitute the char-

acter types, and the functions by and through which characters act out the story, effectively creating the plot sequence. For Propp all folk tales consisted of variations upon this basic structure. He isolated four basic classes of folk tale: those concerned with success at the end of a long struggle; those concerned with the successful conclusion of a difficult task; those concerned with both of these classes; and those concerned with neither. Such broad divisions are of course open to question, and it is this fact which has proven so fruitful in the structuralist attempt to produce a science of narration. The reason for this is that Propp's analytical method has proven to be most attractive to structuralists precisely because in one crucial particular it matches one of the fundamental premises of structuralism itself. This aspect is Propp's attempt to reduce the heterogeneous richness of the folk tale to a fundamental set of rules. These rules form a sort of "deep structure" which can be discerned in all folk tales in his equivalent of the structuralist assumption that, ultimately, a structural homology rooted in the human mind is responsible for narrative. Such a position offered structuralists interested in narrative a model which allowed them not only to compare different narratives, but also to read all narratives as the surface results of a single imperative. Nevertheless Propp cannot be considered to be a fully fledged structuralist of this kind since he did not develop a METALANGUAGE of his own in which to conceptualize his analyses. This remained for those who followed his method but who perhaps found it to be insufficiently couched in scientistic terminology. Propp generalized at the points at which later narratologists move onto different conceptual levels. Thus he tended to analyze the incidents which interested him in the same kind of language employed by the TEXTS he read and it was this methodology which was to be supplanted in the work of structuralists such as Claude BREMOND.

Accordingly, it has been argued by Fredric JAMESON (1989) that Propp therefore organized his material into a single overriding narrative which subsumes all of the folk tale narratives he analyzed. It is this which constitutes a problem for structuralists, who wish to achieve an objective science of narrative. In any event, Propp's analysis came at the moment of a shift in theories of literature: he enacted a movement away from readings which operate in terms of simple representation.

Reading

Jameson, Fredric 1981 (*1989*): *The Political Unconscious: Narrative as a Socially Symbolic Act.*
Propp, Vladimir 1968: *The Morphology of the Folk Tale.*

PAUL INNES

psychoanalysis and psychoanalytic criticism

In an encyclopedia article written in 1922, FREUD (1922, p. 235) supplies a lucid description of the discipline he founded. Psychoanalysis is, he writes, the name given to "a procedure for the investigation of mental processes which are almost inaccessible in any other way." It is a therapeutic method for the treatment of neurotic disorders. Finally, it is a body of psychological data "which is gradually being accumulated into a new scientific discipline."

Although it was developed primarily as a clinical method for the treatment of individuals, Freud's new scientific discipline has always had a variety of other applications. Freud (1913) described it as having claims to scientific interest which made the psychoanalytic method extensible to nonclinical disciplines as diverse as philology, biology, sociology, and education, as well as to the science of AESTHETICS. His professed aversion to totalizing philosophies and system-building notwithstanding, Freud was always prone to the most wide-ranging speculations, and the literary-artistic domain was in his view one which came within the remit of psychoanalysis. Freud's WRITINGS abound in literary allusions and references, mainly to classical German authors such as Goethe and Schiller. There is a certain IRONY here in that whereas Freud is often seen as one of the cardinal thinkers of the modern, his own tastes remain resolutely classical and traditional.

Freud believed that the writer and psychoanalyst draw on the same or similar sources, and that intuition is endorsed by LACAN when he remarks (Lacan, 1965, p. 9) that Marguerite Duras "knows without me what I teach" and that the writer "precedes" the analyst. Literary models have had a productive role in the history of psychoanalysis. The early "cathartic method" of therapy (Breuer and Freud, 1893–5; see FREUD) contains an obvious allusion to classical theories of tragic drama and the theory of the OEDIPUS COMPLEX itself originates in memories of Sophocles and Greek mythology. One of the reasons that Freud was so attracted to Jensen's *Gradiva*, a "Pompeian fantasy" published in 1903, was no doubt that it can be read as a psychiatric study which describes the return of the repressed, for the hero's infatuation with a sculpture proves to derive from repressed childhood memories (Freud, 1907). The manner in which Freud applies his method of dream interpretation to the dreams and delusions of Jensen's fictional character reveals, however, one of the characteristic weaknesses of classical psychoanalytic criticism, namely its surrender to the realist fallacy and its inability to recognize the materiality of the TEXT. There is no challenge to an unproblematically mimetic view of the expressive correspondence between TEXT and author, text and reality or even character and reality.

A number of Freud's papers are devoted to aesthetic topics. These range from studies of fiction (1919, 1927), of Shakespeare (1913), and of Dostoievsky (1927) to two major essays on the visual arts (1910, 1914a) and to briefer but more general considerations on creative writing (1908). In general, Freud displays little interest in the formal properties of the works he discusses and is less concerned with the science of aesthetics than with the psychology of creativity and the psychopathology of creative artists. As Freud (1914b, p. 36) himself puts it, psychoanalysis moves "from the interpretation of dreams to the analysis of works of imagination and ultimately to the analysis of their creators."

Artistic creativity is usually seen as a parallel with the fantasy activity of the child. At the most basic level, fiction provides a form of wish fulfillment for both author and, thanks to the mechanisms of identification, reader. Thus, stories in which women readily fall in love with a first-person hero are readily recognizable as a form of ego gratification (Freud, 1908). Most psychoanalytic criticism relies to a degree upon the theory of sublimation, or the diversion of the sexual instinct toward nonsexual aims. The classical examples are artistic creation and intellectual inquiry, which is often seen as a sublimation of the sexual curiosity of childhood. The theory of sublimation provides, for example, the metapsychological underpinnings for the Leonardo essay (Freud, 1910). Sublimation is not, however, the most coherent notion in Freud's metapsychology, being partly a metaphor drawn from chemistry (where it refers to the vaporization of a solid without the intermediate formation of a liquid) and partly an allusion to an aesthetics of the sublime, and its mechanisms are never described by Freud with any great clarity. While sublimation is held to be a basic property of the aesthetic, Freud is also forced to admit that there is something unknowable about creativity and accepts in his discussion of Dostoievsky that "Before the problem of the creative artist, analysis must lay down its arms" (1928, p. 177). To that extent, Freud is still clinging to a romantic notion of genius.

Classical psychoanalytic criticism is an author and content-based criticism based mainly upon thematic readings. As a theorist of OBJECT-RELATIONS puts it, Freud's writings about ART and literature deal with "general psychological problems expressed in works of art and shows, for instance, how the latent content of universal infantile anxieties is symbolically expressed in them" (Segal, 1952, p. 185). Given that psychoanalysis operates with a fairly small number of SYMBOLS, most of them pertaining to the Oedipal triangle and its effects, its application to the literary domain can be very reductive.

Biography tends to be the dominant mode of classical psychoanalytic criticism, the prototype being Freud's study of Leonardo da Vinci. Here, Freud seeks to demonstrate that both the artist's sexuality and his works relate to the childhood memory or fantasy of a bird opening his lips with its tail (an image of both suckling and passive oral intercourse; the enigmatic smile of the *Mona Lisa* is read as an emblem of the satisfaction obtained from both activities). Freud claims to rediscover that motif in Leonardo's most famous paintings. Freud was extremely fond of his "analytic novel," but it is fatally flawed by reliance upon inaccurate material. Freud believed he was writing about a vulture – a bird with rich mythological connotations relating to the maternal image – but was using a faulty translation. Leonardo's bird was in fact a banal kite, a bird quite devoid of mythological importance.

Marie Bonaparte's study of the life and work of Edgar Allan Poe is a good example of analytic psychobiography (Bonaparte, 1933). The *Tales*, which are grouped by Bonaparte into "cycles" centered upon maternal and paternal figures, are seen as providing an equivalent to the MANIFEST CONTENT of a dream; analytic interpretation of them can supply the LATENT CONTENT. The latent content is then related back to the known biographical data to produce an exercise in psychobiography. Thus "The purloined letter" is read in terms of

the author's identification with the Minister, representing a hated but feared father and illustrating the author's nostalgia for a maternal phallus. The result is a characteristic combination of an investigation of the individual artist's psyche and a search for supposed universals. A certain circularity is inevitable as biographical details are pressed into service to confirm the analytic interpretation. In a much briefer study, Hanna Segal (1952, p. 190) interprets the whole of *A la Recherche du temps perdu* as a product of Proust's acute awareness that "all creation is really a re-creation of a once loved and once whole, but now lost and ruined world and self," and concludes that the wish to create is rooted in the depressive position and the wish to make reparation to the ruined object.

A much more sophisticated version of psychobiography is provided by Charles Mauron's "psychocriticism" (1954; a good English-language account is given in Bersani, 1984), which is influenced by both Freudian and KLEINian models. Racine's plays and career are interpreted in terms of maternal and paternal imagos. Thus, the Oedipal love object of the theater is a counterbalance to the cruel mother of Jansenism and its austere mysticism. Racine eventually renounces the stage, and the Jansenist mother figure is victorious over the weak king figure with whom the playwright attempts to identify. Racine's theater is ultimately a failed attempt to make the transition from an obsessional relation with the mother to a classic Oedipal pattern. Although Mauron does rely upon a psychobiographical framework, his ability to combine an exemplary close reading of Racine and analytic insight allows him to avoid the more crudely reductive aspects of the genre, and to reveal patterns of desire that provide an effective basis for a formal textual organization. Critic and playwright are particularly well matched in that the very formal and repetitive nature of Racinian tragedy lends itself well to a search for a restricted number of SYMBOLS, while the classical concentration on the passions is eminently amenable to an analysis of the fluctuations of desire.

Other variants on classical psychoanalytic criticism adopt a slightly different approach and successfully exploit other areas of Freud's *oeuvre*. The French critic Marthe Robert (1972) skillfully mines the short paper on "Family romance" (Freud, 1909) to produce a broad narrative typology and even an account of the desire to write fiction. Freud uses "family romance" to refer to the Oedipal fantasies in which children construct a different relationship with their parents, imagining that they are the offspring, not of their real father and mother, but of kings and queens, or warding off sibling rivalry with fantasies that their brothers and sisters are illegitimate. Robert applies this fantasy structure to *Robinson Crusoe* and *Don Quixote*, viewed as prototypical novels, and constructs a typology of bastard and foundling, of fictional structures based respectively on the self-creation of the hero and the omnipotence of wishes. A very different typology, but one which again relates Oedipal structures to literary structures, is supplied by Harold BLOOM's thesis about poetry and the anxiety of influence (Bloom, 1984). The anxiety of influence is seen as an equivalent to the experience of the UNCANNY; the young poet comes to recognize in his work the influence of precursors with whom he must wrestle in order to emerge as a "strong poet" capable of absorbing and creating his precursors without dying as a poet. Tradition is likened to the repressed material in the psychic life of individuals, and relations between poetic generations as a form of TRANSFERENCE. Bloom's Freud is a very literary figure, cast in the role of a strong poet.

Given the emphasis of psychoanalysis on the importance of childhood memories and experiences, which are obviously relevant to both Robert and Bloom, it is strange that so little analytic writing is devoted to children's literature, though this may simply reflect the traditional neglect of the genre. A signal exception is Bettelheim's classic reading (1976) of fairy tales as depicting stages of development and metaphors for unconscious conflicts, and illustrating strategies for negotiating problems like aggression, sexuality, and death. More recently, the object-relations approach adopted by Margaret and Michael Rustin (1987) has resulted in an attractive study of the construction of fantasies and internal objects in children's literature which successfully combines analytic and sociologial insights.

While traditional psychoanalytic criticism continues to be written, it is often held in poor regard by critics influenced by the general trends within modern literary theory and by the broad movement from FORMALISM to STRUCTURALISM and POST-STRUCTURALISM. The DEATH OF THE AUTHOR, as proclaimed by BARTHES and FOUCAULT, has undercut the support for traditional psychobiography (though it is important to note that Bloom's schema

requires the revival of the author) and few professional critics would now adopt Bonaparte's "life and works" approach. Increasingly the emphasis is placed upon the text, its operations and its productivity, rather than on the author, while characterological studies have been largely eclipsed.

The interdisciplinarity of modern literary studies makes it increasingly difficult to speak of psychoanalytic criticism as such. Psychoanalysis is now part of a wide tissue of INTERTEXTUALITY, taking in DERRIDA's DECONSTRUCTIONist dialogs with Freud, mingling with strands of FEMINIST CRITICISM and the work of theorists like KRISTEVA, and merging, in the work of MACHEREY, with ALTHUSSER's MARXISM to generate symptomatic readings of the silences of literary texts which attempt to uncover an ideological UNCONSCIOUS.

Recent psychoanalytic criticism tends to be influenced primarily by LACAN and to stem originally from French sources. A major stage in the introduction of these developments into the Anglo-American sphere was the appearance of the important issue of *Yale French Studies* (no. 55–56, 1977), edited by FELMAN and devoted to "Literature and psychoanalysis. The question of reading: otherwise." Lacan himself remains surprisingly close to traditional psychoanalytic views and often simply appropriates literary texts for the defense and illustration of psychoanalytic theory. *Hamlet*, for instance, is seen by Lacan as illustrating "a decadent form of the Oedipus situation, its decline" (1959, p. 45), while Poe's "Purloined letter," which has become a *locus classicus* for Lacanian literary theory, is read as an allegory of the workings of letter and signifier.

Lacan has, however, undoubtedly been the major influence in the emergence of a new psychoanalytic approach to the literary domain, thanks largely to his foregrounding of the cultural and symbolic function of language, his hints at a poetics of a linguistically structured unconscious which is as adept at rhetoric as any poet. The stress on reading in the proposed "return to Freud" also has an obvious appeal to those trained in the literary traditions of close reading and HERMENEUTICS. One of the less happy aspects of the critical appropriation of Lacan has been the emergence of an almost purely literary version of psychoanalysis which is increasingly divorced from the clinically based work of practicing analysts. There is also a tendency to reduce the history of psychoanalysis to the work of Freud and Lacan, and to ignore the broader tradition.

Freud's psychoanalysis has also become part of literary DISCOURSE. Felman reads his work on transference in parallel with the fiction of Henry James, while CIXOUS (1976) literally stages psychoanalysis in an emotionally powerful dramatization of the Dora case (Freud, 1905), which is in part a feminist interrogation of psychoanalysis. The effects of this breaking down of genre boundaries can also be seen at the level of critical discourse. Increasingly, the emphasis is placed upon "theoretical fictions" as very broad definitions of textuality and discourse tend to eliminate almost all reference to the extratextual or social dimension. Sarah Kofman, who is heavily influenced by Derrida's deconstuctionism, detects a parallel between Freud's analytic constructs and the delusions of his patients, and strongly endorses Freud's self-deprecating description of his science as being no more than a provisional construct which is equivalent to a mythology or fiction (Kofman, 1974). Bowie reaches similar conclusions in his fine study of Freud, Proust, and Lacan, arguing that the demolition of the "increasingly dilapidated partition between 'theory' and 'fiction'" has created "a wide terrain of near-synonymy between the two terms" (Bowie, 1987, p. 5). The blurring of the fiction-theory partition does spare the critic the problem of how to address the more embarrassing aspects of Freud's speculative forays into anthropology, and the confusions of the Leonardo essay become distinctly less thorny if it can be read as personal mythology. It is, on the other hand, difficult to reconcile such readings with Freud's more positivist and even scientistic statements and ambitions. And if it can legitimately be claimed that Proust, Freud, and Lacan are "portraitists of the mental life" (Bowie, 1987, p. 7), it might also be argued that reports of the demise of the author and psychological criticism have been greatly exaggerated.

Reading

Bersani, Leo 1984: *A Future for Astyanax: Character and Desire in Literature.*

Bettelheim, Bruno 1976: *The Uses of Enchantment.*

Bloom, Harold 1984: *The Anxiety of Influence: A Theory of Poetry.*

Bonaparte, Marie 1933: *The Life and Work of Edgar Allan Poe.*

Bowie, Malcolm 1987: *Freud, Proust and Lacan: Theory as Fiction.*

Cixous, Hélène 1976b: *Portrait of Dora.*

Freud, Sigmund 1905b: "Fragment of an analysis of a case of hysteria."

——— 1907: "Delusions and dreams in Jensen's *Gradiva.*"

——— 1908b: "Creative writers and day-dreaming."

——— 1910c: *Leonardo da Vinci and a Memory of His Childhood.*

——— 1913: "The claims of psychoanalysis to scientific interest."

——— 1914a: "The Moses of Michelangelo."

——— 1914b: "On the history of the psychoanalytic movement."

——— 1919: "The uncanny."

——— 1923c: "Two encyclopedia articles."

——— 1927: "Dostoievsky and parricide."

Kofman, Sarah 1974: *Freud and Fiction.*

Lacan, Jacques 1959: "Desire and the interpretation of desire in *Hamlet.*"

——— 1965: "Hommage fait à Marguerite Duras, du Ravissement de Lol V. Stein."

Mauron, Charles 1954: *L'Inconscient dans la vie et l'oeuvre de Racine.*

Rustin, Margaret and Michael 1987: *Narratives of Love and Loss.*

Segal, Hanna 1952: "A psychoanalytic approach to aesthetics."

Wright, Elizabeth 1984: *Psychoanalytic Criticism: Theory in Practice.*

DAVID MACEY

punk A term used since the late 1960s to describe, first, a form of pop music and, later, its associated youth SUBCULTURE. As a musical description, punk was originally deployed by American writers to describe a form of rough, aggressive, teenage rock and roll. The term (which derived from criminal street slang) described a sound (harsh, guitar-drive), an attitude ("get out of my way!"), and a form of production (cheap, do-it-yourself). When British musicians began to make a similar sort of music in the mid-1970s (often directly influenced by American bands) journalists gave them the same label. In Britain, though, punk took on other connotations (see Savage, 1992). Punk groups like the Sex Pistols and the Clash were more self-conscious about their shock effect, and more aware of the cultural power of visual images. And it was these – spiky, dyed hair; rips and tears and safety pins; "forbidden" signs of sex and power and fascism; a deliberate ugliness (see Hebdige, 1979) – that were adopted by working-class youths across Britain, thus inspiring both local music-making scenes and a national punk subculture which became a mocking commentary on the Queen's Silver Jubilee. The punk look may have ended up as a tourist attraction, the punk sound just another style export, but the punk attitude continues to be an important, anarchical strand of popular music culture.

Reading
Hebdige, Dick 1979: *Subculture: The Meaning of Style.*
Savage, Jon 1992: *England's Dreaming.*

SIMON FRITH

Putnam, Hilary (1926–) American philosopher. Putnam has held positions at Princeton, Massachusetts Institute of Technology (MIT), and Harvard, and has made important contributions in various areas of metaphysics and epistemology, including the philosophies of mind, logic, and language. A central concern of Putnam's earlier work was the theory of reference. He rejected verificationist accounts, according to which the meaning of a sentence can be completely given by a statement of its verification conditions (see LOGICAL. POSITIVISM). According to the rejected view, any shift in our theoretical PARADIGM dramatic enough to change such verification criteria would effectively change the meanings of the relevant theoretical terms. Putnam observes that the reference of theoretical terms can remain constant even across fundamental changes in our theories about objects: the developments in chemistry which revealed that water is H_2O did not change the *meaning* of "water," but rather our *beliefs* about the microstructure of water (see "The meaning of 'meaning,'" in Putnam, 1975, vol. 2). He therefore proposes that the references of theoretical terms are partly determined by the *objects* (for example, water) which play a causal role in the phenomena described by the theory. Since independent objects help to fix the content of our beliefs, this causal theory of reference committed Putnam to a strong version of realism.

Since 1976, however, Putnam has been best known for his rejection of "metaphysical realism," in favor of his alternative, "internal realism" (see Putnam, 1981; 1987; and 1990). Metaphysical realism holds that the world is made up of a fixed totality of determinate, theory-independent objects, and that there is a single true description of that world, whether we can discover it or not. A theory is true only if it corresponds to the way theory-independent objects really are. The standard to which metaphysical realism holds our theorizing, then, is that of a God's-Eye View of the world. Putnam argues that this standard is ultimately incoherent.

The fundamental insight which reveals this incoherence is what Putnam calls the "phenomenon of . . . conceptual relativity" (Putnam, 1990, p. x). Theories do not simply reflect theory-independent facts, but conceptualize those facts. Such conceptualizations are conventional and relativistic in the sense that we can equally well use different schemes to understand the world. Putnam argues both that this element of convention is ineliminable from our theories, and also that there is no way to draw a clear line between the conventional and factual contributions to knowledge. Since any description of the world is already infected with convention, we are left with no way to characterize the world as it is "in itself," or to give any clear sense to the metaphysical realist ideal of a God's-Eye View on an independent world.

Conceptual relativity does not imply relativism, however. From the fact that different conceptual schemes can be used to interpret the world, it does not follow that every scheme is as good as any other. Putnam points out that any argument for such wholesale relativism is self-refuting. To insist that relativism might still be *true*, even though unwarranted, is just to make an assertion about how things "really" are, and thus to assume the God's-Eye perspective Putnam rejects as incoherent.

Putnam replaces the metaphysical realist appeal to an "external," God's-Eye perspective with his "internal" realism, which insists that our notions of truth and rationality are deeply interconnected. We understand truth not in terms of correspondence to completely theory-independent objects, but rather in terms of a theory's satisfaction of the epistemological standards internal to our theoretical practices. Conversely, our conception of rationality is bound up with truth, since rational standards bring us into theoretical projects which attempt to "get things right." For Putnam, a statement is true if it can be warranted by knowers with more or less our cognitive powers and standards, given that epistemic conditions were good enough. This account must be qualified because our cognitive standards evolve over time, but this HISTORICITY does not mean that different cognitive standards are all equally good (or bad). Such norms are subject to *reform*, in the sense that the future growth of knowledge (guided by those very norms) may lead us to see their limitations, and to revise them so as to lead to theories with better "fit" to our overall experience and background beliefs.

Despite appearances, this internal realism is not completely unrelated to Putnam's earlier realism (see Ebbs, 1992 for a stronger version of this idea). His early causal theory also insisted on an interconnection between reference to objects and our theoretical beliefs. Thus, even in his early period Putnam did not conceive of objects in absolute independence from what our theories have to say about them. From this point of view, Putnam's move to internal realism can be seen as an attempt to reform and clarify his initial realist intuitions, thereby saving what was coherent about them from the Scylla of metaphysical realism and the Charybdis of relativism. *See also* LANGUAGE, PHILOSOPHY OF.

Reading
Putnam, Hilary 1975 (*1979*): *Philosophical Papers.*
——1981: *Reason, Truth, and History.*
——1983a: *Philosophical Papers.* Vol. 3, *Realism and Reason.*
——1987: *The Many Faces of Realism.*
——1990: *Realism with a Human Face.*
Rorty, Richard 1993: "Putnam and the relativist menace."
Philosophical Topics, 20, 1992: "The philosophy of Hilary Putnam."

R. LANIER ANDERSON

Q

Quine, Willard van Orman (1908–) American philosopher. Quine spent his career at Harvard, beginning in the 1930s. His works include important contributions in logic, PHILOSOPHY OF LANGUAGE, metaphysics, and epistemology, and are widely known for the controversial doctrines of indeterminacy of translation, inscrutability of reference, and ontological relativity. These three positions are deeply related to one another, and to Quine's rejection of the analytic/synthetic distinction.

Quine argued against Rudolf Carnap's project of rational reconstruction of science, which strove to separate genuine disagreements from pseudo-problems by giving a rigorous characterization of the rules of evidence assumed by investigators. According to Carnap, various linguistic frameworks might serve for the formulation of genuine questions, but each must have specific rules determining how such questions could be resolved by evidence (see Ricketts, 1982). This picture of rationality essentially distinguishes between analytic and synthetic truths. Analytic truths are established by the assumption of the framework, and are thus revisable only in response to the considerations of convenience proper to framework choice. Synthetic truths respond to empirical evidence.

Quine argues that this analytic/synthetic distinction is unsustainable. Carnap's simple stipulation of analytic sentences does nothing to elucidate the *general* notion of analyticity, because it defines analyticity only for one framework. Moreover, such stipulation presupposes the idea of linguistic frameworks which the appeal to analyticity was supposed to clarify. Quine also insists that purported analytic truths are not fundamentally distinct from synthetic claims when it comes to theory revision. Since empirical theories are underdetermined by their evidence, we always have various options for revising a disconfirmed theory. In particular, we could maintain some favorite (synthetic) theory in the face of recalcitrant evidence by forfeiting some of the "analytic" sentences (logic, rules of evidence, etc.) through which the theory implies the unwanted empirical consequence.

The notion of analyticity might also be defended by appeal to a clear notion of meaning. A sentence would be analytic if it were true simply by virtue of the meanings of its words. Quine, however, finds meaning itself indeterminate. He formulates these worries through the thought experiment of radical translation, the project of producing a translation manual for a language hitherto completely isolated from our own. A successful manual would correlate native expressions with English expressions of the same meaning, and the mutual isolation of the two languages guarantees that any resulting clarification of the notion of meaning will be independent of antecedent assumptions. Unfortunately, Quine argues, a field linguist could adopt any number of substantially different translation manuals, each consistent with all native speech dispositions. Some sentences, of course, are closely tied to sensory stimulations. Thus, the linguist may find that natives assent to the sentence "Gavagai" in the presence of rabbits, and dissent from it in their absence. She might then translate "Gavagai" by "Lo, a rabbit." Most sentences, however, are standing sentences, for which patterns of assent and dissent do not change on the basis of stimulation (for example, "There have been black cats"). The linguist translates such sentences through "analytical hypotheses" about the appropriate translations for the parts (words) of sentences like "Gavagai" (see Quine 1960, pp. 68–72). She supposes, for example, that "gavagai" means "rabbit," and uses this conjecture to translate standing sentences containing that word. Ultimately, she constructs her own native sentences to test native reaction to her emerging translation manual.

According to Quine, these analytical hypotheses are plagued by indeterminacy. Rabbits are present when and only when undetached collections of rabbit parts and temporal stages of rabbits are. These other phrases thus seem equally good as translations of "gavagai." If we could ask questions about, for example, whether this "gavagai" is the same as that, then we might resolve this indeterminacy; but in radical translation, any rendering of some native expression as "same as" is itself in question. The same native expression might be translated by "This is the *same* rabbit *as* that," or by "This undetached rabbit part *belongs with* that." Different syntactic STRUCTURES are reciprocally related, so that changes in the translations of one kind of word can be offset by adjustments in the translations of another, preserving all native speech dispositions. Incompatible translation manuals therefore produce equally good renderings of the native language. In fact, we learn our own language through these same empirical methods, and given that we all speak the *same* language, any facts about that language must be publicly accessible by such means. Since these methods do not suffice to determine a translation manual, translation is indeterminate: there is no fact of the matter about the meanings of standing sentences.

Similar considerations support the doctrines of inscrutability of reference and ontological relativity. Not only is the meaning of sentences including the word "gavagai" indeterminate, but also the reference of the term itself eludes specification. If there were a fixed interpretation for the logical particles concerned with the individuation of objects, then we could precisely specify which objects our terms refer to. But there is no such privileged interpretation of our logical vocabulary. Therefore, any theory can be reinterpreted so as to change its basic ontology, given corresponding adjustments in the theory's "apparatus of individuation" (Quine, 1969, p. 39). Under such a transformation, there will still be a difference between rabbits and undetached rabbit parts. This, however, shows only that the logical syntax of the theory generates two different "nodes" (Quine, 1992, p. 31) to which we can assign objects. Absent any fixed interpretation of the apparatus of individuation, we can assign rabbits and their undetached parts to either node indiscriminately. Thus, no terms have an absolute reference, and fundamental ontology itself is relative to our choice of a translation manual.

It may now seem that Quine has not departed from Carnap after all. Just as the commitments of Carnap's investigator were understood relative to a choice of linguistic framework, so a Quinean's ontology is fixed relative to a choice of translation manual. This appearance is deceptive, however. Quine insists that it makes no sense to think of investigators standing back from their language and theory to make a choice among alternative frameworks or ontologies. We are always already within our language/theory, and our investigations make sense only as understood from this internal point of view. Epistemology itself must therefore become natural science (see Quine, 1969, pp. 69–90). *See also* EMPIRICISM; LOGICAL POSITIVISM.

Reading

Barrett, R., and Gibson, R., eds 1990: *Perspectives on Quine.*
Davidson, D., and Hintikka, J., eds 1969: *Words and Objections.*
Hylton, Peter 1982: "Analyticity and the indeterminacy of translation."
Quine, W.V.O. 1953b (*1980*): *From a Logical Point of View.*
——— 1960: *Word and Object.*
——— 1969: *Ontological Relativity and Other Essays.*
Ricketts, Thomas G. 1982: "Translation, rationality, and epistemology naturalized."
Solomon, Miriam 1989: "Quine's point of view."

R. LANIER ANDERSON

R

race and racism   In *Racial Theories* (1987) Michael Banton has summarized theories about "race" as they have been formulated in Europe and North America during the nineteenth and twentieth centuries: "Perhaps the central question which people have asked," he suggests, "is: why are they not like us?" The knowledge of those described as "they" may have been a group of whom the questioners had limited or inaccurate knowledge, with the question becoming more meaningful as the questioners began to think of the world as composed of a number of different groups of which they themselves were one. The first comprehensive answer conceptualized "race" as lineage: if they were not like us, it was because they belonged to a species which had acquired special characteristics owing to either divine intervention or its distinctive environmental experience. As Banton points out, this answer is flawed since it does not adequately explain how environment affected the transmission of inherited characteristics (1987, pp. 167–8). A second answer was that people were different because from time immemorial they constituted different racial types. The weakness of this explanation was that it failed to account for evolution. The third answer suggested that people were different because genetic variability, mutation, genetic drift, or natural selection created subspecies which in time became separate species. As Banton argues, although this offered a satisfactory explanation of physical differentiation, it could not account for cultural differentiation (1987, p. 168). For an understanding of such differentiation, economic, ideological, and historical factors need to be considered. Similarly, these factors help explain the ways in which "differences" are theorized along racial lines.

"Race," therefore, as a concept is problematic. Robert Miles cogently argues against the notion that there exist distinct "races." He suggests three reasons for this. First, the extent of genetic variation within any population is usually greater than the average difference between populations. Second, while the frequency of occurrence of possible forms taken by genes does vary from one "race" to another, any particular genetic combination can be found in almost any "race." Third, owing to interbreeding and large-scale migrations, the distinctions between "races" identified as dominant gene frequencies are often blurred (Miles, 1982, p. 16). It is for these reasons that the term "race" appears in quotation marks throughout this entry.

If "race" is an imagined concept, racism most certainly is not. Miles has provided the best definition of racism to date, but it requires some modification and critical appraisal. Miles argues that racism presumes a process of racialization whereby social relations between people are structured by the signification of human biological and/or cultural characteristics in such a way as to define and construct differentiated social collectivities. Distinguishing biology from culture is important. In certain instances, biological racism may be more predominant than cultural racism (e.g. the nineteenth-century notion of "scientific racism," which classified black Africans, for example, as a distinct and inferior stock or species); in others, cultural racism may be pre-eminent (e.g. situations where people are thought "odd" or "peculiar," and therefore threatening, because of their cultural practices).

Sometimes, there may be a matrix of biological and cultural racism. Take, for example, the racist term "Paki," in common use in Britain. Relatively unrelated to Pakistan, it has become a generic term for anyone who is perceived to be from a specific alien stock *and/or* is believed to engage in certain alien cultural practices, based, for example, around religion, dress or food.

Racism, Miles continues, entails a view of social groups as having a "natural," unchanging origin and status and as being inherently different and possessing negatively evaluated characteristics and/or inducing negative consequences for other collectivities (Miles, 1989, pp. 75 and 79). As far as "evaluated characteristics" are concerned, while I agree that this definition encompasses certain forms of racism, I believe, following Smina Akhtar (personal correspondence), that it precludes other forms. For example, "negatively evaluated characteristics" include such instances of racist DISCOURSE as "black children are not as clever as white children," but exclude such seemingly positive statements as "black children are good at sports" (Akhtar's examples). Tony Woodiwiss has argued that all stereotypes are negative, while Miles has stated that he has few difficulties in considering the latter statement as an incidence of racist discourse (personal correspondence); however, such a statement can be and often is, irrespective of intention, "seemingly positive" and can be temporarily enhancing. In the long run all stereotypes tend to be negative and ultimately damaging. While "black children are good at sports" is "seemingly positive" and can lead to individual and/or short-term group enhancement (an unmerited place in the school football team for the individual or enhanced status for the group as a whole in an environment where prowess at sport is highly regarded?), it is potentially racist and likely to have racist consequences. This is because, like most stereotypes, it is distorted and misleading and typically appears as part of a discourse which works to justify black children's exclusion from academic activities. Distinguishing between "seemingly positive" and "ultimately damaging" discourse is important. People of Asian origin tend to be stereotyped as having a "strong culture," an attribute which is used to pathologize people of African Caribbean origin, who are in turn stereotyped as having a weak CULTURE or as having no culture at all. While this may serve to enhance the status of the former at the expense of the latter, in the context of racist discourse it can result in accusations that the former are failing to integrate or are "taking over," which can lead to violence and other forms of hostility. Similarly, Jewish people are sometimes characterized as being an intelligent and/or a superior "race," a seemingly positive description but one which can also lead to allegations that they are part of a conspiracy to take over the world, a notion which was in part responsible for the holocaust.

Miles argues that the term "racism" should be used to refer exclusively to an ideological phenomenon and not to accompanying practices. One reason that he gives for this is that exclusionary practice can result from both intentional and unintentional actions (1989, p. 78); thus the given example, "black children are good at sport" could be unintentionally racist. However, the fact that racist discourse is unintentional does not detract from its capacity

to embody racism. For its recipients, effect is far more important than intention. Miles gives two other reasons for separating IDEOLOGY from exclusionary practices. First, such practices do not presuppose the nature of the determination; for example, the disadvantaged postion of black people is not necessarily the result of racism. Second, there is a dialectical relationship between exclusion and inclusion. To exclude is simultaneously to include and vice versa, for example, overrepresentation of the children of African Caribbean parents in "special schools" for the educationally subnormal (ESN) in the 1960s resulted from both exclusion from "normal schools" and inclusion in the ESN schools. I do not see the purpose of this attempt at exclusivity. The fact that the "disadvantaged position of black people is not necessarily the result of racism" is addressed by Miles's own theoretical approach, that is, a class-based analysis which also recognizes other bases of unequal treatment. Therefore this recognition does not warrant the attention that Miles affords it. Second, the simultaneous inclusion of black people entailed by exclusion is by and large a negative inclusion, as in Miles's own example of ESN schools.

In an attempt to formulate a definition of racism, I will borrow from Miles's definition of ideology, as "any discourse which, as a whole (but not necessarily in terms of all its component parts) represents human beings, and the social relations between human beings, in a distorted and misleading manner" (p. 42), combining this definition with my modification of Miles's description of racism to include "seemingly positively evaluated characteristics" (Akhtar's suggestion).

Racism is thus reformulated as entailing a process of racialization whereby social relations between people are structured by the signification of human biological and/or cultural characteristics in such a way as to define and construct differentiated social collectivities. Such groups are assumed to have a natural, unchanging origin and status. They are seen as being inherently different and causing negative consequences for other groups and/or as possessing certain *evaluated* characteristics. Since these evaluated characteristics are stereotypes, they are likely to be distorted and misleading. If they are at first seemingly positive rather than negative, they are likely to be ultimately negative.

I would agree with Miles that, notwithstanding the fact that ideologies are inserted in practices (Althusser, 1971, p. 156), it is possible to make an *analytical* distinction between ideologies and practices and that there is no logical correlation between cognition and action (Miles, 1989, p. 77). However, the distinction is of limited use, both analytically and politically, because it is only when ideologies are expressed and/or actioned that there is any need to attend to them or indeed to worry about them.

The above discussion of racism has of necessity been somewhat abstract. In order to *understand* the phenomenon, it needs to be situated economically, ideologically, historically and geographically. It takes different forms at different historical conjunctures and is justified in different ways according to prevailing circumstances. Notwithstanding the fact that there are features common to all forms of racism, there is in fact a variety of racisms (Miles, 1989, pp. 64–5; see also Hall, 1980, p. 337; and Gilroy, 1982, p. 281). Thus the above definition of racism needs to be context-specific.

"Race" and Racism in British History   The formalization of the concept "race" in the English language can be traced back to 1508 (*Oxford English Dictionary*), when it began to take on a specifically economic connotation with the burgeoning development of the slave trade (Williams, 1964). For most of that century, however, it was used to refer to a class or category of persons or things; there was no implication that these classes or categories were biologically distinct. During the seventeenth century a historical dimension was added, and some English men, interested in their historical origins, developed the view that they were descendants of a German "race" and that the Norman invasion of the eleventh century had led to the domination of the Saxons by an "alien race." This interpretation of history gave rise to a conception of "race" in the sense of lineage back to the Saxons. Distinction, however, was based on separate history rather than biological differences. During the late eighteenth and nineteenth centuries, the term finally became associated with physical traits both within the boundaries of Europe and beyond (Miles, 1982, pp. 10–11), and, in the United States in particular, there were plenty of statements asserting the inferiority of black people (Banton, 1983, p. 45). By 1850, Banton suggests that the evidence indicates the probability that "a significant section of the English upper class subscribed to a rudimentary racial philosophy of history" (1977, p. 25).

By the end of the nineteenth century, the ideology of the "inferiority" of the colonial subjects and the consequent "superiority" of the British "race" was available to all. There were a number of reasons for this. First of all, important social and economic changes had occurred. Britain had been transformed into a predominantly urban, industrial nation (Lorimer, 1978, p. 107). The introduction of cheap popular fiction with imperial themes (Miles, 1982, pp. 110 and 119) was facilitated by the construction of a particular kind of reading public through state education (basic education as from the 1870 Education Act) and through technical developments (Williams, 1961, pp. 168–72; see also Richards, 1989). In addition, missionary work was seen as "civilizing the natives." In fact, a whole plethora of imperial themes permeated POPULAR CULTURE in the late Victorian era (Cole, 1992a, pp. 36–42).

While the "inferiority" of Britain's imperial subjects was perceived secondhand, the indigenous racism of the period was anti-semitic. From the 1880s there was a sizable immigration of destitute Jewish people from the Russian progroms, and this fueled the preoccupation of politicians and commentators about the health of the nation, the accompanying fear of the degeneration of "the race," and the subsequent threat to imperial and economic HEGEMONY. In 1905 the Liberal government passed the Aliens Act which forbade further Jewish immigration. The Act did not exclude "Jews" by name – just as modern legislation does not refer specifically to Asian, black, and other minority ethnic people (Cole, 1993). Anti-semitism directed at the Jewish "race" was not merely the province of the ruling elite. Ten years earlier (1895) the Trades Union Congress (TUC) had convened a special conference at which it compiled a list of questions to be asked of all Members of Parliament. These questions were described as a "labour program" and included demands for the nationalization of land, minerals, and the means of production; old age pensions; adequate health and safety facilities; the abolition of the House of Lords; workers' industrial injury compensation; the eight-hour day; the reform of the Poor Law system; and the restriction of Jewish immigration (Cohen, 1985, pp. 75–6). Robert Blatchford, a founding member and representative of the Manchester and Salford Independent Labour Party (ILP) and one of the leading socialist journalists of his generation, queried the "racial results likely to follow on the infusion of so much alien blood into the British stock" (Howell, 1983). As Cohen argues, "it was a common theme amongst many socialists that England was eugenically doomed if it carried on sending its own citizens to the colonies while receiving Jews from Europe" (Cohen, 1985, p. 80). Having said this, it is important to note that anti-semitism was not based merely on the stereotype of the poor Jew – a member of the lower social orders – threatening to pollute the racial purity of the British "race," but also on the ideology of the "Jewish-capitalist conspiracy" and attempts at world domination (Cole, 1992a, part 1).

Following the 1914–18 war, it was emigration rather than immigration which dominated the agenda (Branson, 1975; Mowat, 1968; Stevenson, 1984). However, this did not prevent the state from renewing anti-alien legislation throughout the 1920s. By the 1930s the focus had shifted to a concern about falling birth rates, in the light of both worries about "race" preservation and the efforts of dictators in Italy and Germany to increase birth rates in those countries (Mowat, 1968, pp. 517–18).

It is within the context of these historical antecedents that the Beveridge Report of 1942, one of the key documents informing the founding of the welfare state, was written. Here are the links between welfare and "race", and indeed GENDER and nation. For example, the argument in favor of child allowances was: "with its present rate of reproduction the British race cannot continue, means of reversing the recent course of the birth rate must be found" (paragraph 413). Women were assigned the role of baby-machines in the service of capitalism and British culture and were told: "In the next thirty years housewives as Mothers have vital work to do in ensuring the adequate continuance of the British Race and British Ideals in the world" (paragraph 117).

The clearest example of Beveridge's own deep chauvinism can be seen in his essay "Children's allowances and the Race." In it he stated:

> Pride of race is a reality for the British as for other peoples . . . as in Britain today we look back with pride and gratitude to our ancestors, look back as a nation or as individuals two hundred years and more to the generations illuminated by Marlborough or Cromwell or Drake, are we not bound also to look forward, to plan society now so that there may be no lack of men or women of the quality of those earlier days, of the best of our breed, two hundred and three hundred years hence? (Cohen, 1985, pp. 88–9)

The modern era   The response to large-scale immigration of Asian, black, and other minority ethnic people in the postwar period after 1945 is dealt with extensively in historical and sociological literature. Briefly, this has been a history of increasing numerical exclusion as the need for migrant labor subsided, along with attempts at assimilation, integration, cultural pluralism, and assimilation again of those already here. All this has taken place within the context of problematizing Asian and black cultures (Cole, 1992a, b).

As far as party politics is concerned, the "race relations policy" of the Labour Party fluctuated considerably, varying from the relatively progressive manifesto of 1983, which proposed the need for an emergency program of action (which included the appointment of a senior minister to lead the offensive against racial disadvantage and a strengthened Race Relations Act) to that of 1987 which was more cautious (and tended to subsume the interests of Asian and black people under a notion of benefits to the "whole community") (Layton-Henry, 1992, pp. 162 and 169–70).

A constant political factor since 1962 has been the parties' defensive stance on immigration and their fear of the adverse electoral consequences of the immigration question. While both major parties supported controls, it was the Conservatives who tended to dictate immigration policy, aided and abetted by the media, in particular the tabloid press, which has formed and shaped public opinion in support of their policies. Thatcherism and its legacy have been of central importance. The ideology of "the free market" and nationalism, heralded by this new era of the "Radical Right," has served to promote the interests of capital, and, at the same time, to further marginalize and intensify the problematization of Asian, black, and other minority ethnic people (Cole, 1992a, chapter 6; 1992b). As soon as Mrs Thatcher became leader of the party, she decided that it should harden its attitude toward immigration, and at the 1975 annual conference, the Shadow Home Secretary, William Whitelaw, promised an end to "immigration as we have seen it in these postwar years" (ibid., p. 183). This contributed dramatically to the electoral demise of the National Front in the 1979 election and culminated in the Nationality Act of 1981. Thus immigration policy has been toughened up and the overall effect of the ascendancy of the "Radical Right" has entailed decidedly negative consequences for the Asian, black, and other minority ethnic communities of Britain.

Reading

Althusser, L. 1971: *Lenin and Philosophy and Other Essays.*

Balibar, E. 1991: "Racism and politics in Europe today."

Banton, M. 1977: *The Idea of Race.*

——1983: *Racial and Ethnic Competition.*

——1987: *Racial Theories.*

Cohen, S. 1985: "Anti-semitism, immigration controls and the welfare state."

Cole, M. 1992a: "Racism, history and educational policy: from the origins of the welfare state to the rise of the Radical Right."

——1992b: "British values, liberal values, or values of justice and equality."

——1993: "'Black and ethnic minority' or 'Asian, black and other minority ethnic': a further note on nomenclature."

Gilroy, P. 1982: "Steppin out of Babylon – race, class and autonomy."

Hall, S. 1980: "Race, articulation and societies structured in dominance."

Howell, D. 1983: *British Workers and the Independent Labour Party 1888–1906.*

Layton-Henry, Z. 1992: *The Politics of Immigration.*

Lorimer, Douglas A. 1978: *Colour, Class and the Victorians: English Attitudes to the Negro in the Mid-Nineteenth Century.*

Miles, R. 1989: *Racism.*

——1982: *Racism and Migrant Labour.*

Mowat, C.L. 1968: *Britain Between the Wars.*

Richards, J. 1989: *Imperialism and Juvenile Literature.*

Sewell, T. 1992: *Black Tribunes: Race and Representation in British Politics.*

Williams, E. 1964: *Capitalism and Slavery.*

Williams, R. 1961: *The Long Revolution.*

MIKE COLE

race–class–gender analysis A method of interpreting texts that attends to the complex intersection of race, class, and gender oppressions in the production of social structure and human subjectivity. The term "TEXT" here is broadly construed, including literary texts, popular cultural texts (televised narratives, for example), political DISCOURSES, social practices, and social structure itself. Race–class–gender analysis has multiple roots in three scholarly traditions: black, Marxist, and feminist inquiry. Each of these traditions, however, originally defined its problematic (its framework of ideas and concomitant problems) exclusively in terms of only one of the three components: black scholars tended to isolate RACE, Marxists isolated CLASS, and feminists isolated GENDER as the primary axis of socially constructed difference and oppression, and consequently as the primary category of inquiry and analysis. There were important precursors to race–class–gender analysis in the early 1970s, including prominently the socialist-

feminist critique of classical Marxist theory as inadequate to explain women's work, and subsequently the development of socialist-feminist theories to account for the relationship of gender and class (see Barrett, 1980). Also, Lillian Robinson's essays in feminist literary criticism, collected in *Sex, Class, and Culture* (1978), urge feminists to commit themselves to the problems of race and class. Properly speaking, however, race–class–gender analysis is the invention of women of color, their creative response to the fact that their experiences, histories, and cultural production (including the production of theory) have been excluded, ignored, effaced, marginalized, and trivialized everywhere in academia, as much by scholars proclaiming themselves to be radically subversive as by traditional conservators of the status quo. Race–class–gender analysis was developed by feminists of color in order to reinterpret their own lives and theorize their own standpoint (Collins, 1990).

In the early 1970s, black feminist theorists worked with notions of the "double" or "triple oppression" of black women, their subjection to both racist oppression as black people and patriarchal oppression as women. Racism and sexism combine, particularly through racial and sexual divisions and stratifications of labor, resulting in the assignment of most black women to the impoverished classes. Discourses of race efface sex, while discourses of sex efface race, either rendering women of color invisible or marking them as always somehow different, anomalous and therefore marginal. While constructing "women of color" as a distinct social entity and promoting the visibility of women of color in all spheres of social life, theories of double and triple oppression quickly proved inadequate, however, in part because they were analytically reductive and in part because of their undesirable political consequences. For one thing, they tended to reify destructive stereotypes, characterizing women of color as the ultimate victims, "sturdy black bridges" whose magnificent, astonishing achievement is that they survive at all (Chigwada, 1987). They also did little to resolve conflicts between black feminists and those multiple others who logically were and should practically have been their allies. The analytical separation of race, class, and gender oppressions neatly coincided with social practices of racism, sexism, and classism to produce oppositional movements that were dominated by identity politics, tended toward separatism, and inadequately addressed black women's needs. In disputes concerning which type of oppression could legitimately be considered primary and how to rank and order types of oppression into hierarchies – disputes which decided how movements set political agendas and distributed resources – black women were frequently cast as a desirable prize and pressured to "choose sides." The first anthology of black feminist writings published in the United States, Toni Cade (Bambara)'s *The Black Woman* (1970), attempted to rewrite the terms of these debates, expressing resentment of both the racism of white feminism and the sexism of black nationalism. Throughout the 1970s, black feminist theory was addressed to multiple audiences, including white women and black men, but increasingly became constructed as a transaction among women of color, an intellectual and political enterprise authored by and for themselves.

Although race–class–gender analysis had been implicit in the work of nineteenth-century black feminists such as Frances Harper and Anna Julia Cooper (work that was "lost" to several generations of twentieth-century cultural critics), the first explicit articulation of contemporary race–class–gender theory was the Combahee River Collective's manifesto, "A Black Feminist Statement" (1977):

> The most general statement of our politics at the present time would be that we are actively committed to struggling against racial, sexual, heterosexual, and class oppression and see as our particular task the development of integrated analysis and practice based upon the fact that the major systems of oppression are interlocking. The synthesis of these oppressions creates the conditions of our lives. As black women we see Black feminism as the logical political movement to combat the manifold and simultaneous oppressions that all women of color face.

The language of the collective's statement is revealing. Clearly, the emphasis is on oppression, the single most repeated word. Race, class, and gender are not merely categories for analysis, variables to be manipulated by the analyst, or "differences" that might either be described, subordinated to another variable, or set aside in order to generalize. Instead, race, class, and gender are the fundamental hierarchies which create oppressive social relations, relations of inequality in which the sub-

ordination of one group constitutes and is the necessary condition for the privilege of another. Forms of oppression are neither separable nor "additive," but "interlocking," "manifold and simultaneous." As Dill and Zinn (1990) explain, "they operate in complex and confounding ways" as each black woman "experiences the effects of these hierarchies and her location in them as a whole. She cannot divide her life into component parts and say which status has the greatest impact at any given moment." Rather than constructing a single, monolithic "black" or "female experience," commitment to race–class–gender analysis reveals the diversity and variety of black women's situations, locations, and positions in historically specific social formations. Race–class–gender analysis is firmly and finally committed to a transformative political agenda, to intervention in and transformation of the oppressive economic, political, and labor relations that exist among social groups. Analyses of CULTURE, especially of cultural representations, are only valuable to the extent that they inform practice, contributing concretely to political struggles against RACISM, sexism, heterosexism, and capitalism.

Race–class–gender analysis yields finely nuanced studies of history, culture, and IDEOLOGY that are particularly useful for rendering visible the agency of oppressed people. The work of Hazel Carby, who is associated with the Centre for Contemporary Cultural Studies in Birmingham, exemplifies the achievements of race–class–gender analysis by the late 1980s. In *Reconstructing Womanhood* (1987), Carby examines the disarticulation by late nineteenth-century Afro-American women of dominant sexual ideologies and their production of an alternate discourse in which black womanhood was rearticulated in liberatory terms. Carby's project necessarily entailed critique of both the androcentricity of constructions of nineteenth-century black American experience and the racism inherent in contemporary white feminist constructions of interracial "sisterhood," which Carby finds nonviable in light of the historical failure of white women to form progressive alliances with black women against racism (see also Carby, 1982). She concludes with an argument for a practice of CULTURAL STUDIES attentive to contradiction and discontinuity and critically aware of itself as a SIGNIFYING practice, itself a sign and site for the production of ideology. Other useful entries into this dynamic line of inquiry include Bryan, Dadzie, and Scafe's history of black experience in Great Britain, *The Heart of the Race* (1985), and Evelyn Glenn's history of three generations of Japanese-American women, *Issei, Nissei, War Bride* (1986).

Race–class–gender analysis is not a method restricted to the study of women of color, although the primary site for its production so far has been the black feminist movement. While race–class–gender analysis is marginalized in both the academy as a whole and even in WOMEN'S STUDIES (Dill and Zinn), it has important implications for every aspect of cultural studies. Not only black women but also everyone else is located in a social structure organized by race, class, and gender; everyone is categorized – empowered and/or disempowered – by these intersecting systems of privilege and inequality; and each and every significant social practice, whether material or discursive, has some relation, whether of opposition or complicity or both, to them.

See also FEMINIST CRITICISM; MARXISM; RACE AND RACISM; WOMEN'S STUDIES.

Reading
Bambara, Toni Cade 1970: *The Black Woman.*
Barrett, Michèle 1980: *Women's Oppression Today: Problems in Marxist Feminist Analysis.*
Bryan, B., Dadzie, S., and Scafe, S. 1985: *The Heart of the Race.*
Carby, Hazel 1982: "White women listen! Black feminism and the boundaries of sisterhood."
——— 1987: *Reconstructing Womanhood: The Emergence of the Afro-American Woman Novelist.*
Chigwada, W. 1987: "Not victims, not superwomen."
Collins, Patricia Hill 1990: *Black Feminist Thought.*
Combahee River Collective 1977 (*1982*): "A black feminist statement."
Dill, Bonnie Thornton, and Zinn, Maxine Bacca 1990: "Race and gender: revisioning social relations."
Glenn, Evelyn 1986: *Issei, Nissei, War Bride: Three Generations of Japanese American Women in Domestic Service.*
Robinson, Lillian S. 1978: *Sex, Class, and Culture.*

GLYNIS CARR

Ransom, John Crowe (1888–1974) American critic and poet. Ransom coined the term NEW CRITICISM (in *The New Criticism*, 1941) and was one of its chief formative influences, particularly in *The World's Body* (1938). It was Ransom more than anyone else who gave the movement its aggressively anti-scientific bias, arguing that science had increasingly reduced the world to abstractions and ART "must invest it again with body." His aim was

an "ontological" criticism which would explore the relationship between poetic language and "the dense, particular, individual world of objects." This resulted in his most influential critical concept, the distinction between a TEXT's "structure," its extractable rational argument, and its "texture," its presentation of the heterogeneous density of the natural world. The fullest embodiment of texture was metaphor, which, like all the New Critics, Ransom found represented in its highest form in metaphysical POETRY.

Reading
Fekete, John 1978: *The Critical Twilight.*
Magner, James 1971: *John Crowe Ransom: Critical Principles and Preoccupations.*
Wellek, René 1986g: "John Crowe Ransom."
Young, Thomas, ed. 1986: *John Crowe Ransom: Critical Essays and a Bibliography.*

IAIN WRIGHT

Raymond, Marcel (1897–) Swiss literary critic. Raymond, whose *From Baudelaire to Surrealism* (1933) inspired a group of phenomenological literary critics called the GENEVA SCHOOL, defined modern literature as the flowering of an anti-rationalist, anti-classical tradition that emphasized a quasi-mystical search for reality, the manipulation of poetic form to express new modes of vision, and an authorial consciousness fusing subjective and objective experience. The critic's task is to recognize and reproduce the workings of that consciousness.

See also POULET, GEORGES; RICHARD, JEAN-PIERRE.

Reading
Grotzer, Pierre, ed. 1979: *Albert Béguin et Marcel Raymond: Colloque de Cartigny sous la Direction de Georges Poulet, Jean Rousset, Jean Starobinski, Pierre Grotzer.*
Lawall, Sarah N. 1968a: "Marcel Raymond."
Miller, J. Hillis 1966 (*1991*): "The Geneva School."
Raymond, Marcel 1933 (*1961*): *From Baudelaire to Surrealism.*

SARAH N. LAWALL

reader, implied *See* IMPLIED READER

reader-response criticism Originating in the late 1960s (see Stanley FISH), reader-response criticism constitutes an attempt to overcome some of the limitations of the New Critical, formalist, and structuralist approaches to the study of literature by diverting the critic's attention from TEXT to reader. This shift coincided with, but happened independently of, a transition from the structuralist focus on studying the SIGN SYSTEMS underlying a literary text to a poststructuralist view of the text as a site for a seemingly endless proliferation and subversion of meanings.

Like POSTSTRUCTURALISM, reader-response criticism distrusts the notion of a reified, autonomous, and pregiven text that NEW CRITICISM, FORMALISM, and STRUCTURALISM propagated. As opposed to poststructuralism, however, reader-response criticism continues to think within the framework of a more traditional version of HERMENEUTICS: reader-response criticism assumes that all perception necessarily entails interpretation, and that therefore our relationship to a literary text is inevitably a hermeneutic construct (with its own blind spots).

In and by itself, reader-response criticism constitutes not a homogeneous but a highly diverse and controversial movement. Much of audience-oriented criticism would agree that what reading a literary text *does* is more important than what it *means*, although it will not agree on much else. The individual strands of audience-related criticism derive from disparate philosophical traditions, and they study different aspects of the reader–text relation.

The conventional approach to mapping the vast ground of audience-oriented criticism consists of asking the question: what reader? Reader-response criticism comprises a multitude of readers such as the mock reader, a role that the reader is invited to play for the duration of the reading (Walker Gibson); the narratee, the imagined person to whom the narrator addresses his DISCOURSE (Gerald Prince); the contemporary reader, that conglomerate of received ideas which forms the horizon of expectations against which a text is read – by accounting for how horizons of expectations and consequently readings change over time, the question of reading is brought into historical perspective (Hans Robert Jauss); the ideal reader, the perfectly insightful reader who commands an intricate system of internalized codes, conventions, and procedures – in other words, LITERARY COMPETENCE – and is therefore able to understand the writer's every move (Jonathan CULLER); the superreaders, a group of informants who, on the basis of crucial deviations of style and "ungrammaticalities" that form stumbling blocks in the reading, highlight the literariness of language (Michael Riffaterre); the informed reader who, by adopting certain shared assumptions about a literary text, becomes part of an INTERPRETIVE COMMUNITY (Stanley Fish); and, finally, the IMPLIED READER, a network of response-inviting structures in the text (Wolfgang ISER).

All these types of readers are mere philosophical propositions, theoretical generalizations, and should by no means be equated or confused with actual readers reading. They are heuristic constructs intended to generate a set of notions for understanding certain isolated aspects of the text–reader relation.

Moreover, most of these reader constructs are essentially deterministic entities: either the reader is dominated by the text, and an ideal reader is posited, or unrestricted power over the text is accorded to him or her, "and the text is reduced to an indeterminate Rorschach blot" (Kuenzli, 1980, p. 48). One possible way out of this predicament is opened up by Wolfgang Iser's theory of aesthetic response which centers on the interactions between text and reader: Iser holds that meaning resides nowhere but in the *convergence* of text and reader.

Most of the various reader-response theories have meanwhile been converted into methods for practical LITERARY CRITICISM. For this very reason, reader-response criticism posits a challenging alternative to the arid self-referentiality inherent in much of poststructuralist criticism. Moreover, reader-response criticism has supplied us with a new and original teaching angle (even if its pedagogical benefits, which were first explored by Louise M. Rosenblatt, have been curiously neglected by the profession at large). And yet reader-response criticism is still riddled with certain unsolved methodological dilemmas.

One of its major shortcomings consists of the fact that reader-response criticism, by evading the question of the individual reading SUBJECT, does not allow for a gendered reader: reading is seen as a hermeneutic act, and as such as trans-historical and gender-neutral. What is at stake here is the problem of how to account for the effects the structures in a literary text have on the activities in which an actual reader engages when processing a text. Attention will have to be called to the open-endedness of all our hermeneutic endeavors as well as the intricacies and contingencies of subject formation. What we need is a theory which comprises both these aspects of reading, and subsequently, a method that will enable us to analyze how the precarious mode of existence of a literary work on the one hand, and on the other, the vicissitudes of subject formation act upon one another during the individual reading.

Another problem inherent in the reader-oriented project consists of the fact that negotiating a literary text is conceived of as a cognitive, conscious, and fundamentally *rational* activity. Reading, however, contains yet another aspect. Side by side with the cognitive and basically rational level of reading there exists an unconscious, emotional, and maybe even irrational level of assimilation. Like the cognitive level, this second level originates with and is to some extent delimited by literary language, by the text. In other words, any literary text comprises rhetorical devices, layers, linguistic strategies, and points of view. These structures guide the hermeneutic and *conscious* acts of making sense of literature, as well as the *unconscious* acts of TRANSFERENCE AND COUNTERTRANSFERENCE that take place between text and reader.

What we need is a comprehensive theory of reading, one that will remain faithful to the actual experience of reading and that can still be converted into a method for analyzing readers and texts. Such a theory will have to allow for the open-endedness of subject formation, and it will have to take account of both levels of reading, the cognitive as well as the unconscious.

Reading

Cooper, C.R., ed. 1985: *Researching Response to Literature and the Teaching of Literature: Points of Departure.*
Culler, J. 1982a: "Reading as a woman." *On Deconstruction: Theory and Criticism after Structuralism.*
Fetterley, J. 1978: *The Resisting Reader: A Feminist Approach to American Fiction.*
Freund, E. 1987c: *The Return of the Reader: Reader-Response Criticism.*
Kuenzli, R.E. 1980: "The intersubjective structure of the reading process: a communication-oriented theory of literature."
Rosenblatt, L.M. 1978: *The Reader, the Text, the Poem: The Transactional Theory of the Literary Work.*
Seldon, R. 1985: "Reader-oriented theories."
Suleiman, S.R. 1980: "Introduction: varieties of audience-oriented criticism."
Tompkins, J. 1980: "An introduction to reader-response criticism."

EVELYNE KEITEL

readerly texts *See* WRITERLY AND READERLY TEXTS

reading, symptomatic *See* SYMPTOMATIC READING

real *See* IMAGINARY/SYMBOLIC/REAL

realism, classic *See* CLASSIC REALISM

realism, socialist *See* SOCIALIST REALISM

realization *See* ENACTMENT/REALIZATION

record industry The record industry is routinely ignored in media studies, but it has more claim than the cinema, press, or television to have changed the experience of everyday life. We now take it for granted that sounds are stored on tape or disc, that they are readily available, that they no longer need to be performed anew on each listening occasion. On the one hand, this means that music is no longer something special. We not only assume now that we can hear recorded sounds from any time and any place (a 1930s recording of Billie Holiday; sacred music from contemporary Thailand; the Sex Pistols' "classic" "Anarchy in the UK" but also that we can listen to these sounds at any time and in any place (the bathroom, the beach, working, shopping, driving). Music, in short, is no longer an *event*. On the other hand, this means that music, *our* music, is individually a commodity, and we are often therefore possessed by it: musical taste seems to express something emotionally real about ourselves that the enjoyment of other media does not.

Before Bell and Edison's experiments with the telephone and the phonograph at the end of the nineteenth century, to hear a disembodied voice was to hear voice of God (or of some other supernatural being), and it is easy to forget how the phonograph, as a street and fairground gimmick, helped accustom people to the magic of electricity, moving pictures, radio, and television. The record industry was at the forefront of many of the issues that have defined the making of twentieth-century mass culture: the transformation of domestic space into something both public and private; the complex collusion of manufacturers of hardware (the electrical and electronic goods industries) and the suppliers of software (the owners of musical rights and talents); the competitive dependency of the various media on each other (in the 1920s and 1930s, for example, the radio and record industries both competed with each other for people's leisure time and became entirely dependent on each other); and the shifting strategies of "cultural imperialism" (the pioneers of recording took their machinery across the world like missionaries, but sold their equipment by using local sounds; the revolutionary technology in spreading the same sounds around the globe – and the trade is not just from West to East or from North to South – was the portable cassette player, which, among other things, made piracy the central issue of the international record business). (For an account of the record industry as an industry, see Frith, 1981, part 2.)

The record industry has changed not just the way we listen to music also how we hear it – it has changed our understanding of what music can and should be. What differentiates recording from memory or musical score as a musical storage system is its ability to reproduce, every time, the details of a musical *performance*. Recording, in short, made possible the remarkable twentieth-century impact of Afro-American musics, and changing recording techniques further shifted musical expectations: electrical recording made possible new forms of musical "perfection." In the end, indeed, tape (and digital) recording freed our experience of "music" from any original happening at all (most "recorded" music today is actually assembled from sounds performed, often in a computer, at quite different times and in quite different places). We are left with a contradiction, an industry that sells us something – a "record" of a performance – that we all know did not exist. And this is as true of "classical" music (which has always been central to the record industry's production and sales policies) as it is of "pop."

Reading
Frith, Simon 1981: *Sound Effects*.

SIMON FRITH

reduction, phenomenological   *See* PHENO-MENOLOGICAL REDUCTION

Reich, Wilhelm (1899–1957) An Austro-American psychoanalyst and apostle of sexual freedom, Reich had the unique distinction of having been expelled from both the International Psychoanalytic Association and the German Communist Party.

Reich became a member of the Vienna Psychoanalytic Society in 1920 when he was still a medical student and rapidly established a reputation as an expert on technique. Reich was also one of the first generation of Freudian revisionists, replacing FREUD's definition of sexuality with a much narrower and more biological notion of "the genital" and arguing that all neuroses were accompanied by a disturbance of genitality and an absence of orgastic potency. In Reich's view, psychic health was dependent upon orgastic potency, or the capacity to experience sexual excitation in a natural act.

A rather less controversial innovation was the notion of character armor and character analysis (Reich, 1933). Originally a metaphor for the resistance of the ego, "character" was extended by Reich to refer to systematic defensive attitudes which appear to resist conventional analysis and interpretation, and which persist depite the content verbalized during treatment. In a character neurosis, defensive conflicts appear not in the form of identifiable symptoms, but as character traits or modes of behavior. Character armor develops in response to anti-sexual pressures arising within the authoritarian family, which is held together by the repressive power of the father.

Throughout the early 1930s Reich was active in sexual politics in Vienna and then Berlin, helping to establish sex-hygiene clinics offering contraceptive advice and seeking to promote orgastic potency. In an attempt to reconcile Freud and MARX, Reich now argued (1935) that, just as MARXISM expressed a growing consciousness of economic exploitation, psychoanalysis represented an emerging consciousness of the social repression of sex. The history of psychoanalysis was the history of the removal of sexual repression.

In 1939, Reich emigrated to the United States, where he spent the remainder of his career. His earlier political views gave way to what can only be described as mysticism. The last decades of his life were spent in an attempt to describe and even capture the mysterious cosmic energy he called orgone. Reich was finally imprisoned for renting a fraudulent therapeutic device, namely an Orgone Energy Accumulator, and died in prison.

Reich's reputation had always been controversial. Vilified by more orthodox psychoanalysts

(Chasseguet-Smirgel and Grunberger, 1976), he enjoyed great popularity with the theorists of the counterculture of the late 1960s (Reiche, 1968). The emphasis on biological genitality and heterosexuality in his work, as well as his failure to consider sexual difference, make it seem much less attractive to a era marked by FEMINISM and gay liberation.

Reading
Chasseguet-Smirgel, Janine, and Grunberger, Béla 1976: *Reich or Freud? Psychoanalysis and Illusion.*
Reich, Wilhelm 1933: *Character Analysis.*
——1935: *The Sexual Revolution.*
Reiche, Reimut 1968: *Sexuality and the Class Struggle.*
Robinson, Alan A. 1970: *The Sexual Radicals.*

DAVID MACEY

reification   From the Latin *res* (thing) and *facere* (to make), the term literally means *to make a thing*. In Marxist terminology, reification is a specific form of ALIENATION in which the consciousness of the individual is so overwhelmed by his or her identification with the means and fruits of production and the artificial designation of value that the dialectical *process* of identity is arrested, a psychological closure taking place that denies individual growth, as well as any meaningful social interaction. Hence human beings lose their humanity and become fixed properties in the assumption of capital, wholly defined by their purpose and utility in the capitalist drama.

An analysis of reification is implicit in MARX's discussion of commodity fetishism (*capital*), or the social dynamics constituted by the production of a commodity in a capitalist economy. According to Marx, capital exploits the worker in that he becomes a mere instrument in the production of value, a tool of the capitalist. The ultimate tragedy and the deciding factor in this game of subjection, however, is the worker's acceptance of his thinglike identity: The social character of men's labor appears to them as an objective characteristic, a social natural quality of the labor product itself. . . . To the producers the social relations connecting the labors of one individual with that of the rest appear not as direct social relations between individuals at work, but as what they really are, thinglike relations between persons and social relations between things (Marx, 1977, p. 72).

The worker identifies himself with the product to the extent that the *thing* that is being produced and consumed constitutes his identity and the nature of his interactions with others. Besides the fact that the baker is not an individual with distinct hopes, dreams, and aspirations, but merely the man who bakes the bread to sustain the productivity and utility of the engineer, the logic of such an abstract identification limits his relationship with others, for the man who makes bread can have little in common with the man who makes sophisticated machinery.

Discussion of reification has been central to Marxist theory, especially that of Lukács, the Frankfurt school, and the New Left, but it is, of course, integral to any philosophical examination of the dichotomy between appearance and reality. The dialectical process of history, as well as individual identity, is a process toward transcendence. To *define* is ultimately to *confine*, and to deny growth and change. A favorite topic of notable twentieth-century theorists (de SAUSSURE, BARTHES, DERRIDA, DE MAN, etc.), one can, none the less, trace discussion of the implications of *naming* or *defining* and the insidious and psychologically manipulative properties of language back to Plato's theory of forms (*The Republic*, book X).
See also ALIENATION; ESTRANGEMENT.

MARY ELLEN BRAY

relative autonomy   A category advanced by ALTHUSSER in "Contradiction and overdetermination" (1965, pp. 87–128), in an attempt to wrest historical materialism from the economic determinism inherent in the orthodox BASE AND SUPERSTRUCTURE topography.

Taking his cue from reflections by ENGELS and GRAMSCI, Althusser sought to reconcile economic "determination in the last instance" with the "specific effectivity of the superstructures" by radically revising the traditional model. Any SOCIAL FORMATION was a global structure, encompassing three regional structures – the economic, the political, and the ideological – each of which enjoyed "relative autonomy" *vis-à-vis* the others. Accordingly, the political and ideological levels of the SOCIAL FORMATION were not to be regarded as the secondary effects of a primordial cause or the superstructural phenomena of an infrastructural essence. At once determined and determinant, they formed the "conditions of existence" of the economic mode of production. This did not, however, license pluralism. The superstructures were not sheerly independent. Any social formation comprised a complex totality, a "structure in dominance," containing a dominant structure which organized the hierarchy and interrelations of the regional structures. And although the economic structure was not invariably *dominant*, it was always ultimately *determinant*, since it allocated dominance (in precapitalist societies, for example, to the ideological or political structures).

Althusser's proposals possessed considerable appeal for Marxists, since they permitted analysis of politics and CULTURE to proceed unconstrained by economic reductionism or ESSENTIALISM; and a fertile literature emerged in their wake. However, critics increasingly came to query the coherence of the category, arguing that politics and IDEOLOGY were *either* autonomous *or* determined; Althusser's formula had failed to square a circle from which the only exit was "post-Marxism" (Hindess and Hirst, 1977; Laclau and Mouffe, 1985). Others (see Geras, 1987, pp. 48–50) have charged Althusser's detractors with a spurious rigor, vindicating the kindred notion of "conditional autonomy."

Reading
Althusser, L. 1965 (*1990*): *For Marx.*
Geras, N. 1986: "Post Marxism?."
Hindess, B., and Hirst, P. 1977: *Mode of Production and Social Formation.*
Laclau, E., and Mouffe, C. 1985: *Hegemony and Socialist Strategy.*

GREGORY ELLIOTT

relativity, ontological *See* ONTOLOGICAL RELATIVITY

Renaissance studies The Renaissance was traditionally considered the era of rebirth, a rallying of the human spirit after the "dark ages" blotted out the accomplishments of the great empires of Greece and Rome; the cradle of HUMANISM, an age of discovery, and a pinnacle of artistic, intellectual, and literary accomplishment. As the era that saw the recovery of the philosophy, drama, literature, and political treatises of classical antiquity, and developed its aesthetic and rhetorical forms in imitation of these models, the Renaissance was considered the repository of the moral, political, and philosophical truths of classical learning – and thus it was credited with regenerating, safeguarding, and furthering the essential tenets of Western

civilization. The epoch has been cast as an era of human self-discovery, and credited with the optimistic realization of human potential – ideas that perhaps reveal more about post-ENLIGHTENMENT POSITIVISM than Renaissance humanism. Yet even more recent schools of critical thought that view much of this traditional picture as an idealized construction indicate, in renaming the era, the degree to which it is still considered to be the root of contemporary Western CULTURE and identity: "the early modern period."

To the scholars of the vast amount of literature in English generated in the sixteenth and seventeenth centuries, Renaissance studies is the study of the *English* Renaissance (although it is traditional to acknowledge the Continent – especially fifteenth-century Italy – as the source of the intellectual and philosophical currents that develop in England). The invention of the movable-type press, and the subsequent increase in the availability of printed material leading to a general increase in literacy across Europe; the recovery of Classical texts that provided new inspirational models, spurring an explosion of literary activity; the rediscovered arts and sciences of poetry, philosophy, rhetoric, and logic; the "new worlds" discovered through scientific and geographic exploration; and the advent of a new philosophical movement, humanism, which primarily valued education – these inventions, discoveries, events, and developments resulted in a prolific explosion in arts and letters, considered a pinnacle of achievement for the English language and its poets, rhetoricians, and philosophers.

Still another result of the rise of a print culture in sixteenth- and seventeenth-century England is that an immense amount of written and printed matter has survived, not only the lyric poems and the countless sonnets that circulated in aristocratic circles, but also a vast body of popular literature: ballads, broadsides, pamphlets, and play scripts – those written artifacts of a flourishing new artistic and commercial enterprise, the English theater. Much documentation has also survived: baptism, marriage, and burial records; legislative accounts of lawsuits, land sales, and commercial transactions; letters, diaries, and household accounts. That it is possible for "the Renaissance" to appear familiar, knowable, might be a tautology of the historic moment; the kinds and quantities of historical evidence which were generated and which survive make it possible to know much about the period. Yet the relationship of that material evidence to literary study – and how literature responds to the influence of historical forces – are vexed questions. Indeed, for much of the twentieth century, scholars denied the "influence" of history upon literature, viewing literary TEXTS in splendid isolation from the circumstances in which they were created. In the literature of the Renaissance – the lyric poetry, the sonnets of Sidney and Spenser, the plays of Shakespeare – generations of NEW CRITICS found fertile ground to practice their methodologies, viewing the works as self-contained verbal icons best "understood" by close reading and attention to patterns of theme, SYMBOL, and imagery.

Attention to the works of William Shakespeare has tended to dominate Renaissance studies, and changes in the study of Shakespeare point to the major developments in the discipline as a whole. Until quite recently, a handful of names sufficed to define the field: the "Silver Poets" of the early sixteenth century – Thomas Wyatt, Henry Howard, John Davies, and later, Edmund Spenser and Philip Sidney; the "metaphysical poets" John Donne and George Herbert, and playwright Thomas Middleton, once T.S. Eliot had recovered them from obscurity in the 1920s and 1930s; Shakespeare's "great" contemporaries, Christopher Marlowe and Ben Jonson; and especially Shakespeare, the master poet whose works embodied both formalist perfection and humanist significance. By aesthetic criteria that frequently elided the difference between poetry and theatrical art, that were often antipathetic to the physical and material conditions of the Renaissance theater, and that deemphasized the unstable processes by which theatrical texts were recorded and disseminated in the period, the plays of Shakespeare came to be regarded as unified literary masterpieces that transcended time, location, and nationality, capturing all that was truest, most enduring, and universal in the human condition.

Virtually every one of these assumptions has been dismantled by the philosophical, literary, and epistemological questions posed by CULTURAL STUDIES. From the first undermining of post-Enlightenment certainties about the primacy of the rational mind and its capability for knowing objective, unchanging truths, to the first challenges to the presumption that literary CANONS are formed from the impartial recognition of a universal standard of value – to the exploration of alternative voices, histories, values – cultural studies and recent CRITICAL THEORIES have proved uniquely suited

to undermining the universalist-formalist claims that had been the basis of traditional Renaissance studies. Inspired to some extent by the political activism of the late 1960s and early 1970s, informed by Marxist-style examinations of the material realities of history, and encouraged by the feminist, civil rights, and anti-war movements to a new awareness of the oppressions, injustices, and exclusions of Western civilization, a generation of scholars ventured to challenge the (presumably) ahistorical, politically neutral aesthetic models of established critical practice. The literary MARXISM of Frederic Jameson and Walter BENJAMIN supplied ideological and philosophical support, as did Louis ALTHUSSER's meditations on IDEOLOGY and consciousness. Michel FOUCAULT's theories about how power circulates in society encouraged literary scholars and historians to a new perception of the ways in which art functions in the social realm that produces it: representing specific historic situations and conflicts, now subverting, now affirming the dominant ideological CODES of its moment. Scholars grew more conscious of the distinction between literature and dramatic art, considering more carefully the difference between static literary texts and the circumstances and conditions of theatrical performance – and appreciating more accurately early modern English drama's unique status as an ephemeral popular form, dependent for its livelihood on a wildly heterogeneous cross-section of London's social composition at a time of unprecedented religious, social, familial, and economic disruption.

If anything united this coalition of (mostly North American and British) academics in the early 1980s (when the transition from "the Renaissance" to "early modern studies" began), it was a shared fascination with reading the Renaissance against its historical moment, keen interest in evaluating the production, circulation, and dissemination of literary art in its material culture, and a desire to place into focus what that culture had consigned to its margins. A new breed of social historians (Christopher Hill, Lawrence Stone, Keith Wrightson) gleaned data about daily activities that made it possible to foreground previously unrecorded lives and disregarded issues: CLASS, GENDER, RACE, LITERACY. Practitioners of new and challenging DISCOURSES like FEMINIST CRITICISM, NEW HISTORICISM, PSYCHOANALYSIS and POSTSTRUCTURALISM transgressed traditional disciplinary boundaries to borrow tools, methodologies, and resources from the social sciences, anthropology, ethnography, linguistics. The influence of DECONSTRUCTION prompted questions about the referential reliability of cherished texts, even of language itself. And as they shattered traditional aesthetic criteria and critical certitude, scholars acknowledged their own "embeddedness" in the present cultural moment and their own concerns, recognizing the difficulty (if not the impossibility) of accurately comprehending the ideological forces of the past, and abandoning the traditional stance of critical objectivity to signal their own political investments and positions.

From its earliest inceptions, these new ways of reading and writing about the Renaissance registered conflicts where there had previously been HEGEMONY, seeing ruptures where unities had previously been established. No longer repositories of essential human values, treatises on "man" and the "human condition," the plays of Shakespeare and Jonson, the poetry of John Donne and Thomas Wyatt, all could be read as "extraordinarily sensitive register[s] of the complex struggles and harmonies of culture" – or so claimed Stephen Greenblatt, whose *Renaissance Self-Fashioning* (1980) helped to craft one of the most significant new methodologies of the decade. New Historicism purposed a more complete vision of "history," one that accounted for contradictions, exclusions, exceptions, and silences, as previous readings, inspired by a monolithic history of ideas, could not. Less a doctrine than a "set of themes, preoccupations, and attitudes," New Historicism (or its now-preferred appellation, CULTURAL MATERIALISM), examines literary and dramatic art against other discursive forms and objects of cultural production – historical documents, pamphlets, ballads, court masques, royal progresses, maps, visual art – seeking "bizarre overlappings" and "surprising coincidences" (Veeser, 1989). By the mid 1980s, titles proliferated that confidently affirmed the extent of this critical revisioning: *Radical Tragedy* (Dollimore, 1984); *Rewriting the Renaissance* (Ferguson, Quilligan, and Vickers, 1986); *Political Shakespeare* (Dollimore and Sinfield, 1985). The polemical introductions and prefaces of these and other works (Holderness, 1988; Howard and O'Connor, 1987) pledged to revolutionize readings and ways of reading; to raise new and profound questions about the status, value, and claim of literary texts. New understandings of early modern printing techniques, editorial practices, and

authorship placed texts themselves under scrutiny, raising doubts about the reliability of transmission and authorial integrity of many Renaissance works – including Shakespeare's (Taylor and Warren, 1983; De Grazia, 1991). Works and authors long considered "lesser" or obscure were opened to interrogation (Beaumont and Fletcher, Thomas Heywood, John Webster), while a strong feminist presence further expanded the canon by bringing to attention works of forgotten women writers (Elizabeth Carey, Lady Mary Wroth). Feminist readings developed from their first attempts to acknowledge and describe – often optimistically – the place of women in Renaissance life and art (Bamber, 1982; Lenz, Greene, and Neely, 1980); to more skeptical appraisals of the tenacity of "patriarchal structures" in the era (Erickson, 1985; Jardine, 1983), to more theoretical discussions of the gendering of identity and its representation (Callaghan, 1989; Traub, 1992). Gay perspectives contributed significant reconsiderations of the homoerotics of the Renaissance theater, the works of Marlowe, and Shakespeare's sonnets (Bray, 1982; Orgel, 1989), while postcolonial awareness urged new attention to the discourses of racial and ethnic difference and imperialism in works as peripheral as Jonson's *Masque of Blackness* and as canonical as *The Tempest* or *Othello*. And media, performance, and FILM STUDIES opened an important new dimension, providing a conceptual framework and vocabulary to theorize the works of Shakespeare – and other Renaissance dramatists – in theatrical performance, on film, and as artifacts of present POPULAR CULTURE.

Some objections have been raised to these attempts to intepret Renaissance literature and drama through the comprehension of the political elements of the historical moment and the material, social, economic, and technological circumstances that produce, value, and disseminate it. Disapproving voices from the intellectual Right – including Washington columnist George Will and former US Secretary of Education William Bennett – have decried New Historicism and other innovations as vaguely Marxist plots that threaten to "politicize" both art and the academy. Allan Bloom (1987) and Roger Kimball (1991) cautioned against the assault upon the traditional canon led by a generation of "tenured radicals," whose perception of literature as a register of social and historic conflicts erased distinctions between timeless literature and unremarkable texts. Renaissance specialist Richard

Levin's critiques of feminist and cultural materialist poetics, published in *PMLA* (1988 and 1990), sparked a controversy that required an entire anthology to chronicle (Kamps, 1991), and pointed to a nostalgia among some scholars in the field for standard literary analysis and aesthetic appreciation. Responses to such challenges typically claim that the criteria of aesthetic excellence that formed literary canons are "always already" political, molded by a patriarchal, white, elitist culture intent on preserving its status quo; that critics whose opinions are sanctioned by the dominant thought systems and values of a culture only appear to be "above" ideology and partisanship (Howard, 1994); that the ideological function of art was no more neutral in the early modern era than in the twentieth century. Recent developments in Renaissance studies have not occurred without failings, excesses, and lapses of vision, such as the sectarian quarrels that divide some critics into factions (for example, a deepening rift between historicists and feminists, or the disdain of some critics for analysis of drama in performance). Scholars who favor more traditional practices complain of being marginalized and underrated, pointing to a strain of insularity within the profession, and, at worst, a tendency to acclaim the derivative and merely fashionable. Despite its rhetoric of diversity, the predominant figures of the academic left remain principally white and male. And given the conservative nature of many of the institutions and structures of the academy, and the privileged status of those who teach in it, claims of radical commitment from university professors can risk appearing either wistful or incongruous. Yet despite these and other controversies, at the midpoint of its second decade of substantial revisioning, the study of this significant body of literature and its remarkable, conflicted, and astonishingly well-documented historical moment signals continued momentum and vitality.

See also FORMALISM; GENDER; HUMANISM; PATRIARCHY.

Reading
De Grazia, Margreta, and Stallybrass, Peter 1993: "The materiality of the Shakespeare text."
Drakakis, John 1985: *Alternative Shakespeares.*
Goldberg, Jonathan 1983: *James I and the Politics of Literature: Jonson, Shakespeare, Donne and their Contemporaries.*
Greenblatt, Stephen, ed. 1982: *The Forms of Power and The Power of Forms in the English Renaissance.*
——and Gunn, Giles, eds 1992: *Redrawing the Boundaries: The Transformation of English and American Studies.*

Jordon, Constance 1990: *Renaissance Feminism: Literary Texts and Political Models.*
Kahn, Coppelia and Schwartz, Murray M., eds 1980: *Representing Shakespeare: New Psychoanalytic Essays.*
McLuskie, Kathleen 1989: *Renaissance Dramatists.*
Montrose, Louis Adrian 1979–80: "The purpose of playing: reflections on a Shakespearean anthropology."
Tennenhouse, Leonard 1986: *Power on Display: The Politics of Shakespeare's Genres.*
Thompson, Marvin and Ruth, eds 1989: *Shakespeare and the Sense of Performance: Essays in the Tradition of Performance Criticism in Honor of Bernard Beckerman.*
Wayne, Valerie 1991: *The Matter of Difference: materialist feminist criticism of Shakespeare.*

JEAN PETERSON

reproductive technologies The new reproductive technologies employ a myriad of methodologies including the use of donor sperm, donor eggs, fertilization outside of the human body (*in vitro* fertilization), analysis and manipulation of genetic components, zygote transfers, and ultimately introduction of the embryo back into the womb. It is surprising that this trade and commerce of the conceptus has evoked only a mild tremor in the social arena. Granted, its significance has been overshadowed by more immediate concerns, such as current environmental and political upheavals, however, twentieth-century science has initiated a rupture in the biology of human nature which challenges the very notion of lineage. Entrance into this putative age of the "motherless child" underscores separateness as an organic reality. Perhaps this is an era where the mirror will reflect a being whose attachments are contractual and whose progenitors may be found as entries in gamete banks, anononymous donors of a genetic code.

Proponents of biotechnology range from feminist legal authorities, claiming the territory for women's autonomy rights, to physicians attempting to give infertility a disease status. Opponents of the practice include those who perceive further manipulation of a uniquely female experience and the inevitable commodification of human life. For a world which groans under the weight of population growth and for an animal which must endure the pathos of its "body sense," the current trends in reproductive strategies are unsettling.

A central tenet in this discussion is that the new reproductive technologies focus on the "use" of the body and its most fundamental activity: the joining of two sets of genetic information, rearranged through chance, which code for another unique individual. Embedded in this rather scant description of reproduction is a set of emergent qualities that coalesce and structure the human capacity for realizing self. This realization is not easily accessible through the methods of medical science, philosophy, theology, or law, but persists as a dynamic amalgam of often irreducible components. Consideration of the issue thus relies on a diverse set of interpretative measures. The ultimate action required is enmeshed in an attempt to apprehend the potential consequences of these technologies for values associated with the creation of well-being.

A brief examination of the cases using the new reproductive technologies, especially contract motherhood, uncovers a radical shift in human relations. The issue is circumscribed by at least three major foci: the continued social devaluation of women and children by giving pregnancy and birth a market value; the strengthening of women as autonomous agents of choice; and the reconfiguration of lived experience via foundational changes in cultural perspectives.

According to the first claim, a woman's relation to her reproductive life has become increasingly derivative. Medical technology and its reproductive interventions have promoted an understanding of pregnancy that has quietly begun to disrupt the narrative of birth. A medicalized language of the woman's body and the value written into it is being generated by a *techne* that suppresses deeply personal images of the human being. The capacity for reproduction, once integrally bound to a particular woman, can now be alienated from her self, objectified, priced, and purchased according to market demand. The ranking and use of a woman's body become criteria for exchange similar to prostitution. Although this analogy appears startling, analysis of both activities, commercialized motherhood and prostitution, reveal that women provide their bodies for economic gain from acts that were once reserved for an individual's most intimate self. Proponents of these engagements state that women choose to control their own reproductive and sexual agency. With regard to surrogate motherhood, it has been argued that the gestational or contractual mother freely enters into the arrangement. However, this argument has been called into question. First, it ignores the power differentials present among people in society. The fact that most surrogate mothers are motivated by economic factors suggests that the fee creates a situation that is potentially coercive. Socioeconomic

survival, not the women's own needs and interests, is a dominating influence. Second, in a society that appears to place great value on child-bearing, the emphatic pronatalist standpoint compounds the erasure of women's worth outside of the breeding arena and creates a diminished self-esteem in the childless woman, thus her willingness to conform and contract for a child.

This perspective implies that biotechnology has splintered moral categories, and, more specifically, that the practices of embryo transfer and contract pregnancy carry elements that subvert the validity of a woman's emotional responses to pregnancy and birth. Adoption of these practices requires a careful plan of inquiry focused on the misuse of a woman's body and the intrusions into the constitution of a newborn child. Perhaps becoming an object transferred at birth via a bill of sale, an entity subject to property rights by the contract holder, may not be in the best interest of the individual or that of a self-reflective society.

In contrast to the commodification of life argument, it has been claimed that the issue is not commercialization but redefinition of women as rational moral agents capable of assuming responsibility for the consequences of their actions. Carmel Shalev states that women have long been "imprisoned by the subjectivity of their wombs." Their shadow life in the male-dominated socioeconomic order suppresses a woman's control of her bodily resources and the use of her birth power for economic gain. Shalev suggests that considerable economic activity is already invested in the biological and nonbiological parent–child relationships by medical professionals, lawyers, and social workers, and that now is the time to imbue women with the power to negotiate the economic value of their reproductive labor. Central to this argument is the contention that a woman's faculty of reason should not be abrogated by the emotional facets of her physiology. The autonomy vested in a woman's reproductive decisions provides a buffer against the "technical control of reproduction by detached parties for economic and political ends." Opinions from other groups collude with the possibility that traditional motherhood is not the only reproductive option. *In vitro* fertilization and contract motherhood should open the way for informed respectful deliberation on reproduction. The assumption that human beings are free to choose new descriptions for self, spirit, and nature underpins these perspectives and provides an avenue for conscious departure from a deeply ingrained norm. This line of reasoning proceeds to venture that diversity in the circumstances of birth enriches the human experience. Novel technological options will evoke new norms and responsibilities within the context of social relations, which may be effectuated through contract.

The issue emerging from this continuum of reproductive strategies is one of "not knowing." The cultural implications of "taking motherhood apart" remain hidden from society, family, and the individual. Only recently have the gender imbalances of the postindustrial world been articulated, and only recently has the psychological scaffold of a child's origins been implicated in the firmament of mental health. However, it is not merely a woman's cultural socialization or a child's early conditioning that is at stake; it is the entire concept of "mother," which was formerly an inalienable truth. A woman giving birth was the actual mother, not a variation on this theme. Current nomenclature for "mother" includes a list of qualifiers that define a peculiar partitioning of the woman-with-child. The *genetic mother* is the woman responsible for contributing 23 chromosomes packaged within the ovum subsequently fertilized; the *gestational mother* carries the emotional and physical risks and supplies the tissues required to maintain the pregnancy; the *contractual* or *social mother* provides postnatal nurturance and economic support. Certainly the conceptual ideal of motherhood has become fractured and this is not simply a semantic problem.

Language here expresses underlying assumptions and contributes to the formation of novel attitudes and dispositions. Linguistic choices are thus significant agents of change, and control of the language has become a primary struggle within the emergence of reproductive technology. Even the phrase "reproductive technology" implies the use of machine parts, gametes as reproductive units or replaceable objects to be catalogued and parceled to the consumer, a utilitarian approach to taming the passions, an undermining of a critical moment in human relations. In this context, the issue of reproductive technology offers a potential explosion in the very definition of connection. It is important to examine the narrative of this cultural infusion, the idea as it becomes word, and the word flesh. Is the woman's body the experimental vessel within which we must shape this new story? How will it be read? What is the quality of this knowledge? Ethicists, scientists, feminists, theologians, attorneys – what tale will they tell? Will it be a matter of aligning language with the world, connecting our senses to the naming of new intellectual associations, new forces of utterance that may retire our former notions of self as if they were old tools that no longer have any truth value?

It is not even a debate between nature and CULTURE. Our conception of "just what something is" emerges from an expanded sense of origin. However, what if, via genetic manipulation of embryos, "foreign" genes are inserted into the embryo? The resultant genetic structures are not a natural origin for this "human being"; rather, they are products of a material reconstruction. More nearly perfect entities perhaps, more evolutionarily resilient, they are thus real challenges for natural selection; but should there be a pause here – a deletion of the qualifier natural, since certainly as a reproductive success this is not "nature's" doing?

If the new technolanguage moves outside a system of discourse which formerly situated the physical and metaphorical concept of mother within the female body, what may be the significance of this movement? The being emerging from the birth canal, conceived in this other's womb, carries the sign of separation, and now total disconnection. If language serves as an opening to the interior of a human being and body language begins in the womb (see Kristeva, 1974a, pp. 27–8), that archaic semiotic space where chaos coalesces into form, then it may be that the "vocabulary" of the newborn is richly tied to the voice and motion of the birth mother. Perhaps these sensory cues are an imprinting not measurable by analysis but existent in that metaphysical space underpinning being. Conversely, what is foundational here? Must the motives for "knowing" ourselves from genetic lineage, from pregnancy and birth be questioned? Is this just another facet of social conditioning to be discarded as the DECONSTRUCTION of reproduction? What philosophy will be suitable to evaluate this special area of knowledge, this establishment of embryo transport and reproductive commerce? To date, only the ethicists approach the problem with vigor. However, their mode of investigation is often confined to a competing individual rights model which is subsumable under the exercise of personal freedom, the pursuit of one's perceived interests. The impact of this cultural change cannot be successfully delineated using the narrative of moral rights, cost–benefit ratios, and decision analysis. Medical and health science attempts to separate from the social fabric in order that tidy technical solutions to formidable epistemic complexities may be found. Molecular biology, used as a technology, presents the ability to divert human biological and cultural evolution. Former representations of the female body as women's reproductive singularity become reimagined and transformed at an unprecedented rate. Whether this practice is a further disintegration of social relations, an erasure of intimate bodily experiences as valid determinants of the human being, or simply another face of Eve has yet to be determined.

Reading

Bonnicksen, Andrea L. 1989: *In Vitro Fertilization: Building Policy from Laboratories to Legislatures.*

Glover, Jonathan 1989: *Ethics of New Reproductive Technologies: The Glover Report to the European Commission.*

Harris, John 1992: *Wonderman and Superman: The Ethics of Human Biotechnology.*

Holmes, Helen Bequaert, ed. 1992: *Issues in Reproductive Technology I: An Anthology.*

Levine, Carol, ed. 1993: *Taking Sides: Clashing Views on Controversial Bioethical Issues.*

Rodin, Judith, and Collins, Aila, eds 1991: *Women and New Reproductive Technologies: Medical, Psychosocial, Legal, and Ethical Dilemmas.*

KATHLEEN CREED-PAGE

residual   *See* DOMINANT/RESIDUAL/EMERGENT

response   *See* CALL AND RESPONSE

Rich, Adrienne (1929–) US poet and feminist critic. Already a canonical poet when she came out as a radical lesbian feminist in the 1970s, Rich has been uniquely situated as a feminist spokesperson: she can be neither marginalized, patronized, nor dismissed by the establishment she opposes. To read Rich's cultural criticism is to have one's finger on the pulse of a major artery of contemporary US FEMINISM: initially radical, then giving way to a sophisticated RACE–CLASS–GENDER analysis that questions its own previous construction of a universal female identity as the basis of feminist alliance. *Of Women Born* (1976) exposes contradictions between (oppressive) ideologies and (potentially liberating) experiences of motherhood. *On Lies, Secrets, and Silence* (1979) explores issues

central to radical feminism: women's creativity and its thwarting, the revolutionary potential of woman bonding, and barriers to it such as RACISM and homophobia. In *Blood, Bread and Poetry* (1986), Rich scrutinizes the historical and cultural specificity of her own identity as a political poet and asks readers to do the same: to locate ourselves at specific intersections of race, class, gender, and national identities, for it is there that we experience the contradictions that blind us or frighten us into collaboration with systems of oppression. In *What is Found There* (1993), Rich continues the work begun in *Blood*, but with a strengthened commitment to international and postcolonial issues. As a literary critic, Rich "re-visions" the past, revaluing the work of women, poor, immigrant, and postcolonial artists as well as canonical figures, and tests the limits of reading and writing as tools of liberation. In Rich's work on women writers, Patrocinio Schweickart discerns a model of feminist reading. Rich's essay, "Compulsory heterosexuality and lesbian existence," merits special attention as a cornerstone of lesbian studies: here Rich rejects the assumption that heterosexuality is "natural," arguing instead that it is a socially constructed institution oppressive to all.

See also LESBIAN FEMINISM; RACE–CLASS–GENDER.

Reading

Rich, Adrienne 1976: *Of Women Born: Motherhood as Experience and Institution.*

——1979: *On Lies, Secrets, and Silence: Selected Prose, 1966–1978.*

——1986: *Blood, Bread, and Poetry: Selected Prose, 1979–1985.*

——1993: *What is Found There: Notebooks on Poetry and Politics.*

Schweickart, Patrocinio 1984 (*1986*): "Reading ourselves: toward a feminist theory of reading."

GLYNIS CARR

Richard, Jean-Pierre (1922–) French literary critic. Equally indebted to Georges POULET and Gaston BACHELARD, Richard distinguishes himself among GENEVA SCHOOL critics by his emphasis on the material world of the mental landscape (its organization by visual themes and motifs) rather than on the implied metaphysical experience of the author (Poulet's *cogito*). He consistently visualizes this interior landscape (*paysage*) as a metaphor for personal experience, "an order of things . . . a being-there" (Richard, 1979). Subjectivity in literature is expressed objectively by a unique arrangement of SYMBOLS whose metamorphoses define a "concrete principle of organization . . . around which a world is constituted and deployed" (Richard, 1961). Richard's work after the more purely phenomenological analyses of *Literature and Feeling* (1954) and *Poetry and Profundity* (1955) applies a psychoanalytic perspective to this thematic symbolism, describing the exploratory relationship of SUBJECT and world as the "self-discovery of a complex and unique libido" (Richard, 1979).

Richard's earlier work is closer to Geneva school practice in its emphasis on an author's quest for psychic unity. Like Poulet, he marshals data drawn from the complete writings to construct a delicately perceptive and consummately organized essay following progressive shifts and changes in the author's existential career. Succeeding literary landscapes project various modes of existence to be matched against an underlying, dimly felt (prereflexive) sense of harmony with the world. The essay on Paul Verlaine (Richard, 1955) describes the poet's instinct for nuances and fleeting, liminal experience as a "faded quality" that is authentically Verlaine and cannot be rejected without destroying his sense of self – and his art. Richard's later work (for example, the books on Mallarmé and Proust) replaces such evaluations with a discreet psychoanalytic framework.

Microreadings (1979–84) marks a shift from broader initial themes to a starting point in "myopic" but revelatory details; *The State of Things* (1990) treats the writing of eight lesser-known contemporary writers as "territories" to be described in material or sensuous terms. Throughout his work, Richard counts on the "sensuous logic" possessed by every human being – by each "reading body" or *corps lisant* (1979) – to provide the link between words and world, and the recognition of another's material imagination.

See also PHENOMENOLOGY; PSYCHOANALYTIC CRITICISM.

Reading

Lawall, S.N. 1968: "Jean-Pierre Richard."
Magowan, Robin 1964: *Jean-Pierre Richard and the Criticism of Sensation.*
Mathieu, Jean-Claude 1986: "Les cinq sensations de J.-P.R."
Miller, J. Hillis 1966 (*1991*): "The Geneva School."
Richard, Jean-Pierre 1954: *Littérature et Sensation* (Literature and Feeling).
——1955a: *Poésie et profondeur.*
——1955b (*1980*): "Verlaine's Faded Quality."
——1961: *L'Univers imaginaire de Mallarmé.*
——1974: *Proust et le monde sensible.*
——1979: *Microlectures* (Microreadings).
——1984: *Pages Paysages: Microlectures II.*
——1990: *L'Etat des Choses: Études sur Huit Écrivains d'Aujourd'hui.*

SARAH N. LAWALL

Richards, Ivor Armstrong (1893–1979) English critic. Richards was the founding father of modern English LITERARY CRITICISM. As a young lecturer in the newly created English faculty at Cambridge in the 1920s, he invented and provided a theory of PRACTICAL CRITICISM, a method of close linguistic analysis which, further elaborated by his pupils William EMPSON and F.R. LEAVIS and then by the American New Critics, became the dominant mode of academic criticism throughout the English-speaking world.

However, to see Richards primarily as the inventor of a technique, or as a kind of formalist, is to misunderstand both his project and the reasons for its extraordinarily wide and enduring influence. Richards was fundamentally a culture theorist, a propagandist, and his literary criticism was almost a by-product. The key to his ideas lies in a nonliterary work, *The Meaning of Meaning* (with C.K. Ogden, 1923), which is at root a melodramatically pessimistic vision of the state of CULTURE after the 1914–18 war. It portrays the world as being in near chaos, and diagnoses the root causes not as spiritual or economic, but as linguistic. Modern man is mentally confused and cannot make sense of his world because "words are at present a very imperfect means of communication" and muddled communication is the basis of all our ills. Advances in modern psychology mean, however, that "there is no longer any excuse for vague talk about Meaning, and ignorance of the ways in which words deceive us . . . a Science of Symbolism has become possible." This what *The Meaning of Meaning* set out to establish, first of all by insisting on a rigorous (and dubious and damaging) distinction between the scientific or "referential" uses of language and the "emotive" uses, of which poetry is seen as the highest form. "We need a spell of purer science and purer poetry before the two can again be mixed," as Richards proclaimed in *Principles of Literary Criticism* (1924).

Principles of Literary Criticism has the appearance of a technical work on the psychology of reading.

However, it too is at root an alarmist vision of postwar history. Modern man lives in chaos, an experiential chaos: everywhere around him Richards found confusion and "nervous strain" caused by the disappearance of the reassurances of religion, by the failure of science to provide a secure substitute, and by the mass media. "The extent to which second-hand experience of a crass and inchoate type is replacing ordinary life [Richards is talking about the cinema] offers a threat which has not yet been realised," and the arts, especially poetry, can save us from this degeneration by offering us a model of highly ordered experience, of mental "balance" and "reconciliation." This will, however, require a fundamental rethinking of CRITICAL THEORY because it is currently dominated by a false notion of the aesthetic: "All modern aesthetics rests upon an assumption which has been strangely little discussed, the assumption that there is a distinct kind of mental activity present in what are called aesthetic experiences." Much of Richard's book is accordingly a polemic against such notions and the idea that beauty is an esoteric mystery. There is no special "æsthetic state" or "pure art value": experiences of beauty "are only a further development, a finer organisation of ordinary experiences," and we need a "psychological theory of value" to explicate that organization: "critical remarks are a branch of psychological remarks."

All this was vigorous and refreshing at the time, and Richards's polemic served a useful purpose in chasing off the remnants of what he called the "poetry for poetry's sake" school. Disappointingly, though, the psychology with which he replaces them now looks crude, a stimulus-and-response behaviorism, and a theory that the most valuable poetry is that in which "appetencies and aversions" are brought into the highest balance in the individual reader's mind. None of this has stood the test of time very well. The basic model is too crudely mechanical and neurological ("the mind is a system of impulses"), and the psychology is too individualistic (Richards said, "To extend this individual morality [of balanced impulses] to communal affairs is not difficult," but it is, and he never does it). Above all, the central notion of "balance" was never adequately defined, and when he attempted to do so, he seemed to be recommending an ethic of passivity and Confucian quietism. This turned out to be particularly damaging when, often in cruder forms, it became the key evaluative term of NEW CRITICISM.

Practical Criticism (1929) was Richards's most influential book, precisely because it was a practical one. He argued, in what sounds like a self-criticism of some of the wilder theorizings of *Principles*, "No theory of poetry can be trusted which is not too intricate to be applied," and settled down instead to detailed close analysis of how actual readers read and how actual poems work. The book is a record of experiments at Cambridge in which he asked students to comment on short unidentified poems, followed by his analysis of the ways in which they understood or misunderstood them. This resulted in a classification of the various "difficulties" that can hamper good reading – sentimentality, stock responses, doctrinal adhesions, and so on. Misapprehensions of the ways in which METAPHOR works was identified as a major difficulty, and Richards began to sketch a theory of metaphor which was to prove highly influential (particularly for the New Critics: John Crowe RANSOM and Cleanth BROOKS, for example, were later to argue that metaphor is the key to poetry's operations). Equally influential and valuable was Richards's attempt to separate the multiple levels of meaning in literary TEXTS. "The all-important fact for the study of literature," he argued, "is that there are several kinds of meaning," and sense, feeling, tone, and intention were singled out as the main ones. From this argument much of the subtle semantic analysis characteristic of later criticism – notably Empson's concept of AMBIGUITY – derives. The continuing usefulness of these attempts at "improvement in communication" – or what Richards calls the study of "the possibilities of human misunderstanding" – is undoubted, and survive despite the book's most obvious weakness, its discussion of the "problem of belief" (how to evaluate texts whose values we do not share). This section, which shows Richards at his most unrealistic and fanciful, results from his almost paranoid distrust of science, and from the consequent insistence on the rigid distinction between literature and science which has distorted so much twentieth-century CRITICAL THEORY, and led him to the conclusion that beliefs in literature are "emotive" rather than "intellectual" and that "the question of belief or disbelief, in the intellectual sense, never arises when we are reading well." Like his attempt in *Science and Poetry* (1926) to assert that poetry does not make statements but "pseudo-statements" whose truth is irrelevant, this now seems simply mistaken. Like so many twentieth-century apologists for poetry, Richards's crusading attempt to defend literature against POSITIVISM ended up denying it any purchase on the world and exiling it again to the closed aesthetic realm from which he had set out to liberate it.

Richards published two other notable critical works in the next few years, *Coleridge on Imagination* (1934), another impassioned defense of poetry as "the supreme use of language," and *The Philosophy of Rhetoric* (1936), which is perhaps his most balanced and sober linguistic theory. Nevertheless, he was turning more and more to pedagogical projects and in the late 1930s "decided to back out of literature as a subject" and devoted himself mainly to educational theorizing and his campaign to promote Basic English as a means to improved international understanding.

See also NEW CRITICISM; EMPSON, SIR WILLIAM.

Reading
Brower, Reuben, Vendler, Helen, and Hollander, John 1973: *I.A. Richards: Essays in his Honor.*
McCallum, Pamela 1983: *Literature and Method: Towards a Critique of I.A. Richards, T.S. Eliot and F.R. Leavis.*
Russo, John 1989: *I.A. Richards: His Life and Work.*
Wellek, René 1986h: "I.A. Richards."

IAIN WRIGHT

Ricoeur, Paul (1913–) French philosopher. Ricoeur has been a participant in almost all the major debates in postwar continental philosophy. After early studies in German EXISTENTIALISM and PHENOMENOLOGY, Ricoeur took up the challenge of STRUCTURALISM and PSYCHOANALYSIS in the 1960s. He emerged with an influential hermeneutic reading of Freudian psychoanalysis, *Freud and Philosophy* in 1965, where he argued that a philosophical reading must simultaneously situate the text that it studies and be willing to be transformed by it. FREUD is read as a philosophical cotraveller of MARX and NIETZSCHE, the holy trinity of the "HERMENEUTICS of suspicion." Warning of the dangers of reducing the Freud–Marx–Nietzsche combine to the vulgar matrices of pansexualism, economics, and biologism, Ricoeur advocated instead the liberatory potential of these thinkers. All these projects are to be understood as extensions of consciousness and not as detractive dismissals of consciousness. They seek to impose Spinoza's lesson: the slave's understanding of his slavery leads to the rediscovery of freedom within the constraints of necessity. Ricoeur's theory of interpretation was further developed in *The Conflict of Interpretations* (1969).

Ricoeur's hermeneutics is an attempt to mediate between semantics and SEMIOTICS. Ricoeur does not believe, as the poststructuralists do, that the structuralist project has come to an end. SAUSSURE, according to Ricoeur, seeks to demonstrate neither the arbitrariness of the SIGN in itself nor the impossibility of reference. What Saussure offers instead, in Ricoeur's understanding, is the intelligibility of the synchronic model for posing certain kinds of disciplinary questions. Though Ricoeur has no problems with the synchronic model of differential relations in phonology, he is not convinced that the transference of the same model into semantics is unproblematic. In *The Rule of Metaphor* (1977) he studies the three different levels of DISCOURSE: the word, the sentence, and the TEXT. In so doing, Ricoeur privileges the interactive theory of METAPHOR over the substitution theory of metaphor. Theories of metaphor, he argues, should not make a fetish of the linguistic sign, but should seek to explain the larger units of discourse. Metaphors are not be found in dictionaries but in discourse. Metaphorical meaning can then be understood as a mode of predication rather than as a semantic deviation from literal meaning. Ricoeur's debate with DERRIDA on metaphor takes up precisely these points. Ricoeur indicts Derrida for working with a sign-based model of metaphor. In *Time and Narrative* (1983–8) Ricoeur's earlier attempt to work out a model of metaphor that is linked to mimesis (imitation) and muthos (employment) serves as a basis for a new model of linguistic reference.

Reading
Clark, S.H. 1990: *Paul Ricoeur.*
Ricoeur, Paul 1969 (*1974*): *The Conflict of Interpretations: Essays in Hermeneutics.*
——1970: *Freud and Philosophy: An Essay on Interpretation.*
——1978: *The Rule of Metaphor: Multi-disciplinary Studies of the Creation of Meaning in Language.*
——1984–8: *Time and Narrative.* 3 vols.

SHIVA KUMAR SRINIVASAN

Right, New *See* NEW RIGHT

ritual All human societies practice ritual, which can be defined as repeated sequences of standardized symbolic acts in which humans seek outcomes mediated by supernatural forces. Ritual may be conducted by specially qualified individuals (for example, priests, diviners, sorcerers) or by ordinary individuals. Rituals may be public events or conducted secretly. Rituals may be conducted to preserve the status quo or to bring change. Rituals may seek the intervention of deities, dead ancestors, impersonal forces, or other sources of supernatural power. Whatever the form, occasion, goal, or participants, rituals are composed of specified acts performed according to known rules within a known set of applications. As Durkheim demonstrated, a key prerequisite for ritual is a culturally defined boundary between two domains, "profane" (ordinary) and sacred. Ritual is a process for crossing that boundary. At the outset a ritual shifts the setting, objects, acts, and participants to the sacred. Subsequent acts transpire in the sacred zone, and, at the end, the ritual returns the setting to ordinary space. There are other means of crossing into the sacred – donning special clothes or entering a sacred locality, for example – but ritual is probably the most common. Religion is of course a heavy employer of ritual, though with its theology, administrative activities, social groups, etc., its scope is much greater than ritual. Rituals are also conducted outside what society may define as religion. Further, magic may not use ritual if the process only taps supernatural power without moving the actor(s) into a sacred context. Ritual behavior has attracted sustained attention from many scholarly disciplines literally for centuries. In the nineteenth century the advent of ethnographic study of exotic societies stimulated a genre of study that continues to flourish. Throughout, the operant assumption is that meanings expressed in ritual and the larger cultural context in which ritual is performed comprise a coherent system. Decoding SYMBOLIC meanings is complicated by frequent symbolic inversions: good becomes evil, black becomes white. Comparing ritual between CULTURES is often illuminating.

An early benchmark in the study of ritual is William Robertson Smith's 1889 analysis of the totemic feast, in which clan members consume the totemic animal that at all other times is taboo. As with subsequent analyses, Smith's inquiry focused on why what is taboo becomes permissible, on the symbolic meaning of the component acts, on the composition of attendees and officiants, on the sequencing of the acts, and on the linkages between ritual elements and the society in profane (ordinary) times.

Emile DURKHEIM expanded on Smith's analysis, examining the functions of the ritual in attaching individuals to the collective whole, acualizing the collective conscious that composed society. Others built on Durkheim's work, notably A.R. Radcliffe-Brown who, among other things, pointed out the similarity between ritual sequences and the structure of spoken sentences, both of which convey meaning and messages. The twentieth century has seen a flourishing of studies in ritual sequence, symbolism, and performance in many scholarly fields including psychology (notably FREUD and JUNG), metalanguage (LÉVI-STRAUSS), and performance (V. Turner).

Reading
Durkheim, Emile 1915 (*1968*): *Elementary Forms of the Religious Life*.
Lévi-Strauss, Claude 1962 (*1976*): *The Savage Mind*.
Munn, Nancy D. 1973: "Symbolism in a ritual context: aspects of symbolic action."
Smith, William Robertson 1889 (*1957*): *Religion of the Semites: The Fundamental Institutions*.
Turner, Victor W. 1982: *From Ritual to Theatre: The Human Seriousness of Play*.

THOMAS C. GREAVES

Rodney, Walter (1942–80) Walter Rodney was one of Guyana's best-known social historians and scholar/activists. His life was a relatively short one but its impact on the world was indisputably significant. Walter Rodney's passion for knowledge could be seen from early in his life when he won an exhibition to attend Guyana's premiere government secondary school at the time – Queen's College. From there Rodney moved on to do his undergraduate work at the University of the West Indies, Mona Campus, Jamaica, where he received a first class honors degree in history. Walter Rodney then traveled to London on a scholarship, where he completed his doctoral degree at the School of Oriental and African Studies, London University, when he was only 24 years old.

Rodney's doctoral dissertation was published in 1970 by Oxford University Press as *A History of the Upper Guinea Coast 1545 to 1800*. This book was later published by Monthly Review Press after his death. *A History of the Upper Guinea Coast* remains a formidable work on the historiography of that section of the West African coast between Gambia and Cape Mount. It was an attempt to recover Upper Guinea before the advent of European influence and subjugation, by carefully analyzing its intricate and constantly changing social, economic, and political relationships.

From London Rodney took his first teaching appointment in Tanzania, at the University of Dar es Salaam, from 1966 to 1968. He later returned to the history department at the University of the West Indies, Jamaica in 1968, from which he was unceremoniously expelled that same year because of his political activism and social and political critique of Jamaican social structure (see Lewis, 1991 for details). From this experience Rodney published his second book, *The Groundings with my Brothers*, in 1969. *Groundings* is a collection of speeches which Rodney shared with the Jamaican populace, along with some reflections on such issues as African history and CULTURE and its relevance to the Caribbean, Black Power, and the contribution of Rastafari to the Jamaican society.

Rodney returned to the University of Dar es Salaam in 1968 until 1974, where he once again vigorously joined the political and intellectual life of that celebrated African institution of scholarship and debate on matters of Third World underdevelopment. It was during these years, at the height of national liberation struggles, that Rodney wrote his most famous book, *How Europe Underdeveloped Africa*, published in 1972. This book was a scathing and often didactic attack on European colonization, exploitation, and plunder of resources on the African continent, which Rodney concluded was responsible for the impoverishment of the entire region. Rodney's last book *A History of the Guyanese Working People, 1881–1905*, was published posthumously by Johns Hopkins Press in 1981. In this book the author returned to the themes he had begun to explore in his work on Upper Guinea. His project here was to excavate the social and political matrix of nineteenth-century Guyanese society, the extent to which slavery and indentureship atomized the working class along racial and ethnic lines, and the nature of working-class politics which sought to transcend these artificial and divisive strategies of European capitalism.

Walter Rodney's epistemological position was quite clear. He believed that history should become a conscious part of the material experiences of a people and inform their political aspirations. He saw the role of the historian as a conduit of historical information for the benefit of the broad mass of workers and peasants. This was his notion of popular history – a history which was not merely archival but essentially connected to the quotidian struggle of ordinary people. This injunction is manifested in his attempt to provide children with some sense of their history in a fictionalized but historically grounded account of an Ashante migrant to Guyana in his monograph *Kofi Baadu Out of Africa*, published in 1980. He always articulated the notion that the intellectual should be attached to the struggle at some point. His own life followed that example.

In 1974 Walter Rodney and his family returned to Guyana from Tanzania. He had been promised the job of professor of history at the University of Guyana, but the decision to hire him was rescinded by the Board of Governors. This board was largely government controlled. The government was widely felt to be opposed to Rodney's politics and to his activism. Rodney, however, elected to remain in Guyana, founding the Working Peoples' Alliance (WPA) in 1974. Rodney and the WPA engaged in defending the interests of the Guyanaese working class, and was openly critical of those "who seek to deprive that class of political hegemony." This strategy was described by Rodney as "critical exposure." Walter Rodney was politically engaged in this struggle until his assassination on June 13, 1980. He was killed in a bomb blast while sitting in a parked car near to the area where he was born. Of his death the Barbadian novelist George Lamming remarked, "He was not the first victim of political murder in Guyana, but the radical nature of his commitment as a teacher and activist, the startling promise that his life symbolized, made his death something of a novel tragedy." The anniversary of Walter Rodney's death is often used by academics, political activists, and other organic intellectuals in the Caribbean to renew the commitment to the ideals by which this historian lived his short life.

Reading

Lewis, Linden 1991: "The groundings of Walter Rodney."
Rodney, Walter 1969: *The Groundings with My Brothers.*
——1970: *A History of the Upper Guinea Coast, 1545–1800.*
——1972: *How Europe Underdeveloped Africa.*
——1980: *Kofi Baadu Out of Africa.*
——1981: *A History of the Guyanese Working People, 1881–1905.*
——1990: *Walter Rodney Speaks: The Making of an African Intellectual.*

LINDEN LEWIS

Rohe, Ludwig Mies van der *See* MIES VAN DER ROHE

Romantic studies   The history of LITERARY CRITICISM and theoretical declaration related to English Romanticism begins with the major poets of that period. Formally and informally, in prose, POETRY, letters, and reported conversations, Blake, Wordsworth, Coleridge, Byron, Shelley, and Keats commented profoundly on their individual work and on the substance of poetry in general. In addition to the explicit assertions formulated in *Preface to Lyrical Ballads, Biographia Literaria,* and the *Defence of Poetry,* the Romantic poets were obviously preoccupied with the process of conceptualization and demonstration related to mythopoeic experience. Subtly, the Classical references to poeta, poesis, and poema became integrated categories at this time: creator, creative process, and created object did not compete for artistic attention, but rather were holistically aligned into comprehensive patterns of balance and tension. Philosophic and aesthetic ideas related to skepticism, dialectical progress and perfection, art for art's sake, the sublime, organic form, and the central role of imagination were in the forefront of attention. In essence, Romantic writers proposed their claims in the configuration of a heroic struggle to defend poetic conceptions about the self and imagination against critics who would deny such claims.

During the nineteenth century, reactions to the grand assertions of Romantic poets ranged from overwhelming admiration for their work to polite acknowledgement, and, in some instances, included distinct hostility to their poetry as well as to the conduct of their personal lives. In the first half of the twentieth century, poets like T.S. ELIOT and W.B. Yeats were vitally important in establishing modern skeptical and affirmative reactions to Romantic poetry that would strongly affect ensuing critical and theoretical thinking. Representing a classical tradition and its rejection of Romantic self-indulgence, Eliot's concerns about imaginative excess reach forward and influence certain poststructuralist arguments. As a counterbalance, Yeats embodies modern aspects of the Romantic struggle for imagination and self-definition that supports other poststructuralist positions. In sum, both poets extend Romantic energies by emphasizing thematic and stylistic innovation; spontaneity in thought and feeling, but guided by acute awareness of poetic convention, tradition, and a religious, spiritual, or mythic past; an incorporation of external nature, including landscape and cityscape, that surpasses mere description by centering on imagistic power related to thought and feeling; and an implicit or explicit reference to the quest for human perfectibility that is inherently accompanied by the curse of human imperfection. Perhaps more crucial than anything else that the twentieth century inherited is the weighty concept of revolutionary imaginative freedom that leads not to mythopoeic anarchy, but rather to creative responsibility within freedom.

Additionally, radical philosophical formulations by NIETZSCHE, Bergson, Husserl, HEIDEGGER, and SARTRE analytically and provocatively point out the intellectual and aesthetic struggle that MODERNITY acquired from the Romantics, accepting and insisting upon the inherent dangers that are associated with deep subjectivity and the emphasis on expressive individual freedom. Early on, cautionary voices like that of Eliot repeatedly launched sound objections to the broad sweep of the existing Romantic tendencies noted above, acknowledging their powerful, seductive influence. Appropriately, they criticized the temptation toward solipsism, narcissism, the loss of objectivity, and the weakening of traditional humanistic and spiritual values, in both literature and all phases of human experience. About the same time, other persuasive literary thinkers sought to establish a NEW CRITICISM that focused intensely on the art work as a unique object of perception, and largely ignored historical-biographical matters. Under the rigorous language analysis called FORMALISM, previously developed by SAUSSURE, JAKOBSON, and others, which complements New Criticism, the hostile viewpoint of early critics toward Romantic "excess" is qualified or muted so that the work is independently judged against certain distinct literary standards of value based on organic interrelationships within a TEXT such as the reader discovers through examination of language, structure, and meaning. Of special concern to the New Critics are the patterns of AMBIGUITY, ambivalence, TENSION, PARADOX, and IRONY revealed through word choice, imagery, imagistic clusters, and SYMBOLS that might reveal authorial intention(s). Although the primary conceptual direction behind this movement in criticism began to wane after 1960, these major contributions to a strict exploration of Romantic poetry have continued to affect the evolving course of literary DISCOURSE.

From 1960 to the present, the English-speaking literary world has witnessed an eruption of interest in the romantic writers. Led by M.H. Abrams,

H. BLOOM, N. FRYE, G. Hartman, and F. KERMODE, close inquiry into the claims and accomplishments of the Romantic period have provoked significant theoretical developments grounded in EXISTENTIALISM, PHENOMENOLOGY, PSYCHOANALYSIS, and STRUCTURALISM. Aesthetically and intellectually, Romanticism presents itself as an enormously complex literary background from which controversial ideas related to language, imagination, and political, religious, and social thought can unfold. Growing out of and distilling 150 years of critical and scholarly thinking, decisive theoretical positions have recently emerged to inform the pattern of Romantic discourse. Falling under the rubric of POSTSTRUCTURALISM, these authoritative studies include DECONSTRUCTION, psychoanalysis, and READER-RESPONSE CRITICISM, on the one hand, and FEMINISM, MARXISM, and NEW HISTORICISM, on the other, which span an investigative range from highly problematic, imaginative arguments to rather determined and ideological positions. The suggestion here is that the ancient struggle between Classicism and Romanticism is currently perpetuated through debates over "context" and "text." It is valuable to recognize that both extremes are designed to undermine provocatively the traditional expectations about the nature of the writer, the reader, and the text, in what could be seen as enacting a kind of Heisenbergian principle of "literary indeterminacy."

If structuralism rigorously analyzes the formal relationship between elements in a text (linguistic, acoustic, imagistic, etc. that lead, in a formalist analysis, to unified meaning), it is apparent that a poststructuralist or deconstructive approach can logically reverse the proposed claims by questioning the seemingly unbiased methods and theories upon which structuralism depends. Such radical "transvaluation of values" systematically reveals the tenuous, deceptive certitudes behind all critical approaches to literature and thought, including its own. Each writer, text as subject, and reader acts independently and uniquely according to the individual dictates of present consciousness, and only memory, complacent familiarity, and vague intuition give us the illusion of objectivity and some "higher truth" than that of personal perception. In particular, deconstructive, psychoanalytic, and reader-response criticism indicates that authority is not found in some abiding feature of WRITING or reading; rather, it is found in becoming alert to consciousness as performative agent in a constant

struggle to define its own "textual integrity." Exploring the theoretical underground they have discovered are such challenging literary thinkers as H. Bloom, S. DE BEAUVOIR, P. DE MAN, J. DERRIDA, M. FOUCAULT, J. KRISTEVA, J. Hillis Miller, and J. LACAN, to name the most prominent among many. They reverse, revise, and often reestablish (but on an entirely unique level) the arguments gleaned from a Romantic past that forcefully acts on our present state of literary and social awareness. Remarkably, a high proportion of major contemporary critics, scholars, and philosophers have found in Romanticism a shaping influence on the twentieth century that urges trenchant responses.

For example, if feminist theorists seek to recover and establish women writers from the Romantic period or examine the conscious and unconscious forms of feminine identity projected through male writers, a concentrated investigation could include representations of women's physicality, psychological particulars of gender experience, status of discourse, and social or economic dependency. The central question has to do with the means whereby inclusive feminine reality in relation to human identity is established by a writer, particularly when there is firm evidence of oppression caused by a system of patriarchal thinking and behavior, as indicated in studies undertaken by M. Jacobus, M. Levinson, B. Johnson, and A. Ostriker. The momentous effort of feminism, then, must be that of deconstructing an overriding scheme of male values, which should create an intense and prolonged argument with traditional Romanticists.

Similarly, Marxism and New Historicism examine closely the distinctive cultural, economic, legal, political, religious, and social circumstances that surround a writer and become embedded revelations, wittingly or not, in creative literature. For Marxists, of course, a powerful text can become a vital expression of individual and CLASS conflict based on the strictures of oppressive and exploitative situations, and while New Historicists prefer to avoid any one ideological bias, they also base their work on precise historical indicators that might inform and determine literary meaning. T. Bennett, T. Clark, A. Lui, and J. McGann apply methods of analysis that have enriched and complicated positively our theoretical understanding of the material basis underpinning Romantic poetry.

Other directions in literary analysis, such as psychoanalytic and reader-response criticism, tend to emphasize a precise regard for the SIGNS,

METAPHORS, and symbols in language that both consciously or unconsciously appear in the form of narrative substance and can be identified with authorial design. Of necessity, the verbal behavior of an author encourages us to speculate upon possible motivations behind WRITING (the author's), within the TEXT (the fictional characters'), and beyond the text (the reader's), as layer upon layer of intentionality comes under investigation. Here, every text and every reading are remarkable preparations for another text and another reading. Like the mind itself, textual accountability is continually in process, and writer–text–reader are all responsible for discovering the various strategies and distinctive features related to human consciousness. Theorists ranging from G. BACHELARD and J. Lacan to D. Bleich, S. FISH, and J. Tompkins have stimulated avenues of thinking that are then related to Romanticism by critics such as M. Cooke, S. Curran, F. Ferguson, K. Johnston, and S. Wolfson.

Not yet exhausted, but obviously and repeatedly acknowledged by the Romantic poets and their commentators, is the theoretical realm that can be termed "the imaginary world of the imagining self," an area of "truth" (not absolute, but at least existential) that can formally be established for writer, text, and reader, and which unqualifiedly occupies a central site in literary conceptualization. Such exploration has less to do with conventional theories of imagination than it does with problematic, even seemingly quirky, processes that deal with the facticity of imagining. As a mental action in writing and reading, imagining reveals what is "true" as grounded in our emotions, intellects, and experiences with the real phenomena of the world, and for our purposes, especially literary phenomena. Imagining becomes the serious play area of the inquisitive, critical, and creative mind that refuses merely to convert process into product, becoming into being; instead, the struggle for, not over, imaginative power proceeds endlessly, and its final formulation always hovers tantalizingly in front of, not behind us.

As noted formerly, the Romantic poets themselves were obviously preoccupied with such issues germane to the composition of and reception to the aesthetic object. However, what can be seen as unique, albeit in some measure expected, about the most recent perspectives on Romanticism is the notion that the historical inheritance from literature and philosophy forms a parlance attempting to be "correct" about its subject while simultaneously undermining and revising its own preconceptions: if we think that the Romantic poets were "right" in poetically projecting ahead to an approximate forecast of the modern condition and temperament, we are also "wrong" in thinking circularly that no further aesthetic or intellectual contest is demanded of them or of us. Their works stand as a constant "invitation to the voyage," in the words of Gaston Bachelard.

We should not consider "Romanticism" as a concept that is defined permanently, but rather as an evolving phenomenon that can be tested constantly by personal experience. The way we interpret and understand poets like Blake, Wordsworth, Coleridge, Byron, Shelley, Keats, and other Romantic writers depends wholly on our unique historical perception of the world and the self. Most importantly, participating vicariously in these poets' imaginary worlds, enhanced by the theories invented and applied to them, may bring us closer to the dynamic process whereby we understand better our own "romantic" sensibility in conjunction with its present reality. Perhaps Shelley's Demogorgon is right – "The deep truth is imageless" – but such a divine and romantic assertion should not prevent us from pursuing truth modestly.

Reading

Abrams, M.H. 1971: *Natural Supernaturalism: Tradition and Revolution in Romantic Literature.*

Bloom, Harold, de Man, Paul, Derrida, Jacques, Hartman, Geoffrey, and Miller, J. Hillis 1979: *Deconstruction and Criticism.*

Chase, Cynthia 1986: *Decomposing Figures: Rhetorical Readings in the Romantic Tradition.*

de Man, Paul 1976 (*1984*): *The Rhetoric of Romanticism.*

Ferguson, Frances 1992: "Romantic studies."

Jacobus, Mary 1990: *Romanticism, Writing, and Sexual Difference: Essays on the Prelude.*

Johnston, Kenneth R., et al. 1990: *Romantic Revolutions: Criticism and Theory.*

Manning, Peter J. 1990: *Reading Romantics: Texts and Contexts.*

McGann, Jerome J. 1983: *The Romantic Ideology.*

Mellor, Anne K., ed. 1988: *Romanticism and Feminism.*

Rajan, Tillotama 1990: *The Supplement of Reading: Figures of Understanding in Romantic Theory and Practice.*

Simpson, David 1979: *Irony and Authority in Romantic Poetry.*

Wolfson, Susan 1986: *The Questioning Presence: Wordsworth, Keats, and the Interrogative Mode in Romantic Poetry.*

JOHN V. MURPHY

Rorty, Richard (1931–) American philosopher who, having trained and practiced in the tradition of analytic philosophy (where he was well respected for work in the philosophy of mind and language), became important for CRITICAL THEORY by repudiating that tradition to embrace a neopragmatism which converges with contemporary continental theory on many major issues. Chief among these are anti-essentialism and anti-foundationalism, the HISTORICITY of human thought, the creation of "truth," and the ineluctable hermeneutic and linguistic dimension of experience. Rorty combines these radical philosophical themes with a defense of bourgeois liberalism.

RICHARD SHUSTERMAN

Rosen, Charles (1927–) US concert pianist, musicologist, critic, and cultural historian. Rosen's unique combination of talents has made him into an exemplary figure in modern interdisciplinary studies. His writing on music is informed by both a historian's understanding of composition and performance as social acts, and a performer's fingertip knowledge of musical meaning as it emerges, develops, and crystallizes over time.

Rosen was born in New York City and attended the Juilliard School of Music until the age of eleven. Thereafter his piano teachers were Moriz Rosenthal and his wife, Hedwig Kanner-Rosenthal. In 1951 he made his recital debut in New York and was awarded a doctorate at Princeton for a dissertation on eighteenth-century French drama. His extensive discography ranges from Bach and Haydn to Boulez and Elliott Carter, and includes luminous accounts of Beethoven's last six sonatas (1972) and Diabelli variations (1977). His writings include *The Classical Style* (1971), *Schoenberg* (1976), *Sonata Forms* (1980), *Romanticism and Realism* (1984) (with Henri Zerner), and *The Romantic Generation* (1995). There exists also a large corpus of occasional writings, as yet uncollected, including many program and liner notes and a remarkable sequence of review articles, often written for the *New York Review of Books*, on a wide variety of cultural topics.

Rosen's music criticism is informed by a keen sense of drama at all levels of argument and analysis. Whether he is discussing the social conditions in which sonata form was consolidated in the late eighteenth century, the clash between different styles inside "Romantic" musical culture, or the buildup and discharge of tension during a single symphonic movement, his attention is always drawn to the placing and timing of key events within complex processes of development. *The Classical Style* is a masterpiece in which precise textual observation is combined with bold speculative criticism, and it is Rosen's dramaturgical imagination that holds these two elements together. The symphonic procedures of Haydn and Mozart, for example, are contrasted in their different approaches to intrigue and resolution:

> In one respect, Haydn's technique of expansion in the recapitulation is less sophisticated than Mozart's, as it consists of a periodic return to the first theme, largely unaltered, as a springboard for quasi-sequential developments, while Mozart is able to expand the phrase, or the individual member of the larger form, as he expands the whole. But this distinction cannot be made a reproach to Haydn, as he has deliberately contracted the phrases of the exposition in preparation for the great expansion of the second half of the movement: the recapitulation seems to be made up of separate small bits of the exposition, like a mosaic, but the spirit that put the pieces together had a tough, dynamic conception of the total controlling rhythm that even Mozart could rarely attain outside opera. (Rosen, 1971, pp. 160–1)

Beethoven in his late keyboard works is seen making an apparently anachronistic return to earlier "Baroque" fugue and variation forms in order to resolve tensions that he himself had introduced into the sonata argument proper. And Schoenberg's later career is presented as a conflict between serialism itself and the melodic structures that were still necessary to organize long stretches of musical time: "The attempt to create 'melodies' against the grain of serialism restored the necessary tension that had gone out of tonality" (Rosen, 1976, p. 111). Rosen's musical criticism is also notable for the unembarrassed directness with which he writes about the emotional content of these unfolding dramas: the grief that finds expression in the twenty-fifth of Bach's Goldberg variations, the terror in Mozart's G minor quintet and late G minor symphony, or the hallucinated anxiety in Schoenberg's *Erwartung* are described with rare candor and eloquence.

What makes Rosen's approach particularly instructive for modern CULTURAL STUDIES is the rigor with which he incorporates comparison – between works, styles, epochs, art forms – into his arguments. Not only does he turn aside gracefully to, say, Marvell and Poussin in discussing Haydn's pastoralism, or to Marivaux and Goldoni in characterizing Mozart the dramatist, but he also suggests new ways in which different art forms can become intelligible to each other. In Rosen's writing, the technical language of musical analysis is constantly animated by another language, more general but still nuanced and precise, in which the dynamic and temporal complexities of art works become articulable. He writes about the difficulties, tensions, and paradoxes with which artists, irrespective of their chosen medium, grapple, and about the new comparative perspectives which come into view once this common ground has been recognized. Writing about the dramatic imperative in art, Rosen is himself a compelling dramatist of artistic ideas.

Reading
Rosen, C. 1971: *The Classical Style: Haydn, Mozart, Beethoven.*
——1976: *Schoenberg.*
——1980: *Sonata Forms.*
——and Zerner, H. 1984: *Romanticism and Realism: The Mythology of Nineteenth-Century Art.*
——1995: *The Romantic Generation.*

MALCOLM BOWIE

Rosenberg, Harold (1906–78) American art critic. Although emerging from much the same milieu as Clement GREENBERG, Rosenberg took a poetic rather than an academic approach in his description of abstract expressionism – he is the Thomas Gainsborough of art criticism to Greenberg's Sir Joshua Reynolds. His view of the Art of Ashile Gorky, Jackson Pollock, and Barnett Newman, for example, focused attention on the action of its making rather than on the resulting surface, finding in their work a break in the tradition of the new and an awakening of the consciousness of self.
See also AVANT-GARDE.

Reading
Rosenberg, Harold 1959: *The Tradition of the New.*
——1964 (*1966*): *The Anxious Object: Art Today and Its Audience.*
——1962: *Ashile Gorky: The Man, the Times, the Idea.*

GERALD EAGER

Roszak, Theodore (1933–) American writer. Best known for *The Making of a Counter Culture* (1969), a work linking an indigenous American critical tradition (as represented, for example, by Paul GOODMAN) with ideas drawn from the European New Left to create a romantically inspired anti-science philosophy. In subsequent books and articles he has continued to develop this critique of technology and the scientific style of mind which he claims is responsible for the inhuman character and destructive potential of modern societies.
See also COUNTERCULTURE; GOODMAN, PAUL.

Reading
Roszak, T. 1968 (*1971*): *The Making of a Counter Culture: Reflections on the Technocratic Society and Its Youthful Opposition.*
——1972: *Where the Wasteland Ends: Politics and Transcendence in Postindustrial Society.*

COLIN CAMPBELL

Rousseau, Jean-Jacques (1712–78) French author. Rousseau was a prolific writer who made important contributions to autobiography, educational theory, the novel, and political philosophy. His most important writings include *Discours sur les sciences et les arts* (1750), *Discours sur l'origine de l'inégalité* (1755), *Julie, ou la Nouvelle Héloïse* (1761), *Emile* (1762), *Du Contrat social* (1762), *Les Confessions* (1781–8), and *Les Rêveries du promeneur solitaire* (1782). Rousseau's ideas about language – especially about relationships between speech and WRITING – have been of major importance to Claude LÉVI-STRAUSS and Jacques DERRIDA, whose *Of Grammatology* (1967) is in part a history of the "age of Rousseau." Jean Starobinski's scholarship on Rousseau has been exceptionally influential in recent reassessments of Rousseau's thought.

Reading
Starobinski, Jean 1957 (*1988*): *Jean-Jacques Rousseau: Transparency and Obstruction.*

MICHAEL PAYNE

Russian formalism A trend in LITERARY CRITICISM in Russia during the first third of the twentieth century. It was distinguished from previous trends in criticism by the fact that it made the analysis of literary TEXT the center of its critical investigations and emphasized the predominant significance of form and striving for the discovery of the immanent laws of language and literature. Historically, Russian formalism developed in two stages: the initial, *Sturm und Drang* period from the mid-1910s to the mid-1920s, and the classic stage of the second half of the 1920s.

Russian formalism originated in the practices of OPOYAZ (the Society for Studies of Poetic Language) in St Petersburg and was closely associated with Russian futurism. The members of OPOYAZ included V. SHKLOVSKY, B. Eikhenbaum, and O. Brik among others. Also close to OPOYAZ were Yu. TYNYANOV, B. Tomashevsky, V. Vinogradov, and S. Berenstein. Russian formalism emerged as a reaction to the impressionism of symbolist criticism and the academic eclecticism of preceding literary movements. The meetings and discussions held by members of OPOYAZ began in the immediate pre-1914–18 war years. The results of these discussions were published between 1916 and 1919 in three slim volumes titled *Collections of Articles on the Theory of Poetic Language* (*Sborniki po teorii poeticheskogo yazyka*). This collection, which can be considered the birthplace of many formalist ideas (or containing the germination of many future formalist ideas) became a turning point in the development of literary criticism not only in Russia but also in Europe and America, in that the contributing scholars turned their attention to studying literature as an immanent structure rather than a representation of historical reality.

In developing their views, the members of OPOYAZ were influenced by theories of language, literature, and CULTURE proposed in the works of Russian scholars A. Potebnya and A. Veselovsky. From Veselovsky, the founder of historical poetics, formalists borrowed the notion of independence of the subject of literary investigation from extrinsic elements: religion, philosophy, morals, etc. The influence of A. Potebnya, the proponent of linguistic poetics in Russia, was even more pronounced. Potebnya's parallels between the general structure of literary work and elements of the word became the precursors of the formalist concepts. Russian futurism, with its notions of a "self-sufficient word" and neologistic, "beyonsense" language, provided the fertile soil for the initial formalist investigations. In their early works, like Shklovsky's "Art as device" and Eikhenbaum's "How Gogol's *Overcoat* is made," formalists rejected methods of cultural-historical, psychological, and sociological schools of criticism and began to approach literary work as a SYSTEM of devices: a work of ART is a sum of literary devices, a device is only a SUBJECT of literary studies, a work of art has no connections with either the personality of its creator or with life and the ideology in which it was created; the development of literature is accomplished by the "automatization" of devices and

"estrangement." According to Shklovsky, the artist's task consisted of the destruction of old, automatized poetic forms by isolating literary objects from their usual context.

The new form, created by an artist, removes objects of everyday life (*byt* in Shklovsky's term) from their usual contexts and makes them "strange," thus forcing readers to react to them as though they perceive them for the first time in their lives (destroying the automatism of their perception enabling them to see an object and not simply to recognize it).

Another important contribution to literary poetics was the formalists' discussion of the structure of literary plot in which they distinguished two components: *fabula* (story) and *siuzhet* (plot *per se*). By *fabula*, formalists understood the totality of events and literary motifs ordered according to their temporal succession (as they would occur in reality) and, as Tomashevsky stressed, according to their logical causality. *Suzhet* was seen as the totality of the same events and motifs in the sequence in which they are arranged in a literary TEXT. Thus, *suzhet* was the liberation of events from temporal contiguity and causal dependency and their teleological redistribution in a literary work. *Fabula* was equated with material and served an artist as a mere pretext for plot construction, a process governed not by external causes but by internal, formal laws.

Russian formalism assumed its classic form in the mid-1920s when OPOYAZ was disbanded (in 1923) and its members merged with the Moscow Linguistic Circle led by Grigory Vinokur and Roman JAKOBSON. At that time, the "Formal school" or "method" in literary criticism (which gave the identification to the entire trend) was officially established on the basis of the postfuturist journal *LEF*, the leading organ of constructivism in Soviet art.

The cornerstone of Russian formalist theory was an attempt to overcome the dualism of form and content, which they tried to accomplish by developing the notion of form as the only expression of specificity of art and by "content" as a nonartistic category. The members of Russian formalism limited the notion of form to mostly "poetic language" which, in their opinion, possessed "immanent" laws of development and was independent of other nonliterary "rows." Proceeding from a KANTIAN concept of beauty (which they acquired from the rejected criticism of a symbolist critic, A. Bely), the formal school considered that the reflection of reality, with its problems and ideas, was not the task of art. An artist created forms which by themselves transmitted his or her emotional experiences.

The most important change which Russian formalists initiated in literary studies was their effort to transfer the emphasis onto studying the poetic language as such: the interplay of verbal forms, TROPES, sounds, syntactic constructions, etc. An artistic image was perceived as merely a "device of poetic language." Composition appeared as a certain sequence in positioning of narrative segments, a parallel was drawn between devices of plot construction and elements of poetic syntax (repetitions, parallelisms, etc.). Studying literature using "precise" statistical, linguistic methods produced remarkable results and allowed one to explore previously unexplored questions: stylistic forms of speech and language (Vinogradov); rhyme, meter, and composition of the verse (Zhirmundsky); the relationship between the semantic and verse construction (Tynyanov); syntax and intonation (B. Eikhenbaum); rhythm and meter (Tomashevsky); language intonations of the futurists (Vinokur); *fabula* and plot (V. Shklovsky); systematic description of the fairy tale (V. PROPP); principles of phonologic studies of verse and stylistic semantics (Jakobson).

In the late 1920s, formalists advanced their earlier concepts of literary work. The most important development in this respect was Tynyanov and Jakobson's article "Problems in studies of literature and language" in 1928. Tynyanov replaced the early formalist notion of a literary work as a sum total of devices with that of a system and started to consider literature in its totality. The elements of literary work were no longer summed up but instead related to each other. They comprehended devices not separately but through a dynamic relation between themselves and the entire literary system. Each literary work was considered a minimal system which existed as a variable in a higher system which in turn was a variable in the ultimate cultural system of systems. The next step was to consider the inner literary system in the context of literary life, that is, a concrete social milieu which in turn was systematic. The methodology of Russian formalism was called "functional poetics."

In the late 1920s, Tynyanov and Propp introduced the notion of literary function which meant that the same elements of literature during different literary epochs had equal significance. The dis-

cussion of these questions led later to SEMIOTICS. The further development of Russian formalism created a broader understanding of form and content in their unity, especially in the works of such scholars as M. BAKHTIN and R. Jakobson, as well as in studies of the Tartu school led by Yu. Lotman which tried to broaden the functional poetics by including in their analytical method the connections between the artistic text and history of literature, CLASS, and national culture, etc.

In late 1928, formalism came under attack from the emerging influence of socialist realism, which demanded that literature be the Communist Party's instrument of propaganda of socialist ideology and saw formalist insistence on the autonomy of literature as dangerous. The formalist approach was opposed to Marxist-Leninist principles of literary criticism, which became the basis of socialist realism (the only acceptable method of Soviet arts). Individual members of the formal school were forced to renounce their mistakes: Shklovsky's public denunciation of formalist principles in 1930 signified the official death of formalism.

Prohibited in its home country, formalism continued its life in Western movements, like the Anglo-American New Criticism. The formalists' claim of the autonomy of literary studies and their insistence on the methodological privacy of a metaliterary approach found their complete realization in the Structuralism and semiotics of the second half of the twentieth century.

See also FOREGROUNDING; FORMALISM; JAKOBSON; SHKLOVSKY; SYSTEM; TYNYANOV.

Reading

Bakhtin, M.M., and Medvedev, P.N. 1978: *The Formal Method in Literary Scholarship: A Critical Introduction to Sociologist Poetics.*

Erlich, Victor 1965 (*1981*): *Russian Formalism. History-Doctrine.*

Gorman, David 1992: *A Bibliography of Russian Formalism in English.*

Jackson, R., and Rudy, S., eds 1985: *Russian Formalism. A Retrospective Glance.*

Jameson, Frederick 1972: *The Prison House of Language: A Critical Account of Structuralism and Russian Formalism.*

Pomorska, Krystyna 1968: *Russian Formalist Theory and Its Poetic Ambiance.*

Stacy, R.H. 1974: *Russian Literary Criticism: A Short History.*

Steiner, Peter 1984: *Russian Formalism: A Metapoetics.*

Thompson, E.M. 1971: *Russian Formalism and Anglo-American Criticism: A Comparative Study.*

SLAVA I. YASTREMSKI

S

Said, Edward William (1935–) Literary and cultural theorist. Born in Jerusalem, Palestine, Edward Said attended schools in Jerusalem, Cairo, and Massachusetts, and since 1963 has been Parr Professor of English and Comparative Literature at Columbia University.

Since Said's first book, *Joseph Conrad and the Fiction of Autobiography* (1966), his thinking has embraced three broad imperatives: first, to articulate the cultural position and task of the intellectual and critic. Said's formulations in this area, influenced by FOUCAULT, provided a crucial impetus to the NEW HISTORICISM in the 1980s, which was in part a reaction against the tendency of American adherents of STRUCTURALISM and POSTSTRUCTURALISM to isolate literature from its various contexts or to reduce those contexts to an indiscriminate "textuality." Said's second concern has been to examine Western DISCOURSES about the Orient in general and Islam in particular. His own origin has defined a third, more immediately political commitment: to bring to light the Palestinian struggle to regain a homeland. Some regard him as a model of the politically engaged scholar, while others view his enterprise as incoherent. Rather than follow a strictly chronological pattern, this account of Said's work will pursue the three lines indicated above.

In *Beginnings* (1975) Said adapts insights from the Italian philosopher Giambattista Vico's *New Science* (1744) to distinguish between "origin," as divine, mythical, and privileged, and "beginning," which is secular and humanly produced. An "origin," as in classical and neoclassical thought, is endowed with linear, dynastic, and chronological eminence, centrally dominating what derives from it. In contrast, a beginning, especially as embodied in much modern thought, encourages orders of dispersion, adjacency, and complementarity (1975, pp. xii, 373). Said defines beginning as its own method, as a first step in the intentional production of meaning, and as the production of difference from preexisting traditions. For beginning to comprise such an activity of subversion, it must be informed by an inaugural logic which authorizes subsequent texts; it both enables them and limits what is acceptable (1975, pp. 32–4).

Drawing on insights of Vico, Valéry, NIETZSCHE, SAUSSURE, Lévi-Strauss, Husserl, and Foucault, Said argues that the novel represents the major form of "beginning" in Western literary culture. In postmodernist literature, beginning embodies an effort to achieve knowledge and art using a "violently transgressive" language.

The problematics of language lie at the heart of "beginnings." With DERRIDA, Foucault, and DELEUZE, Said rejects Lévi-Strauss's notion that language has a "center": rather, meaning is produced within a political and cultural power structure. Certain forms of writing establish rules of admissibility (1975, pp. 16, 377). Given their exposure of the hierarchical and often oppressive SYSTEM of language, Said places Foucault and Deleuze within the "adversary epistemological current" running through Vico, MARX, LUKÁCS, and FANON. Following Foucault, he defines WRITING as the act of "taking hold" of language, which means beginning again rather than taking up language at the point ordained by tradition (1975, pp. 13, 378–9).

A dilemma, however, haunts this enterprise. Said sees MARX, Darwin, FREUD, and Foucault as "passionate radicals" who viewed beginnings not as events but as types or forces (CLASS, UNCONSCIOUS, EPISTEME). He also sees the later French theorists BARTHES, Foucault, Derrida, and LACAN as accounting for reality in terms of impersonal agencies (1975, pp. 51, 373–4). According to Said, criticism should be a constant reexperiencing of beginning, promoting not authority but noncoercive and communal activity (1975, pp. 379–80). However, it is not clear how Said reconciles the "impersonal" accounts of the world offered by the "radicals" he cites with the possibility of effective individual endeavor.

It is precisely CRITICAL THEORY's retreat into a "labyrinth of textuality," whereby it betrays its "insurrectionary" beginnings in the the 1960s, which motivates Said's central arguments in *The World, the Text, and the Critic* (1983). He sees both the "radical" factions of the academy and the traditional humanists as having sold out to the "principle of non-interference" and the ethic of professionalism, a self-domestication concurrent with the rise of Reaganism (1983, pp. 3–4). Contemporary criticism is now politically irrelevant, merely affirming the values of a Eurocentric, dominative, and elitist culture (1983, pp. 25–6).

Said redefines the TEXT as "worldly," as implicated in real social and political conditions: its most important feature is the fact of its production (1983, p. 50), the specific conditions of which generate its capacity to produce meaning. As opposed to critical hypostatizations of semantic "undecidability," texts constrain their own interpretation by placing themselves, intervening in given ideological and aesthetic conjunctures. Texts are marked by an interplay between their speech and the contours of its projected reception. Moreover, as texts dislodge and displace other texts, they are essentially facts of power, not of democratic exchange (1983, pp. 39–40, 45). Hence texts can be opposed neither to the world nor to speech as the privileged bearer of worldly connections. In short, "Texts are a system of forces institutionalized by the reigning CULTURE at some human cost to its various components" (1983, pp. 48–9, 53).

As implied in the foregoing statement, Said views "culture" as intrinsically hierarchical, defining it as a hegemonic environment in which certain modes of thought prevail. Said is indebted here to Foucault's view of culture as an institution which perpetually reinforces itself by differentiation, or domestication, of what is external to it (1983, pp. 8–9, 11–12). Hence Said sees culture as that which fixes the range of meanings of "home," "belonging," and "community"; beyond these are anarchy and homelessness. It is within this opposition that Said, as hinted in *Beginnings*, wishes to carve out a space of "in-betweenness" within civil society for the intellectual and critic. He sees the circumstances of Auerbach's composition of *Mimesis* (1968) as prototypical of the critic's position between "filiation" and "affiliation": written in exile from its author's own culture, Auerbach's text was enabled by a critically important ALIENATION from the Western cultural tradition even as it affirmed that tradition (1983, pp. 5–8). Echoing ARNOLD, whose ultimate identification of culture with state authority he rejects, Said suggests that the "function of

criticism at the present time" is to stand between the dominant culture and the totalizing forms of critical systems (p. 5). He articulates this in terms of the notions of filiation (given ties of family, home, class, and country) and affiliation (an acquired allegiance to an alternative system of values). Said argues that many modernist writers such as Joyce and ELIOT, having experienced the failure of filiative ties, turned to compensatory affiliation with something broader than the parameters of their original situation.

Nevertheless, the passage from filiation to affiliation can itself be coercive, the latter reproducing the generational and hierarchical securities of the former (1983, pp. 15–20, 25). This is what has happened in academia, the university experience effectively rehearsing filiative discipline. Critics can either engage in organic complicity with the resulting Eurocentric model for the humanities or they can adopt an oppositional stance which opens up to scrutiny the social and political world (1983, p. 24). The identity of the criticism Said advocates lies precisely in its difference from other cultural activities and totalizing systems of thought and method. This "secular" criticism focuses on local and worldly situations, opposing itself to the production of massive hermetic or transcendent systems (1983, pp. 26, 291). Said characterizes such criticism not only as oppositional but also ironic, inasmuch as, to remain criticism, it must resist its own integration into fixity or dogma. The task of criticism is to combat every form of tyranny, domination, and abuse; to promote noncoercive knowledge in the interests of human freedom and to articulate possible alternatives to the prevailing orthodoxies of culture and system (1983, 29–30). While Said regards Vico and Swift as protoypes of such opposition, his characterization of Swift as "anarchic in his sense of the range of alternatives to the status quo" might well be applied to himself.

Interestingly, Said traces the emergence of Eurocentrism to Renan's transference of authority from divinely authorized texts to an ethnocentric philology which diminished the status of semitic languages and the "Orient." This theme is developed in *Orientalism* (1978), where Said examines the vast tradition of Western "constructions" of the Orient. Orientalism has been a "corporate institution" for coming to terms with the Orient, for authorizing views about it and ruling over it. Central to Said's analysis is that the Orient is actually a production of Western discourse, a means of self-definition of Western culture as well as justifying imperial domination of oriental peoples (1978, p. 3). Said concentrates on the modern history of British, French, and American engagement with primarily the Islamic world.

Given his crucial treatment of Orientalism as a discourse, his aim is not to show that this edifice of language somehow distorts a "real" Orient, but rather to display it indeed as a language, with an internal consistency, motivation, and capacity for representation resting on a relationship of power and HEGEMONY over the Orient. The book is also an attempt to display Orientalism as but one complex example of the politically and ideologically rooted nature of all discourse (1978, p. 14). Using a vast range of examples, from Aeschylus's play *The Persians* through Macaulay, Renan, and Marx, to Gustave von Grunbaum and the *Cambridge History of Islam*, Said attempts to examine the stereotypes and distortions through which Islam and the East have been consumed. These stereotypes include: Islam as a heretical imitation of Christianity (1978, pp. 65–6); the exotic sexuality of the Oriental woman (1978, p. 187); and Islam as a uniquely unitary phenomenon and a culture incapable of innovation (1978, pp. 296–8). Said's analyses stress the situational peculiarities of individual writers who, in contrast to Foucault, he regards as having a "determining imprint" (p. 23).

Said suggests that twentieth-century electronic and postmodern America reinforces dehumanized portrayals of the Arabs, a tendency aggravated by the Arab–Israeli conflict and intensely felt by Said himself as a Palestinian. In *The Question of Palestine* (1979), Said, a member of the Palestine National Council, attempts to place before the American reader a historical account of the Palestinian experience and plight. *Covering Islam* (1981) reveals how media representations "produce" Islam, reducing its adherents to anti-American fanatics and fundamentalists. Said's later book *Culture and Imperialism* (1993) continues the themes raised in *Orientalism*, extending its compass to discourses on Africa, India, and the Far East as well as Conrad, Jane Austen, and Camus – all of which are shown as participants in a vast system of cultural imperial domination. Said's uniqueness as a cultural critic lies in the range of his interests which allows him to explore the nexus of connections between literature, politics, and religion in a global rather than a national or Eurocentric context.

See also ISLAMIC STUDIES.

Reading
McGowan, J. 1991: "The literary left: Jameson, Eagleton, Said."
Sprinker, M., ed. 1992: *Edward Said: A Critical Reader.*

M.A.R. HABIB

Santayana, George (1863–1952) Spanish-born American philosopher. Born in Madrid, Santayana was brought to America at the age of eight and a half. He was educated at the Boston Latin School and Harvard College. After two years of graduate study in Germany, he returned to America and took his doctorate in philosophy from Harvard in 1889. He was afterwards an instructor and later professor of philosophy at Harvard until his retirement at the age of 48 in 1912. He then returned permanently to Europe to devote himself to writing. Santayana lived in Oxford during the 1914–18 war, and afterward in Paris and Monaco. During the early 1920s he settled permanently in Rome. Always a bachelor, Santayana lived by a strict routine, rising and retiring early, and devoting the full morning to writing. By the end of a long life, he had produced an astonishing number of books and articles on philosophical subjects, as well as poetry, plays, essays, literary criticism, autobiography (*Persons and Places*, 1944–53), and a best-selling novel (*The Last Puritan*, 1935). Santayana began his career as one of the neo-traditionalist or Harvard poets, but by the time of the publication of his final book of new poems, *A Hermit of Carmel and Other Poems* (1901), he decided to abandon poetry and devote himself to philosophy.

Santayana's first prose book, *The Sense of Beauty* (1896) – the radical thesis of which is that beauty is the objectification of pleasure – has become a classic in AESTHETICS; however, it was the appearance of *The Life of Reason: Or the Phases of Human Progress* (five volumes, 1905–6) that firmly established his reputation as a thinker. Fundamental to this work is Santayana's adherence to the classical Greek ideal of the "life of reason," an anti-romantic view that the best and most satisfying life depends upon self-knowledge and the self-discipline necessary to a rational harmony of the passions: the Aristotelian ideal of *sophrosune* or moderation. It is an example of Santayana's belief that the truest philosophy long preceded the present era, and that the best modern thinking is that which most effectively reflects the insights of the great ancients, particularly the Greeks, who long ago discovered the essential truths.

Subsequent to the *Life of Reason* was the development of Santayana's complete philosophical SYSTEM, something that in his earlier years he had not conceived of producing. This philosophical system is expressed most fully in the four-volume *Realms of Being* (1927–40). To each of the four realms – Essence, Matter, Truth, and Spirit – Santayana devoted an individual volume. The system is preceded and introduced by a separate technical work, *Scepticism and Animal Faith* (1923), which, in a compressed form, sets forth the concepts most fully articulated in *Realms of Being*.

The four realms are not regions or elements of being, but rather types or features thereof. The realm of essence comprises an infinite number of real but nonexistent and therefore immutable and indestructible forms. Unlike Plato's essences or forms, Santayana's are utterly passive. All efficacy resides in the realm of matter, the unformed and unconscious source of all power and existence. The selection and embodiment of essences by matter makes possible substance, the formed physical world. Though matter falls into habits, there is no rational purpose in nature, and there are no unalterable laws; all is contingent. Spirit (consciousness or mind) is epiphenomenal, dependent upon matter for its being. Like essences, spirit is impotent; it is only the psyche or vital physical organism become self-aware. In death, the psyche is vitiated and individual spirit or consciousness annihilated. Because matter in itself is unconscious, and because spirit derives from and depends upon a vital material organism, there can be no disembodied spirits, no afterlife, and no God.

The realm of truth is constituted by all those essences that become actualized as substance. Truth is, therefore, completely commonplace, though infinitely complex. From the point of view of human life, however, some truths are immensely more important than others. Our knowledge of the truth results from our intuition of essences *symbolic* of reality; we can never perceive the reality itself. Santayana's view, therefore, may be described as modified skepticism: though we can never perceive reality *per se*, we must none the less believe that the perceptible world exists, which we do through "animal faith." Santayana is, therefore, philosophically a materialist and a naturalist. Except in so far as consciousness is temporarily allied to some physical organism, nature is unconscious and indifferent to human interests. The life of reason requires that we accept and live in accord with this truth.

Though Santayana's writings have been largely neglected since his death, his views on American democracy and culture continue to exert significant influence on students of American civilization. Today, a modest revival of interest in Santayana has been heralded by a new critical edition of his works.

Reading

Dawidoff, Robert 1992: *The Genteel Tradition and The Sacred Rage: High Culture vs. Democracy in Adams, James, and Santayana.*
Lachs, John 1988: *George Santayana.*
McCormick, John 1987: *George Santayana: A Biography.*
Price, Kenneth M., and Leitz, Robert C. III, eds 1991: *Critical Essays on George Santayana.*
Sprigge, Timothy L.S. 1974: *Santayana: An Examination of His Philosophy.*

WILLIAM G. HOLZBERGER

Sapir, Edward (1884–1939) American linguist and anthropologist. Sapir was born in Germany, but his family emigrated to the United States when he was five. While studying at Columbia University he met Franz BOAS, who encouraged Sapir to study Native American languages and cultures. For 15 years Sapir worked in Ottowa, researching the indigenous peoples of Canada. He then taught at the Universities of Chicago and Yale.

Sapir did important work in phonology and historical linguistics, and on the classification of the indigenous languages of America. His name is sometimes linked with that of Benjamin Lee WHORF though statements rejecting the "Whorf hypothesis" can be found in his writings. Sapir also contributed significantly to anthropology, notably on the relation between CULTURE and society, and to Jewish studies. He read widely in psychiatry and PSYCHOANALYSIS, and wrote papers on the relation between culture and personality. His poems appeared in many places, and he wrote several musical works.

Sapir's introductory textbook *Language* (Sapir, 1921), is an elegant and attractive book that is still often recommended as an introduction to linguistics. Although Sapir and Leonard Bloomfield are usually regarded as the main architects of structuralist linguistics in North America (see LANGUAGE THEORIES), Sapir's broader range of scholarly interests meant that much of his influence was in anthropology and CULTURAL STUDIES, while Bloomfield's was stronger in linguistics. History has been kinder to Sapir, however: students nowadays tend to hear about the strengths of Sapir's work and the weaknesses of Bloomfield's. This is largely because Bloomfield avoided psychology, thinking it unscientific, whereas Sapir reveled in it. In circles where the buzzword is "cognitive," Sapir is frequently mentioned as an important intellectual forerunner.

Sapir combined scholarly rigor with a rare humanist breadth of interest and understanding. For appreciations of his work, see Koerner (1984).

Reading
Koerner, K. 1984: *Edward Sapir: Appraisals of His Life and Work.*
Sapir, E. 1921: *Language.*
——1949: *Selected Writings in Language, Culture and Personality.*

RAPHAEL SALKIE

Sartre, Jean-Paul (1905–80) French philosopher and writer, closely associated with the philosophy of EXISTENTIALISM. He is also known for his plays and novels in which philosophical issues are often to the fore. Later in life he became increasingly absorbed in theoretical and practical politics. Important influences on him are Descartes, KANT, Husserl, HEGEL, JASPERS, and HEIDEGGER.

In *Being and Nothingness* (1943) he addressed philosophical problems regarding the universal aspects of the individual human consciousness and its relation to the world, but later in life became increasingly concerned with questions of social anthropology, the relations of groups, and believed that his ideas must become more socially responsible, which led him to attempt a *rapprochement* of existentialism and MARXISM.

Sartre, following Husserl, accepts that the distinguishing feature of consciousness is "intentionality": conscious awareness is always directed to an object of attention. He rejects the idealism latent in Husserl's PHENOMENOLOGY and insists that the object of one's attention in a conscious act must be something that is not-consciousness. He suggests, as had Heidegger, that the world has significance for us only through our concrete being-in-the-world as actors with specifically human concerns, purposes, and needs. Such a world is logically prior, and is in no way inferior to the scientific world and metaphysical speculation which aim at a view of the world stripped of the distorting contingencies of the human perspective, one that is a passive pure disinterested spectatorial account of things, delivering the truth about the world as it is in itself; such an alienating view is parasitic on the world that emerges from our being-in-the-world.

Sartre insists that consciousness, being-for-itself, is not a thing at all, but defines itself through its negation (nothingness) in not being the non-human thing, being-in-itself, of which it is conscious. The interdependence of consciousness and a significant world undercuts dualism and the problem of our knowledge of the reality of the external world. Similarly our knowledge of other minds is presupposed in certain aspects of our consciousness of ourselves as a being-for-others, whereby we are aware of ourselves as an object of consciousness for others. These three modes of being are Sartre's complete and uneliminable list of ontological categories.

Sartre concludes that we are forced to be free. Human consciousness is what it is not, and is not what it is. We have no fixed predetermining essence, no prior "real selves," but rather make ourselves what we are only through what we do. We alone are responsible for what we choose to do and cannot pass the responsibility to any external authority in an attempt to escape our freedom; but it does not follow that we can act only irrationally. To act in "bad faith" is to attempt to evade our freedom while at root knowing that we cannot. Although conditioned by the "facticity" or circumstances of our situation, we have always the possibility of choice. To live in full awareness of our freedom is to act with authenticity. Only in death does an assessment of what kind of person someone is become fully legitimate.

In *Nausea* (1938) the existence and nature of the world in its full particularity are not intelligible or explicable: things are said to be "absurd" or "superfluous." Particular things exist and have features which are not deducible from their falling under essences or universal concepts; the categorization of a thing as falling into a class of things gives no intelligible explanation of the existence and the individualizing features of a thing. Particulars are ultimately unknowable and science is a simplifying fiction. Nonexistent ideal objects, such as triangularity, are completely determined and made intelligible by their defining essence; they are all and only what follows from their essence. *Nausea* describes a nightmare world in which things are starkly revealed as slipping out of being captured by our organizing categories and in which contingent causal laws break down.

Sartre's promised book on ETHICS failed to

materialize. However, one ethical consequence might be the duty upon us not to reify THE OTHER, by "The Look," as a being-in-itself, for in that way we fix others and deny their freedom. Nevertheless, it is difficult for us to resist this temptation because in fixing others as things we simultaneously undermine the other's ability to fix ourselves.

Reading
Danto, Arthur C. 1975: *Sartre*.
Hayman, Ronald 1986: *Writing Against: A Biography of Sartre*.
Howells, Christina, ed. 1992: *The Cambridge Companion to Sartre*.
Schilpp, P.A., ed. 1981: *The Philosophy of Jean-Paul Sartre*.
Warnock, Mary 1965: *The Philosophy of Sartre*.
                                             JOHN SHAND

Saussure, Ferdinand de (1857–1913) French theorist who became professor of linguistics at the University of Geneva. His *Course in General Linguistics* (*1983*), which was collated after his death by his colleagues and students, is considered a landmark text in the development of linguistics as a science, and as the foundation of STRUCTURALISM and SEMIOTICS.

Saussure's insight is that language is a system which is constituted by a relation of difference. There is an irreducible difference between the signified (the real-world object) and the signifier (the lexical item which refers to the object). The theory of the linguistic SIGN which he derives from this initial distinction states that the sign is the arbitrary relation between signifier and signified. What comprises a sign system such as a language is the difference between the signs, not any natural relation of signifier to signified. The sign has meaning only in its difference from other signs. The investigation of these differential relations is to be the sole province of the science of linguistics. This theory has the advantage of realizing that meaning is socially produced, rather than simply given.

Saussure is aware that the kind of science he envisages would require to be synchronic in its approach rather than diachronic, that is, it would pay attention to the state of a language at any one moment rather than to its historical evolution (see SYNCHRONY/DIACHRONY). The method by which this is to be achieved is the distinction between LANGUE/PAROLE. The utterance of an individual, *parole*, is assumed to be simply the product of the generality of the language available at that time,

and so is ignored in favor of the commonality itself, *langue*. Saussure's method therefore privileges the abstract *langue* over the individual *parole*. This is wholly in keeping with the structuralist impulse which powers his work, since the intention is to discover objectively verifiable laws. The relationship between the two is assumed to be stable. In fact, Saussure moves beyond this premise to a reference to a sort of collective unconscious which ultimately underpins all linguistic activity, a claim which is similar to that made later by Claude LÉVI-STRAUSS and structural linguists and literary theorists.

Given these concerns, it is unsurprising that his project almost completely ignores the problem of historical change: in fact, he goes so far as to acknowledge this and to privilege his science of linguistics over the merely contingent. It is this maneuver which constitutes the moment of his production of structural linguistics in opposition to the historical grammarians who were his predecessors and contemporaries. The symptom of this founding movement is a relatively simplistic approach to the problems posed for his assumptions by the written world – the literary text (see Derrida, 1976). In the chapter on the aims of linguistics, he concentrates on the verbal, but recommends that the written should not be neglected. This relegates written records to the status of secondhand witnesses, and privileges verbal communication because of the presence of the person making the utterance. For Saussure, linguistics should discover the fundamental logic which operates permanently and universally in all languages.

The structuralist assumption that such laws exist is obvious here. However, the vocabulary which he utilizes reveals more than this: his project is a moralizing one. The linguist is to denounce errors, to eradicate them, presumably in the name of an all-encompassing structure. And the object of his attack is the written word, which he sees as ossifying linguistic structure. He treats the written sign as unnaturally stable in its appearance, which of course ignores changes in orthography. He asserts that the visual has more psychological impact than the auditory, and so a literary language gives even more "unwarranted" attention to the written. The structuralist concern with the scientifically objective, the concretely definable, here produces a moralism which ultimately can be seen as an attempt to replace God with Structure. In his linguistics Saussure destroyed once and for all the notion that meaning is somehow derived from an ultimate guarantor, a transcendental locus. However, he also attempted to assert that nevertheless there is something which exists at a fundamental level (perhaps in the biological makeup of the human brain, which structures the functions of the human mind, as in later forms of structuralism). This something is an ultimate structure and his call for a linguistic science which will once and for all define all language use is predicated upon this assumption. It also makes his linguistics course read like nostalgia for the lost presence which it has revealed to be an empty space, and this is one of the points with which DE-CONSTRUCTION develops.

The structuralists who come after Saussure do not take his work at face value, but rather utilize it as a point for departure. Thus, for example, Roman JAKOBSON sees Saussurean linguistics as unnecessarily programmatic. Jakobson criticizes Saussure's privileging of one term of the many BINARY OPPOSITIONS he uses, such as his insistence on *langue* over *parole*. But, in common with other structuralists, he does not disagree with Saussure over the fundamental interests of his work, accepting his positing of a structure which ultimately defines all linguistic usage. Despite his interrogation of the uses Saussure makes of binary opposition in his theory, Jakobson does not question the concept itself. In this way Saussure's work serves to provide structuralism with most of its basic concepts, even as they engage with their denial of some of the uses he himself makes of these concerns. Similarly, some of the implications of Saussure's work have been picked up by POSTSTRUCTURALISM, implications which went unnoticed by the structuralists themselves. In particular, the notion of the arbitrary sign which is structured by difference produces a whole theory of the dissemination of meaning which marks a radical departure from Saussure's structural impulse. In this way the theoretical shift which he marks continues to resonate in CULTURAL THEORY.

Reading
Culler, Jonathan 1975 (*1989*): *Structuralist Poetics*.
Derrida, Jacques 1967a (*1976*): *Of Grammatology*.
Hawkes, Terence 1977: *Structuralism and Semiotics*.
Jakobson, Roman 1990a: *On Language*.
Saussure, Ferdinand de 1972 (*1983*): *A Course in General Linguistics*.

PAUL INNES

school, Chicago   *See* CHICAGO SCHOOL

school, Frankfurt   *See* FRANKFURT SCHOOL

school, Geneva   *See* GENEVA SCHOOL

Schorer, Mark (1908–77) American critic, biographer, novelist, and short-story writer. Best known for his biographies of Sinclair Lewis and D.H. Lawrence, Schorer was also influential for his explorations of the relation between fiction and biography, and for his demonstrations that NEW CRITICISM's methods of close verbal analysis could be applied to the novel as well as to POETRY. In his most widely quoted essay, "Technique as discovery" (1947), he explored the relationship between the novelist's moral insight and his or her command of narrative technique.

IAIN WRIGHT

science, philosophy of   What is the status of scientific truth claims? Can they purport to hold good for all time across vastly differing contexts of language, CULTURE, and society? That is to say: is science in the business of providing valid explanations of physical objects and events whose nature remains constant despite such deep-laid shifts of cultural perspective? Or is it not rather the case – as currently argued by relativists, pragmatists, and "strong" sociologists of knowledge – that those contexts provide the only means of understanding why science has taken such diverse forms (and come up with such a range of competing "truths") throughout its history to date?

These questions are of interest not only to philosophers and historians of science but also, increasingly, to cultural and critical theorists influenced by the widespread "linguistic turn" across various disciplines of thought. They are often linked with the issue of ontological relativity, that is, the argument – deriving principally from W.V.O. QUINE's famous essay "Two dogmas of empiricism" – that there exist as many ways of describing or explaining some given phenomenon as there exist ontological schemes or SYSTEMS for redistributing predicates over the entire range of sentences held true at any particular time. According to this holistic view there is no means of drawing a firm, categorical line between synthetic and analytic propositions, or matters of empirical (contingent) truth which might always be subject to revision in the light of further evidence, and on the other hand those so-called logical "laws of thought" whose truth is assumed to be a matter of *a priori* necessity and hence – by definition – valid for all possible contexts of inquiry. With the collapse of this distinction, so Quine argues, we must also let go of the idea that philosophy of science might yet come up with an adequate method for linking observation sentences to theories (or vice versa) through a clear-cut set of logical procedures. For in a holist perspective those sentences can possess meaning – that is to say, be assigned determinate truth values – only as a function of their role within the entire existing "fabric" or "web" of beliefs, or the entire set of truth claims ("empirical" and "logical" alike) that currently happen to command widespread assent. This is really to say that there are no such determinate truth values since theories are always at some point "under-determined" by the best evidence to hand, while that evidence is always "theory-laden" – or committed to some prior ontological scheme – right down to the level of its basic data as given in first-hand observation sentences. Thus for Quine it follows that one must apply a principle of strict ontological parity as between (for instance) Homer's gods, centaurs, numbers, set-theoretical classes, and brick houses on Elm Street. Any preference in the matter – and Quine admits readily that he has a whole range of such preferences – must in the end come down to one's particular choice of ontological scheme.

There are many other sources of this relativist trend in contemporary philosophy of science. They include Thomas KUHN's highly influential account of the way that science alternates between periods of "normal" and "revolutionary" activity, the former characterized by broad agreement on what counts as a proper (constructive and disciplined) approach to certain well-defined problems, the latter by a sense of impending crisis – and an absence of agreement on even the most basic principles – which heralds the transition to a new epoch. Here, as with Quine, it is taken for granted that all the components of a given scientific "PARADIGM" – from observation sentences to high-level theories – are intelligible only in terms of the prevailing consensus, or according to the overall framework of beliefs that provides its own (strictly immanent) criteria of truth, progress, theoretical consistency, evidential warrant, and so forth. However, it then becomes difficult – if not impossible – to explain how we could ever gain insight into scientific world

views other than our own; or again, how historians of science could ever claim to understand the *reasons* (that is, the scientific grounds) for some decisive paradigm shift, as distinct from the various short-term cultural, social, or historical factors that may have played some part in bringing them about. Hence Quine's recourse to the idea of "radical translation" as a means of (purportedly) bridging this otherwise insuperable gulf between different observation languages or ontological schemes. Hence also the difficulties that Kuhn confronted in his 1969 Postscript to *The Structure of Scientific Revolutions* (1970) when responding to his critics on the issue of relativism and its self-disabling consequences. For it is far from clear that these difficulties are in any way resolved by his Quinean (radical-empiricist) line in the face of such strong counterarguments.

This problem is yet more acute with the kinds of ultrarelativist position adopted by proponents of the present-day "linguistic turn" in its fully fledged (postmodern) guise. Thus it is sometimes claimed – for instance by Richard RORTY – that our best model for interpreting the process of scientific paradigm change is what happens when poets and novelists come up with striking new "metaphors we can live by," or again, when strong-revisionist literary critics interpret such metaphors after their own fashion. Then again there are those – Paul FEYERABEND chief among them – who espouse an anarchistic philosophy of science which rejects all appeals to truth, logic, reason, consistency, experimental proof, etc. According to this view the idea of scientific "progress" is nothing more than a piece of bogus mythology, one that takes hold through our myopically equating "truth" with what currently counts as such according to this or that (self-authorized) "expert" community. It is much better, Feyerabend thinks, to have done with this misplaced reverence for science and instead take account of the various factors – social, political, psychological, careerist, and so forth – which have always played a decisive role in the history of scientific thought. We can then see how mixed were the motives (and often how random or opportunist the methods) which gave rise to some so-called discovery or advance that is nowadays treated as a textbook example of its kind. This will bring two great benefits, as Feyerabend sees it. First, it will help to demythologize science – to remove some of its false prestige – and thereby open it up to criticism from other (that is non-

"expert" but socially and ethically more responsive) quarters. Second, it will encourage scientists to become more adventurous in framing risky conjectures or in pursuing novel and hererodox lines of thought.

There are various explanations that might be adduced for the current appeal of such ideas. One is the widely held view that philosophy of science can no longer have recourse to any version of the logical positivist (or logical empiricist) distinction between truths of observation on the one hand and self-evident (tautologous) truths of reason on the other. There are similar problems – so it is argued – with the appeal to deductive-nomological (or covering-law) theories, those which would seek to account for observational data by bringing them under some higher-level (metalinguistic) order of logical entailment relations. Here again the way is open for skeptics like Quine to argue that any such distinction will always be drawn according to some preferred ontological scheme, some language or culture-specific set of descriptive or explanatory priorities. One alternative that has enjoyed wide favor, not least among practicing scientists, is Karl POPPER's hypothetico-deductive account, whereby the measure of a theory's claim to genuine scientific status is not so much its truth as established by the best current methods of experimental testing, but its openness to falsification by those same methods. This account has the signal advantage of explaining how a great many scientific theories that once enjoyed widespread credence eventually have turned out to be mistaken, or – as with Newton's conceptions of absolute space and time – "true" relative only to a certain restricted spatio-temporal domain. It thus meets the criticism of those like Feyerabend, who would exploit such evidence to the point of denying that notions of truth have any role to play in the history and philosophy of science.

Nevertheless, there are difficulties with Popper's position, among them its reliance on underspecified criteria of what should count as a decisive falsification (or as grounds for rejecting some candidate hypothesis) in any given case. In other words, the methodology of "conjecture and refutation" – as Popper describes it – amounts to just a minor inverted variation on the positivist or logical-empiricist theme. Moreover, so his critics maintain, Popper has made illicit use of this dubious methodology in order to attack what he sees as the pseudoscientific pretensions of MARXISM and other such "histor-

icist" trends in the sociological, interpretative, or humanistic disciplines. If there is one type of argument that always draws fire from the present-day cultural relativists, it is the idea that science should enjoy any privileged truth-telling status, any method or set of validity conditions that would place it apart from those other (on its own terms) less rigorous or rationally accountable modes of knowledge. Such is the distinction standardly drawn between the "context of discovery" for scientific truth claims and the "context of justification" wherein those claims are subject to testing by the best available criteria of experimental warrant, theoretical consistency, causal-explanatory yield, and so forth. However, this distinction is rejected by those who maintain – whether on grounds of "ontological relativity" or in pursuit of the so-called strong program in SOCIOLOGY OF KNOWLEDGE – that truth is just a product of localized beliefs whose origin should be sought in their cultural context or in the sociobiographical history (the professional interests, careerist motives, childhood experiences, religious convictions, etc.) of the scientists who held them.

The poet W.H. Auden nicely epitomized this genre in its vulgar form: "A penny life will give you all the facts." More sophisticated, though no less sophistical variants would include Feyerabend's well-known claim that in the case of Galileo versus Cardinal Bellarmine and the church authorities it was not so much an issue of truth – that is, of the heliocentric hypothesis as against the geocentric – but simply a question of who had the better argument on rhetorical, social, or political grounds. Thus if Bellarmine sought to promote the interests of communal stability and peace, while Galileo can be shown to have fudged certain details (observational data) in order to preserve his theory, then the church comes off rather better on balance and – so Feyerabend advises – should even now stick to its doctrinal position and not lean over to accommodate the present-day scientific orthodoxy. Other versions of this argument (if rarely pushed to such a provocative extreme) are often to be found in the current literature on history and sociology of science. What they all have in common is the nominalist persuasion that "truth" is just a term honorifically attached to those items of belief that have managed to prevail, by whatever strategic or rhetorical means, in this contest for the high ground of scientific "knowledge" and "progress." Other sources include the "social construction of reality" thesis (taken up in philosophy of science by writers like Barry Barnes and David Bloor); the skeptical GENEALOGY of power/knowledge essayed across a range of disciplines by Michel FOUCAULT; and the argument of postmodernist thinkers such as Jean-François LYOTARD that science is just one among a range of incommensurable language games (cognitive, ethical, historical, political, etc.) and no longer exerts any privileged claim on knowledge or truth.

We have seen already how such skepticism extends to philosophies of science that invoke some form of deductive warrant from covering-law theories or hypotheses framed with a view to experimental proof or refutation. However, the same sorts of objection have also been brought against inductivist arguments, that is, those which take the opposite route, seeking to derive generalized descriptive or explanatory accounts from observed regularities in this or that physical domain. David Hume was of course the first to remark upon the problems that arise in offering any adequate (that is, more than "commonsense" or probabilistic) defense of inductive procedures. As he saw it, our ideas of causality came down to just a matter of regular succession, contiguity, and "constant conjunction," or our indurate belief that if one event normally follows another in the order of phenomenal experience, then this must be due to some intrinsic causal nexus or relationship between them. This fallacy (*post hoc, propter hoc*) was for Hume the product of a manifest *non sequitur*, albeit one so deeply embedded in our everyday as well as scientific habits of thought as to leave little hope of effective reform. More recently the "puzzle of induction" has been restated in various elaborate and ingenious guises, some of them due to the philosopher Nelson Goodman. Even where not thus intended, they have all served to reinforce the widespread trend toward skeptical or relativist philosophies of science which assimilate "truth" to the shifting currency of in-place consensus belief.

However, these arguments have not gone unopposed, as indeed one might expect, given their strongly counterintuitive character and our natural disposition – as Hume recognized – to attribute something more to scientific truth claims than mere lazy-mindedness or force of habit. The challenge has come from various quarters, among them the Critical Realist school of thought, whose chief proponent is Roy Bhaskar, himself much influenced by the work of Rom Harré. Central to their case is a "stratified" conception of reality, knowledge, and human interests where distinctions may

be drawn between, on the one hand, a realm of "intransitive" objects, processes, and events – that is, those which must be taken to exist independently of human conceptualization – and on the other hand, a "transitive" realm of knowledge-constitutive interests which are properly subject to critical assessment of their ethical and socio-political character. To conflate these realms – so Bhaskar argues – is the cardinal error of relativist philosophies and one that leads to disabling consequences in both spheres of inquiry. Thus it relativizes "truth" (in the natural and human sciences alike) to whatever form of DISCOURSE, or *de facto* regime of instituted power/knowledge, happens to prevail in some given discipline at some given time. It also undermines any critical questioning of scientific projects, investigations, or research programs that would argue in terms of their ethical implications or their consequences for human individual and collective well-being. Such criticism can have no purpose, no grounds or justification, if it fails to take adequate (realistic) account of what science can or might achieve on the basis of present knowledge and research.

So Bhaskar has a twofold reason for maintaining his "transitive"/"intransitive" distinction. It is necessary, first, as a condition of possibility for science and also (*a fortiori*) for the history and philosophy of science. That is to say, these projects would be simply unintelligible in the absence of a presupposed object domain which is *not* just a construct out of our various (for example, linguistic, discursive, historical, or cultural) schemes. Where the relativists err is in confusing *ontological* with *epistemological* issues. Thus they take the sheer variety of truth claims advanced (and very often subsequently abandoned) down through the history of scientific thought as evidence that no truth is to be had, and that nothing could justify such claims aside from their own "internalist" perspective on issues of truth, realism, progress, adequate explanation, etc. And so indeed it must appear if, as in WITTGENSTEIN's resonant but not very helpful phrase, "the limits of my language [for which read "discourse," "paradigm," "conceptual scheme," or whatever] are the limits of my world." However, this conclusion holds only on the mistaken premise – as Bhaskar sees it – that *ontology* (questions like "what things exist?" "what are their real attributes, structures, generative mechanisms, causal dispositions, etc.?") is synonymous with *epistemology* ("how does such knowledge come about?", "according to what criteria?" "within what limits of human cognitive grasp or knowledge-constitutive interest?"). From this follows his second main point against the relativists: that by confusing these questions they deprive criticism of any effective purchase on the way that science has actually developed to date and the extent to which, within practical limits, its potential may be harnessed for the communal good.

These objectives both find expression in the title of Bhaskar's best-known book, *Scientific Realism and Human Emancipation*. Here he argues that relativist (or anti-realist) doctrines may well start out with the laudable aim of opposing that narrowly positivist conception of science which excludes any concern with ethical issues by reducing truth to a matter of purely instrumental (or means–end) rationality. However, their proposed alternative is not much better, amounting as it does to a species of cognitive skepticism devoid of critical content and lacking any basis for informed evaluative judgment. Thus it simply reproduces all the well-worn puzzles – like Hume's problem of induction – which result from a reified conception of the physical object domain joined to a passive spectator theory of knowledge. Bhaskar is not alone among recent philosophers of science in arguing the case for a return to causal–explanatory modes of understanding. Wesley Salmon offers numerous convincing examples of advances that have resulted from the achievement of a deeper, more adequate grasp of precisely such underlying causal mechanisms. These advances include, for instance, the capacity to define and measure heat in terms of the mean kinetic energy of molecules; the understanding of electrical conductivity as the passage of free electrons; or the characterization of the color "blue" as that which pertains to wavelengths within a given frequency range (as distinct, say, from Plato's idea that blue objects were perceived as such on account of their participating in the Form or the Essence of blueness).

Thus the case for causal realism, in Nicholas Rescher's words, is that "every objective property of a real thing has consequences of a dispositional order," even if, as he readily concedes, they "cannot be surveyed *in toto*." The latter is in fact not so much a concession as a further strong argument for the realist case. That is, our chief evidence for the mind-independent status of real-world objects is precisely their possession of attributes, properties, causal dispositions, etc. which may turn out to be

not what we expect according to our present state of knowledge. In that case, as Rescher shrewdly points out, the relativist "argument from error" (namely, that scientists have often been wrong in the past so could just as well be wrong all the time) is one that fails to stand up. It is not so much an argument against scientific realism as an argument against "the ontological finality of science as we have it." Thus Caesar did not know – could not have known – that the metal of his sword contained tungsten carbide and that this was an explanatory factor in its fitness for the purpose intended. Moreover we can now give additional reasons (molecular and subatomic) for the fact that certain metals or metallic compounds possess certain well-tried physical qualities.

Nor are such claims in any way confounded by the high probability – indeed near-certainty – that future science will come up with yet further, more detailed or depth-ontological explanations. This does not alter the knowledge we have that our current explanation is better (more adequate) than anything available to Caesar. (See especially Muntz, 1985; Ruben, 1982; and Lipton, 1993.) That is to say, we have rational warrant for supposing that the objects, theories, and causal postulates used in our own best constructions are closer to the truth than what Caesar (or the scientific experts of his time) might have counted an adequate hypothesis. No doubt it is true that any gaps or shortcomings in our present state of knowledge might yet be revealed by some further advance – some improvement in the means of observation or the powers of theoretical synthesis – which rendered that knowledge either obsolete or henceforth restricted in its range of application. The most obvious example is that of Newtonian physics in the wake of relativity theory, where classical conceptions of gravity or absolute space and time continue to play an explanatory role, albeit under certain limiting conditions or in certain specified regions of inquiry.

Such instances are often adduced in support of the standard relativist claim, namely, that there exist as many ways of construing the phenomena as there exist scientific theories, paradigms, ontologies, conceptual schemes, and so forth. Nevertheless, this argument misses the point in two crucial respects. First, it fails to note that Einstein's general theory of relativity itself has recourse to an absolute value – the speed of light – which then serves as an invariant measure for assigning all loci in the space–time continuum. Thus it is wrong

– little more than a play on words – to confuse "relativity" in this well-defined sense with the kinds of all-out ontological or epistemic relativism which Einstein strenuously sought to avoid. And second, such arguments ignore the extent to which past theories are often not so much discredited *en bloc* as conserved and refined by continual scientific elaboration and critique.

Sometimes this occurs when previously well-established items of knowledge are shown to possess only a partial truth or a power of explanation that is no longer adequate for present purposes. Such would be true of, for instance, those advances in the fields of particle physics or molecular biology which built upon the work of earlier physicists, chemists, and biologists, but which reconfigured the object domain by opening up new regions of depth-ontological inquiry. At other times this process may operate (so to speak) in reverse, starting out with some relatively abstract conjecture regarding the existence of as yet unobservable entities, and then seeking to verify its claims by experiment or further research. Thus, as Newton-Smith notes, the term "electron" was at first a "predicate . . . introduced [by Roentgen] with the intention of picking out a kind of constituent of matter, namely that responsible for the cathode-ray phenomenon." Thereafter it not only "entered the vocabulary" of theoretical physics, as a relativist might choose to phrase it, but also attained the status of a necessary postulate and then (with Rutherford's pioneering work) that of an entity whose passage could be tracked and whose causal-explanatory role placed its existence beyond reasonable doubt. The same is true of a range of other items – such as molecules, genes, DNA proteins, and viruses – which have likewise exhibited a power to explain what previously lacked any adequate account. This is the chief virtue of a realist approach, according to Rescher: that it pays due regard to the prior claims of a "non-phenomenal order from which the phenomena themselves emerge through causal processes." For otherwise, lacking such grounds, we should have absolutely no reason to think that electrons (or molecules, genes, viruses, etc.) exerted any greater claim upon our credence than phlogiston, magnetic effluxes, or the luminiferous ether.

At this point the relativist will answer – most likely with reference to Kuhn – that those grounds are indeed lacking since there is no guarantee of the meaning invariance of terms from one theory to the next. If it is true (as Kuhn thinks, following Quine) that all terms are "theory-laden," object languages and observation statements included, and moreover that theories are radically "underdetermined" by the evidence, then it follows that scientists perceive different objects under different theoretical descriptions. Thus, for instance, the ancient atomists were in no sense talking about the "same" entities as those later physicists (from Dalton to the present) who have themselves come up with such a diverse range of models, metaphors, "elementary" particles, etc., as to render their theories strictly "incommensurable." Again, to take one of Kuhn's best-known examples: Priestley and Lavoisier each laid claim to have discovered the chemical process of combustion, although the latter based his account – correctly, as we now think – on the existence of a hitherto unknown element named "oxygen," while the former adhered to the phlogiston theory and produced experimental results which fully confirmed it. Therefore, where Lavoisier detected the existence of oxygen, Priestley talked about "dephlogistated air," along with a whole set of congruent hypotheses and reasonings on the evidence that amounted to a counterpart theory with similar explanatory scope. Kuhn offers many such examples, among them the difference of views between Aristotle and Galileo regarding what we now – after Galileo – perceive as the gravity-induced motion of a pendulum, but what Aristotle "saw" as matter seeking out its rightful (cosmological) place in the order of the elements.

This is all taken by Kuhn's relativist followers (and arguably by Kuhn himself) to justify a stance of thoroughgoing cognitive skepticism *vis-à-vis* the issue of scientific truth and progress. Even so, there are obvious problems with any strong version of the incommensurability thesis. One is the straightforward logical point that we could be in no position to mount such a claim unless we were able to recognize the differences between two rival theories, or possessed at least some minimal ground of comparison on which they could be said to diverge. After all, as Andrew Collier remarks, "nobody bothers to say that astrology is incompatible with monetarism or generative grammar with acupuncture." There is also the fact – well-attested by numerous examples from the history of science – that knowledge accrues around certain topics *across and despite* the widest differences of theoretical framework, ontological scheme, research paradigm, or whatever. Thus it does make sense to think of modern (post-Dalton) atomic and particle physics as belonging to a line of descent from the ancient atomists, even though the latter may be said to have inhabited a different "conceptual universe," and to have advanced their ideas on a purely speculative basis, devoid of genuine scientific warrant. What enables us to draw this distinction is precisely our knowledge of the growth of knowledge, our ability to grasp those salient respects in which the current understanding of atomic or subatomic structures differs from – and has indeed advanced far beyond – the ancient atomists' conceptions.

Thus the Quinean/Kuhnian thesis of radical meaning variance gives rise to some awkward, not to say nonsensical conclusions. It would require us to believe not only that the Greek atomists were talking about something completely different, but also that later physicists, such as Dalton, Rutherford, Einstein, and Bohr, were themselves working on such disparate assumptions as to rule out any meaningful comparision between them. One might perhaps be tempted to adopt this outlook in other, more extravagant cases, like Anaximander's idea of the earth as "a slab-like object suspended in equilibrium at the centre of the cosmos." (I take this example from Rescher.) Even here, though, it can reasonably be argued that we have grounds for thinking Anaximander wrong – and subsequent thinkers right – with respect to a given planetary body (the earth) whose structure, properties, and place in the solar system are now much better understood. The same would apply to a great deal of early science, including Aristotle's theory of matter as composed of a mixture, in various proportions, of the four "elements" (earth, air, fire, and water), along with the "humours" supposedly produced by their manifold possible combinations. The trouble with such a theory is not that the evidence fails to bear it out, but, on the contrary, that it is perfectly compatible with any kind of "evidence" that might turn up. In Popper's terms it is so vaguely framed as to lack the falsification criteria – or the grounds for its own subsequent disproof – which mark the distinction between science and pseudoscience.

However, there is a stronger argument that avoids the above-noted problems with Popper's account. This is the causal-realist theory, according to which scientific explanations are chiefly concerned with the properties of things themselves – with their structures, effects, "transfactually efficacious" powers (Bhaskar), etc. – rather than the various

propositions or logics of inquiry that purport to account for them. Thus, in Bhaskar's words: "if there is a *real reason*, located in the nature of the stuff, such as its molecular or atomic structure, then water *must* tend to boil when it is heated." It is worth noting that this proposed shift from a descriptive-analytic to a causal-explanatory approach is one that finds a parallel in recent linguistic philosophy, notably Saul Kripke's influential work *Naming and Necessity* (1980). In both cases it entails the argument that certain words – those denominating "natural kinds" – possess reference by virtue of their capacity to pick out certain corresponding objects, substances, or real-world entities. These words ("proper names" in Kripke's nonstandard usage of that term) are defined as such through a chain of transmission which at each stage relates them back to their referent, itself "baptized" in a first (inaugural) act of naming and thereafter subject to various modifications or refinements in the light of newly acquired scientific knowledge. Kripke's chief aim in all this is to avoid the kinds of problems that arise with descriptivist theories (like those advanced by FREGE and Russell), which make truth values a function of reference, and reference, in turn, a function of those meanings (or senses) that attach to a given term. It is then a short step to Quinean and other such forms of wholesale ontological relativism, reached by rejecting any clear-cut distinction between analytic (logically necessary) and synthetic (empirical or factual) propositions. For Kripke, conversely, there is an order of *a posteriori* necessary truths which explain the way things stand in reality and with our knowledge of them as expressed in the form of propositions about natural-kind terms.

Bhaskar again provides some pertinent examples from the scientific field. Thus: "if there is something, such as the possession of the same atomic or electronic configuration, which graphite, black carbon and diamonds share, then chemists are rationally justified in classing them together – the reason is that structure." He also makes the point rather neatly with regard to the standard textbook instance of a deductive syllogism: "All men are mortal. Socrates is a man. Therefore, Socrates is mortal." According to Bhaskar's causal-realist view this becomes: "in virtue of his genetic constitution, if Socrates is a man, he must die." That is, we have grounds, experiential as well as scientific, for asserting the order of necessity here quite apart from the syllogistic structure that identifies a well-formed deductive inference. The same would apply to propositions about other natural-kind terms, for instance (to repeat) that *water* tends to boil when heated, that electrical *conductors* are characterized by the passage of free electrons when a current is applied, or that the *blueness* of an object consists in its reflecting light in the region of wavelength 4400A. These are all cases of what Kripke would call *a posteriori* necessity. Their names denote precisely those sorts of occurrent phenomena – structures, qualities, causal dispositions, etc. – which on the one hand require our having found out about them from experience or scientific investigation, while on the other hand belonging to their intrinsic (necessary) character as *just that kind* of phenomenon. As Bhaskar would claim, it is just this kind of knowledge that enables us to make sense of science, along with the history and philosophy of science.

Of course there are always counterexamples which the skeptic can adduce by way of contending that science deals only with hypothetical entities or with constructs out of this or that preferred ontology, conceptual scheme, etc. Such doubts attach most often to objects (or quasi-objects) at the leading edge of current speculative thought, as with the various postulated items – from electrons to mesons and quarks – that have figured in the history of modern particle physics. There is also the question of how far science may create (rather than "discover") such putative realia with its own ever more resourceful techniques for manipulating the materials at its disposal. (Examples might be drawn from the field of recombinant DNA technology, the new range of particles observed – or produced – with the advent of high-energy accelerator programs, or from the filling-out of Mendeleev's periodic table with elements previously unknown in nature.) Even so, it is true – as Ian Hacking remarks in his book *Representing and Intervening* – that such proteins, particles, or elements are possessed of both structural and causal-explanatory attributes which define their role within an ongoing project of scientific research. Thus some new particle may well start out as a purely speculative construct, a hypothesis required in order to balance the equations or to fill the gap in an otherwise attractive and powerful unifying theory. However, its existence will remain matter for conjecture until that hypothesis can be proven, perhaps by the arrival of an electron microscope with higher powers of resolution, or an accelerator capable of achieving the required velocity. In that case, as Hacking more succinctly concludes, "if you can bounce electrons off it, it is real."

Such arguments would of course carry little weight with cultural or literary theorists, for whom realism of any variety is an option scarcely to be thought of. In these quarters it has become an article of faith – whether derived from Saussure, Foucault, Rorty, or Lyotard – that "truth" is a wholly linguistic or discursive construct, and "science" just the name that attaches to one (currently prestigious) language game or discourse. Hence their inordinate fondness for loose analogies with those branches of "postmodern" science that may be thought to exhibit (in Lyotard's parlance) a sublime disregard for ideas and values like truth, rationality, or progress. This new kind of science, "by concerning itself with such things as undecidables, the limits of precise control, conflicts characterized by incomplete information, *'fracta,'* catastrophes, and pragmatic paradoxes, is theorizing its own evolution as discontinuous, catastrophic, nonrectifiable, and paradoxical." And (Lyotard again) since "the reserve of knowledge – language's reserve of possible utterances – is inexhaustible," therefore it is no longer a question of truth (of that which pertains to the cognitive or constative phrase regimes), but rather a question of the sheer "performativity," the power of suasive utterance, that enables scientists to pick up research grants, plug into information networks, and so forth. In so far as this "increases the ability to produce proof," so likewise it "increases the ability to be right." Thus Lyotard comes out pretty much in agreement with Feyerabend. In his opinion the best (indeed the only) criterion for scientific "progress" is that which seeks to multiply discursive differentials, to judge (so far as possible) "without criteria," and thereby do away with all those authoritarian constraints imposed by notions of scientific "truth" and "method."

With Foucault one can see yet more clearly what results from an ultranominalist stance coupled to a deep suspicion of science and all its works. In *The Order of Things* (1973) this approach takes the form of an "archaeological" questing back into the various discourses, EPISTEMES or STRUCTURES of linguistic representation that have characterized the natural and human sciences alike. Their history is marked – so Foucault contends – by a series of ruptures, or "epistemological breaks," which make it strictly impossible to compare them in point of scientific truth, accuracy, scope, or explanatory power. The only meaningful comparisons to be drawn are those which operate (in Saussurian terms) on a structural-synchronic axis, that is to say, between the various disciplines that constitute the field of accredited knowledge at any given time. Foucault's chief interest is in those ambivalent regions of inquiry – midway between the physical and the human sciences – where issues of truth are most deeply bound up with questions of an ideological or HERMENEUTIC nature. Thus he tends to avoid the "hard" disciplines of (for example) physics or chemistry in favor of those – like philology, economics, and biology – that can plausibly be treated as interpretative constructs out of this or that dominant (period-specific) "discourse." So it is that Foucault's self-professed "archaeology of the human sciences" can also lay claim to a generalized validity for branches of knowledge outside and beyond what would normally fall within that sphere.

The most famous passage from *The Order of Things* is also that which most vividly displays Foucault's extreme anti-realist, conventionalist, or nominalist viewpoint. It is taken from one of Borges's riddling parabolic fictions, and purports to reproduce a Chinese encyclopedia entry wherein "animals" are classified as follows: "(a) belonging to the Emperor, (b) embalmed, (c) tame, (d) sucking pigs, (e) sirens, (f) fabulous, (g) stray dogs, (h) included in the present classification, (i) frenzied, (j) innumerable, (k) drawn with a very fine camel-hair brush, (l) *et cetera*, (m) having just broken the water pitcher, (n) that from a long way off look like flies." Foucault treats this as an object lesson in the fact of ontological relativity, an index of the culture-bound, parochial character of even our deepest-laid concepts and categories. Thus "[i]n the wonderment of this taxonomy, the thing we apprehend in one great leap, the thing that, by means of the fable, is demonstrated as the exotic charm of another system of thought, is the limitation of our own, the stark impossibility of thinking *that*."

Three responses seem to be in order here. First: the *possibility* of thinking such exotic thoughts is demonstrated clearly enough by the existence of Borges's fable, Foucault's commentary on it, and our (that is, the readers') capacity to perceive it as just such an instance of wild or zany categorization. However, second: we do so on the understanding that this is, after all, a piece of fabulous contrivance,

a fiction invented by Borges (and cited by Foucault) with the purpose of offering an "exotic" slant on our naturalized habits of thought and perception. In that case (third) it is an error – a confusion everywhere manifest in *The Order of Things* – to argue from the mere possibility of thinking such starkly "impossible" thoughts (whatever this might mean) to the idea that *all* our concepts, categories, ontological commitments, and so forth are likewise fictive constructions out of one such "arbitrary" discourse or another. Nevertheless, this is exactly the premise that underwrites Foucault's entire project, from his early structuralist-inspired "archaeology" of knowledge to the Nietzschean-genealogical approach that characterized his post-1970 works. It is perhaps best seen as a *reductio ad absurdum* of that anti-realist line of argument which begins by locating truth in propositions about things, rather than in the things themselves, and which ends – as with Quine, Kuhn, Rorty, Lyotard, et al. – by holistically relativizing "truth" to whatever sorts of language game happen to enjoy that title. In other words, it presses right through with that rejection of *de re* in favor of *de dicto* necessity which then turns out to undermine the very grounds of science as a truth-seeking enterprise. This irony indeed finds pointed expression in the title of Foucault's book. For on his account there cannot exist any "things" – any extra-discursive objects, entities, kinds or categories of thing – whose various "orderings" by language or discourse would render his thesis intelligible.

It is worth noting that there may be a common source for some of these issues that have recently emerged in both French and Anglo-American philosophy of science. It is to be found in the work of Pierre Duhem (1861–1916), a thinker whom Quine has acknowledged as a major influence, and whose name is standardly coupled with his own in discussions of the Duhem–Quine thesis with regard to ontological relativity. Duhem, it is worth recalling, was a physicist who specialized in thermodynamics, as well as a philosopher-historian of science, and a practicing Catholic. Hence his belief that science was not in the business of providing ultimate explanations, but should rather confine itself to a conventionalist account of those truths that held good with respect to some given (ontology-relative) conceptual scheme. In this way he could keep science from encroaching upon matters of religious faith. In France there is a clearly marked line of descent which runs from Duhem, via Gaston

BACHELARD, to that structuralist "revolution" across various disciplines which achieved its high point in the 1960s and 1970s. Structural linguistics was at this time seen as converging with that movement in philosophy of science, represented most notably by Bachelard, which likewise sought to define the conditions under which a discipline could properly assert some claim to theoretical validity. However, this is now treated as a bygone episode in the history of thought, a distant prelude to the dawning awareness that science, like philosophy, is just one "discourse" among others, a language game with its own favored idioms and metaphors, but without any privilege in point of epistemological rigor or truth. Since these include (as in Wittgenstein) the "language game" of religious belief, it may not be fanciful to trace the line back to Duhem's attempt at a negotiated truce between science and Catholic doctrine. (Incidentally this might also cast a revealing light on Feyerabend's treatment of the issue between Galileo and Cardinal Bellarmine.)

If Bachelard is remembered nowadays, it is chiefly for works like *The Psychoanalysis of Fire* (1964), his essays in reflection on those modes of metaphoric or creative reverie that stand, so to speak, at the opposite pole from the scientific language of concept and rational inference. What is thereby forgotten – one might say repressed – is the fact that these writings were themselves a part of his epistemological project, his attempt to distinguish more clearly between the two realms of thought. It is a plain misreading of Bachelard's work to extract from it the modish doctrine that "all truth claims are fictions," "all concepts just sublimated metaphors," or "'science' merely the name we attach to some currently prestigious language game." On the contrary: Bachelard's aim was to prevent such promiscuous leveling of the difference – the more than contingent, linguistic, or localized (culture-specific) difference – between scientific epistemologies on the one hand and poetic-metaphorical "reverie" on the other. Thus what Bachelard meant by his term "epistemological break" was a decisive rupture with prescientific modes of thought, one that marked the crucial stage of advance to an adequate conceptualization of some given domain. It retains this significance, if more problematically, in Louis ALTHUSSER's structural-Marxist account of the science/IDEOLOGY distinction. However, for Foucault the idea of an "epistemological break" has been relativized to the point where it means nothing more than a random shift in the prevailing (discursively produced) "order of things."

That Saussure should nowadays be routinely coopted by adepts of this ultrarelativist view is, to say the least, something of an irony, given his methodological concerns and his desire to set linguistics on the path toward a genuine (structural-synchronic) science of language. Such was indeed the main source of its appeal for that earlier generation of theorists who saw in it, as likewise in Bachelard's work, a means of articulating the difference between METAPHOR and concept, ideology and science, natural (everyday) language on the one hand and theoretical discourse on the other. In both cases, however, Saussure and Bachelard, these claims were lost from view with the postmodern turn toward an out-and-out conventionalist theory of science, knowledge, and representation which treated such ideas as merely a species of "metalinguistic" delusion. Thus Bachelard was read – or standardly invoked – as arguing that all scientific concepts could in the end be traced back to their subliminal source in some privileged metaphor or image cluster. Saussure's theoretical commitments counted for nothing in comparison with the prospects that were opened up by treating all theories (his own presumably among them) as "constructed in" or "relative to" some localized SIGNIFYING practice. It could then be maintained, without fear of contradiction on reasoned philosophical grounds, that literary critics were among the vanguard party in a coming "revolution" of the instituted order of discourse, an event whose signs they were able to read from their knowledge that "reality" was merely the figment of a naturalized (though in fact merely "arbitrary") relation between signifier and signified.

The problems with this doctrine are those that have bedeviled every version of the relativist argument from Protagoras down. That is to say, if we redefine "true" as "true relative to L" (where L is taken to denote some language, paradigm, conceptual scheme, "INTERPRETATIVE COMMUNITY," or whatever), then there is no way of counting *any* belief false just so long as it can claim – or could once claim – some measure of communal assent. From this it follows *ex hypothese* that all beliefs are true by their own cultural lights, or according to their own immanent criteria as manifest in this or that linguistically mediated "form of life." Every single truth claim that was ever entertained by a community of like-minded knowers must count as valid when referred to the language game, vocabulary, or belief system then in place. Thus for instance it was once *true* – not just an artifact of limited knowledge or erroneous "commonsense" perception – that the fixed planets were seven in number; that the sun rotated about the earth; that combustion entailed the release of a colourless, odourless, intangible substance called phlogiston, rather than the uptake of oxygen; and that no fixed-wing aircraft could possibly get off the ground since the necessary lift could be generated only by a bird-like flapping motion, or perhaps – as Leonardo da Vinci was the first to suggest – a rotary-blade arrangement of the helicopter type. In each case and numerous others besides (one could multiply examples at leisure), the belief in question is no less true, or no more demonstrably false, than those other beliefs that are nowdays widely (even universally) taken for matters of scientific fact. What counts is their suasive efficacy as measured by the current norms of "science" as a going enterprise, a rhetorical activity where truth is defined in performative (not constative) terms, and where any distinction between concept and metaphor turns out to be merely – like the word "concept" itself, not to mention the concept of "metaphor" – a species of repressed or sublimated metaphor. Therefore it follows, supposedly, that all truth talk, whether in the natural or the more theory-prone human sciences, comes down to a choice of the right sort of metaphor (or the optimum rhetorical strategy) for conjuring assent from others engaged in the same communal enterprise.

Scientists (and at least some philosophers of science) have understandably considered this an implausible account of how advances come about through the joint application of theory and empirical research. Hence, as I have argued, the recent emergence of anti-conventionalist or causal-realist approaches which offer a far better understanding of our knowledge of the growth of knowledge. After all, there seems rather little to be said for a philosophy of science that effectively leaves itself nothing to explain by reducing "science" to just another species of preferential language game, rhetoric, discourse, conceptual scheme, or whatever. The current revival of realist ontologies (along with the return to "natural-kind" theories of reference) betokens a break with this whole misdirected – as it now appears – line of thought. In a longer purview it simply takes up the position attributed to Aristotle by his commentator Themistius: namely, the

principle that "that which exists does not conform to various opinions, but rather the correct opinions conform to that which exists."

See also CRITICAL THEORY; DISCOURSE; LANGUAGE, PHILOSOPHY OF.

Reading
Althusser, Louis 1990: *"Philosophy and the Spontaneous Philosophy of the Scientists" and Other Essays.*
Bachelard, Gaston 1964: *The Psychoanalysis of Fire.*
——1968: *The Philosophy of No: A Philosophy of the New Scientific Mind.*
——1971: *The Poetics of Reverie.*
Barnes, Barry 1985: *About Science.*
Bhaskar, Roy 1986: *Scientific Realism and Human Emancipation.*
——1993: *Dialectic: The Pulse of Freedom.*
Bloor, David 1976: *Knowledge and Social Imagery.*
Collier, Andrew 1994: *Critical Realism: An Introduction to Roy Bhaskar's Philosophy.*
Duhem, Pierre 1954: "The physics of a believer," in *The Aims and Structure of Physical Theory.*
Feyerabend, Paul 1975: *Against Method.*
——1992: *Farewell to Reason.*
Foucault, Michel 1973: *The Order of Things: An Archaeology of the Human Sciences.*
Fuller, Steve 1989: *Philosophy of Science and Its Discontents.*
Goodman, Nelson 1983: *Fact, Fiction and Forecast.*
Gutting, Gary 1989: *Michel Foucault's Archaeology of Scientific Reason.*
Hacking, Ian 1983: *Representing and Intervening.*
Harding, Sandra G. 1976: *Can Theories Be Refuted? Essays on the Duhem–Quine Thesis.*
Harré, Rom 1972: *The Philosophies of Sciences.*
——1983: *Great Scientific Experiments.*
——1986: *Varieties of Realism: A Rationale for the Social Sciences.*
Hollis, Martin, and Lukes, Steven, eds 1982: *Rationality and Relativism.*
Kripke, Saul 1980: *Naming and Necessity.*
Kuhn, Thomas 1970: *The Structure of Scientific Revolutions.*
Laudan, Larry 1990: *Science and Relativism: Some Key Controversies in the Philosophy of Science.*
Lecourt, Dominique 1975: *Marxism and Epistemology: Bachelard, Canguilhem and Foucault.*
Lepin, J., ed. 1984: *Scientific Realism.*
Lipton, Peter 1993: *Inference to the Best Explanation.*
Lyotard, Jean-François 1988: *The Differend: Phrases in Dispute.*
Mackie, J.L. 1974: *The Cement of the Universe: A Study of Causation.*
Margolis, Joseph 1991: *The Truth About Relativism.*
Muntz, Peter 1985: *Our Knowledge of the Growth of Knowledge.*
Newton-Smith, W.H. 1981: *The Rationality of Science.*
Papineau, David 1978: *For Science in the Social Sciences.*
Popper, Karl 1934: *The Logic of Scientific Discovery.*
——1957: *The Poverty of Historicism.*
Quine, W.V.O. 1953b: *From a Logical Point of View.*
Rescher, Nicholas 1987: *Scientific Realism: A Critical Reappraisal.*
Ruben, David-Hillel 1982: *Explaining Explanation.*

Salmon, Wesley C. 1984: *Scientific Explanation and the Causal Structure of the World.*
——1989: *Four Decades of Scientific Explanation.*
Smith, Peter J. 1981: *Realism and the Progress of Science.*
CHRISTOPHER NORRIS

Screen   The most important journal of film criticism in English. Founded in 1969, it has a rich history filled with shifts of focus, editorial control, and ownership. Its history begins almost two decades before the inaugural issue, when in 1950 the BRITISH FILM INSTITUTE (BFI) founded the Society for Education in Film and Television (SEFT), a grant-in-aid body which later parented *Screen.* SEFT established several initial publications out of which grew the journal *Screen Education*, founded in 1959 as a source of articles on film education, film theory, and the film industry. Ten years later, SEFT reestablished the journal under a new title, *Screen.* With its new name came a change of focus; no longer singly dedicated to articles on education, the journal confronted controversial issues in television and FILM STUDIES. At first, *Screen* included a separate section entitled "Educational Notes," but after just three issues, SEFT established *Screen Education Notes*, a separate publication that became *Screen Education* in 1974.

For eight years, SEFT supported both journals: *Screen* for its work in film theory, and *Screen Education* for its articles on teaching film. During this time, *Screen* focused on the relationship between SEMIOLOGY, MARXISM, and PSYCHOANALYSIS, and despite forging a reputation as a leading critical journal – compared by some to *Cahiers du Cinéma* – the editorial board split over the journal's shifting focus. Four board members – Edward Buscombe, Christine Gledhill, Alan Lovell, and Christopher Williams – voiced their objections in a 1976 article entitled "Psychoanalysis and film"; the article was ostensibly about *Screen*'s treatment of psychoanalysis, but their concerns – among them that "controversial intellectual choices [were] made to appear unproblematic" and that the writing was "full of ambiguities and uncertainties" – were much deeper. The four resigned in 1976. Writing for *American Film* years later, Colin MacCabe, a board member from 1973 to 1981, supported their criticisms and, though he suggested that in their final years of that decade changes to *Screen* reflected some of their criticisms, MacCabe admits that during these years he too grew disillusioned with the journal.

In the early 1980s *Screen* entered another phase.

Faced with limited funds, SEFT incorporated *Screen Education* back into *Screen.* The *Screen* of this decade was no more immune to criticism than it had been in 1976. Michael Pursell, writing for *Literature/Film Quarterly* in 1986, coined the term "Screenspeak" to describe the journal's style, accusing *Screen* of knowingly excluding, by wanton use of technical vocabulary and a blindness to alternative interpretations, the people for whom it claimed to write.

The most recent change to *Screen* came in 1990, when the BFI dissolved SEFT; the journal's ownership and editorial offices now moved to the John Logie Baird Centre at the University of Glasgow, and the Oxford University Press began publishing the quarterly journal. The journal now includes several new sections, "Reports and debates" and "Reviews," and assumes a more academic tone, reflecting the editors' desires to "redefine 'the academic'" and "to attempt to re-establish the usefulness of academic, even scholarly work," aims which they announced in their Spring 1990 editorial.
TARA G. GILLIGAN

scriptible and *lisible*   *See* WRITERLY AND READERLY TEXTS

Scrutiny   Challenging a strict academic response to literature and intent upon developing an understanding of the movements of British civilization in their day, a group of young Cambridge research assistants founded *Scrutiny* in 1932. Despite their own connection with the academic setting, the journal's founders identified a need for a publication free from the confines of the academy, which could promote the exchange of ideas crucial to a comprehension of British CULTURE – literary and non-literary. Their interests were overwhelmingly British and they saw their project as a British counterpart to the American *New Republic.* Their approach was radical; literature represented to them a means of preserving the British cultural and moral society. With the publication of criticism, they hoped to present a legitimate analysis of both the practical and the political influences of literature and to present their cause to the "public of Common Readers," as they wrote in their manifesto. They believed that a select group of academics – "self-appointed sponsors of society" were their words – drowned out the voices of the public, their intended audience, and in their first publication invited readers to respond. Critics of the journal, however, claim that the editors of *Scrutiny* never escaped elitism and, in fact, assumed a literary background equal to their own.

For its 21 years of publication, *Scrutiny* contained critical articles on literature, art, and contemporary life; book reviews, and, whenever possible, original composition. The quarterly journal had no financial sponsor and depended on subscriptions and limited advertising revenue, and could provide no payment to contributors. In October 1953 the last issue of *Scrutiny* was published, a decision which F.R. LEAVIS, one of the founding editors, describes as having been "narrowly evaded" several times in the preceding decade. The 1939–45 war disrupted publication patterns, and made correspondence with contributors difficult. Despite its struggles, however, the journal survived until 1953; by then, when the editors finally found it necessary to abandon their project, *Scrutiny* had left its mark on the study of British LITERARY CRITICISM.

TARA G. GILLIGAN

Scruton, Roger   (1944–)   Professor of AESTHETICS and philosopher, associated with the conservative wing of the British NEW RIGHT as editor of *The Salisbury Review* and prolific author of works of "dogmatics," cultural criticism, and journalism. Scruton's conservatism – arising from a sense of belonging "to some continuing and pre-existing social order" and the realization that this is "all-important" in determining what to do – originally found its "principal enemy" in LIBERALISM. His HEGELian defense of the authority of the state and the institutions which nourish it was thus fashioned in opposition to doctrines of individual autonomy, natural rights, the "obsession" with freedom, the market, the "rot of pluralism," and the claims of democracy. Latterly he suggested a reconciliation of social conservatism and economic liberalism in the light of Hayek's social epistemology and the experience of post-Communist Central Europe.

Reading
Scruton, R. 1980 *(1984)*: *The Meaning of Conservatism.*
——1988: "The New Right in Central Europe."
——1991: "What is conservatism?"

JOHN CALLAGHAN

Searle, John Rogers   (1932–)   American philosopher. Searle's best-known work is his theory of speech or elocutionary acts, which is an elaboration on J.L. AUSTIN's theory of performative utterances. Searle groups elocutionary acts into five categories: assertives (which are either true or false); directives (which are intended to make the listener do something); commissives (which commit the speaker to do something); expressives (which reveal the psychological state of the speaker); declaratives (which make things happen). All elocutionary acts fall into one or more of these categories.

Reading
Searle, John R. 1969: *Speech Acts: An Essay in the Philosophy of Language.*
——1979: *Expression and Meaning: Studies in the Theory of Speech Acts.*
——1983: *Intentionality: An Essay in the Philosophy of Mind.*

MICHAEL PAYNE

semiotics (semiology)   The science of SIGNS. Although the term "semiology," which was coined by SAUSSURE (1915, p. 16), has been commonly used in Europe, "semiotics" is now in general use on both sides of the Atlantic. Semiotics originated in ancient attempts by Hippocrates and Galen to understand the relationships between the body and the mind and to relate symptoms to diseases. Nothing less than the links between BODY, mind, and CULTURE – as these constitute themselves as SIGNS – determine the field of semiotics (Danesi, 1994, pp. xi–xii). This does not mean, however, that semiotics is about everything. Umberto Eco (1967, p. 7) has wittily defined semiotics as the study of everything that can be *taken* as a sign. "A sign is everything which can be taken as significantly substituting for something else. This something else does not necessarily have to exist or to actually be somewhere at the moment when a sign stands in for it. Thus *semiotics is in principle the discipline studying everything which can be used in order to lie.* If something cannot be used to tell a lie, conversely it cannot be used to tell the truth: it cannot in fact be used to tell at all. I think that the definition of a theory of the lie should be taken as a fairly comprehensive program for a general semiotics." Eco then proceeds to map the field of semiotics as consisting of 19 areas of contemporary research, ranging from spontaneous natural processes of communication to complex cultural systems: zoosemiotics; olfactory signs; tactile communication; CODES of taste; paralinguistics; medical semiotics;

kinesics and proxemics; musical codes; formalized languages; written languages; unknown alphabets; secret codes; natural languages; visual communication; systems of objects; plot structure; TEXT theory; cultural codes; aesthetic texts; mass communication; and rhetoric. Although BARTHES (1964, p. 11) attempted to invert Saussure's declaration and to absorb semiology into a translinguistics, linguistics now appears to be a subset of semiotics. Current work in semiotics has managed to accommodate the two principal strands of its origin in America in the writings of C.S. PEIRCE (1839–1914) and in Europe in the lectures of Saussure (1857–1913).

Reading
Barthes, Roland 1964 (*1967*): Elements of Semiology.
Eco, Umberto 1976: *A Theory of Semiotics.*
Hawkes, Terence 1977 (*1983*): *Structuralism and Semiotics.*
Sebeok, Thomas A. 1994: *An Introduction to Semiotics.*
                                                    MICHAEL PAYNE

shifters/deictics Items whose reference varies. The word *this*, for instance, may be used to pick out something near the speaker, to refer back to something previously mentioned, or to refer to the TEXT itself. How the three uses of the word are related to each other remains controversial.

JAKOBSON (1957) first used the term *shifter*. Currently the term *deictic* is more widely used. Deictic elements have been intensively studied in text and DISCOURSE analysis and by literary theorists, partly because of their behavior in direct and indirect reported speech.

Reading
Jakobson, R. 1957 (*1971*): "Shifters, verbal categories and the Russian verb."
Levinson, S.C. 1983: "Deixis."
                                                    RAPHAEL SALKIE

Shklovsky, Viktor (1893–1984) Russian Soviet writer, critic, and literary theorist, one of the founding members of OPOYAZ (the Society for Studies of Poetic Language) and the leading representative of RUSSIAN FORMALISM. Shklovsky's career began in the first decade of the twentieth century when he published such early theoretical works as *The Resurrection of the Word*, based on artistic practices of Russian futurists (V. Khlebnikov, V. Mayakovsky, and A. Kruchenykh), who declared language rather than reality the true material of their works.

It is not surprising, therefore, that Shklovsky's works of that period are focused on the discussion of the "self-sufficient word," the stylistic innovations, and poetic specificity of Russian futurists. In 1916 Shklovsky became a cofounder of OPOYAZ and thus one of the leaders of the "formal school" in LITERARY CRITICISM.

Shklovsky was among the first literary critics who viewed verbal art primarily as a construction, establishing the laws of plot development and considering these laws as the sum total of devices by means of which the work of art is constructed. The analysis of these devices, the principles of connections between images, of the "resurrection of the word" renewed by construction becomes the center of Shklovsky's attention in such articles as "About poetry and beyonsense language" and "Potebnya," both 1916. From 1919 Shklovsky dedicated his efforts to the development of the theory of prose. The topics of his investigations range from the analysis of elements and laws of plot development in individual works of literature ("How *Don Quixote* is made" and "Parodic novel. Sterne's *Tristam Shandy*") to the discussion of literary genres ("Mystery novella" and "Mystery novel") and trends in literature ("Ornamental prose" dedicated to the analysis of works of a symbolist poet and writer Andrey Bely), culminating in theoretical works such as "Art as device" and "The connection between devices of plot construction and general stylistic devices," which became cornerstones for the formalist movement. All these essays were collected in a book *On the Theory of Prose* (1925), which is often considered Shklovsky's most important work. Shklovsky maintained that art represented reality not through content but through form. The form is the sum total of devices such as retardation, parallelism, contrast, etc. One of the most interesting discoveries Shklovsky made in the area of the analysis of literary devices was the theory of "estrangement." According to Shklovsky, the word in a literary work is freed from customary, petrified, fixed combinations; and it reveals its inner form that allows for the restoration of the word's primary expressive meaning. Thus the word in art represents the world as if seen anew, as if it is born for the very first time.

In addition to his contribution to literary theory, Shklovsky was also a pioneer of Russian cinema as a critic and script writer (he wrote the scripts for Lev Kuleshov's *By the Law*, *Third Meshchanskaya Street*, and *Captain's Daughter*). In *Literature and*

Cinematography (1923), Shklovsky provided an early theoretical foundation for cinematic art as distinguished from theater. He also supplied the first substantial analysis of the early works of Sergey EISENSTEIN, based on the principle of montage of attractions.

Shklovsky was an original and prolific prose writer as well. His novels, *Sentimental Journey* (1923), *Zoo: Letters not about Love, or The Third Eloise* (1923), and *Hamburg Count* (1928), although based on autobiographical principles, bear an unmistakable resemblance to his theoretical works: short aphoristic phrases connected by associations, which are often hidden so that the reader must discover them in order to grasp the meaning. The associative nature of Shklovsky's fragmentary narrative is based on a wealth of historical knowledge which cements the text and does not allow it to fall apart. Shklovsky uses quotations extensively, documents that become a kind of a montage of facts, creating a mosaic of a given historical period in his novels.

In the 1930s formalism came under attack from the official socialist realist critics. Shklovsky was forced publicly to denounce his position ("The Monument to the Scientific Mistake," 1930) and to start writing socially useful works about such official Soviet writers as M. Sholokhov, N. Ostrovsky, M. Gorky, investigating the correspondence between the social and ideological milieu and the literary work created within its surroundings. Only in the 1970s was Shklovsky able to return to his early ideas of literary genre, in a book called *The Bow-String: On Incompatibility of the Compatible.* See also RUSSIAN FORMALISM.

Reading
Galan, F.W. 1984: "Film as poetry and prose: Viktor Shklovsky's contribution in poetics of cinema."
Gunn, Daniel 1984: "Making art strange: a commentary on defamiliarization."
Hodgson, Peter 1985: "Viktor Shklovsky and the formalist legacy: initiation/stylization in narrative fiction. A *Festschrift* in honor of Victor Erlich."
Rosenberg, Karen 1985: "The concept of originality in formalist theory. A *Festschrift* in honor of Victor Erlich."
Shklovsky, V. 1925 (*1991*): *Theory of Prose.*
SLAVA I. YASTREMSKI

Showalter, Elaine (1941–) US feminist literary critic. Elaine Showalter has been a major proponent of American FEMINIST CRITICISM. She coined the term GYNOCRITICS and penned several of the most important statements of gynocritical theory and method; not surprisingly, her numerous studies of British and US women writers' literary history rank among the fullest realizations of gynocritical ideals. In *A Literature of Their Own* (1977), Showalter provides a framework for understanding British women's literary history, dividing it into three stages, each subject to what Frederick Jameson would call a "cultural dominant": Feminine before 1880, Feminist between 1880 and 1920, and Female since 1920. The difference between *A Literature of Their Own* and Showalter's later history of US women writers, *Sister's Choice* (1991), reveals the flexibility of gynocritics, and especially its remarkable response to early criticism that it was racist. While Showalter's first book focused exclusively on GENDER without considering the issues of RACE and nationality that would become so important by the late 1980s, the introduction to *Sister's Choice* draws heavily on Afro-American literary theory, particularly notions of the essential hybridity and double-voicedness of literary TEXTS, and subsequent chapters attempt a racially desegregated US women's literary history. Showalter's essay, "A criticism of their own," discusses the similar trajectories of Afro-American and feminist criticisms, as well as potential bases for alliance and solidarity. Here, as in earlier essays, some of which are collected in her edited anthology, *The New Feminist Criticism* (1985), Showalter's histories of critical movements are provocative and useful. Showalter has consistently defended feminist pluralism and argued that feminist DISCOURSE must necessarily remain heterogeneous. She deals with her detractors graciously and even-handedly, as when she includes Barbara Smith's critique of RACISM in her work in *The New Feminist Criticism* and alters her own critical practice in response. Her witty essay, "Critical cross-dressing: male feminists and the woman of the year" (1983), deserves special notice as an intervention in the debate about men in feminism.
See also FEMINIST CRITICISM; GYNOCRITICS.

Reading
Showalter, Elaine 1977: *A Literature of Their Own: British Women Novelists From Brontë to Lessing.*
——1983: "Critical cross-dressing: male feminists and the woman of the year."
——1989: "A criticism of our own: autonomy and assimilation in Afro-American and feminist literary theory."
——1991: *Sister's Choice.*

——ed. 1985: *The New Feminist Criticism: Essays on Women, Literature, and Theory*.
——ed. 1989: *Speaking of Gender*.

GLYNIS CARR

sign   Something that stands for something else (*aliquid stat pro aliquo*) the relation between something and something else, or the perception (or misperception) of a relation between something and something else. In the first of these definitions the sign stands for something that is absent, past, or yet to come (such as the portents of a storm or a disaster). In the second definition, the sign and what it signifies form at one extreme a dyadic relationship (as in Linnaeus's attempt to give a different name to each distinct object in nature) or at the other extreme, according to SAUSSURE, a purely arbitrary relationship. The third definition assumes a triad of sign, signified, and perceiver, as in Augustine's famous formulation in *De Doctrina Christiana*. A sign is a thing which causes us to think of something beyond the impression the thing itself makes upon the senses (see Jackson, 1972). The American philosopher C.S. PEIRCE brilliantly elaborates on this definition in "Some consequences of four incapacities," arguing that ultimately all thoughts are signs.

Although the sign is basic to all theories of language, especially to the science of SEMIOTICS, it is a notoriously unstable term and concept. Usually assumed to be an element of visual communication, the word "sign" for Saussure refers strictly to an *image acoustique*, which is at least an oxymoron or at best a synesthesiac term that baffles even Saussure's most careful commentators (Harris, pp. 58–9). Such fascinating oddities as this in Saussure's *Course in General Linguistics* have led DERRIDA to detect a phonocentric prejudice in Saussure by which he disparages WRITING as a monstrous intrusion on spoken language. Before Derrida went to work on Saussure and the sign, Jacques LACAN had appropriated both for psychoanalytic theory, and the Danish linguist Louis HJELMSLEV had begun to expand on Saussure's conviction that language is a SYSTEM or STRUCTURE of forms, not substances, by arguing that linguistic units are neither sounds nor meanings, but rather their interplay or relation. For Lacan signs do not come singly but in signifying chains. Furthermore he proposed, in an apparent reversal of Saussure, that it is the signifier itself that generates the signified.

Returning, in the wake of Lacan and Hjelmslev, to Saussure's theory of the sign, Derrida found a fundamental inconsistency between the arbitrariness of the sign and the presumed secondary, dependent, or monstrous role of writing in relation to speech. Derrida's proposal for a science of writing – GRAMMATOLOGY – and his argument that the sign itself, like all human structures, is subject to DECONSTRUCTION in order to reveal previously disguised or ignored assumptions, constitute one of the most powerful critiques of the sign as a supposedly stable, elemental unit of language.

Reading
Derrida, Jacques 1967a (*1976*): *Of Grammatology*.
Ducrot, Oswald, and Todorov, Tsvetan 1972 (*1979*): *Encyclopedic Dictionary of the Sciences of Language*.
Harris, Roy 1987 (*1991*): *Reading Saussure*.
Hjelmslev, Louis 1961: *Prolegomena to a Theory of Language*.
Jackson, B.D. 1972: "The theory of signs in St Augustine's *De Doctrina Christiana*."
Peirce, C.S. 1868 (*1958*): "Some consequences of four incapacities."
Saussure, Ferdinand de 1972 (*1983*): *Course in General Linguistics*.

MICHAEL PAYNE

signifying   A term central to BLACK CULTURAL STUDIES, which derives from the numerous tales and toasts about the Signifying Monkey, a folk trickster figure said to have originated during slavery in the United States. In most of these narratives, the Monkey manages to dupe the powerful Lion by signifying, a verbal strategy of indirection that exploits the gap between the denotative and figurative meanings of words. Clarifying the inadequacy of standard dictionary meanings, signifying directs attention to the connotative, context-bound significance of words, which is accessible only to those who share the unique cultural values of a given black speech community. The term "signifying" itself currently carries a range of metaphorical and theoretical meanings in black cultural studies that stretch far beyond its literal scope of reference. In his highly influential book, *The Signifying Monkey* (1988), Henry Louis Gates, Jr, expands the term to refer not merely to a specific vernacular strategy but also to a TROPE of double-voiced repetition and reversal that exemplifies the distinguishing property of black DISCOURSE. Thus redefined, the trope of signifying authorizes Gates's ambitious construction of a theory of black literary intertextuality grounded in the vernacular tradition.

Reading

Gates, Henry Louis, Jr 1988a: *The Signifying Monkey.*
Mitchell-Kernan, Claudia 1972: "Signifying, loud-talking and marking."
Smitherman, Geneva 1977: *Talkin and Testifyin: The Language of Black America.*

MADHU DUBEY

Signs   Established in 1975 by Catherine Stimpson and a group of feminist scholars from Barnard College, *Signs* has since its inception been an interdisciplinary journal intended to provide a forum for new scholarship about women. Originally designed to challenge mainstream scholarship, it has, in the course of 20 years of publication, provided the context for social and historical change, and in doing so has itself become a mainstream journal. Its very structure has allowed for this shift; over the years, its editors have remained sensitive to the continually changing field of feminist research, and have solicited scholarship from important thinkers whose work is at the edge of historical and cultural change. *Signs* devotes each of its quarterly issues to a specific field: the social sciences, the humanities, the natural sciences, or work and professions. Initially, only the first and fourth issues in each yearly volume were to focus on general themes, but since then the editors of *Signs* have presented themes in the other two issues as well. The first theme issue addressed the concept of "power," but a later issue focused on the interdisciplinary nature of computers.

In their manifesto, the first editors of *Signs* conceived of the journal as a "process over time"; perhaps their most effective tool for ensuring that their journal remained responsive to changing modes of feminist scholarship was their establishment of a rotating editorial board. With the first rotation – each editorial term lasts five years – the *Signs* editorial offices moved in 1980 to Stanford, where Barbara Charlesworth Gelpi of the English department, and six of her colleagues, channeled the already prospering journal into new areas of research, to continue what Stimpson and her team, in their final editorial, presented as a change in new scholarship about women. Still understanding the journal as a "process," the new editorial board's aim was to recognize the multiplicity of feminisms and to continue to promote feminist scholarship as a vital bridge between academic disciplines and social realities.

With the editorial rotation in 1985, *Signs* moved into the hands of Jean O'Barr, a political scientist at Duke University. She and her colleagues at Duke and the University of North Carolina's Women's Studies Research Center, of which she was also the director, explored a new set of feminist themes. O'Barr, responsible for the issue on computers, further developed the interdisciplinary nature of feminist studies. In 1990 the current editors – for the first time from different disciplines – took over *Signs*. Operating out of the Center for Advanced Feminist Studies at the University of Minnesota, Ruth-Ellen Boetcher Joeres, a historical sociologist, and Barbara Laslett, a scholar of German literature, introduced a new feature to the journal. This section, called "Forum," is devoted to academic DISCOURSE and is intended to reflect what Joeres and Laslett identify as a "multivocality" in feminist issues. Eager to see a renewal of the energy which sparked the inception of *Signs*, the two promise to transform the diverse field of feminist scholarship, always aware of its critical balance between providing an alternative to mainstream scholarship and becoming a part of it.

TARA G. GILLIGAN

social formation   This term is used by most theorists (including MARX and ENGELS) to designate a certain type of society such as feudal or bourgeois. It is given a more specific import in the tradition of structuralist Marxist theorists, which includes Maurice Godelier, Louis ALTHUSSER, Barry Hindess, and Paul Hirst. As opposed to the humanist readings of Marx offered by LUKÁCS, GRAMSCI, and others, which stress the role of human agency and history in social development, the structuralist Marxists have contended that what Marx primarily points the way to is a "scientific" structural analysis of social formations. Althusser views MARXISM as a new science of the history of social formations. These are not centered on human agencies; rather, they comprise a structure of hierarchies relatively autonomous but determined "in the last instance" by the economic substructure. Some of these theorists have attempted to distinguish between the usage of "social formation" and "society"; however, Althusser's understanding of "social formation" as the total complex of superstructure and economic infrastructure contains perhaps the most potential for the practical application of this term.

Reading
Althusser, L. 1965 (*1970*): *For Marx*.
Hindess, B., and Hirst, P. 1977: *Mode of Production and Social Formation*.

M.A.R. HABIB

socialist realism This aesthetic achieved predominance in Russia from around 1930 to 1956. Both prior to and beyond the Bolshevik revolution of 1917, Russia witnessed a series of heated debates, between Lenin, Trotsky, formalists, futurists, and constructivists, over the connection between ART and political commitment. This subsumed such questions as Party control of the arts, the need to create a proletarian culture, the relations between socialism and its bourgeois cultural inheritance, and the formulation of an appropriate socialist aesthetic. A Communist Party resolution of 1925 refused to stand behind any one literary faction. However, by the time of the first Soviet Writers' Congress of 1934 socialist realism emerged, in an atmosphere of Stalinist repression of all other factions, as the victorious official Party aesthetic, sanctioned by Maxim Gorki, N. Bukharin, and especially A.A. Zhdanov, Secretary of the Central Committee of "ideology."

Zhdanov defined socialist realism as the portrayal of "reality in its revolutionary development." Such art, he argued, must contribute to the project of ideological transformation and education of the working class. Other features of socialist realism, as designated by its various proponents, were an emphasis on factuality, the integration of scientific and technical detail, the application of later nineteenth-century realist techniques to Soviet heroes, and the literary projection of a socialist future.

Socialist realism traced its authority back through Lenin's notions of *partinost* (partisanship) and literature as a *reflection* of reality to the statements of MARX and ENGELS themselves, especially Engels's comments on the importance of expressing "typical" individuals and forces. Even so, this alleged lineage is somewhat misleading. While Marx and Engels certainly saw literature as performing an ideological function, they stressed its highly mediated connection with economic formations and Engels spoke of its "relative autonomy." Although it is true that they both praised realism, they did not centralize it in any coherent interventionist formulation. In fact, the first generation of Marxist theorists such as Antonio Labriola (1843–1904) and Georgi Plekhanov (1856–1918) articulated essentially contemplative accounts of the connection between art and social reality. It was only with Lenin and Trotsky that literature was ascribed an interventionist and partisan function in a broader revolutionary approach. However, the interventionism championed by both men was complex and flexible, qualified by its reference to particular historical circumstances. The more immediate impulses behind socialist realism included *Proletkult*, a left-wing group of writers led by A.A. Bogdanov (1873–1928), who, dedicated to creating a proletarian culture which would displace bourgeois art, viewed art as an instrument of class struggle. The Association of Proletarian Writers (VAPP; later RAPP) also insisted on achieving Communist cultural HEGEMONY. These movements, though, were merely prefaces to the official triumph of socialist realism. This triumph, embodied in the Writers' Union Congress of 1934, was essentially a result of the adoption under Stalinism of a more politically committed artistic attitude.

For all its crudities, socialist realism found a powerful if ambivalent advocate in Gyorgy LUKÁCS (1885–1971), whose version of realism elaborated Engels's notion of typicality. While Lukács opposed the modernism and experimentalism of Bertolt BRECHT (1898–1956), the latter also claimed to be a socialist realist, equating realism with the expression of what is typical in human relationships. In the 1930s Brecht's work evoked considerable hostility among the Marxist faithful, though he has subsequently been accepted as a major aesthetician. In the post-Stalinist period socialist realism declined and has been widely subjected to criticism. *See also* MARXISM AND MARXIST CRITICISM.

Reading
Laing, D. 1978: *The Marxist Theory of Art*.
Robin, R. 1992: *Socialist Realism: An Impossible Aesthetic*.
Zhdanov, A.A. 1950: *On Literature, Music and Philosophy*.

M.A.R. HABIB

sociology of knowledge Broadly defined, an approach which seeks to understand what counts (or has counted) as "knowledge" in various disciplines of thought by examining their sociohistorical origins and the way that they have evolved in response to external pressures, incentives, societal demands, modes of ideological conditioning, etc. More specifically (and controversially), it is the claim by exponents of the "strong program" in sociology of knowledge that such interests in effect go all the way down and determine the parameters of "knowledge" or "truth" for members of some given INTERPRETATIVE COMMUNITY, professional guild, scientific research enterprise, etc. Thus it follows that we should attach little or no credence to "internalist" (that is, intradisciplinary) explanations of our "knowledge of the growth of knowledge," or to the kinds of validating criteria that scientists, philosophers, and others have advanced by way of asserting their specialized credentials. Rather, we should reject the very terms of that distinction between (so-called) internal and external perspectives. Such talk merely serves to dissimulate the real operations of power, social interest, or capital investment that standardly adopt such a self-promoting rhetoric of pure, disinterested seeking after truth.

This approach has been most influential in the human and social sciences, where of course it is working very largely on home ground, that is to say, with methods of inquiry developed within those same disciplines. Karl Mannheim was the first to advance such claims on a systematic basis and to apply the term "sociology of knowledge" with full programmatical intent. Its sources also include the MARXIST tradition of *Ideologiekritik*; the work of Max Weber and other sociologists in the classical (mainly German) line of descent; the FRANKFURT SCHOOL approach to CRITICAL THEORY as elaborated in the writings of ADORNO, HORKHEIMER, and HABERMAS; and, later, the "archaeology" (or "GENEALOGY") of discursive power/knowledge formations essayed by Michel FOUCAULT. Where these thinkers divide is chiefly on the issue of just how far such an argument can or should be pressed. That is to say, what remains of the "disciplines" in question if skeptics like Foucault – or subscribers to the "strong program" in history and PHILOSOPHY OF SCIENCE – are justified in rejecting their every last criterion of truth, method, empirical warrant, and progress as attained through adequate (internal) procedures of rigorous self-monitoring, etc.? At the limit such skepticism appears to be self-refuting since it undermines even its own more confident assertions with regard to their *real* (as opposed to their professed) motivating values and interests.

Thus Adorno, in his essay on Mannheim, argued powerfully against any form of wholesale sociological reduction. This was despite having devoted much of his work to a detailed and strenuous dialectical critique of POSITIVISM in the natural sciences and what he saw as its various distorting effects upon the philosophic discourse of MODERNITY. The disadvantage of all such social-relativist arguments is that they can easily lean over into the kind of all-out epistemological and ethical skepticism which sees no difference between truth and falsehood (or justice and injustice) except as determined by this or that set of culture-specific interests and priorities. Where this confusion enters – most obviously in the case of an "anarchist" philosopher of science like Paul FEYERABEND – is in simply ignoring the crucial distinction between *context of discovery* and *context of justification*. The former is concerned with all those motivating factors – sociological, religious, psychobiographical, careerist, and so forth – which may well have influenced a scientist's thinking at some crucial point. The latter is concerned with those quite separate issues that arise when a theory or hypothesis is subject to debate – to the process of properly scientific elaboration and critique – according to the best currently available criteria.

At this point, predictably, the skeptic will respond by arguing:

(i)   that the history of science is very largely the history of dead or discredited theories;

(ii) that we have no reason to suppose that our current theories will fare any better;

(iii) that the criteria of scientific truth, method, and validity are themselves equally open to challenge or radical revision; and

(iv) that for all these reasons the "internalist" approach should now give way to a fully fledged sociological perspective; and therefore

(v)   we shall need to abandon any thought of distinguishing between the "context of discovery" and the "context of justification," for this can now be seen, so the argument goes, as just another ploy by which scientists (and philosophers of science) have sought to maintain their privileged role as arbiters of ultimate truth.

Thus for instance it has been argued, with a fair show of evidence, that Newton's conception of absolute space and time followed not so much from empirical observation or the rigorous requirements of his theory as from a prior (theological) framework of belief allied to a deeply conservative sense of cosmopolitical order. A similar case has been made for Einstein's long-running disagreement with Niels Bohr over the philosophy of quantum mechanics, unwilling as he (Einstein) was to accept its more radically heterodox or disturbing implications. This argument is pushed to a perverse extreme – what many would consider a *reductio ad absurdum* – in Feyerabend's view that Galileo was scientifically out on a limb with his heliocentric hypothesis, and moreover that Cardinal Bellarmine had the better of the argument in placing the interests of social stability over those of mere "scientific" truth. Nothing could more clearly illustrate the epistemological and ethical confusions that arise when sociologists of knowledge lay claim to a competence – or a right to disenfranchise the competence of others – beyond their own (quite legitimate) sphere of interest.

This presumption goes under various names. Among them may be counted POSTMODERNISM (with its aim of debunking all the erstwhile legitimizing "grand narratives" of truth, progress, enlightenment, science, critique, etc.) and the current neopragmatist fashion for reducing such values to the level of consensus belief or suasive rhetoric. (The literary critic Stanley FISH is one who has carried this latter line of argument to a high point of sophisticated, not to say sophistical, art.) However, it has also provoked some cogent counterargument from thinkers concerned to resist what they see as the widespread drift toward forms of disabling value relativism. The most effective opposition at present has come from critical realist philosophers of science such as Rom Harré and Roy Bhaskar; also from those (like Jürgen HABERMAS) who have attempted to argue dialectically through and beyond such wholesale challenges to the philosophic discourse of modernity. Sociology of knowledge is perhaps best defined as the region of interdisciplinary debate where these issues are nowadays pursued with maximum vigor and scope for deep-laid differences of view.

See also BOURDIEU, PIERRE; KUHN, THOMAS; SCIENCE, PHILOSOPHY OF.

Reading
Adorno, T.W., et al. 1976: *The Positivist Dispute in German Sociology.*
Barnes, Barry 1974: *Scientific Knowledge and Sociological Theory.*
Bloor, David 1976: *Knowledge and Social Imagery.*
Gilbert, Margaret 1989: *On Social Facts.*
Habermas, Jürgen 1971: *Knowledge and Human Interests.*
Latour, Bruno, and Woolgar, Steve 1986 (*1979*): *Laboratory Life: The Construction of Scientific Facts.*
Mannheim, Karl 1975 (*1939*): *Ideology and Utopia.*
Muntz, Peter 1985: *Our Knowledge of the Growth of Knowledge.*
Weber, Max 1948: *From Max Weber: Essays in Sociology.*
Woolgar, Steve, ed. 1988: *Knowledge and Reflexivity: New Frontiers in the Sociology of Knowledge.*

CHRISTOPHER NORRIS

Sontag, Susan (1933–) Since the middle 1960s, Susan Sontag has been one of the most individual and provocative of commentators on contemporary CULTURE. To all appearances thoroughly American in her upbringing and intellectual training – she was born in New York City, grew up in Arizona and California, and was educated at the Universities of Chicago and Harvard – Susan Sontag quickly distinguished herself by the passionate and mobile erudition of her concern with European culture, especially the culture associated with modernism. Her first book, *Against Interpretation and Other Essays* (1966) established a characteristically robust voice and critical posture, especially in the title essay's polemic against the depleting violence practiced by the act of interpretation on the particularity of ART. The sketch of the ironic sensibility of contemporary mass culture in "Notes on camp" in the same volume has been influential among theorists of POSTMODERNISM. Her studies of avant-gardism, pornography, and cinema in *Styles of Radical Will* (1969), the culture of images in *On Photography* (1977), and the metaphorical distortions and transformations of illness in *Illness as Metaphor* (1978) and *AIDS and Its Metaphors* (1989) reveal the same attentiveness to particulars and restless impatience with institutionalized forms of knowledge and explanation. Like Roland BARTHES, of whose work she is a great admirer, she prefers the lightness and plasticity of the short essay to the solemnity of the academic treatise. Her work argues tirelessly for the ethical seriousness of the aesthetic sensibility, as a mode of consciousness that maintains the possibility of human enlargement and transformation.

Reading
Sayres, Sohnya 1990: *Susan Sontag: The Elegiac Modernist.*
Sontag, Susan 1966: *Against Interpretation, and Other Essays.*
—— 1969: *Styles of Radical Will.*
—— 1977: *On Photography.*
—— 1978: *Illness as Metaphor.*
—— 1980: *Under the Sign of Saturn.*
—— 1982: *A Susan Sontag Reader.*
—— 1989: *AIDS and Its Metaphors.*

STEVEN CONNOR

South Asian studies   South Asian studies, like its other geographical area counterparts, is largely an artifact of the North American and European academy's approach to scholarship in history, economics, linguistics, and the social sciences following the 1939–45 war. As the most senior of the colonial projects to extend into the twentieth century, the Indian subcontinent is the subject of a broad and well-established body of literature in a variety of disciplines constituting what is now understood to be South Asian studies.

In the period immediately following the 1939–45 war, scholarly inquiry and writing relating to non-Western cultures tended to be departmentalized as reflections of changing colonial groupings and political structures. As the colonial era collapsed in Asia, Indo-China and the Dutch East Indies became Southeast Asia; China, Japan, and Korea became East Asia, with India, Pakistan (and later Bangladesh), and Sri Lanka becoming South Asia.

Contemporary scholarship in South Asian studies is the academic heir to the earlier discipline of Indology which, from its eighteenth-century origins, focused primarily upon historical and literary subjects. As the British imperial administrative structure grew through the nineteenth and early twentieth centuries, Indology expanded beyond its historical and linguistic-literary foci into a broader range of social science disciplines, often in response to colonial administrative needs and prerogatives.

As the conceptual framework of "postwar" evolved into "postcolonial," this existing body of historical, ethnographic, economic, and linguistic research has increasingly been viewed by contemporary critics as informed by and representative of an essentially elitist hegemonic point of view. Much of this postcolonial critique uses as a theoretical base Abdel-Malik's "Orientalism in crisis" (1963) and Edward SAID's more widely read *Orientalism* (1978) which set the parameters for current DISCOURSE on the ideologies underlying our historical and cultural perceptions of the "Orient" (Said concentrated primarily on the Middle East), particularly in relation to the colonial project.

In the first half of the twentieth century the salient characteristic of scholarship relating to India and the subcontinent was its almost total dependency upon documentation and studies undertaken by colonial administrations (Alvares, 1991). The singular, attenuated origin of these historical sources, spanning a period of 300 years of writing

about South Asia, has prompted the creation of a new, confrontational historiography known as SUBALTERN STUDIES. Borrowing conceptually from GRAMSCI, the subaltern history represents the displaced or unwritten narrative of the dominated classes of imperial India (Guha and Spivak, 1982). This history argues, for example, that our understanding of the creation of the independent states of India and Pakistan is based upon the simplistic dichotomy of British colonial overlord versus a small group of Indian nationalists (Ghandi, Nehru, Jinna), exclusive of the role of resistance played by the subaltern classes.

Central to this critical discourse is the purposeful rejection of a traditionally disinterested, disengaged, and objective historiography in favor of a "DECONSTRUCTION" of history in which an attempt is made to expose and demystify the elements of IDEOLOGY and HEGEMONY embedded in the writing of South Asia's historical narrative (Spivak, 1982). The oppositional critical posture of the subaltern scholars, many of whom represent the first generation of South Asian intellectuals to become educated in a postcolonial, postindependence period, is a self-conscious attempt to establish an integrative alternative, open to nontraditional sources and methodologies, to the established narrative.

The products of the new historiographic approaches emerging within South Asian studies often reveal an orientalist structure which establishes a secular "West" contrasted with a somewhat idealized religious Asian subcontinent in which such progressive developments as a fully developed democratic state remain a "failed experiment" (Lele in Breckenridge and van der Veer, 1993). This pervasive theme of the assignation of failure emerges as a key problematic of the postcolonial historiography of South Asia, that is, the issue of why, given their numerical superiority and the long duration of their struggle against the colonial oppressor, the Indian people became a subaltern class (Guha, 1988).

As efforts to capture the subaltern voice have intensified within South Asian studies, methodological debate has also emerged. The propriety of nontraditional methods of research and the utilization of unusual sources of primary material represent a continuing challenge to contemporary scholarship. This methodological latitude has resulted in projects which have crossed the traditional historical and ethnographic boundaries previously defining "area studies" by appropriating philosophical (FOUCAULT via Said) and literary (DERRIDA via Spivak) critical perspectives on issues of culture and narrative. These studies constitute what ALTHUSSER characterizes as an "epistemological break"; a fundamentally new *paradigm* for intellectual inquiry relating to the history and cultures of South Asia.

Another significant dimension of postcolonial scholarship relating to South Asia is the tracing of the juxtaposition of a politically dominant Europe (or West) against a necessarily subservient India back to its roots in HEGEL's treatment of India (Halbfass, 1988). Such examinations of Europe's philosophical HISTORICITY have highlighted the broader role that a purposefully defined, subservient and exotic Orient, with South Asia as a central subject, plays in allowing a dominant, rationally defined Occident to exist.

This European construction of a Western "self" contrasted with a South Asian "OTHER" remains a focal point for contemporary intellectual historians' discourse on the interplay and mutual influence of European and Indian thought. In addition to the dreamlike "Idealism of the imagination" attributed to India by Hegel, theoretical writings of MARX, Mill, and Weber also offer a construction of India as a prerational "Empire of the Imaginary" (Inden, 1990) against which a rational, positivist West can be contrasted and defined. It is Inden's theory that this antithetical South Asian "other" remains embedded in scholarship in a variety of disciplines – anthropology, economics, and political philosophy – thus limiting the "agency" of modern South Asian intellectuals and the evolution of Indian political and cultural institutions.

The role of the literary creations of the *Raj* – British India as a beneficent, paternalistic, even sentimental force – is critical to understanding the cultural contexts within which South Asian studies evolved in the latter half of the twentieth century (Chakravarty, 1989). The unapologetically racist "white man's burden" informing nineteenth-century England's unequal encounter, as exemplified by Kipling, with their imperial subjects became, in the twentieth century, the disillusioned LIBERALISM of E.M. Forster.

The body of nineteenth- and twentieth-century popular fiction in English relating to South Asia represents, in the aggregate, a narrative of sustained stereotypes cumulatively evolved over the three centuries of the colonial project in India. The "inscrutable" Oriental of the nineteenth century

became more primal and predictable in the twentieth; a superstitious native character was transformed into an essentially religious, even spiritually transcendent cultural icon, uneducated but wise, with characteristics often previously portrayed as effeminate now idealized as pacific (Nandy, 1983). From Kipling through Ghandi, the extent to which these stereotypes, which were woven into the "official" colonial administrative historical sources of scholarship about South Asia, continue to undergird and inform postcolonial perspectives is a central tenet of the critique of ORIENTALISM.

As the empire was transformed into the Commonwealth, the cultural and intellectual legacies of the Raj mentality, particularly in examinations of early South Asian civilizations, continued to provide a sometimes unconscious subtext for the characterization of the religious, social, and linguistic traditions and subsequent influences of Vedic and pre-Vedic Indian civilizations. The earliest examples of British scholarship emanating from the subcontinent focused on religious and linguistic "histories" of Hinduism and Sanskrit. The implications of the long-term colonial interest in the linguistic "mapping" of the subcontinent extend into the present day. The sociolinguistic issue of the "NATURALIZATION" of the English language within the Indian experience has emerged as an intersection of debate and scholarship. The role of the language of the colonial suppressors in contrast or confrontation with the use of the vernacular languages of the subcontinent remains a volatile political issue in India with deep and often disparate nationalistic implications.

The orientalist enterprise also embraced the study of Indian literatures. This critical tradition, beginning with eighteenth-century treatises on Vedic civilizations, utilized an ENLIGHTENMENT conception of literature (as, for example, an "ordered" body of work in an indigenous language), while maintaining an adherence, over time, to prevailing European intellectual themes. Again, contemporary critics hold that this colonial representation of the "native" literatures of the subcontinent, although often appropriating an objective, disinterested positivist posture, in fact was unable to escape the European assertion of political and cultural dominance in Asia (Dharwadker, in Breckenridge and van der Veer, 1993).

In general, postcolonial scholarship in the multiple disciplines constituting South Asian studies has been shaped by a hybrid mixture of influences.

MARXISM maintains a central prominence within economics and other social sciences, with Gramsci holding a particularly visible presence in studies dealing with issues of CULTURE and CLASS. Also evident among the theoretical and critical bases of South Asianists is the influence of the structuralist and poststructuralist work of DERRIDA, FOUCAULT, ALTHUSSER, and BARTHES. The most salient of these influences is that of Foucault, whose framing devices of power and knowledge as well as his overall penchant for demystification, has provided a theoretical foundation, vocabulary, and an aggressive methodological stance for much of the postcolonial discourse relating to South Asia.

Finally, as alternative narratives emerge for South Asian studies, there are those who are mindful of the inherent danger of creating a separatist intellectual project which, in a mirror image of its colonial predecessor, is disdainful of the interdependence of the contrasting voices of the suppressor and the suppressed (Said, in Guha and Spivak, 1987). This issue of exclusivity will continue to influence future standards of method and interpretation in this increasingly eclectic and prolific field of inquiry.

Reading
Abdel-Malik, Anouar 1963: "Orientalism in crisis."
Alvares, Claude 1991: *Decolonizing History: Technology and Culture in India, China, and the West, 1492 to the Present Day.*
Breckenridge, Carol, and van der Veer, Peter 1993: *Orientalism and the Postcolonial Predicament: Perspectives on South Asia.*
Chakravarty, Suhash 1991: *The Raj Syndrome: A Study in Imperial Perceptions.*
Guha, Ranajit 1982: *Subaltern Studies: Writings on South Asian History and Society.*
——and Spivak, Gayatari 1988: *Selected Subaltern Studies.*
Halbfass, Wilhelm 1988: *India and Europe: An Essay in Understanding.*
Inden, Ronald 1990: *Imagining India.*
Nandy, Ashis 1983: *The Intimate Enemy: Loss and Recovery of Self Under Colonialism.*
Said, Edward W. 1978: *Orientalism.*

JAMES P. RICE

Southern Agrarians An American political movement of the late 1920s and 1930s. Several of its leaders, such as John Crowe RANSOM and Allen TATE, were literary critics, and the movement played a crucial role in American literary studies since they subsequently went on to become the chief ideologists of NEW CRITICISM. The movement idealized the Old South as an organic society and as an antidote to the dehumanizing forces of science, industrialism, and secularism. Like T.S. ELIOT, whom they greatly revered, they are best described as radical conservatives: Tate aimed to turn the Agrarians into an academy of "Southern positive reactionaries" and wanted their main manifesto, *I'll Take My Stand* (1930), to be entitled "Tracts against Communism." The Agrarians advocated a return to the land and an ideal of subsistence farming (see *Who Owns America?* 1936), but by 1937 its leaders were disillusioned and decided that the northern capitalist-industrialist economy could not be reformed and that their philosophy could best be promulgated by a university-based literary critical movement. Ransom founded *The Kenyon Review*, and the New Critical campaign, with all its associated summer schools, textbooks, and student primers, was born.

See also FUGITIVES; NEW CRITICISM; RANSOM, JOHN CROWE; TATE, ALLEN.

Reading
Conkin, P.K. 1988: *The Southern Agrarians.*
Fekete, John 1977: *The Critical Twilight.*
O'Brien, Michael 1988: "A heterodox note on the southern renaissance."
Stewart, J.L. 1965: *The Burden of Time: The Fugitives and Agrarians.*

IAIN WRIGHT

speech acts A speech act is an utterance which constitutes all or part of an act. For example, in saying (or writing) "I bet you a pound that your baby will be a girl," I am engaging in the act of betting. Other obvious speech acts include promises and warnings.

The theory of speech acts was developed by the Oxford philosopher J.L. AUSTIN in the 1930s and was the subject of 12 William James Lectures which Austin delivered at Harvard University in the United States in 1955. The publication of these lectures (Austin, 1962) and of John SEARLE's (1969) subsequent development of the theory brought it to the attention of linguists (Sadock, 1974; Sinclair and Coulthard, 1975; Hymes, 1967/1986; Schegloff, 1968/1986), language teachers, psychologists (Bruner, 1975; Bates, 1976), and literary theorists, to whom its appeal was immediate. The influence of speech-act theory remains strongest in cross-cultural pragmatics (Blum-Kulka et al., 1989), in communicative language teaching (Widdowson, 1978), and in some literary theories (Petrey, 1990).

The reason why many nonphilosophers found speech-act theory so appealing was their feeling that here at last was a "natural language philosophy" concerned with the actual use of everyday language rather than with the truth or falsity of a restricted set of invented sentences. By the 1930s, when Austin began to work on the notion of speech as action, the truth-oriented logical positivists had achieved such a reduction in the number of "factually significant" sentences that any hope of extending the methods of logic to deal with a major part of natural language looked unlikely to be fulfilled.

Austin writes against the background of "the descriptive fallacy" (1962, p. 3), the belief that the purpose of any declarative sentence is to describe a state of affairs correctly – leading to truth – or incorrectly – leading to falsity. In fact, Austin insists, there are many declarative sentences which do not describe, and in the case of which it makes no sense to ask whether they are true or false, namely those used in the making of speech acts. Austin calls such sentences "performatives," and uses the term "constatives" for sentences which describe. Only constatives are true or false; performatives are "happy" or "unhappy," depending on whether the circumstances in which they are uttered are appropriate. These performatives, then, have "felicity conditions," whereas only constatives have "truth conditions."

Having drawn this distinction, however, Austin sets about breaking it down by showing that (i) constatives can be unhappy in the sense that their presuppositions and implications may not be fulfilled; (ii) performatives can be false in the sense of "conflicting with the facts"; and (iii) every utterance is in fact a speech act. This is because, although no verb naming the speech act being performed – a "speech-act verb" – need be included in it, any speech act is expandable into an utterance having such a verb in it.

Consider the utterance "Fire." This may function as the speech act of warning, and if it does, it is expandable into the explicit form "I warn you that there is a fire." By this argument, every apparently constative utterance is expandable into the speech-act "statement," since any utterance can be prefaced by "I state that." Therefore all linguistic behavior can be considered speech action. In addition to its "propositional content," any utterance has a particular "force" and all that remains to do is to classify these forces.

Searle (1969) attempts a classification into sets of rules for the performance of particular speech acts. For example, the rules for promising specify that what is being promised must (i) be a future action, (ii) which the promisee would like to happen, (iii) and which it is not obvious that the promisor would do anyway, (iv) but which s/he intends to do, (v) and is, having promised, obliged to do. Searle (1969, pp. 66–7) provides rules for several other speech acts, and draws on these in explaining how speakers are able to use and comprehend "indirect speech acts."

In many cases the form of a speech act conflicts with its function. For example, what looks like a promise ("I promise to have you locked up if you do that") may strike us as having quite a different force, in this example probably "warning." We know that this cannot be a proper promise because one of the rules for promising is broken, in so far as we must assume that the hearer would not prefer being locked up to not being locked up. We also know that it is a warning because one of the rules for warning is adhered to, namely the rule that what is being warned against must be something the hearer would not like to happen.

Searle, unlike Austin, claims that the theory of meaning *is* the theory of speech acts, and to make this claim more palatable he provides a set of rules for the speech acts of referring and predicating. However, these incorporate all of the difficulties faced by traditional theories of truth, and both Austin, explicitly, and Searle, implicitly, remain wedded to a theory of truth conditionally derived from literal meaning.

This aspect of speech-act theory has tended to be overlooked outside philosophy itself, where, it is possible to argue, the influence of the theory can lead to insufficient emphasis being placed on the "what" of a given speech act: it is obviously as important to understand *what* is being promised as it is to understand that a promise is being made.

Furthermore, it is not clear that the utterances that form naturally occurring DISCOURSE actually conform to clearly definable conditions or rules. A contrasting view considers the recognition of "speech acts" to be based on the interactants' common knowledge of each other, of the situation, and of the surrounding discourse. On this basis, interactants infer the attitude that a speaker is likely to have to propositions, and the exploration of "propositional attitudes" has become central in philosophically oriented work on language and cognition (see Lycan, 1990).

A still more radical view holds that it is impossible to consider a "proposition" in isolation from a "force" and vice versa (Quine, 1960). From this view, the act of betting is not isolatable from its content, and the act, if the notion makes sense at all, mentioned at the beginning of this entry is the act of "betting you a pound that your baby will be a girl." Comparatively, the "attitude," if the notion makes sense at all, expressed in any utterance of the form, "I believe that x" is not the attitude of believing, but the attitude of believing that x. It is then tempting to conceive of "meaning," not as a property of propositions, but as a full-blown, if fleeting, relationship between a time, a language user, a set of circumstances, and an utterance (Davidson, 1984; Lewis, 1970).

Reading
Austin, J.L. 1962: *How to do Things with Words.*
Blum-Kulka, S., House, J., and Kasper, G., eds 1989: *Cross-Cultural Pragmatics: Requests and Apologies.*
Levinson, S.C. 1980: "Speech act theory: the state of the art."
Searle, J. 1969: *Speech Acts.*
——1975. "Indirect speech acts."

KIRSTEN MALMKJÆR

state apparatus, ideological *See* IDEOLOGICAL
STATE APPARATUS

Steiner, George (1929–) American literary critic. George Steiner is one of the most distinctive figures of twentieth-century criticism. During a long and distinguished career, he, probably more than any other contemporary intellectual, has reflected in a serious, provocative, and far-reaching manner on what precisely it is to be a critic in the modern world, and why it is still a role – and, he would also say, a responsibility – worth preserving. Born in Paris, emigrating to the United States in 1940, Steiner was educated at the Universities of Chicago, Harvard, and Oxford. Since 1969 he has been an extraordinary Fellow of Churchill College, Cambridge, and, since 1974, Professor of English and comparative literature at the University of Geneva. In 1994 he became Weidenfeld visiting professor of European comparative literature at the University of Oxford.

The critic, according to Steiner, can fulfill three tasks: first, to "feel ahead," reminding the reader

that the TEXT stands in a complex, provisional relation to time; second, to "connect," acting as intermediary and custodian of the work of the writer; third, and most important of all, to "judge" the ART of one's own age. The project, addressed most vividly in the essay "Humane literacy" in *Language and Silence* (1967), is to "engage the presence" of the text, to do one's best to read "as total human beings, by example of precision, fear and delight." "LITERARY CRITICISM," he argued at the beginning of *Tolstoy or Dostoevsky* (1960), "should arise out of a debt of love." Steiner's own work has always been characterized by an intense and insistent commitment to personal feeling, making his writing, in both form and content, as much the result of "risks of the heart" as of intellectual reflection.

The task of the critic is to mediate: "only through the critic's constant and anguished recognition of the distance which separates his craft from that of the poet, can such mediation be accomplished." It is a theme that runs like a thread through all of Steiner's most important essays and books. In *Real Presences* (1989), responding to the radical doubt in POSTSTRUCTURALISM, Steiner insists that the critic is answerable to a text "in a very specific sense, at once moral, spiritual and psychological." To communicate the aesthetic experience requires "tact, technical authority and control of a rare order" which, claims Steiner, runs the risk of embarrassment; such embarrassment, he adds, "in bearing witness to the poetic, to the entrance into our lives of the mystery of otherness in art . . . is of a metaphysical-religious kind."

One of Steiner's most important critical concerns (and one he shares with one of his most significant intellectual influences, Walter BENJAMIN) is the task, and implications, of translation. In his major work, *After Babel* (1975), Steiner presents the practice and possibility of translation as the most formidable of all cultural problems. Translation is portrayed as a universal ingredient in all acts of comprehension. He criticizes reductive approaches to the study of language which seek to "cure" it of its fictiveness and AMBIGUITY. He suggests, as an alternative, a more adequate conception which strives to accommodate and appreciate, rather than exclude and deny, the "slippery, ambiguous, altering, subconscious or traditional contextual reflexes" of language. These maligned qualities of language are, he insists, vital to our survival:

Ours is the ability, the need, to gainsay or "un-say" the world, to image and speak it otherwise. In that capacity in its biological and social evolution, may lie some of the clues to the question of the origins of human speech and the multiplicity of tongues. It is not, perhaps, "a theory of information" that will serve us best in trying to clarify the nature of language, but a "theory of misinformation". (1975, p. 228)

Language, he goes on to argue, is essentially "fictive" because "the enemy is 'reality'":

We secrete from within ourselves the grammar, the mythologies of hope, of fantasy, of self-deception without which we would have been arrested at some rung of primate behaviour or would, long since, have destroyed ourselves. It is our syntax, not the physiology of the body or the thermodynamics of the planetary system, which is full of tomorrows . . . We speak, we dream ourselves free of the organic trap. (1975, p. 238)

Steiner's most provocative anxiety, expressed in an extraordinarily varied range of essays, novels, and academic texts, is that the atrocities of the 1914–18 war and the Holocaust have threatened, if not dealt a fatal blow to, the entire Western tradition of "humane literacy." A central question, addressed time and again by Steiner, is why do the humanities not civilize? His phrase, in *Language and Silence*, about the cry in the poem perhaps seeming more real than the cry in the street, sustains, in the publications that followed, a melancholic echo. He warned of a creeping banality produced by mass culture, a culture without privacy or memory. *In Bluebeard's Castle* (1971) he considers the possibility that so-called high culture's abstract speculation may infect human consciousness with an *ennui* out of which may fester a fascination with savagery. A "decent" alternative for CULTURE, one which Steiner, in theory, has always found difficult to resist, is silence, the tacit admission that the civilizing power of a culture based on "the word" is an illusion (the most obvious influence here for Steiner is T.W. ADORNO).

Steiner's own criticism has continued to struggle with the PARADOX of making the claims of silence heard. He has come, for some, to resemble the last critic, the critic who reflects on the death of the critical tradition in a post-Auschwitz world. This critic writes books on how books may become redundant, and on how professional criticism may be discouraged. There is certainly a Steiner for whom criticism is but "a eunuch's shadow," an activity lived "at second-hand." There is also, however, a Steiner for whom criticism is one of the most decent, most precious of activities, a powerful affirmation of a humanist agenda. This critic reads great literature as though it has upon him "an urgent design." Steiner is both of these critics; he embodies their contradictory natures. In doing so, he represents a peculiarly *modern* reading of the critic.

Reading
Howe, Irving 1973: "Auschwitz and high mandarin."
Steiner, George 1984: *George Steiner: A Reader.*
Tanner, Tony 1980: "A Preface to A.H."

GRAHAM MCCANN

story/plot A distinction drawn by narrative theorists across a range of otherwise diverse schools and cultural-linguistic backgrounds. (Thus, for instance, *fabula/suzhet* were the terms adopted by RUSSIAN FORMALISM; *histoire/discours* in the idiom of French narratologists such as Gérard GENETTE and the early Roland BARTHES.) Though recently developed to a high point of sophisticated treatment, this distinction is basically quite simple and will strike most readers – as it did E.M. Forster in his book *Aspects of the Novel* – as a matter of intuitive self-evidence. The fictional *story* can best be defined as the sequence of episodes, actions, or events as they might have occurred if removed from the realm of fictive or novelistic DISCOURSE and rearranged (so to speak) on a real-time basis of "one thing after another." That is, story concerns those elements of chronology, causality, temporal sequence, human acts and their subsequent outcome, etc. that we interpret in accordance with our everyday (non-fictive) knowledge and experience of the world. *Plot* may be defined, in contrast, as the sum total of narrative devices by which a novelist contrives to reorder these basic story-line components and thus create a heightened degree of interest, variety, or suspense. Some works of fiction (for example, novels in the realist or naturalistic mode) will tend to manifest no great discrepancy between story and plot, since their aim is to create a sense of verisimilitude by reproducing the quotidian (real-world) conditions of temporal and causal sequence. Others – from *Tristram Shandy* to TEXTS in the modernist, postmodernist, and experimental genres – go various ways around to complicate the plot/story relationship and resist any reading that would seek (naively) to collapse the difference between them.

Many critics have contributed to refining and developing the terms of this seminal distinction. Indeed, it has always played a crucial part in the formalist theory of literature, beginning with Aristotle's remarks about the various kinds of plot structure ("simple" or "complex") to be found in ancient Greek tragic drama, and taken up again whenever critics have returned to the Aristotelian idea of poetics as an orderly, methodical, or scientific quest for the characteristic forms and modalities of literary discourse. What is most impressive about later work in this field – from the Russian formalist school of the 1920s to French (or French-influenced) NARRATOLOGY of the 1950s to the 1990s – is the degree of conceptual precision attained in its analysis of the various transformational structures used in the passage from story to plot. Thus, for instance, Genette provides an object lesson in the shrewd deployment of analytic categories – tense structure, deviant chronology, patterns of narrative parallelism, repetition, prolepsis, and so forth – which genuinely serves to deepen and extend our awareness of the complexities involved. At the same time this very sophistication of method has raised new problems with regard to the plot/story dualism. Clearly there is a sense in which any attempt to extricate the one from the other – to reconstruct the story line as if it somehow existed apart from (or prior to) its narrative emplotment – must soon encounter obstacles. After all, it is surely mistaken to suppose that the novelist started out with some straightforward story-telling purpose in mind, and then worked it up into a complicated form for the keener delectation of super-subtle readers or exegetes. More than that, there is something decidedly naive – and counter to formalist principle – in the idea that story relates to plot in much the same way as content to form or narrative material to its elaboration in fully fledged artistic or novelistic guise. If there is one central doctrine that unites all varieties of formalist aesthetic, it is the argument against such misconceived and crudely reductive dichotomies.

Deconstructionist critics – Jonathan CULLER for one – have had much to say about the problems that result from this conflict of method and principle. Thus Culler points out that there are two different logics, two modes of intelligibility, required in the reading of narrative texts. On the one hand, when reading for the story, it is matter of suspending disbelief, construing events *as if* they pertained to the real-world order of temporal succession or unilinear cause and effect, and thereby consenting to the fictive illusion which affords our more usual (nontheoretical) kinds of readerly enjoyment. On the other hand, when reading for the plot, we have to recognize that this is not at all the way in which narrative actually works. It then becomes apparent, paradoxically enough, that effects are causes of (what we took to be) causes and that causes are effects of (what we took to be) effects. According to the story-line version, Oedipus is punished with blindness, exile, and death as a result – a causal consequence – of his having killed his father Laius and married his mother Jocasta. However, on a formalist (plot-oriented) reading in the deconstructive mode, this logic is subjected to a point-for-point reversal, whereby Oedipus is constrained to kill his father and marry his mother in order that the play should lead up to a suitably tragic conclusion.

Or again, take the question, much debated by literary critics, of just why Hamlet delays so long in exacting revenge against Claudius, given that (on his own submission) he has adequate motive, cause, and opportunity. Attending to the "story" mostly means seeking some depth-psychological or character-based account of how the drama unfolds from one crisis to the next. In formalist terms, however, such purported "explanations" are entirely beside the point. Hamlet is not a "character" with motives, desires, Oedipal hang-ups, or obscure psychological depths. Rather he is a name to which we standardly impute a number of functional (plot-determined) traits, among them the markers "introvert," "brooding," "mother-fixated," "incapable of decisive action," etc. So when it is asked why Hamlet delays for so long, then the answer, quite simply, is that this is a five-act play in the established revenge–tragedy tradition, and that if he did not delay then the plot would collapse somewhere around the middle of Act One. The same would apply to those novels – Jane Austen's protypically – whose outcome equates the heroine's good fortune with her finding a suitable marriage partner after various ill-advised choices along the way. According to the story-line account, those choices and that outcome can all be construed as resulting understandably from what went before, that is, from certain crucial episodes and events combined with certain traits in the heroine's character which first predisposed her to fix on the wrong man and then, in the wisdom of hindsight, to place her affections elsewhere. However, this account can just as well be run in reverse. Then it is a matter of generic expectation (or plot requirement) that the novel should conclude with a happy marriage; that this should stand in marked contrast to those previous upsets to her sense of self-esteem; and therefore that the novel's *dénouement* should retroactively dictate the whole course of foregoing actions, choices, and events.

Hence Culler's point about the "double logic" – the conflict or interference of narrative codes – that results from our attempting to read simultaneously for the story and the plot. It is a point also made, if in more oblique fashion, by postmodernist writers like Italo Calvino who contrive all manner of vertiginous effects (or techniques of textual *mise-en-abîme*) by switching constantly from one level to the other. The result, as in Calvino's novel *If on a Winter's Night A Traveller*, is to create a perpetual uncertainty in the reader about just where those levels merge or intersect, and just what role s/he (the reader) occupies in relation to her or his fictive surrogates in the text. If Calvino thus preempts every last move of a formalist (or a deconstructive) reading, then the same might be said of Sterne's *Tristram Shandy* or Cervantes's *Don Quixote*. Indeed, as many critics have noted, the "anti-novel" has a history going back as far as – if not further than – its mainstream realist counterpart. Nor perhaps should one expect otherwise, given the pattern of curious metaleptic reversals (the disruption of chronology and cause–effect sequence) that appears at every turn in these attempts to differentiate narrative "story" and "plot." *See also* FORMALISM; NARRATOLOGY; STRUCTURALISM.

Reading

Brooks, Peter 1984: *Reading for the Plot*.
Calvino, Italo 1992: *If on a Winter's Night a Traveller*.
Culler, Jonathan 1981: *The Pursuit of Signs*.
Genette, Gérard 1980: *Narrative Discourse: An Essay in method*.
Lodge, David 1981: *Working with Structuralism*.
Rimmon-Kenan, Shlomith 1983: *Narrative Fiction*.
Todorov, Tzvetan 1981: *Introduction to Poetics*.

                                        CHRISTOPHER NORRIS

Strauss, Leo (1899–1973) German émigré political philosopher and historian of political thought.

He studied at the Universities of Marburg and Hamburg, where he came into contact with Edmund Husserl and the young Martin HEIDEGGER. He left Germany in 1932 for France and England. He later went to the United States, where he was professor of political science at the University of Chicago from 1949 to 1968. It is estimated that he graduated approximately 100 doctoral students. When Strauss died in 1973, eulogies poured forth. His students compared him to Socrates – he was a man to be experienced. They were enchanted, delighted, excited, captivated, confused, awestruck, mildly stunned, even dizzy. There are now second- and third-generation Straussians, as they are known in the profession. They all share the same devotion and ardent faith in the teaching of Strauss. What is the source of all this excitement?

Strauss wrote some 15 books and 80 articles on the history of political thought from Socrates to NIETZSCHE. His best-known books are listed below. Strauss was no ordinary historian of ideas. He believed that all the wise or ancient philosophers in the West shared the same set of beliefs about man, politics, goodness, and truth. However, this was a secret wisdom, which was guarded by seven seals. Strauss was convinced that the truth was dangerous and that all wise men shared his view. As a result, he concluded that all of the great books in the history of political thought contained an exoteric or public teaching as well as an esoteric or private message. The former was a salutary teaching or noble lie intended for the consumption of the many, whereas the latter was the dangerous truth intended only for the few. There is no doubt that much of Strauss's appeal has its source in his seductive combination of elitism and secrecy. Strauss confessed that he was himself an esoteric commentator on esoteric texts (1968, p. 27). In light of all this secrecy, is it possible to penetrate his thought? Some of his disciples say that this is not possible. I believe that Strauss is fairly simple to understand. In my view, the most important key to his thought is his interpretation of Plato.

Strauss is considered by his disciples as well as his critics to be a follower of Plato, whom he regarded as the personification of ancient wisdom. However, Strauss's understanding of Plato is radically at odds with the usual view. On close examination, Strauss's Plato turns out to be a postmodern follower of Nietzsche. Strauss regarded Thrasymachus (not Socrates) as Plato's true spokesman (1964, p. 77). According to Strauss, Plato must have known that there are absolutely no grounds for our cherished moral beliefs. As Thrasymachus teaches, justice is nothing more than the advantage of the stronger: those in power decide what counts as true, right, and good. Truth and goodness are therefore a function of power. Strauss follows Thrasymachus in thinking that the just man is a fool who has fallen prey to the fictions invented by power. In Strauss's view, however, the world needs to be populated by such fools; this is why Plato silences Thrasymachus but does not refute him. According to Strauss, the bulk of the *Republic* is a pious fraud intended for the consumption of the herd. The truth is a luxury intended only for the few who hunger for the reality behind the myths and illusions of the cave. Strauss insists that though the truth is dark, even "sordid," it is still the erotic object of the philosopher's quest. But there is the rub. It seems to me that if we accept Nietzsche's premises we must also accept his conclusion – if the truth is dark, then we must renounce it and live according to the humanizing illusions, the life-giving myths we create for ourselves. By accepting Nietzsche's premises and rejecting his conclusion, Strauss cultivates an elite that is more vulgar than it is wise.

Reading
Bloom, Allan 1987: *The Closing of the American Mind.*
Drury, Shadia B. 1988: *The Political Ideas of Leo Strauss.*
Strauss, Leo 1952: *Persecution and the Art of Writing.*
———— 1953: *Natural Right and History.*
———— 1959: *What is Political Philosophy?*
———— 1964: *The City and Man.*
———— 1968: *On Tyranny.*

SHADIA B. DRURY

structuralism   A method of inquiry which proceeds from the premise that cultural activity can be approached and analyzed objectively as a science. Structuralists attempt to discern the elements in their area of specialization which correspond to a unitary organization. Once these elements are found, they are located in a web-like relationship to one another. The relationships constitute the overall structure which is assumed to be ultimately at the root of the cultural phenomenon under discussion. Once this structure is discovered in the rigor of its composition, all activity in the field can be explained in its terms.

Structuralism is usually considered to have begun with the linguistics of Ferdinand de SAUSSURE,

although it was the Russian structural linguist Roman JAKOBSON who gave the movement its name. Saussure called for a science of signification, SEMIOTICS, of which linguistics was to be the privileged example. For Saussure, all linguistic practice (including nonverbal) could theoretically be analyzed in terms of a deeper structure rooted ultimately in the biology of the human mind. He found that meaning is structured as a relation of difference between elements, that a word has its meaning not because of what it refers to, but because it does not mean the same as other words. The linguistic SIGN is structured as a relation between the signified (the referent) and the signifier (the lexical unit). Signs are structured in relation to each other in accordance with the principle of differential relations, but are also organized in a further relation. This relation is the one which constitutes BINARY OPPOSITIONS, relations between opposites which are charged with important meanings in human CULTURE. Saussure saw this deeper structure as constituting a sort of ideal speech community which overdetermined the utterance of an individual (see LANGUE/PAROLE). It was the *langue* itself which interested him, and he saw no point in analyzing the *parole*. He theorized that this type of relationship between a communal root and an individual practice was at the root of all cultural practice, and his insight had a profound effect on the structuralists who followed him. Structuralist theorists in fields such as CULTURAL ANTHROPOLOGY, NARRATOLOGY, and linguistics all proceed upon assumptions very similar to his.

The linguistic theory of Roman Jakobson developed from a meeting of structuralism and RUSSIAN FORMALISM. However, he did not simply accept Saussure's privileging of *langue* over *parole*, since his own interest was in the operation of an individual's *parole*. This included, for Jakobson, the description of the phoneme, the sound unit which is a meaningful part of the linguistic SIGN in conversation. The reason for the importance Jakobson placed upon *parole* was his interest in the way in which language functions in practice. This interest developed from his days with the PRAGUE LINGUISTIC CIRCLE to his later work in the United States.

It was in this later phase that he was influenced by the work of the American semiotic theorist C.S. PEIRCE. Peirce's theorizing of the three types of linguistic sign (icon, index, and SYMBOL) helped to make Jakobson more aware of the relations inherent in the practice of signification, a major development in structural linguistics from Saussure's denigration of *parole* in favor of *langue*. Peirce's dynamic model provided Jakobson with an improved model.

In addition to these variations from Saussure, Jakobson made more of a distinction implicit in Saussure's work, between METAPHOR AND METONYMY. Jakobson saw these two figures as constituting a binary opposition which is at the root of literary practice. From these two fundamental elements of his work, Jakobson drew out a practice of LITERARY CRITICISM which he used in analyses that are regarded as the epitome of structuralist literary criticism. He used his structural linguistics to pick out the semantic and phonemic correspondences which structure the literary text, coming to the conclusion that this was how all texts were constructed.

At the same time as Jakobson was developing his theories, the French anthropologist Claude LÉVI-STRAUSS was similarly concerned with the way in which meaning is produced. Proceeding from structuralist assumptions similar to those of Jakobson, Lévi-Strauss investigated the relations between the myths of various indigenous American societies. He found that they operated in a homologous pattern which could not be coincidental. He could only explain this by recourse to a coherent theory of the production of mythic meaning. For Lévi-Strauss, there were fundamental meanings which were represented in all of the mythic cycles he analyzed. These meanings were based upon basic narrative patterns which he found to be present in all of the Indian myths. He saw these narrative patterns as composed of the binary oppositions theorized by Saussure. He thought that these patterns were features rooted ultimately in the structure of the human mind, based upon the biology of the brain and the neural network.

Later structuralist developments in narratology and semiotics were based upon a fusion of the work of Jakobson and Lévi-Strauss. One recurring element is that the work of the structuralist theorist results in an objective theory which can then be applied to all texts. This is the project of theorists such as A.J. GREIMAS, Gérard GENETTE, and Claude BREMOND.

It is also the initial intent of Roland BARTHES at the beginning of *S/Z* (1990). Barthes's book, however, marks the development of POSTSTRUCTURALISM, in that his attempt to codify Balzac's short story results in a radical interspersing of his own comments with Balzac's text. The result is that there is an undoing of the boundaries between literary text and critical text, a movement which destroys any pretension to scientific objectivity of the kind claimed by structuralism.

This maneuver complements the analysis of Saussurean linguistics in Jacques DERRIDA (1976), the moment which marks the development of DECONSTRUCTION. Derrida follows Saussure's insight into the way in which the linguistic sign is constructed. However, he questions Saussure's own theorizing of binary oppositions. He undoes binary oppositions by showing that they depend upon their force for an assumption that certain meanings are associated with the other element in the opposition. Thus the pair is not mutually exclusive: the one will always be contaminated with elements of the other. Derrida moves on to consider the consequences of his analysis for theoretical discourse, especially with regard to the TROPES utilized in philosophy. By doing so, he links his concern with linguistics with his interest in philosophy. He applies his insights into structural linguistics to philosophy by searching philosophical texts for the same meanings he finds in Saussure's linguistics. The reason for this is that he considers Saussure's linguistics to represent a nostalgic longing for presence, especially since Saussure denigrates the written sign in favor of the purely verbal. By a series of rigorous readings of philosophical texts, readings which he conducts in the manner of a literary critic, he shows that the Western metaphysical tradition also privileges presence. Structuralism thus provides the initiator of deconstruction with the very tools he needs, which is one characteristic of the method of deconstruction itself. Derrida sets up a binary opposition between the literary and the philosophical only to deconstruct it. He shows that philosophical texts utilize literary motifs to such an extent that they cannot logically be said to be something which is not at all literary in the manner of a structural opposition: he deconstructs this assumption. His initial maneuver regarding structuralism therefore provides the basis for his analysis of Western metaphysics, and the analytical method he uses is the same in both cases. For Derrida, deconstruction is the name of both this maneuver and the impetus to put into question philosophy's assumption of presence, a questioning which can take on the character of a political strategy.

Deconstruction has not ended the protect of

structuralism: rather, it utilizes it as part of its own maneuvers in the way that Derrida uses Saussure. The reason for this is that some of structuralism's insights are still considered fundamental in the history of the humanities, whether or not individual theorists accept its claims to be a universal science. Structuralism developed at a historical moment when many certainties were being questioned, for example, in the evolutionary sciences. Saussure's linguistics put paid to the notion that meaning is rooted ultimately in some transcendental essence which exists outside social practice. By noting that meaning is structured in a closed sign-system, Saussure effectively cut off signification from a metaphysical basis, from God. The consequences of this maneuver, which he himself may not have realized, were that cultural practices could be analyzed purely as social constructs, and that structuralism could take the place of a science which explained such phenomena objectively. In a sense therefore, structuralism constituted a form of materialist practice.

Nevertheless, there are reasons why structuralists never quite attained the scientific objectivity they claimed. It is because of such factors that deconstruction and poststructuralism developed. These later cultural movements came from a realization that structuralist practice could in fact be constructing the very relationships it claimed to be finding in texts, myths, or linguistic utterances. Thus structuralism is a reading practice rather than a science which somehow locates structures already existing in the area being investigated. The example of Barthes shows that the attempt to define exhaustively the features of even a realist short story is bound to fail. Barthes's categories, his CODES, break down into subcategories, multiple readings, dispersals of meaning over wide areas of connotation. Structuralist literary criticism fails to contain these meanings, to define the text once and for all. Barthes's book exemplifies structuralist practice at its most intense and its most unsuccessful. Even as he tries to isolate coherent meanings to uncover the structure which is assumed to be at the heart of Balzac's short story, Barthes finds meanings multiplying out of control.

Following on from this situation, it is possible to see structuralism itself as in fact constituting an attempt to control meanings, to define texts in accordance with preexisting assumptions. The experience of Barthes and Derrida with regard to the explosion of meaning from the structuralist

framework has profound implications for the structuralist project as a whole. For deconstructionists and poststructuralists, the construction of an objective science is ultimately impossible, precisely because objectivity is impossible. Accordingly, structuralism can be seen to impose its own reading upon a text.

Such a conclusion accords neatly with openly materialist readings of the project of structuralism. By attempting to define meanings by reference to an ultimate structure which exists prior to history and the social in the structure of the human mind itself, structuralism tries to escape contingency. Saussure's linguistics not only remove God from the play of meaning, but they also attempt to replace God with Structure. It is the moment of Saussure's initial discovery of the precisely social nature of signification which is of interest to materialists. His collapsing of that discovery back into an essentialist structure is seen as a retrograde movement, and one which is precisely ideological. There is therefore a fundamental contradiction inherent in the structuralist impulse, a conflict between a historicizing movement which seeks to detach meaning from transcendent being, and an ahistoricizing tendency to root meaning in a sort of deep structure.

It is not only structuralist linguists and literary theorists who provide examples of the problem of an essentialism: structural psychologists do so also. The linkage between structural linguistics and psychology was made explicit by Jakobson in a call for an interdisciplinary approach by which psychology would take into account developments in structuralist approaches in other areas. The psychologist who produced such a linkage was to apply the methods of structural linguistics to the way in which meaning is developed psychologically. The implications of the structuralist claim to be an objective universal science are quite clear here: Jakobson assumes that structural linguistics has uncovered the laws by which language operates. Moreover, since those laws are based upon the deeper structure of the human mind, they should be equally applicable to the areas covered by psychology.

In a similar manner this very area was explored by Jean PIAGET. Piaget was interested in the development of the intellect during childhood and also the progression of epistemology itself. His approach to these two problems was based upon an assumption common to both: that the laws discernible in his structuralist developmental psychology were fundamental also to epistemology in general. In other words, the laws he attempted to isolate as the basis for the development of the human intellect were also the laws of epistemology. He utilized a form of structural linguistics in order to uncover these laws, which he stressed as fundamental to the way in which the human being thinks.

The relationship between structural linguistics and psychology provides an example of the interdisciplinary techniques made possible by the emergence of structuralism. The reason for this, of course, was that the differing disciplines shared the same assumptions at the root of their structuralist approach. Nevertheless, this movement helped sow the seeds of the more sophisticated poststructuralist concerns with such forms of interdisciplinary work, another area in which the successors of structuralism owe some of their developments to maneuvers made by structuralists themselves.

The production of a general science of signification which is not limited solely to verbal communication is the result of this interdisciplinary approach. SEMIOTICS developed from the structuralist impulse by and through Jakobson's integration with the work of Peirce. The result has been the emergence of semiotic theoreticians such as Umberto Eco. For these theorists, language serves as the example *par excellence* of the operation of a sign system, and provides the model for discussion of all other sign systems. However, this discussion is not simply subservient to linguistics. In fact, conclusions drawn from study of other sign systems, for example, gesture or socially constituted phenomena such as traffic signs, can be utilized to modify the study of the sign systems of language. In this respect, semiotics attempts rigorously to achieve the status of a science of signs, following on from the structuralist impetus to objectivity.

Overall, structuralism must be seen in terms of its relations with other movements as well as in terms of its own internal relations. There were disagreements within structuralism which proved useful in developing it further, such as Jakobson's development of structural linguistics in directions contrary to that envisaged by Saussure. The movements which followed it, poststructuralism and deconstruction, while they utilize structuralism as a starting point, develop out of it in a way that has seen them labeled as different from their parent movement. Jakobson still considered his work to be structuralist, since he ultimately agreed with the fundamental impetus to objectivity claimed by

the movement. Despite his differences, in other words, he accepted the basic ideals. Nevertheless, deconstruction and poststructuralism do not accept the basic ideals, and the institutional consequences of this denial have been profound.

Structuralism was accepted in academic circles despite its relative iconoclasm, compared at least with the religious HUMANISM of the European and American academic establishment in the period of structuralism's development. The reason for this acceptance was that, although structuralism needed no God, it still constituted a form of humanism. This may at first be considered to be a strange effect of a movement which, after all, claimed to be a science. However, the humanism came in the form of structuralism's acceptance that the structure of the human being was at the root of all of the phenomena it attempted to describe. Materialist critics denounce this as ahistorical: deconstructionists see it as a longing after lost presence. Both criticisms point to an area of convergence between structuralism and the humanities it sought to replace, and it is this which explains the success of the movement in the academic institution. The way in which structuralists very quickly took over the discipline of linguistics and turned it into a science of structural linguistics is the prime example of this movement.

Moreover, despite the relatively radical claims made by poststructuralists, the maneuver made by structuralism in gaining its own ascendancy is worth recalling. It may be possible to see poststructuralism as replicating this maneuver, especially with regard specifically to deconstruction. The reason for this is that it is possible to practice a form of deconstruction which is not in fact very challenging, at least in its relations with the literary-philosophical tradition which Derrida tried to turn on its head. The maneuver of deconstruction can be made without the politics of an onslaught on presence. Deconstruction can be reduced to simply another technique of literary criticism, one which is spectacular, to be sure, but nevertheless ultimately one which can pressed into service on behalf of an academic institution which does not accord with the impetus of Derrida's initial moment. This critique has been leveled at the uses made of deconstruction in the United States, although it has relevance for a discussion of structuralism also. Structuralism as a movement has not finished, as can be seen from the preponderance of structural linguists. The onslaught of deconstruction has had little effect on the areas traditionally covered by its parent: the question "Why not?" has to be asked. The reason may be that the attempt to produce an objective science of structure gained a great deal of strength from the moment of its success in the academy. The very structure of the education system has soaked up the structuralist challenge to the extent that the movement permeates so many disciplines that its effects endure.

Reading
Barthes, Roland 1973 (1990): S/Z.
Bremond, Claude 1973: Logique du Récit.
Derrida, Jacques 1967a (1976): Of Grammatology.
Genette, Gérard 1980: Narrative Discourse: An Essay on Method.
——— 1982a: Figures of Literary Discourse.
Greimas, A.J. 1966: Semantique Structurale.
——— 1970: Du Sens.
——— 1987: On Meaning: Selected Writings in Semiotic Theory.
Jakobson, Roman 1990a: On Language.
Lévi-Strauss, Claude 1971 (1981): The Naked Man.
Propp, Vladimir 1958: Morphology of the Folktale.
Saussure, Ferdinand de 1913 (1983): Course in General Linguistics.

PAUL INNES

structuralism, genetic *See* GENETIC STRUCTURALISM

structure The sum total of stable connections of a literary work which provide for its wholeness and identity with itself, that is, the preservation of basic qualities without external or internal changes. Since the Middle Ages the notion of structure has been used as one of the ways to define form (form as structure, as the organization of the content). In the twentieth century, the analysis of structural relationships and connections occupied an important place in the analysis of language, literary and art works, and CULTURE in general. In contemporary science, the notion of structure usually corresponds to notions of SYSTEM and organization, which characterize the entire manifestation of an object (its components, connections between the elements, their functions, etc.). Structure expresses only those elements which remain stable, relatively unchanging, in various transformations of the system. Organization includes both the structural and the dynamic characteristics of the system which provide for its directed functioning.

An important contribution to the development of the notion of structure was made by structural linguistics, the founders of which were Jan Baudouin de Courtenay and Ferdinand de SAUSSURE. Structural linguistics aimed at a scientifically precise (almost mathematical) analysis of language. The starting point of this analysis was the notion of the structure of language. In general terms, structure represents the inner connections lying in the basis of language, which determine the way readers or listeners directly perceive the substance or "matter" of language: the systems of sounds and meanings.

In the 1920s RUSSIAN FORMALISM applied the notion of structure to the literary work as a whole. By structure they meant the composition of a literary work, its internal and external organization, the type of connection between its composing elements. Structure provided for the wholeness of an art work and its ability to express, to transmit its content. Russian formalist critics made it their primary task to study "how a literary work is made." The system of devices that comprise a literary work inevitably led to the work's structure and the laws of its composition.

Russian formalists and their followers in the PRAGUE LINGUISTIC CIRCLE perceived structure as a special methodological principle of LITERARY CRITICISM. No matter how unique the structure of any concrete literary work is, it inevitably has some common feature with the principles of structure of another work of the same genre, type, and kind of ART. Structure turns out to be a carrier of not only individually meaningful formal characteristics of a given art work, but also of common expressions of genre, type, general style, the artistic trend of literature in its totality as an art and as an objectified creative activity.

Reading
Lotman, Jurij 1977: The Structure of the Artistic Text.
Rowe, J.C. 1990: "Structure."
Serge, Cesare 1979: Structures and Time. Narration, Poetry, Models.
Wellek, René 1963: "Concepts of form and structure in 20th-century criticism."

SLAVA I. YASTREMSKI

structure, decentered *See* DECENTERED STRUCTURE

structure of feeling First used by Raymond WILLIAMS in his *A Preface to Film* (with Michael

Orrom, 1954), developed in *The Long Revolution* (1961), and extended and elaborated throughout his work, in particular *Marxism and Literature* (1977), Williams first used this concept to characterize the lived experience of the quality of life at a particular time and place. It is, he argued, "as firm and definite as 'structure' suggests, yet it operates in the most delicate and least tangible part of our activities." Later he describes structures of feeling as "social experiences *in solution*." Thus a "structure of feeling" is the CULTURE of a particular historical moment, though in developing the concept, Williams wished to avoid idealist notions of a "spirit of the age." It suggests a common set of perceptions and values shared by a particular generation, and is most clearly articulated in particular and artistic forms and conventions. The industrial novel of the 1840s would be one example of the structure of feeling which emerged in middle-class consciousness out of the development of industrial capitalism. Each generation lives and produces it own "structure of feeling," and while particular groups might express this most forcibly, it extends unevenly through the culture as a whole. In later formulations of the concept, however, Williams stresses "the complex relation of differentiated structures of feeling to differentiated classes," and the area of tension between "IDEOLOGY" and "experience."
See also CULTURAL MATERIALISM; WILLIAMS, RAYMOND.

JENNY BOURNE TAYLOR

studies, biblical *See* BIBLICAL STUDIES

studies, black cultural *See* BLACK CULTURAL STUDIES

studies, Canadian *See* CANADIAN STUDIES

studies, Caribbean *See* CARIBBEAN STUDIES

Studies, Centre for Contemporary Cultural *See* CENTRE FOR CONTEMPORARY CULTURAL STUDIES

studies, eighteenth-century *See* EIGHTEENTH-CENTURY STUDIES

studies, film *See* FILM STUDIES

studies, Irish *See* IRISH STUDIES

studies, Islamic *See* ISLAMIC STUDIES

studies, Japanese *See* JAPANESE STUDIES

studies, Latin American *See* LATIN AMERICAN STUDIES

studies, Native American *See* NATIVE AMERICAN STUDIES

studies, postcolonial *See* POSTCOLONIAL STUDIES

studies, post-Soviet *See* POST-SOVIET STUDIES

studies, Renaissance *See* RENAISSANCE STUDIES

studies, Romantic *See* ROMANTIC STUDIES

studies, South Asian *See* SOUTH ASIAN STUDIES

studies, subaltern *See* SUBALTERN STUDIES

studies, translation *See* TRANSLATION STUDIES

studies, Victorian *See* VICTORIAN STUDIES

studies, women's *See* WOMEN'S STUDIES

style The number and variety of definitions of "style" are daunting (Bailey and Burton, 1968, Introduction and pp. 147–53): an honorific applied to aesthetically pleasing writing, ornament and embellishment of content, authorial expressiveness, the unity of form and content, verbal details of diction, imagery, syntax, and sound, and so on. The rise of STYLISTICS has encouraged a definition more susceptible to linguistic use, particularly focusing on (i) the linguistic features of TEXTS (see Dupriez, 1991); and (ii) the patterning of those features. For examples, John Haynes (1989) treats style as choice, "the study of distinctions; looking at what was said against what might have been said" in relation to its contexts (p. 8). However, style is also "tendencies in a text, or in a type of text," the "verbal habits" or recurrences in a text, an author's works, or a genre (and by implication in a historical period or nation). Haynes uses almost half of his book in explaining the language as a SYSTEM in order to confirm his approach to style.

John Childs (1986) focuses upon the specific and the patterning choices of the self-referential POETRY of Pound's *Cantos*. But he places his discussion of fragmentation, deletion, condensation, and coupling within linguistic frames of LANGUE/PAROLE, norm and deviation, form and content, of defamiliarization and foregrounding, that is, within the language system of rules of production (expansion, conversion) which readers share, in which they are competent. For example, he shows how the difficult concluding lines of Canto 1 are construable within English-language sentence structure following the linguistic principles of deletion and condensation (pp. 28–30). Like Haynes, Childs perceives "a dialectic between a semantic matrix [shared cultural and literary conventions] and the transformation of that matrix into a given text" (p. 26), the linguistic result of which is explicitly determinable.

Though they conceptualize the whole range of language from the inherited patterns of genre, period, and nation to specific choices in drama or poetry, and their mutual relationships, both Haynes and Childs emphasize specific texts. The recent sophistication of quantitative analysis is making it increasingly possible to describe more accurately the style of an author, a genre, a period, and a nation. The fields of reader response and pragmatics are developing for the study of DISCOURSE and SPEECH ACTS, the interaction of language and its users, texts and contexts – style as linguistic devices which serve social perspectives and trigger diverse responses (of which Haynes and Childs are actively aware though they do not employ the labels).

These developments in the linguistic definition and analysis of style are not without criticism. Talbot Taylor (1980) attacks as elusive and unconvincing the explanations of the cause–effect relation between form and meaning underlying the theories of style offered by a range of linguists – JAKOBSON, Riffaterre, the generativists, and Dillon.

See also ALIENATION EFFECT; AMBIGUITY; APORIA; CLASSIC REALISM; COMPLEXITY; CONNOTATION/DENOTATION; DECENTERED STRUCTURE; DEFAMILIARIZATION; DOMINANT; FOREGROUNDING; GENDER; INTERNATIONAL STYLE; IRONY; JOUISSANCE; MANIFEST/LATENT CONTENT; MASCULINITY; METAPHOR AND METONYMY; ORGANIC UNITY; POSTMODERNISM; SHIFTERS/DEICTICS; SOCIALIST REALISM; STORY/PLOT; STRUCTURE; STRUCTURE OF FEELING; SYMBOL; SYNTAGMATIC/PARADIGMATIC; TENSION; TRAGEDY, TROPE.

Reading

Bennett, James R. 1993a: "Style."
Brienza, Susan 1987: *Samuel Beckett's New Worlds: Style in Metafiction.*
Childs, John Steven 1986: *Modernist Form: Pound's Style in the Early Cantos.*
Dupriez, Bernard 1991: *Gradus: Dictionary of Literary Devices.*
Haynes, John 1989: *Introducing Stylistics.*
Padhi, Bibhu 1987: *The Modes of Style in Lawrence's Fiction.*
Taylor, Talbot J. 1980: *Linguistic Theory and Structural Stylistics.*

JAMES R. BENNETT

style, international See INTERNATIONAL STYLE

stylistics The movement to be explicit, accurate, and systematic in the study of TEXTS by the application of linguistic theories and methods is called linguistic stylistics or stylistics. Although the study of texts through linguistics reaches back to the early years of the twentieth century and even to classical rhetoric – *schemes* and TROPES, historical philology, Slavic formalism, the NEW CRITICISM, French *stylistique* (the French interest in language has been sustained since the sixteenth century), German *Stilforschung* – its modern organization begins in the 1960s. The Indiana Conference on Style (1958; edited by Sebeok, 1960), Milic's quantitative study of Swift and his bibliography (1967), the creation of the journals *Style* (1967) and *Language and Style* (1968), the Bailey–Burton bibliography (1968), Ohmann's *Shaw* (1969), Bailey's and Dolezel's *Statistics and Style* (1969), collections of essays edited by Donald Freeman (1970) and Seymour Chatman (1971), the collection *The Computer and Literary Studies* edited by Aitken, Bailey, and Hamilton-Smith (1973), and Nils Enkvist's *Linguistic Stylistics* (1973) are some of the pathfinders in English. On the Continent: H. Meschonnic, *Pour la Poétique* (1970–75), D. Alonso, *Pluralità e correlazione in poesia* (1971), and E. Riesel and E. Schendels, *Deutsche Stilistik* (1975) illustrate the extensive early writings there. It was also an intellectually vigorous time of exploring diverse idealist and functionalist linguistic models – transformational grammar, case grammar, generative semantics, text grammar, SPEECH-ACT theory, and systemic/levels and categories. (The idealists/formalists, such as Noam CHOMSKY, Morris Halle, and Paul Kiparsky, treat grammar as distinct in principle, language-specific, not derivable from linguistic behavior; to the functionalists, such as M.A.K. Halliday, Ruquaiya Hasan, and Geoffrey Leech, the structure of grammar is determined by its use.)

In "An approach to the study of style," Spencer and Gregory (1964) offered a holistic program based upon their belief that the student of literature "ought to be trained in the study of both language and literature." They conceived the analysis of texts in five steps largely deriving from the functionalist levels and categories theories of Halliday:

(i) contextualization, placing the text in search of collective characteristics or norms:
   (a) historical-cultural – the personal, rhetorical, social, generic, and ideological circumstances; and
   (b) linguistic – period, dialect, subject matter, spoken and written, and degree of formality;
(ii) detailed description of the language in search of individual characteristics (deviations from norms):
   (a) syntax – hypotaxis and parataxis; and
   (b) lexis – collocation, imagery, markers;
(iii) interrelation of parts to whole;
(iv) description of whole;
(v) comparisons with other texts as controls.

Their explanation of the potential precision, explicitness, and comprehensiveness of their model, that it provides techniques of description, facts about language and texts, and more sensitive responses

to language and literature, offered a sketch of the the discipline of stylistics that was to develop in the following years. For example, *The Literary Stylistics of French* (Bellard-Thomason, 1992) in many ways parallels Spencer and Gregory. They were prescient also in their recognition of the importance of joining two or more disciplines in research and teaching, for this collaboration has become the central feature of contemporary CULTURAL STUDIES.

The potential precision, comprehensiveness, and flexibility of their and other conceptions of textual analysis were embraced by the journal *Style* from its inception and expressed in its annual bibliography of stylistic studies. Beginning with its 1979 bibliography this classification became standard: 1. Bibliographies; 2. General Theory; 3. Culture, History, and Style (period, nation, genre): 3.1 Theory, 3.2 Practice, 3.2.1 Diction, Vocabulary, Imagery, Tropes, 3.2.2 Syntax, 3.2.3 Prosody, 3.2.4 Beyond the Sentence and Line: Discourse, 3.2.5 Studies on Several Linguistic Levels; 4. Habitual Usage (author) (the same system as above is repeated); 5. Individual Choice (the text) (again the same system); 6. Individual Response (the reader) (and again). As the journal stated at the time, its aim was to "facilitate communication world-wide, by minimizing private and obscure terminology and methods and by maximizing connections and relationships."

This taxonomy allows for studies of small linguistic details, while reminding critics of the contexts within which they work. Obversely, it embraces large generic, national, and cultural studies, but reminds critics of the discipline of method and rigor of evidence essential to credibility.

One of the most optimistic expressions of the application of linguistics to the study of literature is *Linguistic Perspectives on Literature* (Ching et al., 1980). They perceived in 1980 "a new phase of linguistic investigation of literature" that would produce "a revolutionary kind of insight into the nature of literature, language, and man himself." Their thesis is "that the creative principles of human language are centrally, not peripherally, located in the semantics and AESTHETICS of human literature and that the ordinary linguistic competence now being formalized in LANGUAGE THEORY offers powerful and unique perspectives on the extraordinary imaginative interplay between writer, text, and reader now dominating the concerns in literary theory" (p. 4). However, this idealist project is presented eclectically, each model valuable in so far as it accomplishes its descriptive and interpretative goals.

The confidence of such advocates for stylistics seems confirmed by such books as *Language Crafted* (Austin, 1984), but through rigorously restricted goals. "LITERARY COMPETENCE" is set aside as a separate through allied discipline. "At best, stylistic evidence may combine with data from other sources – biographical, historical, metrical, or 'new critical' – to elucidate" meaning. Austin operates from the fundamental linguistic assumption, derived from numerous empirical studies, that the same text produces considerable agreement about a work among diverse readers, and that readers share reactions to literary texts because they share an inventory of techniques, a competence for analyzing linguistic and particularly syntactic behavior. He spends a chapter, for example, explaining deviant syntax in POETRY ("Anyone lived in a pretty how town") within the SYSTEM of, rather than exceptions to, the language in which it was written. Thus an ultimate purpose of stylistic analysis is that of explaining the relationship between readers' syntactic competence and their experience of a text, discovering the means by which language's role in shaping that experience is exercised. To give order to this purpose, he establishes four standards for a comprehensive theoretical framework which he then applies to literary analysis (delimit the material to be examined, set forth a clearly defined model, evaluate the capacity of the model to analyze texts insightfully, and consider the implications for associated texts and fields). For example, he shows why the syntax of Shelley's *Laon and Cythna* is not functional and why that of *Adonais* is.

While these organizing and stabilizing developments were occurring in stylistics, countercurrents known by various labels as STRUCTURALISM, POSTSTRUCTURALISM, READER-RESPONSE, and DECONSTRUCTION were questioning the assumptions that stylists were making about the determinable nature of texts and readers. Austin meets the challenges of Jacques DERRIDA and Stanley FISH head on by denying the impossibility of understanding while accepting the impossibility of certitude. The SYSTEM of rules underlying languages and the various particular grammars chosen for literary analysis presuppose the discoverability of stable, though not necessarily unitary, meanings for each literary text.

Austin sets forth what in the syntax of a poem contributes to the meaning of the poem, but the meaning he recognizes as derived from multiple, complex contexts. Other stylisticians are exploring agreements and disputes between stylistics and the expanding and destabilizing theoretical currents of the 1960s to the 1990s. DISCOURSE stylistics has been developing with the same aim of syntactical studies – "to be sufficiently detailed, explicit and retrievable for other analysts, working on the same text" (Carter and Simpson, 1989). Nevertheless, these analysts are acutely aware of the difficulties for a discipline grounded in linguistics, as contexts, especially nonlinguistic contexts, are conjoined with linguistic contexts, when it "becomes difficult to undertake analysis which is sufficiently principled to promote linguistic descriptive progress" (pp. 14–15).

A conference held in Glasgow (addresses published as *The Linguistics of Writing*, Fabb et al., 1987) consciously contrasted itself to the 1958 conference in Indiana, by declaring it "no longer possible to consider questions about language and literature without taking into account the social and political context in which all forms of discourse operate." Another difference is the emphasis upon "WRITING," all kinds of writing, rather than the traditional literature which the 1958 critics assumed as their SUBJECT. A third is the conception of writing as unstable and uncertain, opposed to the idealized certainty and confidence of linguistics. (Some of the contributors to the book treat linguistics as a form of writing susceptible to linguistic, literary, historical, and social scrutiny. For example, one examined Roman JAKOBSON's famous "Closing statement" in *Style in Language* in relation to international political circumstances such as the Cold War.)

The Glasgow conference grappled with the role of a determinable stylistics in the context of recent theoretical diversity, indeterminacy, and doubt. The debate will continue, as linguists recognize. "Neither the general theory [of language structure] nor . . . particular grammars are fixed for all time" (Chomsky); "Disagreement discloses antinomies and tensions within the field discussed and calls for novel exploration" (Roman Jakobson in Sebeok).

See also AESTHETICS; AUSTIN, J.L.; BAKHTIN, MIKHAIL; BENVENISTE, EMILE; BLACK AESTHETIC; BROOKS, CLEANTH; BURKE, KENNETH; CHOMSKY, NOAM; CODES; CONTENT ANALYSIS; CRITICAL THEORY; DAVIDSON, DONALD; DE MAN, PAUL; DECONSTRUCTION; DEFAMILIARIZATION; DERRIDA, JACQUES; DISCURSIVE PRACTICES; ELIOT, T.S.; EMPSON, WILLIAM; ENCODING/DECODING; FORMALISM;

FOWLER, ROGER; GENERATIVE GRAMMAR; GENETTE, GÉRARD; GENRE ANALYSIS; GREIMAS, A.J.; INTERTEXTUALITY; ISER, WOLFGANG; JAKOBSON, ROMAN; KERMODE, FRANK; LANGUAGE, PHILOSOPHY OF; LANGUAGE THEORIES; LANGUE/PAROLE; LINGUISTIC CRITICISM; LITERARY COMPETENCE; LITERARY CRITICISM; MUKAROVSKY, JAN; NARRATOLOGY; NEW CRITICISM; PEIRCE, C.S.; PHENOMENOLOGY; POSTSTRUCTURALISM; PRACTICAL CRITICISM; PRAGUE LINGUISTIC CIRCLE; RANSOM, JOHN CROWE; READER-RESPONSE CRITICISM; RICHARDS, I.A.; RUSSIAN FORMALISM; SAUSSURE, FERDINAND DE; SEMIOTICS, SHKLOVSKY, VIKTOR; SIGN; SPEECH ACTS; STRUCTURALISM; SYNCHRONY/DIACHRONY; TATE, ALLEN; TRANSLATION STUDIES; WIDDOWSON, HENRY.

Reading

Austin, Timothy 1984: *Language Crafted: A Linguistic Theory of Poetic Syntax.*
Bailey, Richard W., and Burton, Dolores 1968: *English Stylistics: A Bibliography.*
Bennett, James R. 1986: *A Bibliography of Stylistics and Related Criticism, 1967–1983.*
——1993b: "Stylistics."
Carter, Ronald, and Simpson, Paul 1989: *Language, Discourse and Literature: An Introductory Reader in Discourse Stylistics.*
Ching, Marvin, Haley, Michael, and Lunsford, Ronald, eds 1980: *Linguistic Perspectives on Literature.*
Chomsky, Noam 1957: *Syntactic Structures.*
Fabb, Nigel, Attridge, Derek, Durant, Alan, and MacCabe, Colin, eds 1987: *The Linguistics of Writing: Arguments Between Language and Literature.*
Halliday, M.A.K., and Hasan, Ruquaya 1985: *Language Context and Text: A Social Semiotic Perspective.*
Milic, Louis T. 1967: *Style and Stylistics: An Analytical Bibliography.*
Saussure, Ferdinand de 1916 (*1966*): *Course in General Linguistics.*
Sebeok, Thomas, ed. 1960: *Style in Language.*
JAMES R. BENNETT

subaltern studies Contemporary Indian historiography. The Italian activist and Marxist, Antonio GRAMSCI, used "subaltern" in his prison writings of the 1930s to refer to socially subordinated groups that, by definition, lacked the unity and organization of those in power. Borrowing the term in the early 1980s, Marxist Indian revisionist historiographers use it to refer to all those "of inferior rank" – a group with even less formal institutional access to political power than Gramsci's European working classes of the 1930s.

Its focus on subaltern groups sharply distinguishes subaltern studies from two dominant and mutually opposed historiographic traditions in India: that of European colonizers and Indian nationalists, who themselves contested the Eurocentrism of the former. Despite this difference, from the perspective of subaltern studies the colonial and Indian nationalist approaches share a middle-class orientation, and a consequent inability to assign Indian subaltern groups any but the most secondary roles in history, to see them as anything but a passive, naive, potentially anarchic and unstable entity in urgent need of guidance from above. In its counternarrative of Indian history, subaltern studies has taken on a dual task: a study of the gaps and closures of official Indian nationalist accounts to understand why nationalism failed to address subalternity; and the project of recovering archival material, including forms of popular and non-print culture, that indicates specific subaltern interventions in the nineteenth and twentieth centuries.

The eight volumes of essays published to date by the collective are marked by an interdisciplinary approach incorporating CULTURAL STUDIES as well as the social sciences; and a sustained reformulation of such Marxist concepts such as HEGEMONY and historical periodization in terms relevant to the Third World.

Recent work by the collective has responded to the call from Indian feminists, such as Susie Tharu and Gayatri C. Spivak, that the figure of the subaltern be gendered and that patriarchal as well as colonial and class-based oppressions be examined. A second critique comes also from Spivak, who identifies herself as a strong admirer of the project but questions the collective's occasional essentializing of the subaltern in the effort to construct its counterhistory. While the larger question here, about ways of conceptualizing agency, will no doubt continue to be addressed as the project continues, the innovativeness and rigor of subaltern studies has already generated excitement among postcolonial scholars in India and elsewhere.

See also GRAMSCI, ANTONIO; MARXIST CRITICISM; POSTCOLONIAL STUDIES; SOUTH ASIAN STUDIES.

Reading

Guha, Ranajit, ed. 1982–94: *Subaltern Studies: Writings on South Asian History and Society.*
Prasad, Madhava 1992: "On the question of a theory of (Third World) literature."
Spivak, Gayatri C. 1987 (*1988*): "Subaltern studies: deconstructing historiography."
APARAJITA SAGAR

subcultures   The concept refers to the distinctive values and processes of particular groups within wider cultural and social formations. Subcultural analysis has been particularly important in work on the variety of postwar youth cultures and has emphasized the active construction of cultural meanings and spaces by subordinate, often working-class, groups in various institutional and everyday contexts.

A curious or concerned or envious interest in those perceived as not respectable or, in a later vocabulary, deviant has been part of the work of novelists, social commentators, journalists, and others since the beginnings of urban capitalism. From Mayhew, Dickens, and Booth to Tom Wolfe there has been detailed commentary upon patterns of behavior, forms of dress, styles of music, modes of speech, and much else. Within the new discipline of sociology there was a notable series of studies from the CHICAGO SCHOOL exploring a range of marginal groups within the city, including hobos and youth "gangs," though this formulation drew attention to particular groups rather than broader cultural patterns. A later trajectory of work in the sociology of deviance on both sides of the Atlantic argued that dominant groups (including the media, judiciary, and police) had power to label groups as "deviant" from preferred norms, with effects upon the ways in which such groups are signified and understood, and also live their own identities.

Subcultural studies have treated the activities, forms, and values which they analyzed as fairly coherent attempts to make sense of and pursue strategies within given social locations. In the 1960s and 1970s work was concerned with the forms of youth cultures and cultural patterns within education, workplaces, sport, and elsewhere. It reclaimed in a positive light behavior and attitudes often dismissed as delinquent, abnormal, or symptomatic of educational failure. Instead these were studied with empathy and sometimes as imminently political though in unfamiliar forms: as ways of coping but also as celebration, protest, or resistance.

Methodologically the studies varied considerably while sharing an emphasis on meanings against a then dominant quantitative POSITIVISM. Sometimes informed by their authors' own experiences, analyses drew variously upon media and other usually hostile public accounts; upon semiological analysis of cultural forms, styles and languages; and upon participant observation and ethnography. A widely cited article by Cohen argued that three levels of work were required: the historical location of the "problematic of a particular class fraction"; structural and semiotic analysis; phenomenological attention to ways in which the subculture is lived out. Others drew attention to the importance of the age stage in a cultural life cycle. However, the shared frame of reference has usually been derived from MARXISM in situating subordinate, usually working-class, groups within dominant social processes, while also being concerned with the cultural, "imagined" forms through which their position was explained, resisted, or (for Willis, ironically) celebrated.

Cumulatively the work was valuable for a generation and beyond in its close sympathetic attention to forms of working-class culture and the detailed strategies of (mainly male) youth, and in its registration of struggles not recognized as such by orthodox social democratic or Marxist politics. If at present it is less resonant, this is partly because of the relative fading from visibility of "youth subcultures" as seen from the 1950s into the 1980s, due to complex changes in class structure, patterns of employment and unemployment, and in the organization of "leisure" industries, activities, and spaces.

A variety of problems have been noted in subcultural analyses. Empirically, the boundaries and shape of distinctive subcultures are not easily drawn, and now forms of mixing and hybridity receive more notice. It is difficult to analyze the complexity of the dominant CULTURES (of society, the "parent" generation of a class culture, an institution such as a school, sometimes all of these), within and against which "sub" cultures mark their presence. There are issues about both power and method in the analyst's close reading of the cultural forms of others, and in the social relations of participant observation and ethnography. Elements of "resistance" may have been exaggerated, at times romanticized, for example in the playing down of aggression and RACISM. Particularly sharp protest has been registered against the implicit tendency of subcultural frameworks to marginalize GENDER and celebrate MASCULINITY, writing out the forms of existence of young women, and also misleadingly overlooking the existence and centrality of relatively conventional, less spectacular behavior. All these issues, in conjunction with the erosion or complex qualification of a Marxist framework through an address to issues of gender and "RACE" have tended to reposition what was once the centrality of subcultural analysis within sociology, work on education, consumption, and music, and in the emerging field of CULTURAL STUDIES. However, the main assertion of this work, that groups which are made to appear marginal or unsuccessful make their own sense of the worlds in which they live, through various cultural forms within complex relations of power, remains extremely important in different kinds of study (for instance, media audiences). Attention to the cultural forms and processes of many other (for example, most middle-class) groups remains absent from most current work, though less so now in the related sphere of documentary representation.

Reading

Becker, H. 1963: *The Outsiders: Studies in the Sociology of Deviance*.
Brake, M. 1985: *Comparative Youth Cultures*.
Clarke, G. 1982: *Defending Ski-Jumpers: A Critique of Theories of Youth Subcultures*.
Cohen, P. 1972 (*1993*): "Subcultural conflict and working-class community."
Hall, S., Clarke, J., Jefferson, T., and Roberts, B., eds 1976: *Resistance through Rituals*.
Hebdige, D. 1979: *Subculture: the Meaning of Style*.
McRobbie, A. 1991: *Feminism and Youth Culture*.
Willis, P. 1977: *Learning to Labour*.

MICHAEL GREEN

subject   The origins of a term which is increasingly used throughout the human sciences are somewhat obscure, but it is possible to trace the notion of the subject back to KANT or even Descartes. In current usage, the term is a reaction against the privileging of the self or the individual in humanist thought. The concept is largely the product of the work of LACAN, for whom the subject is radically distinct fom the ego, which is viewed as an illusory product of the MIRROR-STAGE, and ALTHUSSER, who employs it to analyze how human individuals become subjects, thanks to the imaginary effects of IDEOLOGY. The general tendency is to regard the subject as the effect of a STRUCTURE rather than as its source or origin. The subject does not speak and is not the origin of meaning; the subject is, rather, spoken by law and CULTURE. The signifier is primary, the subject being little more than a support for the exchange of signifiers. The very AMBIGUITY of the term "subject" explains something of its appeal and productivity. It is both a grammatical term and a political-legal term (as in "British subject"); it can be both active

("subject of") and passive ("subject or subjected to").

DAVID MACEY

subject of the enunciation (also **subject of the enounced**)   A pair of terms introduced by Emile BENVENISTE, the French linguist and theoretician of DISCOURSE, whose work has exerted a profound influence on developments in poststructuralist thought. This distinction is best understood if we consider the case of a first-person reflexive (self-referring) utterance like Descartes's *cogito, ergo sum* ("I think, therefore I am"). That is to say, the act of thought is such as to exclude any possible doubt about the present existence of the thinking subject. This would create a logical contradiction, a failure to perceive the strict order of necessity that leads from the indubitable premise ("I think") to the existential consequent ("I am"). From this minimal but bedrock certainty one can then proceed, so Descartes argues, to establish the reality of an external world proof against all the demons of skeptical doubt, for instance, the idea that I might be dreaming when I think myself awake, or that I might be the victim of some wholesale illusion perpetrated by a malign demiurge.

Early commentators on Descartes were quick to point out some of the problems with his argument in its strong (that is, its purportedly logico-deductive) form. Thus there is nothing in the nature of "thinking" *per se* – no absolute or privileged link between the *cogito* and the *sum* – that would rule out the substitution of other (logically equivalent) formulas such as *ambulo, ergo sum* ("I walk, therefore I am"). To this it may perhaps be responded that there is at any rate a manifest performative CONTRADICTION – a linguistic or discursive impossibility – in my uttering (or thinking) the phrase "I think" while denying that there exists (or can be known to exist) any "I" that is simultaneously engaged in that same act of thought. This is where Benveniste's distinction enters to complicate the picture yet further. According to him the Cartesian argument fails, along with its performative (SPEECH-ACT) variant, as a result of the slippage that occurs between the two orders of enunciative modality in its original formulation. Simply put, the SUBJECT who says "I think" is not to be confused with the subject whose existence is posited in that same act of thought. Thus the surface plausibility of Descartes's claim requires that we ignore the underlying structure – the linguistic, discursive, or logico-grammatical form – which emerges on closer inspection, for this allows of no such confident appeal to the unitary, self-possessed subject of knowledge and truth. Rather it confronts us with the sheer *impossibility* that thought should ever coincide with itself (or the *cogito* attain a lucid awareness of its own indubitable being) in a moment of pure, unmediated access beyond all the vagaries of language and representation. It is precisely within language – or "discourse," in Benveniste's specific usage of that term – that we perceive this ineluctable gap that opens up between the "subject of the enunciation" and the "subject of the enounced."

Hence Benveniste's theory has a great attraction for those in the poststructuralist camp who proclaim the demise of the Cartesian "subject-presumed-to-know," along with the entire post-Cartesian tradition of epistemological (or "foundationalist") thought. This argument receives its most extreme, often obscure and riddling, formulations in the work of the French psychoanalyst Jacques LACAN. His avowed purpose is to rescue FREUD's discovery of the UNCONSCIOUS from its various *déformations professionelles* at the hands of ego psychologists and other such perverters of the Freudian truth. Thus Lacan offers his own rewriting of Descartes's original dictum: no longer *cogito, ergo sum* but *cogito, ergo sum ubi cogito, ibi nonsum* ("where I think 'I think, therefore I am,' that is just where I am not"). By this and other pieces of cryptic wordplay Lacan seeks to remind us that the ego is not master in its own house; that the unconscious is (very literally) "structured like a language"; and moreover, that Freud's "royal road" to a knowledge of the unconcious and its effects lay through the region of puns, jokes, AMBIGUITIES, PARAPRAXES (slips of the tongue), and other such mazy detours of the signifier. The "I" is nothing more than an epiphenomenon of discourse, a DEICTIC (or pronominal SHIFTER) which marks the subject's insertion into an order – that of the Lacanian SYMBOLIC – whose workings elude the utmost powers of conscious or reflective grasp. Thus psychoanalysts who persist vainly in the quest for self-knowledge on their patients' (or indeed their own) part are thereby shown up as unwitting dupes of an illusory desire whose origin lies in the Cartesian obsession with "clear and distinct ideas." It is, to say the least, a singular IRONY that Benveniste's elegant and finely honed distinction should be taken up, via Lacan,

into a poststructuralist discourse that on principle finds no room for such virtues.

Reading
Barthes, Roland 1977: *Roland Barthes by Roland Barthes*.
Benveniste, Emile 1971: *Problems of General Linguistics*.
Lacan, Jacques 1977: *Ecrits: A Selection*.
CHRISTOPHER NORRIS

superstructure   *See* BASE AND SUPERSTRUCTURE

symbol   A communicational vehicle, usually verbal or visual, where sender and reader share a learned, arbitrary association between the signal and a conventional meaning. Symbolic communication is pervasive among humans, forming the basis not only of most social life, but also of virtually all human CULTURES and creativity. Indeed the richness of human mental life – language, values, theories, ART, literature, religion, philosophy, kinship, complex social differentiation, etc. – requires elaborate symboling. To a lesser degree symbols are also used by other species (for example, gorillas, chimpanzees). In humans, complex, coherent layered systems of symbols are universal, capable of triggering powerful subconscious responses.

Reading
Douglas, Mary 1966: *Purity and Danger: An Analysis of the Concepts of Pollution and Taboo*.
Patterson, Francine, and Linden, Eugene 1981: *The Education of Koko*.
THOMAS C. GREAVES

symbolic   *See* IMAGINARY/SYMBOLIC/REAL

symptomatic reading   A strategy for the interpretation of theoretical texts employed by ALTHUSSER (Althusser and Balibar, 1965, Part I), and based upon the FREUDian analyst's technique for uncovering the "latent content" behind the "manifest content" of dreams and PARAPRAXES. According to Althusser, TEXTS are governed by their "problematic," which determines not only the questions posed and the answers given, but also the problems omitted by them. Given that this theoretical "UNCONSCIOUS" is present in, yet absent from, any particular segment of the text, only a symptomatic reading can (re)construct it. The Althusserian model was adapted and developed for the reading of fictional texts by MACHEREY (1966) and EAGLETON (1978).

Reading
Althusser, L., and Balibar, E. 1965 (*1990*): *Reading Capital.*
Eagleton. T. 1978 (*1982*): *Criticism and Ideology.*
Macherey, Pierre 1966 (*1978*): *A Theory of Literary Production.*

GREGORY ELLIOTT

synchrony/diachrony A BINARY OPPOSITION utilized by Ferdinand de SAUSSURE to denote two different methods of describing time relationships in language analysis. In his case, the structural linguistics he devised privileged a synchronic approach over a diachronic one. That is, he viewed the state of a language as it existed at a single moment in its history rather than in terms of its development over a period of time. Saussure's synchronic approach allowed him to view the internal relations which constituted a language, and the theory he produced from this position is generally regarded as the first truly structuralist analysis.

Reading
Culler, Jonathan 1989 (*1975*): *Structuralist Poetics.*
Saussure, Ferdinand de 1983 (*1913*): *Course in General Linguistics.*

PAUL INNES

syntagmatic/paradigmatic A BINARY OPPOSITION introduced by Ferdinand de SAUSSURE to denote two relations in language. A syntagmatic analysis pays attention to the ways in which the words used in a particular sentence relate to one another. A paradigmatic analysis is concerned with the way that such vocabulary relates to other words which could have been used but were not. The paradigmatic associations are present by default, as it were, and are Saussure's way of dealing with the concept of connotative associations. The opposition between the two methods is laid open by DERRIDA (1976) in his DECONSTRUCTION of Saussurean linguistics.

Reading
Culler, Jonathan 1975 (*1989*): *Structuralist Poetics.*
Derrida, Jacques 1967a (*1976*): *Of Grammatology.*
Saussure, Ferdinand de 1913 (*1983*): *Course in General Linguistics.*

PAUL INNES

system A term used by TYNYANOV and JAKOBSON who, arguing with SHKLOVSKY, redefined literary work as an aesthetic "system" rather than a "sum total of literacy devices. "System" was viewed as a hierarchical set of interdependent variables which exists in dynamic integration, changing all the time. An individual work of ART was considered a system of the first order, existing in a higher system of a literary trend or a historical period, which in turn was a variable in the ultimate cultural system of systems.
See also TYNYANOV; JAKOBSON.

Reading
Lefevere, André 1991: "The dynamics of the system: convention and innovation in literary history."
Totosy de Zepanek, Steven 1992: "Systemic approaches to literature: an introduction with selected bibliography."

SLAVA I. YASTREMSKI

T

taboo Violating a taboo produces supernatural consequences. While some taboos proscribe behaviors, others are restrictions required in order for supernatural protections to continue. Probably all societies have taboos. Taboos may reflect unspoken anxieties generated by the demands or contradictions of social STRUCTURE, or simply enhance public acts or set individuals such as shamans or elites apart.

Reading
Freud, Sigmund 1913 (*1950*): *Totem and Taboo*.
THOMAS C. GREAVES

Tate, Allen (1899–1979) American critic. One of the chief ideologists of NEW CRITICISM, Tate was chiefly responsible for bringing into it the ideas of T.S. ELIOT, especially his notions of tradition (embodied for Tate in the Old South and orthodox religion) and the DISSOCIATION OF SENSIBILITY. In his criticism (particularly in his concept of TENSION) Tate sets out to demonstrate that poetry provides a special kind of knowledge, superior to the "abstract" knowledge of science and similar to Eliot's idea of the unified sensibility, in which intellect and feeling are harmonious and provide a model for the "cultivation of our total human powers."
See also ELIOT, T.S.; FUGITIVES; NEW CRITICISM; SOUTHERN AGRARIANS; TENSION.

Reading
Squires, Radcliffe, ed. 1972: *Allen Tate and His Work: Critical Evaluations*.
Stewart, John Lincoln 1965: *The Burden of Time: The Fugitives and Agrarians*.
Wellek, René 1986i: "Allen Tate."
IAIN WRIGHT

technologies, reproductive *See* REPRODUCTIVE TECHNOLOGIES

Tel Quel A journal published in Paris from 1960 to 1982 that under the editorial direction of novelist Philippe Sollers, which became a key source of AVANT-GARDE work in literature and CRITICAL THEORY. Concerned with the relations between art and politics, the *Tel Quel* group explored new conceptions of language and the SUBJECT, seeking to establish WRITING – *écriture* – as having its own specific and necessary revolutionary force. Influential in its emphasis on textual practices valued as breaking with the given social ordering of subjectivity (the "limit texts" of writers such as Sade or Artaud), the journal published important theoretical work on TEXTUALITY, notably by Roland BARTHES, Julia KRISTEVA, and Jacques DERRIDA.

Reading
Forrest, Philippe 1995: *Histoire de Tel Quel 1960–1982*.
Kauppi, Niilo 1990: *Tel Quel: La constitution sociale d'une avant-garde*.
Suleiman, Susan Robin 1989: "As is."
STEPHEN HEATH

television Much of present-day television analysis emerges from the initial work of Raymond WILLIAMS and Marshall McLuhan. Williams's *Television: Technology and Cultural Form* (1974) places the emergence of television as an invention of applied technology within the context of larger societal and economic transformations in the West. By historicizing television as well as questioning the social effects of programming, Williams creates a framework and vocabulary from which to examine television and its programs.

One of Williams's most influential ideas is that television is experiencing "a significant shift from the concept of sequence as *programming* to the concept of sequence of *flow*" (p. 89) where textual material constantly moves from one image to the next. This sequential description of "flow" continues to be an important way to discuss television, especially in the age of MTV, CNN, and the Home

Shopping Network, where images are increasingly "detextualized."

John Ellis (1982) problematizes Williams's notion of "flow," preferring to discuss television's tendency for "segmentation." Ellis argues that television programming presents "rapid alternation between scenes . . . rather than any sustained progression" (p. 120), presenting "segments in larger or smaller conglomerations" of images (p. 122). For Ellis, the narrative of television is a matter of succession rather than consequence. Williams's idea of "flow" is also echoed in Neil Postman's (1994) statement that "television is a worldview without the word 'because' in it . . . [with] no beginning . . . [and] no end"; instead, it is "all 'ands' " (pp. 68–9). Though both Postman and Ellis challenge and expand Williams's idea, his framework remains vital in their discussion of television.

McLuhan's controversial *Understanding Media* (1964) also discusses media as part of a larger cultural and societal change. McLuhan views the prominence of various forms of media as a shift toward the "cool" abstract and impersonal values created by the media over the "hot" passionate and egocentric values of print. He sees society returning to an emphasis on the privileging of the spoken word over the written. McLuhan's incorporation of television into this oral tradition is problematic since television is not solely an audio experience, and in later work he attempted to further examine and expand his incorporation of television into such a framework. McLuhan's conceptions of television produced critical responses, but was, overall, not as influential as Williams in this area.

During the 1980s and 1990s television studies have been greatly influenced by the development of diverse strands of literary theory. Contemporary criticism, represented by a variety of approaches such as SEMIOTICS, READER-RESPONSE, FEMINIST, MARXIST, DECONSTRUCTION, and PSYCHOANALYTIC, has provided a further framework from which to examine television. By placing television and its representations of CULTURE in a textual vocabulary, it has allowed television to be seen as a site for "serious" academic investigation, while still highlighting the differences between a television program, a piece of literature, and a film. Robert C. Allen's (1992) *Channels of Discourse* collects an interesting overview of essays examining television from a variety of contemporary critical approaches. More specifically, Gregory Ulmer (1989) utilizes Derrida's GRAMMATOLOGY to situate current academic DISCOURSE in the age of television, while John Fiske (1987) adopts a "viewer-centered" approach to examine how television can promote "oppositional cultural capital."

The influence of contemporary criticism has also allowed a broader examination of how television represents those on the "margins," especially women, people of color, and homo/bisexuals. Feminist television criticism has addressed the representation of women on television as well as broader questions concerning the construction of GENDER and sexuality in the media. Helen Baehr and Gillian Dyer's *Boxed In: Women And Television* (1987) examines primarily British television culture, focusing on how it is used in the production of dominant images of women and how various programs can both negate the challenges of feminism as well as offer opposition to the dominance of PATRIARCHY. Elayne Rapping (1994) offers a varied look at the portrayal of women in various American media, especially television programs aimed primarily at women.

In terms of RACE, there has not been as much written as perhaps there should be. Issues concerning the televisual representations of race are increasingly foregrounded as television in the West attempts a more "multicultural" perspective and in the postcolonial world at large the divisions between nations become blurred. Prabha Krishman and Anita Dighe (1990) look at the portrayal of women on Indian television where discourses of colonialism become intertwined with issues of gender. Linda K. Fuller (1992), Sut Jhally and Justin Lewis (1992), and Henry Louis Gates (1989) have all written about the immensely popular American program *The Cosby Show*, examining the global ramifications of an affluent black sitcom family becoming a quintessential role model. Amelia Simpson's *Xuxa* (1993) specifically addresses the Brazilian television icon, Xuxa, and her children's program, which Simpson argues privileges certain ideas of beauty which are racially coded.

The emerging field of queer studies has just begun to examine television. One such study is Alexander Doty's *Making Things Perfectly Queer* (1993); he undertakes the task of revealing the implicit "queerness" of mass culture as a means of confronting the dominant discourses of homophobia and heterosexism present in television.

With the popularity of the rubric of POSTMODERNISM in the academy, some critics have explored television's relation to this cultural condition. Jim

Collins's essay in the revised edition of *Channels of Discourse* (Allen, 1992) places television in the larger framework of postmodern AESTHETICS, using David Lynch's *Twin Peaks* as the "cultural phenomenon that epitomizes the multiple dimensions of televisual postmodernism" (p. 341). Andrew Goodwin (1992) attempts a postmodern analysis of MTV, utilizing a historical materialist standpoint to engage in the politics and IDEOLOGY embodied in the images of music television. Many of the leading postmodern theorists, such as Fredric Jameson and Jean BAUDRILLARD, also address the role of media images in the emergence of a postmodern world view.

Much of the work on television discussed above falls under the heading of CULTURAL STUDIES. In relation to television, cultural studies have been critical in developing the interdisciplinary approach required to theorize television within POPULAR CULTURE. However, David Morley (1992) critiques the work of cultural studies on television as being solely humanities and arts-based and not interdisciplinary enough. Despite acknowledgements that television cannot be reduced to a textual phenomenon, Morley feels that most studies remain "text-centric."

Though such a critique is valid in some respects, writers such as Fiske are attempting to negotiate television in relation to the "TENSION" existing between "institutions, offices, agencies, academics . . . nations, races [and] genders" (p. 6) which Morley feels is crucial for adequate theorization. A text such as Douglas Kellner's *Television and the Crisis of Democracy* (1990) specifically attempts what Morley suggests. Kellner situates television within the institutional and systemic framework of present-day US culture, expanding upon the work of such theorists as Max HORKHEIMER and Theodor ADORNO.

The works addressed in this entry reveal only a minority of the work which has been undertaken on the subject of television. However, perhaps the most valuable aspect of an entry such as this one is that it reveals the work which remains. Issues of race, CLASS, and gender, and their representations in television, must continue to be theorized and criticisms such as Morley's must be noted as we continue our studies in television and media.
See also CULTURAL STUDIES; POSTMODERNISM; WILLIAMS, RAYMOND.

Reading
Allen, Robert C. 1987 (*1992*): *Channels of Discourse, Reassembled.*

Baehr, Helen, and Dyer, Gillian, eds 1987: *Boxed In: Women and Television.*
Casmore, Ellen 1994: *. . . And there was Television.*
Doty, Alexander 1993: *Making Things Perfectly Queer: Interpreting Mass Culture.*
Ellis, John 1982: *Visible Fictions: Cinema, Television, Video.*
Fiske, John 1987: *Television Culture.*
Fuller, Linda K. 1992: *The Cosby Show: Audiences, Impact and Implications.*
Gates, Henry Louis 1989: "TV's black world turns – but stays unreal."
Goodwin, Andrew 1992: *Dancing in the Distraction Factory: Music, Television and Popular Culture.*
Jhally, Sut, and Lewis, Justin 1992: *Enlightening Racism: The Cosby Show, Audiences, and the Myth of the American Dream.*
Kellner, Douglas 1990: *Television and the Crisis of Democracy.*
Krishman, Prabha, and Dighe, Anita 1990: *Affirmation and Denial: Construction of Femininity on Indian Television.*
Lewis, Justin 1991: *The Ideological Octopus: An Exploration of Television and Its Audience.*
McLuhan, Marshall 1964 (*1965*): *Understanding Media.*
Morley, David 1992: *Television, Audiences and Cultural Studies.*
Postman, Neil 1994: "Interview with Neil Postman."
Rapping, Elaine 1994: *Media-tions: Forays into the Culture and Gender Wars.*
Seiter, Ellen, Borchers, Hans, Kreutzner, Gabriele, and Warth, Eva-Maria, eds 1989: *Remote Control: Television, Audiences and Cultural Power.*
Simpson, Amelia 1993: *Xuxa: The Mega-Marketing of Gender, Race and Modernity.*
Ulmer, Gregory 1989: *Teletheory: Grammatology in the Age of Video.*
Williams, Raymond 1974: *Television: Technology and Cultural Form.*

KENNETH J. URBAN

tension   A term used by Allen TATE to denote the coexistence in POETRY of "extension" (literal meaning) and "intension" (metaphorical meaning). (Compare CONNOTATION/DENOTATION.) More broadly, it was used in NEW CRITICISM to describe the pattern of structured conflict or resolved contradictions (for example, "between the formality of the rhythm and the informality of the language" (R.P. Warren), or between the abstract and the concrete) which the New Critics regarded as the essential characteristic of the best poetry.

Reading
Lee, Brian 1966: "The New Criticism and the language of poetry."
Tate, Allen 1969: *Essays of Four Decades.*

IAIN WRIGHT

text   In one sense "text" is simply a neutral term for any cultural object of investigation, whether a piece of WRITING, a ritual activity, a CITY, or a mode of knowledge. Thus in literary theory "text" is commonly used in place of such generic designations as "lyric" or "novel" in order to leave open the question of whether what is being examined is generically specifiable. Virginia Woolf's *The Waves*, for example, sets out to confound the distinction between the lyric and the novel; and Shakespeare's *The Winter's Tale* is simultaneously (perhaps deliberately) a tragedy, a comedy, and a romance. Similarly, Lévi-Strauss's *Tristes tropiques* employs novelistic techniques even though it is ostensibly an anthropological text. In other uses of the term, however, "text" can be not at all innocent but heavily loaded with meaning. Although DERRIDA's infamous remark that "There is nothing outside the text" (1967a (*1976*), p. 227) has been mistaken as a denial that there is anything other than language, even its more credible interpretation – that if one tries to go to ROUSSEAU's biography in order to understand something that he has written, one is still dealing with written records of his life that were mostly written by him – still, the claim has far-reaching implications. For KRISTEVA (1974a (*1984*), pp. 99–106) texts are generated by complex psychosocial-biological processes that allow meaning first to be constituted and then disrupted or exceeded, by materiality, for example, which is initially (for her) outside meaning.

Reading
Derrida, Jacques 1967a (*1976*): *Of Grammatology*.
Kristeva, Julia 1974a (*1984*): *Revolution in Poetic Language*.
                                                    MICHAEL PAYNE

Textual Practice   When Terence Hawkes from the University of Wales at Cardiff, along with an international editorial board, set out to produce the first volume of *Textual Practice*, he was wary about its future. Hawkes's introductory editorial begins with the disclaimer that, while there is never any good time to start a new journal, 1987 seemed an especially gloomy year for such purposes, for "the academic world in general feels itself to be under attack." And yet, Hawkes concluded his remarks with the assertion that "there was never a time when [a journal] such as *Textual Practice* was more necessary."

The journal, which focuses primarily on literary TEXTS, while managing to keep sight of the broader study of textuality across disciplines, serves its purpose well. The role of *Textual Practice* has proven to be one of both the observer and the active participant, challenging existing STRUCTURES in textual criticism; the articles in the journal are by and about major critics of the day. The lead article in the first issue, for instance is "The end of English," by Terry EAGLETON; the focus of the essay, in which he dwells on the effect of the influential journal *SCRUTINY*, is the struggle between the study of "English" as a subject and CRITICAL THEORY, which sparks the interest of today's scholars. Eagleton ends with the claim that "the only conflict which finally matters is between the internationalism of late capitalist consumerism, and the internationalism of its political antagonist." The article, besides being reminiscent of some of Hawkes's earlier writings, is an appropriate lead into *Textual Practice*; this same sort of concern for literature and its relation to other textual forms recurs in each volume.

Textual Practice is now published by Routledge three times each year; articles and reviews makes up the bulk of these issues, although the occasional letter makes its way into the journal. Periodically, the journal strays slightly from its typical form to incorporate a special project; once, in 1991, it published a bibliography of DERRIDA's works between 1962 and 1990. In 1988 *Textual Practice* devoted four articles to a study of Donald DAVIDSON's work, including a piece by Christopher NORRIS, Hawkes's colleague at the University of Wales at Cardiff, who serves as review editor and frequent contributor. Two years later it devoted an entire issue (with the exception of a few reviews) to the exploration of lesbian and gay cultures, for which Joseph Bristow served as guest editor.

Despite Hawkes's forecasts, *Textual Practice* has provided lively academic DISCOURSE on the movements in literary theory and other related fields. *Textual Practice* was not "self-evidently doomed" from the start, as Hawkes wrote in those early pages; rather, it has helped set the pace for textual studies.

                                                    TARA G. GILLIGAN

theater   For the greater part of the twentieth century, Anglo-European theories of drama and performance were associated with several questions of mostly Aristotelian derivation: whether the primary function of drama should be to delight or to instruct; to what extent drama truly holds "the mirror up to nature;" whether the essence of drama lies in the "TEXT" or in the performance; whether it is possible to achieve a "total theater" in which the constituent elements of character, PLOT, music, gesture, and spectacle are inseparable; whether such key Aristotelian concepts as catharsis or hamartia are relevant to modern tragedy, or, for that matter, whether the received generic and structural categories – tragedy, comedy, climax, dénouement, and so forth – are relevant to the study of any drama, modern or otherwise.

Dramatic theory during the last decades of the twentieth century variously adopted, interrogated, and reformulated this inheritance. It sought to reevaluate received theater history without focusing merely on the periods traditionally centered by scholars and practitioners, the ancient Greek, the European Renaissance, and the European Modern. Because new research into theater historiography has challenged and reconfigured the received criteria for determining artistic "value," scholars have become at once more cautious and more open in designating what might qualify as the "significant" theatrical activity of particular periods. As a consequence of this recent openness concerning the range and constitution of performance art, increasing attention has been turned toward forms once ignored (popular and folk arts, regional and amateur theaters); toward types of performance or "symbolic action" (Clifford Geertz) which have not traditionally been examined by students of theater; toward the conditions and social contexts of theatrical production; and toward the ideological underpinnings of performing texts.

As a result, contemporary theater studies have cumulatively produced not only impressive theoretical discussions of stagecraft but also, more important, a complex critical apparatus capable of decoding all "symbolic action" and thus of intervening in what is thought of as the contemporary, postmodernist crisis of spectacle and representation. It should be noted that, in spite of this diversification, and in spite of several decades of intensive study of non-Western arts (as opposed, that is, to non-Western critical traditions), Anglo-European studies occupy a hegemonic position in dramatic theory as it is practiced today.

Before reviewing the most recent trends in dramatic theory and criticism, it is necessary to consider the state of contemporary performance art itself. Contemporary Western criticism is in many ways a response to the crisis of survival confronting the theater in an age in which cultural production has been overwhelmingly technologized and commodified. As television, film, and video technology drive the theater into increasingly marginal and inadequately funded performance spaces, even commercial stages have struggled to survive the onslaught of mass communication. Oddly enough, in spite of over a century of experimentation with theatrical space and dramatic technique, much theater practiced commercially today in the West seems conventionally designed for a proscenium stage, using more or less realistic characterization, dialogue, and plot. Such apparent devotion to convention may be seen as a defensive strategy which enables the commercial theater to maintain the kind of permanence available to extinct or rare species: by adopting the role of a performing museum, the theater participates in the commodification of nostalgia and thereby earns at least a fraction of the income generated by dinosaurs or the colonial fashion industry. Opera and contemporary musicals, for example, are able (especially when performed in "restored" prewar theaters) to compete in the open market with music television; ticket prices for popular musicals and rock concerts are roughly comparable. To a lesser extent, folk theaters and revivals of "classics" (such as Greek tragedies or Ibsen) are able to claim various forms of institutional subsidy in their capacity as repositories of Western heritage. Consider the continuing popularity of Shakespeare, which, albeit tenuous, generates income sufficient enough to allow Shakespearean companies to experiment occasionally, and even, once in a while, to stage new plays.

It is useful to distinguish "commercial" theater from the "AVANT-GARDE" performance art of critically acclaimed artists, whose work is seen to challenge the "official," commercial theater at the same time that it enjoys another kind of "official" sanction and approbation, that granted by critics, scholars, and funding organizations. To some extent, the established CANON of modern theater consists of artists who form a kind of official underground; whose work is recognized to have influenced that of other artists and to have contributed to the acknowledged theoretical debates of the century; whose names are often unknown to the public at large even when their work has been adapted and assimilated into POPULAR CULTURE; and whose work is, in spite of such obscurity, somewhat capable of generating institutional sponsorship. To name only the most obvious: Henrik Ibsen; August

Strindberg; Anton Chekhov; Konstantin Stanis-
lavsky; Vsevolod Meyerhold; Vladimir Mayakovsky;
Edward Gordon Craig; John Millington Synge;
George Bernard Shaw; Antonin Artaud; Jean
Anouilh; Friedrich Dürrenmatt; Stanislaw Witkie-
wicz; Erwin Piscator; Bertolt BRECHT; Jean Genet;
Luigi Pirandello; Sean O'Casey; Eugene Ionesco;
Samuel Beckett; Harold Pinter; Brendan Behan;
Augusto Boal; Dario Fo; Jerzy Grotowski; Peter
Brook – a list of notables which draws attention to
the relentless if unsurprising eurocentrism and male
orientation of dramatic theory and practice. Virtually every artist deemed worthy of inclusion in this
canon has been preoccupied with the question of
MODERNITY and has advocated the development of
a theatrical aesthetic appropriate to a postindustrial
age, to what Walter BENJAMIN described as "the
age of mechanical reproduction." Their experimentation with theatrical form has generated a complex of discussions concerning all aspects of
theatrical creativity and production: "authorship;"
spectatorship; genre; language; silence and articulation; gesture; space; design; cultural politics;
philosophies and techniques of acting; and, centrally, AESTHETICS and IDEOLOGY. (See Bentley, 1968
and Carlson, 1984. Also, for a critique of the ways
in which the idea of the avant-garde is privileged
in theatre historiography, see Alan Woods's essay
in Postlewait and McConachie, 1989.)

However, the range of theatrical activity practiced
globally today far exceeds what is visible in the
West on financially competitive stages or those
which are supported by the cultural apparatuses
of the state. Theaters in most parts of the world
function not only in such "official," economically
protected spaces, but also, and more frequently,
in informal or underground sites, often without
budgets or formal stages and often at enormous
political risk. Grass-roots "people's theater" groups,
which have always flourished by the thousand all
over the world, provide powerful examples of
oppositional cultural politics in action, and, in their
contemporary form, also of postindustrial, anti-
consumer society aesthetics. Operating outside and
against the established structures of power in the
societies they inhabit, such groups participate at
several levels in struggles for cultural and political
emancipation and self-determination: revivals of
local arts, customs, histories, and languages, as
well as economic and political organizing against
poverty, racial and sexual oppression, and other
violations of human rights.

Collectively, "people's theater" groups constitute an international movement in performance arts
which is comparable in aesthetic scope to film and
considerably more effective as political activism.
The International Popular Theatre Alliance was
formed during the 1980s to create a network among
such groups and to draw critical attention to their
work. The Alliance focused specifically on "Third
World" theaters, but it is clear that underground
theaters perform everywhere; indeed, many influential artists of the official Western canon (Meyerhold, Mayakovsky, Brecht, Piscator) drew upon
the work of grass-roots groups to develop theories
of political theater. Among several projects which
have in recent years earned international recognition are the Kamiriithu Community Educational
and Cultural Centre of Kenya; the early work of
Václav Havel in the former Czechoslovakia; the
Jamaican Sistren Collective; John McGrath's 7:84
theater company in England and Scotland; the Jana
Natya Manch in India; the Philippines Educational
Theater Association; and, in the United States, El
Teatro Campesino, Teatro de la Esperanza, and
the San Francisco Mime Troupe (see van Erven,
1988 and 1992).

Grass-roots political theaters share with the "official" avant-garde described above a critical attitude towards contemporary CULTURE; both seek,
in playwright Howard Brenton's words, to "disrupt the spectacle" of modern life and to expose its
many cultural contradictions. Because such theaters
so often function without official sponsorship, and
because, as Benjamin has argued, they tend to assimilate or "enter into debate" with newer artistic
forms and with contemporaneity at large, experimental theaters (whether in the official or invisible
underground) may be especially capable of with-
standing the technological age, perhaps even of
protecting theater from extinction. Both draw upon
a vast variety of performance techniques, including agitational propaganda, slogan art, cartooning,
acrobatics and juggling, cabaret, puppetry and mask,
male and female impersonation, and dance.
Unsurprisingly, the artistic flexibility and inven-
tiveness of such groups have reconfigured the collapsing boundaries between art, political activism,
and entertainment.

In the West, alternative and oppositional theaters
have often operated in a shifting middle ground
between the underground, avant-garde, and commerce. The activist movements of the 1960s and
1970s – protests against war, capitalism, and impe-

rialism; agitation for racial and sexual emancipation – encouraged the emergence of new playwrights as well as the development of politically specific collectives. In the United States and Britain, several NEW LEFT theaters proliferated during these decades, initially staging agitational propaganda and consciousness-raising plays in small venues and later moving to bigger stages. African-American, feminist, and gay theaters have been especially prolific and innovative, not only remapping the boundaries between "high" and POPULAR CULTURE but also shaping – as the recent increase in published collections of plays testifies – what should become the canon of late twentieth-century drama in English. Since the mid-1980s, black British, Chicana/o, Native American, and Asian American artists and groups have begun to attract belated critical notice. To name, once again, only the best known of the interventionist playwrights and companies to emerge in the postwar era: Lorraine Hansberry; Amiri Baraka; Ed Bullins; Adrienne Kennedy; August Wilson; Ntozake Shange; Anna Deavere Smith; the Negro Ensemble Company; the Free Southern Theatre; Caryl Churchill; Pam Gems; the Omaha Magic Theater; the Spiderwoman Theater Workshop; Monstrous Regiment; Harvey Fierstein; Martin Sherman; Joe Orton; Split Britches; WOW Cafe; Theatre Rhinoceros; Gay Sweatshop; Mustapha Matura; Caryl Phillips; Benjamin Zephaniah; Jacqueline Rudet; Hanif Khureishi; Hanay Geiogamah; the Native American Theatre Ensemble; Luis Valdez; Jorge Huerta; National Teatros of Aztlán; Frank Chin; the Theatre for Asian American Performing Artists.

Contemporary critical interest in oppositional DISCOURSE and theater has been stimulated in large measure by the challenge posed by underground and avant-garde groups. A new generation of political criticism has engaged the racial and sexual politics of theater history and performance texts, and has drawn upon the work of International Situationism, with its analysis of the "society of the spectacle," to explore the performance of cultural opposition in society at large. These and other interests have been theorized and extensively developed, particularly in the United States, where studies of Renaissance theater initially played a key role in redefining the terrain of dramatic criticism (see RENAISSANCE STUDIES). During the 1980s theater studies were substantially transformed following the publication of controversial discussions of CRITICAL THEORY and performance. Recent

theorists have drawn upon several interpretative methodologies, including SEMIOTICS, DECONSTRUCTION, PSYCHOANALYTIC CRITICISM, and PHENOMENOLOGY. Semiotic and structuralist theory have provided theater criticism with a means to analyze performance as an encoded SYSTEM of shifting SIGNS in which the various elements of the performance, including the audience, are brought into a continual play of transformational possibilities. Deconstruction has further enabled analysis of the means by which theater continually dismantles its own systems of signification in a play of shifting subjectivities and unstable signs which undermines the performance's claims to represent reality. Discussions of the politics of realism and deconstruction in postmodernist theaters have especially engaged theorists of RACE and GENDER. Psychoanalytic theory has been widely influential in feminist theater criticism, particularly in post-LACANian considerations of spectatorship. (For overviews, see Reinelt and Roach, 1992, and Carlson, 1984. For specific discussions, consult Elam, 1980, and Pavis, 1983, on semiotics; Austin, 1990, and Case, 1990, on deconstruction, psychoanalytic theory, and feminist performance studies; and Wilshire, 1982, and States, 1985, on phenomenology and theater.)

New research into theater history has been particularly important in completing the theatrical record and enabling the emergence of buried voices (see Postlewait and McConachie, 1989). Some of the most complex and provocative studies have been developed by those scholars and practitioners who have engaged the vast array of questions concerning the politics of race, CLASS, gender, and sexuality posed by transatlantic CULTURAL STUDIES: the materialities of cultural production and more generally of SIGNIFYING practices; the possibility of oppositional discourse in an era of mass media and CONSUMER CULTURE; the "imagined communities" of nation, race, ethnicity; the condition of LIMINALITY and border-crossing; the positionalities of power, oppression, and resistance (see Reinelt and Case, 1991; Reinelt and Roach, 1992; Postlewait and McConachie, 1989; and Case, 1990). Theorists as well as practitioners of African-American performance arts have produced not only comprehensive and influential studies of the origins and development of black theater and performative aesthetics, but also, until the 1990s, the only systematic theorizing of ethnicity and race (see Harrison, 1972; Hill, 1980; Fabre, 1983; essays by

Sandra Richards in Reinelt and Roach, 1992, and by James V. Hatch in Postlewait and McConachie, 1989). Studies of feminism and theater have contributed to the study of theater history and historiography, radicalizing analysis of the semiotics of performance, the aesthetics of oppositional cultural production, and the analysis of body politics (see Case, 1990; Austin, 1990; Dolan, 1991). Studies of gay and lesbian theaters, and gay and lesbian performance art itself, have extended the feminist interrogation of sexuality and cultural politics, effectively redefining the scope of what constitutes performative action (see especially Dolan, 1991; and Case, 1990).

Anthropologically oriented discussions of performance rituals, developed most notably by Richard Schechner, have contributed to general understanding of the central role of theater and performance in cultural self-constitution, and have also influenced specific ethnographic studies of non-Western performance arts. Although this has led to some Western dabbling in non-Western theaters, both internationalism and interculturalism remain inadequately theorized (see Marranca and Dasgupta, 1991; and Schechner, 1985). The twentieth-century avant-garde has, of course, frequently turned to the non-West; many approaches to non-Western performance art are derived from modernist interests in primitivism. Artaud, for example, looked to the Orient for a means to enslave spectators with the inner truths of their own "erotic obsessions," "savagery," and "even ... cannibalism." However, theater professionals and critics often seem unaware, even in this day and age, of the problematic racialism of discourses which seek in the non-West a means of psychic self-realization through RITUAL (the implicit contrast being between the purported inability of Western industrialism to articulate the spiritual or psychic and the purported expertise of the Orient in matters immaterial).

Such a legacy will have to be thoroughly reviewed and problematized before theater studies can begin to theorize anew questions of race and nation. In spite of the challenges posed by black and postcolonial cultural theory and many oppositional theaters, and in spite of the manifold successes of theater historians in recovering performance histories marginalized by institutionalized racism, theorists of drama and performance have not responded with any vigor to questions of race, ethnicity, or cultural nationalism. However, with the emergence of new artists and groups which challenge the presumed stability of such categories as West or non-West, it becomes increasingly evident that the performance of HYBRIDITY and interculturalism will concern scholars for many years to come.

Reading

Austin, Gayle 1990: *Feminist Theories for Dramatic Criticism.*

Bentley, Eric, ed. 1968: *The Theory of the Modern Stage: An Introduction to Modern Theatre and Drama.*

Carlson, Marvin 1984: *Theories of the Theatre: A Historical and Critical Survey from the Greeks to the Present.*

Case, Sue-Ellen, ed. 1990: *Performing Feminisms: Feminist Critical Theory and Theatre.*

Dolan, Jill 1988 (*1991*): *The Feminist Spectator as Critic.*

Elam, Keir 1980: *The Semiotics of Theatre and Drama.*

Fabre, Genevieve E. 1983: *Drumbeats, Masks, and Metaphor: Contemporary Afro-American Theatre.*

Harrison, Paul Carter 1972: *The Drama of Nommo: Black Theater in the African Continuum.*

Hill, Errol, ed. 1980: *The Theatre of Black Americans.*

Marranca, Bonnie and Dasgupta, Gautam, eds 1991: *Interculturalism and Performance: Writings from PAJ.*

Pavis, Patrice 1983: *Languages of the Stage: Essays in the Semiology of Theatre.*

Postlewait, Thomas, and McConachie, Bruce A., eds 1989: *Interpreting the Theatrical Past: Essays in the Historiography of Performance.*

Reinelt, Janelle G. and Case, Sue-Ellen, eds 1991: *The Performance of Power: Theatrical Discourse and Politics.*

——and Roach, Joseph R., eds 1992: *Critical Theory and Performance.*

Schechner, Richard 1985: *Between Theatre and Anthropology.*

States, Bert O. 1985: *Great Reckonings in Little Rooms: On the Phenomenology of Theatre.*

van Erven, Eugene 1988: *Radical People's Theatre.*

——1992: *The Playful Revolution: Theatre and Liberation in Asia.*

Wilshire, B. 1982: *Role Playing and Identity: The Limits of Theatre As Metaphor.*

MEENAKSHI PONNUSWAMI

theories, language *See* LANGUAGE THEORIES

theory, critical *See* CRITICAL THEORY

theory, cultural *See* CULTURAL THEORY

Thompson, Edward Palmer (1924–93) English historian and socialist intellectual. While teaching in adult education he produced a major study of William Morris and his politics (1955). His celebrated and influential *The Making of the English Working Class* (1963) drew on wide-ranging scholarship in analyzing the formation of CLASS and class consciousness through work, religion, popular customs, and political activity. Thompson's work consistently stressed the power of human agency, and also distinctively English traditions of thought and practice. Moving from the Communist Party to help found the NEW LEFT in 1967, he engaged ever more combatively with French structuralist accounts of Marxist theory. Prolific historical writing (for example, *Whigs and Hunters*, 1975) and editing (*The Unknown Mayhew*, 1971) appeared alongside vigorous and distinctive interventions in political and intellectual debates. His force and skill as a polemicist were increasingly evident in assaults upon business management practice in universities (*Warwick University Limited*, 1970) and on left theoreticism (*The Poverty of Theory*, 1978), then in speeches, articles, and books connected with campaigns for nuclear disarmament (for example, *The Heavy Dancers*, 1985). A book on Blake, published posthumously, again vividly located an English author, in enormous detail, within the social world and political traditions of his time.

Reading
Kaye, H.J., and McLelland, K. 1990: *E.P. Thompson, Critical Perspectives.*
Thompson, E.P. 1955 (*1977*): *William Morris: Romantic to Revolutionary.*
——1963: (*1980*): *The Making of the English Working Class.*
——1993: *Witness Against the Beast: William Blake and the Moral Law.*
MICHAEL GREEN

totemism   A term that classifies together a number of different phenomena. In its widest sense, it refers to a population divided into groups, each of which is associated with a class of animate or inanimate objects (its totem). The term may refer to simple heraldic SYMBOLism or to complex SYSTEMS of religious and magical observances. The totem has variously been seen as a social emblem which represents and maintains the solidarity and continuity of the social group, or as a means of conceptualizing the natural, animal world in terms of the social world, the diversity of species constituting a conceptual support for social differentiation.

Reading
Durkheim, Emile 1912 (*1968*): *The Elementary Forms of the Religious Life.*
Lévi-Strauss, Claude 1962a (*1963*): *Totemism.*
JANET MACGAFFEY

tragedy   Chaucer's famous definition of tragedy as

> a certain storie,
> As olde books maken us memorie,
> of hym that stood in great prosperitee,
> And is yfallen out of high degree,
> Into myserie, and endeth wrecchedly

echoes Aristotle's "virtuous man brought from prosperity to adversity." Aristotle, whose theory of tragedy remained the relevant aesthetic standard for the writing and judgment of tragedy from the late Middle Ages through the eighteenth century, favors "an air of design" in what brings about the suffering in the fall of the hero. The most important part of tragedy for Aristotle is, perhaps surprisingly, not the character but the structure of the tragic action, for in this way the dialectic between fate and the character's doomed, if dignified, responses can be dramatized. The plot, being "the soul of tragedy," is famously defined by a beginning, a middle, and an end complicated by a reversal or peripeteia. The structure and closure of the action achieves in the audience – to allay Plato's fears of incitement to immorality – a vicarious emotional discharge, a catharsis of fear and pity. Incidentally, the notion of a curative narrative resulting in a catharsis or recognition identifies Aristotle as one of the central influences without whom PSYCHOANALYSIS would be unthinkable. The connection between tragedy as aesthetic form and psychoanalytic transference has been concisely articulated in Hannah Arendt's insightful phrase, "The tragic hero becomes knowledgeable by re-experiencing what has been done in the way of suffering, and in . . . resuffering the past, the network of individual acts is transformed into an event, a significant whole."

The SUBJECT of tragedy enclosed by an aesthetic form attains a moral dimension: according to Aristotle it is "serious, complete, and of a certain magnitude." Indeed, Aristotle's aesthetic principles finally assign to tragedy an affirmative existential and political function for the unexpendable value of the individual in society. Both classical and Shakespearean tragedy confirm the solidity of existing orders by subjecting them to a crisis, while comedy much more than tragedy points out the fundamentally fragile nature of social and individual identity.

Aristotle's theory of tragedy is modeled on Sophocles' *Oedipus Rex*, an account, as were all tragedies of the fifth century (with the exception of Aeschylus's *Persians*), of an ancient legend or myth. These antecedent, mostly orally transmitted forms of "tragic" tales may be conceived, Richard Sewall argues, as responses to "the original unreason, the terror of the irrational" and to "the irreducible facts of suffering and death." Sewall's observation seems confirmed by the survival of the chorus in classical tragedy. The chorus echoes the RITUAL festivals and religious cults in Greek cities performed to honor Dionysus, the god of the death and rebirth of the cycles of life, or as NIETZSCHE saw it, the "procreative lust" of the "life force." To Nietzsche, whose *Birth of Tragedy* remains one of the most original and influential interpretations of the genre, "all the famous characters of the Greek stage, Prometheus, Oedipus, etc., are only masks of the original hero." The steadily diminishing size and function of the choral parts, from Aeschylus to Euripides, demonstrates not only the death of tragedy, as Nietzsche argued, but also its diminishing religious significance associated with the early forms of tragic ritual.

One usually considers Aeschylus, the oldest known tragedian, as the most religious: his tragic plot is set in motion by primeval forces of darkly uncertain intent. Each character's desire in *The Oresteia*, "to check the curse cried on the house of Atreus" for example, only perpetuates the curse itself, and the characters are represented as caught in an inescapable net. In Aeschylus' successor Sophocles, the tragic flaw is more individualized; tragic necessity becomes, as FREUD later claimed with famous reference to Oedipus, a psychological destiny inscribed in humankind from earliest childhood. Unlike Orestes in Aeschylus, who subjects his will to cosmic powers, Sophocles' Oedipus displays a temporary if illusory independence, for not only does he survive the curse of the gods, but with his self-punishment he wrests out of the hands of fate, as it were, his own individual guilt and responsibility. In Euripides, the third of the three classical tragedians, the cosmic frame is either entirely absent, or itself, as Lionel Abel points out, in catastrophic disarray.

Such a development of tragedy from cosmology to IRONY is traceable either in the classical CANON itself or historically from Agamemnon to Arthur Miller's Willy Loman. Although the protagonists of tragedy reflect the current political and social structures – depicting as they do either the death of a king or the death of a salesman – the one constant of the tragic experience is a kind of suffering which the protagonist and the audience experience as disproportionate to its cause or to his flaw. According to James Joyce, in a famous passage from *Portrait of the Artist as a Young Man*, tragic suffering inspires pity through the sense of a shared humanity, while "the secret cause" inspires fear. The two contrary emotions may account for the fact, as Adrian Poole points out, that "the experiences which tragedies represent are such as at one and the same time most urgently demand and resist explanation." Indeed, the grounds of tragic pathos are, as Job blasphemously suggests, more just than God. Tragedy as a literary response, in any case, is not so much a representation of suffering as it is a protest or complaint against the unfathomable secrecy of its cause or reason. In this sense, the very length and unabated passion of Job's complaint could be interpreted not only as as an indictment of God's guilt, but also as a fundamental constituent of human nature.

As an aesthetic form, tragedy is itself a frame of SYMBOLic containment and closure of suffering and the questions it raises, hence the possibility of a cathartic resolution, however precarious, of moral TENSIONS and emotions. Aristotle's theory underwent numerous reiterations and refinements which culminate in HEGEL's theory of tragedy. While Hegel's notion of tragedy as a collision of equally justified powers, of good with good (as Aeschylus had already said) offers insight into tragedy as a profound crisis of values, the ethical or aesthetic sublation of that collision in an eternal justice offers that crisis, in turn, a final aesthetic resolution. Murray Krieger has pointed out that Hegel's fundamentally classical theory cannot, however, represent our own time, "the self-conscious modernism . . . characterized by fragmentation rather than by the ever-uniting synthesis which Hegel tried valiantly, if vainly, to impose upon it as its salvation." Similar critiques of the AESTHETIC, chiefly in Kierkegaard's and Nietzsche's philosophies, account for an ensuing critical tradition effective to this time, in which Aristotelian tragedy is seen in terms of an aesthetic illusion veiling as it reveals the incomprehensible phenomenon of human suffering. Such a view may be motivated rather by a tragic sense of life than inspired by close reading of tragedies. As Walter Kaufmann demonstrates, for example, BRECHT's attempts to dispell the aesthetic illusion by an ALIENATION EFFECT overlook the many rhetorical ways – the masks being the most obvious, or the play within the play in Hamlet, for example – to reflect on problems of representation in tragedy.

Stephen Booth's critique of the term suggests its opaque qualities: "the word by which the mind designates (and thus in part denies) its helplessness before a concrete, particular, and thus undeniable demonstration of the limits of human understanding." Even if such self-reflective faculties are always operative in the complexities of tragedy as a literary genre – Shakespeare's *Hamlet* is perhaps the best example, although even Aeschylus' *Agamemnon* would serve as a demonstration – it was Kierkegaard who subjected the term to substantive revaluation. Responding to Hegel's sublation of individual right in a universal order, Kierkegaard raised the suffering of the individual (Abraham on the way to sacrifice Isaac), in so far as it constitutes an incomprehensible or incommunicable situation, beyond Hegel's universals. For Kierkegaard, the classical tragic hero who willingly sacrifices himself for an ethical cause belies true suffering; he provides "a trim, clean, and, as far as possible, faultless edition of himself, readable by all," and goes a dancing step in comparison with Kierkegaard's "knight of faith." Kierkegaard's critique of the readable relegates us to the radically different, unreadable quality of individual suffering itself.

Though long read as an exemplification of pious patience in suffering, Job may demonstrate on several levels the paradox between individual suffering and the dubious nature of its aesthetic or theological containment. Yet, to imagine Job entirely without these contexts would be to echo his wife's advice, "curse God, and die," or to arrive at a modernist conception of the term tragedy. Here, nostalgic for the loss of any form of containment, cultural, aesthetic, or spiritual, T.S. ELIOT, for example, situates his anonymous speaker in a waste land, complaining, "I can connect / Nothing with nothing." A notable contemporary of Eliot's, Robinson Jeffers, who rewrote Euripidean tragedy, assigns his characters a tragic role precisely because any jurisdiction, whether ethical or poetic,

is unavailable, or, for that matter, insignificant in the face of a Darwininan conception of the universe where human life disappears in the indiscriminate sameness of all existence.

If these are only some examples, many more could be and have been adduced to demonstrate the existence of literary forms of tragedy in our time: Dostoevsky, Chekhov, Ibsen, SARTRE, Silone, Conrad, to name only a few. One might want to insist that the ironic or solipsistic nature of suffering in modern literature may not be deserving of the moral and aesthetic values associated with tragedy, and that for these specific experiences other terms, such as tragicomedy (Beckett's *Waiting for Godot*, for example) or the notion of an absurd theater, would have to be employed. Indeed, if the anonymity of pain suffered by modern characters were in any sense symptomatic of a fundamental human loneliness, the dramatic forms of tragedy attempted to redeem the individual's anonymity through the genre of drama, which, constituting a shared experience with an audience, may either symbolize the presence of diviner auditors or substitute for their absence. Modern tragedy, by contrast, particularly if it is offered in the individualized experience of the novel or the lyric, or if its structure undermines PLOT, declares such acts of social, let alone metaphysical, connection no longer possible. The autonomy of these genres implies increasingly the absence of social, moral, or cosmic contexts for suffering. The pain of the individual can thus not easily be valorized as tragic. For Georg Lukács just this autonomy and anonymity constitutes the tragic: "loneliness is the very essence of tragedy" and therefore, "The language of the absolutely lonely man is lyrical, monological." The dramatic, dialogic form of drama thus contradicts the essence of tragedy. Indeed, not only Aristotle's notions of the serious, the magnitude of the fall of the hero, but also more than these, the coherence of plot itself assigns a value to pain. The notion of "suffering" itself suggests a temporality and a narrative, and hence the possibility of a response. Modern representations of tragedy, for example, the stories of Kafka, the poetry of Paul Celan, or Samuel Beckett's theater, redress in their formal and thematic discontinuities and their subversions of genre the fundamental question of the sharability of pain itself.

Aristotle's disparaging remarks about the "episodic," defined as acts that "succeed one another without probable or necessary sequence," prefigure modern texts. Illustrating the importance of action as an organizing principle in tragedy, he refers to "the parallel in painting, where the most beautiful colors laid on without order will not give one the same pleasure as a simple black-and-white sketch of a portrait." The pleasure that such colors laid on without order allegedly fail to give may result from their attempts to valorize the disorder of the episodic, accidental nature of life. Tragedy in the classical sense, however, as Raymond Williams has argued, is possible only "when fully connecting meanings were available." One can see here that Euripides' tragedies already implied such a critique of connecting meanings.

The representation of disorder encounters, of course, the paradox of representing the unrepresentable. One of the most complex responses to this paradox occurs in Theodor ADORNO's notion of aesthetic autonomy as simultaneously removed from and indifferent to suffering while at the same time, as an image of the autonomy of suffering, owing it its gravity. The significance of such a valorization of the autonomous aesthetic work as capable of tragic content might well begin to point ways beyond what Raymond Williams has called the IDEOLOGY implicit in the academic tradition of tragedy. The significance of a new definition of tragedy, according to Williams, is to integrate suffering into a continuing sense of life. Failure to establish such connections would "admit a strange and particular bankruptcy, which no rhetoric of tragedy can finally hide."

Reading

Booth, Steven 1983: *King Lear, Macbeth, Indefinition and Tragedy.*
Brereton, Geoffrey 1968: *Principles of Tragedy.*
Cavell, Stanley 1987: *Disowning Knowledge in Six Plays of Shakespeare.*
Draper, R.P. 1980: *Tragedy: Developments in Criticism.*
Kaufmann, Walter 1968: *Tragedy and Philosophy.*
Krieger, Murray 1973: *The Tragic Vision.*
Nietzsche, Friedrich 1967: *The Birth of Tragedy.*
Nussbaum, Martha C. 1968: *The Fragility of Goodness: Luck and Ethics in Greek Tragedy and Philosophy.*
Poole, Adrian 1987: *Tragedy: Shakespeare and the Greek Example.*
Sewall, Richard B. 1980: *The Vision of Tragedy.*
Williams, Raymond 1966: *Modern Tragedy.*

HAROLD SCHWEIZER

transcendental philosophy Transcendental philosophy is characterized by the attempt to ground the possibility of certainty in a conception of the human being as a detached knower or agent, and by the related commitment to the primacy of scientific knowledge over other modes of knowing and relating to the world. As such, transcendental philosophy is a foundationalist project committed to characterizing and vindicating precisely the conception of the human SUBJECT which is criticized by POSTMODERNISM. Transcendental philosophy is widely acknowledged to have been initiated and most significantly influenced by KANT. He was the first thinker to maintain a rigorous distinction between "transcendent" and "transcendental," where the former term signifies that which lies beyond the scope of human thought and experience, and the latter term refers to those most fundamental and unchanging characteristics of human subjectivity which serve as "the conditions for the possibility" of coherent experience generally and scientific knowledge in particular. In Christian medieval thought, God had been conceived as the transcendent; Kant's turn to the transcendental conditions for the possibility of coherent human experience and certain knowledge brings with it a rejection of the idea, advanced by the likes of Aquinas and Descartes, that God's existence could be demonstrated cognitively in addition to being an article of faith. For Kant, what had previously been conceived as the transcendent cannot be known but at best can be thought; the prospects for certain knowledge are limited to mathematics and nature as experienced concretely. In developing his conception of human subjectivity in *The Critique of Reason* (1781/7), Kant thought that he had exhibited the timeless, ahistorical, transcultural, and essentially incorporeal features of human experience which make absolutely certain knowledge possible; and he thought that the human subject's ability both to establish scientific knowledge and think beyond the limits of such knowledge made it possible for the subject to establish ethical commitments and aesthetic judgments which, while not purely objective, are necessitated by the nature of thought and hence are neither arbitrary nor historically relative.

Almost invariably, subsequent work in transcendental philosophy explicitly acknowledges its debt to Kant, indeed to such an extent that it would be difficult to separate the spirit of Kant's work from any philosophical endeavor that falls under the rubric of "transcendental philosophy." Transcendental philosophy after Kant has been concerned with precisely those tasks which Kant set for himself:

the refutation of skepticism regarding the existence of the external word and other minds, as well as the vindication of objective scientific knowledge.

In the twentieth century no thinker has done more in the service of these aims than the German philosopher Edmund Husserl. With his emphasis on phenomenological, transcendental, and eidetic reductions as the necessary methodological steps towards the disclosure of the transcendental domain, Husserl seeks to vindicate the Western scientific project by establishing it upon the foundation of the human knower conceived as the transcendental ego; in making this turn to the transcendental ego, Husserl places intentional acts, with their act–noema structure, at the methodological core of all scientific investigation.

More recent work in transcendental philosophy has devoted itself primarily to an examination of the nature and possibility of transcendental arguments. Transcendental arguments are arguments which seek to establish the necessary conditions for the possibility of something being the case and for the possibility of saying truly that something is the case. The emphasis which has been placed on conceptual schemes in this work on transcendental arguments has led some contemporary thinkers into a debate concerning the very possibility of alternative conceptual frameworks. The argument in favor of alternative conceptual frameworks maintains that whatever concepts may be fundamental to our ability to know ourselves and the world, there are necessarily other, alternative, conceptual frameworks which could render experience coherent. Kant believed that the subject invariably operates with fixed forms of space and time and with a set of 12 specific concepts or "categories" in establishing knowledge; for example, he believed that Euclidean geometry exhibits rigorous certainty precisely because it describes the form of our necessary experience of spatiality or "outer sense," and he similarly believed that arithmetic is certain because it describes the form of our internal time consciousness or "inner sense." The argument for alternative conceptual frameworks rejects this commitment to a rigid and unchanging set of forms of experience, and it leaves open the possibility that the conceptual schemes we employ are subject to variation. In particular, developments in mathematics (such as non-Euclidean geometries) and physics (discoveries regarding the heterogeneity of space and of time) have led to a radicalization of Kant's own "Copernican revolution," so that arithmetic and

Euclidean geometry have come to be accepted as idealized distortions of actual (and possible) human experience. This reflection on the features of human experience which contribute to our vision of what is real has led a variety of contemporary thinkers to include the particularity of cultural perspective, as well as the influence of language and the BODY, among the "conditions for possibility" which underlie coherent experience and knowledge claims. While thinkers like Thomas KUHN remain open to the possibility of incommensurable ways of experiencing the world, thinkers such as Donald DAVIDSON and Richard RORTY have sought to argue that the notion of alternative conceptual frameworks is essentially incoherent, generally on the grounds that the possibility of such alternative schemes would entail the impossibility of those schemes determining the content of our experience.

Reading

Davidson, Donald 1974 (*1984*): "On the very idea of a conceptual scheme."
Genova, A.C. 1984: "Good transcendental arguments."
Kant, Immanuel 1781/7 (*1929*): *Critique of Pure Reason*.
Körner, Stephan 1967: "The impossibility of transcendental deductions."
Mohanty, J.N. 1985: *The Possibility of Transcendental Philosophy*.
Rorty, Richard 1972 (*1982*): "The world well lost."
Strawson, P.F. 1959: *Individuals: An Essay in Descriptive Metaphysics*.
Stroud, Barry 1968: "Transcendental arguments."

GARY STEINER

transference (counter) In psychoanalytic theory, transference refers to the actualization of unconscious wishes or prototypes, particularly within the analytic situation (Laplanche and Pontalis, 1967, p. 455). Infantile prototypes, memories, or desires are transferred or projected on to the analyst, and are experienced with a feeling of great immediacy. The process usually entails the identification of the analyst with an important figure from childhood. The term is also sometimes used more generally to refer to all aspects of the patient's relationship with the analyst. Countertransference describes the analyst's unconscious reaction to the analysand, and especially to his or her transference.

Initially, FREUD took the view that transference was a form of displacement of effect or emotional charges on to the person of the analyst, and that it was to be analyzed and treated like any other symptom. Tranferences were new editions or facsimiles of the impulses and fantasies aroused in analysis (Freud, 1905, p. 116). The material appearing in the transference was repetitive, tended to block the emergence of new associations, and could be seen as a form of resistance. Indeed, Freud held (1905) that the inconclusive analysis of the patient known as "Dora" was a direct result of his failure to analyze the transference. In later papers, Freud still refers to transference as an obstacle to analysis, but also comes to recognize that transference manifestations are the only thing that makes possible the actualization of repressed or forgotten emotions (Freud, 1912).

LACAN initially (1951) describes transference in terms of a quasi-HEGELian dialectic of identifications; he later (1977) relates it to the fantasy – found in both the analytic and the pedagogic situation – of a "subject presumed to know."

Reading

Freud, Sigmund 1905b: "Fragment of an analysis of a case of hysteria."
——1912: "The dynamics of the transference."
Lacan, Jacques 1951: "Intervention on transference."
——1977: *The Four Fundamental Concepts of Psychoanalysis.*
Laplanche, J., and Pontalis, J.-B. 1967: *The Language of Psychoanalysis.*

DAVID MACEY

transformation A grammatical rule which changes one sentence into another: for example, the question transformation changes "Ruby can operate an electric drill" into "Can Ruby operate an electric drill?"

In GENERATIVE GRAMMAR transformations operate on abstract grammatical structures. So the question transformation changes the structure (noun phrase – auxiliary verb – verb phrase) into (auxiliary verb – noun phrase – verb phrase).

Transformations were an important innovation in early generative grammar, so much so that the theoretical framework as a whole was sometimes called "transformational grammar." In later work transformations became less central.

See also CHOMSKY, NOAM; GENERATIVE GRAMMAR; HARRIS, ZELLIG.

Reading

Radford, A. 1988: *Transformational Grammar.*
Salkie, R. 1990: *The Chomsky Update: Linguistics and Politics.*

RAPHAEL SALKIE

translation studies A term in use since the early 1970s to describe the study of the processes of translation beyond the purely linguistic. Some scholars maintain that translation studies is now a discipline in its own right, and the proliferation of books, journals, conferences, international associations, degree programs, and chairs appears to confirm that view. Translation studies is closely related to intercultural studies, since the object of study is to examine systematically the processes of transfer of TEXTS across cultural boundaries, and the resulting implications for both source and target cultural SYSTEMS.

Current work in translation studies evolved largely as a reaction against (i) the marginalization of translation in literary studies; (ii) the decontextualized approach of much work on translation within linguistics. Its development has also been assisted by growing recognition of the significance of translation as a factor for cultural change, and the role played by translations in CANON formation and in the evolution of literary genres.

The move toward translation studies as distinct from the long history of pragmatic statements on the nature and difficulties of translating, from the Romans onwards, can be traced to developments in computer translation techniques in the period immediately after the 1939–45 war and to the work of Eugene Nida, who endeavored to introduce scientific analysis into the translation of the Bible. The key issues emerging from these forms of translation were definitions of untranslatability and the problematization of the nature of equivalence between languages. J. Catford (1965) tried to distinguish between linguistic and cultural untranslatability, arguing that linguistic untranslatability is due to differences of lexicon and syntax between source and target languages, while cultural untranslatability is due to the absence in the receiving CULTURE of a relevant situational feature in the source culture. Nida (1960; 1964) distinguished between two types of equivalence, formal and dynamic. He proposed formal equivalence as focusing on the form and content of a text, in contrast to dynamic equivalence, which focused on equivalent effect between receivers in source and target cultures. Such distinctions offered an alternative perspective on the traditional distinction made by translators following Cicero and St Jerome between word for word and sense for sense translation, open to a wide range of interpretations. By the early 1970s the debate on the nature of equivalence was extensive, but was superseded by a new approach that took the notion of equivalent effect much further, with emphasis directed away from the source and toward the receiving culture.

That approach was polysystems theory, propounded by Evan-Zohar (1976; 1978) and Toury (1978; 1980) in Tel-Aviv and taken up by a group of scholars working in the Netherlands and Belgium (Holmes, Lambert, Lefevere, Van den Broek, and Van Leuven). Polysystems theory linked translation directly to cultural history by focusing on the reception of the text in the target cultural system. It also offered a model for describing and measuring the impact of translated texts on the target culture, giving rise to what has become a major branch of translation studies, the history of translation in theory and practice.

Although deriving from a structuralist model, polysystems theory parallels developments in reception theory and DECONSTRUCTION. Translation studies from the 1980s onwards has seen a move toward greater integration of trends in literary theory, CULTURAL STUDIES, and linguistics. The so-called Manipulation Group (Hermans, Bassnett, Lambert, and Lefevere) has stressed the ideological implications of translation, looking at the role played by cultural politics in determining not only which texts are translated in a given literary system, but also why and how they are translated. In the United States, the translation workshop approach developed in Iowa has moved closer to the historical research into translation practice going on in institutions like SUNY, Binghamton, and Amherst, Massachussetts. In Germany, the Göttingen school has begun systematically to examine the history of translated literary texts between German and English, paying special attention to the role played by editors and compilers of anthologies. Outside Europe, translation studies is increasingly linked to developments in postcolonial theory, where the old-style dominance of the source text or "original" is called into question. The Brazilian "cannibalistic" school of translation studies, led by the de Campos brothers, exemplifies this new approach, which studies the question of the reappropriation of the original by a new, liberated culture with metaphors of cannibalism and diabolical transformation.

The range of developments in the broad field of translation studies now includes: a growing number of philosophical studies deconstructing the concept of the original and the problems of meaning, interpretation, and relevance (Derrida, 1985 (in Graham, 1985); Benjamin, 1989; Gutt, 1990); translation and DISCOURSE analysis (Blum-Kulka, 1981; Snell-Hornby, 1988; Hatim and Mason, 1990; Baker, 1992); translation as intercultural transfer, a highly charged activity that throws into question assumptions about universals, cultural individuality, and hierarchies of literary development (Kittel, 1990; Frank, 1991; Venuti, 1992). As the subject increases in importance, there has been a notable increase in textbooks on the teaching of translation, and further work on translation and interpreting, translation and bilingualism, translation and psychology, all of which bring translation studies closer to the pragmatics of teaching and practicing translation.

A major development in translation studies from the mid-1980s is work on issues of GENDER and translation. Of particular significance is the Canadian school (Brisset, Brossard, Godard, de Lotbinière-Harwood, and Simon) which uses feminist theory to investigate the inbetweenness of translation, rejecting bipolarity between source and target texts, parallel to the rejection of a BINARY OPPOSITIONal model of gender differentiation.

Translation studies as a field of study is distinct from practical training programs for translators. It can be seen as a branch of literary and cultural history, which examines the factors of textual transfer and compares the reception of texts in both source and target cultures. The pattern of work from the mid-1970s has been a shift away from FORMALISM toward an emphasis on ideology and the role played by translators in shaping individual literary systems.

Reading

Bassnett, Susan 1991: *Translation Studies*.

Bassnett, Susan, and Lefevere, André 1990: *Translation, History and Culture*.

Benjamin, Andrew 1989: *Translation and the Nature of Philosophy*.

Biguenet, John, and Schulte, Rainer, eds 1989: *The Craft of Translation*.

Catford, J.C. 1965: *A Linguistic Theory of Translation*.

Delisle, Jean 1988: *Translation: An Interpretive Approach*.

Evan-Zohar, Itamar 1978: *Papers in Historical Poetics*.

Gentzler, Edwin 1993: *Contemporary Translation Theories*.

Graham, J.F. 1985: *Difference and Translation*.

Hatim, Basil, and Mason, Ian 1990: *Discourse and Translation*.

Hermans, Theo, ed. 1985: *The Manipulation of Literature*.

Holmes, James, ed. 1970: *The Nature of Translation: Essays on the Theory and Practice of Literary Translation*.

——1988: *Translated! Papers on Literary Translation and Translation Studies*.

House, J. and Blum-Kulka, S., eds 1986: *Interlingual and Intercultural Communication: Discourse and Cognition in Translation and Second Language Acquisition Studies.*

Kittel, Harold, and Frank, Armin Paul 1991: *Interculturality and the Historical Study of Literary Translation.*

Lefevere, André 1992: *Translation, Rewriting and the Manipulation of Literary Fame.*

Nida, Eugene 1964: *Towards a Science of Translating.*

Nida, Eugene, and Taber, E. 1969: *The Theory and Practice of Translating.*

Snell-Hornby, Mary 1988: *Translation Studies: An Integrated Approach.*

Toury, Gideon 1980: *In Search of a Theory of Translation.*

Van Leuven-Zwart, Kitty, and Naaijkens, Tom, eds 1991: *Translation Studies: The State of the Art.*

Venuti, Lawrence 1992: *Rethinking Translation: Discourse, Subjectivity, Ideology.*

SUSAN BASSNETT

Trilling, Lionel (1905–75) American literary critic and essayist. A Columbia professor linked to the *Partisan Review* group of "New York intellectuals," he expressed the cultural anxieties of a rational LIBERALISM under threat from modern irrationalisms, seeking reasonable compromises between self and society. Like LEAVIS, but far less dogmatically, he engaged in MORAL CRITICISM and placed LITERARY CRITICISM at the center of liberal CULTURE. His critical studies of ARNOLD and Forster admire their flexibly tolerant attitudes. His essays, notably in *The Liberal Imagination* (1950), explore the relationships between literature, morality, and politics; some also consider subtly the cultural implications of FREUD's work.

Reading

Boyers, Robert 1977: *Lionel Trilling: Negative Capability and the Wisdom of Avoidance.*

Chace, William M. 1980: *Lionel Trilling: Criticism and Politics.*

CHRIS BALDICK

trope   A term in the art of rhetoric usually defined as an instance of the use of words to mean something other than what they normally mean. Although this definition is firmly established in the Western rhetorical tradition that descends from Quintillian and Cicero, it is now common to observe that such a definition uncritically assumes that there is a normal use of words that can be distinguished from the figurative or the tropological. An inescapable historical problem in understanding tropes is that, particularly during the European Renaissance, the art of rhetoric as a practical field of study for politicians, lawyers, and poets developed rapidly and usually independently from critical reflection on the nature of language. By the sixteenth century the general availability of printed books made possible a thriving market for rhetorical handbooks, of which Erasmus's *De copia* (1521) is justly the most famous. As with all dictionaries and encyclopedias, however, these handbooks, by defining and exemplifying rhetorical tropes, tended to rigidify them and to create the mistaken view that normal language is something other than tropological. Furthermore, they tended to perpetuate Quintillian's favoring of METAPHOR over METONYMY and a general Renaissance preference for imagery over other figures. In his brilliant examination of the consequences of insufficient reflection on these assumptions, DERRIDA (1982, pp. 255–6) turns to the nineteenth-century text by Pierre Fontanier, *Les Figures du discours* (1821), which epitomizes the ubiquitous "metaphorical lexis" in philosophy, to the effect that word and idea, thought and speech are necessarily divided. Were this true, no language could be unmetaphorical.

Some of the more important tropes that appear in classical and Renaissance rhetorics are briefly defined below by quotation from classical or Renaissance rhetoricians. However, when contemporary theorists, such as BLOOM, Derrida, de MAN, and Miller use these terms, they often redefine them on the basis of critical reflection on their usual definitions.

Allegory: "A fictional narration to present the truth by presenting images of the truth." (Scaliger: Sonnino, p. 98)

Antiphrasis: "For single words when one by one we mean its opposite." (Susenbrotus: Sonnino, p. 131)

Catachresis: "The practice of adapting the nearest available term to describe something for which no proper term exists. . . . Therefore it differs from a metaphor which changes the proper term into another one." (Susenbrotus: Sonnino, p. 16)

Hyperbole: "An elegant straining of the truth which may be employed either for exaggeration or attenuation. . . . We may say more than the actual facts." (Quintillian: Sonnino, p. 68)

Irony: "We understand something the

Metaphor: opposite of what is actually said."
(Quintillian: Sonnino, p. 105)
"The commonest and by far the most beautiful of tropes. . . . A noun or verb is transferred from the place to which it properly belongs to another where there is no literal term or the transferred is better than the literal." (Quintillian: Sonnino, pp. 181–2)

Metonymy: "A noun is substituted for a noun in such a way that we substitute the cause of the thing . . . for the thing itself. . . . We do this in several ways, substituting the container for the thing contained. . . . , an author for his work, . . . the sign for the thing signified." (Susenbrotus: Sonnino, pp. 184–5)

Prosopopoeia: "[We] attribute any human quality, as reason or speech, to dumb creatures or other insensible things and do study to give them a human person . . . by way of fiction." (Puttenham: Sonnino, p. 55)

Synecdoche: "When we understand one thing for another . . . the whole for the part, . . . the species for the genus." (Erasmus: Sonnino, p. 172)

Several of these definitions seem about to undermine the linguistic assumptions on which they rest.

Reading
Bloom, Harold 1973: *The Anxiety of Influence: A Theory of Poetry.*
De Man, Paul 1971a: *Blindness and Insight: Essays in the Rhetoric of Contemporary Criticism.*
Derrida, Jacques 1982a: "White mythology: metaphor in the text of philosophy."
Miller, J. Hillis 1991: *Hawthorne and History: Defacing It.*
Sonnino, Lee A. 1968: *A Handbook to Sixteenth-Century Rhetoric.*

MICHAEL PAYNE

Tugendhat, Ernst (1930–) German philosopher; professor at the Freie Universität in Berlin. In his landmark work, *The Concept of Truth in Husserl and Heidegger* (1970), Tugendhat contrasts Husserl's intentionality based conception of truth with the senses of truth which HEIDEGGER develops before and after his "turning," and he demonstrates the fundamentally decisionistic (and hence nihilistic) character of truth in Heidegger's *Being and Time*. In his other major work, Tugendhat develops a theory of rationality which rejects "object-centered" philosophies of language in favor of an analysis of meaning in terms of linguistic usage; as part of this theory he argues for a version of a consensus theory of truth, according to which the decisions made by the most experienced members of the relevant community serve as the proper measure for moral justification.

Reading
Tugendhat, Ernst 1970: *Der Wahrheitsbegriff bei Husserl und Heidegger.*
—— 1976 (*1982*): *Traditional and Analytic Philosophy.*
—— 1979 (*1986*): *Self-consciousness and Self-determination.*
GARY STEINER

Tynyanov, Yury (1894–1943) Russian literary scholar and novelist, one of the leading representatives of RUSSIAN FORMALISM. Tynyanov's critical works can be divided into those dealing with the historical aspects of language and literature and those dealing with literary theory. In his historical works, collected later into his book of essays *Archaists and Innovators* (1929), the center of Tynyanov's attention was the conflict between various artistic trends for what he called "a new vision." In his theoretical works, Tynyanov continued Potebnya's studies of the distinction between poetic language and the language of prose (*Problems of Poetic Language*, 1924). Tynyanov's contribution to the studies of poetic language consisted of the discovery of the "dynamism" of poetic language which anticipated the views of some Marxist theorists like G. LUCÁCS, on the one hand, and first Czech and later French and American structuralists on the other.
See also RUSSIAN FORMALISM; SYSTEM.

Reading
Eagle, Herbert 1981: "Verse as semiotic system: Tynjanov, Jakobson, Mukarovsky, Lotman extended."
Hammarberg, Gitta 1984: "A reinterpretation of Tynyanov and Jakobson on prose (with some thoughts on the Bakhtin and Lotman connection). In honor of Ladislav Matejko."
Tynyanov, Yu. 1981: *The Problems of Verse Language.*
SLAVA I. YASTREMSKI

U

uncanny, the   FREUD's essay on "The uncanny" (1919) is an exploration of what he terms a relatively neglected province of the AESTHETIC, and concentrates upon works of ART that provoke feelings of unease, dread, or horror. Freud explores the semantics and etymology of the German terms *unheimlich* ("uncanny") and *heimlich* ("homely," "familiar") and reaches the conclusion that the uncanny relates to a domain in which the apparent antonyms are actually synonymous and refer to an experience which is at once uncanny and familiar. The "uncanny familiar" is a fairly obvious expression of ambivalence, but Freud is also influenced here by his reading of the philologist Karl Abel's theories about the antithetical meaning of primal words and the thesis that dreams and ancient languages often have only a single word to describe two contraries (Freud, 1910a). The AMBIGUITY of the *heimlich/unheimlich* doublet can thus be related on a philological basis to the survival in the UNCONSCIOUS of primitive elements and to the thesis that the uncanny is an instance of the animistic view of the universe. In that sense, the uncanny represents the emergence of something which was once familiar (animism) and which has been repressed and alienated from the mind.

Freud's second approach centers on a thematic reading of Hoffman's stories "The sandman" and "The Devil's elixir." It is also a highly selective reading. Freud concentrates on elements which can be related to fear of castration (severed limbs, the children's eyes which the sandman magically removes and carries off to feed his children). The uncanny can now be associated with a male neurotic claim that there is something uncanny about the female genitals, a theme also explored in the brief paper on Medusa's head (Freud, 1922). That *unheimlich* place is of course the entrance to the original home (*Heim*) of all human beings. It was once a familiar place, and the prefix *un* is an index of its repression.

Despite its brevity, "The uncanny" continues to exert a considerable fascination for writers exploring the relationship between PSYCHOANALYSIS and literature (Kofman, 1974), as well as feminist writers, many of whom are critical of the selectivity of Freud's reading. Thus CIXOUS (1976a) notes that Freud dismisses as irrelevant the figure of the doll which becomes animated in Hoffman's tale; she in contrast argues, in terms similar to those used by Todorov (1970) in his discussion of the fantastic, that it is precisely the blurring of the animate/inanimate that produces the frisson of the uncanny. KRISTEVA (1980) exploits Freud's essay to construct her own notion of the abject, which describes the experience of a primal fear of the SUBJECT's abolition within the maternal BODY, and argues that this fear predates castration anxiety.

Reading
Cixous, Hélène 1976a: "Fiction and its phantoms: a reading of Freud's *Das Unheimliche*."
Freud, Sigmund 1910a: "The antithetical meaning of primal words."
——1919: "The uncanny."
——1922: "Medusa's Head."
Kofman, Sarah 1974: *Freud and Fiction*.
Kristeva, Julia 1980a (*1982*): *Powers of Horror*.
Todorov, Tzvetan 1970: *The Fantastic: A Structural Approach to a Literary Genre*.

DAVID MACEY

unconscious, collective   *See* COLLECTIVE UNCONSCIOUS

unconscious, the   Although the notion of unconscious thoughts or impulses has a long history in both philosophy and psychology (see Ellenberger, 1970), the modern concept of the unconscious derives from the theory and practice of PSYCHOANALYSIS, as defined by FREUD and his followers. A distinction should be made between Freudian usage and the notion of a collective unconscious, as elaborated by JUNG.

Freud uses both the adjective "unconscious," which describes phenomena that are not within the field of consciousness at any given moment, and the noun "the unconscious." The latter term is used in a topographical sense to refer to one of the three SYSTEMS that constitute the psychical apparatus, the others being the preconscious and conscious systems. After the introduction, from 1920 onwards (see in particular Freud, 1923a), of the second or so-called structural topography of id, ego, and superego, Freud tends to revert to the adjectival usage, though the id does display many of the characteristics previously ascribed to the unconscious. The term "id" (German *Es*) is borrowed from Groddeck (1923), a psychiatrist close to the Viennese psychonalytic milieu; Groddeck himself claims to have taken the term from NIETZSCHE.

The topographical concept of a systemic unconscious is operative in Freud's earliest works and especially in his great study of dreams (Freud, 1900), but it is in a metapsychological paper of 1915 that he provides the clearest description of what is to be understood by the unconscious (Freud, 1915). The unconscious is a necessary concept because it alone can explain a number of "gaps" in conscious life; these include PARAPRAXES such as slips of the tongue, obsessions, and symptoms, and of course dreams, "the royal road" to the discovery of the unconscious. Phenomena such as posthypnotic suggestion and the practice of psychoanalysis itself provide further evidence for its existence. On the basis of these and related phenomena, Freud posits the existence of unconscious mental processes.

The content of the unconscious consists of elements which are unacceptable to the conscious mind, and which have been censored or repressed. The unconscious also contains survivals of the infantile residues of early stages of development; it is often described as being primitive or archaic and Freud argues that is in part a phylogenetic inheritance which contains elements of humanity's earliest experiences. That inheritance is also said to contain primal fantasies or scenes (including observation of parental sexual intercourse, castration, and seduction), which together form an unconscious nucleus constituted from a hypothetical process of primal repression. More importantly, the content of the unconscious consists of representatives or images of the basic instincts or drives (sexual drives and instincts of self-preservation; after the turning point of 1920, a death drive is also introduced and described as a desire to return

to an inanimate state). The drives themselves, which exist at the interface between the psychic and thesomatic, can never become an object of consciousness, and it follows that the unconscious is known only through its manifestations. Its primary manifestations are mainly dreams, although symptoms, fantasies, and obsessions are also indications of its existence.

The unconscious SYSTEM is characterized by a number of special features. Its instinctual representations or wishful impulses do not acknowledge the existence of negation or the principle of non-contradiction. They are dominated by the primary processes of CONDENSATION/DISPLACEMENT and are timeless. Unlike the mechanisms of the conscious-preconscious system, they take no account of external reality, which is replaced with internal reality. The system is further characterized by the free circulation of cathexis, or of the quantities of psychic energy attached to ideas and representations. Unconscious processes are subject to the pleasure principle; this is the mechanism which seeks to reduce excitation and to restore a degree of equilibrium to the system.

While all psychoanalytic literature can in some sense be regarded as making a contribution to the theory of the unconscious, by far the most extensive reformulation is that proposed by Jacques LACAN. In a famous passage of his "Rome discourse" of 1953, Lacan (1977, p. 50) describes the unconscious as a censored chapter in the history of the subject. It has been censored or occupied by a falsehood. The truth has, however, been written down elsewhere: in "monuments" or, in other words, in the nucleus of a neurosis where the symptom reveals the STRUCTURE of a language; in inscriptions which have to be deciphered, in the documents of childhood memories, in the individual's stock of words and character traits, and in the few traces that have been preserved by the need to connect the distorted chapter to those surrounding it.

Lacan describes the unconscious as being structured like a language on a number of grounds, not least the standard view that psychoanalysis is a talking cure with language as its sole medium. On the one hand, symptoms and unconscious formations like the DREAM-WORK exhibit the same formal properties as rhetorical figures like METAPHOR AND METONYMY, which can be likened to condensation and displacement respectively. On the other hand, the findings of linguistics, and SAUSSURE in particular, reveal structures analogous to those found in the formations of the unconscious. Dream images are accordingly described by Lacan as signifiers.

Although Lacan's reformulation of the concept of the unconscious is persuasive and has been enormously influential, it is not always easy to reconcile it with Freud, for whom language is a phenomenon specific to the consciousness-perception system.

Reading

Ellenberger, Henri F. 1970: *The Discovery of the Unconscious: The History and Development of Dynamic Psychiatry*.
Freud, Sigmund 1900: *The Interpretation of Dreams*.
—— 1915: "The unconscious."
—— 1923a: *The Ego and the Id*.
Groddeck, Georg 1923 (*1935*): *The Book of the Id*.
Lacan, Jacques 1977: *Ecrits: A Selection*.
Leclaire, Serge, and Laplanche, Jean 1966 (*1972*): "The unconscious: a psychoanalytic study.'

DAVID MACEY

unheimlich   *See* UNCANNY, THE

unity, organic   *See* ORGANIC UNITY

urban culture   The processes of worldwide urbanization have consistently stimulated attempts to analyze distinctive cultural features of urban life. They have differed sharply in their focus and method, articulating various stages of urbanization and successive intellectual debates and preoccupations.

An early set of comparisons, often of a strongly moral kind, was drawn between the urban world and that of the countryside. Ruralism became part of an implicit anti-urbanism, as in some early twentieth-century constructions of "Englishness." In sociology, Toennies and others followed the work of many earlier Romantic writers in distinguishing the closeness and community of rural *Gemeinschaft* from the impersonality and ALIENATION of *Gesellschaft*. As cities grew, attracting waves of migration, they exhibited ever more sharply contrasting and varied social worlds, so that broad ideal typical contrasts were replaced by studies of different localities, groups, and SUBCULTURES. Closely focused work typified much of the CHICAGO SCHOOL, the community studies of the 1950s and after, and then the radical action analyses stemming from the 1960s. Carefully descriptive and empirical writing looked at particular life patterns within the inequality and diversity of large conurbations. These were in turn challenged by a larger-scale structural analysis of the workings of capital mobility and the state in the recomposition of cities, as in seminal though contrasting Marxist work by Castells and by Harvey. To the previous research concerns of a subdiscipline of "urban sociology" were added attention to land values, the politics of city government and new urban protest movements, and a heightened interest in uneven development.

Elsewhere BENJAMIN had developed a series of fragmentary, dense, and fascinating exploratory "readings" of urban settings, illuminating such topics as the arcade or the male *flâneur*'s right to stroll and look on the CITY's streets. The city is written by him as a place of contradiction, fantasy, and dream. His work exemplifies the complexity and difficulty of modernism, itself seen by WILLIAMS as made possible in its concerns and forms by emigration to dislocated spaces within the "imperial and capitalist metropolis." In Berman's highly original text, connections were made between various cities and TEXTS and between modernist art, modernization, and MODERNITY. That such accounts may be gender-blind or masculinist has been increasingly emphasized by such feminists as Wilson, who suggests ways in which cities may be positive sites for women and not only places of danger.

Extensive recent changes in capitalist cities have been a major theme in analyses both skeptical and celebratory of POSTMODERNISM. Typical issues have been urban architecture, the heightened emphasis on consumption spaces, SIGNS and spectacle, gentrification, and the working-up of cities as imaginaries in a competition for tourism and business investment. Recent work has also questioned the suitability of cities as convivial living spaces (often with Los Angeles as model or warning), or as coherent entities in a decentered era of accelerated global movement. While the history of thinking about cities has been constantly interrupted by such doubts, urban changes (different political strategies in defense of "places," intraurban conflicts, new lived crossovers and hybridities between groups and cultural forms in city spaces) continue to provoke prolific and cogent work currently developing in various directions not easily reconciled. Urban culture remains almost an impossible object of study, but an extremely interesting one.

Reading

Benjamin, W. 1969: *Charles Baudelaire or the Lyric Poet of High Capitalism*.

Berman, M. 1983: *All That is Solid Melts into Air: The Experience of Modernity.*

Castells, M. 1977: *The Urban Question*.

Harvey, D. 1989: *The Condition of Postmodernity*.

Savage, M., and Warde, A. 1993: *Urban Sociology, Capitalism and Modernity*.

Sennett, R., ed. 1969: *Classic Essays on the Culture of Cities.*

Williams, R. 1973: *The Country and the City*.

Wilson, E. 1991: *The Sphinx in the City*.

Zukin, S. 1995: *The Culture of Cities*.

MICHAEL GREEN

V

value in literature In the present state of the argument it would be rash to attempt a definition of literary value. To do so would entail the bold claim that one had already settled the more general problem of value. These remarks fall roughly under two headings: first, some observations, far from exhaustive, on the ways the problem is now being discussed; and secondly some speculations of a more literary variety, perhaps less arid though probably no less contentious.

The writhing subtleties of axiological debate, once the concern of philosophers, are now proper to literary-critical DISCOURSE. The old assumptions were that some things, some attitudes, some books, were more valuable than others, and that if there were disputes about which were the valuable things, attitudes, books, there was little disposition to argue that such evaluations should be preceded by questions of what philosophical foundations they might depend upon. However, the wall between the SUBJECTS has been at least partly demolished. Some philosophers roam freely across the literary terrain, and some literary critics sound or wish to sound more like philosophers. Many of them even seem to be suffering a certain loss of interest in literature, even of confidence in its existence. They want to know not only what and where it is, but also whether, if it does exist, it has value and of what kind. This worry provides an occasion for discourses of many other sorts than those formerly associated with LITERARY CRITICISM. These deviations or defections or derelictions arise in part from a moral uncertainty about whether what used to be unequivocally and honorifcally called *literature* may be, in its effects, an evil rather than a good thing.

How then can one hope to evaluate it, or confirm former valuations that persisted for so long without satisfactory testing, without considering it in the broader contexts now thought appropriate? And so the philosophical issue of value has of late become one of the preoccupations of literary theorists. Most agree that the subject is difficult, and nobody has produced completely persuasive answers to the questions it now seems necessary to put.

Value, in the literary-critical world, used to be either taken for granted or considered off limits in so far as the supposedly value-free discourse of the sciences was what, for the sake of academic respectability if for no better reason, literary study should be seen to aspire to. Such were the assumptions of the old-style philology, and more recently of early STRUCTURALISM. However, there was another reason: it used to be assumed that what could be said in analyzing a "verbal icon" was itself a tacit demonstration of its positive value, so that in practice brute enquiries about the nature of that value, and whom it counted as such, were simply not made. So Barbara Herrnstein Smith, in the most impressive of modern philosophico-literary critical treatises on the subject, can speak of the long exile of the topic of value from American criticism, especially since Northrop FRYE's powerful polemical Introduction to his *Anatomy of Criticism* (1957), and suggest that it was not recalled till much later. Perhaps that somewhat overstates the case, not only because Yvor Winters, like F.R. LEAVIS in England, was always confident of, if not always constant or wholly persuasive in, his evaluations, and would have regarded it as absurd to question whether the values he found in POETRY were there already or had to be inserted; but also because a great many other people, professional and nonprofessional, some teachers, some mere readers, more simply assumed that there were valuable books, and even that some books were more valuable than others, just as some pictures and some jewels and some cups and saucers and, for that matter, some restaurants and some footballers and some friends were, when it came to the point, more valuable than others.

In the 30-odd years that divided the books of Frye and Smith, there seem to have been few other works which took the question of value seriously. John Ellis, in his *Theory of Literary Criticism* (1974) maintained that value was "centrally part" of the definition of literature, though he shied away from the idea of "aesthetic value:" "It is essential to begin by saying that great works of literature are those that are particularly successful in performing as works of literature, rather than by assuming that they have a quality called aesthetic value, which we must then try to locate" (p. 88). What one seeks, according to Ellis, are the "facts" of the work's structure that relate to performance; this will not help to establish criteria, but descriptive analysis of a work "is the only possible approach to the question of its value. The critic investigates value empirically; he does not determine it, and his investigations have to do with whatever relates to the ability of literary texts to function as literary texts." That remark would be entirely vacuous if its author were not sure he knew what a "literary" TEXT was, and of course Ellis was sure. He explains that literary texts are distinguished from others in that "they are used by society in such a way that the text is not taken as specifically relevant to the immediate context of its origin," whereas "ordinary pieces of language . . . function in the context in which they originate" (p. 44). However, this rule would introduce into the category of literature (which is the way value, according to this view, is asserted) matter that is not usually regarded as literature at all: statutes, for instance. Ellis's criteria for literature are perhaps more persuasively described thus: as weeds are weeds, however diverse their structures and properties, only because we agree to distinguish them by this name from the plants we choose to nurture, so texts are literary if members of the language community agree to call them so, and not if they do not.

Ellis was writing before this agreement began to break down, and professional circles began to dissociate themselves from common linguistic practice, at any rate when being very professional (for the slack colloquial habit of saying that one poem or lecture or whatever is more valuable, "greater," "more profound," etc. than another will persist in unguarded moments). Back in 1974 Ellis knew, or imagined he knew, what it was that literary criticism could properly undertake to work on, and so could proceed to explain how it should do so; but nobody can now be so confident about what is to be described or analyzed, and so evaluated, or how those inquiries are to be conducted.

John Reichert, in *Making Sense of Literature* (1977) took a not very different view of the evaluator's role. "When we say that a work is good in

some respects, and provide the right sort of reasons for our judgment, we are describing the work, and our description may be true or false" (p. 174). It is by means of such descriptions that we make evaluations; and by evaluations we promote understanding, if, presumably, the descriptions are true. Really, for Reichert, evaluating a work is an act identical with that of making sense of it by a new description. The work under consideration may very well have already been highly valued and often interpreted or described, as in a case he considers at length, that of *Huckleberry Finn*. An examination of some of the descriptions accorded this novel allows him to ask a final rhetorical question: "What impels and gives point to criticism's pursuit of ever more refined and true ways of making sense of a novel like *Huckleberry Finn* if not a desire to get its value rightly placed and understood?" (p. 203). Clearly Reichert accepts that the prior esteem in which a work is held is evidence of a value which is somehow already there, if not yet "rightly placed" or described. He also thinks we can progressively improve on existing descriptions of it, so confirming that it is a literary work, as well as reaffirming or reinforcing its value. The value of the book is somehow there in the book, waiting for somebody, or preferably a succession of people, to come and uncover it. The expression "a novel like *Huckleberry Finn*" seems vague and unsteady, but it must mean something like "works which the community agrees to call 'literary' and which it credits with some appropriate value." It is of such works that one can hope for further descriptions, for progressive knowledge and possibly higher and more accurate valuations. The question whether this would be true not only of "a novel like *Huckleberry Finn*" but equally of "a novel like" one of Zane Grey's, which can now be freely posed, did not then present itself to the theorist, even though Reichert's book is not very old. Nevertheless, the assumptions that there is somehow there, in the text, a value to be elicited, and that we can proceed as if the sheep and the goats, the plants and the weeds, were already firmly differentiated, are assumptions now vigorously contested.

No doubt there were other significant treatments of the question in these interim years. Mention of Ellis and Reichert will hint at the change that has come over us: we may call the views of Ellis and Reichert typically modern, as opposed to what are probably thought of as postmodern understandings of the question. The latter variety is represented by Herrnstein Smith's *Contingencies of Value* (1988), originally subtitled *Postaxiological Perspectives in Literary Theory*, which was changed to *Alternative Perspectives*. . . . Smith's main thesis is by now well known: all value is "radically contingent" and "the value of not only any artwork or other object but that of any utterance is also contingent, and aesthetic judgments . . . are no different in this respect from any other type of utterance, including so-called factual or scientific statements." She is clear that value is not a fixed attribute or inherent quality of things but rather "an effect of multiple, continuously changing, and continuously interacting variables, or, to put it another way, the product of the dynamics of a system, specifically an economic system" (p. 30). Fluctuation in the economies of communities and persons explain the wide differences of valuation that occur between communities, persons, and epochs.

It is a matter of importance to this author – and it is probably the most compelling reason for the question of value having been so insistently raised in recent years – that valuations can be manipulated or imposed. It is possible for an institution to perpetuate not only itself but also its valuations, and perhaps it needs to do one to do the other; thus, despite the incursion of various rebels or outsiders, the academic community "produces generation after generation of subjects for whom the objects and texts thus labeled ['as works of art and literature'] do indeed perform the functions thus privileged, thereby ensuring the continuity of mutually defining canonical works, canonical functions; and canonical audiences" (p. 44). And here she refers us to, and endorses, certain French Marxist pronouncements about Literature as an Ideological Form. Smith appears to be persuaded of the truth of Pierre BOURDIEU's thesis: that the legitimation of certain kinds of ART or CULTURE as superior is a means of reinforcing the idea of the natural superiority of the social CLASS that esteems them; and that such condemnations of POPULAR CULTURE as ADORNO's are a "reactionary response" to the "increasing contemporary destratification of cultural arenas and practices" (p. 76). Attempts like those of I.A. RICHARDS and Herbert Gans to show that in one way or another "HIGH" CULTURE is more effective in the provision of gratification than "low" culture; that the difference can somehow be measured; and that people can be educated to achieve the superior gratification, are dismissed. It is true that we can "acculturate" the young,

persuade them that it is a good thing to acquire an understanding of and a taste for Beethoven's quartets, Quattrocento painting, Shakespeare's late tragedies, or wine; however, there is no way of comparing the quantity of such pleasures with the amount of gratification to be gained from listening to Elvis Presley records, or watching television soap operas, and drinking beer out of cans. All value is contingent, and to behave as if it were not so is to exercise over others a power unjustly derived from privilege and status.

Terry EAGLETON has developed similar points in a somewhat different way, feeling a need to demonstrate that the culture of a particular class, dependent as it is on "aesthetic IDEOLOGY" (a concept at present under attack from Marxist and deconstructionist alike) is historically inseparable from bourgeois HEGEMONY; the PARADOX, as he sees it, is that a class that in his view really cares very little about art has nevertheless used it in this fraudulent way. As we have seen, Smith argues, from different premises, that assumptions about value in the arts have similar political implications.

To evaluate Smith's book – its value would in any case be complexly contingent – one would need to say a great deal more about it. The present issue is this matter of the political uses of attributed literary value. Smith at one point – and this is representative of her sympathies – signifies her approval of the views expressed by the Nigerian-born writer Chinweiza in a letter to the *Times Literary Supplement* (*TLS*). Chinweiza said that his purpose was not "to thrust a black face among the local idols of Europe which, to our grave injury, have been bloated into 'universality'" – and he specifies such local idols as Shakespeare, Aristophanes, Dante, Milton, Dostoevsky, Joyce, Pound, Sartre, Eliot, etc. – but "rather . . . to help heave them out of the way . . . by making it clear that we have among our own the equals and betters of these chaps." Smith calls this "genuine evaluative conflict." However, Geoffrey Galt Harpham (*Raritan*, Summer, 1989) points out that when Hume says Milton is better than Ogilvy, or Rorty that Liberalism is better than theocracy, Smith brands them as oppressors. This looks like a direct hit, to which a fashionable cause has exposed the usually more circumspect author.

It may here be relevant to comment on an essay by Susan Stuart on New York and Philadelphia subway graffiti. It is clear that the practitioners and connoisseurs of this art exist outside the limits of that part of society which is interested in, and, as some say, supported by, "high" art. That members of the higher culture have appropriated graffiti and sold them in galleries is not the point; that kind of appropriation has been going on for a long time. More interesting are the activities of those who remain within the culture of graffiti, to whom the WRITING of graffiti is an art that not only calls for some daring and self-assertion in the practitioner, but also has its mysteries, on which learned studies might be, indeed have been, written. Outside the graffiti community itself the "aesthetic" product of its members is normally valued at zero, treated indeed as mere dirt, which municipalities spend millions of dollars cleaning up. Inside it is differentiated into schools and methods, provided with its own peculiar art-historical terminology. By the mere fact of its existence on the blank expensive surfaces of the city, it constitutes a critique of the world of property which cultivates, possesses, and values forms of art in which the graffiti community, though violently critical of that overbearing world, are no more interested than Chinweiza is in Sartre or Aristophanes.

We can make certain inferences from Smith's attitude to Chinweiza's preferences, and from the existence of an organized SUBCULTURE of graffiti. First, it is surely intelligible and acceptable that there should coexist cultures of opposition, each with its own CANON and its own kind of commentary. I take this to be a firm, not a soppy, liberal attitude, and find support, though at a remove, in some remarks of Bernard WILLIAMS on the claim of another philosopher that "a properly untendentious description of the world would not mention any values, that our values are in some sense imposed or projected on to our surroundings." "That discovery," says Williams, "if that is what it is, can be met with despair, as can the loss of a teleologically significant world. But it can also be seen as a liberation, and a radical form of freedom may be found in the fact that we cannot be forced by the world to accept one set of values rather than another" (Williams, 1985, p. 128).

Much depends, of course, on that parenthetical "if that is what it is," and also on whether it is true that "we cannot be forced." Even so, those who, like the friend cited by Williams's friend, find that they can "survive on a diet of masterpieces," need complain of no shortage of food, and if others prefer not to call them masterpieces, or would rather reserve that kind of praise for their own kind of thing, pop songs or horror movies or Zane Grey novels, that should be all right with those who enjoy a diet of masterpieces and equally all right with the fans of Zane Grey. Each party, it may be said, imposes or projects different values on the world. There are rock classics and horror movie classics, also an ample diet and amply financed, for those who choose it.

However, that way of talking fails to answer the charge that the diet of masterpieces is provided by a kitchen that dispenses oppression to others, as when the police would like to get their hands on the graffiti writers. More generally, the educational system which, at higher levels, serves or has served the masterpiece lovers rather than the connoisseurs of graffiti, is weighted against the projections of the less powerful – blacks, women, the young – to whom our way of doing things can look like colonial exploitation. There, for instance, are the young, already with their own culture of television and folk rock and comic books, an innocent tribe to which institutionalized elders bring their pseudoreligions, their values, their canonical books, which are alien and possibly even corrupting; it is as if, in exploiting them, the powerful also gave them their intellectual and aesthetic diseases, harmless to the donors, perhaps fatal to them. It is her sympathy with this kind of argument that induces Smith to categorize Chinweiza's remark as genuine evaluative conflict and Hume's as illicit and oppressive. If she had given unbiased thought to Chinweiza she might have noticed that his attitude mirrors the very attitudes of which she complains, in omitting serious comment on what is rejected, and in attempting to set up a rival canonical HEGEMONY.

The graffiti writers are a little different, presumably having formed no intention to take over politically; but even their kind of protest seems to require a variety of institutional support – the continuance of their art has called for and gained the support of their own organized scholarship and commentary. And of course their institution and their culture are parasitic upon the larger apparatus in which they exist by defacing. Literary revolutionaries are less willing to accept that their kind of thing can coexist with the official culture; like Chinweiza, they want to heave white male writers out of their way, and seek to promote a black canon, a feminist canon, anyway a new canon, proclaiming quite openly the need to overthrow the institutional canons and replace them with something else they find more congenial politically. The project may seem extravagant and implausible, but then revolutionary programs tend to look like that. The project is certainly political, for it is to take over the institution, the institution being regarded as an important instrument of social and political power. The new regime will still have a canon because the old one is held to have been successfully authoritarian and therefore a good model. The new canon will be supported by methods based on those which, as it was argued, made the old one oppressive. Nor can it be seriously maintained that absolutely no canonical directives would be issued, for every reading list is a canon of sorts.

Generally speaking, such arguments make literary value entirely contingent on the political preferences of the evaluator. A subtler argument, favored by some Marxists, maintains that the value of a particular text must be sought in the relationship between that text and its concealed ideological context – that is, in the *non dit* and its relation to what it actually said. However, that argument rests on the assumption that what is "not said" must invariably be ideological. This is an assumption that readers of poetry in any language may wish to dispute. To accept it is to accept that literary value resides in a "political UNCONSCIOUS" which the ingenious analytical labors of the commentator can penetrate; he or she will then discourse on the transactions between this unconscious and the conscious text. This gives ideology its proper importance, but it does not seem greatly to clarify the issue of value. We learn that value is dynamic, transactional, contingent, and must be sought by analysis of a more subtle and extensive sort than was envisaged by, say, Ellis, with his value-discovering descriptions. It reinforces the notion that the problem cannot properly be stated in such exclusively literary terms, terms which ignore its full dimension. It begs the question by assuming a priori, in what can only be a demonstration of false consciousness, the existence of autonomous literary value.

Victims of their own unconscious ideologies, literary persons may nevertheless want to approach the issue of value in terms not prescribed by those who pity or despise them. They might recall what may be described as an axiological *locus classicus* in one of their canonical texts, Shakspeare's *Troilus and Cressida* (ll.ii). The scene in a way balances one in the previous act, when the Greek commanders had a long and useless debate about why, after seven years of war, they had achieved none of their aims. They attributed this failure to a dereliction from the values of a transcendentally ordained hierarchical system. Now we hear the Trojan leaders considering whether they should go on with a war that they too are finding unsatisfactory and costly. The Greeks have proposed a straight deal: hand Helen over and there will be no further demands; the war can stop. Priam asks Hector for his views, and Hector gives it as his opinion that the Greek terms should be accepted. The war has already cost a deal of blood; the Trojans have lost a tenth of their men, all "to guard a thing not ours nor worth to us . . . the value of one [life]." He can see no merit "in that reason which denies/The yielding of her up." Troilus replies:

> Fie, fie, my brother!
> Weigh you the worth and honour of a king
> So great as our dread father's in a scale
> Of common ounces?

It is goldsmith's talk, and it is not about weighing Helen's worth, but Priam's – that is, Priam's honor. Another brother, the priest Helenus, replies that their father surely ought to be reasonable, and not like Troilus. Troilus answers this with contempt: it is reasonable, he points out, to run away from danger, reason is the enemy of honor, to be reasonable in this matter, as in war, is to be dishonored. But Hector brings the discussion back to the simple issue of economic value: "Brother, she is not worth what she doth cost/ The keeping." Whereupon Troilus introduces more abstract axiological considerations. "What is aught but as 'tis valued?" he asks, and Hector answers:

> But value dwells not in particular will;
> It holds his estimate and dignity
> As well wherein 'tis precious of itself
> As in the prizer. 'Tis mad idolatry
> To make the service greater than the god;
> And the will dotes that is attributive
> To what infectiously itself affects,
> Without some image of the affected merit.

In other words, there is intrinsic value (in Helen's case very small) as well as the value imparted to an object by a "prizer." The will that supposes its own desire for an object to be the sole source of its value, believing that this desire is not itself influenced by a preunderstanding of the inherent merit of the thing desired, is simply narcissistic stupidity. Troilus answers this argument of Hector's with a parable: if today he were to marry a wife – a choice guided by his will (a word at this time often almost synonymous with "desire") – he could not honorably dispose of her if later his will should come to "distaste what it elected." The Trojans gained the incomparable Helen in exchange for "an old aunt."

Why keep we her? The Grecians keep our aunt.
Is she worth keeping? Why, she is a pearl,
Whose price hath launch'd above a thousand ships
And turn'd crown'd kings to merchants.
If you'll avouch 'twas wisdom Paris went –
As you must needs, for you all cried "go, go" –
If you'll confess he brought home worthy prize –
As you must needs, for you all clapp'd your hands,
And cried "Inestimable!" – why do you now
The issue of your proper wisdoms rate,
And do a deed that never fortune did,
Beggar the estimation which you priz'd
Richer than sea or land?

The economic pull on this discussion is obvious. Hector associates value with the word "estimate," and though the hendiadys suggests that "dignity" and "estimate" are not easily separated, he also speaks of things as being precious in themselves as well as in the "prizer," the appraiser. Troilus uses the same sort of language but on the other side of the case, and without conceding that value dwells elsewhere than in particular will: Helen, he says, is a pearl of price, a worthy prize, inestimable. "Estimation" and "prize" are repeated, and it seems that for Troilus the argument comes down to this: once one has agreed to place a high value on an object, it will be a diminution not of the value of the object but of one's own worth to seek to devalue it, to "beggar the estimation which you prized" so highly. Some of the attributed value sticks to the object, though it will be calculated in terms of a loss of personal worth in the prizer who changes his mind or will or desire.

When Cassandra interrupts the discussion Hector asks whether her dire divinations might persuade Troilus to be more reasonable. However, Troilus replies, quite reasonably, that considerations of success or failure make no difference to his position, which it would be a loss of honor, of personal worth, to give up. This point is endorsed by Paris, who says his reason for wanting to keep Helen is not that he enjoys sleeping with her; the reason is that for the family of Priam to give her back would constitute a derogation from their "great worths." Hector then remarks magisterially that Troilus and Paris argue like young men whose reason is so dominated by passion that they cannot tell right from wrong. He adds that Helen's first contractual duty is, by the law of nature and of nations, to her deserted husband, the implication being that, if there seems to be a question of the Trojans losing personal value, they should reflect that they have done so already by their original interference with the husband's right. If Helen means a loss of face, that loss was suffered long ago when she was kidnapped, and it makes no sense to fear that the loss could be repeated if they let Helen go. Hector then brings the argument to a sudden end by simply giving in, saying that although he has expressed his opinion "in way of truth," he accepts after all that their dignities depend on their keeping Helen. It is a strange submission, unnecessarily conceding or appropriating the arguments he has been resisting, as if the whole thing had been a merely academic debate in which he defended a cause not really his. Of course he had to give in, after all the war did continue, but we are far from persuaded that the other side had the best of the argument, which, like the one in the Greek camp, remains without satisfactory resolution; everything went on just as before, or worse than before, as if these discussions of degree and value were, as I have said, merely academic, as if everybody's business, namely war and politics and sex, was essentially, as Thersites keeps on saying, a matter of vanity and ambition to which ethical considerations did not apply except hypocritically, or perhaps academically.

One curious aspect of this unique scene is that until the law is mentioned at the end of it, there is no attempt to refer to any transcendent SYSTEM or sanction of value other than an institutional and unexamined code of honor or "dignity" or "worth." Troilus is clear that the value of anything depends upon a purely human economy, determined by the worth one attributes to oneself, which, as the language of the play repeatedly informs us, must ultimately depend on what others think about one; it is thus dependent on opinion, and evaluated by such essentially irrational criteria as military courage. Value is strictly a matter of opinion, of *doxa*, not of truth; the valuation of an object depends on a complex of superstitions and ideological constraints.

Troilus's position is complicated by many allusions to taste and distaste, all increasing the weight of the notion that the choice, by will or desire, of the valued object is a matter of the lower senses, taste and touch (even as he speaks he is in a ferment of desire for Cressida), yet not subject to revision when those senses are satisfied; it would be dishonorable, a loss of personal worth, to allow mere disrelish to alter a valuation once made, however transient its basis. (Later he discovers that although he is "true" – constant to the choice he willed – Cressida is not; she is an advocate of contingency.) Hector's economy is different. From a reasonable view, he thinks, there is a discrepancy between Helen's value, at any rate at the moment, and her cost, and he argues the Trojans should cut their losses. His point about the law of nature and nations comes in largely as an afterthought.

As often in Shakespeare, we find that much of the effect derives not from overt argument but from the insistence of a special vocabulary: worth, worthy, unworthy, estimation, estimate, inestimable, prize, price, pearl, opinion, truth, honor. The scene cannot offer, any more than we can, a definite solution to the problem of value it raises; it merely shows how complicated it must be in the particular case considered, how dependent on prior and unquestioned assumptions; and it ends with the ostensibly more commonsensical and influential debater, the advocate of rationality, weakly giving up. The questions simply spread out like a stain; the value of Helen is a matter inseparable from the worth and dignity of Priam, and so forth. That kings become merchants for her sake is meant to be a compliment, though it could be read otherwise. Other characters in the play go to some trouble to show us that Helen is not, in the sense of the word they accept, worth very much, and is herself, no more than Cressida, "honorable" – honor being, as applied to women, entirely a matter of chastity and fidelity, to be lost in a moment. This is of course important, for the women also have exchange value, and are used as commercial counters, Helen in exchange for an aunt (Troilus thinks this a real bargain), Cressida for Antenor (Troilus likes this deal much less). These women could be called passive victims of rape, Helen snatched from her husband for Paris, Cressida forced into the Greek camp for use by Diomedes; and rape, by violating female honor, is, on the prevailing system, a destroyer of value. Women are not "precious in themselves," though their beauty may create an appearance to the contrary; their value lies in what men think about them, that is, in opinion.

Economies and polities are fueled by opinion. It seems from the Shakespearean debate that this position, possibly modified by some idea of things as precious in themselves – truly precious – was held in the sixteenth century, and we seem to be in much the same position, differently described, at present. We behave in the ordinary way as if things were capable of being precious in themselves, though admitting, on reflection, that opinion, which includes self-esteem, governs all valuations. We will further allow that it cannot be merely one's own private opinion that does so; for that opinion will be affected by tacit or explicit agreements within our particular community. A great many people place a high value, and spend a great deal of money, on automobile number plates with distinctive characteristics of one sort or another; or on vintage cars or matchboxes or stamps. Many more do not, but this does not affect the devotees' notion of their value, which is reflected in the price they, unlike most other people, would be willing to pay for them. Of other things it is possible to say they had a value before they were traded; gold, obviously, had useful properties such as ductility, a capacity to form useful alloys, and so forth, which are intrinsic and not dependent on the fluctuating price at which it is traded; and those who exchange it probably have, somewhere in their heads, what Hector called "some image of th'affected merit." A "fine" piece of eighteenth-century furniture, worth thousands of pounds, is also called valuable because of the way it is made, the combination of woods, the elegance of the design and the workmanship of the marquetry or whatever. These qualities contribute to the exchange value of the auction room but exist independently of it, and it is hard to think that anybody who cared about how others valued them would profess to believe that as between such a piece and some piece of modern plastic junk furniture the difference of value, as distinct from price, was merely a matter of opinion; nor would the question value for what or in what contingency be very sensible, since it hardly needs saying that the value of the eighteenth-century chest is zero if it is judged by its usefulness as a chest; it will be too valuable for daily use.

Of course the quasi-inherent value of such a thing is much more evident to an expert than to the uninformed passerby, and the expert may be thought to confer its "attributive" value, his image of the affected merit being so much sharper than the ignorant glance could achieve. Here we may attend again to our supposedly wicked ways with literature. It is a simple truth that the more you know about a particular kind of thing, the better able you are to appraise, prize, estimate its wood, its design, its marquetry, and its place among other artifacts of a similar kind. This is true also of "canonical" literature; the expression implies not only a favored view of a particular work, but also the membership of that work in a larger group of works also esteemed. To believe that canons are in themselves oppressive, that oppression is a constitutive element in canons, you must have a false image of them. This is not to say that the attributive value of their contents is one that everybody is obliged to accept. If people want to know about them because they have heard that they too can acquire an image of their merit, they can do so without coercion, just as they may in respect of matchboxes and rock music. Anybody with teaching experience will know that you can no more force unwilling students to place a high value on canonical works of literature, to gain the knowledge necessary to that act, than you can persuade me, if I am unwilling, to place a high value on rare stamps or matchboxes.

What, to put the matter at its lowest, are the benefits of knowing something about a literary canon, in something the same way as experts know a lot about, and many examples of, Chippendale furniture? The fact is that you must know about a great many interrelated things to value any one thing, and the benefits accruing from that knowledge are palpable, even if they include an element of self-esteem. Readers who know the works of Wallace Stevens – his "canon" – in some depth will understand some of the late short poems – like "The planet on the table" or "Of mere being" – as valuable or "great" poems, while those who come upon them in isolation may see them as rather trivial. The phenomenon is equally familiar in canons more largely conceived.

The point is simple: that membership of a corpus of poetry affects the value of the components as perceived by those who know the corpus, though not by those who ignore it. This observation applies to canons of greater extent. It says more about how canons work than it does about the intrinsic value of their constituents, but it does also say that valuations vary not only with varying degrees of knowledge of a particular object but also with varying degrees of knowledge of a canonical context; and it also implies that it is wrong to complain that the higher valuations come from an economically privileged group. The privilege derives from knowledge, not money. It is simply a group that knows more about this poetry, and perhaps about poetry in general, as some know more about graffiti or B movies. This is the difference between those who have an image of the affected merit and those who have not; and there seems little reason why those who have should worry about the strictures of the others, or envy them the merits they may prefer to affect. Like Bernard Williams, we should rejoice in such freedom rather than yield to despair.

Admittedly this fails to answer the big question, in what sense is there merit independent of effect, or whether you can have one without the other. Although they do seem to go together, we habitually speak of them as distinct, entertaining the notion of a good picture we do not actually like, liking objects we would, if pressed, admit not to have much merit, and so on. And it cannot be without importance that we all know how to use appropriate, inexact language about the value of artifacts when talking informally, careless of the constraints imposed by considerations of axiology, or even of postaxiology.

Reading
Eagleton, Terry 1990: *The Ideology of the Aesthetic.*
Ellis, John 1974: *Theory of Literary Criticism.*
Kermode, Frank 1988: *History and Value.*
Reichert, John 1977: *Making Sense of Literature.*
Smith, Barbara Herrnstein 1988: *Contingencies of Value.*
                                        FRANK KERMODE

van der Rohe, Ludwig Mies *See* MIES VAN DER ROHE, LUDWIG

Vattimo, Gianni (1936–) Italian philosopher and cultural theorist, associated chiefly with the postmodern (counter-ENLIGHTENMENT) turn in recent philosophical thought. Vattimo is cheerfully eclectic in his range of sources, drawing upon HEGEL, NIETZSCHE, WITTGENSTEIN, the later HEIDEGGER, a selective (not to say opportunist) reading of DERRIDA, and also on the strain of neopragmatist (or "POSTANALYTIC") PHILOSOPHY exemplified by Richard RORTY. From these he derives the idea of "weak thinking" (*pensiero debole*), a thinking that on principle renounces such Enlightenment values as truth, reason, critique, dialectics, argumentative validity, etc. Much better, he urges, that we should henceforth cultivate the postmodern virtue – the philosophic line of least resistance – which aims at a broad-based pluralist consensus beyond such obsolete and pointless grounds of dispute. He therefore subscribes to a version of the END OF PHILOSOPHY argument, albeit a version less portentous than Heidegger's depth-ontological brooding on the epochal closure of Western metaphysics.

Reading
Vattimo, Gianni 1988: *The End of Modernity.*
——1993: *The Adventure of Difference: Philosophy After Nietzsche and Heidegger.*

CHRISTOPHER NORRIS

Venturi, Robert (1925–) American architect and author of two influential studies of modern architecture. In the first study, *Complexity and Contradiction in Architecture* (1966), Venturi finds that many modern architects have come to blindly idealize simplicity, accepting Ludwig MIES VAN DER ROHE's epigrammatic statement about his own work – "less is more" – as a guiding principle of architectural design. Venturi responds to this with his counterepigram – "less is a bore" – arguing instead for a richness and exuberance in architectural expression, like that frequently found in examples of Mannerist, baroque, and Rococo architecture. Venturi also suggests at the conclusion of this study that the vitality of main street and commercial strips could be a source of ideas for architects, as it had been for artists associated with the POP ART movement. In his second study, *Learning from Las Vegas: The Forgotten Symbolism of Architectural Form* 1972 (*1977*), written with Denise Brown and Steven Izenour, Venturi examines in detail the landscape of the main street, and particularly of a strip, in Las Vegas, a small CITY which presents an exaggerated picture of urban signage and sprawl. The parking lots and billboards, the service stations and fastfood restaurants, the hotels and casinos of Las Vegas provide an ideal TEXT for Venturi to analyze the "messy vitality" that he prefers in the experience of architecture to an "obvious unity." An important lesson learned from this text is that ordinary buildings with explicit ornament attached to them – the "decorated shed" – serve architecture and the modern experience better than the

"high art" modern architecture, which treats the whole structure as an expressive ornament. Venturi puts this lesson in the language of literary theory, pointing out that modern architecture has tended to ignore DENOTATION, which applied ornament can provide, and has emphasized CONNOTATION, which transforms buildings into big ornaments. So Venturi gives a new and unexpected twist to the meaning of Adolph Loos's statement that the "ornament is crime." Venturi has used the lessons of Las Vegas and the ideas of COMPLEXITY and CONTRADICTION in his own architectural practice from, for example, the Guild House, Philadelphia, 1960–3, to the Sainsbury Wing, National Gallery, London, 1989–91. The oversized and nonfunctional television antenna on top of the Guild House serves as a sculptural SYMBOL of the activity which is important in the lives of the elderly residents of this building. The colossal applied columns which are spaced at increasing intervals along the facade of the Sainsbury Wing act as symbolic SIGNS that link this extension to the colonnade and applied pilasters of the main structure, as well as to nearby Nelson's Column. The Guild House and the Sainsbury Wing show the development of Venturi's work, and also illustrate the shifting currents and tastes in architecture from the 1960s to the 1990s. Venturi is no longer an architect of regional interest, but one of international importance; and he is no longer reviled as a "Pop architect," but respected as a founding father of postmodern architecture.

Reading
Venturi, Robert 1966: *Complexity and Contradiction in Architecture.*
——Brown, Denise Scott, and Izenour, Steven 1972 (*1977*): *Learning from Las Vegas: The Forgotten Symbolism of Architectural Form.*

GERALD EAGER

Verfremdung   See ALIENATION

Verfremdungseffekt   See ALIENATION EFFECT

Victorian studies   Until quite recently, most accounts of the CULTURE of Britain during the reign of Queen Victoria (1837–1901) began by acknowledging the persistence of clichés about what "Victorianism" means: sexual prudishness, earnestness of spirit, middle-class smugness and stuffiness, self-righteousness, moral conservatism, class prejudice, Anglo-ethnocentrism. These largely pejorative views were fostered by such writers as Lytton Strachey (in *Eminent Victorians*, 1918). Cultural historians have come to understand that, although the clichés held some truth, a larger reality was that the Victorian age found British society in a struggle over important issues that today are associated with modernist – even postmodernist – developments in politics, philosophy, the arts, and religion.

During the industrial revolution (c. 1760 to the mid-nineteenth century), the invention of the blast furnace, textile looms, the spinning jenny, and the steam engine; the development of a merchant fleet, roads, and canals; and a rising capitalist economy led to massive restructuring of British society. By 1826 about two-thirds of those who had farmed had moved to the cities to seek work in the factories. Craftsmen were replaced with machines. Commerce in textiles enriched England and contributed to the creation of a worldwide empire. Nevertheless, sweat shops and exploitation of those in need of work, especially women and children, opened the gap between the poor and the affluent in a dangerous way. A struggle for political control among the aristocracy, landowners, and the new middle class(es) and laborers developed.

Scientific advances challenged long-held assumptions about the individual's relationship with others, and about religious beliefs. Geologists, such as Charles Lyall in *Principles of Geology* (1830–3) maintained that the earth was created not a biblical 6,000 years in the past, but eons in the past. Charles Darwin offered convincing evidence in *The Origin of Species* (1859) for a theory that mankind evolved from primates (contradicting the traditional view derived from Genesis). Astronomers extended knowledge of the universe to almost incomprehensible distances and moved the earth from the center of the cosmos to a remote place on the edge of the galaxy. To many, each of these scientific advances seemed to reduce human importance drastically.

Voices in philosophy and theology added further challenges to traditional religious beliefs about the central place of humanity in the scheme of the universe. Auguste Comte (1798–1857) founded POSITIVISM, which gained a wide audience; his followers argued that sense perceptions are the only admissible basis of human knowledge. LOGICAL POSITIVISM insisted upon the primacy of observation

when assessing truth, and the doctrine that metaphysical and subjective arguments not based upon observable data are meaningless. Jeremy Bentham's utilitarianism gained even more popular acceptance, its major tenet being that any behavior or act must be judged on the basis of its utility in bringing the "greatest happiness to the greatest number" of people. Utilitarians argued that all humans are self-interested, but humankind's supreme gift is reason: emotion, intuitions, beliefs (even religious beliefs) are irrational and should be repressed. Education is the *sine qua non* in helping reason to see where true individual self-interest lies. The "higher criticism," fostered by a group of scientifically-minded scholars, added to the consternation of traditional Judeo-Christian believers; its practitioners studied the Bible as a historical TEXT and not necessarily as a divinely inspired book.

Politically, the power of the crown and landowners was ebbing, but not without struggle, as is dramatized in George Eliot's *Middlemarch* (1871–2). The Reform Bill of 1832 extended the right to vote to all men owning property worth £10 or more; in 1867 a Second Reform Bill extended the vote to the working classes. However, with rapid urbanization and industrialization also came massive poverty, growing CLASS tensions and struggles, clashes over the directions the newly mandated educational system should take, questions about the needs of women and feminist rights, an uneasiness about moral certitude, and a sense of a world having lost its way.

Yet, in this caldron of uncertainty paradoxically mixed with a sense of national destiny, some began to argue and search for answers to questions – philosophic, political, social, religious – that foreshadow pressing issues being debated 100 years later at the close of the twentieth century.

Indeed the hallmark of the Victorian age might well be seen – if any unifying mark exists other than Victoria's 64-year reign – as the whirlwind of change that overtook England during this era. Some, like the historian and statesman Thomas Babington Macaulay (1800–59), argued that industrialization, an expanding empire, and growing participation in government by the middle classes were resulting in great economic progress and a more comfortable life for the average Briton. To an extent, this view was true. However, other voices, like those of Elizabeth Barrett Browning, Thomas Carlyle, John Ruskin, and Matthew ARNOLD, offered a more somber reading of the age. It rapidly became clear that the English were not living in a progressive world.

Modern commentators have come to describe Victoria's reign as divided into three (or four) periods.

The first Reform Bill (1832) – which eliminated "rotten boroughs" (depopulated rural regions whose representatives continued to be sent to Parliament, usually representing views of powerful landowners) – is often identified as the actual beginning of the Victorian age. The age's initial period is said to run to about the time of the Great Exhibition of the Works of All Nations (1851), housed in the Crystal Palace, history's first prefabricated public building. The 1830s and 1840s witnessed a gradual recognition of and attempts at coming to grips with the squalor and poverty engendered among the newly formed working class by the industrial revolution, with social unrest, and recognition of the challenges to traditional beliefs.

A mid-Victorian period followed (c. 1851–c. 1880), which, too, was a time of problems but also one of great prosperity. Great Britain experienced economic boom times, built the world's strongest economy, and became the world's prime banker and leading supplier and shipper of manufactured goods. The middle class expanded and many lived in growing comfort; some economic benefits even trickled down to the working class. The Second Reform Bill (1867) doubled the electorate, expanding the franchise to include the middle class and town workers – but not women or the poor. Religious controversy became an absorbing concern as proponents of utilitarianism – with obvious successes in applying their theories to political and social problems – argued the irrelevance of belief, while scientists like Thomas Huxley popularized the Darwinian theories of natural selection, and the troubling question of human identification with primates. The work of geologists, extending the origin of the earth further backward through time with their research into "the riddle of the rocks," and astronomers in expanding knowledge of galactic space (and the earth's disconcertingly diminishing importance in the scheme of the universe) added to the bewilderment of many believers.

A third period (1880–90) gave rise to new challenges to British faith in progress and the nation's destiny as the world's dominant power: the emergence of Bismarck's Germany and a post-Civil War America offered growing competition in industrial production and trade while the United States' development of farm-rich prairie lands forced lower grain prices and competition upon English farmers. A growing trade union movement made the new Labour Party a political force, with some Labour leaders flirting with various shades of socialism, including the communist theories of Karl Marx and Friedrich Engels. A tendency on the part of writers like Samuel Butler to ridicule such Victorian giants as Tennyson and Gladstone, as well as the self-righteous morality of the British middle class, emphasized a growing sense of disease, which intensified during the 1890s (often identified as the fourth period of Victorianism). In this decade the artists of the aesthetic movement consciously cultivated a sense of decadent languor and melancholic sophistication; quite representative of the work of these years were Oscar Wilde's *The Picture of Dorian Gray* (1891) and *Salome* (1893), and the poems of Ernest Dowson. Many artists in the *fin-de-siècle* years stressed a sense of *moral decay* and a feeling of the old gods failing.

However, galloping cultural change is not the only characteristic of Victorianism which modern scholars see as being related to the postmodern period of the twentieth century. Many issues which overtook the Victorians, and which the Victorians addressed with thoughtful vigor, have since 1970 reappeared or been reemphasized as crucial problems in contemporary life.

An apt example is what the Victorians called "the woman question." Ironically, at a time when the world of upper-class men was dominated by the idea of utility, upper-class women were relegated to a life of subservience and pursuit of trivial refinements – needlework, flower arrangement, sketching – or charitable work among the nearby poor. The upper middle-class woman's place became one of devotedly nurturing her husband, home from the wars of business. Coventry Patmore in a well-intentioned paean to family sacredness and the woman's dominant place in the home made her *The Angel in the House* (1854–62). Ironically, however, to deprive women of their humanity by sanctifying them dehumanized them to a status of subservience and actual serfdom. Women of the working class had far different lives: as a cheap source of labor from families squeezed by poverty, they worked long hours for little pay in the fields, mills, and factories, mines, and handicraft shops. Dora Spenlow in Dickens's *David Copperfield* (1849–50) stands as a dramatization of the refined but trapped woman, while Stephen Blackpool's Rachael in Dickens's *Hard Times* (1854) offers insight into the working-class woman's life.

However, a healthy countermovement was put into action by the will and example of a number of women: Florence Nightingale, Harriet Martineau, George Eliot, and Elizabeth Barrett Browning. John Stuart Mill's work, *The Subjection of Women* (1869), was influential in raising public consciousness against the tyranny of Victorian family life. And popular novelists such as William Thackeray and Thomas Hardy repeatedly created far more realistic portraits of women than Patmore's *Angel in the House* by dramatizing the lives of nonconforming heroines like Becky Sharp of Thackeray's *Vanity Fair* (1847–8) and Bathsheba Everdene of Hardy's *Far from the Madding Crowd* (1874), who had sexual passions, ambition, and intellectual aspirations.

A second major issue paralleling Victorian and modern cultures is debate over the direction education must take. For the Victorians the principle tension, as dramatized in Dickens's *Hard Times*, was between the need for a technical education of "hard facts" that prepared youth for jobs in industry and the arguments of thinkers like John Henry Newman and Matthew Arnold on behalf of a LIB-ERAL education, one of "ideas" which challenge the individual's mind and spirit. In contemporary times the argument centers not only on debate between the liberal and technical education, but between traditionalists and the agenda put forward by the "politically correct" in Western societies on behalf of feminism, MULTICULTURALISM, and relativist philosophies.

Yet another parallel between the two eras exists in the power struggle, both economic and political, waged as part of the capitalistic versus socialistic agendas. Adam Smith in *An Inquiry into the Nature and Causes of the Wealth of Nations* (1776) provided the classic statement of pure *laissez-faire* capitalism; Karl Marx, joined by his friend Friedrich Engels, proposed its diametric economic (and political) opposite, communism. Smith argued that, since society in a changing world could no longer survive under traditional authoritarian rules, the marketplace itself, based upon two central laws, actually provided a new mechanism for governing. The two laws of the marketplace – individual self-interest and competition – act upon each other and become self-balancing, thus guaranteeing the survival of a healthy society. Marx proposed that history demonstrated humanity to be an inex-

orable class struggle between the proletariat and bourgeois classes and eventually, because of its inequities and imperfections, capitalism itself would be swept away. Victorian writers such as Thomas Carlyle in *Past and Present* (1834) could be seen to justify positions set forth by Adam Smith, while those opposed, like William Morris in *The Earthly Paradise* (1868), argued against capitalism and on behalf of more collectivist, socialistic political policies. But John Stuart Mill in his brilliant *Principles of Political Economy* (1848) contended that the laws set forth by classical economists applied not to distribution, only to production; and so he provided a rationale for a balance between socialism and capitalism, a synthesis that has dominated much of British and Western economic direction since the mid-nineteenth century.

A fourth issue, religious belief versus unbelief, remains a torrid one today, much as it was in Victorian debates over agnosticism, skepticism, Comte's religion of humanity, and traditional beliefs. At its best the debate was undertaken during the 1870s by the Metaphysical Society, a group composed of remarkable thinkers, including Cardinal Henry Manning, Thomas Huxley, Tennyson, John Ruskin, and Gladstone: individuals whose commitment to meeting in debate over a period of years emphasizes the importance of the issue in Victorian times.

A renewed inquiry during the 1990s into Victorian social, political, philosophical, and theological thought resulted in attempts to reformulate questions about contemporary cultural concerns with an eye to Victorian models in framing the discourse. This inquiry led to a heightened appreciation of Victorian use of forms in the arts, and a renewed respect for the intellectual rigor of the debates that marked the years of Victoria's reign.

Reading

Altick, Richard D. 1973: *Victorian People and Ideas: A Companion for the Modern Reader of Victorian Literature.*

Auerbach, Nina 1982: *Women and the Demon: The Life of a Victorian Myth.*

Briggs, Asa 1989: *Victorian Things.*

Buckley, Jerome H. 1966: *The Triumph of Time: A Study of the Victorian Concepts of Time, History, Progress and Decadence.*

Culler, A. Dwight 1986: *The Victorian Mirror of History.*

David, Deidre 1987: *Intellectual Women and Victorian Patriarchy.*

Houghton, Walter E. 1957: *The Victorian Frame of Mind 1830–1870.*

Knoepflmacher, U.C., and Tennyson, G.B., eds 1977: *Nature and the Victorian Imagination.*

Scott, Patrick, and Fletcher, Pauline, eds 1990: *Culture and Education in Victorian England.*

Showalter, Elaine 1990: *Sexual Anarchy: Gender and Culture at the Fin de Siècle.*

Wheeler, Michael 1991: *Death and the Future Life in Victorian Literature and Theology.*

Willey, Basil 1977: *Nineteenth Century Studies.*

Young, G.M. *Victorian England: Portrait of an Age.*

JOHN J. JOYCE

Voloshinov, Valentin Nikolaevich (1894–1936) Russian writer on language and literature: see BAKHTIN, Mikhail.

W

Warhol, Andy (1928?–87) American painter, film maker, publisher, and entrepreneur. Andy Warhol was the most iconic figure in POP ART. Starting out as a successful commercial artist in the 1950s, he entered the gallery world in 1962 with his pictures of Campbell's soup tins. Warhol, though, was less interested in using pop imagery in his ART than in replicating its production processes (his studio was named The Factory) and its marketing devices (see Warhol and Hackett, 1980). Warhol's influence on POPULAR CULTURE itself was thus immense; he gave artists an aesthetic justification for self-promotion, and pop stars a way of interpreting the sales process as art. David Bowie, among others, celebrated him in song, but of all musicians Madonna probably owes the most to Warhol's example of how to make commerce art.

Reading
Warhol, Andy, and Hackett, Pat 1980: *Popism: The Warhol 60s.*

SIMON FRITH

West, Cornel (1953–) Afro-American philosopher of religion and cultural critic. Following studies at Harvard (AB, 1973) and Princeton (PhD, 1980), West has been located at several institutions of higher learning, most notably Union Theological Seminary, Yale, the University of Paris, and Princeton. In 1994 he joined the faculties of the Department of Afro-American Studies and the Divinity School at Harvard. His position as an honorary chairperson of the Democratic Socialists of America is indicative of his self-avowed role as an "organic intellectual."

The uniqueness and power of his philosophical perspective derive from his effort to draw together, in creative synthesis, several seemingly disparate traditions of theory and practice: prophetic Christianity, historicist pragmatism, progressive MARXISM, and African-American critical thought. As West interprets these traditions, each in its own way provides support for the two ethical principles that pervade all his thought, the dignity of the individual and radical democracy.

Prophetic Christianity is epitomized by West in three themes: the *imago Dei* (a basis for revolutionary egalitarianism); fallenness (a ground for radical democracy); and the kingdom of God (a source of hope). From pragmatism, particularly that of John Dewey, West appropriates a strong anti-metaphysical bent, leading him to stress the need for constant political struggle in a history that is inevitably burdened with tragedy, but within which the possibility for liberation is a constant hope.

West distinguishes progressive Marxism from Leninism and Stalinism in its democratic sensibilities (Rosa Luxemburg) and its attention to culturally specific forms of HEGEMONY and counter-hegemony (Antonio GRAMSCI). The heuristic virtue of Marxist social analysis, in West's judgment, is its focus on the dynamic interconnections that conjoin dominant social structures and oppositional forces.

Yet, while West draws deeply from these religious and philosophical traditions, he affirms that the primary root of his thought and practice is the African-American (or "New World African") community which, given its unique history, is as much a source of prophetic criticism of authoritarian domination, particularly in the form of white supremacy, as Euro-American MODERNITY. However, he carefully distinguishes his perspective from both black conservativism and black LIBERALISM, identifying himself as an African-American socialist Christian. Moreover, he rejects both the Romanticism of African-American exceptionalists and the self-denigration of Afro-American assimilationists on behalf of a kind of HUMANISM that acknowledges the special historical character and struggles of the African-American community. Given prevailing social and cultural circumstances, West has recently expressed special concern for the nihilism – the deep sense of meaninglessness – pervasive throughout the lower classes of African-Americans, and for the crisis of leadership – the lack of moral vision – that extends throughout the African-American political and intellectual elite.

West associates his work with postmodernist movements, particularly in their divergence from Eurocentric modes of thought and practice and their receptivity to radical forms of heterogeneity and difference. Even so, he distinguishes his own perspective from those kinds of POSTMODERNISM that result in sheer moral relativism and political indifference. Hence he calls upon the "new cultural politics of difference" to engage in an extensive critique of capitalist civilization and the collaborative empowerment of all those classes of persons who have been subjugated and oppressed by that dominant system. In his assessment, a genuinely prophetic politics would move beyond both the hegemony of Eurocentrism and the cacophony of MULTICULTURALISM toward a new form of thoroughgoing democracy.

Reading
West, Cornel 1982: *Prophesy Deliverance! An Afro-American Revolutionary Christianity.*
—— 1989: *The American Evasion of Philosophy: A Genealogy of Pragmatism.*
—— 1993a: *Race Matters.*
—— 1993b: *Keeping Faith: Philosophy and Race in America.*
DOUGLAS STURM

Western Europe, European cultural studies in   *See* EUROPEAN CULTURAL STUDIES IN WESTERN EUROPE

Whorf, Benjamin Lee (1897–1941) American linguist and anthropologist. Trained as a chemical engineer, Whorf spent his working life in the insurance business. His lifelong interest in language led him to study linguistics under Edward SAPIR, and his publications aroused great interest. His main writings were reissued posthumously in *Language, Thought, and Reality* (1956).

Whorf is best known for his view that the language you speak influences the way you think. This view is known as the Whorf hypothesis: since Sapir on occasion expressed similar views, it is sometimes called the Sapir–Whorf hypothesis. Whorf's interest in this area arose out of his insurance work, where part of his job was to study fire prevention. He noticed that certain rigid patterns of thought persistently led people to ignore fire risks, and he tried to relate these rigid thought patterns to linguistic STRUCTURES.

Whorf went on to study the language of the Hopi Indians, and was struck by the world view that seemed to him to be embodied in the structure and vocabulary of the language, which looked so different from the world view of English and what he called "Standard Average European" languages. He went on to publish several papers claiming that the world view encoded in each language determines the way its speakers perceive and interpret the world.

The Sapir–Whorf hypothesis is best seen as combining two separate claims: linguistic *determinism* and linguistic *relativity* (see Slobin, 1979, pp. 174–85). Linguistic determinism holds that language determines thought; linguistic relativity says that the relationship between language and thought varies in different languages. It is possible to support determinism without believing in relativity: for example, Chomsky's belief in universal grammar could be described as determinism without relativity (see CHOMSKY, Noam).

Whorf seems to have supported both determinism and relativity, though there are passages in his work which merely express the weaker claim that language influences rather than determines thought. The strong Sapir–Whorf hypothesis does not seem tenable. If it were true, translation between languages should be impossible much of the time: but translation is clearly possible, though not necessarily easy, most of the time. Later work also cast doubt on some of Whorf's claims about Hopi (see Malotki, 1983).

If the strong form of the hypothesis is not tenable, the weak form is not very interesting. It is easy to show connections between language and thought: but extrapolating from these to the claim that the influence is one-way is rather pointless. Later research in psycholinguistics tended to concentrate on universals of language and thought, rather than stressing variation as Whorf did.

One reason why the Sapir–Whorf hypothesis has remained alive is that a discussion of it makes a convenient essay task for first-year undergraduates in linguistics. The lessons that students should be encouraged to draw, however, are not about language and thought but about scientific hypotheses. A hypothesis should first be precise enough to be testable. Second, when tested, it should look as if it might be correct. If it turns out to be incorrect, we may still have learned interesting things from disproving it. Whorf's hypothesis seems to fail on all three grounds. (For a more positive assessment see Fishman, 1982.)

Reading

Fishman, J. 1982: "Whorfianism of the third kind: ethnolinguistic diversity as a worldwide societal asset."
Malotki, E. 1983: *Hopi Time: A Linguistic Analysis of the Temporal Concepts in the Hopi Language.*
Slobin, D. 1971 (*1979*): *Psycholinguistics.*
Whorf, B.L. 1956: *Language, Thought and Reality: Selected Writings.*

RAPHAEL SALKIE

Widdowson, Henry George (1935–) British applied linguist. Widdowson worked for the British Council in Sri Lanka and Bangladesh, and lectured at the Universities of Indonesia and Edinburgh before becoming professor of English for speakers of other languages at the University of London Institute of Education in 1977. One of the most influential educational linguists in Britain, he has written prolifically on "communicative language teaching" and the use of literature in language teaching.

Reading

Widdowson, H.G. 1978: *Teaching Language as Communication.*
——1984: *Explorations in Applied Linguistics II.*
——1990: *Aspects of Language Teaching.*
——1992: *Practical Stylistics.*

KIRSTEN MALMKJÆR

Williams, Bernard (1929–) British philosopher. A broad range of intellectual concerns gives Williams's analytically inspired philosophical work unusual reach and depth: he is adept at discussing Greek tragedy as well as the philosophical implications of modern natural science. Much of Williams's recent work has grown out of his attacks on traditional moral philosophy, in which he is critical of both the utilitarian and KANTian traditions.

For example, in "Persons, character, and morality" (Williams, 1981, essay 1) Williams argues that neither of these strands of ethical thought can grasp the importance of "ground projects," those commitments which give us a reason to go on living. If our ground projects were to conflict with the demands of a Kantian or utilitarian moral standard, we would be morally required to give up those commitments – and yet they are required for us to care enough about going on to do anything at all. In "Moral luck" and "Conflicts of values" (Williams,

1981, essays 2 and 4) he argues that it is to a large extent a matter of luck whether what one does is rationally justified, and that there is not only a plurality of "the most basic values" but also in fact a real incommensurability between them.

Ethics and the Limits of Philosophy (Williams, 1985) brings together various strands of these and other criticisms of traditional ethical theories, and explores the territory beyond moral theory itself. Ethical thought needs to be liberated from "morality," that subspecies of ETHICS best expressed in the Kantian attempt to uncover a realm of obligation beyond the reach of luck, and from "theory," which is not the only kind of reflection, not the only way to combat prejudice, and which trades in "thin" rather than "thick" ethical notions – the latter exemplified by "brutality" and "courage," which (unlike the more general notion of "moral obligation") "seem to express a union of fact and value" and typically offer reasons for action (Williams, 1985, pp. 129f.). Philosophical theory often undoes our confidence in such thick notions, but this says more about the limits of philosophy than about their importance. Our best hope in ethics is to seek thick ethical concepts that survive reflection and social practices that use these concepts.

The ground for much of Williams's work, both critical and constructive, is what might be called his nonmoralistic moral psychology, and his method of inquiry therefore gives a primacy to "life as it is actually experienced" rather than to philosophical or prephilosophical "intuitions" (Williams, 1981, p. 37; Williams, 1985, chapter 6). His later work, *Shame and Necessity* (Williams, 1993), both applies and extends his earlier psychological inquiries. Williams sees the Greeks as neither "primitives" whom we have transcended nor members of a past golden age; though our distance from them is not to be forgotten, many aspects of their thought are closer to us than we might have imagined. Thus the Homeric epics and Greek tragedy, for example, offer a psychology usefully freed from moral constraints – unlike the psychology of Plato and Aristotle (let alone Kant or the utilitarians). They also offer an understanding of human action free from the idea that our ethical interests in those actions accord in some way or other with the way the world is: "We know that the world was not made for us, or we for the world" (Williams, 1993, p. 166).

As he himself noted (Williams, 1993, p. 9), in some important ways Williams's work is reminiscent of NIETZSCHE: at the heart of his psychology there is a questioning of the project of self-unification and the power the moral and the ideal seems to have over us. Williams none the less explicitly distances himself from Nietzsche's comments about politics (Williams, 1993, pp. 10f.). And yet there is another, perhaps even more important difference: Nietzsche claimed that modern natural science had not yet "de-deified" nature enough, and so would be skeptical of Williams's claim that modern natural science can offer us an "absolute conception of the world" (Williams, 1985, chapter 8). Nietzsche was thereby led to a perspectivism more radical than that of Williams, whose apparently unshakable commitment to some form of scientific realism also distinguishes him from contemporary thinkers following the path of Richard RORTY. For Williams, modern natural science is decidedly not "just one more story" about the way the world is.

Reading

Altham, J., and Harrison, R., eds 1995: *World, Mind, and Ethics: Essays on the Ethical Philosophy of Bernard Williams*.

Smart, J.J.C. and Williams, B. 1973: *Utilitarianism: For and Against*.

Williams, B. 1973: *Problems of the Self: Philosophical Papers 1956–1972*.

—— 1981: *Moral Luck: Philosophical Papers 1973–1980*.

—— 1985: *Ethics and the Limits of Philosophy*.

—— 1993: *Shame and Necessity*.

JEFFREY S. TURNER

Williams, Raymond (1921–88) British cultural critic. One of the most significant socialist intellectuals in postwar British history, Raymond Williams's work had a major influence on CULTURAL THEORY and history from the late 1950s. He was born in the Welsh border village of Pandy, the son of a railway signalman, and after a local schooling went to Trinity College, Cambridge, in 1939, from which he was called up from 1941 to 1945. After leaving Cambridge he worked in adult education from 1946 until 1961, when he returned to Cambridge as a Fellow of Jesus College, where he stayed for the rest of his working life. He always saw himself as an active socialist, and as a "Welsh European" occupying the "border country" between different cultural and social worlds. His writing ranges across cultural and literary history, studies of drama and society, theories of cultural formations and institutions, and the changing social significance of language and the media. He also wrote fiction alongside and in dialog with his theoretical work.

Williams's work both grows out of and against the dominant cultural traditions that he analyzed. *Culture and Society* (1958) emphasized the notion of CULTURE as *process* – not simply the highest products of a society, the great works of an individual genius – and traced a history of the cultural critique of industrial capitalism (which, he argued, was profoundly politically contradictory) from Burke and Cobbett, through Ruskin, ARNOLD, Morris, ELIOT, and LEAVIS. Its sequel, *The Long Revolution* (1961), emphasized and developed the broader definition of culture as a way of life. It analyzed the evolving history of cultural forms and institutions in Britain over the previous 200 years and developed a theoretical framework within which to explore this process of dynamic change. Here Williams develops his concepts of STRUCTURES OF FEELING and DOMINANT, RESIDUAL, AND EMERGENT cultures to help understand the complex ideological negotiations which might exist at any particular moment and the uneven ways these structures of feeling shift historically, and both dominant and oppositional forms emerge.

These concepts, elaborated and developed throughout his work, became central to what Williams was to later term CULTURAL MATERIALISM. He argued that cultural forms are not simply the effect of a primary economic process but also actively constitute that process, and that cultural struggle and the acknowledgement of the diversity of cultural identity are central to any genuinely democratic society. Thus studies of the politics of language are crucial to this analysis: *The Long Revolution* traces the development of standard English as a key process in the establishment of the HEGEMONY of a dominant metropolitan culture; *Keywords* (1976) teases out these questions in a more intricate way by looking at the complex history of specific notions and concepts. Also crucial is his analysis of the broadcast media; he refuted both technological determinism, whereby mass communications become a monolithic agent of control, and the elitist perception of users of the media as "telly-glued masses," manipulated by the state and consumer capitalism.

Raymond Williams's work flourished on TENSION, COMPLEXITY, and CONTRADICTION – between "HIGH" and "POPULAR" CULTURE, between tradition and MODERNITY, between a sense of cultural roots and the experience of their dislocation, between public and private, region and metropolis. As in his analysis of the changing meanings of rural and

urban life, *The Country and the City* (1973), he wanted to analyze the structural formation of economic and cultural divisions and identities, without losing sight of the lived experience in which these identities are embodied, or the "resources of a journey of hope" which can look optimistically toward the future, as he does in *Towards 2,000*. "Community" is a key word throughout his writing, but it is a shifting term: it is made up of the combination of relations, place, mutual recognition, shared experience, and class identity.
See also CULTURAL MATERIALISM; DOMINANT/RESIDUAL/EMERGENT; STRUCTURE OF FEELING.

Reading
Raymond Williams 1958: *Culture and Society*.
——1961: *The Long Revolution*.
——1979: *Politics and Letters*.

JENNY BOURNE TAYLOR

Winnicott, Donald Woods (1896–1971) British pediatrician, child psychiatrist, and psychoanalyst associated with the OBJECT-RELATIONS school and influenced by KLEIN.

Winnicott often remarked that there is no such thing as a baby, meaning that a baby cannot exist outside a relationship with a carer. The successful development of the child depends upon the provision of a facilitating environment by a "good enough" mother – the choice of terminology reflects an attempt to avoid an idealization of the maternal function. Good enough mothering permits a gradual development toward independence; its absence may result in the creation of a false self which colludes with environmental demands and hides the true self.

Winnicott is noted for the introduction into psychoanalytic thought of the notion of the transitional object. Typically, this is a material object such as a blanket to which the child develops a powerful emotional attachment. It allows the child to begin the transition from the initial oral relationship with the mother to true object-relations. As it is the child's first "not-me possession," the transformational object permits an initial spatial differentiation between me and not-me.

Reading
Davis, Madeleine, and Wallbridge, David 1980: *Boundary and Space: An Introduction to the Work of D.W. Winnicott*.

Winnicott, D.W. 1958: *Collected Papers: Through Paediatrics to Psycho-analysis*.

DAVID MACEY

Wittgenstein, Ludwig (1889–1951) Philosopher, born in Vienna, studied at Cambridge University with Bertrand Russell and G.E. Moore. He received his PhD in 1929 and was appointed a Fellow of Trinity College in 1930. While never losing touch with academic life, he was never comfortable with it and constantly sought refuge, spending many years away from Cambridge. Much of his philosophical work was done outside academic environments, and he often felt the need to stop or completely give up his work in favor of other things. He spent six years (1920–26) teaching classes of Austrian school children (mainly ages 9 and 10), an experience that resulted in the publication, in 1926, of a small dictionary *Wörterbuch für Volksschulen*, which he developed for use by his pupils. Shortly thereafter he spent two years helping plan and build a house for his sister. While such sojourns and desires to leave academic philosophy continued throughout his life, he was constantly pulled back to Cambridge to lecture, and his influence and reputation grew greatly through these lectures. He was, however, dissatisfied with his efforts and often remarked that he was doing nothing but harm and that he was teaching others nothing but a new jargon. Only two of his works (other than the dictionary) were published during his lifetime, *Tractatus Logico-Philosophicus* (1922) (titled by Moore) and "Some remarks on logical form" (1929). His central work *Philosophical Investigations* (which he began writing while living in a small hut in Norway in 1936) was published posthumously in 1953. Several other influential works also published posthumously include *Remarks on the Foundations of Mathematics* (1956), *Zettel* (1967), *On Certainty* (1969), all named and organized by editors.

It is sometimes convenient to distinguish between an early and a late Wittgenstein, where the first refers to his work in logic and the *Tractatus*, and the second looks at the *Investigations* and his concerns with language. While convenient, such a perspective can be misleading. Wittgenstein does speak of "grave mistakes" in his first work, but he does not repudiate that work or cease to be interested in its topics. Rather he situates these "earlier" concerns within his broadened and continuing thoughts about language. (He had hoped, in fact, to have both works published together within the same cover.) These two TEXTS each exhibit a transcendental (Kantian) spirit in their approach and the questions they ask. In the *Tractatus*, Wittgenstein attempts to show that the conditions that make possible our saying things meaningfully lie in the formal structures of logic, in the logic of language. In the *Investigations*, he wonders about the conditions that make possible those things we are interested in, and attempts to show the contexts and conditions that make possible logical inquiry and anything else humans do. Each work has a concern with the nature of philosophy, the limits and character of language, and the possibilities and conditions of the human.

In his texts, Wittgenstein attempts to give his ideas a proper literary form, and the way in which things are written is of importance to him. Numbered remarks populate his writings and the system of their arrangement is closely tied to what they express. The *Tractatus* indicates this concern through the topics of saying and showing, whereas the *Investigations* approaches it through an emphasis on language games and forms of life. Both texts have been cited as intriguing examples of the marriage of form and content. The *Investigations*, in particular, has been seen as a masterful "feat of WRITING," with its careful attention to grammar, its use of dashes, parentheses, and expression of many voices; all to produce a text of multiple perspectives and possibilities of interpretation which show different pictures of the landscape of language that Wittgenstein finds himself investigating.

Philosophical Investigations attempts to reveal the indispensable nature of the "ordinary" for philosophical inquiry. Wittgenstein says in the *Investigations* that philosophy's task (his task) "is to bring words back from their metaphysical to their everyday use." He is therefore often labeled an ordinary language philosopher and that is not without justification. However, such a label seems often given to oppose him to metaphysical or abstract inquiry. That reading is deceptive as neither conception of Wittgenstein is accurate without the other, for he may just as usefully be labeled a philosopher of metaphysical language as one of ordinary language . . . What "has to be accepted," the (metaphysical) given, for Wittgenstein, is found in the (ordinary) things we do and say, in our forms of life and language games. We must not in our philosophical inquiries forget the training and ordinary ways of speaking we have been given by our elders.

The temptation, however, is to leave behind or clean up that life and language given to us by others in order to expose supposed hidden truths or metaphysical realities. This, says Wittgenstein, is a natural temptation, a temptation resulting from our ways of using ordinary language. Much of the value and confusion of ordinary language is found in understanding the TENSIONS between such language and the desire to leave or correct it. It is in the systematic orderings of ordinary language that we discover the kind of object anything is. Grammar expresses essence for Wittgenstein and metaphysical investigations are inseparable from investigations of the ordinary. Proper philosophical inquiry, says Wittgenstein, is a descriptive enterprise, stating what we already know but are in need of reminding – reminders which emphasize what it is that makes possible what we are doing and saying. Philosophy is not to seek explanations or advance any kind of theory, but rather present the possibilities and the conditions of talk and action, with the hope of untying the intellectual knots that have resulted from lack of attention to language use. Humans are naturally and easily misled by the expressions they use. This results mainly from restricted and partial considerations about what we say, the fixing of our attention on a single or simple conception or theory (a "one-sided diet"), and not asking what makes possible that perspective. ("The basic evil of Russell's logic, as also of mine in the *Tractatus*, is that what a proposition is is illustrated by a few commonplace examples, and then presupposed as understood in full generality" (1989, p. 10).) When we concentrate on questions about the possibilities of language and being for long enough, we find ourselves confronted with what we do and what we say, for example, stating a fact, constructing a building, painting a picture, counting with five apples, teaching how to count with five apples, pointing to five apples. Each of these is an example of ordinary things we do and sets the context and conditions that make possible what we can meaningfully say. They are examples of what Wittgenstein calls forms of life; our physical ways of being, over which we have no choice – the ways we naturally are – but that we distinguish and identify (name) by our words, our ability to speak, by particular language-games.

Wittgenstein's emphasis on and attention to the ordinary and his resistance to explanation and theory as part of proper philosophical inquiry naturally produce criticism from many, especially those scientifically inclined in their thinking. If it is finally "grammar" that expresses essence and it is the systematic ordering of our ordinary language that philosophy must remind us of, then must there not be something on which grammar depends, something objective which science can discover? What value does science have for the philosopher? Is there not value in scientific theory and explanation? Wittgenstein responds that science helps the philosopher by making the imagining of human possibilities easier by discovery of facts. As to the spirit of those questions that suggests philosophy ought to become science or be founded on it, or give way to discovery of objective facts, he reminds us that the very questions being asked here are framed, and must be so, in language; they have to be expressed in ordinary language, if there is anything to be asked. To say, as he tried in the *Tractatus*, "This is how things are" is to still be unclear about what the conditions are that make such an assertion possible. And the initial approach to understanding those conditions is to remember that the claim itself is a proposition, an English sentence, and that we need to ask how the sentence is to be applied, how it is used in our everyday language. For that is where we got it from and nowhere else, and we were trained to use it in certain ways. None of this simple give and take, question and response, will satisfy the scientifically inclined or correctly capture Wittgenstein's writing or its unsettling character. None the less, it might be useful to say that possibly the greatest philosophical wonder confronted and engendered by Wittgenstein is the simple fact that there are creatures who use language. In many important ways this is the fact at which he wants us to be most amazed and the one he himself found most amazing and wondrous. In that spirit he is first and foremost a philosopher of (human) language.

Reading

Cavell, Stanley 1969: "The availability of Wittgenstein's later philosophy."
Finch, Henry Le Roy 1971: *Wittgenstein – The Early Philosophy.*
——1971: *Wittgenstein – The Later Philosophy.*
Malcolm, Norman 1959: *Wittgenstein: A Memoir.*

RICHARD FLEMING

Wittig, Monique (1935–) French feminist and writer. Wittig's work attempts to overturn the present SYSTEM in order to create new sets of relations, expressed in "new language" – one derived from the feminine. This language, Wittig believes, will be found in the gaps and silences of male language and " 'his'tory," in the zero, the O, the perfect circle that you invent" (1969, p. 164). Wittig offers perhaps the clearest example of *écriture féminine.* Her WRITING practice attempts to make the categories of sex and GENDER obselete, in particular by the destabilization of "I" signalled by the splitting of the subject: I/I, symbolizing a new language where the "I" relinquishes its position of power, and refuses the appropriation of the other. *See also* LESBIAN FEMINISM.

Reading

Wittig, Monique 1969 *(1971): Les Guerillères.*
——1973 *(1975): The Lesbian Body.*
——1986: "The mark of gender."

DANIELLE CLARKE

Wollstonecraft, Mary (1759–97) The reputation of Mary Wollstonecraft has been intimately connected with the growth of the modern feminist movement. Since the 1960s she has been the subject of six full-length biographies and a bibliography, while editions of her major works have proliferated. There is interest in both her life and her writings. These included novels, histories, reviews, children's books, pedagogical and political treatises, and a travel book, as well as *A Vindication of the Rights of Woman* (1792), for which she is most famous. In this book she made daring claims for the extension of the ENLIGHTENMENT rights of men to women, by arguing against the sentimental emphasis on the difference between men and women and asserting instead an intellectual and spiritual equality which women should be allowed to prove through proper education. The trivial and sexualized character she admitted that she saw in women, and which Rousseau and other male theoreticians described as natural was, she insisted, the result of cultural construction. *The Vindication* was quite well received by the public of 1792, but in the following years attitudes toward it and its author changed radically, owing to the strengthening of conservative opinion and the extraordinary exposure of Wollstonecraft's life by her husband, William Godwin, in his loving but imprudent *Memoirs of the Author of A Vindication of the Rights of Woman* (1798). From that time onward her life – her fraught loves of another struggling girl, Fanny Blood, who died after childbirth; of the married painter, Henry Fuseli; of the American entrepreneur, Gilbert Imlay, which led to the birth of her first daughter and to her two suicide attempts; and finally of the philosopher, Godwin, whom she married just before the birth of her second daughter Mary – was coupled firmly with the message of her works. The result was that feminism and sexual license became fused in the public mind. Wollstonecraft was immediately attacked as an unsexed female and a whore. Her book was revealed in numerous novels as the sexual corrupter of young girls. George Eliot, writing in 1855, was surprised to find the *Vindication* a rational and moral book at odds with the improper reputation of its author.

Although she was a felt presence in the lives of many feminist thinkers, Victorian feminism, aiming at political and social influence for women, was on the whole frightened by Wollstonecraft's sexualized image. When the late nineteenth-century movement wished to reclaim her as one of the first feminists, there was an effort to separate her writing from her licentious reputation, and works of the time denied many of the embarrassing details of her personal life. Even in the twentieth century her feminist views were denigrated from disgust at her life: in 1947, in *Modern Woman, the Lost Sex*, Ferdinand Lundberg and Marynia Farnham found both her life and her views the result of a severe case of penis envy. Since the 1960s, however, in conjunction with the new feminist movement, Wollstonecraft has become an attractive figure precisely because of the boldness and nonconformity of her personal stand, although some biographers have clearly felt too great a discrepancy between the unhappy emotional life and the rational work. Some feminist commentators, reading against the grain, have found the rational language of *A Vindication* too much a collusion with male DISCOURSE. The edition of her complete works in 1989, including the first publication of her translations and reviews for the *Analytical Review*, allows judgment of her output as a whole and helps her to be seen as one of the earliest feminist critics as well as one of the pivotal figures in the development of modern political feminism.

Reading

Ferguson, M., and Todd, J. 1984: *Mary Wollstonecraft.*
Poovey, Mary 1984: *The Proper Lady and the Woman Writer: Ideology as Style in the Works of Mary Wollstonecraft, Mary Shelley, and Jane Austen.*
Sapiro, V. 1992: *Mary Wollstonecraft.*
Tomalin, Claire 1974: *The Life and Death of Mary Wollstonecraft.*
Wardle, Ralph 1951: *Mary Wollstonecraft.*

JANET TODD

womanism An alternative term for black feminism, coined and defined by Alice Walker in *In Search of Our Mothers' Gardens* (1984). In an attempt to articulate a feminist consciousness both indigenous to black CULTURE and distinct from white American and European versions of feminism, Walker derived the term "womanist" from the black vernacular word "womanish." As opposed to "girlish," the expression "womanish" evokes the qualities of independence, audacity, responsibility, and tough capability that, according to Walker and other black feminists, have enabled black women to resist their history of racial and sexual oppression in the United States. Walker uses the term "womanism" not only to clarify black women's exclusion from and rejection of the white middle-class definition of FEMININITY, but also to project a feminist program that might integrate the aims of sexual and racial emancipation. A nonseparatist IDEOLOGY that refuses to privilege sexual over racial or CLASS oppression, womanism is committed to promoting the unity and liberation of the entire black community.

Reading

Ogunyemi, Chikwenye Okonjo 1985: "Womanism: the dynamics of the contemporary black female novel in English."
Walker, Alice 1984: *In Search of Our Mothers' Gardens.*

MADHU DUBEY

women's studies The term "women's studies" is used in two major ways: as a synonym for FEMINIST CRITICISM and scholarship generally, and as the name for that ensemble of university departments, research centers, professional organizations, journals, presses, conferences, and other academic "houses" specifically dedicated to promoting such scholarship. Women's studies has frequently been called the "academic arm of the feminist movement." Whether located inside or outside traditional educational institutions, women's studies is envisaged as a "safe space" for feminist intellectuals, designed to facilitate the personal and intellectual growth of its participants and challenge the sexism of society at large. Catherine Stimpson (1986) summarizes three specific major goals of women's studies: "teaching the subject of women properly; ending sex discrimination in education at all levels, from pre-kindergarten to postdoctoral study; and integrating feminist activism with feminist thought" (pp. 12–13). Additionally, the goal of proper teaching raises a complex set of other, related issues:

content (what is taught), pedagogy (how it is taught), subjects (the questions asked in classroom and laboratory), and theory and method (how questions are answered and research conducted; what counts as knowledge).

Although the first classes in women's studies were taught in the 1960s in Britain and the United States, the history of women's studies extends much further back, beginning perhaps with Christine de Pisan (c. 1364–1431), a French noblewoman who argued that women have the same capacity for learning and right to be educated as men, and including such advocates of women's education as Mary Wollstonecraft in the eighteenth century and Margaret Fuller in the nineteenth. However, while the argument for women's education that was finally successful at the end of the nineteenth century was concerned with making women better companions for men and better suited to fulfill their designated roles in PATRIARCHY, the architects of women's studies argued that feminist scholarship and teaching must be not only *about* women, but also *for* women – specifically, for women's liberation from male dominance.

A number of historical developments converged in the 1960s to make women's studies, with its avowedly radical mission, possible: demographic changes affecting higher education generally, the free university movement, and widespread political dissent (including anti-colonial movements internationally and the black civil rights and women's liberation movements in the United States, where women's studies is most extensively developed). In the 1960s higher education was undergoing democratization, an opening of its doors to classes of people formerly excluded *de jure* or *de facto*. After three decades of setbacks for women in their struggle for higher education, their rate of enrollment and appointment to teaching positions in Western universities was again on the rise, as was that of black and working-class people as well. The intellectual climate was extremely receptive to change, as scholars in every discipline explored new theories and methods. The developments of DECONSTRUCTION in literary studies and revisionist social history, or the study of history from the point of view of ordinary people, are perhaps the most powerful examples of the kinds of sweeping intellectual innovation that characterized the academy in the 1960s. However, even scholars in the sciences revealed signs of skepticism toward received tradition, as in Thomas KUHN'S *The Structure of Scientific Revolutions* (1962), which demonstrated the contingent and provisional status of scientific knowledge. By the 1980s this PARADIGM shift pervading academia would be recognized as a "crisis of knowledge," suggesting a mandate to reform old disciplines, wedge open spaces for new ones, or even surpass disciplinarity altogether. The advent of POSTMODERNISM inevitably supported the formation of women's studies, but equally influential were the more immediately political calls for "relevance" in education, by which was meant that institutions of higher learning should cease to be the handmaidens of the repressive state and instead serve grass-roots struggles for freedom and democracy.

Many of the new female academics also participated in New Left politics; their participation in the Civil Rights movement must especially not be underestimated. As in the nineteenth century, when abolitionism became the hotbed of feminism, the young discipline of black studies and the freedom schools run by such organizations as the Student Non-Violent Coordinating Committee (SNCC) and the nationalist Black Panthers were the original models for women's studies. The first women's studies courses were not taught in universities, but at Susan Koppelman's School for Women in Boston and the New Orleans Free School, affiliated with Students for a Democratic Society (SDS), in 1966, and the British Anti-University in 1968. Many free school ventures have been launched since then, but most such projects have been short-lived, both because funds have been chronically lacking and because most women pursue educational programs in order to obtain professional or vocational certification (see Bunch and Pollack, 1983). Throughout the 1970s, countless women joined informal study and consciousness-raising groups in which nonhierarchical, cooperative methods of learning were developed, techniques that have had a considerable impact on feminist pedagogy in academia. Since the 1970s the independent, free school model of women's studies is still usefully employed, often in connection with artists' colonies and organizations providing direct services to women, as when shelters for battered women conduct reading groups for clients and volunteers. Although the primary location of women's studies did not ultimately become the free university, women's studies outside academia can claim some noteworthy achievements, such as the publication by the Boston Women's Health Collective of *Our Bodies, Ourselves* (1976;

1984), a book that has educated at least two generations of women about sexuality, reproduction, and health.

Within established academic structures, the growth of women's studies has been phenomenal. Stimpson (1986) reports that in 1969–70 a mere 17 courses about women were offered in the United States, but by 1973 there were more than 2,000 courses and 80 women's studies programs; by 1980 the number of women's studies courses had swelled to over 20,000 and the number of programs to 350; by 1982 universities offered a staggering 30,000 courses in women's studies. The National Women's Studies Association Task Force for the Association of American Colleges counted 621 women's studies programs in 1991, with 68 percent of all universities offering them. Extensive networks have rapidly developed for the exchange of information and ideas. Numerous collections of course outlines have been published, beginning with *Female Studies*, a ten-volume series sponsored in the 1970s first by the MLA Commission on the Status of Women and then by the Clearinghouse on Women's Studies of the Feminist Press. Early on, the sheer bulk of new courses forced an abandonment of the comprehensiveness and interdisciplinary scope attempted in *Female Studies*; in the 1980s book-length collections of syllabi and course designs would continue to appear, but be more narrowly focused, as in Paul Lauter's *Reconstructing American Literature* (1983). In the 1990s feminist teachers have shared syllabi electronically, via the "Women's Studies List" (WMST-L), an Internet discussion group. Between the mid-1970s and mid-1990 archives and research centers have been established at a dizzying rate. Some are independently funded, like the community-based Lesbian Herstory Archives in New York or the Institute for Research in History and the Center for Women's Policy Studies in Washington, D.C. Others, like The Bunting Institute at Radcliffe, or centers at Wellesley and Memphis State, rely on a combination of university subsidy, federal grants, and foundation money. International centers exist too, including the International Research and Training Institute for the Advancement of Women, funded by the United Nations, the Association of African Women for Research and Development, and the Asian and Pacific Centre for Women and Development (for an extensive directory, see Albrecht and Brewer, 1990). Feminist caucuses and professional organizations have been formed within scholarly societies at every level, from the regional to the international, and new organizations founded, such as the National Women's Studies Association in 1977, which sponsors one of many annual conferences in women's studies. Fellowships, prizes, and chairs have been endowed; and journals and presses proliferated. The Feminist Press, begun by Florence Howe and Paul Lauter in 1970, was one of the first feminist presses and remains one of the most important, although there are now numerous others, including the Kitchen Table: Women of Color, Crossing, and Pergamon presses. Indeed, virtually every major publisher, including all the university presses, now has an established women's studies series or division, and a staggering number of women's studies journals are also now in print, including prominently *Signs, Feminist Studies, Women's Studies, Sage, Gender and Society*, and *Women's Studies International Forum*. Clearly, the rapid pace with which women's studies has become legitimized indicates that urgent needs were being met.

The first and most urgent of those needs was to sate an enormous hunger for information about women and analysis of women's lives, to develop ways of knowing that did not, to paraphrase historian Gerda Lerner, leave out half of humanity. Women's studies has been incredibly productive, generating an enormous body of scholarship with paradigmatic implications for every discipline. Scholarship and curriculum revision have proceeded hand in hand, as women's studies practitioners first seemed to ask what Mary DALY called "non-questions about non-data," and then moved to make women visible and reinterpret women's roles in history and contributions to culture. Just as early work in black studies was envisaged as a necessary corrective to the demeaning representation of black people in the dominant racist culture – a means of demonstrating the street slogan, "Black is Beautiful" – early work in women's studies began with critique of the stereotyped and derogatory representation of women in male dominant culture, with analysis of the ideological charge of "images of women," especially their destructive psychological impact as oppression is internalized. An early anthology of feminist LITERARY CRITICISM, Susan Koppelman [Cornillon]'s *Images of Women in Literature* (1972), reveals this moment well, even as it gestures toward the next phase of women's studies work: the title of one contributor's essay is "Why aren't we writing about ourselves?"

By the mid-1980s this process of curriculum revision would be theorized as a progression through distinct stages, beginning with the exclusion of women from the disciplines and ending with the complete transformation of disciplinary materials, theories, and methods. In 1985 literary scholars GILBERT AND GUBAR articulated a four-stage process: critique, recovery, reconceptualization, and reassessment (see also Tetreault, 1985). *Critique* consists of analyzing the absence of women as both SUBJECTS and objects of inquiry, as well as understanding androcentric epistemologies that pose exclusively male subjects and points of view as universal and distribute sexist biases throughout the disciplinary field. *Recovery* consists of refocusing women's historical experience and their agency as producers of culture; it is frankly compensatory and separatist, for it seeks to understand women's experience and cultural production on their own terms. Gerda Lerner's *Black Women in White America* (1972), Nancy Cott's *Root of Bitterness* (1972), and Nochlin and Harris's *Women Artists, 1550–1950* (1979) all exemplify recovery, since they document the presence of women in history and begin to form alternative CANONS. Because androcentric epistemologies are premised on the exclusion of women, recovery not only produces new information, but also forces the development of alternative perspectives and *reconceptualization* of paradigms, theories, and methods. New categories of analysis are furnished and old theories are revised. Much feminist work on women's psychology is in this vein, for example, the revision of Freudian theory in the 1970s by such scholars as Juliet MITCHELL and Nancy CHODOROW or the revision of Kohlberg's androcentric model of ethical development by Carol Gilligan in 1982. *Reassessment* entails the nonsexist reintegration of men and women, as both subjects and objects of inquiry. Reassessment tends to focus on gender relations and uses both revised androcentric theories and new gynocentric ones to develop explanations that are truly universal. In the 1990s reassessment is still mainly imagined, a goal toward which women's studies strives, even as it is transformed from within by women of color.

Just as white feminist scholarship antagonized and criticized androcentric work, it has itself been challenged for uncritically accepting and reproducing racist premises and paradigms. The title of an important landmark in black women's studies speaks volumes: *All the Women are White, All the Blacks are Men, But Some of Us are Brave: Black Women's Studies* (Hull, Scott, and Smith 1982). This multidisciplinary collection of essays on the theory, methods, and materials of black women's studies condemns the racism of a feminist practice that excludes and marginalizes black women, scrutinizes the problematic political position of black women scholars in the postmodern academy, speculates about the radical possibilities of black feminist teaching, and distributes a large body of material to support such teaching. It also reprints the crucially influential manifesto, "A black feminist statement," in which the Combahee River Collective rejects one-dimensional theories of sexism, racism, and class oppression, arguing instead that a radically oppositional black feminist practice can only be developed in tandem with theories that begin by assuming a complex intersection of race, class, and gender oppressions in black women's lives. Such RACE–CLASS–GENDER analysis has had a powerful influence on white women's studies and androcentric black studies and ethnic studies, and has even inspired a considerable reexamination of white males – whose history and cultural production continue to be most frequently and thoroughly studied in the academy as a whole. A similar process of critique, recovery, reconceptualization, and reassessment and a similar commitment to race–class–gender analysis have also characterized the development of Chicana, Asian-American, and Native American women's studies. The Memphis State University Center for Research on Women has sponsored a great deal of this work; their extensive databases and series of working papers are incisive tools. In addition, the ground-breaking anthologies, Morgana and Anzaldua's *This Bridge Called My Back* (1981), Anzaldua's *Making Face, Making Soul, Haciendo Caras* (1990), and Butler and Walter's *Transforming the Curriculum: Ethnic Studies and Women's Studies* (1991), measure three decades in the development of a practice of women's studies committed both to multicultural diversity and anti-racism.

Because women's studies has been so incredibly productive, it is beyond the scope of this discussion to summarize adequately its achievements within each of the disciplines, but such overviews are provided in *The Impact of Feminist Research in the Academy* (Farnham, 1987) for anthropology, history, religious studies, psychology, science, economics, political science, literature, and sociology in the mid-1980s. Generally, one can say that women's studies has firmly distinguished between sex and gender and established gender as a legitimate category of analysis. Women's studies has documented the oppression of women in every sphere of social life; raised public awareness about a number of issues including violence against women and the feminization of poverty; helped create awareness of and respect for women's multiple roles in the economy and of a "gender gap" in politics; and promoted knowledge of women's agency in history and achievements in the arts. Women's studies has pioneered new pedagogical techniques and research methodologies that integrate theory and praxis (see Bowles and Klein, 1983; Cullley and Portuges, 1985; and Weiler, 1988). Finally, women's studies has had a tremendous impact on public policy, as in the virtual redefinition of rape in the courts since the 1960s. Ironically, though, women's studies has had little impact on the academy in which most of its work is performed.

Because the dominant mode of reading in the academy is eclectic and relativistic, women's studies has been easily absorbed and possibly neutralized: it has become simply one mode among many for describing and interpreting the social world. Although women's studies is unevenly developed in the various disciplines, making only crude generalizations possible, it is safe to say that not a single discipline has interpreted the findings of feminist scholarship as a mandate for thorough reform. Although scholarly publications in journals about women have burgeoned, for example, they remain proportionally the same as they were in 1966, and other indicators too, such as the content and organization of introductory textbooks in most disciplines, reveal that "by and large male-biased disciplinary frameworks remain firmly entrenched" (DuBois et al., 1985, p. 181). The collective dream, articulated by Adrienne Rich (1973), that academic feminists could radically transform academia into a place where women's work and lives are treated with the same seriousness as are those of men has not yet been realized, while the history of backlash against women's studies suggests that steady progress toward this goal, however slow, cannot be assured.

In the 1970s opposition to women's studies took the form of firings, negative tenure decisions, and cuts in funding to programs at individual schools. In the 1980s, which saw a resurgence of political conservativism, funds were cut at the national level and a media campaign was launched against women's studies by the religious right, characterizing it as a "takeover" of college campuses by "feminazis," man-hating lesbian guerrillas disguised by a thin veneer of "ersatz scholarship."

However, dealing with backlash is only one of the problems facing women's studies in the 1990s. More serious is a cluster of issues which indicate the need for greater inclusivity and diversity in women's studies. Since its beginnings, women's studies has been a site of political and ideological diversity, yet despite the creative possibilities diversity allows, it is often feared and suppressed as a source of conflict. In the 1970s, for example, there was considerable conflict between LIBERAL and radical feminists about whether or not women's studies should represent itself as overtly feminist, or even "political." That is, while most practitioners agreed that the generation of knowledge is always somehow charged with political significance, there was disagreement about whether women's studies practitioners must also engage in activism outside academia. Is it sufficient, for example, merely to study wife-battering, or must one's research also have an immediate, direct, and quantifiable impact on battered women's lives? This conflict was played out as a battle over how women's studies should be named ("Sex Role Studies," "Female Studies," "Feminist Studies," and of course, "Women's Studies" were all possibilities). In the 1980s the question of naming was reopened as the role of men in feminism was debated. Some programs welcomed men and men's studies, renaming this cooperative effort "Gender Studies." Other programs resisted this movement, claiming that work on men and MASCULINITY should not compete for the increasingly limited resources available to women's studies. There is no disagreement, however, about the need to recruit and retain faculty members of color, which is universally considered a major desideratum, along with enhanced cooperation with ethnic studies programs, as women's studies continues to be embarrassed and frustrated by its dominance by white women. Similarly, international ties need to be established or, where they exist, strengthened, especially in the United States, where intellectual and cultural provincialisms are deeply ingrained habits. The curriculum should be revised to reflect these commitments.

Other problems result from the lack of a unifying IDEOLOGY for women's studies, which has been a central and unresolved problem since its inception. Two related questions are important here: whether or not women's studies is a discipline, and whether or not "mainstreaming" should be women's studies' overriding goal (Bowles and Klein, 1983). For either project to succeed, women's studies needs to establish itself as authoritative, yet it is fundamentally a movement committed to anti-authoritarianism. The conflict between the democratizing tendency of women's studies and its reproduction of the authoritarian structures of patriarchy is nowhere seen more clearly than in struggles over governance, which have been particularly thorny and divisive, sometimes even destroying whole programs. Should women's studies be governed by faculty and administrators only, or should students and women in the community also be empowered to shape programs? Can programs preserve their autonomy, including the right to experiment with unorthodox structures of governance? Can they prevent administrative interference, yet simultaneously cultivate administrative support? Can practitioners recognize and deal creatively with conflicts rooted in difference of status, conflicts between tenured and untenured faculty women, for example, or between faculty and graduate and undergraduate students? To what extent can nonhierarchical, consensual structures of administration be created, and how can practitioners resolve the contradictions and paradoxes that arise when such experiments collide with established or required institutional procedures? How, for example, can teachers attempt to create an egalitarian classroom climate and then assign grades?

Finally, women's studies shares certain problems with academics generally, problems which the rapid growth of women's studies and its commitment to interdisciplinary inquiry have only exacerbated. Chief among these is the enormous expansion of knowledge, how to cope with the burgeoning scholarship and proliferation of theories and methods. Although women's studies has produced fine tools and guides for research, including *Feminist Periodicals, Feminist Collections*, and *New Books on Women and Feminism* (all produced by the University of Wisconsin Women's Studies Librarian), *Women's Studies Abstracts*, and Susan Searing's *Introduction to Library Research in Women's Studies* (1985) for undergraduates, it lacks the equivalent of, say, Harner's *Literary Research Guide* in English. Such tools, of course, do not solve the greater problem of how to find the time and energy, not only to read, but also to think – broadly and freely. It is desirable that scholars in

women's studies, along with scholars everywhere else in academia, resist the temptation to manage this proliferation of knowledge by becoming more and more narrowly specialized, more and more indifferent to the complex relationships between branches of study, the possibilities of cross-fertilization between them, and how they are located in, shaped by, and in turn shape the world at large. *See also* FEMINIST CRITICISM; PATRIARCHY; RACE–CLASS–GENDER ANALYSIS.

Reading
Albrecht, Lisa, and Brewer, Rose M., eds 1990: *Bridges of Power: Women's Multicultural Alliances.*
Anzaldua, Gloria, ed. 1990: *Making Face, Making Soul, Haciendo Caras: Creative and Critical Perspectives by Women of Color.*
Bowles, Gloria, and Klein, Renate Duelli, eds 1983: *Theories of Women's Studies.*
Bunch, Charlotte, and Pollack, Sandra, eds 1983: *Learning Our Way: Essays in Feminist Education.*
Butler, Johnnella E., and Walter, John C., eds 1991: *Transforming the Curriculum: Ethnic Studies and Women's Studies.*
Culley, Margo, and Portuges, Catherine, eds 1985: *Gendered Subjects: The Dynamics of Feminist Teaching.*
DuBois, Ellen Carol, et al. 1985: *Feminist Scholarship: Kindling in the Groves of Academe.*
Farnham, Christie, ed. 1987: *The Impact of Feminist Research in the Academy.*
Gilbert, Sandra M., and Gubar, Susan, eds 1985b: *A Classroom Guide to Accompany The Norton Anthology of Literature by Women.*
Hull, Gloria T., Scott, Patricia Bell, and Smith, Barbara, eds 1982: *All the Women are White, All the Blacks are Men, But Some of Us are Brave: Black Women's Studies.*
Morgana, Cherrie, and Anzaldua, Gloria eds 1981: *This Bridge Called My Back: Writings by Radical Women of Color.*
National Women's Studies Association Task Force for the Association of American Colleges 1991: *Liberal Learning and the Women's Studies Major: A Report to the Profession.*
Rich, Adrienne 1973 (*1979*): "Toward a woman-centered university."
Stimpson, Catherine R. with Cobb, Nina Kressner 1986: *Women's Studies in the United States.*
Tetreault, Mary Katy Thompson 1985: "Feminist phase theory: An experience-derived evaluation model."
Weiler, Kathleen 1988: *Women Teaching for Change: Gender, Class and Power.*

GLYNIS CARR

Woolf, Virginia (1882–1941) British feminist writer. The history of Virginia Woolf's reception as one of the twentieth century's major feminist voices is tortuous and healthily problematic. Considerable reason for at least one feature of what is a complicated case history may be found within the patriarchal critical tradition. Male critics have been either historically incapable of registering, or variously reluctant to recognize and weigh, the feminism that informs or drives her writing (and not simply feminism: theorists in LESBIAN FEMINISM carry the issue even farther from the purlieus of the PATRIARCHY). E.M. Forster (1941), who might have known *differently*, advised readers that there were spots of feminism all over Woolf's work, as if, as has been remarked, feminism were a disease, like chicken pox. Forster saw and admitted that, as an elderly male, he was unfitted to pass judgment on the subject, but none the less had his cake and ate it too. Nor were male critics entirely alone. Q.D. Leavis (1938), for example, could only choke on what she saw to be privilege and elitism in Woolf's position and a belle-lettrist frivolity in her style.

However, when in the 1960s and 1970s a number of events conjoined – the feminist revolution in North America; publication of Quentin Bell's biography, the subsequent issue of the letters and diaries – Woolf found the kind of acclaim that a few critics and many women readers (among them those, from all social classes, whose letters to her may be read in the Monks House Papers at Sussex University) had all along seen to be her due. She was a radical voice, in a great tradition that embraces Mary WOLLSTONECRAFT and, as now might be added, Simone de BEAUVOIR and Julia KRISTEVA, and a more obscure tradition written by Margaret Paston, or Judith Shakespeare and company: Margaret Cavendish, Dorothy Osborne, Anne Finch, Laetitia Pilkington, Maria Edgeworth, etc. By no manner of means was the new critical climate without controversy, both within and without the feminist debate. The issues are numerous but seem most yieldingly to focus where AESTHETICS and social history are embroiled.

That Virginia Woolf was a "lady" of Victorian birth is something she wisely never sought to evade. Lady into woman was an emancipatory metamorphosis too far to be completely negotiable for her. No more could the twentieth become discontinuous with the nineteenth century, dramatic caesurae, such as the Great War of 1914–18, notwithstanding. Woolf's hero/heroine Orlando might effect a truly startling transition from man into woman, but there was no question that Virginia Woolf could become, let us say, another Katherine Mansfield (hence in some measure her ambivalent fascination

and rivalry with Mansfield). Everything precluded it, not least her entrenched prejudices about the underworld of bohemia. (It is symptomatic that, for example, Woolf wrote for Bruce Richmond's *Times Literary Supplement* (*TLS*), not A.R. Orage's *New Age*; her version of modernism is strictly English, in spite of post-impressionism, and, in a sense, deeply traditional.) Still less could she begin to speak for the working class. (Her honesty and good sense regarding her ignorance of working-class CULTURE informs most notably her introduction to *Life As We Have Known It*, 1931.) She was born into a connection which Annan (1955), unwittingly and inappropriately borrowing a phrase from George Meredith's *The Ordeal of Richard Feverel* (1859), has identified as that most oxymoronic of cultural phenomena (more *moronic* than *oxy*?) "the intellectual aristocracy." By this Annan meant a network of upper middle-class, generally Oxbridge (and predominantly Cambridge) related, interconnected families whose sires and scions held sway at the universities, upon the bench, and, *inter alia*, in the administration of the British Empire. Woolf herself did not attend a university. It was a matter at once of grievance and considerable satisfaction to her, in her conception of herself as an "outsider." She found her schooling in the library of her father, the muscularly agnostic alpinist, editor, biographer, critic, literary historian, and philosopher, Leslie Stephen, and, briefly enough, at the knee of such women as Clara Pater, and the inspiration of others, like Jane Harrison. Cambridge was *the* university to which she did not go, and it was through Cambridge, where her more privileged brothers studied, that she met the young men, including her future husband, who were together to form what became known as the Bloomsbury Group. Bloomsbury's AESTHETICS derived from or were cogently mediated by G.E. Moore, whose emphasis upon the value of aesthetic enjoyment as an end in itself fitted comfortably with Paterian ideas and, subsequently, postimpressionist theory, which Clive Bell and, more substantially, Roger Fry were to cultivate, and which finds expression in Woolf's own criticism and theorizing about an impersonal, autonomous, epiphanic, and transcendental (but relentlessly secular) literary art.

A major critical maneuver, by feminists such as Marcus (1982), was to wrench Woolf from this background, to deny it, and the process, in some measure since redressed and readdressed, proved for the most part a vitally useful dislocation. It also helped liberate Woolf from the chimerae of sickbed, sofa, and ivory tower to which even Forster, to say nothing of F.R. LEAVIS, had variously confined her. (Raymond WILLIAMS, for his part, had no difficulty in accounting rather positively for the phenomenon of Bloomsbury, as a dissenting fraction of the upper class, or for Woolf's aesthetic of the momentary – but then he skirted the question of her feminism.) With or without Bloomsbury, however, the issue of Woolf's ideas about pure and impure ART remains problematic, for those ideas were also more fundamentally socially conditioned. Her will toward obliquity, as well as being grounded in rhetorical and aesthetic theory, was, by her own acknowledgement, governed by notions of good manners and polite conversation, as cultivated, for example, at the Victorian tea-table. In a work of high symbolism like, for example, *To the Lighthouse* (1927), a considered obliquity is essential and enriching. Carried far enough it will carry the price of obscurity. Carried into ostensibly polemical writing, such as *A Room of One's Own* (1929) and the visionary *Three Guineas* (1938) (which in a revolutionary and profoundly controversial way binds feminism and pacificism together), it may be, some have argued (notably Elaine SHOWALTER), that it has been carried too far. This possibility has provided the crux in a major debate concerning Woolf's rhetorical strategies, their literary and sociopolitical effectiveness, the nature of feminist DISCOURSE, and the issue of self-censorship (upon which contentious question consult, for example, Rosenbaum (1992). Toril Moi and, subsequently, Silver (1991a and b) have been prominent among critics engaged upon these issues, while the theories of Sandra GILBERT and Susan GUBAR, concerning "feminine 'swerves'" and conversational style have helped nourish fruitfully charitable readings of Woolf's maneuvers, such as those by Cuddy-Keane (forthcoming).

Feminist readings of Woolf's novels and criticism have anchored her work in "the real world," as Zwerdling (1986) has termed it, and freed her for us from the constraints of her FORMALISM. An important materialist position has been forcefully argued by Barrett (1979), while Abel (1989) has, with great acuity, written from the viewpoint of PSYCHOANALYSIS. The major subjects of Woolf's fictions are now seen to be the patriarchy and the family (see notably *To the Lighthouse*, and *The Years* (1937)), identity and the self (see *Mrs Dalloway* (1925), and, especially, *The Waves* (1931)), war

(see for an oblique approach, *Jacob's Room* (1922), *Mrs Dalloway*, the "Time passes" section in *To the Lighthouse*, and *Between the Acts* (1941)), empire (see *Mrs Dalloway* and *The Waves*), the nature of time, consciousness, memory and history, and language itself (she could talk of a linear verbal art in terms of statuary, an art that was "eyeless" and monumental). Woolf owed considerable debts to the writings of James Joyce, whose work she none the less famously condemned, and to T.S. ELIOT whose *The Waste Land* she typeset by hand for the Hogarth Press's first English edition of that poem. As a novelist-critic she developed and promoted her own blend of impressionism and psychological realism (see Erich AUERBACH), opposing, notably, the "impure" "materialism" of her Edwardian contemporaries. Many of her key essays explore and develop ideas from which her fictional experiments grew, though once again the obliquity of her essay style has for some critics obscured the view. Woolf's feminist position naturally led for her to a revisory CANON. Her theories of reading, as expressed in *The Common Reader* (1925, 1932) collections and numerous other essays, anticipate much in current READER-RESPONSE CRITICISM, down to the ideas of Stanley FISH concerning "reading communities."

From misread aesthete, Virginia Woolf has been reread, especially since 1970, to achieve a status scarcely less elevated than that of Shakespeare, as a cultural icon of the age.

Reading
Abel, Elizabeth 1989: *Virginia Woolf and the Fictions of Psychoanalysis*.
Barrett, Michèle 1979: "Introduction." *Women and Writing*.
Bell, Quentin 1972: *Virginia Woolf: A Biography*.
Rosenbaum, S.P., ed. 1992: *Women & Fiction: The Manuscript Versions of "A Room of One's Own."*
Williams, Raymond 1978 (*1980*): "The Bloomsbury fraction."
Zwerdling, Alex 1986: *Virginia Woolf and the Real World*.
ANDREW MCNEILLIE

writerly and readerly texts   (usual translations of French *scriptible* and *lisible*.) A pair of terms introduced by Roland BARTHES in his book *S/Z*, a brilliant and meticulous (almost sentence-by-sentence) close reading of Balzac's novella *Sarrasine*. The readerly, or "classic realist," TEXT is one that observes all those cultural CODES and conventions which the reader expects of a well-made narrative. It can thus be consumed (so to speak) without remainder as a piece of straightforward mimetic DISCOURSE whose fictive or textual status is forgotten for the sake of just enjoying the story or following the fortunes of its various protagonists. The writerly text, on the other hand, is one that permits of no such easy escape route into the naive pleasures of that realist illusion which Barthes identifies with the workings of bourgeois IDEOLOGY. It is the kind of text that resists mere passive consumption – or which holds out against those conformist habits of response – by refusing the reader a stable, self-assured subject position from which he or she can share in the author's omniscient view of characters and events. This it does by disrupting those various narrative codes (the proairetic, hermeneutic, semic, cultural, and symbolic) which weave and intersect at every point in the text and whose breakdown generates a "scandal" in the naturalized order of meaning and representation. At the limit such writing would aspire to the condition of an infinitized "freeplay" of SIGNS, a domain of intertextual traces and allusions where the author function is dissolved into an open polyphony of surrogate voices.

For Barthes – as for other French literary theorists in the late 1960s, Philippe Sollers among them – this ideal is attained (or most nearly attained) by a text like Joyce's *Finnegans Wake* (1939). What is here in prospect is a writing that transgresses all the orthodox values – of coherence, linear plot structure, extratextual reference, character interest, social and historical specificity, etc. – imposed by the generic conventions of the novel as a high bourgeois artform. Those conventions operate (so Barthes argues) in the manner of all such mythic ideologies, that is, by transforming "CULTURE" into "nature," or passing off as timeless, transcendent truths what in fact are mere items of class-based "commonsense" belief or products of some localized cultural *doxa*. *S/Z* may thus be seen as marking the point of transition from those early works of Barthes (like *Mythologies*, 1957) which adopted a broadly structuralist approach in demystifying bourgeois sign SYSTEMS to the later (post-1970) phase which produced such influential essays as "The death of the author" and "From work to text."

The *lisible/scriptible* distinction enjoyed a high profile among literary theorists during the decade or so of intensive poststructuralist debate that followed the book's publication. However, it also gave rise to some problems fairly typical of the heady rhetoric which characterized that period of endlessly deferred textual "revolutions that as yet

have no model." These included the somewhat mandarin idea of "SIGNIFYING practice" as a substitute for real-world engagement; the dubious appeal to texts like *Finnegans Wake* as somehow more "radical" than texts with an overtly critical, progressive, or social-realist content; and the fondness for typecast generic oppositions – like writerly *versus* readerly – which left no room for more subtle or nuanced approaches. "Bliss was it in that dawn to be alive," sure enough, but a bliss rather oddly out of touch with events off-page.

See also NARRATOLOGY; POSTSTRUCTURALISM; TEXTUALITY.

Reading
Barthes, Roland 1975: *S/Z*.
——1977a: *Image–Music–Text*.
Culler, Jonathan 1983: *Roland Barthes*.
Mowitt, John 1992: *Text: The Genealogy of An Antidisciplinary Object*.

CHRISTOPHER NORRIS

writing   A concept that figures prominently in the thought of DERRIDA, BARTHES, FOUCAULT, CIXOUS, and other theorists. Before the advent of sound recordings, writing differed from speech in that it was the form of language that did not rely on the presence of the one who used it. Because it makes possible the preservation and transmission of DISCOURSE, writing has been highly prized but also surprisingly condemned. For Plato it is a threat to memory, and for SAUSSURE it is a monstrous imposition on speech. If spoken language is one step removed from thought, then writing may be thought a supplement to a supplement. Cixous, however, observes that because a piece of writing continues to produce an apparently unlimited number of readings and rewritings, it persists in deferring any definitive sense of meaning. Women, she argues, have a privileged position in relation to writing. *Of Grammatology* is Derrida's manifesto for launching a new science of writing in order to challenge concealed assumptions about speech that have important implications for Western metaphysics and CULTURE.

Reading
Cixous, Hélène 1975a (*1987*): "Sorties: out and out: attacks/ways out/forays."
Derrida, Jacques 1967a (*1976*): *Of Grammatology*.
——1967b (*1978*): *Writing and Difference*.

MICHAEL PAYNE

Y

Yates, Frances Amelia (1899–1981) Renaissance historian who, after an unconventional early education, began to live on small family resources as a private scholar. Her first academic appointment, in 1941, was to the staff of the Warburg Institute, which had escaped from Germany in 1933 but was not yet part of the University of London.

Frances Yates's London MA thesis on sixteenth-century French social drama led her to the religio-political refugee language teachers of Elizabethan England, particularly John Florio (1553?–1625), the subject of her first book (1934) and his father, as well as to the Italian heretical philosopher, Giordano Bruno (1548–1600). In *A Study of Love's Labour's Lost* (1936) she attempted to revise current views of Florio's influence on Shakespeare, seeing the opposition of poetic and pedantic language as a chief theme of the play and proposing for it a relevance to contemporary religious thought.

In 1937 these interests brought her into contact with the Warburg and kept her associated with it until her death. She learned to apply the pragmatic, encyclopedic, historical approach and European outlook of its members to her lifelong preoccupation with the religious, cultural, and intellectual milieu of Elizabethan England. Her influential essay on Queen Elizabeth I as Astraea (1947), later issued (1975) with her other studies of Renaissance imperial aspirations as expressed in SYMBOLism, WRITINGS, ART, and pageantry, owed much to Aby Warburg (1866–1929) and Fritz Saxl (1890–1948). So did her book *The Valois Tapestries* (1959). She was also much indebted to D.P. Walker (1914–85), particularly in *The French Academies of the Sixteenth Century* (1948), in which she explored French mystical encyclopedism and its attempts to foster a harmony of all knowledge for the betterment of the *vita activa*.

These studies, published by the Warburg, had already given Frances Yates a high if narrow reputation when she embarked on the phase of her work that was to make her more widely known, though not until she was in her mid-sixties. In 1949 she began to occupy herself again with Bruno, with the aim of explaining the nature, antecedents, and historical significance of his thought. Having perceived the importance of Bruno's acknowledged debt to Ramon Lull (c. 1233–c. 1315), she first studied Lull's project for a true and fundamental logic which could be applied to all arts and sciences. She also emphasized Bruno's appraisal of Jewish *Kabbalah*, in which he followed Pico della Mirandola (1463–94). Bruno's references to the mythical Egyptian magus Hermes Trismegistus, an important Platonic witness in Renaissance eyes, especially Marsilio Ficino's (1433–99), led her to emphasize the significance of Hermes for Bruno's belief in a sun-centered universe. To her Bruno's reading of the Copernican cosmology was Hermetic, vitalistic, and visionary, the hieroglyph of a magical religion which would restore world harmony. The supposed argument of *Giordano Bruno and the Hermetic Tradition* (1964), that Bruno was the precursor of the scientific revolution, the so-called Yates thesis, gave rise to controversy and opposition from historians of science. *The Art of Memory* (1966) was, however, generally accepted and recognized as important for the understanding of Renaissance rhetoric and poetics. It traced the ancestry and influence of Bruno's system of artificial memory, designed to strengthen the mind's natural mnemonic powers. Having their origin in classical oratory, as she showed, such schemes took on a universal character in the Renaissance.

The works of Frances Yates's last decade, such as *Theatre of the World* (1969), *The Rosicrucian Enlightenment* (1972), *Shakespeare's Last Plays* (1975), and *The Occult Philosophy in Elizabethan England* (1979), developed themes and preoccupations from these books. They were severely criticized, especially for the boldness of the claims advanced for the importance of particular individuals, notably John Dee (1527–1609) and Robert

Fludd (1574–1637), and intellectual currents. Her place as a highly individual, powerful, and lasting influence on the study of Renaissance thinking, belief, and modes of expression, as well as Renaissance literature (a concept she repudiated), is nevertheless secure.

Reading

Merkel, I., and Debus, A.G., eds 1988: *Hermeticism and the Renaissance: Intellectual History and the Occult in Early Modern Europe.*

Vickers, B., ed. 1984: *Occult and Scientific Mentalities in the Renaissance.*

Yates, F.A. 1984: *Collected Essays.*

J.B. TRAPP

Z

Žižek, Slavoj (1949–) Slovenian philosopher and cultural theorist. One of the most important influences on Žižek's prolific and diverse writing has been the thought of Jacques LACAN. Without becoming in the least a slavish disciple of Lacan, Žižek has productively amplified and developed Lacanian thought in ways that were uniquely but briefly anticipated by Louis ALTHUSSER. In his helpful Preface to Žižek's *The Sublime Object of Ideology*, Ernesto Laclau has distinguished the Slovenian reception of Lacan from that in Anglo-Saxon, French, and Latin cultures. In Slovenia the emphasis has been on the political and philosophical implications of Lacanian PSYCHOANALYSIS. Along with several colleagues at the Institute for Sociology in Ljubljana, Žižek has employed Lacanian theory in dealing with the mechanisms of political IDEOLOGY and in analyzing traditional philosophical texts, especially those of HEGEL and KANT. A distinctive feature of Žižek's writing is his determination to be provocative – to open up discussion and to stimulate new work – rather than to be reductively definitive. His own influence has very quickly become widespread in CULTURAL STUDIES, film theory, psychoanalysis, and philosophy. Žižek's boldest intellectual efforts in numerous books – which are at once learned, profound, playful, and politically committed – have been in crossing the divide that has often been thought impassable between psychoanalysis and MARXISM, ART and ideology, traditional philosophy and POPULAR CULTURE.

Reading
Žižek, Slavoj 1989: *The Sublime Object of Ideology.*
——1993: *Tarrying with the Negative: Kant, Hegel, and the Critique of Ideology.*

MICHAEL PAYNE

Bibliography

Abbate, C. 1991: *Unsung Voices: Opera and Musical Narrative in the Nineteenth Century*. Princeton, NJ: Princeton University Press.

Abel, Elizabeth 1989: *Virginia Woolf and the Fictions of Psychoanalysis*. Chicago: University of Chicago Press.

Abdel-Malik, Anouar 1963: "Orientalism in crisis." *Diogenes*, 44 (Winter), 103–40.

Abelove, Henry, Barale, Michele Aina, and Halperin, David M., eds 1993: *The Lesbian and Gay Studies Reader*. New York: Routledge.

Abercrombie, N., Hill, S., and Turner, B.S. 1980: *The Dominant Ideology Thesis*. London: Allen & Unwin.

Abrams, M.H. 1953: *The Mirror and the Lamp*. New York: Oxford University Press.

——1971: *Natural Supernaturalism: Tradition and Revolution in Romantic Literature*. New York: Norton.

——1993: *A Glossary of Literary Terms*. New York: Harcourt Brace Jovanovich.

Achinstein, Peter, and Barker, Stephen, eds 1969: *The Legacy of Logical Positivism*. Baltimore, MD: Johns Hopkins University Press.

Ackerman, Robert John 1976: *The Philosophy of Karl Popper*. Amherst: University of Massachusetts Press.

Adorno, Theodor W. 1931 (*1977*): "The actuality of philosophy," *Telos*, 31.

——1932 (*1984*): "The idea of natural history," *Telos*, 60.

——1933 (*1989*): *Kierkegaard: Construction of the Aesthetic*. Minneapolis: University of Minnesota Press.

——1936 (*1977*): "Adorno to Benjamin, 18 March 1936." In Ernst Bloch et al., *Aesthetics and Politics*. London: Verso.

——1951 (*1978*): *Minima Moralia. Reflections from Damaged Life*, trans. E.F.N. Jephcott. London: New Left Books.

——1955 (*1982*): *Prisms*. Cambridge, MA: MIT Press.

——1956 (*1982*): *Against Epistemology*, trans. Willis Domingo. Oxford: Blackwell.

——1966 (*1973*): *Negative Dialectics*. London: Routledge.

——1970a (*1984*): *Aesthetic Theory*. London: Routledge.

——1970b: *Gesammelte Schriften*, 23 vols, ed. Rolf Tiedemann. Frankfurt am Main: Suhrkamp Verlag.

——1991: *The Culture Industry: Selected Essays on Mass Culture*. London: Routledge.

Adorno, Theodor W. and Horkheimer, Max 1944 (*1973*): *Dialectic of Enlightenment*, trans. John Cumming. London: Allen Lane; New York: Herder and Herder.

Adorno, Theodor W. et al. 1950: *The Authoritarian Personality*. New York: Harper and Brothers.

——1976: *The Positivist Dispute in German Sociology*, trans. G. Adey and D. Frisby. London: Heinemann.

Agger, B. 1992: *Cultural Studies as Critical Theory*. London: Falmer Press.

Ahmad, Aijaz 1992: *In Theory: Classes, Nations, Literatures*. London: Verso.

Ahmed, Akbar S. 1992: *Postmodernism and Islam*. London: Routledge.

Ahmed, Leila 1992: *Women and Gender in Islam*. New Haven, CT: Yale University Press.

Aida, T. 1991: "The concept of communication in Mead's theory – a critique on the conventional concept of communication." In *Journal of the Faculty of Law*, Komazawa University, 49, 1–29.

Aitmatov, Chingiz 1993: "The intellectual crisis, the demise of totalitarism, and the fate of literature," *World Literature Today*, 67:1.

Aksyonov, Vassily 1993: "Distrophy of the 'thick' and *Bespredel* of the 'thin' (literary notes)," *World Literature Today*, 67:1.

Al-Azmeh, Aziz 1993: *Islams and Modernities*. London: Verso.

Albrecht, Lisa, and Brewer, Rose M. eds 1990: *Bridges of Power: Women's Multicultural Alliances*. Philadelphia, PA: New Society Publishers.

Ali, A. Yusuf 1934 (*1983*): *The Holy Qur'an: Text, Translation and Commentary*. Baltimore, MD: Amana Corporation.

Allen, Paula Gunn, ed. 1983: *Studies in Native American Literature: Critical Essays and Course Designs*. New York: MLA.

Allen, Robert C. 1987 (*1992*): *Channels of Discourse Reassembled*. Chapel Hill: University of North Carolina Press.

Alter, Robert 1981: *The Art of Biblical Narrative*. New York: Basic Books.

——1985: *The Art of Biblical Poetry*. New York: Basic Books.

Alter, Robert, and Kermode, Frank 1987: *The Literary Guide to the Bible*. Cambridge, MA: Harvard University Press.

Altham, J., and Harrison, R., eds 1995: *World, Mind, and Ethics: Essays on the Ethical Philosophy of Bernard Williams*. Cambridge: Cambridge University Press.

Althusser, Louis 1964 (*1971*): "Freud and Lacan," trans. Ben Brewster. In *Lenin and Philosophy and Other Essays*. London: New Left Books.

—— 1965a (*1979*): "Marxism is not a historicism," trans. Ben Brewster. In *Reading "Capital."* London: Verso.

—— 1965b (*1970*): *For Marx*, trans. Ben Brewster. New York: Vintage; London and New York: Verso, 1990.

—— 1970 (*1971*): "Ideology and ideological state apparatuses." In *Lenin and Philosophy and Other Essays*, trans. Ben Brewster. London: New Left Books.

—— 1971: *Lenin and Philosophy and Other Essays*; trans. Ben Brewster. London: New Left Books.

—— 1972: "Ideology and ideological state apparatus." In *Education: Structure and Society*, ed. B. Cosin. Harmondsworth: Penguin.

—— 1976a: *Essays in Self-Criticism*, trans. Grahame Lock. London: New Left Books.

—— 1976b (*1983*): "Note on the ISAs," *Economy and Society*, 12:4, 455–65.

—— 1984 (*1993*): *Essays on Ideology*, trans. Ben Brewster and Grahame Lock. London: Verso.

—— 1990: *"Philosophy and the Spontaneous Philosophy of the Scientists" and Other Essays*, trans. Gregory Elliott. London: Verso.

—— 1992 (*1993*): *The Future Lasts a Long Time and The Facts*, trans. Richard Veasey. London: Chatto & Windus.

Althusser, Louis, and Balibar, Etienne 1965 (*1979*): *Reading "Capital,"* trans. Ben Brewster. London and New York: Verso.

Altick, Richard D. 1973: *Victorian People and Ideas: A Companion for the Modern Reader of Victorian Literature*. New York: W.W. Norton.

Alvares, Claude 1991: *Decolonizing History: Technology and Culture in India, China, and the West, 1492 to the Present Day*. Goa: The Other India Press.

Aman, Kenneth, ed. 1991: *Ethical Principles for Development: Needs, Capacities or Rights?* Upper Monclair, NJ: Institute for Critical Thinking, Monclair State University.

Amin, Samir 1990: *Maldevelopment: Anatomy of a Global Failure*. London: Zed Books.

Anderson, P. 1974a (*1985*): *Passages from Antiquity to Feudalism*. London: Verso.

—— 1974b (*1986*): *Lineages of the Absolutist State*. London: Verso.

—— 1976 (*1989*): *Considerations on Western Marxism*. London: Verso.

—— 1983 (*1984*): *In the Tracks of Historical Materialism*. Chicago: University of Chicago Press.

—— 1992a: *English Questions*. London: Verso.

—— 1992b: *A Zone of Engagement*. London: Verso.

Andreev, A. 1993/4: "'Trety put,' ili Bestsennyi dar Atlantidy. (Opyt noveishego filosofsko-poliklinicheskogo issledovaniya)," *Novoe literaturnoe obozrenie*, 6.

Ansell-Pearson, Keith 1991: *Nietzsche contra Rousseau: A Study of Nietzsche's Moral and Political Thought*. Cambridge: Cambridge University Press.

Anyon, J. 1980: "Social class and the hidden curriculum of work," *Journal of Education*, 162:1, 67–92.

—— 1981: "Schools as agencies of social legitimation," *International Journal of Political Education*, 4, 195–218.

Anzaldua, Gloria, ed. 1990: *Making Face, Making Soul, Haciendo Caras: Creative and Critical Perspectives by Women of Color*. San Francisco: aunt lute foundation.

Anzieu, Didier 1975 (*1986*): *Freud's Self-Analysis*, trans. Peter Graham. London: Hogarth.

Apel, Karl-Otto 1980: *Toward a Transformation of Philosophy*. London: Routledge & Kegan Paul.

Appadurai, Arjun 1990: "Disjuncture and difference in the global cultural economy," *Public Culture*, 2:2, 1–23.

Appiah, Kwame Anthony 1985 (*1987*): "The uncompleted argument: Du Bois and the illusion of race." In *"Race," Writing, and Difference*, ed. Henry Louis Gates, Jr. Chicago: University of Chicago Press.

—— 1992: *In My Father's House: Africa in the Philosophy of Culture*. New York: Oxford University Press.

Apple, M. 1993: *Official Knowledge: Democratic Education in a Conservative Age*. New York: Routledge.

Arato, A., and Gebhardt, E., eds 1978: *The Essential Frankfurt School Reader*. Oxford: Blackwell.

Arberry, A.J. 1950: *Sufism: An Account of the Mystics of Islam*. London: George Allen & Unwin.

—— 1955: *The Koran Interpreted: A Translation*. London: George Allen & Unwin.

Aristotle (*1955*): *The Ethics of Aristotle*, trans. J.A.K. Thomson. London: George Allen & Unwin.

—— (*1946*): *The Politics of Aristotle*, trans. Ernest Barker. Oxford: Clarendon Press.

Arkhangel'sky, A. 1993: "pRoza mira," *Novy mir*, 1.

Arnold, A. James 1981: *Modernism and Negritude: The Poetry and Poetics of Aimé Césaire*. Cambridge, MA: Harvard University Press.

Arnold, Matthew 1978: "God and the Bible." In *Selected Poems and Prose*, ed. Miriam Allot. New York: Dutton.

Aronson, David 1994: "Why Tolerance?" in "Multiculturalism and diversity," *National Forum*, 74, 28–31.

Ascroft, Bill et al., eds 1989: *The Empire Writes Back: Theory and Practice in Postcolonial Literatures*. London: Routledge.

Atack, Margaret 1986: "The other: feminist," *Paragraph*, 8, 25–39.

Attfield, Robin 1983 (*1991*): *The Ethics of Environmental Concern*. Athens: University of Georgia Press.

—— 1987: *A Theory of Value and Obligation*. London and New York: Croom Helm.

—— 1995: *Value, Obligation and Meta-ethics*. Amsterdam and Atlanta: Rodopi.

Atwood, Margaret 1972: *Surfacing*. Toronto: McClelland & Stewart.

—— 1972: *Survival: A Thematic Guide to Canadian Literature*. Toronto: House of Anansi.

Auerbach, Erich 1959: *Scenes from the Drama of European Literature*. New York: Meridian Books.

—— "Figura." In *Scenes from the Drama of European Literature*. New York: Meridian Books.

—— 1961: *Introduction to Romance Languages and Literature*. New York: Capricorn.

—— 1968: *Mimesis*. Princeton, NJ: Princeton University Press.

Auerbach, Nina 1982: *Woman and the Demon: The Life of a Victorian Myth*. Cambridge, MA: Harvard University Press.

Auffret, Dominique 1991: *Alexandre Kojève: La Philosophie, l'état, la fin de l'histoire*. Paris: Grasset.

Aumont, Jacques 1983a: "Montage Eisenstein, I: Eisensteinian concepts," trans. Lee Hildreth, *Discourse: Journal for Theoretical Studies in Media and Culture*, 5 (Spring).

—— 1983b: "Montage Eisenstein, II: Eisenstein taken at his word," trans. Lee Hildreth, *Discourse: Journal for Theoretical Studies in Media and Culture*, 5 (Spring).

Austin, Gayle 1990: *Feminist Theories for Dramatic Criticism*. Ann Arbor: University of Michigan Press.

Austin, J.L. 1962: *Sense and Sensibilia: How To Do Things With Words*. Oxford: Oxford University Press.

—— 1979: *Philosophical Papers*, 3rd edn. Oxford: Oxford University Press.

Austin, Timothy 1984: *Language Crafted: A Linguistic Theory of Poetic Syntax*. Bloomington: Indiana University Press.

Avena, Thomas, ed. 1994: *Life Sentence: Writers, Artists, and AIDS*. San Francisco, CA: Mercury House.

Ayer, A. J. 1936 (*1987*): *Language, Truth and Logic*. Harmondsworth: Penguin.

——, ed. 1959: *Logical Positivism*. New York: Free Press; London: Allen & Unwin.

Azami, M. M. 1978: *Studies in Early Hadith Literature*. Indianapolis: American Trust Publications.

Bacciocco, Edward, Jr 1974: *The New Left in America: Reform to Revolution 1956–1970*. Stanford, CA: Hoover Institution Press.

Bachelard, Gaston 1934 (*1985*): *The New Scientific Spirit*, trans. Arthur Goldhammer. Boston, MA: Beacon Press.

—— 1957 (*1969*): *The Poetics of Space*, trans. Maria Jolas. Boston, MA: Beacon Press.

—— 1961 (*1988*): *The Flame of a Candle*, trans. Joni Caldwell. Dallas, TX: The Dallas Institute of Humanities and Culture Publications.

—— 1934 (*1964*): *The Psychoanalysis of Fire*, trans. A.C.M. Ross. Boston, MA: Beacon Press.

—— 1940 (*1968*): *The Philosophy of No: A Philosophy of the New Scientific Mind*. New York: Orion Press.

—— 1971: *The Poetics of Reverie*, trans. Daniel Russell. Boston, MA: Beacon Press.

Baehr, Helen, and Dyer, Gillian, eds 1987: *Boxed In: Women and Television*. London: Pandora Press.

Bahti, Timothy 1986: "Ambiguity and indeterminacy: the juncture," *Comparative Literature*, 36, 209–23.

Bailey, Richard W., and Burton, Delores 1968: *English Stylistics: A Bibliography*. Cambridge, MA: MIT Press.

Baker, Houston A., Jr 1980: *The Journey Back*. Chicago: University of Chicago Press.

—— 1988: *Afro-American Poetics: Revisions of Harlem and the Black Aesthetic*. Madison: University of Wisconsin Press.

Bakhtin, Mikhail 1929 (*1984*): *Problems of Dostoevsky's Poetics*, ed. and trans. C. Emerson. Minneapolis: University of Minnesota Press.

—— 1965 (*1984*): *Rabelais and His World*, trans. Helene Iswolsky. Bloomington: Indiana University Press.

—— 1975 (*1981*): *The Dialogic Imagination: Four Essays*, trans. C. Emerson and M. Holquist. Austin, TX: University of Texas Press.

—— 1979 (*1986*): *Speech Genres and Other Late Essays*, ed. C. Emerson and M. Holquist, trans. V.W. McGee. Austin, TX: University of Texas Press.

Bakhtin, M.M. and Medvedev, P.N. 1978: *The Formal Method in Literary Scholarship: A Critical Introduction to Sociologist Poetics*, trans. A.J. Wehrle. Baltimore, MD: Johns Hopkins University Press.

Bal, Mieke 1987: *Lethal Love: Feminist Literary*

Readings of Biblical Love Stories. Bloomington: Indiana University Press.

—— 1991: *Reading "Rembrandt": Beyond the Word-Image Opposition.* Cambridge: Cambridge University Press.

Balazs, Bela 1945: (*1970*): *Theory of the Film.* New York: Dover.

Baldick, Chris 1983: *The Social Mission of English Criticism 1848–1932.* Oxford: Clarendon Press.

Balfour, Ian 1988: *Northrop Frye.* Boston, MA: Twayne.

Balibar, Etienne 1965 (*1990*): "The basic concepts of historical materialism," trans. Ben Brewster. In L. Althusser and E. Balibar, *Reading "Capital."* London: Verso.

—— 1974: *Cinq études du matérialisme historique.* Paris: François Maspero.

—— 1976 (*1977*): *On the Dictatorship of the Proletariat,* trans. Grahame Lock. London: Verso.

—— 1985: *Spinoza et la politique.* Paris: Presses Universitaires de France.

—— 1991a: *Ecrits pour Althusser.* Paris: Editions la Découverte.

—— 1991b: "Racism and politics in Europe today," *New Left Review.*

—— 1993a: *Masses, Classes, Ideas,* trans. James Swenson. London: Routledge.

—— 1993b (*1995*): *The Philosophy of Marx,* trans. Chris Turner. London: Verso.

Balibar, Etienne, and Wallerstein, Immanuel 1988 (*1991*): *Race, Nation, Class,* trans. Chris Turner. London: Verso.

Ballester, Ros 1992. *Seductive Farms: Woman's Amatory Fiction from 1684 to 1740.* Oxford: Clarendon Press.

Bambara, Toni Cade 1970: *The Black Woman.* New York: New American Library.

Bamber, Linda 1982: *Comic Women, Tragic Men: A Study of Gender and Genre in Shakespeare.* Stanford, CA: Stanford University Press.

Bann, Stephen, and Bowlt, John E., eds 1973: *Russian Formalism.* Edinburgh: Scottish Academic Press.

Bantock, G. 1975: "Towards a theory of popular education." In *Curriculum Design,* ed. M. Golby, J. Greenwald, R. West. London: Croom Helm and the Open University Press.

Banton, M. 1977: *The Idea of Race.* London: Tavistock.

—— 1983: *Racial and Ethnic Competition.* Cambridge: Cambridge University Press.

—— 1987: *Racial Theories.* Cambridge: Cambridge University Press.

Barnes, Barry 1974: *Scientific Knowledge and Sociological Theory.* London: Routledge & Kegan Paul.

—— 1982: *T.S. Kuhn and Social Science.* London: Macmillan.

—— 1985: *About Science.* Oxford: Blackwell.

Barrett, Michèle 1979: "Introduction." *Women and Writing.* London: The Women's Press.

—— 1980 (*1988*): *Women's Oppression Today: Problems in Marxist Feminist Analysis.* London: Verso/ New Left Books.

—— 1993: "Althusser's Marx, Althusser's Lacan." In *The Althusserian Legacy,* ed. E.A. Kaplan and M. Sprinker. London: Verso.

Barrett, R., and Gibson, R., eds 1990: *Perspectives on Quine.* Oxford: Blackwell.

Barry, N. 1987: *The New Right.* London: Croom Helm.

Barthes, Roland 1953 (*1967*): *Writing Degree Zero,* trans. Annette Lavers and Colin Smith. London: Cape.

—— 1953 (*1957, 1982*): *Mythologies,* trans. Annette Lavers. London: Granada.

—— 1961 (*1991*): "The photographic message." In *Image, Music, Text,* trans. Stephen Heath. New York: Noonday Press.

—— 1963 (*1977*): *On Racine,* trans. Richard Howard. New York: Octagon Books.

—— 1964 (*1967*): *Elements of Semiology,* trans. Annette Lavers and Colin Smith. New York: Hill and Wang.

—— 1966 (*1987*): *Criticism and Truth,* trans. K.P. Keuneman. London: Athlone Press.

—— 1967a (*1977*): "The death of the author," trans. Stephen Heath. In *Image, Music, Text.* London: Fontana.

—— 1967b: "Seven photo models of *Mother Courage,*" *Drama Review,* 12:1 (Fall), 44–55.

—— 1970 (*1982*): *The Empire of Signs.* New York: Hill and Wang.

—— 1970 (*1975*): *S/Z,* trans. Richard Miller. Oxford: Blackwell.

—— 1973 (*1976*): *The Pleasure of the Text,* trans. Richard Miller. London: Jonathan Cape.

—— 1977a (*1991*): *Image, Music, Text,* trans. Stephen Heath. New York: Noonday.

—— 1977b: *Roland Barthes by Roland Barthes,* trans. Richard Howard. London: Macmillan.

—— 1977c (*1978*): *A Lover's Discourse: Fragments,* trans. Richard Howard. New York: Hill and Wang.

—— 1978: *Image, Music, Text,* trans. Stephen Heath. New York: Hill and Wang.

—— 1980 (*1981*): *Camera Lucida,* trans. Richard Howard. New York: Hill and Wang.

—— 1982: *A Barthes Reader,* ed. Susan Sontag. London: Fontana.

—— 1987 (*1992*): *Incidents,* trans. Richard Howard. Berkeley: University of California Press.

Bartlett, Thomas, et al., eds 1988: *Irish Studies: A General Introduction.* Dublin: Gill & Macmillan.

Bassin, Mark 1992: "Geographical determinism in fin-de-siècle Marxism: Georgii Plekhanov and

the environmental basis of Russian history."
Geographers, 82, 3–22.

Bassnett, Susan 1990: *Comparative Literature: A Critical Introduction*. Oxford: Blackwell.

—— 1991: *Translation Studies*. London: Routledge.

Bassnett, Susan, and Lefevere, André 1990: *Translation, History and Culture*. London: Pinter.

Bataille, Georges 1928 (*1979*): *The Story of the Eye*, trans. Joachim Neugroschel. London: Marion Boyars.

—— 1943 (*1988*): *Inner Experience*, trans. Lesley Anne Boldt. Albany: State University of New York Press.

—— 1949 (*1988*): *The Accursed Share*, trans. Robert Hurley. New York: Zone Books.

—— 1957a (*1962*): *Eroticism: Death and Sensuality*, trans. Mary Dalwood. London: John Calder.

—— 1957b (*1985*): *Literature and Evil*, trans. Alistair Hamilton. London: Marion Boyars.

—— 1985: *Visions of Excess: Selected Writings 1927–1939*, trans. Allan Stoekl, C.R. Lovitt, and D.M. Leslie. Manchester: Manchester University Press.

Bates, E. 1976: *Language and Context: The Acquisition of Pragmatics*. New York: Academic Press.

Bates, Ronald 1971: *Northrop Frye*. Toronto: McClelland and Stewart.

Bateson, F.W. 1951: "Contributions to a dictionary of critical terms. II: Dissociation of sensibility," *Essays in Criticism*, 1, 302–12.

Bateson, Mary Catherine 1984 (*1988*): *With a Daughter's Eye: A Memoir of Margaret Mead and Gregory Bateson*. New York: Washington Square Press.

Baudelaire, Charles 1845 (*nd*): "The painter of modern life." In *The Painter of Modern Life and Other Essays*, trans. Jonathan Mayne. New York: Da Capo Press.

Baudrillard, Jean 1968: *Le Système des objets*. Paris: Gallimard.

—— 1970: *La Société de consommation*. Paris: Denoël.

—— 1972 (*1981*): *For a Critique of the Political Economy of the Sign*, trans. Charles Levin. St Louis, MO: Telos Press.

—— 1973 (*1975*): *The Mirror of Production*, trans. Mark Poster. St Louis, MO: Telos Press.

—— 1976 (*1993*): *Symbolic Exchange and Death*, trans. Iain Hamilton Grant. London: Sage.

—— 1979 (*1990*): *Seduction*, trans. Brian Singer. London: Macmillan.

—— 1981 (*1983*): *Simulacra and Simulations*, trans. Paul Foss, Paul Patton, and Philip Beitchman. New York: Semiotext(e).

—— 1988: *Selected Writings*, ed. Mark Poster. Cambridge: Polity.

—— 1990 (*1993*): *The Transparency of Evil: Essays on Extreme Phenomena*. London: Verso.

—— 1991: *La Guerre du Golfe n'a pas lieu*. Paris: Gallimard.

Baynes, K., Bohman, J., and McCarthy, T., eds 1987: *After Philosophy: End or Transformation?* Cambridge, MA: MIT Press.

Bazin, André 1967 (*1971*): *What is Cinema?* 2 vols, trans. Hugh Gray. Berkeley: University of California Press.

—— 1971: *Jean Renoir*, ed. François Truffaut, trans. W.W. Halsey and William Simon. New York: Delta.

Beauvoir, S. de 1949 (*1974, 1984*): *The Second Sex*, trans. H.M. Parshley. Harmondsworth: Penguin.

—— 1963 (*1987*): *Force of Circumstance*, trans. Richard Howard. Harmondsworth: Penguin.

Becker, Howard S. 1963: *The Outsiders. Studies in the Sociology of Deviance*. New York: Free Press of Glencoe.

—— 1974: "Art a collective action," *American Sociological Review*, 39.

—— 1982: *Art Worlds*. Berkeley: University of California Press.

Beetham, David 1991: *The Legitimation of Power*. London: Macmillan.

Bell, Daniel 1979: *The Cultural Contradictions of Capitalism*. 2nd edn. London: Heinemann.

Bell, David 1987: "The art of judgement." *Mind*, 96.

—— 1990: *Husserl*. London: Routledge.

Bell, Quentin 1972: *Virginia Woolf: A Biography*, 2 vols. London: Hogarth Press.

Bellamy, R., and Schecter, D. 1993: *Gramsci and the Italian State*. Manchester: Manchester University Press.

Belsey, Catherine 1985: *The Subject of Tragedy: Identity and Difference in Renaissance Drama*. London: Methuen.

Bender, John 1987: *Imagining the Penitentiary: Fiction and Architecture of Mind in Eighteenth-Century England*. Chicago: Chicago University Press.

—— 1992: "A new history of the Enlightenment?" In *The Profession of Eighteenth-Century Literature: Reflections on an Institution*. Baltimore, MD: Johns Hopkins University Press.

Benevolo, Leonardo 1993: *The European City*. Oxford: Blackwell.

Benhabib, Seyla M. 1992: *Situating the Self: Gender, Community and Postmodernism in Contemporary Ethics*. Cambridge: Polity Press.

Benjamin, Andrew 1989: *Translation and the Nature of Philosophy*. London: Routledge.

—— 1991: *Thinking Art: Beyond Traditional Aesthetics*. London: ICA Books.

——, ed. 1989 and 1992: *Judging Lyotard*. Oxford: Blackwell; London: Routledge.

Benjamin, Walter 1913 (*1972*): "Metaphysics of youth." In Benjamin 1972, II.

——— 1919 (*1972*): "The concept of art criticism in German Romanticism." In Benjamin 1972, I.

——— 1924–5 (*1972*): "Goethe's *Elective Affinities.*" In Benjamin 1972, I.

——— 1928a (*1977*): *The Origin of German Tragic Drama.* London: Verso.

——— 1928b (*1979*): "One-way street." In Benjamin 1979.

——— 1929 (*1979*): "Surrealism: the last snapshot of the European intelligentsia." In Benjamin 1979.

——— 1934 (*1973*): "The author as producer." In *Understanding Brecht.* London: Verso and New Left Books.

——— 1936 (*1968*): "The work of art in the age of mechanical reproduction." In Benjamin 1968.

——— 1938–9 (*1985*): "Central Park." *New German Critique*, 34.

——— 1940 (*1968*): "Theses on the philosophy of history." In Benjamin 1968.

——— 1968: *Illuminations.* London: Fontana.

——— 1969: *Charles Baudelaire or the Lyric Poet of High Capitalism.* London: New Left Books.

——— 1972: *Gesammelte Schriften*, 7 vols, ed. Rolf Tiedemann and Herman Schweppenhauser. Frankfurt am Main: Suhrkamp Verlag.

——— 1973: *Understanding Brecht.* London: New Left Books.

——— 1979: *One-Way Street and Other Writings.* London: Verso.

Bennett, James R. 1986: *A Bibliography of Stylistics and Related Criticism, 1967–1983.* New York: Modern Language Association.

——— 1993a: "Style." In *The New Princeton Encyclopedia of Poetry and Poetics*, ed. O. Preminger et al. Princeton, NJ: Princeton University Press, 1225–7.

——— 1993b: "Stylistics." In *The New Princeton Encyclopedia of Poetry and Poetics*, ed. O. Preminger et al. Princeton, NJ: Princeton University Press, 1227–9.

Bennett, Tony 1979: *Formalism and Marxism.* London: Methuen.

——— 1990: *Outside Literature.* London and New York: Routledge.

Bennington, Geoffrey 1985: *Lyotard: Writing the Event.* Manchester: Manchester University Press.

Bentley, Eric, ed. 1968: *The Theory of the Modern Stage: An Introduction to Modern Theatre and Drama.* Harmondsworth: Penguin.

——— 1981: *The Brecht Commentaries, 1943–1980.* New York: Grove Press; London: Eyre Methuen.

——— 1990: "The influence of Brecht." In *Reinterpreting Brecht: His Influence on Contemporary Drama and Film*, ed. Pia Kleber and Colin Visser. Cambridge: Cambridge University Press.

Benton, Mike 1989: *The Comic Book in America.* Dallas, TX: Taylor Publishing.

Benton, T. 1984: *The Rise and Fall of Structural Marxism.* London: Macmillan.

Benveniste, Emile 1966 (*1971*): *Problems of General Linguistics*, trans. Mary E. Meek. Miami: Miami University Press.

——— 1969 (*1973*): *Indo-European Language and Society.* London: Faber & Faber.

Berghe, Pierre L. van den 1973: "*Pluralism.*" In *Handbook of Social and Cultural Anthropology*, ed. J. Honigmann. New York: Rand McNally.

Bergson, Henri 1900 (*1980*): "Laughter." In *Comedy: An Essay on Comedy by George Meredith and Laughter by Henri Bergson*, ed. Wylie Sypher. Baltimore, MD: Johns Hopkins University Press.

Berlin, Brent, and Kay, Paul 1969: *Basic Color Terms: Their Universality and Evolution.* Berkeley: University of California Press.

Berman, Marshall: 1982 (*1983*): *All That is Solid Melts into Air: The Experience of Modernity.* London: Verso.

Bernal, Martin 1987: *The Black Athena: The Afroasiatic Roots of Classical Civilization.* New Brunswick, NJ: Rutgers University Press.

Bernstein, Leonard 1976: *The Unanswered Question: Six Talks at Harvard.* The Charles Eliot Norton Lectures. Cambridge, MA: Harvard University Press.

Bernstein, R.J., ed. 1985: *Habermas and Modernity.* Cambridge: Polity Press.

Bernstein, Richard 1983: *Beyond Objectivism and Relativism.* Philadelphia, PA: University of Pennsylvania Press.

Bersani, Leo 1984: *A Future for Astyanax: Character and Desire in Literature.* New York: Columbia University Press.

Bethurum, Dorothy, ed. 1961: "Patristic exegesis in the criticism of medieval literature." In *Critical Approaches to Medieval Literature, Selected Papers from the English Institute, 1958–59.* New York: Columbia University Press.

Bettelheim, Bruno 1976 (*1986*): *The Uses of Enchantment.* Harmondsworth: Penguin.

Bhabha, Homi K. 1991: "'Race,' time and the revision of modernity." *Oxford Literary Review*, 13.

——— 1994: *The Location of Culture.* London: Routledge.

Bhaskar, Roy 1975: *A Realist Theory of Science.* Hassocks: Harvester.

——— 1986: *Scientific Realism in Human Emancipation.* London: Verso.

——— 1989: *Reclaiming Reality: A Critical Introduction to Contemporary Philosophy.* London: Verso.

——— 1993: *Dialectic: The Pulse of Freedom.* London: Verso.

Biguenet, John, and Schulte, Rainer, eds 1989: *The Craft of Translation.* Chicago: Chicago University Press.

Blackham, H.J. 1961: *Six Existentialist Thinkers: Kierkegaard, Nietzsche, Jaspers, Marcel, Heidegger, Sartre.* London: Routledge.

Blais, Marie-Claire 1966: *A Season in the Life of Emmanuel.* New York: Farrar, Straus, and Giroux.

Blake, Nigel, and Kay Pole, eds 1983 (*1984*): *Dangers of Deterrence.* London: Routledge & Kegan Paul.

—— 1984: *Objections to Nuclear Defence.* London: Routledge & Kegan Paul.

Bleicher, Joseph 1980: *Contemporary Hermeneutics: Hermeneutics as Method, Philosophy and Critique.* London: Routledge.

Bloch, E. 1986: *The Principle of Hope,* trans. Neville Plaice, Stephen Plaice, and Paul Knight. 3 vols, Oxford: Blackwell.

—— 1988: *Natural Law and Human Dignity,* trans. Dennis J. Schmidt. Cambridge, MA: MIT Press.

—— 1991: *Heritage of Our Times,* trans. Neville Plaice and Stephen Plaice. Oxford: Polity Press.

Bloch, Ernst, et al. 1977 (*1980*): *Aesthetics and Politics,* trans. and ed. Ronald Taylor. London and New York: Verso.

Bloom, Allan 1987: *The Closing of the American Mind.* New York: Simon & Schuster.

Bloom, Harold 1961: *The Visionary Company.* New York: Doubleday.

—— 1973 (*1984*): *The Anxiety of Influence: A Theory of Poetry.* New York and Oxford: Oxford University Press.

—— 1975a: *Kabbalah and Criticism.* New York: Continuum.

—— 1975b: *A Map of Misreading.* New York: Oxford University Press.

—— 1982: *The Breaking of the Vessels.* Chicago: University of Chicago Press.

—— 1991: *The Book of J.* London: Faber.

Bloom, Harold, de Man, Paul, Derrida, Jacques, Hartman, Geoffrey, and Miller, J. Hillis 1979: *Deconstruction and Criticism.* New York: Seabury.

Bloomfield, L. 1933: *Language.* New York: Holt, Rinehart & Winston.

Bloor, David 1976: *Knowledge and Social Imagery.* London: Routledge & Kegan Paul.

Blum-Kulka, S., House, J., and Kasper, G., eds 1989: *Cross-Cultural Pragmatics: Requests and Apologies.* Norwood, NJ: Ablex.

Blumenberg, Hans 1983: *The Legitimacy of the Modern Age.* Cambridge, MA: MIT Press.

Blundell, Valda, Shepherd, John, and Taylor, Ian, eds 1993: *Relocating Cultural Studies: Developments in Theory and Research.* London: Routledge.

Boas, Franz 1911: *The Mind of Primitive Man.* New York: Macmillan.

Bohr, Niels 1934: *Atomic Theory and the Description of Nature.* Cambridge: Cambridge University Press.

Boland, Eavan 1989: *A Kind of Scar: The Woman Poet in a National Tradition.* Dublin: Attic Press.

Bolton, Richard, ed. 1989 (*1992*): *The Contest of Meaning: Critical Histories of Photography.* Cambridge: MIT Press.

Bonaparte, Marie 1933 (*1949*): *The Life and Work of Edgar Allan Poe.* London: Imago.

Bonnicksen, Andrea L. 1989: *In Vitro Fertilization: Building Policy from Laboratories to Legislatures.* New York: Columbia University Press.

Bookchin, Murray 1980 (*1991*): *Toward an Ecological Society.* Montreal: Black Rose Books.

Booth, Steven 1983: *King Lear, Macbeth, Indefinition and Tragedy.* New Haven, CT: Yale University Press.

Booth, Wayne 1974: *A Rhetoric of Irony.* Chicago: University of Chicago Press.

Bordwell, David 1993: *The Cinema of Eisenstein.* Cambridge, MA: Harvard University Press.

Borges, Jorge Luis 1974. *Obras Completas.* Buenos Aires: Emece.

Boswell, John 1982 (*1990*): "Revolutions, universals, and sexual categories." In *Hidden from History: Reclaiming the Gay and Lesbian Past,* ed. Martin Duberman, Martha Vicinius, and George Chauncey, Jr. New York: Meridian.

Bottomore, T.B. 1965: (*1991*): *Classes in Modern Society.* London: Harper/Collins.

Bouchard, D.F., ed. 1977: *Language, Countermemory, Practice: Selected Essays and Interviews by Michel Foucault.* Oxford: Blackwell.

Bourdieu, Pierre 1958 (*1962*): *The Algerians,* trans. A.C.M. Ross. Boston, MA: Beacon Press.

—— 1976: "The school as a conservative force: scholastic and cultural inequalities." In *Schooling and Capitalism,* ed. R. Dale, G. Esland, M. MacDonald. London: Routledge & Kegan Paul and the Open University Press.

—— 1977: *Outline of a Theory of Practice.* Cambridge: Cambridge University Press.

—— 1980 (*1990*): *The Logic of Practice.* Oxford: Polity Press.

—— 1984: *Distinction: A Social Critique of the Judgement of Taste.* Cambridge MA: Harvard University Press.

—— 1990: *In Other Words.* Oxford: Policy Press.

—— 1992: *Les règles de l'art. Genèse et structure du champ littéraire.* Paris: Editions du Seuil.

—— 1993: *The Field of Cultural Production,* ed. Raphael Johnson. Cambridge: Polity Press.

Bouza Alvarez, Fernando 1992: *Del escribano a la biblioteca. La Civilización escrita europea en la alta edad moderna (Siglos XV–XVII).* Madrid: Editorial Sintesis.

Bové, Paul 1990: "A conversation with William V. Spanos," *boundary 2,* 17, 1–39.

Bowie, Andrew 1990 (*1993*): *Aesthetics and Subjec-*

tivity: From Kant to Nietzsche. Manchester: Manchester University Press.

Bowie, Malcolm 1987: *Freud, Proust and Lacan: Theory as Fiction*. Cambridge: Cambridge University Press.

—— 1991: *Lacan*. London: Fontana.

Bowles, Gloria, and Klein, Renate Duelli, eds 1983: *Theories of Women's Studies*. London: Routledge & Kegan Paul.

Bowles, S., and Gintis, H. 1976: *Schooling in a Capitalist America*. New York: Basic Books.

Boyers, Robert 1977: *Lionel Trilling: Negative Capability and the Wisdom of Avoidance*. Columbia, MO: University of Missouri Press.

Boyle, D.G. 1969: *A Students' Guide to Piaget*. Oxford: Pergamon.

Bracey, John H., Jr, Meier, August, and Rudwick, Elliott, eds 1970: *Black Nationalism in America*. New York: Bobbs-Merrill.

Braithwaite, Edward Kamau 1978: *The Development of Creole Society in Jamaica: 1770–1820*. Oxford: Clarendon Press.

Brake, M. 1985: *Comparative Youth Cultures*. London: Routledge.

Bramwell, Anna 1989: *Ecology in the 20th Century. A History*. New Haven, CT: Yale University Press.

Brantlinger, P. 1990: *Crusoe's Footprints*. London: Routledge.

Braudel, Fernand 1949 (*1973*): *The Mediterranean and the Mediterranean World in the Age of Philip II*. New York: Harper & Row.

—— 1958 (*1972*): "History and the social sciences: the *longue durée*." In *Economy & Society in Early Modern Europe*, ed. P. Burke. London: Routledge & Kegan Paul.

—— 1979 (*1981–4*): *Civilization and Capitalism, 15th–18th Century*. New York: Harper & Row.

Braverman, Harry 1974: *Labor and Monopoly Capital*. New York: Monthly Review Press.

Bray, Alan 1982 (*1988*): *Homosexuality in Renaissance English*. Boston: Gay Men's Press.

Brecht, Bertold 1978: *Brecht on Theatre*. London: Methuen.

Breckenridge, Carol, and van der Veer, Peter 1993: *Orientalism and the Postcolonial Predicament: Perspectives on South Asia*. Philadelphia, PA: University of Pennsylvania Press.

Bremond, Claude 1973: *Logique du récit*. Paris: Seuil.

Brenkman, John 1993: "Multiculturalism and criticism." In *English Inside and Out: The Place of Literary Criticism*, ed. Susan Gubar and Jonathan Kamholtz. New York: Routledge.

Brereton, Geoffrey 1968: *Principles of Tragedy*. Coral Gables: University of Miami Press.

Breuer, Joseph, and Freud, Sigmund 1893–5 (*1953–74*): *Studies on Hysteria*. In *The Complete Psychological Works of Sigmund Freud*, trans. James Strachey. 24 vols, Vol. 2. London: Hogarth Press, and the Institute of Psychiatry.

Bridgewater, Patrick 1972: *Nietzsche in Anglosaxony*. Leicester: Leicester University Press.

Brienza, Susan 1987: *Samuel Beckett's New Worlds: Style in Metafiction*. Norman: University of Oklahoma Press.

Briggs, Asa 1989: *Victorian Things*. Chicago: University of Chicago Press.

Bristow, Joseph, and Wilson, Angie, eds 1993: *Activating Theory: Lesbian, Gay, Bisexual Politics*. London: Lawrence & Wishart.

Brooker, Peter 1988: *Bertold Brecht: Dialectics, Poetry, Politics*. London: Croom Helm.

Brooks, Cleanth 1947 (*1968*): *The Well-Wrought Urn*. London: Methuen.

Brooks, Peter 1984: *Reading for the Plot*. New York: Alfred Knopf.

Brower, Reuben, Vendler, Helen, and Hollander, John 1973: *I.A. Richards: Essays in His Honor*. New York: Oxford University Press.

Brown, James Robert 1991: *The Laboratory of the Mind: Thought Experiments in the Natural Sciences*. London: Routledge.

—— 1994: *Smoke and Mirrors: How Science Reflects Reality*. London: Routledge.

Brown, Peter 1982: *Society and the Holy in Antiquity*. Los Angeles: University of California Press.

—— 1988: *The Body and Society: Men, Women and Sexual Renunciation in Early Christianity*. London: Faber.

Bruner, J. 1975: "The ontogenesis of speech acts," *Journal of Child Language*, 2, 1–19.

Bruns, Gerald 1992: *Hermeneutics Ancient and Modern*. New Haven, CT, and London: Yale University Press.

Bryan, B., Dadzie, S., and Scafe, S. 1985: *The Heart of the Race*. London: Virago.

Bryson, Norman 1981 (*1986*): *Word and Image: French Painting of the Ancient Regime*. Cambridge: Cambridge University Press.

—— 1983 (*1988*): *Vision and Painting: The Logic of the Gaze*. New Haven, CT: Yale University Press.

—— 1984: *Tradition and Desire: From David to Delacroix*. Cambridge: Cambridge University Press.

—— 1989: *Looking at the Overlooked: Four Essays on Still-Life*. Cambridge: Rection Press.

Buck-Morss, Susan 1977: *The Origin of Negative Dialectics: Theodor W. Adorno, Walter Benjamin, and the Frankfurt Institute*. New York: Macmillan Free Press.

—— 1989: *Dialectics of Seeing: Walter Benjamin and the Arcades Project*. Cambridge, MA: MIT Press.

Buckley, Jerome H. 1966: *The Triumph of Time: A Study of the Victorian Concepts of Time, History, Progress and Decadence*. Cambridge, MA: Harvard University Press.

Buckley, Vincent 1959: *Poetry and Morality: Studies in the Criticism of Matthew Arnold, T.S. Eliot and F.R. Leavis*. London: Chatto & Windus.

Bujic, B., ed. 1988: *Music in European Thought, 1851–1912*. Cambridge: Cambridge University Press.

Bullock, Alan, and Shock, Maurice, eds 1957: *The Liberal Tradition: From Fox to Keynes*. New York: New York University Press.

Bulmer, M. 1984: *The Chicago School of Sociology*. Chicago: University of Chicago Press.

Bunch, Charlotte, and Pollack, Sandra, eds 1983: *Learning Our Way: Essays in Feminist Education*. Trumansburg, NY: The Crossing Press.

Burgin, Victor 1986: "Re-reading Camera Lucida." In *The End of Art Theory: Criticism and Postmodernity*. Atlantic Highlands, NJ: Humanities Press.

Burke, Kenneth 1966: *Language as Symbolic Action*. Berkeley: University of California Press.

Burke, Peter 1978: *Popular Culture in Early Modern Europe*. New York: Harper & Row.

Burke, Sean 1992: *The Death and Return of the Author*. Edinburgh: Edinburgh University Press.

Burton, Humphrey 1994: *Leonard Bernstein*. New York: Doubleday.

Bulter, C. 1994: *Early Modernism: Literature, Music, and Painting in Europe, 1900–1916*. Oxford: Oxford University Press.

Butler, J. 1990: *Gender Trouble. Feminism and the Subversion of Identity*. London: Routledge.

Butler, Johnnella E., and Walter, John C., eds 1991: *Transforming the Curriculum: Ethnic Studies and Women's Studies*. Albany, NY: State University of New York Press.

Buttjes, D. 1981: *Landeskundliches Lernen im Englischunterricht*. Paderborn: Schoningh.

—— 1989: "Landeskunde-Didaktik und Landeskundliches Curriculum." In *Handbuch Fremdsprachenunterricht*, ed. K.R. Bausch et al. Tübingen: Francke.

Buttjes, D. and Byram, M., eds 1991: *Mediating Languages and Cultures*. Clevedon: Multilingual Matters.

Byg, Barton 1990: "*History Lessons*: Brecht's Caesar novel and the film by Straub/Huillet." *In Essays on Brecht (Brecht Yearbook 15)*, ed. Marc Silberman et al. College Park, MD: International Brecht Society.

Byram, M., ed. 1994: *Culture and Language Learning in Higher Education*. Clevedon: Multilingual Matters.

Cabral, Amilcar 1973: *Return to the Source: Selected Speeches of Amilcar Cabral*. New York: Monthly Review Press.

Cage, John Milton 1961: *Silence*. Wesleyan University Press.

Cain, A. ed. 1991: *Enseignement/Apprentissage de la civilisation en cours de langue*. Paris: Institut National de Recherche Pedagogique.

Cairns, David, and Richards, Shaun 1988: *Writing Ireland: Colonialism, Nationalism and Culture*. Manchester: Manchester University Press.

Calinescu, Matei 1987: *Five Faces of Modernity: Modernism, Avant-Garde, Decadence, Kitsch, Postmodernism*. Durham, NC: Duke University Press.

Callaghan, Dympna 1989: *Woman and Gender in Renaissance Tragedy*. Atlantic Highlands, NJ: Humanities Press.

Callinicos, A. 1976: *Althusser's Marxism*. London: Pluto Press.

Calvino, Italo 1992: *If On a Winter's Night a Traveller*, trans. W. Weaver. London: Minerva.

Cameron, Peter 1994: *The Weekend*. New York: Farrar, Straus & Giroux.

Campenhausen, Hans von 1972: *The Formation of the Christian Bible*. Philadelphia, PA: Fortress.

Campos, C., Higman, F., Mendelson, D., and Nagy, G. 1988: *L'Enseignement de la civilisation française dans les universités d'Europe*. Paris: Didier.

Canovan, Margaret 1992: *Hannah Arendt: A Reinterpretation of Her Political Thought*. Cambridge: Cambridge University Press.

Carby, Hazel 1982: "White women listen! Black feminism and the boundaries of sisterhood." In *The Empire Strikes Back*, ed. Centre for Contemporary Cultural Studies. London: Hutchinson.

—— 1987: *Reconstructing Womanhood: The Emergence of the Afro-American Woman Novelist*. New York: Oxford University Press.

Carlson, Marvin 1984: *Theories of the Theatre: A Historical and Critical Survey from the Greeks to the Present*. Ithaca, NY and London: Cornell University Press.

Carroll, Joseph 1982: *The Cultural Theory of Matthew Arnold*. Berkeley: University of California Press.

Carson, Rachel 1962 (*1972*): *Silent Spring*. Harmondsworth: Penguin.

Carter, Ronald, and Simpson, Paul 1989: *Language, Discourse and Literature: An Introductory Reader in Discourse Stylistics*. London: Unwin Hyman; Boston: Routledge & Kegan Paul.

Carver, T. 1990: *Friedrich Engels, his Life and Thought*. New York: St Martin's Press.

——, ed. 1991: *The Cambridge Companion to Marx*. Cambridge: Cambridge University Press.

Case, Sue-Ellen, ed. 1990: *Performing Feminisms:*

Feminist Critical Theory and Theatre. Baltimore, MD: Johns Hopkins University Press.

Casey, John 1966: *The Language of Criticism*. London: Methuen.

Casmore, Ellen 1994: *And There Was Television*. London: Routledge.

Cassirer, Ernst 1932 (*1951*): *The Philosophy of the Enlightenment*. Princeton, NJ: Princeton University Press.

Castells, M. 1977: *The Urban Question*. London: Edward Arnold.

Castillo, Debra A. 1992: *Talking Back. Toward a Latin American Feminist Literary Criticism*. Ithaca, NY: Cornell University Press.

Castle, Terry 1986: *Masquerade and Civilisation in Eighteenth-Century Culture and Fiction*. Stanford, CA: Stanford University Press.

Castoriadis, Cornelius 1984: *Crossroads in the Labyrinth*, trans. Martin H. Ryle and Kate Soper. Brighton: Harvester Press.

——1987: *The Imaginary Institution of Society*, trans. Kathleen Blamey. Cambridge: Polity Press.

——1991: *Philosophy, Politics, Autonomy*, trans. David A. Curtis. Oxford: Oxford University Press.

——1993: *Political and Social Writings*, 3rd edn, trans. David A. Curtis. Minneapolis: University of Minnesota Press.

Catford, J.C. 1965: *A Linguistic Theory of Translation*. London: Oxford University Press.

Caute, David 1988: *The Year of the Barricades: A Journey Through 1968*. New York: Harper & Row.

Cavell, Stanley 1965: "Austin at criticism," *Philosophical Review*, 74, 204–19.

——1969: "The availability of Wittgenstein's later philosophy." In *Must We Mean What We Say?* New York: Scribners.

——1971: *The World Viewed: Reflections on the Ontology of Film*. New York: Viking.

——1972: *The Senses of Walden*. New York: Viking.

——1979a: *The Claim of Reason*. New York: Oxford University Press.

——1979b: *The World Viewed*. New York: Viking.

——1987: *Disowning Knowledge in Six Plays of Shakespeare*. Cambridge: Cambridge University Press.

Caygill, Howard 1989: *Art of Judgement*. Oxford: Blackwell.

Centre for Contemporary Cultural Studies 1982: *The Empire Strikes Back*. London: Hutchinson.

Certeau, Michel de 1984: *The Practice of Everyday Life*. Berkeley: University of California Press.

Césaire, Aimé 1939 (*1983*): *Cahier d'un retour au pays natal. [Notebook of a Return to My Native Land.]* In *The Collected Poetry (1939–1976)*, trans. Clayton Eshelman and Annette Smith. Berkeley: University of California Press.

——1972: *Discourse on Colonialism*. Cambridge, MA: MIT Press.

Chace, William M. 1980: *Lionel Trilling: Criticsm and Politics*. Stanford, CA: Stanford University Press.

Chakravarty, Suhash 1991: *The Raj Syndrome: A Study in Imperial Perceptions*. New Delhi: Penguin Books.

Chalmers, A. 1978 (*1987*): *What is This Thing Called Science?* Milton Keynes: Open University Press.

Cham, Mbye B., and Andrade-Watkins, Claire, eds 1988: *Blackframes: Critical Perspectives on Black Independent Cinema*. Cambridge, MA: MIT Press.

Chartier, Roger 1988: *Cultural History: Between Practices and Representations*. Oxford: Polity Press.

——1994: *The Order of Books. Readers, Authors, and Libraries in Europe between the Fourteenth and Eighteenth Centuries*. Oxford: Polity Press.

Chase, Cynthia 1986: *Decomposing Figures: Rhetorical Readings in the Romantic Tradition*. Baltimore, MD: The Johns Hopkins University Press.

Chasseguet-Smirguel, J. 1981: *Female Sexuality, New Psychoanalytic Views*. London: Virago.

Chasseguet-Smirgel, Janine, and Grunberger, Béla 1976 (*1985*): *Reich or Freud? Psychoanalysis and Illusion*, trans. Claire Pajaczkowska. London: Free Press Association Books.

Chigwada, W. 1987: "Not victims, not superwomen," *Spare Rib*, 183.

Childs, John Steven 1986: *Modernist Form: Pound's Style in the Early Cantos*. Cranbury, NJ and London: Associated University Presses.

Chilton, P., ed. 1985: *Language and the Nuclear Arms Debate: Nukespeak Today*. London and Dover, NH: Pinter.

Ching, Marvin, Haley, Michael, and Lunsford, Ronald, eds 1980: *Linguistic Perspectives on Literature*. London and Boston: Routledge & Kegan Paul.

Chinweizu, Onwuchekwa Jemie, and Madubuike, Ihechukwu, 1983: *Toward the Decolonization of African Literature*, Vol. 1. Washington, DC: Howard University Press.

Chodorow, Nancy 1978: *The Reproduction of Mothering: Psychoanalysis and the Sociology of Gender*. Berkeley: University of California Press.

——1989: *Feminism and Psychoanalytic Theory*. New Haven, CT: Yale University Press.

Chomsky, Noam 1957: *Syntactic Structures*. The Hague: Mouton.

——1964a: *Current Issues in Linguistic Theory*. The Hague: Mouton.

——1964b: "Review of *Verbal Behavior* by B.F. Skinner." In *The Structure of Language*, ed. J. Fodor and J. Katz. Englewood Cliffs, NJ: Prentice-Hall.

Chomsky, Noam 1965: *Aspects of the Theory of Syntax.* Cambridge, MA: MIT Press.
——1986: *Knowledge of Language.* New York: Praeger.
——1987: *On Power and Ideology.* Boston, MA: South End Press.
——1988: *Language and Problems of Knowledge.* Cambridge, MA: MIT Press.
——1991a: *Deterring Democracy.* London: Verso.
——1991b: *Knowledge of Language.* New York: Praeger.
Chow, Rey 1993: *Writing Diaspora: Tactics of Intervention in Contemporary Cultural Studies.* Bloomington: Indiana University Press.
Cioffi, Frank 1963: "Intention and interpretation in criticism," *Proceedings of the Aristotelian Society,* n.s. 44, 85–106.
Citron, M.J. 1993: *Gender and the Musical Canon.* Cambridge: Cambridge University Press.
Cixous, Hélène 1975a (*1987*): "Sorties: out and out: attacks/ways out/forays." In *The Newly Born Woman,* trans. Betsy Wing. Manchester: Manchester University Press.
——1975b (*1981*): "The Laugh of the Medusa," trans. Keith Cohen and Paula Cohen. In *New French Feminisms,* ed. Elaine Marks and Isabelle de Courtivron. Brighton: Harvester.
——1976a: "Fiction and its phantoms: a reading of Freud's *Das Unheimliche,*" *New Literary History,* 7, 525–48.
——1976b (*1979*): "Portrait of Dora," trans. A. Barrows. In *Benmusa Directs: Portrait of Dora and the Singular Life of Albert Nobbs.* London: John Calder.
——1991: *"Coming to Writing" and Other Essays,* ed. Deborah Jenson. Cambridge, MA: Harvard University Press.
Clark, John G. 1989: "The place of alchemy in Bachelard's oneiric criticism." In *The Philosophy and Poetics of Gaston Bachelard,* ed. Mary McAllester. Washington, DC: Center for Advanced Research in Phenomenology and University Press of America, 133–47.
Clark, K., and Holoquist, M. 1984: *Mikhail Bakhtin.* Cambridge: Harvard University Press.
Clark, Kenneth 1956: *The Nude.* New York: Pantheon.
Clark, S.H. 1990: *Paul Ricoeur.* London and New York: Routledge.
Clark, T.J. 1973: *The Absolute Bourgeois: Artists and Politics in France 1848–1851.* Greenwich, CT: New York Graphic Society Ltd.
——1973 (*1984*): *Image of the People: Gustave Courbet and the 1848 Revolution.* Princeton, NJ: Princeton University Press.
——1985: *The Painting of Modern Life: Paris in the Art of Manet and His Followers.* New York: Alfred A. Knopf.

Clarke, G. 1982: *Defending Ski-Jumpers: A Critique of Theories of Youth Subcultures.* Birmingham: Department of Cultural Studies, University of Birmingham.
Clarke, J. 1991: *New Times and Old Enemies: Essays on Cultural Studies and America.* London: Harper Collins.
Clement, Wallace, and Williams, Glen, eds 1989: *The New Canadian Political Economy.* Montreal: McGill-Queen's University Press.
Clingham, Greg (forthcoming): *Writing Memory: Textuality, Authority, and Johnson's "Lives of the Poets."* Cambridge: Cambridge University Press.
Cohen, Margaret 1993: *Profane Illumination: Walter Benjamin and the Paris of Surrealist Revolution.* Berkeley: University of California Press.
Cohen, P. 1972 (*1993*): "Subcultural conflict and working-class community." In *Extracts in Studying Culture,* ed. A. Gray and J. McGuigan. London: Edward Arnold.
Cohen, S. 1985: "Anti-semitism, immigration controls and the welfare state," *Critical Social Policy,* 13, Summer.
Cohn, Ruby 1969: *Currents in Contemporary Drama.* Bloomington: Indiana University Press.
Cole, M. 1992a: "Racism, history and educational policy: from the origins of the welfare state to the rise of the radical right. University of Essex: unpublished PhD dissertation.
——1992b: "British values, liberal values, or values of justice and equality: three approaches to education in multicultural Britain." In *Cultural Diversity and the Schools.* Vol. 3. *Equity or Excellence? Education and Cultural Reproduction,* ed. J. Lynch, C. Modgil, and S. Modgil. London: Falmer Press.
——1993: "'Black and ethnic minority' or 'Asian, black and other minority ethnic': a further note on nomenclature." *Sociology,* 27:4.
Coleman, A.D. 1976: "The directorial mode: notes towards a definition." In *Photography in Print,* ed. Vicki Goldberg. Albuquerque: University of New Mexico Press.
Collard, Cyril 1989 (*1993*): *Savage Nights,* trans. William Rodarmor. Woodstock, NY: Overlook Press.
Colletti, L. 1975: "Marxism and the dialectic," *New Left Review,* 93, 3–29.
Collier, Andrew 1994: *Critical Realism: An Introduction to Roy Bhaskar's Philosophy.* London: Verso.
Collingwood, R.G. 1945 (*1972*): *The Idea of Nature.* Oxford: Clarendon Press.
Collini, Stefan 1988: *Arnold.* Oxford: Oxford University Press.
Collins, Patricia Hill 1990: *Black Feminist Thought.* New York: Routledge.
Combahee River Collective 1977 (*1982*): "A black feminist statement." In *All the Women Are White,*

All the Blacks Are Men, But Some of Us Are Brave: Black Women's Studies, ed. Gloria T. Hull, Patricia Bell Scott, and Barbara Smith. Old Westbury, NY: The Feminist Press.

Conklin, P.K. 1988: *The Southern Agrarians*. Knoxville: University of Tennessee Press.

Connell, R.W. 1987: *Gender and Power: Society, the Person and Sexual Politics*. Cambridge: Polity Press.

Connolly, William, ed. 1984: *Legitimacy and the State*. Oxford: Basil Blackwell.

Connor, Steven 1989: *Postmodernist Culture: An Introduction to Theories of the Contemporary*. Oxford: Blackwell.

Cook, David 1985: *Northrop Frye: A Vision of the New World*. New York: St Martin's Press.

Cook, V. 1988: *Chomsky's Universal Grammar: An Introduction*. Oxford: Basil Blackwell.

Cooper, C.R., ed. 1985: *Researching Response to Literature and the Teaching of Literature: Points of Departure*. Norwood, NJ: Ablex Publishing Corporation.

Cooper, David E. 1987: *Philosophy and the Nature of Language*. Westport, CT: Greenwood Press.

——1990: *Existentialism: A Reconstruction*. Oxford: Blackwell.

Copeland, Roger 1987: "Shades of Brecht," *American Theatre*, 3:11, 12–19, 45.

Corner, J. 1980 (*1986*): "Codes and cultural analysis." In *Media, Culture and Society: A Critical Reader*, ed. R. Collins, J. Curran, N. Garnham, P. Scannell, P. Schlesinger, and C. Sparks. London: Sage.

Cortes, Carlos 1994: "Limits to pluribus, limits to unum: unity and diversity and the great American balancing act." In "Multiculturalism and diversity," *National Forum*, 74, 6–9.

Coulthard, M. 1977: *An Introduction to Discourse Analysis*. London: Longman.

Coupland, Nikolas, ed. 1987: *Styles of Discourse*. London: Croom Helm.

Couvalis, George 1989: *Feyerabend's Critique of Foundationalism*. Aldershot: Avebury.

Coward, R. 1984: *Female Desire: Women's Sexuality Today*. London: Paladin.

Coward, Rosalind, and Ellis, John 1977: *Language and Materialism*. London and Boston: Routledge & Kegan Paul.

Cragg, Kenneth 1984: *Muhammad and the Christian*. New York: Orbis Books.

——1988: *Readings in the Qur'an*. London: Collins.

——1985: *The Call of the Minaret*. New York: Orbis Books.

Craig, David 1975: *Marxists on Literature: An Anthology*. Harmondsworth: Penguin.

Crane, R.S. 1953: *The Languages of Criticism and the Structure of Poetry*. Toronto: University of Toronto Press.

Crane, R.S., ed. 1952: "The critical monism of Cleanth Brooks." In *Critics and Criticism: Ancient and Modern*. Chicago: University of Chicago Press.

Cranston, Maurice 1971: *The New Left: Six Critical Essays on Che Guevara, Jean-Paul Sartre, Herbert Marcuse, Frantz Fanon, Black Power, R.D. Laing*. New York: Philosophical Library.

Crary, Johnathon 1990 (*1992*): *Techniques of the Observer: On Vision and Modernity in the 19th Century*. Cambridge, MA: MIT Press.

Crawford, Robert 1992: *Devolving English Literature*. Oxford: Clarendon Press.

Creighton, Donald 1956: *John A. Macdonald*, 2 vols. Toronto: Macmillan.

Crilly, Anne, dir. 1989: *Mother Ireland*. Derry: Derry Film and Video.

Cuddy-Keane, Melba (forthcoming): "The rhetoric of feminist conversation: Virginia Woolf and the trope of the twist."

Cudjoe, Selwyn 1992: "C.L.R. James misbound," *Transition*, 58, 124–36.

Culler, A. Dwight 1966: *The Victorian Mirror of History*. New Haven, CT: Yale University Press.

Culler, Jonathan 1973: "The linguistic basis of structuralism." In *Structuralism: An Introduction*, ed. D. Robey. Oxford: Oxford University Press.

——1975 (*1989*): *Structuralist Poetics*. London: Routledge & Kegan Paul.

——1981a: "Stanley Fish and the righting of the reader." In *The Pursuit of Signs: Semiotics, Literature, Deconstruction*.

——1981b: *The Pursuit of Signs: Semiotics, Literature, Deconstruction*. London: Routledge & Kegan Paul.

——1982a: "Reading as a woman." In *On Deconstruction: Theory and Criticism After Structuralism*. London: Routledge & Kegan Paul.

——1982b: *On Deconstruction: Theory and Criticism After Structuralism*. London: Routledge & Kegan Paul.

——1983: *Roland Barthes*. London: Fontana.

——1988: *Framing the Sign: Criticism and Its Institutions*. Oxford: Blackwell.

Culley, Margo, and Portuges, Catherine, eds 1985: *Gendered Subjects: The Dynamics of Feminist Teaching*. Boston, MA: Routledge & Kegan Paul.

Curriculum Development Centre 1980: *Core Curriculum for Australian Schools*. Canberra: Curriculum Development Centre.

Curtis, James 1989: *Mind's Eye, Mind's Truth: FSA Photography Reconsidered*. Philadelphia, PA: Temple University Press.

Daly, Mary 1978: *Gyn/Ecology: The Metaethics of Radical Feminism*. Boston, MA: Beacon Press.

——1984: *Pure Lust*. Boston, MA: Beacon Press.

Daly, Mary 1992: *Outercourse: The Be-Dazzling Voyage: Containing Recollections from my Logbook of a Radical Feminist Philosopher (Be-ing an account.)* San Francisco: Harper.

Damrosch, Leo, ed. 1992: *The Profession of Eighteenth-Century Literature: Reflections on an Institution.* Madison: University of Wisconsin Press.

Danesi, Marcel 1994: "Introduction: Thomas A. Sebeok and the science of signs." In Thomas A. Sebeok, *An Introduction to Semiotics.* London: Pinter.

Daniels, Les 1991: *Marvel: Five Fabulous Decades of the World's Greatest Comics.* New York: Harry N. Abrams.

Danto, Arthur C. 1975: *Sartre.* London: Fontana.

Darnton, Robert 1990: *The Kiss of Lamourette: Reflections in Cultural History.* New York: Norton.

Dasenbrock, Reed Way 1992: "Teaching multicultural literature." In *Understanding Others: Cultural and Cross-Cultural Studies and the Teaching of Literature,* ed. Joseph Trimmer and Tilly Warnock. Urbana, IL: National Council of Teachers of English.

Dash, J. Michael 1989: "Introduction." In *Caribbean Discourse: Selected Essays,* trans. J. Michael Dash. Charlottesville: University Press of Virginia.

David, Diedre 1987: *Intellectual Women and Victorian Patriarchy.* Ithaca, NY: Cornell University Press.

Davidson, Donald 1974 (*1984*): "On the very idea of a conceptual scheme." In *Inquiries into Truth and Interpretation.* Oxford: Clarendon Press.

——1980: *Essays on Actions and Events.* Oxford: Clarendon Press.

——1984a: *Inquiries into Truth and Interpretation.* Oxford: Clarendon Press.

——1984b: "On the very idea of a conceptual scheme." In *Inquiries into Truth and Interpretation.* Oxford: Clarendon Press, 183–98.

Davidson, D., and Hintikka, J., eds 1969: *Words and Objections.* Dordrecht: D. Reidel.

Davis, Madeleine, and Wallbridge, David 1980: *Boundary and Space: An Introduction to the Work of D.W. Winnicott.* London: Karnac.

Davis, Natalie Zemon 1975: *Society and Culture in Early Modern France.* Stanford, CA: Stanford University Press.

——1976: "Women's history in transition: the European case," *Feminist Studies,* 3, 83–103.

Dawidoff, Robert 1992: *The Genteel Tradition and the Sacred Rage: High Culture vs. Democracy in Adams, James, and Santayana.* Chapel Hill: University of North Carolina Press.

Deane, Seamus 1985: *Celtic Revivals.* Winston-Salem, NC: Wake Forest University Press.

——, ed. 1991: *The Field Day Anthology of Irish Writing,* 3 vols. Derry: Field Day Publications.

de Bolla, Peter 1988: *Harold Bloom: Towards Historical Rhetorics.* London: Routledge.

——1989: *The Discourse of the Sublime: Readings in History, Aesthetics, and the Subject.* New York and Oxford: Basil Blackwell.

De Grazia, Margreta 1991: *Shakespeare Verbatim: The Reproduction of Authenticity and the 1790 Apparatus.* Oxford: Clarendon Press.

De Grazia, Margreta, and Stallybrass, Peter 1993: "The materiality of the Shakespeare text," *Shakespeare Quarterly,* 44, 255–83.

de Man, Paul 1971a (*1989*): *Blindness and Insight: Essays in the Rhetoric of Contemporary Criticism.* New York: Oxford University Press; London: Routledge.

——1971b: "The literary self as origin: the work of Georges Poulet." In *Blindness and Insight: Essays in the Rhetoric of Contemporary Criticism.* New York: Oxford University Press.

——1976 (*1984*): *The Rhetoric of Romanticism.* New York: Columbia University Press.

——1979: *Allegories of Reading: Figural Language in Rousseau, Nietzsche, Rilke, Proust.* New Haven, CT, and London: Yale University Press.

——1984: *The Rhetoric of Romanticism.* New York and London: Columbia University Press.

——1986: *The Resistance to Theory.* Minneapolis: University of Minnesota Press.

Deleuze, Gilles 1962 (*1983*): *Nietzsche and Philosophy,* trans. Hugh Tomlinson. London: Athlone Press.

——1991: *Cinema,* trans. Hugh Tomlinson and Robert Galeta. 2 vols. Minneapolis: University of Minnesota Press.

Deleuze, Gilles, and Guatarri, Félix 1980 (*1988*): *A Thousand Plateaus,* trans. Brian Massumi. Minneapolis: University of Minnesota Press.

——1991 (*1994*): *What is Philosophy?* London: Verso.

Delisle, Jean 1988: *Translation: An Interpretive Approach.* Ottawa and London: University of Ottawa Press.

Delpit, L.D. 1988: "The silenced dialogue: power and pedagogy in educating other people's children," *Harvard Educational Review,* 58, 280–98.

Denham, Robert D. 1978: *Northrop Frye and Critical Method.* University Park: Pennsylvania University Press.

——1987: *Northrop Frye: An Annotated Bibliography of Primary and Secondary Sources.* Toronto: University of Toronto Press.

Derrida, Jacques 1962 (*1978*): *Edmund Husserl's "Origin of Geometry:" An Introduction,* trans. John P. Leavey. Pittsburgh, PA: Duquesne University Press.

——1967a (*1976*): *Of Grammatology,* trans. Gayatri Chakravorty Spivak. Baltimore, MD: Johns Hopkins University Press.

——1967b (*1978*): *Writing and Difference*, trans. Alan Bass. Chicago: Chicago University Press.

——1967c (*1973*): *Speech and Phenomena and Other Essays on Husserl's Theory of Signs*, trans. David B. Allison. Evanston: Northwestern University Press.

——1972a (*1981*): *Positions*, trans. Alan Bass. Chicago: Chicago University Press.

——1972b (*1982*): *Margins of Philosophy*, trans. Alan Bass. Chicago: University of Chicago Press.

——1974 (*1986*): *Glas*, trans. John P. Leavey and Richard Rand. Lincoln: University of Nebraska Press.

——1977: "Limited Inc abc," *Glyph*, 2, 162–254.

——1978a: "An Hegelianism without reserve: from restricted to general economy in Georges Bataille." In *Writing and Difference*, trans. Alan Bass. London: Routledge and Kegan Paul.

——1978b (*1979*): *Spurs: Nietzsche's Styles*, trans. Barbara Harlow. Chicago and London: University of Chicago Press.

——1979: "Living on: borderlines." In *Deconstruction and Criticism*, ed. Harold Bloom et al. London: Routledge & Kegan Paul, 75–176.

——1980 (*1987*): *The Post Card: From Socrates to Freud and Beyond*, trans. Alan Bass. Chicago and London: University of Chicago Press.

——1982a: "White mythology: metaphor in the text of philosophy." In *Margins of Philosophy*, trans. Alan Bass. Chicago: University of Chicago Press.

——1982b (*1988*): *The Ear of the Other*, ed. Christie MacDonald, trans. Peggy Kamuf and Avital Ronell. Lincoln: University of Nebraska Press.

——1984: "No apocalypse, not now (seven missiles, seven missives)," *Diacritics*, 14:2, 20–31.

——1992: "Force of law: the mystical foundation of authority." In *Deconstruction and the Possibility of Justice*, ed. Drucilla Cornell et al. London: Routledge.

——1993 (*1994*): *Spectres of Marx: The State of the Debt, the Work of Mourning, and the New International*, trans. Peggy Kamuf. London: Routledge.

Descartes, R. 1951 (*1960*): *Meditations*, trans. L.J. Lafleur. Indianapolis: Bobbs-Merrill.

Descombes, Vincent 1979 (*1980*): *Modern French Philosophy*, trans. L. Scott-Fox and J.M. Harding. Cambridge: Cambridge University Press.

Devitt, M., and Sterelny, K. 1987: *Language and Reality: An Introduction to the Philosophy of Language*. Oxford: Basil Blackwell.

Devonish, Hubert 1986: *Language and Liberation: Creole Language Politics in the Caribbean*. London: Karia Press.

Dews, P., ed. 1986: *Autonomy and Solidarity: Interviews with Jürgen Habermas*. London: Verso.

——1987: *Logics of Disintegration: Post-structuralist Thought and the Claims of Critical Theory*. London: Verso.

Diacritics, 14:2, 1984: Special number on the topic of nuclear criticism.

Diamond, Elin 1988: "Brechtian theory/feminist theory," *Drama Review*, 32:1 (Spring), 82–94.

Diawara, Manthia 1992: *African Cinema: Politics and Culture*. Bloomington: Indiana University Press.

Diggins, Patrick 1992: *The Rise and Fall of the American Left*. New York: Norton.

Dill, Bonnie Thornton, and Zinn, Maxine Bacca 1990: "Race and gender: Revisioning social relations." Research Paper #11. Memphis, TN: Center for Research on Women, Memphis State University.

Dilthey, Wilhelm 1976: *Selected Writings*, ed. and trans. H.P. Rickman. Cambridge: Cambridge University Press.

Diop, C. A. 1974: *The African Origin of Civilization*. New York: Lawrence Hill.

Dirven, R., and Fried, V., eds 1987: *Functionalism in Linguistics*. New York: Harper & Row.

Docherty, David 1990: *Violence in Television Fiction*. London: Libbey.

Docherty, Thomas, ed. 1993: *Postmodernism: A Reader*. Hemel Hempstead: Harvester/Wheatsheaf.

Dolan, Jill 1988 (*1991*): *The Feminist Spectator as Critic*. Ann Arbor: University of Michigan Press.

Dolezel, Lubomir 1982: "Mukarovsky and the idea of poetic truth," *Russian Literature*, 12:3.

Dollimore, Jonathan 1984 (*1986*): *Radical Tragedy: Religion, Ideology and Power in the Drama of Shakespeare and His Contemporaries*. Hemel Hempstead: Harvester.

——1985: "Introduction: Shakespeare, cultural materialism, and the new historicism." In *Political Shakespeare: New Essays in Cultural Materialism*, ed. Jonathan Dollimore and Alan Sinfield. Ithaca, NY: Cornell University Press.

——1986a: "Homophobia and sexual difference." *Oxford Literary Review*, 8, 5–12.

——1990: "Shakespeare, cultural materialism, feminism and Marxist humanism," *New Literary History*, 21:3, 471–93.

Dollimore, Jonathan, and Sinfield, Alan, eds 1985: *Political Shakespeare*. Manchester: Manchester University Press.

Donoghue, Denis 1976: *The Sovereign Ghost: Studies in Imagination*. New York: Ecco Press.

Dort, Bernard 1990: "Crossing the desert: Brecht in France in the eighties." In *Re-interpreting Brecht: His Influence in Contemporary Drama and Film*, ed. Pia Kleber and Colin Visser. Cambridge: Cambridge University Press.

Doty, Alexander 1993: *Making Things Perfectly Queer: Interpreting Mass Culture*. Minneapolis: University of Minnesota Press.

Douglas, Mary T. 1963: *The Lele of the Kasai*. Oxford: Oxford University Press.

——1966 (*1985*): *Purity and Danger*. London: Ark Paperbacks.

——1970 (*1973*): *Natural Symbols: Explorations in Cosmology*. New York: Vintage Books.

Douglas, Mary T., and Isherwood, B. 1979: *The World of Goods*. New York: Basic Books.

Drakakis, John, ed. 1985: *Alternative Shakespeares*. London and New York: Methuen.

Draper, R.P. 1980: *Tragedy: Developments in Criticism*. London: Macmillan.

Draper, Theodore 1970: *The Rediscovery of Black Nationalism*. New York: Viking Press.

Dreyfus, H.L., ed. 1982: *Husserl, Intentionality, and Cognitive Science*. Cambridge, MA: MIT Press.

——1991: *Being-in-the-World: A Commentary on Heidegger's "Being and Time," Division I*. Cambridge, MA: MIT Press.

Dreyfus, H.L., and Rabinow, P. 1982: *Michel Foucault: Beyond Structuralism and Hermeneutics*. Brighton: Harvester Press.

Driver, Harold E. 1962: *The Contribution of A.L. Kroeber to Culture Area Theory and Practice*. Baltimore, MD: Waverly.

Drury, Shadia B. 1988: *The Political Ideas of Leo Strauss*. New York: St Martin's Press.

——*Alexandre Kojève: The Roots of Postmodern Politics*. New York: St Martin's Press.

Dry, Helen 1992: "Foregrounding: an assessment." In *Language in Context: Essays for Robert E. Longacre*, ed. Shin Ja Hwang and William Morrifield. Dallas, TX: Summer Institute of Linguistics.

D'Souza, Dinesh 1992: *Illiberal Education: The Politics of Race and Sex on Campus*. New York: Vintage Books.

Dubiel, Helmut 1978 (*1985*): *Theory and Politics: Studies in the Development of Critical Theory*. Cambridge, MA: MIT Press.

DuBois, Ellen Carol et al. 1985: *Feminist Scholarship: Kindling in the Groves of Academe*. Urbana: University of Illinois Press.

DuBois, W.E.B. 1903 (*1969*): *The Souls of Black Folk*. New York: New American Library.

——1935 (*1964*): "The propaganda of history." In *Black Reconstruction in America*. Cleveland, OH: Meridian Books.

Ducrot, Oswald, and Todorov, Tsvetan 1972 (*1979*): *Encyclopedic Dictionary of the Sciences of Language*, trans. Catherine Porter. Baltimore, MD: Johns Hopkins University Press.

Duhem, Pierre 1954: "The physics of a believer." In *The Aims and Structure of Physical Theory*, trans. Philip Wiener. Princeton, NJ: Princeton University Press.

Dummett, Michael 1973: *Frege's Philosophy of Language*. London: Duckworth.

Dunsby, J., and Whittal, A. 1988: *Music Analysis in Theory and Practice*. London: Faber Music.

Dupriez, Bernard 1991: *Gradus: Dictionary of Literary Devices*. Toronto: University of Toronto Press.

Durham, M. 1992: *Sex and Politics: The Family and Morality in the Thatcher Years*. London: Macmillan.

During, S., ed. 1993: *The Cultural Studies Reader*. London: Routledge.

Durkheim, Emile 1893 (*1984*): *The Division of Labor in Society*, trans. W.D. Halls. New York: Free Press.

——1895 (*1938*): *Rules of the Sociological Method*, trans. S. Solovay and J. Mueller. Chicago: University of Chicago Press.

——1897 (*1951*): *Suicide*, trans. J. Spaulding and G. Simpson. New York: Free Press.

——1912, 1915 (*1968*): *The Elementary Forms of the Religious Life*, trans. J.W. Swain. New York: Free Press.

Durkheim, Emile, and Mauss, Marcel 1903 (*1963*): *Primitive Classification*. Chicago: University of Chicago Press.

Dworkin, Ronald 1986: *Law's Empire*. London: Fontana.

——, ed. 1977: *The Philosophy of Law*, London: Oxford University Press.

Eagle, Herbert 1981: "Verse as semiotic system: Tynjanov, Jakobson, Mukarovsky, Lotman extended," *SEEJ*, 25:4.

Eagleton, Terry 1976: *Marxism and Literary Criticism*. London: Methuen.

——1978 (*1982*): *Criticism and Ideology*. London and New York: Verso.

——1982: *The Rape of Clarissa*. Minneapolis: University of Minnesota Press.

——1983 (*1985*): *Literary Theory: An Introduction*. Oxford: Blackwell.

——1986a: "Marxism, structuralism and post-structuralism." In *Against the Grain*. London: Verso.

——1986b: "Capitalism, modernism and postmodernism." In *Against the Grain*. London: Verso.

——1986c: *Against the Grain: Essays 1975–1985*. London: Verso.

——1990: *The Ideology of the Aesthetic*. Oxford: Basil Blackwell.

——1991: *Ideology: An Introduction*. London: Verso.

——1993: *The Crisis of Contemporary Culture.* Oxford: Clarendon Press.

Eagleton, Terry, Jameson, Fredric, and Said, Edward W. 1990: *Nationalism, Colonialism, and Literature.* Minneapolis: University of Minnesota Press.

Ebert, Teresa 1991: "The 'difference' of postmodern feminism," *College English*, 53:8, 886–904.

——1993: "Ludic feminism, the body, performance, and labor: Bringing *materialism* back into feminist cultural studies," *Cultural Critique*, 5–50.

Ebbs, Gary 1992: "Realism and rational inquiry," *Philosophical Topics*, 20, 1–33.

Echevarría, Roberto G., and Pupo-Walker, Enrique, eds 1995: *The Cambridge History of Latin America.* 3 vols. Cambridge: Cambridge University Press.

Eckersley, Robyn 1992: *Environmentalism and Political Theory. Toward an Ecocentric Approach.* Albany, NY: State University of New York Press.

Eco, Umberto 1976 (*1979*): *A Theory of Semiotics.* Bloomington: Indiana University Press.

Eddershaw, Margaret 1991: "Echt Brecht? 'Mother Courage' at the Citizens, 1990," *New Theatre Quarterly*, 7, 303–14.

The Eighteenth Century: Theory and Interpretation, Vol. 28. 1987.

Eisenstein, Sergei 1942: *The Film Sense*, trans. Jay Leyda. New York: Harcourt Brace Jovanovich.

——1949: *Film Form*, trans. Jay Leyda. New York: Harcourt Brace Jovanovich.

——1982: *The Nonindifferent Nature.* Cambridge: Cambridge University Press.

Eisenstein, Zillah 1981: *The Radical Future of Liberal Feminism.* New York: Longman.

Eisner, Will 1985: *Comics & Sequential Art.* Tamarac, FL: Poorhouse Press.

Elam, Keir (*1980*): *The Semiotics of Theatre and Drama.* London and New York: Methuen.

Eldridge, R. 1992: "'Reading for life:' Martha C. Nussbaum on philosophy and literature," *Arion*, 2:1, 187–97.

Elias, Norbert 1983: *The Court Society.* Oxford: Basil Blackwell.

Eliot, T.S. 1921 (*1975*): "The metaphysical poets." In *Selected Prose*, ed. Frank Kermode. London: Faber.

——1948: *Notes Towards the Definition of Culture.* London: Faber.

——1960: "Religion and literature." In *Selected Essays*. New York: Harcourt Brace.

Ellenburger, Henri F. 1970: *The Discovery of the Unconscious: The History and Development of Dynamic Psychiatry.* New York: Basic Books.

Elliott, G. 1987: *Althusser: The Detour of Theory.* London: Verso.

——, ed. 1994: *Althusser: A Critical Reader.* Oxford: Blackwell.

Ellis, John 1974: *The Theory of Literary Criticism.* Berkeley: University of California Press.

——1982: *Visible Fictions: Cinema, Television, Video.* London: Routledge.

Ellmann, Mary 1968: *Thinking About Women.* New York: Harcourt.

Ellmann, Maud 1987: *The Poetics of Impersonality: T.S. Eliot and Ezra Pound.* Brighton: Harvester.

Elton, G.R. 1991: *Return to Essentials: Some Reflections on the Present State of Historical Study.* Cambridge: Cambridge University Press.

Empson, William 1930 (*1973*): *Seven Types of Ambiguity.* London: Penguin.

——1951: *The Structure of Complex Words.* London: Chatto & Windus.

Engel, Marian 1976: *Bear.* Toronto: McClelland & Stewart.

Engels, F. 1939 (*1970*): *Herr Eugen Düring's Revolution in Science (Anti-Düring)*, trans. E. Burns. New York: International Publishers.

——1940a: *On Historical Materialism.* New York: International Publishers.

——1940b (*1973*): *Dialectics of Nature*, trans. C. Dutt. New York: International Publishers. (First published 1925.)

——1968: "Letter to J. Bloch." In K. Marx and F. Engels, *Selected Works.* London: Lawrence & Wishart.

——1972 (*1985*): *The Origin of the Family, Private Property and the State*, introd. Michèle Barrett. Harmondsworth: Penguin.

——1975: *Socialism: Utopian and Scientific*, trans. E. Aveling. New York: International Publishers.

Epstein, Mikhail 1993: "After the future: on the new consciousness in literature." In *Late Soviet Culture. From Perestroika to Novostroika*, ed. T. Lahusen and G. Kuperman. Durham, NC: Duke University Press.

Eribon, D. 1992: *Michel Foucault.* London: Faber.

Erickson, Peter 1985: *Patriarchal Structures in Shakespeare's Drama.* Berkeley: University of California Press.

——1991: "What multiculturalism means," *Transition*, 55, 105–14.

Erikson, E.H. 1950: *Childhood and Society.* London: Imago.

——1959: *Identity and the Life Cycle.* New York: International University Press.

Erlich, Victor 1965 (*1981*): *Russian Formalism. History–Doctrine.* New Haven, CT: Yale University Press.

Esslin, Martin 1959 (*1971*): *Brecht: The Man and His Work.* Garden City, NY: Anchor Books.

Evans, M. 1981: *Lucien Goldmann.* Brighton: Harvester Press.

Evan-Zohar, Itamar 1978: *Papers in Historical Poetics*. Tel Aviv: Porter Institute for Poetics and Semiotics.

Ewen, David 1960: *Leonard Bernstein*. New York: Bantam Books.

Fabb, Nigel, Attridge, Derek, Durant, Alan, and MacCabe, Colin, eds 1987: *The Linguistics of Writing: Arguments Between Language and Literature*. New York: Manchester University Press/Methuen.

Fabre, Genevieve E. 1983: *Drumbeats, Masks and Metaphor: Contemporary Afro-American Theatre*. Boston, MA: Harvard University Press.

Fairbairn, W.R.D. 1952: *An Object Relations Theory of the Personality*. New York: Basic Books.

Famia, J.V. 1981: *Gramsci's Political Thought: Hegemony, Consciousness and the Revolutionary Process*. Oxford: Oxford University Press.

Fanon, Frantz 1952 (*1989*): *Black Skin, White Masks*, trans. Charles Lam Markmann. New York: Grove Press.

——1959 (*1988*): *A Dying Colonialism*, trans. Haakon Chevalier. New York: Grove Press.

——1961 (*1988*): *The Wretched of the Earth* (Preface by Jean-Paul Sartre), trans. Constance Farrington. New York: Grove Press.

——1964 (*1988*): *Toward the African Revolution*, trans. Haakon Chevalier. New York: Grove Press.

Farnham, Christie, ed. 1987: *The Impact of Feminist Research in the Academy*. Bloomington: Indiana University Press.

Fekete, John 1977 (*1978*): *The Critical Twilight*. London: Routledge & Kegan Paul.

Felman, Shoshana 1977: "Turning the screw of interpretation." *Yale French Studies*, 55/56, 94–207.

——1987: *Jacques Lacan and the Adventure of Insight: Psychoanalysis in Contemporary Culture*. Cambridge, MA, and London: Harvard University Press.

Ferguson, Frances 1984: "The nuclear sublime," *Diacritics*, 14:2, 4–10.

——1992: "Romantic studies." In *Redrawing the Boundaries*, ed. Stephen Greenblatt and Giles Gunn. New York: Modern Language Association.

Ferguson, Margaret W., Quilligan, Maureen, and Vickers, Nancy J., eds 1985: *Rewriting the Renaissance: The Discourses of Sexual Difference in Early Modern Europe*. Chicago: University of Chicago Press.

Ferguson, Russell, et al., eds 1990: *Out There: Marginalization and Contemporary Cultures*. Cambridge, MA: MIT Press/New York: New York Museum of Contemporary Art.

Fernandéz Moreno, César, and Ortega, Julio, eds 1980: *Latin America in its Literature*, trans. Mary G. Berg. New York: Holmes and Meier.

Fetterly, J. 1978: *The Resisting Reader: A Feminist Approach to American Fiction*. Bloomington: Indiana University Press.

Feyerabend, P. 1975 (*1993*): *Against Method: Outline of an Anarchistic Theory of Knowledge*. London: New Left Books and Verso.

——1981a: *Realism, Rationalism and Scientific Method* (*Philosophical Papers*, Volume 1). Cambridge: Cambridge University Press.

——1981b: *Problems of Empiricism* (*Philosophical Papers*, Volume 2). Cambridge: Cambridge University Press.

——1991: *Three Dialogues on Knowledge*. Oxford: Blackwell.

——1992: *Farewell to Reason*. London: Verso.

Field Day Theatre Company 1986: *Ireland's Field Day*. Notre Dame, IN: University of Notre Dame Press.

Finch, Henry Le Roy 1971: *Wittgenstein – The Early Philosophy*. New York: Humanities Press.

——1977: *Wittgenstein – The Later Philosophy*. New York: Humanities Press.

Fine, Arthur 1986: *The Shaky Game: Einstein, Realism, and Quantum Theory*. Chicago: University of Chicago Press.

Fine, M. 1987: "Silencing in public schools," *Language Arts*, 64:2, 157–74.

Finnegan, Ruth 1977: *Oral Poetry: Its Nature, Significance, and Social Context*. Cambridge: Cambridge University Press.

Firestone, Shulamith 1970 (*1971*): *The Dialectic of Sex*. New York: Bantam.

Fischer, Michael 1989: *Stanley Cavell and Literary Skepticism*. Chicago: University of Chicago Press.

Fish, S. 1967: *Surprised by Sin: The Reader in Paradise Lost*. New York: St Martin's Press.

——1980: *Is There a Text in This Class? The Authority of Interpretive Communities*. Cambridge, MA: Harvard University Press.

——1989a: *Doing What Comes Naturally: Change, Rhetoric and the Practice of Theory in Literary and Legal Studies*. Oxford: Clarendon Press.

——1989b: "Being interdisciplinary is so very hard to do." In *Profession 89*. New York: Modern Language Association.

Fishman, J. 1982: "Whorfianism of the third kind: ethnolinguistic diversity as a worldwide societal asset," *Language in Society*, 11, 1.

Fiske, John 1987: *Television Culture*. London: Methuen.

——1989: *Understanding Popular Culture*. Boston, MA: Unwin Hyman.

Fitzpatrick, Peter, and Hunt, Alan, eds 1987: *Critical Logal Studies*. Oxford: Blackwell.

Fleming, Richard 1993: *The State of Philosophy: A Reading in Three Parts of Stanley Cavell's The Claim of Reason*. Lewisburg, PA: Bucknell University Press.

Fleming, Richard, and Duckworth, William, eds 1989: *John Cage at Seventy-Five. Bucknell Review*. Lewisburg, PA: Bucknell University Press.

Fleming, Richard, and Payne, Michael, eds 1987: *The Senses of Stanley Cavell. Bucknell Review*. Lewisburg, PA: Bucknell University Press.

Floistad, G., ed. 1987: *Contemporary Philosophy: A New Survey*, Vol. 5: *African Philosophy*. The Hague: Martinus Nijhoff.

Fodor, Jerry, and LePore, Ernest 1991: *Holism: A Shopper's Guide*. Oxford: Basil Blackwell.

Fontana, B. 1993: *Hegemony and Power*. Minneapolis: University of Minnesota Press.

Foot, Philippa 1978: *Virtues and Vices*. Oxford: Basil Blackwell.

Fordham, Frieda 1953 (*1970*): *An Introduction to Jung's Psychology*. Harmondsworth: Penguin.

Forrest, Philippe 1995: *Histoire de Tel Quel 1960–1982*. Paris: Seuil.

Forster, E.M. 1941 (*1951*): "Virginia Woolf." In *Two Cheers for Democracy*. London: Edward Arnold.

Foster, David William, ed. 1992: *Handbook of Latin American Literature*. 2nd edn. New York: Garland.

Foster, George 1960: *Culture and Conquest*. New York: Wenner-Gren Foundation for Anthropological Research.

Foster, Hal, ed. 1983 (*1991*): *The Anti-Aesthetic: Essays on Postmodern Culture*. Seattle, WA: Bay Press.

Foster, Richard 1962: *The New Romantics: A Reappraisal of the New Criticism*. Bloomington: Indiana University Press.

Foucault, Michel 1963 (*1976*): *The Birth of the Clinic*. London: Tavistock.

—— 1969 (*1986*): "What is an author?" trans. Josué V. Harari. In *The Foucault Reader*, ed. Paul Rabinow. Harmondsworth: Penguin.

—— 1971a (*1977*): "Nietzsche, genealogy, history." In *Language, Counter-memory, Practice*, ed. Donald F. Bouchard. Ithaca, NY: Cornell University Press; Oxford: Basil Blackwell.

—— 1971b: "Orders of discourse," *Social Science Information*, 10:2, 7–30.

—— 1973: *The Order of Things: An Archaeology of the Human Sciences*. New York: Vintage Books; London: Tavistock.

—— 1974: *The Archaeology of Knowledge*. London: Tavistock.

—— 1975 (*1977*): *Discipline and Punish: The Birth of the Prison*. London: Allen Lane.

—— 1976 (*1990*): *The History of Sexuality*, 3 vols. Vol. 1, *An Introduction*, trans. by Robert Hurley. New York: Vintage Books.

—— 1977a (*1980*): "Truth and power." In *Power/Knowledge: Selected Interviews and Other Writings, 1972–1977*, ed. Colin Gordon, trans. Colin Gordon et al. New York: Pantheon Books.

—— 1977b: "Preface to transgression." In *Language, Counter-Memory, Practice: Selected Essays and Interviews*, trans. Donald F. Bouchard and Sherry Simon. Oxford: Blackwell.

—— 1978: "Politics and the study of discourse," *Ideology*.

—— 1980a: "Two lectures." In *Power/Knowledge: Selected Interviews and Other Writings 1972–1977*, ed. Colin Gordon. New York: Pantheon.

—— 1980b: *Power/Knowledge: Selected Interviews and Other Writings 1972–1977*, ed. Colin Gordon. New York: Pantheon.

—— 1986a: "What is Enlightenment?" In Paul Rabinow, ed. *The Foucault Reader*. Harmondsworth: Penguin.

—— 1986b: "Kant on enlightenment and revolution," *Economy and Society*, 15:1, 88–96.

—— 1986c: "*Nietzsche, genealogy, history*." In *The Foucault Reader*, ed. Paul Rabinow. Harmondsworth: Penguin.

—— 1987: *Death and the Labyrinth: The World of Raymond Roussel*. London: Athlone Press.

—— 1988a: "Power, moral values, and the intellectual: an interview," *History of the Present*, 4, 1–2, 11–13.

—— 1988b: "On problematization," *History of the Present*, 4, 1–2, 11–13.

—— 1988c: "Questions of method: an interview with Michel Foucault." In *After Philosophy: End or Transformation?* ed. K. Baynes, J. Bohman, and T. McCarthy. London: MIT Press, 100–117.

—— 1989a: "The archaeology of knowledge." In S. Lotringer, ed. *Foucault Live (Interviews 1966–84)*. New York: Semiotext(e), 45–56.

—— 1989b: "The order of things." In S. Lotringer, ed. *Foucault Live (Interviews 1966–84)*. New York: Semiotext(e), 1–10.

—— 1989c: "An historian of culture." In S. Lotringer, ed. *Foucault Live (Interviews 1966–84)*. New York: Semiotext(e), 73–88.

Fowler, R. 1981: *Literature as Social Discourse: The Practice of Linguistic Criticism*. London: Batsford.

—— 1986: *Linguistic Criticism*. New York: Oxford University Press.

—— 1991: *Language in the News*. London: Routledge.

Fowler, R., Hodge, R., Kress, G., and Trew, T. 1979: *Language and Control*. London: Routledge & Kegan Paul.

Fox, Martin, ed. 1988: *Print*, 17:6, 59–206.

Fox, Richard G. 1991: *Recapturing Anthropology*. Santa Fe, NM: School of American Research Press.

Frank, Manfred 1972: *Das Problem "Zeit" in der deutschen Romantik, Zeitbewußtsein und Bewußtsein von Zeitlichkeit in der frühromantischen Philosophie und in Tiecks Dichtung*. Munich: Winkler.

——1977 (*1990*): *Das Individuelle-Allgemeine. Textstrukturierung und interpretation nach Schleiermacher (The Individual-Universal. Text-Structuration and Interpretation Following Schleiermacher)*. Frankfurt: Suhrkamp.

——1979 (*1980*): "The infinite text;" trans. Michael Schwerin. In *Glyph 7. The Strasbourg Colloquium: Genre: A Collection of Papers*. Baltimore, MD: Johns Hopkins University Press.

——1984 (*1989*): *Was Ist Neo-Strukturalismus?* Frankfurt: Suhrkamp (*What Is Neo-structuralism?*; trans. Sabine Wilke and Richard Gray. Minneapolis: Minnesota University Press.)

——1986: *Die Unhintergehbarkeit von Individualität. Reflexionen über Subjekt, Person, und Individuum aus Anlaß*.

——1987 (*1992*): "Is self-consciousness a case of *présence à soi*? Towards a meta-Critique of the recent French critique of metaphysics," trans. Andrew Bowie. In *Derrida: A Critical Reader*, ed. David Wood. Oxford: Blackwell Publishers.

——1989a: *Einführung in die frühromantische Ästhetik (Introduction to Early-Romantic Aesthetics)*. Frankfurt: Suhrkamp.

——1989b: *Das Sagbare und das Unsaghare (The Sayable and the Unsayable)*. Frankfurt: Suhrkamp.

——1990: *Das Sagbare und das Unsaghare. Studien zur deutsch–französischen Hermeneutik und Texttheorie*. Frankfurt: Suhrkamp.

——1991: *Selbstbewußtsein und Selbsterkenntnis. Essays zur analytischen Philosophie der Subjektivität*. Stuttgart: Reclam.

——1992: *Stil in der Philosophie (Style in Philosophy)*. Stuttgart: Reclam.

Franke, Robert, G. 1993: "Beyond good doctor, bad doctor: AIDS fiction and biography as a developing genre," *Journal of Popular Culture* (Winter), 93–101.

Franklin, John Hope 1957 (*1989*): "The new negro history." In *Race and History: Selected Essays 1938–1988*. Baton Rouge: Lousiana State University Press.

Franklin, Phyllis, ed. 1993: "Multiculturalism: the task of literary representation in the twenty-first century," *Profession 93*. New York: Modern Language Association.

Franklin, S., Lury, C., and Stacey, J. 1991: *Off-Centre: Feminism and Cultural Studies*. London: Harper Collins.

Frege, Gottlob 1952: "On sense and reference." In P.T. Geach and M. Black, eds. *Translations from the Philosophical Writings*. Oxford: Blackwell.

——1977: *Logical Investigations*, trans. P.T. Geach. Oxford: Blackwell.

Freire, Paolo 1972: *Pedagogy of the Oppressed*. New York: Herder & Herder.

French, Philip 1980: *Three Honest Men: Edmund Wilson, F.R. Leavis, Lionel Trilling*. Manchester: Carcanet.

Freud, Sigmund 1896 (*1974*): "The aetiology of hysteria." In *The Standard Edition of the Complete Psychological Works of Sigmund Freud*, trans. James Strachey; 24 vols (Hereafter abbreviated *SE*). Vol. 3, 187–222. London: Hogarth Press and Institute of Psycho-Analysis.

——1900: *The Interpretation of Dreams. SE*, vols 4–5.

——1901a: *The Psychopathology of Everyday Life. SE*, vol. 6.

——1901b: "On dreams." *SE*, vol. 5, 629–714.

——1905a: "Three essays on the theory of sexuality," *SE*, vol. 7, 1–246.

——1905b: "Fragment of an analysis of a case of hysteria." *SE*, vol. 7, 1–122.

——1905c (*1960*): *Jokes and Their Relationship to the Unconscious. SE*, vol. 8.

——1907: "Delusions and dreams in Jensen's *Gradiva*." *SE*, vol. 7, 1–122.

——1908a: "On the sexual theories of children." *SE*, vol. 9, 205–26.

——1908b: "Creative writers and day-dreaming." *SE*, vol. 9, 141–54.

——1910a: "The antithetical meaning of primal words." *SE*, vol. 11, 153–62.

——1910b: "A special type of choice of object made by men." *SE*, vol. 11, 163–276.

——1910c: "Leonardo da Vinci and a memory of his childhood." *SE*, vol. 11, 59–138.

——1912: "The dynamics of the transference." In *SE*, vol. 2, 97–100.

——1913: "The claims of psychoanalysis to scientific interest." *SE*, vol. 13, 163–90.

——1914a: "The Moses of Michelangelo." *SE*, vol. 13, 209–38.

——1914b: "On the history of the psychoanalytic movement." In *SE*, vol. 14, 1–66.

——1915: "The unconscious." *SE*, vol. 14, 159–216.

——1918: "The taboo of virginity." *SE*, vol. 11, 191–208.

——1919: "The uncanny." *SE*, vol. 17, 217–52.

——1920: *Beyond the Pleasure Principle, SE*, vol. 18, 1–64.

——1922: "Medusa's head." *SE*, vol. 18, 273–6.

——1923a: *The Ego and the Id. SE*, vol. 19, 1–66.

——1923b: "The infantile genital organization: an

interpolation into the theory of sexuality." *SE*, vol. 19, 173–82.

——1923c: "Two encyclopedia articles." *SE*, vol. 18, 235–54.

——1924: "The dissolution of the Oedipus complex." *SE*, vol. 19, 173–82.

——1925 (*1977*): "Some psychical consequences of the anatomical distinction between the sexes." In *On Sexuality. Three Essays on the Theory of Sexuality and Other Works*, ed. A. Richards. Harmondsworth: Penguin.

——1926: "The question of lay analysis." *SE*, vol. 20, 177–250.

——1927: "Dostoievsky and parricide." *SE*, vol. 21, 173–94.

——1930: *Civilization and Its Discontents*, *SE*, vol. 21, 59–146.

——1931 (*1977*): "Female sexuality." In *On Sexuality. Three Essays on the Theory of Sexuality and Other Works*, ed. A. Richards. Harmondsworth: Penguin.

——1933: *New Introductory Lectures in Psychoanalysis. SE*, vol. 22, 1–182.

——1938: "An outline of psychoanalysis." *SE*, vol. 23, 139–208.

——1974: *The Freud/Jung Letters*; trans. Ralph Manheim and R.F.C. Hull; ed. William MacGuire. London: Hogarth Press and Routledge & Kegan Paul.

——1985: *The Complete Letters of Sigmund Freud to Wilhelm Fliess 1887–1904*, trans. and ed. Jeffrey Moussaieff Masson. Cambridge, MA: Harvard University Press.

Freund, E. 1987a: "Literature in the reader: Stanley Fish and affective poetics." In *The Return of the Reader: Reader-Response Criticism*. London: Methuen.

——1987b: "The peripatetic reader: Wolfgang Iser and the aesthetics of reception." In *The Return of the Reader: Reader-Response Criticism*. London: Methuen.

——1987c: *The Return of the Reader: Reader-Response Criticism*. London: Methuen.

Friedan, Betty 1963: *The Feminine Mystique*. New York: Norton.

——1981: *The Second Stage*. New York: Summit Books.

Friedman, M. ed. 1956: *Studies in the Quantity Theory of Money*. Chicago: University of Chicago Press.

——1962: *Capitalism and Freedom*. Chicago: University of Chicago Press.

Friedman, M., and Friedman, R. 1980: *Free to Choose*. London: Secker & Warburg.

Frisby, David 1985: *Fragments of Modernity: Theories of Modernity in the Work of Simmel, Kracauer and Benjamin*. Cambridge: Polity Press.

Frith, Simon 1981: *Sound Effects*. New York: Pantheon.

Fromm, Erich 1932 (*1978*): "The method and function of an analytical social psychology: notes on psychoanalysis and historical materialism." In *The Essential Frankfurt School Reader*, ed. Andrew Arato and Eike Gebhardt. Oxford: Blackwell.

Frye, Northrop 1957: *Anatomy of Criticism*. Princeton, NJ: Princeton University Press.

——1980: *Creation and Recreation*. Toronto: University of Toronto Press.

——1982: *The Great Code: The Bible and Literature*. New York: Harcourt.

Fuegi, John 1972: *The Essential Brecht*. Los Angeles, CA: Hennessey & Ingalls.

Fueler, Linda K. 1992: *The Cosby Show: Audiences, Impact and Implications*. Westport, CT: Greenwood Press.

Fuentes, Carlos 1992: *The Buried Mirror. Reflections on Spain and the New World*. Boston, MA: Houghton-Mifflin.

Fukuyama, Francis 1992: *The End of History and the Last Man*. New York: Free Press.

Fuller, Steve 1989: *Philosophy of Science and Its Discontents*. Boulder, CO: Westview Press.

Fuss, Diana, ed. 1991: *Inside/Out: Lesbian Theories, Gay Theories*. New York: Routledge.

Gabrielli, Francesco 1984 (*1957*): *Arab Historians of the Crusades*. Berkeley: University of California Press.

Gadamer, Hans-Georg 1960 (*1993*): *Truth and Method*, trans. J. Weinsheimer and D.G. Marshall. London: Sheed & Ward.

——1975 (*1989*): *Wahrheit und Methode*. Tübingen: J.C.B. Mohr.

——1976: *Philosophical Hermeneutics*, trans. and ed. D.E. Linge. Berkeley: University of California Press.

——1981: *Reason in the Age of Science*, trans. F.G. Lawrence. Cambridge, MA: WIT Press.

——1986a: *Hermeneutik II. Wahrheit und Methode 2 (Hermeneutics II. Truth and Method 2)*. Tübingen: J.C.B. Mohr.

——1986b: *The Relevance of the Beautiful and Other Essays*, trans. N. Walker; ed. R. Bernasconi. Cambridge: Cambridge University Press.

——1989: "Text and interpretation." In *Dialogue and Deconstruction*, ed. D.P. Michelfelder and R.E. Palmer. Albany: State University of New York Press.

Gaita, R. 1983: "Values, human good, and the unity of a life," *Inquiry*, 26, 407–24.

Galan, F.W. 1984: "Film as poetry and prose: Viktor Shklovsky's contribution in poetics of cinema," *Essays in Poetics: The Journal of the British Neo-Formalist School*, 9:1.

Gallop, Jane 1988: *Thinking Through the Body*. New York: Columbia University Press.

Gamble, A. 1988: *The Free Economy and the Strong State*. London: Macmillan.

Gandelman, Claude 1988: "The dialectic functioning of Mukarovsky's semiotic model." In *The Prague School and Its Legacy: In Linguistics, Literature, Semiotics, Folklore, and the Arts*, ed. Y. Tobin. Amsterdam: Benjamins.

Gane, M. 1983: "On the ISAs episode," *Economy and Society*, 12.4, 431–55.

Garza Cuaron, Beatriz 1991: *Connotation and Meaning*, trans. C. Broad. Berlin: Mouton de Guyter.

Gates, Henry Louis, Jr 1978: "Preface to blackness: text and pretext". In *Afro-American Literature: The Reconstruction of Instruction*, ed. Dexter Fisher and Robert B. Stepto. New York: Modern Language Association.

—— 1985 (*1992*): "Writing 'race' and the difference it makes." In *Loose Canons: Notes on the Cultural Wars*. New York: Oxford University Press.

—— 1988a: *The Signifying Monkey*. Oxford: Oxford University Press.

—— 1988b: Foreword to Anna Julia Cooper. *A Voice from the South*. New York: Oxford University Press.

—— 1990 (*1992*): "The master's pieces: on canon formation and the African American tradition." In *Loose Canons: Notes on the Cultural Wars*. New York: Oxford University Press.

—— 1992: *Loose Canons: Notes on the Cultural Wars*. New York: Oxford University Press.

—— 1989: "TV's black world turns – but stays unreal," *New York Times*, November 12.

—— 1993: "Beyond the culture wars: identities in dialogue." In *Multiculturalism: The Task of Literary Representation in the Twenty-First Century. Profession 93*, ed. Phyllis Franklin; New York: Modern Languages Association.

Gauss, Kathleen McCarthy, and Grundberg, Andy 1987: *Photography and Art: Interactions Since 1946*. New York: Abbeville Press.

Gay Left Collective, eds 1980: *Homosexuality: Power and Politics*. London: Allison & Busby.

Gay, Peter 1967: *The Enlightenment: An Interpretation*, 2 vols. London: Weidenfeld & Nicolson.

—— 1988: *Freud: A Life for Our Time*. London: Dent.

Gayle, Addison, Jr, ed. 1971 (*1972*): *The Black Aesthetic*. New York: Doubleday.

Geertz, Clifford 1973 (*1993*): *The Interpretation of Cultures*. New York: Basic Books. (London: Fontana.)

—— 1989: *Works and Lives: The Anthropologist as Author*. Oxford: Polity Press.

Geis, Deborah R. 1990: "Wordscapes of the body:

performative language as *Gestus* in Maria Irene Fornes's plays," *Theatre Journal*, 42, 291–307.

Gelb, I.J. 1963: *A Study of Writing: The Foundations of Grammatology*. Chicago: University of Chicago Press.

Gendzier, Irene L. 1973: *Frantz Fanon: A Critical Study*. New York: Pantheon Books.

Genette, Gérard 1980: *Narrative Discourse: An Essay on Method*. Oxford: Blackwell.

—— 1982a: *Figures of Literary Discourse*. Oxford: Blackwell.

—— 1982b: *Palimpsestes: la littérature au second degré*. Paris: Seuil.

Gennep, Arnold van 1908 (*1960*): *The Rites of Passage*, trans. M. Vizedom and G. Caffee. Chicago: University of Chicago Press.

Genova, A.C. 1984: "Good transcendental arguments," *Kant-Studien*, 75, 469–95.

Gentzler, Edwin 1993: *Contemporary Translation Theories*. London: Routledge.

Geoghagen, Vincent 1981: *Reason and Eros: The Social Theory of Herbert Marcuse*. London: Pluto Press.

Geras, N. 1972 (*1986*): "Althusser's Marxism: an account and assessment." In *Literature of Revolution*. London: Verso.

—— 1986: "Post Marxism?" *New Left Review*, 163, 40–82.

Geuss, Raymond 1981: *The Idea of a Critical Theory: Habermas & the Frankfurt School*. Cambridge: Cambridge University Press.

Geyer, R.F. 1992: *Alienation, Society and the Individual*. New Brunswick, NJ: Transaction Publishers.

Gibbins, Peter 1987: *Particles and Paradoxes: The Limites of Quantum Logic*. Cambridge: Cambridge University Press.

Gibbons, John, ed. 1994: *Language and the Law*. Harlow: Longman.

Gibbons, Luke 1988: "Coming out of hibernation? The myth of modernity in Irish culture." In *Across the Frontiers*.

Giddens, Anthony 1973 (*1980*): *The Class Struggle of the Advanced Societies*. London: Hutchinson.

—— 1990: *Consequences of Modernity*. Stanford: Stanford University Press.

Giddens, Anthony, and Held, David, eds 1982: *Classes, Power, and Conflict: Classical and Contemporary Debates*. Berkeley: University of California Press.

Gilbert, Margaret 1989: *On Social Facts*. London: Routledge.

Gilbert, Sandra M., and Gubar, Susan 1979: *The Madwoman in the Attic: The Woman Writer and the Nineteenth-Century Literary Imagination*. New Haven, CT: Yale University Press.

—— 1988: *No Man's Land: The Place of the Woman*

Writer in the Twentieth Century, 2 vols. New Haven, CT: Yale University Press.

——, eds 1979: *Shakespeare's Sisters: Feminist Essays on Women Poets*. Bloomington: Indiana University Press.

——, eds 1985a: *The Norton Anthology of Literature by Women: The Tradition in English*. New York: Norton.

——, eds 1985b: *A Classroom Guide to Accompany the Norton Anthology of Literature by Women*. New York: Norton.

——, eds 1986: *The Female Imagination and the Modernist Aesthetic*. New York: Gordon & Breach.

Gill, Roma, ed. 1974: *William Empson: The Man and His Work*. London: Routledge & Kegan Paul.

Gill, S. ed. 1993: *Gramsci, Historical Materialism and International Relations*. Cambridge: Cambridge University Press.

Gilligan, Carol 1982 (*1993*): *In a Different Voice*. Cambridge, MA and London: Harvard University Press.

Gilroy, Paul 1982: "Steppin out of Babylon – race, class and autonomy." In *The Empire Strikes Back*, ed. University of Birmingham, Centre for Contemporary Cultural Studies. London: Hutchinson.

——1987: *There Ain't No Black in the Union Jack: The Cultural Politics of Race and Nation*. London: Hutchinson.

——1993: *The Black Atlantic: Modernity and Double Consciousness*. London: Verso.

Ginzburg, Carlo 1980: *The Cheese and the Worms: The Cosmos of a Sixteenth-Century Miller*. Baltimore, MD: Johns Hopkins University Press.

Girard, René 1977: *Violence and the Sacred*, trans. Patrick Gregory. Baltimore, MD: Johns Hopkins University Press.

——1984: *Deceit, Desire, and the Novel: Self and Other in Literary Structure*, trans. Yvonne Freccero. Baltimore, MD: Johns Hopkins University Press.

——1986: *The Scapegoat*, trans. Yvonne Freccero. London: Athlone Press.

——1987a: *Job: The Victim of His People*, trans. Yvonne Freccero. London: Athlone Press.

——1987b: *Things Hidden Since the Foundation of the World*, trans. Stephen Bann. Palo Alto, CA: Stanford University Press.

Giroux, H. 1983: *Theory and Resistance in Education*. New York: Bergin & Garvey.

Glasgow University Media Group 1976: *Bad News*. London: Routledge.

Glenn, Evelyn 1986: *Issei, Nissei, War Bride: Three Generations of Japanese American Women in Domestic Service*. Philadelphia: Temple University Press.

Glissant, Edouard 1981 (*1989*): *Caribbean Discourse: Selected Essays*, trans. J. Michael Dash. Charlottesville: University Press of Virginia.

Glover, Jonathan 1977: *Causing Death and Saving Lives*. Harmondsworth: Penguin.

——1989: *Ethics of New Reproductive Technologies: The Glover Report to the European Commission*. Illinois: Northern Illinois University Press.

Gluck, M. 1985: *Georg Lukács and His Generation*. Cambridge, MA: Harvard University Press.

Godbout, Jacques 1968: *Knife on the Table*. Toronto: McClelland & Stewart.

Goldberg, David Theo 1993: *Racist Culture: Philosophy and the Politics of Meaning*. Oxford: Blackwell.

Goldberg, Jonathan 1983: *James I and the Politics of Literature: Jonson, Shakespeare, Donne and Their Contemporaries*. Baltimore, MD: Johns Hopkins University Press.

Goldberg, Vicki, ed. 1981 (*1988*): *Photography in Print*. Albuquerque: University of New Mexico Press.

Goldmann, Lucien 1956 (*1964*): *The Hidden God*, trans. P. Thody. London: Routledge & Kegan Paul.

——1967 (*1970*): "The sociology of literature: status and problems of method." In *The Sociology of Art and Literature*, ed. M.C. Albrecht et al. London: Duckworth.

——1977: *Lucács and Heidegger: Towards a New Philosophy*. London and Boston, MA: Routledge & Kegan Paul.

Gombrich, Ernst 1950 (*1995*): *The Story of Art*. London: Phaidon Press.

——1960 (*1969*): *Art and Illusion: A Study in the Psychology of Pictorial Representation*. London: Phaidon Press.

——1963 (*1971*): *Meditations on a Hobby Horse and Other Essays on the Theory of Art*. London: Phaidon Press.

——1966 (*1978*): *Norm and Form: Studies in the Art of the Renaissance I*. London: Phaidon Press.

——1971: *Ideas of Progress and Their Impact on Art*. New York: Cooper Union School of Art and Architecture.

——1972 (*1978*): *Symbolic Images: Studies in the Art of the Renaissance II*. London: Phaidon Press.

——1979: *The Sense of Order: A Study in the Psychology of Decorative Art*. Oxford: Phaidon Press.

——1982: *The Image and the Eye: Further Studies in the Psychology of Pictorial Representation*. Oxford: Phaidon Press.

——1991: *Topics of Our Time, Twentieth Century Issues in Learning and in Art*. London: Phaidon Press.

Gombrich, Ernst, and Eribon, Didier 1993: *Looking for Answers: Conversations on Art and Science*. London: Harry N. Abrams.

Goodman, Nelson 1978: *Ways of Worldmaking*. Indianapolis: Hackett Publishing.

——1983: *Fact, Fiction and Forecast*, 4th edn. Indianapolis: Bobbs-Merrill.

Goodman, P. 1960 (*1966*): *Growing up Absurd*. New York: Vintage Books.

Goodman, P., Perls, F., and Hefferline, R. 1951: *Gestalt Therapy*. New York: Dell Publishing.

Goodrich, Peter 1987: *Legal Discourse: Studies in Linguistics, Rhetoric and Legal Analysis*. London: Macmillan.

Goodwin, Andrew 1992: *Dancing in the Distraction Factory: Music Television and Popular Culture*. Minneapolis: University of Minnesota Press.

Goody, Jack 1977: *The Domestication of the Savage Mind*. Cambridge: Cambridge University Press.

——1987: *The Interface Between the Written and the Oral*. Cambridge: Cambridge University Press.

Goody, Jack and Watt, Ian 1968: "The consequences of literacy." In *Literacy in Traditional Societies*, ed. Jack Goody. Cambridge: Cambridge University Press.

Gorman, David 1992: "A bibliography of Russian formalism in English." *Style*, 26:4.

Goslan, Richard 1993: *René Girard and Myth: An Introduction*. New York: Garland.

Gracia, Jorge J.E., ed. 1986: *Latin American Philosophy in the Twentieth Century. Man, Values, and the Search for Philosophical Indentity*. Buffalo, NY: Prometheus Books.

Gradenwitz, Peter 1987: *Leonard Bernstein: The Infinite Variety of a Musician*. New York: St Martin's Press.

Graff, Gerald 1979: "What Was New Criticism?" In *Literature Against Itself: Literary Ideas in Modern Society*. Chicago: University of Chicago Press.

——1987: *Professing Literature: An Institutional History*. Chicago: University of Chicago Press.

Graff, Gerald, and Robbins, Bruce 1992: "Cultural criticism." In *Redrawing the Boundaries: The Transformation of English and American Literary Studies*, ed. Stephen Greenblatt and Giles Gunn. New York: Modern Language Association.

Graff, Harvey 1982: *Literacy and Social Development in the West: A Reader*. Cambridge: Cambridge University Press.

Graham, J.F. 1985: *Difference and Translation*. Ithaca and London: Cornell University Press.

Gramsci, A. 1957 (*1968*): *The Modern Prince and Other Writings*, trans Q. Hoare. London: Lawrence & Wishart.

——1929–35 (*1971*): *Selections from the Prison Notebooks*, trans. Q. Hoare and G.N. Smith. London: Lawrence & Wishart.

——1977: *Selections from Political Writings*, trans.

J. Mathews; ed. Q. Hoare. New York: International Publishers.

Grandy, R., and Warner, R. 1986: *Philosophical Grounds of Rationality*. Oxford University Press.

Grant, George 1965: *Lament for a Nation*. Toronto: McClelland and Stewart.

Gray, A. and McGuigan, J., eds 1993: *Studying Culture: An Introductory Reader*. London: Edward Arnold.

Gray, Piers 1982: *T.S. Eliot's Intellectual and Poetic Development 1909–1922*. Brighton: Harvester.

Green, André 1986: *On Private Madness*. London: Hogarth Press and the Institute of Psychoanalysis.

Green, Geoffrey 1982: *Literary Criticism and the Structures of History: Erich Auerbach and Leo Spitzer*. Lincoln: University of Nebraska Press.

Green, M., ed. 1987: *Broadening the Context: English and Cultural Studies*. London: John Murray.

Greenberg, Clement 1961 (*1968*): *Art and Culture*. Boston, MA: Beacon Press.

——1964: *Post Painterly Abstraction*. Los Angeles: Los Angeles County Museum of Art.

——1971: "Counter Avant-Garde," *Art International*, 15.

——1986: *The Collected Essays and Criticism*, ed. John O'Brien. 2 vols. Chicago: University of Chicago Press.

Greenblatt, Stephen 1980: *Renaissance Self-Fashioning: From More to Shakespeare*. Chicago: University of Chicago Press.

——, ed. 1982: *The Forms of Power and the Power of Forms in the Renaissance*. Norman: University of Oklahoma Press and Pilgrim Books.

——1988: *Shakespearean Negotiations*. Oxford: Oxford University Press.

——1990: "Resonance and wonder." In *Learning to Curse: Essays in Early Modern Culture*. New York: Routledge, Chapman, and Hall.

——1991: *Marvellous Possessions: The Wonder of the New World*. Oxford: Oxford University Press.

Greenblatt, Stephen, and Gunn, Giles, eds 1992: *Redrawing the Boundaries: The Transformation of English and American Studies*. New York: Modern Language Association.

Greenleaf, W.H. 1965: *Oakeshott's Philosophical Politics*. London: Longman.

Greer, Germaine 1970: *The Female Eunuch*. London: MacGibbon & Kee.

——1979: *The Obstacle Race: The Fortunes of Women Painters and Their Work*. New York: Farrar, Strauss, and Giroux.

——1982: "Tulsa Center for the Study of Women's Literature – What we are doing and why we are doing it," *Tulsa Studies in Women's Literature*, 1:1, 5–26.

——1984: *Sex and Destiny: The Politics of Human Fertility*. New York: Harper & Row.

——, ed. 1988: *Kissing the Rod: An Anthology of Seventeenth-Century Women's Verse*. London: Virago.

Greimas, A.J. 1966: *Semantique structurale*. Paris: Larousse.

——1970: *Du Sens*. Paris: Seuil.

——1973: "Les Actants, les acteurs et les figures." In *Semiotique narrative et textuelle*, ed. Chabrol. Paris: Larousse.

——1987: *On Meaning: Selected Writings in Semiotic Theory*. London: Pinter.

Griaule, M. 1965: *Conversations with Ogotemmeli: An Introduction to Dogon Religious Ideas*. London: Oxford University Press.

Grice, Paul 1989: *Studies in the Ways of Words*. Cambridge, MA: Harvard University Press.

Grieder, Alfons 1986: "Gaston Bachelard – 'phénoménologue' of modern science," *Journal of the British Society for Phenomenology*, 17:2, 107–23.

Grimm, Reinhold, and Hermand, Jost, eds 1989: *From the Greeks to the Greens. Images of the Simple Life*. Madison: University of Wisconsin Press.

Groddeck, Georg 1923 (*1935*): *The Book of the Id*. London: C.W. Daniel.

Gros Louis, Kenneth R.R., ed. 1974 (*1982*): *Literary Interpretations of Biblical Narratives*. 2 vols. Nashville, TN: Abington Press.

Grossberg, L. 1989: "The formation(s) of cultural studies," *Strategies*, 2, 114–49.

Grossberg, L., Nelson, L., and Treicher, P., eds 1992: *Cultural Studies*. London: Routledge.

Grosskurth, Phyllis 1986: *Melanie Klein*. London: Hodder and Stoughton.

Grosz, Elizabeth 1989: *Sexual Subversions: Three French Feminists*. Sydney: Allen & Unwin.

Grotzer, Pierre, ed. 1979: *Albert Béguin et Marcel Raymond: Colloque de Cartigny sous la direction de Georges Poulet, Jean Rousset, Jean Starobinski, Pierre Grotzer*. Paris: Corti.

Grundmann, Rainer 1991: *Marxism and Ecology*. Oxford: Clarendon Press.

Grundy, S. 1987: *Curriculum: Product or Praxis*. Lewes: Falmer.

Gudkov, L., and Dubin, B. 1993: "Bez napryazheniya . . . Zametki o kul'ture perekhodnogo perioda," *Novy mir*, 2.

Guha, Ranajit 1982–94: *Subaltern Studies: Writings on South Asian History and Society*, 8 vols. New Delhi: Oxford University Press.

Guha, Ranajit, and Spivak, Gayatari 1988: *Selected Subaltern Studies*. New York: Oxford University Press.

Guignon, Charles, ed. 1993: *The Cambridge Companion to Heidegger*. Cambridge: Cambridge University Press.

Guillaume, Alfred 1977 (*1954*): *Islam*. Harmondsworth: Penguin.

Guillory, John 1983: "The ideology of canon-formation: T.S. Eliot and Cleanth Brooks," *Critical Inquiry*, 10, 173–98.

Gunew, S. ed. 1990: *Feminist Knowledge, Critique and Construct*. London and New York: Routledge.

Gunn, Daniel 1984: "Making art strange: a commentary on defamiliarization," *Georgia Review*, 38:1.

Gunn, Thom 1992: *The Man with Night Sweats*. New York: Farrar, Straus & Giroux.

Gutting, Gary 1989: *Michel Foucault's Archaeology of Scientific Reason*. Cambridge: Cambridge University Press.

——, ed. 1980: *Paradigms and Revolutions: Appraisals and Applications of Thomas Kuhn's Philosophy of Science*. Notre Dame, IN: University of Notre Dame Press.

Guyer, Paul 1979: *Kant and the Claims of Taste*. Harvard University Press.

Habermas, Jürgen 1962 (*1989*): *The Structural Transformation of the Public Sphere: An Inquiry into a Category of Bourgeois Society*, trans. T. Burger and F. Lawrence. Cambridge, MA: MIT Press.

——1968 (*1981*): *Knowledge and Human Interests*, trans. Jeremy J. Shapiro. London: Heinemann.

——1975: *Legitimation Crisis*. Cambridge: Polity Press.

——1979: *Communication and the Evolution of Society*, trans. Thomas McCarthy. London: Heinemann.

——1980 (*1985*): "Modernity – an incomplete project." In *Postmodern Culture*, ed. H. Foster. London: Pluto Press.

——1983a: (*1992*): *Moral Consciousness and Communicative Rationality*, trans. C. Lenhardt and S. Weber Nicholson. Cambridge: Polity Press.

——1983b: "Modernity – an incomplete project." In *Postmodern Culture*, ed. H. Foster. London: Pluto Press.

——1984: *The Theory of Communicative Action*. Vol. 1. *Reason and the Rationalization of Society*, trans. T. McCarthy. Cambridge: Polity Press/ Basil Blackwell.

——1985 (*1987*): *The Philosophical Discourse of Modernity*; trans. Frederick Lawrence. Cambridge: Polity Press.

——1986: "Taking aim at the heart of the present." In *Foucault: A Critical Reader*, ed. D.C. Hoy. Oxford: Blackwell, 103–8.

——1987: *The Theory of Communicative Action*. Vol. 2. *Lifeworld and System*, trans. T. McCarthy. Cambridge: Polity Press/Basil Blackwell.

Hacking, I. 1975: *Why Language Matters to Philosophy*. Cambridge: Cambridge University Press.

——1983: *Representing and Intervening*. Cambridge: Cambridge University Press.

Hacking, I., ed. 1981: *Scientific Revolutions*. Oxford: Oxford University Press.

Haegeman, L. 1991: *Introduction to Government and Binding Theory*. Oxford: Basil Blackwell.

Halbfass, Wilhelm 1988: *India and Europe: An Essay in Understanding*. Albany: State University of New York Press.

Hall, David D. 1989: *Worlds of Wonder, Days of Judgment: Popular Belief in Early New England*. Cambridge, MA: Harvard University Press.

Hall, Stuart 1980a: "Encoding/decoding." In *Culture, Media, Language*, ed. S. Hall, D. Hobson, A. Lowe, and P. Willis. London: Hutchinson.

—— 1980b: "Race, articulation and societies structured in dominance." In *Sociological Theories: Race and Colonialism*, ed. UNESCO. Paris: UNESCO.

—— 1980c: "Cultural studies: two paradigms," *Media, Culture, and Society*, 2, 55–72.

—— 1981: "Notes on deconstructing 'the popular.'" In *People's History and Socialist Theory*, ed. R. Samuel. London: Routledge.

—— 1982: "The rediscovery of 'ideology;' return of the repressed in media studies." In *Culture, Society and the Media*; ed. M. Gurevich et al. New York: Methuen, 56–90.

—— 1985a: "Signification, representation, ideology: Althusser and the post-structuralist debates," *Critical Studies in Mass Communication*, 2:2, 91–114.

—— 1985b: "The toad in the garden: Thatcherism amongst the theorists." In *Marxism and the Interpretation of Culture*, ed. C. Nelson and L. Grossberg. Urbana: University of Illinois Press.

—— 1988: *The Hard Road to Renewal: Thatcherism and the Crisis of the Left*. London: Verso.

—— 1990: "Cultural Identity and Diaspora." In *Identity: Community, Culture, Difference*, ed. Jonathan Rutherford. London: Lawrence & Wishart.

——, ed. 1992: *Understanding Modern Societies: An Introduction*. Vol. 1. *Formations of Modernity*. Vol. 2. *Political and Economic Forms of Modernity*. Vol. 3. *Social and Cultural Forms of Modernity*. Vol. 4. *Modernity and Its Futures*. Cambridge: Polity Press/Open University.

Hall, S., Clarke, J., Jefferson, T., and Roberts, B. eds 1976: *Resistance through Rituals*. London: Hutchinson.

Hall, S., Critcher, C., Jefferson, T., Clarke, J., and Roberts, B. 1978: *Policing the Crisis: Mugging, the State and Law and Order*. London: Macmillan.

Hall, S., Hobson, D., Lowe, A., and Willis, P. 1980: *Culture, Media, Language*. London: Hutchinson.

Hallen, Barry, and Sodipo, J.O. 1986: *Knowledge, Belief & Witchcraft: Analytic Experiments in African Philosophy*. London: Ethnographica.

Halliday, M.A.K. 1978: *Language as Social Semiotic*. London: Edward Arnold.

—— 1985: *An Introduction to Functional Grammar*. London: Edward Arnold.

Halliday, M. A. K., and Hasan, Ruquaya 1985: *Language Context and Text: A Social Semiotic Perspective*. Geelong, Victoria: Deakin University Press.

Halperin, David M. 1989: "Is there a history of sexuality?" *History and Theory*, 28, 257–64.

Hamilton, A. C. 1990: *Northrop Frye: Anatomy of His Criticism*. Toronto: University of Toronto Press.

Hamilton, Richard 1982: *Collected Words, 1953–1982*. London: Thames & Hudson.

Hammarberg, Titta 1984: "A reinterpretation of Tynyanov and Jakobson on prose (with some thoughts on the Bakhtin and Lotman connection). In honor of Ladislav Matejko." In *Language and Literary Theory*, ed. B. Stolz, I. Titunik, and L. Dolezel. Ann Arbor: University of Michigan Press.

Hammond, Gerald 1983: *The Making of the English Bible*. New York: Philosophical Library.

Hammond, M., Howarth, J., and Keat, R. 1991: *Understanding Phenomenology*. Oxford: Blackwell.

Hanfling, Oswald 1981: *Logical Positivism*. Oxford: Blackwell.

Haraway, Donna 1985 (*1990*): "A Manifesto for cyborgs: science, technology, and socialist feminism in the 1980s." In *Feminism/Postmodernism*, ed. Linda J. Nicholson. New York: Routledge.

Harding, Sandra G. 1976: *Can Theories Be Refuted? Essays on the Duhem–Quine Thesis*. Dordrecht: D. Reidel.

Hardt, H. 1992: *Critical Communication Studies: Communications, History and Theory in America*. London: Routledge.

Hardt, Michael 1993: *Gilles Deleuze: An Apprenticeship in Philosophy*. London: University College London Press.

Hare, R.M. 1981: *Moral Thinking*. Oxford: Clarendon Press.

Hargreaves, A. 1989: *Curriculum and Assessment Reform*. Oxford: Basil Blackwell.

Harker, Dave 1985: *Fakesong. The Manufacture of British Folksong. 1700 to the Present Day*. Milton Keynes: Open University Press.

Harlow, Barbara 1987: *Resistance Literature*. London: Methuen.

Harré, Rom 1972: *The Philosophies of Sciences*. London: Oxford University Press.

—— 1983: *Great Scientific Experiments*. London: Oxford University Press.

—— 1986: *Varieties of Realism: A Rationale for the Social Sciences*. Oxford: Basil Blackwell.

Harris, John 1992: *Wonderman and Superman: The Ethics of Human Biotechnology*. Oxford: Oxford University Press.

Harris, Leonard, ed. 1983: *Philosophy Born of Struggle: Anthology of Afro-American Philosophy from 1917*. Dubuque, IO: Kendall/Hunt.

Harris, Marvin 1968: *The Rise of Anthropological Theory*. New York: Crowell.

Harris, Roy 1987 (*1991*): *Reading Saussure*. La Salle, IL: Open Court.

Harris, Wilson 1983: *The Womb of Space: The Cross Cultural Imagination*. Westport, CT: Greenwood.

Harris, Z. 1951: *Methods in Structural Linguistics*. Chicago: University of Chicago Press.

—— 1951 (*1972*): "Review of *Selected Writings* by Edward Sapir." Reprinted in *Edward Sapir: Appraisals of His Life and Work*, ed. K. Koerner. Amsterdam: John Benjamins.

—— 1952: "Discourse analysis," *Language*, 28.

—— 1982: *A Grammar of English on Mathematical Principles*. New York: Wiley.

Harrison, B. 1979: *An Introduction to the Philosophy of Language*. London: Macmillan.

Harrison, Paul Carter 1972: *The Drama of Nommo: Black Theater in the African Continuum*. New York: Grove Press.

Hart, H.L.A. 1983: *Essays in Jurisprudence and Philosophy*. Oxford: Clarendon Press.

Harten, Hans-Christian, and Harten, Elke 1989: *Die Versöhnung mit der Natur. Gärten, Freiheitsbäume, republikanische Wälder, heilige Berge und Tugendparks in der Französischen Revolution*. Reinbek: Rowohlt Verlag.

Hartman, Geoffrey, ed. 1979: *Deconstruction and Criticism*. New York: Seabury.

—— 1981: *Saving the Text: Literature/Derrida/Philosophy*. Baltimore, MD: Johns Hopkins University Press.

Hartman, Geoffrey, and Budick, Sanford, eds 1986: *Midrash and Literature*. New Haven, CT: Yale University Press.

Hartz, Louis 1955: *The Liberal Tradition in America: An Interpretation of American Political Thought Since the Revolution*. New York: Harcourt, Brace & World.

Harvey, D. 1989: *The Condition of Postmodernity*. Oxford: Basil Blackwell.

Hassan, Ihab 1971 (*1982*): *The Dismemberment of Orpheus: Toward a Postmodern Literature*. New York: Oxford University Press; 2nd rev. edn, Madison: University of Wisconsin Press.

—— 1975: *Paracriticisms: Seven Speculations of the Times*. Urbana: University of Illinois Press.

—— 1980: *The Right Promethean Fire: Imagination, Science, and Cultural Change*. Urbana: University of Illinois Press.

—— 1987: *The Postmodern Turn: Essays in Postmodern Theory and Culture*. Columbus: Ohio State University Press.

Hatim, Basil, and Mason, Ian 1990: *Discourse and Translation*. London: Longman.

Haug, W.F. 1986: *Critique of Commodity Aesthetics*. Cambridge: Polity.

Hawkes, Terence 1977 (*1983*): *Structuralism and Semiotics*. London: Methuen; Routledge.

Hayman, Ronald 1986: *Writing Against: A Biography of Sartre*. London: Weidenfeld & Nicolson.

Haynes, John 1989: *Introducing Stylistics*. London: Unwin Hyman.

Healy, Thomas 1992: *New Latitudes: Theory and English Renaissance Studies*. London: Edward Arnold.

Hebdige, D. 1979: *Subculture: The Meaning of Style*. London: Routledge.

Hederman, Mark, and Kearney, Richard, eds 1982 (*1987*): *The Crane Bag Book of Irish Studies*. 2 vols. Dublin: Blackwater Press (vol. 1); Wolfhound Press (vol. 2).

Hegel, G.W.F. 1821 (*1991*): *Elements of the Philosophy of Right*, ed. Allen W. Wood; trans. H.B. Nisbet. Cambridge: Cambridge University Press.

—— 1899 (*1956*): *The Philosophy of History*, trans. J. Sibree. New York: Dover Publications.

Heidegger, Martin 1927 (*1980*): *Sein und Zeit*; Tübingen: Max Niemeyer; trans. J. Macquarrie and E. Robinson, *Being and Time*. Oxford: Basil Blackwell.

—— 1947 (*1993*): "A letter on humanism," trans. Grank A. Capuzzi and J. Glenn Gray. In *Basic Writings*, ed. D.F. Krell. London: Routledge.

—— 1950 (*1962*): "Letter to Husserl." In *Husserliana*, Vol. I. The Hague: Nijhoff.

—— 1959 (*1982*): *Unterweg zur Sprache*; Pfullingen: Neske, trans. Peter Hertz, *On the Way to Language*. New York: Harper.

—— 1967: *What Is a Thing?* trans. W.B. Barton, Jr and Vera Deutsch. South Bend, Indiana: Regnery & Gateway.

—— 1971: *Poetry, Language, Thought*, trans. A. Hofstadter. New York: Harper & Row.

—— 1972: *On Time and Being*, trans. J. Stambaugh. New York: Harper & Row.

—— 1975 (*1982*): *The Basic Problems of Phenomenology*, trans. A. Hofstadter. Bloomington: Indiana University Press.

—— 1978: *Basic Writings*, ed. and trans. D.F. Krell. London: Routledge & Kegan Paul.

Heidsieck, François 1971: *L'Ontologie de Merleau-Ponty*. Paris: Presses Universitaires de France.

Heilbrun, Carolyn 1973: *Toward a Recognition of Androgyny*. New York: Knopf.

Heisenberg, Werner 1956 (*1958*): *Physics and Philosophy: The Revolution in Modern Science.* New York: Harper & Row.

Held, David 1980 (*1989*): *Introduction to Critical Theory: Horkheimer to Habermas.* Cambridge: Polity Press.

Held, Virginia, ed. 1993: *Feminist Morality.* Chicago: University of Chicago Press.

Hermand, Jost 1991: *Grüne Utopien in Deutschland. Zur Geschichte des ökologischen Bewusstseins.* Frankfurt am Main: Fischer Taschenbuch Verlag.

Hermans, Theo 1985: *The Manipulation of Literature.* London: Croom Helm.

Hernadi, Paul 1972: *Beyond Genre: New Directions in Literary Classification.* Ithaca, NY: Cornell University Press.

Herr, Cheryl 1986: *Joyce's Anatomy of Culture.* Urbana University of Illinois Press.

——1994: "A state o'chassis: mobile capital, Ireland, and the question of postmodernity." In *Irishness and (Post)Modernism*; ed. John S. Rickard. *Bucknell Review.* Lewisburg, PA: Bucknell University Press.

Hill, Claude 1975: *Bertolt Brecht.* Boston, MA: Twayne.

Hill, Errol, ed. 1980: *The Theater of Black Americans.* 2 vols. Englewood Cliffs, NJ: Prentice Hall.

Himmelfarb, Gertrude 1989: "Some reflections on the new history," *American Historical Review,* 94, 661–70.

Hindess, B. and Hirst, P. 1977: *Mode of Production and Social Formation.* London: Macmillan.

Hinshelwood, R.D. 1989: *A Dictionary of Kleinian Thought.* London: Free Association Books.

Hirk, Aritha van 1981: *Tent Peg.* Toronto: McClelland and Stewart.

Hirsch, E. D. 1987: *Cultural Literacy: What Every American Needs to Know.* Boston, MA: Houghton Mifflin.

——1994: *The Dictionary of Cultural Literacy.* Boston, MA: Houghton Mifflin.

Hirschberg, Stuart 1992: *One World, Many Cultures.* New York: Macmillan.

Hirschkop, K. and Shepherd, D., eds 1989: *Bakhtin and Cultural Theory.* Manchester: Manchester University Press.

Hirst, P. 1976 (*1979*): "Althusser and the theory of ideology." In *On Law and Ideology.* London: Macmillan.

——1979: *On Law and Ideology.* London: Macmillan.

Hitchcock, Henry-Russell, and Johnson, Philip 1932 (*1966*): *The International Style.* New York: W. W. Norton.

Hjelmslev, Louis 1943 (*1961*): *Prolegomena to a Theory of Language,* trans. F. J. Whitfield. Madison: University of Wisconsin Press.

Hobbes, T. 1651 (*1991*): *Leviathan.* Cambridge: Cambridge University Press.

Hodgson, Marshall 1974: *The Venture of Islam.* Chicago and London: University of Chicago Press.

Hodgson, Peter 1985: "Viktor Shklovsky and the formalist legacy: initiation/stylization in narrative fiction. A *Festschrift* in honor of Victor Erlich." In *Russian Formalism. A Retrospective Glance,* ed. R. Jackson and S. Rudy. New Haven, CT: Yale University Press.

Hofstadter, Richard 1955: *The Age of Reform: From Bryan to F.D.R.* New York: Vintage/Random House.

Hoggart, R. 1958: *The Uses of Literacy.* Harmondsworth: Penguin.

——1970: *Speaking to Each Other.* 2 vols. London: Chatto & Windus.

——1988: *Life and Times.* 3 vols. London: Chatto & Windus.

Holderness, Graham 1988: *The Shakespeare Myth.* Manchester: Manchester University Press.

Hollander, John 1981: *Rhyme's Reason.* New Haven, CT: Yale University Press.

Hollier, Denis, ed. 1979: *Le Collège de sociologie: Textes de Georges Bataille et autres.* Paris: Gallimard.

Hollingdale, R.J. 1973: *Nietzsche.* London: Routledge & Kegan Paul.

Hollis, Martin, and Lukes, Steven, eds 1982: *Rationality and Relativism.* Cambridge, MA: MIT Press; Oxford: Basil Blackwell.

Holmes, Helen Bequaert, ed. 1992: *Issues in Reproductive Technology I: An Anthology.* New York and London: Garland Publishing.

Holmes, James 1970: *The Nature of Translation: Essays on the Theory and Practice of Literary Translation.* The Hague: Mouton.

——1988: *Translated! Papers on Literary Translation and Translation Studies.* Amsterdam: Rodopi.

Holt, Thomas 1986: "Introduction: whither now and why?" In *The State of Afro-American History,* ed. Darlene Clark Hine. Baton Rouge: Lousiana State University Press.

Holub, R.C. 1991: *Jürgen Habermas: Critic in the Public Sphere.* London: Routledge.

Honner, John 1987: *The Description of Nature: Niels Bohr and the Philosophy of Quantum Physics.* Oxford: Clarendon Press.

Honneth, Axel 1985: *Critique of Power: Stages of Reflection of a Critical Theory of Society,* trans. Ken Bayes. Cambridge, MA: MIT Press.

——1993: "Conceptions of 'civil society,'" *Radical Philosophy,* 64, 19–22.

hooks, bell 1984: *Feminist Theory: From Margin to Center.* Boston, MA: South End Press.

——1989: *Talking Back: Thinking Feminist/ Thinking Black*. Boston, MA: South End Press.

——1990: *Yearning: Race, Gender and Cultural Politics*. Boston, MA: South End Press.

——1992: *Black Looks: Race and Representation*. Boston, MA: South End Press.

Hookway, Christopher 1985: *Peirce*. London: Routledge.

Hörisch, Jochen 1988: *Die Wut des Versstehens*. [*The Rage of Interpretation*.] Frankfurt: Suhrkamp.

Horkheimer, Max 1930: *Anfange der burgerklichen Geschichtsphilosophie*. Stuttgart: Kohlhammer.

——1938 (*1972*): "Traditional and critical theory." In *Critical Theory: Selected Essays*. New York: Herder and Herder.

——1947 (*1974*): *Eclipse of Reason*. New York: Seabury Press.

——1962 (*1967*): "Schopenhauer today." In *The Critical Spirit: Essays in Honor of Herbert Marcuse*, ed. Kurt H. Wolff and Barrington Moore, Jr.

——1972: "Die gegenwartige Lage der Sozialphilosophie und die Aufgaben eines Instituts für Sozialforschung." In *Sozialphilosophische Studien*; ed. Werner Brede. Frankfurt am Main: Fischer.

Hosek, Chavia, and Parker, Patricia, eds 1985: *Lyric Poetry: Beyond New Criticism*. Ithaca, NY: Cornell University Press.

Houghton, Walter E. 1957: *The Victorian Frame of Mind, 1830–1870*. New Haven, CT: Yale University Press.

Hourani, Albert 1991: *Islam in European Thought*. Cambridge: Cambridge University Press.

House, J. and Blum-Kulka, S. 1986: *Interlingual and Intercultural Communication: Discourse and Cognition in Translation and Second Language Acquisition Studies*. Tübingen: Gunter Narr.

Householder, Fred 1971: *Linguistic Speculations*. Cambridge: Cambridge University Press.

Houtondji, Paulin 1983: *African Philosophy: Myth or Reality*. Bloomington: Indiana University Press.

Howard, Jean E. 1994: *The Stage and Social Struggle in Early Modern England*. London: Routledge.

Howard, Jean E., and Connor, Marion F. eds 1987: *Shakespeare Reproduced: The Text in History and Ideology*. London and New York: Methuen.

Howard, Richard 1980: *Alone with America: Essays on the Art of Poetry in the United States Since 1950*. New York: Atheneum.

Howe, Irving 1973: "Auschwitz and high mandarin." In *The Critical Point: On Literature and Culture*. New York: Horizon Press.

Howell, D. 1983: *British Workers and the Independent Labour Party 1888–1906*. Manchester: Manchester University Press.

Howells, Christina, ed. 1992: *The Cambridge Companion to Sartre*. Cambridge: Cambridge University Press.

Hoy, D.C., ed. 1986. *Foucault: A Critical Reader*. Oxford: Basil Blackwell.

——1988: "Foucault: modern or postmodern?" In *After Foucault: Humanistic Knowledge, Postmodern Challenges*; ed. J. Arac. London: Rutgers University Press, 12–41.

Hoy, David Couzens, and McCarthy, Thomas 1994: *Critical Theory*. Oxford: Blackwell.

Hudson, W. 1982: *The Marxist Philosophy of Ernst Bloch*. London: Macmillan Press.

Hull, Gloria T., Scott, Patricia Bell, and Smith, Barbara, eds 1982: *All the Women are White, All the Blacks are Men, But Some of Us are Brave: Black Women's Studies*. Old Westbury, NY: The Feminist Press.

Hume, D. 1748 (*1987*): *An Enquiry Concerning Human Understanding*, ed. L.A. Selby-Bigge. Oxford: Clarendon Press.

Humm, Maggie 1986: *Feminist Criticism: Women as Contemporary Critics*. New York: St Martin's Press.

Hunt, Geoffrey 1987: "The development of the concept of civil society in Marx," *History of Political Thought*, 8, 263–76.

Hunt, Lynn 1991: "History as gesture; or, the scandal of history." In *Consequences of Theory: Selected Papers from the English Institute, 1987–88*, ed. Jonathan Arac and Barbara Johnson. Baltimore, MD: Johns Hopkins University Press.

Hurka, Thomas 1993: *Perfectionism*. New York and Oxford: Oxford University Press.

Hurston, Zora Neale 1935 (*1978*): *Mules and Men*, Part II. Bloomington: Indiana University Press.

Hurtig, Mel 1985: *The Canadian Encyclopedia*. Edmonton: Hurtig Publishers.

Husemann, H. 1994: "From NIMBY *Landeskunde* to IMBY cultural studies." In *Culture and Language Learning in Higher Education*, ed. M. Byram. Clevedon: Multilingual Matters.

Husserl, E. 1900–1 (*1970*): *Logical Investigations*, trans. J. Findlay. London: Routledge & Kegan Paul.

——1913 (*1962*): *Ideas: General Introduction to Pure Phenomenology*, trans. W. Boyce-Gibson. New York: Collier.

——1936 (*1970*): *The Crisis of European Sciences and Transcendental Phenomenology*, trans. D. Carr. Evanston: Northwestern University Press.

——1950 (*1977*): *Cartesian Meditations*, trans. D. Cairns. The Hague: Nijhoff.

——1965: *Phenomenology and the Crisis of Philosophy*, trans. Q. Lauer. New York: Harper & Row.

——1975: *The Paris Lectures*, trans. P. Koestenbaum. The Hague: Nijhoff.

Hutchins, Loraine, and Kaahumanu, Lani, eds

1991: *Bi Any Other Name: Bisexual People Speak Out*. Boston, MA: Alyson.

Hylton, Peter 1982: "Analyticity and the indeterminacy of translation," *Synthese*, 52, 167–84.

Hymes, D. 1967 (*1986*): "Models of the interaction of language and social setting." In *Directions in Sociolinguistics: The Ethnography of Communication*, ed. J.J. Gumpertz and D. Hymes. Oxford: Basil Blackwell.

——1972: "On communicative competence." In *Sociolinguistics*. Harmondsworth: Penguin.

Hyppolite, J. 1963: *Sens et Existence dans la Philosophie de Maurice Merleau-Ponty*. Oxford: Clarendon Press.

——1974: *Genesis and Structure of Hegel's Phenomenology of Spirit*, trans. S. Cherniak and J. Heckman. Evanston, IL: Northwestern University Press.

Iggers, Georg G. 1973: "Historicism." In *Dictionary of the History of Ideas*, ed. Philip P. Wiener. New York: Charles Scribner Sons.

Ikegami, Y. 1981: *Linguistics of Doing and Becoming*. Tokyo: Taishukan.

——1982: *Poetics of Language*. Tokyo: Iwanami.

——1983: *Poetics and Cultural Semiology*. Tokyo: Chikuma.

——1991: *The Empire of Signs, Semiotic Essays on Japanese Culture*. Amsterdam: Beijamins.

Illich, Ivan 1973: *Tools for Conviviality*. New York: Harper & Row.

Inden, Ronald 1990: *Imagining India*. Oxford: Blackwell.

Indian Voices: The First Convocation of American Indian Scholars: 1967. San Francisco: Indian Historian Press.

Ingarden, R. 1931 (*1973*): *The Literary Work of Art*, trans. G. Grabowicz. Evanston, IL: Northwestern University Press.

——1964 (*1979*): "Artistic and aesthetic values." In *Aesthetics*, ed. H. Osborne. Oxford: Oxford University Press.

Inglis, Fred 1993: *Cultural Studies*. Oxford: Blackwell Publishers.

Institute for Social Research 1936: *Studien über Autorität und Familie*. Paris: Felix Alcan.

International Council for Canadian Studies: 1992: *International Dictionary of Canadian Studies*. Ottawa: ICCS.

Iqbal, Sir Mohammad 1934 (*1984*): *The Reconstruction of Religious Thought in Islam*. New Delhi: Kitab Bhavan.

——1915 (*1978*): *The Secrets of the Self*, trans. R.A. Nicholson. Lahore: Ashraf Publications.

Irigaray, Luce 1974 (*1985*): *Speculum of the Other Woman*, trans. Gillian G. Gill. Ithaca, NY: Cornell University Press.

——1977a (*1991*): "The poverty of psychoanalysis," trans. David Macey and Margaret Whitford. In *The Irigaray Reader*. Oxford: Blackwell.

——1977b (*1985*): *This Sex Which Is Not One*, trans. Catherine Porter. Ithaca, NY: Cornell University Press.

Iser, Wolfgang 1974: *The Implied Reader: Patterns of Communication in Prose Fiction from Bunyan to Beckett*. Baltimore, MD: Johns Hopkins University Press.

——1978: *The Act of Reading: A Theory of Aesthetic Response*. Baltimore, MD: Johns Hopkins University Press.

——1980: "Interaction between text and reader." In *The Reader in the Text: Essays on Audience and Interpretation*, ed. Susan Suleiman and Inge Crosman. Princeton, NJ: Princeton University Press.

——1980: "The reading process: a phenomenological approach." In *Reader-Response Criticism*, ed. Jane Tompkins. Baltimore, MD: Johns Hopkins University Press.

Israel, J. 1971: *Alienation, from Marx to Modern Sociology*. Atlantic Highlands, NJ: Humanities Press.

Jackson, B.D. 1972: "The theory of signs in St Augustine's *De Doctrina Christiana*." In *Augustine*, ed. R. Markus. Garden City, NY: Doubleday.

Jackson, R. and Rudy, S., eds 1985: *Russian Formalism: A Retrospective Glance*. New Haven, CT: Yale University Press.

Jackson, Richard L. 1988: *Black Literature and Humanism in Latin America*. Athens: University of Georgia Press.

Jacobs, Joanne 1994: "Multiculturalism: giving an appreciation of patriotism," *Tallahassee Democrat*, May 21, 13A.

Jacobus, Mary 1990: *Romanticism, Writing, and Sexual Difference: Essays on the Prelude*. Oxford: Clarendon Press.

Jakobson, Roman 1957 (*1971*): "Shifters, verbal categories and the Russian verb." In *Selected Writings*, Vol. 2. The Hague: Mouton.

——1971: 'On realism in art'. In *Readings in Russian Formalist Poetics*, ed. K. Pomorska and L. Mateika. Cambridge: MIT Press.

——1990a: *On Language*. Cambridge, MA, and London: Harvard University Press.

——1990b: *Selected Writings*. 4 vols. The Hague: Mouton.

Jakobson, Roman, and Jones, Lawrence G. 1970: *Shakespeare's Verbal Art in Th'Expence of Spirit*. The Hague: Mouton.

James, C.L.R. 1936 (*1971*): *Minty Alley*. London: New Beacon Books.

—— 1937 (*1973*): *World Revolution 1917: The Rise and Fall of the Communist International.* Connecticut: Hyperion Press.

—— 1938: *The Black Jacobins: Toussaint L'Ouverture and the Saint Domingo Revolution.* New York: Dial Press.

—— 1948 (*1980*): *Notes on Dialectics: Hegel, Marx, Lenin.* Connecticut: Lawrence Hill.

—— 1953 (*1986*): *Mariners, Renegades and Castaways: The Story of Herman Melville and the World We Live In.* London: Allison & Busby.

—— 1962 (*1984*): *Party Politics in the West Indies.* Trinidad: Imprint Caribbean.

—— 1963 (*1983*): *Beyond a Boundary.* New York: Pantheon.

—— 1977: *The Future in the Present.* London: Allison & Busby.

James, C.L.R., Dunayevskaya, Raya, and Boggs, Grace Lee 1953 (*1986*): *State Capitalism and World Revolution.* Chicago: Charles H. Kerr.

James, Henry 1987: *The Critical Muse: Selected Literary Criticism,* ed. Roger Gard. Harmondsworth: Penguin.

Jameson, Fredric 1971 (*1974*): *Marxism and Form.* Princeton, NJ: Princeton University Press.

—— 1972: *The Prison House of Language: A Critical Account of Structuralism and Russian Formalism.* Princeton, NJ: Princeton University Press.

—— 1979 (*1988*): "Marxism and historicism." In *The Ideologies of Theory: Essays 1971–1986.* Vol. 2, *Syntax of History.* Minneapoli: University of Minnesota Press.

—— 1981 (*1989*): *The Political Unconscious: Narrative as a Socially Symbolic Act.* London: Routledge; Methuen.

—— 1984: "Postmodernism, or the cultural logic of late capitalism," *New Left Review,* 146, 53–92.

—— 1990: *Late Marxism: Adorno, or, The Persistence of Dialectic.* London: Verso.

Jardine, Alice 1985: *Gynesis: Configurations of Woman and Modernity.* Ithaca, NY: Cornell University Press.

Jardine, Alice, and Smith, Paul, eds 1987: *Men in Feminism.* London: Methuen.

Jardine, Lisa 1983: *Still Harping on Daughters: Women and Drama in the Age of Shakespeare.* Hemel Hempstead: Harvester Wheatsheaf.

Jarvis, Robert 1984: *The Illogic of American Nuclear Strategy.* Ithaca, NY: Cornell University Press.

Jaspers, Karl 1950: *The Perennial Scope of Philosophy,* trans. R. Mannheim. London: Routledge.

—— 1951: *The Way to Wisdom,* trans. R. Mannheim. New Haven, CT: Yale University Press.

—— 1969–71: *Philosophy,* trans. E.B. Ashton. 3 vols. Chicago: University of Chicago Press.

Jay, Martin 1973: *The Dialectical Imagination: A History of the Frankfurt School and the Institute of Social Research 1923–50.* London: Heinemann.

—— 1984a: *Marxism and Totality.* Berkeley: University of California Press.

—— 1984b: *Adorno.* London: Fontana.

Jayawardena, Kumari 1986: *Feminism and Nationalism in the Third World.* London: Zed Books.

Jaye, Michael, and Watts, Ann Chalmers 1981: *Literature and the Urban Experience.* New Brunswick, NJ: Rutgers University Press.

Jencks, Charles 1991: *The Language of Post-Modern Architecture.* 6th edn. London: Academy Editions.

Jenkins, Richard 1992: *Pierre Bourdieu.* London: Routledge.

Jenks, Chris 1993: *Culture.* London: Routledge.

Jhally, Sut, and Lewis, Justin, 1992: *Enlightening Racism: The Cosby Show, Audiences, and the Myth of the American Dream.* San Francisco, CA: Westview Press.

Johnson, Barbara 1980: *The Critical Difference: Essays in the Contemporary Rhetoric of Reading.* Baltimore, MD: Johns Hopkins University Press.

—— 1990: *A World of Difference.* Baltimore, MD: Johns Hopkins University Press.

Johnson, Philip 1947 (*1978*): *Mies Van Der Rohe.* New York: The Museum of Modern Art.

Johnson, Richard 1984: *What Is Cultural Studies Anyway?* Birmingham: CCCS.

Johnson, Robert 1983: *We: Understanding the Psychology of Romantic Love.* San Francisco, CA: Harper & Row.

Johnson, Kenneth R. et al. 1990: *Romantic Revolutions: Criticism and Theory.* Bloomington: Indiana University Press.

Jones, LeRoi, and Neal, Larry, eds 1968: *Black Fire.* New York: Morrow.

Jordon, Constance 1990: *Renaissance Feminism: Literary Texts and Political Models.* Ithaca, NY and London: Cornell University Press.

Journal of the Midwest Modern Language Association 1991: "Cultural studies and New Historicism," 24:1 (special issue).

Jung, C.G. 1953: "Two essays on analytical psychology." In *The Collected Works,* Vol. 7. Princeton, NJ: Princeton University Press.

—— 1963: *Memories, Dreams, Reflections.* New York: Pantheon Books.

—— 1969a: "The structure and dynamics of the psyche." In *The Collected Works,* Vol. 8. Princeton, NJ: Princeton University Press.

—— 1969b: *The Collected Works,* Vol. 9, Parts I & II. Princeton, NJ: Princeton University Press.

—— 1970: "The development of personality." In *The Collected Works,* Vol. 17. Princeton, NJ: Princeton University Press.

Kabbani, Rana 1989: *Letter to Christendom*. London: Verso.

Kadarkay, A. 1991: *Georg Lukács: Life, Thought, and Politics*. Oxford: Blackwell.

Kaetz, James P., ed. 1994: "Multiculturalism and diversity," *National Forum*, 74, 2–40.

Kagame, Alexis 1956 (*1975*): *La Philosophie bantou-rwandaise de l'être*. Brussels: Académie Royale des Sciences Coloniales.

Kagarlitsky, Boris 1993: "A step to the left, a step to the right." In *Late Soviet Culture. From Perestroika to Novostroika*, ed. Th. Lahusen and G. Kuperman. Durham, NC, and London: Duke University Press.

Kahn, Coppelia, and Schwartz, Murray M. eds 1980: *Representing Shakespeare: New Psychoanalytic Essays*. Baltimore, MD: Johns Hopkins University Press.

Kamps, Ivo 1991: *Shakespeare Left and Right*. London: Routledge.

Kandiyoti, Deniz, ed. 1991: *Women, Islam and the State*. Philadelphia, PA: Temple University Press.

Kant, Immanuel 1781/7 (*1929*): *Critique of Pure Reason*, trans. Norman Kemp Smith. New York: St Martin's Press.

——1785 (*1948*): *The Moral Law: Kant's Groundwork of the Metaphysic of Morals*, trans. H.J. Paton. London: Hutchinson.

——1790 (*1988*): *Kritik der Urteilskraft*, ed. Wilhelm Weischedel. Frankfurt: Suhrkamp; [trans. J.C. Meredith. *Critique of Judgement*. Oxford: Oxford University Press.]

Kaplan, C. 1986: "The feminist politics of literary theory." In *Sea Changes: Essays on Culture and Feminism*. London: Verso.

Kaplan, E.A., and Sprinker, M., eds 1993: *The Althusserian Legacy*. London: Verso.

Kaplan, Steven L., ed. 1984: *Understanding Popular Culture: Europe from the Middle Ages to the Nineteenth Century*. Berlin: De Gruyter.

Katz, Barry 1982: *Herbert Marcuse and the Art of Liberation*. London: Verso.

Kaufmann, Walter 1950 (*1974*): *Nietzsche: Philosopher, Psychologist, Antichrist*. Princeton, NJ: Princeton University Press.

——1968: *Tragedy and Philosophy*. Princeton, NJ: Princeton University Press.

Kauppi, Niilo 1990: *Tel Quel: La constitution sociale d'une avant-garde*. Helsinki: Societas Scientiarum Fennica (Commentationes Scientiarum Socialium, No. 43).

Kaye, H.J., and McLelland, K. 1990: *E.P. Thompson, Critical Perspectives*. Oxford: Basil Blackwell.

Keane, John 1988a: *Democracy and Civil Society*. London: Verso.

——, ed. 1988b: *Civil Society and the State: New European Perspectives*. London: Verso.

Kearney, Richard 1988: *Transitions: Narratives in Modern Irish Culture*. Manchester: Manchester University Press.

Kellner, Douglas 1984: *Herbert Marcuse and the Crisis of Marxism*. London: Macmillan.

——1989: *Jean Baudrillard: From Marxism to Postmodernism and Beyond*. Cambridge: Polity Press.

——1990: *Television and the Crisis of Democracy*. Boulder, CO: Westview Press.

Kelman, Mark 1985 (*1992*): *A Guide to Critical Legal Studies*. Cambridge, MA: Harvard University Press.

Kerman, J. 1985: *Musicology*. London: Fontana.

Kermode, Frank 1957: *The Romantic Image*. London: Routledge & Kegan Paul.

——1967: *The Sense of an Ending: Studies in the Theory of Fiction*. New York: Oxford University Press.

——1975: *The Classic*. London: Faber.

——1979: *The Genesis of Secrecy: On the Interpretation of Narrative*. Cambridge, MA: Harvard University Press.

——1983: *The Art of Telling*. Cambridge, MA: Harvard University Press.

——1985: *Forms of Attention*. Chicago: University of Chicago Press.

——1988: *History and Value*. Oxford: Clarendon Press.

——1990a: *An Appetite for Poetry*. Cambridge, MA: Harvard University Press.

——1990b: "New ways with Bible stories." In *Poetry, Narrative, History*. Oxford: Blackwell.

——1990c: *Poetry, Narrative, History*. Oxford: Blackwell.

Kermode, F., Fenden, S., and Palmer, K. 1974: *English Renaissance Literature: Introductory Lectures*. London: Gray Mills.

Kesteloot, Lilyan 1963 (*1974*): *Black Writers in French. A Literary History of Negritude*, trans. Ellen Conroy Kennedy. Philadelphia, PA: Temple University Press.

Kimball, Roger 1990: *Tenured Radicals: How Politics Has Corrupted Higher Education*. New York: Harper & Row.

King, R. 1973: "Paul Goodman." In *The Party of Eros: Radical Social Thought and the Realm of Freedom*. New York: Dell Publishing.

Kirszner, Laurie G., and Mandell, Stephen R. eds 1994: *Common Ground: Reading and Writing about America's Cultures*. New York: St Martin's Press.

Kitses, Jim 1969: *Horizons West*. London: British Film Institute and Secker & Warburg.

Kittel, Harold, and Frank, Armin Paul 1991: *Interculturality and the Historical Study of Literary Translation*. Berlin: Erich Schmidt Verlag.

Kleber, Pia, and Visser, Colin, eds 1990: *Re-interpreting Brecht: His Influence on Contemporary Drama and Film*. Cambridge: Cambridge University Press.

Kleberg, Lars, and Lovgren, H., eds 1987: *Eisenstein Revisited: A Collection of Essays*. Stockholm: Almquist and Wiksell.

Klein, Melanie 1975a: *Guilt and Reparation and Other Works 1921–45*. London: Hogarth Press and Institute of Psychoanalysis.

——1975b: *Envy and Gratitude and Other Works 1946–1963*. London: Hogarth Press and Institute of Psychoanalysis.

——1975c: *The Psychoanalysis of Children*. London: Hogarth Press and Institute of Psychoanalysis.

——1975d: *Narrative of a Child Analysis*. London: Hogarth Press and Institute of Psychoanalysis.

Klein, Richard 1990: "The future of nuclear criticism," *Yale French Studies*, 77, 76–100.

Klinkowitz, Jerome 1988: *Rosenberg, Barthes, Hassan: The Postmodern Habit of Thought*. Athens: University of Georgia Press.

Klusacek, Allan and Morrison, Ken, eds 1993: *A Leap in the Dark: AIDS Art and Contemporary Culture*. Quebec: Véhicule Press.

Knoepflmacher, U.C., and Tennyson, G.B., eds 1977: *Nature and the Victorian Imagination*. Berkeley: University of California Press.

Kockelmans, J., ed. 1980: *Phenomenology: The Philosophy of Edmund Husserl and Its Interpretations*. New York: Anchor.

Koelb, Clayton, and Noakes, Susan 1988: *The Comparative Perspective on Literature. Approaches to Theory and Practice*. Ithaca, NY: Cornell University Press.

Koerner, K. 1984: *Edward Sapir: Appraisals of His Life and Work*. Amsterdam: John Benjamins.

Kofman, Sarah 1974 (*1991*): *Freud and Fiction*, trans. Sarah Wykes. Cambridge: Polity Press.

Kogan, Pauline 1969: *Northrop Frye: High Priest of Clerical Obscurantism*. Montreal: Progressive Books and Periodicals.

Kohnke, Klaus Christian 1991: *The Rise of Neo-Kantanism*, trans. R.J. Hollingdale. Cambridge: Cambridge University Press.

Kojève, Alexandre 1947 (*1977*): *Introduction to Hegel. Lectures on "The Phenomenology of Mind,"* ed. Allan Bloom, trans. James H. Nichols. Ithaca, NY: Cornell University Press.

Kolakovski, Leszek 1972: *Positivist Philosophy: From Hume to the Vienna Circle*. London: Penguin.

Kolko, Gabriel 1984: *Main Currents in Modern American History*. New York: Pantheon.

Körner, Stephan 1967: "The impossibility of transcendental deductions," *Monist*, 51, 317–31.

Kostelantez, Richard 1988: *Conversing with Cage*. New York: Limelight Editions.

Kostelleck, Reinhart 1979 (*1985*): *Futures Past: The Semantics of Historical Time*. Cambridge, MA: MIT Press.

Kostof, Spiro 1985: *A History of Architecture: Settings and Rituals*. New York: Oxford University Press.

Kracauer, Siegfried 1947 (*1960*): *Theory of Film: The Redemption of Physical Reality*. New York: Oxford University Press.

Kramer, Hilton 1973: *The Age of the Avant-Garde: An Art Chronicle of 1956–72*. New York: Farrar, Straus, and Giroux.

Kramer, J. 1983: *English Cultural and Social Studies*. Stuttgart: Metzler.

——1990: *Cultural and Intercultural Studies*. Frankfurt a. M.: Peter Lang.

——1994: "Cultural studies in English studies: a German perspective." In *Culture and Language Learning in Higher Education*. Ed. M. Byram. Clevedon: Multilingual Matters.

Kramer, L. 1990: *Music as Cultural Practice 1800–1900*. Berkeley: University of California Press.

Krauss, Rosalind 1981 (*1985*): "The originality of the avant-garde," *October*, 18.

——1984: "A note on photography and the simulacral," *October*, 31, 49–68.

——1985: *The Originality of the Avant-Garde and Other Modernist Myths*. Cambridge, MA: MIT Press.

——1993: *The Optical Unconscious*. Cambridge, MA: MIT Press.

Krieger, Murray 1973: *The Tragic Vision*. Baltimore, MD: Johns Hopkins University Press.

Kripke, Saul 1980: *Naming and Necessity*. Cambridge, MA: Harvard University Press; Oxford: Blackwell.

Krishman, Prabha, and Dighe, Anita 1990: *Affirmation and Denial: Construction of Femininity on Indian Television*. New Delhi: Sage Publications.

Kristeva, Julia 1967: "Word, dialogue and novel," trans. Alice Jardine, Thomas Gora, and Léon Roudiez. In *The Kristeva Reader*, ed. Toril Moi. Oxford: Basil Blackwell.

——1969: *Sémiotiké. Recherches pour une sémanalyse*. Paris: Seuil.

——1970: *Le Texte du roman*. The Hague: Mouton.

——1974a (*1984*): *Revolution in Poetic Language*, trans. Leon S. Roudiez. New York: Columbia University Press.

——1974b: *About Chinese Women*, trans. Anita Barrows. London: Marion Boyars.

——1977 (*1986*): "Why the United States?" In *The Kristeva Reader*, ed. Toril Moi. Oxford: Blackwell, 272–91.

——1979 (*1986*): "Women's time." In *The Kristeva Reader*, ed. Toril Moi. Oxford: Basil Blackwell, 187–213.

Kristeva, Julia 1980a (*1982*): *Powers of Horror*, trans. Leon S. Roudiez. New York: Columbia University Press.
—— 1980b (*1984*): *Desire in Language: A Semiotic Approach to Literature and Art*, trans. Thomas Gora, Alice Jardine, and Leon S. Roudiez. New York: Columbia University Press.
—— 1986: *The Kristeva Reader*, ed. Toril Moi. Oxford: Blackwell.
—— 1989: *Black Sun*, trans. Leon S. Roudiez. New York: Columbia University Press.
—— 1990a: *Lettre ouverte à Harlem désir*. Marseille: Rivages.
—— 1990b: *Les Samuraïs*. Paris: Fayard.
Kroeber, A.L. 1917: "The superorganic," *American Anthropologist*, 19, 163–213.
—— 1923 (*1948*): *Anthropology*. New York: Harcourt Brace.
—— 1944: *Configurations of Culture Growth*. Berkeley: University of California Press.
—— 1952: *The Nature of Culture*. Chicago: University of Chicago Press.
—— 1957 (*1963*): *Style and Civilization*. Ithaca, NY: Cornell University Press.
Kroeber, A.L., and Kluckhohn, Clyde 1952: *Culture: A Critical Review of Concepts and Definitions*. New York: Vintage.
Kroeber, Theodora 1970: *Alfred Kroeber: A Personal Configuration*. Berkeley: University of California Press.
Kroetsch, Robert 1970: *Studhorse Man*. Toronto: McClelland and Stewart.
Kruger, Loren 1994: "'Stories from the production line:' modernism and modernization in the GDR production play," *Theatre Journal*, 46, 489–505.
Krupat, Arnold 1985: *For Those Who Come After: A Study of Native American Autobiography*. Berkeley: University of California Press.
—— 1989: "The dialogic of Silko's *Storyteller*." In *Indian Literatures*, ed. Gerald Vizenor. Norman: University of Oklahoma Press.
Kuenzli, R.E. 1980: "The intersubjective structure of the reading process: a communication-oriented theory of literature." *Diacritics*, 10, 47–56.
Kuhn, T.S. 1957: *The Copernican Revolution: Planetary Astronomy in the Development of Western Thought*. Cambridge, MA: Harvard University Press.
—— 1962 (*1970*): *The Structure of Scientific Revolutions*. Chicago: University of Chicago Press.
—— 1977: *The Essential Tension: Selected Studies in Scientific Tradition and Change*. Chicago: University of Chicago Press.
Kushner, Tony (interviews by Lynn Jacobson) 1989: "American Brecht," *American Theatre*, 6:7, 46–52, 122–3.

Kuspit, Donald 1993: *The Cult of the Avant-Garde Artist*. Cambridge: Cambridge University Press.
Kustanovich, Konstantin 1993: "Erotio glasnost: sexuality in recent Russian literature," *World Literature Today*, 67:1.

Lacan, Jacques 1932 (*1975*): *De la psychose paranoïaque dans ses rapports avec la personalité*. Paris: Seuil.
—— 1948 (*1977*): "Aggressivity in psychoanalysis." In *Ecrits: A Selection*, trans. Alan Sheridan. London: Tavistock, 8–29.
—— 1949 (*1977*): "The mirror-stage as formative of the function of the I as revealed in psychoanalytic experience." In *Ecrits: A Selection*, trans. Alan Sheridan. London: Tavistock, 8–29.
—— 1951 (*1982*): "Intervention on transference." In *Jacques Lacan and the Ecole Freudienne: Feminine Sexuality*, trans. Jacqueline Rose; ed. Juliet Mitchell and Jacqueline Rose. London: Macmillan, 61–73.
—— 1953 (*1977*): "The function and field of speech and language in psychoanalysis." In *Ecrits: A Selection*, trans. Alan Sheridan. London: Tavistock.
—— 1957 (*1977*): "The agency of the letter in the unconscious, or reason since Freud." In *Ecrits: A Selection*, trans. Alan Sheridan. London: Tavistock, 146–78.
—— 1958 (*1977*): "On a question preliminary to any possible treatment of psychosis." In *Ecrits: A Selection*, trans. Alan Sheridan. London: Tavistock, 178–225.
—— 1958 (*1982*): "The meaning of the phallus," trans. Jacqueline Rose. In *Feminine Sexuality: Jacques Lacan and the Ecole Freudienne*, ed. Juliet Mitchell and Jacqueline Rose. London: Macmillan.
—— 1959: "Desire and the interpretation of desire in *Hamlet*," trans. James Hulbert. *Yale French Studies*, 55/56, 1–52.
—— 1960 (*1977*): "Subversion of the subject and dialectic of desire." In *Ecrits: A Selection*, trans. Alan Sheridan. London: Tavistock, 178–225.
—— 1965: "Hommage fait à Marguerite Duras, du ravissement de Lol V. Stein," *Cahiers Renaud-Barreult*, 53, 7–13.
—— 1966: *Ecrits*. Paris: Seuil.
—— 1968: *The Language of the Self: The Function of Language in Psychoanalysis*, ed. and trans. A. Wilden. Baltimore, MD: Johns Hopkins University Press.
—— 1973 (*1977*): *The Four Fundamental Concepts of Psychoanalysis*, trans. Alan Sheridan. London: Hogarth Press and Institute of Psychoanalysis.
—— 1975 (*1988*): *The Seminar of Jacques Lacan*. Book 1, *Freud's Papers on Technique, 1953–54*,

trans. John Forrester. Cambridge: Cambridge University Press.

——1977: *Ecrits: A Selection*, trans. Alan Sheridan. London: Hogarth Press and Institute of Psychoanalysis.

——1978 (*1988*): *The Seminar of Jacques Lacan. Book 2, The Ego in Freud's Theory and in the Technique of Psychoanalysis*, trans. Sylvana Tomaselli. Cambridge: Cambridge University Press.

——1981: *Le Séminaire de Jacques Lacan. Livre Trois, Les Psychoses. 1955–1956*. Paris: Seuil.

LaCapra, Dominick 1985: *History and Criticism*. Ithaca, NY: Cornell University Press.

LaCapra, Dominick, and Kaplan, Steven L., eds 1982: *Modern European Intellectual History: Reappraisals and New Perspectives*. Ithaca, NY: Cornell University Press.

Lachs, John 1988: *George Santayana*. Twayne's United States Authors Series. Boston, MA: Twayne Publishers.

Laclau, E., and Mouffe, C. 1985: *Hegemony and Socialist Strategy: Towards a Radical Democratic Politics*, trans. Winston Moore and Paul Cammack. London and New York: Verso.

Lacoue-Labarthe, Philippe 1989: *Typography: Mimesis, Philosophy, Politics*, ed. and trans. Christopher Fynsk. Cambridge, MA: Harvard University Press.

——1990: *Heidegger, Art and Politics: The Fiction of the Political*, trans. Chris Turner. Oxford: Blackwell.

Lado, R. 1964: *Language Teaching*. New York: McGraw-Hill.

Lafrance, Guy, ed. 1987: *Gaston Bachelard*. Ottawa: University of Ottawa Press.

Laing, D. 1978: *The Marxist Theory of Art*. Boulder, CO: Harvester/Westview Press.

Lakatos, I. 1974: "Falsification and the methodology of scientific research programmes." In *Criticism and the Growth of Knowledge*, ed. I. Lakatos and A. Musgrave. Cambridge: Cambridge University Press.

Lakatos, I., and Musgrave, A., eds 1970: *Criticism and the Growth of Knowledge*. Cambridge: Cambridge University Press.

Lampe, G.W.H., ed. 1969: *The Cambridge History of the Bible*. Vol. 2. *The West from the Fathers to the Reformation*. New York: Cambridge University Press.

Lampert, Laurence 1993: *Nietzsche and Modern Times: A Study of Bacon, Descartes and Nietzsche*. New Haven, CT, and London: Yale University Press.

Landry, Donna 1990: *Muses of Resistance: Laboring-Class Women's Poetry in Britain, 1739–1796*. Cambridge: Cambridge University Press.

Lang, P.H. 1941: *Music in Western Civilization*. New York: W.W. Norton.

Lange, F.A. 1974: *The History of Materialism*, trans. E.C. Thomas. New York: Arno Press.

Laplanche, Jean, and Pontalis, J.-B. 1967 (*1973*): *The Language of Psychoanalysis*, trans. Donald Nicholson-Smith. London: Hogarth Press and Institute of Psychoanalysis.

Larrain, J. 1979: *The Concept of Ideology*. London: Hutchinson.

Lash, Scott, and Urry, John 1987: *The End of Organized Capitalism*. Cambridge: Polity.

Latour, Bruno, and Woolgar, Steve 1979 (*1986*): *Laboratory Life: The Construction of Scientific Facts*. Princeton, NJ: Princeton University Press.

Latynina, Yuliya 1993: "Dedal i Gerkules, ili Neskol'ko rassuzhdenii o pol'ze literatury," *Novy mir*, 5.

Laudan, Larry 1990: *Science and Relativism: Some Key Controversies in the Philosophy of Science*. Chicago: University of Chicago Press.

Laughlin, Karen 1990: "Brechtian theory and American feminist theatre," In *Re-interpreting Brecht: His Influence on Contemporary Drama and Film*, ed. Pia Kleber and Colin Visser. Cambridge: Cambridge University Press.

Laurence, Margaret 1965: *The Stone Angel*. Toronto: McClelland & Stewart.

Lauter, Paul 1990: "The literatures of America: a comparative discipline." In *Redefining American Literary History*, ed. A. LaVonne Brown Ruoff and Jerry W. Ward, Jr. New York: Modern Language Association.

Lavers, A. 1982: *Roland Barthes: Structuralism and After*. London: Methuen.

Lawall, Sarah N. 1968a: "Marcel Raymond." In *Critics of Consciousness: The Existential Structures of Literature*. Cambridge, MA: Harvard University Press.

——1968b: "Georges Poulet." In *Critics of Consciousness: The Existential Structures of Literature*. Cambridge, MA: Harvard University Press.

——1968c: "Marcel Raymond." In *Critics of Consciousness: The Existential Structures of Literature*. Cambridge, MA: Harvard University Press.

——1968d: "Jean-Pierre Richard." In *Critics of Consciousness: The Existential Structures of Literature*. Cambridge, MA: Harvard University Press.

Lawrence, D.H. 1985: *A Study of Thomas Hardy and Other Essays*, ed. Brian Steele. Cambridge: Cambridge University Press.

Lawton, D. 1989: *Education, Culture and the National Curriculum*. Sevenoaks: Hodder and Stoughton.

Layton, Robert, ed. 1989: *Conflict in the Archaeology of Living Traditions*. London: Hyman.

Layton-Henry, Z. 1992: *The Politics of Immigration*. Oxford: Blackwell.

Leavis, F.R. 1943 (*1948*): *Education and the University*. Cambridge: Cambridge University Press.

—— 1948 (*1972*): *The Great Tradition: George Eliot, Henry James, Joseph Conrad*. Harmondsworth: Penguin.

—— 1986: *Valuation in Criticism and Other Essays*, ed. G. Singh. Cambridge: Cambridge University Press.

Leavis, Q.D. 1938 (*1975*): "Review of *Three Guineas* by Virginia Woolf," *Scrutiny*, September. In *Virginia Woolf: The Critical Heritage*; ed. Majumdar and McLaurin. London: Routledge & Kegan Paul.

Leclaire, Serge, and Laplanche, Jean 1966 (*1972*): "The unconscious: a psychoanalytic study," trans. P. Coleman, *Yale French Studies*, 48, 118–75.

Le Corbusier 1929 (*1971*): *The City of To-morrow and Its Planning (Urbanisme)*, trans. F. Etchells. London: Architecturial Press.

—— 1960: *Creation is a Patient Search*. New York: Frederick A. Praeger.

Lecourt, D. 1975: *Marxism and Epistemology: Bachelard, Canguilhem and Foucault*. London: New Left Books.

Ledbetter, Steven, ed. 1988: *Sennets and Tuckets: A Bernstein Celebration*. Boston, MA: David R. Godine.

Le Dœuff, Michèle 1989 (*1991*): *Hipparchia's Choice: An Essay Concerning Women, Philosophy, etc.*, trans. Trista Selous. Oxford: Blackwell.

Lee, Brian 1966: "The New Criticism and the language of poetry." In *Essays on Style and Language*, ed. Roger Fowler. London: Routledge & Kegan Paul.

Lee, Dennis 1968: *Civil Elegies*. Toronto: House of Anansi.

Lee, Keekok 1989: *Social Philosophy and Ecological Scarcity*. London: Routledge.

Lee, Martyn J. 1993: *Consumer Culture Reborn, the Cultural Politics of Consumption*. London: Routledge.

Lefebvre, H. 1982: *The Sociology of Marx*, trans. N. Guterman. New York: Columbia University Press.

Lefevere, André 1991: "The dynamics of the system: convention and innovation in literary history." In *Convention and Innovation in Literature*, ed. Theo D'hoen, Rainer Grubel, and Helmut Lethen. Amsterdam: Benjamins.

—— 1992: *Translation, Rewriting and the Manipulation of Literary Fame*. London: Routledge.

Lehman, David 1990: "The not-so-new formalism," *Michigan Quarterly Review*, 29:1.

Lehman, W., ed. 1967: *A Reader in Nineteenth-Century Indo-European Historical Linguistics*. Bloomington: Indiana University Press.

Leiderman, N., and Lipovetsky, M. 1993: "Zhizn posle smerti, ili Novye svedeniya o realizme," *Novy mir*, 7.

Leighton, Mike, ed. 1992: *Eighteenth-Century Studies: The Rights of Man*. Pretoria: HSRC Publishers.

Leitch, Vincent B. 1994: "Cultural studies." In *The Johns Hopkins Guide to Literary Theory and Criticism*, ed. Michael Groden and Martin Kreiswirth. Baltimore, MD: Johns Hopkins University Press.

Lemelin, Roger 1969: *The Town Below*. Toronto: McClelland & Stewart.

Lemon, Lee T., and Reis, Marion J., eds 1965: *Russian Formalist Criticism: Four Essays*. Lincoln: Nebraska University Press.

Lenin, V.I. 1987: *Introduction to Marx, Engels, Marxism*. New York: International Publishers.

Lentricchia, Frank 1980: *After the New Criticism*. Chicago: University of Chicago Press; London: Athlone Press.

Lenz, Carolyn Ruth, Greene, Gayle, and Neely, Carol Thomas, eds 1980: *The Woman's Part: Feminist Criticism of Shakespeare*. Urbana: University of Illinois Press.

LePan, Douglas 1953: "A country without a mythology." In *The New Oxford Book of Canadian Verse in English*, ed. Margaret Atwood. Toronto: Oxford University Press.

Lepin, J. ed. 1984: *Scientific Realism*. Berkeley and Los Angeles: University of California Press.

LePore, Ernest 1986: *Truth and Interpretation: Perspectives on the Philosophy of Donald Davidson*. Oxford: Basil Blackwell.

Le Roy Ladurie, Emmanuel 1975 (*1979*): *Montaillou, the Promised Land of Error*, trans. Barbara Bray. New York: Vintage.

Lerner, Gerda 1971: *The Woman in American History*. Menlo Park, CA: Addison-Wesley.

Levin, Bob 1988: "Comics," *Spin*, 4:5, 40–5.

Levin, Harry 1972: *Refractions, Essays in Comparative Literature*. Oxford: Oxford University Press.

Levin, Richard 1988: "Feminist thematics and Shakespearean tragedy," *PMLA*, 103, 125–38.

—— 1990: "The poetics and politics of Bardicide," *PMLA*, 105, 491–504.

Levine, Carol, ed. 1993: *Taking Sides: Clashing Views on Controversial Bioethical Issues*. Hartford, CT: Dushkin.

Levine, Kenneth 1986: *The Social Context of Literacy*. London: Routledge & Kegan Paul.

Levine, Lawrence W. 1977: *Black Culture and Black Consciousness: Afro-American Folk Thought from Slavery to Freedom*. Oxford: Oxford University Press.

—— 1988: *Highbrow/Lowbrow. The Emergence of Cultural Hierarchy in America*. Cambridge, MA: Harvard University Press.

Levine, N. 1975: *The Tragic Deception: Marx Contra Engels*. Oxford: Clio Books.

Levins, Richard, and Lewontin, Richard 1985: *The Dialectical Biologist*. Cambridge: Harvard University Press.

Levinson, S.C. 1980: "Speech act theory: the state of the art." In *Language Teaching and Linguistics: Abstracts*, 13, 5–24.

——1983: "Deixis." Chapter 2 of *Pragmatics*. Cambridge: Cambridge University Press.

Lévi-Strauss, Claude 1949 (*1969*): *The Elementary Structures of Kinship*, trans. James Herle Bell, Richard von Sturmer, and Rodney Needham. London: Eyre & Spottiswoode.

——1950 (*1987*): *Introduction to the Work of Marcel Mauss*. London: Routledge & Kegan Paul.

——1955 (*1973*): *Tristes tropiques*, trans. J. and D. Weightman. London: Cape.

——1962a (*1963*): *Totemism*, trans. Rodney Needham. Boston, MA: Beacon Place.

——1962b (*1970*): "History and dialect." In *The Savage Mind*. Chicago: University of Chicago Press.

——1970: *The Savage Mind*. Chicago: University of Chicago Press.

——1971 (*1981*): *The Naked Man*. London: Jonathan Cape.

Levitas, R. 1986: *The Ideology of the New Right*. Cambridge: Polity Press.

Lewis, D.K. 1970 (*1983*): "General semantics." In *Philosophical Papers*, Vol. 1. Oxford: Oxford University Press.

Lewis, Gordon K. 1968: *The Growth of the Modern West Indies*. New York: Monthly Review Press.

——1983: *Main Currents in Caribbean Thought: The Historical Evolution of Caribbean Society in Its Ideological Aspects 1492–1900*. Baltimore, MD: Johns Hopkins University Press.

Lewis, Justin 1985: "Decoding television news." In *Television in Transition*; ed. P. Drummond and R. Peterson. London: British Film Institute.

——1991: *The Ideological Octopus: An Exploration of Television and Its Audience*. London: Routledge.

Lewis, Linden 1991: "The groundings of Walter Rodney," *Race and Class*, 33:1, 71–82.

Leyh, Gregory, ed. 1992: *Legal Hermeneutics: History, Theory, and Practice*. Berkeley: University of California Press.

Likhachev, D. 1993: "O russkoi intelligantsii," *Novy mir*, 2.

——1994: "Kul'tura kak tselostnaya sreda," *Novy mir*, 8.

Lindley, David 1985: *Lyric*. New York: Methuen.

Lings, Martin 1983: *Muhammad: His Life Based on the Earliest Sources*. Vermont: Inner Traditions International.

Lipietz, Alan 1987: *Mirages and Miracles: The Crisis of Global Fordism*. London: Verso.

Lippard, Lucy R. 1970: *Pop Art*. London: Thames & Hudson.

Lipset, Seymour Martin 1992: *Continental Divide: The Values and Institutions of the United States and Canada*. New York: Routledge.

Lipton, Peter 1993: *Inference to the Best Explanation*. London: Routledge.

Liu, Alan 1989: "The power of formalism: the New Historicism," *ELH*, 56:5.

Livingstone, Marco, ed. 1991: *Pop Art*. London: Royal Academy of the Arts.

Lloyd, David 1993: *Anomalous States: Irish Writing and the Post-Colonial Moment*. Durham, NC: Duke University Press.

Lloyd, Geoffrey E. R. 1993: *Demystifying Mentalities*. Cambridge: Cambridge University Press.

Locke, J. 1964 (*1975*): *An Essay Concerning Human Understanding*. London: Fontana/Collins.

Lodge, David 1981: *Working with Structuralism*. London: Routledge & Kegan Paul.

Longley, Edna 1990: *From Cathleen to Anorexia: The Breakdown of Irelands*. Dublin: Attic Press.

Lonsdale, Roger, ed. 1989: *Eighteenth-Century Women Poets: An Oxford Anthology*. Oxford: Clarendon Press.

Lord, Albert 1968: *The Singer of Tales*. Cambridge, MA: Harvard University Press.

Lord, Barry 1974: *The History of Painting in Canada: Towards a People's Art*. Toronto: NC Press.

Lorde, Audre 1981: "An open letter to Mary Daly." In *This Bridge Called My Back: Writings by Radical Women of Color*, ed. Cherrie Moraga and Gloria Anzaldua. Watertown, MA: Persephone Press.

Lorimer, Douglas A. 1978: *Colour, Class and the Victorians: English Attitudes to the Negro in the Mid-Nineteenth Century*. Leicester: Leicester University Press.

Lotman, Jurij 1977: *The Structure of the Artistic Text*. Ann Arbor: University of Michigan Press.

Lotman, Yury 1977: *Analysis of the Poetic Text*. Ann Arbor: University of Michigan Press.

Lovejoy, Arthur O. 1936: *The Great Chain of Being: A Study of the History of an Idea*. Cambridge, MA: Harvard University Press.

——1960: *The Revolt Against Dualism: An Inquiry Concerning the Existence of Ideas*. LaSalle, IL: Open Court.

——1961: *Reflections on Human Nature*. Baltimore, MD: Johns Hopkins University Press.

Lovell, T. 1980: *Pictures of Reality*. London: British Film Institute.

——1985: *Consuming Fiction*. London: Verso.

Lowenthal, Leo 1942–3: "Radio and popular music." In *Radio Research*, ed. P.F. Lazensfeld and F. Stanton. New York: Duell, Sloan & Pearce.

Lowie, Robert H. 1937: *The History of Ethnological Theory*. New York: Holt, Rinehart & Winston.

Lubac, Henri de 1959–64: *Exegèse médieval: Les quatre sens de l'écriture*. 4 vols. Paris: Aubier.

Lucretius 1951 (*1986*): *On the Nature of the Universe*, trans. R. E. Latham. Harmondsworth: Penguin.

Lukács, Gyorgy [Georg] 1910 (*1974*): *The Soul and the Forms*. London: Merlin; Cambridge, MA: MIT Press.

——1937, 1962 (*1983*): *The Historical Novel*, trans. H. and S. Mitchell. Lincoln and London: University of Nebraska Press.

——1958 (*1963*): *The Meaning of Contemporary Realism*. London: Merlin Press.

——1916 (*1971a*): *The Theory of the Novel*, trans. A. Bostock. London: Merlin Press.

——1923 (*1971b*): *History and Class Consciousness*, trans. R. Livingstone. London: Merlin Press.

——1975. *The Young Hegel*, trans. R. Livingstone. London: Merlin Press.

——1980. *Essays on Realism*, trans. D. Fernbach. Cambridge, MA: MIT Press.

Lunn, Eugene 1982: *Marxism and Modernism: An Historical Study of Lukács, Brecht, Benjamin and Adorno*. Berkeley: University of California Press.

Lycan, W.G., ed. 1990: *Mind and Cognition: A Reader*. Oxford: Basil Blackwell.

Lynch, James 1993: *Multicultural Education in a Global Society*. New York: Falmer Press.

Lyotard, Jean-François 1971: *Discours, figure*. Paris: Klincksieck.

——1974 (*1993*): *Economie libidinale*. Paris: Minuit; trans. Iain Hamilton Grant, *Libidinal Economy*. London: Athlone Press.

——1979 (*1989*): *La Condition postmoderne: Rapport sur le savoir*. Paris: Minuit; trans. Geoffrey Bennington and Brian Massumi, *The Postmodern Condition: A Report on Knowledge*. Minneapolis: University of Minnesota Press (1979); Manchester: Manchester University Press.

——1982 (*1984*): "Answering the question: What is postmodernism?" In *The Postmodern Condition: A Report on Knowledge*. Minneapolis: Minnesota University Press.

——1984 (*1988*): *Le Différend*. Paris: Minuit; trans. Georges van den Abbeele, *The Differend: Phrases in Dispute*. Manchester: Manchester University Press.

——1985: *La Faculté de juger*. Paris: Minuit.

——1986 (*1993*): *Le Postmoderne expliqué aux enfants: Corréspondance, 1982–1985*. Paris: Galilée; trans. Don Barry et al., *The Postmodern Explained to Children: Correspondence, 1982–1985*. Manchester: Manchester University Press.

——1988 (*1991*): *L'Inhumain: causeries sur le temps*. Paris: Galilée; trans. Geoffrey Bennington and Rachel Bowlby, *The Inhuman: Reflections on Time*. Cambridge: Polity Press.

——1991 (*1994*): *Leçons sur l'Analytique du sublime: Kant, critique de la faculté de juger, sections 23–29*. Paris: Galilée; trans. Elizabeth Rottenberg, *Lessons on the Analytic of the Sublime: Kant's Critique of Judgement Sections 23–29*. Stanford, CA: Stanford University Press.

——1993: *Political Writings*, trans. Bill Readings and Kevin Paul Geiman. London: UCL Press.

Lyotard, Jean-François, and Thébaud, Jean-Loup 1979 (*1985*): *Au Juste*. Paris: Christian Bourgeois; trans. Wlad Godzich, *Just Gaming*. Manchester: Manchester University Press.

McAllester, Mary 1990: "On science, poetry and the 'honey of being:' Bachelard's Shelley." In *Philosophers' Poets*; ed. David Ward. London: Routledge, 153–76.

——1991: *Gaston Bachelard: Subversive Humanist*. Madison: University of Wisconsin Press.

McArthur, Colin 1972: *Underworld USA*. London: British Film Institute and Secker & Warburg.

MacCabe, Colin 1978: *James Joyce and the "Revolution of the Word."* London: Macmillan.

——1979: "On discourse," *Economy and Society*, 8:3, 279–307.

McCallum, Pamela 1983: *Literature and Method: Towards a Critique of I.A. Richards, T.S. Eliot, and F.R. Leavis*. Dublin: Gill & Macmillan.

McCarthy, T. 1984: *The Critical Theory of Jürgen Habermas*. Cambridge: Polity Press.

McClary, S. 1991: *Feminine Endings: Music, Gender, and Sexuality*. Minneapolis: University of Minnesota Press.

McCloud, Scott 1993: *Understanding Comics*. Northampton, MA: Tundra Publishing.

McCole, John 1993: *Walter Benjamin and the Antinomies of Tradition*. Ithaca, NY: Cornell University Press.

McCormick, John 1987: *George Santayana: A Biography*. New York: Alfred A. Knopf.

——1989: *Reclaiming Paradise. The Global Environmental Movement*. Bloomington: Indiana University Press.

MacDonell, D. 1986: *Theories of Discourse: An Introduction*. Oxford and New York: Blackwell.

McDowell, Deborah 1989: "Reading family matters." In *Changing Our Own Words*, ed. Cheryl A. Wall. New Brunswick, NJ: Rutgers University Press.

McDowell, W. Stuart 1976: "Actors on Brecht: the Munich years," *Drama Review*, 20:3, 101–16.

Macey, David 1988: *Lacan in Context*. London: Verso.

—— 1993: *The Lives of Michel Foucault*. London: Hutchinson.

McGann, Jerome J. 1983: *The Romantic Ideology*. Chicago: University of Chicago Press.

McGowan, J. 1991: "The literary left: Jameson, Eagleton, Said." In *Postmodernism and Its Critics*. Ithaca, NY, and London: Cornell University Press.

McGuire, Randall H. 1992: "Archaeology and the first Americans," *American Anthropologist*, 94, 816–36.

Machado, Arlindo 1981: "Eisenstein: a radical dialogism," *Dispositio: American Journal of Semiotic and Cultural Studies*, 6:17–18 (Summer–Fall).

Macherey, Pierre 1965: "A propos du processus d'exposition du *Capital*." In L. Althusser et al., *Lire le Capital I*. Paris: François Maspero.

—— 1966 (*1978*): *A Theory of Literary Production*; trans. G. Wall. London and Boston, MA: Routledge & Kegan Paul.

—— 1979: *Hegel ou Spinoza*. Paris: François Maspero.

—— 1989: *Comte: La Philosophie et les sciences*. Paris: Presses Universitaires de France.

—— 1990 (*1994*): *A quoi pense la littérature?* Paris: François Maspero.

—— 1995: *The Object of Literature*, trans. David Macey. Cambridge: Cambridge University Press.

Macherey, Pierre, and Balibar, Etienne 1974 (*1993*): "On literature as an ideological form;" In *Contemporary Marxist Literary Criticism*; trans. Ian McLeod, John Whitehead, and Ann Wordsworth; ed. Francis Mulhern. London: Longman.

MacIntyre, Alasdair 1967: *A Short History of Ethics*. London: Routledge & Kegan Paul.

—— 1980 (*1985*): *After Virtue: A Study in Moral Theory*. London: Duckworth; Notre Dame, IN: Notre Dame University Press.

—— 1988: *Whose Justice? Which Rationality?* London: Duckworth; Notre Dame, IN: Notre Dame University Press.

—— 1990: *Three Rival Versions of Moral Enquiry: Encyclopedia, Genealogy, and Tradition*. Notre Dame, IN: Notre Dame University Press.

McKenzie, D.F. 1986: *Bibliography and the Sociology of Texts*. Panizzi Lectures 1985. London: The British Library.

McKeon, Michael 1987: *Origins of the English Novel, 1660–1740*. Baltimore, MD: Johns Hopkins University Press.

Mackie, J. 1974: *The Cement of the Universe: A Study of Causation*. Oxford: Clarendon Press.

—— 1978: *Ethics*. Harmondsworth: Penguin.

MacKinnon, Catharine 1979: *Sexual Harassment of Working Women: A Case of Sex Discrimination*. New Haven, CT: Yale University Press.

—— 1987: *Feminism Unmodified: Discourses on Life and Law*. Cambridge, MA: Harvard University Press.

—— 1989: *Toward a Feminist Theory of the State*. Cambridge, MA: Harvard University Press.

—— 1993: *Only Words*. Cambridge, MA: Harvard University Press.

McLellan, D. 1973 (*1977*): *Karl Marx: His Life and Thought*. New York: Harper & Row.

—— 1975: *Karl Marx*. New York: Viking Press.

—— 1977 (*1978*): *Engels*. New York: Viking Press.

—— 1986: *Ideology*. Milton Keynes: Open University Press.

McLuhan, Marshall 1964: *Understanding Media: The Extensions of Man*. London: Routledge & Kegan Paul.

McLuskie, Kathleen 1989: *Renaissance Dramatists*. Atlantic Highlands, NJ: Humanities Press.

McManmon, John 1990: "Formalism, structuralism, poststructuralism, and text," *Christianity and Literature*, 40:1.

McRobbie, A. 1991: *Feminism and Youth Culture*. London: Macmillan.

—— 1994: *Postmodernism and Popular Culture*. London: Routledge.

Magee, Bryan 1973 (*1982*): *Karl Popper*. London: Woburn Press.

Magner, James 1971: *John Crowe Ransom: Critical Principles and Preoccupations*. The Hague: Mouton.

Magowan, Robin 1964: *Jean-Pierre Richard and the Criticism of Sensation*. Detroit: Wayne State University Press.

Majumdar, Swapan 1987: *Comparative Literature, Indian Dimensions*. Calcutta: Papyrus.

Malcolm, Norman 1989: *Wittgenstein: A Memoir*. London: Oxford University Press.

Malotki, E. 1983: *Hopi Time: A Linguistic Analysis of the Temporal Concepts in the Hopi Language*. The Hague: Mouton.

Mann, Paul 1991: *The Theory-Death of the Avant-Garde*. Bloomington: Indiana University Press.

Mannheim, Karl 1924 (*1972*): "Historicism." In *Essays on the Sociology of Knowledge*, ed. and trans. Paul Kecskemeti. London: Routledge & Kegan Paul.

—— 1929 (*1954*): *Ideology and Utopia: An Introduction to the Sociology of Knowledge*, trans. Louis Wirth and Edward Shils. New York: Harcourt.

Manning, Peter J. 1990: *Reading Romantics: Texts and Contexts*. New York: Oxford University Press.

Marcus, Jane 1982 (*1987*): "Taking the bull by the udders: sexual difference in Virginia Woolf – a conspiracy theory." In *Virginia Woolf and Bloomsbury: A Centenary Celebration*, ed. Jane Marcus. London: Macmillan.

Marcuse, Herbert 1928 (*1969*): "Contribution to a phenomenology of historical materialism." *Telos*, 4.

—— 1937 (*1968*): "The affirmative character of culture." In *Negations: Essays in Critical Theory*. Boston, MA: Beacon Press.

—— 1941 (*1960*): *Reason and Revolution: Hegel and the Rise of Social Theory*. Boston, MA: Beacon Press.

—— 1955 (*1966*): *Eros and Civilization: A Philosophical Inquiry into Freud*. Boston, MA: Beacon Press.

—— 1964: *One-Dimensional Man: Studies in the Ideology of Advanced Industrial Society*. Boston, MA: Beacon Press.

—— 1969: *An Essay on Liberation*. Boston, MA: Beacon Press.

—— 1972: *Counter-Revolution and Revolt*. Boston, MA: Beacon Press.

—— 1977 (*1978*): *The Aesthetic Dimension: Towards a Critique of Marxist Aesthetics*. Boston, MA: Beacon Press.

Margolis, Joseph 1991: *The Truth About Relativism*. Oxford: Basil Blackwell.

Marmor, Andrei 1992: *Interpretation and Legal Theory*. Oxford: Clarendon Press.

Marranca, Bonnie, and Dasgupta, Gautam, eds 1991: *Interculturalism and Performance: Writings from PAJ*. New York: Performing Arts Journal Publications.

Martin, J. 1984: *Marxism and Totality*. Berkeley: University of California Press.

Martin, Tony 1972: "C.L.R. James and the race/class question," *Race*, 14:2, 183–93.

Martinich, A., ed. 1990: *The Philosophy of Language*. Oxford: Clarendon Press.

Maruyama, K. 1981: *The Thought of Saussure*. Tokyo: Iwanami.

—— 1984: *The Fetishism of Culture*. Tokyo: Keiso.

—— 1987: *Language and Unconsciousness*. Tokyo: Kodansha.

——, ed. 1985: *The Dictionary of Saussure*. Tokyo: Taishukan.

Marx, Karl 1954 (*1965*): *Capital: A Critique of Political Economy*, trans. Samuel Moore and Edward Aveling. London: Lawrence & Wishart. (First published 1867.)

—— 1959 (*1981*): *Economic and Philosophic Manuscripts of 1844*. London: Lawrence & Wishart.

—— 1963 (*1964*): *Early Writings*, trans. and ed. T.B. Bottomore. New York: McGraw-Hill.

—— 1975: *Early Writings*, ed. L. Colletti. Harmondsworth: Pelican/*New Left Review*.

—— 1976: *Preface and Introduction to A Contribution to the Critique of Political Economy*. Peking: Foreign Languages Press.

—— 1977: *Selected Writings*, ed. D. McLellan. Oxford: Oxford University Press.

Marx, Karl, and Engels, Frederick 1932 (*1976*): *The German Ideology*, trans. C. Dutt, W. Lough, and C.P. Magill. In Marx and Engels, *Collected Works*, vol. 5, *1845–7*. London: Lawrence & Wishart.

—— 1952 (*1973*): *Manifesto of the Communist Party*, trans. S. Moore. Moscow: Progress Publishers.

—— 1956 (*1980*): *The Holy Family, or Critique of Critical Criticism: Against Bruno Bauer and Company*, trans. R. Dixon and C. Dutt. Moscow: Progress Publishers. (First published 1845.)

—— 1957 (*1975*): *On Religion*. Moscow: Progress Publishers.

—— 1968: *Selected Works in One Volume*. London: Lawrence & Wishart.

—— 1970 (*1982*): *The German Ideology: Part One*. London: Lawrence & Wishart.

—— 1973: *Feuerbach: Opposition of the Materialist and Idealist Outlooks: The First Part of "The German Ideology."* London: Lawrence & Wishart. (First published 1845.)

Marx, Werner 1971: *Heidegger and the Tradition*. Evanston, IL: Northwestern University Press.

Marxist-Feminist Literature Collective 1978: *The Sociology of Literature: Proceedings of the Essex Conference on the Sociology of Literature, July 1977*, ed. F. Barker et al. Colchester: University of Essex.

Masolo, D.A. 1994: *African Philosophy in Search of Identity*.

Masson, Jeffrey Moussaieff 1984: *The Assault on Truth: Freud's Suppression of the Seduction Theory*. New York: Farrar, Straus, and Giroux.

Mast, Gerald, Cohen, Marshall, and Braudy, Leo, eds 1974 (*1992*): *Film Theory and Criticism*. New York: Oxford University Press.

Matejka, L., ed. 1978: *Sound, Sign and Meaning. Quinquagenary of the Prague Linguistic Circle*. Michigan Slavic Contributions, 6. Ann Arbor: Department of Slavic Languages and Literatures.

Matejka, L. and Titunik, I.R., eds 1976: *Semiotics of Art; Prague School Contributions*. Cambridge, MA: MIT Press.

Matejka, Ladislav, and Pomorska, Krystyna, eds 1980: *Readings in Russian Poetics: Formalist and Structuralist Views*. Cambridge, MA: MIT Press.

Mathews, Robin, and Steele, John 1970: "The universities: take over the mind." In *Close the 49th Parallel, Etc.: The Americanization of Canada*; ed. Ian Lumsden. Toronto: University of Toronto Press.

Mathieu, Jean-Claude 1986: "Les cinq sensations de J.-P. R." In *Territoires de l'imaginaire: pour Jean-Pierre Richard/ Textes réunis par Jean-Claude Mathieu*. Paris: Seuil.

Mauron, Charles 1954 (*1969*): *L'Inconscient dans la vie et l'oeuvre de Racine*. Paris: Jose Corti.

Mauss, Marcel, and Hubert, H. 1902–3 (*1972*): *A General Theory of Magic*, trans. R. Brain. London: Routledge & Kegan Paul.

——1923 (*1990*): *The Gift: The Form and Reason for Exchange in Archaic Societies*; trans. W.D. Halls. London: W.W. Norton.

——1979: *Sociology and Psychology*, trans. B. Brewster. London: Routledge & Kegan Paul.

May, Charles E. 1989: "Metaphoric motivation in short fiction: 'In the beginning was the story.'" In *Short Story: Theory at the Crossroads*, ed. Susan Lohafer and Jo Ellyn Clarey. Baton Rouge: Louisiana State University Press.

Mbiti, John S. 1969: *African Religions and Philosophy*. New York: Praeger.

Mead, G.H. 1934 (*1962*): *Mind, Self and Society*. Chicago: University of Chicago Press.

Mead, Margaret 1928: *Coming of Age in Samoa: A Psychological Study in Primitive Youth for Western Civilization*. New York: Morrow.

——1930: *Growing Up in New Guinea: A Comparative Study of Primitive Education*. New York: Morrow.

——1935: *Sex and Temperament in Three Primitive Societies*. New York: Morrow.

——1949: *Male and Female: A Study of the Sexes in a Changing World*. New York: Morrow.

——1964: *Anthropology, a Human Science: Selected Papers, 1939–1960*. Princeton, NJ: Van Nostrand.

——1970: *Culture and Commitment: A Study of the Generation Gap*. Garden City, NY: Natural History Press.

——1972 (*1975*): *Blackberry Winter: My Early Years*. New York: Morrow.

——1977: *Letters from the Field: 1925–1975*. New York: Harper & Row.

Medvedev, P.N. 1928 (*1978*): *The Formal Method in Literary Scholarship: A Critical Introduction to Sociological Poetics*, trans. A.J. Wehrle. Baltimore, MD: Johns Hopkins University Press.

Meinecke, Friedrich 1936 (*1972*): *Historicism: The Rise of a New Historical Outlook*, trans. J.E. Anderson, with revisions by H.B. Schimdt. London: Routledge & Kegan Paul.

Mellor, Anne K., ed. 1988: *Romanticism and Feminism*. Bloomington: Indiana University Press.

Melotti, U. 1977: *Marx and the Third World*; trans. P. Ransford. London Macmillan.

Mercer, Kobena, ed. 1988: *Black Film/ British Cinema, ICA Document 7*. London: ICA.

Merkel, I. and Debus, A.G. eds 1988: *Hermeticism and the Renaissance. Intellectual History and the Occult in Early Modern Europe*. Washington, DC: The Folger Shakespeare Library; London and Toronto: Associated University Press.

Merleau-Ponty, M. 1942a, 1945, 1962 (*1981*): *Phenomenology of Perception*, trans. C. Smith. London: Routledge & Kegan Paul.

——1942b (*1963*): *The Structure of Behavior*, trans. A.L. Fisher. Boston, MA: Beacon Press.

——1947 (*1969*): *Humanism and Terror*, trans. J. O'Neill. Boston, MA: Beacon Press.

——1955 (*1973*): *Adventures of the Dialectic*, trans. Joseph Bien. Evanston, IL: Northwestern University Press.

——1964a: "Eye and mind." In *The Primacy of Perception*; trans. James Edie. Evanston, IL: Northwestern University Press.

——1964b (*1968*): *The Visible and the Invisible*, trans. Alphonso Lingis. Evanston, IL: Northwestern University Press.

Mernissi, Fatima 1991: *The Veil and the Male Elite: A Feminist Interpretation of Women's Rights in Islam*, trans. Mary Jo Lakeland. New York: Addison-Wesley.

Meschonnic, Henri 1992: "Modernity, modernity." *New Literary History*, 23.

Messer-Davidow, Ellen 1987: "The philosophical bases of feminist literary criticism." *New Literary History*, 19:1, 65–104.

Meszaros, I. 1970: *Marx's Theory of Alienation*. London: Merlin Press.

Metcalf, William 1982: *Understanding Canada*. New York: New York University Press.

Mews, Siegfried, ed. 1989: *Critical Essays on Bertolt Brecht*. Boston, MA: G.K. Hall.

Meyer, L.B. 1956: *Emotion and Meaning in Music*. Chicago: University of Chicago Press.

Meynell, H.A. 1981: *Freud, Marx, and Morals*. London: Macmillan.

Midgley, Mary 1979: *Beast and Man, The Roots of Human Nature*. Hassocks, Sussex: Harvester Press.

Midwinter, E. 1975: "Curriculum and the EPA community school." In *Curriculum Design*, ed., M. Golby, J. Greenwald, and R. West. London: Croom Helm and the Open University Press.

Miles, R. 1982: *Racism and Migrant Labour*. London: Routledge & Kegan Paul.

——1989: *Racism*. London: Routledge.

Milic, Louis T. 1967: *Style and Stylistics: An Analytical Bibliography*. New York: Free Press.

Miller, J. Hillis 1965: *Poets of Reality*. Cambridge, MA: Harvard University Press.

——1966 (*1991*): "The Geneva school." In *Theory Now and Then*. Durham, NC: Duke University Press.

——1971 (*1991*): "Geneva or Paris: Georges Poulet's 'Criticism of Identification.'" In *Theory Then and Now*. Durham, NC: Duke University Press.

——1982: "Hommage à Georges Poulet," *MLN*, 97:5, v–xii.

Miller, J. Hillis 1991: *Hawthorne and History: Defacing It*. Oxford: Basil Blackwell.

Miller, Timothy F. and Poirier, Suzanne, eds 1993: *Writing AIDS: Gay Literature, Language, and Analysis*. New York: Columbia University Press.

Millett, Kate 1970 (*1971*): *Sexual Politics*. New York: Avon Books.

Milosz, Czeslaw 1983: *The Witness of Poetry*. Cambridge, MA: Harvard University Press.

Mitchel, W.O. 1947: *Who Has Seen the Wind*. Toronto: Macmillan of Canada.

Mitchell, Cristopher, ed. 1988: *Changing Perspectives in Latin American Studies: Insights from Six Disciplines*. Stanford, CA: Stanford University Press.

Mitchell, Juliet 1966 (*1984*): *The Longest Revolution: On Feminism, Literature, and Psychoanalysis*. New York: Pantheon.

——1974: *Psychoanalysis and Feminism*. London: Allen Lane; New York: Random House.

Mitchell, Juliet, and Rose, J. 1982 (*1985*): *Feminine Sexuality. Jacques Lacan and the École Freudienne*. Basingstoke and London: Macmillan.

Mitchell-Kernan, Claudia 1972: "Signifying, loud-talking and marking." In *Rappin' and Stylin' Out: Communication in Urban Black America*, ed. Thomas Kochman. Urbana: University of Illinois Press.

Moers, Ellen 1976: *Literary Women: The Great Writers*. New York: Doubleday.

Mohanty, Chandra Talpade et al., eds 1991: *Third World Women and the Politics of Feminism*. Bloomington: Indiana University Press.

Mohanty, J.N. 1985: *The Possibility of Transcendental Philosophy*. Dordrecht: Martinus Nijhoff.

——1989: *Transcendental Phenomenology*. Oxford: Blackwell.

Moi, Toril 1985: *Sexual/Textual Politics: Feminist Literary Theory*. London and New York: Methuen.

——1994: *Simone de Beauvoir: The Making of an Intellectual Woman*. Oxford: Blackwell.

Moked, G. 1988: "Objective features of text-analysis according to Mukarovsky: a brief survey and some critical remarks." In *The Prague School and Its Legacy: In Linguistics, Literature, Semiotics, Folklore, and the Arts*. Amsterdam: Benjamins.

Monette, Paul 1988: *Borrowed Time: An AIDS Memoir*. San Diego, CA: Harcourt Brace Jovanovich.

Montrose, Louis 1979–80: "The purpose of playing: reflections on a Shakespearean anthropology," *Helios*, 7, 51–74.

——1986: "Renaissance literary studies and the subject of history," *English Literary Renaissance*, 11:1, 5–12.

——1992: "New historicisms." In *Redrawing the Boundaries: The Transformation of English and American Literary Studies*, ed. Stephen Greenblatt and Giles Gunn. New York: Modern Language Association.

Moore, G.E. 1903 (*1959*): *Principis Ethica*. Cambridge: Cambridge University Press.

Moore, Stephen D. 1990: *Literary Criticism and the Gospels: The Theoretical Challenge*. New Haven, CT: Yale University Press.

Moore, S. W. 1993: *Marx Versus Markets*. University Park. PA: Penn. State University Press.

Morgan, Lewis H. 1877 (*1963*): *Ancient Society. Researches in the Lines of Human Progress from Savagery through Barbarism to Civilization*, ed. E.B. Leacock. Cleveland and New York: World.

Morgana, Cherrie, and Anzaldua, Gloria, eds 1981: *This Bridge Called My Back: Writings by Radical Women of Color*. Watertown, MA: Persephone Press.

Morley, D. 1992: *Television, Audiences and Cultural Studies*. London: Routledge.

Morrison, K.R.B. 1994a: *Implementing Cross-Curricular Themes*. London: David Fulton.

——1994b: "Habermas, pedagogy and the school curriculum"; paper presented at the Educational Conference *Innovations in Education*. Penang, Malaysia: University of Science.

Moses, Wilson Jeremiah 1978: *The Golden Age of Black Nationalism, 1850–1925*. Hamden, CT: Archon Books.

Mowat, C.L. 1968: *Britain between the Wars*. London: Methuen.

Mowitt, John 1992: *Text: The Genealogy of an Antidisciplinary Object*. Durham, NC: Duke University Press.

Mudimbe, V.Y. 1973: *Entretailles*. Paris: Editions Saint Germain-des-Prés.

——1974: *L'Autre Face du royaume*. Lausanne: L'Age d'Homme.

——1976: *Before the Birth of the Moon*. New York: Simon and Schuster.

——1982: *L'Odeur du père*. Paris: Présence Africaine.

——1988: *The Invention of Africa: Gnosis, Philosophy, and the Order of Knowledge*. Bloomington: Indiana University Press.

——1991: *Parables and Fables*. Madison: University of Wisconsin Press.

Muecke, D.C. 1970: *Irony*. London: Methuen.

Mueller, Roswitha 1989: *Bertolt Brecht and the Theory of Media*. Lincoln: University of Nebraska Press.

Mukarovsky, Jan 1976 (*1977*): *The Word and Verbal Art: Selected Essays by Jan Mukarovsky*, trans. and ed. John Burbank and Peter Steiner. New Haven, CT, and London: Yale University Press.

—— 1978: *Structure, Sign, and Function: Selected Essays by Jan Mukarovsky*, trans. and ed. John Burbank and Peter Steiner. New Haven, CT, and London: Yale University Press.

Mukerji, Chandra, and Schudson, Michael, eds 1991: *Rethinking Popular Culture: Contemporary Perspectives in Cultural Studies*. Berkeley: University of California Press.

Mulhall, Stephen 1994: *Stanley Cavell: Philosophy's Recounting of the Ordinary*. London: Oxford University Press.

Mulhern, Francis 1979: *The Moment of "Scrutiny."* London: New Left Books.

—— 1994: "Message in a bottle: Althusser in literary studies." In *Althusser: A Critical Reader*, ed. Gregory Elliott. Oxford: Blackwell.

——, ed. 1992: *Contemporary Marxist Literary Criticism*. London and New York: Longman.

Müller-Vollmer, Kurt 1986: *The Hermeneutics Reader*. Oxford: Oxford University Press.

Mumford, Lewis 1961: *The City in History: Its Origins, Its Transformations, Its Prospects*. London: Oxford University Press.

Munn, Nancy D. 1973: "Symbolism in a ritual context: aspects of symbolic action." In *Handbook of Social and Cultural Anthropology*; ed. J. Honigmann. Chicago: Rand McNally.

Muntz, Peter 1985: *Our Knowledge of the Growth of Knowledge*. London: Routledge & Kegan Paul.

Murray, M. 1978: *Heidegger and Modern Philosophy*. New Haven, CT: Yale University Press.

Museum of Broadcasting 1985: *Leonard Bernstein: The Television Work*. New York: Museum of Broadcasting.

Musgrove, Frank 1974: *Ecstasy and Holiness. Counter Culture and the Open Society*. London: Methuen.

Myers, Eugene A. 1964: *Arabic Thought and the Western World*. New York: Frederick Ungar.

Naïr, S. and Lowy, M. 1973: *Goldmann*. Paris: Seghers.

Nandy, Ashis 1983: *The Intimate Enemy: Loss and Recovery of Self Under Colonialism*. Oxford: Oxford University Press.

National Women's Studies Association Task Force for the Association of American Colleges 1991: *Liberal Learning and the Women's Studies Major: A Report to the Profession*. Washington, DC: Association of American Colleges.

Nattiez, J.-J. 1990: *Music and Discourse: Toward a Semiology of Music*. Princeton, NJ: Princeton University Press.

Neal, Larry 1971 (*1972*): "The black arts movement." In *The Black Aesthetic*, ed. Addison Gayle, Jr. New York: Doubleday.

Nelson, Emmanuel S. ed. 1992: *AIDS: The Literary Response*. New York: Twayne.

Nettleford, Rex 1978: *Caribbean Cultural Identity: The Case of Jamaica*. Los Angeles: The Center for Afro-American Studies.

Neville, Richard 1970: *Play Power*. London: Cape.

New Encyclopedia Britannica. 15th edn. 1993: Chicago: Encyclopedia Publications.

Newhall, Beaumont 1937 (*1982*): *The History of Photography*. New York: Museum of Modern Art.

Newman, Karen 1991: *Fashioning Femininity and English Renaissance Drama*. Chicago: Chicago University Press.

Newton-Smith, W.H. 1981: *The Rationality of Science*. London: Routledge & Kegan Paul.

Ngugi wa Thiong'o 1986: *Decolonising the Mind: The Politics of Language in African Literature*. Nairobi: Heinemann.

Nichols, Bill 1989: "Form wars: the political unconscious of formalist theory," *South Atlantic Quarterly*, 88:2.

Nicholls, Peter 1989: "Old problems and New Historicism," *Journal of American Studies*, 23, 423–34.

Nida, Eugene 1964: *Towards a Science of Translating*. Leiden: E.J. Brill.

Nida, Eugene, and Taber, E. 1969: *The Theory and Practice of Translating*. Leiden: E. J. Brill.

Nietzsche, Friedrich 1872 (*1967*). *The Birth of Tragedy*, trans. Walter Kaufmann. New York: Vintage.

—— 1873–6 (*1983*): *Untimely Meditations*, trans. R.J. Hollingdale. Cambridge: Cambridge University Press.

—— 1878–80 (*1986*): *Human, All Too Human*, Vols. I and II, including *Assorted Opinions and Maxims* and *The Wanderer and His Shadow*, trans. R. J. Hollingdale. Cambridge: Cambridge University Press.

—— 1881 (*1982*): *Daybreak*, trans. R.J. Hollingdale. Cambridge: Cambridge University Press.

—— 1882 (*1974*): *The Gay Science*, trans. Walter Kaufmann. New York: Vintage Books.

—— 1883–92 (*1976*): *Thus Spoke Zarathustra*, trans. Walter Kaufmann. In *The Portable Nietzsche*. New York: Penguin.

—— 1886 (*1968*): *Beyond Good and Evil*, trans. Walter Kaufmann. In *Basic Writings of Nietzsche*. New York: Vintage.

—— 1887 (*1968*): *On the Genealogy of Morals*, trans. Walter Kaufmann. In *Basic Writings of Nietzsche*. New York: Vintage.

—— 1888/95 (*1976*): *The Antichrist*, trans. Walter Kaufmann. In *The Portable Nietzsche*. New York: Penguin.

—— 1901 (*1968*): *The Will to Power*, trans. Walter Kaufmann and R.J. Hollingdale. New York: Vintage.

Nietzsche, Friedrich 1980: *Sämtliche Werke* [Complete Works]; ed. F. Colli & M. Montinari. Berlin: Walter de Gruyter.

Nkrumah, Kwame 1964: *Consciencism: Philosophy and Ideology for Decolonization and Development with Particular Reference to the African Revolution*. London: Heinemann.

Noe, K. 1985: "Language and praxis." In *The Philosophical Series*. Vol. 2, *The Experience, Language and Recognition*, ed. S. Omori et al. Tokyo: Iwanami.

Norman, R. 1980: *Hegel, Marx and Dialectic*. Hassocks, Sussex: Harvester.

Norris, Christopher 1978: *William Empson and the Philosophy of Literary Criticism*. London: Athlone Press.

—— 1982: *Deconstruction: Theory and Practice*. London: Methuen.

—— 1983: *The Deconstructive Turn: Essays in the Rhetoric of Philosophy*. London: Methuen.

—— 1985: *The Contest of Faculties: Philosophy and Theory after Deconstruction*. London: Methuen.

—— 1987: *Jacques Derrida*. London: Fontana.

—— 1988: *Paul de Man: Deconstruction and the Critique of Aesthetic Ideology*. London and New York: Routledge.

—— 1989: *Deconstruction and the Interests of Theory*. London: Pinter.

—— 1990: *What's Wrong with Postmodernism: Critical Theory and the Ends of Philosophy*. Baltimore, MD: Johns Hopkins University Press.

—— 1991: *Spinoza and the Origins of Modern Critical Theory*. Oxford: Blackwell.

—— 1992: *Uncritical Theory: Postmodernism, Intellectuals and the Gulf War*. London: Lawrence & Wishart.

—— 1993: *The Truth about Postmodernism*. Oxford: Blackwell.

Norris, Christopher, and Mapp, Nigel, eds 1993: *William Empson: The Critical Achievement*. Cambridge: Cambridge University Press.

Norton, Bryan G. 1992: "Epistemology and environmental values," *The Monist*, 75, 208–26.

Novick, Peter 1988: *That Noble Dream: The "Objectivity Question" and the American Historical Profession*. Cambridge: Cambridge University Press.

Nozick, Robert 1974: *Anarchy, State and Society*. Oxford: Basil Blackwell; New York: Basic Books.

Nussbaum, Felicity 1989: *The Autobiographical Subject: Gender and Ideology in Eighteenth-Century England*. Baltimore, MD: Johns Hopkins University Press.

Nussbaum, Felicity, and Brown, Laura, eds 1987: *The New Eighteenth Century: Theory, Politics, English Literature*. New York and London: Methuen.

Nussbaum, Martha C. 1986: *The Fragility of Goodness: Luck and Ethics in Greek Tragedy and Philosophy*. Cambridge: Cambridge University Press.

—— 1990: *Love's Knowledge: Essays on Philosophy and Literature*. New York and Oxford: Oxford University Press.

—— 1992: "Reply to Richard Eldridge," *Arion*. 2:1, 198–207.

—— 1993: "Non-relative virtues: an Aristotelean approach." In *The Quality of Life*, ed. Martha Nussbaum and Amartya Sen. Oxford: Clarendon Press, 242–69.

—— 1994: *The Therapy of Desire: Theory and Practice in Hellenistic Ethics*. Princeton, NJ: Princeton University Press.

Oakeshott, Michael 1962 (*1991*): *Rationalism in Politics*. Indianapolis: Liberty Fund.

—— 1975: *On Human Conduct*. Oxford: Clarendon Press.

Oakland, J. 1993: "Definition and methodology. The civilization debate and practice in Norway." *Les Cahiers de l'Observatoire*, 6, 33–48.

O'Brien, G.D. 1975: *Hegel on Reason and History*. Chicago: University of Chicago Press.

O'Brien, Michael 1988: "A heterodox note on the southern renaissance." In *Rethinking the South*. Baltimore, MD: Johns Hopkins University Press.

Ogunyemi, Chikwenye Okonjo 1985: "Womanism: the dynamics of the contemporary black female novel in English." *Signs: Journal of Women in Culture and Society*, 11, 68–80.

O'Hear, Anthony 1980: *Karl Popper*. London: Routledge & Kegan Paul.

Ohmann, Richard 1976: *English in America: A Radical View of the Profession*. New York: Oxford University Press.

Okrent, Mark 1988: *Heidegger's Pragmatism: Understanding, Being, and the Critique of Metaphysics*. Ithaca, NY: Cornell University Press.

O'Neill, Onora 1989: *Constructions of Reason*. Cambridge: Cambridge University Press.

Ong, Walter J. 1982: *Orality and Literacy: The Technologizing of the Word*. New York and London: Methuen.

Open University 1989 (*1990*): *Popular Culture*. Milton Keynes: Open University Press.

Orgel, Stephen 1989: "Nobody's perfect: or why did the English stage take boys for women?" *South Atlantic Quarterly*, 88, 7–29.

Ormiston, Gayle L., and Schrift, Alan D. 1990: *The Hermeneutic Tradition: From Ast to Ricoeur*. Albany: SUNY Press.

Ortega, Julio 1985: *Critica de la Identidad. La Pregunta por el Perú en su Literatura*. Mexico City: Fondo de Cultura Economica.

Oruka H. Odera. 1990a: *Trends in Contemporary African Philosophy*. Nairobi: Shirikon.
——1990b: *Sage Philosophy: Indigenous Thinkers and Modern Debates about African Philosophy*. Nairobi: Shirikon.
Ostriker, Alicia 1993: *Feminist Revision and the Bible*. Oxford: Blackwell.
Owen, Louis 1993: *Other Destinies: Understanding the American Indian Novel*. Norman: University of Oklahoma Press.
Owen, Roger C. 1967: *The North American Indian: A Source Book*. New York: Macmillan.
Owusu, Kwesi, ed. 1988: *Storms of the Heart: An Anthology of Black Arts and Culture*. London: Camden Press.

Padhi, Bihhu. 1987: *The Modes of Style in Lawrence's Fiction*. Troy, NY: Whitston.
Palmer, Richard 1969: *Hermeneutics: Interpretation Theory in Schleiermacher, Dilthey, Heidegger, and Gadamer*. Evanston, IL: Northwestern University Press.
Papineau, David 1978: *For Science in the Social Sciences*. London: Macmillan.
Parfit, Derek 1984: *Reasons and Persons*. Oxford: Clarendon Press.
Park, R.E., Burgess, E.W., and McKenzie, R.D. 1925 (*1967*): *The City*. Chicago: University of Chicago Press.
Parkin, Frank 1971: *Class Inequality and Political Order*. London: MacGibbon.
——1979: *Marxism and Class Theory: A Bourgeois Critique*. New York: Columbia University Press.
Parkinson, G.H.R., ed. 1968: *The Theory of Meaning*. London: Oxford University Press.
Parry, Milman 1971: *The Making of Homeric Verse*. London: Clarendon Press.
Pasanen, Outi 1986: "Postmodernism: an interview with William V. Spanos," *Arbeiten aus Anglistik und Amerikanistik*, 11.
Pastore, Judith Laurence, ed. 1993: *Confronting AIDS through Literature: The Responsibilities of Representation*. Urbana: University of Illinois Press.
Patterson, Francine, and Linden, Eugene 1981: *The Education of Koko*. New York: Holt, Rinehart, & Winston.
Patterson, Michael 1994: "Brecht's legacy." In *The Cambridge Companion to Brecht*, ed. Peter Thomson and Glendyr Sacks. Cambridge: Cambridge University Press.
Patton, Cindy 1990: *Inventing AIDS*. New York: Routledge.
Pavis, Patrice 1983: *Languages of the Stage: Essays in the Semiology of Theatre*. New York: Performing Arts Journal Publications.

Payne, Michael 1991: "Canon: New Testament to Derrida." *College Literature*, 18:2, 5–21.
——1993: *Reading Theory: An Introduction to Lacan, Derrida, and Kristeva*. Oxford: Blackwell.
Paynter, J. et al., eds 1992: *Companion to Contemporary Musical Thought*. London: Routledge.
Paz, Octavio 1985: *One Earth, Four or Five Worlds. Reflections on Contemporary History*, trans. Helen R. Lane. San Diego, CA: Harcourt Brace Jovanovich.
Peatman, J.G. 1942–3: "Radio and popular music." In *Radio Research*; ed. P.F. Lazersfeld and F. Stanton. New York: Duell, Sloan & Pearce.
Pêcheux, M. 1975 (*1982*): *Language, Semantics and Ideology*, trans. Harbans Nagpal. London: Macmillan.
Peck, Dale 1993: *Martin and John*. New York: St Martin's Press.
Peck, J., ed. 1987: *The Chomsky Reader*. London: Serpents Tail.
Peirce, C.S. 1868 (*1958*): "Some consequences of four incapacities." In *Charles S. Peirce: Selected Writings*, ed. Philip P. Wiener. New York: Dover.
——1958: *Charles S. Peirce: Selected Writings*, ed. Philip P. Wiener. New York: Dover.
Pepper, David 1993: *Eco-Socialism From Deep Ecology to Social Justice*. London: Routledge.
Perloff, Marjorie 1990: *Poetic License: Essay on Modernist and Postmodernist Lyric*. Evanston, IL: Northwestern University Press.
Peterson, R.A. 1976: *The Production of Culture*.
Petrey, S. 1990: *Speech Acts and Literary Theory*. London and New York: Routledge.
Petrucci, Armando 1986: *La scrittura. Ideologia e rappresentazione*. Turin: Piccola Biblioteca Einaudi.
Philosophical Topics, 20, 1992: "The philosophy of Hilary Putnam."
Piaget, Jean 1950: *The Psychology of Intelligence*. London: Routledge & Kegan Paul.
——1953a: *Logic and Psychology*. Manchester: Manchester University Press.
——1953b: *The Origin of Intelligence in the Child*. London: Routledge & Kegan Paul.
——1959: *The Language and Thought of the Child*. London: Routledge & Kegan Paul.
Pines, Jim, and Willeman, Paul, eds 1989: *Questions of Third Cinema*. London: British Film Institute.
Pinkney, Alphonso 1976: *Red, Black and Green: Black Nationalism in the United States*. Cambridge: Cambridge University Press.
Polanyi, Karl 1957: "Economy as instituted process." In *Trade and Market in the Early Empires*, ed. K. Polanyi et al. Glencoe, IL: Free Press.
Pomorska, Krystyna 1968: *Russian Formalist Theory and Its Poetic Ambiance*. The Hague: Mouton.

Poole, Adrian 1987: *Tragedy: Shakespeare and the Greek Example*. Oxford: Basil Blackwell.

Poovey, Mary 1984: *The Proper Lady and the Woman Writer: Ideology as Style in the Works of Mary Wollstonecraft, Mary Shelley, and Jane Austen*. Chicago: University of Chicago Press.

Popov, Yevgeny 1993: "The silhouette of truth," *World Literature Today*, 67:1.

Popper, Karl 1934 (*1937*): *The Logic of Scientific Discovery*. New York: Harper and Row; London: Hutchinson.

——1945a and 1957 (*1960*): *The Poverty of Historicism*. New York: Harper and Row; Basic Books.

——1945b (*1966*): *The Open Society and Its Enemies*. 2 vols. London: Routledge & Kegan Paul.

——1982: *Quantum Theory and the Schism in Physics*. London: Unwin Hyman.

Porcher, L. 1986: *La Civilisation*. Paris: Clé International.

Porter, John 1965: *The Vertical Mosaic*. Toronto: University of Toronto Press.

Postlewait, Thomas, and McConachie, Bruce A., eds 1989: *Interpreting the Theatrical Past: Essays in the Historiography of Performance*. Iowa City: University of Iowa Press.

Postman, Neil 1994: "Interview with Neil Postman," *Spin* (January), 66–9, 87.

Poulantzas, N. 1975: *Classes in Contemporary Capitalism*. London: New Left Books.

Poulet, Georges 1949–68a (*1956*): *Studies in Human Time*, trans. Elliott Coleman. Baltimore, MD: Johns Hopkins University Press.

——1949–68b (*1959*): *The Interior Distance*, trans. Elliott Coleman. Baltimore, MD: Johns Hopkins University Press.

——1963 (*1977*): *Proustian Space*; trans. Elliott Coleman. Baltimore, MD: Johns Hopkins University Press.

——1969: "Phenomenology of reading." *New Literary History*, 1, 53–65.

——1971: *La Conscience critique*. Paris: Corti.

Prasad, Madhava 1992: "On the question of a theory of (Third World) literature," *Social Text*, 31/32, 57–82.

Prawer, Siegbert 1973: *Comparative Literary Studies: An Introduction*. London: Duckworth.

Preminger, Alex, et al. *The New Princeton Encyclopedia of Poetry and Poetics*. Princeton, NJ: Princeton University Press.

Prendergast, Christopher 1992: *Paris and the Nineteenth Century*. Oxford: Blackwell.

Price, Kenneth M., and Leitz, Robert C. III, eds 1991: *Critical Essays on George Santayana*. Boston, MA: G.K. Hall.

Pritchett, James 1993: *The Music of John Cage*. London: Cambridge University Press.

Progoff, Ira 1973: *Jung, Synchronicity and Human Destiny*. New York: Dell.

Propp, Vladimir 1958 (*1968*): *Morphology of the Folktale*, trans. L. Scott. Bloomington: Indiana Research Centre in Anthropology; Austin: University of Texas Press.

Pryse, Marjorie 1985: "Zora Neale Hurston, Alice Walker, and the 'ancient power' of black women." In *Conjuring: Black Women, Fiction and Literary Tradition*, ed. Marjorie Pryse and Hortense J. Spillers. Bloomington: Indiana University Press.

Pudovkin, V.I. 1933: *Film Technique*, trans. Ivor Montagu. London: Newnes.

Puren, C. 1988: *Histoire des méthodologies*. Paris: Nathan.

Putnam, Hilary 1975 (*1979*): *Philosophical Papers*. 2 vols. Cambridge: Cambridge University Press.

——1981: *Reason, Truth, and History*. Cambridge: Cambridge University Press.

——1983a: *Philosophical Papers*. Vol. 3, *Realism and Reason*. Cambridge: Cambridge University Press.

——1983b: *Realism and Reason*. Cambridge: Cambridge University Press.

——1987: *The Many Faces of Realism*. La Salle, IL: Open Court.

——1990: *Realism with a Human Face*, ed. James Conant. Cambridge, MA: Harvard University Press.

——1992: *Renewing Philosophy*. Cambridge: Harvard University Press.

Quine, W.O. 1953a (*1980*): "Two dogmas of empiricism." In *From a Logical Point of View*. Cambridge, MA: Harvard University Press.

——1953b (*1980*): *From a Logical Point of View*. New York: Harper and Row; Cambridge, MA: Harvard University Press.

——1960: *Word and Object*. Cambridge, MA: MIT Press.

——1969: "*Ontological Relativity*" *and Other Essays*. New York: Columbia University Press.

——1990 (*1992*): *Pursuit of Truth*. Cambridge, MA: Harvard University Press.

Radford, A. 1988: *Transformational Grammar*. Cambridge: Cambridge University Press.

Radway, J. 1984 (*1987*): *Reading the Romance*. London: Verso.

Radnitzky, Gerard, and Andersson, Gunnar, eds 1978: *Progress and Rationality in Science*. Dordrecht: Reidel.

Radway, Janice 1984: *Reading the Romance: Women, Patriarchy, and Popular Literature*. Chapel Hill: University of North Carolina Press.

Rahman, Fazlur 1982: *Islam and Capitalism*, trans. Brian Pearce. Austin: University of Texas Press.

Rajan, Tilottama 1980: *Dark Interpreter: The Discourse of Romanticism*. Ithaca, NY: Cornell University Press.

——1990: *The Supplement of Reading: Figures of Understanding in Romantic Theory and Practice*. Ithaca, NY: Cornell University Press.

Rajchmann, J., and West, C., eds 1985: *Post Analytic Philosophy*. New York: Columbia University Press.

Rama, Angel 1985: *La critica de la cultura en América Latina*, ed. Tomás Eloy Martinez and Saul Sosnowski. Caracas: Biblioteca Ayacucho.

Ramberg, Bjorn T. 1989: *Donald Davidson's Philosophy of Language: An Introduction*. Oxford: Basil Blackwell.

Rapping, Elaine 1994: *Media-tions: Forays into the Culture and Gender Wars*. Boston, MA: South End Press.

Rasmussen, D.M. 1990: *Reading Habermas*. Oxford: Basil Blackwell.

Rasputin, Valentin 1993: "'Motherland' is not an abstract notion," *World Literature Today*, 67:1.

Raulet, G. 1983: "Strucuralism and post-structuralism: an interview with Michel Foucault," *Telos*, 55, 195–211.

Rawls, John 1971 (*1972*): *A Theory of Justice*. Oxford: Clarendon Press.

Raymond, Marcel 1933 (*1961*): *From Baudelaire to Surrealism*, trans. G.M. New York: Wittenborn, Schultz.

Readings, Bill (*1991*): *Introducing Lyotard: Art and Politics*. London: Routledge.

Redner, Harry 1986: *The Ends of Philosophy*. London: Croom Helm.

Reich, Wilhelm 1933 (*1972*): *Character Analysis*. New York: Farrar, Straus and Giroux.

——1935 (*1972*): *The Sexual Revolution*, trans. Theodore P. Wolfe. London: Vision Press.

Reiche, Reimut 1968 (*1970*): *Sexuality and the Class Struggle*. London: New Left Books.

Reichert, John 1977: *Making Sense of Literature*. Chicago: University of Chicago Press.

Reinelt, Janelle 1990: "Rethinking Brecht: deconstruction, feminism and the politics of form." In *Essays on Brecht (Brecht Yearbook 15)*, ed. Marc Silberman et al. College Park, MD: International Brecht Society.

Reinelt, Janette, and Case, Sue-Ellen, eds 1991: *The Performance of Power: Theatrical Discourse and Politics*. Iowa City: University of Iowa Press.

Reinelt, Janelle G., and Roach, Joseph R., eds 1992: *Critical Theory and Performance*. Ann Arbor: University of Michigan Press.

Renan, Ernest 1863 (*1955*): *The Life of Jesus*, trans. J.H. Holmes. New York: Random House.

Rescher, Nicholas 1987: *Scientific Realism: A Critical Reappraisal*. Dordrecht: D. Reidel.

Révauger, J-P. 1993a: "Civilization and culture: towards a synthesis." *Les Cahiers de l'Observatoire*, 6, 21–32.

——1993b: *Civilization: Theory and Practice*. Grenoble: Université Stendhal.

Revill, David 1992: *The Roaring Silence: John Cage: A Life*. New York: Arcade Publishing.

Rich, Adrienne 1973 (*1979*): "Toward a woman-centered university." In *On Lies, Secrets, and Silence: Selected Prose, 1966–1978*. New York: Norton.

——1976: *Of Women Born: Motherhood as Experience and Institution*. New York: Norton.

——1979: *On Lies, Secrets, and Silence: Selected Prose, 1966–1978*. New York: Norton.

——1980: "Compulsory heterosexuality and lesbian existence." In *Women, Sex and Sexuality*, ed. C.R. Stimpson and E. Spector Person. Chicago: University of Chicago Press.

——1986: *Blood, Bread, and Poetry: Selected Prose, 1979–1985*. New York: Norton.

——1993: *What Is Found There: Notebooks on Poetry and Politics*. New York: Norton.

Richard, Jean-Pierre 1954: *Littérature et sensation*. Paris: Seuil.

——1955a: *Poésie et profondeur*. Paris: Seuil.

——1955b (*1980*): "Verlaine's faded quality;" trans. Sarah Lawall. *Denver Quarterly*, 15:3, 27–43.

——1961: *L'Univers imaginaire de Mallarmé*. Paris: Seuil.

——1974: *Proust et le monde sensible*. Paris: Seuil.

——1979: *Microlectures*. Paris: Seuil.

——1984: *Pages Paysages: Microlectures II*. Paris: Seuil.

——1990: *L'Etat des choses: études sur huit écrivains d'aujourd'hui*. Paris: Gallimard.

Richards, I.A. 1929 (*1964*): *Practical Criticism*. London: Routledge & Kegan Paul.

Richards, J. 1989: *Imperialism and Juvenile Literature*. Manchester: Manchester University Press.

Richman, Michele 1982: *Reading Georges Bataille: Beyond the Gift*. Baltimore, MD: Johns Hopkins University Press.

Ricketts, Thomas G. 1982: "Translation, rationality, and epistemology naturalized," *Journal of Philosophy*, 86, 113–36.

Ricoeur, P. 1969 (*1974*): *Le Conflit des interprétations. Essais d'herméneutique*. Paris: Seuil; [*The Conflict of Interpretations*, ed. D. Ihde. Evanston, IL: Northwestern University Press.]

——1970: *Freud and Philosophy: An Essay on Interpretation*, trans. Denis Savage. New Haven, CT: Yale University Press.

——1978: *The Rule of Metaphor: Multi-disciplinary Studies of the Creation of Meaning in Language*, trans. Robert Czerny with Kathleen McLaughlin and John Costello. London: Routledge & Kegan Paul.

Ricoeur, P. 1984–6: *Time and Narrative*, trans. Kathleen McLaughlin and David Pellauer. 3 vols. Chicago and London: University of Chicago Press.

Ricoeur, P., and Gadamer, H-G. 1982 (*1991*): "The conflict of interpretation: debate with Hans-Georg Gadamer." In *A Ricoeur Reader: Reflection and Imagination*, ed. M.J. Valdes. Hemel Hempstead: Harvester Wheatsheaf.

Riffaterre, Michael 1979 (*1983*): *Text Production*, trans. Terese Lyons. New York: Columbia University Press.

Rigby, S.H. 1992: *Engels and the Formation of Marxism*. Manchester: Manchester University Press.

Rimmon-Kenan, Shlomith 1983: *Narrative Fiction*. London: Methuen.

Riquelme, J.P. 1980: "The ambivalence of reading," *Diacritics*, 10, 47–56.

Roberts, David 1991: *Art and Enlightenment: Aesthetic Theory After Adorno*. Lincoln: University of Nebraska Press.

Robbins, Derek 1991: *The Work of Pierre Bourdieu*. Milton Keynes: Open University Press.

Robin, R. 1992: *Socialist Realism: An Impossible Aesthetic*, trans. C. Porter. Palo Alto, CA: Stanford University Press.

Robins, R. 1967: (*1990*): *A Short History of Linguistics*. London: Longman.

Robinson, Alan A. 1970: *The Sexual Radicals*. London: Maurice Temple.

Robinson, Lillian S. 1978: *Sex, Class, and Culture*. New York: Methuen.

Robinson, Maxime 1961 (*1980*): *Muhammad*, trans. Anne Carter. New York: Pantheon.

——1966 (*1978*): *Islam and Capitalism*, trans. Brian Pearce. Austin: University of Texas Press.

Rockmore, T. 1992: *Irrationalism: Lukács and the Marxist View of Reason*. Philadelphia, PA: Temple University Press.

Roderick, R. 1986: *Habermas and the Foundations of Critical Theory*. London: Macmillan.

Rodin, Judith, and Collins, Aila, eds 1991: *Women and New Reproductive Technologies: Medical, Psychosocial, Legal, and Ethical Dilemmas*. New Jersey: Lawrence Erlbaum.

Rodney, Walter 1969: *The Groundings with My Brothers*. London: Bogle-L'Ouverture Publications.

——1970: *A History of the Upper Guinea Coast. 1545–1800*. Oxford: Oxford University Press.

——1972: *How Europe Underdeveloped Africa*. London: Bogle-L'Ouverture Publications.

——1980: *Kofi Baadu Out of Africa*. Guyana: Guyana National Lithographic.

——1981: *A History of the Guyanese Working People, 1881–1905*. Baltimore, MD, and London: Johns Hopkins University Press.

——1990: *Walter Rodney Speaks: The Making of an African Intellectual*. New Jersey: Africa World Press.

Rodnyanskaya, Irina 1993: "Gipsovyi veter. O filsofskoi intosikatsii v tekushchei slovesnosti," *Novy mir*, 12.

Roemer, Kenneth 1983: *Native American Renaissance*. Berkeley: University of California Press.

Roger, P. 1986: *Roland Barthes, Roman*. Paris: Grasset.

Rohner, Ronald P., and Rohner, Evelyn C. 1969: "Franz Boas and the Development of North American Ethnology and Ethnography." In *The Ethnography of Franz Boas*; ed. R. Rohner. Chicago: University of Chicago Press.

Rolston, Holmes, III, 1988: *Environmental Ethics, Duties to and Values in the Natural World*. Philadelphia, PA: Temple University Press.

Rorty, Richard, ed. 1970 (*1971*): *The Linguistic Turn*. Chicago: University of Chicago Press.

——1972 (*1982*): "The world well lost." In *Consequences of Pragmatism (Essays: 1972–1980)*. Minneapolis: University of Minnesota Press.

——1980: *Philosophy and the Mirror of Nature*. Oxford: Blackwell.

——1989: *Contingency, Irony, and Solidarity*. Cambridge: Cambridge University Press.

——1991: "Texts and lumps." In *Objectivity, Relativism, and Truth*. Cambridge: Cambridge University Press, 78–92.

——1993: "Putnam and the relativist menace," *Journal of Philosophy*, 90, 443–61.

Rose, Gillian 1978: *The Melancholy Science: An Introduction to the Thought of Theodor W. Adorno*. London: Macmillan.

——1981: *Hegel Contra Sociology*. London: Athlone Press.

Rose, Mark 1993: *Authors and Owners: The Invention of Copyright*. Cambridge, MA: Harvard University Press.

Rosen, Charles 1971: *The Classical Style: Haydn, Mozart, Beethoven*. London: Faber & Faber.

——1976: *Schoenberg*. Glasgow: Fontana/Collins.

——1980: *Sonata Forms*. New York and London: Norton.

Rosen, Charles, and Zerner, H. 1984: *Romanticism and Realism: The Mythology of Nineteenth-Century Art*. New York: Viking.

Rosenbaum, S.P., ed. 1992: *Women & Fiction: The Manuscript Versions of "A Room of One's Own."* Oxford: Shakespeare Head Press/Blackwell Publishers.

Rosenberg, Harold 1959: *The Tradition of the New*. New York: Horizon Press.

——1962: *Arshile Gorky: The Man, the Time, the Idea*. New York: Horizon Press.

——1964 (*1966*): *The Anxious Object: Art Today and Its Audience*. New York: Horizon Press.

Rosenberg, Karen 1985: "The concept of originality in formalist theory. A *Festschrift* in honor of Victor Erlich." In *Russian Formalism. A Retrospective Glance*, ed. R. Jackson and S. Rudy. New Haven, CT: Yale University Press.

Rosenblatt, L.M. 1978: *The Reader, the Text, the Poem: The Transactional Theory of the Literary Work*. Carbondale, IL: Southern Illinois University Press.

Rossi, Pietro, ed. 1988: *La memoria del sapere: Forme di conservazione e strutture organizzative dell'Antichita a oggi*. Rome/Bari: Laterza.

Roszak, T. 1968 (*1971*): *The Making of a Counter Culture: Reflections on the Technocratic Society and Its Youthful Opposition*. London: Faber.

——1972: *Where the Wasteland Ends: Politics and Transcendence in Postindustrial Society*. Garden City, NY: Doubleday.

Roudinesco, Elisabeth 1986: *Jacques Lacan & Co.: A History of Psychoanalysis in France 1925–1985*, trans. Jeffrey Mehlman. London: Free Association Books.

Rousseau, George, ed. 1972: *Organic Form: The Life of an Idea*. London: Routledge & Kegan Paul.

Rousseau, George S., and Porter, Roy, eds 1988: *Sexual Underworlds of the Enlightenment*. Chapel Hill: University of North Carolina Press.

Rowe, J.C. 1990: "Structure." In *Critical Terms for Literary Studies*, ed. F. Lentricchia and T. McLaughlin. Chicago: University of Chicago Press.

Roy, Gabrielle 1947 (*1969*): *The Tin Flute*. Toronto: McClelland & Stewart.

Ruben, David-Hillel 1982: *Explaining Explanation*. London: Routledge.

Rubin, Gayle 1975: "The traffic in women." In *Toward an Anthropology of Women*, ed. Rayna R. Reiter. New York: Monthly Review Press.

Ruoff, A. LaVonne Brown 1990: *American Indian Literatures: An Introduction, Bibliographic Review, and Selected Bibliography*. New York: Modern Language Association.

Russo, John 1989: *I.A. Richards: His Life and Work*. Baltimore, MD: Johns Hopkins University Press.

Russell, B. 1934: *The Meaning of Marx: A Symposium*. New York: Farrar & Rinehart.

——1946: *Is Materialism Bankrupt?: Mind and Matter in Modern Science*. Girard, KA: Haldeman-Julius Publications.

——1956: *Logic and Knowledge*. London: Allen & Unwin.

Rustin, Margaret, and Rustin, Michael 1987: *Narratives of Love and Loss*. London: Verso.

Ruthven, K.K. 1979: *Critical Assumptions*. Cambridge: Cambridge University Press.

——1984: *Feminist Literary Studies: An Introduction*. Cambridge: Cambridge University Press.

——1993: *Nuclear Criticism*. Melbourne: Melbourne University Press.

Ryan, M. 1982: *Marxism and Deconstruction: A Critical Articulation*. Baltimore, MD: Johns Hopkins University Press.

Sadock, J. 1974: *Towards a Linguistic Theory of Speech Acts*. New York: Academic Press.

Said, Edward 1975 (*1985*): *Beginnings: Intention and Method*. New York: Columbia University Press.

——1978 (*1979*): *Orientalism*. New York: Random House and Vintage.

——1979 (*1980*): *The Question of Palestine*. New York: Random House.

——1981: *Covering Islam*. New York: Pantheon.

——1983: *The World, the Text, and the Critic*. Cambridge, MA: Harvard University Press.

——1993 (*1994*): *Culture and Imperialism*. London: Chatto & Windus; New York: Alfred A. Knopf.

Salkie, Raphael 1990: *The Chomsky Update: Linguistics and Politics*. London: Unwin Hyman.

Salmon, Wesley C. 1984: *Scientific Explanation and the Causal Structure of the World*. Princeton, NJ: Princeton University Press.

——1989: *Four Decades of Scientific Explanation*. Minneapolis: University of Minnesota Press.

Salomon, Barbara, ed. 1992: *Other Voices Other Vistas: Short Stories from Africa, China, India, Japan, and Latin America*. New York: New American Library.

Salvadori, Massimo, ed. 1972: *European Liberalism*. New York: John Wiley.

Salvaggio, Jerry L. 1979: "Between formalism and semiotics: Eisenstein's film language," *Dispositio: American Journal of Semiotic and Cultural Studies*, 4.

Samson, Anne 1992: *F.R. Leavis*. Hemel Hempstead: Harvester Wheatsheaf.

Sandel, Michael 1982: *Liberalism and the Limits of Justice*. Cambridge: Cambridge University Press.

Sapir, E. 1921: *Language*. New York: Harcourt Brace.

——1949: *Selected Readings in Language, Culture and Personality*, ed. D. Mandelbaum. Berkeley: University of California Press.

Sarat, Austin, and Kearns, Thomas R., eds 1991: *The Fate of Law*. Ann Arbor: University of Michigan Press.

Sartre, Jean-Paul 1937 (*1957*): *The Transcendence of the Ego*, trans. F. Williams and R. Kirkpatrick. New York: Noonday.
—— 1938 (*1965*): *Nausea*. London: Penguin.
—— 1940: *L'Imaginaire*. Paris: Gallimard.
—— 1943 (*1958*): *Being and Nothingness*, trans. Hazel Barnes. London: Methuen.
—— 1946 (*1990*): *Existentialism and Humanism*, trans. Philip Mairet. London: Methuen.
—— 1948 (*1983*): *What Is Literature?* trans. B. Frechtman. London: Methuen.
—— 1961 (*1967*): "Preface to Frantz Fanon, *The Wretched of the Earth*," trans. Constance Farrington. Harmondsworth: Penguin.
Saussure, Ferdinand de 1972 (*1983*): *A Course in General Linguistics*, trans. R. Harris. London: Duckworth; 1916 (*1966*): trans. Wade Buskin. New York: McGraw.
Savage, Jon 1992: *England's Dreaming*. London: Faber.
Savage, M., and Warde, A. 1993: *Urban Sociology, Capitalism and Modernity*. London: Macmillan.
Sayres, Sohnya 1990: *Susan Sontag: The Elegiac Modernist*. London: Routledge.
Schechner, Richard 1985: *Between Theater and Anthropology*. Philadelphia: University of Pennsylvania Press.
Schegloff, E.A. 1968 (*1986*): "Sequencing in conversational openings." In *Directions in Sociolinguistics: The Ethnography of Communication*, ed. J.J. Gumpertz and D. Hymes. Oxford: Basil Blackwell.
Scheler, M. 1916 (*1954*): *Der Formalismus in der Ethick und die materiale Wertethik*. Bern: Francke.
Schilpp, P.A., ed. 1957: *The Philosophy of Karl Jaspers*. New York: Tudor.
—— ed. 1981: *The Philosophy of Jean-Paul Sartre*. La Salle, IL: Open Court.
Schimtt, R. 1967: "Phenomenology." In *The Encyclopedia of Philosophy*, ed. P. Edwards. New York: Macmillan and Free Press.
Schleiermacher, Friedrich 1977: *Hermeneutik und Kritik* (Hermeneutics and Critique); ed. Manfred Frank. Frankfurt: Suhrkamp.
Scholem, Gershom 1975 (*1982*): *Walter Benjamin: The Story of a Friendship*. London: Faber.
Scholes, Robert 1969: *Elements of Poetry*. New York: Oxford University Press.
Scholte, Bob 1973: "The structural anthropology of Claude Lévi-Strauss." In *Handbook of Social and Cultural Anthropology*, ed. J. Honigmann. New York: Rand McNally.
Schubnell, Matthias 1993: "'What other story?': Mythic subtexts in Leslie Silko's 'Storyteller,'" *Nebraska English Journal*, 38, 40–8.
Schulman, Sarah 1990: *People in Trouble*. New York: Dutton.

Schultz, H.J., and Rhein, P.H. 1973: *Comparative Literature. The Early Years*. Chapel Hill: University of North Carolina Press.
Schwartz, Richard B., ed. 1990: *Theory and Tradition in Eighteenth-Century Studies*. Carbondale: Southern Illinois University Press.
Schwartz, Steven, ed. 1977: *Naming, Necessity, and Natural Kinds*. Ithaca, NY: Cornell University Press.
Schwartz, W. 1989: "Some remarks on the development, poetic range and operational disposition of Mukarovsky's term 'semantic gesture.'" In *Issues in Slavic Literary and Cultural Theory*, ed. K. Eimermacher, P. Grzybek, and G. Witte. Bochum: Brockmyer.
Schweickart, Patrocinio 1984 (*1986*): "Reading ourselves: Toward a feminist theory of reading." In *Gender and Reading: Essays on Readers, Texts, and Contexts*, ed. Elizabeth A. Flynn and Patrocinio P. Schweickart. Baltimore, MD: Johns Hopkins University Press.
Schweitzer, D. and Seyer, R.F., eds 1989: *Alienation Theories and Alienation Strategies*. Middlesex: Science Reviews.
Scott, Joan Wallach 1988: *Gender and the Politics of History*. New York: Columbia University Press.
—— 1989: "History in crisis?" *American Historical Review*, 94, 680–92.
Scott, Patrick, and Fletcher, Pauline, eds 1990: *Culture and Education in Victorian England*. Lewisburg, PA: Bucknell University Press.
Scruton, R. 1980 (*1984*): *The Meaning of Conservatism*. London: Macmillan.
—— 1988: "The New Right in Central Europe." *Political Studies*, 36:4, 638–53.
—— 1991: "What is conservatism?" In *Conservative Texts: An Anthology*. London: Macmillan.
Searle, J. 1969: *Speech Acts: An Essay in the Philosophy of Language*. Cambridge: Cambridge University Press.
—— 1975: "Indirect speech acts." In *Syntax and Semantics*, Vol. 3, ed. P. Cole and J. Morgan. New York: Academic Press.
—— 1979: *Expression and Meaning: Studies in the Theory of Speech Acts*. Cambridge: Cambridge University Press.
—— 1983: *Intentionality: An Essay in the Philosophy of Mind*. Cambridge: Cambridge University Press.
Sebeok, Thomas, ed. 1960: *Style in Language*. Cambridge, MA: MIT Press.
—— 1994: *An Introduction to Semiotics*. London: Pinter.
Segal, Hanna 1952 (*1986*): "A psychoanalytic approach to aesthetics." In *The Work of Hanna Segal: A Kleinian Approach to Clinical Practice*. London: Free Association Books and Maresfield Library.

——1979: *Klein*. London: Fontana.

Seigel, J.E. 1993: *Marx's Fate: The Shape of a Life*. University Park, PA: Penn. State University Press.

Seiter, Ellen, Borchers, Hans, Kreutzner, Gabriele, and Warth, Eva-Maria, eds 1989: *Remote Control: Television, Audiences and Cultural Power*. London: Routledge.

Sekula, Allen 1975: "On the invention of photographic meaning." In *Photography in Print*, ed. Vicki Goldberg. Albuquerque: University of New Mexico Press.

Seldon, R. 1985: "Reader-oriented theories." In *A Reader's Guide to Contemporary Literary Theory*. Brighton: Harvester Press.

Selivanova, Svetlana 1993: "From the seventies to the nineties," *World Literature Today*, 67:1.

Sellers, Susan 1991: *Language and Sexual Difference: Feminist Writing in France*. London: Macmillan.

Semenov, Oleg 1993: "Iskusstvo li – iskusstvo nashego stoleitiya?" *Novy mir*, 8.

Senghor, Léopold Sédar, ed. 1948: *Anthologie de la nouvelle poésie nègre et malgache*. Paris: Presses Universitaires de France.

Sennett, R., ed. 1969: *Classic Essays on the Culture of Cities*. New York: Appleton-Century-Crofts.

Serge, Cesare 1979: *Structures and Time. Narration, Poetry, Models*. Chicago: University of Chicago Press.

Serequberhan, Tsenay 1994: *The Hermeneutics of African Philosophy: Horizon and Discourse*. New York: Routledge.

——ed. 1992: *African Philosophy: The Essential Reading*. New York: Paragon.

Sevaldsen, J. 1993: "Civilization as comparative politics." *Les Cahiers de l'Observatoire*, 6, 9–20.

Sewall, Richard B. 1980: *The Vision of Tragedy*. Stanford, CA: Stanford University Press; New Haven, CT: Yale University Press.

Sewell, T. 1992: *Black Tribunes: Race and Representation in British Politics*. London: Lawrence & Wishart.

Shaw, C.R. 1930 (*1966*): *The Jack-Roller: A Delinquent Boy's Own Story*. Chicago: University of Chicago Press.

Shiach, Morag 1989a: "Their 'symbolic' exists, it holds power – we, the sowers of disorder, know it only too well." In *Between Feminism and Psychoanalysis*, ed. Teresa Brennan. London: Routledge.

——1989b: *Discourse on Popular Culture*. Cambridge: Polity Press.

——1991: *Hélène Cixous: A Politics of Writing*. London: Routledge.

Shilts, Randy 1987: *And the Band Played On: Politics, People and the AIDS Epidemic*. New York: St Martin's Press.

Shinoda, K. 1989: *Roland Barthes*. Tokyo: Iwanami.

Shklovsky, V. 1925 (*1991*): *Theory of Prose*, trans. Benjamin Sher. Elmwood Park, IL: Dalkey Archive Press.

Short, M. 1973: "Some thoughts on foregrounding and interpretation," *Language and Style*, 6.

Showalter, Elaine 1977: *A Literature of Their Own: British Women Novelists from Brontë to Lessing*. Princeton, NJ: Princeton University Press.

——1983: "Critical cross-dressing: Male feminists and the woman of the year," *Raritan*, 3, 130–49.

——1989: "A criticism of our own: Autonomy and assimilation in Afro-American and feminist literary theory." In *The Future of Literary Theory*, ed. Ralph Cohen. New York: Routledge.

——1990: *Sexual Anarchy: Gender and Culture at the Fin de Siècle*. New York: Viking Press.

——1991: *Sister's Choice*. New York: Oxford University Press.

——1993: "American gynocriticism," *American Literary History*, 5:1, 111–28.

——ed. 1985: *The New Feminist Criticism: Essays on Women, Literature, and Theory*. New York: Pantheon.

——ed. 1989: *Speaking of Gender*. London: Routledge.

Shreider, Yu 1993: "Mezhdu molokhom i mamonoi," *Novy mir*, 5.

——1994: "Tsennosti, kotorye my vybiraem," *Novy mir*, 1.

Shusharin, D. 1994: "Vozvrashchenie v kontekst," *Novy mir*, 7.

Silberman, Marc 1993: "A postmodernized Brecht?" *Theatre Journal*, 45, 1–19.

Silver, Brenda 1991a: "The authority of anger: *Three Guineas* as case study," *Signs*, 16.

——1991b: "Textual criticism as feminist practice: or, who's afraid of Virginia Woolf Part II." In *Representing Modernist Texts*, ed. George Bernstein. Ann Arbor: University of Michigan Press.

Silverman, H.J., ed. 1991: *Gadamer and Hermeneutics*. London: Routledge.

Simonson, Rick, and Walker, Scott, eds 1988: "Introduction." In *Multicultural Literacy*. St Paul, MN: Graywolf Press.

——1988: *Multicultural Literacy*. St Paul, MN: Graywolf Press.

Simpson, Amelia 1993: *Xuxa: The Mega-Marketing of Gender, Race and Modernity*. Philadelphia, PA: Temple University Press.

Simpson, David 1979: *Irony and Authority in Romantic Poetry*. London: Macmillan.

Simpson, Lewis, ed. 1976: *The Possibilities of Order: Cleanth Brooks and His Works*. Baton Rouge: Louisana State University Press.

Sinclair, J. McH., and Coulthard, R.M. 1975: *Towards an Analysis of Discourse*. London: Oxford University Press.

Sinfield, Alan 1992: *Faultlines: Cultural Materialism and the Politics of Dissident Reading*. Oxford: Oxford University Press.

Singer, June 1972: *Boundaries of the Soul: The Practice of Jung's Psychology*. New York: Doubleday.

Singer, Peter 1979: *Practical Ethics*. Cambridge: Cambridge University Press.

——ed. 1986: *Applied Ethics*. Oxford: Oxford University Press.

Slobin, D. 1971 (*1979*): *Psycholinguistics*. Glenview, IL: Scott, Foresman.

Smalley, Beryl 1984: *The Study of the Bible in the Middle Ages*. Oxford: Basil Blackwell.

Smart, Barry 1983: *Foucault, Marxism, and Critique*. London: Routledge.

——1985: *Michel Foucault*. London: Tavistock.

Smart, J.J.C., and Williams, B. 1973: *Utilitarianism: For and Against*. Cambridge: Cambridge University Press.

Smith, Barbara Herrnstein 1988: *Contingencies of Value*. New York: Oxford University Press.

Smith, David Lionel 1991: "The black arts movement and its critics." *American Literary History*, 3, 93–110.

Smith, Gary, ed. 1988: *On Walter Benjamin: Critical Essays and Reflections*. Cambridge, MA: MIT Press.

——1989: *Walter Benjamin: Philosophy, Aesthetics, History*. Chicago: University of Chicago Press.

Smith, Iris 1991: "Brecht and the mothers of epic theatre," *Theatre Journal*, 43, 491–505.

Smith, M.G. 1965: *The Plural Society in the British West Indies*. Berkeley: University of California Press.

Smith, Peter J. 1981: *Realism and the Progress of Science*. Cambridge: Cambridge University Press.

Smith, Roth C. 1985: "Bachelard's logosphere and Derrida's logocentrism: is there a differance [sic]?" *French Forum*. 10, 225–34.

Smith, Valerie 1989: "Gender and Afro-Americanist literary theory and criticism." In *Speaking of Gender*, ed. Elaine Showalter. New York: Routledge.

Smith, William Robertson 1889 (*1957*): *Religion of the Semites: The Fundamental Institutions*. New York: Meridian Books.

Smitherman, Geneva 1977: *Talkin and Testifyin: The Language of Black America*. Boston, MA: Houghton Mifflin.

Smyth, J. 1991: *Teachers as Collaborative Learners*. Buckingham: Open University Press.

Snell-Hornby, Mary 1988: *Translation Studies; An Integrated Approach*. Amsterdam: John Benjamins.

Solé, Carlos A., ed. 1989: *Latin American Writers*. 3 vols. New York: Charles Scribners' Sons.

Solich, Wolfgang 1993: "The dialectic of mimesis and representation in Brecht's *Life of Galileo*," *Theatre Journal*, 45, 49–54.

Sollers, Walter 1989: *The Invention of Ethnicity*. New York: Oxford University Press.

Solomon, J. Fisher 1988: *Discourse and Reference in the Nuclear Age*. Norman, OK: University of Oklahoma Press.

Solomon, Miriam 1989: "Quine's point of view," *Journal of Philosophy*, 86, 113–36.

Solomon, Robert C. 1972: *From Rationalism to Existentialism*. New York: University Press of America.

——1988: *Continental Philosophy Since 1750*. Oxford: Oxford University Press.

Solzhenitsyn, A. 1994: " 'Russkii vopros' k kontsu XX veka," *Novy mir*, 7.

Sonnino, Lee A. 1968: *A Handbook to Sixteenth-Century Rhetoric*. London: Routledge & Kegan Paul.

Sontag, Susan 1966: *Against Interpretation and Other Essays*. New York: Farrar, Straus & Giroux.

——1969 (*1988*): *Styles of Radical Will*. New York: Farrar, Straus & Giroux.

——1973 (*1977*): *On Photography*. New York: Farrar, Straus & Giroux.

——1978: *Illness as Metaphor*. New York: Farrar, Straus & Giroux.

——1980: *Under the Sign of Saturn*. New York: Farrar, Straus & Giroux.

——1982: *A Susan Sontag Reader*; ed. Elizabeth Hardwick. Harmondsworth: Penguin.

——1986: "The way we live now." In *The Best American Short Stories of the Eighties*; ed. Shannon Ravenel. New York: Houghton.

——1989: *AIDS and Its Metaphors*. New York: Farrar, Straus & Giroux.

Soper, K. 1986: *Humanism and Anti-Humanism*. London: Hutchinson.

Speirs, Ronald 1987: *Bertolt Brecht*. New York: St Martin's Press.

Sperber, D., and Wilson, D. 1986: *Relevance: Communication and Cognition*. Oxford: Basil Blackwell.

Spiegelberg, H. 1960 (*1982*): *The Phenomenological Movement*. The Hague: Nijhoff.

Spiegelman, J., Khan, P.V.I., and Fernandex, T. 1991: *Sufism, Islam and Jungian Psychology*. Arizona: Falcon Press.

Spitz, David 1982: *The Real World of Liberalism*. Chicago: University of Chicago Press.

Spivak, Gayatri C. 1987a: *In Other Worlds: Essays in Cultural Politics*. New York: Methuen.

——1987b (*1988*): "Subaltern studies: deconstructing historiography." In *Selected Subaltern Stud-*

ies, ed. Ranajit Guha and Gayatri C. Spivak. Delhi: Oxford University Press.

——1994: *Outside in the Teaching Machine*. London: Routledge.

Sprigge, Timothy L.S. 1974: *Santayana: An Examination of His Philosophy*. London, and Boston, MA: Routledge & Kegan Paul.

Sprinker, M. 1987: *Imaginary Relations: Aesthetics and Ideology in the Theory of Historical Materialism*. London: Verso.

——, ed. 1992: *Edward Said: A Critical Reader*. Cambridge, MA, and Oxford: Blackwell.

Squires, Radcliffe, ed. 1972: *Allen Tate and His Work: Critical Evaluations*. Minneapolis: University of Minnesota Press.

Stacy, R.H. 1974: *Russian Literary Criticism: A Short History*. Syracuse, NY: Syracuse University Press.

Stafford, Barbara Maria 1991: *Body Criticism: Imaging the Unseen in Enlightenment Art and Medicine*. Cambridge, MA: MIT Press.

Starobinski, Jean 1957 (*1988*): *Jean-Jacques Rousseau: Transparency and Obstruction*, trans. Arthur Goldhammer. Chicago: University of Chicago Press.

States, Bert O. 1985: *Great Reckonings in Little Rooms: On the Phenomenology of Theatre*. Berkeley, CA, and London: University of California Press.

Steiner, George 1960 (*1977*): *Tolstoy or Dostoevsky: An Essay in Contrast*. London: Faber; New York: Viking.

——1967: *Language and Silence*. London: Faber.

——1971: *In Bluebeard's Castle: Some Notes Towards the Redefinition of Culture*. London: Faber.

——1975: *After Babel*. London and New York: Oxford University Press.

——1978: *Heidegger*. New York: Viking.

——1984: *George Steiner: A Reader*. Harmondsworth: Penguin.

——1989: *Real Presence*. London: Faber.

Steiner, P., ed. 1982: *The Prague School, Selected Writings, 1929–1946*. University of Texas Press Slavic Series, 6. Austin: University of Texas Press.

Steiner, Peter 1984: *Russian Formalism: A Metapoetics*. Ithaca, NY: Cornell University Press.

Sternberg, Meir 1985: *The Poetics of Biblical Narrative: Ideological Literature and the Drama of Reading*. Bloomington: Indiana University Press.

Steward, Julian H. 1973: *Alfred Kroeber*. New York: Columbia University Press.

Stewart, John Lincoln 1965: *The Burden of Time: The Fugitives and Agrarians*. Princeton, NJ: Princeton University Press.

Stimpson, Catherine R., with Cobb, Nina Kressner

1986: *Women's Studies in the United States*. New York: Ford Foundation.

Stocking, George, ed. 1974: *The Shaping of American Anthropology, 1883–1911: A Franz Boas Reader*. New York: Basic Books.

Stone, Merlin 1976: *When God Was a Woman*. New York: Dial Press.

Stout, J. 1984: "Virtue among the ruins: an essay on MacIntyre," *Neue Zeitschrift für Systematische Theologie und Religionsphilosophie*, 26, 256–73.

Stove, David C. 1982: *Popper and After: Four Modern Irrationalists*. Oxford: Pergamon.

Strauss, Leo 1952: *Persecution and the Art of Writing*. Chicago: University of Chicago Press.

——1953: *Natural Right and History*. Chicago: University of Chicago Press.

——1959: *What is Political Philosophy?* New York: Free Press.

——1963 (*1991*): *On Tyranny*. New York: Free Press.

——1964: *The City and Man*. Chicago: University of Chicago Press.

Strawson, P.F. 1959: *Individuals: An Essay in Descriptive Metaphysics*. London: Methuen.

Street, Brian 1984: *Literacy in Theory and Practice*. Cambridge: Cambridge University Press.

Striedter, Jurij 1989: *Literary Structure, Evolution, and Value. Russian Formalism and Czech Structuralism*. Cambridge, MA, and London: Harvard University Press.

Stroud, Barry 1968: "Transcendental arguments," *Journal of Philosophy*, 65, 241–56.

Stuckey, Sterling 1972: *The Ideological Origins of Black Nationalism*. Boston, MA: Beacon Press.

Suleiman, S.R. 1980: "Introduction: varieties of audience-oriented criticism." In *The Reader in the Text. Essays on Audience and Interpretation*, ed. S.R. Suleiman and I. Crosman. Princeton, NJ: Princeton University Press.

——1989: "As is." In *A New History of French Literature*, ed. Denis Hollier. Cambridge, MA: Harvard University Press.

Suvin, Darko 1984: *To Brecht and Beyond: Soundings in Modern Dramaturgy*. Brighton: Harvester Press; Totowa, NJ: Barnes and Noble Books.

Swann, Bian, ed. 1983: *Smoothing the Ground: Essays on Native American Oral Literature*. Berkeley: University of California Press.

Symons, T.H.B. 1975: *To Know Ourselves: The Report of the Commission on Canadian Studies*. Ottawa: Association of Universities and Colleges of Canada.

Takeuchi, Y. 1981: *The Theory of Culture*. Tokyo: Iwanami.

Takeuchi, Y., and Maruyama, K. 1982: "Language, sign and society," *Thought*, 693, 1–29.

Tanner, Tony 1980: "A preface to A.H." In George Steiner, *The Portage to San Cristobal of A.H.* Cambridge: Granta.
—— 1992: *Venice Desired*. Oxford: Blackwell.
Tate, Allen 1969: *Essays of Four Decades*. Chicago: Swallow Press.
Taylor, C. 1975: *Hegel*. Cambridge: Cambridge University Press.
Taylor, Gary, and Warren, Michael 1983: *The Division of the Kingdom: Shakespeare's Two Versions of King Lear*. Oxford: Oxford University Press.
Taylor, Talbot J. 1980: *Linguistic Theory and Structural Linguistics*. Oxford and New York: Pergamon Press.
Teigas, Demetrius 1995: *Knowledge and Hermeneutic Understanding: A Study of the Habermas–Gadamer Debate*. Lewisburg, PA: Bucknell University Press.
Tempels, Placide 1969: *Bantu Philosophy*. Paris: Présence Africaine.
Tennenhouse, Leonard 1986: *Power on Display: The Politics of Shakespeare's Genres*. New York and London: Methuen.
Tester, Keith 1992: *Civil Society*. London: Routledge.
Tetreault, Mary Katy Thompson 1985: "Feminist phase theory: An experience-derived evaluation model," *Journal of Higher Education*, 56:4, 363–84.
Therborn, G. 1980: *The Ideology of Power and the Power of Ideology*. London and New York: Verso.
Thieme, J.P. 1957 (*1982*): "The Indo-European language." *Scientific American*, October. Repr. in *Human Communication*, ed. W.S.-Y. Wang. San Francisco: W.H. Freeman.
Thompson, E.M. 1971: *Russian Formalism and Anglo-American Criticism: A Comparative Study*. The Hague: Mouton.
Thompson, E.P. 1955 (*1977*): *William Morris: Romantic to Revolutionary*. New York: Pantheon.
—— 1963 (*1980*): *The Making of the English Working Class*. Harmondsworth: Penguin.
—— 1978: *The Poverty of Theory and Other Essays*. London: Merlin Press.
—— 1993: *Witness Against the Beast: William Blake and the Moral Law*. Cambridge: Cambridge University Press.
Thompson, J.B. 1984: *Studies in the Theory of Ideology*. Cambridge: Polity Press.
Thompson, Kenneth 1982: *Emile Durkheim*. Chichester: Ellis Horwood.
Thompson, Kristin 1981: "Eisenstein's *Ivan the Terrible*: a neoformalist analysis," *Dispositio: American Journal of Semiotic and Cultural Studies*, 6:17–18 (Summer–Fall).
Thompson, Marvin, and Thompson, Ruth, eds 1989: *Shakespeare and the Sense of Performance: Essays in the Tradition of Performance Criticism*

in Honor of Bernard Beckerman. Newark, NJ: University of Delaware Press.
Thomson, Peter, and Sacks, Glendyr, eds 1994: *The Cambridge Companion to Brecht*. Cambridge: Cambridge University Press.
Tillyard, E.M.W. 1943: *The Elizabethan World Picture*. London: Chatto & Windus.
Timms, Edward, and Kelly, David 1985: *Unreal City: Urban Experience in Modern European Literature and Art*. Manchester: Manchester University Press.
Tobin, Y., ed. 1988: *The Prague School and Its Legacy, in Linguistics, Literature, Semiotics, Folklore, and the Arts*. Linguistic and Literary Studies in Eastern Europe, 27. Amsterdam: John Benjamins.
Todd, Janet 1988: *Feminist Literary History*. Cambridge: Polity.
—— 1989: *The Sign of Angelica: Women, Writing and Fiction 1660–1800*. London: Virago.
Todorov, Tzvetan 1967: *Littérature et signification*. Paris: Larousse.
—— 1970 (*1982*): *The Fantastic: A Structural Approach to Literary Genre*, trans. Richard Howard. Cleveland, OH: Case Western Reserve University Press.
—— 1971: *Poétique de la prose*. Paris: Seuil.
—— 1981a: *Introduction to Poetics*, trans. R. Howard. Brighton: Harvester Press.
—— 1981b (*1984*): *Mikhail Bakhtin: The Dialogical Principle*, trans. W. Godzich. Manchester: Manchester University Press.
Tokar, Brian 1987 (*1992*): *The Green Alternative. Creating an Ecological Future*. San Pedro, CA: R. & E. Miles.
Tokieda, M. 1941: *The Principle of the Study of the Japanese Language*, Vol. 1. Tokyo: Iwanami.
—— 1955: *The Principle of the Study of the Japanese Language*, Vol. 2. Tokyo: Iwanami.
Tomalin, Claire 1974: *The Life and Death of Mary Wollstonecraft*. New York: Harcourt Brace Jovanovich.
Tompkins, J. 1980: "An introduction to reader-response criticsm." In *Reader-Response Criticism*, ed. J. Tompkins. Baltimore, MD: Johns Hopkins University Press.
Tong, Rosemarie 1989: *Feminist Thought: A Comprehensive Introduction*. Boulder, CO: Westview Press.
Torrance, J. 1977: *Estrangement, Alienation, and Exploitation: A Sociological Approach*. New York: Columbia University Press.
Totosy de Zepanek, Steven 1992: "Systemic approaches to literature: an introduction with selected bibliography." In *Canadian Review of Comparative Literature*, 19:1–2.
Toury, Gideon 1980: *In Search of a Theory of Trans-*

lation. Tel Aviv: Porter Institute for Poetics and Semiotics.

Traub, Valerie 1992: *Desire and Anxiety: Circulations of Sexuality in Shakespearean Drama*. London: Routledge.

Trilling, Lionel 1950 (*1979*): *The Liberal Imagination*. New York: Harcourt Brace Jovanovich.

—— 1956 (*1978*): *A Gathering of Fugitives*. New York: Harcourt Brace Jovanovich.

Trinh T Minh ha 1989: *Woman, Native, Other: Writing Postcoloniality and Feminism*. Bloomington: Indiana University Press.

Troeltsch, Ernst 1923 (*1979*): *Christian Thought: Its History and Application*. Westport, CT: Hyperion Press.

Truffaut, François 1978 (*1994*): *The Films in My Life*, trans. Leonard Mayhew. New York: Da Capo Press.

Tugendhat, Ernst 1970: *Der Wahrheitsbegriff bei Husserl und Heidegger*. Berlin: de Gruyter.

—— 1979 (*1986*): *Self-Consciousness and Self-Determination*, trans. Paul Stern. Cambridge, MA: MIT Press.

—— 1976 (*1982*): *Traditional and Analytic Philosophy*, trans. P.A. Gorner. Cambridge: Cambridge University Press.

—— 1992: *Philosophische Aufsätze* (*Philosophical Essays*). Frankfurt: Suhrkamp.

Turner, Bryan S. 1974: *Weber and Islam*. London: Routledge & Kegan Paul.

Turner, Victor W. 1982: "Liminal to liminoid in play, flow, and ritual." In *From Ritual to Theatre, The Human Seriousness of Play*. New York: Performing Arts Journal Publications.

—— 1982: *From Ritual to Theatre, The Human Seriousness of Play*. New York: Performing Arts Journal Publications.

—— 1986: *The Anthropology of Performance*. New York: PAJ Publications.

Tynyanov, Yury 1981: *The Problems of Verse Language*; trans. M. Sosa and B. Harvey. Ann Arbor, MI: Ardis.

Ulanov, Ann 1971: *The Feminine in Jungian Psychology and in Christian Theology*. Evanston, IL: Northwestern University Press.

Ulmer, Gregory 1989: *Teletheory: Grammatology in the Age of Video*. London: Routledge.

UNESCO 1982: *Cultural Industries. A Challenge for the Future of Culture*. Paris: UNESCO.

Unger, Roberto Mangabeira 1986: *The Critical Legal Studies Movement*. Cambridge, MA: Harvard University Press.

Urban Life 1983: Special issue: "The Chicago school: the tradition and the legacy," 11:4.

Urmson, J.O. 1965: "J.L. Austin," *Journal of Philosophy*, 62, 499–508.

Vachek, J. 1966: *The Linguistic School of Prague; an Introduction to its Theory and Practice*. Bloomington: Indiana University Press.

Vachek, J., and Duskova, L., eds 1983: *Praguiana, Some Basic and Less Known Aspects of the Prague Linguistic School*; Linguistic and Literary Studies in Eastern Europe, 12. Amsterdam: John Benjamins.

van Dijk, T.A. 1985: *Handbook of Discourse Analysis*. 4 vols. London: Academic Press.

van Erven, Eugene 1988: *Radical People's Theatre*. Bloomington Indiana University Press.

—— 1992: *The Playful Revolution: Theatre and Liberation in Asia*. Bloomington: Indiana University Press.

Van Leuven-Zwart, Kitty, and Naaijkens, Tom, eds 1991: *Translation Studies: The State of the Art*. Amsterdam: Rodopi.

Van Reijen, Willem, and Veerman, Dick 1988: "An interview with Jean-François Lyotard," *Theory, Culture and Society*, 5, 277–309.

Vattimo, Gianni 1985 (*1988*): *The End of Modernity*, trans. J.R. Snyder. Cambridge: Polity Press.

—— 1993: *The Adventure of Difference: Philosophy After Nietzsche and Heidegger*, trans. Cyprian Blamires. Cambridge: Polity Press.

Veeser, H. Aram, ed. 1989: *The New Historicism*. London and New York: Routledge.

Vendler, Helen 1988: *The Music of What Happens: Poems, Poets, Critics*. Cambridge: Harvard University Press.

Venturi, Robert 1966: *Complexity and Contradiction in Architecture*. New York: The Museum of Modern Art.

Venturi, Robert, Brown, Denise Scott, and Izenour, Steven 1972 (*1977*): *Learning from Las Vegas: The Forgotten Symbolism of Architectural Form*. Cambridge, MA: MIT Press.

Venuti, Lawrence 1991: *Rethinking Translation: Discourse, Subjectivity, Ideology*. London: Routledge.

Viala, Alain 1985: *Naissance de l'écrivain. Sociologie de la littérature à l'âge classique*. Paris: Editions de Minuit.

Vickers, B., ed. 1984: *Occult Mentalities in the Renaissance*. Cambridge: Cambridge University Press.

Vizenor, Gerald, ed. 1989 (*1993*): *Narrative Chance: Postmodern Discourse on Native American Indian Literatures*. Norman: University of Oklahoma Press.

Vogel, Harold L. 1986 (*1990*): *Entertainment Industry Economics*. Cambridge: Cambridge University Press.

Voloshinov, V.N. 1926 (*1976*): *Freudianism: A Marxist Critique*, trans. I.R. Titunik; ed. N.H. Bruss. New York: Academic Press.

—— 1929 (*1973*): *Marxism and the Philosophy of*

Language, trans. L. Matejka and I.R. Titunik. New York: Seminar Press.

Von Franz, Marie-Louise 1973: *Interpretation of Fairy Tales*. Zurich: Spring Publications.

Waal Malefijt, Annemarie de 1974: *Images of Man: A History of Anthropological Thought*. New York: Knopf.

Wachterhauser, B.R., ed. 1994: *Hermeneutics and Truth*. Evanston, IL: Northwestern University Press.

Waelhens, Alphonse de 1951: *Une Philosophie de l'ambiguité: L'Existentialisme de Maurice Merleau-Ponty*. Louvain: Publications Universitaires de Louvain.

Walker, Alice 1984: *In Search of Our Mothers' Gardens*. New York: Harcourt Brace Jovanovich.

Wallace, Michelle 1992: *Black Popular Culture*. Seattle, WA: Bay Press.

Wallerstein, Immanuel 1991: *Unthinking Social Science: The Limits of Nineteenth-Century Paradigms*, Part V: "Revisiting Braudel." Cambridge: Polity Press.

Walliman, I. 1981: *Estrangement: Marx's Concept of Human Nature and the Division of Labor*. Westport, CT: Greenwood Press.

Wallon, Henri 1984: *The World of Henri Wallon*; ed. Gilbert Voyat. New York: Aronson.

Wallraff, Charles F. 1970: *Karl Jaspers: An Introduction to His Philosophy*. Princeton, NJ: Princeton University Press.

Walzer, Michael 1983: *Spheres of Justice: A Defence of Pluralism and Equality*. Oxford: Blackwell.

—— 1987: *Interpretation and Social Criticism*. Cambridge, MA: Harvard University Press.

Wardle, Ralph 1951: *Mary Wollstonecraft*. Lawrence: University of Kansas Press.

Warhol, Andy, and Hackett, Pat 1980: *Popism, the Warhol '60s*. New York: Harcourt Brace Jovanovich.

Warnke, G. 1987: *Gadamer: Hermeneutics, Tradition and Reason*. Cambridge: Polity Press.

Warnock, Mary 1965: *The Philosophy of Sartre*. London: Hutchinson.

—— 1970: *Existentialism*. Oxford: Oxford University Press.

Warren, Austin, and Wellek, René 1968: *Theory of Literature*. New York: Harvest.

Waters, Lindsay, and Godzich, Wlad, eds 1989: *Reading De Man Reading*. Minneapolis: University of Minnesota Press.

Watney, Simon 1987: *Policing Desire: Pornography, AIDS, and the Media*. Comedia.

Watson, George 1962: "The mid-century scene." In *The Literary Critics*. Harmondsworth: Penguin.

Watt, W. Montgomery 1987 (*1962*): *Islamic Philosophy and Theology*. Edinburgh: Edinburgh University Press.

Wayne, Valerie 1991: *The Matter of Difference: Materialist Feminist Criticism of Shakespeare*. Ithaca, NY: Cornell University Press.

Weber, Carl 1980: "Brecht in eclipse?" *Drama Review*, 24:1, 115–24.

Weber, Jean Jacques 1983: "The foreground–background distinction: a survey of its definitions and applications," *Language and Literature*, 8:1–3.

Weber, Max 1921 (*1968*): *Economy and Society*. 3 vols. New York: Bedminster Press.

—— 1922a (*1948*): "Wirtschaft und Gesellschaft." In *From Max Weber: Essays in Sociology*, ed. and trans. H. Gerth and C. Wright Mills. London: Routledge & Kegan Paul.

—— 1922b (*1953*): "The three types of political rule."

—— 1962: *The City*. New York: Collier.

Webster, Grant 1979: *The Republic of Letters*. Baltimore, MD: Johns Hopkins University Press.

Weeks, Jeffrey 1977 (*1990*): *Coming Out: Homosexual Politics in Britain from the Nineteenth Century to the Present*. London: Quartet.

Weiler, Kathleen 1988: *Women Teaching for Change: Gender, Class and Power*. South Hadley, MA: Bergin & Garvey Publishers.

Weisheimer, J.C. 1985: *Gadamer's Hermeneutics: A Reading of Truth and Method*. New Haven, CT: Yale University Press.

Weisheimer, Joel 1991: *Philosophical Hermeneutics and Literary Theory*. New Haven, CT: Yale University Press.

Weisstein, Ulrich 1974: *Comparative Literature and Literary Theory*. Bloomington: Indiana University Press.

Wellek, René 1963: "Concepts of form and structure in twentieth-century criticism." In *Concepts of Criticism*. New Haven, CT: Yale University Press.

—— 1969: *The Literary Theory and Aesthetics of the Prague School*. Ann Arbor, MI: Department of Slavic Languages and Literatures, University of Michigan.

—— 1970: *Discriminations: Further Concepts of Criticism*. New Haven, CT: Yale University Press.

—— 1986a: *English Criticism 1900–1950*. (*A History of Modern Criticism 1750–1950*, Vol. 5.) New Haven, CT: Yale University Press.

—— 1986b: "Cleanth Brooks." In *American Criticism, 1900–1950*. (*A History of Modern Criticism 1750–1950*, Vol. 6.) New Haven, CT: Yale University Press.

—— 1986c: *American Criticism 1900–1950*. (*A History of Modern Criticism 1750–1950*, Vol. 6.) New Haven, CT: Yale University Press.

—— 1986d: "T.S. Eliot." In *English Criticism, 1900–1950*. (*A History of Modern Criticism 1750–1950*, Vol. 5.) New Haven, CT: Yale University Press.

——1986e: "William Empson." In *English Criticism 1900–1950*. (*A History of Modern Criticism 1750–1950*, Vol. 5.)

——1986f: "New criticism." In *American Criticism, 1900–1950*. (*A History of Modern Criticism 1750–1950*, Vol. 6.) New Haven, CT: Yale University Press.

——1986g: "John Crowe Ransom." In *American Criticism, 1900–1950*. (*A History of Modern Criticism 1750–1950*, Vol. 6.) New Haven, CT: Yale University Press.

——1986h: "I.A. Richards." In *English Criticism 1900–1950*. (*A History of Modern Criticism 1750–1950*, Vol. 5.)

——1986i: "Allen Tate." In *American Criticism, 1900–1950*. (*A History of Modern Criticism 1750–1950*, Vol. 6.)

West, Cornel 1982: *Prophesy Deliverance! An Afro-American Revolutionary Christianity*. Philadelphia, PA: Westminster Press.

——1989: *The American Evasion of Philosophy: A Genealogy of Pragmatism*. Madison: University of Wisconsin Press.

——1993a: *Race Matters*. Boston, MA: Beacon Press.

——1993b: *Keeping Faith: Philosophy and Race in America*. New York: Routledge.

West, Cornel, and Rajchman, John, eds 1985: *Post-Analytical Philosophy*. New York: Columbia University Press.

Wheeler, Michael 1991: *Death and the Future Life in Victorian Literature and Theology*. Cambridge: Cambridge University Press.

White, A., and Stallybrass, P. 1986: *The Politics and Poetics of Transgression*. Ithaca, NY: Cornell University Press.

White, Hayden 1975 (*1986*): "Historicism, history, and the figurative imagination." In *Tropics of Discourse: Essays in Cultural Criticism*. Baltimore, MD: Johns Hopkins University Press.

White, James Boyd 1985: *Hercules's Bow: Essays on the Rhetoric and Poetics of the Law*. Madison: University of Wisconsin Press.

Whitford, Margaret 1991: *Luce Irigaray: Philosophy in the Feminine*. London: Routledge.

Whitmont, Edward 1969: *The Symbolic Quest – Basic Concepts of Analytical Psychology*. New York: C.G. Jung Foundation.

Whittock, Trevor 1980: "Eisenstein on Montage Metaphor." In *Generous Converse: English Essays in Memory of Edward Davis*, ed. B. Green. Cape Town: Oxford University Press.

Whitty, G. 1985: *Sociology and School Knowledge*. London: Methuen.

Whorf, B.L. 1956: *Language, Thought and Reality: Selected Writings*, ed. J.B. Carroll. Cambridge, MA: MIT Press.

Widdowson, H.G. 1978: *Teaching Language as Communication*. Oxford: Oxford University Press.

——1984: *Explorations in Applied Linguistics II*. Oxford: Oxford University Press.

——1990: *Aspects of Language Teaching*. Oxford: Oxford University Press.

——1992: *Practical Stylistics*. London: Longman.

Wiebe, Rudy 1973: *The Temptations of Big Bear*. Toronto: McClelland & Stewart.

Wiget, Andrew 1985: *Native American Literature*. Boston, MA: Twayne.

Wilcox, Helen, ed. 1990: *The Body and the Text: Hélène Cixous, Reading and Teaching*. Hemel Hempstead: Harvester.

Wiley, N., ed. 1987: *The Marx–Weber Debate*. Newbury Park, CA: Sage Publications.

Willett, John 1959: *The Theatre of Bertolt Brecht: A Study from Eight Aspects*. Norfolk, CT: James Laughlin (New Directions).

——, ed. 1964: *Brecht on Theatre: The Development of an Aesthetic*. New York: Hill & Wang.

——1984: *Brecht in Context*. London: Methuen.

Willey, Basil 1977: *Nineteenth Century Studies*. New York: Columbia University Press.

Willey, Thomas E. 1978: *Back to Kant: The Revival of Kantianism in German Social and Historical Though*. Detroit: Wayne State University Press.

Williams, Bernard 1973: *Problems of the Self: Philosophical Papers 1956–1972*. Cambridge: Cambridge University Press.

——1981: *Moral Luck: Philosophical Papers 1973–1980*. Cambridge: Cambridge University Press.

——1985: *Ethics and the Limits of Philosophy*. London: Fontana.

——1993: *Shame and Necessity*. Berkeley: University of California Press.

Williams, E. 1964: *Capitalism and Slavery*. London: Deutsch.

Williams, Patricia J. 1991: *The Alchemy of Race and Rights*. Cambridge, MA: Harvard University Press.

Williams, Raymond 1958 (*1993*): *Culture & Society: Coleridge to Orwell*. London: Hogarth Press.

——1961: *The Long Revolution*. Harmondsworth: Penguin; London: Chatto and Windus.

——1966: *Modern Tragedy*. Stanford, CA: Stanford University Press.

——1973: *The Country and the City*. London: Chatto & Windus.

——1974: *Television and Cultural Form*. New York: Shocken Books.

——1976 (*1988*): *Keywords*. London: Fontana.

——1977: *Marxism and Literature*. Oxford: Oxford University Press.

——1978 (*1980*): "The Bloomsbury fraction." In *Problems in Materialism and Culture*. London: Verso.

Williams, Raymond 1979a (*1980*): "Base and super-structure in Marxist cultural theory." In *Problems in Materialism and Culture*. London: Verso.
—— 1979b: *Politics and Letters*. London: New Left Books.
—— 1980: *Problems in Materialism and Culture*. London: Verso.
—— 1981: *Culture*. London: Fontana.
—— 1989: *The Politics of Modernism: Against the New Conformists*. London: Verso.
Williamson, Allan 1984: *Introspection and Contemporary Poetry*. Cambridge: Harvard University Press.
Willingham, John 1989: "The New Criticism then and now." In *Contemporary Literary Theory*, ed. D. Atkins and L. Morrow. Amherst: University of Massachusetts Press.
Willis, P. 1979: *Learning to Labour*. London: Saxon House.
—— 1990: *Common Culture*. Milton Keynes: Open University Press.
Wilshire, B. 1982: *Role Playing and Identity: The Limits of Theatre as Metaphor*. Bloomington: Indiana University Press.
Wilson, Daniel J. 1980: *Arthur O. Lovejoy and the Quest for Intelligibility*. Chapel Hill: University of North Carolina Press.
Wilson, E. 1991: *The Sphinx in the City*. London: Virago.
Wimsatt, W.K., and Beardsley, Monroe C. 1946 (*1954*): "The intentional fallacy." In *The Verbal Icon*. Lexington, KY: University of Kentucky Press.
—— 1949 (*1954*): "The affective fallacy." In *The Verbal Icon*. Lexington, KY: University of Kentucky Press.
Winkler, Earl R., and Coombs, Jerrold R., eds 1993: *Applied Ethics: A Reader*. Oxford: Blackwell Publishers.
Winner, Thomas 1987: "Text and context in the aesthetic theories of Jan Mukarovsky." In *Text and Context: Essays to Honor Nils Ake Nilsson*, ed. P. Jensen, B. Lonquist, F. Bjorling, L. Kleberg, and A. Sjoberg. Stockholm: Almquist & Wiksell.
Winnicott, D.W. 1958: *Collected Papers: Through Paediatrics to Psycho-analysis*. London: Tavistock.
Wiredu, Kwasi 1980: *Philosophy and an African Culture*. Cambridge: Cambridge University Press.
Witte, Bernd 1985 (*1991*): *Walter Benjamin: An Intellectual Biography*. Detroit: Wayne State University Press.
Wittgenstein, L. 1958 (*1969*): *Philosophical Investigations*, trans. G.E.M. Anscombe. New York: Macmillan.
—— 1989: *Remarks on the Philosophy of Psychology*, vol. 1. Oxford: Basil Blackwell.

Wittig, Monique 1969 (*1971*): *Les Guerillères*, trans. David Le Vay. New York: Viking.
—— 1973 (*1975*): *The Lesbian Body*, trans. David Le Vay. London: Peter Owen.
—— 1986: "The mark of gender." In *The Poetics of Gender*, ed. Nancy K. Miller. New York: Columbia University Press.
Wolfson, Susan 1986: *The Questioning Presence: Wordsworth, Keats, and the Interrogative Mode in Romantic Poetry*. Ithaca, NY: Cornell University Press.
Wollen, Peter 1969 (*1972*): *Signs and Meaning in the Cinema*. London: British Film Institute and Secker & Warburg.
Wolin, Richard 1982: *Walter Benjamin: An Aesthetic of Redemption*. New York: Columbia University Press.
Wood, David, ed. 1992: *Derrida: A Critical Reader*. Oxford: Blackwell.
Wood, Ellen Meiksins 1990: "The uses and abuses of 'civil society.'" In *The Socialist Register 1990*, ed. Ralph Miliband, Leo Panitch, and John Saville. London: Merlin Press.
Woodmansee, Martha, and Jaszi, Peter, eds 1994: *The Contruction of Authorship. Textual Appropriation in Law and Literature*. Durham, NC: Duke University Press.
Woods, R. 1977: "Discourse analysis: the work of Michel Pêcheux," *Ideology and Consciousness*, 2, 57–79.
Woolf, Virginia 1927 (*1977*): *To the Lighthouse*. London: Grafton.
—— 1938: *Three Guineas*. London: Hogarth Press.
Woolgar, Steve, ed. 1988: *Knowledge and Reflexivity: New Frontiers in the Sociology of Knowledge*. London: Sage.
Worcester, Kent 1992: "A Victorian with the rebel seed: C.L.R. James and the politics of intellectual engagement." In *Intellectuals in the Twentieth-Century Caribbean*, Vol. 1, ed. Alistair Hennessy. London: Macmillan Education.
Wright, Elizabeth 1984: *Psychoanalytic Criticism: Theory in Practice*. London: Methuen.
—— 1989: *Postmodern Brecht: A Re-Presentation*. London: Routledge.
Wright, Erik Olin 1985: *Classes*. London: New Left Books.
—— 1989: *The Debate on Classes*. London: Verso.

Yates, F.A. 1984: *Collected Essays*. 3 vols. London: Routledge.
Young, G.M. 1977: *Victorian England: Portrait of an Age*. New York: Oxford University Press.
Young, M.F.D., ed. 1971: *Knowledge and Control*. Basingstoke: Collier-Macmillan.
Young, Nigel 1977: *An Infantile Disorder? The Crisis*

and Decline of the New Left. Boulder, CO: Westview.

Young, T.D. 1985: "The fugitives: Ransom, Davidson, Tate." In *The History of Southern Literature*, ed. L.D. Rubin et al. Baton Rouge: Louisiana State University Press.

Young, Thomas, ed. 1986: *John Crowe Ransom: Critical Essays and a Bibliography.* Baton Rouge: Louisiana State University Press.

Young-Bruehl, Elisabeth 1982: *Hannah Arendt: For Love of the World.* New Haven, CT: Yale University Press.

Yúdice, George, Franco, Jean, and Flores, Juan, eds 1992: *On Edge. The Crisis of Contemporary Latin American Culture.* Minneapolis: University of Minnesota Press.

Zan, Yigal 1989: "The scientific motivation for the structural analysis of folktales," *Fabula: Journal of Folktale Studies,* 30: 3–4.

Zarate, G. 1993: *Représentations de l'etranger et didactique des langues.* Paris: Didier.

Zavala, Iris 1992: *Colonialism and Culture. Hispanic Modernisms and the Social Imaginary.* Bloomington: Indiana University Press.

Zea, Leopoldo, ed. 1986: *América Latina en sus ideas.* Mexico City: Siglo Veintiuno.

Zea, Leopoldo et al. 1985: *El problema de la identidad latinoamericana.* Mexico City: Universidad nacional autónoma de México.

Zhdanov, A.A. 1950: *On Literature, Music and Philosophy.* London and New York: Lawrence & Wishart.

Žižek Slavoj 1989: *The Sublime Object of Ideology.* London: Verso.

——1993: *Tarrying with the Negative: Kant, Hegel, and the Critique of Ideology.* Durham, NC: Duke University Press.

Zuidervaart, Lambert 1991: *Adorno's Aesthetic Theory: The Redemption of Illusion.* Cambridge, MA: MIT Press.

Zukin, S. 1995: *The Culture of Cities.* Oxford: Blackwell.

Zwerdling. Alex 1986: *Virginia Woolf and the Real World.* Berkeley, Los Angeles, London: University of California Press.

Index

This index lists only references to concepts, persons, and terms where significant commentary can be found or where cross-references can be easily located.